MW00623775

The Art of War in World History

BY THE SAME AUTHOR

Mirrors of a Disaster: The Spanish Military Conquest of America. Watertown, Mass.: Blue Crane Books, forthcoming.

The Kurdish Tragedy. London: Zed Press, forthcoming.

Atlas of Diasporas, with J. P. Rageau. Baltimore: Penguin Books, forthcoming.

The Stubborn March: Poems. Watertown, Mass.: Blue Crane Books, 1992.

Minorities in the Age of Nation-States, ed. London: Pluto Press, 1988.

Terrorism and Guerrilla Warfare. London: Saqi Books, 1987.

Strategic Atlas: A Comparative Geopolitics of the World's Powers, with J. P. Rageau. New York: HarperCollins, 1987; rev. eds., 1990, 1993.

The Armenians: From Genocide to Resistance, with Yves Ternon. London: Zed Press, 1983.

Guerrilla Strategy: A Historical Anthology from the "Long March" to Afghanistan, ed. Berkeley: University of California Press, 1982.

The Struggle for Africa: Great Power Strategies. London: Macmillan, 1982.

Report from Afghanistan. Baltimore: Penguin Books, 1982.

Food without Frontiers: An International Cookbook. London: Pluto Press, 1982.

People without a Country: The Kurds and Kurdistan, ed. London: Zed Press, 1981.

Revolution in the Third World: Myths and Prospects. New York: Viking, 1977; rev. ed. (Baltimore: Penguin Books), 1989.

The Palestinian Resistance. Baltimore: Penguin Books, 1972.

Peasants of North Vietnam. Baltimore: Penguin Books, 1970.

Armed Struggle in Africa. New York: Monthly Review Press, 1969.

Gérard Chaliand

THE ART OF WAR
IN WORLD HISTORY

FROM ANTIQUITY TO
THE NUCLEAR AGE

University of California Press

BERKELEY
LOS ANGELES
LONDON

The publisher gratefully acknowledges the contribution provided by the General Endowment Fund of the Associates of the University of California Press.

In memory of my father, who taught me so much and who gave me his taste for learning.

University of California Press
Berkeley and Los Angeles, California

University of California Press, Ltd.
London, England

© 1994 by
The Regents of the University of California

Library of Congress Cataloging-in-Publication Data

Anthologie mondiale de la stratégie. English
    The art of war in world history : from antiquity to the nuclear
age / [compiled by] Gérard Chaliand.
        p.   cm.
    Includes bibliographical references.
    ISBN 0-520-07963-9 (alk. paper). — ISBN 0-520-07964-7 (pbk. :
alk. paper)
    1. Military art and science—History.   2. Military history.
I. Chaliand, Gérard, 1934–   .   II. Title.
U27.A6713   1994
355'.009—dc20

                                                         92-20153
                                                         CIP

Printed in the United States of America
9 8 7 6 5 4 3 2 1

The paper used in this publication meets the minimum requirements of
American National Standard for Information Sciences—Permanence of
Paper for Printed Library Materials, ANSI Z39.48-1984. ∞

CONTENTS

List of maps xvii
Foreword by Lucien Poirier xix
Preface to the American edition xxv
Preliminary Note xxix

Warfare and Strategic Cultures in History
by Gérard Chaliand 1

1. THE ANCIENT NEAR EAST

The Kadesh Inscription (c. 1295 B.C.)
The Battle of Kadesh 49

Deuteronomy (eighth–sixth centuries B.C.)
The Conduct of War 59

The Dead Sea Scrolls (first century B.C.?)
The War Rule 61

2. GREECE AND ROME

Thucydides (c. 460–c. 399 B.C.)
The Dispute over Corcyra 67
Pericles' Reply to the Spartan Ultimatum 77

Xenophon (c. 426–c. 354 B.C.)
The Expedition of Cyrus 82
The Duties of a Cavalry Commander 102

Polybius (c. 202–c. 120 B.C.)
The Battle of Lake Trasimene 112
The Battle of Cannae 116

Julius Caesar (c. 101–44 B.C.)
The Siege of Massilia   125
The Battle of Pharsalus   132

Sallust (c. 86–c. 35 B.C.)
Guerrilla Warfare   138

Josephus (c. A.D. 37–c. 100)
The Organization of the Roman Army   150

Onasander (first century A.D.)
The General   154

Plutarch (c. A.D. 46–c. 120)
An Absolute Disaster   157

Tacitus (c. A.D. 55–c. 120)
War and the Germans   165
Germanicus's Campaigns on the Rhine   168

Arrian (c. A.D. 92–175)
The Battle of Issus   174
The Battle of Gaugamela   180
The War against Porus   188

Cassius Dio (c. A.D. 155–235?)
The Battle of Actium   197

Flavius Vegetius (late fourth century A.D.)
Dispositions for Action   201

3. CHINA

Sun Zi (fourth century B.C.)
The Art of War   221

Shang Yang (fourth century B.C.)
The Book of Lord Shang   239

Ssu-ma Ch'ien (c. 145–c. 86 B.C.)
Lord Shang   245
Tien Tan   252
Lien Po and Lin Hsiang-ju   255
Chang Liang, Marquis of Liu   264
The Marquis of Huai-yin (Han Hsin)   274

4. INDIA

Kautilya (fourth century B.C.?)
The Six-fold Policy 287
The Work of an Invader 321
Concerning a Powerful Enemy 324
Strategic Means to Capture a Fortress 327

5. BYZANTIUM

Procopius (c. A.D. 500–565?)
The Persian War 335
The Gothic War 341

Maurikios (c. A.D. 539–602)
Strategy 348

Leo VI (A.D. 865–912)
Tactics 356

Liutprand (c. A.D. 920–972)
The Use of Greek Fire against the Rus 376

Kritovoulos (c. 1410–?)
The Fall of Constantinople 378

6. THE ARAB WORLD

The Koran (seventh century)
On Holy War 387

Al-Muttaqi' al-Hindi (1477–1567)
Sayings Ascribed to the Prophet 388

Al-Bukhari (810–870)
Sayings Ascribed to the Prophet 391

Al-Tabari (c. 838–923)
Abu Bakr on the Rules of War 392
Conquest 393
The Battle of Kadisaya 394
The Battle of Karbala' 395

Ibn al-Athir (1160–1233)
The Battle of Hittin 400

Baha' ad-Din Ibn Shaddad (1145–1234)
The Fall of Acre 405

Ibn Hudhayl al-Andalusi (fourteenth century)
Principles of War 410

Ibn Khaldun (1332–1406)
Bedouins and Sedentary People 415
The Admiralty 416
Methods of Waging War Practiced by the Various Nations 420

7. PERSIA

Kai Ka'us Ibn Iskandar (c. 1020–1085)
On Giving Battle to an Enemy 429
The Art of Controlling an Armed Force 431

Nizam al-Mulk (1018–1092)
The Book of Government 434

Al-Rawandi (thirteenth century)
Conduct of War, Conduct of Battle 441

Nasir al-Din al-Tusi (1201–1274)
The Use of War 444

Mubarakshah (c. 1150–1224)
The Rules of War and Bravery 447

Sa'di (c. 1209–1291)
On War 451

8. THE OTTOMAN EMPIRE

Ottoman Chronicle (fourteenth century)
The Origin of the Janissaries 455

Busbecq (1522–1592)
The Sultan in the Field 457

9. MONGOLIA AND CENTRAL ASIA

Ibn al-Athir (1160–1233)
The Coming of the Mongols 463

John of Plano Carpino (c. 1182–1252)
How Mongols Fight 465
How to Fight Mongols 470

Ata Malik al-Juwayni (1226–1283)
The Mongols in Iran 475

Timur (1336–1405)
The Conquest of Dehli 479

Babur (1483–1530)
The Conquest of Hindustan 491

10. LIMITED WARS IN THE WEST

Jean Froissart (c. 1337–1404?)
The Battle of Crécy 501

Hernán Cortés (1485–1547)
The Siege of Tenochtitlán 508

Francisco de Jerez (c. 1497–?)
The Capture of Atahuallpa 531

Niccolò Machiavelli (1469–1527)
Of Different Kinds of Troops 535
The Art of War 536
War and Political Strategy 538
On the Object of War and the Use of Victory 545

Francesco Guicciardini (1483–1540)
The Perfection of the French Artillery 547

Walter Raleigh (1554–1618)
Sea Warfare and the Defense of England 550

Richard Hakluyt (c. 1553–1616)
The Destruction of the Spanish Armada 553

Duc de Richelieu (1585–1642)
On Sea Power 556

Sébastien de Vauban (1633–1707)
General Rules or Maxims for Attacking a Fortress 560
Treatise on the Attack and Defense of Fortresses 563

Raimondo de Montecuccoli (1608–1681)
Military Considerations 566

Jean de Folard (1669–1752)
On Column Order 570
On Defensive War 571
On Mountain War 574

Peter the Great (1672–1725)
"Testament" 577

Maurice de Saxe (1696–1750)
Reveries on the Art of War 580

Frederick the Great (1712–1786)
Military Instructions for the Generals 596

Henry Lloyd (1729–1783)
Armies, Ancient and Modern 609

Jacques de Guibert (1743–1790)
Introduction to the Essai général de tactique 623

11. THE AGE OF TOTAL WARS

Lazare Carnot (1753–1823)
On the Defense of Fortified Places 629
To Michaud, Commander of the Army of the Rhine 637
The Current Campaign on the Northern Frontiers 638

Horatio Nelson (1758–1805)
The Trafalgar Memorandum 641

Duke of Wellington (1769–1852)
Two Letters 643

Napoleon (1769–1821)
Maxims (1) 646
Maxims (2) 649
Geopolitics (from the memoirs of Las Cases) 651

Denis Davydov (1784–1839)
On Guerrilla Warfare   653
Why Partisan War Suits Russia   657

J. F. A. Le Mière de Corvey (1770–1832)
On Partisans and Irregular Forces   662

Carl von Clausewitz (1780–1831)
On the Nature of War   671

Henri Jomini (1779–1869)
Statesmanship in Its Relation to War   724
Strategy   736
Strategic Combinations   740
Epitome of Strategy   742

Thomas Bugeaud (1784–1849)
On Pacification   744

Shaka (c. 1787–1828)
The Zulu Army (from the diary of Henry Francis Fynn)   747

Charles Ardant du Picq (1821–1870)
Confidence, the Soul of Victory   754

William T. Sherman (1820–1891)
The March to the Sea   760

Helmuth von Moltke (1800–1891)
On Strategy   767

Friedrich Engels (1820–1895)
The Spirit of Resistance   770
Erosion by the Waves of Popular Warfare   774
War to the Knife   778

Friedrich Ratzel (1844–1904)
The Spatial Growth of States   782
The Sea and Sea-going Peoples   784

Alfred Thayer Mahan (1840–1914)
Naval Strategy   787

Colmar von der Goltz (1843–1916)
The Nation in Arms   808

Joseph Gallieni (1849–1916)
The Conquest of Madagascar   813

Alfred Schlieffen (1833–1913)
Present-day War   816

Charles Callwell (1859–1928)
Counterinsurgency   819

Halford J. Mackinder (1861–1947)
The Geographical Pivot of History   821
The Round World and the Winning of the Peace   825

Julian Corbett (1854–1922)
Strategical Terms and Definitions   830

Friedrich von Bernhardi (1849–1930)
On War of Today   843

Jean Colin (1864–1917)
The New Conditions of War   865

Ferdinand Foch (1851–1929)
Principles of War   868

V. I. Lenin (1870–1924)
Advice of an Onlooker   871

Leon Trotsky (1879–1940)
The Armored Train   874

T. E. Lawrence (1885–1935)
Guerrilla Warfare   880

Giulio Douhet (1869–1930)
Command of the Air   891

William Mitchell (1879–1936)
The Aeronautical Era   897

Hugh Trenchard (1873–1956)
The War Object of an Air Force   905

James Connolly (1868–1916)
On Street Fighting   911

Mikhail Tukhachevsky (1893–1937)
Counterinsurgency   914
Mounting Threats   916

J. F. C. Fuller (1878–1966)
Tank Warfare   921

Basil Liddell Hart (1895–1970)
The Strategy of Indirect Approach   927

Raoul Castex (1878–1968)
The Significance and Limits of Geography   932

Charles de Gaulle (1890–1970)
The Army of the Future   937

Winston Churchill (1874–1965)
"Blood, Toil, Tears, and Sweat"   941

Adolf Hitler (1889–1945)
War and Colonization in the East   943
Proclamation to the German People   945

Heinz Guderian (1888–1954)
Tank Attack   949

Erwin Rommel (1891–1944)
Rules of Desert Warfare   957

Alexander de Seversky (1894–1974)
The Challenge to America   962

Nicholas Spykman (1893–1943)
Heartland and Rimland   966

Mohandas K. Gandhi (1869–1948)
The Way of Nonviolence   974

Mao Ze-dong (1893–1976)
Strategy in China's Revolutionary War   976

12. THE NUCLEAR ERA

Bernard Brodie (1910–1978)
War in the Atomic Age   991

Albert Wohlstetter (b. 1912)
The Delicate Balance of Terror   1004

Thomas C. Schelling (b. 1921)
The Diplomacy of Violence   1013

André Beaufre (1902–1975)
Indirect Strategy in the Nuclear Age   1023

Henry Kissinger (b. 1923)
Defense Policy and Strategy   1041

Lucien Poirier (b. 1918)
Elements of a Theory of Crisis   1056

Pierre M. Gallois (b. 1911)
The Social Dimension of Strategy   1065

Principal subjects covered   1071

MAPS

Pages xxx–xliii

1. The geopolitics of ancient and medieval Eurasia
2. The first four decades of Muslim expansion
3. The conquests of the Mongols and of Timur (Tamerlane)
4. The great Muslim empires
5. The founding of European empires
6. The colonial expansion of Europe
7. "Rimlands" and "heartland"
8. Recent urban uprisings

FOREWORD

Lucien Poirier

This anthology is not only an unparalleled corpus of information and an aid to failing memory; it is also and above all a reliable and liberating guide for research: as it reveals the unsuspected dimensions of the thesaurus and explores the whole spectrum of the varieties of strategic thinking, it leads us to acknowledge that we are enclosed in our local culture, prisoners of our heritage, slaves of our mental habits. Ranging "from the origins to the nuclear age," it compels us to widen our narrow perspectives on conflicts and strategic action and open ourselves up to the universal.

Yet compiling an anthology means making choices. It is also means excluding, and most collections, in whatever area, are defined at least as much by what they reject as by what they include. On what criteria are these choices to be based? Doubtless the global view adopted by Chaliand seems to make his task easier. However, that simply poses the question of choice differently; it does not solve it. Certainly, of course, like each of his readers—and this is not the least obstacle to the *power* of a work of this sort—our selector has his favorite authors; like any creation of the imagination, an anthology is also a matter of taste. Chaliand does not conceal his, and I know that, among men of war, he prefers the "irregulars"—Genghis Khan, Cortés, Lawrence of Arabia. I even suspect that he might have only a modest amount of respect for the grand and carefully calculated military science of men like Eugene of Savoy, Frederick, Napoleon, and Moltke—to mention only a few of the leading figures among the great masters of military strategy. I doubt whether he is very taken with the high-powered performances of those hair-splitters the nuclear strategists, far too nominalist for a man of the ground. Unfortunately, the "irregulars" were long disdained by the professionals, and the literature has little to say about marginals: how do you theorize about irregularity?

We may legitimately indulge our tastes in creating an anthology and putting our stamp on it, but we must nonetheless overcome our lack of appetite for a few authors, embalmed in glory, who have exhausted their charms, notwithstanding that they may be required reading for undergraduates. Their prestige lay in their power to ask questions and in the pedagogical virtues of works that were innovative in their time, but after forming generations of practitioners, they no longer excite the intellect of experts who are in turn called upon to innovate. Since Chaliand also has in mind enlightened apprentices and amateurs, however, overcoming his manifest tastes, he pays proper respect to the great masters: they are all there in his list.

This concession to good usage made, he takes a greater gamble by adopting very ambitious selection criteria. The first is not obvious: it is first necessary to agree on the domain of strategic literature. Chaliand does not hesitate and gives the concept of strategy the widest possible meaning. He covers the whole field of thought open to men when they have to think and act to solve the problems posed by conflicts in society. His object is man, individually and collectively, against man; more precisely, the way in which he writes and the languages he has created to record his experience of conflicts, to express all manner of thinking about, calculating, and employing armed force in collective action, in the trial of opposing political wills.

All varieties of conflict and all strategic modes have been the objects of discourse. Whether descriptive or normative, literature has overlooked no information on man engaged in the work of continuous creation, which is what the politico-strategic undertaking is. Everything has been said about the mental and physical operations that make weapons into the—often necessary, and often excessive—instruments of changes in, or even transformations of, social and political systems. And it is from the chaotic profusion of these writings that Chaliand takes extracts, chosen not only for their significance, for the light they cast on strategy as object and for what they can teach us, but also for the accents of writing to which, as the poet that he continues basically to be, he is so sensitive. His anthology is one of authors who, whether theoreticians or practitioners, historians or analysts, refugees from every discipline applicable to knowledge of conflicts and praxeology, constitute the long lines and schools of armchair students or men with experience on the ground whose disparate works become organized before the reader's very eyes into a genealogy of strategy.

After portraying the first dimension of his project by selecting significant texts that place *homo strategicus* "in all his relations" (in Jacques de Guibert's words), Chaliand is under an obligation, to be consistent, to explore, with a cosmopolitan eye, the strategic cultures of every continent and over the very long run—what amounts to the universal history of the literature of war, from its very beginnings in the ancient east. Although it is true that from the time of our own Renaissance, the European art of war and European writers on war spread their paradigms and models all over the world, to the point where they misled us as to their universality, ethnocentrism has become untenable since

1945. It has become a commonplace to refer to the interdependence of peoples and the merging of cultures. We have seen the emergence of a universal consciousness sensitized by the diffusion of technical progress, better informed about the risks of war, the demented proliferation of weaponry, and the implications of nuclear power, as well as being attentive to the endemic conflicts that are more or less controlled and regulated by fear of the ultimate catastrophe, and finally obsessed by the organization of a less unstable and safer interstate system. Everything in this shift in attitudes to deal with the globalization of the great issues of our time has conspired to mobilize academic and military experts, along with policies, in the quest for less irrational solutions to disputes and promoting the establishment of an international order acceptable to all. As strategic questions thus everywhere moved to the forefront of concerns, new and relevant responses had to be found.

But, as in every area of innovation and creation, invention did not exclude the quest for what, in the strategic baggage left by those who had gone before, could be useful and capable of guiding the process of creative imagination, if only by the comparative critical analysis of past experiences recovered through a process of literary reconstitution. To the extent that the heritage could still stimulate and guide the new strategic problematic—by making it possible to refine concepts and discern the regularities, or constants, of thought and action—making an inventory of strategic cultures and assessing their respective contributions to the understanding of *homo strategicus,* and his tools and conduct in action, proved necessary. But, faced with the complexity of the questions posed to the *new strategic thought,* such an inventory and assessment could only reveal their heuristic powers on condition that they were freed from the straitjacket of Eurocentricity and took into account the common heritage of humanity.

I have indicated elsewhere how, over the years and in every culture, the universal body of strategic thought and practice on which experts have drawn since 1945 to find aids to invention was built up. It is that corpus that Chaliand reassembles here, using his own judgment and taste to weigh the legacy of each strategic culture, and repairing what he rightly considers injustices of omission or incomprehension. We may be familiar with the writings of the Greeks and the Romans, but the highly elaborated thought of the Byzantines is already less familiar to us. Even less well known, except among Islamicists, is that of the Arabs and Berbers. There are very few writings relating to the Mongols and the peoples of Central Asia, and Chaliand is right to cite them, given the considerable role that men from the steppe have played in history. As for the political and military literature of the Persians, Turks, and Indians, I imagine, to judge from my own reactions, that many readers will be surprised by its abundance, but so far as I know our European masters did not borrow much from it. Similarly, except for Sun Zi and Mao Ze-dong, the Chinese whom Chaliand presents are hardly ever mentioned by our writers. As for the extensive catalogue of writers who have filled the libraries of Europe and America from the fifteenth century down to our own day, he reassures us: here we are in well-known country! That is surely where our attentive reader will be awaiting our selector. But how can he be criticized when he takes good care not to omit any of the great names of theorists or practitioners? Neither land nor maritime nor aerial strategy is neglected; nor any of their varieties: wars with absolute or limited goals in the classical age, total or colonial wars in the industrial age, revolutionary wars and nuclear strategies in our own day, direct and indirect strategies, crisis management and so on—nothing is overlooked.

Naturally, Chaliand includes geopolitics and geostrategy in his list. On this point I note that in his Introduction he adopts a novel perspective: "The area between the Caspian Sea and Manchuria can also be considered as both the zone of turbulence and the true heartland of the Eurasian world for 2,000 years. Through this new vision, geopolitics recovers its historical depth." And further on: "Looked at in a long-term perspective, what seems to characterize the history of the Eurasian landmass is not the opposition between sea power and continental power but the opposition between sedentary areas and nomad invasions." In these two assertions, he seems to be revealing the key to his anthology, the criterion of choice that enables him to go beyond our age-old ethnocentrism and justifies him in giving pride of place to *noncenter* authors whom we have too long ignored.

It is time to conclude: every preface always postpones too much, and too weightily, the pleasure of getting to the meat of the reading. Once he has added that a quarter of the work has not previously been published in French, it only remains for the prefacer to retire. Let the reader then embark on the adventure of discovery. With this anthology, the first of its type in terms of its abundance and design, Chaliand was taking a gamble. He has triumphed. The prefacer risks nothing in predicting that this new and considerable work will long remain an irreplaceable tool for the researcher. It will also be a powerful stimulant for anyone curious about man: he is here shown in one of the constant applications of his desire to create, in his thousand and one ways of *operating* with the forces of armed violence; both ever-changing and always the same through the variations of language and strategy. Strategy, long neglected by the human and social sciences, now at last has an honorable status. It is to be met with everywhere today, but is often very ill-treated and misused. We should be grateful to Gérard Chaliand, who knows the power but also the shortcomings of words, for his skill in choosing the fundamental texts out of the profusion of very uneven works, the ones that, through the long gropings of thought applied to action reveal both the regularities and the peculiarities of strategy. He thus introduces us into the workshop of strategy, inviting us to follow the work of a language and writing seeking their forms to uncover their object. It is a work that is forever being recommenced to state the postures adopted by man before the eternal prevalence of violence; to state how he learned to accommodate himself to the tyranny of arms and how, with and despite them, he knew how to and could *do something.*

PREFACE TO THE AMERICAN EDITION

It is a great pleasure for me to see *The Art of War in World History* published in the United States, a country that, since 1970, has been my second home, and where I have both relatives and lasting friends.

This anthology encompasses not only the makers of Western strategy, from Machiavelli to the nuclear era, and the Greco-Roman writers familiar to us, but the great strategic traditions of Byzantium, China, India, and the Muslims.

As with any other anthology, this one cannot be made complete, and to be sure there are other authors, both ancient and modern, who would have been worth including. But I had to make choices and have decided to privilege many non-Western authors who are, if we except Sun Zi, unjustly unknown.

Two or three centuries of almost absolute superiority have led the West to forget the Arab conquests, the Mongol invaders, and the Ottoman power that was so threatening from the fourteenth to the seventeenth centuries. The writings of the Byzantine emperors Maurikios (Maurice) and Leo VI, the Indian *Arthashastra,* and Sun Zi's *Art of War* are among the major contributions to strategy. In these writings, the reader should note the following factors: (1) the emphasis on the indirect approach, so dramatically opposed to the European and American traditions of the past two centuries; and (2) the elaboration of a military ethnology of the enemy. To this must be added a conscious effort of adaptation to the enemy's strategic culture in order to respond to it adequately. This perfectly illustrates the old saying "Know your enemy."

It is particularly important in societies where history is not widely taught to become familiar with the strategic cultures of other societies and the history of strategy. Insulated and without threatening neighbors, the United States has long been able to ignore the classic need to deal with international relations. Besides, it has not experienced disaster. In that respect, the U.S. experience is almost unique.

The United States has consequently tended to consider peace the normal state of affairs and external war as a crusade that should lead to complete victory.

The United States, including its elite, has long been characterized by a relative ignorance of foreign cultures and ideologies. The world of international relations in which the United States has participated since World War II has required a series of difficult adaptations. However, owing to its global superiority and to its capacity to adapt, the United States—apart from the Vietnam War—has been successful in dealing with the conceptual and practical challenges it has faced. In spite of its financial cost, the Cold War has been won. And if domestic affairs were in better shape today, this triumph, which involves not only drastic changes in central Europe but also the collapse of Soviet communism and the dissolution of the USSR, would be complete.

In a world that is becoming increasingly integrated economically, and at the same time politically multipolar and consequently more complex, the solutions to political, economic, demographic, and migratory crises will have to be handled with greater subtlety. Political problems are not technical problems, and pragmatic solutions are inadequate, particularly when the use of force is not part of the agenda.

It is more crucial than ever to understand the historical context that may be at the root of present or future crises. Their management requires a knowledge of foreign strategic cultures from both military and political standpoints.

The Gulf War, for instance, was superbly won—success being evaluated above all in terms of allied losses—but it brought to the fore the social dimension of strategy: which is the extreme vulnerability of public opinion among Westerners, both American and European.

The fear of a terrorist threat was sufficient partially to paralyze Western countries. Business discouraged its executives from flying. The specter of war was feared more than war itself. Today fighting troops are psychologically less vulnerable than civilians watching TV far from the battlefield.

This phenomenon is all the more important as most crises and conflicts now take place in the minds of populations that have long been fairly secure and prosperous but are today aging.

Not so long ago, a U.S. historian pointed out the (relative) decline of this country, corroborated by statistics. At the beginning of the century, the United States manufactured 32 percent of world industrial production. That figure is now closer to 20 percent. Military spending has been tremendous. Negative factors have multiplied in the past few decades in both economic and social areas, particularly in education. However, the short twentieth century beginning in 1914 and ending in 1991 (with the collapse of Soviet communism and the USSR) has been dominated by the United States. The American system based on dynamic free enterprise has prevailed. Today, the United States, provincial as it may be, is probably the only country that simultaneously learns from the rest of the world while also serving as a teacher. On those grounds, it might be called the only universal state—besides being the greatest military power.

However, the race for power and hegemony seems to depend more and more on economic growth, technological innovations, and the capacity to adapt than on the military.

What is the strategic future of the United States going to be? Are we going to witness tougher competition between Japan (and soon other countries in the Far East), the EEC, and the United States? Whatever happens, the United States, with a free trade zone including probably both Canada and Mexico (i.e., almost 350 million people), will be in a favorable position at the turn of the century.

In the meantime, the emergence of a state or a group of states in Eurasia that could threaten the security of the United States is very unlikely.

We should nevertheless bear in mind that the concept of security now has to include the dimensions of demography, migrations, and domestic social conflicts. In the next two or three decades, are we going to witness problems of alliances between the various countries of the Far East (Japan, China, Korea), Europe, Russia, and the United States? Who, eventually, will be allied with whom? What new threats will arise from the emergence of China as a major power? The future world will not be, as during the Cold War (the Sino-Soviet conflict aside), a stable world in terms of alliances.

It is also possible to imagine an alternative—namely, the relative decline of the nation-state, while multinational business grows and intermingles more and more. This trend already seems to be under way. But to what extent will it alter the classic world of interstate relations in which we have been living up to now? In any case, some polarities will remain and the United States is going to be the center of one of them.

Whatever happens, provided it remains efficient and still capable of social integration, of restoring a high educational level, and of widening its cultural scope, the United States will be in a splendid position to face the first quarter of the coming century victoriously.

ACKNOWLEDGMENTS

I should like to thank Lucien Poirier, Maurice Prestat, Pierre Vidal-Naquet, Maxime Rodinson, Walter Laqueur, Jean-Paul Charnay, Pierre M. Gallois, Dominique Moïsi, and Jean Klein; Ahmad Salamatian, who contributed greatly in the choice of Persian texts; Colonel Georges Reynaud of the Ecole supérieure de guerre; my friend Jean-Pierre Rageau; Eric J. Grove, a British naval strategist and an expert on Julian Corbett; Edward Luttwak, who brought Hugh Trenchard's memorandum to my attention; the Royal Institute of International Affairs and its library in London for their help; and, especially, Hubert de Leffe, director of the library of the Ecole supérieure de guerre; Hervé

Coutau-Begarie, as usual; Juliette Minces for her critical reading of the Introduction; and Tony Berrett for his excellent translations from the French.

I particularly want to acknowledge the contribution of Arnaud Blin. Without him, the English version of the book would not have been possible. His seriousness, his dynamism, and his research skills have been invaluable. Lastly, I want to thank Peter Dreyer and Tony Hicks for their outstanding editing of this work and Monica McCormick of the University of California Press for her efficiency and her kindness.

Gérard Chaliand

Paris, 1992

PRELIMINARY NOTE

Some readers of this anthology will not find texts that they would have liked to see here. Homer, for example, is not here, and not because he does not naturally belong in an anthology of this type; nor, among the historians of antiquity, is Appian, who so well evokes the Roman Civil War. Villehardouin and Joinville are also absent. More examples could easily be given. It will perhaps come as a surprise to find no strategic works from Japan. The fact is that there is no Japanese treatise of the quality of that of Sun Zi. The Chinese art of war long remained the model in Japan. The few works translated into English or French are only treatises on the individual behavior of samurai in the spirit of Bushido, the samurai code of conduct (see Musahi Myamoto, Traité des cinq roues [Paris: Albin Michel, 1987]).

However, such as it is, this anthology is the only one of its kind on the market, either in French or in any other language, and that it is available is thanks to Guy Schoeller, editor of the Bouquins series, who gave immediate backing for my proposal.

In 1991, the Fondation Nationale pour les Etudes de Défense awarded this book the Castex Prize for the best book of the year on strategy.

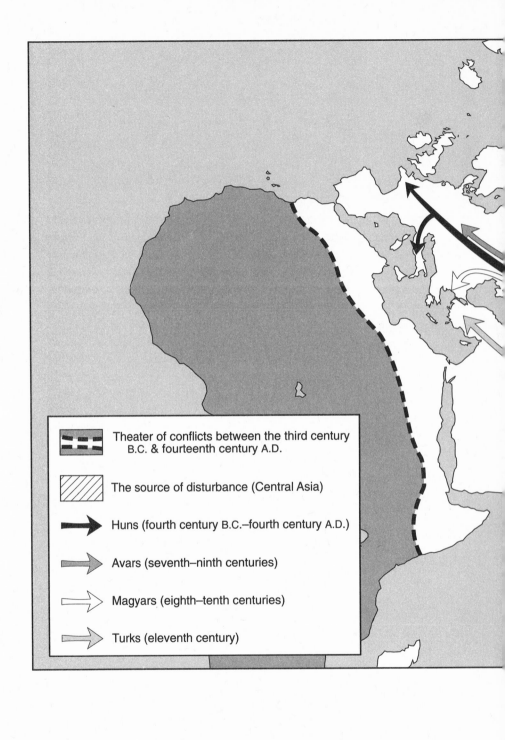

Theater of conflicts between the third century B.C. & fourteenth century A.D.

The source of disturbance (Central Asia)

Huns (fourth century B.C.–fourth century A.D.)

Avars (seventh–ninth centuries)

Magyars (eighth–tenth centuries)

Turks (eleventh century)

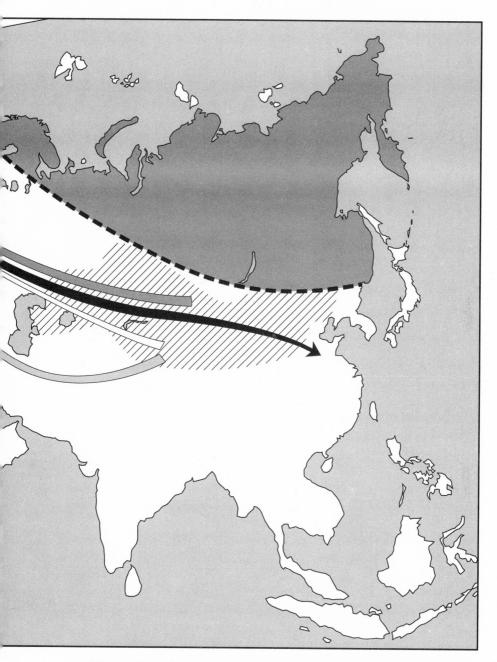

1. The geopolitics of ancient and medieval Eurasia. From the beginning of history down to the fourteenth and fifteenth centuries A.D., Eurasia and North Africa were the main theaters of war. From the fourth century B.C. until the fourteenth century A.D., and sometimes beyond, Central Asian nomads were a constant threat to societies all the way from China to Byzantium and Europe.

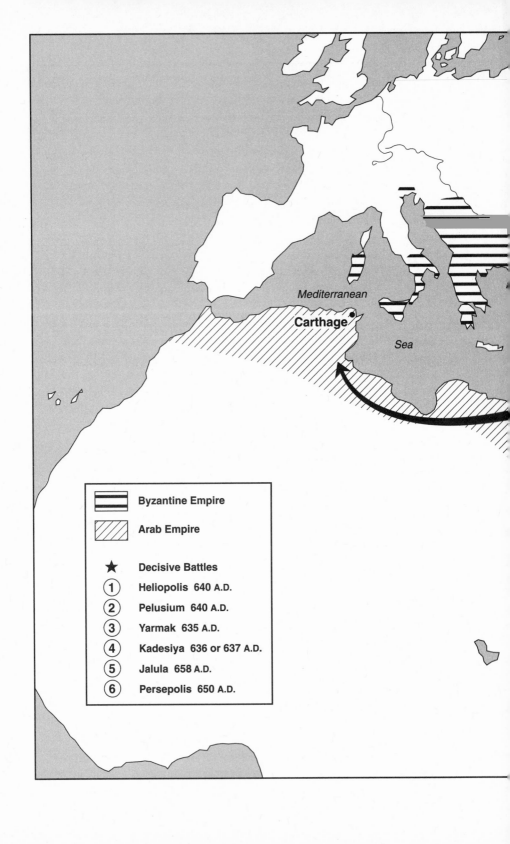

Mediterranean

Carthage

Sea

	Byzantine Empire
	Arab Empire

★	**Decisive Battles**
①	**Heliopolis** 640 A.D.
②	**Pelusium** 640 A.D.
③	**Yarmak** 635 A.D.
④	**Kadesiya** 636 or 637 A.D.
⑤	**Jalula** 658 A.D.
⑥	**Persepolis** 650 A.D.

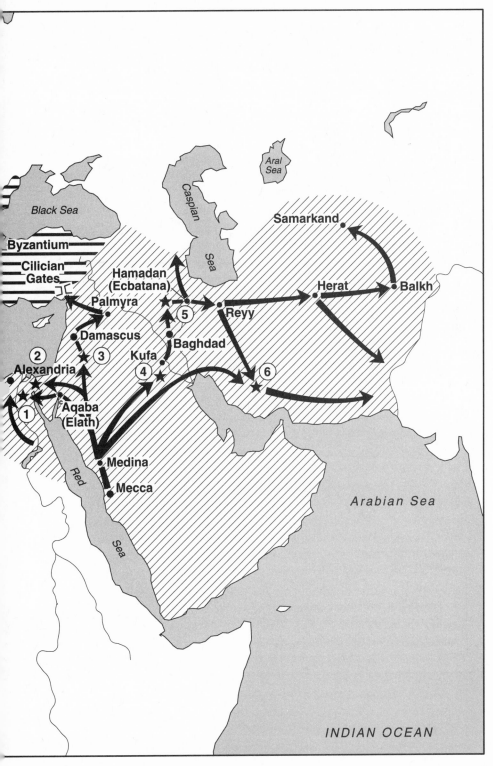

2. The first four decades of Muslim expansion.

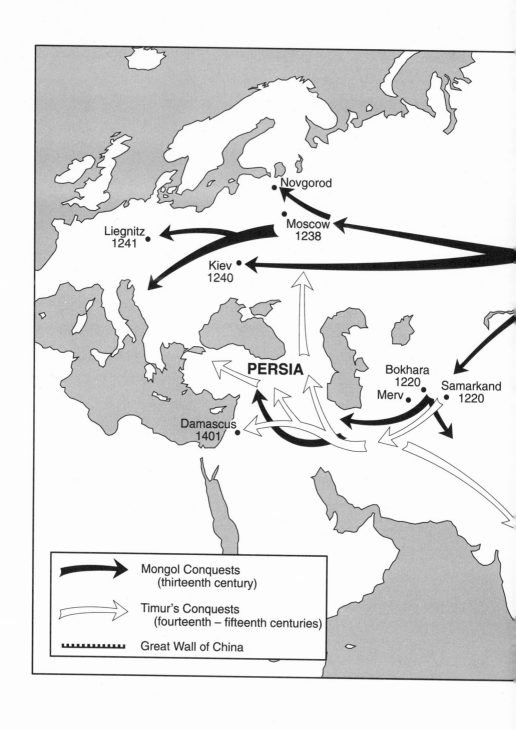

Novgorod

Moscow
1238

Liegnitz
1241

Kiev
1240

PERSIA

Bokhara
1220

Merv

Samarkand
1220

Damascus
1401

	Mongol Conquests (thirteenth century)
	Timur's Conquests (fourteenth – fifteenth centuries)
▪▪▪▪▪▪▪▪▪▪▪	Great Wall of China

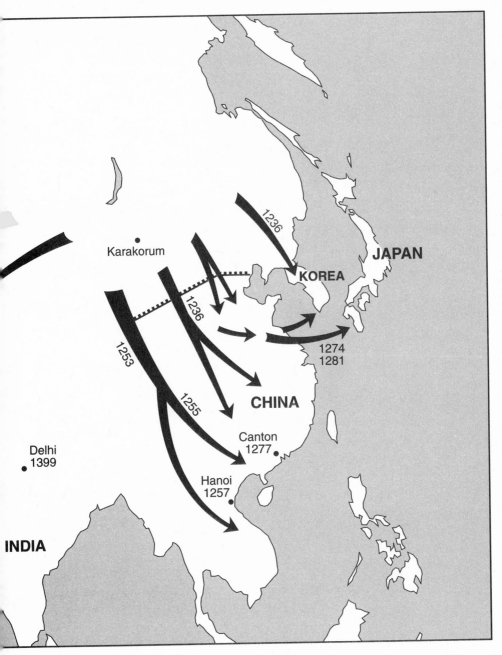

3. The conquests of the Mongols and of Timur (Tamerlane). Baghdad was sacked in 1258 by the Mongols and twice later by Timur.

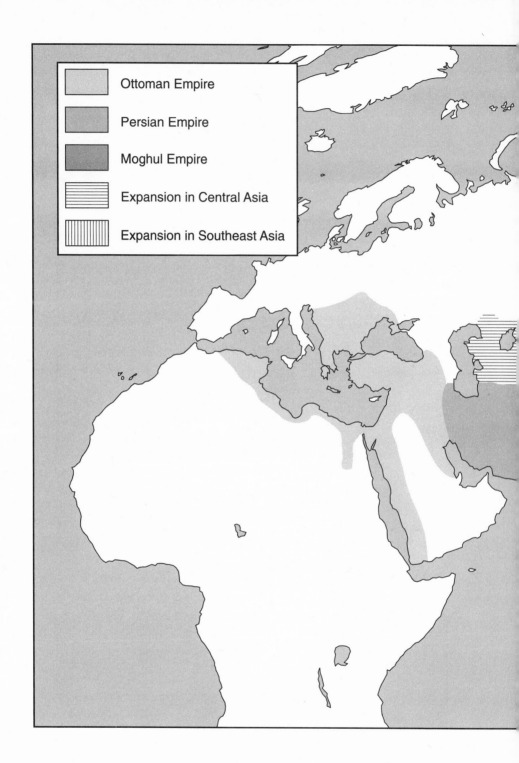

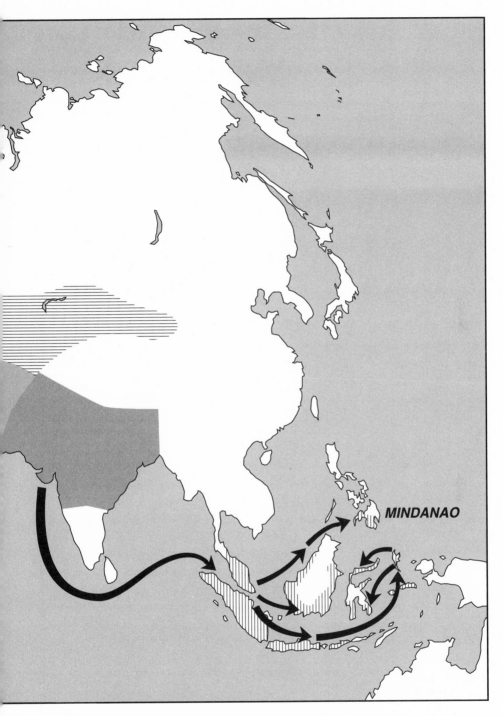

4. The great Muslim empires. The Spaniards came into conflict with Muslims in Mindanao in the Philippines. Islam also expanded in both East and West Africa.

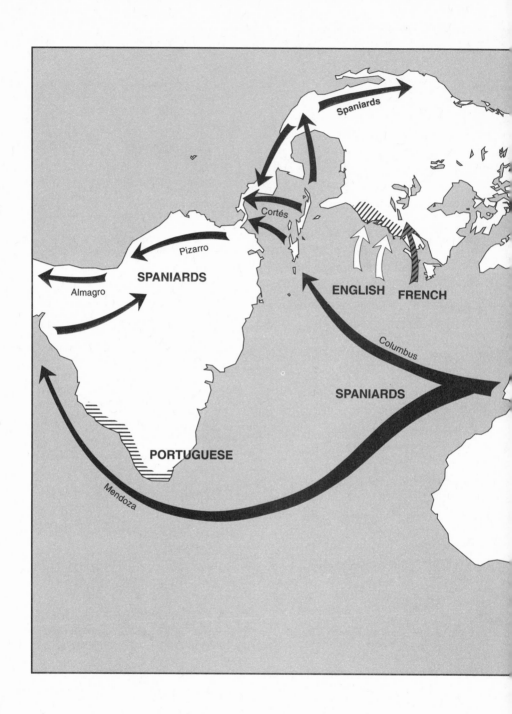

RUSSIANS

5. The founding of European empires: Spanish and Portuguese expansion to the Americas and Russian conquest of Siberia in the sixteenth century; English and French expansion in North America in the seventeenth century.

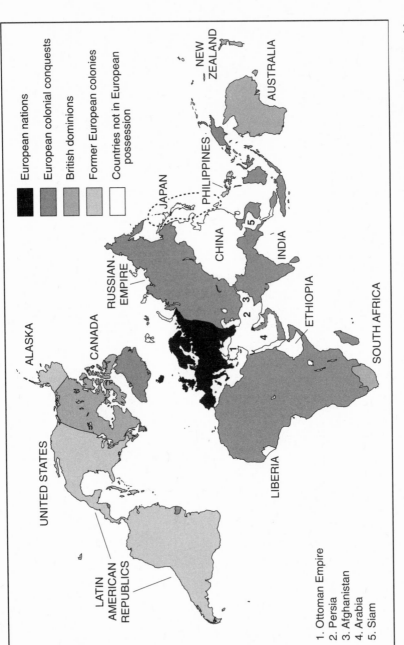

6. The colonial expansion of Europe. The impact of Europe from the sixteenth century to the beginning of the twentieth was worldwide. In the Far East, only Japan, China, and Siam (Thailand) were not colonized (although China granted large concessions in its maritime provinces and cities to the European powers and lost two million square kilometers to Russia). The Ottoman Empire survived until 1918; thereafter only Turkey remained independent. Persia was semi-independent. Unconquered Afghanistan was a buffer state. In the Arab world, only Yemen and Arabia were not conquered. In Africa, only Liberia and Ethiopia (Abyssinia) remained independent; Italy would occupy Ethiopia from 1935 to 1941.

Legend:
- European nations
- European colonial conquests
- British dominions
- Former European colonies
- Countries not in European possession

1. Ottoman Empire
2. Persia
3. Afghanistan
4. Arabia
5. Siam

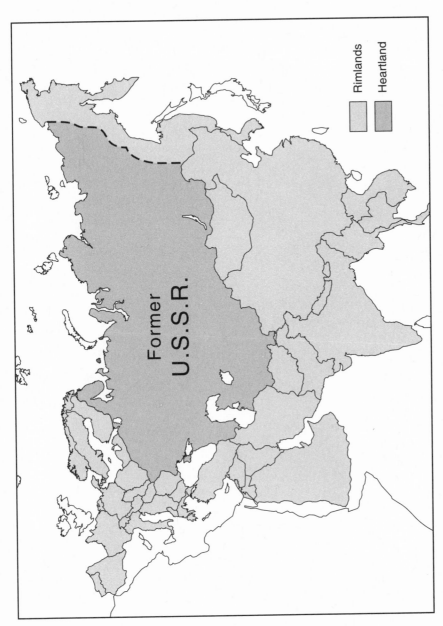

7. "Rimlands" and "heartland" according to Nicholas Spykman. This view contributed greatly to the policy of containment of the USSR during the Cold War.

Rimlands

Heartland

Former
U.S.S.R.

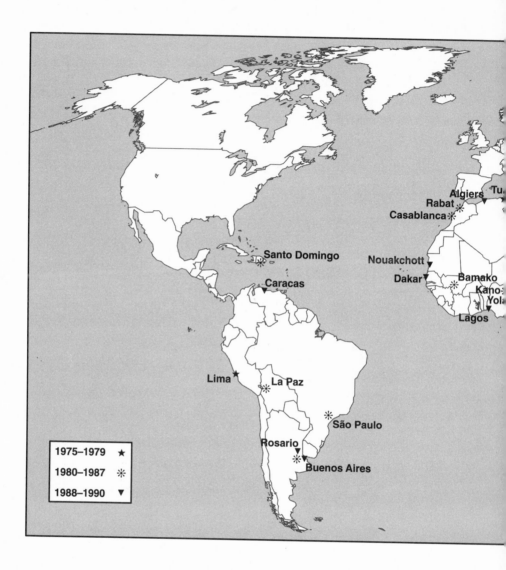

1975–1979 ★
1980–1987 ✳
1988–1990 ▼

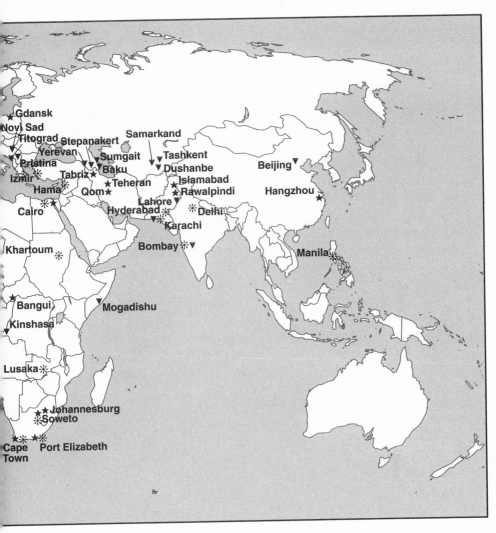

8. Recent urban uprisings. Such uprisings are likely to occur with increasing frequency in the South and may also occur in the North. They are expressions of sociopolitical crisis in overcrowded megalopolises.

WARFARE AND STRATEGIC CULTURES IN HISTORY

Gérard Chaliand

Opposite the entrance in the Velázquez room in the Prado Museum in Madrid hangs the *Surrender of Breda,* also known as *Las Lanzas,* which the artist painted in about 1634–35, when triumphant Spain was just beginning its decline.

The scene depicted by Velázquez shows a flat, water-covered landscape stretching as far as the eye can see, under a lowering, gray-flecked sky. In the foreground, the composition is so skillful that it creates the impression of a sea of humanity whereas a close look reveals only about twenty faces. On the left, the Dutch; on the right, the Spaniards, in a tighter group, with the array of lances in serried ranks behind them. Very close up is a horse's croup. Everyone has dismounted. In the center are two figures: Justius of Nassau and Ambrogio Spinola. Justius is bowing and presenting the keys of the fortress to the victor. Spinola is also bowing and putting his right hand on his opponent's shoulder in an exquisite gesture of forbearance. He is about to speak a few words worthy of a gentleman. Both sides belong to the same world. Doubtless they would be dining together that evening.[1]

This is a picture of war, of a particular war, within shared conventions, accepted by both sides, even if populations were subjected to reprisals or exactions.

The town of Breda, besieged and taken by the Dutch in a surprise move in 1590, had been so well transformed into a fortress that it came to be known as the "bastion of Flanders." Thirty-four years later, in the context of one of those conflicts that could, with long periods of quiescence, stretch out over two generations, the Spaniards laid siege to it. Taking advantage of the lie of the land, and resorting to their usual tactic, the Dutch opened their dikes and flooded the region. But, in less than a year, the fortress had to capitulate. The commander of the Spanish forces, a Genoan in the service of the Hapsburgs, offered the besieged very honorable terms of surrender. "They must be treated

---

1. Three centuries later, in the film *La Grande Illusion,* Jean Renoir portrayed the same aristocratic relationship between a German and a Frenchman.

as brave fighting men and come out in good order with all their weapons. The infantry, with flags flying and drums beating . . . , the cavalry with banner in the wind and mounted as if on campaign."

That was on 5 June 1624. At the court of Spain, there was rejoicing. And yet, a quarter of a century later, the Netherlands won its independence and Spanish hegemony in Europe, which had lasted almost a century and a half, gave way to the long hegemony of France over the continent.

Since the last quarter of the sixteenth century, the Netherlands had been fighting Spain, the hegemonic power of the time, with the Hapsburgs ruling over half of western Europe and a large part of the Americas. In the sixty or so years that the war between Spain and the United Provinces lasted, there was only one large-scale battle. The art of war then, as in the eighteenth century, consisted above all in besieging and attacking fortified places; the whole aim was to carry on operations prudently and avoid battles, which were too costly in men. Maneuvers and feints designed to cut the enemy's communications were the chosen weapon, the aim being to wear down the enemy's will or exhaust his financial resources.

Velázquez's painting depicts a period. It expresses a long tradition in which wars in Europe had only limited objectives and were not designed, as they were after the French Revolution, to annihilate the opponent's armed forces in a decisive battle.

And yet, wars of religion have the implacable character of wars of ideas, and in a theater close by, at the very time when Velázquez was painting the *Surrender of Breda,* the terrible Thirty Years' War was unfolding at the expense of the people, a bloodletting that affected Germany for many years after, so well summed up by Grimmelshausen in his picaresque tale *Simplicissimus:*

> Unger und Durst, auch Hitz und Kält,
> Arbeit und Armuth, wie es fällt.
> Gewaltthat, Ungerechtigkeit,
> Treiben wir Landsknecht allezeit.[2]

> Hunger and thirst, cold and heat,
> Work and want, as is meet.
> Injustice and violent crime
> We soldiers commit all the time.

---

2. Grimmelshausen, *Der Abenteurlicher Simplicius Simplicissimus,* bk. 1, ch. 16. "This couplet was not misleading, but quite accurate, for all they did was eat and drink, endure hunger and thirst, wallow in debauch, kill and be killed, shoot and be shot, torture and be tortured, hunt and be hunted, terrorize and be terrorized, rob and be robbed, pillage and be pillaged, spread misery and suffer it. In short, everywhere, cause havoc and ruin and suffer havoc and ruin," says the author.

The art of war in seventeenth-century Europe comprised lengthy campaigns, and sieges were its key feature. In fact, the picture that we have of warfare in the eighteenth century (when, indeed, battles were very costly in terms of men) originated in a much earlier period: from the time of the Renaissance and in almost every country, war was carried on by mercenaries. Under Louis XIV, "nationals" were incorporated because they were cheaper.

Conserving manpower and wearing down the enemy were counterparts to the price paid by civilian populations. These wars had their share of atrocities. The sack of Malines in 1568 was total, the Spanish troops not having been paid: it even included churches and convents, which were theoretically sacrosanct.

CHANGING PERCEPTIONS OF WAR

The strategist is concerned with the ways and means of coercing the enemy and imposing his will on him. Conversely, he rarely poses the problem, which is one of considerable interest for the historical perspective, of the *nature of warfare.*

Today, mention of war—at least in the northern hemisphere—summons up both fear of nuclear apocalypse and the painful reminder of the two great wars of the first half of the century. The qualitative change brought about by nuclear energy underlies the feeling of rejection of a general war. Such a war seems less likely than ever, although it is difficult to imagine that the human species can forever continue to behave so rationally.

But the phenomenon of war, as a manifestation of collective violence in history, cannot be analyzed on the basis of today's sensitivities and moral judgments.

Arnold Toynbee sought, with the help of a series of examples drawn from ancient history, to show that a halt or breakdown of civilization invariably accompanies each new improvement in the art of warfare. Nothing could be less certain, especially in modern history. The opposite is not certain either over the long haul. It should be noted, however, that Toynbee is looking at violence only from a strictly moral angle. Examining the fate of rulers who had come to the throne by violence, he develops the hypothesis of the "suicidal importunity of a sword that has been sheathed after tasting blood. The *polluted* weapon will not rust in its scabbard but must ever be itching to leap out again. . . . The would-be saviour who first had recourse to this could now find no rest until his *sin* of seeking *salvation* along a path of crime has been *atoned for* by the agency of the very weapon which he once so perversely used."[3]

3. *War and Civilization,* extracts from *A Study of History* selected by A. V. Fowler (New York: Oxford University Press, 1950). Emphasis added.

The Judeo-Christian world, of whose criminals Macbeth is one of the prototypes, cannot account for the fate of illegitimate rulers through the ages, any more than warlike activity, when it is offensive, automatically disqualifies the conqueror morally. And if there are societies that are permanently warlike, can it not be said that Europe is in the forefront of such societies?

For the most part, wars have not been wars of extermination. Formerly, victory meant the appropriation of goods, slaves, and land. Extermination involved only particular categories of conflict, and the annihilation of the adversary theorized by Clausewitz as the goal of military operations was in itself only a phase in the ever-changing conception of warfare.

Today, when, since the advent of nuclear energy, it is possible to envisage an archaeology of warfare (possibly only a provisional one), what must be stressed is how much the French Revolution completely transformed the very conception and nature of warfare for a century and a half.

By resorting to the "*levée en masse,*" a logical consequence of the idea of popular sovereignty, the French Revolution and, subsequently, the Empire, radically democratized an occupation hitherto reserved to professional armies composed largely of mercenaries, a term that from the Renaissance to the eighteenth century had no pejorative implications.

Modern nationalism, a new idea based on the concept of the nation-state and popular sovereignty, leads naturally to mass warfare. [4] With Napoleon began the era of what Clausewitz calls "absolute war," the "decisive" battle in which the aim is to exterminate the enemy's armed forces. Gradually, armies became exclusively national affairs, and compulsory military service was introduced. The considerable advances in firepower associated with the advances of industrialization, the growing bitterness of national antagonisms, reminiscent of the religious conflicts of the sixteenth century, and the diabolization of the enemy in wars of ideas made the wars of the first half of the twentieth century total wars. The development of propaganda during World War I, engendered by democratization, aimed to bind the rear and the front together in a common effort, in which the outcome of prolonged conflicts depended more and more on industrial capacities. World War II accentuated the total character of warfare. In the Spanish Civil War, the destruction of Guernica symbolically prefigured the reversal that was under way, with civilians becoming targets as much as, if not more than, soldiers, as Coventry, Dresden, Tokyo, Hiroshima, and Nagasaki were subsequently to show. In fact, reverting to a tradition long abandoned in Europe, an attempt was made to terrorize civilian populations and destroy their morale, in addition to attacking purely military targets. Europeans emerged from World War I with a feeling of disgust, tempered in the

4. Itself rendered technically possible by the introduction of the divisional system.

victors by the often bitter scent of victory, and strengthened in the defeated by a painful feeling of frustration. After World War II, in which Europe collapsed, pacifism spread. The attitude of some French conscripts during the Algerian war of independence and of some Americans in Vietnam is evidence of this. Soviet conscripts behaved similarly in Afghanistan. But it is not possible to analyze warfare historically simply in terms of the criteria of sensitivity that we have today. Executions, for example, were public in parts of Europe before World War I and drew excited crowds there, as they still do in some other parts of the world. The great change in western Europe seems to have crystallized during World War I; the officer caste began to give way to more democratic recruitment; other ranks no longer accepted being looked upon as cannon fodder. War ceased to be perceived as a game: the cost in suffering was too high. Human life was considered more precious than in earlier times. Other, demographically younger peoples outside Europe, many of whom did not directly experience the severe losses of the two world wars, and who have virtually no reason to be satisfied with the current world status quo, may have different sentiments.

THE NATURE OF WARFARE: A TYPOLOGY

For a long time, at different periods and in various societies, warfare took on a *ritual* character. Its ritualization manifested itself, for example, when two rival groups designated champions to settle a conflict: David and Goliath, or the Horatii and the Curiatii. Sparta and Argos fought through chosen champions; out of six hundred, three survived (Herodotus *Histories* 1.82). The high Middle Ages in the West were a significant period in this respect. As Jacques Duby writes, battles were organized as the ultimate recourse to the judgment of God: "Their role was to compel heaven to declare itself, to reveal its plans, to show once and for all, clearly and indisputably, on what side right lay. Battles, like oracles, partook of the sacred." Battles were duels; the two sides fought until one of them conceded defeat. God had then given his verdict. Until the beginning of the twelfth century, this procedure was virtually unchallenged: "The greatest princes had no hesitation in offering battle to anyone challenging their authority."

"Here there was no surprise, no ambush, but a long ritual preparation, as is appropriate when approaching a sacrament. The two adversaries were about to present themselves before the tribunal of God. . . . On the field of battle of Tinchebray, in 1106, Henry, the son of [William] the Conqueror, was readying himself; against him, his brother, Robert Courthose; and the duchy of Normandy and the kingdom of England were the stake. Henry proffered his prayer in justification and propitiation, a plea in his own behalf: 'I am going into battle only to come to the aid of the desolated people; I implore the Creator of all things from the bottom of my soul that in today's battle He may grant victory to the one whom He has chosen to secure protection and rest for His people.'"[5]

Among the Aztecs, a warrior people whose empire was built up through a series of conquests, the goal of warfare, along with the aim of increasing tribute enriching the hegemonic group, was less to cause casualties among the enemy than to procure prisoners to be sacrificed to the gods. The enemy was defeated when the leaders had been seized or when his temple was destroyed, a sign that his gods were less potent.

In the course of its internecine struggles, the wars of Western feudalism were fought economically and ritualistically, the purpose often being to take knights prisoner in order to make them pay ransom. Even later, in the Renaissance, the conception of war held by the condottieri was close to one of chivalry, in that both, aiming to secure ransom, sought not to annihilate the enemy but to capture him. The sudden arrival in Italy in 1494 of troops equipped with artillery belonging to Charles VIII of France was something completely new.[6] The same is true of the Swiss squares that, at the very beginning of the fourteenth century, gave back to the infantry an importance it had lost for a thousand years, thanks to their cohesion (the squares were formed on a cantonal basis, so that everybody knew everybody else). Unlike other soldiers of the time, the Swiss gave no quarter. No prisoner, whatever his rank, was spared. In the seventeenth century, Gustavus Adolphus of Sweden was the first to break with the strategy of his time; he sought frontal battle. Once he had improved the firepower of his forces, largely made up—at least at the beginning of his great campaign—of Swedish nationals (and Finns), he did not waste time with sieges and sought a decisive engagement in open countryside. He fought as many as three battles in seven months, something unprecedented in his time.

In fact, the dogma of the "decisive" battle, according to which the aim is the annihilation of the enemy's armed forces, lasted approximately a century and a half (from Napoleon Bonaparte to 1945). But military historians in the second half of the nineteenth and the first half of the twentieth centuries traced the pattern of the decisive battle to a much earlier period of history, without making much effort to distinguish the nature of the warfare within which the allegedly "decisive" battle was being fought. If we limit ourselves to what the British and Americans call grand strategy, only battles whose historic military

---

5. Jacques Duby, *La Bataille de Bouvines* (Paris: Gallimard, 1982), pp. 14–15.
6. See Guicciardini, pp. 547–49 below.

and political results are decisive should be considered decisive. In that sense, the conquest of Constantinople in 1453 by the Turks and the Arab victories at the River Yarmak and Kadisaya in 636, which—fought against Byzantium in the case of the former and against the Persians in the case of the latter—gave them possession of Syria and Iraq, were decisive battles.

Difficult and complex though it may be, it is important to develop a typology of wars, starting from the observation that there have been many different concepts of warfare and its nature in history. If we exclude the wars of primitive societies, which were determined by subsistence and demography and were probably not very costly in lives (because of concern for survival), we can try and sketch out a loose typology of wars, as follows:

Ritualized wars. These usually occur within a given society or neighboring societies in conflicts that are not wars to the death. Generally, they are the mark of societies that are still archaic or traditional.

Wars with limited objectives. Are these a modern variant of ritualized warfare? It is worth asking the question. In any event, they occur within a world in which the code of behavior, values, and institutional and social framework are implicitly accepted. Dynastic disputes, for example, do not seek to change the world—that is, the established order.

Conventional wars of conquest. These have infinitely greater predatory objectives and seek to coerce the opponent, no lasting compromise being possible short of military victory. They may involve annihilating the enemy or be satisfied with subduing him.

Mass wars. These wars (which Clausewitz calls "absolute"), the advent of which was marked by the French Revolution, reached their culmination in World War I and, especially, World War II. Such wars aim at the annihilation of the enemy's armed forces in battle and, increasingly, the collapse of the civilian population through the massive use of terror (summary executions, mass deportations, bombardments).

Wars without quarter. Over history, the two most cruel types of war have been civil wars, which in the early nineteenth century came to be called "wars of ideas." The wars of religion in the late sixteenth and early seventeenth centuries are a classic example. Civil wars are the hardest-fought and, proportionally, result in the most victims: the Thirty Years' War; the French wars of religion; the Civil War in the United States (1861–65), which caused more casualties than the Franco-Prussian War (1870–71); the Civil War in Russia (1918–20); the Civil War in Spain (1936–39); or the religious conflicts in India between Hindus and Muslims following partition (1947–48). If strategy consists in weighing an issue in relation to the risks it carries, civil wars are the most irrational of wars; the costs usually far exceed the value of what is being fought over. However the conflict in Lebanon (1975–91) is interpreted (civil war or conflict between quasi-nations, as Maxime Rodinson would have it), the overall result of this fighting with no local victor is out of all proportion to any theoretically rational cost/benefit analysis.

War waged against a race seen as radically different is the other type of war without quarter. Conflicts between nomads and sedentary populations can be put in this category. The sudden irruption of the Mongols west and south of central Asia in the thirteenth century and colonial conquests, from America to Africa, are classic examples. The war waged in the east by Hitler's forces (not to mention the extermination of Jews and Gypsies, both nonterritorial minorities) was of the same type, Poles, Ukrainians, and Russians, indeed all Slavs, being destined to become slave labor or to disappear, in part to open up living space.

To use different language, the sharpest conflict is that of the Same against the Same, just exceeding in intensity that against the Other who is radically Other because his essence is perceived as Other.

CONCEPTS OF WARFARE IN THE WEST

There is a great difference between wars with limited objectives and the total warfare of the industrial age, which flows from the concept of the nation-state; a great difference between ritualized wars and the devastating clash of radically different societies or the frenzied fury of civil wars. Similarly, the combatant—mercenary, conscript, or volunteer—almost always corresponds to the particular type of warfare.

Battles were more frequent in the eighteenth century, despite the fact that they were then avoided where possible, than during the century between the battles of Mühlberg in 1547 and Breitenfeld in 1631. For over a century, the only two large-scale battles in western Europe were those of Nieuwpoort (the Netherlands, 1600) and the White Mountain (Bohemia, 1621). It was the age of the long siege. In a few decades, the answer had been discovered to cannon, which in 1453 had brought about the fall of Constantinople, whose high medieval walls were ill-suited to resisting gunpowder. [7] Under the influence of Italian engineers, Errard de Bar-le-Duc, and the Netherlander Simon Stevinus, the art of fortification was rethought: low, thick walls with bastions gave the advantage back to the defense. The adaptation occurred quickly. The can-

---

7. In the same year, 1453, it was the cannon that enabled Charles VII to put an end to the long English occupation of Aquitaine.

non, briefly triumphant, for example, with Charles VIII in Italy in 1494, was countered by innovations in fortification. The cost of mercenary forces and the consequent professional prudence of their captains (who hesitated to risk their destruction) also explain why these dynastic wars with limited objectives were so long, so indecisive, and thus so disastrous for civilian populations, which were systematically plundered. The regularly paid and well-disciplined army of the United Provinces, which saved the country from ruin in its long conflict with the Hapsburgs, was the sole exception.

The wars of seventeenth and eighteenth centuries were aimed at exhausting the opponent's economic resources. From the time of the formation of national states in the fifteenth century, war was in fact waged largely by mercenaries, and mercenaries came from all over Europe: Swiss, Germans, Italians, Croatians, and Hungarians fought indiscriminately in the armies of France and the Hapsburgs. Gustavus Adolphus's army, which, for the seventeenth century, looked like a national army, was in fact made up of a core of Swedes and large numbers of Finns, Scots, and Germans. Generals themselves placed themselves successively at the service of rival rulers: until the eighteenth century, there was nothing unusual in being successively an officer with the Hapsburgs, the czar of Russia, and the king of Sweden. The great Condé himself (1621–86) went into Spanish service at the time of the Fronde.

It was rulers that one served, the state being a dynastic one. Identities were religious in the seventeenth century, as they had been in the previous one, and it was often more important to a French Protestant to be free to practice his religion in Germany or Holland than to continue being a subject of the king of France.

Aristocratic values survived for a long time, at least until the American and French Revolutions, and sometimes until the beginning of the twentieth century in other European countries, such as the Austro-Hungarian empire. Other ranks, under the orders of warrant officers enforcing rigid discipline (Prussian drill) based on corporal punishment, were looked upon in this context as an inferior species.

LONG-TERM GEOPOLITICS:
NOMAD/SEDENTARY CONFLICTS AND THE
ANTAGONISM BETWEEN ISLAM
AND CHRISTIANITY

For anyone looking at the history of Europe over the long term, a history built on the Judeo-Christian and Greco-Roman heritages, the prime adversary, from the seventh and eighth centuries to the sixteenth century at least, was Islam. In the course of its prodigious initial expansion, Arab Islam in less than a century seized control of half the largely Hellenized, Romanized, and Christian Mediterranean and reached the Iberian peninsula, whose reconquest, begun in 1085 with the taking of Toledo, was only completed in 1492. In Europe, this Muslim expansion was followed by a second thrust by the Ottomans between the fourteenth and sixteenth centuries: the Balkans and a considerable part of the countries along the Danube were conquered after a series of defeats inflicted on Christian armies: Kossovo, 1389; Nicopolis, 1396; Mohács (Hungary), 1526. Vienna itself was besieged in 1529 (and was to be a second time in 1683, when it was only saved by the intervention of the Pole Jan Sobieski). As for the Mediterranean, it remained a disputed zone until the battle of Lepanto in 1571 and well beyond. The final collapse of the Ottomans in the Balkans took almost a century, between 1821 when Greece declared its independence and the Balkan Wars of 1911–12. A massive exchange of populations (on criteria that were not linguistic or national but religious) between Greece and Mustafa Kemal's Turkey, following the latter's victory (1922–23), closed this period. Such a perspective reflects European history over the long term, but if we look at universal history, other phenomena appear that make short shrift of some of our received ideas.

Historians, generally more interested in national histories, when not concerned with the ancient Greek and Roman world, have too often neglected the role and impact of nomads.[8] According to a view generally accepted today, there has throughout history been a fundamental antagonism between maritime powers and continental ones. Since the beginning of the twentieth century, geopoliticians have repeatedly stressed this antagonism. Doubtless this assessment is valid for modern history since the sixteenth and seventeenth centuries, but it is untrue of the two millennia that separate the fourth century B.C. and the fourteenth century A.D., notwithstanding the battle of Salamis and Rome's efforts to become a maritime power. The fundamental antagonism in Eurasia between the fourth century B.C. and the fourteenth century was that between nomads and sedentary peoples.

From the Huns, who raided China even before the Han dynasty, to the Mongols, who seized control of it in the thirteenth century, the Eurasian landmass, from China to central and even western Europe, continuously felt the turbulence of central Asia: China, Persia, the Fertile Crescent, Asia Minor, Russia, Ukraine, Poland, and, beyond, the plain of Pannonia and western Europe (the

8. With a few exceptions: see René Grousset, *L'Empire des steppes* (Paris: Payot, 1965) and D. Sinor, ed., *The Cambridge History of Early Inner Asia* (Cambridge: Cambridge University Press, 1989).

battle of Châlons) were affected. One after the other, Scythians, Huns, Avars, Magyars, Turks, and Mongols—all archers on horseback—made brutal onslaughts into the Eurasian theater.

In fact, the steppes of central Asia can be compared to a vast inland sea, whence, in successive waves for over 2,000 years, nomad raids erupted. The area between the Caspian Sea and Manchuria can also be considered both a "zone of turbulence" and the true heartland of the Eurasian world for some 2,000 years. Through this new vision, geopolitics recovers its historical depth.

Over the period stretching from the fourth century B.C. to the fourteenth century, this zone of turbulence affected China under the Han and succeeding dynasties, until the advent of the Ming, with varying degrees of seriousness. The Yuan dynasty established by Kublai Khan was Mongol, although, after the conquest, it gradually became sinicized. The Manchu dynasty, which seized power in 1644, represented a new victory of the nomads. The longest-lasting threat was that of the Hun tribes (Hsiung-nu); the most devastating was that of the Mongols in the thirteenth century, which even affected Vietnam, Burma, and Korea on China's periphery. Two attempts by the Mongols to land in Japan failed, mainly because of bad weather.

This zone of turbulence had a continuous influence on Persia, where invasions by Turks and Mongols followed one another. Iran was separated from central Asia only by the fluid barrier of the Oxus (Amu Darya). Byzantium, too, was threatened many times between the sixth century and its fall by waves of nomads from the steppes of central Asia—Huns, Avars (sixth century), Magyars, and Seljuk Turks—until the final assault by the Ottoman Turks that led to the fall of Constantinople in 1453.

The impact of the nomads was also felt further west: in Russia, Ukraine, Poland, and the Pannonian plain. On the eve of the fall of the Roman empire, the Huns arrived with Attila, after ravaging Russia, Poland, and Germany as far as the plain of Châlons in eastern France. The Hungarians (ninth century), with the Bulgars (seventh–ninth centuries) and the Finns, constituted the most westerly outpost of the world of the steppes. As for the Mongols, who built up the largest empire the world has ever seen, their irresistible advance westward was only halted in the mid thirteenth century by the death of the great khan Ogadei.

Apart from this area of turbulence, which, in terms of its duration and its impact, was the most significant in world history, a second such nomad area, that of the Bedouin of Arabia, played a vital role. In less than a century, between the death of Muhammad in 632 and their arrival in Spain in 712, the Arabs, motivated and sustained by the Muslim faith, defeated Byzantium in Syria, conquered Iran, seized Egypt and the Maghreb, and reached the Indus and the foothills of the Himalayas.

With slight setbacks, notably in the Iberian peninsula, Islam continued to expand between the eighth and seventeenth centuries in both Asia and Africa: it made inroads in central Asia, where a significant number of steppe nomads were converted, sometimes, like the Turks, when they advanced into sedentary areas. (Gradually speakers of Turkic languages from central Asia seized political and military power, which had initially been monopolized by the Arabs.) The Muslim advance reached as far as Sinkiang. India, where Islam had already made converts, was invaded in 1525 by Muhammad Babur (1483–1530), who had himself been driven out of Transoxiana by Uzbeks, initially toward Afghanistan. The dynasty of the Great Moghuls was thus born, and the subcontinent had been almost entirely conquered when the British arrived. Meanwhile, the Muslim advance continued toward Malaysia, Borneo, Java, Celebes, and Sarawak, and reached Mindanao, the southernmost of the Philippine islands, where it was once again halted, this time in Asia, by the Spaniards.[9]

Finally, Islam, which had already penetrated black Africa in the ninth and tenth centuries in the Sahel, moved vigorously southward in both the east and the west in a continuous movement.

There is one last large-scale nomadic expansion to be mentioned in the period from the eighth to the eleventh centuries, that of the nomads of the sea, the Vikings, whose impact on France, England, and later Sicily, albeit important, was less significant than the role these Scandinavian warrior-sailors played in the creation of Kievan Rus, sailing up the rivers of Russia, marking their passage at Novgorod, and traveling down the Volga. Some of them entered the service of Byzantium, where they were called Varangians.

Thus, looked at in a long-term perspective, what seems to characterize the history of the Eurasian landmass is not the opposition between sea power and continental power but the opposition between sedentary areas and nomad invasions. The ancient settled centers were China, India, Persia, Mesopotamia, Asia Minor, Egypt, Greece, Syria-Palestine, Italy, and, later, the Europe growing from the Carolingian nucleus. They were founded around rivers or oases and in the long run ended up triumphing over the nomads.

THE THEATER OF CONFLICTS BECOMES WORLDWIDE: WESTERN IMPERIALISM

A change began in the sixteenth century, reaching its peak between 1850 and 1950; the theater of conflict, which had essentially been Eurasia, including only

---

9. Today about 4 or 5 percent of the population of the Philippines are Muslim, mostly in the western part of Mindanao. They have waged an armed struggle for autonomy.

Africa north of the Sahara, gradually expanded to embrace the whole world. The Spaniards attacked Cuba and Santo Domingo and used these as jumping-off points to conquer Mexico, Yucatan, and Guatemala. Then, from Central America, it was the turn of Peru and Colombia. Chile and La Plata were soon invested too. Christianization followed military conquest. The Portuguese, who also succeeded in sailing round the south of Africa, established themselves in Brazil.

In the sixteenth century too, thanks to the Cossacks, the Russians, only recently liberated from the long Mongol domination, made a prodigious advance and seized the whole of southern Siberia as far as the Sea of Okhotsk. This first European push in the sixteenth century, by sea in the west and by land in the east, was followed by a second one in the seventeenth and eighteenth centuries. The Dutch installed themselves in Indonesia, and before long the British did likewise in India. The Ottomans were constantly retreating before the Russians and the Hapsburgs in the eighteenth century. Both the British and the French were present in North America.

The third push occurred in the nineteenth century after Europe had settled the problems emerging from the Napoleonic era. Gradually, and then faster in the last quarter of the nineteenth century, virtually the whole of Asia and Africa was occupied militarily and colonized by Europeans: India, Indochina, Australia, New Zealand, Algeria, Tunisia, Egypt, and all of Africa south of the Sahara, except for Abyssinia and Liberia.

The Russian empire, which had made deep inroads into the Ottoman conquests north of the Black Sea (in the Crimea) in the eighteenth century, launched a series of offensives in the following century in the Caucasus against Kajar-ruled Persia, the Muslims of central Asia (Uzbeks, Turkmens, Tajiks), and the Manchu imperial possessions along the Ussuri River and in northern Manchuria.

At the beginning of the twentieth century, Europeans occupied Morocco and Libya. Following World War I, Britain and France carved out "mandates" in the Near East, hitherto under Ottoman rule.

In terms of geopolitics, the centuries between 1492 (when Columbus reached America) and 1945 marked both the globalization of the theater of conflict and the hegemony of Europeans—the Americans being their heirs. The maritime dimension of the globe only assumed its full importance in the fifteenth century, just as the nomads were losing their military superiority.

Modern nationalism, the major ideology of the nineteenth century, which Europe had helped spread through the influence of the French Revolution, was turned against it by the peoples it had subjugated. Nationalism harbors the death of empires: starting on the American continent, this movement of emancipation gradually spread to cover the entire planet. Meiji Japan successfully evaded the white peril. The peoples dominated by the Ottoman and Hapsburg empires gained their emancipation, or aspired to it, after World War I. Mustafa Kemal's Turkey succeeded in avoiding the semicolonial status that the Allies had been preparing for it. After World War II, the colonial empires disappeared, a development that eventually affected the Soviet empire in 1988–91.

AGAINST SOME RECEIVED IDEAS

Contrary to widespread belief, warfare has not always had as its objective the annihilation of the opposing force through a decisive battle. In fact, the very term *decisive* is worth reexamining; the taking of Constantinople, for example, was more decisive in its consequences than the battle of Austerlitz or the battle of Cannae, even though these were perhaps more striking affairs.

In the framework of European history looked at as a whole (that is, based on Christendom and not on the medieval opposition between the Church of Rome and the Eastern Churches or on the opposition deriving from the Reformation), the major antagonism opposed Europe to Islam (and vice versa). This antagonism was obviously sharpest in regions where domination and confrontation lasted longest: Spain and the Balkans on the Christian side (during World War I, the Armenians suffered a general deportation and mass liquidation, what today we would call genocide). Muslims suffered the domination of czarist Russia in the nineteenth century and of the USSR in the twentieth, both in central Asia and in part of the Caucasus. It should be noticed that the pressure of Islam, long ago felt in Europe, has conversely been acutely felt more recently in India. It was British interference that put an end to almost three centuries of Muslim rule in India, and that at independence gave power to the Hindus, while a significant proportion of Muslims opted for partition.

Modern nationalism, born at the end of the eighteenth century in France and developed in Europe through the nineteenth century to become, in the twentieth, the quasi-universal ideology based on the model of the nation-state, has tended to push into the background the fact that in the framework of dynastic states, most European armies up to the mid seventeenth century, and even beyond, consisted of mercenaries from many parts of Europe. Without denying the importance of nationalism, it is worth stressing how excessive the nationalist reinterpretation of the high Middle Ages has been. Moralizing criteria such as those used by Montesquieu and Toynbee to condemn war or bring out the causes of decay often misguidedly survive in assessments of the decline of empires. Roman "virtue," for example, is largely a myth, invented for use in the secondary schools of yesteryear. Rome, like all empires, resorted to cruelty, and we pay little heed to how her adversaries saw things (the reverse occurs in studies of the Mongols; there it is the defeated who tell the story). Sallust puts these words into a letter he attributes to Mithridates, king of Pontus, writing to Arsaces, king of Persia, proposing an alliance against the Romans:

> Do you not realise that the Romans, blocked by the Atlantic from expanding to the west, have turned their armies in this direction? That from the start everything they own has been snatched from others—home, wives, land, and empire? That they were once refugees, homeless and fatherless? Thus they are now the scourge of the world, who know no reason human or divine. They pillage and destroy friends and allies, near and far, weak and strong, and consider all who will not agree to become slaves, and particularly monarchs, as their enemies. For few wish for liberty, the majority desiring no more than justice from their masters. We are suspected of being their rivals, who will in due time exact vengeance on them. Look at yourself: you have the great city of Seleuceia, and the kingdom of Persia with its legendary riches. Yet what do you expect from them except treachery now and war later? The Romans turn their weapons against everyone, particularly those whose defeat will yield the most spoil; by daring the deceit, by breeding war from war they have become great: in this way they overwhelm and put an end to everything. . . . [To defeat the Romans] is not difficult if you in Mesopotamia and we in Armenia surround an army that is without provisions, without support, and has remained safe hitherto only by good luck and our own shortcomings. And you will win fame as one who went out to help great kings and overcame the robbers who plundered the globe.[10]

Cold-blooded cruelty is the political use of calculated terrorism. Its aim is first to engender a collapse of the spirit of resistance, then a feeling of inevitability. At one point or another in their growth, all empires—among them Rome, the Ottomans, and Europeans overseas—have resorted to it. The political limits of terrorism are reached when conditions acceptable in the framework of what is recognized as such at a given time have been worked out for the subject populations. Such was the case with the status of non-Muslims in the Ottoman empire, which was felt to be tolerable until the birth of modern nationalism. In almost every case, the victor's "generosity" is above all the expression of his diplomatic farsightedness.

Our Western-centeredness, in the military domain, leads us to treat the contributions of other societies as of no consequence. It took the unexpected victory of Mao Ze-dong to bring about a rediscovery of Sun Zi. European mili-

10. *Sallust: Fragments of the "Historia" and Pseudo-Sallust: Letter to Arsaces* (London: London Association of Classical Teachers, 1970). The "great kings" Arsaces is urged to help are Mithridates himself and Tigranes, king of Armenia, a kingdom then at its height.

military superiority, so patent between Napoleon's Egyptian campaign and World War II, led to neglect of the study of non-Western military thought. Between the fall of Rome and the seventeenth century, however, if we exclude Machiavelli, the outstanding strategic thinking was Byzantine and Chinese. India, too, occupies a place of honor, with Kautilya's *Arthashastra*. More than in other disciplines, we are backward as regards matters military outside the West, above all because Orientalists and experts on overseas societies have rarely looked at military problems. Another reason is that because these societies were defeated or in decline, they were often looked down on. However much one may admire the prodigious work devoted to war as a historical phenomenon by Hans Delbrück, one cannot but be struck by his academic narrow-mindedness in dismissing the Mongols in the thirteenth century in three lines, on the pretext that they did not develop anything new in strategic thinking—as if theory simply limped along behind reality.[11] Despite their importance, the lightning expansion of the Arabs in the seventh century and of the Ottomans between the fourteenth and sixteenth centuries, the Chinese military tradition, and the strategies that made possible the survival of the Byzantine empire for a thousand years after the fall of Rome have been little studied compared to the numerous writings devoted to rather unimportant European captains.[12] Because he fought the Aztecs, Cortés is held to be a negligible "irregular" in most academic military studies. Yet he has the rare merit of being at once a political and military leader, a strategist (the siege of Tenochtitlán was an operation on both land and water) and tactician who also classically doubled as heroic war chief.[13]

Until the introduction and, above all, the improvement and spread of firearms—that is to say, until very recently, given that the real transition occurred with Frederick the Great of Prussia—the superiority of armies did not lie principally in the quality of their weaponry. Apart from the skill of the commander, organization, capacity to maneuver, cohesion, and morale were almost always decisive. As is shown by the battle of Cannae and some of Napoleon's victories, numbers did not always carry the day either, provided that the imbalance was made up for by some other factor. In that sense, it is interesting to take a look at the modes of organization and strategic concepts

11. Delbrück, *Geschichte der Kriegskunst im Rahmen der politischen Geschichte* (7 vols.; Berlin, 1919), trans. W. J. Renfroe as *History of the Art of War within the Framework of Political History* (Westport, Conn.: Greenwood Press, 1975).

12. See John Bagot Glubb, *The Great Arab Conquests* (London: Hodder & Stoughton, 1963), and J.-P. Charnay, *L'Islam et la guerre* (Paris: Fayard, 1986) on Muslim military history. The Chinese art of war is dealt with in F. A. Kierman, Jr., and J. K. Fairbank, eds., *Chinese Ways in Warfare* (Cambridge, Mass.: Harvard University Press, 1974).

13. See Gérard Chaliand, *Mirrors of a Disaster: The Spanish Military Conquest of America* (Watertown, Mass: Blue Crane Books, forthcoming).

of other societies—in short, at other strategic cultures. For too long, from the nineteenth century to the period after World War I, the strategy of indirect approach (see p. 927 below) was generally neglected in Europe. The quest for the decisive blow, firepower, and the spirit of unrestricted attack met their limits in World War I, but it took colonial defeats in Asia and the lessons of revolutionary wars to bring about a rethinking of indirect strategy, which is today all the more important because it is almost the sole form conflicts have been allowed to take since the nuclear stalemate.

SUN ZI'S CONCEPTUAL BREAKTHROUGH

Sun Zi was the author of the oldest known treatise on the art of war, a Chinese masterpiece unequaled until modern times. In Sun Zi's work, war is looked at neither from a moral standpoint nor as either accidental or inevitable. In a considerable advance on the military theorists of other societies (except for the Greek historian Thucydides),[14] Sun Zi presents war as an essential aspect of statecraft and an activity lending itself to rational analysis, one to which peace gives meaning. Sun Zi and Clausewitz agree that war is in the last analysis a political matter. The Chinese treatise begins thus: "The art of war is of vital importance to the state. It is a matter of life and death; a road either to safety or to ruin. Hence it is a subject of inquiry which can on no account be neglected."

Sun Zi does not limit himself to military matters seen from a technical (and hence superficial) angle, but endeavors to bring out the essence of strategy and its link with policy. He embraces and synthesizes the general principles that should guide the conduct of a conflict, placing the greatest stress on the morale and cohesion of the troops and the importance of "the harmony of the people with their leaders." His doctrine stresses the importance of knowledge of the adversary, how he views things, and his modus operandi: "What is of extreme importance is to attack the enemy's strategy." He devotes a great deal of space to deception, to manipulating the enemy while maintaining steadfastness and discipline in one's own forces. For Sun Zi, strategy is based on intelligence of the other, knowledge of his weaknesses, and undermining his morale so as to deliver a final blow to an enemy already in disarray.

As an undogmatic theorist, Sun Zi recognizes the importance of the ability to adapt to the unforeseen: "And as water has no constant form, there are in war no constant conditions." He also adds that there should be no fear of disobeying the ruler's orders if the situation on the ground so requires. With such

14. See Thucydides, *History of the Peloponnesian War*, translated by Rex Warner (Baltimore: Penguin Books, 1954).

a bold assertion, especially at a time when despotism was the rule, Sun Zi was not questioning the political dimensions of conflict ("good rulers deliberate on plans, good generals execute them"), but the rigid directives of rulers lacking the means to assess a concrete situation. The courage and skill of a commander are measured also by his capacity to disobey orders when he is firmly convinced that he holds the tactical key to a situation.

Far from advocating war or even battle, Sun Zi considers that a conflict is best kept short, or else the victor himself risks being exhausted. He advises against sieges and advocates mobile warfare using the element of surprise. He recommends exploiting the enemy's weaknesses, using what we today call psychological warfare: "Avoid force, strike where he is weak." This last factor is vital, and rarely has so much emphasis been put on rumor, deception, creating a fifth column, sowing discord among the enemy, and subverting and corrupting his leaders. These tactics are that much easier when dealing with mercenary troops, generals with doubtful loyalties, and conflicts whose outcome is of no great importance except for the dynasty or ruler embarking on it.

Sun Zi's art of war is essentially a brilliant conceptualization of conflicts with limited objectives and a masterpiece of universal relevance on the use of the indirect approach strategy. One cannot fail to note that in his implicit conception of warfare, none of the factors that determine the outcome of the most deadly conflicts—civil wars and wars to the death between societies with radically opposed values—are to be found. Sun Zi's intellectual universe is naturally one in which war occurs within a single society, with relatively limited means, and ends within a framework of generally accepted rules. In that sense, the war that Sun Zi writes of is close in its motivations, objectives, and means to medieval conflicts or the dynastic wars with limited objectives of seventeenth- and eighteenth-century Europe. With Sun Zi, we are neither in the terrible world of religious and national wars nor in the climate of terror created by clashes between radically different societies—wars to death such as those of the conquistadores in America and the sweeping inroads of nomads that China was soon to experience, against which, after the time of Sun Zi, it built the Great Wall.

WARFARE IN THE ANCIENT WORLD

To kings and nobles of the ancient world (from the second millennium B.C. on), the chariot was both a symbol of power and the supreme weapon. The chariot was used by the Egyptians, in the ancient Near East, in ancient India, by the Chinese at the time of the Warring States, and by the Mycenaean or Homeric Greeks, and it was the key means of attack in battle. Mounted on two wheels and drawn by two horses, it usually carried three warriors: a driver, an archer, and, in the back, someone whom the Assyrian texts call "the third man," whose role was to protect the other two with a large shield. Cavalry was, of course, used for offensive action. Behind, as always in larger numbers, came the infantry, divided into heavy infantry and light infantry, some using missile weapons—bows and slings—and some thrusting weapons—spears and swords. The body was protected by a helmet, a breastplate, and greaves. Siege weapons made their appearance at a very early date. The Assyrians used mobile screens of solid wickerwork, beneath which they sheltered as they moved toward the walls of a city to fire their arrows. Wheeled machines carried large battering rams to make breaches. Ladders were used for the assault. The Assyrians were probably the best-organized armed force in the ancient Near East. Their use of terror (although it is sometimes excessively attributed to them) seems to have been very widespread everywhere, in order to deter any later resistance, and the defeated paid dearly for their loss: enslavement was the least of evils for a conquered population, which was usually deported.

In about the seventh century B.C., the Spartan phalanx made its appearance in Greece. Foot soldiers played a growing role after they learned to maneuver in groups. The phalanx improved with time. Epaminondas of Thebes made a tactical innovation by strengthening the left wing in depth to annihilate the right wing of the enemy, which usually moved forward faster than the left wing (because of the position of the shield). This oblique arrangement secured victory at Leuctra (371 B.C.) against the Spartans and was also subsequently typical of the Macedonian order of battle. On the wings, the very numerous Macedonian cavalry and the light infantry countered moves by the enemy to outflank the main body. The Macedonian phalanx, armed with long pikes held in both hands, was more powerful than a Spartan phalanx armed with the short one-handed pike. Lightly armed infantrymen, peltasts or targeteers, covered the flanks of the phalanx and also engaged in skirmishing. The cavalry, although without stirrups, were important and sometimes decisive, and sieges—too often neglected in the history of battles—also played a considerable role.[15] Well before the fifth century B.C., the catapult, the battering ram, towers, and galleries on wheels were already being used. Later, the Romans improved the order of battle: Roman legionnaires, infantrymen armed with javelins and swords, marched into battle in thin order in two successive waves, a third being held in reserve. This system reached its peak at the time of the Civil War (c. 48–44 B.C.).[16]

15. See, for example, the account of the siege of Tyre in Quintus Curtius, bk. 4.

16. See Yvon Garlan, *War in the Ancient World: A Social History,* trans. J. Lloyd (London: Chatto & Windus, 1975). On Rome, see Edward Luttwak, *The Grand Strategy of the Roman Empire* (Baltimore: Johns Hopkins University Press, 1976).

In Europe (but not in China, where the cavalry played a much more important role because of the impact of nomads), the infantryman was supreme for a thousand years (from the seventh century B.C. to the fourth century A.D.). When, in A.D. 376, the Roman legions were crushed by German cavalry, the infantry was replaced as the shock force by Byzantine horsemen, called cataphracts. It was another thousand years before the infantry recovered its leading role in the fourteenth century with the Swiss in western Europe, and above all in the Balkans with the janissaries, the Ottomans' shock troops.

For a long time, weaponry remained more or less unchanged, with some variations and improvements (better-smelted steels, bows with greater range, etc.). The pike was the shock weapon of men organized in groups; the sword, the individual shock weapon. Missile weapons included the bow, the sling, and, later, the crossbow. The use of horses in fighting and sometimes elephants or dromedaries completed a panoply that lasted three or four thousand years until the appearance and spread of firearms.

What in fact was important was the organization and cohesion of fighting forces and the combination of missile weapons and thrusting weapons. The skill and sometimes the genius of the leader were, of course, decisive. Great captains were rarely military theorists (the opposite was generally true). The result is that throughout history, until recently, war was generally better fought than studied. It is true that many Greek treatises on tactics (for example, those of Arrian and Aelian) have been lost, but the literature on use of the siege in warfare is considerable, including the writings of Aeneas the tactician, Athenaeus, Biton, Heron of Alexandria, and Apollodorus. Among the Romans, Vegetius (fourth century A.D.) was late. Concrete instances of strategy have to be sought in the historians: in this respect, Thucydides, Xenophon, Polybius, Arrian, Tacitus, and Sallust are more than precious. Sometimes in less famous historians, such as Cassius Dio, there are exceptional fragments. Cassius Dio's description of the naval battle of Actium, in which Octavian, the future emperor Augustus, defeated Antony in 31 B.C. is admirable.

Fundamentally, throughout history, armies seem to have had two ways of fighting. One was through attack and retreat and envelopment, as practiced by the nomads of central Asia (archers on horseback) and the Arabs at the time of the first wave of conquest in the seventh century. The other was by charging in line to create a breach, as with the Macedonian phalanx, the Roman legions, and the Frankish armies at the very beginning of the Crusades, when they were fighting in accordance with the medieval tactics of the West.

The treatment of the defeated varied even in ancient times from society to society and depending on circumstances. It ranged from almost total destruction, as with the Assyrians and Timur, who practiced full-blown terrorism, to partial destruction accompanied by enslavement, the most common treatment, or partial destruction followed by coexistence, the conquerer implanting himself on the conquered society. Alexander's campaigns fall into the last category, and the Muslims also took this approach in building their empires. Often it was the demographic factor (the number of the defeated) that determined this last sort of treatment.

The military side of Greek and Roman antiquity is generally quite well known to us, but for other societies, except for a few experts, we have little to guide us. I shall now sketch the broad outlines of the strategic cultures of a few societies that will be discussed in the pages that follow.

CHINA AND ITS STRATEGIC CULTURE

Three observations, of varying importance depending on the period, but all fundamental, must be made regarding the military aspect of Chinese history.

In the north was a frontier that was under almost constant threat from warrior nomads (except for isolated periods, such as the mid seventh and late tenth centuries) from the fourth century B.C. to the seventeenth century A.D. These incursions, which were sometimes invasions, began at the time of the Warring States and grew in intensity after the unification of China in 221 B.C., a few years before the rise of the Han dynasty (202 B.C.–A.D. 221). In less than half a century, between 138 and 90 B.C., there were over twenty large-scale raids and invasions by the Huns (Hsiung-nu). Not only did all Chinese dynasties have, with varying degrees of urgency, to fight the nomads from the north;[17] China was twice conquered by them. The Mongols, led by Kublai Khan, established the Yuan dynasty, which lasted for a century (1279–1363). They were overthrown by the Ming, but the Mongol threat, which followed that of the nomads generically called Huns, continued to hover over China until the sixteenth century. In 1550, Altan Khan's Mongols reached the gates of Beijing. In 1620, that Mongol threat was replaced by that of the Manchus, who in 1644 overthrew the Ming and held power until the establishment of the Chinese republic in 1912.

It is impossible to overestimate the defensive aspect of Chinese strategic thinking, which inspired the building of the Great Wall (even though China did make use of offense at certain periods). The closing in on itself that resulted led China, not only to a vision that was self-centered, as with all empires, but to a stance that was simultaneously defensive and disdainful of the non-Chinese world.

---

17. In 138 B.C., Chang Ch'ien, a contemporary of the historian Ssu-ma Ch'ien, was sent by the Han emperor as ambassador to the king of Bactria to try and make an alliance with countries in the Huns' rear.

Already by the fourth and third centuries B.C., Chinese troops had adapted to the necessities of war against nomadic mounted archers. Cavalry played an important role in China even before the Han, while logistical problems led to the multiplication of strongpoints that were not castles as such but fortified towns, in which the administration and trade were concentrated.

Starting in the fourteenth century A.D., another threat appeared, this time from the sea. Raids by Japanese pirates along the coast increased under the Ming, especially in the sixteenth century. The Ming established a new version of the Great Wall in the shape of a series of fortified strongholds from Korea in the north to Annam in the south, and a large fleet was mobilized, but it was not possible to think of an offensive given the threat of the nomads in the north, and the Ming ended up opting for depopulation of the coastal areas, with the resulting collapse of maritime trade. This Chinese "defensive withdrawal" embraced an area larger than the whole of Europe excluding Russia.

Another aspect of Chinese military history that is sometimes overlooked is the constant effort by the central government to cope with peasant revolts or provincial crises, upheavals that sometimes even precipitated the fall of a dynasty. The fact that some of the empire's military operations were directed against the population it administered—which is not peculiar to China—recalls one of the often neglected functions of armies: to restore order. (For much of the nineteenth century after the congress of Vienna, the British and French armies intervened frequently to maintain or restore order in the metropoles.) During the period between 750 and 950 A.D., Chinese military problems were internal: the T'ang put an end to regionalism and at the same time pursued an offensive policy. Historians noted that in 751 the Arabs defeated the T'ang, without always realizing that, at the time of the battle of Talas, the Chinese forces were as far from their bases as the Muslim ones were from theirs. Chinese troops who had covered 2,000 miles and were in the steppes of Turkestan, with an overextended supply chain, were far from enjoying favorable conditions.

The occupation and administration of China's eighteen provinces were a considerable accomplishment, and it is wise to remember that China was the largest and longest-lasting empire that the world has known, built on a homogeneous society constructed around shared values. Unified China was virtually self-sufficient for almost ten centuries before maritime trade with the states of southeast Asia began to grow significantly.

The last essential military factor in classical Chinese history is the advance to the south and southwest that brought about a shift of the heart of Chinese society from its original northern home.

The military policy of the Chinese empire, founded on force of arms, political intelligence, and the social organization instituted by the mandarin bureaucracy, oscillated, depending on what was required, between annihilating the enemy and, more often, a so-called pacification policy. After the Han period, given the political importance of the mandarins, military virtues were given little emphasis, at least in official Confucian ideology. The model was the educated man rather than the soldier (unlike in Japan, for example). Nonetheless, the military, conceived of as the fighting arm of policy, continued to play a fundamental role, in thinking as well as in practice. In fact, it is surely in the two great defensive empires (defensive in the sense of being above all anxious to preserve what they had), China and Byzantium, that strategic thinking was richest and most stimulating, in antiquity as in the Middle Ages.

BYZANTIUM AND THE ART OF WAR

The eastern part of the Roman empire, which lasted for a thousand years after the fall of Rome (how many empires have lasted so long?), was its more populous half. Apart from Rome, the biggest cities of the empire were Constantinople, Alexandria, Antioch, and Tarsus. In the course of its long existence, the Byzantine empire successfully resisted the attacks of the Huns, the Avars, the Arabs, the Bulgars, and the Kievan Russians, and survived the Crusaders before falling in 1453.

Under Justinian (527–65 A.D.), the Byzantine empire took the offensive, after defeating the Sassanids of Iran. The small but excellent forces of Belisarius, almost 40 percent of whom were horsemen (archers on horseback), triumphed over the Vandals of North Africa. Narses conquered central and southern Italy by defeating the Ostrogoths. Byzantine superiority lay in combining the use of mounted archers (taken over from the Avars), heavy cavalry (cataphracts) armed with lances, and infantry. Domination of the Mediterranean gave Byzantium a further advantage when it was necessary to send reinforcements. For a brief moment, the Roman empire was almost wholly restored to its former territorial extent, but such far-flung borders were scarcely tenable in the face of rising perils. Byzantium was almost constantly threatened, often on two fronts. Before long, the empire embraced only what it was able successfully to defend.

From the reign of the emperor Maurikios (582–602) on, the empire's policy was mainly defensive, and this was to remain its strategy for centuries to come. Byzantium pursued above all a defensive policy in the face of threats, or at best an offensive defensive policy.[18] The reforms introduced by Maurikios were of great importance: he ensured the security of the frontiers through a

---

18. That is to say, taking the offensive for defensive motives, the purpose being more to maintain a status quo or ward off a threat than to extend domination.

system of distributing land to the soldiers of the themes. The theme system, which rested on local forces, made it possible to contain foreign intervention long enough for reinforcements to arrive. A strategic reserve was built up, and lines of fortified strongpoints were constructed in sensitive areas. A chain of over fifty fortresses defended the Danube, for example.

As a theorist, Maurikios condemned the line system, and for battle advocated, not penetration through shock, but envelopment, doubtless having learnt the lessons of the tactics used by the nomads from the steppes. Byzantine conceptions of war were much more developed than those of the feudal West. As against the direct approach of the Franks, whose heavy cavalry used shock tactics, the Byzantines preferred an indirect strategy, and, like every threatened empire, thought of war in all its dimensions. Diplomacy played a major role; war was only a last resort, and if it came to that, attempts were made to seek allies in the enemy's rear. The Byzantine empire was more of a sea power even than Rome. Reinforcements were sent by sea rather than by land, as, for example, when Heraclius (610–41) was fighting the Sassanids, in a remarkable campaign of envelopment and attack from the rear.

Byzantine sailors, whose dromonds (biremes) covered the Mediterranean, had a considerable asset in Greek fire, invented in 673 and used successfully against Muslim fleets in 677 and again in 717–18, at the time of the siege of Constantinople by the Arabs, and later against the Kievan Russians in 941 and 1043.

Made up of patient prudence, stratagems, knowledge of the enemy, and sometimes the use of terror, as against the Bulgars under Basil II in the tenth century, the Byzantine art of war as practiced between the seventh and tenth centuries can be likened to that of Sun Zi: there was the same idea that war is a phenomenon that lends itself to rational analysis, the same strategy of wearing down and demoralizing the enemy. There was none of the chivalry and ritual of western Europe, where strategic thinking was at best in its infancy.

What is exceptional in Maurikios, as later in Leo VI, is that the enemy, instead of being abstract, as in classical strategic treatises, is described and analyzed in terms of his behavior, his virtues, his weaknesses, and his manner of fighting. Never in the history of strategy has the famous advice "Know your enemy" been applied with such seriousness and so concretely.[19] It is difficult for us to grasp how new the idea was that it was necessary to understand the strategic cultures of different opponents in order to be in a better position to thwart them. Different enemies require different solutions.

---

19. In his *Germania,* Tacitus sketches an ethnology of the Germans, but, not being a strategist, he does not explain how to fight them. Curiously, in the thirteenth century, it was the inspired Franciscan Giovanni of Plano Carpino who, dealing with the Mongols, rediscovered the importance of knowing one's enemy. So, later, did Ibn Khaldun.

In the sixth and seventh centuries, Byzantium fought the Huns and Avars and adapted to the fighting techniques of mounted archers. In the seventh century, the empire was simultaneously fighting the Avars and the Slavs in the Balkans. In the east, the fight was against the Sassanids, not to annihilate them—as was the aim with the nomads and the Slavs—but to ensure respect for a zone of influence.

Just when the Byzantine and Sassanid empires were exhausted by a long conflict, the Muslim threat made its appearance. Following the death of the Prophet, the Arabs embarked on a lightning expansion. In less than fifteen years, Iran collapsed, while Byzantium lost Syria-Palestine and Egypt. Halted at the Cilician Gates, the Arabs sought to challenge the Byzantine empire for supremacy at sea. But Byzantium resisted, and in 717–18, the last Arab siege of Constantinople was a failure. The true bastion of Christianity in the seventh century was the Byzantine empire. The halt that it put to the Arab advance in 718 was far more important than the victory of 732 at Poitiers. After the fall of Constantinople in 1453, the Muslims were able to advance as far as Vienna (1529).

In his *Taktika*, the emperor Leo VI (who paraphrased both Onasander and Maurikios) introduced a number of new features; it was also a treatise that, like Vegetius's, constituted a summation of the strategic thinking that had preceded it: "Analyzing the causes of the success of Islam and how to put an end to it, [Leo] was led to think comparatively about the organization of the empire, the mode of recruitment of the soldiers and their integration into society and on the situation of a state engaged in constant warfare," writes Georges Dagron.[20]

Emperor Leo's thinking about this new adversary with a universal appeal, quite unlike the barbarians of the steppes, led him, a century before the Crusades, to envisage the idea of a war in the name of Christendom.

In Nicephorus Phocas's work on guerrilla warfare, we can see how, for over two centuries, Byzantine horsemen protected the Cilician frontier against Islam. Such horsemen, patrolling the borders of the empire with their own special esprit de corps, were later also to be found under the Hapsburg empire in the shape of Hungarian hussars, Croatian pandours, and Albanian stradiots, waging the same mounted war of harassment against the Ottomans. This military frontier *(Militärgrenze)* guard created in the sixteenth century, often with refugees from the Balkans, was only dissolved in 1869.

Before long, other threats appeared: the Hungarians, the Kievan Russians, and, above all, the Bulgars. The war against the Bulgars was the main business

---

20. Nicephorus II, Phocas, *Le Traité sur la guérilla (De velitatione)*, trans. with commentary by Georges Dagron (Paris: Ed. du CNRS, 1986), p. 85.

of the reign of Basil II (976–1025). Defense became chronically bipolar: in the west the frontier along the Danube was under pressure from the Bulgars; in the east, there was the Muslim threat in Anatolia. The decline of Byzantium began at the end of the tenth century, but the empire had enough wind and resources to survive almost four hundred years longer.

On land as on sea, the Byzantine empire established its supremacy over a period of at least six centuries under a series of remarkable emperors.[21] In the ninth century A.D., a series of innovations in defensive siegecraft was introduced. The number of surrounding walls was increased; outworks were interposed; the height and, above all, the thickness of walls was increased, and walls were built with standard blocks, cemented, and reinforced with metal joints; and round towers (more resistant to battering rams than angle towers) were constructed with salients and recesses, all protected by wider and deeper ditches.

These innovations manifest a quite remarkable military art, whose true originality is too little known.[22] This is partly because the Byzantine empire was long unjustly scorned because of its religious disputes; however, such disputes were for at least a thousand years just as much a feature of both the Catholic Church and Islam.

THE BEGINNINGS OF ISLAM

The initial expansion of the Arabs following the death of Muhammad in 632 was prodigious. A political and military empire was organized in the space of a few decades based on a religion with a universal vocation. Part of this drive came from the fact that Islam provides religious justification for war. The notion of the jihad, a holy war waged on behalf of God, like that of *shahid,* martyrdom for the faith, is to be found more than once in the Koran: "And call not those who are slain in the way of Allah 'dead'. Nay, they are living, only ye perceive not" (2.154).[23] With the introduction of Islam, the faith and discipline

21. Heraclius I (610–41); Leo III, the Isaurian (717–41); Basil I (867–86), who restored the border on the Euphrates; Romanus I, Lecapenus (919–44), who reconquered Armenia; Nicephorus Phocas (963–69); John I, Tzimisces (969–76); Basil II, Bulgaroctonus (976–1025); and Alexis I, Comnenus (1081–1118).

22. Contemporary works of relevance include Nicephorus Uranus's *Tactics* and Kekaumenos's *Strategikon;* see J. F. Haldon, *Some Aspects of Byzantine Military Technology from the Sixth to the Tenth Century* (London, 1975).

23. *The Meaning of the Glorious Koran,* trans. M. M. Pickthall (New York, 1953), 2: 154. On the jihad, see E. Khadduri, *War and Peace in the Law of Islam,* (Baltimore, 1955). On Muslims at war, see also the *Encyclopaedia of Islam* (London: Luzac, 1934).

born of the Koranic precepts were added to the individual qualities of the Bedouin fighter. This was not an army of mercenaries, ready to mutiny as soon as it was not paid, but of volunteers, soldiers of God. In terms of numbers, the alliance between the various tribes of Arabia certainly made it possible to put ten or fifteen thousand men in line, and it must be remembered that, under Justinian, Belisarius undertook his victorious campaign against the Vandals and the Goths with fifteen thousand soldiers. The proverbial individual warrior qualities of the Bedouin are well known. "The nomads live an isolated life. They are not defended by walls. Therefore, they provide their own defense. They always carry weapons and are ever on the watch; they watch carefully for the least sign of danger, putting their trust in their fortitude and their strength. Fortitude has become a character quality of theirs, and courage their second nature," writes Ibn-Khaldun.

As sons of the desert, the Arabs won their victories largely because they fought their decisive battles against Persia and Byzantium in the desert: "The key to all the early operations, against Persia and against Syria alike, is that the Persians and Byzantines could not move in the desert, being mounted on horses. The Muslims were like a sea-power cruising off shore," Glubb Pasha observes.[24] Rather like the Norse and Danish pirates who raided England, the Arabs were at first afraid to move far "inland." Raiding fringe areas, the "shores" of the desert, they hastened back to their own element when danger threatened. Except for the "battle of the Bridge" in 635, when the Arabs made the mistake of crossing the Euphrates and fighting with their backs to the river, the Persians were always engaged on the desert side. When, after a prolonged resistance, the Byzantine armies collapsed at the battle of the River Yarmak in 636, a sandstorm helped the Muslim forces.

Less than half a dozen years after the death of the Prophet, the mobile and highly motivated armies of the Muslims had conquered both the forces of Byzantium in Syria-Palestine (Yarmak, 636) and the Persians at Kadisiya (636). Penetration into Mesopotamia began; Damascus had already fallen into the hands of the Muslims in 635. On the one side, they advanced as far as Antioch, at the foot of the Taurus mountains, and on the other as far as Ctesiphon on the Tigris (in 641). By 638, they appeared irresistible. Byzantium was able to counterattack and retain control of Asia Minor, but Muslim expansion continued eastward, toward the borders of central Asia and India, and westward into Egypt. Given the maritime superiority of the Byzantine empire, the conquest of Egypt, at least in the Nile Delta, might have been very difficult. But the Byzantine patriarch, who himself had continuously oppressed the Copts,

---

24. J. B. Glubb, *The Great Arab Conquests* (London: Hodder and Stoughton, 1963).

chose to submit after a single defeat in battle. By 641, the Arabs controlled Egypt from the east bank of the Nile, except for Alexandria, which submitted in 642.

The conquest of Persia continued on two fronts: along a line in the south from Basra to Ahvaz[25] and a northern line, running from the Tigris, by way of the foothills of the Zagros mountains, to Nehavend (642). Following their victory at Nehavend, the Arabs occupied Ecbatana (Hamadan), and the Persians fought no further large-scale battles. Nevertheless, resistance continued, tenaciously, and the Persians, once Islamized, were the first to reassert their identity.

The Arabs suffered a reverse in the Sudan but moved victoriously toward Tripoli, which they took in 643. In a dozen years (632–44), from the reign of the caliphs Abu Bakr and 'Umar on, there was a period of uninterrupted expansion, and these successes had to do with the fact that the conquered populations were not subjected to systematic forced conversions. Provided that they paid tribute, the "peoples of the book" (Jews and Christians) could continue to practice their faiths. Two of the greatest empires in the world had been defeated, and the Arab conquests proved durable.

Although the Arab expansion was halted in the north by the barrier of the Caucasus, it spread to east and northwest Africa. North Africa was, at least nominally, under the suzerainty of the Byzantine empire, but the Arabs had provided themselves with a fleet by 650, and Byzantine naval supremacy was strongly challenged from 655 on. In 652, the last Sassanid ruler disappeared.[26]

After the assassination of the caliph 'Uthman in 656, civil war broke out over the succession ('Ali's candidacy, etc.). In fact, the great Arab caliphate reached what was almost its military apogee in a quarter of a century (632–56). Schisms and heresies shook the Arab empire, but it nevertheless resumed its advance across North Africa, against tenacious Berber resistance, after the assassination of 'Ali in 661. In 711 the strait of Gibraltar was crossed, and in a decade almost the whole of the Iberian peninsula had been conquered. Constantinople was besieged, unsuccessfully, for a first time in 670 and again in 717. In the east, by the end of the seventh century, the Muslim conquest had reached central Asia (713) and the barrier of the Indus (710). In fewer than fifty years, the Arabs had conquered a vast empire, which, militarily, lasted for two and a half centuries. Only Alexander had previously achieved such vast conquests, but his were much less durable. Muslim expansion, the bulk of which occurred between 632 and 680, profoundly transformed the world.

---

25. This was the same route that the Iraqi armies took in 1980.

26. It was not until the sixteenth century that a new Persian dynasty, the Safavids, established itself.

THE TURKS

The Islamization of the Turks, warriors from the steppes, gave a new military impetus to the Muslim world. The Seljuk Turks took Baghdad in 1055 and in 1071 won a great victory over the Byzantine emperor Romanus IV at Manzikert. Between 1078 and 1084, they secured control of Syria-Palestine. By the beginning of the fourteenth century, the Ottoman empire was a formidable military power. Despite the resistance of Byzantium, the Ottomans established themselves in the Balkans and won a series of victories there.

The Seljuks were the first Muslims that the crusaders encountered. Turkish cavalry tactics were in the tradition of the archer-horsemen of the steppes: harassment of the enemy with volleys of arrows and attempts to envelop him. Once the enemy was seriously weakened by means of arrows, the Turks closed in on horseback with swords or maces. The first clash between crusaders and Muslims took place at Dorylaea in 1097. After being put in danger, the first body of crusaders was saved by the arrival of a second. But Bohemond of Taranto, a Norman, quickly realized the need to adapt to Turkish tactics.[27]

What emerges from the subsequent history of the Crusades is the great difference between the crusaders who were established in the Holy Land, who knew their adversary and had adapted to him, and those Franks who had only recently arrived on a crusade, often for the first time, who out of feudal bravura sought dazzling, dramatic action without being properly organized, for which they often paid dearly.

THE MONGOLS AND THE WORLD EMPIRE

In the thirteenth century, the Mongols burst like thunder over the whole of the Eurasian landmass. The unity of the Mongols was achieved by Genghis Khan in 1207. The first invasions of sedentary nations began almost at once: the Chinese world (1209–16), followed by the Muslim world (Khwarizm, a Muslim state comprised of Turkestan, Persia, and parts of Afghanistan, fell in 1219–21) and eastern Europe (1219–23). After the death of Genghis Khan in 1227, his son Ogadai (r. 1229–41) conquered northern China and the Russian plain and penetrated as far as central Europe. It is not surprising that nomadic herdsmen (sheep are essential to the Mongols) and hunters, dependent on their mobility, their skill and their frugality, should be fine warriors. What

---

27. It was only after 1150 that the great Kurdish warrior Saladin achieved the unity of Syria and Egypt and was able to defeat his Frankish enemies.

made them exceptional was the organization achieved by Genghis. The vast empire, which retained its unity until 1259 (the date of the great Khan Möngke's death), was subject to a single law, the *yasa* proclaimed by Genghis.

Victory rapidly followed victory: Beijing fell in 1215; Bukhara and Samarkand in 1220. A reconnaissance raid through Armenia and Georgia reached into southern Russia in 1223. After the death of Genghis Khan, the conquest continued. Baiju defeated the Seljuk sultanate. Another general, Subotaï, defeated the Turks and Volga Bulgars (1236–39) and, between 1237 and 1240, seized Riazan, Vladimir, and Kiev one after the other.

In 1241, Hungarian forces were crushed, as were Polish and German ones. Only the death of the great khan Ogadai saved central Europe, as the Mongol troops were nearing Vienna. Baghdad was taken in 1258, and Damascus in 1260.

In the Far East, Kublai Khan (1215–94) seized Song China, and Mongol troops reached as far as Burma and Tonkin; they even made two attempts to land in Japan.

Mongol strength was based on strict, extremely mobile organization. A Mongol army transported its own supplies, and the leaders of mounted columns had very wide autonomy. Their coordination over vast distances (between 1219 and 1221, Mongol raids covered 6,500 kilometers, from the Altai mountains to Tbilisi) and their capacity to concentrate were quite extraordinary: their flanking or encircling maneuvers, unexpected by infinitely more static adversaries, were quite prodigious. For a century, the Mongols held sway over China (the Yuan dynasty), and for over two centuries, over Russia. The "Pax mongolica" enabled European envoys and traders to travel in complete safety into previously insecure regions for almost one hundred and fifty years.

The chronicles of the defeated—Chinese, Persians, Arabs, Armenians, Georgians, and Russians—naturally record only the terrifying aspect of the Mongol irruption and tell us rather little about the Mongols' organization. It is observers and eyewitnesses of the Mongol empire once it was organized who tell us most about their military organization.

Units were organized on a decimal system.[28] Initially, the Mongol armies consisted entirely of light cavalry. Each man had four or five horses and was equipped with two bows, a short one, to be used while moving on horseback, and a longer, more accurate one. However, before long the demands of warfare against Chinese and Persians modified and improved these forces. The Mongols learned from the Muslims how to use siege equipment and engineering units.[29] At least in the beginning, the Mongols also pushed forward

28. A regiment (*mingham*) consisted of a thousand men; ten regiments constituted a division or army corps (*tumen*); a Mongol army usually comprised three *tumen*, or thirty thousand men.

29. The Mongols used Muslim siege engines, the most advanced then in existence, against the southern Song in 1268–73.

successive waves of captives when besieging a city, who were sacrificed to fill the ditches.

Campaigns were minutely prepared; information, naturally, was vital. There was also psychological warfare: people were promised the end of their oppression or freedom of worship, or they were guaranteed their lives if they surrendered without resistance.

The task of coordinating army corps and armies fell to special couriers, who were continually at the ready. The Mongols always had light troops a day ahead as scouts. The normal order of battle included five lines, each of a single rank, with long intervals between lines—sometimes over a hundred meters. The first two lines were made up of heavy, armored cavalry, equipped with hooked spears (to unhorse the adversary), swords, and maces. The next three lines were made up of light cavalry without armor, equipped with bows. When battle was joined, the light cavalry passed through the spaced-out lines of heavy cavalry and, as they rained down volley after volley of arrows at point-blank range, elements of this cavalry enveloped the enemy's wings. Sometimes, a column would take the enemy from behind by surprise. Once disorganized, the enemy's forces suffered the shock of the heavy cavalry, which completed the breach, leaving a way out for the defeated opponents so as to massacre them more conveniently in the pursuit. Maneuvers were signaled by raising or lowering standards, which was done in close coordination, based on relentless discipline. The Mongol army would very often feign a retreat, which might last for days, until the scattered and exhausted enemy fell into an ambush.

The defeated enemy was always annihilated, either in pursuit, however long it might take, or in an ambush that caught an enemy with exhausted horses in a trap. The Mongol cavalry, for its part, had three or four remounts for each horseman. Combined with the endurance and frugality of nomads, this meant that the latter were vastly more mobile than any of their opponents. This extreme mobility provided security, and Mongol reconnaissance was so elaborate that in a century no chronicler reports any attack or counterattack taking the Mongols by surprise.

It is interesting to note that instinctively, but also thanks to the organizing genius of Genghis Khan, his successors, and their generals, in a considerable advance (they had everything except artillery), the Mongols employed the same tactics of mobility, dispersal, concentration, and pursuit to complete the annihilation of the enemy that Napoleon, an irregular of genius, subsequently rediscovered after a long tradition of limited-goal strategy.

A little more than a century after the death of Genghis, another nomad from the steppes, this time a Muslim, Timur, or Tamerlane, took up the task of bringing together the legacy of the great Mongol. In Persia, the Mongol khanate was weakened, and by about 1370, the Ottomans were advancing in

Asia Minor, but Timur crushed the forces of the Ottoman sultan Bayazid I at Ankara in 1402. He used terror more systematically, but his political ideas seem to have been less coherent than those of the earlier Mongol great khans.

THE OTTOMANS

Once the counteroffensive of the Crusades was over, the Ottomans, whose dynasty began in 1299, moved into the Balkans, despite Byzantium, and seized Adrianople in 1361. The Armenian kingdom of Cilicia, long associated with the crusaders, was crushed in 1375. In 1389, an army consisting of Serbs, Bulgars, Albanians, Poles, and Hungarians were defeated at Kossovo in Serbia. The crusader knights were beaten at Nicopolis in 1396. When he crushed the forces of Bayazid I near Ankara in 1402, Timur gave the Byzantine empire one last respite, but the cannon triumphed over the walls of Constantinople in 1453. The Greek empire of Trebizond disappeared in 1461. Ottoman power was at its zenith between about 1451 and 1566, after when it experienced a relative decline up to 1683.

In 1456, the Hungarian voivode János Hunyadi was defeated at Belgrade, but the Albanian leader Skanderbeg, who was supported by Venice, held out against the Ottoman advance between 1443 and 1468. In 1474, the Crimea was invaded, and in 1514–15, the Ottomans conquered Azerbaijan and Kurdistan. Three years later, Syria and Egypt were attacked; Baghdad was taken, and the Ottoman sultan assumed the title of caliph. In 1526, a Hungarian army was crushingly defeated at Mohács, and Budapest fell in 1540. Although the first siege of Vienna had failed in 1529, the Ottoman empire occupied the Balkans and the countries along the Danube and embarked on a long struggle against the Hapsburgs. The coast of Arabia (Aden, 1539) and North Africa as far as Algeria (1516) also passed into Ottoman hands.

Unlike most armies of the period, the permanent core of the Ottoman forces received regular pay. The elite were rewarded by revenues charged to lands, but the fiefs were not hereditary and the sultan thus maintained complete power over his dignitaries. Militarily, the Ottoman empire was the strongest power of the time.

The elite troops, the janissaries (*yeniçeri*, "new army"), formed a permanent body of highly disciplined professionals; originally they were volunteers who were forbidden to marry, but, with time, their ranks were swollen by the forcible recruitment of boys, often selected from among the Christian subjects of the empire. These were brought up in the Muslim faith and exclusively trained to the profession of arms. Each platoon of janissaries was made up of ten men, and ten platoons formed a company, or *oda*. In the fourteenth century, these elite troops numbered some five thousand men; later their numbers tripled. In the early centuries, cavalry armed with bows protected the janissaries' flanks. By the beginning of the sixteenth century, the Ottoman army was over 100,000 strong and possessed powerful artillery. Campaigns were usually short and lasted predominantly from May to October. The classical Ottoman disposition placed infantry battalions in the center and the cavalry on the wings, arrayed in a concave formation to attempt an enveloping maneuver. A battle was a succession of rapid attacks followed by withdrawals and feints to dislocate or weaken the enemy's lines.[30]

Although not made up of professional sailors like the Venetians, the Ottoman fleet was formidable and was only defeated at Lepanto in 1571 by a coalition of some of the fleets of Christendom.

THE WEST FROM THE FOURTEENTH
TO THE SIXTEENTH CENTURIES

In the Middle Ages in the West, warfare was a codified, ritual activity, essentially reserved to nobles—at least as regards the major arm, the cavalry.[31] This superiority of horse over foot soldier was as much social as strictly military. In 1315, at Morgarten, a reversal occurred: the Swiss infantry cut Leopold I of Austria's cavalry to pieces. The pike was an effective weapon provided the Swiss square retained its cohesion: the first four ranks lowered their weapons, and the rear ranks replaced those who fell in the front ones. Early on, the square was strictly defensive; later, it became offensive. The Swiss reigned as the supreme infantry for almost two centuries. It may be that this innovation is to be attributed to the cantonal democracy forged by these hardy mountain-dwellers. In the West, the Swiss infantry was the first disciplined force since Rome.

It was not until 1515 that the Swiss were defeated by the French artillery, at Marignano. Before long, the Swiss were being rivaled by German landsknechts, who defeated them at La Biocca in 1522. The number of free companies of mercenaries, predominantly made up of Germans, Frenchmen, and Italians, began to increase. By the end of the fifteenth century, the arquebus was coming into use, and in the sixteenth century, the musket. Infantry once again became decisive in western Europe, as it had become once again with the janissaries in the Ottoman empire.

30. In the seventeenth century, when the Ottoman empire was in decline, the Hapsburg general Raimondo de Montecuccoli recommended the following tactics as best adapted to blocking Muslim troops: fire regulated by rank so as to be continuous; using the best troops on the flanks; banning heavy cavalry from letting itself be drawn into any pursuit (it must cover the infantry's flanks throughout the battle). He defeated the Ottoman army in 1664.

31. Michael Howard's *War in European History* (London: Oxford University Press, 1976) is a masterpiece of clarity and conciseness on warfare in Europe from the Middle Ages to the present.

Strategic innovations were relatively few in number.[32] The most original was the use by the Hussite general Jan Zizka in Bohemia of light artillery mounted on trolleys, which could themselves be used as defensive structures (1420–24), against the Catholic German armies. This artillery was employed in conjunction with bows, crossbows, pikes, and maces.

However, wars waged with mercenaries were expensive, and their limited objectives meant that battles were avoided, as was especially the case with the condottieri. In the sixteenth century, the inadequacy of firepower compared to the advances of fortification (which the Italian engineers Sangallo and San Michele had improved in the course of the century) rendered a bold strategy against a system of fortified places impotent. The Spanish *tercios* became the most remarkable infantry force in the sixteenth and early seventeenth centuries. The great captain Gonsalvo de Cordoba combined arquebuses and pikes in equal proportions, and the firepower of the *tercio* (a 3,000-man infantry regiment) was considerable for the time.

For almost a hundred years, from the second third of the sixteenth century to the first third of the seventeenth, there were almost no battles in western Europe. Operations were aimed at exhausting the enemy's treasury and living off the enemy's land. This dilatory strategy sought to wage war cheaply through maneuvers and sieges and by striking at the enemy's communications. Operations stopped for the winter. These interminable wars ravaged rural populations especially (as in the Thirty Years' War).

Maurice of Nassau, the commander of the forces of the United Provinces (the independent Netherlands), was one of the most important generals of the time. Thanks to the system of fortifications established by Simon Stevinus, and by paying his forces regularly, he secured remarkable results both in siege warfare and in battle itself (Nieuwpoort, 1600). He also correctly assessed the growing importance and potential of firepower, which became decisive only in the second half of the eighteenth century.[33] The United Provinces created the professional army in western Europe.

However, outside the European theater, major developments were under way as the sixteenth century began. The Portuguese and Spanish discoveries of the Americas were being followed in a single movement by the Spanish conquest of Mexico and Peru.

Although regarded as secondary even by modern analysts, these conquests are extremely interesting from a military point of view. They foreshadowed

32. Inventions of this period included the bronze cannonball (1463), the pistol (1483), and the incendiary ball (1487).

33. The adoption of firearms occurred very gradually from the first third of the fifteenth century to the mid seventeenth century; they came to be decisive only in the second half of the eighteenth century.

later colonial conquests in the eighteenth and nineteenth centuries and showed the fragility of centralized states and empires, like Peru, that rested on the authority of a ruler regarded as a god. Aside from the disunity of the Indians, the Spaniards' success is largely explained by their different concept of warfare, their superior weaponry, their unity and determination, and the fact that they had cavalry, but the role played by epidemics in the case of Mexico was also extremely important. Guatemala, Colombia, Argentina, and Chile were also being conquered, and it was the societies without an organized state that resisted Spanish penetration best and longest, as they were more difficult to disrupt (for example, the Araucans in Chile and the Chichimecs in northern Mexico). Once the leaders of the highly hierarchical societies of the Aztecs and the Incas were removed, they collapsed in disarray.

While western Europeans, and more specifically Iberians, were invading the American continent, the Russians were resuming the initiative, driving back the Mongols, and then, with the help of the Cossacks, occupying southern Siberia all the way to the sea. Under the pressure of European maritime expansion, the theater of conflict began to become worldwide in the sixteenth century.

THE SEVENTEENTH AND
EIGHTEENTH CENTURIES

Gustavus Adolphus (1594–1632), the greatest general of his time, ordered a general levy in 1612. His army, at least initially, was overwhelmingly composed of Swedes. He created a new instrument by tackling the organization and training of military officers and concerning himself with tactical improvements: more mobile artillery, better muskets, and, finally, coordinating shock troops with firepower. The cavalry recovered its former importance.

Thanks to Richelieu, the end of the Thirty Years' War in 1648 marked the beginning of France's long military domination of the continent, which lasted until the battle of Waterloo.

Until the beginning of the sixteenth century, the navy had been scarcely more mobile than land forces, but it now began to assume growing importance. As Michael Howard points out, cannon played a key role in the development of naval warfare:

Until the fifteenth century war at sea was an extension of war at land. The object in battle was to close with the enemy vessel, board it, and overwhelm the crew. The most effective warship was thus, as it had been throughout antiquity, the oared galley, independent of wind or tide for its propulsion and carrying armed forces to board, fight and capture the enemy. . . .

... With guns mounted along flush decks, even merchantmen [under sail] could more than hold their own against war galleys whose guns could only be mounted in prow and stern. So for a time the distinction between warship and merchantman almost disappeared. It was to reappear in the eighteenth century when gun power became all important and warships had to crowd on board as many guns as the decks would hold if they were to take their place in the battle line; but in the meantime it was hardly worth putting a ship to sea unless it could both carry a cargo *and* fight. It was a period when war, discovery, and trade were almost interchangeable terms.[34]

The Dutch chiefly, but also the English and the French, dominated the seas following the Thirty Years' War. It was only at the end of the eighteenth century, and decisively following the battle of Trafalgar in 1805, that Britain, having defeated its rivals, emerged as mistress of the seas for a century and a half.

It was not until the second half of the seventeenth century that a number of European rulers—and especially the king of France—acquired a capacity to control their countries' resources. The state began to exercise its prerogatives more tightly, and it is only from this period that rulers began to have standing armies that could be used both for defense against the foreigner and as an instrument of domestic control. France went furthest in this direction, although Oliver Cromwell (1599–1658), a military innovator, was able to create an army with a cavalry that was both regularly paid and disciplined. These two features were exceptional at the time, and, combined with an offensive posture and a judicious combination of firepower and shock tactics, gave Cromwell sufficient superiority, to which was added a militant religious ideology.

Thus it can be said that the European art of war only really began to flower in the second half of the seventeenth century. On the continent, the state played a considerable part in this; in England, protected by its island position, the state, like the army, had a smaller role.

The dynastic state consolidated itself in the fifteenth century. It gained depth—that is, control—in the second half of the seventeenth century, especially in France, and, in its administrative capabilities, foreshadowed the time when, at the end of the eighteenth century, it sprang up fully armed, a concept with formidable military consequences.

France played a key role when the power of Spain and the Hapsburgs was declining. The conditions required for the exercise of military power were put in place by Richelieu and brought to fruition by Michel Le Tellier and, under Louis XIV, by his son, Louvois. Not only was the largest standing army the

---

34. Howard, *War in European History* (Oxford University Press, 1963), pp. 40–41.

world had ever seen created (by 1680, France had some 300,000 men in line), but a civilian bureaucracy (war commissioners) to administer the army was established. The French pattern of an organized and administered professional army was copied by other powers in western Europe.[35] Vauban exemplifies the military creativity of the time.

In the second half of the seventeenth century, besides Charles XII of Sweden, a number of highly talented commanders began to appear, among them Turenne, Condé, Montecuccoli, Eugene of Savoy, Marshal Luxembourg, and Marlborough. Wars nevertheless remained the affair of kings. In the course of the following century, when dynastic conflicts with limited objectives developed in Europe, wars were fought on the cheap if possible (battles being very costly in lives)[36] in campaigns lasting no more than five or six months, complicated by the need to move a large magazine train. Frederick II of Prussia was the great military figure of the eighteenth century, when firepower finally took on a decisive role in battle.

Jacques de Guibert (1743–90) had, however, already heralded a new type of warfare in his *Essai général de tactique*. Classical strategy was transformed in the second part of the eighteenth century. Artillery had been improved in terms of mobility and standardized by Jean de Gribeauval (1715–89); the divisional system and, soon after, under the influence of Guibert, the mixed order were introduced. Deep order was preferred to thin order because now it was offensive shock and no longer the defensive line that was sought.[37] A light infantry composed of *voltigeurs* was created.[38] Yet it was not technical innovations that were mainly responsible for revolutionizing warfare,[39] but the new idea of the sovereign nation promulgated by the French Revolution. The *levée en masse*, mass conscription, now made its appearance in western Europe's most populous country.

TOWARD TOTAL WAR

With the French Revolution, war ceased to be the affair of dynasties and became that of nations. This signaled the beginning of a period, lasting a century

35. French influence on the Prussian army of the Hohenzollern was further promoted by the Huguenot refugees in the Protestant German states following the revocation of the Edict of Nantes in 1685.

36. Marlborough, although the victor, lost a third of his men at Malplaquet in 1709, and Frederick the Great lost half his at Kunersdorf in 1758.

37. Jean Charles de Folard (1669–1752) had been a strong advocate of the attacking column.

38. Small units that moved where needed, which broke with the rigid order of the armies of the eighteenth century.

39. The geographical campaign map, for example, appeared in the late eighteenth century.

and a half, of what Clausewitz called "absolute wars," which we have gradually come to call total wars.

The political and social upheavals in France had profound repercussions on military organization after 1793. The army was based on the national state, which became the expression of the nation: the nation was mobilized. By January 1794, there were over half a million men under arms. War had changed nature: it was now all-out war.

Napoleon, who inherited the conditions created by the French Revolution, organized the army, as Howard puts it, "according to a pattern which was to be adopted by all European forces for the next century and a half; one which made possible almost unlimited decentralization under a single supreme command."[40] With Napoleon, for a variety of reasons, there came to an end almost four centuries of Western strategy that had most commonly been dilatory. Generals like Gustavus Adolphus, Cromwell, Turenne, Prince Eugene, and Marlborough did, of course, seek battle, but Napoleon systematically sought it with intention of delivering a decisive blow. The aim of strategy became to crush the opposing forces utterly. Napoleon not only compelled a decision by concentrating his troops, through rapid forced marches,[41] at what was deemed the decisive point, but pursued the defeated enemy to ensure a complete rout.

It was the catastrophe of Jena in 1806 that precipitated the Prussian military renaissance (typified by Scharnhorst, Gneisenau, Boyen, and Clausewitz) and the ideas that underlay it. Only a patriotic army could alter things, but the dangerous ideas of the Revolution were precisely the ones that the dynasties and aristocracies of Europe wanted to stifle.[42] The Prussian command succeeded in breaking with the practice of reserving access to an officer's career exclusively to the nobility. After 1813, Prussian patriotism manifested itself, and the grand coalition of all the sovereigns of Europe ended up victorious. But the art of war continued to be marked by the personality of Napoleon, which, willy-nilly, fascinated both Clausewitz and the Swiss Antoine de Jomini.

Both the Prussians and the Russians retained large armies. By 1821, however, Britain, protected by its maritime superiority, had reduced its troops from

---

40. Howard, *War in European History*, p. 83. The Napoleonic army was divided into army corps, themselves made up of two or three divisions of ten thousand men each. Two battalions made up a regiment, two regiments a brigade, and two brigades a division.

41. The load carried by a soldier was considerably reduced; he no longer camped in a tent, he bivouacked under his coat.

42. The other ranks in all European armies, except the French, continued to be made up of marginal men looked down on by aristocratic officers; the two worlds rubbed shoulders without ever communicating except through warrant officers. These relations continued to prevail in most armies until the beginning of the twentieth century.

685,000 to 100,000 men, half of them in the colonies. For half a century, apart from the Crimean War (1853–56), the British army—like the French army between 1830 and 1870—devoted much effort to maintaining order domestically and in the colonies.

The nineteenth century was the century of industrialization and the rise of new powers, especially of Germany and, to a lesser extent, of Russia and the United States. The military power of the United States did not yet reflect its capacities, but the American Civil War was nonetheless the first modern, industrial war, with railroads playing a key role (as did maritime communications).

In the nineteenth century, the population of Europe rose from 185 to 400 million. The populations of Germany and Great Britain tripled; that of the United States increased almost fifteenfold as a result of immigration. Among the great nations, only France stagnated demographically. Thanks to its domination of the seas, unchallenged after 1805, Britain was the world's leading financial, industrial, and colonial power until 1890, the year when the industrial power of the United States overtook that of the leading continental European industrial power, Germany.

The military innovations of the nineteenth century, as already pointed out, had largely to do with industrialization and scientific advances. Railroads revolutionized the movement of men and matériel, the concentration of troops and logistics. Firepower underwent a total transformation after 1870: the rifle and the rifled musket had already been introduced; now came the breech-loading gun; advances in artillery; and the Gatling machine gun (1863) and the Maxim (1884), two vital weapons in colonial conquest; which all favored well-organized defensive tactics. Sanitary conditions gradually changed after the Crimean War (1853–56). Up to that time, the overwhelming majority of casualties in war (five to one) were actually caused by epidemics or the consequences of wounds, rather than being deaths in battle. By the end of the century, this proportion had been reversed. The electric telegraph altered the relationship between the front and the rear, which, at a time of increasingly assertive and aggressive nationalisms, became more and more involved in war, as war came increasingly to be seen as a national affair.

One of the century's military innovations was the establishment by Prussia of a new type of general staff, a political and military instrument whose influence was to be decisive until the middle of the twentieth century. Gerhard von Scharnhorst laid the groundwork for the general staff, but it really took shape with its total reform by Helmuth von Moltke. By 1821, there were already 56 officers in the great general staff and the offices directly associated with it. Under Moltke, the general staff enjoyed virtual autonomy from the Ministry of War (by 1883, the general staff and the military cabinet had become administratively independent of the Ministry of War). The general staff paid special attention to military theory, and there was frequent rotation between the great general staff and general staff officers so as to circulate and stimulate creative ideas.[43]

Entry to the Military Academy was by examination. Those who graduated (50 out of a total of 150 by the end of the century) were assigned to the great general staff for two years, during which they were responsible for organizing maneuvers, map exercises, and war games (*Kriegspielen*). After that, three or four of the probationers became permanent members of the general staff. The rest occupied the posts assigned to them and received rapid promotion. On the eve of the Franco-Prussian war in 1870, most Prussian senior officers had undergone such training.

The long French military hegemony, which had lasted since the second half of the seventeenth century, had ended. After 1871, every state in continental Europe copied the Prussian system. Three decades later, so did Britain and the United States.

However, technology had brought about more radical changes than the best-informed general staffs foresaw. Contrary to predictions, World War I was a long one. Notwithstanding the primacy assigned to attack, defense often proved necessary. New weaponry had rendered war static and costly in men and resources.[44] In the last analysis, leaving mortality aside, the factors that were ever more important were industrial and financial means. On that account, the Allied coalition, backed by the United States, could not lose.

During World War I, along with mass propaganda, a series of new weapons made their appearance: the submarine, the tank (which was to have its heyday in World War II) and the airplane. From beginning to end, warfare at sea played a vital role. War now involved mass mobilization, and became increasingly the preserve of experts in certain areas (air war, naval war, tanks, etc.).

In World War II, the Germans used tactics based on mobility (Heinz Guderian), initially demoralizing their enemies, who were still fighting the previous war, with a combination of tanks and airpower. Basil Liddell Hart and J. F. C. Fuller, Franz Eimansberger and Charles de Gaulle, had

43. Walter Görlitz, *History of the German General Staff, 1657–1945*, trans. B. Battershaw (New York: Greenwood, 1953).

44. "A regiment of field guns could in 1914 deliver on to a target area of a few hundred square yards more destructive power in an hour than had been fired by all the guns on both sides in the whole course of the Napoleonic wars" (Howard, *War in European History*, p. 120). Half a century or so later, U.S. aviation dropped more bombs on North Vietnam alone than the belligerents had used during the whole of World War II.

more or less preached in the wilderness in favor of mechanized forces, but at least Marshal Hugh Trenchard (unlike Giulio Douhet) was successful in getting many of his views accepted and, in the shape of the RAF, equipped Britain with an instrument that held off the Luftwaffe in 1940.

One of the features of World War II in military terms was the fact (dimly perceived in Spain because of the internecine character of the conflict) that populations themselves had become a target, almost as much as military forces themselves. It was not just that whole groups were exterminated because of the Nazis' racist ideology; the populations of the belligerent countries themselves constituted a domestic front, which had to be broken. That was the purpose of the terrorist-type air raids on Coventry, Tokyo, and Dresden (200,000 dead) and of the use of two atomic bombs on Hiroshima and Nagasaki (130,000 dead).

The appearance of nuclear power marked a qualitative change, which meant a total rethinking of strategic problems. Fraught with uncertainties, conflict remained latent, hanging on mutual deterrence. From the beginning of the Cold War in 1947–48, the military situation was frozen in the key theater, Europe. It is worth stressing that the Cold War ended in 1989–91 without recourse to the military, not even as a threat.

STRATEGY AND ITS UNCERTAINTIES

Generally speaking, strategy is based on understanding the relations of force, but grand strategy requires a more precise definition: it relates to the use of force to achieve a political decision; it is the art of organizing violence in the conduct of war—and nonwar, of the kind we have today.

According to Clausewitz, strategy is a matter of "compelling the enemy to accept our will"; according to André Beaufre, it is "the art of the dialectic of wills employing force to resolve a conflict." One can easily see how essential psychology is in this dialectic of wills. What is the element, the situation that will compel the enemy to bend? For example, in 1812, during the Russian campaign, Napoleon failed to break the will of Czar Alexander. The taking of Moscow was not enough, and neither were the losses that Field Marshal Kutuzov suffered at Borodino. The czar, becoming ever more mystical, was beginning to identify Napoleon with the Antichrist. It was Saint Petersburg and the court that needed to be hit, not the despised rabble of mujiks. Similarly, the American aerial escalation and bombing of North Vietnam between 1965 and 1972 did not make Hanoi bend.

The collapse of the adversary can be attained through a panoply of means organized by an overall vision. This is what I call the assessment and organization of the strategic field and maneuver in the broad sense, and these remain constantly dependent on a "dialectic of uncertainties."

Patterns may vary according to the margin of maneuver or freedom of action (to use Xenophon's expression) that one has. It may be conflict aiming at victory through annihilation of the adversary (Napoleon), a technique used whenever one of the protagonists feels he can, without excessive risk, achieve it by concentrating his forces at what is deemed to be a vulnerable point for the enemy; or it may be the indirect approach, aiming to wear down the adversary in terms of morale and matériel and militarily through dispersal and/or harassment, without committing all one's forces in one blow. This pattern has often been used in Asia. It involves a temporal dimension in two aspects: duration and seizing the favorable moment—a dynamic element requiring surprise and speed. The first pattern uses attack, although it may involve a combination of defense and attack. The latter tends to use attack far less systematically and endeavors to enlarge the theater of confrontation.

Choices are naturally made in the light of constraints, uncertainties, objectives, circumstances sometimes, and strategic cultures. The strategic culture of the United States, for example, as manifested in the first half of the century, was based on the concept of total victory and unconditional surrender, the legacy of a tradition in which war settled a conflict situation once and for all. That is a concept very far removed from that of Europe, where peace and war are the result of an ever-shifting balance.

Tactics is the use of military means on the ground. Operational strategies relate to the articulation between logistical and tactical factors and the objectives set.

In conventional strategy, especially that of direct approach, the objective sought was the disruption of the opposing forces either by a frontal breakthrough or by enveloping the enemy's wings.

It is hard today, when technological advance is so rapid that theories are outdated as fast as weapons, to imagine how slow changes in warfare were before the fifteenth century. In some periods, the state of technology gave the superiority to defense; in others, to attack. In Europe, after several centuries during which the system of strongpoints was essential and determined operations, a return to mobile warfare and concentration for a breakthrough only came with the French Revolution and the Napoleonic Empire. But the development of firepower in the late nineteenth and early twentieth centuries rendered a breakthrough difficult, if not almost impossible. The improvement in mechanized forces restored the advantage to attack.

Even though the art of warfare obeys certain principles, it remains variable, since the conditions under which it operates are changing all the time. It is necessary both to rely on experience and to invent the relevant response to new conditions and all their uncertainties. "All theorists . . . limit themselves to saying what the input data and output product are of mental processes about which they remain silent. They put themselves inside a black box, and neither we nor they know how it works to process assimilated knowledge and events into a decision calculated to attain a goal. What method does one use to choose the most effective ones?"[45]

As for atomic strategy, which has been essentially speculative since the surrender of Japan in 1945, the destructive power of its weapons and their accuracy are developing all the time. The essential factor in deterrence is uncertainty, itself founded on the credibility of the threat—or the response. So far, deterrence has been successful. Conventional forces have had to be maintained, since nuclear weapons could only be used as a last resort. With time, this last resort itself moved from the theory of massive retaliation to that of graduated response. Atomic weaponry is thus simply added to other weapons without eliminating any of them, and today, for example, with the introduction of the shoulder-mounted Stinger missile, the infantryman is more formidable than ever in a conventional conflict such as a guerrilla war.

"Weapons of mass destruction open up the prospect of a historic revolution, at the end of which the very essence of interstate relations will be different," wrote Raymond Aron, foreseeing that relations between states equipped with a formidable destructive capacity might one day perhaps not lead classically to open war.[46] It seems that this is, at least provisionally, the case in the northern hemisphere. The changes in the status quo in central and eastern Europe in 1989–91 were not owing to any military pressure. They were the result of the development of communications, which reinforced the feeling of failure in the Eastern bloc, showing that shortages and the absence of freedoms are the fruit of political and economic bankruptcy.

INDIRECT STRATEGIES

Apart from a few regional conventional wars (between India and Pakistan, Israel and the Arab countries, in Korea, between Iran and Iraq, in the Falklands), many conflicts in the contemporary world are settled by indirect strate-

45. Lucien Poirier, postface to Jean Colin, *Les Transformations de la guerre* (Paris: Economica, 1988.

46. Raymond Aron, *Peace and War: A Theory of International Relations* (Melbourne, Fla.: Krieger, 1981).

gies. In the phase of decolonization, revolutionary warfare played a considerable role, to which the West did not always know how to adapt.[47] Guerrilla warfare is a technique of irregulars, based on surprise and harassment, designed
to weaken a regular army; revolutionary war seeks, by the same political and
military means, to organize the population in order to seize power. Ideas of
liberation and modern nationalism and organizational techniques enabled the
colonized and semicolonized to free themselves by violence—or by other
means—from the grip of the West. The legitimacy of colonial rule was challenged in the metropoles themselves. In the end, as a result of the weariness of
metropolitan public opinion and the opposition of a section of that opinion,
or because the game was not worth the candle for many rulers, liberation
movements have often won out politically.[48] In the world of "neither war nor
peace" of the Cold War, there were local wars like the Korean War and crises
like the Berlin one. Psychological warfare has become more and more often
the substitute for actual war. Crisis management (Berlin, 1961; Cuba, 1962),
propaganda, disinformation, manipulation, and diabolization of the enemy,
along with espionage, made up the arsenal of East-West competition. The
dominated countries of Asia and Africa, seeking their own emancipation,
turned its own principles against the West, provoking a feeling of guilt in many
Westerners. André Beaufre put the central psychological point of East-West
rivalry in a nutshell when he wrote in 1963 that the key thing was "to restore
the prestige of Western civilization."[49] But that prestige could only be restored
after the West had decolonized and renounced the most shocking forms of its
rule over what was called the Third World. In this respect, it was difficult to
use the ideology of human rights as a counterattack by the West against totalitarian regimes so long as it was flagrantly abused by the very people who ought
to have been upholding it. Over that same period, the failure of communist
countries, China as much as the Soviet Union, became patent in the eyes of
most people. With the independence of the countries of Asia and Africa and
the emergence of what was conventionally called the Third World, a North-
South dimension was added to East-West competition. Or, to be less
schematic, autonomous political forces made their appearance, inspired by regional powers. These are by nature destabilizing, since they are not satisfied
with the status quo. The direct use of terrorism or indirect support for orga-

---

47. G. Chaliand, ed., *Stratégies de la guérilla: De la longue marche à nos jours* (Paris: Gallimard,
1984); English translation: *Guerrilla Strategies: An Historical Anthology from the Long March to
Afghanistan* (Berkeley: University of California Press, 1982).

48. There are exceptions, notably in the case of the communist guerrillas in Malaysia, Greece,
and the Philippines, who were defeated or have so far been kept at bay (in the case of the Philippines).

49. André Beaufre, *Introduction à la stratégie* (Paris: Armand Colin, 1963).

nizations using it, often as their sole technique, has been (and may again become) one of the violent forms of psychological warfare and coercive diplomacy by some of those states (Iraq, Syria, Libya, and Iran in particular).[50]

The indirect strategy may be military, but today it usually is not. It is a platitude today to observe that generalized war, like real peace, ended with World War II. Indeed, it may legitimately be asked whether the period that in Europe separates the Franco-Prussian War from World War I can be called a period "of peace" in the territories then being colonized. What is essential is to grasp clearly that the indirect strategy expects results above all from means other than military ones. More than ever, it depends on firmness of mind and will: psychological warfare (of which terrorism is only the most violent form), propaganda, and disinformation. With the emergence of mass warfare at the beginning of the twentieth century and the appearance of nuclear weapons, a "reversal of vulnerabilities" (to employ Pierre Gallois's phrase) between civilians and soldiers to some extent occurred. While piecemeal operations, rapid interventions, and so on have become the job of small, highly professional units, the risks of generalized war and the attitude adopted to deal with it must take account of a public opinion, which is infinitely more vulnerable. Apart from nuclear weapons, the proliferation of chemical weapons with powerful vectors presents a new threat. The militarization of space is a new factor with considerable consequences.[51]

CONCLUSION

In a context in which we are both in the midst of change and, consequently, in a state of permanent crisis, accelerations in change sometimes affect more, even when they represent a victory (such as the changes in central Europe and the nations that formerly constituted the USSR in 1989–91), than the maintenance of the status quo to which one had lazily become used. Competition today is global: technological, industrial, economic, financial, and military.[52]

The very concept of security is usually envisaged in an overly conservative and anachronistic sense. We need, for example, to integrate into the concept of security, taken in its global sense, the demographic dimension of the South-

50. The most radical Muslims see the West and the values it represents as their main enemy.

51. The American SDI program played a significant role in the Soviet Union's concern to slow down the arms race.

52. Japanese businesses spend a lot of time preparing a project (discussing, examining, convincing) and then move very rapidly to implementation, which is close to the military way of doing things.

North relationship, which is noticeable today but will be sharper tomorrow in both North America and Europe.[53] The aging of the population, birth rates, immigration, and achieving relative political and social peace become as important, if not more so, than many narrowly military aspects of defense. As for the South, and especially Africa, the combination of population growth and the suburbanization of megalopolises suggests that we shall be seeing new urban disturbances there in the near future.

Strategies today need to be more refined than ever, since conflict situations are increasingly complex and multifaceted and more than ever call for clear-sightedness in the perception of threats and determination in tackling them, while military force and capacity to respond remain the indispensable guarantors of security.

∾ ∾ ∾ ∾

At the end of his account of the Punic Wars, Polybius, who was present with Scipio Africanus at the destruction and burning of defeated Carthage, writes:

> Scipio, when he looked upon the city as it was utterly perishing and in the last throes of its complete destruction, is said to have shed tears . . . [realizing] that this [had] happened to Ilium [Troy], once a prosperous city, to the empires of Assyria, Media, and Persia, the greatest of their time, and to Macedonia itself. . . . And when Polybius, speaking freely, for he was his teacher, asked him what he was thinking, they say that without any attempt at concealment he named his own country, for which he feared when he reflected on the fate of all things human.

The order to put the city to the torch had been given by Scipio, and Polybius adds that he remembers something else Scipio said at that time. Turning to Polybius and taking his hand, he is supposed to have observed: "A glorious moment, Polybius, but I have a dread foreboding that some day the same doom will be pronounced upon my own country."[54]

53. In 1900, Europe and North America accounted for one-third of the world's total population. Today it is only 17 percent.
54. Polybius, *Histories*, bk. 38.

PART 1

THE ANCIENT NEAR EAST

THE KADESH INSCRIPTION
(C. 1295 B.C.)

Aside from the battle of Megiddo in 1468 B.C. under Pharaoh Thutmose III, the battle of Kadesh is the earliest famous battle of which there is historical evidence. It was fought in northern Syria between the Egyptians and the Hittites, and the outcome was indecisive. Fifteen years later, the two sides signed a treaty recognizing their respective zones of influence, accepting that neither could inflict a decisive defeat on the other. Apart from its lyrical beauty, the story of the battle of Kadesh, when seen as a military report, is the very model of a false communiqué. At the time, the first requirement was to exalt the ruler/hero.

THE BATTLE OF KADESH

> His majesty was a youthful lord,
> Active and without his like;
> His arms mighty, his heart stout,
> His strength like Mont in his hour.
> Of perfect form like Atum,
> Hailed when his beauty is seen;
> Victorious over all lands,
> Wily in launching a fight.
> Strong wall around his soldiers,
> Their shield on the day of battle;
> A bowman without his equal,
> Who prevails over vast numbers.
> Head on he charges a multitude,
> His heart trusting his strength;

From "The Kadesh Battle Inscriptions of Ramses II," in *Ancient Egyptian Literature: A Book of Readings* (3 vols.), edited by Miriam Lichtheim (Berkeley: University of California Press, 1973–80), 2: 62–71. Copyright © 1976 by the Regents of the University of California.

Stout-hearted in the hour of combat,
Like the flame when it consumes.
Firm-hearted like a bull ready for battle,
He heeds not all the lands combined;
A thousand men cannot withstand him,
A hundred thousand fail at his sight.
Lord of fear, great of fame,
In the hearts of all the lands;
Great of awe, rich in glory,
As is Seth upon his mountain;
[Casting fear] in foreigners' hearts,
Like a wild lion in a valley of goats.
Who goes forth in valor, returns in triumph,
Looking straight and free of boasting;
Firm in conduct, good in planning,
Whose first response is ever right.
Who saves his troops on battle day,
Greatly aids his charioteers;
Brings home his followers, rescues his soldiers. . . .

Now his majesty had made ready his infantry and his chariotry, and the Sherden in his majesty's captivity whom he had brought back in the victories of his strong arm. They had been supplied with all their weapons, and battle orders had been given to them. His majesty journeyed northward, his infantry and his chariotry with him, having made a good start with the march in year 5, second month of summer, day 9. His majesty passed the fortress of Sile, being mighty like Mont in his going forth, all foreign lands trembling before him, their chiefs bringing their gifts, and all rebels coming bowed down through fear of his majesty's might. His majesty's army traveled on the narrow paths as if on the roads of Egypt.

Now when days had passed over this, his majesty was in Ramessemeramun, the town which is in the Valley of the Pine, and his majesty proceeded northward. And when his majesty reached the hill country of Kadesh, his majesty went ahead like Mont, the lord of Thebes. He crossed the ford of the Orontes with the first army, "Amun-gives-victory-to-Usermare-sotpenre," and his majesty arrived at the town of Kadesh.

Now the vile Foe from Khatti had come and brought together all the foreign lands as far as the end of the sea. The entire land of Khatti had come, that of Nahrin also, that of Arzawa and Dardany, that of Keshkesh, those of Masa, those of Pidasa, that of Irun, that of Karkisha, that of Luka, Kizzuwadna, Carchemish, Ugarit, Kedy, the entire land of Nuges, Mushanet, and Kadesh. He had not spared a country from being brought, of all those distant lands, and their chiefs were there with him, each one with his infantry and chariotry, a great number without equal. They covered the mountains and valleys and were like locusts in their multitude. He had left no silver in his land. He had stripped it of all its possessions and had given them to all the foreign countries in order to bring them with him to fight.

Now the vile Foe from Khatti and the many foreign countries with him stood concealed and ready to the northeast of the town of Kadesh, while his majesty was alone by himself with his attendants, the army of Amun marching behind him, the army of Pre crossing the ford in the neighborhood south of the town of Shabtuna at a distance of 1 *iter* from where his majesty was, the army of Ptah being to the south of the town of Ironama, and the army of Seth marching on the road. And his majesty had made a first battle force from the best of his army, and it was on the shore of the land of Amor. Now the vile Chief of Khatti stood in the midst of the army that was with him and did not come out to fight for fear of his majesty, though he had caused men and horses to come in very great numbers like the sand—they were three men to a chariot and equipped with all weapons of warfare—and they had been made to stand concealed behind the town of Kadesh.

Then they came forth from the south side of Kadesh and attacked the army of Pre in its middle, as they were marching unaware and not prepared to fight. Then the infantry and chariotry of his majesty weakened before them, while his majesty was stationed to the north of the town of Kadesh, on the west bank of the Orontes. They came to tell it to his majesty, and his majesty rose like his father Mont. He seized his weapons of war; he girded his coat of mail; he was like Baal in his hour. The great horse that bore his majesty was "Victory-in-Thebes" of the great stable of *Usermare-sotpenre,* beloved of Amun.

Then his majesty drove at a gallop and charged the forces of the Foe from Khatti, being alone by himself, none other with him. His majesty proceeded to look about him and found 2,500 chariots ringing him on his way out, of all the fast troops of the Foe from Khatti and the many countries with him—Arzawa, Masa, Pidasa, Keshkesh, Irun, Kizzuwadna, Khaleb, Ugarit, Kadesh and Luka, three men to a team acting together.

> No officer was with me, no charioteer,
> No soldier of the army, no shield-bearer;
> My infantry, my chariotry yielded before them,
> Not one of them stood firm to fight with them.
> His majesty spoke: "What is this, father Amun?
> Is it right for a father to ignore his son?
> Are my deeds a matter for you to ignore?

Do I not walk and stand at your word?
I have not neglected an order you gave.
Too great is he, the great lord of Egypt,
To allow aliens to step on his path!
What are these Asiatics to you, O Amun,
The wretches ignorant of god?
Have I not made for you many great monuments,
Filled your temple with my booty,
Built for you my mansion of Millions-of-Years,
Given you all my wealth as endowment?
I brought you all lands to supply your altars,
I sacrificed to you ten thousands of cattle,
And all kinds of sweet-scented herbs.
I did not abstain from any good deed,
So as not to perform it in your court.
I built great pylons for you,
Myself I erected their flagstaffs;
I brought you obelisks from Yebu,
It was I who fetched their stones.
I conveyed to you ships from the sea,
To haul the lands' produce to you.
Shall it be said: 'The gain is small
For him who entrusts himself to your will'?
Do good to him who counts on you,
Then one will serve you with loving heart.
I call to you, my father Amun,
I am among a host of strangers;
All countries are arrayed against me,
I am alone, there's none with me!
My numerous troops have deserted me,
Not one of my chariotry looks for me;
I keep on shouting for them,
But none of them heeds my call.
I know Amun helps me more than a million troops,
More than a hundred thousand charioteers,
More than ten thousand brothers and sons
Who are united as one heart.
The labors of many people are nothing,
Amun is more helpful than they;
I came here by the command of your mouth,
O Amun, I have not transgressed your command!"

Now though I prayed in the distant land,
My voice resounded in Southern On.

I found Amun came when I called to him,
He gave me his hand and I rejoiced.
He called from behind as if near by:
"Forward, I am with you,
I, your father, my hand is with you,
I prevail over a hundred thousand men,
I am lord of victory, lover of valor!"
I found my heart stout, my breast in joy,
All I did succeeded, I was like Mont.
I shot on my right, grasped with my left,
I was before them like Seth in his moment.
I found the mass of chariots in whose midst I was
Scattering before my horses;
Not one of them found his hand to fight,
Their hearts failed in their bodies through fear of me.
Their arms all slackened, they could not shoot,
They had no heart to grasp their spears;
I made them plunge into the water as crocodiles plunge,
They fell on their faces one on the other.
I slaughtered among them at my will,
Not one looked behind him,
Not one turned around,
Whoever fell down did not rise.

And the wretched Chief of Khatti stood among his troops and chariots,
Watching his majesty fight all alone,
Without his soldiers and charioteers,
Stood turning, shrinking, afraid.
Then he caused many chiefs to come,
Each of them with his chariotry,
Equipped with their weapons of warfare:
The chief of Arzawa and he of Masa,
The chief of Irun and he of Luka,
He of Dardany, the chief of Carchemish,
The chief of Karkisha, he of Khaleb,
The brothers of him of Khatti all together,
Their total of a thousand chariots came straight into the fire.
I charged toward them, being like Mont,
In a moment I gave them a taste of my hand,
I slaughtered among them, they were slain on the spot,
One called out to the other saying:
"No man is he who is among us,
It is Seth great-of-strength, Baal in person;
Not deeds of man are these his doings,

They are of one who is unique,
Who fights a hundred thousand without soldiers and chariots,
Come quick, flee before him,
To seek life and breathe air;
For he who attempts to get close to him,
His hands, all his limbs grow limp.
One cannot hold either bow or spears,
When one sees him come racing along!"
My majesty hunted them like a griffin,
I slaughtered among them unceasingly.

I raised my voice to shout to my army:
"Steady, steady your hearts, my soldiers;
Behold me victorious, me alone,
For Amun is my helper, his hand is with me.
How faint are your hearts, O my charioteers,
None among you is worthy of trust!
Is there none among you whom I helped in my land?
Did I not rise as lord when you were lowly,
And made you into chiefs by my will every day?
I have placed a son on his father's portion,
I have banished all evil from the land.
I released your servants to you,
Gave you things that were taken from you.
Whosoever made a petition,
'I will do it,' said I to him daily.
No lord has done for his soldiers
What my majesty did for your sakes.
I let you dwell in your villages
Without doing a soldier's service;
So with my chariotry also,
I released them to their towns;
Saying, 'I shall find them just as today
In the hour of joining battle.'
But behold, you have all been cowards,
Not one among you stood fast,
To lend me a hand while I fought!
As the *ka* of my father Amun endures,
I wish I were in Egypt,
Like my fathers who did not see Syrians,
And did not fight them [abroad]!
For not one among you has come,
That he might speak of his service in Egypt!
What a good deed to him who raised monuments

In Thebes, the city of Amun,
This crime of my soldiers and charioteers,
That is too great to tell!"

Behold, Amun gave me his strength,
When I had no soldiers, no chariotry;
He caused every distant land to see
My victory through my strong arm,
I being alone, no captain behind me,
No charioteer, foot soldier, officer.
The lands that beheld me will tell my name,
As far as distant lands unknown.
Whoever among them escaped from my hand,
They stood turned back to see my deeds.
When I attacked their multitudes,
Their feet were infirm and they fled;
All those who shot in my direction,
Their arrows veered as they attacked me.

Now when Menena my shield-bearer saw
That a large number of chariots surrounded me,
He became weak and faint-hearted,
Great fear invading his body.
He said to his majesty: "My good lord,
Strong ruler, great savior of Egypt in wartime,
We stand alone in the midst of battle,
Abandoned by soldiers and chariotry,
What for do you stand to protect them?
Let us get clear, save us, Usermare-sotpenre!"
His majesty said to his shield-bearer:
"Stand firm, steady your heart, my shield-bearer!
I will charge them as a falcon pounces,
I will slaughter, butcher, fling to the ground;
Why do you fear these weaklings
Whose multitudes I disregard?"
His majesty then rushed forward,
At a gallop he charged the midst of the foe,
For the sixth time he charged them.
I was after them like Baal in his moment of power,
I slew them without pause.

Now when my soldiers and chariotry saw
That I was like Mont, strong-armed,
That my father Amun was with me,

Making the foreign lands into chaff before me,
They started coming one by one,
To enter the camp at time of night.
They found all the foreign lands I had charged
Lying fallen in their blood;
All the good warriors of Khatti,
The sons and brothers of their chiefs.
For I had wrecked the plain of Kadesh,
It could not be trodden because of their mass.
Thereupon my soldiers came to praise me,
Their faces [bright] at the sight of my deeds;
My captains came to extol my strong arm,
My charioteers likewise exalted my name:
"Hail, O good warrior, firm of heart,
You have saved your soldiers, your chariotry;
You are Amun's son who acts with his arms,
You have felled Khatti by your valiant strength.
You are the perfect fighter, there's none like you,
A king who battles for his army on battle day;
You are great-hearted, first in the ranks,
You heed not all the lands combined.
You are greatly victorious before your army,
Before the whole land, it is no boast;
Protector of Egypt, curber of foreign lands,
You have broken the back of Khatti forever!"

Said his majesty to his infantry,
His captains and his chariotry:
"What about you, my captains, soldiers,
My charioteers, who shirked the fight?
Does a man not act to be acclaimed in his town,
When he returns as one brave before his lord?
A name made through combat is truly good,
A man is ever respected for valor.
Have I not done good to any of you,
That you should leave me alone in the midst of battle?
You are lucky to be alive at all,
You who took the air while I was alone!
Did you not know it in your hearts:
I am your rampart of iron!
What will men say when they hear of it,
That you left me alone without a comrade,
That no chief, charioteer, or soldier came,
To lend me a hand while I was fighting?
I crushed a million countries by myself

On Victory-in-Thebes, Mut-is-content, my great horses;
It was they whom I found supporting me,
When I alone fought many lands.
They shall henceforth be fed in my presence,
Whenever I reside in my palace;
It was they whom I found in the midst of battle,
And charioteer Menena, my shield-bearer,
And my household butlers who were at my side,
My witnesses in combat, behold, I found them!"
My majesty paused in valor and victory,
Having felled hundred thousands by my strong arm.

At dawn I marshaled the ranks for battle,
I was ready to fight like an eager bull;
I arose against them in the likeness of Mont,
Equipped with my weapons of victory.
I charged their ranks fighting as a falcon pounces,
The serpent on my brow felled my foes,
Cast her fiery breath in my enemies' faces,
I was like Re when he rises at dawn.
My rays, they burned the rebels' bodies,
They called out to one another:
"Beware, take care, don't approach him,
Sakhmet the Great is she who is with him,
She's with him on his horses, her hand is with him;
Anyone who goes to approach him,
Fire's breath comes to burn his body!"
Thereupon they stood at a distance,
Touching the ground with their hands before me.
My majesty overpowered them,
I slew them without sparing them;
They sprawled before my horses,
And lay slain in heaps in their blood.

Then the vile Chief of Khatti wrote and worshiped my name like that of Re, saying: "You are Seth, Baal in person; the dread of you is a fire in the land of Khatti." He sent his envoy with a letter in his hand [addressed] to the great name of my majesty, greeting the Majesty of the Palace: "Re-Harakhti, The Strong-Bull-beloved-of-Maat, the Sovereign who protects his army, mighty on account of his strong arm, rampart of his soldiers on the day of battle, King of Upper and Lower Egypt: *Usermare-sotpenre*, the Son of Re, the lion lord of strength: *Ramesse, Beloved of Amun*, given life forever":

"Your servant speaks to let it be known that you are the Son of Re who came from his body. He has given you all the lands together. As for the land of Egypt and the land of Khatti, they are your servants, under your feet. Pre, your august father, has given them to you. Do not overwhelm us. Lo, your might is great, your strength is heavy upon the land of Khatti. Is it good that you slay your servants, your face savage toward them and without pity? Look, you spent yesterday killing a hundred thousand, and today you came back and left no heirs. Be not hard in your dealings, victorious king! Peace is better than fighting. Give us breath!"

Then my majesty relented in life and dominion, being like Mont at his moment when his attack is done. My majesty ordered brought to me all the leaders of my infantry and my chariotry, all my officers assembled together, to let them hear the matter about which he had written. My majesty let them hear these words which the vile Chief of Khatti had written to me. Then they said with one voice: "Very excellent is peace, O Sovereign our Lord! There is no blame in peace when you make it. Who could resist you on the day of your wrath?" My majesty commanded to hearken to his words, and I moved in peace southward.

His majesty returned in peace to Egypt with his infantry and his chariotry, all life, stability, and dominion being with him, and the gods and goddesses protecting his body. He had crushed all lands through fear of him; his majesty's strength had protected his army; all foreign lands gave praise to his fair face.

DEUTERONOMY
(eighth–sixth centuries B.C.)

Deuteronomy, or the Second Book of Laws, is made up of sayings attributed to Moses. It is the fifth and last book of the Pentateuch, and takes up and develops a new version of Moses' precepts to the Jewish people.

THE CONDUCT OF WAR

When thou goest forth to battle against thine enemies, and seest horses, and chariots, and a people more than thou, thou shalt not be afraid of them: for the LORD thy God is with thee, which brought thee up out of the land of Egypt. And it shall be, when ye draw nigh unto the battle, that the priest shall approach and speak unto the people, and shall say unto them, Hear, O Israel, ye draw nigh this day unto battle against your enemies: let not your heart faint; fear not, nor tremble, neither be ye affrighted at them; for the LORD your God is he that goeth with you, to fight for you against your enemies, to save you. And the officers shall speak unto the people, saying, What man is there that hath built a new house, and hath not dedicated it? let him go and return to his house, lest he die in the battle, and another man dedicate it. And what man is there that hath planted a vineyard, and hath not used the fruit thereof? let him go and return unto his house, lest he die in the battle, and another man use the fruit thereof. And what man is there that hath betrothed a wife, and hath not taken her? let him go and return unto his house, lest he die in the battle, and another man take her. And the officers shall speak further unto the people, and they shall say, What man is there that is fearful and faint-hearted? let him go and return unto his house, lest his brethren's heart melt as his heart. And it shall be, when the officers have made an end of speaking unto the people, that they shall appoint captains of hosts at the head of the people.

Deuteronomy, ch. 20, in *The Modern Reader's Bible*, edited by Richard G. Moulton (New York: Macmillan, 1944).

When thou drawest nigh unto a city to fight against it, then proclaim peace unto it And it shall be, if it make thee answer of peace, and open unto thee, then it shall be, that all the people that is found therein shall become tributary unto thee, and shall serve thee. And if it will make no peace with thee, but will make war against thee, then thou shalt besiege it: and when the LORD thy God delivereth it into thine hand, thou shalt smite every male thereof with the edge of the sword: but the women, and the little ones, and the cattle, and all that is in the city, even all the spoil thereof, shalt thou take for a prey unto thyself; and thou shalt eat the spoil of thine enemies, which the LORD thy God hath given thee. Thus shalt thou do unto all the cities which are very far off from thee, which are not of the cities of these nations. But of the cities of these peoples, which the LORD thy God giveth thee for an inheritance, thou shalt save alive nothing that breatheth: but thou shalt utterly destroy them; the Hittite, and the Amorite, the Canaanite, and the Perizzite, the Hivite, and the Jebusite; as the LORD thy God hath commanded thee: that they teach you not to do after all their abominations, which they have done unto their gods; so should ye sin against the LORD your God.

When thou shalt besiege a city a long time, in making war against it to take it, thou shalt not destroy the trees thereof by wielding an axe against them; for thou mayest eat of them, and thou shalt not cut them down; for is the tree of the field man, that it should be besieged of thee? Only the trees which thou knowest that they be not trees for meat, thou shalt destroy and cut them down; and thou shalt build bulwarks against the city that maketh war with thee, until it fall.

THE DEAD SEA SCROLLS
(first century B.C.?)

"The War Rule" was discovered in 1947 at Qumran, near the Dead Sea, and translated into English for the first time in 1954. It was probably written during the beginning of Roman rule in Palestine.

THE WAR RULE

When the battle formations are marshalled facing the enemy, formation facing formation, seven Priests of the sons of Aaron shall advance from the middle gates to the place between the formations. They shall be clothed in vestments of white cloth of flax, in a fine linen tunic and fine linen breeches; and they shall be girdled with fine cloth of flax embroidered with blue, purple, and scarlet thread, a many-coloured design worked by a craftsman. And on their heads they shall wear mitred turbans. These shall be battle raiment; they shall not take them into the Sanctuary.

The first Priest shall advance before the men of the formation to strengthen their hand for battle, and the six other Priests shall hold in their hands the trumpets of Summons, and the trumpets of the Reminder, and the trumpets of Alarm [for massacre], and the trumpets of Pursuit, and the trumpets of Withdrawal. And when the Priests advance to the place between the formations, seven Levites shall accompany them bearing in their hands seven rams' horns; and three officers of the Levites shall walk before the Priests and Levites. The Priests shall sound the two trumpets of Sum[mons for the gates of] war to open fifty shields [wide] and the foot-soldiers shall advance, fifty from one gate [and fifty from the other. With them shall advance] the officers of

From "The War Rule," in *The Dead Sea Scrolls in English*, translated by G. Vermes (Baltimore: Penguin Books, 1962), 133–35. Copyright © 1962 by G. Vermes. Reproduced by permission of Penguin Books Ltd.

the Levites, and they shall advance with every formation according to all this R[ule].

[The Priests shall sound the trumpets, and two divisions of foot-]soldiers [shall advance] from the gates [and shall] station [themselves] between the two [formations] . . . the trumpets shall sound to direct the slingers until they have cast seven times. Afterwards, the Priests shall sound for them the trumpets of Withdrawal and they shall return to the flank of the first formation to take up their position.

Then the Priests shall sound the trumpets of Summons and three divisions of foot-soldiers shall advance from the gates and shall station themselves between the formations; the horsemen shall be on their flanks, to right and to left. The Priests shall sound a sustained blast on the trumpets for battle array, and the columns shall move to their [battle] array, each man to his place. And when they have taken up their stand in three arrays, the Priests shall sound a second signal, soft and sustained, for them to advance until they are close to the enemy formation. They shall seize their weapons, and the Priests shall then blow a shrill staccato blast on the six trumpets of Massacre to direct the battle, and the Levites and all the blowers of rams' horns shall sound a mighty alarm to terrify the heart of the enemy, and therewith the javelins shall fly out to bring down the slain. Then the sound of the horns shall cease, but the Priests shall continue to blow a shrill staccato blast on the trumpets to direct the battle until they have thrown seven times against the enemy formation. And then they shall sound a soft, a sustained, and a shrill sound on the trumpets of Withdrawal.

It is according to this Rule that the Priests shall sound the trumpets for the three divisions. With the first throw, the [Priests] shall sound [on the trumpets] a mighty alarm to direct the ba[ttle until they have thrown seven times. Then] the Priests [shall sound] for them on the trumpets [of Withdrawal a soft, sustained, and a shrill sound, and they shall return] to their positions in the formation.

[Then the Priests shall blow the trumpets of Summons and the two divisions of foot-soldiers shall advance from the gates] and shall stand [between the formations. And the Priests shall then blow the trumpets of] Massacre, [and the Levites and all the blowers of rams' horns shall sound an alarm, a mighty blast, and therewith] they shall set about to bring down the slain with their hands. All the people shall cease their clamour but the Priests shall continue to blow the trumpets of Massacre to direct the battle until the enemy is smitten and put to flight; and the Priests shall blow to direct the battle.

And when they are smitten before them, the Priests shall sound the trumpets of Summons and all the foot-soldiers shall rally to them from the midst of the front formations, and the six divisions, together with the fighting division, shall take up their stations. Altogether, they shall be seven formations: twenty-eight thousand fighting men and six thousand horsemen.

All these shall pursue the enemy to destroy him in an everlasting destruction in the battle of God. The Priests shall sound for them the trumpets of Pursuit, and they shall deploy against all the enemy in a pursuit to destruction; and the horsemen shall thrust them back on the flanks of the battle until they are utterly destroyed.

And as the slain men fall, the Priests shall trumpet from afar; they shall not approach the slain lest they be defiled with unclean blood. For they are holy, and they shall not profane the anointing of their priesthood with the blood of nations of vanity.

PART 2

GREECE AND ROME

THUCYDIDES

(c. 460–c. 399 B.C.)

*Along with Polybius, Thucydides was undoubtedly the greatest historian of
antiquity. He wrote a history of the Peloponnesian War (in which he himself
fought) between Athens, then at the height of its naval power, and Sparta
and its allies.*

THE DISPUTE OVER CORCYRA

All this year, after the battle and the one following, the Corinthians being vexed
at the war with the Corcyræans, applied themselves to the building of galleys,
and to the preparing of a fleet, the strongest they were able to make, and to
procure mariners, offering the inducement of pay, out of Peloponnesus itself,
and out of all other parts of Greece. The Corcyræans, having intelligence of
these preparations, began to fear, and (because they had never been in league
with any Grecian city, nor were in the roll of the confederates, either of the
Athenians or Lacedæmonians,) thought it best now, to go to the Athenians
and to become their allies, and try if they could procure any aid from them.

   This being perceived by the Corinthians, they also sent their ambassadors
to Athens, lest the addition of the Athenian navy, to that of the Corcyræans,
might hinder them from carrying the war as they desired. On the assembly at
Athens being met, they proceeded to plead against each other, and the Corcyræans spake to this effect:

   "Men of Athens, it is but just, that such as come to implore the aid of their
neighbours, (as we now do) and cannot pretend by any great benefit or league,
some precedent merit, should, before they go any farther, make it appear
principally, that what they seek is profitable, or if not so, yet is not prejudicial at least, to those that are to grant it: and next, that they will be constantly

From Thucydides, *History of the Peloponnesian War*, translated by Thomas Hobbes (Oxford:
Henry Slatter and Joseph Vincent, 1841), [bk. 1,] 25–39.

thankful for the same. But if they can clearly prove none of these, then not to take it ill if their suit be rejected. And the Corcyræans being fully persuaded that they can make these sure to you, have therefore sent us hither, desiring you to add them to the number of your confederates. But it has happened that our policy has been, both unreasonable in respect of our suit to you, and also for the present unprofitable to our own selves. For having ever till now, been unwilling to be joined in league with any one, we are now not only suitors for league to others, but also left destitute by that means of friends in this our war with the Corinthians. And that which before we thought wisdom, namely, not to enter into league with others, because we would not at the discretion of others enter into danger, has proved to be weakness and imprudence. Wherefore, though we alone repulsed the Corinthians in the late battle by sea, yet since they are set to invade us with greater preparation out of Peloponnesus, and the rest of Greece; and seeing with our own single power we are not able to prove superior in the contest; and since also the danger, in case they subdue us, would be very great, it is both necessary that we seek the succours both of you and whomsoever else we can; and we are also to be pardoned, though we boldly cross our former custom of not having to do with other men, proceeding not from malice, but error of judgment.

"Now if you yield unto us in what we request, this supplying of our wants will on your part be honourable, for many reasons. First, in this respect, that you will lend your help to such as have suffered, and not to such as have committed the injustice. And next, considering that you receive into league such as have at stake their whole fortune, you will confer a favour, where it will be stored up in constant remembrance. Besides this, the greatest navy but your own, is ours: consider then, what rarer good luck, or what greater grief to your enemies can befall you, than that that power which you would have prized above any money or other requital, should come voluntarily, and without all danger or cost present itself to your hands; bringing with it reputation amongst most men, a grateful mind from those you defend, and strength to yourselves. All which have not happened to many at once. And few there be of those that sue for league, that come not rather to receive strength and reputation, than to confer it on those on whom they call. If any here think that the war wherein we may do you service will not take place, he is in an error, and sees not how the Lacedæmonians through fear of you, are already inclined to war; and that the Corinthians, having much influence with them, and enemies to you, first take us, in the way to the invasion of you hereafter, that we may not, through our common hatred, mutually withstand them, and that they may not miss being before hand in one of two things, either to weaken us, or to strengthen their own selves. It must therefore be your part, we offering, and you accepting the league, to be before hand with them, and to anticipate plotting, rather than to counterplot against them.

"If they say that it is unjust that you receive their colony, let them learn, that all colonies, so long as they receive no wrong from their mother city, so long they honour her; but when they suffer injury from her, they then become alienated; for they are not sent out to be the slaves of them that stay, but to be their equals. That they have done us the injury, is manifest; for when we offered them a judicial trial of the controversy touching Epidamnus, they chose to prosecute their charges rather by arms than judgment. Now let that which they have done unto us who are their kindred, serve you for some argument, not to be seduced by their demands, and when they ask your aid, not at once and without hesitation to grant it. For he that hath to repent the least often of having conferred favours on his enemies will pass his life most secure.

"As for the articles between you and the Lacedæmonians, ye will not violate them by receiving us into your league, because we are in league with neither party. For there it is said, that whosoever is confederate of neither party may be allowed to join himself to either party he may think fit. And sure it were very unreasonable, that the Corinthians should have the liberty to man their fleet out of the cities comprised in the league, and out of any other parts of Greece, and not the least out of places in your dominion; and that they should exclude us from the league now before us, and also from all other help from whencesoever, and then should impute it to you as a fault that you grant our request; but we shall take it for a greater that you grant it not. For therein you will reject us that are invaded and be none of your enemies; and them who are your enemies and make the invasion, you will not only not oppose, but also suffer to raise forces in your dominions contrary to justice; whereas you ought in truth, either not to suffer them to hire mercenaries in your states, or else to send us succours also, in such manner as you shall think good yourselves; but especially by openly taking us into your league, and aiding us. Many advantages, as we said in the beginning, we shew unto you, but this for the greatest, that the same persons are your enemies also, (as well as ours), which is the firmest bond of alliance, and these not weak ones, but able to hurt those who secede from them, and as we offer you a naval, not a land power, the declining of them is not the same; nay, rather your principal aim, if it could be done, should be, to let none at all have shipping but yourselves; or, at least, if that cannot be, to make such your friends, as are best furnished therewith.

"If any man now think thus, that what we have spoken is indeed profitable, but fears, if it were admitted, the league were thereby broken, let that man consider, that his fear joined with strength, will make his enemies fear; and his confidence, having (if he rejects us) so much the less strength, will cause the less fear to enemies of strength. Let him also remember that he is now deliberating, no less concerning Athens than Corcyra; wherein he forecasteth not the best (considering the present state of affairs) when he makes it a question, whether against a war at hand, and all but already on foot, he should join unto it, or not, that city which with most important advantages, or disadvantages, is made friend or enemy. For it lieth so conveniently for the voyage along the shore to Italy and Sicily, that it can both hinder any fleet coming to Peloponnesus from thence, and convoy any going hence thither; and is also for all other purposes most commodious. And to comprehend all in brief, both with regard to the whole and each particular, that ye may learn not to abandon us by this: for Greece having but three navies of any account, yours, ours, and that of Corinth, if you suffer the other two to join in one, by letting the Corinthians first seize us, you will have to fight by sea at one time both against the Corcyræans and the Peloponnesians; whereas by making league with us, you will, with your fleet augmented, have to deal against the Peloponnesians alone."

Thus spake the Corcyræans; and after them the Corinthians thus:

"The Corcyræans in their oration having made mention not only of your taking them into league, but also, that we wrong them, and that they are unjustly warred on; it is also necessary for us first to answer concerning both those points, and then afterwards to proceed to the rest of what we have to say, to the end you may first more thoroughly know our demands, and that you may not from want of consideration reject their necessitous request. Whereas they allege in defence of their refusing to enter league with other cities, that the same hath proceeded from motives of prudence; the truth is, that they took up that custom, not from any virtue, but deliberate wickedness; as being unwilling to call any confederate for a witness of their evil actions, and to be put to blush by calling them. Besides, their city being by situation independent, affords them this power, that when they do any man a wrong, they themselves are the judges of the same, and not men appointed by consent. For going seldom forth against other nations, they admit into their harbours such as of necessity put in. And in this consisteth their specious pretext for not admitting confederates; not because they would not accompany others in doing evil, but because they had rather do it alone; that where they were strong, they might oppress; and when there should be none to observe them, they might have the more, and that they might escape the shame when they took any thing. But if they had been honest men, (as they themselves say they are) by how much the more unapproachable they are, so much the more means they have, by giving and taking what is due, to make their honesty appear.

"But they are not such, neither towards others, nor towards us; for though our colonists, they have not only been ever in revolt, but now they also make war upon us, and say they were not sent out to be injured by us; but we say again, that we did not send them forth to be insulted by them, but to be their leaders and to be treated with fitting respect. Our other colonies any how both honour and love us much, and it is manifest that if we are agreeable to the greater part, that these have no just cause to be offended alone; and that without some manifest wrong, we should not have had any colour of reason to war against them. But even had we been in error, it had been praiseworthy in them, to have given way to our passion, as it had been also dishonourable in us to have pressed too heavily on their moderation. But through pride and wealth they have done us wrong, both in many other things, and also in this; that Epidamnus being ours, which whilst it was vexed with wars, they never claimed; as soon as we came to relieve it, was forcibly seized by them, and still retained.

"They say now, that before they took it, they offered to put the cause to trial of judgment; with respect to which you ought not to think him worthy of credit who invites another to this, when he himself hath the advantage, and is sure already of what he offereth to plead for; but rather he that before his trial makes the deeds agree with his words: whereas these men offered not this specious pretence of a judicial trial, before they had besieged the city, but after, when they saw we meant not to put up with it. And now hither they are come, not content to have been faulty in that business themselves, but to get you not into their confederacy, but into their conspiracy: and to receive them for this reason, that they are enemies to us. But they should have come to you then, when they were most in safety; not now, when we have the wrong, and they the danger; and when you that never partook of their power, must impart unto them your aid; and having been free from their faults, must have an equal share from us of the blame. They should communicate their power before-hand, that mean to make common the issue of the same; and they that share not in the crimes, ought also to have no part in the consequences of them.

"Thus it appears that we come, for our parts, with well founded complaints; whereas the proceedings of these other are nothing else but violence and rapine. And now we shall shew you likewise, that you cannot receive them in point of justice. For although it be in the treaty, that the states who had formed no alliance with any of the parties, should be at liberty to join either of them they please; yet it holds not for such as do so, to the detriment of either; but only for those that having separated themselves from neither part, want protection, and bring not a war with them instead of peace to those (if they be wise) that receive them; which ye will suffer, unless ye be persuaded by us. For you shall not only be auxiliaries unto these; but to us, instead of confederates, enemies. For if you go with them, it follows, that we must beat off them and you too. You would act most uprightly by standing out of both our ways; and if not, then by taking our parts against the Corcyræans, (for between the Corinthians and you there are articles of peace, but with the Corcyræans you never had so much as a truce,) and not to constitute a new law of harbouring one another's rebels. For neither did we give our votes against you, when the Samians revolted, though the rest of Peloponnesus was divided in opinion as to whether we ought to aid them; but plainly alleged, that every one should have liberty to proceed against their own revolting confederates. And if you shall once aid and receive the doers of wrong, it will be seen, that they will come over as fast from you to us; and you will set up a law, not so much against us as against yourselves.

"These are the just claims we had to shew you, conformable to the law of the Grecians. And now we come to matter of advice, and claim of favour; which (being not so much your enemies as to hurt you, nor such friends as in turn to make use of you) we say, ought on the present occasion, to be granted us by way of requital: for when you had want of long ships against the Æginetæ, before the Median war, you had twenty lent unto you by the Corinthians; which benefit of ours, and that other against the Samians, when by us it was that the Peloponnesians did not aid them, was the cause both of your victory against the Æginetæ, and of the punishment of the Samians. And these things were done for you in a season, when men going to fight against their enemies, neglect all things but victory. For they think him a friend who serves them, even though before he had been an enemy, and him an enemy who stands in their way, though he may happen to have been a friend; for even their nearest interests men manage worse through eagerness of present contention.

"Which benefits considering, (the younger learning them from the elder,) be you pleased now to requite us in the like manner. And have not this thought, that though in what we have spoken there be equity, yet if the war should arise, the profit would be found in the contrary. For advantage followeth those actions most wherewith we do the least wrong; besides that, the event of the war, wherewith the Corcyræans frightening you, go about to draw you to injustice, is yet obscure, and not sufficient to excite you to a manifest and decided hostility with the Corinthians: but it were rather prudent for you indeed to take away our former jealousies concerning the Megareans. For the last obligation done in season, though but small, is able to cancel an accusation of much greater moment. Neither suffer yourselves to be drawn on, by the greatness of the navy which now shall be at your service; for to do no injury to our equals is a firmer power than that addition of strength, which (puft up by present appearances) men are to acquire with danger.

"And since we are come into the same condition, in which once before we said at Lacedæmon, that every one ought to proceed, as he shall think good, against his own confederates, we claim that liberty now of you; and that you who have been helped by our votes, will not hurt us now by yours: but render like for like, remembering that now is that occasion, wherein he that aideth us, is our greatest friend; and he that opposeth us, our greatest enemy. And do not receive these Corcyræans into league against our wills, nor defend them in their injuries. These things if you grant us, you will both do as is fit, and also advise the best for your own selves."

This was the purport of what was spoken by the Corinthians.

Both parties having been heard, and the Athenian people twice assembled; in the former assembly they approved no less of the reasons of the Corinthians than of the Corcyræans; but in the latter, they changed their minds; not so as to make a league with the Corcyræans both offensive and defensive, that the friends and enemies of the one, should be so of the other, (for then if the Corcyræans should have required them to go against Corinth, the peace had been broken with the Peloponnesians) but made it only defensive, that if any one should invade Corcyra or Athens, or any of their confederates, they were then mutually to assist one another. For they expected, that even thus they should grow to war with the Peloponnesians, and were therefore unwilling to let Corcyra, that had so great a navy, fall into the hands of the Corinthians; but rather, as much as in them lay, desired to bring them into collision against each other; that if need required, they might have to do with the Corinthians and others that had shipping, when they should be weakened to their hands. And the island seemed also to lie conveniently for passing into Italy and Sicily.

With this design the people of Athens received the Corcyræans into league; and when the Corinthians were gone, sent ten galleys not long after to their aid. The commanders of them were Lacedæmonius, the son of Cimon; Diotimus, the son of Strombichus; and Proteas, the son of Epicles; and had orders not to fight with the Corinthians unless they invaded Corcyra, or offered to land there, or in some other place of theirs: which if they did, then with all their might to oppose them. These orders they gave that they might not break the peace concluded with the Peloponnesians. So these galleys arrived at Corcyra.

The Corinthians, when they were ready, made towards Corcyra with a hundred and fifty sail, viz. of the Eleans ten, of the Megareans twelve, of the Leucadians ten, of the Ambraciots twenty-seven, of the Anactorians one, and ninety of their own. The commanders of these were men chosen out of the said several cities, for the several parts of the fleet which they sent in; and over those of Corinth, was Xenocleides, the son of Euthycles, with four others. After they had come to land upon the coast of the continent over against Corcyra, sailing from Leucas, they came to anchor at Cheimerium, in the country of Thesprotis. In this place is a haven, and above it, farther from the sea, the city of Ephyre, in that part of Thesprotis, which is called Elæatis; and near to it, the lake Acherusia discharges itself into the sea, and into that (having first passed through Thesprotis,) the river Acheron, from which it takes the name. Also the river Thyamis flows here, which divides Thesprotis from Cestrine, between which two rivers, projects the promontory of Cheimerium. To this part of the continent the Corinthians came to anchor and encamped.

The Corcyræans, understanding that they were advancing against them, having filled a hundred and ten galleys under the conduct of Miciades, Æsimides, and Eurybatus, encamped in one of the islands called Sybota. And the ten galleys of Athens were also with them. But their land forces were on the promontory of Leucimna, and with them a thousand men of arms of the Zacynthians that came to aid them. The Corinthians also had in the continent the aid of many Barbarians; for those on this part of the continent have been at all times their friends.

The Corinthians, after they were ready, and had taken aboard three days' provision, put off by night from Cheimerium intending to fight; and about break of day as they were sailing, descried the galleys of the Corcyræans, which were also put off into the open sea and sailing against them. As soon as they had sight one of another, they put themselves into order of battle. On the right wing of the Corcyræans were placed the galleys of Athens; and the rest of the line they themselves formed, being divided into three squadrons under three commanders, one under each. This was the order of the Corcyræans. The Corinthians had on their right wing the galleys of Megara, and of Ambracia; in the centre, other their confederates in order; and on the left, opposite to the Athenians, and right wing of the Corcyræans, they were themselves placed with such galleys as were the best sailers.

The standard being on either side lifted up, they fought, having come to close quarters, having on both sides many men at arms on the decks, and many archers and slingers, but after the old fashion, being as yet (as to their fleet) somewhat unskilfully fitted up. The battle was not so skilfully as hardly contested, bearing, for the most part, a great resemblance to a fight at land. For after they had once run their galleys up aboard one of another, they could not for the number and throng be easily separated again, but relied for the victory especially upon their men at arms on the decks, who kept up a close and steady fight, whilst their galleys remained without motion. There were not breakings through the line, but they fought it out with courage and strength, rather than with skill; insomuch as the battle was in every part not without much tumult and disorder; in which the Athenian galleys, being always at hand where the Corcyræans were pressed, kept the enemy in fear, but yet began no assault, because their commanders stood in awe of the previous orders of the Athenian people. The right wing of the Corinthians was chiefly distressed, for the Corcyræans with twenty galleys had made them turn their backs, and chased them scattered in disorder to the continent; and sailing to their very camp, went on land, burnt their abandoned tents, and pillaged their baggage; so that in this part the Corinthians and their confederates were vanquished, and the Corcyræans had the victory. But on the left wing, where the Corinthians were themselves, they were far superior; because the Corcyræans had twenty galleys of their number, which was at first less than that of the Corinthians, absent in the chase of the enemy. And the Athenians, when they saw the Corcyræans were in distress, now aided them more openly, whereas at first they had abstained from making a direct assault upon any. But when once they fled outright, and the Corinthians pressed upon them, then every one fell to the business without making any difference any longer: and matters came at last to such a pitch of distress, that they engaged one another, Corinthians and Athenians.

The Corinthians, when their enemies fled, did not tow off, by lashing them on, the hulls of the galleys they had waterlogged; but made after the men, rowing up and down to kill rather than to take alive; and through ignorance (not knowing that their right wing had been discomfited) slew also some of their own friends. For the galleys of either side being many, taking up a large space of sea, after they were once mixed together in close contest they could not easily discern who were of the victors, and who of the vanquished party. For this was the greatest naval battle, in number of ships, that ever had been before, of Grecians against Grecians. When the Corinthians had chased the Corcyræans to the shore, they turned to the broken galleys and bodies of their dead, which for the greatest part they recovered and brought to Sybota, where also lay the land forces of the Barbarians that were come to aid them. This Sybota is a desert haven of Thesprotis. When they had done this they again re-united themselves and sailed against the Corcyræans; and they likewise with such galleys as they had fit for the sea, remaining of the former battle, together with those of Athens, put forth to meet them, fearing lest they should attempt to land upon their territory. By this time the day was far spent, and the Pæan had been sung for the charge, when suddenly the Corinthians began to row astern: for they had descried twenty Athenian galleys sent from Athens to aid the former ten, for fear lest the Corcyræans (as was the case) should be overcome, and those ten galleys of theirs be too few to help them.

When the Corinthians therefore first descried these galleys, suspecting that they were from Athens, and more in number than they saw, fell back by degrees. But the Corcyræans (because these galleys were more out of their sight) descried them not, but wondered why the Corinthians rowed astern, till at last some saw them and gave notice of their approach, and then they also retired. For by this time it was dark, and the Corinthians turned about the heads of their galleys, and finished the engagement. And thus they parted, and the battle ended at night. The Corcyræans lying at Leucimna, these twenty Athenian galleys, under the command of Glauco, the son of Leager, and Andocides, the son of Leogoras, passing through the midst of the floating carcases and wreck, soon after they were descried, arrived at the camp of the Corcyræans, in Leucimna. The Corcyræans at first, (being night) were afraid they had been enemies, but knew them afterwards; so they anchored there.

The next day, both the thirty galleys of Athens, and as many of Corcyra as were fit for service, sailed towards the haven in Sybota, where the Corinthians lay at anchor, to see if they would fight. But the Corinthians, when they had put off from the land, and arranged themselves in the open sea, remained quiet, not meaning of their own accord to begin the battle; both because they saw the supply of fresh galleys from Athens, and that many difficulties happened to them, both about the safe custody of the prisoners aboard, and also because being in a desert place, there were no means of repairing their ships; but they considered about the voyage homewards, how they could get there, lest the Athenians, thinking the peace already broken, in that they had fought against each other, should not suffer them to depart.

They therefore thought fit to put some men on board a small boat without the herald's staff, and to send them to the Athenians to sound them: and having sent them, they spoke thus:

"Men of Athens, Ye act unjustly in beginning the war, and violating the treaty: for whereas we go about to punish our enemies, ye stand in our way, and bear arms against us. If therefore ye be resolved to hinder our going against Corcyra, or what place else we please, both put an end to the peace, and laying hands first upon us that are here, use us as enemies."—Thus said they: and the Corcyræans, as many of the army as heard them, cried out immediately to take and kill them. But the Athenians made answer thus: "Men of Peloponnesus, neither do we begin the war, nor break the peace; but we have come to aid these our confederates, the Corcyræans; if you wish therefore to go any where else, we hinder you not; but if against Corcyra, or any place belonging to it, we will not suffer you, as far as we are able."

When the Athenians had given this answer, the Corinthians made ready to sail home, and set up a trophy in Sybota of the continent. And the Corcyræans also, both took up the wreck, and the dead bodies, which were carried towards them by the current and the wind, which, arising during the night, dispersed them every way; and, as having had the victory, set up a trophy likewise in the Sybota of the islands. And each claimed the victory on these grounds: the Corinthians set up a trophy, because in the battle they had had the superiority all day until night, so as to get most of the wrecks and dead bodies, and had taken no less than a thousand prisoners, and rendered unserviceable about seventy galleys. And the Corcyræans set up a trophy, because they had destroyed thirty galleys of the Corinthians, and had after the arrival of the Athenians, picked up the wreck and dead bodies that drove to them by the wind:

and because the day before, on sight of the Athenians, the Corinthians had rowed astern, and gone away from them: and because, when the Athenians had come, the Corinthians came not from Sybota out to encounter them. Thus each side claimed the victory.

PERICLES' REPLY TO THE
SPARTAN ULTIMATUM

At length, when the last ambassadors from Lacedæmon were arrived, namely, Rhamphius, Melesippus, and Agesander, and spake nothing of that which formerly they were wont, but only this, "That the Lacedæmonians desire that there should be peace, which may be had, if you will suffer the Grecians to be governed by their own laws," the Athenians called an assembly, and propounding their opinions among themselves, thought good, after they had debated the matter, to give them an answer once for all. And many stood forth, and delivered their minds on either side, some for the war, and some that this act concerning the Megareans ought not to stand in their way to peace, but that they should abrogate it. And Pericles, the son of Xantippus, the principal man at that time of all Athens, and most powerful both in speech and action, gave his advice in such manner as follows:

"Men of Athens, I still hold the same opinion, not to give way to the Peloponnesians, although I know that men have not the same feelings in the war itself, which they have when they are incited to it, but change their opinions with the events, and I see also that I must now advise the same things, or very nearly the same as before; and I require of you, with whom my counsel may have effect, that if we miscarry in aught, to render your aid to support what is either decreed by common consent, or if we prosper, not attribute it to your own wisdom. For it often happens with the events of actions no less than with the purposes of man, to proceed with uncertainty: which is also the cause that when any thing happens contrary to our expectation, we are wont to lay the fault on fortune. That the Lacedæmonians, both formerly, and especially now, take counsel how to do us mischief, is manifest. For whereas it is said, [in the articles of the treaty,] that in disputed matters, we shall give and receive trials of judgment, and in the mean time, either side hold what they possess, they never yet sought any such trial themselves, nor do they accept of the same offered by us. They wish to clear themselves of their accusations by war rather than by words: and come hither no more now to expostulate, but to command. For they command us to arise and depart from before Potidæa, and to restore

From Thucydides, *History of the Peloponnesian War*, translated by Thomas Hobbes (Oxford: Henry Slatter and Joseph Vincent, 1841), [bk. 1,] 91–96.

Ægina to the liberty of its own laws, and to abrogate the act concerning the Megareans: and they that come last command us to restore all the Grecians to their liberty. Now let none of you conceive that we shall go to war for a trifle, by not abrogating the act concerning Megara, about which they principally hold forth that for the abrogation of it the war shall not take place; nor retain in your minds any feeling of self blame, as if a small matter moved you to the war: for even this small matter contains the trial and constancy of your resolution; wherein if you give way to them, you will hereafter have their commands laid upon you as to some greater matter, as men that for fear will obey them likewise in that. But by a stiff denial, you will make it evident to them, that they must hold intercourse with you hereafter on terms of more equality.

"Resolve therefore forthwith, either to yield them obedience, before you receive damage; or if we must have war, (which for my part I think is best,) be the pretence weighty or light, not to give way, nor keep what we possess in fear. For the greatest and the least claim, imposed by equals upon their neighbours, before judicial trial, by way of command, amounts to the same degree of subjection. As for the war, how both we and they be furnished, and why we are not likely to be less fully prepared than they, by hearing the particulars, you shall now understand. The Peloponnesians are men that live by their labour, without money, either individually or in a common exchequer. Besides, in long wars, and by sea, they are without experience; for the wars which they have had one against another, have been but short, through poverty; and such men can neither man their fleets, nor yet send out their armies by land very often, because they would have to be absent from all that is their own, and maintain themselves on their own private resources; and be besides kept out from the use of the sea. It must be superabundant revenues, not forced contributions, that support wars, and such as live by their labour are more ready to serve the wars with their bodies than with their money. For they feel confident that their bodies will outlive the danger, but their money they are by no means confident that they shall not expend before their object be gained; especially if the war, as it is likely, should last long. So that the Peloponnesians and their confederates, though for one battle they be able to stand out against all Greece besides, yet to maintain a war against such as have their preparations of another kind, they are not able; inasmuch as not having one and the same council, they can speedily perform nothing upon the moment: and having equality of vote, and not being of the same race, every one will press his particular interest, whereby nothing is like to be fully executed. For some will desire most to take revenge on some enemies, and others least to hurt what is their own; and being long before they can assemble, they take the less part of their time to debate the common business, and the greater to despatch their own private affairs. And each one thinks not that owing to his neglect he will injure the public welfare, but thinks that it is the duty of somebody else to look to that instead of him; not observing how that by the same idea held by every one singly, the common welfare is jointly ruined.

"But their greatest hinderance of all will be their want of money, which being raised slowly, their actions must be full of delay; but the opportunities of war are not wont to wait. As for their fortifying places here, and as for their navy, they are matters not worthy fear. For it were a hard matter for a city equal to our own, in time of peace to fortify in that manner, much less in the country of an enemy, and we no less fortified against them. And if they formed a fort here, though they might be excursions, and by the receiving of our fugitives, annoy some part of our territory; yet the thus building a fort would not be able to hinder us from sailing into their territories, and from taking revenge with our fleet, which is the thing wherein our strength lies. For we have more experience in land service by use of the sea, than they have in sea service by use of the land. Nor will they attain the knowledge of naval affairs easily. For you, though applying yourselves to it immediately from the time of the Persian war, have not yet attained it fully. How then should husbandmen, not seamen—whom also we will not suffer to apply themselves to it, by their being kept continually blockaded with numerous fleets—perform any thing of consequence? Indeed, against a few ships they might venture, encouraging their want of knowledge by numbers; but awed by many they will not stir; and not by applying themselves to it, will be yet more unskilful, and thereby more cowardly. For knowledge of naval matters is an art as well as any other, and not to be attended to at idle times as a by-job, but requiring, rather, that whilst it is learning, nothing else should at the same time be done as by-work.

"But if they should even remove any of the money at Olympia and Delphi, and therewith, by greater wages, go about to draw from us the foreigners employed in our fleet; this indeed, if when we ourselves and the Metics went on board ship, we could not match them, were a dangerous matter. But now we can both do this, and, which is the strongest point, we have steersmen, and other men necessary for the service of a ship, both more and better of our own citizens, than are in all the rest of Greece. Besides that on account of the risk, not any of these foreigners would be willing to leave his own place of residence; and with less hope at the same time of [victory,] for a few days' high pay, take part with the other side. In this manner, or like to this, seems to me to stand the case of the Peloponnesians: whereas ours is both free from what in theirs I have reprehended, and has many great advantages besides. If they invade our territory by land, we will invade theirs by sea; and when we have wasted part of Peloponnesus, and they all Attica, the damage done will not be found to be equal. For they, unless by the sword, can gain no other territory instead of that we shall destroy: whereas for us there is other land, both in the islands and the continent: for the dominion of the sea is a matter of the greatest advantage. Consider but this; if we dwelt in the islands, who would have been less liable to attack? We must therefore now, forming our plans and ideas as near as we can in accordance with that kind of situation, lay aside the care of our fields and dwellings, and applying ourselves to guarding the city and to the sea; not for the loss of them, out of passion give battle to the Peloponnesians, far more in number than ourselves; (for though we should give them an overthrow, we should have to fight again with as many more: and if we should experience any reverse, we should lose the help of our confederates, which are our strength; for when we become unable to lead expeditions against them, they will revolt:) nor bewail ye the loss of fields or houses, but of men's bodies; for men acquire these, but these do not acquire men. And if I thought I should persuade you, I would advise you to go out, and destroy them yourselves, and shew the Peloponnesians that you will never yield them obedience for the sake of such things as these.

"There be many other things that lead me to expect victory, in case you do not at the same time that you are in this war strive to enlarge your dominion, and do not also add to it other dangers of your own seeking; for I am afraid of our own errors more than of their designs, but they shall be spoken of in a future discourse, during the prosecution of the war itself. For the present, let us send away these men with this answer: 'that the Megareans shall have the liberty of our fairs and ports, if the Lacedæmonians will also desist from forbidding us and our confederates to dwell among them. For neither our act concerning Megara, nor their banishment of strangers, is forbidden in the articles. Also that we will let the Grecian cities be free, if they were so when the peace was made; and if the Lacedæmonians will also give leave to their confederates to use their freedom, not as shall serve the turn of the Lacedæmonians, but as they themselves shall every one think good. Also, that we will submit to judicial trial according to the articles, and will not begin the war, but will repel those that do.' For this is both just, and becoming to the dignity of this city to return as our answer. Nevertheless you must know, that of necessity we must go to war; and the more willingly we embrace it, the less likely to fall upon us shall we have our enemies; and that out of the greatest dangers, as well to cities as to private men, arise the greatest honours. For our fathers, when they supported the attack of the Medes, did—not only from resources inferior to what we now have, nay, abandoning even what they had—by wisdom rather than fortune, by courage rather than strength, both repel the Barbarian, and advance this state to the height it is now at. Of whom we ought not now to come short, but rather to repel our enemies by every means, and do our best to deliver the state, unimpaired and whole to those who come after us."

Thus spake Pericles. The Athenians, thinking he advised them what was best, decreed as he would have them; answering the Lacedæmonians according to his direction, both in all particulars as he had spoken, and generally; that they would do nothing on command, but were ready to come to a decision concerning what they charged them with, upon equal and fair terms, by means of a judicial trial. So the ambassadors went home, and after these they sent them no more.

XENOPHON
(c. 426–c. 354 B.C.)

Xenophon was a pupil of Socrates and served in the cavalry before leaving Athens shortly after Sparta's victory in 404 at the end of the Peloponnesian War. In 401 he was in Persia with Greek mercenaries working for Cyrus the Younger, who was trying to seize the throne from his elder brother. But Cyrus was killed, and the Greeks had to make a retreat, after losing three of their commanders in a trap. Xenophon was elected head of the expedition and led a 2,500-km retreat lasting eighteen months, fighting the whole way.

Nothing is more difficult than making an orderly retreat when one is being harassed in unfavorable terrain, and the Anabasis, *or Retreat of the* Ten Thousand, *provides an exemplary account of this. Subsequently, after serving with Sparta, Xenophon wrote some of his works (inter alia the* Hellenica*) at Scillus, near Olympia, before returning to Athens. By then he was sixty years old, but he went on to write the* Hipparchicus, *a treatise on cavalry, and the* Cyropaedia, *a tale of the education of Cyrus the Great, king of Persia in the sixth century* B.C.

THE EXPEDITION OF CYRUS

Here they staid three days, both on account of the wounded, and because they found plenty of provisions, as wheat-meal, wine, and a great quantity of barley for horses; which was laid up for the satrap of the country. The fourth day they descended into the plain, where, when Tissaphernes had overtaken them with the army under his command, he taught them how necessary it was to encamp in the first village they came to, and to march no longer fighting: for some being wounded, some employed in carrying those that were so, and oth-

From Xenophon, *The Expedition of Cyrus*, in *The Whole Works of Xenophon*, translated by Ashley Cooper et al. (New York: Bangs, Brother, & Co., 1855), [bk. 3,] 229–32, [bk. 4] 235–48.

[82]

ers in carrying the arms of the latter, great numbers were not in a condition to fight. But when they were encamped, and the Barbarians, coming up to the village, offered to skirmish, the Greeks had greatly the advantage of them; for they found a great difference between sallying from their camp to repulse the enemy, and being obliged to march fighting, whenever they were attacked. When the evening approached it was time for the Barbarians to retire; because they never encamped at a less distance from the Greeks than sixty stadia, for fear these should fall upon them in the night. A Persian army being then subject to great inconveniences, for their horses are tied, and generally shackled, to prevent them from running away; and if an alarm happens, a Persian has the housing to fix, his horse to bridle, and his corslet to put on, before he can mount. All these things cannot be done in the night without great difficulty, particularly if there is an alarm. For this reason they always encamped at a distance from the Greeks. When these perceived they designed to retire, and that the word was given, they in the enemy's hearing received orders to make ready to march; whereupon the Barbarians made a halt; but when it grew late they departed; for they did not hold it expedient to march and arrive at their camp in the night.

When the Greeks plainly saw they were retired, they also decamped, and marching away, advanced about sixty stadia. The two armies were now at so great a distance from one another, that the enemy did not appear either the next day or the day after. But on the fourth, the Barbarians having got before the Greeks in the night, possessed themselves of an eminence that commanded the road through which the Greeks were to pass. It was the brow of a hill, under which lay the descent into the plain. As soon as Cheirisophus saw this eminence possessed by the enemy, he sent for Xenophon from the rear, and desired him to bring up the targeteers to the front. Xenophon did not take these with him, (for he saw Tissaphernes advancing with his whole army) but riding up to him himself, said, "Why do you send for me?" Cheirisophus answered, "You see the enemy have possessed themselves of the hill that commands the descent, and unless we dislodge them it is not possible for us to pass: but," adds he, "why did you not bring the targeteers with you?" Xenophon replied, because he did not think proper to leave the rear naked, when the enemy was in sight: "but," says he, "it is high time to consider how we shall dislodge those men." Here Xenophon observing the top of the mountain that was above their own army, found there was a passage from that to the hill where the enemy was posted. Upon this he said, "O Cheirisophus! I think the best thing we can do is to gain the top of this mountain as soon as possible; for if we are once masters of that, the enemy cannot maintain themselves upon the hill. Do you stay with the army; if you think fit, I will go up to the hill; or do you go, if you desire it, and I will stay here." Cheirisophus answered, I give you your choice; to this Xenophon replied, that as he was the younger man, he chose to go: but desired he would send with him some troops from the front, since it would take a great deal of time to bring up a detachment from the rear. So Cheirisophus sent the targeteers that were in the front: Xenophon also took those that were in the middle of the square. Besides these, Cheirisophus ordered the three hundred chosen men, who attended on himself in the front of the square, to follow him.

After that they marched with all possible expedition. The enemy, who were upon the hill, the moment they saw them climb the mountain, advanced at the same time, striving to get there before them. Upon this occasion there was a vast shout raised both by the Greek army, and that of Tissaphernes, each encouraging their own men. And Xenophon, riding by the side of his troops, called out to them, "Soldiers! think you are this minute contending to return to Greece, this minute to see your wives and children: after this momentary labour we shall go on without any further opposition." To whom Soteridas, the Sicyonian, said, "We are not upon equal terms, O Xenophon! for you are on horseback, while I am greatly fatigued with carrying my shield." Xenophon hearing this, leaped from his horse, and thrust him out of his rank; then, taking his shield, marched on as fast he could. He happened to have a horseman's corslet on at that time which was very troublesome. However, he called to those who were before to mend their pace, and to those behind, who followed with great difficulty, to come up. The rest of the soldiers beat and abused Soteridas, and threw stones at him, till they obliged him to take his shield, and go on. Then Xenophon remounted, and led them on horseback, as far as the way would allow; and, when it became impassable for his horse, he hastened forward on foot. At last they gained the top of the mountain, and prevented the enemy.

Hereupon the Barbarians turned their backs, and fled every one as he could, and the Greeks remained masters of the eminence. Tissaphernes and Ariæus with their men, turning out of the road, went another way, while Cheirisophus with his forces came down into the plain, and encamped in a village abounding in every thing. There were also many other villages in this plain, near the Tigris, full of all sorts of provisions. In the evening the enemy appeared on a sudden in the plain, and cut off some of the Greeks who were dispersed in plundering; for many herds of cattle were taken, as the people of the country were endeavouring to make them pass the river. Here Tissaphernes and his army attempted to set fire to the villages; whereby some of the Greeks were disheartened, from the apprehension of wanting provisions if he burned them. About this time Cheirisophus and his men came back from relieving their companions, and Xenophon being come down into the plain, and riding through the ranks, after the Greeks were returned, said, "You see, O Greeks!

the enemy already acknowledge the country to be ours; for when they made peace with us, they stipulated that we should not burn the country belonging to the king, and now they set fire to it themselves, as if they looked upon it no longer as their own. But wherever they leave any provisions for themselves, thither also they shall see us direct our march. But, O Cheirisophus! I think we ought to attack these burners, as in defence of our country." Cheirisophus answered, "I am not of that opinion. On the contrary, let us also set fire to it ourselves, and by that means they will give over the sooner."

When they came to their tents, the soldiers employed themselves in getting provisions, and the generals and captains assembled, and were in great perplexity; for on one side of them were exceeding high mountains, and on the other a river so deep, that when they sounded it with their pikes, the ends of them did not even appear above the water. While they were in this perplexity, a certain Rhodian came to them, and said, "Gentlemen, I will undertake to carry over four thousand heavy-armed men at a time, if you will supply me with what I want, and give me a talent for my pains." Being asked what he wanted, "I shall want," says he, "two thousand leather bags. I see here great numbers of sheep, goats, oxen, and asses: if these are flayed, and their skins blown, we may easily pass the river with them. I shall also want the girths belonging to the sumpter-horses: with these," adds he, "I will fasten the bags to one another, and hanging stones to them, let them down into the water instead of anchors, then tie up the bags at both ends, and when they are upon the water, lay fascines upon them, and cover them with earth. I will make you presently sensible," continues he, "that you cannot sink, for every bag will bear up two men, and the fascines and the earth will prevent them from slipping."

The generals, hearing this, thought the invention ingenious, but impossible to be put in practice; there being great numbers of horse on the other side of the river to oppose their passage, and these would at once break all their measures. The next day the army turned back again, taking a different road from that which leads to Babylon, and marched to the villages that were not burned, setting fire to those they abandoned, insomuch that the enemy did not ride up to them, but looked on, wondering which way the Greeks meant to take, and what their intention was. Here, while the soldiers were employed in getting provisions, the generals and captains re-assembled, and ordering the prisoners to be brought in, inquired concerning every country that lay round them. The prisoners informed them that there was to the south a road that led to Babylon and Media, through which they came: another to the east, leading to Susa and Ecbatana, where the king is said to pass the summer and the spring; a third to the west over the Tigris, to Lydia and Ionia; and that the road which lay over the mountains to the north, led to the Carduchians. This people, they said, inhabited those mountains, and that they were a warlike nation, and not subject to the king; and that once the king's army, consisting of one and twenty thousand men, penetrated into their country, whence not one of them returned, the roads being hardly passable. But that whenever there was a peace subsisting between them and the governor residing in the plain, there was an intercourse between the two nations.

The generals, hearing this, kept those prisoners by themselves from whom they received the intelligence of each country, without discovering what route they designed to take. However, they found there was a necessity to pass the mountains, and penetrate into the country of the Carduchians: for the prisoners informed them, that, as soon as they had passed through it, they should arrive in Armenia, which was a spacious and plentiful country, and of which Orontas was governor: whence they might, without difficulty, march which way so-ever they pleased. Upon this they offered sacrifice to the end that when they found it convenient they might depart, (for they were afraid the pass over the mountains might be possessed by the enemy,) and commanded the soldiers, as soon as they had supped, to get their baggage ready, then all to go to rest, and march upon the first order.

. . . When the Greeks came to the place, where the river Tigris is, both from its depth and breadth, absolutely impassable, and no road appeared, the craggy mountains of the Carduchians hanging over the river, the generals resolved to march over those mountains: for they were informed by the prisoners, that, after they had passed them, they would have it in their power to cross the head of the Tigris, in Armenia, if they thought proper; if not, to go round it. The source of the Euphrates also was said not to be far distant from that of the Tigris: and, indeed, the distance between these two rivers is in some places but small. To the end, therefore, that the enemy might not be acquainted with their design of penetrating into the country of the Carduchians, and defeat it, by possessing themselves of the eminences, they executed it in the following manner: when it was about the last watch, and so much of the night was left, as to allow them to traverse the plain while it was yet dark, they encamped; and, marching when the order was given, came to the mountains by break of day. Cheirisophus commanded the vanguard with his own people, and all the light-armed men; and Xenophon brought up the rear with the heavy-armed, having none of the light-armed, because there seemed no danger of the enemy's attacking their rear, while they were marching up the mountain. Cheirisophus gained the top before he was perceived by the enemy: then led forward; and the rest of the army, as fast as they passed the summit, followed him into the villages, that lay dispersed in the valleys and recesses of the mountains.

Upon this, the Carduchians left their houses, and, with their wives and children, fled to the hills, where they had an opportunity of supplying themselves with provisions in abundance. The houses were well furnished with all sorts of brass utensils, which the Greeks forbore to plunder: neither did they pursue the inhabitants, in hope, by sparing them, to prevail upon the Carduchians, since they were enemies to the king, to conduct them through their country in a friendly manner: but they took all the provisions they met with, for they were compelled to it by necessity. However, the Carduchians paid no regard to their invitations, nor showed any other symptoms of a friendly disposition; and when the rear of the Greek army was descending from the top of the mountains into the villages, it being now dark, (for as the way was narrow, they spent the whole day in the ascent of the mountains, and the descent from thence into the villages,) some of the Carduchians, gathering together, attacked the hindmost, and killed and wounded some of them with stones and arrows. They were but a few in number, for the Greek army came upon them unawares. Had the enemy been more numerous at that time, great part of the army had been in danger. In this manner they passed the night in the villages: the Carduchians made fires all round them upon the mountains, and both had their eyes upon one another.

As soon as it was day, the generals and the captains of the Greeks assembled, and resolved to reserve only those sumpter-horses upon their march that were necessary and most able, and to leave the rest, and dismiss all the slaves they had newly taken: for the great number of sumpter-horses and slaves retarded their march; and many of their men, by having charge of these, were unfit for action. Besides, there being so many mouths, they were under a necessity of providing and carrying double the quantity of provisions. This being resolved, they gave orders to have it put in execution.

While, therefore, they were upon their march after dinner, the generals placed themselves in a narrow pass, and, whatever they found reserved by the soldiers, contrary to order, they took it away: and the men submitted, unless any of them happened privately to have retained some boy or beautiful woman he was fond of. In this manner they marched that day, sometimes fighting, and sometimes resting themselves. The next day there was a great storm: however, they were obliged to go on; for their provisions failed them. Cheirisophus led the van, Xenophon brought up the rear. Here, the ways being narrow, the enemy made a brisk attack upon them, and, coming up close, discharged their arrows, and made use of their slings; so that the Greeks, sometimes pursuing, and sometimes retreating, were obliged to march slowly: and Xenophon often ordered the army to halt, when the enemy pressed hard upon them. Upon one of these orders, Cheirisophus, who used to stand still on the like occasions, did not stop, but marched faster than usual, and ordered the men to follow. By this it appeared there was something extraordinary, but they were not at leisure to send to him to inquire the cause of this haste; so that the march of those in the rear had the resemblance more of a flight than a retreat. Here fell a brave man, Cleonymus, a Lacedæmonian, who was wounded in the side by an arrow, that made its way both through his shield and his buff coat. Here also fell Basias, an Arcadian, whose head was pierced quite through with an arrow. When they arrived at the place, where they designed to encamp, Xenophon immediately went as he was to Cheirisophus, and blamed him for not stopping, but obliging the rear to fly and fight at the same time. "Here we have lost two brave and worthy men," says he, "without being able either to bring them off, or to bury them." To this Cheirisophus answered, "Cast your eyes upon those mountains, and observe how impassable they all are. You see there is but one road, and that a steep one. It is, you may observe, possessed too by a great multitude of men, who stand ready to defend it. For this reason, I marched hastily, without staying for you, that, if possible, I might prevent the enemy, and make myself master of the pass; for our guides assure us there is no other road." Xenophon replied, "I have two prisoners: for, when the enemy molested us in our march, we placed some men in ambush, which gave us time to breathe, and, having killed some of them, we were also desirous of taking some alive, with this view, that we might have guides who were acquainted with the country.

The prisoners, therefore, being brought before them, they questioned them separately, whether they knew of any other road than that which lay before them. One of them said he knew no other, though he was threatened with divers kinds of torture. As he said nothing to the purpose, he was put to death in the presence of the other. The survivor said, this man pretended he did not know the other road, because he had a daughter married to a man who lived there; but that he himself would undertake to conduct us through a road that was passable even for the sumpter-horses. Being asked whether there was any difficult pass in that road, he said there was a summit, which, if not secured in time, would render the passage impracticable. Upon this it was thought proper to assemble the captains, the targeteers, and some of the heavy-armed men; and, having informed them how matters stood, to ask them whether any of them would show their gallantry, and voluntarily undertake this service. Two of the heavy-armed men offered themselves: Aristonymus of Methydria, and Agasias of Stymphalus, both Arcadians. But Callimachus of Parrhasie, an Arcadian, and Agasias, had a contest who should undertake it. The latter said that he would go, and take with him volunteers out of the whole army. "For I am well assured," says he, "if I have the command, many of the youth will follow me." After that they asked if any of the light-armed men, or of their officers, would also be of the party. Upon which Aristeas of Chios, presented himself. He had, upon many occasions of this nature, done great service to the army.

The day was now far advanced; so the generals ordered these to eat something, and set out, and delivered the guide to them bound. It was agreed that if they made themselves masters of the summit, they should make it good that night, and as soon as it was day, give them notice of it by sounding a trumpet; and that those above should charge that body of the enemy that was posted in the passage that lay before them, while those below marched up to their assistance with all the expedition they were able. When things were thus ordered, they set forward, being about two thousand in number. And, notwithstanding it rained most violently, Xenophon marched at the head of the rear-guard towards the passage before them, in order to draw the attention of the enemy that way, and conceal as much as possible the march of the detachment. When Xenophon, with the rear-guard, came to a valley which they were to pass, in order to climb the ascent, the Barbarians rolled down vast round stones, each a ton in weight, with others both larger and smaller. These being dashed against the rocks in their fall, the splinters were hurled every way, which made it absolutely impossible to approach the road. Some of the captains despairing to gain this passage, endeavoured to find out another, and employed themselves in this manner till it was dark. When they imagined they could retire without being seen, they went away to get their supper; for the rear-guard had not dined that day. However, the enemy continued to roll down stones all night, as was perceived by the noise they made in their fall. In the meantime, those who marched round with the guide, surprised the enemy's guard as they were sitting round a fire; and having killed some of them, and forced others down the precipice, they staid there, thinking they had made themselves masters of the summit. But in this they were mistaken, for there was still an eminence above them, near which lay the narrow way, where the guard sat. There was indeed a passage from the post they had taken, to that the enemy were possessed of, in the open road. Here they remained that night.

As soon as it was day, they put themselves in order, and marched in silence against the enemy; and, there being a mist, came close to them before they were perceived. When they saw one another, the trumpet sounded, and the Greeks, shouting, made their attack. However, the Barbarians did not stand to receive them, but quitted the road, very few of them being killed in the flight: for they were prepared for expedition. Cheirisophus and his men hearing the trumpet, immediately marched up the passage which lay before them. The rest of the generals took bye-paths, each of them where he happened to be, and, climbing as well as they could, drew up one another with their pikes; and these were the first who joined the detachment that had gained the post. Xenophon, with one half of the rear guard, marched up the same way those who had the guide went, this road being the most convenient for the sumpter-horses; the other half he ordered to come up behind the baggage. In their march they came to a hill that commanded the road, and was possessed by the enemy, whom they were either to dislodge, or to be severed from the rest of the Greeks. The men indeed, might have gone the same way the rest took, but the sumpter-horses could go no other. Encouraging, therefore, one another, they made their attack upon the hill in columns, not surrounding it, but leaving the enemy room to run away, if they were so disposed. Accordingly, the Barbarians seeing our men marching up the hill, every one where he could, without discharging either their arrows or their darts upon those who approached the road, fled, and quitted the place. The Greeks, having marched by this hill, saw another before them also possessed by the enemy. This they resolved to attack likewise; but Xenophon, considering that if he left the hill they had already taken without a guard, the enemy might repossess it, and from thence annoy the sumpter-horses as they passed by them; (for the way being narrow, there was a long file of them.) He therefore left, upon this hill, Cephisodorus, the son of Cephisiphon, an Athenian, and Archagoras, a banished Argive, both captains; while he with the rest marched to the second hill, and took that also in the same manner. There yet remained a third, by much the steepest. This was the eminence that commanded the post where the guard was surprised at the fire, the night before, by the detachment. When the Greeks approached the hill, the Barbarians quitted it without striking a stroke: so that every body was surprised and suspected they left the place, fearing to be surrounded and besieged in it. But the truth was, that seeing from the eminence what passed behind, they all made haste away with a design to fall upon the rear.

Xenophon, with the youngest of his men, ascended to the top of this hill, and ordered the rest to march slowly after, that the two captains, who were left behind, might join them: and that when they were all together, they should choose some even place in the road, and there stand to their arms. He had no sooner given his orders than Archagoras, the Argive, came flying from the enemy, and brought an account, that they were driven from the first hill, and that Cephisodorus and Amphicrates, and all the rest who had not leaped from the rock and joined the rear, were slain. The Barbarians, after this advantage, came to the hill opposite to that where Xenophon stood; and Xenophon treated with them, by an interpreter, concerning a truce, and demanded the dead. They consented to deliver them, provided he agreed not to burn their villages. Xenophon came into this. While the other part of the army approached, and these were employed in treating, all the men moved from the post they were in towards the same place. Upon this the enemy made a stand, and when the Greeks began to descend from the top of the hill to join those who were drawn up in order of battle, they advanced in great numbers, and with tumult; and, after they had gained the top of the hill, which Xenophon had quitted, they rolled down stones, and broke the leg of one of our men. Here Xenophon's armour-bearer deserted him, taking away his shield: but Eurylochus of Lusia, an Arcadian, and one of the heavy-armed men, ran to his relief, and covered both himself and Xenophon with his shield, while the rest joined those who stood ready drawn up.

And now the Greeks were altogether, and quartered there, in many fine houses, where they found provisions in abundance: for there was so great a plenty of wine, that they kept it in plastered cisterns. Here Xenophon and Cheirisophus prevailed upon the Barbarians to deliver up their dead in exchange for the guide. These, as far as they were able, they buried with all the honours that are due to the memory of brave men. The next day they marched without a guide, and the enemy, both by fighting with them, and seizing all the passes, endeavoured to hinder them from advancing. Whenever, therefore, they opposed the vanguard, Xenophon, ascending the mountains from behind, endeavoured to gain some post that commanded the enemy, and by this means opened a passage for those who were in the van: and, when they attacked the rear, Cheirisophus ascended the hills, and endeavouring also to get above the enemy, removed the obstruction they gave to the march of the rear. Thus they were very attentive to relieve one another. Sometimes also the Barbarians, after the Greeks had ascended the eminences, gave them great disturbance in their descent, for they were very nimble; and, though they came near to our men, yet still they got off, having no other arms but bows and slings. They were very skilful archers; their bows were near three cubits in length, and their arrows above two. When they discharged their arrows, they drew the string by pressing upon the lower part of the bow with their left foot. These arrows pierced through the shields and corslets of our men, who, taking them up, made use of them instead of darts, by fixing thongs to them. In these places the Cretans were of great service. They were commanded by Stratocles, a Cretan.

This day they staid in the villages situate above the plain that extends to the river Centrites, which is two hundred feet broad, and the boundary between Armenia and the country of the Carduchians. Here the Greeks rested themselves. This river is about six or seven stadia from the Carduchian mountains. Here, therefore, they staid with great satisfaction, having plenty of provisions, and often calling to mind the difficulties they had undergone; for, during the seven days they had marched through the country of the Carduchians, they were continually fighting, and suffered more than from all the attempts of the king and Tissaphernes. Looking upon themselves, therefore, as freed from these hardships, they rested with pleasure. But, as soon as it was day, they saw a body of horse on the other side of the river, completely armed, and ready to oppose their passage; and, above the horse, another of foot drawn up upon an eminence, to hinder them from penetrating into Armenia. These were Armenians, Mygdonians, and Chaldæans, all mercenary troops, belonging to Orontas and Artuchus. The Chaldæans were said to be a free people, and warlike; their arms were long shields and spears. The eminence upon which they were drawn up, was about three or four hundred feet from the river. The only road the Greeks could discover, led upwards, and seemed to have been made by art. Over against this road the Greeks endeavoured to pass the river: but, upon trial, they found the water came up above their breasts; that the river was rendered uneven by large slippery stones; and that it was not possible for them to hold their arms in the water; which, if they attempted, they were borne away by the stream, and, if they carried them upon their heads, they were exposed to the arrows, and the other missive weapons of the enemy. They retired, therefore, and encamped on the banks of the river.

From hence they discovered a great number of armed Carduchians, who were got together upon the mountain, in the very place where they had encamped the night before. Here the Greeks were very much disheartened, seeing on one side of them a river hardly passable, and the banks of it covered with troops to obstruct their passage, and, on the other, the Carduchians ready to fall upon their rear, if they attempted it. This day, therefore, and the following night, they remained in the same place under great perplexity. Here Xenophon had a dream: he thought he was in chains, and that his chains breaking asunder of their own accord, he found himself at liberty, and went withersoever he pleased. As soon as the first dawn of day appeared, he went to Cheirisophus, and told him he was in hopes every thing would be well, and acquainted him with his dream. Cheirisophus was pleased to hear it: and, while the morn advanced, all the generals who were present offered sacrifice, and the very first victims were favourable. As soon therefore as the sacrifice was over, the generals and captains departing ordered the soldiers to get their breakfast. While Xenophon was at breakfast, two young men came to him, for it was well known that all persons might have free access to him at his meals; and, that, were he even asleep, they might wake him, if they had any thing to communicate concerning the operations of the war. These youths informed him, that while they were getting brush-wood for the fire, they saw on the other side of the river, among the rocks that reached down to it, an old man, and a woman with some maid-servants, hiding something, that looked like bags full of clothes, in the hollow of a rock. That, seeing this, they thought they might securely pass the river, because the place was inaccessible to the enemy's horse. So they undressed themselves, and taking their naked daggers in their hands, proposed to swim over; but the river being fordable, they found themselves on the other side before the river came up to their middle, and having taken the clothes, repassed it.

Xenophon hearing this made a libation himself, and ordered wine to be given to the youths to do the same, and that they should address their prayers to the gods, who had sent the dream, and discovered the passage to complete their happiness. After the libation, he immediately carried the two youths to Cheirisophus, to whom they gave the same account. Cheirisophus, hearing this, made libations also. After that, they gave orders to the soldiers to get their baggage ready. Then, assembling the generals, they consulted with them in what manner they should pass the river with most advantage, and both overcome those who opposed them in front, and secure themselves against the others, who threatened their rear. And it was resolved that Cheirisophus should lead the van, and pass over with one half of the army, while the other staid with Xenophon: and that the sumpter-horses, with all those that attended the army, should pass in the middle. After this disposition was made, they began their march. The two youths led the way, keeping the river on their left. They had about four stadia to go before they came to the ford.

As they marched on one side of the river, several bodies of horse advanced on the other opposite to them. When they came to the ford, and to the bank of the river, the men stood to their arms, and first Cheirisophus, with a garland upon his head, pulled off his clothes, and, taking his arms, commanded all the rest to do the same; he then ordered the captains to draw up their companies in columns, and march some on his left hand, and some on his right. In the meantime the priests offered sacrifice, and poured the blood of the victims into the river; and the enemy, from their bows and slings, discharged a volley of arrows and stones, but none of them reached our men. After the victims appeared favourable, all the soldiers sung the pæan and shouted, all the women answered them; for the men had many mistresses in the army.

Immediately Cheirisophus, with his men, went into the river; and Xenophon, taking those of the rear-guard, who were most prepared for expedition, marched back in all haste to the passage opposite to the road that led to the Armenian mountains, making a feint as if his design was to pass the river in that place, and intercept the horse that were marching along the bank of it. The enemy, seeing Cheirisophus with his men passing the river with great ease, and Xenophon with his forces marching back in all haste, were afraid of being intercepted, and fled with precipitation to the road that led from the river up into the country. Having gained that road, they continued their march up the mountains. As soon as Lycius, who had the command of the horse, and Æschines, who commanded the targeteers belonging to Cheirisophus, saw the enemy flying with so much haste, they pursued them, the rest of the soldiers crying out to them that they would not be left behind, but would march up the mountain in a body. When Cheirisophus had passed the river with his forces, he did not pursue the horse, but marched along the bank against the other body of the enemy that was posted upon the upper ground. These, finding themselves abandoned by their horse, and seeing our heavy-armed men coming up to attack them, quitted the eminence that commanded the river.

Xenophon therefore perceiving every thing went well on the other side, returned in all haste to the army that was passing over; for, by this time the Carduchians were seen descending into the plain, as if they designed to fall upon the rear. Cheirisophus had now possessed himself of the eminence, and Lycius, while he was pursuing the enemy, with a few of his men, took part of their baggage that was left behind, and in it rich apparel, and drinking cups. The baggage of the Greeks, with those who had charge of it, was yet passing; when Xenophon, facing about, drew up his men against the Carduchians. He ordered all the captains to divide their several companies into two distinct bodies of twenty-five men each, and to extend their front to the left, and that the captains with the leaders of these distinct bodies should march against the Carduchians, while the hindmost men of every file posted themselves upon the bank of the river.

Now the Carduchians, when they saw the rear reduced to a few by the departure of those who had the charge of the baggage, advanced the faster, singing as they came on. Upon this, Cheirisophus, seeing all on his side was secure, sent the targeteers, the slingers, and archers to Xenophon, with directions to do whatever he commanded: but he, as soon as he saw them coming down the hill, sent a messenger to them with orders to halt, as soon as they came to the river; and that, when they saw him begin to pass it with his men, they should come forward in the water on each side opposite to him, the darters with their fingers in the slings of their darts, and the archers with their arrows on the string, as if they designed to pass over, but not advance far into the river. At the same time he ordered his own men, when they came near enough to the enemy to reach them with their slings, and the heavy-armed men struck their shields with their pikes, to sing the pæan, and rush at once upon the enemy: and, when they were put to flight, and the trumpet from the river sounded a charge, to face about to the right, and that the hindmost men of every file should lead the way, and all make what haste they could to the river, which they were to pass in their ranks, that they might not hinder one another; telling them that he should look upon him as the bravest man, who first reached the opposite side.

The Carduchians, seeing those who remained, but few in number, (for many even of those who had orders to stay, were gone, some to take care of the sumpter-horses, some of their baggage, and others of other things) came up boldly towards them, and began to use their slings and bows. But, when the Greeks, singing the pæan, ran forward to attack them, they did not stand to receive them, (for though they were well enough armed for a sudden onset, and retreat upon the mountains they inhabited, yet they were not all so to fight hand to hand.) In the meantime the trumpet sounded, upon which the enemy fled much faster than before; and the Greeks, facing about, passed the river in all haste. Some of the enemy seeing this, ran back to the river, and wounded a few of our men with their arrows; but many of them, even when the Greeks were on the other side, were observed to continue their flight. In the meantime those who had met them in the river, carried on by their courage, advanced unseasonably, and repassed it after Xenophon and his men were on the other side; by this means some of them also were wounded.

The army having passed the river about noon, drew up in their ranks, and, in this manner, marched at once over the plain of Armenia, intermixed with hills of an easy ascent, making no less than five parasangs: for there were no villages near the river, by reason of the continual wars with the Carduchians. However at last they came to a large village, that had a palace in it belonging to the satrap, and upon most of the houses there were turrets: here they found provisions in abundance. From this place they made, in two days' march, ten parasangs, till they were advanced above the head of the Tigris. From thence they made fifteen parasangs in three days' march, and came to the river Teleboas. The river, though not large, was beautiful, and had many fine villages on its banks: this country was called the western part of Armenia. The governor of it was Teribazus, who had behaved himself with great fidelity to the king, and, when he was present, no other, lifted the king on horseback. This person rode up towards the Greeks with a body of horse, and, sending his interpreter, acquainted them that he desired to speak with their commanders. Upon this the generals thought proper to hear what he had to say, and advancing within hearing, asked him what he wanted. He answered that he was willing to enter into a league with them upon these terms: that he should not do any injury to the Greeks, or they burn the houses, but have liberty to take what provisions they wanted. The generals agreed to this: so they concluded a league upon these conditions.

From thence they advanced through a plain, and in three days' march made fifteen parasangs, Teribazus following them with his forces at the distance of about ten stadia, when they came to a palace, surrounded with many villages, abounding in all sorts of provisions. While they lay encamped in this place, there fell so great a snow in the night, that it was resolved the next morning the soldiers, with their generals, should remove into the villages, and quarter there, for no enemy appeared; and the great quantity of snow seemed a security to them. Here they found all sorts of good provisions, such as cattle, corn, old wines exceeding fragrant, raisins and legumens of all kinds. In the meantime, some of the men, who had straggled from the camp, brought word that they had seen an army, and that in the night many fires appeared. For this reason the generals thought it not safe for the troops to quarter in the villages at a distance from one another: so resolved to bring the army together. Upon this they re-assembled, and it was determined to encamp abroad. While they passed the night in this camp, there fell so great a quantity of snow, that it covered both the arms and the men as they lay upon the ground; the sumpter-horses also were so benumbed with the snow, that it was with difficulty they were made to rise. It was a miserable sight to see the men lie upon the ground still covered with snow. But, when Xenophon was so hardy as to rise naked, and rive wood, immediately another got up, and taking the wood from him, cleft it himself. Upon this they all rose up, and making fires, anointed themselves; for they found there many sorts of ointments, which served them instead of oil, as hog's-grease, oil of sesame, of bitter almonds, and of turpentine. There was also found a precious ointment made of all these.

After this they determined to disperse themselves again in the villages, and quarter under cover. Upon which the soldiers ran with great shouts and pleasure to the houses and provisions; but those who had set fire to the houses, when they left them before, were justly punished by encamping abroad, exposed to the inclemency of the weather. From hence they sent that night a detachment to the mountains, where the stragglers said they had seen the fires, under the command of Democrates of Temenus, because he was ever thought to give a true account of things of this nature, reporting matters as they really were. At his return he said he had seen no fires, but, having taken a prisoner, he brought him with him. This man had a Persian bow and quiver, and an Amazonian battle-axe; and, being asked of what country he was, he said he was a Persian, and that he went from the army of Teribazus to get provisions. Upon this they asked him of what numbers that army consisted, and with what intention it was assembled. He answered, that Teribazus, besides his own army, had mercenary troops of Chalabians and Taochians; and, that his design was to attack the Greeks in their passage over the mountains, as they marched through the defile, which was their only road.

The generals, hearing this, resolved to assemble the army, and, leaving a guard in the camp under the command of Sophænetus of Stymphalus, they immediately set forward, taking the prisoner with them for their guide. After they had passed the mountains, the targeteers, who marched before the rest, as soon as they discovered the enemy's camp, ran to it with shouts, without staying for the heavy-armed men. The Barbarians, hearing the tumult, did not stand their ground, but fled. However some of them were killed, and about twenty horses taken, as was also the tent of Teribazus, in which they found beds with silver feet, and drinking cups, with some prisoners, who said they were his bakers and cupbearers. When the commanders of the heavy-armed were informed of all that passed, they determined to return in all haste to their own camp, lest any attempt should be made upon those they had left there; and immediately ordering a retreat to be sounded, they returned, and arrived there the same day.

The next day they resolved to march away with all the haste they could, before the enemy should rally their forces, and possess themselves of the pass. Their baggage therefore being presently ready, they set forward through a deep snow with many guides; and having the same day passed the eminence upon which Teribazus designed to attack them, they encamped. From thence they made three marches through a desert, and came to the Euphrates, which they passed, the water coming up to their navel. It was said the sources of this river were not far off. From thence they made, in three days' march, fifteen parasangs, over a plain covered with deep snow. The last day's march was very grievous, for the north wind, blowing full in their faces, quite parched and benumbed the men. Upon this one of the priests advised to sacrifice to the wind, which was complied with, and the vehemence of it visibly abated. The snow was a fathom in depth, insomuch that many of the slaves and sumpter-horses died, and about thirty soldiers. They made fires all night, for they found plenty of wood in the place where they encamped; and those who came late, having no wood, the others who were before arrived, and had made fires, would not allow them to warm themselves till they had given them a share of the wheat, or of the other provisions they had brought with them. By this exchange they relieved one another's wants. In the places where the fires were made, the snow being melted, there were large pits which reached down to the ground; this afforded an opportunity of measuring the depth of the snow.

From thence they marched all the next day through the snow, when many of them contracted the bulimy. Xenophon, who commanded the rear, seeing them lie upon the ground, knew not what their distemper was: but being informed by those who were acquainted with it, that it was plainly the bulimy, and that, if they ate any thing, they would rise again, he went to the baggage, and, whatever refreshments he found there, he gave some to those who were afflicted with this distemper, and sent persons able to go about, to divide the rest among others, who were in the same condition: and as soon as they had eaten something, they rose up, and continued their march. During which, Cheirisophus came to a village, just as it was dark, and, at a fountain, without the walls, [he] found some women and girls, who belonged to it, carrying water. These inquired who they were? The interpreter answered, in Persia[n], that they were going to the satrap from the king. The women replied, that he was not there, but at a place distant about a parasang from thence. As it was late, they entered the walls together with the women, and went to the bailiff of the town. Here Cheirisophus encamped with all that could come up. The rest, who were unable to continue their march, passed the night without victuals or fire, by which means some of them perished: and a party of the enemy following our march, took some of the sumpter-horses that could not keep pace with the rest, and fought with one another about them. Some of the men also, who had lost their sight by the snow, or whose toes were rotted off by the intenseness of the cold, were left behind. The eyes were relieved against the snow by wearing something black before them, and the feet against the cold, by continual motion, and by pulling off their shoes in the night. If any slept with their shoes on, the latchets pierced their flesh, and their shoes stuck to their feet: for when their old shoes were worn out, they wore carbatines made of raw hides. These grievances therefore occasioned some of the soldiers to be left behind; who, seeing a piece of ground that appeared black, because there was no snow upon it, concluded it was melted; and melted it was by a vapour that was continually exhaling from a fountain in a valley near the place. Thither they betook themselves, and, sitting down, refused to march any further. Xenophon, who had charge of the rear, as soon as he was informed of this, tried all means to prevail upon them not to be left behind, telling them that the enemy were gotten together in great numbers and followed them close. At last he grew angry. They bid him kill them, if he would, for they were not able to go on. Upon this, he thought the best thing he could do, was, if possible, to strike a terror into the enemy that followed, lest they should fall upon the men that were tired. It was now dark, and the enemy came on with great tumult, quarrelling with one another about their booty. Upon this, such of the rear-guard as were well, rising up, rushed upon them; while those who were tired, shouted out as loud as they could, and struck their shields with their pikes. The enemy, alarmed at this, threw themselves into the valley through the snow, and were no more heard of.

Then Xenophon, with the rest of the forces, went away, assuring the sick men, that, the next day some people should be sent to them: but before they had gone four stadia, they found others taking their rest in the snow, and covered with it, no guard being appointed. These they obliged to rise, who acquainted him, that those at the head of the army did not move forward. Xenophon, hearing this, went on, and sending the ablest of the targeteers before, ordered them to see what was the occasion of the stop. They brought word that the whole army took their rest in that manner. So that Xenophon and his men, after they had appointed such guards as they were able, passed the night there also without either fire or victuals. When it was near day, he sent the youngest of his men to oblige the sick to get up and come away. In the meantime Cheirisophus sent some from the village to inquire into what condition the rear was. These were rejoiced to see them, and having delivered their sick to them to be conducted to the camp, they marched forward; and, before they had gone twenty stadia, they found themselves in the village where Cheirisophus was quartered. When they came together, they were of opinion that the army might quarter in the villages with safety. So Cheirisophus staid in the place he was in, and the rest went to the several villages that were allotted to them.

Here Polycrates, an Athenian, one of the captains, desired he might have leave to absent himself; and, taking with him those who were most prepared for expedition, he made such haste to the village that had fallen to Xenophon's lot, that he surprised all the inhabitants, together with their bailiff, in their houses. He found here seventeen colts, that were bred as a tribute for the king; and also the bailiff's daughter, who had not been married above nine days. However, her husband being gone to hunt the hare, was not taken in any of the villages. Their houses were under ground; the mouth resembling that of a well, but spacious below; there was an entrance dug for the cattle, but the inhabitants descended by ladders. In these houses were goats, sheep, cows, and fowls, with their young. All the cattle were maintained within doors with fodder. There was also wheat, barley, and legumens, and beer in jars, in which the malt itself floated even with the brims of the vessels, and with it reeds, some large and others small, without joints. These, when any one was dry, he was to take into his mouth and suck. The liquor was very strong, when unmixed with water, and exceeding pleasant to those who were used to it.

Xenophon invited the bailiff of this village to sup with him, and encouraged him with this assurance, that his children should not be taken from him, and that, when they went away, they would leave his house full of provisions in return for those they took, provided he performed some signal service to the army, by conducting them, till they came to another nation. The bailiff promised to perform this, and, as an instance of his good-will, informed them where there was wine buried. The soldiers rested that night in their several quarters in the midst of plenty, keeping a guard upon the bailiff, and having an eye at the same time upon his children. The next day Xenophon, taking the bailiff along with him, went to Cheirisophus, and, in every village through which he passed, made a visit to those who were quartered there; and found them everywhere feasting and rejoicing. They all would force him to sit down to dinner with them, and he every where found the tables covered with lamb, kid, pork, veal, and fowls; with plenty of bread, some made of wheat, and some of barley. When any one had a mind to drink to his friend, he took him to the jar, where he was obliged to stoop, and, sucking, drink like an ox. The soldiers gave the bailiff leave to take whatever he desired; but he took nothing; only wherever he met with any of his relations, he carried them along with him.

When they came to Cheirisophus, they found them also feasting, and crowned with garlands made of hay, and Armenian boys, in Barbarian dresses, waiting on them. To these they signified by signs what they would have them do, as if they had been deaf. As soon as Cheirisophus and Xenophon had embraced one another, they asked the bailiff, by their interpreter, who spoke the Persian language, what country it was. He answered, Armenia. After that they asked him for whom the horses were bred. He said for the king, as a tribute. He added that the neighbouring country was inhabited by the Chalybians, and informed them of the road that led to it. After that Xenophon went away, carrying back the bailiff to his family, and gave him the horse he had taken some time before, which was an old one, with a charge that he should recover him for a sacrifice (for he had heard he was consecrated to the sun), being afraid that, as he was very much fatigued with the journey, he should die. At the same time he took one of the young horses for himself, and gave one of them to each of the generals and captains. The horses of this country are less than those of Persia, but have a great deal more spirit. Upon this occasion the bailiff taught us to tie bags to the feet of the horses and beasts of burden, when they travelled through the snow, for, without them, they sunk up to their bellies.

After they had staid here eight days, Xenophon delivered the bailiff to Cheirisophus, to serve him as a guide, and left him all his family, except his son, a youth just in the flower of his age. This youth he committed to the charge of Episthenis of Amphipolis, with a design to send him back with his father, if he conducted them in a proper manner. At the same time they carried as many things as they could into his house, and, decamping, marched away. The bailiff conducted them through the snow unbound. They had now marched three days, when Cheirisophus grew angry with him for not carrying them to some villages. The bailiff said there were none in that part of the country. Upon this Cheirisophus struck him, but did not order him to be bound: so that he made his escape in the night, leaving his son behind him. This ill treatment and neglect of the bailiff was the cause of the only difference that happened between Cheirisophus and Xenophon during their whole march. Episthenis took an affection to the youth, and, carrying him into Greece, found great fidelity in him.

After this they made seven marches at the rate of five parasangs each day, and arrived at the river Phasis, which is about one hundred feet in breadth. From thence they made, in two marches, ten parasangs; when they found the Chalybians, Taochians, and Phasians posted upon the passage that led over the mountains to the plain. As soon as Cheirisophus saw the enemy in possession of that post, he halted at the distance of about thirty stadia, that he might not approach them while the army marched in a column; for which reason he ordered the captains to bring up their companies in the front, that the army might be drawn up in a line.

When the rear guard came up, he called the generals and captains together, and spoke to them in this manner. "The enemy, you see, are masters of the pass over the mountains. We are therefore now to consider in what manner we may charge them with the greatest advantage. It is my opinion, that while the soldiers get their dinner, we should consult among ourselves, whether it will be most proper to attempt the passage to-day, or stay till to-morrow." "My advice is," says Cleanor, "that, as soon as we have dined, we should take our arms, and attack the enemy; for, if we defer it till to-morrow, this delay will inspire those who observe us with confidence, and their confidence will, in all probability, draw others to their assistance."

After him Xenophon said, "This is my sense of the matter. If we are obliged to fight, we ought to prepare ourselves to fight with all possible bravery; but if we propose to pass the mountain in the easiest manner, we are to consider by what means we may receive the fewest wounds, and lose the fewest men. The mountain that lies before us, reaches above sixty stadia in length, and, in all this extent, no guard appears to be posted any where, but only in this part. For which reason I should think it more for our advantage to endeavour to surprise some unguarded place upon the mountain, and, if possible, prevent their seizing it, than to attack a post already fortified, and men prepared to resist; for it is easier to climb a steep ascent, without fighting, than to march upon plain ground, when the enemy are posted on both sides of us. We can also better see what lies before us in the night, when we are not obliged to fight, than in the day time, when we are; and the roughest way is easier to those who march without fighting, than an even way to those whose heads are exposed to the darts of an enemy. Neither do I think it impossible for us to steal such a march, since we may have the advantage of the night to conceal us, and may take so great a circuit as not to be discovered. I am also of opinion, that, if we make a false attack upon the post which is possessed by the enemy, we shall, by that means, find the rest of the mountain more unguarded; for this will oblige them to keep all their forces in a body. But why do I mention stealing? Since I am informed, O Cheirisophus! that among you Lacedæmonians, those of the first rank, practise it from their childhood, and that, instead of being a dishonour, it is your duty to steal those things which the law has not forbidden: and to the end you may learn to steal with the greatest dexterity and secrecy imaginable, your laws have provided that those who are taken in a theft, shall be whipped. This is the time, therefore, for you to show how far your education has improved you, and to take care that, in stealing this march, we are not discovered, lest we smart severely for it."

Cheirisophus answered, "I am also informed, that you Athenians are very expert in stealing the public money, notwithstanding the great danger you are exposed to, and that your best men are the most expert at it, that is, if you choose your best men for your magistrates. So this is a proper time for you also to show the effects of your education." "I am ready," replies Xenophon, "to march with the rear-guard, as soon as we have supped, in order to possess myself of the mountain. I have guides with me: for our light-armed men have, in an ambuscade, taken some of the marauders, that follow the army. By these I am informed that the mountain is not inaccessible, but that goats and oxen graze upon it, so that, if we are once masters of any part of it, it will be accessible also to our sumpter-horses. Neither do I believe the enemy will keep their post, when they see we are masters of the summit, and upon an equality with themselves; because they are now unwilling to come down to us upon equal ground." But Cheirisophus said, "Why should you go, and leave the charge of the rear? Rather send others, unless any offer themselves to this service." Upon this Aristonymus of Methydria presented himself with his heavy-armed men; and Aristeus of Chius, and Nicomachus of Oete, both with their light-armed. And it was agreed that, when they had possessed themselves of the summit, they should light several fires. When these things were settled, they went to dinner. After which Cheirisophus led the whole army within ten stadia of the enemy, as if he had absolutely resolved to march that way.

Supper being ended, and night coming on, those who had orders marched away, and made themselves masters of the top of the mountain. The others went to rest where they were. The enemy finding our men were possessed of that post, remained under arms, and made many fires all night. As soon as it was day, Cheirisophus, after he had offered sacrifice, led his forces up to the road, while those who had gained the summit attacked the enemy: great part of whom staid to defend the pass, and the rest advanced against those who were masters of the eminence. But before Cheirisophus could come up to the enemy, those upon the summit were engaged; where our men had the advantage, and drove the enemy before them. In the meantime, the Greek targeteers ran on from the plain to attack those who were ready drawn up to receive them, and Cheirisophus at the head of the heavy-armed men, followed as fast as was consistent with a regular march. However, the enemy that were posted in the pass, when they saw those above give way, fled also; when great numbers of them were slain, and many of their bucklers taken, which the Greeks, by cutting them to pieces, rendered useless. As soon as they had gained the ascent, they offered sacrifice, and having erected a trophy, marched down into the plain, where they found villages well stored with all sorts of provisions.

THE DUTIES OF A CAVALRY COMMANDER

On marches, the commander of cavalry ought constantly to consider how he may give rest to the backs of his horses, and afford relief to the riders as they proceed, whether by riding at a moderate pace, or by dismounting and walking at a moderate pace. In maintaining this moderate pace you will not fail, if you pay proper attention to the matter; for every man can judge from himself, so as not to be unaware when others are over-fatigued. When, however, you

From Xenophon, *Hipparchicus*, in *Xenophon's Minor Works*, translated by J. S. Watson (London: George Bell & Sons, 1877), [chs. 4–5,] 312–17, [chs. 7–8,] 320–27.

are marching to any particular place, and it is uncertain whether you may fall in with the enemy, you must let the tribes rest only in turns, for it would be dangerous if the enemy should come upon you when all your men are dismounted. If, again, you have to march through narrow passes, you must lead on your men, at the word of command, in single file; if you come into broad roads, you must, at the word of command, extend the front of each tribe; and when you come forth into open plains, you must form all the tribes in a solid body; for it is well to execute these movements even for the sake of exercise, and it is more agreeable, as you pursue your route, to vary the modes of marching in the different companies.

When you march out of the beaten road, and over difficult ground, it will be very proper, not only in a hostile but in a friendly country, that some of the inferior officers should ride on in advance of each tribe; who, if they meet with impassable woods, may seek unobstructed ways, and point out to the rest of the cavalry where they must direct their march, so that whole companies may not stray from one another. If you march in expectation of encountering dangers, it is the part of a prudent commander to see that extraordinary scouts go before the ordinary ones to ascertain the position of the enemy. It is proper, also, both with reference to attacking and for keeping on guard, that at the crossing of rivers the soldiers should wait for one another, that those who get over last may not fatigue their horses by hastening after their leader. Almost all officers know the propriety of this, but there are not many willing to take the trouble of constantly attending to it.

It is the duty of a commander of cavalry in time of peace, also, to study to acquire an exact knowledge, as well of the enemy's country, as of his own; and if he cannot obtain such knowledge personally, he may keep about him men that are well acquainted with the several parts of both countries; for a leader who knows the roads is a totally different person from one who is ignorant of them; and, in forming plans against the enemy, he who has a knowledge of the country has a vast advantage over him who is a stranger to it. When you are procuring spies, too, before a war is actually begun, you ought to take care that they may be taken from towns friendly to both parties, and from merchants; for all towns receive as friends those who bring anything with them; and such persons are sometimes useful as pretended deserters. You ought never to trust to your spies, however, so far as to neglect to keep on your guard, but you should always be as well prepared as if the enemy were reported to be approaching; for however trustworthy the spies may be, it may be difficult for them to bring information in time, since many obstacles occur in war.

The enemy will be least likely to observe the march of cavalry out of the camp, if it be conducted by notice communicated from man to man rather than by announcement made by a herald or by a written order. Besides leading out the troops, too, by notice from man to man, it will be proper to appoint captains of ten, and captains of five under the captains of ten, that each may have to give orders to as few as possible, and also that the captains of five may extend the front of the troop by bringing forward their men, as they may do without confusion, whenever there is occasion.

Whenever it is necessary to guard against surprise, I always recommend watches to be set, and sentinels to be posted, with secrecy; for thus, while they are a security to their friends, they are rendered as it were an ambush for the enemy. The watch themselves, too, when they are concealed, are less liable to surprise, and much more to be dreaded by the enemy; for though the enemy may know that there are advanced guards somewhere, yet, if they know not where they are, or what is their number, their ignorance deprives them of all feeling of security, and compels them to regard every spot with suspicion; while guards posted openly show them at once what they have to fear, and how far they may be free from apprehension. He also that has parties on guard posted secretly, will be able, by sending out a small party openly in advance of those that are concealed, to endeavour to draw the enemy into an ambush. Another way of occasionally surprising the enemy, also, is to post parties that are visible behind those that are concealed; and this may be as effective in deceiving an antagonist as the method previously mentioned. It is indeed the part of a prudent commander never to expose himself to danger, except when he has previously made it clear that he will have the advantage over his adversaries. But for him to offer favourable opportunities of which the enemy may take advantage, may be justly considered rather a betrayal of his party, than a display of fortitude. It is judicious, moreover, to make an attack on the enemy in the part where he is weakest, though that part may be at some distance; for to endure the fatigue of a long march is less dangerous than to contend against a superior force. Should the enemy advance between two fortified places that are friendly to you, it will be well, even though they are far superior to you in number, to attack them on that wing on which you may approach them unobserved; or it will be well even to attack them on both wings at once; for, whenever one of your parties has to retire, the other, riding up on the opposite side, may throw the enemy into confusion and assist in bringing off their friends.

That it is proper to endeavour to learn the state of the enemy's affairs by means of scouts, has been long ago said; but I think it best of all for the general himself to watch the enemy, if he can, from some safe position, and observe whether they commit any error. Whatever may be taken from them secretly, too, it is well to send a competent detachment to bring off; and whatever can be snatched from them openly, it is proper to despatch troops openly to seize.

If, again, when the enemy are on the march, any part of their force, weaker than your own, is detached from the main body, or strays from it through too great self-confidence, you must not fail to take advantage of such an opportunity; but you must always take care to pursue such weaker body with a force stronger than itself. You may also, by giving your attention, profit by the following observations in regard to animals. Since birds and beasts of prey, which are inferior in intellect to man, as kites for instance, will seize on whatever is left unguarded, and retreat to a place of safety before they are captured, and wolves will hunt cattle that are without protection, or steal such as are in places unwatched, and if a dog comes in pursuit of one of them, he will, if the dog is weaker than himself, attack him, or, if he is stronger, will kill the animal that he is carrying, and make off; and since wolves, too, when they think themselves stronger than those who are keeping guard, appoint some of their number to drive off the guard, and others to carry away the cattle, and thus secure subsistence for themselves; does it not become man, when beasts can carry off their prey with so much cunning, to show himself wiser than beasts, which are themselves caught by the art of man?

Contrivances for Deceiving the Enemy

A man who has the charge of cavalry ought also to know in what distance a horse can overtake a person on foot, and at what distance slow horses may escape from such as are swifter. It becomes a commander of cavalry to understand, too, on what kinds of ground foot are preferable to horse, and when horse are preferable to foot. He should be fertile also in contrivances, and know how to make a small body of cavalry appear large, and a large one appear but small; how to make the enemy imagine that he is absent when he is present, and present when he is absent; and how, not only to conceal the state of things among the enemy from his own men, but, by concealing the movements of his own men from the enemy, to attack them unawares. It is an excellent artifice, also, to contrive, when you are weaker than the enemy, to strike terror into them, that they may not attack you; and, when you are stronger, to create a false confidence in them, that they may come to a battle; for thus you yourself are least likely to suffer loss, and are in the best condition to take advantage of any error on the part of the enemy.

That I may not be thought to prescribe what is impossible, I will explain how that which appears most difficult in such proceedings may be accomplished. Security from failure, then, when attempting to pursue or retreat, a knowledge of the strength of his horses will give. But how can he obtain this knowledge? By observing, in the mock fights during peace, how the horses hold out in pursuit and retreat. When you wish your cavalry to appear numerous, let it be your first consideration whether there be a fair opportunity for doing so, that you may not attempt to deceive the enemy when you are close upon them; for it is safer to try such deceit at a distance, and it is more likely to be successful. You must then bear in mind that horses appear numerous when they are in a close body, on account of the size of the animal, but that, when they are scattered about, they are easily counted. Your cavalry may also be made to appear more numerous than they are, if you station the grooms between the horsemen, holding spears, if possible, or, if not, something resembling spears, in their hands; and this you may do whether you exhibit the cavalry standing still, or whether you are leading it along, for the mass of a troop must thus always appear greater and denser. Should you, on the other hand, wish a large number to seem small, it is plain that, if there be grounds at hand to admit of concealment, you may keep some of your men on the open parts, and place others out of sight, and thus disguise their number; but if the country is entirely open, you must range your men by tens in single file, and lead them on with an interval between the files, and you must make the men of each ten immediately in front of the enemy hold their lances erect, while the rest keep them down and out of sight. To alarm the enemy you may adopt pretended ambuscades, may feign to send succour to this or that quarter, or may circulate false reports. The enemy, however, are always boldest when they hear that their adversaries have plenty of trouble or occupation. . . .

The Qualifications Necessary to a General

It belongs, doubtless, to every commander to be prudent; but the commander of the cavalry of the Athenians ought to be far superior to others, both in showing respect for the gods and in military qualifications, as he has enemies bordering on his country who have as many cavalry as himself, and a large force of heavy-armed infantry. Should he then attempt to invade the enemy's country without the support of the other troops of the state, he would have to maintain a perilous contest against the enemy's cavalry and infantry with his cavalry only. Should the enemy, on the other hand, invade the country of the Athenians, they would not come, in the first place, without other cavalry united with their own, and, in the second place, without such a number of infantry that they would consider all the Athenians together unable to oppose them in the field. If, however, the whole people should go forth against such an enemy, with a resolution to defend their territory, favourable hopes might be entertained; for the cavalry, if their commander pays due attention to them, will be, with the help of the gods, superior to those of the enemy; the infantry will not be inferior to theirs in number, nor will they have the disadvantage in bodily strength, while in their minds they will be even more ambitious of distinction, if, under the favour of the gods, they be properly exercised. On their ancestors, certainly, the Athenians pride themselves no less than the Bœotians. But should the people turn their thoughts towards the sea, and think it sufficient to save merely their walls, as at the time when the Lacedæmonians invaded the country in conjunction with all the other Greeks, and should they appoint the cavalry to defend the parts outside the walls, and to hazard a contest, themselves alone, against all the invaders, I think that in that case there would be need, above all, of powerful support from the gods, and that it will be proper, in addition, for the commander of the cavalry to be an extremely accomplished leader; for he will require great judgment to act against an enemy far more numerous than his own troops, and great boldness to take advantage of an opportunity whenever one may present itself.

It is necessary also, as it appears to me, that he should be able to sustain personal fatigue; for otherwise, having to contend at his peril with an army before him, to which not even the whole state would be willing to oppose itself, it is evident that he would have to submit to whatever those stronger than himself chose to impose upon him, and would be able to make not even a semblance of defence. But if he should protect the grounds without the walls, with such a number of men as would suffice to watch the motions of the enemy, and be able to retreat into a place of safety after having observed whatever might be requisite, (and a small number may be not less able to reconnoitre than a larger one,) and those who are too timid to trust either to themselves or their horses may be as well qualified for going out to watch, and returning to their friends, as others, (for fear appears to be a powerful incentive to keeping guard), and a commander might perhaps accordingly decide rightly in taking guards from these; but if, when he has with him those who are not wanted for the guard, he considers that he has an army, it will certainly appear to him but a small one, for it will be altogether too weak to make head against the enemy in the field. But if he employs them as flying parties, he may find their force, as it would appear, quite sufficient for that duty. It behoves him, however, as it seems to me, to keep his men always ready for action, and to be on the watch for any secret movement of the enemy's army, in case that they should be guilty of any error. The more numerous an army is, indeed, the more faults the men are accustomed to commit; for they either scatter themselves about for the purpose of getting provisions, or, marching with too little regard to order, some go before, and others fall behind, farther than is proper. Such negligences you should not suffer to be committed with impunity, (for if you do so, the whole country will be one camp,) taking good care, however, if you undertake any expedition, to make a hasty retreat before the great body of the enemy can come to the aid of their party.

An army on the march often comes into roads in which a large number of men can do no more than a small one; and at the crossings of the rivers it is possible for a commander who is on the alert, and who pursues with caution, to manage in such a manner that he may attack as many of his adversaries at once as he pleases. Sometimes it is advantageous, too, to make attacks on the enemy when they are at their morning or evening meal, or when they are rising from their beds; for at all such times the troops are unarmed, the infantry for a shorter, and the cavalry for a longer time. On their sentinels and outposts you should never cease to make attempts; for these are always few in number, and are sometimes stationed far away from the main body. Should the enemy guard such posts well, it will not be amiss to pass them secretly, and penetrate into the enemy's ground, relying on the support of the gods, and after having first ascertained what force is at each station, and the exact spots where they are placed; for no prize is so honourable as the capture of an enemy's advanced guard. Guards, indeed, are very easily deceived; since they are ready to pursue whatever small force they see, imagining that this is a part of their duty. You must have a care, however, as to the direction of your retreat, that it may not be on that side where the enemy will come to the succour of their party.

Further Admonitions

Those, however, who would be able to annoy a much stronger army than their own, ought to have so much the advantage over their enemies in military skill, that they themselves may appear accomplished in all kinds of equestrian exercises, and their adversaries utterly unpractised in them. The first requisite to this is, that those who are to engage in predatory excursions should be so inured to the fatigue of riding, that they may be prepared to endure every sort of military exertion; for horses and men that are unaccustomed to such duty would appear like women going to fight against men. But those who are taught and accustomed to leap across ditches, to vault over walls, to spring up on eminences, to descend from them with safety, and to ride at full speed down steep grounds, will have as much advantage over those who are unpractised in such exercises as winged animals have over those that can only walk. Those, again, whose feet are hardened with exercise will be as superior on rough ground to those who are not habituated to it, as persons who are sound in their limbs are to those who are lame; and those who are acquainted with the face of a country will as much surpass those who are unacquainted with it, in advancing and retreating, as those who have sight would surpass the blind. A commander should understand, moreover, that horses in good condition are such as are well fed, but at the same time exercised so effectually that they will not lose their wind under fatigue. And as bits and housings for horses can be useful only when they are fitted with straps, a commander of cavalry should never be without straps; for he may at a small expense put those who are in want of them in an efficient condition.

Should any officer think that he shall have too much trouble if he must thus exercise his cavalry, let him reflect that those who exercise themselves in gymnastic games undergo far greater labour and trouble than those who practise equestrian exercises to the utmost degree; for the greater part of gymnastic exercises are performed with extreme exertion, but most of those of an equestrian kind with pleasure. Should a man pray, indeed, to become a winged animal, there is no human accomplishment that would bring him so near to the object of his wishes as horsemanship. To gain a victory in the field of battle is far more glorious than to gain one in a pugilistic contest; for the state has a share in such honour, and it is through success in war that the gods, for the most part, crown communities with prosperity; so that I know not why it is proper to practise any kind of exercises more than those of a warlike nature. We may consider, also, that it is only through being inured to toil that the pirates are enabled to live on the property of those who are far stronger then themselves. On land, too, it is not the part of those who reap the fruit of their own grounds, but of those who are in want of sustenance, to commit depredations on others; for they must either cultivate the ground themselves, or live on the produce of the labour of others, since by no other means is it possible either to secure life or enjoy peace.

You must likewise bear in mind that you must never, when you make an attack with cavalry on a superior force, leave any ground behind you which is difficult for the horses to cross; for to be unhorsed is fare more perilous to him who is retreating than to him who is pursuing.

I would wish to remind you, also, that you ought to be very cautious in the following respects; for there are some commanders who, when they are going against an enemy to whom they think themselves superior, set out with a very small force, so that they often suffer what they hoped to inflict; and, when they proceed against an enemy to whom they are quite certain that they are inferior, they take with them all the troops that they can command. But I am of opinion that you ought to act in a quite contrary manner; when a commander leads out his troops in the expectation that he shall conquer, I think that he should not spare his force, whatever he has; for to have obtained an overwhelming victory has never been a cause of repentance to any leader. But when he makes an attempt upon an enemy far superior in number, and foresees that, after doing his utmost, he will still be obliged to retreat, I assert that, in such a case, it is much better for him to lead a few of his men, than the whole of them, to the charge, but that he should take the flower of his force, the best of his men, and the best of his horses; for, being of that description, they will be able to execute any enterprise, and secure a retreat, with most safety. But when he leads all his force against a superior enemy, and wishes to retreat, it must happen that those who are on the slowest horses will be overtaken, while others will fall off from unskilfulness in riding, and others will be intercepted through the difficulties of the ground; for it is hard to find any large extent of ground exactly such as you would wish. They may also, from being numerous, run against each other, impede one another's progress, and do much damage. But good horses and men will be able to escape from the hands of the enemy, especially if the commander contrive to threaten the pursuers with that portion of his cavalry that has remained behind. For this purpose, pretended ambushes are serviceable; and it will be useful for him also to discover at what point some of his own party may show themselves with safety so as to retard the course of the pursuers. It is manifest, too, that where exertion and expedition are required, a smaller number will have the advantage over a larger, rather than a larger over a smaller; not that I say that the smaller number will be more efficient and expeditious because it is smaller, but that it is easier to find a small number who will take care of themselves and their horses, and who will practise horsemanship with skill, than a large one.

If it even happen that a commander has to contend with a body of cavalry exactly equal in number to his own, I think that it will not be amiss for him to form two troops out of each tribe, of which the phylarch may command one, and the other whosoever appears best qualified. The latter leader may follow with his troop, for a time, at the rear of the troop under the phylarch; and when the enemy come close up, he may, at the word of command, ride forward to attack them; for by this method I think that they will cause more alarm to the enemy, and will be more difficult to withstand. Should both the leaders also have infantry with them, and should these be concealed behind the cavalry, and, discovering themselves suddenly, close with the enemy, they seem likely to contribute much more by that means to secure a victory; for I see that what is unexpected, if it be good, gives people much more pleasure, and, if it is something formidable, causes them much more alarm. This any person may very well understand, who reflects how much those are startled that fall into an ambuscade, even though they be much superior in numbers; and how much greater terror, when two armies are encamped opposite to one another, is felt during the first days after their meeting. To order these matters, however, is not difficult; but to secure men who will act against the enemy with prudence, fidelity, zeal, and courage, requires great ability in a commander; for he ought to be qualified to speak and to act in such a manner that those who are under his command may feel convinced that it is advantageous for them to obey him, to follow him as their leader, and to engage the enemy under his direction, and that they may feel a desire for praise, and a resolution to persevere in whatever course they adopt.

If, on any occasion, when two camps lie face to face, or two fortresses belonging to the opposite parties, there occur returns to the charge, and pursuits, and retreats of the cavalry in the space between them, both parties are for the most part accustomed, in such cases, to advance slowly on returning to a charge, and then to ride over the intermediate space at full speed. But if any commander, letting it be supposed that he will act thus, nevertheless, on wheeling about, charges with speed and retires with speed, he may thus, as is apparent, do most damage to the enemy, and consult best for his own safety, riding forward quickly while he is near the strength of his own side, and retreating quickly from before the strength of the enemy. If he could contrive to leave unobserved, too, four or five of the best horses and men of each troop, they would be of great weight in charging the enemy as they are returning to the attack.

POLYBIUS

(C. 202–C. 120 B.C.)

Polybius, a Greek who entered the service of Rome, was born at Megalopolis in Arcadia. He underwent military training and was taken as a hostage to Rome as one of the leaders of the Achaean League. His exile lasted from 167 to 150, during which time he moved in patrician circles and traveled to southern Italy, Spain, and Gaul. Called upon by Scipio Africanus, he was present at the destruction of Carthage in 146 and took part in Scipio's expedition to Spain.

Polybius was a great traveler, and his writings are accurate and carefully documented. The outstanding historian of Roman imperialism, he recounts and analyzes the story of the triumph of Rome over Carthage and Roman expansion in the Hellenistic east. The battle of Cannae in 216 B.C. was Hannibal's greatest victory, a classic of envelopment by the wings—and that despite the fact that the Carthaginians were numerically inferior; it was often the subject of later reflection (there are also accounts of it by Appian and Livy).

THE BATTLE OF LAKE TRASIMENE

. . . Having crossed the marshes . . . Hannibal found Flaminius in Etruria encamped under the walls of Arretium. For the present he pitched his camp close to the marshes, to refresh his army, and to investigate the plans of his enemies and the lie of the country in his front. And being informed that the country before him abounded in wealth, and that Flaminius was a mere mob-orator and demagogue, with no ability for the actual conduct of military affairs, and was moreover unreasonably confident in his resources; he calculated that, if he passed his camp and made a descent into the district beyond, partly for fear

From *The Histories of Polybius*, translated by Evelyn S. Shuckburgh (London: Macmillan, 1889), 1: 238–43.

of popular reproach and partly from a personal feeling of irritation, Flaminius would be unable to endure to watch passively the devastation of the country, and would spontaneously follow him wherever he went; and being eager to secure the credit of a victory for himself, without waiting for the arrival of his colleague, would give him many opportunities for an attack.

And in making these calculations Hannibal showed his consummate prudence and strategical ability. For it is mere blind ignorance to believe that there can be anything of more vital importance to a general than the knowledge of his opponent's character and disposition. As in combats between individuals or ranks, he who would conquer must observe carefully how it is possible to attain his object, and what part of his enemy appears unguarded or insufficiently armed,—so must a commander of an army look out for the weak place, not in the body, but in the mind of the leader of the hostile force. For it has often happened before now that, from mere idleness and lack of energy, men have let not only the welfare of the state, but even their private fortunes fall to ruin: some are so addicted to wine that they cannot sleep without bemusing their intellects with drink; and others so infatuated in their pursuit of sensual pleasures, that they have not only been the ruin of their cities and fortunes, but have forfeited life itself with disgrace. In the case of individuals, however, cowardice and sloth bring shame only on themselves; but when it is a commander-in-chief that is concerned, the disaster affects all alike and is of the most fatal consequence. It not only infects the men under him with an inactivity like his own; but it often brings absolute dangers of the most serious description upon those who trust such a general. For rashness, temerity, and uncalculating impetuosity, as well as foolish ambition and vanity, give an easy victory to the enemy. And are the source of numerous dangers to one's friends: for a man who is the prey of such weaknesses falls the easiest victim to every stratagem, ambush or ruse. The general then who can gain a clear idea of his opponent's weaknesses, and direct his attack on the point where he is most open to it, will very soon be the victor in the campaign. For as a ship, if you deprive it of its steerer, falls with all its crew into the hands of the enemy; so, in the case of an army in war, if you outwit or out-manoeuvre its general, the whole will often fall into your hands.

Nor was Hannibal mistaken in his calculations in regard to Flaminius. For no sooner had he left the neighbourhood of Faesulae, and, advancing a short way beyond the Roman camp, made a raid upon the neighbouring country, than Flaminius became excited, and enraged at the idea that he was despised by the enemy: and as the devastation of the country went on, and he saw from the smoke that rose in every direction that the work of destruction was proceeding, he could not patiently endure the sight. Some of his officers advised that they should not follow the enemy at once nor engage him, but should act on the defensive, in view of his great superiority in cavalry; and especially that they should wait for the other Consul, and not give battle until the two armies were combined. But Flaminius, far from listening to their advice, was indignant at those who offered it; and bade them consider what the people at home would say at the country being laid waste almost up to the walls of Rome itself, while they remained encamped in Etruria on the enemy's rear. Finally, with these words, he set his army in motion, without any settled plan of time or place; but bent only on falling in with the enemy, as though certain victory awaited him. For he had managed to inspire the people with such confident expectations, that the unarmed citizens who followed his camp in hope of booty, bringing chains and fetters and all such gear, were more numerous than the soldiers themselves.

Meanwhile Hannibal was advancing on his way to Rome through Etruria, keeping the city of Cortona and its hills on his left, and the Thrasymene lake on his right; and as he marched, he burned and wasted the country with a view of rousing the wrath of the enemy and tempting him to come out. And when he saw Flaminius get well within distance, and observed that the ground he then occupied was suited to his purpose, he bent his whole energies on preparing for a general engagement.

The route which he was following led through a low valley enclosed on both sides by long lines of lofty hills. Of its two ends, that in front was blocked by an abrupt and inaccessible hill, and that on the rear by the lake, between which and the foot of the cliff there is only a very narrow defile leading into this valley. Making his way to the end of the valley along the bank of the lake, Hannibal posted himself with the Spanish and Libyan troops on the hill immediately in front of him as he marched, and pitched a camp on it; but sent his Balearic slingers and light-armed troops by a détour, and stationed them in extended order under the cover of the hills to the right of the valley; and by a similar détour placed the Gauls and cavalry under the cover of hills to the left, causing them also to extend their line so far as to cover the entrance of the defile running between the cliff and lake into the valley.

Having made these preparations during the night, and having thus enclosed the valley with ambuscades, Hannibal remained quiet. In pursuit of him came Flaminius, in hot haste to close with the enemy. It was late in the evening before he pitched his camp on the border of the lake; and at daybreak next morning, just before the morning watch, he led his front maniples forward along the borders of the lake into the valley with a view of engaging the enemy.

The day was exceedingly misty: and as soon as the greater part of the Roman line was in the valley, and the leading maniples were getting close to him, Hannibal gave the signal for attack; and at the same time sent orders to the troops lying in ambush on the hills to do the same, and thus delivered an assault upon the enemy at every point at once. Flaminius was taken completely by surprise: the mist was so thick, and the enemy were charging down from the upper ground at so many points at once, that not only were the Centurions and Tribunes unable to relieve any part of the line that was in difficulties, but were not even able to get any clear idea of what was going on: for they were attacked simultaneously on front, rear, and both flanks. The result was that most of them were cut down in the order of march, without being able to defend themselves: exactly as though they had been actually given up to slaughter by the folly of their leader. Flaminius himself, in a state of the utmost distress and despair, was attacked and killed by a company of Celts. As many as fifteen thousand Romans fell in the valley, who could neither yield nor defend themselves, being habituated to regard it as their supreme duty not to fly or quit their ranks. But those who were caught in the defile between the lake and the cliff perished in a shameful, or rather a most miserable, manner: for being thrust into the lake, some in their frantic terror endeavoured to swim with their armour on, and presently sank and were drowned; while the greater number, wading as far as they could into the lake, remained there with their heads above water; and when the cavalry rode in after them, and certain death stared them in the face, they raised their hands and begged for quarter, offering to surrender, and using every imaginary appeal for mercy; but were finally despatched by the enemy, or, in some cases, begged the favour of the fatal blow from their friends, or inflicted it on themselves. A number of men, however, amounting perhaps to six thousand, who were in the valley, defeated the enemy immediately in front of them; but though they might have done much to retrieve the fortune of the day, they were unable to go to the relief of their comrades, or get to the rear of their opponents, because they could not see what was going on. They accordingly pushed on continually to the front, always expecting to find themselves engaged with some of the enemy: until they discovered that, without noticing it, they were issuing upon the higher ground. But when they were on the crest of the hills, the mist broke and they saw clearly the disaster which had befallen them; and being no longer able to do any good, since the enemy was victorious all along the line, and in complete possession of the ground, they closed their ranks and made for a certain Etrurian village. After the battle Maharbal was sent by Hannibal with the Iberians and light-armed troops to besiege the village; and seeing themselves surrounded by a complication of dangers, they laid down their arms and surrendered on condition of their lives being spared. Such was the end of the final engagement between the Romans and Carthaginians in Etruria. . . .

THE BATTLE OF CANNAE

... through all that winter and spring [of 216 B.C.] the two armies remained encamped facing each other. But when the season for the new harvest was come, Hannibal began to move from the camp at Geronium; and making up his mind that it would be to his advantage to force the enemy by any possible means to give him battle, he occupied the citadel of a town called Cannae, into which the corn and other supplies from the district round Canusium were collected by the Romans, and conveyed thence to the camp as occasion required. The town itself, indeed, had been reduced to ruins the year before: but the capture of its citadel and the material of war contained in it, caused great commotion in the Roman army; for it was not only the loss of the place and the stores in it that distressed them, but the fact also that it commanded the surrounding district. They therefore sent frequent messages to Rome asking for instructions: for if they approached the enemy they would not be able to avoid an engagement, in view of the fact that the country was being plundered, and the allies all in a state of excitement. The Senate passed a resolution that they should give the enemy battle: they, however, bade Gnaeus Servilius wait, and despatched the Consuls to the seat of war. It was to Aemilius that all eyes turned, and on him the most confident hopes were fixed; for his life had been a noble one, and he was thought to have managed the recent Illyrian war with advantage to the State. The Senate determined to bring eight legions into the field, which had never been done at Rome before, each legion consisting of five thousand men besides allies. For the Romans, as I have stated before, habitually enrol four legions each year, each consisting of about four thousand foot and two hundred horse; and when any unusual necessity arises, they raise the number of foot to five thousand and of the horse to three hundred. Of allies, the number in each legion is the same as that of the citizens, but of the horse three times as great. Of the four legions thus composed, they assign two to each of the Consuls for whatever service is going on. Most of their wars are decided by one Consul and two legions, with their quota of allies; and they rarely employ all four at one time and on one service. But on this occasion, so great was the alarm and terror of what would happen, they resolved to bring not only four but eight legions into the field.

With earnest words of exhortation, therefore, to Aemilius, putting before him the gravity in every point of view of the result of the battle, they despatched him with instructions to seek a favourable opportunity to fight a decisive battle with a courage worthy of Rome. Having arrived at the camp and united

From *The Histories of Polybius,* translated by Evelyn S. Shuckburgh (London: Macmillan, 1889), 1: 263–75.

their forces, they made known the will of the Senate to the soldiers, and Aemilius exhorted them to do their duty in terms which evidently came from his heart. He addressed himself especially to explain and excuse the reverses which they had lately experienced; for it was on this point particularly that the soldiers were depressed and stood in need of encouragement. "The causes," he argued, "of their defeats in former battles were many, and could not be reduced to one or two. But those causes were at an end; and no excuse existed now, if they only showed themselves to be men of courage, for not conquering their enemies. Up to that time both Consuls had never been engaged together, or employed thoroughly trained soldiers: the combatants on the contrary had been raw levies, entirely unexperienced in danger; and what was most important of all, they had been so entirely ignorant of their opponents, that they had been brought into the field, and engaged in a pitched battle with an enemy that they had never once set eyes on. Those who had been defeated on the Trebia were drawn up on the field at daybreak, on the very next morning after their arrival from Sicily; while those who had fought in Etruria, not only had never seen the enemy before, but did not do so even during the very battle itself, owing to the unfortunate state of the atmosphere.

But now the conditions were quite different. For in the first place both Consuls were with the army: and were not only prepared to share the danger themselves, but had also induced the Consuls of the previous year to remain and take part in the struggle. While the men had not only seen the arms, order, and numbers of the enemy, but had been engaged in almost daily fights with them for the last two years. The conditions therefore under which the two former battles were fought being quite different, it was but natural that the result of the coming struggle should be different too. For it would be strange or rather impossible that those who in various skirmishes, where the numbers of either side were equal, had for the most part come off victorious, should, when drawn up all together, and nearly double of the enemy in number, be defeated."

"Wherefore, men of the army," he continued, "seeing that we have every advantage on our side for securing a victory, there is only one thing necessary,—your determination, your zeal! And I do not think I need say more to you on that point. To men serving others for pay, or to those who fight as allies on behalf of others, who have no greater danger to expect than meets them on the field, and for whom the issues at stake are of little importance,—such men may need words of exhortation. But men who, like you, are fighting not for others, but themselves,—for country, wives, and children; and for whom the issue is of far more momentous consequence than the mere danger of the hour, need only to be reminded: require no exhortation. For who is there among you who would not wish if possible to be victorious; and next, if that may not be, to die with arms in his hands, rather than to live and see the outrage and death of those dear objects which I have named? Wherefore, men of the army, apart from any words of mine, place before your eyes the momentous difference to you between victory and defeat, and all their consequences. Enter upon this battle with the full conviction, that in it your country is not risking a certain number of legions, but her bare existence. For she has nothing to add to such an army as this, to give her victory, if the day now goes against us. All she has of confidence and strength rests on you; all her hopes of safety are in your hands. Do not frustrate those hopes: but pay back to your country the gratitude you owe her; and make it clear to all the world that the former reverses occurred, not because the Romans are worse men than the Carthaginians, but from the lack of experience on the part of those who were then fighting, and through a combination of adverse circumstances." With such words Aemilius dismissed the troops.

Next morning the two Consuls broke up their camp, and advanced to where they heard that the enemy were entrenched. On the second day they arrived within sight of them, and pitched their camp at about fifty stades' distance. But when Aemilius observed that the ground was flat and bare for some distance round, he said that they must not engage there with an enemy superior to them in cavalry; but that they must rather try to draw him off, and lead him to ground on which the battle would be more in the hands of the infantry. But Gaius Terentius being, from inexperience, of a contrary opinion, there was a dispute and misunderstanding between the leaders, which of all things is the most dangerous. It is the custom, when the two Consuls are present, that they should take the chief command on alternate days; and the next day happening to be the turn of Terentius, he ordered an advance with a view of approaching the enemy, in spite of the protests and active opposition of his colleague. Hannibal set his light-armed troops and cavalry in motion to meet him, and charging the Romans while they were still marching, took them by surprise and caused a great confusion in their ranks. The Romans repulsed the first charge by putting some of their heavy-armed in front; and then sending forward their light-armed and cavalry, began to get the best of the fight all along the line: the Carthaginians having no reserves of any importance, while certain companies of the legionaries were mixed with the Roman light-armed, and helped to sustain the battle. Nightfall for the present put an end to a struggle which had not at all answered to the hopes of the Carthaginians. But next day Aemilius, not thinking it right to engage, and yet being unable any longer to lead off his army, encamped with two-thirds of it on the banks of the Aufidus, the only river which flows right through the Apennines,—that chain of mountains which forms the watershed of all the Italian rivers, which flow either west to the Tuscan sea, or east to the Hadriatic. This chain is, I say, pierced by the Aufidus, which rises on the side of Italy nearest the Tuscan Sea, and is discharged into the Hadriatic. For the other third of his army he caused a camp to be made across the river, to the east of the ford, about ten stades from his own lines, and a little more from those of the enemy; that these men, being on the other side of the river, might protect his own foraging parties, and threaten those of the enemy.

Then Hannibal, seeing that his circumstances called for a battle with the enemy, being anxious lest his troops should be depressed by their previous reverse, and believing that it was an occasion which required some encouraging words, summoned a general meeting of his soldiers. When they were assembled, he bid them to look round upon the country, and asked them, "What better fortune they could have asked from the gods, if they had had the choice, than to fight in such ground as they saw there, with the vast superiority of cavalry on their side?" And when all signified their acquiescence in such an evident truth, he added: "First, then, give thanks to the gods: for they have brought the enemy into this country, because they designed the victory for us. And, next to me, for having compelled the enemy to fight,—for they cannot avoid it any longer,—and to fight in a place so full of advantages for us. But I do not think it becoming in me now to use many words in exhorting you to be brave and forward in this battle. When you had had no experience of fighting the Romans this was necessary, and I did then suggest many arguments and examples to you. But now seeing that you have undeniably beaten the Romans in three successive battles of such magnitude, what arguments could have greater influence with you in confirming your courage than the actual facts? Now, by your previous battles you have got possession of the country and all its wealth, in accordance with my promises: for I have been absolutely true in everything I have ever said to you. But the present contest is for the cities and the wealth in them: and if you win it, all Italy will at once be in your power; and freed from your present hard toils, and masters of the wealth of Rome, you will by this battle become the leaders and lords of the world. This, then, is a time for deeds, not words: for by God's blessing I am persuaded that I shall carry out my promises to you forthwith." His words were received with approving shouts, which he acknowledged with gratitude for their zeal; and having dismissed the assembly, he at once formed a camp on the same bank of the river as that on which was the larger camp of the Romans.

Next day he gave orders that all should employ themselves in making preparations and getting themselves into a fit state of body. On the day after that he drew out his men along the bank of the river, and showed that he was eager to give the enemy battle. But Aemilius, dissatisfied with his position, and seeing that the Carthaginians would soon be obliged to shift their quarters for the sake of supplies, kept quiet in his camps, strengthening both with extra guards. After waiting a considerable time, when no one came out to attack him, Hannibal put the rest of the army into camp again, but sent out his Numidian horse to attack the enemy's water parties from the lesser camp. These horsemen riding right up to the lines and preventing the watering, Gaius Terentius became more than ever inflamed with the desire of fighting, and the soldiers were eager for a battle, and chafed at the delay. For there is nothing more intolerable to mankind than suspense; when a thing is once decided, men can but endure whatever out of the catalogue of evils it is their misfortune to undergo.

But when the news arrived at Rome that the two armies were face to face, and that skirmishes between advanced parties of both sides were daily taking place, the city was in a state of high excitement and uneasiness; the people dreading the result, owing to the disasters which had now befallen them on more than one occasion; and foreseeing and anticipating in their imaginations what would happen if they were utterly defeated. All the oracles preserved at Rome were in everybody's mouth; and every temple and house was full of prodigies and miracles: in consequence of which the city was one scene of vows, sacrifices, supplicatory processions, and prayers. For the Romans in times of danger take extraordinary pains to appease gods and men, and look upon no ceremony of that kind in such times as unbecoming or beneath their dignity.

When he took over the command on the following day, as soon as the sun was above the horizon, Gaius Terentius got the army in motion from both the camps. Those from the larger camp he drew up in order of battle, as soon as he had got them across the river, and bringing up those of the smaller camp he placed them all in the same line, selecting the south as the aspect of the whole. The Roman horse he stationed on the right wing along the river, and their foot next them in the same line, placing the maniples, however, closer together than usual, and making the depth of each maniple several times greater than its front. The cavalry of the allies he stationed on the left wing, and the light-armed troops he placed slightly in advance of the whole army, which amounted with its allies to eighty thousand infantry and a little more than six thousand horse. At the same time Hannibal brought his Balearic slingers and spearmen across the river, and stationed them in advance of his main body; which he led out of their camp, and, getting them across the river at two spots, drew them up opposite the enemy. On his left wing, close to the river, he stationed the Iberian and Celtic horse opposite the Roman cavalry; and next to them half the Libyan heavy-armed foot; and next to them the Iberian and Celtic foot; next, the other half of the Libyans, and, on the right wing, the Numidian horse. Having now got them all into line he advanced with the central companies of the Iberians and Celts; and so arranged the other companies next these in regular gradations, that the whole line became crescent-shaped, diminishing in depth toward its extremities: his object being to have his Libyans as a reserve in the battle, and to commence the action with his Iberians and Celts.

The armour of the Libyans was Roman, for Hannibal had armed them with a selection of the spoils taken in previous battles. The shield of the Iberians and Celts was about the same size, but their swords were quite different. For that of the Roman can thrust with as deadly effects as it can cut, while the Gallic sword can only cut, and that requires some room. And the companies coming alternately,—the naked Celts, and the Iberians with their short linen tunics bordered with purple stripes, the whole appearance of the line was strange and terrifying. The whole strength of the Carthaginian cavalry was ten thousand, but that of their foot was not more than forty thousand, including the Celts. Aemilius commanded on the Roman right, Gaius Terentius on the left, Marcus Atilius and Gnaeus Servilius, the Consuls of the previous year, on the centre. The left of the Carthaginians was commanded by Hasdrubal, the right by Hanno, the centre by Hannibal in person, attended by his brother Mago. And as the Roman line faced the south, as I said before, and the Carthaginian the north, the rays of the rising sun did not inconvenience either of them.

The battle was begun by an engagement between the advanced guard of the two armies; and at first the affair between these light-armed troops was indecisive. But as soon as the Iberian and Celtic cavalry got at the Romans, the battle began in earnest, and in the true barbaric fashion: for there was none of the usual formal advance and retreat; but when they once got to close quarters, they grappled man to man, and, dismounting from their horses, fought on foot. But when the Carthaginians had got the upper hand in this encounter and killed most of their opponents on the ground,—because the Romans all maintained the fight with spirit and determination,—and began chasing the remainder along the river, slaying as they went and giving no quarter; then the legionaries took the place of the light-armed and closed with the enemy. For a short time the Iberian and Celtic lines stood their ground and fought gallantly; but, presently overpowered by the weight of the heavy-armed lines, they gave way and retired to the rear, thus breaking up the crescent. The Roman maniples followed with spirit, and easily cut their way through the enemy's line; since the Celts had been drawn up in a thin line, while the Romans had closed up from the wings towards the centre and the point of danger. For the two wings did not come into action at the same time as the centre: but the centre was first engaged, because the Gauls, having been stationed on the arc of the crescent, had come into contact with the enemy long before the wings, the convex of the crescent being towards the enemy. The Romans, however, going in pursuit of these troops, and hastily closing in towards the centre and the part of the enemy which was giving ground, advanced so far, that the Libyan heavy-armed troops on either wing got on their flanks. Those on the right, facing to the left, charged from the right upon the Roman flank; while those who were on the left wing faced to the right, and, dressing by the left, charged their right flank, the exigency of the moment suggesting to them what they ought to do. Thus it came about, as Hannibal had planned, that the Romans were caught between two hostile lines of Libyans—thanks to their impetuous pursuit of the Celts. Still they fought, though no longer in line, yet singly, or in maniples, which faced about to meet those who charged them on the flanks.

Though he had been from the first on the right wing, and had taken part in the cavalry engagement, Lucius Aemilius still survived. Determined to act up to his own exhortatory speech, and seeing that the decision of the battle rested mainly on the legionaries, riding up to the centre of the line he led the charge himself, and personally grappled with the enemy, at the same time cheering on and exhorting his soldiers to the charge. Hannibal, on the other side, did the same, for he too had taken his place on the centre from the commencement. The Numidian horse on the Carthaginian right were meanwhile charging the cavalry on the Roman left; and though, from the peculiar nature of their mode of fighting, they neither inflicted nor received much harm, they yet rendered the enemy's horse useless by keeping them occupied, and charging them first on one side and then on another. But when Hasdrubal, after all but annihilating the cavalry by the river, came from the left to the support of the Numidians, the Roman allied cavalry, seeing his charge approaching, broke and fled. At that point Hasdrubal appears to have acted with great skill and discretion. Seeing the Numidians to be strong in numbers, and more effective and formidable to troops that had once been forced from their ground, he left the pursuit to them; while he himself hastened to the part of the field where the infantry were engaged, and brought his men up to support the Libyans. Then, by charging the Roman legions on the rear, and harassing them by hurling squadron after squadron upon them at many points at once, he raised the spirits of the Libyans, and dismayed and depressed those of the Romans.

It was at this point that Lucius Aemilius fell, in the thick of the fight, covered with wounds: a man who did his duty to his country at that last hour of his life, as he had throughout its previous years, if any man ever did. As long as the Romans could keep an unbroken front, to turn first in one direction and then in another to meet the assaults of the enemy, they held out; but the outer files of the circle continually falling, and the circle becoming more and more contracted, they at last were all killed on the field; and among them Marcus Atilius and Gnaeus Servilius, the Consuls of the previous year, who had shown themselves brave men and worthy of Rome in the battle. While this struggle and carnage were going on, the Numidian horse were pursuing the fugitives, most of whom they cut down or hurled from their horses; but some few escaped into Venusia, among whom was Gaius Terentius, the Consul, who thus sought a flight, as disgraceful to himself, as his conduct in office had been disastrous to his country.

Such was the end of the battle of Cannae, in which both sides fought with the most conspicuous gallantry, the conquered no less than the conquerors. This is proved by the fact that, out of six thousand horse, only seventy escaped with Gaius Terentius to Venusia, and about three hundred of the allied cavalry to various towns in the neighbourhood. Of the infantry ten thousand were taken prisoners in fair fight, but were not actually engaged in the battle: of those who were actually engaged only about three thousand perhaps escaped to the towns of the surrounding district; all the rest died nobly, to the number of seventy thousand, the Carthaginians being on this occasion, as on previous ones, mainly indebted for their victory to their superiority in cavalry: a lesson to posterity that in actual war it is better to have half the number of infantry, and the superiority in cavalry, than to engage your enemy with an equality in both. On the side of Hannibal there fell four thousand Celts, fifteen hundred Iberians and Libyans, and about two hundred horse.

The ten thousand Romans who were captured had not, as I said, been engaged in the actual battle; and the reason was this. Lucius Aemilius left ten thousand infantry in his camp that, in case Hannibal should disregard the safety of his own camp, and take his whole army on to the field, they might seize the opportunity, while the battle was going on, of forcing their way in and capturing the enemy's baggage; or if, on the other hand, Hannibal should, in view of this contingency, leave a guard in his camp, the number of the enemy in the field might thereby be diminished. These men were captured in the following circumstances. Hannibal, as a matter of fact, did leave a sufficient guard in his camp; and as soon as the battle began, the Romans, according to their instructions, assaulted and tried to take those thus left by Hannibal. At first they held their own: but just as they were beginning to waver, Hannibal, who was by this time gaining a victory all along the line, came to their relief, and routing the Romans, shut them up in their own camp; killed two thousand of them; and took all the rest prisoners. In like manner the Numidian horse brought in all those who had taken refuge in the various strongholds about the district, amounting to two thousand of the routed cavalry.

The result of this battle, such as I have described it, had the consequences which both sides expected. For the Carthaginians by their victory were thenceforth masters of nearly the whole of the Italian coast which is called Magna Graecia. Thus the Tarentines immediately submitted; and the Arpani and some of the Campanian states invited Hannibal to come to them; and the rest were with one consent turning their eyes to the Carthaginians: who, accordingly, began now to have high hopes of being able to carry even Rome itself by assault.

On their side the Romans, after this disaster, despaired of retaining their supremacy over the Italians, and were in the greatest alarm, believing their own lives and the existence of their city to be in danger, and every moment expecting that Hannibal would be upon them. For, as though Fortune were in league with the disasters that had already befallen them to fill up the measure of their ruin, it happened that only a few days afterwards, while the city was still in this panic, the Praetor who had been sent to Gaul fell unexpectedly into an ambush and perished, and his army was utterly annihilated by the Celts. In spite of all, however, the Senate left no means untried to save the State. It exhorted the people to fresh exertions, strengthened the city with guards, and deliberated on the crisis in a brave and manly spirit. And subsequent events made this manifest. For though the Romans were on that occasion indisputably beaten in the field, and had lost reputation for military prowess; by the peculiar excellence of their political constitution, and the prudence of their counsels, they not only recovered their supremacy over Italy, by eventually conquering the Carthaginians, but before very long became masters of the whole world.

JULIUS CAESAR
(c. 101–44 b.c.)

*Gaius Julius Caesar was military tribune in 71 b.c. He played an ambiguous
role in the conspiracy of Catiline and became triumvir with Pompey and
Crassus and consul in 59. Between 57 and 50, he campaigned in Belgium,
Gaul, and England, crossed the Rhine, and was victorious in Gaul. After the
death of Crassus, civil war broke out between the supporters of Caesar and
Pompey in 49. The latter, who controlled the sea, crossed over to Greece,
and Caesar thereupon attacked Pompey's legions in Spain, in a campaign
of which the siege of Massilia (Marseilles) was an episode. In 48 he won a
decisive victory over Pompey at Pharsalus in Thessaly. After Pompey's
murder, Caesar waged war against Pompey's sons and followers in Africa
and Spain (47–45). He was sole master of the Roman world when he was
assassinated in 44 b.c.*

Caesar was a politician with the brain of a strategist. The Civil War, *of
which he was either the author or the inspiration, is a work of value from a
military perspective.*

THE SIEGE OF MASSILIA

. . . the Massiliotes had brought old ships out of the dockyard to replenish their
fleet and had worked hard at repairing them and fitting them out; they had
plenty of steersmen and rowers for them. They had added fishing boats, which
they had decked over to protect the rowers against missiles, and these they
filled with archers and ballistic engines. When the fleet was ready they embarked, amid the tears and prayers of all the old men, mothers and young girls,
who begged them to rescue their city in its dire need. Their courage and

From Caesar, *The Civil War*, translated by Jane F. Mitchell (Harmondsworth, England: Penguin Books, 1976), 81–92. Copyright © 1967 by Jane F. Mitchell. Reproduced by permission of Penguin Books Ltd.

confidence were as great as when they had fought before; for it is a common fault in human nature that the unseen and unknown provoke excessive confidence or excessive fear, and so it happened on this occasion. The arrival of Lucius Nasidius had filled the people with optimism and enthusiasm. When they got a suitable wind they left harbour and joined Nasidius at Taurois, which is one of their forts. There they prepared the ships for action, screwed up their resolution to fight again, and discussed their plans. The Massiliotes held the right of the line, Nasidius the left.

Brutus hurried there also. He had a larger fleet than before, for to those made at Arelate on Caesar's orders had been added six captured from the Massiliotes. These Brutus had repaired and completely fitted out during the preceding days. And so, exhorting his men to scorn the men they had already conquered, since they had defeated them already when their force was undamaged, he advanced, full of confidence and courage, against the enemy. From the camp of Gaius Trebonius and from all the high ground it was easy to look into the city and to see how all the men of military age who had remained in the town, all the older men, and the wives and children, were stretching up their hands to heaven in the public squares or at look-out points or on the wall, or were going to the temples of the immortal gods and prostrating themselves in front of the statues of the gods and begging for victory. There was no one who was not convinced that all his future fortunes depended on the result of that day; for all the best warriors and the men most highly esteemed from every age-group had been called out by name and had responded to entreaties and gone on board ship. As a result, if the Massiliotes should suffer a reverse, they could not see that there would be any possibility left even of attempting a resistance; whereas, if they were victorious, they could rely for the protection of the State on their own resources and on help from outside.

When the battle started, the courage of the Massiliotes left nothing to be desired. They remembered the injunctions their people had given them a little while before. They fought in the belief that they would have no second chance, and that those who jeopardized their lives in the battle would not, they thought, anticipate by very long the fate of the rest of the citizens, who would have to submit to the same fortune of war, should the city be captured. Our ships gradually became separated, and this gave the enemy an opportunity to make use of the skill of their steersmen and the manoeuvrability of their ships; and whenever our men took an opportunity of fastening on a ship with grappling irons, they would come in from all directions to rescue their comrades from difficulties. They also acquitted themselves well in hand-to-hand fighting, along with the Albici, and did not fall far short of our men in courage. At the same time, volleys of missiles were being hurled from the smaller boats standing off at a distance, and these inflicted many wounds unexpectedly on our men, who had not foreseen this and were embroiled in the battle. Two triremes had sighted the ship of Decimus Brutus, which could easily be recognized from its ensign, and bore down on it from different directions. Brutus, however, had just enough forewarning to make an effort and propel his ship a little way ahead of them. The two triremes collided at speed so hard that both were severely damaged by the impact, and in fact one had its beak broken off and began to founder. Observing this, the ships of Brutus's fleet which were nearest the spot attacked the crippled ships and soon sank them both.

Nasidius's ships, on the other hand, were of no help and quickly withdrew from the battle; for their crews had not the sight of their homeland nor the injunctions of their kinsfolk to urge them on into mortal danger. And so none of that contingent of ships was lost. Of the Massiliote fleet, five were sunk, four captured and one fled with those of Nasidius, all of which made for Hither Spain. One of the remaining ships had been sent ahead to Massilia to convey the news. On its approach, the whole population poured out to hear the result; and when they heard it, there was such consternation that it seemed as if at the same time the city itself had been taken by the enemy. None the less, the people set themselves to do all that remained to be done for the defence of the city.

The legionaries who were engaged on the right-hand part of the siege-works observed that they would obtain substantial protection against the frequent sallies of the enemy if they built a tower of brickwork there close up against the wall as a sort of fort and place of refuge. At first they made only a small, low structure, against sudden onslaughts. Into this they would retire; from this, whenever there was an exceptionally vigorous attack, they would defend themselves; from this they would sally out to repel and pursue the enemy. The tower was thirty feet square, but the walls were five feet thick. Later, however, their natural intelligence told them (experience, as usual, being instructive) that it could be extremely useful if this tower was built up high. This was done in the following manner.

When the tower was built up as high as the first floor, they built this flooring into the walls in such a way that the ends of the beams were covered by the brickwork of the walls, so that there should be no parts projecting on which enemy firebrands could take hold. Above this timber-work, they built up the sides with bricks as high as the protection afforded by siege-hut and screens allowed; then above that they put two beams across, not far from the ends of the walls, on which to support the wooden framework that was going to act as a roof for the tower. On top of these beams they put joists across at right angles and fastened these with tie-beams. They made the joists rather longer so that they stuck out beyond the ends of the walls, to provide something on which to hang the coverings to ward off and repel blows, while the walls were being built up inside this wooden frame. The top of this woodwork they covered with bricks and clay, to prevent the enemy damaging it with fire, and they laid pads of rag on top of that again, so that javelins from ballistas should not break through the timber or blows from catapults dislodge the brickwork.

They also made three fenders four feet broad out of anchor-cables to fit along the length of the walls of the tower, and fastened these so that they hung from the projecting ends of the joists on the three sides of the tower that were exposed to the enemy; for their experience elsewhere had taught them that this was the one type of covering that no missile or ballistic engine could penetrate. Now, once that part of the tower which was completed had been roofed over and protected against all enemy missiles, they removed the siege-huts to other parts of the works. Then they began to poise and lift up the roof of the tower, all in a piece, by leverage from the flooring of the first storey. When they had raised it as far as the cover provided by the fenders permitted, they went on, concealed and protected by these shields, building up the walls with bricks, and levering the roof up farther to allow room for working. When it seemed to be time to make a second storey, they built in beams, as before, protected by the outside brickwork, and above this flooring they again raised up the roof and the fenders. In this way, safely and without casualties or danger, they built six storeys, and left apertures where it seemed suitable in the course of building for discharging missiles from ballistic engines.

When they were certain that from this tower they could protect all the surrounding works, they began making a covered gallery sixty feet long, of boards two feet square, to be taken from the brick tower up to a bastion of the enemy's wall. The structure of the gallery was as follows. First, two beams of equal length were laid on the ground four feet apart, and on these were fixed posts five feet high. They joined these together with wooden stays forming a slight gable, on which to lay the timbers for roofing the gallery, and laid on top boards two feet square which they fastened with plates and bolts. At the edge of the roof of the gallery and at the ends of the timbers they fixed poles with a square section, about three inches square. These were to hold the bricks which were to be laid on top of the gallery.

When the gallery had been gabled and methodically built up in this way, and the timbers had been laid on the stays, it was covered with bricks and clay, as a protection against fire thrown from the wall. Hides were laid over the bricks, so that water could not be discharged on the bricks from pipes and split them up. The hides themselves were covered with pads of rags as a protection against fire and stones. They completed the whole of this work, under the protection of screens, as far as the bastion, and suddenly, when the enemy were off their guard, they used a naval trick and put the rollers under the gallery, bringing it right up to the bastion so that it lay alongside the building.

Dismayed at this sudden calamity, the inhabitants pushed up with levers the largest rocks they could manage and sent them toppling down from the edge of the bastion on to the gallery. The strength of the construction stood up to the impact and anything that fell on the gable of the gallery rolled off. Seeing this, they changed their tactics; they filled barrels with firewood and pitch, lit them and rolled them down from the wall on to the gallery. The barrels rolled and fell off, and as they fell at the sides they were pushed away from the construction with poles and forks. Meanwhile, under the gallery, the soldiers were using crowbars to pull apart the stones which held together the foundations of the bastion. Some of our troops kept up a protective fire from the brick tower with javelins and missile engines; the enemy were driven back from the wall and the bastion and were not given free scope to defend the wall. When several of the stones in the wall under the bastion had been withdrawn, part of the bastion suddenly collapsed, and the rest began keeling over on top of it. The enemy were thrown into consternation at this breach in their city and all rushed out of the gates unarmed, wearing white bands and stretching out their hands in supplication to the officers and the army.

This new development put a complete stop to military operations. The troops left their action stations and came eagerly to see and hear. When the enemy reached the officers and the army, they all flung themselves down at their feet, and begged them to await the arrival of Caesar. They said, "We see our city taken, the siege-works complete, the bastion undermined; and so we are abandoning the defence. When Caesar does arrive, if we do not carry out orders at his behest, there can be no hindrance to the immediate sack of the city. If the bastion collapses completely, there is no possibility of restraining your troops from bursting into the town in search of plunder and destroying it." These and other pleas of the same sort, as one might expect from skilled orators, were delivered with much weeping and so as to excite much compassion.

The officers were touched by this appeal and withdrawing their men from the siege-works they suspended the siege, leaving only a guard on the works. Yielding to compassion, they thus established an informal truce and waited for Caesar's arrival. No missiles were launched from the wall, and none from our side; everyone relaxed their conscientiousness in attending to duty, as if the job was done. For Caesar, in a dispatch, had strongly impressed on Trebonius that he was not to allow the city to be stormed by force, in case the combined effects of resentment against the rebels, the contempt displayed towards themselves and their prolonged labours should inflame the soldiers' feelings to such a degree that they should kill all the men of military age. This indeed they were threatening to do, and it was only with difficulty that they were being restrained at this time from breaking into the town. They bitterly resented the fact that through Trebonius's fault, as it seemed, they were not taking over the town.

The enemy, however, were not acting in good faith. They were merely seeking the time and opportunity for trickery. A few days later, when our men were relaxed and off guard, some of them away, others resting after their long labours on the siege-works, with their weapons all put away and covered up, the enemy suddenly burst out of the gates at midday and set fire to the siege-works.

There was a strong following wind, which spread the fire, so that the siege-wall, the screens, the "tortoise," the tower, the missile engines all went up in flames at once and were all consumed before it could be seen how it had happened. This sudden blow stung our men to action; they snatched up such weapons as they could, and more men rushed out of the camp to join them. They charged at the enemy as they fled, but were prevented from pursuing them by showers of arrows and missiles from the town wall; meanwhile the enemy rallied close to the wall and there without hindrance set fire to the gallery and brickwork tower. And so the work of many months perished in a moment, thanks to the faithlessness of the enemy and the strength of the wind. The Massiliotes tried to repeat their exploit on the following day. They had the same wind, and with even greater boldness they sallied out fighting and brought large quantities of firebrands against the other tower and siege-wall. But whereas our men had previously relaxed all their earlier watchfulness, they had now made preparations for defence, warned by the events of the day before. The result was that they killed many of the enemy and drove the rest back into the town before they could achieve their object.

Trebonius began to reorganize and rebuild those siege-works which had been destroyed. His men worked with increased zeal, for they had seen the utter collapse of the contrivances that had cost them so much work and they were stung by the thought that their courage would be held up to ridicule as a result of this criminal breach of truce. There were no materials left at all that could be collected to make a siege-wall, since all the timber for a long way around in the territory of Massilia had been felled and carried off. They therefore began to build a wall using a novel and unexampled method of construction. They built two walls of brick, six feet thick and with a timber roof between them; this made a siege-wall of about the same width as the old wall of piled timbers had been. Where the space between the walls or the weakness of the structure seemed to demand it, they drove piles into the ground between the walls and laid cross-beams on these to strengthen the wall. The timber roofing was covered with wickerwork, which was plastered with clay. The soldiers, with a roof over them, walls to the right and left and a screen in front, were able to bring up whatever was needed for the construction without danger. The work proceeded quickly; the good sense and hardiness of the troops soon repaired the loss of their prolonged labours. Gateways were left in the wall at suitable places to allow them to sally out.

The enemy saw that the siege-works, which they had hoped were incapable of repair except at the expense of a great deal of time and effort, had been so far restored after a few days' work that there was no scope for treachery or for breaking out, and no way left at all of injuring the men with missiles or damaging the works by fire. They realized also that that whole part of the city which was accessible from land could be surrounded in the same way with a wall and towers, so that it would be impossible even for them to stand their ground on their own defences, since our army seemed to have built its walls practically on the walls of the town and we were near enough to throw missiles. Besides, they were unable to make use of their ballistic engines, in which they had placed great hopes, because we were too near; and they were aware that, given the chance of fighting on equal terms from walls and towers, they could not match the valour of our men. They therefore had recourse again to surrender on the same terms as before. . . .

Massilia Capitulates

The Massiliotes were worn down by all sorts of trouble. They had begun to suffer from an extreme shortage of grain; they had twice been defeated in a naval battle; their frequent sallies had been routed; besides, they were assailed by severe pestilence, the result of long confinement and abnormal diet—for they were all subsisting on old stocks of millet and rotten barley, which they had long ago obtained and stored as a public reserve for just such an emergency; a bastion had been thrown down and a large part of the wall undermined; and they had given up hope of help from the provinces and the armies, which they learned had come into Caesar's power. They decided therefore to surrender, in earnest. However, a few days before, Lucius Domitius had learned the intentions of the Massiliotes and had got together three ships, two of which he assigned to his adherents; he embarked on one himself and set off, as soon as he got stormy weather. He was observed by ships which had been sent out by Brutus, according to daily routine, and were keeping watch by the harbour. They lifted anchor and began following. Domitius's own ship held steadily on its course in flight and with the help of the storm soon went out of sight, but the other two, alarmed at meeting our ships, went back into harbour. The Massiliotes, obeying orders, brought their weapons and catapults out of the town, took the ships out of the harbour and dockyards, and handed over the money from their treasury. After this Caesar, sparing them rather because of the age and fame of the city than because of any services to himself, left two legions there as a garrison and sent the rest to Italy. He himself set off for Rome.

THE BATTLE OF PHARSALUS

Pompey, whose camp was on a hill, kept drawing up his line of battle by the lower spurs of the mountain, always, as it seemed, waiting to see if Caesar would offer battle on unfavourable ground. Caesar, judging that Pompey could in no way be enticed out to battle, decided to move his camp from there and keep constantly on the march. His aim was, by moving camp and going to various places, to make it easier to get corn and at the same time to try to get some opportunity en route for battle, as well as to tire out Pompey's army, which was unaccustomed to exertion, by daily marches. Having taken this decision, he gave the signal for departure, and the tents were already struck when he observed that Pompey's line had advanced a little farther forward from the rampart than was its daily habit, so that is appeared possible to fight without being in an unfavourable position. Caesar then said to his men, when the column was already going through the gates, "We must postpone our march for the time being and think of battle, just as we have always desired. Our spirits are ready for battle; we shall not easily find another chance." Then he led the troops out quickly, without kit.

Pompey also, as was learned later, had decided at the insistence of all his men to settle the issue by battle. Indeed he had even said in the council of war during the preceding days that Caesar's army would be routed before the two lines came to grips. The majority were surprised at this. "I know that what I promise is almost incredible," he said, "but listen to my tactical plan, so that you may go to battle with the more confidence. I have advised the cavalry, when the armies come within fairly close range, to attack Caesar's right wing on its exposed flank, surround the line in the rear and thus throw his army into confusion and rout it before a missile is thrown from our side at the enemy. They have undertaken to do so, and in this way we shall bring the war to an end without danger to the legions and almost without bloodshed. It is not difficult, in view of our superiority in cavalry." He exhorted them also to be prepared in spirit for what was to come and, since the opportunity for battle,

From Caesar, *The Civil War*, translated by Jane F. Mitchell (Harmondsworth, England: Penguin Books, 1976), 149–55. Copyright © 1967 by Jane F. Mitchell. Reproduced by permission of Penguin Books Ltd.

which had often been in their thoughts, was being offered, not to let their conduct and prowess belie the expectations of the rest.

Labienus spoke next. He belittled Caesar's forces and extolled Pompey's plan to the skies, saying: "Do not think, Pompey, that this is the army which conquered Gaul and Germany. I took part in all the battles and I am not giving an unconsidered opinion on something I know nothing about. A very small part of that army survives; the greater part has perished, as it must needs have done in so many battles; the unhealthiness of the autumn in Italy carried off a good many; many have gone home; many were left behind on the mainland of Italy. Have you not heard that cohorts were formed out of those who stayed behind at Brundisium because of sickness? The forces you see were made up to strength from the levies of the last few years in Cisalpine Gaul and most of them are from the colonies in Transpadane Gaul. Besides, such good men as the army contained perished in the two battles at Dyrrachium." He then swore that he would not re-enter the camp except as a victor and he urged the others to swear likewise. Pompey praised him and took the same oath; and none of the rest hesitated to swear. After this, the council broke up, with everyone full of joy and hope; and they were already mentally anticipating victory, since it seemed that the assurance given by so experienced a general on a matter of such moment could not be mistaken.

When Caesar approached Pompey's army, he observed his line drawn up as follows. On the left wing were the two legions which had been handed over by Caesar in accordance with the decree of the Senate at the beginning of the troubles. One was named the First, the other the Third. Pompey himself was there. Scipio was holding the centre of the line with his legions from Syria. The legion from Cilicia together with the Spanish cohorts which, as we said, were brought over by Afranius, was stationed on the right wing. Pompey believed that these were his strongest troops. The rest he had stationed between the centre and the wings and had made up 110 cohorts. There were 45,000 men, plus about 2,000 time-expired veterans from the special-duty corps of the earlier armies who had come to join him. These he dispersed throughout the battle-line. The remaining seven cohorts he had posted to guard the camp and the near-by forts. His right wing was protected by a stream with steep banks, and he had therefore put all the cavalry, archers and slingers on the left wing.

Caesar, keeping his previous order of battle, had stationed the Tenth legion on the right wing and the Ninth on the left, although the latter had been sorely depleted by the battle at Dyrrachium. To it he added the Eighth legion, so as almost to make one legion out of two, and ordered them to cooperate. He had eighty cohorts stationed in the line, totalling 22,000 men. He had left two cohorts to guard the camp. He had put Antony on the left wing, Sulla on the right and Gnaeus Domitius in the centre. He himself took up his position opposite

Pompey. At the same time, he observed the dispositions described above, and fearing that his right wing might be surrounded by the large numbers of the Pompeian cavalry, he quickly took one cohort from each legion from his third line and formed them into a fourth line, which he stationed opposite the cavalry. He gave them their instructions, and warned them that that day's victory would depend on the valour of those cohorts. He also ordered the third line and the army as a whole not to charge without his command, saying that he would give the signal with his flag when he wished them to do so.

In giving the usual address of encouragement to the troops, in which he related the good service they had done him at all times, he recalled above all that he could call the troops to witness the earnestness with which he had sought peace, his attempts to negotiate through Vatinius by personal interviews and, through Aulus Clodius, with Scipio, and his efforts at Oricum to negotiate with Libo for the sending of envoys. It had never been his wish to expose his troops to bloodshed, nor to deprive the State of either army. After this speech, at the insistence of his troops, who were afire with enthusiasm, he gave the signal by trumpet.

In Caesar's army there was a recalled veteran named Crastinus, who in the previous year had been chief centurion of the Tenth legion in his service, a man of outstanding valour. When the signal was given, he said: "Follow me, you who were formerly in my company, and give your general the service you have promised. Only this one battle remains; after it, he will recover his position, and we our freedom." Looking at Caesar, "General," he said, "today I shall earn your gratitude, either dead or alive." So saying, he ran out first from the right wing, followed by about 120 crack troops, volunteers from the same century.

Between the two armies there was just enough space left for them to advance and engage each other. Pompey, however, had told his men to wait for Caesar's onset, and not to move from their positions or allow the line to be split up. He was said to have done this on the advice of Gaius Triarius, with the intention of breaking the force of the first impact of the enemy and stretching out their line, so that his own men, who were still in formation, could attack them while they were scattered. He also thought that the falling javelins would do less damage if the men stood still than if they were running forward while the missiles were discharged. Moreover, Caesar's troops, having run twice the distance, would be out of breath and exhausted. It appears to us that he did this without sound reason, for there is a certain eagerness of spirit and an innate keenness in everyone which is inflamed by desire for battle. Generals ought to encourage this, not repress it; nor was it for nothing that the practice began in antiquity of giving the signal on both sides and everyone's raising a war-cry; this was believed both to frighten the enemy and to stimulate one's own men.

Our men, on the signal, ran forward with javelins levelled; but when they observed that Pompey's men were not running to meet them, thanks to the practical experience and training they had had in earlier battles they checked their charge and halted about half-way, so as not to approach worn out. Then after a short interval they renewed the charge, threw their javelins and, as ordered by Caesar, quickly drew their swords. Nor indeed did the Pompeians fail to meet the occasion. They stood up to the hail of missiles and bore the onset of the legions; they kept their ranks, threw their javelins, and then resorted to their swords. At the same time the cavalry all charged forward, as instructed, from Pompey's left wing, and the whole horde of archers rushed out. Our cavalry failed to withstand their onslaught; they were dislodged from their position and gave ground a little. Pompey's cavalry thereupon pressed on the more hotly and began to deploy in squadrons and surround our line on its exposed flank. Observing this, Caesar gave the signal to the fourth line which he had formed of single cohorts. They ran forward swiftly to the attack with their standards and charged at Pompey's cavalry with such force that none of them could hold ground. They all turned, and not only gave ground but fled precipitately to the hilltops. Their withdrawal left all the archers and slingers exposed, and, unarmed and unprotected, they were killed. In the same charge the cohorts surrounded the Pompeians who were still fighting and putting up a resistance on the left wing, and attacked them in the rear.

At the same time Caesar gave the order to advance to the third line, which had done nothing and had stayed in its position up till then. As a result, when fresh and unscathed troops took the place of the weary, while others were attacking from the rear, the Pompeians could not hold out, and every one of them turned tail and fled. Caesar was not wrong in thinking that the victory would originate from those cohorts which had been stationed in a fourth line to counteract the cavalry, as he had declared in cheering on his men; for it was by these first that the cavalry were repulsed, it was by these that the slingers and archers were massacred, and it was by these that the Pompeian left wing was surrounded and the rout started. When Pompey, however, saw his cavalry routed, and observed that part of his forces on which he most relied in a state of panic, having no confidence in the rest he left the field; he rode straight to the camp and said to the centurions he had posted on guard at the praetorian gate, loudly, so that the soldiers could hear: "Watch the camp and defend it strenuously, if there should be any reverse. I am going round to the other gates to make sure of the guard on the camp." So saying, he went to his tent, doubting his chances of success and yet awaiting the outcome.

The Pompeians were driven back in their retreat inside the rampart. Caesar, thinking that they should be given no respite in their panic, urged his men to take advantage of the generosity of fortune and storm the camp. Even though it was extremely hot—for the engagement had gone on until midday—his men were ready to undertake any toil, and obeyed his order. The camp was being zealously defended by the cohorts left to guard it, and more fiercely still by the Thracian and native auxiliaries. For the troops who had fled from the field, terrified and exhausted, mostly dropped their weapons and military standards and had more thought for continuing their flight than for the defence of the camp. Nor indeed could those who had taken up their position on the rampart hold out any longer against the hail of missiles. Overcome by their wounds, they abandoned their posts and at once, led by their centurions and tribunes, fled to the hilltops near the camp.

In Pompey's camp could be seen artificial arbours, a great weight of silver plate laid out, tents spread with fresh turf, those of Lucius Lentulus and several others covered with ivy, and many other indications of extravagant indulgence and confidence in victory; so that it could readily be judged that they had had no fears for the outcome of the day, in that they were procuring unnecessary comforts for themselves. Yet these were the men who taunted Caesar's wretched and long-suffering army with self-indulgence, although the latter had always been short of all kinds of necessities. When our men were already inside the rampart, Pompey got a horse, removed his general's insignia, rushed out of the camp by the rear gate and galloped off to Larissa. He did not stop there, but with a few of his men whom he had picked up in his flight he went on through the night without stopping, accompanied by thirty cavalrymen, until he reached the sea. There he embarked on a grain-ship, with, it was said, frequent laments that he should have been so grossly mistaken, that he appeared almost to have been betrayed by the very group of men whom he had hoped would secure victory but who had in fact started the flight.

Once Caesar had taken possession of the camp, he urged the soldiers not to let preoccupation with plundering render them incapable of attending to the tasks that remained. They obeyed, and he began building fortifications round the hill. Since the hill had no water, Pompey's men had no confidence in this position and leaving the mountain they all began retreating towards Larissa over its foothills. Caesar observed what they intended to do, and dividing his own forces he ordered part of the legions to stay behind in Pompey's camp and sent part back to his own camp; he took four legions with him and started along a more convenient route, to intercept the Pompeians. After advancing six miles he drew up his battle line. Observing this, the Pompeians halted on a hill, close under which ran a river. Caesar spoke encouragingly to his troops and though they were tired with continual exertion all during the day, and night was already approaching, he constructed a fortification cutting off the river from the hill, so that Pompey's men should not be able to get water during the night. When this was complete, the Pompeians sent a deputation and began to negotiate a surrender. A few of the senatorial order who had joined them sought to save themselves by fleeing during the night.

At dawn Caesar ordered all those who had settled on the hill to come down from the higher ground on to the plain and throw down their weapons. They did this without demur; then they threw themselves to the ground with their hands outstretched, weeping, and begged him for their lives. He reassured them, told them to get up, and spoke briefly to them about his own leniency, to alleviate their fears. He spared them all and charged his own soldiers to see to it that none of them suffered any physical violence or lost any part of his property. These matters taken care of, he ordered the other legions to come from the camp to join him, and the ones which he brought with him to go back to camp and rest in their turn. He arrived at Larissa on the same day.

SALLUST
(c. 86–c. 35 B.C.)

Sallust was one of the great Roman historians; his Conspiracy of Catiline
has rather overshadowed his Jugurthine War *(c. 40), a model of writing on
the tactics of the weak against the strong and the fighting of a guerrilla war of
attrition and harassment. The* Jugurthine War *lasted from 110 to 104 B.C.*

   *Sallust was at Caesar's side when the Civil War broke out in early 49 B.C.
He accompanied him to Africa and, in 46, became the first governor of the
new province of Africa created by Caesar. After the death of his patron, he
left politics and devoted himself to his writing. Most of his* History *is lost. He
was among the earliest Latin historians and, with the* Jugurthine War, *one
of the most important.*

GUERRILLA WARFARE

. . . Numidia had fallen to Metellus, a man of spirit, and, although he was an
opponent of the popular party, of a consistently unblemished reputation.
When he first entered upon his term of office, thinking that his colleague
shared with him all the other business he devoted his attention to the war
which he was going to conduct. Accordingly, being distrustful of the old army,
he enrolled soldiers, summoned auxiliaries from every hand, got together
arms, weapons, horses, and other munitions of war, as well as an abundance
of supplies; in short, he provided everything which commonly proves useful
in a war of varied character and demanding large resources. Furthermore,
in making these preparations the senate aided him by its sanction, allies, Latin
cities, and kings by the voluntary contribution of auxiliaries; in short,
the whole state showed the greatest enthusiasm. Therefore, after everything
was prepared and arranged to his satisfaction, Metellus left for Numidia,

From *Sallust,* translated by J. C. Rolfe (Cambridge, Mass.: Harvard University Press, 1940),
227–67. Reprinted by permission of the publishers and the Loeb Classical Library.

bearing with him the high hopes of the citizens, which were inspired not only by his good qualities in general, but especially because he possessed a mind superior to riches; for it had been the avarice of the magistrates that before this time had blighted our prospects in Numidia and advanced those of the enemy.

But when Metellus reached Africa, the proconsul Spurius Albinus handed over to him an army that was weak, cowardly, and incapable of facing either danger or hardship, readier of tongue than of hand, a plunderer of our allies and itself a prey to the enemy, subject to no discipline or restraint. Hence their new commander gained more anxiety from the bad habits of his soldiers than security or hope from their numbers. Although the postponement of the elections had trenched upon the summer season and Metellus knew that the citizens were eagerly anticipating his success, yet, notwithstanding this, he resolved not to take the field until he had forced the soldiers to undergo the old-time drill and training. For Albinus, utterly overcome by the disaster to his brother Aulus and the army, had decided not to leave the province; and during that part of the summer when he retained the command he had kept the soldiers for the most part in a permanent camp, except when the stench or need of fodder had compelled him to change his position. But his camps were not fortified, nor was watch kept in military fashion; men absented themselves from duty whenever they pleased. Camp followers and soldiers ranged about in company day and night, and in their forays laid waste the country, stormed farmhouses, and vied with one another in amassing booty in the form of cattle and slaves, which they bartered with the traders for foreign wine and other luxuries. They even sold the grain which was allotted them by the state and bought bread from day to day. In short, whatever disgraceful excesses resulting from idleness and wantonness can be mentioned or imagined were all to be found in that army and others besides.

But in dealing with these difficulties, as well as in waging war, I find that Metellus showed himself a great and prudent man, so skilful a course did he steer between indulgence and severity. For in the first place he is said to have removed the incentives to indolence by an edict that no one should sell bread or any other cooked food within the camp, that sutlers should not attend the army, and that no private soldier should have a slave or a pack animal in camp or on the march; and he set a strict limit on other practices of the kind. Moreover he broke camp every day for cross-country marches, fortified it with a palisade and moat just as if the enemy were near, and set guards at short intervals and inspected them in person attended by his lieutenants. On the march too he was now with those in the van, now in the rear, often in the middle of the line, to see that no one left the ranks, that they advanced in a body about the standards, and that the soldiers carried food and arms. In this way, rather by keeping them from doing wrong than by punishing them, he soon restored the temper of his army.

Jugurtha meanwhile learned through messengers what Metellus was about, and at the same time received word from Rome that his opponent was incorruptible. He therefore began to lose heart in his cause and for the first time attempted to arrange a genuine surrender. Accordingly, he sent envoys to the consul with tokens of submission, merely asking that his own life and those of his children be spared and leaving all else to the discretion of the Roman people. But Metellus had already learned from experience that the Numidians were a treacherous race, of fickle disposition, and fond of a change. He therefore separated the envoys and approached them one by one. When by gradually sounding them he found that they could be used for his design, he induced them by lavish promises to deliver Jugurtha into his hands, alive if possible; or dead, if he could not be taken alive. But publicly he bade them take back a reply in accordance with the king's wishes.

A few days later the consul with his army alert and ready for battle invaded Numidia, where he found nothing to indicate a state of war; the huts were full of men, and cattle and farmers were to be seen in the fields. The king's officers came out to meet him from the towns and villages, offering to furnish grain, transport provisions—in short, to do everything that they were ordered. None the less, exactly as if the enemy were close at hand, Metellus advanced with his line protected on all sides, and reconnoitred the country far and wide, believing that these indications of submission were a pretence and that the enemy were seeking an opportunity for treachery. Accordingly, he himself led the van with the light-armed cohorts as well as a picked body of slingers and archers, his lieutenant Gaius Marius with the cavalry had charge of the rear, while on both flanks he had apportioned the cavalry of the auxiliaries to the tribunes of the legions and the prefects of the cohorts. With these the light-armed troops were mingled, whose duty it was to repel the attacks of the enemy's horsemen, wherever they might be made. For Jugurtha was so crafty, so well acquainted with the region and so versed in military science, that it was not certain whether he was more dangerous when absent or when present, at peace or making war.

Not far from the route which Metellus was taking lay a town of the Numidians called Vaga, the most frequented emporium of the entire kingdom, where many men of Italic race traded and made their homes. Here the consul stationed a garrison, both to see whether the inhabitants would accept his overtures and because of the advantages of the situation. He gave orders too that grain and other necessaries of war should be brought together there, believing, as the circumstances suggested, that the large numbers of traders would aid his army in getting supplies and serve as a protection to those which he had already prepared.

While this was going on, Jugurtha with even greater insistence sent suppliant envoys, begged for peace, and offered Metellus everything except his life and that of his children. These envoys too, like the former ones, the consul persuaded to turn traitors and sent home, neither refusing nor promising the king the peace for which he asked and meanwhile waiting for the envoys to fulfil their promises.

When Jugurtha came to compare the words of Metellus and his actions, he realized he was being attacked with his own weapons; for ostensibly peace was offered him but in reality the bitterest warfare was on foot. His principal city had been taken from him, the country was now familiar to the enemy, the loyalty of his subjects was being undermined. He was therefore compelled to try the fortune of battle. Accordingly, having reconnoitred the enemy's march, he was led to hope for victory from the nature of the country, and after assembling the greatest possible forces of all kinds, he got in advance of Metellus' army by obscure by-paths.

In that part of Numidia which the partition had given to Adherbal there was a river flowing from the south called the Muthul, and about twenty miles from it was a naturally desolate and uncultivated range of hills running parallel with the river. From about the middle of this range an elevation branched off and extended for a long distance, clothed with wild olive, myrtles, and other varieties of trees which grow in a dry and sandy soil. The intervening plain was uninhabited from lack of water except the parts along the river, which were covered with shrubs and frequented by cattle and farmers.

On this hill then, which flanked the Romans' line of march, as I have said, Jugurtha took his position with his line greatly extended. He gave the command of the elephants and a part of the infantry to Bomilcar and told him what his plan was. He placed his own men nearer the mountain with all the cavalry and the flower of his infantry. Then going about to the various squads and companies, he admonished and besought them to be mindful of their old time valour and victories, and to defend themselves and their country from the greed of the Romans. They were to fight, he said, with men whom they had already vanquished and sent under the yoke; their leader was changed but not their spirit. For his own part, he had provided for his men everything that a leader ought: that on higher ground and prepared for action they might fight against men taken by surprise; that they might not have to fight few against many or untrained against better soldiers. Therefore they must be ready and eager to attack the Romans when the signal was given, for that day would either crown all their toil and victories, or would be the beginning of the utmost wretchedness. He also addressed them individually and recalled his favours to the mind of every soldier whom he had ever rewarded with money or honour for any deed of arms, and pointed out the recipient to his comrades. Finally, by promises, threats or entreaties he incited one man after another, each in a different way according to his disposition, when meanwhile Metellus, unaware of the enemy and coming down the mountain with his army, caught sight of them. At first the Roman wondered what the unusual appearance of things meant, for the Numidians with their horses had taken their places amid the woods, and while because of the lowness of the trees they were not entirely covered, yet it was difficult to make out just what they were, since the men and their standards were concealed both by the nature of the place and by disguise. But the consul soon detected the ambuscade, halted his army for a space, and then made a change in its formation. His right flank, which was nearest the enemy, he strengthened with three lines of reserves. Between the maniples he placed the slingers and archers, while on the wings he stationed all the cavalry. Then after exhorting the soldiers briefly, as the time demanded, he led his army down into the plain, just as he had drawn it up, with those who had been in the van now forming the flank.

When Metellus saw that the Numidians remained quiet and did not come down from the hill, he feared that at that season of the year and because of the scarcity of water his army might be exhausted by thirst. He therefore sent his lieutenant Rutilius with the light-armed cohorts and a part of the cavalry towards the river, with instructions to occupy in advance a position for the camp; for he thought that the enemy would try to delay his progress by frequent assaults on the flank, and since they put little trust in their arms, that they would try the effect of fatigue and thirst upon his soldiers. Then, as the circumstances and situation demanded, he advanced slowly in the same order in which he had come down from the mountain, keeping Marius behind what had been the front line, while he himself was with the cavalry on the left wing, which had now become the van.

As soon as Jugurtha saw that Metellus' rear had passed by the first of his own men, he stationed a force of about two thousand infantry on the mountain at the point from which the Romans had just come, so that if his opponents should give ground, they might not have this refuge and protection in their rear. Then he suddenly gave the signal and launched his attack. Some of the Numidians cut down the hindermost Romans, while a part attacked them on the right and left, pressing on with vigour and energy and throwing the ranks into general confusion. For even those who had withstood the charge with a stout heart were baffled by this irregular manner of fighting, in which they were only wounded from a distance, without having the opportunity of striking back or of joining in hand to hand conflict. Jugurtha's horsemen, following the instructions given them beforehand, whenever a squadron of the Roman cavalry began to attack them, gave way; not, however, in a body or in one direction, but dispersing as widely as possible. Thus even if they had been unable to check the enemy's pursuit, with their superior numbers they cut off the stragglers in the rear or on the flanks. If the hill proved to be more favourable for their flight than the plains, there too the horses of the Numidians, being acquainted with the ground, easily made their escape amid the thickets, while the steep and unfamiliar ground proved a hindrance to our men.

Thus the aspect of the whole affair was confused, uncertain, horrible and lamentable. Separated from their comrades, some of our men gave way, others attacked. They could neither follow the standards nor keep their ranks; but wherever each man had been overtaken by danger, there he stood his ground and defended himself. Arms and weapons, men and horses, Numidians and Romans were mingled in confusion. There was no opportunity for advice nor command; chance held sway everywhere.

In this way a considerable part of the day had passed and the outcome of the battle was still uncertain. Finally, when all the Romans were growing wearied from their exertions and the heat, Metellus noticed that the Numidians also were attacking with less vigour. He therefore gradually united his soldiers, reformed the ranks, and opposed four legionary cohorts to the enemy's infantry, the greater part of which through fatigue had taken refuge on the higher ground. At the same time he begged and implored his men not to weaken or allow a fleeing enemy to win the victory; he pointed out that the Romans had no camp or fortress as a refuge, but must rely wholly upon their arms. Meanwhile Jugurtha in his turn was not quiet, went about and encouraged his men, and endeavoured to renew the battle; in person with the flower of his troops he tried every device, aided his men, charged the enemy where they wavered, and by attacks at long range held at bay those whom he had found to be unshaken.

Thus did these two men, both great commanders, struggle with each other; personally they were on an equality but they were ill matched in their resources; for Metellus had valiant soldiers but an unfavourable position, while Jugurtha had the advantage in all except his men. At last the Romans, realizing that they had no place of refuge and that the foe gave them no opportunity for fighting (and it was already evening), charged up the hill as they had been ordered and broke through. Losing that position, the Numidians gave way and fled. A few were killed; the greater number were saved by their quickness and the Romans' lack of familiarity with the country.

In the meantime Bomilcar, who had been put in command of the elephants and a part of the infantry by Jugurtha, as I have already said, when Rutilius had passed him, slowly led his forces down into the plain; and while the lieutenant was hastily making his way to the river, to which he had been sent on, Bomilcar drew up his line quietly, as the circumstances demanded, continuing to keep an eye on the enemy's movements in all parts of the field. When he found that Rutilius had encamped and was now easy in mind, while the din from Jugurtha's battle increased, he feared that the lieutenant, if he knew the critical condition of his countrymen, might go to their aid. Accordingly, wishing to intercept the enemy's march, he extended his line, which he had drawn up in close order through distrust of his soldiers' courage, and in that formation approached Rutilius's camp.

The Romans on a sudden became aware of a great cloud of dust, for the bushes which covered the ground cut off their view. At first they thought that the wind was blowing up the dry soil; but later, as they saw that the cloud remained unchanged and came nearer and nearer as the line advanced, they realized the truth, and hastily catching up their arms, took their places before the camp, as they were ordered. Then, when they were at close quarters, both sides charged with loud shouts. The Numidians stood their ground only so long as they thought the elephants could protect them; but when they saw that the brutes became entangled in the branches of the trees and were thus separated and surrounded, they took to flight. The greater number, after throwing away their arms, escaped unhurt, thanks to the hill and the night, which was now close at hand. Four elephants were taken, and all the rest to the number of forty were killed. But although the Romans were wearied by their march, by the work on the camp, and by the battle, yet because Metellus was later than they expected, they went to meet him in order of battle on the alert; for the craft of the Numidians admitted of no relaxation or carelessness. It was now dark night, and at first, when the armies were not far apart, the sound, as of a hostile force approaching, caused fear and confusion on both sides; and the mistake might have led to a deplorable catastrophe, had not the horsemen who were sent out by both sides to reconnoitre discovered what the situation was. Thereupon in place of fear a sudden joy arose. The exultant soldiers called out to one another, told of their exploits and heard the tales of others. Each man praised his own valiant deeds to the skies. For so it is with human affairs; in time of victory the very cowards may brag, while defeat discredits even the brave.

Metellus remained in the same camp for four days, giving careful attention to the wounded, rewarding good service in the battles with military prizes, and praising and thanking all the troops in a body. He urged them to have like courage for the easy tasks which remained; their fight for victory was at an end, the rest of their efforts would be for booty. Meanwhile, however, he sent deserters and other available spies to find out where in the world Jugurtha was and what he was about, whether he had but few followers or an army, how he conducted himself in defeat. As a matter of fact, the king had retreated to a wooded district of natural strength and was there recruiting an army which in numbers was larger than before, but inefficient and weak, being more familiar with farming and grazing than with war. The reason for this was, that except for the horsemen of his bodyguard not a single Numidian follows his king after a defeat, but all disperse whithersoever they choose, and this is not considered shameful for soldiers. Such are their customs.

Accordingly, when Metellus saw that the king was still full of confidence, and that a war was being renewed which could be carried on only as his opponent chose, he realized that his struggle with the enemy was an unequal one, since defeat cost them less than victory did his own men. He accordingly decided that he must conduct the campaign, not by pitched battles, but in another fashion. He therefore marched into the most fertile parts of Numidia, laid waste the country, captured and burned many strongholds and towns which had been hurriedly fortified or left without defenders, ordered the death of all the adults and gave everything else to his soldiers as booty. In this way he caused such terror that many men were given to the Romans as hostages, grain and other necessities were furnished in abundance, and garrisons were admitted wherever Metellus thought it advisable.

These proceedings alarmed the king much more than the defeat which his men had suffered; for while all his hopes depended upon flight, he was forced to pursue, and when he had been unable to defend favourable positions, he was obliged to fight in those which were unfavourable. However, he adopted the plan which seemed best under the circumstances and ordered the greater part of the army to remain where it was, while he himself followed Metellus with a select body of cavalry. Making his way at night and through by-paths he suddenly fell upon the Roman stragglers when they least expected it; the greater number of them were killed before they could arm themselves, many were taken, not one escaped unscathed. Before aid could be sent from the camp, the Numidians, as they had been ordered, scattered to the nearest hills.

Meanwhile, great joy had arisen at Rome from the news of Metellus' exploits, when it was learned that he conducted himself and treated his army after the fashion of old, that he, though caught in an unfavourable position, had nevertheless won the victory by his valour, was holding possession of the enemy's territory, and had compelled Jugurtha, who had been made insolent by Albinus' incapacity, to rest his hopes of safety on the desert or on flight. The senate accordingly voted a thanksgiving to the immortal gods because of these successes, while the community, which before this had been in fear and anxiety as to the outcome of the war, gave itself up to rejoicing. Metellus' fame was brilliant. He therefore strove the harder for victory, hastened matters in every way, yet was careful not to give the enemy an opening anywhere, remembering that envy follows hard upon glory. Hence the greater his fame, the more caution he showed; after Jugurtha's ambuscade he no longer ravaged the country with his army in disorder; when he required grain or fodder, a number of cohorts stood on guard along with all the cavalry; he led part of the army himself and Marius the rest. But fire did more than plundering to devastate the land. The consul and his lieutenant used to encamp in two places not far apart. When necessity demanded the use of strength, they joined forces; otherwise they acted separately, in order that the enemy's terror and flight might be more widespread.

Meanwhile Jugurtha would follow along the hills, watching for a suitable time or place for battle: he spoiled the fodder and contaminated the springs, which were very few, in the places to which he had heard that the enemy were coming; showed himself now to Metellus, again to Marius; made an attempt on the hindermost in the line and at once retreated to the hills; again threatened others and afterwards others, neither gave battle nor let the enemy rest, but merely prevented them from carrying out their plans.

When the Roman general began to realize that he was being exhausted by the strategy of his opponent, who gave him no chance for battle, he decided to lay siege to a large city called Zama, the citadel of the part of the kingdom in which it was situated. He thought that as a matter of course Jugurtha would come to the aid of his subjects in distress and that a battle would be fought in that place. But Jugurtha, learning from deserters what was on foot, by forced marches outstripped Metellus; he encouraged the townspeople to defend their walls, and gave them the help of a band of deserters, who formed the strongest part of the king's forces because they dared not be treacherous. He promised too that he would come himself in due season with an army. Having made these arrangements, the king withdrew to places as secluded as possible, and presently learned that Marius had been ordered to leave the line of march and go with a few cohorts to forage at Sicca, which was the very first town to revolt from the king after his defeat. Thither Jugurtha hastened by night with the best of his cavalry and engaged the Romans at the gate just as they were coming out. At the same time, in a loud voice he urged the people of Sicca to surround the cohorts in the rear; fortune, he said, gave them the chance for a brilliant exploit. If they took advantage of it, he would be restored to his kingdom and they would live for the future in freedom and without fear. And had not Marius hastened to advance and leave the town, surely the greater part of the townspeople, if not all of them, would have changed their allegiance; such is the fickleness with which the Numidians act. Jugurtha's soldiers were held firm for a time by the king, but when the enemy attacked with greater force they fled in disorder after suffering slight losses.

Marius went on to Zama. That town, situated in an open plain and fortified rather by art than by nature, lacked no essential, and was well supplied with arms and men. Therefore Metellus, making his preparations to suit the circumstances and the locality, completely invested the walls with his army, assigning to each of his lieutenants his special point of attack. Then, upon a given signal, a mighty shout arose from all sides at once, but without in the least frightening the Numidians; ready and eager for action they awaited the fray without disorder and the battle began. The Romans acted each according to his own quality: some fought at long range with slings and stones, others advanced and undermined the wall or applied scaling-ladders, striving to get at grips with the foe. The townsmen met their attacks by rolling down stones upon the foremost and hurling at them beams, pikes, burning pitch mixed with sulphur, and firebrands. Not even those of our men who had remained at a distance were wholly protected by their timidity, for very many of them were wounded by javelins hurled from engines or by hand. Thus the valiant and the craven were in like danger but of unlike repute.

While this struggle was going on at Zama, Jugurtha unexpectedly fell upon the Roman camp with a large force, and through the carelessness of the guards, who were looking for anything rather than a battle, forced one of the gates. Our men were struck with a sudden panic and sought safety each according to his temperament; some fled, others armed themselves, nearly all were killed or wounded. But out of the entire number forty or less remembered that they were Romans. These gathered together and took a position a little higher than the rest, from which they could not be dislodged by the greatest efforts of the enemy, but they threw back the weapons which were thrown at them from a distance, and few against many could hardly miss. But if the Numidians came nearer, they then showed their real quality, charging them with the greatest fury, routing and scattering them.

Meanwhile, Metellus, who was vigorously pressing the attack on the town, heard shouts like the melley of a hostile force behind him; then, wheeling his horse about, he saw that the fugitives were coming his way, which indicated that they were his countrymen. He therefore sent all the cavalry to the camp in haste and ordered Gaius Marius to follow at once with the cohorts of allies, begging him with tears in the name of their friendship and their common country not to allow any disgrace to stain their victorious army, and not to suffer the enemy to escape unpunished. Marius promptly did as he was ordered. As for Jugurtha, he was hampered by the fortifications of the camp, since some of his men were tumbling over the ramparts and others, endeavouring to make haste in the crowded spaces, were getting in each other's way; he therefore, after considerable losses, withdrew to a place of safety. Metellus was prevented by the coming of night from following up his victory and returned to camp with his army.

Accordingly, the next day, before going out to attack the town, Metellus ordered all the cavalry to ride up and down before that part of the camp where the king was likely to attack, assigned to the several tribunes the defence of the gates and their neighbourhood, and then himself proceeded to the town and assailed the wall as on the day before. Meanwhile Jugurtha suddenly rushed upon our men from ambush. Those who were stationed nearest the point of attack were terrified and thrown into confusion for a time, but the rest quickly came to their help. And the Numidians would not have been able to make a long resistance, had not their combination of infantry and cavalry done great execution in the melley; for the Numidian horsemen, trusting to this infantry, did not alternately advance and retreat, as is usual in a cavalry skirmish, but charged at full speed, rushing into and breaking up our line of battle; thus with their light-armed infantry they all but conquered their enemy.

At the same time the contest at Zama continued with great fury. Wherever each of the lieutenants or tribunes was in charge, there was the bitterest strife and no one relied more on another than on himself. The townspeople showed equal courage; men were fighting or making preparations at all points, and both sides were more eager to wound one another than to protect themselves. There was a din of mingled encouragement, exultation, and groans; the clash of arms also rose to heaven, and a shower of missiles fell on both sides. But whenever the besiegers relaxed their assault ever so little, the defenders of the walls became interested spectators of the cavalry battle. As Jugurtha's fortunes shifted, you might see them now joyful, now alarmed; acting as if their countrymen could see or hear them, some shouted warnings, others urged them on; they gesticulated or swayed their bodies, moving them this way and that as if dodging or hurling weapons.

When Marius perceived all this (for he was in charge at that point) he purposely slackened his efforts and feigned discouragement, allowing the Numidians to witness their king's battle undisturbed. When their attention was thus riveted upon their countrymen, he suddenly assaulted the wall with the utmost violence. Our soldiers, mounting on scaling-ladders, had almost reached the top of the wall, when the townsmen rushed to the spot and met them with a rain of stones, firebrands, and other missiles besides. At first our men resisted; then, as ladder after ladder was shattered and those who stood upon them were dashed to the ground, the rest made off as best they could, some few unharmed but the greater number badly wounded. At last night ended the combat on both sides.

After Metellus saw that his attempt was vain, that the town was no nearer being taken, that Jugurtha would not fight except from ambush or on his own ground, and that the summer was now at an end, he left Zama and placed garrisons in such of the towns which had gone over to him as were strongly enough fortified by their situation or by walls. The rest of his army he stationed in the part of our province which lies nearest to Numidia, that they might pass the winter there. But he did not devote that season, as others commonly do, to rest or dissipation, but since the war was making little progress through arms, he prepared to lay snares for the king through his friends and to make their treachery his weapons.

JOSEPHUS

(C. A.D. 37–C. 100)

*Flavius Josephus was appointed governor of Galilee by the Sanhedrin early
in the rebellion of the Jews against Rome (A.D. 66–70). In 67 he was
captured and went over to the enemy, breaking the collective oath kept by
his companions. He was witness to the last years of the Jewish state, being
present in the Roman camp at the fall of Jerusalem and the destruction of
the Temple.* The Jewish War *covers the period from 175 B.C. to A.D. 73.*

THE ORGANIZATION OF THE ROMAN ARMY

The Romans showed remarkable foresight in making their domestic staff useful to them not only in the services of everyday life but also in war. Anyone
who will take a took at the organization of their army in general will recognize
that they hold their wide-flung empire as the prize of valour, not the gift of
fortune. They do not wait for war to begin before handling their arms, nor do
they sit idle in peacetime and take action only when the emergency comes—
but as if born ready armed they never have a truce from training or wait for
war to be declared. Their battle-drills are no different from the real thing; every
man works as hard at his daily training as if he was on active service. That is
why they stand up so easily to the strain of battle: no indiscipline dislodges
them from their regular formation, no panic incapacitates them, no toil wears
them out; so that victory over men not so trained follows as a matter of course.
It would not be far from the truth to call their drills bloodless battles, their battles bloody drills.

They never give the enemy a chance to catch them off their guard; for whenever they invade hostile territory they rigidly refuse battle till they have fortified their camp. This they do not construct haphazard or unevenly, nor do

From Josephus, *The Jewish War*, translated by G. A. Williamson (Harmondsworth, England:
Penguin Books, 1959), 378–81. Copyright © 1959 by G. A. Williamson. Reproduced by permission
of Penguin Books Ltd.

they tackle the job with all their manpower or without organized squads; if the ground is uneven it is thoroughly levelled, then the site is marked out as a rectangle. The inside is divided up ready for the huts. From outside the perimeter looks like a wall and is equipped with towers evenly spaced. In the gaps between the towers they mount quick-loaders, catapults, stone-throwers, and every type of ordnance, all ready to be discharged. Four gates are constructed, one in each length of wall, practicable for the entry of baggage-animals and wide enough for armed sorties, if called for. The camp is divided up by streets accurately marked out; in the middle are erected the officers' huts, and in the middle of these the commander's headquarters, which resembles a shrine. It all seems like a mushroom town, with marketplace, workmen's quarters, and orderly-rooms where junior and senior officers can settle disputes as they arise. The erection of the outer wall and the buildings inside is accomplished faster than thought, thanks to the number and skill of the workers. If necessary a ditch is dug all round, six feet deep and the same width.

The fortifications completed, the men go to their quarters unit by unit in a quiet and orderly manner. All other duties are carried out with attention to discipline and security, wood, food, and water as required being brought in by the units detailed. They do not have supper or breakfast just when they fancy at individual discretion, but all together. Times for sleep, guard-duty, and reveille are announced by trumpet-calls, and nothing whatever is done without orders. At stand-to the private soldiers report by units to their centurions, the centurions go to their tribunes to salute them, and the tribunes accompany all their superior officers to Headquarters, where the commander-in-chief, in accordance with routine, gives them the password and other orders to communicate to their subordinates. They act in the same orderly way on the battle field, changing direction promptly as required, and whether attacking or retreating move as one man.

When camp is to be struck, the trumpet sounds and every man springs to his duty. Following the signal huts are instantly dismantled and all preparations are made for departure. The trumpet then sounds "Stand by to march!" At once they load the mules and wagons with the baggage and take their places like runners lined up and hardly able to wait for the starter's signal. Then they fire the camp, which they can easily reconstruct if required, and which might some day be useful to the enemy. For the third time the trumpets give the same signal for departure, to urge on those who for any reason have been loitering, so that not a man may be missing from his place. Then the announcer, standing on the right of the supreme commander, asks three times in their native language whether they are ready for war. They three times shout loudly and with enthusiasm "Ready," hardly waiting for the question, and filled with a kind of martial fervour raise their right arms as they shout. Then they step off, all marching silently and in good order, as on active service every man keeping his place in the column.

The infantry are armed with breastplate and helmet and carry a blade on each side; of these by far the longer is the one on the left, the other being no more than nine inches long. The general's bodyguard of picked infantry carry lance and buckler, the other units javelin and long shield, together with saw and basket, axe and pick, as well as strap, reaphook, chain, and three days' rations, so that there is not much difference between a foot-soldier and a pack-mule! The trooper carries a long sword on his right hip and an enormous pike in his hand, a shield slanted across his horse's flank, and in a quiver slung alongside three or more darts, broad-pointed and as big as spears. Helmets and breast-plates of infantry pattern are worn by all arms. Equipment is exactly the same for the general's mounted bodyguard as for the other cavalry units. Lots are always drawn for the legion that is to head the column. So much for Roman routine on the march and in quarters, and for the variety of equipment.

In battle nothing is done without plan or on the spur of the moment; careful thought precedes action of any kind, and to the decisions reached all actions must conform. As a result they meet with very few setbacks, and if anything goes wrong the setbacks are easily cancelled out. They regard successes due to luck as less desirable than a planned but unsuccessful stroke, because victories that come of themselves tempt men to leave things to chance, but forethought, in spite of occasional failures, is good practice in avoiding the same mistake. Good things that come of themselves bring no credit to the recipient, but unfortunate accidents that upset calculations have at least this comfort in them, that plans were properly laid.

Military exercises give the Roman soldiers not only tough bodies but determined spirits too. Training methods are partly based on fear; for military law demands the death penalty not only for leaving a post but even for trivial misdemeanours; and the generals inspire more fear than the law, since by rewarding good soldiers they avoid seeming harsh towards the men they punish. So complete is their submission to their superiors that in peace they are a credit to Rome and in the field the whole army is a single body; so knit together are their ranks, so flexible their manoeuvres, so ready their ears for orders, their eyes for signals, their hands for the tasks to be done. Thus it is that they are as quick to act as they are slow to give way, and never was there an engagement in which they were worsted by numbers, tactical skill, or unfavourable ground—or even by fortune, which is less within their grasp than is victory. When planning goes before action, and the plans are followed by so effective an army, who can wonder that in the east the Euphrates, in the west the ocean, in the south the richest plains of Africa, in the north the Danube and the Rhine are the limits of the Empire? One might say with truth that the conquests are less remarkable than the conquerors.

The purpose of the foregoing account has been less to eulogize the Romans than to console their defeated enemies and to deter any who may be thinking of revolt; and possibly those of an enquiring frame of mind who have not studied the matter may find it useful to get an insight into the Roman military set-up. This is all that I propose to say on the subject.

ONASANDER
(first century A.D.)

Onasander, who was of Greek origin, was a contemporary with the emperor Claudius (r. A.D. 41–54). His treatise Strategikos *is about the science of army command. Onasander's influence on Byzantine generals is clear, notably in Leo VI's* Taktika. *Onasander himself seems to owe some debt to Xenophon.*

THE GENERAL

I believe, then, that we must choose a general, not because of noble birth as priests are chosen, nor because of wealth as the superintendents of the gymnasia, but because he is temperate, self-restrained, vigilant, frugal, hardened to labour, alert, free from avarice, neither too young nor too old, indeed a father of children if possible, a ready speaker, and a man with a good reputation.

The general must be temperate in order that he may not be so distracted by the pleasures of the body as to neglect the consideration of matters of the highest importance.

He must be self-restrained, since he is to be a man of so great authority; for the licentious impulses, when combined with the authority which confers the power of action, become uncontrollable in the gratification of the passions.

Vigilant, that he may spend wakeful nights over the most important projects; for at night, as a rule, with the mind at rest, the general perfects his plans.

Frugal, since expensive attendance upon the luxurious tastes of commanders consumes time unprofitably and causes resources to waste away.

Hardened to labour, that he may not be the first but the last of the army to grow weary.

Alert, for the general must be quick, with swiftness of mind darting at every subject—quick, as Homer says, "as a bird, or as thought." For very frequently

From *Aeneas Taciticus Asclepiodorus Onasander,* translated by the Illinois Greek Club (New York: Putnam's; London: Heinemann, 1923), 375–91.

unexpected disorders arise which may compel him to decide on the spur of the moment what is expedient. . . .

Neither too young nor too old; since the young man does not inspire confidence, the old man is feeble, and neither is free from danger, the young man lest he err through reckless daring, the older lest he neglect something through physical weakness. The ideal lies between the two, for physical vigour is found in the man who has not yet grown old, and discretion in the man who is not too young. . . .

A ready speaker; for I believe that the greatest benefit can accrue from the work of a general only through this gift. For if a general is drawing up his men before battle, the encouragement of his words makes them despise the danger and covet the honour; and a trumpet-call resounding in the ears does not so effectively awaken the soul to the conflict of battle as a speech that urges to strenuous valour rouses the martial spirit to confront danger. . . . No city at all will put an army in the field without generals nor choose a general who lacks the ability to make an effective speech.

The general should be a man of good reputation, because the majority of men, when placed under the command of unknown generals, feel uneasy. For no one voluntarily submits to a leader or an officer who is an inferior man to himself. . . .

An illustrious family name we should welcome, if it be present, but if lacking it should not be demanded, nor should we judge men worthy or unworthy of commands simply by this criterion; but just as we test the pedigrees of animals in the light of the things they actually do, so we should view the pedigrees of men also. For it is dangerous to consider what fine thing a general's ancestors have done, rather than what the generals now chosen will do, as if those long dead could still protect us, and as if they would maintain us in our former possessions. . . . Of course, if a general has birth in addition to these other qualities, he is fortunate, but even if he has a famous name without the other qualities, he is useless. It might perhaps be expected that those men who cannot take pride in their ancestors would become even better generals; for men who glory in their forefathers, even if they are themselves failures, believing that the fame of their family is theirs forever are often too careless as administrators, whereas those who have no ancestral renown to begin with, desiring to make up for the obscurity of their lineage by their own zeal, are more eager to take part in dangerous enterprises. . . .

The General's Advisory Council

The general should either choose a staff to participate in all his councils and share in his decisions, men who will accompany the army especially for this purpose, or summon as members of his council a selected group of the most respected commanders, since it is not safe that the opinions of one single man, on his sole judgement, should be adopted. For the isolated decision of one man, unsupported by others, can see no farther than his own ingenuity, but that which has the additional testimony of councillors guarantees against mistake. However, the general must neither be so undecided that he entirely distrusts himself, nor so obstinate as not to think that anyone can have a better idea than his own; for such a man, either because he listens to every one else and never to himself, is sure to meet with frequent misfortune, or else, through never listening to others but always to himself, is bound to make many costly mistakes. . . .

The Necessity of a Reasonable Cause for War

The causes of war, I believe, should be marshalled with the greatest care; it should be evident to all that one fights on the side of justice. For then the gods also, kindly disposed, become comrades in arms to the soldiers, and men are more eager to take their stand against the foe. For with the knowledge that they are not fighting an aggressive but a defensive war, with consciences free from evil designs, they contribute a courage that is complete; while those who believe an unjust war is displeasing to heaven, because of this very opinion enter the war with fear, even if they are not about to face danger at the hands of the enemy. On this account the general must first announce, by speeches and through embassies, what he wishes to obtain and what he is not willing to concede, in order that it may appear that, because the enemy will not agree to his reasonable demands, it is of necessity, not by his own preference, that he is taking the field.

PLUTARCH

(C. A.D. 46–C. 120)

Plutarch was a Greek, born in Boeotia, who lived under the emperors Nero, Trajan, and Hadrian (making him a contemporary of Tacitus's). He was a philosopher, a historian, and a priest of Delphi for thirty years; his work is uneven, but for the strategist, the Parallel Lives *contains some remarkable episodes, such as the story of Crassus's expedition against the Parthians c. 54 B.C., which pitted mounted archers engaged in harassment on unfavorable terrain against heavy infantry seeking to apply shock tactics. Until the time of the Mongol invasions, this type of encounter occurred frequently, although settled peoples switched from infantry to heavy cavalry. Crassus (c. 115–53 B.C.), one of the triumvirs with Pompey and Caesar, and governor of Syria, fought a campaign against Mithridates, king of Pontus, and Tigranes, king of Armenia, before advancing into southern Mesopotamia against the Parthians.*

AN ABSOLUTE DISASTER

... [Crassus] began to march forward into the country by the river's side, with seven legions of footmen, and little lack of four thousand horse, and in manner as many shot and slings lightly armed. There returned to him certain of his scouts that had viewed the country, and told him there was not an enemy to be seen in the field: howbeit that they had found the track of a marvellous number of horse, which seemed as they were returned back. Then Crassus first of all began to hope well: and his soldiers also, they fell to despite the Parthians, thinking certainly that they would not come to battle with them. Yet Cassius his treasurer ever persuaded him the contrary, and thought it better for him to refresh his army a little in one of the cities where he had his garri-

From "Crassus," in *Lives of the Noble Grecians and Romans,* translated by James Amyot and Thomas North, edited by Paul Turner (Carbondale, Ill.: Southern Illinois University Press, 1963), 1: 266–72.

son, until such time as he heard more certain news of the enemies: or else that he would march directly towards Seleucia by the river's side, which lay fit for him to victual himself easily by boats that would always follow his camp, and should be sure besides that the enemies could not environ him behind, so that having no way to set upon them but before, they should have none advantage of them.

Crassus going about then to consult of the matter, there came one Ariamnes unto him, a captain of the Arabians, a fine subtle fellow, which was the greatest mischief and evil, that fortune could send to Crassus at that present time, to bring him to utter ruin and destruction. For there were some of Crassus' soldiers that had served Pompey before in that country, who knew him very well, and remembered that Pompey had done him great pleasures: whereupon they thought that he bare great goodwill to the Romans. But Ariamnes had been laboured at that time by the king of Parthia's captains, and was won by them to deceive Crassus, and to entice him all he could, to draw him from the river and the woody country, and to bring him into the plain field, where they might compass him in with their horsemen: for they meant nothing less than to fight with the Romans at the sword's point.

This barbarous captain Ariamnes coming to Crassus, did highly praise and commend Pompey, as his good lord and benefactor (for he was an excellent spoken man) and extolled Crassus' army, reproving him that he came so slowly forward, tracting time in that sort as he did, preparing himself as though he had need of armour and weapon, and not of feet and hands swift and ready against the enemies: who (for the chiefest of them) had of long time occupied themselves to fly with their best movables, towards the deserts of Scythia and Hyrcania. Therefore if you determine (said he) to fight, it were good you made haste to meet them, before the king have gathered all his power together. For now you have but Surena and Sillaces, two of his lieutenants against you, whom he hath sent before to stay you that you follow him not: and for the king himself, be bold, he meaneth not to trouble you.

But he lied in all. For King Hyrodes had divided his army in two parts at the first, whereof himself took the one, and went to spoil the realm of Armenia, to be revenged of King Artabazes: and with the other he sent Surena against the Romans, not for any contempt he had of Crassus (for it was not likely he would disdain to come to battle with him, being one of the chiefest noblemen of Rome, and to think it more honourable to make war with King Artabazes in Armenia) but I think rather he did it of purpose to avoid the greater danger, and to keep far off, that he might with safety see what would happen, and therefore sent Surena before to hazard battle, and to turn the Romans back again.

For Surena was no mean man, but the second person of Parthia next unto the king: in riches, reputation, valure, and experience in wars, the chiefest of his time among all the Parthians, and for execution, no man like him. Surena, when he did but remove into the country only with his household, had a thousand camels to carry his sumpters, and two hundred coaches of courtesans, a thousand men of arms armed at all pieces, and as many more besides lightly armed: so that his whole train and court made above ten thousand horse. Further, by the tenure of that land he had by succession from his ancestors, his office was at the first proclaiming of any king, to put the royal crown or diadem upon the king's head. Moreover, he had restored King Hyrodes that then reigned, to his crown, who had been before driven out of his realm: and had won him also the great city of Seleucia, himself being the first man that scaled the walls, and overthrew them with his own hands that resisted him. And though he was under thirty years of age, yet they counted him a wise man, as well for his counsel, as his experience, which were the means whereby he overcame Crassus. Who through his rashness and folly at the first, and afterwards for very fear and timorousness, which his misfortune had brought him unto, was easy to be taken and entrapped, by any policy or deceit.

Now this barbarous captain Ariamnes having then brought Crassus to believe all that he said, and drawn him by persuasion from the river of Euphrates, unto a goodly plain country, meeting at the first with very good way, but after with very ill, because they entered into sands where their feet sunk deep, and into desert fields where was neither tree nor water, nor any end of them that they could discern by eye, so that not only extreme thirst and miserable way marvellously amazed the Romans, but the discomfort of the eye also, when they could see nothing to stay their sight upon: that, above all the rest, wrought their extreme trouble. For, neither far nor near any sight of tree, river, brook, mountain, grass, or green herb appeared within their view, but in troth an endless sea of desert sands on every side, round about their camp. Then began they to suspect that they were betrayed.

Again, when news came that Artabazes king of Armenia, was kept in his country with a great war King Hyrodes made upon him, which kept him that he could not according to his promise come to aid him, yet that he wished him to draw towards Armenia, that both their armies being joined together they might the better fight with King Hyrodes, if not, that he would always keep the woody country, marching in those valleys and places where his horsemen might be safe, and about the mountains: Crassus was so wilful, as he would write no answer to it, but angrily told the messenger, that he had no leisure then to hearken to the Armenians, but that afterwards he would be revenged well enough of Artabazes' treason.

Cassius his treasurer was much offended with Crassus for this answer: howbeit perceiving he could do no good with him, and that he took everything in evil part, he said unto him, he would tell him no more. Notwithstanding, taking Ariamnes this captain of the Armenians aside, he rebuked him roundly, and said: O thou wretch, what cursed devil hath brought thee to us, and how cunningly hast thou bewitched and charmed Crassus: that thou hast made him bring his army into this endless desert, and to trace this way fitter for an Arabian captain of thieves, than for a general and Consul of the Romans? Ariamnes being crafty and subtle, speaking gently unto Cassius, did comfort him, and prayed him to have patience, and going and coming by the bands, seeming to help the soldiers, he told them merrily: O my fellows, I believe you think to march through the country of Naples, and look to meet with your pleasant springs, goodly groves of wood, your natural baths, and the good inns round about to refresh you, and do not remember that you pass through the deserts of Arabia and Assyria. And thus did this barbarous captain entertain the Romans awhile: but afterwards he dislodged betimes, before he was openly known for a traitor, and yet not without Crassus' privity, whom he bare in hand, that he would go set some broil and tumult in the enemies' camp.

It is reported that Crassus the very same day came out of his tent not in his coat armour, of scarlet, (as the manner was of the Roman generals) but in a black coat: howbeit, remembering himself, he straight changed it again. It is said moreover, that the ensign bearers when they should march away, had much ado to pluck their ensigns out of the ground, they stuck so fast. But Crassus scoffing at the matter, hastened them the more to march forward, compelling the footmen to go as fast as the horsemen, till a few of their scouts came in, whom they had sent to discover: who brought news how the enemies had slain their fellows, and what ado they had themselves to scape with life, and that they were a marvellous great army, and well appointed to give them battle.

This news made all the camp afraid, but Crassus self more than the rest, so as he began to set his men in battle ray, being for haste in manner besides himself. At the first following Cassius' mind, he set his ranks wide, casting his soldiers into a square battle, a good way asunder one from another, because he would take in as much of the plain as he could, to keep the enemies from compassing them in, and so divided the horsemen into the wings. Yet afterwards he changed his mind again, and straited the battle of his footmen, fashioning it like a brick, more long than broad, making a front, and showing their faces every way. For there were twelve cohorts or ensigns embattled on either side, and by every cohort a company of horse, because there should be no place left without aid of horsemen, and that all his battle should be alike defended. Then he gave Cassius the leading of one wing, his son Publius Crassus the other, and himself led the battle in the middest.

In this order they marched forward, till they came to a little brook called Balissus, where there was no great store of water, but yet happily lighted on for the soldiers, for the great thirst and extreme heat they had abidden all that painful way, where they had met with no water before. There the most part of Crassus' captains thought best to camp all night, that they might in the mean-time find means to know their enemies what number they were, and how they were armed, that they might fight with them in the morning. But Crassus yield-ing to his son's and his horsemen's persuasion, who entreated him to march on with his army, and to set upon the enemy presently: commanded, that such as would eat, should eat standing, keeping their ranks.

Yet on the sodain, before this commandment could run through the whole army, he commanded them again to march, not fair and softly as when they go to give battle, but with speed, till they spied the enemies, who seemed not to the Romans at the first to be so great a number, neither so bravely armed as they thought they had been. For, concerning their great number, Surena had of purpose hid them, with certain troops he sent before: and to hide their bright armours, he had cast cloaks and beasts' skins upon them, but when both the armies approached near the one to the other, and that the sign to give charge was lift up in the air: first they filled the field with a dreadful noise to hear. For the Parthians do not encourage their men to fight with the sound of a horn, neither with trumpets nor howboys, but with great kettle drums hollow within, and about them they hang little bells and copper rings, and with them they all make a noise everywhere together, and it is like a dead sound, mingled as it were with the braying or bellowing of a wild beast, and a fearful noise as if it thundered, knowing that hearing is one of the senses that soonest moveth the heart and spirit of any man, and maketh him soonest besides himself.

The Romans being put in fear with this dead sound, the Parthians straight threw the clothes and coverings from them that hid their armour and then showed their bright helmets and curaces of Margian tempered steel, that glared like fire, and their horses barbed with steel and copper. And Surena also, general of the Parthians, who was as goodly a personage, and as valiant, as any other in all his host, though his beauty somewhat effeminate, in judgement showed small likelihood of any such courage, for he painted his face, and ware his hair after the fashion of the Medes, contrary to the manner of the Parthi-ans, who let their hair grow after the fashion of the Tartars, without combing or tricking of them, to appear more terrible to their enemies.

The Parthians at the first thought to have set upon the Romans with their pikes, to see if they could break their first ranks. But when they drew near, and saw the depth of the Romans' battle standing close together, firmly keeping their ranks: then they gave back, making as though they fled, and dispersed themselves. But the Romans marvelled when they found it contrary, and that it was but a device to environ them on every side. Whereupon Crassus com-manded his shot and light armed men to assail them, the which they did: but they went not far, they were so beaten in with arrows, and driven to retire to their force of the armed men. And this was the first beginning that both feared and troubled the Romans, when they saw the vehemency and great force of the enemies' shot, which brake their armours, and ran through anything they hit, were it never so hard or soft.

The Parthians thus still drawing back, shot all together on every side, not aforehand, but at adventure: for the battle of the Romans stood so near together, as if they would, they could not miss the killing of some. These bowmen drew a great strength, and had big strong bows, which sent the arrows from them with a wonderful force. The Romans by means of these bows were in hard state. For if they kept their ranks, they were grievously wounded: again if they left them, and sought to run upon the Parthians to fight at hand with them, they saw they could do them but little hurt, and yet were very likely to take the greater harm themselves. For, as fast as the Romans came upon them, so fast did the Parthians fly from them, and yet in flying continued still their shooting: which no nation but the Scythians could better do than they, being a matter indeed most greatly to their advantage. For by their flight they best do save themselves, and fighting still, they thereby shun the shame of that their flying.

The Romans still defended themselves, and held it out, so long as they had any hope that the Parthians would leave fighting, when they had spent their arrows or would join battle with them. But after they understood that there were a great number of camels laden with quivers full of arrows, where the first that had bestowed their arrows fetched about to take new quivers: then Crassus seeing no end of their shot, began to faint, and sent to Publius his son, willing him in any case to charge upon the enemies, and to give an onset, before they were compassed in on every side. For it was on Publius' side, that one of the wings of the enemies' battle was nearest unto them, and where they rode up and down to compass them behind. Whereupon Crassus' son taking thirteen hundred horsemen with him (of the which, a thousand were of the men of arms whom Julius Caesar sent) and five hundred shot, with eight ensigns of footmen having targets, most near to the place where himself then was: he put them out in breadth, that wheeling about they might give a charge upon them that rode up and down. But they seeing him coming, turned straight their horse and fled, either because they met in a marisse, or else of purpose to beguile this young Crassus, enticing him thereby as far from his father as they could.

Publius Crassus seeing them fly, cried out, These men will not abide us, and so spurred on for life after them: so did Censorinus and Megabacchus with him (the one a senator of Rome a very eloquent man, the other a stout courageous valiant man of war) both of them Crassus' well approved friends, and in manner of his own years. Now the horsemen of the Romans being trained out thus to the chase, their footmen also would not abide behind, now show themselves to have less hope, joy and courage, than their horsemen had. For they thought all had been won, and that there was no more to do, but to follow the chase: till they were gone far from the army, and then they found the deceit. For the horsemen that fled before them, sodainly turned again, and a number of others besides came and set upon them. Whereupon they stayed, thinking that the enemies perceiving they were so few, would come and fight with them hand to hand.

Howbeit they set out against them their men at arms with their barbed horse, and made their light horsemen wheel round about them, keeping no order at all: who galloping up and down the plain, whirled up the sand hills from the bottom with their horse feet, which raised such a wonderful dust, that the Romans could scarce see or speak one to another. For they being shut up into a little room, and standing close one to another, were sore wounded with the Parthians' arrows, and died of a cruel lingering death, crying out for anguish and pain they felt: and turning and tormenting themselves upon the sand, they brake the arrows sticking in them. Again, striving by force to pluck out the forked arrow heads, that had pierced far into their bodies through their veins and sinews: thereby they opened their wounds wider, and so cast themselves away.

Many of them died thus miserably martyred: and such as died not, were not able to defend themselves. Then when Publius Crassus prayed and besought them to charge the men at arms with their barbed horse, they showed him their hands fast nailed to their targets with arrows, and their feet likewise shot through and nailed to the ground: so as they could neither fly nor yet defend themselves. Thereupon himself encouraging his horsemen, went and gave a charge, and did valiantly set upon the enemies, but it was with too great disadvantage, both for offence, and also for defence. For himself and his men with weak and light staves, brake upon them that were armed with curaces of steel, or stiff leather jacks. And the Parthians in contrary manner with mighty strong pikes gave charge upon these Gauls, which were either unarmed, or else but lightly armed.

Yet those were they in whom Crassus most trusted, having done wonderful feats of war with them. For they received the Parthian's pikes in their hands, and took them about the middles, and threw them off their horse, where they lay on the ground, and could not stir for the weight of their harness: and there were divers of them also that lighting from their horse, lay under their enemies' horse bellies, and thrust their swords into them. Their horse flinging and bounding in the air for very pain threw their maisters under feet, and their enemies one upon another, and in the end fell dead among them. Moreover, extreme heat and thirst did marvellously comber the Gauls, who were used to abide neither of both: and the most part of their horse were slain, charging with all their power upon the men at arms of the Parthians, and so ran themselves in upon the points of their pikes.

At the length, they were driven to retire towards their footmen, and Publius Crassus among them, who was very ill by reason of the wounds he had received. And seeing a sand hill by chance not far from them, they went thither, and setting their horse in the middest of it, compassed it in round with their targets, thinking by this means to cover and defend themselves the better from the barbarous people: howbeit they found it contrary. For the country being plain, they in the foremost ranks did somewhat cover them behind, but they that were behind, standing higher than they that stood foremost (by reason of the nature of the hill that was highest in the middest) could by no means save themselves, but were all hurt alike, as well the one as the other, bewailing their own misery and misfortune, that must needs die without revenge, or declaration of their valiancy.

TACITUS

(C. A.D. 55–C. 120)

Tacitus, who may have been of Gallic origin, was consul under the
emperor Nerva in A.D. 97, and later governor of Asia from 110 to 113.
The Life of Agricola, *written in memory of his father-in-law, one of the*
emperor Diocletian's generals, dates from 98. In his Germania, *Tacitus*
turns ethnologist and gives a detailed description of the military
characteristics of the Germans. He published the Annals *(a work greatly*
superior to the Histories*) c. 117. Despite a deliberately moralistic side, his*
work is full of valuable insights.

WAR AND THE GERMANS

Even iron is not plentiful among [the Germans], as may be inferred from the
nature of their weapons. Swords or broad lances are seldom used; but they
generally carry a spear (called in their language *framea*), which has an iron
blade, short and narrow, but so sharp and manageable, that, as occasion requires, they employ it either in close or distant fighting. This spear and a shield
are all the armor of the cavalry. The foot have, besides, missile weapons, several to each man, which they hurl to an immense distance. They are either
naked, or lightly covered with a small mantle; and have no pride in equipage:
their shields only are ornamented with the choicest colors. Few are provided
with a coat of mail; and scarcely here and there one with a casque or helmet.
Their horses are neither remarkable for beauty nor swiftness, nor are they
taught the various evolutions practiced with us. The cavalry either bear down
straight forward, or wheel once to the right, in so compact a body that none
is left behind the rest. Their principal strength, on the whole, consists in their
infantry: hence in an engagement these are intermixed with the cavalry; so
well accordant with the nature of equestrian combats is the agility of those foot

From Tacitus, *Germania*, in *The Works of Tacitus*, Oxford translation (New York: Harper &
Brothers, 1858), 292–305.

soldiers, whom they select from the whole body of their youth, and place in the front of the line. Their number, too, is determined; a hundred from each canton; and they are distinguished at home by a name expressive of this circumstance; so that what at first was only an appellation of number, becomes thenceforth a title of honor. Their line of battle is disposed in wedges. To give ground, provided they rally again, is considered rather as a prudent stratagem than cowardice. They carry off their slain even while the battle remains undecided. The greatest disgrace that can befall them is to have abandoned their shields. A person branded with this ignominy is not permitted to join in their religious rites, or enter their assemblies; so that many, after escaping from battle, have put an end to their infamy by the halter.

In the election of kings they have regard to birth; in that of generals, to valor. Their kings have not an absolute or unlimited power; and their generals command less through the force of authority than of example. If they are daring, adventurous, and conspicuous in action, they procure obedience from the admiration they inspire. None, however, but the priests are permitted to judge offenders, to inflict bonds or stripes; so that chastisement appears not as an act of military discipline, but as the instigation of the god whom they suppose present with warriors. They also carry with them to battle certain images and standards taken from the sacred groves. It is a principal incentive to their courage, that their squadrons and battalions are not formed by men fortuitously collected, but by the assemblage of families and clans. Their pledges also are near at hand; they have within hearing the yells of their women, and the cries of their children. These, too, are the most revered witnesses of each man's conduct, these his most liberal applauders. To their mothers and their wives they bring their wounds for relief, nor do these dread to count or to search out the gashes. The women also administer food and encouragement to those who are fighting.

Tradition relates, that armies beginning to give way have been rallied by the females, through the earnestness of their supplications, the interposition of their bodies, and the pictures they have drawn of impending slavery, a calamity which these people bear with more impatience for their women than themselves; so that those states who have been obliged to give among their hostages the daughters of noble families, are the most effectually bound to fidelity. They even suppose somewhat of sanctity and prescience to be inherent in the female sex; and therefore neither despise their counsels, nor disregard their responses. . . .

The Germans transact no business, public or private, without being armed: but it is not customary for any person to assume arms till the state has approved his ability to use them. Then, in the midst of the assembly, either one of the chiefs, or the father, or a relation, equips the youth with a shield and javelin. These are to them the manly gown; this is the first honor conferred on youth: before this they are considered as part of a household; afterward, of the state. The dignity of chieftain is bestowed even on mere lads, whose descent is eminently illustrious, or whose fathers have performed signal services to the public; they are associated, however, with those of mature strength, who have already been declared capable of service; nor do they blush to be seen in the rank of companions. For the state of companionship itself has its several degrees, determined by the judgment of him whom they follow; and there is a great emulation among the companions, which shall possess the highest place in the favor of their chief; and among the chiefs, which shall excel in the number and valor of his companions. It is their dignity, their strength, to be always surrounded with a large body of select youth, an ornament in peace, a bulwark in war. And not in his own country alone, but among the neighboring states, the fame and glory of each chief consists in being distinguished for the number and bravery of his companions. Such chiefs are courted by embassies; distinguished by presents; and often by their reputation alone decide a war.

In the field of battle, it is disgraceful for the chief to be surpassed in valor; it is disgraceful for the companions not to equal their chief; but it is reproach and infamy during a whole succeeding life to retreat from the field surviving him. To aid, to protect him; to place their own gallant actions to the account of his glory, is their first and most sacred engagement. The chiefs fight for victory; the companions for their chief. If their native country be long sunk in peace and inaction, many of the young nobles repair to some other state then engaged in war. For, besides that repose is unwelcome to their race, and toils and perils afford them a better opportunity of distinguishing themselves; they are unable, without war and violence, to maintain a large train of followers. The companion requires from the liberality of his chief, the warlike steed, the bloody and conquering spear; and in place of pay he expects to be supplied with a table, homely indeed, but plentiful. The funds for this munificence must be found in war and rapine; nor are they so easily persuaded to cultivate the earth, and await the produce of the seasons, as to challenge the foe, and expose themselves to wounds; nay, they even think it base and spiritless to earn by sweat what they might purchase with blood.

During the intervals of war, they pass their time less in hunting than in a sluggish repose, divided between sleep and the table. All the bravest of the warriors, committing the care of the house, the family affairs, and the lands, to the women, old men, and weaker part of the domestics, stupefy themselves in inaction: so wonderful is the contrast presented by nature, that the same persons love indolence, and hate tranquility!

GERMANICUS'S CAMPAIGNS ON THE RHINE

. . . Germanicus had collected his force and stood prepared to exact a reckoning from the mutineers. Thinking it best, however, to allow them a further respite, in case they should consult their own safety by following the late precedent, he forwarded a letter to Caecina, saying that he was coming in strength, and, unless they forestalled him by executing the culprits, would put them impartially to the sword. Caecina read it privately to the eagle-bearers, the ensigns, and the most trustworthy men in the camp, urging them to save all from disgrace, and themselves from death. "For in peace," he said, "cases are judged on their merits; when war threatens, the innocent and the guilty fall side by side." Accordingly they tested the men whom they considered suitable, and, finding that in the main the legions were still dutiful, with the general's assent they fixed the date for an armed attack upon the most objectionable and active of the incendiaries. Then, passing the signal to one another, they broke into the tents and struck down their unsuspecting victims; while no one, apart from those in the secret, knew how the massacre had begun or where it was to end.

No civil war of any period has presented the features of this. Not in battle, not from opposing camps, but comrades from the same bed—men who had eaten together by day and rested together at dark—they took their sides and hurled their missiles. The yells, the wounds, and the blood were plain enough; the cause, invisible: chance ruled supreme. A number of the loyal troops perished as well: for, once it was clear who were the objects of attack, the malcontents also had caught up arms. No general or tribune was there to restrain: licence was granted to the mob, and it might glut its vengeance to the full. Before long, Germanicus marched into the camp. "This is not a cure, but a calamity," he said, with a burst of tears, and ordered the bodies to be cremated.

Even yet the temper of the soldiers remained savage and a sudden desire came over them to advance against the enemy: it would be the expiation of their madness; nor could the ghosts of their companions be appeased till their own impious breasts had been marked with honourable wounds. Falling in with the enthusiasm of his troops, the Caesar laid a bridge over the Rhine, and threw across twelve thousand legionaries, with twenty-six cohorts of auxiliaries and eight divisions of cavalry, whose discipline had not been affected by the late mutiny.

From Tacitus, *The Histories and The Annals* (4 vols.) translated by Clifford H. Moore and John Jackson (Cambridge, Mass.: Harvard University Press, 1931), 2: 325–61. Reprinted by permission of the publishers and the Loeb Classical Library.

Throughout the pause, which the mourning for Augustus had begun and our discords prolonged, the Germans had been hovering gleefully in the neighbourhood. By a forced march, however, the Roman columns cut through the Caesian Forest and the line of delimitation commenced by Tiberius. By this line they pitched the camp, with their front and rear protected by embankments and the flanks by a barricade of felled trees. Then came a threading of gloomy forests and a consultation which of two roads to follow; the one short and usual, the other more difficult and unexplored, and therefore left unguarded by the enemy. The longer route was chosen, but otherwise all speed was made: for scouts had brought in news that the night was a German festival and would be celebrated with games and a solemn banquet. Caecina was ordered to move ahead with the unencumbered cohorts and clear a passage through the woods: the legions followed at a moderate interval. The clear, starry night was in our favour; the Marsian villages were reached, and a ring of pickets was posted round the enemy, who were still lying, some in bed, others beside their tables, without misgivings and with no sentries advanced. All was disorder and improvidence: there was no apprehension of war, and even their peace was the nerveless lethargy of drunkards.

To extend the scope of the raid, the Caesar divided his eager legions into four bodies, and, for fifty miles around, wasted the country with sword and flame. Neither age nor sex inspired pity: places sacred and profane were razed indifferently to the ground; among them, the most noted religious centre of these tribes, known as the temple of Tanfana. The troops escaped without a wound: they had been cutting down men half-asleep, unarmed or dispersed.

The carnage brought the Bructeri, Tubantes, and Usipetes into the field; and they occupied the forest passes by which the army was bound to return. This came to the prince's ear, and he took the road prepared either to march or to fight. A detachment of cavalry and ten auxiliary cohorts led the way, then came the first legion; the baggage-train was in the centre; the twenty-first legion guarded the left flank; the fifth, the right; the twentieth held the rear, and the rest of the allies followed. The enemy, however, made no move, till the whole line was defiling through the wood: then instituting a half-serious attack on the front and flanks, they threw their full force on the rear. The light-armed cohorts were falling into disorder before the serried German masses, when the Caesar rode up to the men of the twenty-first, and, raising his voice, kept crying that now was their time to efface the stain of mutiny:—"Forward, and make speed to turn disgrace into glory!" In a flame of enthusiasm, they broke through their enemies at one charge, drove them into the open and cut them down. Simultaneously the forces in the van emerged from the forest and fortified a camp. From this point the march was unmolested, and the soldiers, emboldened by their late performances, and forgetful of the past, were stationed in winter quarters.

The news both relieved and disquieted Tiberius. He was thankful that the rising had been crushed; but that Germanicus should have earned the goodwill of the troops by his grants of money and acceleration of discharges—to say nothing of his laurels in the field—there was the rub! However, in a motion before the senate, he acknowledged his services and enlarged on his courage; but in terms too speciously florid to be taken as the expression of his inmost feelings. He expressed his satisfaction with Drusus and the conclusion of the trouble in Illyricum more briefly; but he was in earnest, and his language honest. In addition, he confirmed to the Pannonian legions all concessions granted by Germanicus to his own. . . .

And so, six years after the fatal field, a Roman army, present on the ground, buried the bones of the three legions [annihilated in the Teutoburg Forest in A.D. 9 by the forces of Arminius, chieftain of the Cherusci]; and no man knew whether he consigned to earth the remains of a stranger or a kinsman, but all thought of all as friends and members of one family, and, with anger rising against the enemy, mourned at once and hated.

At the erection of the funeral-mound the Caesar laid the first sod, paying a dear tribute to the departed, and associating himself with the grief of those around him. But Tiberius disapproved, possibly because he put an invidious construction on all acts of Germanicus, possibly because he held that the sight of the unburied dead must have given the army less alacrity for battle and more respect for the enemy, while a commander, invested with the augurate and administering the most venerable rites of religion, ought to have avoided all contact with a funeral ceremony.

Germanicus, however, followed Arminius as he fell back on the wilds, and at the earliest opportunity ordered the cavalry to ride out and clear the level ground in the occupation of the enemy. Arminius, who had directed his men to close up and retire on the woods, suddenly wheeled them round; then gave the signal for his ambush in the glades to break cover. The change of tactics threw our horse into confusion. Reserve cohorts were sent up; but, broken by the impact of the fugitive columns, they had only increased the panic, and the whole mass was being pushed towards swampy ground, familiar to the conquerors but fatal to strangers, when the Caesar came forward with the legions and drew them up in line of battle. This demonstration overawed the enemy and emboldened the troops, and they parted with the balance even.

Shortly afterwards, the prince led his army back to the Ems, and withdrew the legions as he had brought them, on shipboard: a section of the cavalry was ordered to make for the Rhine along the coast of the Northern Ocean. Caecina, who led his own force, was returning by a well-known route, but was none the less warned to cross the Long Bridges as rapidly as possible. These were simply a narrow causeway, running through a wilderness of marshes and thrown up, years before, by Lucius Domitius; the rest was a slough—foul, clinging mud intersected by a maze of rivulets. Round about, the woods sloped gently from the plain; but now they were occupied by Arminius, whose forced march along the shorter roads had been too quick for the Roman soldier, weighted with his baggage and accoutrements. Caecina, none too certain how to relay the old, broken-down bridges and at the same time hold off the enemy, decided to mark out a camp where he stood, so that part of the men could begin work while the others accepted battle.

Skirmishing, enveloping, charging, the barbarians struggled to break the line of outposts and force their way to the working parties. Labourers and combatants mingled their cries. Everything alike was to the disadvantage of the Romans—the ground, deep in slime and ooze, too unstable for standing fast and too slippery for advancing—the weight of armour on their backs—their inability amid the water to balance the pilum for a throw. The Cherusci, on the other hand, were habituated to marsh-fighting, long of limb, and armed with huge lances to wound from a distance. In fact, the legions were already wavering when night at last released them from the unequal struggle.

Success had made the Germans indefatigable. Even now they took no rest, but proceeded to divert all streams, springing from the surrounding hills, into the plain below, flooding the ground, submerging the little work accomplished, and doubling the task of the soldiery. Still, it was Caecina's fortieth year of active service as commander or commanded, and he knew success and danger too well to be easily perturbed. On balancing the possibilities, he could see no other course than to hold the enemy to the woods until his wounded and the more heavily laden part of the column passed on: for extended between mountain and morass was a level patch which would just allow an attenuated line of battle. The fifth legion was selected for the right flank, the twenty-first for the left; the first was to lead the van, the twentieth to stem the inevitable pursuit.

It was a night of unrest, though in contrasted fashions. The barbarians, in high carousal, filled the low-lying valleys and echoing woods with chants of triumph or fierce vociferations: among the Romans were languid fires, broken challenges, and groups of men stretched beside the parapet or straying amid the tents, unasleep but something less than awake. The general's night was disturbed by a sinister and alarming dream: for he imagined that he saw Quintilius Varus risen, blood-bedraggled, from the marsh, and heard him calling, though he refused to obey and pushed him back when he extended his hand. Day broke, and the legions sent to the wings, either through fear or wil-fulness, abandoned their post, hurriedly occupying a level piece of ground be-yond the morass. Arminius, however, though the way was clear for the attack, did not immediately deliver his onslaught. But when he saw the baggage-train caught in the mire and trenches; the troops around it in confusion; the order of the standards broken, and (as may be expected in a crisis) every man quick to obey his impulse and slow to hear the word of command, he ordered the Germans to break in. "Varus and the legions," he cried, "enchained once more in the old doom!" And, with the word, he cut through the column at the head of a picked band, their blows being directed primarily at the horses. Slipping in their own blood and the marsh-slime, the beasts threw their riders, scat-tered all they met, and trampled the fallen underfoot. The eagles caused the greatest difficulty of all, as it was impossible either to advance them against the storm of spears or to plant them in the water-logged soil. Caecina, while at-tempting to keep the front intact, fell with his horse stabbed under him, and was being rapidly surrounded when the first legion interposed. A point in our favour was the rapacity of the enemy, who left the carnage to pursue the spoils; and towards evening the legions struggled out on to open and solid ground. Nor was this the end of their miseries. A rampart had to be raised and mate-rial sought for the earthwork; and most of the tools for excavating soil or cut-ting turf had been lost. There were no tents for the companies, no dressings for the wounded, and as they divided their rations, foul with dirt or blood, they bewailed the deathlike gloom and that for so many thousands of men but a single day now remained.

As chance would have it, a stray horse which had broken its tethering and taken fright at the shouting, threw into confusion a number of men who ran to stop it. So great was the consequent panic (men believed the Germans had broken in) that there was a general rush to the gates, the principal objective being the decuman, which faced away from the enemy and opened the better prospects of escape. Caecina, who had satisfied himself that the fear was groundless, but found command, entreaty, and even physical force, alike powerless to arrest or detain the men, threw himself flat in the gateway; and pity in the last resort barred a road which led over the general's body. At the same time, the tribunes and centurions explained that it was a false alarm.

He now collected the troops in front of his quarters, and, first ordering them to listen in silence, warned them of the crisis and its urgency:—"Their one safety lay in the sword; but their resort to it should be tempered with discre-tion, and they must remain within the rampart till the enemy approached in the hope of carrying it by assault. Then, a sally from all sides—and so to the Rhine! If they fled, they might expect more forests, deeper swamps, and a savage enemy: win the day, and glory and honour were assured." He reminded them of all they loved at home, all the honour they had gained in camp: of disaster, not a word. Then, with complete impartiality, he distributed the horses of the commanding officers and tribunes—he had begun with his own—to men of conspicuous gallantry; the recipients to charge first, while the infantry followed.

Hope, cupidity, and the divided counsels of the chieftains kept the Germans in equal agitation. Arminius proposed to allow the Romans to march out, and, when they had done so, to entrap them once more in wet and broken country; Inguiomerus advocated the more drastic measures dear to the barbarian:—"Let them encircle the rampart in arms. Storming would be easy, captives more plentiful, the booty intact!" So, at break of day, they began demolishing the fosses, threw in hurdles, and struggled to grasp the top of the rampart; on which were ranged a handful of soldiers apparently petrified with terror. But as they swarmed up the fortifications, the signal sounded to the cohorts, and cornets and trumpets sang to arms. Then, with a shout and a rush, the Romans poured down on the German rear. "Here were no trees," they jeered, "no swamps, but a fair field and an impartial Heaven." Upon the enemy, whose thoughts were of a quick despatch and a few half-armed defenders, the blare of trumpets and the flash of weapons burst with an effect proportioned to the surprise, and they fell—as improvident in failure as they had been headstrong in success. Arminius and Inguiomerus abandoned the fray, the former unhurt, the latter after a serious wound; the rabble was slaughtered till passion and the daylight waned.

ARRIAN
(C. A.D. 92–175)

A Greek from Bythynia in Asia Minor, Arrian (Flavius Arrianus) studied under Epictetus at Nicopolis in Epirus before entering the service of Rome. The bulk of his career was under the emperor Hadrian (A.D. 117–32). He was proconsul in Spain and then governor of Cappadocia (131–37), on the marches of the empire, where he drove back the invading Alans in 134. The Anabasis *(written four centuries after the events it recounts) relates the epic of Alexander the Great, who conquered Asia as far as northern India in 334–323 B.C. Arrian was also the author of a* Treatise on Tactics.

THE BATTLE OF ISSUS

. . . [Alexander] was still at Mallus when a report reached him that Darius and the whole Persian army were at Sochi, a place in Assyrian territory about two days' march from the Assyrian Gates. He at once called a meeting of his staff and told them this important news. They urged unanimously an immediate advance. Alexander thanked them and dismissed the meeting, and on the following day moved forward with the evident intention of attack. Two days later he was past the Gates. He took up a position near Myriandrus, and during the night there was a storm of such violent wind and rain that he was compelled to remain where he was, with no chance of breaking camp.

Meanwhile Darius had no apparent intention of making a move; he had chosen for his position a part of Assyria where the country was flat and open, good for cavalry action, and suitable for manoeuvring the vast numbers under his command. Amyntas, son of Antiochus, a deserter from Alexander's army, urged him not to move from such favourable ground, for plenty of space was precisely what the Persian army most needed, its numbers and equipment

From Arrian, *The Life of Alexander the Great,* translated by Aubrey de Sélincourt (Harmondsworth, England: Penguin Books, 1958), 65–73. Copyright © 1958 by Aubrey de Sélincourt. Reproduced by permission of Penguin Books Ltd.

being what they were. Darius took Amyntas' advice, but later, when there was still no sign of Alexander, who had been held up at Tarsus by his illness, and again at Soli, for nearly as long, by the grand parade and religious ceremonies he held there and, finally, by his expedition against the hill tribes of Cilicia, he began to have his doubts. Moreover, Darius was always ready to believe what he found it most agreeable to believe, and on this occasion flattering courtiers, such as always are, and always will be, the bane of kings, had persuaded him into thinking that Alexander no longer wished to advance further into Asia: in fact, that the news of his own approach was the cause of Alexander's hesitation. First one, then another of them blew up the bladder of his conceit by saying that the Persian cavalry would ride over the Macedonian army and trample it to pieces. Only Amyntas opposed them, persistently affirming that Alexander would seek out Darius in any place where he knew him to be, and urging him not to shift his ground. But the worse counsel prevailed—because it told him what at the moment he liked to hear; more than that, there was surely some supernatural power which led Darius to take up a position where he could get little advantage either from his cavalry or his superiority in numbers of men and weight of missiles—a position where he had no chance of dazzling the enemy with the splendour of his great host, but was doomed to make a present of easy victory to Alexander and the Macedonians. Destiny had decreed that Macedon should wrest the sovereignty of Asia from Persia, as Persia once had wrested it from the Medes, and the Medes, in their turn, from the Assyrians.

Darius now moved; he crossed the high ground by what are called the Amanian Gates—the pass across Mount Amanus—and, making for Issus, established himself without being perceived in Alexander's rear. Once in possession of Issus he mutilated and put to death every Macedonian he found left there as unfit for service, and on the following day moved on to the river Pinarus. Alexander, not trusting the report that Darius was in his rear, dispatched a party of the Hetaeri in a galley with orders to sail back to Issus and find out for themselves whether or not it was true. The coast by Issus is deeply indented, and this fact enabled the party in the galley the more easily to see what they wished to see—that the Persians were there. So back they went to Alexander with their news: Darius was indeed at hand.

Alexander now sent for his infantry and cavalry commanders and all officers in charge of allied troops and appealed to them for confidence and courage in the coming fight. "Remember," he said, "that already danger has often threatened you and you have looked it triumphantly in the face; this time the struggle will be between a victorious army and an enemy already once vanquished. God himself, moreover, by suggesting to Darius to leave the open ground and cram his great army into a confined space, has taken charge of operations in our behalf. We ourselves shall have room enough to deploy our infantry, while they, no match for us either in bodily strength or resolution, will find their superiority in numbers of no avail. Our enemies are Medes and Persians, men who for centuries have lived soft and luxurious lives; we of Macedon for generations past have been trained in the hard school of danger and war. Above all, we are free men, and they are slaves. There are Greek troops, to be sure, in Persian service—but how different is their cause from ours! They will be fighting for pay—and not much of it at that; we, on the contrary, shall fight for Greece, and our hearts will be in it. As for our foreign troops—Thracians, Paconians, Illyrians, Agrianes—they are the best and stoutest soldiers in Europe, and they will find as their opponents the slackest and softest of the tribes of Asia. And what, finally, of the two men in supreme command? You have Alexander, they—Darius!"

Having thus enumerated the advantages with which they would enter the coming struggle, Alexander went on to show that the rewards of victory would also be great. The victory this time would not be over mere underlings of the Persian King, or the Persian cavalry along the banks of Granicus, or the 20,000 foreign mercenaries; it would be over the fine flower of the Medes and Persians and all the Asiatic peoples which they ruled. The Great King was there in person with his army, and once the battle was over, nothing would remain but to crown their many labours with the sovereignty of Asia. He reminded them, further, of what they had already so brilliantly accomplished together, and mentioned any act of conspicuous individual courage, naming the man in each case and specifying what he had done, and alluding also, in such a way as to give least offence, to the risks to which he had personally exposed himself on the field. He also, we are told, reminded them of Xenophon and his Ten Thousand, a force which, though not to be compared with their own either in strength or reputation—a force without the support of cavalry such as they had themselves, from Thessaly, Boeotia, the Peloponnese, and elsewhere, with no archers or slingers except a small contingent from Crete and Rhodes hastily improvised by Xenophon under pressure of immediate need—nevertheless defeated the King of Persia and his army at the gates of Babylon and successfully repelled all the native troops who tried to bar their way as they marched down to the Black Sea. Nor did Alexander omit any other words of encouragement such as brave men about to risk their lives might expect from a brave commander; and in response to his address his officers pressed forward to clasp his hand and with many expressions of appreciation urged him to lead them to battle without delay.

Alexander's first order was that his men should eat, while at the same time he sent a small party of mounted men and archers to the narrow pass by the shore to reconnoitre the road by which he would have to return; then, as soon as it was dark, he moved off himself with the whole army to take possession once more of that narrow gateway. About midnight the passage was secured; for the remainder of the night he allowed his men to rest where they were, on the rocky ground, with outposts to keep exact and careful watch, and just before daylight next morning moved forward from the pass along the coast road. The advance was in column so long as lack of space made it necessary, but as soon as the country began to open up he gradually extended his front, bringing up his heavy infantry a battalion at a time, until he was moving in line with his right on the base of the hills and his left on the sea.

During the advance the mounted troops were kept in the rear, but as soon as open ground was reached Alexander ordered battle stations: the picked infantry battalions and the Longshields, under Parmenio's son Nicanor, were sent to the right wing on the nearby rising ground, with Coenus' battalion on their left in close touch with Perdiccas' men, the whole forming a line from right wing to centre—the position of the heavy infantry. On the extreme left were stationed Amyntas' troops, and in touch with them, and working towards the centre, first Ptolemy's battalion, then Meleager's. Command of the infantry on the left was given to Craterus, of the left wing as a whole to Parmenio, whose orders were on no account to leave a gap between his extreme left and the sea; for if he did, they might well be surrounded, as the numerical superiority of the enemy would certainly enable them to outflank the Macedonians.

When Darius received the report that Alexander was moving forward to the attack, he sent some 30,000 mounted troops and 20,000 light infantry across the river Pinarus, to give himself a chance of getting the main body of his army into position without molestation. His dispositions were as follows: in the van of his heavy infantry were his 30,000 Greek mercenaries, facing the Macedonian infantry, with some 60,000 Persian heavy infantry—known as Kardakes— to support them, half on each of their flanks. These troops were drawn up in line, and the ground would not admit of a greater number. Hard on the rising ground on his left, and facing Alexander's right, was another division about 20,000 strong, some portions of which actually worked round to Alexander's rear; for the hills on their left receded to some distance so as to form a sort of bay, the further shore of which (so to put it) curved round back again, bringing the sections which were posted close under the hill to the rear of Alexander's right wing. In the rear of the Greek mercenaries and the Persians supporting them on either flank was the remainder of Darius' army—a great mass of light and heavy infantry. These were organized according to the countries of their origin and drawn up in greater depth than was likely to prove of much service; mere numbers made this unavoidable—indeed, it is on record that the army as a whole was some 600,000 strong.

As soon as Alexander found the ground in front of him opening out a little more, he brought his cavalry—the Thessalian and Macedonian divisions, together with the Hetaeri—up from the rear to the right wing under his own personal command, and at the same time sent the Peloponnesian troops and other allied divisions round to Parmenio on the left. Darius, immediately his main infantry force was in position, recalled by signal the mounted troops which he had sent across the river to cover the movement, and ordered the greater number of them over to his right, to threaten Parmenio, on the seaward side, where the ground was rather more suitable for cavalry manoeuvre; some, however, he sent to the opposite flank under the hills, though, as lack of space at that end of the line made them obviously useless, he soon recalled nearly all of them and ordered them round to the right flank. Darius himself took the centre, the traditional position of the Persian Kings. (The general principle of the Persian order of battle has been explained by Xenophon in his History.)

Nearly all the Persian cavalry had now been transferred to a position on the seaward side facing Alexander's left, and opposing them he had nothing except the Peloponnesians and other allied cavalry; to meet this threat he sent his Thessalian cavalry with all speed to their support, with instructions to conceal their movement from the enemy by passing in the rear of the massed infantry battalions. At the same time, at the other end of the line he threw forward his cavalry patrols, under Protomachus' command, together with the Paeonians under Ariston, and the archers under Antiochus.

The Agrianes under Attalus, supported by a few units of mounted troops and archers, were ordered out towards the high ground at an angle to his main line of advance, thus splitting the right wing of the army into two separate prongs, one designed to engage Darius and the main body of the Persians on the further side of the river, the other the units which had worked round to the hill in the Macedonian rear. In the van of the infantry on the Macedonian left were the Cretan archers and the Thracians, under Sitalces, with the cavalry of the left wing in advance of them; all units had a proportion of foreign mercenaries assigned to them.

Observing a certain weakness on his right and also the danger of being outflanked at that end of his line, Alexander withdrew from the centre two squadrons of the Hetaeri and two others—that, namely, from Anthemus commanded by Peroedes and the so-called Leugaean squadron, under Pantordanus, son of Cleander—and ordered them over to the right, with every precaution to conceal their movement; at the same time he further strengthened his right by a contingent of Agrianes and Greek mercenaries which he drew up in line, and so outflanked the Persian left. The Persians on the hills had made no aggressive move; indeed, when Alexander ordered a raid upon them by a small party of the Agrianes and archers, they had been easily dislodged from their position and had sought safety higher up the mountainside, so that Alexander decided that he could use the men originally intended to deal with them to strengthen his main attacking force. Three hundred mounted men were sufficient to keep an eye on the fugitives.

For a while Alexander's advance was slow and deliberate; every now and then he ordered a halt, giving the impression that time was on his side. Darius made no move as yet to attack, but kept his men in their original dispositions on the river bank. In many places the bank was steep, and any sections of it which seemed less easy to defend he had strengthened with a stockade—at once by this precaution making it clear to Alexander's men that his was a craven spirit.

The two armies were now almost within striking distance. Alexander rode from one end of his line to the other with words of encouragement for all, addressing by name, with proper mention of rank and distinctions, not the officers of highest rank only but the captains of squadrons and companies; even the mercenaries were not forgotten, where any distinction or act of courage called for the mention of a name, and from every throat came the answering shout: "Wait no longer—forward to the assault!"

The Persian army was in full view; still, however, Alexander moved forward in line at a deliberate pace, for a too-rapid advance might have thrown the line out of dressing and caused a break somewhere; but once within range of missiles, Alexander, at the head of his own troops on the right wing, rode at a gallop into the stream. Rapidity was now all in all: a swift attack would shake the enemy, and the sooner they came to grips the less damage would be done by the Persian archers. Alexander's judgement was not at fault: the Persian left collapsed the very moment he was on them—a brilliant local success for the picked troops under his personal command. In the centre, however, things did not go so well: here some of the troops had broken away towards the right and left a gap in the line, and, in contrast with Alexander, who had so swiftly crossed the stream and was already, in close combat, compelling the Persian left to withdraw, the Macedonian centre was much slower off the mark; in a number of places, moreover, the steep banks of the stream prevented them from maintaining a regular and unbroken front, and the result was that Darius' Greek mercenaries attacked precisely at that point in the line where the gap was widest. There was a violent struggle. Darius' Greeks fought to thrust the Macedonians back into the water and save the day for their left wing, already in retreat, while the Macedonians, in their turn, with Alexander's triumph plain before their eyes, were determined to equal his success and not forfeit the proud title of invincible, hitherto universally bestowed upon them. The fight was further embittered by the old racial rivalry of Greek and Macedonian. It was in this phase of the battle that Ptolemy, son of Seleucus, and about 121 Macedonians of distinction met a soldier's death.

Alexander's victorious right wing now swung left towards the centre, hard pressed as it was by Darius' Greeks; they forced them back from the river and then, outflanking the broken enemy left, delivered a flank attack on the mercenaries and were soon cutting them to pieces. The Persian cavalry facing Alexander's Thessalians refused, once the battle had developed, to remain inactive on the further side of the stream, but charged across in a furious onslaught on the Thessalian squadrons. The cavalry action which ensued was desperate enough, and the Persians broke only when they knew that the Greek mercenaries were being cut off and destroyed by the Macedonian infantry, and that Darius himself was in flight. That was the signal for a general rout—open and unconcealed. The horses with their heavily equipped riders suffered severely, and of the thousands of panic-stricken men who struggled in hopeless disorder to escape along the narrow mountain tracks, almost as many were trampled to death by their friends as were cut down by the pursuing enemy. The Thessalians pressed the pursuit without mercy, and the Persian losses in both arms, infantry, and cavalry were equally severe.

The moment the Persian left went to pieces under Alexander's attack and Darius, in his war-chariot, saw that it was cut off, he incontinently fled—indeed, he led the race for safety. Keeping to his chariot as long as there was smooth ground to travel on, he was forced to abandon it when ravines and other obstructions barred his way; then, dropping his shield and stripping off his candys—and even leaving his bow in the war-chariot—he leapt upon a horse and rode for his life. Darkness soon closed in; and that alone saved him from falling into the hands of Alexander, who, while daylight held, relentlessly pressed the pursuit. . . .

THE BATTLE OF GAUGAMELA

. . . Alexander reached Thapsacus in August, during the archonship of Aristophanes in Athens. Two bridges were already across the river. For some time previously Mazaeus, under orders from the Persian King, had been guarding the approaches to the river with a force of 3,000 mounted troops, two-thirds of them Greek mercenaries; and for this reason the Macedonians had not carried their bridge right to the further bank, lest the enemy should attack it at their end. Mazaeus, however, no sooner got wind of Alexander's ap-

From Arrian, *The Life of Alexander the Great*, translated by Aubrey de Sélincourt (Baltimore: Penguin Books, 1958), 96–106. Copyright © 1958 by Aubrey de Sélincourt. Reproduced by permission of Penguin Books Ltd.

proach than he made off at his best speed with all his men, whereupon the two bridges were promptly completed, and Alexander was able to use them to get his army across.

Thence he proceeded north and east, keeping the Euphrates and the Armenian mountains on his left, through Mesopotamia; for once across the river he preferred not to follow the direct route to Babylon, as by this other route supplies of all sorts, including fodder for the horses, would be more readily available; other needs for man and beast could be supplied by the country through which they passed, and, furthermore, the heat would be less intense.

During the march some prisoners were taken—men from Darius' army who had gone off on reconnaissance. They reported that Darius had taken up a position on the Tigris and intended to resist any attempt by Alexander to cross it. The force under his command greatly exceeded in numbers what he had had at the battle of Issus. Alexander's reply to this news was to push on for the Tigris at all speed. However, upon reaching it he found neither Darius nor the guard he had left there; so he crossed without opposition—except from the current, which was swift and made the operation a difficult one. Once over the river, he gave his men a rest.

While the troops were resting, there was an almost total eclipse of the moon, and Alexander offered sacrifice to Moon, Sun, and Earth, the three deities supposed to be concerned in this phenomenon. The opinion of Aristander, the seer, was that the moon's failure was propitious for Alexander and the Macedonians, and that the coming battle would be fought before the month was out; he concluded, moreover, that the sacrifices portended victory.

Alexander now continued his advance through Aturia, keeping the Tigris on his right and the mountains of Gordya on his left. Four days after the crossing of the river a report came in from his scouts that enemy cavalry had been sighted in open ground, but their numbers could not be accurately estimated; Alexander accordingly, before advancing further, made the necessary dispositions for an engagement, and immediately afterwards more scouts rode in; these had had a better view of the enemy force, and declared their belief that it was not above 1,000 strong, whereupon Alexander rode for it at the gallop with the Royal Squadron, one squadron of Hetaeri, and the Paeonian rangers. The main body of the army was ordered to follow at its own pace. The sight of Alexander's rapid approach was too much for the Persian cavalry, who incontinently fled, with Alexander in hot pursuit; most of them got away, but a few, whose horses could not stand the pace, were killed, and a few others were taken alive, horses and all. From these prisoners they learned that Darius was not far off, with a powerful force.

Darius' army had been reinforced by the Sogdians, the Bactrians, and the Indian tribes on the Bactrian border—all under the command of Bessus, satrap of Bactria; their lead had been followed by certain contingents of the Sacae (a branch of the Asiatic Scythians) who, though they owed no allegiance to Bessus, were in military alliance with Persia. These troops were mounted archers, and were commanded by Manaces. The Arachotians and the Indian hillmen were commanded by Barsaentes, satrap of Arachotia; the Areians by their satrap, Satibarzanes; the Parthians, Hyrcanians, and Tapurians, all mounted troops, by Phrataphernes; the Medes, to whom were attached the Cadusians, Albanians, and Sacesinians, by Atropates; all contingents from the neighbourhood of the Persian Gulf by Ocondobates, Ariobarzanes, and Orxines; the Uxians and Susiani by Oxathres, son of Abulites; the Babylonians, to whom were attached the Sitacenians and Carians, by Bupares (these Carians had previously been resettled after a mass transference of population); the Armenians by Orontes and Mithraustes; the Cappadocians by Ariaces; the lowland and Mesopotamian Syrians by Mazaeus. Darius' total force was estimated at 40,000 cavalry, 1,000,000 infantry, 200 scythe-chariots, and a few elephants—the Indian troops from the hither side of the Indus had about fifteen of them.

This was the army which had taken up a position under Darius at Gaugamela, near the river Bumodus, about seventy-five miles from Arbela. The country where it lay was level and open, all places where a broken surface might obstruct the movement of cavalry having been worked on some time previously by the Persian troops, so that all of it was now good going for both chariots and cavalry. The reason for this precaution was the fact that it had been urged upon Darius that much of his trouble at the battle of Issus had been due to lack of space to manoeuvre in—an explanation which Darius was very ready to accept.

On receiving this information from the Persian prisoners, Alexander stayed where he was for four days, to rest his men after their march. He fortified his camp with a ditch and palisade, as he proposed to leave the pack-animals there together with all troops unfit for service, while he himself led to battle the remainder burdened with nothing but their weapons. The order to fall in was given, and at night, about the second watch, the advance began—so timed as to engage the enemy at dawn. The report that Alexander was on the move soon reached Darius, and he, too, ordered his men to battle stations. Meanwhile Alexander was drawing nearer, his troops ready to engage—but the opposing armies were still seven miles apart and had not yet seen each other, as each was screened by a ridge of high ground.

Past the crest of the ridge, just as he was beginning the descent, Alexander had his first sight of the enemy, about four miles away. He gave the order to halt, and sent for his officers—his personal staff, generals, squadron commanders, and officers of the allied and mercenary contingents—to consult upon the plan of action. The alternatives were either to advance at once with the main corps of infantry, as the majority urged him to do, or to accept the advice of Parmenio and stay where they were long enough to enable a careful reconnaissance of the ground to be made; for there might well be reasons for caution—hidden obstructions, concealed trenches or stakes—and, in addition to that, it would be wise to get a more accurate knowledge of the enemy's dispositions. Parmenio's proposal appeared the better of the two; so for the moment there was no further forward move, the troops all remaining in the order in which they were to engage.

Alexander meanwhile carried out a wide reconnaissance with his light infantry and the mounted Hetaeri, minutely examining the whole terrain where the battle would be fought; he then returned and called a second meeting of his officers. There was no need, he said, for any words from him to encourage them to do their duty; there was inspiration enough in the courage they had themselves shown in previous battles, and in the many deeds of heroism they had already performed. All he asked was that every officer of whatever rank, whether he commended a company, a squadron, a brigade, or an infantry battalion, should urge to their utmost efforts the men entrusted to his command; for they were about to fight, not, as before, for Syria or Phoenicia or Egypt, but this time the issue at stake was the sovereignty of the whole Asian continent. What need, then, was there for many words to rouse his officers to valour, when that valour was already in their own breasts? Let him but remind them each for himself to preserve discipline in the hour of danger—to advance, when called upon to do so, in utter silence; to watch the time for a hearty cheer, and, when the moment came, to roar out their battle-cry and put the fear of God into the enemy's hearts. All must obey orders promptly and pass them on without hesitation to their men; and, finally, every one of them must remember that upon the conduct of each depended the fate of all: if each man attended to his duty, success was assured; if one man neglected it, the whole army would be in peril.

With some such brief words of exhortation Alexander addressed his officers, and in reply they begged him to have every confidence in them. Orders were then given for the troops to rest and eat.

Some authorities state that Parmenio went to Alexander's tent and advised a night attack, because the enemy would not be expecting it, and it would naturally cause alarm and confusion. Alexander and Parmenio were not alone in the tent; others were listening, and that, perhaps, was one reason for Alexander's reply: "I will not," he said, "demean myself by stealing victory like a thief. Alexander must defeat his enemies openly and honestly." However, these lofty words probably indicated confidence in danger rather than vanity, and in my own opinion they were based upon perfectly sound sense: night-fighting is a tricky business; unexpected things happen to both sides—to those who have carefully planned the attack as much as to those who are taken off their guard—and often enough the better men get the worst of it, while victory, contrary to everybody's expectation, goes to the weaker side. More often than not Alexander took risks in his battles; but on this occasion he felt the chances of a night attack to be too unpredictable; moreover, the mere fact that it was delivered stealthily and under cover of darkness would save Darius, were he again defeated, the necessity of admitting inferiority, either in himself or in his men; while if they themselves suffered an unexpected reverse, they would be a defeated army in an unfamiliar country among enemies thoroughly at home and surrounded by friends—and of those enemies not a few would be the prisoners of war, who might well attack them at night even after an indecisive victory, not to mention a defeat.

These arguments were sound enough, and I therefore commend Alexander's decision, and approve no less his resounding claim to act openly.

During the night Darius' army kept the same dispositions as on the previous day, the reason for maintaining battle stations being their fear of a night attack, added to the fact that their position had no regular defence works. One thing, at this critical moment, told against the Persians more than anything else: their protracted stand under arms, and the consequent fear, natural enough when lives are at stake, but on this occasion rendered less bearable by the fact that it did not come, as it were, in a flash from the moment's crisis, but had been brooded on hour after hour until their spirit was sapped.

We are informed by Aristobulus that Darius' written orders for the disposition of his troops came into Greek hands after the battle; we know, consequently, what his order of battle was. On his left was the Bactrian cavalry supported by the Daae and Arachotians; in touch with them were mixed Persian cavalry and infantry, followed by Susian, and then by Cadusian contingents. These units composed the left wing of the army as far as the centre. On the right were the contingents from Lowland Syria and Mesopotamia, and the Medes; then, in touch with these, were the Parthians and the Sacae; then the Tapurian and Hyrcanian contingents; lastly, next to the centre, the Albanians and Sacesinians. In the centre, with Darius himself and his kinsmen, were the royal Persian bodyguard with the golden apples on their spear-butts, the Indians, the so-called "stateless" Carians, and the Mardian archers. Uxians, Babylonians, troops from the Persian Gulf, and Sitacenians were drawn up in depth behind them. In advance of the left wing, facing Alexander's right, were the Scythian cavalry, about 1,000 Bactrians and 100 scythe-chariots—the elephants and fifty war-chariots were posted in close support of the Royal Squadron of the King's cavalry. In advance of the Persian right were fifty scythe-chariots and the Armenian and Cappadocian cavalry; the Greek mercenaries—the only troops likely to be a match for the Macedonian infantry—were drawn up facing them in two sections, one on each side of Darius and his Persian guard.

On the right wing of Alexander's army was the mounted brigade of the Hetaeri, led by the Royal Squadron under the command of Cleitus, son of Dropides; in touch with them, and working towards the centre, were the squadrons under the following officers and in the following order: Glaucias, Ariston, Sopolis son of Hermodorus, Heracleides son of Antiochus, Demetrius son of Althaemenes, and Meleager; finally there was the royal squadron commanded by Hegelochus son of Hippostratus. Parmenio's son Philotas was general officer in command of the mounted Hetaeri. Of the infantry, the shock troops of the Longshields were posted in closest touch with the cavalry, and were supported on their own left by the other Longshields units under the command of Nicanor, son of Parmenio; next to them was the brigade of Coenus son of Polemocrates, followed (working towards the left) by the units commanded respectively by Perdiccas son of Orontes, Meleager son of Neoptolemus, Polyperchon son of Simmias, and Amyntas son of Andromenes—the last being commanded by Simmias, as Amyntas had been sent to Macedonia to recruit.

The left of the Macedonian infantry line consisted of the brigade of Craterus son of Alexander—who commanded all the infantry in that sector; in touch with him were the allied cavalry units under Erigyus son of Larichus, supported by the Thessalian cavalry commanded by Philippus son of Menelaus. The Thessalian cavalry extended to the left wing of the army, the whole of which was under the general command of Parmenio son of Philotas. Close about this officer were grouped the mounted troops of Pharsalia, the finest and most powerful unit of the Thessalian cavalry.

Such was the disposition of Alexander's front line, in addition to which he posted reserve formations in order to have a solid core of infantry to meet a possible attack from the rear; the officers of the reserve had orders, in the event of an encircling movement by the enemy, to face about and so meet the threatened attack. One half of the Agrianes, commanded by Attalus and in touch with the Royal Squadron on the right wing, were, together with the Macedonian archers under Briso, thrown forward at an oblique angle, in case it should suddenly prove necessary to extend or close up the front line of infantry, and in support of the archers was the so-called "Old Guard" of mercenaries under Cleander. In advance of the Agrianes and archers were the mounted skirmishers and the Paeonians, commanded by Aretes and Ariston; the mercenary cavalry commanded by Menidas were posted right in the van. The position in advance of the Royal Squadron and other units of the Hetaeri was occupied by the other half of the Agriane contingent and of the archers, supported by Balacrus' spearmen who stood facing the Persian scythe-chariots. Menidas had orders to wheel and attack the enemy in the flank, should they attempt an out-flanking movement.

So much for Alexander's right; on his left, forming an angle with the main body, were the Thracians under Sitalces supported, first, by the allied cavalry under Coeranus and, secondly, by the Odrysian cavalry under Agathon son of Tyrimmes. Right in the van of this sector was the foreign mercenary cavalry commanded by Andromachus son of Hiero. The Thracian infantry had orders to stand guard over the pack-animals. The total strength of Alexander's army was 7,000 cavalry and about 40,000 foot.

The two armies were now close together. Darius and his picked troops were in full view. There stood the Persian Royal Guard, the golden apples on their spear-butts, the Indians and Albanians, the Carians and the Mardian bow-men—the cream of the Persian force, full in face of Alexander as he moved with his Royal Squadron to the attack. Alexander, however, inclined slightly to his right, a move which the Persians at once countered, their left outflank-ing the Macedonians by a considerable distance. Meanwhile in spite of the fact that Darius' Scythian cavalry, moving along the Macedonian front, had already made contact with their forward units, Alexander continued his advance to-wards the right until he was almost clear of the area which the Persians had levelled during the previous days. Darius knew that once the Macedonians reached rough ground his chariots would be useless, so he ordered the mounted troops in advance of his left to encircle the Macedonian right under Alexander and thus check any further extension in that direction. Alexander promptly ordered Menidas and his mercenary cavalry to attack them. A counter-attack by the Scythian cavalry and their supporting Bactrians drove them back by weight of numbers, whereupon Alexander sent in against the Scythians Ariston's Paeonian contingent and the mercenaries. This stroke had its effect, and the enemy gave ground; but the remaining Bactrian units came to the support of the Paeonians and foreign troops and succeeded in rallying the fugitives. A close cavalry action ensued, in which the Macedonians suffered the more severely, outnumbered as they were and less adequately provided with defensive armour than the Scythians were—both horses and men. None the less the Macedonians held their attacks, and by repeated counter-charges, squadron by squadron, succeeded in breaking the enemy formation.

Meanwhile as Alexander moved forward the Persians sent their scythe-chariots into action against him, in the hope of throwing his line into confu-sion. But in this they were disappointed; for the chariots were no sooner off the mark than they were met by the missile weapons of the Agrianes and Ba-lacrus' javelin-throwers, who were stationed in advance of the mounted He-taeri; again, they seized the reins and dragged the drivers to the ground, then surrounded the horses and cut them down. Some few of the vehicles succeeded in passing through, but to no purpose, for the Greeks had orders, wherever they attacked, to break formation and let them through deliberately: this they did, with the result that neither they, the objects of the attack, nor the vehicles themselves suffered any damage whatever. Such as got through were, however, subsequently dealt with by the Royal Guard and the army grooms.

Darius now brought into action the main body of his infantry, and an order was sent to Aretes to attack the Persian cavalry which was trying to outflank and surround the Greek right. For a time Alexander continued to advance in column; presently, however, the movement of the Persian cavalry, sent to the support of their comrades who were attempting to encircle the Macedonian right, left a gap in the Persian front—and this was Alexander's opportunity. He promptly made for the gap, and, with his mounted Hetaeri and all the heavy infantry in this sector of the line, drove in his wedge and raising the battle-cry pressed forward at the double straight for the point where Darius stood. A close struggle ensued, but it was soon over; for when the Macedonian horse, with Alexander himself at the head of them, vigorously pressed the assault, fighting hand to hand and thrusting at the Persians' faces with their spears, and the infantry phalanx in close order and bristling with pikes added its irresistible weight, Darius, who had been on edge since the battle began and now saw nothing but terrors all around him, was the first to turn tail and ride for safety. The outflanking party on the Macedonian right was also broken up by the powerful assault of Aretes and his men.

On this part of the field the Persian rout was complete, and the Macedonians pressed the pursuit, cutting down the fugitives as they rode. But the formation under Simmias and his staff, unable to link up with Alexander to join in the pursuit, was forced to stand its ground and continue the struggle on the spot, a report having come in that the Macedonian left was in trouble. At this point the Greek line was broken, and some of the Indian and Persian cavalry burst through the gap and penetrated right to the rear where the Macedonian pack-animals were. There was some hard fighting; the Persians set about it with spirit, most of their adversaries being unarmed men who had never expected a break-through—at any rate here, where the phalanx was of double strength; moreover, the prisoners joined in the attack. However, the officers in command of the reserves on this sector, the moment the situation was clear, faced about according to orders and appeared in the Persian rear. Many of the Persians, as they swarmed round the baggage-trains, were killed; others did not stay to fight, but made off.

Meanwhile the Persian right, not yet knowing that Darius had fled, made a move to envelop Alexander's left and delivered a flank attack on Parmenio. The Macedonians being caught, as it were, between two fires, Parmenio sent an urgent message to Alexander that his position was serious and that he needed help. Alexander at once broke off the pursuit, wheeled about with his mounted Hetaeri and charged the Persian right at the gallop. Coming first into contact with those of the enemy cavalry who were trying to get away, he was soon heavily engaged with the Parthians, some of the Indians, and the strongest and finest cavalry units of Persia. The ensuing struggle was the fiercest of the whole action; one after another the Persian squadrons wheeled in file to the charge; breast to breast they hurled themselves on the enemy. Conventional cavalry tactics—manoeuvring, javelin-throwing—were forgotten; it was every man for himself, struggling to break through as if in that alone lay his hope of life. Desperately and without quarter, blows were given and received, each man fighting for mere survival without any further thought of victory or defeat. About sixty of Alexander's companions—picked troops of the Hetaeri—were killed; among the wounded were Coenus, Menidas, and Hephaestion himself.

In this struggle Alexander was once again victorious. Such Persians as managed to fight their way through galloped off the field to save their skins.

Alexander was now on the point of engaging the Persian right; but his help was not needed, as in this sector the Thessalian cavalry had fought hardly less magnificently than Alexander himself. The Persians were already in retreat by the time he made contact with them, so he turned back and started once more in pursuit of Darius, continuing as long as daylight served. Parmenio, in chase of his own quarry, was not far behind him. Once across the Lycus, Alexander halted for a brief rest for men and horses, and Parmenio went on to take possession of the Persian camp and all its contents; baggage, elephants, and camels. . . .

THE WAR AGAINST PORUS

. . . Once across the river [Indus], Alexander offered his customary sacrifice and continued his march to Taxila, a large and prosperous town—indeed, the largest between the Indus and the Hydaspes. Here he was courteously received by Taxiles, the governor, and the Indians of the district, and he granted them, in return, as much of the territory bordering on their own as they asked for. He was also visited by representatives from Abisarus, King of the Indian hill-tribes, with his brother and other distinguished personages among them, and by representatives from the local governor Doxareus. All of them brought presents. Here as elsewhere Alexander offered his usual sacrifices, and held public games with contests in athletics and riding; then, after appointing Philip, son of

From Arrian, *The Life of Alexander the Great*, translated by Aubrey de Sélincourt (Baltimore: Penguin Books, 1958), 170–79. Copyright © 1958 by Aubrey de Sélincourt. Reproduced by permission of Penguin Books Ltd.

Machatas, as governor of this district, he proceeded to the Hydaspes, leaving in Taxila any men who were sick and unfit for service.

News had already reached him that Porus with all the troops he could muster was on the other side of the Hydaspes, determined either to prevent his crossing or to attack him should he attempt it. Alexander, accordingly, sent Coenus, son of Polemocrates, back to the Indus with orders to cut into sections the boats which had been used at the crossing of that river and transport them to the Hydaspes; the order was carried out, the smaller vessels being cut in half, the thirty-oared galleys into three, and the sections carried in carts to the bank of the Hydaspes, where they were re-assembled, so that the whole flotilla was once again to be seen, as it had been seen upon the Indus. Then, with the force he had brought to Taxila and 5,000 Indian troops under Taxiles and the local chieftains, he marched for the Hydaspes.

From the position he took up on the bank of this river he was able to see Porus, with all his forces, including his squadron of elephants, on the further side. At the point immediately opposite Alexander, Porus remained on guard in person, and sent pickets, each under command of an officer, to the various other points along the river where a crossing was practicable; for he was determined to stop the Macedonians from getting over. Alexander's answer was by continual movement of his own troops to keep Porus guessing: he split his force into a number of detachments, moving some of them under his own command hither and thither all over the place, destroying enemy possessions and looking for places where the river might be crossed, and putting others under the command of various officers with instructions to keep constantly on the move, now in this direction, now in that. As supplies continued to come in for his army from all parts of the country west of the Hydaspes, it was clear to Porus that he meant to remain in the neighbourhood of the river, until in the course of the winter the water fell sufficiently to enable him to effect a crossing at any one of a number of places. Moreover, the continual movement of Alexander's boats up or down stream, the manufacture of skin floats filled with chaff, and the sight of troops, cavalry, and infantry, constantly massed on the river-bank, gave Porus no chance to relax his vigilance or to concentrate his defensive preparations upon any one point rather than another.

The water was high at that time of year—the summer solstice—in all the Indian rivers, and the current in them swift and turbulent; for there are heavy rains at this season, and these, added to the melting snow from the Caucasus, where most of the rivers rise, greatly increase the volume of water, while during the winter the flow is checked again, the water becomes less turbid, and the level of it drops, so that here and there it is possible to get across. The Indus and the Ganges (and perhaps one other) are never fordable—but what I have said is certainly true of the Hydaspes.

Alexander openly declared his intention of waiting for the season in which the water in the river should fall, if he were prevented from crossing immediately; nevertheless he remained in the neighbourhood and kept a sharp lookout for any possible opportunity of getting his men over by a swift and unexpected movement. It was clear to him that he could not effect the crossing at the point where Porus held the opposite bank, for his troops would certainly be attacked, as they tried to gain the shore, by a powerful and efficient army, well-equipped and supported by a large number of elephants; moreover, he thought it likely that his horses, in face of an immediate attack by elephants, would be too much scared by the appearance of these beasts and their unfamiliar trumpetings to be induced to land—indeed, they would probably refuse to stay on the floats, and at the mere sight of the elephants in the distance would go mad with terror and plunge into the water long before they reached the further side.

The river had to be crossed, so, as it could not be done openly, Alexander determined to attain his object by cunning. Every night he kept moving the greater part of his mounted troops up and down the bank of the river, making as much noise as possible—shouts, war-cries, and every sort of clatter and shindy which might be supposed to precede an attempted crossing. Porus, bringing up his elephants, followed these movements, guided by the noise, and Alexander gradually led him to make these marches, parallel to his own, a regular thing. This went on for some time, until Porus, finding that the Greeks never went beyond shouts and yells, gave it up. Clearly, it was a false alarm; so he ceased to follow the movements of the Greek cavalry and stayed where he was, in his original position, with look-outs posted at various points along the river. Thus Porus, no longer expecting a sudden attempt under cover of darkness, was lulled into a sense of security—and this was Alexander's opportunity.

At a sharp bend in the river there was a projecting spit of land, thickly wooded with different sorts of timber; and just off this promontory lay an uninhabited island, also well wooded. Alexander did not fail to observe the opportunity which this offered: the dense woodland both on the island and on the river-bank beyond it was just the thing to conceal his attempt, so this was the spot where he determined to make the crossing. It was some eighteen miles from his main position, and all along the river he had stationed pickets, close enough to enable them to keep contact with each other both by sight and sound and to hear without difficulty any orders passed from any point along the line. For several nights in succession over a wide area noise and bustle were kept going and fires burning.

The decision once made, Alexander began his preparations openly. Craterus was left in charge of the original position with his own cavalry regiment, the mounted contingents from Arachotia and the Parapamisidae, part of the Macedonian infantry consisting of the brigade of Alcetas and Polyperchon, the local Indian chieftains, and the 5,000 troops under their command. His orders were not to attempt a crossing until Porus had moved from his position to attack Alexander, or until he was sure that Porus was in retreat and the Greeks victorious. "But if," Alexander added, "Porus opposes me with a part only of his force and leaves the rest, together with elephants, where it now is, you must stay where you are; if, on the other hand, he moves his whole contingent of elephants against me, leaving in his present position only some portion of his other forces, then you must lose no time in getting across. The only real danger to our horses, as we put them ashore, is elephants. Nothing else will worry them."

Between the island and the main camp of which Craterus was left in charge, Meleager, Attalus, and Gorgias were posted with the mercenary cavalry and infantry; their instructions, too, were to effect a crossing in sections as soon as they saw that the Indians were fairly engaged. The mounted troops which Alexander selected to operate under his own command consisted of the special squadron of the Hetaeri, the cavalry regiments of Hephaestion, Perdiccas, and Demetrius, the contingents from Bactria and Sogdiana, the Scythian cavalry, and the mounted archers of the Daae; from the infantry units he chose the Longshields, the brigade of Cleitus and Coenus, the archers, and the Agrianes. He took the precaution of moving at some distance from the river, in order to conceal his march to the point where he proposed to cross—the island, namely, and the spit of land opposite to it. To this point the floats had already been conveyed some time previously, and now, under cover of darkness, they were filled with chaff and carefully sewn up. During the night a deluge of rain helped to conceal the preparations for the coming attempt; the clatter of arms, shouted orders, and the commotion they caused could not be heard across the river through the noise of the storm and the claps of thunder. Besides the skin-floats, most of the boats, including the thirty-oared galleys, had already arrived. These had been cut into sections, and were now re-assembled and concealed among the trees.

Just before dawn the rain stopped and the wind fell light. The mounted troops were embarked on the floats, the boats taking as many of the infantry as they would hold, and the crossing began—screened by the island, to prevent discovery by Porus' scouts before the island was passed and the whole flotilla already near the opposite bank. Alexander himself crossed in one of the galleys with half the regiment of Longshields, the remainder following in other galleys. He was accompanied by three officers of his personal guard—Ptolemy, Perdiccas, and Lysimachus—and by Seleucus (the Seleucus who afterwards became King).

Once past the island, the approach to the river-bank was in full view of the enemy patrols, who galloped off with all the speed their horses could muster, to report to Porus. Alexander was the first ashore, and promptly took charge of the troops from the other galleys; the cavalry had had orders to disembark first, and these he proceeded to marshal as each squadron came off the floats. He then moved forward in battle order.

To Alexander this was all strange country, and it so happened that he had, without knowing it, landed on another island, and not on the mainland at all. It was an island of considerable extent—and therefore all the more difficult to recognize as such—and was separated from the mainland beyond by a branch of the river of no very great size. Nevertheless the torrential rain throughout the previous night had increased the volume of water, and the mounted troops were unable to find a practicable place for crossing. For a time they were faced with the disagreeable prospect that all the labour they had gone through would have to be repeated; at last, however, a ford was found, and Alexander led the way over. It was no easy task, as the water in the deepest part was up to the men's armpits and the horses' necks.

Once this second crossing was successfully accomplished, Alexander again marshalled his troops. His picked cavalry and the best of the other mounted regiments he brought round to the right wing, stationing the mounted archers in the van; in the rear of the cavalry he posted the Royal Regiment of Long-shields under Seleucus, then the Royal regiment of the heavy infantry, in close touch with the other Longshields divisions, according to their precedence for that day. The archers, Agrianes, and Javelins took their position on either wing of the main body of infantry. Having thus made his dispositions, he gave orders for the infantry, nearly 6,000 strong, to follow in order of march, while he himself, with only the cavalry (numbering some 5,000) in which he thought he had the advantage over the enemy, moved forward rapidly. Tauron, captain of the archers, was instructed to advance in the rear of the cavalry with all the speed he could make.

The idea in Alexander's mind was that if Porus' army should attack in force he would either settle them straight away by a cavalry charge, or, failing that, fight a delaying action until his infantry could come to his support; if, on the other hand, the Indians proved to be so badly shaken by the bold and unexpected crossing of the river that they took to their heels, he would be able to press hard on the retreating army, and the more men they lost during their withdrawal, the lighter his own task would subsequently be.

There are, however, somewhat conflicting accounts of these operations. According to Aristobulus, Porus' son arrived on the scene with sixty chariots before Alexander effected his second crossing—from the large island, that is; and in view of the fact that the crossing was no easy matter even without opposition, he might have prevented it altogether if his Indians had left their chariots and attacked on foot Alexander's leading troops as they were trying to get on shore. But in point of fact he merely drove past, and permitted Alexander to cross without molestation. Against this force Alexander sent his mounted archers, and it was broken up without difficulty, many of the men being wounded. Other writers state that there was a fight at the actual landing between Alexander's cavalry and a force of Indians commanded by Porus' son, who was there ready to oppose them with superior numbers, and that in the course of the fighting he wounded Alexander with his own hand and struck the blow which killed his beloved horse Bucephalus.

Ptolemy, son of Lagus, gives a different account, which I myself accept. According to him, Porus did, as other writers relate, send his son, but not with only sixty chariots. For it is hardly likely that, on a report from his scouts that either Alexander himself or, at any rate, some portion of his army, had crossed the Hydaspes, he would have sent his own son to oppose the landing with so trivial a force—a force, on the one hand, unnecessarily large for mere reconnaissance and unsuitably equipped for a rapid withdrawal, and, on the other, totally inadequate either to prevent a proposed crossing or to attack an enemy which had already succeeded in getting over. Ptolemy's actual statement is that Porus' son had with him 2,000 mounted troops and 120 chariots when he reached the spot; but Alexander had been too quick for him and had already effected his final crossing from the island. Against this force Alexander first sent his mounted archers, while he himself moved on with the cavalry, thinking that Porus was on the way to engage him with the main strength of his army. This cavalry contingent, posted in the van, preceded the rest of the Greek troops; but as soon as Alexander received an accurate report of the enemies' numbers, he attacked at once, and the Indians, seeing Alexander there in person and his massed cavalry coming at them in successive charges, squadron by squadron, broke and fled. The Indians' losses in the action were some 400 mounted men, Porus' son being himself among the killed; their chariots and horses were captured as they attempted to get away—speed was impossible, and the muddy ground had rendered them useless even during the fight.

The Indians who did succeed in getting away reported to Porus that Alexander had crossed the river in force and that his son had been killed in the action. Porus was faced with a difficult choice, for the troops under Craterus, who had been left behind in Alexander's original position opposite the main Indian army, could now be seen making their way over the river. Swiftly he made up his mind; he determined to move in force against Alexander, and to fight it out with the King of Macedon himself and the flower of his men. Then, leaving behind a small force with a few elephants to spread alarm among Craterus' cavalry as they attempted to land on the river-bank, he marched to meet Alexander with all his cavalry, 4,000 strong, all of his 300 chariots, 200 elephants, and the picked contingents of his infantry, numbering some 30,000 men.

Much of the ground was deep in soft mud, so he continued his advance till he found a spot where the sandy soil offered a surface sufficiently firm and level for cavalry manoeuvre, and there made his dispositions. In the van he stationed his elephants at intervals of about 100 feet, on a broad front, to form a screen for the whole body of the infantry and to spread terror among the cavalry of Alexander. He did not expect that any enemy unit would venture to force a way through the gaps in the line of elephants, either on foot or on horseback; terror would make the horses uncontrollable, and infantry units would be even less likely to make the attempt, as they would be met and checked by his own heavy infantry and then destroyed by the elephants turning upon them and trampling them down. Behind the elephants were the foot-soldiers, though not on a front of equal extent: the various units, forming a second line, were so disposed as to fill the intervals in the line of elephants. There was infantry on both wings as well, outflanking the elephants, and, finally, on both flanks of the infantry were the mounted units, each with a screen of war-chariots.

Noting that the enemy was making his dispositions for battle, Alexander checked the advance of his cavalry to allow the infantry to come up with him. Regiment by regiment they made contact, moving swiftly, until the whole force was again united. Alexander had no intention of making the fresh enemy troops a present of his own breathless and exhausted men, so he paused before advancing to the attack. Meanwhile he kept his cavalry manoeuvring up and down the line, while the infantry units were allowed to rest until they were once more in good heart for battle.

Observation of the Indian dispositions decided him against attempting an assault upon their centre, where the heavy infantry was massed in the intervals of the protecting screen of elephants, and his reluctance to take this course was based precisely upon Porus' own calculations; relying, instead, on his superiority in cavalry, he moved the major portion of his mounted troops towards the enemy's left wing, to make his assault in that sector. Coenus was sent over to the Indians' right with Demetrius' squadron and his own, his orders being that when the enemy moved their cavalry across to their left to counter the massed formations of the Macedonian mounted squadrons, he should hang on to their rear. The heavy infantry was put in charge of Seleucus, Antigenes, and Tauron, with orders not to engage until it was evident that the Indians, both horse and foot, had been thrown into confusion by the Macedonian cavalry.

Once the opposing armies were within range, Alexander launched his mounted archers, 1,000 strong, against the enemy's left wing, hoping to shake it by the hail of their arrows and the weight of their charge, and immediately afterwards himself advanced with the mounted Hetaeri against the Indian left, intent upon making his assault while they were still reeling under the attack of the mounted archers and before their cavalry could change formation from column into mass.

The Indians meanwhile withdrew all the cavalry from other sections of their line, and moved it across to meet and counter Alexander's movement towards their flank, and it was not long before Coenus' men could be seen following, according to orders, close in their rear. The Indians were thereupon compelled to split their force into two; the larger section, containing the best troops, continued to proceed against Alexander, while the remainder wheeled about in order to deal with Coenus. This, of course, was disastrous not only to the effectiveness of the Indians' dispositions, but to their whole plan of battle. Alexander saw his chance; precisely at the moment when the enemy cavalry were changing direction, he attacked. The Indians did not even wait to receive his charge, but fell back in confusion upon the elephants, their impregnable fortress—or so they hoped. The elephant-drivers forced their beasts to meet the opposing cavalry, while the Macedonian infantry, in its turn, advanced against them, shooting down the drivers, and pouring in a hail of missiles from every side upon the elephants themselves. It was an odd bit of work—quite unlike any previous battle; the monster elephants plunged this way and that among the lines of infantry, dealing destruction in the solid mass of the Macedonian phalanx, while the Indian horsemen, seeing the infantry at one another's throats, wheeled to the assault of the Macedonian cavalry. Once again, however, the verve and experience of Alexander's mounted troops were too much for them, and they were forced back a second time on the elephants.

During the action all the Macedonian cavalry units had, by the exigencies of the fighting rather than deliberate orders, concentrated into a single body; and now its successive charges upon this sector or that inflicted heavy losses on the enemy. By this time the elephants were boxed up, with no room to manoeuvre, by troops all round them, and as they blundered about, wheeling and shoving this way and that, they trampled to death as many of their friends as of their enemies. The result was that the Indian cavalry, jammed in around the elephants and with no more space to manoeuvre than they had, suffered severely; most of the elephant-drivers had been shot; many of the animals had themselves been wounded, while others, riderless and bewildered, ceased altogether to play their expected part, and, maddened by pain and fear, set indiscriminately upon friend and foe, thrusting, trampling, and spreading death before them. The Macedonians could deal with these maddened creatures comfortably enough; having room to manoeuvre, they were able to use their judgement, giving ground when they charged, and going for them with their javelins when they turned and lumbered back, whereas the unfortunate Indians, jammed up close among them as they attempted to get away, found them a more dangerous enemy even than the Greeks.

In time the elephants tired and their charges grew feebler; they began to back away, slowly, like ships going astern, and with nothing worse than trumpetings. Taking his chance, Alexander surrounded the lot of them—elephants, horsemen, and all—and then signalled his infantry to lock shields and move up in a solid mass. Most of the Indian cavalry was cut down in the ensuing action; their infantry, too, hard pressed by the Macedonians, suffered terrible losses. The survivors, finding a gap in Alexander's ring of cavalry, all turned and fled.

CASSIUS DIO
(C. A.D. 155–235?)

Born in Nicaea, Bithynia, Cassius Dio rose to be proconsul in Africa and then legate in Dalmatia and Pannonia. He wrote a history of Rome, in Greek, of which only twenty-five of eighty books have been partially preserved. Cassius Dio is one of the very best historians of the third century A.D.

THE BATTLE OF ACTIUM

. . . So the fleets came to grips and the battle began. Each side uttered loud shouts to the men aboard, urging the troops to summon up their prowess and their fighting spirit, and the men could also hear a babel of orders being shouted at them from those on shore.

The two sides used different tactics. Octavian's fleet, having smaller and faster ships, could advance at speed and ram the enemy, since their armour gave them protection on all sides. If they sank a vessel, they had achieved their object; if not, they would back water before they could be engaged at close quarters, and either ram the same ship suddenly a second time, or let it go and turn against others. When they had damaged these as much as they could in a short time, they would seek out fresh opponents over and over again, constantly switching their attack, so that their onslaught always came where it was least expected. They feared their adversaries' long-range missiles no less than their superior strength in fighting at close quarters, and so they wasted no time either in the approach or the clash. They would sail up suddenly so as to close with their target before the enemy's archers could hit them, inflict damage or

From Cassius Dio, *The Roman History: The Reign of Augustus,* translated by Ian Scott-Kilvert (Harmondsworth, England: Penguin Books, 1987), 58–61. Copyright © 1987 by Ian Scott-Kilvert. Reproduced by permission of Penguin Books Ltd.

cause enough confusion to escape being grappled, and then quickly back away out of range.

Antony's tactics, on the other hand, were to pour heavy volleys of stones and arrows upon the enemy ships as they approached, and then try to entrap them with iron grapnels. When they could reach their targets, Antony's ships got the upper hand, but if they missed, their own hulls would be pierced by the rams and they would sink, or else, in the attempt to avoid collision, they would lose time and expose themselves to attack by other ships. Two or three of Octavian's vessels would fall upon one of Antony's, with some inflicting all the damage they could, while the others bore the brunt of the counter-attack.

On the one side the helmsmen and rowers suffered the heaviest casualties, on the other the marines. Octavian's ships resembled cavalry, now launching a charge, and now retreating, since they could attack or draw off as they chose, while Antony's were like heavy infantry, warding off the enemy's efforts to ram them, but also striving to hold them with their grappling-hooks. Each fleet in turn gained the advantage over the other: the one would dart in against the rows of oars which projected from the ships' sides and break the blades, while the other fighting from its higher decks would sink its adversaries with stones and ballistic missiles. At the same time each side had its weaknesses. Antony's ships could do no damage to the enemy as they approached: Octavian's, if they failed to sink a vessel when they had rammed it, would find the odds turned against them once they were grappled.

For a long while the struggle was evenly poised and neither side could gain the upper hand anywhere, but the end came in the following way. Cleopatra, whose ship was riding at anchor behind the battle lines, could not endure the long hours of uncertainty while the issue hung in the balance: both as a woman and as an Egyptian she found herself stretched to breaking-point by the agony of the suspense, and the constant and unnerving effort of picturing victory or defeat. Suddenly she made her choice—to flee—and made the signal for the others, her own subjects. So when her ships immediately hoisted their sails and stood out to sea, a favourable wind having luckily got up, Antony supposed that they were turning tail, not on Cleopatra's orders, but out of fear because they felt themselves to have been defeated, and so he followed them.

At this, dismay and confusion spread to the rest of Antony's men, and they resolved likewise to take whatever means of escape lay open. Some raised their sails, while others threw the turrets and heavy equipment overboard to lighten the vessels and help them to get away. While they were thus engaged, their opponents again attacked: they had not pursued Cleopatra's fleeing squadron, because they themselves had not taken sails aboard and had put out prepared only for a naval battle. This meant that there were many ships to attack each one of Antony's, both at long range and alongside. The result was that the struggle took many forms on both sides and was carried on with the greatest ferocity. Octavian's soldiers battered the lower parts of the ships from stem to stern, smashed the oars, broke off the rudders, and, climbing on to the decks, grappled with their enemies. They dragged down some, thrust others overboard, and fought hand to hand with others, since they now equalled them in numbers. Antony's men forced their attackers back with boat-hooks, cut them down with axes, hurled down stones and other missiles which had been prepared for this purpose, forced down those who tried to scale the ships' sides, and engaged all who came within reach. A witness of the battle might have compared it, if one can reduce the scale, to the spectacle of a number of walled towns or islands set close together being besieged from the sea. Thus one side strove to clamber up the sides of the ships, as it might be up a cliff or fortress, and brought to bear all the equipment which is needed for such an assault, while the others struggled to repel them, using all the weapons and tactics which are known to defenders.

As the fighting remained evenly balanced, Octavian, who found himself in doubt what to do next, sent for fire from his camp. Until then he had been unwilling to use it, since he was anxious to capture Antony's treasure intact. He now resorted to it because he saw that it was impossible to win in any other way and believed that this was the only weapon which would help him. The battle then changed its character. The attackers would approach their targets from many different points at once, bombarding them with blazing missiles and hurling by hand javelins with torches attached to them; from a longer range they would also catapult jars filled with charcoal or pitch. The defenders tried to ward off these missiles one by one, but when some got through, they ignited the timbers and immediately started a blaze, as is bound to happen on a ship. The crews first put out the flames with the drinking water which they carried on board, and when that ran out, they used sea water. If they managed to throw this on the fire in great quantities at once, they could sometimes quench it by the sheer volume of the water. But this was not always possible, since their buckets were few and of no great size. In their confusion they sometimes only half filled them, and in that case instead of reducing the blaze they only increased it, since small quantities of salt water poured on a fire make it burn all the more strongly. So when they found that they were failing to check the flames, they threw on their heavy cloaks and even dead bodies, and for a time these stifled the conflagration, which seemed to die down. But later, and especially when the wind blew strongly, the flames leaped up more violently than ever, fed by their own efforts.

So long as only a section of the ship was on fire, the men would stand close by and jump into it, cutting away some of the planks and scattering others; in some instances the men threw the timbers into the sea, and in others against their adversaries, in the hope that they might cause them some hurt. Others would take up position in the part of the ship that was undamaged, and would ply their long spears and grappling-hooks more desperately than ever, in the hope of making some enemy ship fast to theirs and boarding her, or, if not, setting her alight as well. But when none of the enemy came near enough, since they were guarding against this very possibility, and when the fire spread to the encircling sides of the ship and descended into the hold, they found themselves in the most terrible plight of all. Some, especially the sailors, were overcome by the smoke before the flames ever came near them, while others were roasted in the midst of the holocaust as if they were in ovens. Others were incinerated in their armour as it grew red-hot. Others, again, to avoid such a fate, or when they were half burned, threw off their armour and were wounded by the missiles shot at them from long range, or jumped into the sea and were drowned, or were clubbed by their enemies and sank, or were devoured by sea-monsters. The only men to find a death which was endurable in the midst of such sufferings were those who either killed one another in return for the service, or took their own lives before such a fate could befall them. These were spared the torments I have described, and their corpses were burned on board the ships, as though they were on a funeral pyre.

When Octavian's men saw that the battle had taken this turn, they at first held off from the enemy, since some of the latter could still defend themselves. But when the fire had taken hold of the ships, and the men aboard them, so far from being able to injure an opponent, could no longer even defend themselves, they eagerly sailed up to Antony's vessels in the hope of seizing their treasure, and tried to put out the fires which they themselves had started. The result was that many of them perished, both from the flames and from their own greed.

FLAVIUS VEGETIUS
(late fourth century A.D.)

Flavius Vegetius Renatus probably lived at Constantinople. His Epitoma
rei militaris, *perhaps dedicated to the emperor Theodosius the Great, is a
recapitulation of the whole of Roman military knowledge, summarizing the
observations on the subject of Cato the Censor, Cornelius Celius, Frontinus,
and other writers. These military instructions were a bible in the West right
up to the sixteenth century, although in places they lack originality. Book 3,
the bulk of which is reproduced here, is the most interesting part of the
treatise. Vegetius has the merit of having attempted an epitome of Roman
strategy, tactics, and logistics. He is a theoretician of the direct style on the
battlefield, but advocates that preparatory maneuvers be indirect.*

DISPOSITIONS FOR ACTION

. . . An army too numerous is subject to many dangers and inconveniences. Its
bulk makes it slow and unwieldy in its motions; and as it is obliged to march
in columns of great length, it is exposed to the risk of being continually harassed and insulted by inconsiderable parties of the enemy. The incumbrance
of the baggage is often an occasion of its being surprised in its passage through
difficult places or over rivers. The difficulty of providing forage for such numbers of horses and other beasts of burden is very great. Besides, scarcity of provisions, which is to be carefully guarded against in all expeditions soon ruins
such large armies where the consumption is so prodigious that, notwithstanding the greatest care in filling the magazines, they must begin to fail in a
short time. And sometimes they unavoidably will be distressed for want of water. But, if unfortunately this immense army should be defeated, the numbers

From Flavius Vegetius Renatus, *The Military Institutions of the Romans* (Harrisburg, Pa.: Military Service Pub. Co., 1944; reprint, Westport, Conn.: Greenwood Press, 1985), 69–93, 111–13.

lost must necessarily be very great, and the remainder, who save themselves by flight, too much dispirited to be brought again to action.

The ancients, taught by experience, preferred discipline to numbers. In wars of lesser importance they thought one legion with auxiliaries, that is, ten thousand foot and two thousand horse, sufficient. And they often gave the command to a praetor as to a general of the second rank. When the preparations of the enemy were formidable, they sent a general of consular dignity with twenty thousand foot and four thousand horse. In our times this command was given to a commander of the first order. But when there happened any dangerous insurrection supported by infinite multitudes of fierce and barbarous nations, on such emergencies they took the field with two armies under two consuls, who were charged, both singly and jointly, to take care to preserve the Republic from danger.

In short, by this management, the Romans, almost continually engaged in war with different nations in different parts of the world, found themselves able to oppose them in every quarter. The excellence of their discipline made their small armies sufficient to encounter all their enemies with success. But it was an invariable rule in their armies that the number of allies or auxiliaries should never exceed that of the Roman citizens. . . .

Care to Provide Forage and Provisions

Famine makes greater havoc in an army than the enemy, and is more terrible than the sword. Time and opportunity may help to retrieve other misfortunes, but where forage and provisions have not been carefully provided, the evil is without remedy. The main and principal point in war is to secure plenty of provisions and to weaken or destroy the enemy by famine. An exact calculation must therefore be made before the commencement of the war as to the number of troops and the expenses incidental thereto, so that the provinces may in plenty of time furnish the forage, corn, and all other kinds of provisions demanded of them to be transported.

They must be in more than sufficient quantity, and gathered into the strongest and most convenient cities before the opening of the campaign. If the provinces cannot raise their quotas in kind, they must substitute for them money, to be employed in procuring all things requisite for the service. For the possessions of the subjects cannot be kept secure otherwise than by the defense of arms. . . .

On difficult expeditions the ancients distributed the provisions at a fixed allowance to each man without distinction of rank; and when the emergency was past, the government accounted for the full proportions. The troops should never want wood and forage in winter or water in summer. They should have corn, wine, vinegar, and even salt, in plenty at all times. Cities and fortresses are garrisoned by such men as are least fit for the service of the field. They are provided with all sorts of arms, arrows, slings, stones, onagri [heavy stone-throwing machines] and ballistae for their defense. . . .

Methods to Prevent Mutiny

An army drawn together from different parts sometimes is disposed to mutiny. And the troops, though not inclined to fight, pretend to be angry at not being led against the enemy. Such seditious dispositions principally show themselves in those who have lived in their quarters in idleness and effeminacy. These men, unaccustomed to the necessary fatigue of the field, are disgusted at its severity. Their ignorance of discipline makes them afraid of action and inspires them with insolence.

There are several remedies for this evil. While the troops are yet separated and each corps continues in its respective quarters, let the tribunes, their lieutenants and the officers in general, make it their business to keep up so strict a discipline as to leave them no room to harbor any thoughts but of submission and obedience. Let them be constantly employed either in field days or in the inspection of their arms. They should not be allowed to be absent on furlough. They should be frequently called by roll and trained to be exact in the observance of every signal.

Let them be exercised in the use of the bow, in throwing missile-weapons and stones, both with the hand and sling, and with the wooden sword at the post; let all this be continually repeated and let them be often kept under arms till they are tired. Let them be exercised in running and leaping to facilitate the passing of ditches. And if their quarters are near the sea or a river, let them all, without exception, be obliged in the summer to have frequent practice in swimming. Let them be accustomed to march through thickets, inclosures and broken grounds, to fell trees and cut out timber, to break ground and to defend a post against their comrades who are to endeavor to dispossess them; and in the encounter each party should use their shields to dislodge and bear down their antagonists.

All the different kinds of troops thus trained and exercised in their quarters will find themselves inspired with desire for glory and eagerness for action when they come to take the field. In short, a soldier who has proper confidence in his own skill and strength, entertains no thought of mutiny.

A general should be alert to discover the turbulent and seditious soldiers in the army, legions or auxiliaries, cavalry or infantry. He should endeavor to procure his intelligence not from informers, but from the tribunes, their lieutenants and other officers of undoubted veracity. It would then be prudent in him to separate them from the rest under pretence of detailing them for some service agreeable to them, or by detaching them to garrison cities or castles, but with such address that though he wants to get rid of them, they may think themselves employed by preference and favor. A multitude never broke out into open sedition at once and with unanimous consent. They are prepared and excited by some few mutineers, who hope to secure impunity for their crimes by the number of their associates. But if the height of the mutiny requires violent remedies, it will be most advisable, after the manner of the ancients, to punish the ring-leaders only in order that, although few suffer, all may be terrified by the example. But it is much more to the credit of a general to accustom his troops to submission and obedience by habit and discipline than to be obliged to force them to their duty by the terror of punishment.

Marches near the Enemy

It is asserted by those who have made the profession their study that an army is exposed to more danger on marches than in battles. In an engagement the men are properly armed, they see their enemies before them and are prepared to fight. But on a march the soldier is less on his guard, has not his arms always ready and is thrown into disorder by a sudden attack or ambuscade. A general, therefore, cannot be too careful and diligent in taking necessary precautions to prevent a surprise on the march and in making proper dispositions to repulse the enemy, in case of such event, without loss.

In the first place, he should have an exact description of the country that is the seat of war, in which the distances between places, the nature of the roads, the shortest routes, by-roads, mountains and rivers, should be correctly provided. We are told that the greatest generals have carried their precautions on this head so far that, not satisfied with the simple description of the country wherein they were engaged, they caused plans to be made of it on the spot, that they might regulate their marches by the eye with greater safety. A general should also inform himself of all these particulars from persons of sense and reputation well acquainted with the country by examining them separately at first, and then comparing their accounts in order to come at the truth with certainty.

If any difficulty arises about the choice of roads, he should procure proper and skillful guides. He should put them under a guard and spare neither promises nor threats to induce them to be faithful. They will acquit themselves well when they know it is impossible to escape and are certain of being rewarded for their fidelity or punished for their perfidy. He must be sure of their capacity and experience, that the whole army be not brought into danger by the errors of two or three persons. For sometimes the common sort of people imagine they know what they really do not, and through ignorance promise more than they can perform.

Routes Kept Secret

But of all precautions the most important is to keep entirely secret which way or by what route the army is to march. For the security of an expedition depends on the concealment of all motions from the enemy. The figure of the Minotaur was anciently among the legionary ensigns, signifying that inasmuch as this monster, according to the fable, was concealed in the most secret recesses and windings of the labyrinth [a fabled Cretian maze] so the designs of a general should always be impenetrable. When the enemy has no intimation of a march, it is made with security; but as sometimes the scouts either suspect or discover the decampment, or traitors or deserters give intelligence thereof, it will be proper to mention the method of acting in case of an attack on the march.

The general, before he puts his troops in motion, should send out detachments of trusty and experienced soldiers well mounted, to reconnoiter the places through which he is to march, in front, in rear, and on the right and left, lest he should fall into ambuscades. The night is safer and more advantageous than day for your spies to do their business, for if they are taken prisoners, you have, as it were, betrayed yourself. After this, the cavalry should march off first, then the infantry; the baggage, officers' horses, servants and vehicles follow in the center; and part of the best cavalry and infantry come in the rear, since it is oftener attacked on a march than the front. The flanks of the baggage column, exposed to frequent ambuscades, must also be covered with a sufficient guard to secure them. But above all, the part where the enemy is most expected to attack must be reinforced with some of the best cavalry, light infantry and foot archers.

If surrounded on all sides by the enemy, you must make dispositions to receive them wherever they may come, and the soldiers should be cautioned beforehand to keep their arms in hand, and to be ready in order to prevent the unfavorable effects of a sudden attack.

Men are frightened and thrown into disorder by sudden reverses and surprises which are apt to be of no consequence when foreseen. The ancients were very careful that the servants or followers of the army, if wounded or frightened by the noise of action, might not disorder the troops while engaged, and also to prevent their either straggling or crowding one another too much, which might incommode their own men and give advantage to the enemy. They ranged the baggage, therefore, in the same manner as the regular troops under particular ensigns. They selected from among the servants the most fit and experienced and gave them the command of a number of other servants and boys, not exceeding two hundred, and their ensigns directed them where to assemble the baggage. Proper intervals should always be kept between the baggage and the troops, that the latter may not be embarrassed for want of room in which to fight in case of an attack during the march.

Defensive Measures Vary

The manner and disposition of defense must be varied according to the difference of ground. In an open country you are more liable to be attacked by horse than by foot. But in a woody, mountainous or marshy situation, the danger to be apprehended is from foot. Some of the divisions being apt through negligence to move too fast, and others too slow, great care is to be taken to prevent the army from being broken into parts or from running into too great length, as the enemy would instantly take advantage of the neglect and penetrate the lines without difficulty.

The tribunes, their lieutenants or the masters-at-arms of most experience, must therefore be posted at proper distances, in order to halt those who advance too fast and quicken such as move too slow. The men at too great a distance in the front, on the appearance of an enemy, are more disposed to fly than to join their comrades. And those too far behind, destitute of assistance, fall a sacrifice to the enemy and their own despair. The enemy, it may be concluded, will either plant ambuscades or make his attack by open force, according to the advantage of the ground. Circumspection in examining every place will be a security against concealed danger; and an ambuscade, if discovered and promptly surrounded, will repay the intended mischief with interest.

If the enemy prepare to fall upon you by open force in a mountainous country, detachments must be sent forward to occupy the highest eminences, so that on their arrival they may not dare to attack you under such disadvantage of ground, your troops being posted so much above them and presenting a front ready for their reception. It is better to send men forward with hatchets and other tools in order to open ways that are narrow but safe, without regard to the labor, rather than to run any risk in the best roads. It is necessary to be well posted as to whether the enemy usually make their attempts in the night, at break of day or in the hours of refreshment or rest; and by knowledge of their customs to guard against what we find their general practice. We must also inform ourselves whether they are strongest in infantry or cavalry; whether their cavalry is chiefly armed with lances or with bows; and whether their principal strength consists in their numbers or the excellence of their arms. All of this will enable us to take the most proper measures to distress them and for our advantage.

When we have a design in view, we must consider whether it will be most advisable to begin the march by day or by night; we must calculate the distance to the places we want to reach; and take such precautions that in summer the troops may not suffer for want of water on their march, nor be obstructed in winter by impassable morasses or torrents, as these would expose the army to great danger before it could arrive at the place of its destination.

As it highly concerns us prudently to guard against these inconveniences, so it would be inexcusible not to take advantage of an enemy that fell into them through ignorance or negligence. Our spies should be constantly abroad; we should spare no pains in tampering with their men, and give all manner of encouragement to deserters. By these means we may get intelligence of their present or future designs. And we should constantly keep in readiness some detachments of cavalry and light infantry to fall upon them when they least expect it, either on the march, or when foraging or marauding. . . .

Rules for Encamping

An army on the march cannot expect always to find walled cities for quarters, and it is very imprudent and dangerous to encamp haphazardly without some sort of entrenchment. It is an easy matter to surprise troops while refreshing themselves or dispersed in the different occupations of the service. The darkness of night, the necessity of sleep and the dispersion of the horses at pasture afford opportunities of surprise. A good camp site is not sufficient; we must choose the very best that can be found lest, having failed to occupy a more advantageous post, the enemy should get possession of it to our great detriment.

An army should not encamp in summer near bad water or far from good, nor in winter in a situation without plenty of forage and wood. The camp should not be liable to sudden inundations. The avenues of approach should not be too steep and narrow lest, if invested, the troops should find it difficult to retreat; nor should it be commanded by any eminences from which it may be harmed by the enemy's weapons. After these precautions, the camp is formed square, round, triangular or oblong, according to the nature of the ground. For the form of a camp does not constitute its excellence. Those camps, however, are thought best where the length is one third more than the depth. The dimensions must be exactly computed by the engineers, so that the size of the camp may be proportioned to the number of troops. A camp which is too confined will not permit the troops to perform their movements with freedom, and one which is too extensive divides them too much.

There are three methods of entrenching a camp. The first applies to when the army is on the march and will continue in the camp for only one night. They then throw up a slight parapet of turf and plant it with a row of palisades or caltrops [An instrument with four points so designed that when any three of them are on the ground the fourth projects upward. These are extensively used today for antitank barriers.] of wood. The sods are cut with iron instruments. If the earth is held strongly together by the roots of the grass, they are cut in the form of a brick a foot and one half high, a foot broad and a foot and one half long. If the earth is so loose that the turf cannot be cut in this form, they run a slight trench round the camp, five feet broad and three feet deep. The earth taken from the trench forms a parapet on the inside and this secures the army from danger. This is the second method.

But permanent camps, either for summer or winter, in the neighborhood of an enemy, are fortified with greater care and regularity. After the ground is marked out by the proper officers, each century receives a certain number of feet to entrench. They then range their shields and baggage in a circle about their own colors and, without other tools than their swords, open a trench nine, eleven or thirteen feet broad. Or, if they greatly apprehend the enemy, they enlarge it to seventeen feet (it being a general rule to observe odd numbers). Within this they construct a rampart with fascines or branches of trees well fastened together with stakes, so that the earth may be better supported.

Defensive Works

Upon this rampart they raise a parapet with battlements as in the fortifications of a city. The centurions measure the work with rods ten feet long and examine whether every one has properly completed the portion assigned to him. The tribunes likewise inspect the work and should not leave the place till the whole is finished. And that the workmen may not be suddenly interrupted by the enemy, all the cavalry and that part of the infantry exempted by the privilege of their rank from working, remain in order of battle before the entrenchment to be ready to repel any assault.

The first thing to be done after entrenching the camp, is to plant the ensigns, held by the soldiers in the highest veneration and respect, in their proper places. After this the praetorium is prepared for the general and his lieutenants, and the tents pitched for the tribunes, who have soldiers particularly appointed for that service and to fetch their water, wood, and forage. Then the legions and auxiliaries, cavalry and infantry, have the ground allotted to them to pitch their tents according to the rank of the several corps. Four foot-soldiers of each century and four troopers of each troop are on guard every night. As it seemed impossible for a sentinel to remain a whole night on his post, the watches were divided by the hourglass into four parts, that each man might stand only three hours. All guards are mounted by the sound of trumpet and relieved by the sound of cornet. The tribunes choose proper and trusty men to visit the different posts and report to them whatever they find amiss.

The cavalry furnish the grand guards at night and the outposts by day. They are relieved every morning and afternoon because of the fatigue imposed by this duty upon the men and horses. It is particularly incumbent upon the general to provide for the protection of the pastures and of the convoys of grain and other provisions either in camp or garrison, and to secure wood, water and forage against the incursions of the enemy. This can only be effected by posting detachments advantageously in the cities or walled castles on the roads along which the convoys advance. And if there are no existing fortifications, small forts must be built in proper situations, surrounded with large ditches, for the reception of detachments of horse and foot, so that the convoys will be effectually protected. For an enemy will hardly venture far into a country where he knows his adversary's troops are so disposed as to be ready to encompass him on all sides.

Motives for Plan of Campaign Operations

Readers of this military abridgement will perhaps be impatient for instructions relative to general engagements. But they should consider that a battle is commonly decided in two or three hours, after which usually no further hopes are left for the worsted army. Every plan, therefore, is to be considered, every expedient tried and every method taken before matters are brought to this last extremity. Good officers decline general engagements where the odds are too great, and prefer the employment of stratagem and finesse to destroy the enemy as much as possible in detail and intimidate them without exposing their own forces.

I shall insert some necessary instructions on this head collected from the ancients. It is the duty and interest of the general frequently to assemble the most prudent and experienced officers of the different corps of the army and consult with them on the state of both his own and the enemy's forces. All overconfidence, as being most pernicious in its consequences, must be banished from the deliberations. He must examine which has the superiority in numbers, whether his or the adversary's troops are best armed, which are in the best condition, best disciplined and most resolute in emergencies.

The state of the cavalry of both armies must be inquired into, but more especially that of the infantry, for the main strength of an army consists of the latter. With respect to the cavalry, he must endeavor to find out in which are the greatest numbers of archers or of troopers armed with lances, which has the most cuirassiers and which the best horses. Lastly he must consider the field of battle and to judge whether the ground is more advantageous for him or his enemy. If strongest in cavalry, we should prefer plains and open ground; if superior in infantry, we should choose a situation full of enclosures, ditches, morasses and woods, and sometimes mountainous. Plenty or scarcity of food in either army are considerations of no small importance, for famine, according to the common proverb, is an internal enemy that makes more havoc than the sword.

But the most material point is to determine whether it is most proper to temporize or to bring the situation to a speedy decision by action. The enemy sometimes expect an expedition will soon be over; and if it is protracted to any length, his troops are either reduced by want, induced to return home by the desire of seeing their families or, having accomplished nothing considerable in the field, disperse themselves from despair of success. Thus numbers, tired out with fatigue and disgusted with the service, desert, others betray them and many surrender themselves. Fidelity is seldom found in troops disheartened by reverses. In such case an army which was numerous on taking the field insensibly dwindles away to nothing.

It is essential to know the character of the enemy and of their principal officers—whether they be rash or cautious, enterprising or timid, whether they fight on principle or from chance and whether the nations they have been engaged with were brave or cowardly.

Improving Morale

We must know how far to depend upon the fidelity and strength of auxiliaries, how the enemy's troops and our own are affected and which appear most confident of success, a consideration of great effect in raising or depressing the courage of an army. A speech from the general, especially if he seems under no apprehension himself, may reanimate dejected soldiers. Their spirits revive if any considerable advantage is gained either by stratagem or otherwise, if the fortune of the enemy begins to change or if you can contrive to beat some of their weak or poorly-armed detachments.

But you must by no means venture to lead an irresolute or spiritless army to a general engagement. The difference is great whether troops are raw or veterans, inured to war by recent service or for some years unemployed. For soldiers unused to fighting for a length of time must be considered in the same light as recruits. As soon as the legions, auxiliaries and cavalry are assembled from their several quarters, it is the duty of a good general to have every corps instructed separately in every part of the drill by tribunes of known capacity. He should afterwards form them into one body and train them in all the maneuvers of the line as for a general action. He must frequently drill them himself to try their skill and strength, and to see whether they perform their evolutions with proper regularity and are sufficiently attentive to the sound of the trumpets, the motions of the colors and to his own orders and signals. If deficient in any of these particulars, they must be instructed and exercised till perfect.

But though thoroughly disciplined and complete in their field exercises, in the use of the bow and javelin, and in the evolutions of the line, it is not advisable to lead them rashly or immediately to battle. A favorable opportunity must be watched for, and they must first be prepared by frequent skirmishes and slight encounters. Thus a vigilant and prudent general will carefully weigh in council the state of his own forces and of those of the enemy, as a civil magistrate judging between two contending parties. If he finds himself in many respects superior to his adversary, he must by no means defer bringing on an engagement. But if he knows himself to be inferior, he must avoid general actions and endeavor to succeed by surprises, ambuscades and stratagems. These, when skillfully managed by good generals, have often given them the victory over enemies superior both in numbers and strength.

All arts and trades whatever are brought to perfection by continual practice. How much more should this maxim, true in inconsiderable matters, be observed in affairs of importance! And how much superior to all others is the art of war, by which our liberties are preserved, our dignities perpetuated and the provinces and the whole Empire itself exist.

Handling Raw and Undisciplined Troops

The Lacedaemonians, and after them the Romans, were so aware of this truth that to this science they sacrificed all others. And the barbarous nations even at this day think only this art worth attention, believing it includes or confers all other gains. In short, it is indispensably necessary for those engaged in war not only to instruct soldiers in the means of preserving their own lives, but how to gain the victory over their enemies.

A commander-in-chief therefore, whose power and dignity are so great and to whose fidelity and bravery the fortunes of his countrymen, the defense of their cities, the lives of the soldiers, and the glory of the state, are entrusted, should not only consult the good of the army in general, but extend his care to every private soldier in it. For when any misfortunes happen to those under his command, they are considered as public losses and imputed entirely to his misconduct.

If therefore he finds his army composed of raw troops or if they have long been unaccustomed to fighting, he must carefully study the strength, the spirit, the customs of each particular legion, and of each body of auxiliaries, cavalry and infantry. He must know, if possible, the name and capacity of every officer, tribune, subaltern and soldier. He must make his authority respected and maintain it by severity. He must punish all military crimes with the greatest rigor of the laws. He must have sufficient character to make himself inexorable towards offenders and endeavor to give public examples thereof in different places and on different occasions.

Having once firmly established these regulations, he must watch the opportunity when the enemy, dispersed in search of plunder, think themselves in security, and attack them with detachments of tried cavalry or infantry, intermingled with young soldiers, or such as are under the military age. The veterans will acquire fresh experience and the others will be inspired with courage by the advantages such opportunities will give him. He should form ambuscades with the greatest secrecy to surprise the enemy at the passages of rivers, in the rugged passes of mountains, in defiles in woods and when embarrassed by morasses or difficult roads.

Attacking the Enemy

He should regulate his march so as to fall upon them while taking their refreshments or sleeping, or at a time when they suspect no danger and are dispersed, unarmed and their horses unsaddled. He should continue these tactics till his soldiers have imbibed a proper confidence in themselves. For troops that have never been in action or have not for some time been used to such spectacles, are greatly shocked at the sight of the wounded and dying; and the impressions of fear they receive dispose them rather to fly than fight.

If the enemy makes excursions or expeditions, the general should attack him when fatigued by a long march, fall upon him unexpectedly, or harass his rear. He should detach parties to endeavor to carry by surprise any quarters established at a distance from the hostile army for the collection of forage or provisions. For such measures should be pursued at first as can produce no very bad effects if they should happen to miscarry, but be of great advantage if attended with success. A prudent general will also try to sow dissention among his adversaries, for no nation, no matter how weak in itself, can be completely ruined by its enemies unless its fall be facilitated by its own acts. In civil dissensions men are so intent on the destruction of their private enemies that they are entirely regardless of the public safety.

One maxim must be remembered throughout this work: that no one should ever despair of effecting what has been already accomplished. It may be said that our troops for many years past have not even fortified their permanent camps with ditches, ramparts or palisades. The answer is plain. If those precautions had been taken, our armies would never have suffered by surprises of the enemy both by day and night.

The Persians, after the example of the old Romans, surround their camps with ditches and, as the ground in their country is generally sandy, they always carry with them empty bags to fill with the sand taken out of the trenches and raise a parapet by piling them one on the other. All the barbarous nations range their vehicles round them in a circle, a method which bears some resemblance to a fortified camp. They thus pass their nights secure from surprise.

Restoring Ancient Discipline

Are we afraid of not being able to learn from others what they before have learned from us? At present all this is to be found in books only, although formerly constantly practiced. Inquiries are now no longer made about customs that have been so long neglected, because in the midst of peace, war is looked upon as an eventuality too distant to merit consideration. But former instances will convince us that the reestablishment of ancient discipline is by no means impossible, although now so totally in disuse.

In former ages the art of war, often neglected and forgotten, was as often recovered from books and reestablished by the authority and attention of our generals. Our armies in Spain, when Scipio Africanus [237–183 B.C.; defeated Hannibal at Zama, 202 B.C.] took the command, were in bad condition and had often been beaten under preceding generals. He soon reformed them by severe discipline and obliged them to undergo the greatest fatigue in the different military works, reproaching them by the remark that since they would not wet their hands with the blood of their enemies, they should soil them with the mud of the trenches. In short, with these very troops he afterwards took the city of Numantia and burned it to the ground with such destruction of its inhabitants that not one escaped.

In Africa an army, which under the command of Albinus had been forced to pass under the yoke, was by Metellus brought into such order and discipline, by forming it on the ancient model, that they afterwards vanquished those very enemies who had subjected them to that ignominious treatment. The Cimbri defeated the legions of Caepio, Manilus and Silanus in Gaul, but Marius collected their shattered remnants and disciplined them so effectually that he destroyed an innumerable multitude of the Cimbri, Teutones and Ambrones in one general engagement. Nevertheless it is easier to form young soldiers and inspire them with proper notions of honor than to reanimate troops who have been once disheartened.

Preparations for a General Engagement

Having explained the less considerable branches of the art of war, the order of military affairs naturally leads us to the general engagement. This is a conjuncture full of uncertainty and fatal to kingdoms and nations, for in the decision of a pitched battle consists the fulness of victory. This eventuality above all others requires the exertion of all the abilities of a general, as his good conduct on such an occasion gains him greater glory, as the reverse exposes him to greater danger and disgrace. This is the moment in which his talents, skill and experience show themselves in their fullest extent.

Formerly to enable the soldiers to charge with greater vigor, it was customary to order them a moderate refreshment of food before an engagement, so that their strength might be the better supported during a long conflict. When the army is to march out of a camp or city in the presence of their enemies drawn up and ready for action, great precaution must be observed lest they should be attacked as they defile from the gates and be cut to pieces in detail. Proper measures must therefore be taken so that the whole army may be clear of the gates and form in order of battle before the enemy's approach.

If they are ready before you can have quitted the place, your design of marching out must either be deferred till another opportunity or at least dissembled, so that when they begin to taunt you on the supposition that you dare not appear, or think of nothing but plundering or retiring and no longer keep their ranks, you may sally out and fall upon them while in confusion and surprise. [In ancient warfare the practice prevailed of opponents exchanging vituperations, boasts and threats, as a means of intimidating or angering].

Troops must never be engaged in a general action immediately after a long march, when the men are fatigued and the horses tired. The strength required for action is spent in the toil of the march. What can a soldier do who charges when out of breath? The ancients carefully avoided this inconvenience, but in later times some of our Roman generals, to say nothing more, have lost their armies by unskillfully neglecting this precaution. Two armies, one tired and spent, the other fresh and in full vigor, are by no means an equal match.

Troops' Pre-Battle Sentiment

It is necessary to know the sentiments of the soldiers on the day of an engagement. Their confidence or apprehensions are easily discovered by their looks, their words, their actions and their motions. No great dependence is to be placed on the eagerness of young soldiers for action, for the prospect of fighting is attractive to those who are strangers to it. On the other hand, it would be wrong to hazard an engagement, if old experienced soldiers testify to a disinclination to fight. A general, however, may encourage and animate his troops by proper exhortations and orations, especially if by his prophecies of a favorable result of the approaching action he can persuade them into the belief of an easy victory. With this view, he should lay before them the cowardice or unskillfulness of their enemies and remind them of any former advantages they may have gained over them. He should employ every argument capable of exciting rage, hatred and indignation against the adversaries in the minds of his soldiers.

It is natural for men in general to be affected with some sensations of fear at the beginning of an engagement, but there are without doubt some of a more timorous disposition who are disordered by the very sight of the enemy. To diminish these apprehensions before you venture on action, draw up your army frequently in order of battle in some safe situation, so that your men may be accustomed to the sight and appearance of the enemy. When opportunity offers, they should be sent to fall upon them and endeavor to put them to flight or kill some of their men. Thus they will become acquainted with their customs, arms and horses. The objects with which we are once familiarized are seldom longer capable of inspiring us with terror. . . .

General Maxims

It is the nature of war that what is beneficial to you is detrimental to the enemy and what is of service to him hurts you. It is therefore a maxim never to do, or to omit doing anything as a consequence of his actions, but to consult invariably your own interest only. And you depart from this interest whenever you imitate such measures as he pursues for his benefit. For the same reason it would be wrong for him to follow such steps as you take for your advantage.

The more your troops have been accustomed to camp duties on frontier stations and the more carefully they have been disciplined, the less danger they will be exposed to in the field.

Men must be sufficiently tried before they are led against the enemy.

It is much better to overcome the enemy by imposing upon him famine, surprise or terror than by general actions, for in the latter instance fortune has often a greater share than valor.

Those designs are best of which the enemy are entirely ignorant till the moment of execution. Opportunity in war is often more to be depended on than courage.

To seduce the enemy's soldiers from their allegiance and encourage them to surrender is of especial service, for an adversary is more hurt by desertion than by slaughter.

It is better to have several bodies of reserves than to extend your front too much.

A general is not easily overcome who can form a true judgment of his own and the enemy's forces.

Valor is superior to numbers.

The nature of the ground is often of more consequence than courage.

Few men are born brave; many become so through training and force of discipline.

An army is strengthened by labor and enervated by idleness.

Troops are not to be led to battle unless confident of success.

Novelty and surprise throw an enemy into consternation, but common incidents have no effect.

He who rashly pursues a flying enemy with troops in disorder, seems bent upon throwing away that victory which he had before obtained.

An army unsupplied with grain and other necessary provisions risks being vanquished without striking a blow.

A general whose troops are superior both in number and bravery should engage in the oblong square, which is the first formation.

He who judges himself inferior should advance his right wing obliquely against the enemy's left. This is the second formation.

If your left wing is strongest, you must attack the enemy's right according to the third formation.

The general who can depend on the discipline of his men should begin the engagement by attacking both the enemy's wings at once, the fourth formation.

He whose light infantry is good should cover his center by forming them in its front and charge both the enemy's wings at once. This is the fifth formation.

He who cannot depend either on the number or courage of his own troops, if obliged to engage, should begin the action with his right and endeavor to break the enemy's left, the rest of his army remaining formed in line perpendicular to the front and extended to the rear like a javelin. This is the sixth formation.

If your forces are few and weak in comparison to the enemy, you must make use of the seventh formation and cover one of your flanks either with an eminence, a city, the sea, a river or some protection of that kind.

A general who trusts to his cavalry should choose the proper ground for them and employ them principally in the action.

He who depends on his infantry should choose a situation most proper for them and make full use of them.

When an enemy's spy lurks in the camp, order all your soldiers in the day time to their tents, and he will instantly be apprehended.

On finding that the enemy has notice of your designs, you must immediately alter your plan of operations.

Consult with many on proper measures to be taken, but communicate the plans you intend to put in execution to few, and those only of the most assured fidelity. Or better, trust no one but yourself.

Punishment, and fear thereof, are necessary to keep soldiers in order in quarters; but in the field they are more influenced by hope and rewards.

Good officers never engage in general actions unless induced by opportunity or obliged by necessity.

To distress the enemy more by famine than the sword is a mark of consummate skill.

Many instructions might be given with regard to the cavalry. But as this branch of the service has been brought to perfection since the ancient writers and considerable improvements have been made in their drills and maneuvers, their arms, and the quality and management of their horses, nothing can be collected from those writers' works. Our present mode of discipline is sufficient.

Dispositions for action must be carefully concealed from the enemy, lest they should counteract them and defeat your plans by proper expedients.

PART 3

CHINA

SUN ZI
(fourth century B.C.)

"The art of war is of vital importance to the state," wrote Sun Zi (Sun Tzu). This short treatise sets out principles for the intelligent pursuit of a victorious war based on indirect strategy; economy of means, stratagems, knowledge of the adversary, and psychological action are everything, leaving shock tactics only the job of delivering a well-placed coup de grâce to a totally disoriented enemy. Sun Zi envisages war as taking place in a single society in the framework of generally accepted rules, and as having limited aims. In that sense, we are still before the terrible incursion of the nomads of central Asia, who would soon determine China's defensive strategy behind its Great Wall. Sun Zi had a considerable influence on Chinese and Japanese military traditions. The Art of War *was translated in 1772 by the French Jesuit Joseph Amyot and was a great success, but then was forgotten. Mao Ze-dong's victories drew attention back to this manual of indirect strategy.*

THE ART OF WAR

Sun Tzu said: The art of war is of vital importance to the state.

It is a matter of life and death, a road either to safety or to ruin. Hence it is a subject of inquiry which can on no account be neglected.

The art of war is governed by five constant factors, to be taken into account in one's deliberations, when seeking to determine the conditions obtaining in the field.

These are: (1) The Moral Law; (2) Heaven; (3) Earth; (4) The Commander; (5) Method and Discipline.

From Sun Tzu, *The Art of War*, translated by Lionel Giles (London: Luzac, 1910), reprinted in *Roots of Strategy*, edited by Thomas R. Phillips (London: John Lane the Bodley Head, 1943; reprint, Stackpole Books, 1985), 21–47, 60–63.

The Moral Law causes the people to be in complete accord with their ruler, so that they will follow him regardless of their lives, undismayed by any danger.

Heaven signifies night and day, cold and heat, times and seasons.

Earth comprises distances, great and small; danger and security; open ground and narrow passes; the chances of life and death.

The Commander stands for the virtues of wisdom, sincerity, benevolence, courage and strictness.

By *Method and Discipline* are to be understood the marshaling of the army in its proper subdivisions, the gradations of rank among the officers, the maintenance of roads by which supplies may reach the army, and the control of military expenditure.

These five heads should be familiar to every general; he who knows them will be victorious; he who knows them not will fail.

Therefore, in your deliberations, when seeking to determine the military conditions, let them be made the basis of a comparison, in this wise:

(1) Which of the two sovereigns is imbued with the Moral law?
(2) Which of the two generals has most ability?
(3) With whom lie the advantages derived from Heaven and Earth?
(4) On which side is discipline most rigorously enforced?
(5) Which army is the stronger?
(6) On which side are officers and men most highly trained?
(7) In which army is there the greater constancy both in reward and punishment?

By means of these seven considerations I can forecast victory or defeat.

The general that harkens to my counsel and acts upon it, will conquer—let such a one be retained in command! The general that harkens not to my counsel nor acts upon it, will suffer defeat—let such a one be dismissed! While heeding the profit of my counsel, avail yourself also of any helpful circumstances over and beyond the ordinary rules. According as circumstances are favorable, one should modify one's plans.

All warfare is based on deception. Hence, when able to attack, we must seem unable; when using our forces, we must seem inactive; when we are near, we must make the enemy believe that we are away; when far away, we must make him believe we are near. Hold out baits to entice the enemy. Feign disorder, and crush him.

If he is secure at all points, be prepared for him. If he is superior in strength, evade him. If your opponent is of choleric temper, seek to irritate him. Pretend to be weak, that he may grow arrogant.

If he is taking his ease, give him no rest. If his forces are united, separate them. Attack him where he is unprepared, appear where you are not expected. These military devices, leading to victory, must not be divulged beforehand.

Now the general who wins a battle makes many calculations in his temple ere the battle is fought. The general who loses a battle makes but few calculations beforehand. Thus do many calculations lead to victory, and few calculations to defeat: How much more no calculation at all! It is by attention to this point that I can see who is likely to win or lose.

Waging War

Sun Tzu said: In the operations of war, where there are in the field a thousand swift chariots, as many heavy chariots, and a hundred thousand mail-clad soldiers, with provisions enough to carry them a thousand *li* [2.78 *li* = one mile], the expenditure at home and at the front, including entertainment of guests, small items such as glue and paint, and sums spent on chariots and armour, will reach the total of a thousand ounces of silver per day. Such is the cost of raising an army of 100,000 men.

When you engage in actual fighting, if victory is long in coming, the men's weapons will grow dull and their ardour will be damped. If you lay siege to a town, you will exhaust your strength. Again, if the campaign is protracted, the resources of the state will not be equal to the strain.

Now, when your weapons are dulled, your ardour damped, your strength exhausted and your treasure spent, other chieftains will spring up to take advantage of your extremity. Then no man, however wise, will be able to avert the consequences that must ensue.

Thus, though we have heard of stupid haste in war, cleverness has never been associated with long delays. There is no instance of a country having been benefited from prolonged warfare.

It is only one who is thoroughly acquainted with the evils of war that can thoroughly understand the profitable way of carrying it on. The skillful soldier does not raise a second levy, neither are his supply-wagons loaded more than twice. Bring war material with you from home, but forage on the enemy. Thus the army will have food enough for its needs.

Poverty of the state exchequer causes an army to be maintained by contributions from a distance. Contributing to maintain an army at a distance causes people to be impoverished.

On the other hand, the proximity of an army causes prices to go up; and high prices cause the people's substance to be drained away.

When their substance is drained away, the peasantry will be afflicted by heavy exactions.

With this loss of subsistance and exhaustion of strength, the homes of the people will be stripped bare and three-tenths of their incomes will be dissipated; while Government expenses for broken chariots, worn-out horses, breast-plates and helmets, bows and arrows, spears and shields, protective mantlets, draught-oxen and heavy wagons, will amount to four-tenths of its total revenue.

Hence a wise general makes a point of foraging on the enemy. One cartload of the enemy's provisions is equivalent to twenty of one's own, and likewise a single picul of his provender is equivalent to twenty from one's own store.

Now in order to kill the enemy, our men must be roused to anger; that there may be advantage from defeating the enemy, they must have their rewards.

Therefore in chariot fighting, when ten or more chariots have been taken, those should be rewarded who took the first. Our own flags should be substituted for those of the enemy, and the chariots mingled and used in conjunction with ours. The captured soldiers should be kindly treated and kept. This is called, using the conquered foe to augment one's own strength.

In war, then, let your great object be victory, not lengthy campaigns.

Thus it may be known that the leader of armies is the arbiter of the people's fate, the man on whom depends whether the nation shall be in peace or peril.

Attack by Stratagem

Sun Tzu said: In the practical art of war, the best thing of all is to take the enemy's country whole and intact; to shatter and destroy it is not so good. So, too, it is better to capture an army entire than to destroy it, to capture a regiment, a detachment or a company entire than to destroy them.

Hence to fight and conquer in all your battles is not supreme excellence; supreme excellence consists in breaking the enemy's resistance without fighting.

Thus the highest form of generalship is to baulk the enemy's plans; the next best is to prevent the junction of the enemy's forces; the next in order is to attack the enemy's army in the field; and the worst policy of all is to besiege walled cities.

The rule is, not to besiege walled cities if it can possibly be avoided. The preparation of mantlets, movable shelters, and various implements of war, will take up three whole months; and the piling up of mounds over against the walls will take three months more.

The general, unable to control his irritation, will launch his men to the assault like swarming ants, with the result that one-third of his men are slain, while the town remains untaken. Such are the disastrous effects of a siege.

Therefore the skillful leader subdues the enemy's troops without any fighting; he captures their cities without laying siege to them; he overthrows their kingdom without lengthy operations in the field.

With his forces intact he will dispute the mastery of the empire, and thus, without losing a man, his triumph will be complete. This is the method of attacking by stratagem.

It is the rule in war, if our forces are ten to the enemy's one, to surround him; if five to one, to attack him; if twice as numerous, to divide our army into two.

If equally matched, we can offer battle; if slightly inferior in numbers, we can avoid the enemy; if quite unequal in every way, we can flee from him. Hence, though an obstinate fight may be made by a small force, in the end it must be captured by the larger force.

Now the general is the bulwark of the state: if the bulwark is complete at all points, the state will be strong; if the bulwark is defective, the state will be weak.

There are three ways in which a ruler can bring misfortune upon his army:

(1) By commanding the army to advance or to retreat, being ignorant of the fact that it cannot obey. This is called hobbling the army.

(2) By attempting to govern an army in the same way as he administers a kingdom, being ignorant of the conditions which obtain in an army. This causes restlessness in the soldier's minds.

(3) By employing the officers of his army without discrimination, through ignorance of the military principle of adaptation to circumstances. This shakes the confidence of the soldiers.

But when the army is restless and distrustful, trouble is sure to come from other feudal princes. This is simply bringing anarchy into the army, and flinging victory away.

Thus we may know that there are five essentials for victory: (1) He will win who knows when to fight and when not to fight. (2) He will win who knows how to handle both superior and inferior forces. (3) He will win whose army is animated by the same spirit throughout all ranks. (4) He will win who, prepared himself, waits to take the enemy unprepared. (5) He will win who has military capacity and is not interfered with by the sovereign. Victory lies in the knowledge of those five points.

Hence the saying: If you know the enemy and know yourself, you need not fear the result of a hundred battles. If you know yourself but not the enemy, for every victory gained you will also suffer a defeat. If you know neither the enemy nor yourself, you will succumb in every battle.

Tactical Dispositions

Sun Tzu said: The good fighters of old, first put themselves beyond the possibility of defeat, and then waited for an opportunity of defeating the enemy.

To secure ourselves against defeat lies in our own hands, but the opportunity of defeating the enemy is provided by the enemy himself.

Thus the good fighter is able to secure himself against defeat, but cannot make certain of defeating the enemy.

Hence the saying: One may *know* how to conquer without being able to do it.

Security against defeat implies defensive tactics; ability to defeat the enemy means taking the offensive.

Standing on the defensive indicates insufficient strength; attacking, a superabundance of strength.

The general who is skilled in defense hides in the most secret recesses of the earth; he who is skilled in attack flashes forth from the topmost heights of heaven. Thus on the one hand we have ability to protect ourselves; on the other, a victory that is complete.

To see victory only when it is within the ken of the common herd is not the acme of excellence. Neither is it the acme of excellence if you fight and conquer and the whole empire says, "Well done!"

To lift an autumn hair is no sign of great strength; to see sun and moon is no sign of sharp sight; to hear the noise of thunder is no sign of a quick ear. What the ancients called a clever fighter is one who not only wins, but excels in winning with ease.

Hence his victories bring him neither reputation for wisdom nor credit for courage. He wins his battles by making no mistakes. Making no mistakes is what establishes the certainty of victory, for it means conquering an enemy that is already defeated.

Hence the skillful fighter puts himself into a position which makes defeat impossible, and does not miss the moment for defeating the enemy.

Thus it is that in war the victorious strategist seeks battle after the victory has been won, whereas he who is destined to defeat first fights and afterwards looks for victory.

The consummate leader cultivates the moral law, and strictly adheres to method and discipline; thus it is in his power to control success.

In respect of military method, we have, firstly, Measurement; secondly, Estimation of quantity; thirdly, Calculation; fourthly, Balancing of chances; fifthly, Victory.

Measurement owes its existence to Earth; Estimation of quantity to Measurement; Calculation to Estimation of Quantity; Balancing of chances to Calculation; and Victory to Balancing of chances.

A victorious army opposed to a routed one, is as a pound's weight placed in the scale against a single grain. The onrush of a conquering force is like the bursting of pent-up waters into a chasm a thousand fathoms deep. So much for tactical dispositions.

Energy

Sun Tzu said: The control of a large force is the same in principle as the control of a few men: it is merely a question of dividing up their numbers.

Fighting with a large army under your command is nowise different from fighting with a small one: it is merely a question of instituting signs and signals.

To ensure that your whole host may withstand the brunt of the enemy's attack and remain unshaken—this is effected by maneuvers direct and indirect.

That the impact of your army may be like a grindstone dashed against an egg—that is effected by the science of weak points and strong.

In all fighting, the direct method may be used for joining battle, but indirect methods will be needed in order to secure victory.

Indirect tactics, efficiently applied, are inexhaustible as Heaven and Earth, unending as the flow of rivers and streams; like the sun and moon, they end but to begin anew; like the four seasons, they pass but to return once more.

There are not more than five musical notes, yet the combinations of these five give rise to more melodies than can ever be heard. There are not more than five primary colors, yet in combination they produce more hues than can ever be seen. There are not more than five cardinal tastes, yet combinations of them yield more flavours than can ever be tasted.

In battle, there are not more than two methods of attack—the direct and indirect; yet these two in combination give rise to an endless series of maneuvers. The direct and indirect lead on to each other in turn. It is like moving in a circle—you never come to an end. Who can exhaust the possibilities of their combination?

The onset of troops is like the rush of a torrent which will even roll stones along its course.

The quality of decision is like the well-timed swoop of a falcon which enables it to strike and destroy its victim.

Therefore the good fighter will be terrible in his onset, and prompt in his decision.

Energy may be likened to the bending of a cross-bow; decision, to the releasing of the trigger.

Amid the turmoil and tumult of battle, there may be seeming disorder and yet no real disorder at all; amid confusion and chaos, your array may be without head or tail, yet it will be proof against defeat.

Simulated disorder postulates perfect discipline; simulated fear postulates courage; simulated weakness postulates strength.

Hiding order beneath the cloak of disorder is simply a question of subdivision; concealing courage under a show of timidity presupposes a fund of latent energy; masking strength with weakness is to be effected by tactical dispositions.

Thus one who is skillful at keeping the enemy on the move maintains deceitful appearances, according to which the enemy will act.

By holding out baits, he keeps him on the march; then with a body of picked men he lies in wait for him.

The clever combatant looks to the effect of combined energy, and does not require too much from individuals. Hence his ability to pick out the right men and to utilize combined energy.

When he utilizes combined energy, his fighting men become as it were like unto rolling logs or stones. For it is the nature of a log or stone to remain motionless on level ground, and to move when on a slope; if four cornered, to come to a standstill, but if round-shaped to go rolling down.

Thus the energy developed by good fighting men is as the momentum of a round stone rolled down a mountain thousands of feet in height. So much on the subject of energy.

Weak Points and Strong

Sun Tzu said: Whoever is first in the field and awaits the coming of the enemy, will be fresh for the fight; whoever is second in the field and has to hasten to the battle, will arrive exhausted.

Therefore the clever combatant imposes his will on the enemy, but does not allow the enemy's will to be imposed on him.

By holding out advantages to him, he can cause the enemy to approach of his own accord; or by inflicting damage, he can make it impossible for the enemy to draw near.

If the enemy is taking his ease, he can harass him; if well supplied he can starve him out; if quietly encamped, he can force him to move.

Appear at points which the enemy must hasten to defend; march swiftly to places where you are not expected.

An army may march great distances without distress if it marches through country where the enemy is not.

You can be sure of succeeding in your attacks if you attack places which are not defended. You can insure the safety of your defense if you hold only positions that cannot be attacked.

Hence the general is skillful in attack whose opponent does not know what to defend; and he is skillful in defense whose opponent does not know what to attack.

O divine art of subtlety and secrecy! Through you we learn to be invisible, through you inaudible; and hence hold the enemy's fate in our hands.

You may advance and be absolutely irresistible, if you make for the enemy's weak points; you may retire and be safe from pursuit if your movements are more rapid than those of the enemy.

If we wish to fight, the enemy can be forced to an engagement even though he be sheltered behind a high rampart and a deep ditch. All we need to do is to attack some other place which he will be obliged to relieve.

If we do not wish to fight, we can prevent the enemy from engaging us even though the lines of our encampment be merely traced on the ground. All we need to do is to throw something odd and unaccountable in his way.

By discovering the enemy's dispositions and remaining invisible ourselves, we can keep our forces concentrated while the enemy must be divided.

We can form a single united body, while the enemy must split up into fractions. Hence there will be a whole pitted against separate parts of a whole, which means that we shall be many to the enemy's few.

And if we are thus able to attack an inferior force with a superior one, our opponents will be in dire straits.

The spot where we intend to fight must not be made known; for then the enemy will have to prepare against a possible attack at several different points; and his forces being thus distributed in many directions, the numbers we shall have to face at any given point will be proportionately few.

For should the enemy strengthen his van, he will weaken his rear; should he strengthen his rear, he will weaken his van; should he strengthen his left, he will weaken his right; should he strengthen his right, he will weaken his left. If he sends reinforcements everywhere, he will be everywhere weak.

Numerical weakness comes from having to prepare against possible attacks; numerical strength, from compelling our adversary to make these preparations against us.

Knowing the place and time of the coming battle, we may concentrate from great distances in order to fight.

But if neither time nor place be known, then the left wing will be impotent to succor the right, the right equally impotent to succor the left, the van unable to relieve the rear, or the rear to support the van. How much more so if the furthest portions of the army are anything under a hundred *li* apart, and even the nearest are separated by several *li*.

Though according to my estimate the soldiers of Yüeh exceed our own in number, that shall advantage them nothing in the matter of victory. I say then that victory can be achieved.

Though the enemy be stronger in numbers, we may prevent him from fighting. Scheme so as to discover his plans and the likelihood of their success.

Rouse him, and learn the principle of his activity or inactivity. Force him to reveal himself, so as to find out his vulnerable spots.

Carefully compare the opposing army with our own, so that you may know where strength is superabundant and where it is deficient.

In making tactical dispositions, the highest pitch you can attain is to conceal them; conceal your dispositions and you will be safe from the prying of the subtlest of spies, from the machinations of the wisest brains.

How victory may be produced for them out of the enemy's own tactics— that is what the multitude cannot comprehend.

All men can see these tactics whereby I conquer, but what none can see is the strategy out of which victory is evolved.

Do not repeat the tactics which have gained you one victory, but let your methods be regulated by the infinite variety of circumstances.

Military tactics are like unto water; for water in its natural course runs away from high places and hastens downwards. So in war, the way to avoid what is strong is to strike what is weak.

Water shapes its course according to the ground over which it flows; the soldier works out his victory in relation to the foe whom he is facing.

Therefore, just as water retains no constant shape, so in warfare there are no constant conditions.

He who can modify his tactics in relation to his opponent and thereby succeed in winning, may be called a heaven-born captain.

The five elements [water, fire, wood, metal, and earth] are not always equally prominent; the four seasons make way for each other in turn. There are short days and long; the moon has its periods of waning and waxing.

Maneuvering

Sun Tzu said: In war, the general receives his commands from the sovereign.

Having collected an army and concentrated his forces, he must blend and harmonize the different elements thereof before pitching his camp.

After that, comes the tactical maneuvering, than which there is nothing more difficult. The difficulty of tactical maneuvering consists in turning the devious into the direct, and misfortune into gain.

Thus, to take a long circuitous route, after enticing the enemy out of the way, and though starting after him, to contrive to reach the goal before him, shows knowledge of the artifice of *deviation*.

Maneuvering with an army is advantageous; with an undisciplined multitude, most dangerous.

If you set a fully equipped army in march in order to snatch an advantage, the chances are that you will be too late. On the other hand, to detach a flying column for the purpose involves the sacrifice of its baggage and stores.

Thus if you order your men to roll up their buff-coats, and make forced marches without halting day or night, covering double the usual distance at a stretch, doing a hundred *li* in order to wrest an advantage, the leaders of your three divisions will fall into the hands of the enemy.

The stronger men will be in front, the jaded ones will fall behind, and on this plan only one-tenth of your army will reach its destination.

If you march fifty *li* in order to outmaneuver the enemy, you will lose the leader of your first division, and only half your force will reach its goal.

If you march thirty *li* with the same object, two-thirds of your army will arrive.

We may take it then that an army without its baggage train is lost; without provisions it is lost; without bases of supply it is lost.

We cannot enter into alliances until we are acquainted with the designs of our neighbors.

We are not fit to lead an army on the march unless we are familiar with the face of the country—its mountains and forests, its pitfalls.

We shall be unable to turn natural advantages to account unless we make use of local guides.

In war, practice dissimulation, and you will succeed. Move only if there is a real advantage to be gained.

Whether to concentrate or to divide your troops must be decided by circumstances.

Let your rapidity be that of the wind, your compactness that of the forest. In raiding and plundering be like fire, in immovability like a mountain.

Let your plans be dark and impenetrable as night and when you move, fall like a thunderbolt.

When you plunder a countryside, let the spoil be divided amongst your men; when you capture new territory, cut it up into allotments for the benefit of the soldiery.

Ponder and deliberate before you make a move.

He will conquer who has learnt the artifice of deviation. Such is the art of maneuvering.

The *Book of Army Management* says: On the field of battle the spoken word does not carry far enough: hence the institution of gongs and drums. Nor can ordinary objects be seen clearly enough: hence the institution of banners and flags.

Gongs and drums, banners and flags, are means whereby the ears and eyes of the host may be focussed on one particular point.

The host thus forming a single united body, it is impossible either for the brave to advance alone, or for the cowardly to retreat alone. This is the art of handling large masses of men.

In night-fighting, then, make much use of signal fires and drums, and in fighting by day, of flags and banners, as a means of influencing the ears and eyes of your army.

A whole army may be robbed of its spirit; a commander-in-chief may be robbed of his presence of mind.

Now a soldier's spirit is keenest in the morning; by noonday it has begun to flag; and in the evening his mind is bent only on returning to camp.

A clever general, therefore, avoids an army when its spirit is keen, but attacks it when it is sluggish and inclined to return. This is the art of studying moods.

Disciplined and calm, to await the appearance of disorder and hubbub amongst the enemy—this is the art of retaining self possession.

To be near the goal while the enemy is still far from it, to wait at ease while the enemy is toiling and struggling, to be well fed while the enemy is famished—this is the art of husbanding one's strength.

To refrain from intercepting an enemy whose banners are in perfect order, to refrain from attacking an army drawn up in calm and confident array—this is the art of studying circumstances.

It is a military axiom not to advance uphill against the enemy, nor to oppose him when he comes downhill.

Do not pursue an enemy who simulates flight; do not attack soldiers whose temper is keen.

Do not swallow a bait offered by the enemy. Do not interfere with an army that is returning home.

When you surround an army leave an outlet free. Do not press a desperate foe too hard.

Such is the art of warfare.

Variation of Tactics

Sun Tzu said: In war, the general receives his commands from the sovereign, collects his army and concentrates his forces.

When in difficult country do not encamp. In country where high roads intersect join hands with your allies. Do not linger in dangerously isolated positions. In hemmed-in situations, you must resort to stratagem. In a desperate position, you must fight.

There are roads which must not be followed, armies which must not be attacked, towns which must not be besieged, positions which must not be contested, commands of the sovereign which must not be obeyed.

The general who thoroughly understands the advantages that accompany variation of tactics knows how to handle his troops.

The general who does not understand these may be well acquainted with the configuration of the country, yet he will not be able to turn his knowledge to practical account.

So, the student of war who is unversed in the art of varying his plans, even though he be acquainted with the Five Advantages will fail to make the best use of his men.

Hence in the wise leader's plans, considerations of advantage will be blended together. If our expectation of advantage be tempered in this way, we may succeed in accomplishing the essential part of our schemes.

If, on the other hand, in the midst of difficulties we are always ready to seize an advantage, we may extricate ourselves from misfortune.

Reduce the hostile chiefs by inflicting damage on them; make trouble for them, and keep them constantly engaged; hold out specious allurements, and make them rush to any given point.

The art of war teaches us to rely not on the likelihood of the enemy's not coming, but on our own readiness to receive him; not on the chance of his not attacking, but rather on the fact that we have made our position unassailable.

There are five dangerous faults which may affect a general: (1) Recklessness, which leads to destruction; (2) cowardice, which leads to capture; (3) a hasty temper that can be provoked by insults; (4) a delicacy of honor that is sensitive to shame; (5) over-solicitude for his men, which exposes him to worry and trouble. These are the five besetting sins of a general, ruinous to the conduct of war.

When an army is overthrown and its leader slain, the cause will surely be found among the five dangerous faults. Let them be a subject of meditation.

The Army on the March

Sun Tzu said: We now come to the question of encamping the army, and observing signs of the enemy. Pass quickly over mountains, and keep in the neighborhood of valleys.

Camp in high places. Do not climb heights in order to fight. So much for mountain warfare.

After crossing a river, you should get far away from it.

When an invading force crosses a river in its onward march, do not advance to meet it in mid-stream. It will be best to let the army get across and then deliver your attack.

If you are anxious to fight, you should not go to meet the invader near a river which he has to cross.

Moor your craft higher up than the enemy and facing the sun. Do not move upstream to meet the enemy. So much for river warfare.

In crossing salt-marshes, your sole concern should be to get over them quickly, without any delay.

If forced to fight in a salt-marsh, you should have the water and grass near you, and get your back to a clump of trees. So much for operations in salt-marshes.

In dry, level country, take up an easily accessible position with rising ground to your right and on your rear, so that the danger may be in front, and safety lie behind. So much for campaigning in flat country.

These are the four useful branches of military knowledge which enabled the Yellow Emperor to vanquish four several sovereigns.

All armies prefer high ground to low, and sunny places to dark. If you are careful of your men, and camp on hard ground, the army will be free from disease of every kind, and this will spell victory.

When you come to a hill or a bank, occupy the sunny side, with the slope on your right rear. Thus you will at once act for the benefit of your soldiers and utilize the natural advantages of the ground.

When, in consequence of heavy rains up-country, a river which you wish to ford is swollen and flecked with foam, you must wait until it subsides. Country in which there are precipitous cliffs with torrents running between, deep natural hollows, confined places, tangled thickets, quagmires and crevasses, should be left with all possible speed and not approached.

While we keep away from such places, we should get the enemy to approach them; while we face them, we should let the enemy have them on his rear.

If in the neighborhood of your camp there should be any hilly country, ponds surrounded by aquatic grass, hollow basins filled with reeds, or woods with thick undergrowth, they must be carefully routed out and searched; for these are places where men in ambush or insidious spies are likely to be lurking.

When the enemy is close at hand and remains quiet, he is relying on the natural strength of his position.

When he keeps aloof and tries to provoke a battle, he is anxious for the other side to advance.

If his place of encampment is easy of access, he is tendering a bait.

Movement amongst the trees of a forest shows that the enemy is advancing. The appearance of a number of screens in the midst of thick grass means that the enemy wants to make us suspicious.

The rising of birds in their flight is the sign of an ambuscade. Startled beasts indicate that a sudden attack is coming.

When there is dust rising in a high column, it is the sign of chariots advancing; when the dust is low, but spread over a wide area, it betokens the approach of infantry. When it branches out in different directions, it shows that parties have been sent out to collect firewood. A few clouds of dust moving to and fro signify that the army is encamping.

Humble words and increased preparations are signs that the enemy is about to advance. Violent language and driving forward as if to the attack are signs that he will retreat.

When the light chariots come out and take up a position on the wings, it is a sign that the enemy is forming for battle.

Peace proposals unaccompanied by a sworn covenant indicate a plot.

When there is much running about it means that the critical moment has come.

When some are seen advancing and some retreating, it is a lure.

When soldiers stand leaning on their spears, they are faint from want of food.

If those who are sent to draw water begin by drinking themselves, the army is suffering from thirst.

If the enemy sees an advantage to be gained and makes no effort to secure it, the soldiers are exhausted.

If birds gather on any spot, it is unoccupied. Clamour by night betokens nervousness.

If there is disturbance in the camp, the general's authority is weak. If the banners and flags are shifted about, sedition is afoot. If the officers are angry, it means that the men are weary.

When an army feeds its horses with grain and kills its cattle for food, and when the men do not hang their cooking pots over the camp-fires, showing that they will not return to their tents, you may know that they are determined to fight to the death.

The sight of men whispering together in small knots and speaking in subdued tones points to dissatisfaction amongst the rank and file.

Too frequent rewards signify that the enemy is at the end of his resources; too many punishments betray a condition of dire distress.

To begin by bluster, but afterwards to take fright at the enemy's numbers, shows supreme lack of intelligence.

When convoys are sent with compliments in their mouths, it is a sign that the enemy wishes for a truce.

If the enemy's troops march up angrily and remain facing ours for a long time without either joining battle or taking themselves off again, the situation is one that demands great vigilance and circumspection.

If our troops are no more in number than the enemy, that is amply sufficient; it means that no direct attack can be made. What we can do is simply to concentrate all our available strength, keep a close watch on the enemy, and obtain reinforcements.

He who exercises no forethought but makes light of his opponents is sure to be captured by them.

If soldiers are punished before they have grown attached to you, they will not prove submissive; and, unless submissive, they will be practically useless. If, when the soldiers have become attached to you, punishments are not enforced, they will still be useless.

Therefore soldiers must be treated in the first instance with humanity, but kept under control by means of iron discipline. This is a certain road to victory.

If in training soldiers commands are habitually enforced, the army will be well disciplined.

If a general shows confidence in his men but always insists on his orders being obeyed, the gain will be mutual. . . .

The Use of Spies

Sun Tzu said: Raising a host of a hundred thousand men and marching them great distances entails heavy loss on the people and a drain on the resources of the state. The daily expenditure will amount to a thousand ounces of silver. There will be commotion at home and abroad, and men will drop down exhausted on the highways. As many as seven hundred thousand families will be impeded in their labor.

Hostile armies may face each other for years, striving for victory which is decided in a single day. This being so, to remain in ignorance of the enemy's condition simply because one grudges the outlay of a hundred ounces of silver in honours and emoluments, is the height of inhumanity.

One who acts thus is no leader of men, no present help to his sovereign, no master of victory.

Thus, what enables the wise sovereign and the good general to strike and conquer, and achieve things beyond the reach of ordinary men, is *foreknowledge*.

Now this foreknowledge cannot be elicited from spirits; it cannot be obtained inductively from experience, nor by any deductive calculation.

Knowledge of the enemy's dispositions can only be obtained from other men.

Hence the use of spies, of whom there are five classes: (1) Local spies; (2) inward spies; (3) converted spies; (4) doomed spies; (5) surviving spies.

When these five kinds of spy are all at work, none can discover the secret system. This is called "divine manipulation of the threads." It is the sovereign's most precious faculty.

Having *local spies* means employing the services of the inhabitants of a district.

Having *inward spies,* making use of officials of the enemy.

Having *converted spies,* getting hold of the enemy's spies and using them for our own purposes.

Having *doomed spies,* doing certain things openly for purposes of deception, and allowing our own spies to know of them and report them to the enemy.

Surviving spies, finally, are those who bring back news from the enemy's camp.

Hence it is that with none in the whole army are more intimate relations to be maintained than with spies. None should be more liberally rewarded. In no other business should greater secrecy be preserved. Spies cannot be usefully employed without certain intuitive sagacity.

They cannot be properly managed without benevolence and straightforwardness.

Without subtle ingenuity of mind, one cannot make certain of the truth of their reports. Be subtle! and use your spies for every kind of business.

If a secret piece of news is divulged by a spy before the time is ripe, he must be put to death together with the man to whom the secret was told.

Whether the object be to crush an army, to storm a city, or to assassinate an individual, it is always necessary to begin by finding out the names of the attendants, the aides-de-camp, the door-keepers and sentries of the general in command. Our spies must be commissioned to ascertain these.

The enemy's spies who have come to spy on us must be sought out, tempted with bribes, led away and comfortably housed. Thus they will become converted spies and available for our service.

It is through the information brought by the converted spy that we are able to acquire and employ local and inward spies.

It is owing to his information, again, that we can cause the doomed spy to carry false tidings to the enemy.

Lastly, it is by his information that the surviving spy can be used on appointed occasions.

The end and aim of spying in all its five varieties is knowledge of the enemy; and this knowledge can only be derived, in the first instance, from the converted spy. Hence it is essential that the converted spy be treated with the utmost liberality.

Of old, the rise of the Yin dynasty was due to I Chih, who had served under the Hsia. Likewise, the rise of the Chou dynasty was due to Lü Ya, who had served under the Yin.

Hence it is only the enlightened ruler and the wise general who will use the highest intelligence of the army for purposes of spying, and thereby they achieve great results. Spies are a most important element in war, because on them depends an army's ability to move.

SHANG YANG
(fourth century B.C.)

Shang Yang, a statesman of the western Chinese state of Qin (Ch'in), was the first theoretician of the school later known as Legalism, which took a pessimistic view of society and believed in the need to control it strictly in order to avoid disorder.

THE BOOK OF LORD SHANG

The Method of Warfare

Generally in the method of warfare, the fundamental principle consists in making government measures supremely prevalent. If this is done, then the people concerned will have no disputes, and having no disputes, they will have no thought of self-interest, but will have the interest of the ruler in mind. Therefore, a real king, through his measures, will cause people to be fearful in fights between various cities, but brave in wars against external foes. If people have been trained to attack dangers with energy, they will, as a result, think lightly of death. Should the enemy be routed as soon as the engagement has begun, and should he not stop in his rout, abstain from further pursuit. Therefore does [Sun Zi's?] *Art of War* say: "In a big battle, in the event of victory, pursue the fugitives not further than 10 *li;* in a small battle, in the event of victory, pursue the fugitives not further than 5 *li.*" When hostilities begin, weigh the strength of the enemy; if your organization is not equal to his, do not engage him in battle; if your provisions are not equal to his, do not protract the war; if the enemy is numerically strong, do not invade his territory; if the enemy is in every way your inferior, attack him without hesitation. Therefore it

From *The Book of Lord Shang,* translated by Dr. J. J. L. Duyvendak (London: Arthur Probsthain, 1928; Chicago: University of Chicago Press, 1963), 244-59. Copyright © 1928 by Arthur Probsthain. Reprinted by permission of the University of Chicago Press and Arthur Probsthain.

is said: "The great rule of an army is prudence." By estimating the strength of the enemy and by examining one's own hosts, victory or defeat may be known beforehand.

The army of a real king does not boast of victory, nor does it harbour rancour for defeat. That it does not boast of victory, is because it ascribes it to its clever tactics; that it does not harbour rancour for defeat, is because it knows why it has failed. If the relative strength of the armies is well-matched, the side that has clever leadership will win, and the side that has inferior leadership will lose. If the organization has its origin in the calculations made in the temple, then it will win, whether the leadership is clever or inferior. He who holds victorious tactics will be so strong that he will attain supremacy. If people are submissive and obey their ruler, then the country will become rich and the army victorious, and if this state of affairs is maintained for long, he will surely attain supremacy.

But it is a mistake for an army to penetrate deeply into the enemy's country, in difficult and unsurmountable terrain and cut off in a cul-de-sac; the men will become exhausted, hungry and thirsty as well, and will, moreover, fall victims to disease. This is the way to defeat. Therefore he who intends to direct the people . . . and he who mounts a good horse cannot but be on his guard.

The Establishment of Fundamentals

Generally, in the utilizing of soldiers, there are three stages to victory; prior to the outbreak of hostilities, laws should be fixed; laws being fixed, they should become the custom; when they have become customary, supplies should be provided. These three things should be done within the country before the soldiers can be sent abroad. For performing these three things, there are two conditions; the first is to support the law, so that it can be applied; the second is to obtain the right men in appointments, so that the law can be established. For reliance on masses is said to be the assembling of a mob; reliance on outward appearances is said to be smartness; reliance on fame and sight is said to be deceitfulness. If one relies on any one of these three, one's soldiers may be captured. Therefore is it said: "The strong are unbending, they fight for what they desire. By fighting, their strength develops to the full, and thus they are prepared. In this way, they have no rival in the four seas, and by order prevailing, products are accumulated; by the accumulation of products, it is possible for the rewards to be big." If rewards are uniform, rank will be honoured; if rank is honoured, rewards will bring profit. Therefore is it said: "The army, being based on a state of order, there is a marvellous result; custom, being based on law, ten thousand changes of circumstances are brought about; a condition of supremacy being based upon the mind, it is outwardly manifested in a condition of preparedness. If these three points of view are all taken into consideration, the result will be that the strong may be firmly established." Thus orderly government is the necessary result of strength, and strength again of orderly government; orderly government of riches, and riches again of orderly government; riches of strength and strength again of riches. Therefore is it said: "The way to orderly government and strength is to discuss fundamentals."

Military Defense

A state that has to fight on four fronts values defense, and a state that rests against the sea values attack. For, if a state that fights on four fronts is fond of raising soldiers, it will be in a dangerous position, as it has to resist four neighbours. As soon as a country with four neighbours begins hostilities, four countries mobilize armies; therefore is it said that the country is in a dangerous position. If a state that has to fight on four fronts is unable to raise, from a city of ten thousand houses, an army of more than ten thousand men, then the state will be in a dangerous position. Therefore is it said: "A state that has to fight on four fronts should concern itself with defensive warfare." In defending walled cities, the best way is, with the strength of the worn-out men, to fight the fresh strength of the invaders. It is assaults upon walled cities that wear out the strength of men. So long as the walled cities have not all been razed, the invaders have no means of penetrating the country. This is meant by the saying that the strength of worn-out men should fight the fresh strength of the invading force. But when the walled cities have all been razed and the foreign army thus finds the means of penetrating, then certainly it will be exhausted, and the people within the country will be rested. Fighting with rested strength against those of exhausted strength is said to be: fighting with the strength of fresh men against the worn-out strength of the invading forces. All these are called the misfortunes attendant upon the besieging of walled cities. It is regarded as a misfortune that always, in capturing cities, the strength of the army is worn out. In these three things, misfortune is due, not to insufficient effort, but to mistaken generalship.

The way to hold a city is to have abundant strength. Therefore is it said: "When the invading force musters its levies, mobilize as many as three armies, and divide them according to the number of the chariots of the invading force." Of these three armies, one should be formed of able-bodied men, one of able-bodied women, and one of the old and feeble men and women. These are called the three armies. Cause the army of able-bodied men, with abundant provisions and sharp weapons, to marshall themselves, and to await the enemy; cause the able-bodied women, with abundant provisions and ramparts at their backs, to marshall themselves and to await orders, so as to make, at the approach of the invaders, earthworks as an obstruction, and traps, chevaux-de-frise and pitfalls, to pull down the supporting beams and to tear down the houses, to transport what is transportable, and to burn what is untransportable, so that the invaders are not able to make use thereof in their attack. Cause the army of the old and feeble to guard the oxen, horses, sheep, and swine, and to collect all that is consumable of plants and water, to feed them therewith, so as to obtain food for the able-bodied men and women. But see to it carefully that the three armies do not intermingle. If the able-bodied men mingle with the army of the able-bodied women, they will attach great value to the safety of the women and wicked people will have opportunities for intrigue, with the result that the state will perish. Taking pleasure in the women's company, the men will be afraid of disturbing reports and so not even the brave will fight. If the able-bodied men and women intermingle with the army of the old and feeble, then the old will arouse the compassion of the able-bodied, and the feeble the pity of the strong. Compassion and pity in the heart cause brave people to be more anxious and fearful people not to fight. Therefore is it said: "See to it carefully that the three armies do not intermingle." This is the way to have abundant strength.

Making Orders Strict

If orders are made strict, orderly government is not delayed, and if laws are equable, officials are not wicked. Once the law is fixed, one should not damage it with virtuous words; if men of merit are appointed to office, people will have little to say, but if men of virtue are appointed to office, people will have much to say. The practice of good government begins with making judgments. Where five hamlets are the unit for judgments, supremacy is attained; where ten hamlets are the unit for judgments, there is merely strength. He who procrastinates in creating order will be dismembered. Govern by punishments and wage war by rewards; seek transgressors and do not seek the virtuous. . . . If in the country there are no wicked people, there is no wicked trade in the capital. If affairs are many and secondary things are numerous, if agriculture is relaxed and criminals gain the upper hand, then the country will certainly be dismembered.

If the people have a surplus of grain, cause them to obtain office and rank by means of their cereals; if through their own efforts they can count upon obtaining office and rank, farmers will not be lazy.

If a tube of no more than four inches has no bottom, it can certainly not be filled; to confer office, to give rank and to grant salaries, without regard to merit, is like having no bottom.

If a state, when poor, applies itself to war, the poison will originate on the enemy's side, and it will not have the six parasites, but will certainly be strong. If a state, when rich, does not apply itself to war, the poison is transferred to its own interior, and it will have the six kinds of parasites and will certainly be weak. If the state confers office and gives rank according to merit, it may be said to be planning with complete wisdom, and fighting with complete courage. Such a country will certainly have no equal. If a state confers office and gives rank according to merit, then government measures will be simple and words will be few. This may be said to be abolishing laws by means of the law and abolishing words by means of words. But if a state confers office and gives rank according to the six parasites, then government measures will be complicated and words will arise. This may be said to be bringing about laws by means of the law and causing volubility by means of words. Then the prince will devote himself to talking; officials will be distracted with ruling the wicked; wicked officials will gain their own way, and those who have merit will retire more daily. This may be said to be failure. When one has to observe ten rules, there is confusion; when one has only one to observe, there is order. When the law is fixed, then those who are fond of practising the six parasites perish. If people occupy themselves entirely with agriculture, the state is rich; if the six parasites are not practised, then soldiers and people will, without exception, vie with one another for encouragement and will be glad to be employed by their ruler; the people within the borders will vie with one another to regard it as glorious and none will regard it as disgraceful. Following upon this comes the condition where people will do it because they are encouraged by means of rewards and restrained by means of punishments. But the worst case is when people hate it, are anxious about it, and are ashamed of it; then they adorn their outer appearances and are engaged in talking; they are ashamed of taking a position and exalt culture. In this way they shun agriculture and war, and outside interests being thus furnished, it will be a perilous position for the country. To have people dying of hunger and cold, and to have unwillingness to fight for the sake of profit and emolument, are usual occurrences in a perishing state. The six parasites are: rites and music, odes and history, moral culture and virtue, filial piety and brotherly love, sincerity and faith, chastity and integrity, benevolence and righteousness, criticism of the army and being ashamed of fighting. If there are these twelve things, the ruler is unable to make people farm and fight, and then the state will be so poor that it will be dismembered. If these twelve things come together, then it may be said that the prince's administration is not stronger than his ministers and that the administration of his officials is not stronger than his people. This is said to be a condition where the six parasites are stronger than the government. When these twelve gain an attachment, then dismemberment ensues.

Therefore to make a country prosperous, these twelve things should not be practised, then the state will have much strength and no one in the empire will be able to invade it. When its soldiers march out, they will capture their objective, and, having captured it, will be able to hold it. When it keeps its soldiers in reserve and does not attack, it will certainly become rich. The court officials do not reject any merits, however few they may be, nor do they detract from any merits, however many they may be. Office and rank are obtained according to the acquired merit, and even though there may be sophistical talk, it will be impossible thereby to obtain undue precedence. This is said to be government by statistics. In attacking with force, ten points are gained for every one point undertaken, but in attacking with words, a hundred are lost for every one marched out. If a state loves force, it is said to attack with what is difficult; if a state loves words, it is said to attack with what is easy. If penalties are heavy and rewards few, then the ruler loves his people and they will die for him; if rewards are heavy and penalties light, then the ruler does not love his people nor will they die for him.

If the profit disappears through one outlet only, the state will have no equal; if it disappears through two outlets, the state will have only half the profit; but if the profit disappears through ten outlets, the state will not be preserved. If heavy penalties are clear, there will be great control, but if they are not clear, there will be the six parasites. If the six kinds of parasites come together, then the people are not fit for employment. Therefore, in a prosperous country, when punishments are applied, the people will be closely associated with the ruler, and when rewards are applied they will reap profit.

In applying punishments, light offences should be punished heavily; if light offences do not appear, heavy offences will not come. This is said to be abolishing penalties by means of penalties, and if penalties are abolished, affairs will succeed. If crimes are serious and penalties light, penalties will appear and trouble will arise. This is said to be bringing about penalties by means of penalties, and such a state will surely be dismembered.

A sage-prince understands what is essential in affairs, and therefore in his administration of the people, there is that which is most essential. For the fact, that uniformity in the manipulating of rewards and punishments supports moral virtue, is connected with human psychology. A sage-prince, by his ruling of men, is certain to win their hearts; consequently he is able to use force. Force produces strength, strength produces prestige, prestige produces virtue, and so virtue has its origin in force, which a sage-prince alone possesses, and therefore he is able to transmit benevolence and righteousness to the empire.

SSU-MA CH'IEN

(C. 145–C. 86 B.C.)

Ssu-ma Ch'ien was the author of Shih chi *(Records of the Historian), a work that has been a source of inspiration for many Chinese writers. He was born in Shanxi; his father was "great historian" at Xi'an, the Han capital, and Ssu-ma Ch'ien succeeded him in that office at the age of thirty-eight. His history is a monumental work, comprising twelve annals, ten tables, eight treatises, thirty "hereditary houses," and seventy biographies. When he was forty-seven, Ssu-ma Ch'ien fell into disgrace and was imprisoned and castrated. Two years later, in 96, he was pardoned and became secretary at the imperial palace. He continued his work until 90 B.C.*

LORD SHANG

Lord Shang was descended, through a concubine, from the royal house of Uei. His personal name was Yang, his clan name Kungsun, and his ancestors had been of the royal Chi clan. As a youth he was interested in the study of law and served as clan officer under Kungshu Tso, the prime minister of Wei, who recognized his ability but lacked opportunity to recommend him.

When Kungshu Tso fell ill, King Hui of Wei went in person to inquire after him and asked, "If anything should happen to you, what will become of my state?"

"My clan officer Kungsun Yang, although young, has remarkable gifts," replied Kungshu Tso. "I hope you will entrust affairs of state to him."

The king was silent and prepared to leave. The prime minister sent everyone else away and said, "If you do not mean to take my advice and employ him, then have Yang killed. Don't let him leave the country."

The king agreed to this, and left.

From Szuma Chien, *Records of the Historian,* translated by Yang Hsien-yi and Gladys Yang (Beijing: Foreign Languages Press, 1979), 60–69.

Then Kungshu Tso sent for Yang and told him regretfully, "Today the king asked me to suggest a successor. When I recommended you, I saw disapproval written on his face. So, putting my sovereign's interest first, I urged him to kill you if he would not use your services, and he agreed to do this. You must leave without delay, or you will be caught."

"If the king ignored your advice to employ me," said Yang, "why should he take your advice to have me killed?" And he did not leave.

After this interview King Hui told his followers, "I'm afraid the prime minister is in a bad way. He urged me to entrust affairs of state to Kungsun Yang—how absurd!"

After Kungshu's death, Yang heard that Duke Hsiao of Chin was trying to recruit men of talent to continue the achievements of Duke Mu and recover the territory Chin had lost in the east. He went west to Chin and obtained an audience with the duke through the offices of his favourite eunuch Ching. Yang held forth at great length but Duke Hsiao did not listen and kept dropping off to sleep. The duke afterwards complained to Ching, "Your friend is a fool. How could I use such a man?"

When Ching reproached Yang, the latter said, "I spoke to him about the emperors' way, but he lacks the necessary enlightenment." Five days later, at another audience, he did better, although it still was not what the duke wanted. Duke Hsiao complained once more to Ching, who reproached Yang again.

"I spoke about the kingly way," said Yang, "but he could not accept that either. I must beg for another audience."

This time the duke was pleased with Yang but did not take him into his service. After he had withdrawn, the duke told Ching, "Your protégé is all right. I can talk with him."

"I spoke of the conquerors' way," said Yang, "so now he is thinking of using me. I know how to talk with him next time I see him."

At their next meeting the duke unconsciously moved forward to sit closer to Yang. He spoke with him without wearying for several days.

"How did you make such a good impression?" asked Ching. "My master is delighted."

"I spoke to him first of the emperors' way and the kingly way, drawing comparisons with the Three Dynasties," Yang explained. "But the duke said, 'That would take too long, I cannot wait. A good ruler should make his mark in the world in his lifetime, not wait for a century to achieve the emperors' or the kingly way.' I then told him how to make his state powerful, and he was overjoyed. But he will hardly equal Shang and Chou."

Upon entering Duke Hsiao's employment, Yang asked to introduce reforms, but the duke was afraid of popular discontent.

"Those who hesitate to act win no fame, those who falter in their course achieve nothing," reasoned Yang. "Those who outdo others are condemned by the world. Those who see further than others are mocked by the mob. Fools are blind to what already exists whereas the wise perceive what is yet to come. It is no use consulting the people at the start, but one can enjoy the fruits with them. Those whose virtue is highest do not compromise with the common herd, those whose achievements are greatest do not consult the mob. A wise ruler who knows how to strengthen his state will not abide by old traditions; one who knows how to profit the people will not cling to conventions."

The duke approved.

But Kan Lung [a minister of Chin] said, "Not so. A sage does not teach the people to change their ways, a wise sovereign does not rule by discarding tradition. He who educates the people in accordance with custom succeeds without any trouble; he who rules according to established laws will have competent officers and satisfied subjects."

Yang replied, "Kan Lung talks like one of the vulgar herd. The common run of men cling to conventions, while scholars are smothered by their own learning. They are all adequate at sticking to official routine, but not the sort of people with whom to discuss other matters. The Three Dynasties were each governed according to different traditions, and the Five Conquerors [Duke Huan of Chi, Duke Wen of Tsin, Duke Hsiang of Sung, Duke Mu of Chin, and King Chuang of Chu] each prevailed by different policies. The wise make laws; the foolish keep them. The able alter the conventions; the foolish are bound by them."

[Minister] Tu Chih said, "Never change your way except for a hundredfold profit. Never alter a tool except for a tenfold advantage. We cannot go wrong if we follow the ancient way. We cannot err by keeping to conventions."

"There are many ways of governing," retorted Yang. "To benefit the state we need not follow the ancients. Tang and Wu of old ruled as kings without following the ancients, and the Hsia and Shang Dynasties perished through keeping the conventions unchanged. We must not condemn those who oppose the ancients or praise those who abide by conventions."

"Well said!" approved Duke Hsiao. He appointed Yang adjutant general and laid down new laws.

The people were divided into groups of five and ten households, mutually responsible for each other. Those who failed to denounce a criminal would be cut in two; those who denounced him would be rewarded as if they had beheaded an enemy; those who harboured a criminal would be punished as if they had surrendered to the enemy. Families with two or more grown sons not living in separate households had to pay a double tax. Those who distinguished themselves in war would be rewarded with noble rank according to merit. Those who carried on private feuds would be punished according to their offence. The people had to work hard at the fundamental occupations of farming and weaving, and those who harvested most grain or produced most silk would be exempted from levies. Those who followed subsidiary occupations like trade, or who were idle and poor, would have their wives and sons enslaved. Nobles who failed to distinguish themselves in war would lose their noble status. The social hierarchy was clearly defined and each rank allotted its appropriate land property, retainers, women slaves and clothing. Those who achieved worthy deeds would be honoured; those who did not, even if they were wealthy, could not make a splendid display.

When these reforms were ready to be promulgated, the authorities, fearing that the people would disregard them, set up a wooden pillar thirty feet high at the south gate of the market and offered a reward of ten gold pieces to anyone who would move it to the north gate. The people were sceptical and no one dared move it. Then a reward of fifty gold pieces was offered. A man moved the pillar and received the reward, proving that the authorities meant what they said. After that, the new decrees were issued.

Within a year, the subjects of Chin were flocking to the capital in thousands to complain of the new measures. And then the crown prince broke the law.

"These reforms are not working because those at the top are breaking the law," said Yang. He wanted to penalize the crown prince, but, since the heir apparent could not be punished, his guardian Lord Chien was punished in his stead while his tutor Lord Chia had his face tattooed. From the next day on all the people of Chin obeyed the laws.

By the end of ten years the people were well content. Nothing lost on the road was picked up and pocketed, the hills were free of brigands, every household was comfortably off, men fought bravely in war but avoided private feuds, and villages and towns were well-governed. When some of the citizens who had first complained of the reforms now came to praise them, Yang said, "These are trouble-makers." These men were banished to frontier towns, after which no more discussion of the laws was heard.

Then Yang was promoted to the sixteenth rank, the highest rank in Chin being the twentieth. He led an army to besiege Anyi in Wei, and subjugated the city. Three years later, he built a palace with archways at Hsienyang, and the duke moved his capital there from Yung.

Then fathers, sons and brothers were forbidden to live in one house, small villages and towns were grouped together as counties, with magistrates and vice-magistrates over them. The state was divided into thirty-one of these counties; the old boundaries between the fields were abolished; regular taxation was introduced; and weights and measures were standardized.

Four years later, the prince's guardian Lord Chien broke the law again and his nose was cut off. After five years Chin was so wealthy and powerful that the king of Chou sent sacrificial meat to the duke, and all the states offered congratulations.

The following year Chi defeated the army of Wei at Maling, capturing Crown Prince Shen and killing General Pang Chuan.

The next year Yang advised the duke, "Wei is like a cancer in our heart. Either Wei will annex us, or we must annex Wei. For they lie west of the mountains with their capital at Anyi, separated from us by the Yellow River but possessing all the advantages of the east. They can march west to invade us whenever they please, or hold their land in the east if they are weak. Thanks to Your Majesty's wisdom our state is prospering, whereas Wei was heavily defeated by Chi last year and all their allies have left them. This is the time to attack. When they withdraw, unable to resist us, we can seize the strongholds of the mountains and the Yellow River and control the other states in the east. This is the task for a king!"

The duke, approving, gave him an army to attack Wei, whose king dispatched troops under Lord Ang to resist. When both forces confronted each other, Yang sent Lord Ang this message, "We are old friends, yet now we are commanding hostile armies. I cannot bear the thought of fighting you. Let us meet to pledge our faith and feast together, then withdraw our troops so that our states may live at peace."

Lord Ang agreed to this. The two commanders made a pledge and, as they were drinking together, armed men whom Yang had set in ambush seized Lord Ang. Then the Chin troops fell upon the army of Wei and after routing it returned home. Since Wei had been defeated by both Chi and Chin, King Hui of Wei's resources were exhausted and his territory was dwindling away. In fear he sent an envoy to sue for peace, offering the land west of the Yellow River to the duke of Chin. Then King Hui moved his capital from Anyi to Taliang, saying, "I should have taken Kungshu Tso's advice!"

Upon Yang's return from defeating the Wei army, the duke gave him fifteen towns in Shang and Wu as his fief, and he became known as Lord Shang.

For ten years Lord Shang was prime minister of Chin, and many of the nobles hated him.

Chao Liang [a recluse of Chin] asked for an interview with him, and Lord Shang told him, "I owe this introduction to Meng Lan-kao. May I ask you to be my friend too?"

"I must decline the honour," Chao Liang replied. "Confucius said, 'One who shows his love for the people by recommending good men succeeds. One who assembles inferior men to rule fails.' As an inferior individual, I dare not accept your friendship. I have heard that 'claiming a position not rightly yours is greed, claiming a name not rightly yours is ambition.' Were I to do as you ask, sir, I should be guilty of both greed and ambition. So I dare not accept."

"Do you disapprove of my way of governing Chin?"

"The wise man considers carefully what he is told, the enlightened man looks within, the strong man masters himself. Thus King Shun said, 'He who humbles himself makes himself great.' You should follow the sage king's way, sir, instead of consulting me."

Lord Shang rejoined, "The men of Chin used to be like the barbarian tribes of Jung and Ti, making no distinction between fathers and sons, and all living in the same room. Now I have changed those ways, segregating men and women. I have built palaces with archways like those of Lu and Uei. How would you say I compare with Paili Hsi [a minister of Duke Mu of Chin (659–621 B.C.)] in governing the state?"

"A thousand sheepskins are not as good as one fox fur," replied Chao Liang. "A thousand sycophants are not as good as one outspoken man. King Wu prospered thanks to frank advisers, while King Chow, the last ruler of the Yin Dynasty, lost his state through silencing criticism. If you have no objection to King Wu's way, may I speak frankly without fear of punishment for the rest of my life?"

"As the old saying goes, 'Fair words are flowers, true words are fruit; reproof is medicine, flattery is disease.' By all means speak absolutely frankly. You will be administering medicine to me and I shall be guided by you, sir. Pray don't hesitate."

So Chao Liang said, "Paili Hsi, a borderer of Chu, wanted to come to Chin because he heard that Duke Mu was a good ruler. Since he had no money for the journey, he sold himself as a slave to a native of Chin. He wore rags and tended cattle for over a year till the duke, hearing about him, took him from the herd and raised him above common citizens to the highest position in the land. After he had been prime minister for six or seven years, Chin attacked Cheng in the east, appointed three different rulers of Tsin, and rescued Chu from ruin. He spread enlightenment throughout the state, and the men of Pa [in present-day Szechuan] sent tribute. His virtue spread through all the land and even barbarians submitted to his rule. When Yiu-yu [a famous strategist of Tsin] heard of him, he crossed the frontier to see him. While in office, he rode in a standing, not a sitting chariot, even if he was tired, and never used an awning in hot weather. He toured the country without any equipage or armed retainers. His noble deeds are recorded in the archives, his virtue has influenced later generations. At his death, every man and woman in Chin shed tears, the children stopped singing, the millers stopped chanting as they pounded rice—such was his goodness.

"As for you, sir, you obtained an audience with the king of Chin through his eunuch Ching, which was hardly proper. During your administration you have done nothing for the people, simply building a host of archways and palaces, which is hardly to your credit. You have punished and tattooed the crown prince's tutor and guardian and mutilated the people with harsh penalties, arousing resentment and making enemies. It is more effective for a ruler to influence men than to give them orders, and subjects are quicker to imitate their superiors than to obey their commands; yet you introduce wrong systems and mistaken measures, which is no way to educate the people. You talk and act like a prince, and are pressing the nobles of Chin harder every day. The *Book of Songs* says, 'Even a rat knows what is proper, but some men do not. If a man does not know what is proper, the sooner he dies the better.' Judging by this, you are not likely to live long. For eight years Lord Chien has not ventured out of doors. You killed Chu Huan too and had Lord Chia tattooed. According to the *Book of Songs*, 'He who wins support will prosper, he who loses support will fall.' Your actions are not such as win support.

"You drive out followed by a dozen carriages of retainers and with others full of guards, flanked by strong men, with lancers and halberdiers beside you. You will not stir abroad without all these precautions. The *Book of Documents* says, 'Those who rely on virtue will prosper, those who rely on force will perish.' You are as vulnerable as the morning dew and your expectation of life can hardly be long.

"You would do better to return those fifteen towns, work on some vegetable farm outside the city and urge the duke to honour recluses who live in mountain caves, to care for the old and helpless, to show respect to elders, and to reward and honour men of achievements and virtue; for this would lessen your danger. If you cling to your rich estates, monopolize state power, and arouse the hatred of the common people, then the men of Chin will have ample reason to get rid of you once the duke dies. Your end will come as swift as a kick!"

But Lord Shang ignored his advice.

Five months later Duke Hsiao of Chin died, and the crown prince came to the throne. The followers of his guardian Lord Chien accused Lord Shang of plotting revolt, and officers were sent to arrest him. He fled and sought lodging for the night in a frontier inn but the inn-keeper, not knowing who he was, told him, "According to the laws of Lord Shang, I shall be punished if I take in a man without a permit."

Lord Shang sighed and said, "So I am suffering from my own laws!"

He went to Wei, but the men of Wei would not give him asylum, because his betrayal of Lord Ang and the defeat of their army still rankled. Before he could go elsewhere, they said, "Lord Shang is a traitor to Chin, and Chin is powerful. How can we let him escape through our territory?" So they turned him back.

Once in Chin again, Lord Shang fled to his fief and made his followers raise local troops to attack Cheng in the north. Chin sent an army against him and he was killed at Mienchih. King Hui of Chin had his corpse torn limb from limb by chariots as a warning to others, and decreed, "Let no man rebel like Lord Shang!" His family was wiped out.

The Grand Historian comments: Lord Shang had a cruel nature. His falseness was shown by the way in which he tried to impress the duke with the emperors' way and kingly way, just high-sounding talk in which he had no real interest. His inhumanity was revealed by the way he gained an audience through the duke's favourite, but after he was in power punished Lord Chien, tricked Lord Ang of Wei and turned a deaf ear to Chao Liang's advice. I have read his dissertations on law and government, agriculture and war, which correspond to his actions. The bad end he finally came to in Chin was no more than he deserved. . . .

TIEN TAN

Tien Tan belonged to a distant branch of the royal house of Tien in the state of Chi. During the reign of King Min [323–284 B.C.], he was a minor official in Lintzu.

When Yueh Yi, a general of the state of Yen, defeated the army of Chi, King Min fled from his capital to the city of Chü, while the soldiers of Yen advanced unopposed to conquer Chi. Then Tien Tan fled to Anping and ordered his clansmen to saw off the projecting ends of their chariot-axles and fit iron guards round the stumps. When the troops of Yen took Anping by storm, the men of Chi fled and, in the mêlée on the road, the other chariots' axle ends broke and their occupants were captured. Tien Tan and his kinsmen were the only ones to escape, thanks to their reinforced axles, and they went east to defend Chimo. Alone of all the cities of Chi, Chü and Chimo were holding out against Yen.

As the men of Yen knew that King Min was in Chu, they attacked the city in strength. Nao Chih assassinated the king and defended Chu stubbornly, holding out against the besiegers for several years. Yen's troops then marched east to lay siege to Chimo. Its governor going out to give battle was defeated and killed.

From Szuma Chien, *Records of the Historian,* translated by Yang Hsien-yi and Gladys Yang (Beijing: Foreign Languages Press, 1979), 89–93.

The defenders at once chose Tien Tan to lead them, saying, "In the battle of Anping, Tien Tan's kinsmen escaped because of the iron guards fitted to their axles. He understands warfare." They made him their commander to defend Chimo.

Soon after this, King Chin of Yen died. His successor King Hui had an aversion to Yueh Yi, and when Tien Tan knew this he sowed further dissension between them by declaring, "Chi's king is dead and only two of its cities remain to be taken. But Yueh Yi dares not return for fear of punishment. Under the pretext of subjugating Chi, he is hoping to combine his forces with those of Chi and make himself king here. He is delaying his attack so that the men of Chi may come over to his side. The one thing we fear is that another general might be appointed, for then Chimo must be destroyed."

The king of Yen believed this and made Chi Chieh take over Yueh Yi's command, and Yueh Yi went back to [his native] Chao, to the great indignation of the soldiers of Yen.

Then Tien Tan ordered the citizens of Chimo to sacrifice to their ancestors in the courtyard before each meal, so that birds flocked down to the city to find food, to the astonishment of the besiegers.

"I have been granted a divine revelation," announced Tien Tan. Then he told the citizens, "A man with supernatural powers will be our teacher."

"Can I be that teacher?" cried a soldier, and was running off when Tien Tan stood up and led him to a seat facing east, treating him as a teacher.

"I was fooling, sir," said the soldier. "I have no special powers."

"Hush!" whispered Tien Tan. He treated the man as a teacher with divine powers, and attributed all the orders he gave to his divine teacher. He also declared, "My one fear is lest the soldiers of Yen cut off their captives' noses and place these men in the front ranks against us. For then Chimo is doomed."

The men of Yen, hearing this, acted upon it. And when the defenders saw this mutilation of all who had surrendered, they were so angry that they resisted manfully, determined not to be captured.

To add fuel to the fire Tien Tan also said, "Heaven help us if the invaders dig up the graves outside the city and defile our ancestors!"

When the men of Yen dug up the graves and burned all the corpses, the defenders watching from the city wall wept with redoubled rage, longing to go out and fight.

Now that he knew that his men were ready for battle, Tien Tan himself set to work with them to repair the defences, enrolling his wife and concubine in the ranks and sharing all his food and wine with the soldiers. He ordered the men in armour to keep out of sight while the old, the weak and the women mounted the city walls and an envoy was sent out to treat for surrender. At this a great cheer went up in the enemy ranks.

Tien Tan collected a thousand *yi* of gold from the people and made some wealthy citizens present this sum to the enemy general, saying, "The city is about to surrender. We entreat you to spare our wives, concubines and kinsmen, and let us live in peace!" The Yen general very gladly agreed to this. And the invaders further relaxed their vigilance.

Then Tien Tan assembled more than one thousand bulls, swathed them in red silk, painted them different colours so that they looked like dragons, tied daggers to their horns and tied straw soaked in oil to their tails. At night the straw was set alight and the bulls were let out through dozens of breaches in the city wall. They were followed by five thousand stout fellows. Goaded into fury by their burning tails, the bulls charged the army of Yen, taking the invaders completely by surprise. The flaming torches on their tails cast a lurid light, and to the men of Yen the bulls seemed like so many dragons sowing death and destruction. After them rushed the five thousand, their mouths gagged, followed by the inhabitants, shouting and drumming. The old and infirm beat so loudly on copper vessels that the tumult shook heaven and earth. Yen's forces fell back in terror. And when their general Chi Chieh was killed, the enemy fled in confusion, pursued by the host of Chi. Every town and city they passed threw off Yen's yoke and flocked to Tien Tan's support.

Tien Tan's ranks swelled after each fresh victory, as Yen's grew daily weaker. When at last the enemy was thrown back to the river [the northern boundary of Chi], all Chi's cities—seventy and more—had been recovered. Then Tien Tan invited King Hsiang back from the city of Chü to govern in Lintzu, and the king enfeoffed him Lord of Anping.

The Grand Historian comments: In war, regular tactics are used to fight a battle and surprise tactics to win it. Skilled commanders show endless resourcefulness in devising an infinite variety of tactics, moving endlessly between regular and surprise ones. First passive as a young girl in face of the enemy, then swift as an escaped hare that cannot be overtaken—these were Tien Tan's surprise tactics.

Previously, when Nao Chih assassinated King Min, the citizens of Chü sought out the king's son Fa-chang, whom they found working as a gardener for Taishih Chiao. The daughter of the family had taken pity on him and treated him well. He told her who he was, and they became lovers. After the citizens made him king of Chi to hold Chu against Yen, the girl became his queen with the title of Chief Lady.

When the forces of Yen first entered Chi, they heard that Wang Chu of Houyi was a virtuous man. An order was issued forbidding troops to go within thirty *li* of where he lived, and messengers were sent to him, saying, "The men of Chi speak so highly of your virtue that we will make you a general with a fief of ten thousand households." When Wang Chu declined this offer, the envoys said, "If you do not agree, we shall bring troops to wipe out this district."

"A loyal subject cannot serve two masters, a chaste woman cannot change her husband," replied Wang Chu. "Since the king of Chi ignored my advice I retired to till the fields. Now that our land is conquered I have nothing to live for, and today you are trying to force me to be your general. If I consented, I should be aiding a tyrant. I would rather die in the cauldron than live without virtue."

He tied a halter to a tree and with one leap hanged himself.

When the ministers of Chi heard this they said, "Wang Chu was an ordinary citizen, yet he would not submit to Yen. What an example for those of us who have official positions and government emoluments!" So they went to Chü to find the prince and set him up as King Hsiang. . . .

LIEN PO AND LIN HSIANG-JU

Lien Po was an able general of Chao. In the sixteenth year of King Hui-wen [283 B.C.], he commanded the Chao army against Chi and defeated its troops, taking the city of Yangtsin. Then he was made a chief minister and was known for his prowess to all the states.

Lin Hsiang-ju, a man of Chao, was the steward of Mu Hsien the chief eunuch.

King Hui-wen had come into possession of the jade of Pien Ho, a man of Chu. When King Chao of Chin knew this, he sent an envoy with a letter to the king of Chao, offering fifteen cities in exchange for the jade. The king took counsel with General Lien Po and his chief ministers, who feared that if the jade were sent to Chin they might be cheated and get no cities in return, yet if they refused the soldiers of Chin might attack. They could neither hit on a plan nor find an envoy to take their answer to Chin.

Then Mu Hsien the chief eunuch said, "My steward Lin Hsiang-ju would make a good envoy."

"How do you know?" asked the king.

He replied, "Once I did something wrong and secretly planned to escape to Yen, but my steward stopped me, asking, 'How can you be sure of the king of Yen?' I answered, 'I met him at the frontier with our king, and he privately grasped my hand and offered me his friendship. That is how I know, and why

From Szuma Chien, *Records of the Historian,* translated by Yang Hsien-yi and Gladys Yang (Beijing: Foreign Languages Press, 1979), 139–51.

I mean to go there.' Lin said, 'Chao is strong and Yen is weak, and because you stood well with our lord the king of Yen desired your friendship. But if you now fly from Chao to Yen, for fear of Chao he will not dare to keep you and will have you sent back in chains. Your only possible way out is to bare your shoulder and prostrate yourself before the axe and block for punishment.' I took his advice and Your Majesty pardoned me. To my mind he is a brave, resourceful man, well fitted to be our envoy."

The king thereupon summoned Lin Hsiang-ju and asked him, "Should I accept the king of Chin's offer of fifteen cities in exchange for my jade?"

"Chin is strong, we are weak," replied Lin Hsiang-ju. "We cannot refuse."

"What if he takes my jade but will not give me the cities?"

"If we refuse Chin's offer of cities in exchange for the jade, that puts us in the wrong; but if we give up the jade and get no cities, that puts Chin in the wrong. Of these two courses, the better one is to agree and put Chin in the wrong."

"Who can be our envoy?"

"If Your Majesty has no one else, I will gladly take the jade and go on this mission. If the cities are given to Chao, the jade will remain in Chin. If no cities are given, I shall bring the jade back unscathed."

So the king of Chao sent Lin Hsiang-ju with the jade west to Chin.

The king of Chin sat in his pleasure pavilion to receive Lin Hsiang-ju, who presented the jade to him. The king, very pleased, had it shown to his ladies and attendants, and all his attendants cheered.

Seeing that the king had no intention of giving any cities to Chao, Lin Hsiang-ju stepped forward and said, "There is a blemish on the jade. Let me show it to you, sir."

As soon as the king gave him the jade, Lin Hsiang-ju retreated to stand with his back to a pillar. His hair bristling with fury, he said, "To get this jade, great king, you sent a letter to the king of Chao. When our sovereign summoned his ministers to discuss the matter, they said, 'Chin is greedy and, relying on its strength, hopes to get our jade in return for empty promises. We are not likely to receive the cities.' They were against giving you the jade. It seemed to me, however, that if even fellows in homespun can trust each other, how much more can powerful states. Besides, how wrong it would be to offend mighty Chin for the sake of a piece of jade! So the king of Chao, after fasting for five days, sent me with a letter and the jade to your court. Why? To show the respect and awe in which we hold your great country. Yet on my arrival you received me in a pleasure pavilion and treated me with contempt. You took the jade and passed it among your ladies to make a fool of me. I can see you have no intention of giving Chao those cities in return, so I have taken back the jade. If you use force against me, I will smash my head and the jade against this pillar."

With that, glancing at the pillar, he raised the jade and threatened to smash it.

To save the jade, the king of Chin apologized and begged him to stop, then ordered the officer in charge to look up the map and point out the boundaries of the fifteen cities to be given to Chao.

Lin Hsiang-ju, thinking this was a subterfuge and that Chao would never really get the cities, declared, "The jade of Pien Ho is a treasure known throughout the world, but for fear of Chin the king of Chao dared not withhold it. Before parting with it he fasted for five days. So it is only right, great king, that you too should fast for five days and then prepare a grand court reception. Only then dare I hand it over."

Since he could not seize the jade by force, the king agreed to fast for five days, during which time Lin Hsiang-ju should be lodged in the Kuang-cheng Hostel.

Lin Hsiang-ju suspected that despite his fast the king would not keep his promise to give the cities. So, dressing one of his followers in rags and concealing the jade on his person, he made him hurry back to Chao by paths and byways.

When the king of Chin had fasted for five days, he prepared a grand reception for Chao's envoy.

Lin Hsiang-ju, arriving, announced to the king, "Since the time of Duke Mu of Chin, not one of the twenty-odd princes of your state has kept faith. Fearful of being deceived by Your Majesty and letting my country down, I sent a man back with the jade. He should be in Chao by now. Chin is strong and Chao is weak. When you, great king, sent a single messenger to Chao, we immediately brought the jade here. If your mighty state had first given us fifteen cities, we should not have dared offend you by keeping the jade. I know I deserve death for deceiving you and beg to be boiled in the cauldron. Consider this well with your ministers, great king!"

The king and all his ministers gaped at each other. Some attendants prepared to drag Lin Hsiang-ju away, but the king said, "Killing him now will not get us the jade but would spoil our relations with Chao. Better treat him handsomely and send him back. The king of Chao dare not risk offending Chin for the sake of a piece of jade."

Thereupon he entertained Lin Hsiang-ju in his court, dismissing him when the ceremony was over.

The king of Chao was so pleased with the skill with which Lin Hsiang-ju had saved the state from disgrace that he made him a high councillor on his return. Neither did Chin give the cities to Chao, nor Chao give the jade to Chin.

After this, Chin attacked Chao and took Shihcheng.

The following year twenty thousand men of Chao were killed in another attack. Then the king of Chin sent an envoy to the king of Chao, proposing a friendly meeting at Minchih south of Hsiho. The king of Chao was loath to go, for fear of Chin. But Lien Po and Lin Hsiang-ju reasoned with him saying, "Not to go, sir, would make our country appear weak and cowardly."

So the king went, accompanied by Lin Hsiang-ju.

Lien Po saw them to the frontier, where he bade the king farewell saying, "I reckon that Your Majesty's journey there, the meeting and the journey back should not take more than thirty days. If you fail to return in that time, I suggest that we set up the crown prince as king, to thwart the designs of Chin."

The king, having agreed, went to meet the king of Chin at Minchih.

The king of Chin, merry after drinking, said, "I have heard that the king of Chao is a good musician. Will you play the cithern for me?"

The king of Chao did as he asked. Then the Chin chronicler stepped forward and recorded, "On such-and-such a day the king of Chin drank with the king of Chao and ordered the king of Chao to play the cithern."

Lin Hsiang-ju then advanced and said, "The king of Chao has heard that the king of Chin is a good hand at Chin music. Will you entertain us with a tune on the pitcher?"

The king of Chin angrily refused. But Lin Hsiang-ju went forward to present a pitcher and, kneeling down, requested him to play. Still the king refused.

"I am only five steps from you," cried Lin Hsiang-ju. "I can bespatter you, great king, with the blood from your throat!"

The attendants wanted to kill him, but he glared and shouted so fiercely that they shrank back. Then the king of Chin sullenly beat once on the pitcher, whereupon Lin Hsiang-ju turned to bid the Chao chronicler record, "On such-and-such a date, the king of Chin played the pitcher for the king of Chao."

Then the ministers of Chin said, "We hope Chao will present fifteen cities to the king of Chin."

Lin Hsiang-ju retorted, "We hope Chin will present Hsienyang [the Chin capital] to the king of Chao!"

At this feast, then, the king of Chin was unable to get the better of Chao. Nor dared he make any move because of the strong guard brought by the king of Chao.

Upon their return to Chao after this meeting, Lin Hsiang-ju was appointed a chief minister for his outstanding service, taking precedence over Lien Po.

Lien Po protested, "As a general of Chao I have served the state well in the field and stormed many cities. All Lin Hsiang-ju can do is wag his tongue, yet now he is above me. I'd think shame to work under such a base-born fellow." He swore, "When I meet Lin Hsiang-ju I shall humiliate him!"

When Lin Hsiang-ju got word of this, he kept out of Lien Po's way and absented himself from court on grounds of illness, not wanting to compete for precedence. Once when he caught sight of Lien Po in the distance on the road he drove his carriage another way.

His stewards reproached him saying, "We left our kinsmen to serve you because we admired your lofty character, sir. Now you have the same rank as Lien Po, but when he insults you in public you try to avoid him and look abjectly afraid. This would disgrace even a common citizen, let alone generals and ministers! We are afraid we must beg to resign."

Lin Hsiang-ju stopped them, asking, "Is General Lien Po as powerful in your eyes as the king of Chin?"

"Of course not," they replied.

"If, useless as I am, I lashed out at the mighty king of Chin in his court and insulted his ministers, why should I be afraid of General Lien Po? To my mind, however, were it not for the two of us, powerful Chin would not hesitate to invade Chao. When two tigers fight, one must perish. I behave as I do because I put our country's fate before private feuds."

When word of this reached Lien Po, he bared his shoulders, fastened a switch of thorns to his back and had a protégé conduct him to Lin Hsiang-ju's gate. He apologized, "Contemptible boor that I am, I could not understand your magnanimity, sir!"

They became close friends, ready to die for each other.

That year Lien Po attacked Chi in the east and defeated one of its armies. Two years later he took another city of Chi. Three years later he stormed Fangling and Anyang in Wei. Four years later Lin Hsiang-ju led an army against Chi, but withdrew after reaching Pingyi. The following year Lien Po defeated the army of Chin at Oyu.

Chao Sheh was a tax-collector in Chao. When Lord Pingyuan's family refused to pay the land tax, he punished them in accordance with the law, executing nine of their stewards. In his rage, Lord Pingyuan wanted to kill him.

Chao Sheh reasoned with him, "You are a noble of Chao yet you flout the law, allowing your family to evade taxation. When the law is flouted, the state will grow weak and other states will invade and destroy us; and when Chao is no more, what will become of your wealth? If you, a noble, pay taxes according to the law, society will be at peace, the state of Chao will be strong and secure and you, sir, as a member of the royal house, will not be despised by the world."

Impressed by Chao Sheh's worth, Lord Pingyuan recommended him to the king, who put him in charge of the state revenues, and he managed these so well that the people prospered and the treasury was full.

Then Chin invaded Han and stationed an army at Oyu. The king of Chao summoned Lien Po and asked, "Can we go to their aid?"

Lien Po replied, "The road is long and over very mountainous country. It would be hard."

The king consulted Yueh Sheng, who made the same answer. He then consulted Chao Sheh, who replied, "The way is far and lies through ravines. The combatants would be like two rats fighting in a hole—the braver would win."

Then the king ordered Chao Sheh to lead troops to rescue Han.

When the army was only thirty *li* from Hantan, Chao Sheh issued this order: "Criticism of the plan of campaign will be punished with death."

The men of Chin were stationed west of Wu-an. The roll of their drums when they drilled set the tiles on the roofs of Wu-an vibrating. A scout of the Chao army who urged that they should make haste to rescue the town was executed by Chao Sheh on the spot. Having fortified his camp, he stayed there without advancing for twenty-eight days, simply building more and more ramparts. When a Chin spy came to the camp, Chao Sheh gave him a good meal and sent him away. The spy reported this to his commander, who gloated, "Their army is only thirty *li* from their capital, yet already they have stopped to strengthen their defences. They will never recapture Oyu."

After Chao Sheh had dismissed the spy, he commanded his troops to advance in light marching order at full speed. In two days and one night he reached Oyu and stationed his best archers fifty *li* from the city. No sooner had they dug in than the men of Chin, hearing of their approach, came in full force.

An officer named Hsu Li asked permission to make a suggestion. When Chao Sheh had him brought to his tent, Hsu Li said, "The men of Chin never thought we would get so far. They are in a confident mood. You must mass your troops to resist their attack, or we shall be defeated."

Chao Sheh replied, "I shall take your advice."

"I beg to die by the axe," said Hsu Li.

"Wait until we get to Hantan," was the answer.

Hsu Li gave him some more advice, saying, "The first to take the North Hill will win. The late-comers will be defeated."

Again Chao Sheh agreed and sent ten thousand men to storm the hill. The troops of Chin, coming later, could not retake it. Then Chao Sheh launched an attack and inflicted a heavy defeat on the Chin army, which scattered and fled. Thereupon he raised the siege of Oyu and returned. King Hui-wen of Chao made him the lord of Mafu and promoted Hsu Li to be marshal. So now Chao Sheh ranked equal with Lien Po and Lin Hsiang-ju.

Four years later, King Hui-wen died and King Hsiao-cheng ascended the throne. In the seventh year of his reign, Chin fought Chao at Changping. As Chao Sheh was now dead and Lin Hsiang-ju mortally ill, Lien Po led the troops against Chin. After several defeats he strengthened his defences and refused to give battle. Though repeatedly challenged by Chin, he would not fight.

Then a spy from Chin told the king of Chao, "All Chin fears is that Chao Kuo, son of Chao Sheh, lord of Mafu, may be appointed commander." Because the king believed this, he made Chao Kuo take over Lien Po's command.

Lin Hsiang-ju protested, "If you are sending him because of his father's fame, that is like playing the cithern with fixed frets. All Chao Kuo can do is read his father's treatises: he has no idea how to apply or modify them." But the king did not listen to him and made Chao Kuo commander.

Chao Kuo had studied military science and discussed strategy since boyhood. He was confident that no one in the world was a match for him. Once he even worsted his father Chao Sheh in a discussion on strategy, yet he could not win Chao Sheh's approval. When Chao Kuo's mother asked him why, Chao Sheh said, "War is a matter of life and death, but he makes light of it. I can only hope he never becomes our state's commander. If he does, he will destroy our army."

So when Chao Kuo was about to set out with his troops, his mother wrote to beg the king not to send him. Asked for her reasons, she replied, "When I was first married to his father, who was then a commander, he offered food and wine to dozens of men at his meals and treated hundreds as his friends, distributing his gifts from Your Majesty and others of the royal house among his officers and friends. From the day he took the command he gave no further thought to family affairs. But as soon as Chao Kuo became a commander he put on such airs that none of his officers or men dare look him in the eye. When you give him gold and silk he takes it home, and he looks every day for cheap property to buy. How does he compare with his father, would you say? Since father and son are so different, I hope you will not send him."

"Leave it to me," said the king. "I have made the decision."

Then she asked, "If you must send him, will you spare me from punishment if he does badly?" The king agreed to this.

After Chao Kuo took over from Lien Po, he rescinded all previous orders and appointments. When General Pai Chi of Chin knew this, he made a surprise attack, feigned a retreat, cut Chao's supply route and split the army into two so that both officers and men lost heart. When his army was starving some forty days later, Chao Kuo led picked troops out to fight and the men of Chin shot and killed him. Chao was defeated and hundreds of thousands of its men surrendered, only to be buried alive by Chin. In all, Chao lost four hundred and fifty thousand men.

The following year the Chin army besieged Hantan. For more than a year the capital was under siege and would have fallen if not for help sent from Chu and Wei, who managed to raise the siege. Because Chao Kuo's mother had warned him, the king of Chao did not have her executed.

Five years after the relief of Hantan, Yen attacked Chao on the advice of its minister Li Fu, who said, "All the able-bodied men of Chao were wiped out at

Changping, and their orphans are not yet fully grown." But Lien Po as Chao's commander utterly routed the men of Yen at Hao, killed Li Fu and laid siege to the capital of Yen. To make peace, Yen offered five cities which were accepted. Then Chao gave Lien Po the district of Weiwen as his fief, making him Lord Hsinping and acting chief minister.

When, deprived of his command, Lien Po had returned home from Changping, all his protégés had left him because he was out of power. Upon his reappointment they came back, but he ordered them away.

"Ah, how lacking you are in understanding," they told him. "All friendship in this world follows the rules of the market. When you have power we follow you, when you lose power we leave you. This is only natural. Why should you complain?"

Six years later, Chao sent Lien Po against Fanyang in Wei and he captured it. After the death of King Hsiao-cheng of Chao, his son King Tao-hsiang came to the throne and made Yueh Sheng take over the army command. Lien Po in his anger attacked Yueh Sheng, who fled. Then Lien Po went to Taliang, the capital of Wei. The following year Chao appointed Li Mu commander against Yen, and he took Wusui and Fangcheng.

Lien Po remained many years in Wei but was never trusted there or given a post. Because Chao was so hard pressed by Chin, the king wanted to have him back. Lien Po too was eager to serve his own country again. The king of Chao sent an envoy to see whether Lien Po could still command an army, but an enemy of his named Kuo Kai gave the envoy a large bribe to slander him. When the envoy came to see him, Lien Po ate a whole peck of rice and ten catties of meat, then buckled on his armour and mounted his horse to show that he was still fit for active service.

On his return, however, the messenger told the king, "Though old, General Lien Po still enjoys his food. But in the short time I was with him, he went out three times to relieve himself." Then the king decided he was too old to recall.

When the men of Chu heard that Lien Po was in Wei, they secretly invited him to their state. But as a general of Chu he had no success and sighed, "If only I had some men of Chao under me!" He finally died in Shouchun.

Li Mu was an able general on Chao's northern frontier, who remained in Yenmen in the land of Tai to guard against the Huns. He appointed officers as he saw fit and had all the market taxes sent to his headquarters to meet army expenses. He slaughtered several oxen daily for his troops, trained his men in mounted archery, kept the beacons in readiness, made full use of spies and treated his soldiers handsomely. He enjoined on his men, "When the Huns make a raid, withdraw quickly to the ramparts. Whoever dares engage the enemy will lose his head."

So whenever they were raided by the Huns, they lit the beacon fires and withdrew without fighting. This went on for several years, with no losses incurred. The Huns, of course, considered Li Mu a coward, while even his frontier troops thought him faint-hearted. But when the king of Chao reprimanded him, he carried on as before. Then the king angrily recalled Li Mu, sending someone else to take over the command.

For over a year the Chao troops gave battle every time the Huns raided, and were always defeated with heavy losses. The men of Chao could no longer farm or breed cattle on the frontier. But when asked to go back, Li Mu shut himself behind closed doors, pleading illness, till the king ordered him to get up and take command.

"Very well, if Your Majesty insists," he said. "But only if I can carry on as before."

The king agreed to this. And Li Mu on his return used his old tactics. For several years the Huns could get no advantage, yet still they thought him a coward. And the frontier troops, daily rewarded yet kept out of action, were spoiling for a fight. Then Li Mu chose thirteen hundred chariots, thirteen thousand horsemen, fifty thousand brave fighters, and a hundred thousand archers. Having trained them well, he let cattle and men wander all over the plain. When the Huns made a small raid, he pretended to be defeated and abandoned several thousand men to the enemy. The khan of the Huns, hearing this, attacked in full force. Then Li Mu, resorting to unconventional stratagems, deployed both wings of his army in attacks from right and left and routed and killed more than a hundred thousand of the Hun horsemen. He wiped out the tribes of Tanlan, defeated those of Tunghu, and subjugated those of Linhu. The khan fled and for ten years and more dared not approach the frontier again.

In the first year of King Tao-hsiang of Chao [244 B.C.], as Lien Po had fled to Wei, Li Mu was sent to attack Yen and he captured Wusui and Fangcheng. Two years later Pang Hsuan defeated the army of Yen, killing Chu Hsin. Seven years later Chin defeated Chao, killed its commander Hu Che at Wusui and wiped out a hundred thousand men. Then Li Mu was made commander-in-chief to attack the Chin army at Yi-an, where he routed the men of Chin and forced General Huan Yi to flee. For this he was enfeoffed as lord of Wu-an. Three years later Chin attacked Panwu, but Li Mu defeated its army and resisted Hann and Wei in the south.

In the seventh year of King Chien of Chao, Chin sent Wang Chien to attack Chao, and Li Mu and Szuma Shang were ordered to resist him. Chin bribed the king's favourite, Kuo Kai, to act as its agent and slander both these generals by accusing them of plotting treason. Then the king of Chao sent Chao Tsung and Yen Chu, a general from Chi, to take over Li Mu's command. When

Li Mu refused to give it up, the king sent men to take him by surprise and kill him, while Szuma Shang was also dismissed. Three months later, Wang Chien routed the men of Chao with a surprise attack, killing Chao Tsung and capturing King Chien and General Yen Chu. The state of Chao was thus extinguished.

The Grand Historian comments: A man who knows he must die acts courageously, for it is not hard to die, only hard to face death. When Lin Hsiang-ju prepared to smash the jade on the pillar and lashed out at the attendants of the king of Chin, the worst that could befall him was death. Other men, of course, might have been paralysed with fear, but he summoned up courage to strike awe into the enemy. When later he gave way to Lien Po, he won a name for himself as great as Mount Tai. Truly he was a paragon of resourcefulness and courage combined! . . .

CHANG LIANG, MARQUIS OF LIU

The ancestors of Chang Liang, marquis of Liu, came from the state of Hann. His grandfather Kai-ti served as prime minister to Marquis Chao, King Hsuan-hui and King Hsiang-ai of Hann. His father Ping was prime minister to King Hsi and King Tao-hui. Chang Ping died in the twenty-third year of King Tao-hui [250 B.C.], and twenty years later Hann was conquered by Chin. Chang Liang, still young, held no official position in Hann. At the time of the fall of Hann he still had three hundred slaves, yet when his younger brother died he did not bury him but used his patrimony to find an assassin who would kill the king of Chin to avenge his state, because his grandfather and father had been ministers of Hann during five reigns.

Chang Liang went east to study ceremony at Huaiyang, where he met Lord Tsang-hai and found a strong man whom he armed with an iron hammer one hundred and twenty catties in weight. When the First Emperor of Chin made a tour of the east, Chang Liang and the assassin attacked him at Polangsha, but by mistake struck at his attendant's carriage. In fact, Chang Liang was the cause of the urgent, countrywide search for brigands ordered by the emperor in his rage. But Chang Liang escaped to Hsiapi and went into hiding under an assumed name.

One day he was strolling idly across the bridge at Hsiapi when an old man in rough homespun approached, dropped a shoe under the bridge and, turning to Chang Liang, said, "Boy! Go down, and fetch my slipper!" Chang Liang

From Szuma Chien, *Records of the Historian*, translated by Yang Hsien-yi and Gladys Yang (Beijing: Foreign Languages Press, 1979), 238–52.

was astounded and wanted to hit the fellow. But controlling himself on account of the other's age, he went down to fetch the shoe.

"Put it on for me," ordered the old man. And since Chang Liang had already fetched the shoe, he knelt down to put it on. The old man stretched out his foot for it, then left with a smile while Chang Liang watched in amazement. After going some distance the old man came back. "You can be taught, boy," he said. "Meet me here five days from now at dawn."

Chang Liang, his curiosity aroused, knelt down to answer, "I will."

At dawn five days later he went back to the place. The old man, there before him, said angrily. "What do you mean by keeping an old man waiting? Come earlier five days from now." With that he left.

Five days later Chang Liang went earlier, only to find the old man already there. He was told to come back after another five days.

This time Chang Liang went before midnight. Presently the old man arrived. "That's right!" he said approvingly and handed him a book with the injunction, "Read this and you will become the teacher of kings. Ten years from now you will prosper. Thirteen years from now you will once more encounter me, as the yellow rock at the foot of Mount Kucheng north of the River Chi." Without another word he left and did not appear again.

When day broke Chang Liang examined the book and found it was *The Patriarch Lu Shang's Art of War.* Prizing this work, he pored over it again and again. He remained in Hsiapi as a champion of justice and helped to conceal Hsiang Po after he killed a man.

Ten years later Chen Sheh and the others revolted, and Chang Liang gathered a band of more than a hundred young men. When Ching Chu made himself the acting king of Chu in Liu, Chang Liang decided to join him; but on the way he met Liu Pang, then in command of several thousand men who were conquering the region west of Hsiapi, and he threw in his lot with him. Liu Pang made him a cavalry officer. Chang Liang expounded *The Patriarch's Art of War* to him on several occasions and he approved of the book and made use of its strategies, although Chang Liang found others could not understand them. Struck by Liu Pang's natural genius, he followed him instead of joining Ching Chu.

When Liu Pang went to Hsueh to see Hsiang Liang, who had set up King Huai of Chu, Chang Liang advised Hsiang Liang saying, "You have enthroned a descendant of the royal house of Chu. Lord Cheng of Hengyang of the House of Hann is also a worthy man. If you make him a king you will win another ally."

So Hsiang Liang sent him to find Lord Cheng and make him king of Hann with Chang Liang as his minister. Chang Liang went with the king of Hann and over a thousand men to conquer the territory of Hann in the west, but each time they took a city the army of Chin recaptured it. So they carried on mobile warfare in Yingchuan.

When Liu Pang marched south from Loyang through Huanyuan, Chang Liang led his men to join him and together they captured more than ten cities of Hann and routed Yang Hsiung's army. Then Liu Pang ordered King Cheng of Hann to defend Yangti while he went south with Chang Liang and stormed Wan before advancing west through the Wu Pass. He planned to lead twenty thousand men against the forces of Chin at the Yao Pass, but Chang Liang said, "Don't underestimate the men of Chin—they are still a powerful force. I hear their general is a butcher's son, and tradesmen are easily tempted by gain. Why not entrench yourself here, send a force ahead with provisions for fifty thousand and set up banners on all the hills around to dismay the enemy, while Li Yi-chi goes with rich gifts to bribe him?"

The Chin general did in fact surrender and offered to advance west with Liu Pang against Hsienyang. Liu Pang would have agreed, but Chang Liang warned, "The general is willing to surrender but I doubt if his troops will follow suit. That would put us in a dangerous position. Better strike while they are off their guard." So Liu Pang attacked and defeated the army of Chin, then marched north to Lantien where he routed the Chin forces again. When he reached Hsienyang, Tzu-ying, king of Chin, surrendered.

Liu Pang, entering the Chin palaces, found there hangings, curtains, hounds, horses, treasures and women by the thousand. Tempted to stay there, he ignored the advice of Fan Kuai, who urged him to camp outside.

Chang Liang said, "You are here because Chin did not rule well. And now that you have rid the world of a tyrant, you should trade on frugality. If the moment you enter Chin you indulge in its pleasures, you will just be outdoing the despot. 'Home truths grate on the ears yet are good guides to action; strong medicine tastes bitter yet helps to cure disease.' I hope you will take Fan Kuai's advice." Then Liu Pang withdrew his troops and stationed them at Pashang.

When Hsiang Yu, arriving in Hungmen, decided to attack Liu Pang, Hsiang Po hastened by night to their camp and secretly urged Chang Liang to leave with him.

But Chang Liang said, "I came on behalf of my prince to help Liu Pang. It would not be right to desert him in his hour of danger."

He reported the whole matter to Liu Pang, who asked in consternation, "What shall I do?"

"Do you really intend to oppose Hsiang Yu?" asked Chang Liang.

"A worthless fellow advised me to hold the Pass against the other princes so that I could rule over the whole of Chin. I acted on his advice."

"Do you believe you can defeat Hsiang Yu?"

After quite a long silence he answered, "No, of course not. What shall I do?"

Then Chang Liang urged Hsiang Po to come in and see Liu Pang, who drank a toast to him, promised to link their families by marriage, and asked him to explain to Hsiang Yu that he would never think of betraying him and had simply held the Pass against brigands. So Hsiang Po went back and cleared up this matter, as has been recorded in the account of Hsiang Yu.

In the first month of the first year of Han [206 B.C.], Liu Pang became king of Han ruling over Pa and Shu. He gave Chang Liang a hundred *yi* of gold and two pecks of pearls, all of which Chang Liang presented to Hsiang Po. Liu Pang also sent rich gifts to Hsiang Po through Chang Liang with a request for Hanchung, and since Hsiang Yu agreed Liu Pang obtained this district.

When Liu Pang set off to his kingdom, Chang Liang accompanied him as far as Paochung before he was told to return. He advised Liu Pang saying, "Why not burn the plank road through the mountains? This would show the world you have no intention of marching east again and reassure Hsiang Yu." Liu Pang, having sent him off, went on, destroying the plank road on his way.

Upon his return to Hann, Chang Liang found that King Cheng had not been allowed to go there but had been taken east by Hsiang Yu, because Chang Liang was on the side of Liu Pang. He told Hsiang Yu, "Liu Pang has destroyed the plank road and has no intention of coming east again." He also informed him of the revolt of King Tien Jung of Chi. Then Hsiang Yu set his mind at rest about Liu Pang in the west, and led an army north against Chi. He would not let King Cheng go, however, but made him a marquis and then had him killed at Pengcheng.

Chang Liang fled to join Liu Pang, who by then had marched back and conquered the three states of Chin. Chang Liang, made marquis of Chenghsin, went east with the army of Han to attack Chu.

At Pengcheng the Han army was defeated and Liu Pang retreated to Hsiayi. Unsaddling his horse to squat on the saddle, he said, "I mean to give up all the land east of the Pass to someone who will make common cause with me. Can you suggest anyone?"

Chang Liang stepped forward and said, "Ying Pu, king of Chiuchiang, is an able Chu general who hates Hsiang Yu. Or there is Peng Yueh, who has rebelled with King Tien Jung of Chi in Liang. Both men would serve in this emergency. Of your own generals, Han Hsin alone is capable of great things and can play an independent part. If you mean to give up this territory, give it to these three men. Then Hsiang Yu can be defeated."

Liu Pang sent Sui Ho to win over Ying Pu and another envoy to make an alliance with Peng Yueh. And when King Pao of Wei rebelled, he dispatched

Han Hsin against him with an army. So he conquered Yen, Tai, Chi and Chao. And the final overthrow of Chu was thanks to these three men. Chang Liang's health was poor and he never commanded an army, but in his capacity as an adviser he was constantly with the king.

In the third year of Han, Hsiang Yu beset Liu Pang so hard at Yingyang that in alarm he asked Li Yi-chi how to weaken the power of Chu.

"When Tang conquered King Chieh of the Hsia Dynasty," said Li Yi-chi, "he gave the land of Chi to his descendants. When King Wu conquered King Chow of the Shang Dynasty, he gave Sung to his descendants. But Chin, abandoning virtue and justice, has abolished the ancestral sacrifices of the six princes and disinherited their descendants, leaving them not a single inch of land. If you restore the descendants of the six royal houses and present them with seals, then they, their ministers and their people will acknowledge your virtue and turn towards you in admiration, willing to be your subjects. When you have done such deeds of virtue and justice, you can rule as the overlord and Hsiang Yu will have to submit to your sovereignty."

"Good!" said Liu Pang. "Have the seals cut at once and you can set out with them."

Chang Liang happened to come in before Li Yi-chi left on this mission. Liu Pang who was at his meal called, "Come over here! Someone has proposed a plan to weaken Chu's power." Having told Chang Liang all Li Yi-chi had said, he asked, "What do you think?"

"Who made this plan?" asked Chang Liang. "This will be your ruin!"

"In what way?" asked Liu Pang.

"Give me your chopsticks and let me explain. When Tang conquered the Hsias, he gave Chi to his descendants because he had power of life and death over them. Have you power of life and death over Hsiang Yu?"

"No, I have not."

"Fallacy number one. When King Wu conquered the Shangs, he gave Sung to his descendants because he knew he could cut off the head of the Shang king. Can you cut off Hsiang Yu's head?"

"No, I cannot."

"Fallacy number two. When King Wu took the Shang capital, he honoured Shang Jung's lane, released Chi Tzu from prison and enlarged Pi Kan's grave. Are you in a position to enlarge a sage's grave, honour a good man's lane or a wise man's gate?"

"No, I am not."

"Fallacy number three. King Wu was able to distribute the grain stored at Chuchiao and the money stored at Lutai among the poor. Are you able to distribute grain and money to the poor?"

"No, I am not."

"Fallacy number four. After his conquest of Shang, King Wu converted war chariots into carriages, while shields and spears were laid down and covered with tiger skins to show the world that there would be no more war. Are you in a position to lay down arms, practise the arts of peace and end all wars?"

"No, I am not."

"Fallacy number five. King Wu grazed his horses south of Mount Hua to show that there would be no more unrest. Are you in a position to turn your horses loose?"

"No, I am not."

"Fallacy number six. King Wu pastured his cattle north of Taolin to show that there would be no more transport duty. Are you in a position to do that?"

"No, I am not."

"Fallacy number seven. Itinerant scholars from all over the world have left their homes, ancestral graves and friends to follow you just in the hope of getting a little land. If you restore the six states and enthrone the descendants of the royal houses of Hann, Wei, Yen, Chao, Chi and Chu, all these gentlemen will go back to serve their old masters, returning to their homes, friends and ancestral graves. Then who will help you to win your empire? This is fallacy number eight. Your main task now is to stop Chu from growing stronger. If the six states are restored and follow Hsiang Yu, how can you subjugate Chu? If you really adopt this plan, it will be your ruin."

Liu Pang stopped eating and spat the food out of his mouth. "That fool of a pedant nearly did for me!" he swore. He gave orders at once to have the seals cancelled.

In the fourth year of Han, Han Hsin conquered Chi and wanted to make himself king there. Liu Pang was angry, but Chang Liang persuaded him to give Han Hsin the seal of a king, as is recorded in the account of Han Hsin.

That autumn Liu Pang pursued Hsiang Yu to south of Yangchia; then, being worsted in battle, he entrenched himself in Kuling, but the other commanders failed to come to his aid. Only when he acted on Chang Liang's advice did the reinforcements come, as is recorded in the account of Hsiang Yu.

In the first month of the sixth year of Han, fiefs were given for outstanding services. Chang Liang had never distinguished himself in battle, but the emperor said, "The strategies you planned in your tent won battles for us a thousand *li* away—that is your achievement. Take your choice of any thirty thousand households in Chi."

Chang Liang answered, "After I rebelled at Hsiapi I met you at Liu. Heaven sent me to you, and I am glad that some of the plans I proposed proved useful. I shall be satisfied with the district of Liu as my fief. I cannot accept thirty thousand households." So Chang Liang was made marquis of Liu at the same time as Hsiao Ho and the others were enfeoffed.

That same year, after the emperor had enfeoffed more than twenty men with great achievements to their credit, the others disputed day and night and could not reach agreement, so that the work of enfeoffment was held up. One day in his Southern Palace in Loyang, the emperor looked down from a terrace and saw some generals sitting by the river and talking together.

"What are they discussing?" he asked.

"Don't you know, sir?" replied Chang Liang. "They are plotting rebellion."

"Peace has just been restored. Why should they revolt?"

"You started out as a common citizen but with their help won the empire. Since becoming the emperor you have ennobled close friends like Hsiao Ho and Tsao Shen and punished all your former enemies. Now these officers, comparing their achievements, think you have not land enough to give fiefs to all. They fear you may not ennoble them, or may even punish them for past shortcomings. That is why they are gathering together to plot revolt."

The emperor was disturbed and asked, "What shall I do?"

"Is there any man they all know you abominate?"

"Yung Chih is one of my old confederates, but he keeps plaguing and insulting me. If not for all he's done, I'd kill him."

"Then lose no time in giving Yung Chih a fief. When the others see him enfeoffed, they will rest assured."

So the emperor gave a feast at which he made Yung Chih marquis of Shihfang and ordered the prime minister and chief counsellor to decide on the other fiefs. After this feast the officers were pleased and said, "If even Yung Chih is made a marquis, we need have no worry."

Liu Ching advised the emperor to make his capital within the Pass. The emperor was in two minds about this. At most of his attendants and high ministers came from east of the mountains, they urged him to make Loyang the capital. "East of Loyang there is Chengkao, west Mount Yao and River Min," they said. "With the Yellow River behind and the Yi and Lo Rivers before, it is surely impregnable!"

But Chang Liang objected, "Though Loyang has these advantages, it covers no more than a few hundred *li*, the land is not fertile and the city is open to attack on four sides. It is not strategically situated. Within the Pass, however, we have Mount Yao and the Hanku Pass to the east, the Lung and Shu ranges to the west, and a thousand *li* of fertile fields; while to the south is the wealth of Pa and Shu, to the north the advantage of the Hunnish pastures. With natural barriers on three sides, we need only cope with the barons in the east. So long as they are quiet, ships can sail along the Yellow River and the Wei to all parts of the empire to bring back grain to the capital in the west. And if the barons make trouble, we can sail downstream with supplies and reinforcements. This is truly a mighty stronghold of solid gold, a thousand-*li* wall of bronze, a natural treasure-house! Liu Ching is right."

That same day the emperor drove west in his carriage to make his capital within the Pass, and Chang Liang accompanied him. As his health was poor, Chang Liang practised breath control and ate no grain, not venturing out of his house for a year and more.

The emperor wished to depose the crown prince in favour of Prince Ju-yi of Chao, his son by Lady Chi; but because many of his chief ministers objected, he had not reached a final decision. Empress Lu was alarmed and did not know what to do till someone suggested, "The Marquis of Liu is a shrewd schemer and the emperor trusts him."

Accordingly Empress Lu sent Lu Tse, marquis of Chiencheng, to enlist Chang Liang's help saying, "You have always advised the emperor. Now that he wants to disinherit the crown prince, how can you lie easy on your pillow?"

"When the emperor was in difficulties he used several of my plans," replied Chang Liang. "Now the empire is at peace and, if he wants to substitute his favorite son for the crown prince, this is between his own flesh and blood. A hundred or more ministers like myself can do nothing."

But Lu Tse insisted, "Think of some plan for us!"

"Hard to talk him out of this," was Chang Liang's answer. "But there are four men the emperor has failed to win over. These four men are old and, because they think his manner insulting, they have hidden themselves in the hills and refuse to serve the House of Han. The emperor has a high regard for these men. Now if you spare no expense on gold and rich gifts, get the crown prince to write a letter couched in humble terms, send comfortable carriages for them and an eloquent speaker to press the invitation, it is possible they may come. If they do, you can entertain them as guests, taking them from time to time with you to the palace, where the emperor will notice them, wonder who they are and make inquiries. When he learns that they are these four worthies, that should help your case."

Then Empress Lu made Lu Tse send a messenger with the crown prince's letter, inviting these four men with humble words and rich gifts. Upon their arrival, Lu Tse made them his guests.

In the eleventh year of Han, Ying Pu rebelled. The emperor, who was ill, wanted the crown prince to command the army sent against him. The four worthies said to each other, "We came here to preserve the crown prince. If he commands the army he will be endangered." So they told Lu Tse, "If the crown prince commands the army and is successful that will not improve his position, while if he returns unsuccessful that will be disastrous. Besides, all the generals under him will be redoubtable veterans who helped his father to win the empire. The crown prince at their head will be like a lamb commanding a pack of wolves. As they will not fight well for him, his failure is certain.

"We have heard that whoever loves the mother will fondle her child. Now Lady Chi waits on the emperor day and night so that Prince Ju-yi is always dandled before him, and the emperor has declared that no unworthy son shall ever rule over a son whom he loves. It is obvious that he is going to replace the crown prince. Lose no time, then, in urging Empress Lu to find some chance to plead to the emperor with tears. She can say that Ying Pu is a formidable fighter, a brilliant commander known throughout the world. Since our generals are all the emperor's old comrades-in-arms, setting the crown prince at their head would be like setting a lamb at the head of wolves—they would never obey him. And once Ying Pu knew this, he would march west towards the capital to the roll of drums. Although the emperor is unwell, he should make the effort to lead this campaign and direct his troops from a carriage, for then his generals will not dare to shirk. Hard as it is, the emperor should do this for the sake of his wife and child."

Lu Tse went that same night to see the empress, who did as the four worthies suggested, seizing an opportunity to plead to the emperor with tears in her eyes.

"I suppose the boy is not up to it," said the emperor. "Your old man will have to go!" So he led his army eastwards. The ministers left in charge saw him off at Pashang. Although Chang Liang was ill, he forced himself to get up and see the emperor at Chuyiu.

"I should have accompanied you," he said, "but I am too ill. The men of Chu are swift. Don't risk a head-on clash." He persuaded the emperor to give the crown prince the command of the troops within the Pass.

"Although you are ill," said the emperor, "do your best to help the crown prince from your couch." At this time Shusun Tung was the prince's senior guardian, so Chang Liang acted as the junior guardian.

In the twelfth year of Han the emperor returned after defeating Ying Pu. His illness had grown worse and he was more determined than ever to depose the crown prince. When Chang Liang's advice against this was disregarded, he retired on the pretext of illness. The senior guardian Shusun Tung, quoting precedents ancient and modern, put up such a hard fight for the crown prince that the emperor pretended to agree, though he still meant to change his heir.

One day there was a feast and wine was served. The crown prince came to wait on his father, attended by four old men each over eighty. Their beards and eyebrows were white, their hats and gowns most imposing.

The emperor asked in surprise, "Who are these men?"

Then the four advanced and gave their names as Master Tung-yuan, Scholar Luli, Chili Chi and Master Hsia-huang.

The emperor exclaimed in astonishment, "I tried for several years to get hold of you, yet you always kept away. What are you doing with my son?"

The four men replied, "You insult gentlemen, sir, and are addicted to swearing. Unwilling to put up with humiliation, we ran away in fear. Then we heard that the crown prince was kind, pious and courteous to all, and that the people of the empire are ready to die for him, and so we came."

The emperor said, "Take good care of the crown prince!"

After the four had paid their respects they rose to leave, and the emperor watched them go. He called Lady Chi and pointed them out to her, saying, "I meant to depose the crown prince, but these four men have come to his aid. His feathers are grown, it would be hard to dislodge him. Empress Lu is going to be your mistress now."

Lady Chi shed tears, at which the emperor said, "Dance one of the dances of Chu for me, and I shall sing a song of Chu for you." With that he sang:

> High flies the wild swan,
> Soaring a thousand *li;*
> His feathers grown,
> He sweeps freely across the four seas;
> Sweeps freely across the four seas,
> And what can we do?
> Even our stringed shafts
> Are powerless against him.

He sang this several times while Lady Chi wept and sobbed. Then he rose and left the feast. So thanks to these four men invited at the suggestion of Chang Liang, the crown prince retained his position.

Chang Liang accompanied the emperor on his expedition against Chen Hsi in Tai, he devised the stratagem at Mayi, and it was he who urged that Hsiao Ho be made prime minister. In his leisure he advised the emperor on various matters, but since these were not vital affairs of state they need not be recorded.

Then Chang Liang announced, "My forefathers were ministers of the state of Hann and after the state was overthrown I gave up a fortune to avenge Hann against mighty Chin, causing a great stir in the world. With my ready tongue I became the adviser of an emperor, was given a fief of ten thousand households and made a marquis. This is all a common citizen could desire, and I am satisfied. Now I mean to turn my back on worldly affairs and follow the Master of the Red Pine." He abstained from grain and studied breath control so that he might fly through the air.

When the emperor died, Empress Lu was so grateful to Chang Liang that she insisted on his taking nourishment and said, "A man's life passes as swiftly as a white charger seen through a crack in the door. Why should you mortify yourself in this way?" So Chang Liang had to take food.

Eight years later he died and was given the posthumous title of Marquis of Wen-cheng. His son Pu-yi succeeded to his title.

As for the old man who met him on the bridge at Hsiapi and gave him *The Patriarch Lu Shang's Art of War,* when Chang Liang went north of the Chi River with the emperor thirteen years after their meeting, he found a yellow stone at the foot of Mount Kucheng which he took away and worshipped. After his death this stone was buried with him, and during the summer and winter sacrifices men sacrificed to the stone too. In the fifth year of Emperor Wen, Chang Liang's son Pu-yi was charged with impiety and deprived of his fief.

The Grand Historian comments: Most scholars deny the existence of ghosts and spirits, but admit that marvels take place. The story of Chang Liang's meeting with the old man who gave him the book is certainly a strange one. It was surely the will of Heaven that Chang Liang was so often able to save the first emperor of Han when he was in trouble. The emperor said, "When it comes to scheming in the commander's tent to win a battle a thousand *li* away, I am no match for Chang Liang." So I had always visualized him as a tall, imposing figure, yet when I saw his portrait he looked like a woman or a pretty girl. Confucius said, "Judging by appearances I have been mistaken in the case of Tzu-yu." The same might be said of Chang Liang.

THE MARQUIS OF HUAI-YIN (HAN HSIN)

... After the king of Han had retired to his territory in Shu, Han Hsin fled from Ch'u and joined the forces of Han. Being still a man of no particular renown, he was given a minor position as attendant to guests.

Han Hsin became involved in an offense and was condemned to die. Thirteen other men in the group had already been beheaded and it was Han Hsin's turn next. He raised his head and looked about, when his eye fell upon Lord T'eng. "Has our sovereign no desire to win the world?" he asked. "Why does he deliberately cut off the head of a brave man?"

From *Records of the Grand Historian of China,* vol. 1, *Early Years of the Han Dynasty, 209 to 141* B.C., translated by Burton Watson (New York and London: Columbia University Press, 1961), 209–21. Copyright © 1961 by Columbia University Press, New York. Reprinted by permission of the publishers.

Lord T'eng was struck by his words and saw that he had a brave appearance, and so he did not execute him but set him free. After talking to Han Hsin, and finding him much to his liking, Lord T'eng mentioned him to the king of Han, who made him a commissary colonel, though the king saw nothing unusual in him. Han Hsin several times talked to Hsiao Ho, who regarded him with peculiar respect.

By the time the Han army reached Nan-cheng, it was found that twenty or thirty of the generals had deserted along the way. "Hsiao Ho and others have several times spoken about me to the king," Han Hsin considered to himself, "but the king has no use for me," and with this he too deserted. When Hsiao Ho heard that Han Hsin had run away, he did not wait to ask the king but started after him in person.

Someone reported to the king that Prime Minister Hsiao Ho had deserted. The king flew into a rage and was as distressed as if he had lost his right or left hand. After a day or so Hsiao Ho returned and appeared before the king. The king, half in anger and half in joy, began to curse him. "You deserted, didn't you!" he said. "Why?"

"How would I dare to desert?" replied Hsiao Ho. "I went after a deserter!"

"Who is it you went after?"

"Han Hsin."

The king cursed again. "When my generals were deserting me by the tens you did not pursue one of them. This going after Han Hsin is a lie!"

"Generals are easy enough to get," replied Hsiao Ho, "but men like Han Hsin are the best in the nation. If Your Majesty's ambition is to rule the area of Han for as long as possible, then you have no use for Han Hsin's services. But if you hope to contend for mastery of the world, then Han Hsin is the only man to lay plans with. It is entirely a matter of which course you choose to take."

"My whole ambition is to march east," the king replied. "How could I bear to stay pent up in a place like this forever?"

"Since your plans are aimed at moving east again, if you can make good use of Han Hsin, then he will stay with you. But if you cannot use him properly, then he will eventually desert!"

"For your sake I will make him a general," said the king.

"If you make him no more than a general, he will never stay."

"Then I will make him a major general!"

"That would be most gracious of you," Hsiao Ho replied. The king was about to summon Han Hsin and invest him with the position at once, but Hsiao Ho said, "Your Majesty is inclined to be rather brusque and lacking in ceremony. If you were to call him in and make him a general at once, it would be like ordering a little boy about. This is precisely the reason Han Hsin deserted. If you wish to confer a title on him, you must select an auspicious day, fast and purify yourself, erect an altar and go through the whole ceremony. This is the only way."

The king gave his consent to this. All of the generals were filled with joy, each considering that it was himself who was about to be made a major general. But when the title was conferred, to the astonishment of the entire army, it was upon Han Hsin. After the ceremony of investiture was concluded and Han Hsin had returned to his seat, the king said, "Prime Minister Hsiao Ho has often spoken to me about you, general. What sort of strategy is it that you would teach me?"

Han Hsin expressed his gratitude for the honor and took advantage of the king's inquiry to ask a question of his own. "Anyone who marched east to contend for the empire would have to face Hsiang Yü, would he not?"

"He would," replied the king.

"In Your Majesty's estimation, which of you, Hsiang Yü or yourself, excels in fierceness of courage and depth of kindness?"

The king of Han was silent for a while and then he said, "I am inferior to Hsiang Yü."

Han Hsin bowed once more and commended the king, saying, "Yes, I too believe that you are inferior. But I once served Hsiang Yü, and I would like to tell you what sort of person he is. When Hsiang Yü rages and bellows it is enough to make a thousand men fall down in terror. But since he is incapable of employing wise generals, all of it amounts to no more than the daring of an ordinary man.

"When Hsiang Yü meets people he is courteous and thoughtful, his manner of speaking is gentle and, if someone is ill or in distress, he will weep over him and give him his own food and drink. But when someone he has sent upon a mission has achieved merit and deserves to be honored and enfeoffed he will fiddle with the seal of investiture until it crumbles in his hand before he can bring himself to present it to the man. This sort of kindness deserves to be called merely womanish!

"Now although Hsiang Yü has made himself dictator of the world and subjugated the other nobles to his rule, he has not taken up residence in the area within the Pass, but has made his capital at P'eng-ch'eng. He has gone against the agreement made with the Righteous Emperor and instead given out kingdoms to the nobles on the basis of his own likes and preferences, which has resulted in much injustice. The nobles, seeing that Hsiang Yü has banished the Righteous Emperor and sent him to reside in Chiang-nan, when they return to their own territories in like manner drive out their sovereigns and make themselves rulers of the choicest lands. Hsiang Yü has left death and destruction everywhere he has passed. Much of the world hates him. The common people do not submit to him out of affection, but are awed by his might alone. In name he is a dictator, but in truth he has lost the hearts of the world. Therefore I say that his might can be easily weakened!

"Now if you could only pursue the opposite policy and make use of the brave men of the world, what enemy would not fall before you? If you were to enfeoff your worthy followers with the territories of the empire, who would not submit? If you were to take your soldiers of righteousness and lead them back east where they long to return, who would not flee from your path?

"The three kings of the region of Ch'in were formerly generals of Ch'in and led the sons of Ch'in for several years. The number of men who were killed under their command exceeds estimation. In addition they deceived their men into surrendering to the other nobles and, when they reached Hsin-an, Hsiang Yü treacherously butchered over two hundred thousand soldiers of the Ch'in army who had surrendered, sparing only the three generals Chang Han, Ssu-ma Hsin, and Tung I. Therefore the fathers of Ch'in loath these three men with a passion that eats into their very bones. Now Hsiang Yü has managed by sheer force to make kings of these men, but the people of Ch'in have no love for them. When you entered the Wu Pass, you inflicted not a particle of harm, but repealed the harsh laws of Ch'in and gave to the people a simple code of laws in three articles only, and there were none of the people of Ch'in who did not wish to make you their king. According to the agreement concluded among all the nobles, you ought to have been made king of the area within the Pass, and the people of the area all knew this. And when you were deprived of your rightful position and retired to the region of Han, the people of Ch'in were all filled with resentment. Now if you will raise your army and march east, you can win over the three kingdoms of Ch'in simply by proclamation!"

The king of Han was overjoyed and only regretted that he had been so long in discovering Han Hsin. He proceeded to follow the strategy Han Hsin had outlined and assigned to his generals the areas which each was to attack. In the eighth month the king of Han raised his army, marched east out of Ch'en-ts'ang, and subjugated the three kingdoms of Ch'in.

In the second year of Han the king marched out of the Pass and seized control of Wei and Ho-nan. The kings of Hann and Yin both surrendered to him. Joining the forces of Ch'i and Chao, he attacked Ch'u. In the fourth month he reached P'eng-ch'eng, where his forces were defeated and compelled to retreat in disorder. Han Hsin gathered a second force of troops and joined the king of Han at Jung-yang and once more they attacked Ch'u in the region of Ching and So. As a result of this attack the armies of Ch'u were unable to proceed any further west.

When the Han army was defeated at P'eng-ch'eng and driven back, Ssu-ma Hsin, the king of Sai, and Tung I, the king of Ti, fled from Han and surrendered to Ch'u. Ch'i and Chao also revolted against Han and made peace with Ch'u.

In the sixth month Pao, king of Wei, asked to be allowed to go home and look after his ailing parents but, when he reached his kingdom, he cut off the fords over the Yellow River, revolted against Han, and concluded an alliance with Ch'u. The king of Han dispatched Master Li I-chi in an attempt to dissuade him, but he refused to listen. In the eighth month of this year Han Hsin was made prime minister of the left and sent to attack Wei. The king of Wei concentrated his forces at P'u-fan and blockaded Lin-chin. Han Hsin thereupon planted a dummy army and lined up a number of boats as though he were about to attempt to cross the river at Lin-chin. In the meantime he secretly led another force of men by way of Hsia-yang, where he ferried them across the river on floats and attacked An-i. Pao, the king of Wei, taken completely by surprise, led his troops to oppose Han Hsin but was taken prisoner. Han Hsin subjugated Wei and made it into the province of Ho-tung.

The king of Han dispatched Chang Erh to join Han Hsin and with him lead a force of troops to the northeast to attack Chao and Tai. In the intercalary ninth month they defeated the troops of Tai and took Hsia Yüeh prisoner at Yen-yü. As soon as Han Hsin had conquered Wei and defeated Tai the king of Han hastily sent someone to take command of Han Hsin's best troops and bring them to Jung-yang to help in the blockade against Ch'u.

Han Hsin and Chang Erh with their force of twenty or thirty thousand men prepared to march east through the Ching Gorge to attack Chao. The king of Chao and Ch'en Yü, lord of Ch'eng-an, hearing that the Han forces were about to attack them, gathered an army, ostensibly numbering two hundred thousand, at the mouth of the gorge. Li Tso-ch'e, lord of Kuang-wu, advised Ch'en Yü, saying, "I have heard that the Han general Han Hsin has forded the Yellow River to the west, made the king of Wei and Hsia Yüeh his prisoners, and spilled blood anew at Yen-yü. Now with the help of Chang Erh he has laid his plans and intends to conquer Chao. An army such as his, riding the crest of victory and fighting far from its homeland, cannot be opposed.

"I have heard it said that, when provisions must be transported a thousand miles, the soldiers have a hungry look and, when fuel must be gathered before the mess is prepared, the army seldom sleeps with a full stomach. Now the road through the Ching Gorge is such that two carts cannot drive side by side, nor two horsemen ride abreast. On a march of several hundred miles under such circumstances, their provisions are sure to be in the rear. I beg you to lend me a force of thirty thousand surprise troops which I can lead by a secret route to cut off their supply wagons. In the meantime, if you deepen your moats, heighten your ramparts, strengthen your camp, and refuse to engage in battle, they will be unable either to advance and fight, or to retreat and go back home. With my surprise force I will cut off their rear and see to it that they get no plunder from the countryside, and before ten days are out I will bring the heads of their two commanders and lay them beneath your banners! I beg you to give heed to my plan for, if you do not, you will most certainly find yourself their prisoner!"

But Ch'en Yü was a Confucianist who always spoke of his "soldiers of righteousness" and had no use for tricky schemes or unusual strategies. "I have always heard that in the art of warfare," he said, "if you outnumber the enemy ten to one, you surround him, but if you outnumber him two to one, you engage him in battle. Now although Han Hsin's forces are reputed to be twenty or thirty thousand, they do not in fact exceed three or four thousand. Furthermore, he has marched a thousand miles to attack me, so he must already be thoroughly exhausted. If I were to flee and decline to fight under such circumstances, what would I do in the future when faced with a larger number? The other nobles would call me coward and think nothing of coming to attack me!"

Thus he refused to listen to the lord of Kuang-wu's plan, and the suggestion went unheeded. Han Hsin sent men to spy in secret and when they learned that the lord of Kuang-wu's plan was not being followed, they returned and reported to Han Hsin. He was overjoyed and proceeded without fear to lead his troops down the gorge. When they were still thirty *li* from the mouth of the gorge, he halted and made camp. During the night he sent an order through the camp to dispatch a force of two thousand light cavalry. Each man was to carry a red flag and, proceeding along a secret route, to conceal himself in the mountains and observe the Chao army. "When the Chao forces see me marching out, they are sure to abandon their fortifications and come in pursuit. Then you must enter their walls with all speed, tear down the Chao flags, and set up the red flags of Han in their place," he instructed them. Then he ordered his lieutenant generals to distribute a light meal to the army, saying, "This day we shall defeat Chao and feast together!" None of his generals believed that the plan would work, but they feigned agreement and answered, "Very well."

Han Hsin addressed his officers, saying, "The Chao forces have already constructed their fortifications in an advantageous position. Moreover, until they see the flags and drums of our commanding general, they will be unwilling to attack our advance column for fear that I will see the difficulty of the position and retreat back up the gorge." Han Hsin therefore sent ten thousand men to march ahead out of the gorge and draw up in ranks with their backs to the river that ran through the gorge. The Chao army, observing this from afar, roared with laughter.

At dawn Han Hsin raised the flags of the commanding general, set his drums to sounding, and marched out of the mouth of the Ching Gorge. The Chao army opened their gates and poured out to attack and for a long time the two armies fought together fiercely. At this point Han Hsin and Chang Erh deceptively abandoned their flags and drums and fled to the forces drawn up along the river. The columns along the river opened to receive them, and the battle continued to rage. As Han Hsin had anticipated, the Chao forces finally abandoned their fortifications completely in their eagerness to contend for the Han flags and pursue Han Hsin and Chang Erh. With Han Hsin and Chang Erh in their ranks, however, the army along the river determined to fight to the death and could not be defeated.

In the meantime the surprise force of two thousand cavalry which Han Hsin had sent out, waiting until the Chao forces had abandoned their camp in order to follow up their advantage, rushed into the Chao fortifications, tore down the Chao flags, and set up two thousand red flags of Han in their place. The Chao forces, unable to achieve a victory and capture Han Hsin and the others, were about to return to their fortifications when they discovered that the walls were lined with the red flags of Han. The soldiers were filled with alarm and, concluding that the Han army had already captured the generals of the king of Chao, fled in panic in all directions. Though the Chao generals cut them down on the spot, they could not stop the rout. With this the Han forces closed in from both sides, defeated and captured the Chao army, executed Ch'en Yü on the banks of the Ch'ih River, and took Hsieh, the king of Chao, prisoner.

Han Hsin issued orders to his army that the lord of Kuang-wu was not to be killed, and offered a reward of a thousand catties of gold to the man who could capture him alive. As a result the lord of Kuang-wu was bound by one of the men and led before the commanding general. Han Hsin loosed his bonds, placed him in the seat of honor facing east, and himself took a seat facing west, treating him with the respect due a teacher. The subordinate generals arrived to present their captives and the heads of their victims, and then rested from their labors and joined in congratulating Han Hsin on the victory.

Taking advantage of the opportunity, they began to question Han Hsin. "According to The Art of War, when one fights he should keep the hills to his right or rear, and bodies of water in front of him or to the left," they said. "Yet today you ordered us on the contrary to draw up ranks with our backs to the river, saying 'We shall defeat Chao and feast together!' We were opposed to the idea, and yet it has ended in victory. What sort of strategy is this?"

"This is in The Art of War too," replied Han Hsin. "It is just that you have failed to notice it! Does it not say in The Art of War: 'Drive them into a fatal position and they will come out alive; place them in a hopeless spot and they will survive'? Moreover, I did not have at my disposal troops that I had trained and led from past times, but was forced, as the saying goes, to round up men from the market place and use them to fight with. Under such circumstances, if I had not placed them in a desperate situation where each man was obliged to fight for his own life, but had allowed them to remain in a safe place, they would have all run away. Then what good would they have been to me?"

"Indeed!" his generals exclaimed in admiration. "We would never have thought of that."

Then Han Hsin questioned the lord of Kuang-wu. "I am planning to march north and attack Yen, and from there proceed east to strike at Ch'i. What would be the most effective way to go about it?"

The lord of Kuang-wu, however, declined to answer, saying, "The general of a defeated army, they say, is not qualified to talk of bravery, nor the minister of a lost nation to invent schemes for survival. Now that I am a prisoner taken in defeat, how could I be worthy to weigh such great undertakings?"

Han Hsin replied, "I have heard it said that when Po-li Hsi lived in Yü, Yü was destroyed, but when he lived in Ch'in, Ch'in became a great power. This was not because he was stupid when he was in Yü and wise when in Ch'in. It was only because in one he was employed and in the other he was not; in one he was listened to and in the other ignored. As a matter of fact, if Ch'en Yü had listened to your plan, even I would have become your prisoner. It is only because he did not make use of you that I have the honor of waiting upon you now." Han Hsin continued to press him for an answer, saying, "I shall set all of my ideas aside and do whatever you suggest. I beg you to decline no further!"

"They say," answered the lord of Kuang-wu, "that among the schemes of the wisest man one in a thousand will end in error, while among those of the greatest fool one in a thousand will succeed. Therefore it is said that a sage will find something to choose even from the words of a madman. I am doubtful whether any plan I might suggest would be worthy of consideration, but I beg to exercise the limits of my poor ability.

"Ch'en Yü had a plan which seemed to insure a hundred victories in as many battles, and yet in one morning it proved a failure, his army was defeated before the walls of Ho, and he himself met death on the banks of the Ch'ih. Now you have crossed the Yellow River to the west, made a prisoner of the king of Wei, captured Hsia Yüeh at Yen-yü, in one stroke descended the Ching Gorge and, before the morning was out, defeated Chao's great army of two hundred thousand and executed Ch'en Yü. Your fame resounds throughout the land and your might fills the world with awe. The farmers have left their plowing and cast aside their hoes and, anticipating that your armies will soon be upon them, have donned their finest clothes and are feasting while they may, inclining their ears in wait for your command. Such is the strength of your position.

"On the other hand, your troops are tired and worn out, and in point of fact are not of much use. Now you plan to lead this force of weary and exhausted men and further exhaust them before the stout walls of Yen. Yet, no matter how long you battle, your strength will not be sufficient to overcome them. The hopelessness of your situation will become apparent as your might declines, the days will pass fruitlessly while your supplies grow scarce, and still Yen, weak though it is, will not submit. Ch'i in the meantime will certainly man its frontiers and strengthen its defense and, with Yen and Ch'i supporting each other and refusing to capitulate, the king of Han and Hsiang Yü will continue at a stalemate and their fate will never be decided. This is the weak side of your position. In my humble opinion such a move would be a mistake, for one who is skilled in the use of arms never attacks strength with weakness, but only weakness with strength."

"Then what course should I follow?" asked Han Hsin.

"If I were to suggest a plan for you," replied the lord of Kuang-wu, "I would say the best thing to do would be to halt your army and rest your soldiers. Patrol the land of Chao and comfort the orphans made in today's battle. From the surrounding area have oxen and wine brought each day to feast your officers and banquet your men, and face them north towards the roads of Yen. After that you may dispatch your rhetoricians bearing documents to prove how superior your strength is to that of Yen, and Yen will not dare to turn a deaf ear. When Yen has submitted, you may send your propagandists to the east to talk to Ch'i, and Ch'i too will be obliged by the trend of events to submit, for even her wisest councilors will be able to think of no alternative. In this way you can have your will with the whole empire. In warfare the important thing is to publicize yourself first, and act afterward. Therefore I have suggested this plan."

Han Hsin approved of his plan and set about putting it into action, dispatching an envoy to Yen. Yen bowed before the report of Han Hsin's power and submitted. Han Hsin sent an envoy to report this to the king of Han, at the same time requesting that Chang Erh be made king of Chao to bring peace and order to the land. The king of Han gave his permission and set up Chang Erh as king of Chao.

Ch'u from time to time sent surprise forces across the Yellow River to attack Chao, but Chang Erh and Han Hsin, by moving back and forth through the area, were able to save Chao, step by step gain control of its cities, and eventually dispatch a force of troops to aid the king of Han, who at this time was in Jung-yang surrounded and sorely pressed by the armies of Ch'u. The king of Han escaped south to the area of Yüan and She, where he obtained the aid of Ch'ing Pu, and then fled to safety in Ch'eng-kao. The Ch'u forces once more surrounded and pressed him. In the sixth month the king of Han fled from

Ch'eng-kao, crossed to the east side of the Yellow River and, accompanied only by Lord T'eng, went to join the army of Chang Erh at Hsiu-wu. When he arrived he stopped for a night at the posthouse and at dawn the next day, representing himself as an envoy from the king of Han, hastened into the Chao camp. Chang Erh and Han Hsin being still in bed, he went to their chambers, seized their seals of command, and with these summoned all the subordinate generals and began assigning them to new posts. When Han Hsin and Chang Erh woke up and found that the king of Han had arrived, they were astounded. Thus the king of Han seized the armies of both men, ordering Chang Erh to man and guard the region of Chao, and making Han Hsin his prime minister with orders to form an army from the men of Chao who had not yet been pressed into service and proceed to attack Ch'i.

Han Hsin led his troops east but, before he had crossed the Yellow River at the P'ing-yüan Ford, he received word that the king of Han had sent Li I-chi to bargain with Ch'i and that Ch'i had already submitted. Han Hsin wanted to halt his march, but K'uai T'ung, a rhetorician from Fan-yang, counseled him against this. "You have received a royal order to attack Ch'i. In the meantime the king of Han has independently dispatched a secret envoy to talk Ch'i into submission. But there has been no royal order instructing you to halt, has there? How can you fail to proceed on your mission? Furthermore, this one man, Master Li I-chi, by bowing graciously from his carriage and wagging his meager tongue, has conquered the seventy-odd cities of Ch'i, while you, with your army of thousands, needed a year and over before you could gain control of the fifty-odd cities of Chao. Could it be that what you have done in your several years as a general is not equal to the accomplishments of one wretched Confucianist?"

Persuaded by his arguments, Han Hsin followed his advice and proceeded to cross the Yellow River. Ch'i in the meantime, having heeded Master Li's persuasions, was detaining him with wine and feasts and had at the same time dispersed the defenses which it had prepared against the Han armies. Han Hsin was thus able to attack the Ch'i army at Li-hsia and proceed as far as Lin-tzu. T'ien Kuang, the king of Ch'i, concluding that Master Li had betrayed him, had Master Li boiled alive and then fled to Kao-mi, where he sent an envoy to Ch'u to beg for aid.

After conquering Lin-tzu, Han Hsin proceeded east in pursuit of T'ien Kuang as far as the west of Kao-mi. Ch'u also sent its general Lung Chü with a reputed force of two hundred thousand to aid Ch'i. The king of Ch'i and Lung Chü with their combined armies fought with Han Hsin but, before the armies had closed in battle, someone advised Lung Chü, saying, "The soldiers of Han, battling far from their homeland, will fight to the death. They cannot be opposed in combat. Ch'i and Ch'u, however, are fighting on their own ground and their soldiers may easily run away in defeat. It would be better to strengthen your fortifications and have the king of Ch'i send his trusted ministers to rally the lost cities of Ch'i. If the lost cities hear that their king is still alive and that aid has come from Ch'u, they will certainly revolt against the Han army. The Han soldiers have marched a thousand miles into a strange land. If the cities of Ch'i all turn against them, they will find themselves with no way to get food for their forces, and they can be overcome without a fight."

Lung Chü replied, "I have long known what sort of man Han Hsin is. He is easy enough to deal with. Furthermore, now that I have come to rescue Ch'i, if I were to overcome him without a battle, what merit would I gain from the expedition? But if I fight and beat him, half of Ch'i can be mine. Why should I stop now?"

In the end he engaged Han Hsin in battle, the two armies drawing up on opposite sides of the Wei River. In the night Han Hsin ordered his men to make more than ten thousand bags, fill them with sand, and block the flow of the river upstream. Then he led his army halfway across the river to attack Lung Chü but, pretending to be defeated, fled back to the shore. As Han Hsin had expected, Lung Chü announced delightedly, "I always knew that Han Hsin was a coward!" and forthwith pursued Han Hsin across the river. Han Hsin then ordered his men to break open the dam of sandbags. The water came rushing down so that the large part of Lung Chü's army could not get across the river. With all speed Han Hsin closed in and killed Lung Chü, while the men of Lung Chü's army who had crossed to the east side of the river fled in disorder. T'ien Kuang, the king of Ch'i, fled at the same time. Han Hsin pursued the defeated army as far as Ch'eng-yang, where he captured all the soldiers of Ch'u.

PART 4

INDIA

KAUTILYA
(fourth century B.C.?)

The author of the Arthashastra, *which was written in Sanskrit, is said to have been the Brahman Kautilya (or Chanakya, or Vishnugupta), who is traditionally believed to have overthrown the Nanda dynasty and made Chandragupta Maurya king of Magadha (in what is now Bihar) around 321 B.C. In fact, the work was very possibly written by someone entirely different, perhaps in the third century A.D. or even later. It is divided into fifteen books, ten of which are devoted to diplomacy and war. In ancient India, there was a clear separation between the realms of religion (dharma) and politics (artha), and the* Arthashastra *is a treatise on the art of government, intended for the prince. As such, it is close to the thinking of Machiavelli and Hobbes—shot through with cold realism, devoid of moralizing considerations. It must be regarded as one of the major political and strategic treatises of the ancient world.*

THE SIX-FOLD POLICY

The Circle of States is the source of the six-fold policy.

My teacher says that peace [*sandhi*], war [*vigraha*], observance of neutrality [*asana*], marching [*yana*], alliance [*samshraya*], and making peace with one and waging war with another are the six forms of state policy.

But Vatavyadhi holds that there are only two forms of policy, peace and war, inasmuch as the six forms result from these two primary forms of policy.

While Kautilya holds that, as their respective conditions differ, the forms of policy are six.

Of these, agreement with pledges is peace; offensive operation is war; indifference is neutrality; making preparations is marching; seeking the protection

From Kautilya, *Arthashastra*, translated by R. Shamasastry (1915), 5th ed. (Mysore: Sri Raghuveer, 1956), [bk. 7,] 293–340.

of another is alliance; and making peace with one and waging war with another, is termed a double policy [*dvaidhibhava*]. These are the six forms.

Whoever is inferior to another shall make peace with him; whoever is superior in power shall wage war; whoever thinks, "No enemy can hurt me, nor am I strong enough to destroy my enemy," shall observe neutrality; whoever is possessed of necessary means shall march against his enemy; whoever is devoid of necessary strength to defend himself shall seek the protection of another; whoever thinks that help is necessary to work out an end shall make peace with one and wage war with another. Such is the aspect of the six forms of policy.

Of these, a wise king shall observe that form of policy which, in his opinion, enables him to build forts, to construct buildings and commercial roads, to open new plantations and villages, to exploit mines and timber and elephant forests and at the same time to harass similar works of his enemy.

Whoever thinks himself to be growing in power more rapidly both in quality and quantity [than his enemy], and the reverse of his enemy, may neglect his enemy's progress for the time.

If any two kings, hostile to each other, find the time of achieving the results of their respective works to be equal, they shall make peace with each other.

No king shall keep that form of policy, which causes him the loss of profit from his own works, but which entails no such loss on the enemy; for it is deterioration.

Whoever thinks that in the course of time his loss will be less than his acquisition as contrasted with that of his enemy, may neglect his temporary deterioration.

If any two kings, hostile to each other, and deteriorating, except to acquire equal amount of wealth in equal time, they shall make peace with each other.

That position in which neither progress nor retrogression is seen is stagnation.

Whoever thinks his stagnancy to be of a shorter duration and his prosperity in the long run to be greater than his enemy's, may neglect his temporary stagnation.

My teacher says that if any two kings, who are hostile to each other, and are in a stationary condition, except to acquire equal amount of wealth and power in equal time, they shall make peace with each other.

"Of course," says Kautilya, "there is no other alternative."

Or if a king thinks:

"That keeping the agreement of peace, I can undertake productive works of considerable importance and destroy at the same time those of my enemy; or apart from enjoying the results of my own works, I shall also enjoy those of my enemy in virtue of the agreement of peace; or I can destroy the works of my enemy by employing spies and other secret means; or by holding out such inducements as a happy dwelling, rewards, remission of taxes, little work and large profits and wages, I can empty my enemy's country of its population, with which he has been able to carry his own works; or being allied with a king of considerable power, my enemy will have his own work destroyed; or I can prolong my enemy's hostility with another king whose threats have driven my enemy to seek my protection; or being allied with me, my enemy can harass the country of another king who hates me; or oppressed by another king, the subjects of my enemy will immigrate into my country, and I can, therefore, achieve the results of my own works very easily; or being in a precarious condition due to the destruction of his works, my enemy will not be so powerful as to attack me; or by exploiting my own resources in alliance with any two [friendly] kings, I can augment my resources; or if a Circle of States is formed by my enemy as one of its members, I can divide them and combine with the others; or by threats or favour, I can catch hold of my enemy, and when he desires to be a member of my own Circle of States, I can make him incur the displeasure of the other members and fall a victim to their own fury"—if a king thinks thus, then he may increase his resources by keeping peace.

Or if a king thinks:

"That as my country is full of born soldiers and of corporations of fighting men, and as it possesses such natural defensive positions as mountains, forests, rivers, and forts with only one entrance, it can easily repel the attack of my enemy; or having taken my stand in my impregnable fortress at the border of my country, I can harass the works of my enemy; or owing to internal troubles and loss of energy, my enemy will early suffer from the destruction of his works; or when my enemy is attacked by another king, I can induce his subjects to immigrate into my country," then he may augment his own resources by keeping open hostility with such an enemy.

Or if a king thinks:

"That neither is my enemy strong enough to destroy my works, nor am I his; or if he comes to fight with me like a dog with a boar, I can increase his afflictions without incurring any loss in my own works," then he may observe neutrality and augment his own resources.

Or if a king thinks:

"That by marching my troops it is possible to destroy the works of my enemy; and as for myself, I have made proper arrangements to safeguard my own works," then he may increase his resources by marching.

Or if a king thinks:

"That I am strong enough neither to harass my enemy's works nor to defend my own against my enemy's attack," then he shall seek protection from a king of superior power, and endeavour to pass from the stage of deterioration to that of stagnancy and from the latter to that of progress.

Or if a king thinks:

"That by making peace with one, I can work out my own resources, and by waging war with another, I can destroy the works of my enemy," then he may adopt that double policy and improve his resources.

Thus, a king in the circle of sovereign states shall, by adopting the six-fold policy, endeavour to pass from the state of deterioration to that of stagnation, and from the latter to that of progress.

The Nature of Alliance

When the advantages derivable from peace and war are of equal character, one should prefer peace; for disadvantages, such as the loss of power and wealth, sojourning, and sin, are ever attending upon war.

The same holds good in the case of neutrality and war.

Of the two [forms of policy], double policy and alliance, double policy [i.e., making peace with one and waging war with another] is preferable; for whoever adopts the double policy enriches himself, being ever attentive to his own works, whereas an allied king has to help his ally at his own expense.

One shall make an alliance with a king who is stronger than one's neighbouring enemy; in the absence of such a king, one should ingratiate oneself with one's neighbouring enemy, either by supplying money or army or by ceding a part of one's territory and by keeping oneself aloof; for there can be no greater evil to kings than alliance with a king of considerable power, unless one is actually attacked by one's enemy.

A powerless king should behave as a conquered king [towards his immediate enemy]; but when he finds that the time of his own ascendancy is at hand, due to a fatal disease, internal troubles, increase of enemies, or a friend's calamities that are vexing his enemy, then under the pretence of performing some expiatory rites to avert the danger of his enemy, he may get out [of the enemy's court]; or if he is in his own territory, he should not go to see his suffering enemy; or if he is near to his enemy, he may murder the enemy when opportunity affords itself.

A king who is situated between two powerful kings shall seek protection from the stronger of the two; or from one of them on whom he can rely; or he may make peace with both of them on equal terms. Then he may begin to set one of them against the other by telling each that the other is a tyrant causing utter ruin to himself, and thus cause dissension between them. When they are divided, he may put down each separately by secret or covert means. Or, throwing himself under the protection of any two immediate kings of considerable power, he may defend himself against an immediate enemy. Or, having made an alliance with a chief in a stronghold, he may adopt the double policy [i.e., make peace with one of the two kings and wage war with another]. Or, he may adapt himself to circumstances, depending upon the causes of peace and war in order. Or, he may make friendship with traitors, enemies, and wild chiefs who are conspiring against both the kings. Or, pretending to be a close friend of one of them, he may strike the other at the latter's weak point by employing enemies and wild tribes. Or, having made friendship with both, he may form a Circle of States. Or, he may make an alliance with the Madhyama or the neutral king; and with this help he may put down one of them or both. Or when hurt by both, he may seek protection from a king of righteous character among the Madhyama king, the neutral king, and their friends or equals, or from any other king whose subjects are so disposed as to increase his happiness and peace, with whose help he may be able to recover his lost position, with whom his ancestors were in close intimacy or blood relationship, and in whose kingdom he can find a number of powerful friends.

Of two powerful kings who are on amicable terms with each other, a king shall make alliance with one of them who likes him and whom he likes; this is the best way of making alliance.

The Character of Equal, Inferior and Superior Kings; and Forms of Agreement Made by an Inferior King

A king desirous of expanding his own power shall make use of the six-fold policy.

Agreements of peace shall be made with equal and superior kings: and an inferior king shall be attacked.

Whoever goes to wage war with a superior king will be reduced to the same condition as that of a foot-soldier opposing an elephant.

Just as the collision of an unbaked mud-vessel with a similar vessel is destructive to both, so war with an equal king brings ruin to both.

Like a stone striking an earthen pot, a superior king attains decisive victory over an inferior king.

If a superior king discards the proposal of an inferior king for peace, the latter should take the attitude of a conquered king, or play the part of an inferior king towards a superior.

When a king of equal power does not like peace, then the same amount of vexation as his opponent has received at his hands should be given to him in return; for it is power that brings about peace between any two kings: no piece of iron that is not made red-hot will combine with another piece of iron.

When an inferior king is all submissive, peace should be made with him; for when provoked by causing him troubles and anger, an inferior king, like a wild fire, will attack his enemy and will also be favoured by [his] Circle of States.

When a king in peace with another finds that greedy, impoverished, and oppressed as are the subjects of his ally, they do not yet immigrate into his own territory lest they might be called back by their master, then he should, though of inferior power, proclaim war against his ally.

When a king at war with another finds that greedy, impoverished, and oppressed as are the subjects of his enemy, still they do not come to his side in consequence of the troubles of war, then he should, though of superior power, make peace with his enemy or remove the troubles of war as far as possible.

When one of the two kings at war with each other and equally involved in trouble finds his own troubles to be greater than his enemy's, and thinks that by getting rid of his [enemy's] trouble his enemy can successfully wage war with him, then he should, though possessing greater resources, sue for peace.

When, either in peace or war, a king finds neither loss to his enemy nor gain to himself, he should, though superior, observe neutrality.

When a king finds the troubles of his enemy irremediable, he should, though of inferior power, march against the enemy.

When a king finds himself threatened by imminent danger or troubles, he should, though superior, seek the protection of another.

When a king is sure to achieve his desired ends by making peace with one and waging war with another, he should, though superior, adopt the double policy.

Thus it is that the six forms of policy are applied together.

As to their special application:

When a powerless king finds himself attacked by a powerful king, leading a Circle of States, he should submissively sue for peace on the condition of offering treasure, army, himself or his territory.

Agreement made on the condition that with a fixed number of troops or with the flower of his army, a king should present himself [when called for], is peace termed *atmamisha* ["offering himself as flesh"].

Agreement made on the condition that the commander of the army together with the heir-apparent should present himself [when called for], is peace styled *purushantarasandhi* ["peace with hostages other than the king himself"]; and it is conducive to self-preservation, as it does not require the personal attendance of the king.

Agreement made on the condition that the king himself or some one else should march with the army to some place, as required, is peace termed *adrshtapurush* ["peace with no specified person to serve"]; and it is conducive to the safety of the king and the chiefs of his army.

In the first two forms of the peace, a woman of high rank should be given as a hostage, and in the last, a secret attempt should be made to capture the enemy; these are the forms of peace concluded on the condition of supplying his army.

When, by offering wealth, the rest of the elements of sovereignty are set free, that peace is termed *parikraya* ["price"].

Similarly, when peace is concluded by offering money capable of being taken on a man's shoulders, it is termed *upagrahah* ["subsidy"]; and it is of various forms; owing to distance and owing to its having been kept long, the amount of the tribute promised may sometimes fall in arrears.

Yet as such a burden can tolerably be paid in future, this peace is better than the one with a woman given as a hostage. When the parties making an agreement of peace are amicably united, it is termed *suvarnasandhi* ["golden peace"].

Quite reverse from the former is the peace called *kapala* ["half of a pot"], which is concluded on the condition of paying immense quantity of money.

In the first two, one should send the supply of raw materials, elephants, horses and troops [with a snare to get back]; in the third, money; and in the fourth, one should evade the payment under the plea of loss of result from works; these are the forms of peace concluded on the payment of money.

When by ceding a part of the territory, the rest of the kingdom with its subjects are kept safe, it is termed *adishta* ["ceded"] and is of advantage to one who is desirous of destroying thieves and other wicked persons [infesting the ceded part].

When with the exception of the capital, the whole of the territory, impoverished by exploitation of its resources, is ceded, it is termed *uchchhinnasandhi* ["peace cut off from profit"] and is of advantage to one who desires to involve the enemy in troubles.

When by the stipulation of paying the produce of the land, the kingdom is set free, it is termed *avakraya* ["rent"]. That which is concluded by the promise of paying more than the land yields is called *paribhushana* ["ornament"].

One should wait for an opportunity in the first; but the last two, based upon the payment of the produce, should be made only when one is obliged to submit to power. These are the forms of peace made by ceding territory.

These three kinds of peace [made by supplying the army, money, or territory] are to be concluded by an inferior king in submission to the power of a superior king owing to the peculiar condition of his own works, circumstances, and time.

Neutrality after Proclaiming War or after Concluding a Treaty of Peace; Marching after Proclaiming War or after Making Peace; and the March of Combined Powers

Neutrality or marching after proclaiming war or peace has been explained.

Sthana (keeping quiet), *asana* (withdrawal from hostility), and *upekshana* (negligence) are synonymous with the word *asana* ["neutrality"]. As to the difference between three aspects of neutrality:—Keeping quiet, maintaining a particular kind of policy is *sthana;* withdrawal from hostile actions for the sake of one's own interest is *asana;* and taking no steps or strategic means [against an enemy] is *upekshana.*

When two kings, who, though bent on making conquests, are desirous of peace, are unable to proceed, one against the other, they may keep quiet after proclaiming war or after making peace.

When a king finds it possible to put down by means of his own army, or with the help of a friend, or of wild tribes, another king of equal or superior power, then having set up proper defences against both internal and external enemies, he may keep quiet after proclaiming war.

When a king is convinced that his own subjects are brave, united, prosperous, and able not only to carry on their own works without interference, but also to harass his enemy's works, then he may keep quiet after proclaiming war.

When a king finds that as his enemy's subjects are ill-treated, impoverished and greedy, and are ever being oppressed by the inroads of the army, thieves and wild tribes, they can be made through intrigue to join his side; or that his own agriculture and commerce are flourishing while those of his enemy are waning; or that as the subjects of his enemy are suffering from famine, they will immigrate into his own territory; or that, though his own returns of agriculture and commerce are failing and those of his enemy increasing, his own subjects will never desert him in favour of his enemy; or that by proclaiming war, he can carry off, by force, the grains, cattle and gold of his enemy; or that he can prevent the import of his enemy's merchandise, which was destructive of his own commerce; or that valuable merchandise would come to his own territory, leaving that of his enemy; or that war being proclaimed, his enemy would be unable to put down traitors, enemies, and wild tribes and other rebels, and would be involved in war with them; or that his own friend would in a very short time accumulate wealth without much loss and would not fail to follow him in his march, since no friend would neglect the opportunity of acquiring a fertile land and a prosperous friend like himself—then in view of inflicting injuries on his enemy and of exhibiting his own power, he may keep quiet after proclaiming war.

But my teacher says that, turning against such a king, his enemy may swallow him.

"Not so," says Kautilya, "impoverishment of the enemy who is free from troubles is all that is aimed at [when a king keeps quiet after proclaiming war]. As soon as such a king acquires sufficient strength, he will undertake to destroy the enemy. To such a king, the enemy's enemy will send help to secure his own personal safety." Hence, whoever is provided with necessary strength may keep quiet after proclaiming war.

When the policy of keeping quiet after proclaiming war is found productive of unfavourable results, then one shall keep quiet after making peace.

Whoever has grown in strength in consequence of keeping quiet after proclaiming war should proceed to attack his helpless enemy.

When a king finds that his enemy has fallen into troubles; that the troubles of his enemy's subjects can by no means be remedied; that as his enemy's subjects are oppressed, ill-treated, disaffected, impoverished, become effeminate and disunited among themselves, they can be prevailed upon to desert their master; that his enemy's country has fallen a victim to the inroads of such calamities as fire, floods, pestilence, epidemics [*maraka*] and famine and is therefore losing the flower of its youth and its defensive power—then he should march after proclaiming war.

When a king is so fortunate as to have a powerful friend in front and a powerful ally [*akranda*] in the rear, both with brave and loyal subjects, while the reverse is the case with his enemies both in front and in the rear, and when he finds it possible for his friend to hold his frontal enemy in check, and for his rear-ally to keep his rear-enemy [*parshnigraha*] at bay, then he may march after proclaiming war against his frontal enemy.

When a king finds it possible to achieve the results of victory single-handed in a very short time, then he may march [against his frontal enemy] after proclaiming war against his rear-enemies; otherwise he should march after making peace [with his rear-enemies].

When a king finds himself unable to confront his enemy single-handed and when it is necessary that he should march, then he should make the expedition in combination with kings of inferior, equal, or superior powers. When the object aimed at is of a definite nature, then the share of spoils should be fixed; but when it is of a manifold or complex nature, then with no fixity in the share of the spoils. When no such combination is possible, he may request a king either to supply him with the army for a fixed share, or to accompany him for an equal share of the spoils.

When profit is certain, then they should march with fixed shares of profit; but when it is uncertain, with no fixity of shares.

Share of profit proportional to the strength of the army is of the first kind; that which is equal to the effort made is the best; shares may be allotted in proportion to the profit earned or to the capital invested.

Consideration about Marching against an Assailable Enemy and a Strong Enemy; Causes Leading to the Dwindling, Greed, and Disloyalty of the Army; and Considerations about the Combination of Powers.

When two enemies, one an assailable enemy and another a strong enemy, are equally involved in troubles, which of them is to be marched against first?

The strong enemy is to be marched against first; after vanquishing him, the assailable enemy is to be attacked, for, when a strong enemy has been vanquished, an assailable enemy will volunteer of his own accord to help the conqueror; but not so a strong enemy.

Which is to be marched against—an assailable enemy involved in troubles to a greater degree or a strong enemy troubled to a lesser degree?

My teacher says that, as a matter of easy conquest, the assailable enemy under worse troubles should be marched against first.

Not so, says Kautilya: the conqueror should march against the strong enemy under less troubles, for the troubles of the strong enemy, though less, will be augmented when attacked. True, that the worse troubles of the assailable enemy will be still worse when attacked. But when left to himself, the strong enemy under less troubles will endeavour to get rid of his troubles and unite with the assailable enemy or with another enemy in the rear of the conqueror.

When there are two assailable enemies, one of virtuous character and under worse troubles, and another of vicious character under less troubles, and with disloyal subjects, which of them is to be marched against first?

When the enemy of virtuous character and under worse troubles is attacked, his subjects will help him; whereas, the subjects of the other vicious character and under less troubles will be indifferent. Disloyal or indifferent subjects will endeavour to destroy even a strong king. Hence the conqueror should march against that enemy whose subjects are disloyal.

Which is to be marched against—an enemy whose subjects are impoverished and greedy or an enemy whose subjects are being oppressed?

My teacher says that the conqueror should march against that enemy whose subjects are impoverished and greedy, for impoverished and greedy subjects suffer themselves to be won over to the other side by intrigue, and are easily excited. But not so the oppressed subjects whose wrath can be pacified by punishing the chief men [(*pradhana,* "ringleader") of the state].

Not so, says Kautilya: for though impoverished and greedy they are loyal to their master and are ready to stand for his cause and to defeat any intrigue against him; for it is in loyalty that all other good qualities have their strength. Hence the conqueror should march against the enemy whose subjects are oppressed.

Which enemy is to be marched against—a powerful enemy of wicked character or a powerless enemy of righteous character?

The strong enemy of wicked character should be marched against, for when he is attacked, his subjects will not help him, but rather put him down or go to the side of the conqueror. But when the enemy of virtuous character is attacked, his subjects will help him or die with him.

By insulting the good and commending the wicked; by causing unnatural and unrighteous slaughter of life;

by neglecting the observance of proper and righteous customs; by doing unrighteous acts and neglecting righteous ones;

by doing what ought not to be done and not doing what ought to be done; by not paying what ought to be paid and exacting what ought not to be taken;

by not punishing the guilty and severely punishing the less guilty; by arresting those who are not to be caught hold of and leaving those who are to be arrested;

by undertaking risky works and destroying profitable ones; by not protecting the people against thieves and by robbing them of their wealth;

by giving up manly enterprise and condemning good work; by hurting the leaders of the people and despising the worthy;

by provoking the aged, by crooked conduct, and by untruthfulness; by not applying remedies against evils and neglecting works in hand;

and by carelessness and negligence of himself in maintaining the security of person and property of subjects, the king causes impoverishment, greed, and disaffection to appear among his subjects;

when a people are impoverished, they become greedy; when they are greedy, they become disaffected; when disaffected, they voluntarily go to the side of the enemy or destroy their own master.

Hence, no king should give room to such causes as would bring about impoverishment, greed or disaffection among his people. If however, they appear, he should at once take remedial measures against them.

Which [of the three] is the worst—an impoverished people? greedy people? or disaffected people?

An impoverished people are ever apprehensive of oppression and destruction [by over-taxation, etc.], and are therefore desirous of getting rid of their impoverishment, or of waging war or of migrating elsewhere.

A greedy people are ever discontented and they yield themselves to the intrigues of an enemy.

A disaffected people rise against their master along with his enemy.

When the dwindling of the people is due to want of gold and grain, it is a calamity fraught with danger to the whole of the kingdom and can be remedied with difficulty. The dearth of efficient men can be made up by means of gold and grain. Greed [is] partial and is found among a few chief officers, and it can be got rid of or satisfied by allowing them to plunder an enemy's wealth. Disaffection or disloyalty [viraga] can be got rid of by putting down the leaders; for in the absence of a leader or leaders, the people are easily governed [bhogya] and they will not take part in the intrigues of enemies. When a people are too nervous to endure the calamities, they first become dispersed when their leaders are put down; and when they are kept under restraint, they endure calamities.

Having well considered the causes which bring about peace or war, one should combine with kings of considerable power and righteous character and march against one's enemy.

"A king of considerable power" means one who is strong enough to put down or capture an enemy in the rear of his friend or to give sufficient help to his friend in his march.

"A king of righteous character" means one who does what one has promised to do, irrespective of good or bad results.

Having combined with one of superior power or with two of equal power among such kings, should the conqueror march against his enemy?

It is better to march combined with two kings of equal power; for, if combined with a king of superior power, the ally appears to move, being caught hold of by his superior, whereas in marching with two kings of equal power, the same will be the result, only, when those two kings are experts in the art of intrigue; besides it is easy to separate them; and when one of them is wicked, he can be put down by the other two and made to suffer the consequence of dissension.

Combined with one of equal power or with two of lesser power, should a king march against his enemy?

Better to march with two kings of lesser power; for the conqueror can depute them to carry out any two different works and keep them under his control. When the desired end is achieved, the inferior king will quietly retire after the satisfaction of his superior.

Till his discharge, the good conduct of an ally of usually bad character should be closely scrutinised, either by suddenly coming out at a critical time from a covert position [*sattra*] to examine his conduct, or by having his wife as a pledge for his good conduct.

Though actuated with feelings of true friendship, the conqueror has reason to fear his ally, though of equal power, when the latter attains success in his mission; having succeeded in his mission, an ally of equal power is likely to change his attitude even towards the conqueror of superior power.

An ally of superior power should not be relied upon, for prosperity changes the mind. Even with little or no share in the spoils, an ally of superior power may go back, appearing contented; but some time afterwards, he may not fail to sit on the lap of the conqueror and carry off twice the amount of share due to him.

Having been satisfied with mere victory, the leading conqueror should discharge his allies, having satisfied them with their shares or he may allow himself to be conquered by them instead of attempting to conquer them [in the matter of spoils]; it is thus that a king can win the good graces of his Circle of States.

The March of Combined Powers; Agreement of Peace with or without Definite Terms; and Peace with Renegades

The conqueror should thus over-reach the second element [the enemy close to his territory]: He should engage his neighbouring enemy to undertake a simultaneous march with him and tell the enemy: "Thou march in that direction, and I shall march in this direction; and the share in the spoils is equal."

If the booty is to be equally divided, it is an agreement of peace; if otherwise, it is overpowering the enemy.

An agreement of peace may be made with promise to carry out a definite work [*paripanita*] or with no such promise [*aparipanita*].

When the agreement is to the effect that, "Thou march to that place, and I shall march to this place," it is termed an agreement of peace to carry out a work in a definite locality.

When it is agreed upon that, "Thou be engaged so long, I shall be engaged thus long," it is an agreement to attain an object in a fixed time.

When it is agreed upon that, "Thou try to accomplish that work, and I shall try to finish this work," it is an agreement to achieve a definite end.

When the conqueror thinks that, "My enemy [now an ally] has to march through an unknown country, which is intersected with mountains, forests, rivers, forts and deserts, which is devoid of foodstuffs, people, pastural grounds, fodder, firewood and water, and which is far away, different from other countries, and not affording suitable grounds for the exercise of his army; and I have to traverse a country of quite the reverse description," then he should make an agreement to carry out a work in a definite locality.

When the conqueror thinks that, "My enemy has to work with foodstuffs falling short and with no comfort during the rainy, hot or cold season, giving rise to various kinds of diseases and obstructing the free exercise of his army during a shorter or longer period of time than necessary for the accomplishment of the work in hand; and I have to work during a time of quite the reverse nature," then he should make time a factor of the agreement.

When the conqueror thinks that, "My enemy has to accomplish a work which, not lasting but trifling in its nature, enrages his subjects, which requires much expenditure of time and money, and which is productive of evil consequences, unrighteous, repugnant to the Madhyama and neutral kings, and destructive of all friendship; whereas, I have to do the reverse," then he should make an agreement to carry out a definite work.

Likewise with space and time, with time and work, with space and work, and with space, time, and work, made as terms of an agreement, it resolves itself into seven forms.

Long before making such an agreement, the conqueror has to fix his own work and then attempt to over-reach his enemy.

When, in order to destroy an enemy who has fallen into troubles and who is hasty, indolent, and not foresighted, an agreement of peace with no terms of time, space, or work is made with an enemy merely for mutual peace, and when, under cover of such an agreement, the enemy is caught hold of at his weak points and is struck, it is termed peace with no definite terms [*aparipanita*]. With regard to this there is a saying as follows:

"Having kept a neighbouring enemy engaged with another neighbouring enemy, a wise king should proceed against a third king, and having conquered that enemy of equal power, take possession of his territory."

Peace with no specific end [*akrtachikirsha*], peace with binding terms [*krtashleshana*], the breaking of peace [*krtavidushana*], and restoration of peace broken [*apashirnakriya*], are other forms of peace.

Open battle, treacherous battle, and silent battle [i.e., killing an enemy by employing spies when there is no talk of battle at all] are the three forms of battle.

When, by making use of conciliation and other forms of stratagem and the like, a new agreement of peace is made and the rights of equal, inferior and superior powers concerned in the agreement are defined according to their respective positions, it is termed an agreement of peace with no specific end [other than self-preservation].

When, by the employment of friends [at the Courts of each other], the agreement of peace made is kept secure and the terms are invariably observed and strictly maintained so that no dissension may creep among the parties, it is termed peace with binding terms.

When, having proved through the agency of traitors and spies the treachery of a king, who has made an agreement of peace, the agreement is broken, it is termed the breaking of peace.

When reconciliation is made with a servant, or a friend, or any other renegade, it is termed the restoration of broken peace.

There are four persons who run away from, and return to, their master: one who had reason to run away and to return; one who had no reason either to run away or to return; one who had reason to run away, but none to return; and one who had no reason to run away, but had reason to come back.

He who runs away owing to his master's fault and returns in consideration of [his master's] good nature, or he who runs away attracted by the good nature of his master's enemy and returns finding fault with the enemy, is to be reconciled as he had reason to run away and to return.

Whoever runs away owing to his own fault and returns without minding the good nature either of his old or new master, is a fickle-minded person having no explanation to account for his conduct, and he should have no terms of reconciliation.

Whoever runs away owing to his master's fault and returns owing to his own defects, is a renegade who had reason to run away, but none to return: and his case is to be well considered [before he is taken back].

Whoever returns deputed by the enemy; or of his own accord, with the intention of hurting his old master, as is natural to persons of such bad character; or coming to know that his old master is attempting to put down the enemy, his new master, and apprehensive of danger to himself; or looking on the attempt of his new master to destroy his old master as cruelty—these should be examined; and if he is found to be actuated with good motives, he is to be taken back respectfully; otherwise, he should be kept at a distance.

Whoever runs away owing to his own fault and returns owing to his new master's wickedness is a renegade who had no reason to run away, but had reason to come back; such a person is to be examined.

When a king thinks that, "This renegade supplies me with full information about my enemy's weakness, and, therefore, he deserves to remain here; his own people with me are in friendship with my friends and at enmity with my enemies, and are easily excited at the sight of greedy and cruel persons or of a band of enemies," he may treat such a renegade as deserved.

My teacher says that whoever has failed to achieve profit from his works, lost his strength, or made his learning a commercial article, or is very greedy, inquisitive to see different countries, dead to the feelings of friendship, or has strong enemies, deserves to be abandoned.

But Kautilya says that it is timidity, unprofessional business, and lack of forbearance [to do so]. Whoever is injurious to the king's interests should be abandoned, while he who is injurious to the interests of the enemy should be reconciled; and whoever is injurious to the interests of both the king and his enemy should be carefully examined.

When it is necessary to make peace with a king with whom no peace ought to be made, defensive measures should be taken against that point where he can shew his power.

In restoring broken peace, a renegade or a person inclined towards the enemy should be kept at such a distance that, till the close of his life, he may be useful to the state.

Or, he may be set against the enemy or may be employed as a captain of an army to guard wild tracts against enemies, or thrown somewhere on the boundary.

Or he may be employed to carry on a secret trade in new or old commodities in foreign countries, and may accordingly be accused of conspiracy with the enemy.

Or, in the interests of future peace, a renegade who must be put to death may at once be destroyed.

That kind of wicked character which has from the beginning grown upon a man owing to his association with enemies is, as ever, fraught with danger as constant living in company with a snake;

and is ever threatening with destruction just as a pigeon living on the seeds of *plaksha* (holy fig-tree) is to the *shalmali* (silk-cotton) tree.

When battle is fought in daylight and in some locality, it is termed an open battle; threatening in one direction, assault in another, destruction of an enemy captured while he was careless or in troubles;

and bribing a portion of the army and destroying another portion, are forms of treacherous fight; an attempt to win over the chief officers of the enemy by intrigue, is the characteristic of silent battle.

Peace and War by Adopting the Double Policy

The conqueror may take in the aid of the second member [i.e., the immediate enemy] thus:

Having combined with a neighbouring king, the conqueror may march against another neighbouring king. Or if he thinks that "[my enemy] will neither capture my rear nor make an alliance with my assailable enemy against whom I am going to march; I shall have double the strength with him, i.e., the enemy suing peace; [my ally] will not only facilitate the collection of my revenue and supplies and put down the internal enemies who are causing me immense trouble, but also punish wild tribes and their followers entrenched in their strongholds, reduce my assailable enemy to a precarious condition or compel him to accept the proffered peace, and having received as much profit as he desires, he will endeavour to endear my other enemies to me," then the conqueror may proclaim war against one and make peace with another, and endeavour to get an army for money or money for the supply of an army from among his neighbouring kings.

When the kings of superior, equal or inferior power make peace with the conqueror and agree to pay a greater, or equal, or less amount of profit in proportion to the army supplied, it is termed even peace; that which is of the reverse character is styled uneven peace; and when the profit is proportionally very high, it is termed deception [*atisandhi*].

When a king of superior power is involved in troubles, or is come to grief or is afflicted with misfortune, his enemy, though of inferior power, may request of him the help of his army in return for a share in the profit proportional to the strength of the army supplied. If the king to whom peace is offered on such terms is powerful enough to retaliate, he may declare war; otherwise he may accept the terms.

In view of marching for the purpose of exacting some expected revenue to be utilised in recouping his own strength and resources, an inferior king may request of a superior the help of the latter's army for the purpose of guarding the base and the rear of his territory in return for the payment of a greater share in the profit than the strength of the army supplied deserves. The king to whom such a proposal is made may accept the proposal, if the proposer is of good intentions; otherwise he may declare war.

When a king of inferior power or one who is provided with the aid of forts and friends has to make a short march in order to capture an enemy without waging war or to receive some expected profit, he may request a third king of superior power, involved under various troubles and misfortunes, the help of the latter's army in return for the payment of a share in the profit less than the strength of the army supplied deserves. If the king to whom this proposal is made is powerful enough to retaliate, he may declare war; otherwise he may accept the proposal.

When the king of superior power and free from all troubles is desirous of causing to his enemy loss of men and money in the latter's ill-considered undertaking, or of sending his own treacherous army abroad, or bringing his enemy under the clutches of an inimical army, or of causing trouble to a reducible and tottering enemy by setting an inferior king against that enemy, or is desirous of having peace for the sake of itself and is possessed of good intentions, he may accept a less share in the profit [promised for the army supplied to another], and endeavour to make wealth by combining with an ally if the latter is equally of good intentions; otherwise he may declare war [against that ally].

A king may deceive or help his equal as follows:

When a king proposes peace to another king of equal power on the condition of receiving the help of the latter's army strong enough to oppose an enemy's army, or to guard the front, centre, and rear of his territory, or to help his friend, or to protect any other wild tracts of his territory, in return for the payment of a share in the profit proportionally equal to the strength of the army supplied, the latter may accept the terms if the proposer is of good intentions; otherwise he may declare war.

When a king of equal power, capable of receiving the help of an army from another quarter requests of another king in troubles due to the diminished strength of the elements of sovereignty, and with many enemies, the help of the latter's army in return for the payment of a share in the profit less than the strength of the army supplied deserves, the latter, if powerful, may declare war; or accept the terms otherwise.

When a king who is under troubles, who has his works at the mercy of his neighbouring kings, and who has yet to make an army, requests of another king of equal power the help of the latter's army in return for the payment of a share in the profit greater than the strength of the army supplied deserves, the latter may accept the terms if the proposer is of good intentions; otherwise war may be declared.

When, with desire of putting down a king in troubles due to the diminished strength of the elements of sovereignty, or with the desire of destroying his well-begun work of immense and unfailing profit, or with the intention of striking him in his own place or on the occasion of marching, one, though frequently getting immense [subsidy] from an assailable enemy of equal, inferior, or superior power, sends demands to him again and again, then he may comply with the demands of the former if he is desirous of maintaining his own power by destroying with the army of the former an impregnable fortress of an enemy, or a friend of that enemy, or laying waste the wild tracts of that enemy, or if he is desirous of exposing the army of the ally to wear and tear even in good roads and good seasons, or if he is desirous of strengthening his own army with that of his ally, and thereby putting down the ally, or winning over the army of the ally.

When a king is desirous of keeping under his power another king of superior or inferior power as an assailable enemy and of destroying the latter after routing out another enemy with the help of the latter, or when he is desirous of getting back whatever he has paid [as subsidy], he may send a proposal of peace to another on the condition of paying more than the cost of the army supplied. If the king to whom this proposal is made is powerful enough to retaliate he may declare war; or if otherwise, he may accept the terms; or he may keep quiet allied with the assailable enemy; or he may supply the proposer of peace with his army full of traitors, enemies and wild tribes.

When a king of superior power falls into troubles owing to the weakness of the elements of his sovereignty, and requests of an inferior king the help of the latter's army in return for the payment of a share in the profit proportionally equal to the strength of the army supplied, the latter, if powerful enough to retaliate, may declare war; if otherwise, accept the terms.

A king of superior power may request of an inferior the help of the latter's army in return for the payment of a share in the profit less than the cost of the army supplied; and the latter, if powerful enough to retaliate, may declare war, or accept the terms otherwise.

The king who is sued for peace and also the king who offers peace should both consider the motive with which the proposal of peace is made, and adopt that course of action which on consideration seems to be productive of good results.

The Attitude of an Assailable Enemy;
and Friends That Deserve Help

When an assailable enemy who is in danger of being attacked is desirous of taking upon himself the condition which led one king to be combined with another against himself, or of splitting them from each other, he may propose peace to one of the kings on the condition of himself paying twice the amount of profit accruing from the combination. The agreement having been made, he may describe to that king the loss of men and money, the hardship of sojourning abroad, the commission of sinful deeds, and the misery and other personal troubles to which that king would have been subjected. When the king is convinced of the truth, the amount promised may be paid; or having made that king to incur enmity with other kings, the agreement itself may be broken off.

When a king is inclined to cause to another loss of men and money in the ill-considered undertakings of the latter, or to frustrate the latter in the attempt of achieving large profit from well-begun undertakings; or when he means to strike another at his [another's] own place or while marching; or when he intends to exact subsidy again in combination with the latter's assailable enemy; or when he is in need of money and does not like to trust to his ally, he may, for the time being, be satisfied with a small amount of profit.

When a king has in view the necessity of helping a friend or of destroying an enemy, or the possibility of acquiring much wealth [in return for the present help], or when he intends to utilise in future the services of the one now obliged by him, he may reject the offer of large profit at the present in preference of a small gain in future.

When a king means to help another from the clutches of traitors or enemies or of a superior king threatening the very existence of the latter, and intends thereby to set an example of rendering similar help to himself in future, he should receive no profit either at the present or in the future.

When a king means to harass the people of an enemy or to break the agreement of peace between a friend and a foe, or when he suspects of another's attack upon himself, and when, owing to any of these causes, he wants to break peace with his ally, he may demand from the latter an enhanced amount of profit long before it is due. The latter under these circumstances may demand for a procedure [karma] either at the present or in the future. The same procedure explains the cases treated of before.

The conqueror and his enemy helping their respective friends differ according as their friends are such or are not such as undertake possible, praiseworthy or productive works and as are resolute in their undertakings and are provided with loyal and devoted subjects.

Whoever undertakes tolerable work is a beginner of possible work; whoever undertakes an unblemished work is a beginner of praiseworthy work; whoever undertakes a work of large profits is a beginner of a productive work; whoever takes no rest before the completion of the work undertaken is a resolute worker; and whoever has loyal and devoted subjects is in a position to command help and to bring to a successful termination any work without losing anything in the form of favour. When such friends are gratified by the enemy or the conqueror, they can be of immense help to him; friends of reverse character should never be helped.

Of the two, the conqueror and his enemy, both of whom may happen to have a friend in the same person, he who helps a true or a truer friend overreaches the other; for by helping a true friend he enriches himself, while the other not only incurs loss of men and money and the hardships of sojourning abroad, but also showers benefits on an enemy who hates the benefactor all the more for his gratification.

Whoever of the two, the conqueror and his enemy, who may happen to have a friend in the same Madhyama king, helps a Madhyama king of true or truer friendship, over-reaches the other; for, by helping a true friend, he enriches himself, while the other incurs loss of men and money and the difficulties of sojourning abroad. When a Madhyama king thus helped is devoid of good qualities, then the enemy over-reaches the conqueror, for such a Madhyama king, spending his energies on useless undertakings and receiving help with no idea of returning it, withdraws himself away.

The same thing holds good with a neutral king under similar circumstances.

In case of helping with a portion of the army one of the two, a Madhyama or a neutral king, whoever happens to help one who is brave, skillful in handling weapons, and possessed of endurance and friendly feelings will himself be deceived, while his enemy, helping one of reverse character, will over-reach him.

When a king achieves this or that object with the assistance of a friend who is to receive the help of his army in return later on, then he may send out his various kinds of army—such as hereditary army, hired army, army formed of corporations of people, his friend's army and the army composed of wild tribes—either that kind of army which has experience of all sorts of grounds and of seasons or the army of enemies or of wild tribes, which is far removed in space and time.

When a king thinks that, "Though successful, my ally may cause my army to move in an enemy's territory or in wild tracts, and during unfavourable seasons, and thereby he may render it useless to me," then under the excuse of having to employ his army otherwise, he may help his ally in any other way; but when he is obliged to lend his army, he may send that kind of his army, which is used to the weather of the time of operation, under the condition of employing it till the completion of the work, and of protecting it from dangers. When the ally has finished his work, he should, under some excuse, try to get back his army; or he may send to his ally that army which is composed of traitors, enemies, and wild tribes; or having made peace with ally's assailable enemy, he may deceive the ally.

When the profit accruing to kings under an agreement, whether they be of equal, inferior, or superior power, is equal to all, that agreement is termed peace [*sandhi*]; when unequal, it is termed defeat [*vikrama*]. Such is the nature of peace and war.

Agreement for the Acquisition of a Friend or Gold

Of the three gains, the acquisition of a friend, of gold, and of territory, accruing from the march of combined powers, that which is mentioned later is better than the one previously mentioned; for friends and gold can be acquired by means of territory; of the two gains, that of a friend and of gold, each can be a means to acquire the other.

Agreement under the condition, "Let us acquire a friend," etc., is termed even peace; when one acquires a friend and the other gold or land, it is termed uneven peace; and when one gains more than the other, it is deception.

In an even peace [i.e., agreement on equal terms], whoever acquires a friend of good character or relieves an old friend from troubles, over-reaches the other; for help given in misfortune renders friendship very firm.

Which is better of the two: a friend of long-standing but unsubmissive nature, or a temporary friend of submissive nature, both being acquired by affording relief from their respective troubles?

My teacher says that a long-standing friend of unsubmissive nature is better, inasmuch as such a friend, though not helpful, will not create harm.

Not so, says Kautilya: a temporary friend of submissive nature is better; for such a friend will be a true friend so long as he is helpful; for the real characteristic of friendship lies in giving help.

Which is the better of two submissive friends: a temporary friend of large prospects, or a long-standing friend of limited prospects?

My teacher says that a temporary friend of large prospects is better, inasmuch as such a friend can, in virtue of his large prospects, render immense service in a very short time, and can stand undertaking of large outlay.

Not so, says Kautilya: a long-standing friend of limited prospects is better, inasmuch as a temporary friend of large prospects is likely to withdraw his friendship on account of material loss in the shape of help given, or is likely to expect similar kind of help in return; but a long-standing friend, of limited prospects can, in virtue of his long-standing nature, render immense service in the long run.

Which is better, a big friend, difficult to be roused, or a small friend, easy to be roused?

My teacher says that a big friend, though difficult to be roused, is of imposing nature, and when he rises up he can accomplish the work undertaken.

Not so, says Kautilya: a small friend easy to be roused is better, for such a friend will not, in virtue of his ready preparations, be behind the opportune moment of work, and can, in virtue of his weakness in power, be used in any way the conqueror may like; but not so the other of vast territorial power.

Which is better, scattered troops, or an unsubmissive standing army?

My teacher says that scattered troops can be collected in time, as they are of submissive nature.

Not so, says Kautilya: an unsubmissive standing army is better, as it can be made submissive by conciliation and other strategic means; but it is not so easy to collect in time scattered troops, as they are engaged in their individual avocations.

Which is better, a friend of vast population, or a friend of immense gold?

My teacher says that a friend of vast population is better, inasmuch as such a friend will be of imposing power and can, when he rises up, accomplish any work undertaken.

Not so, says Kautilya: a friend possessing immense gold is better; for possession of gold is ever desirable; but an army is not always required. Moreover, armies and other desired objects can be purchased for gold.

Which is better, a friend possessing gold or a friend possessing vast territory?

My teacher says that a friend possessing gold can stand any heavy expenditure made with discretion.

Not so, says Kautilya: for it has already been stated that both friends and gold can be acquired by means of territory. Hence a friend of vast territory is far better.

When the friend of the conqueror and his enemy happen to possess equal population, their people may yet differ in possessions of qualities such as bravery, power of endurance, amicableness, and qualification for the formation of any kind of army.

When the friends are equally rich in gold, they may yet differ in qualities such as readiness to comply with requests, magnanimous and munificent help, and accessibility at any time and always.

About this topic, the following sayings are current:

Long-standing, submissive, easy to be roused, coming from fathers and grandfathers, powerful, and never of a contradictory nature, is a good friend; and these are said to be the six qualities of a good friend;

that friend who maintains friendship with disinterested motives and merely for the sake of friendship, and by whom the relationship acquired of old is kept intact, is a long-standing friend;

that friend whose munificence is enjoyable in various ways is a submissive friend, and is said to be of three forms: one who is enjoyable only by one, one who is enjoyable by two [the enemy and the conqueror], and one who is enjoyable by all, is the third;

that friend who, whether as receiving help or as giving help, lives with an oppressive hand over his enemies, and who possesses a number of forts and a vast army of wild tribes is said to be a long-standing friend of unsubmissive nature;

that friend who, either when attacked or when in trouble, makes friendship for the security of his own existence is a temporary and submissive friend;

that friend who contracts friendship with a single aim in view and who is helpful, immutable, and amicable, is a friend never falling foul even in adversity;

whoever is of an amicable nature is a true friend; whoever sides also with the enemy is a mutable friend; and whoever is indifferent to neither [the conqueror and his enemy] is a friend to both;

that friend who is inimical to the conqueror or who is equally friendly to the conqueror's enemy is a harmful friend, whether he is giving help or is capable of helping;

whoever helps the enemy's friend, protege or any vulnerable person or a relation of the enemy is a friend common to [both] the enemy [and the conqueror];

whoever possesses extensive and fertile territory and is contented, strong, but indolent, will be indifferent [towards his ally] when the latter becomes despicable under troubles;

whoever, owing to his own weakness, follows the ascendancy of both the conqueror and his enemy, not incurring enmity with either, is known as a common friend;

whoever neglects a friend, who is being hurt, with or without reason, and who seeks help, with or without reason, despises his own danger.

Which is better, an immediate small gain or a distant large gain?

My teacher says that an immediate small gain is better, as it is useful to carry out immediate undertaking.

Not so, says Kautilya: a large gain, as continuous as a productive seed, is better; otherwise an immediate small gain.

Thus, having taken into consideration the good aspects of permanent gain or of a share in a permanent gain, should a king, desirous of strengthening himself, march combined with others.

Agreement of Peace for the Acquisition of Land

The agreement made under the condition, "Let us acquire land," is any agreement of peace for the acquisition of land.

Of the two kings thus entering into an agreement, whoever acquires a rich and fertile land with standing crops over-reaches the other.

The acquisition of rich land being equal, whoever acquires such land by putting down a powerful enemy, over-reaches the other; for not only does he acquire territory, but also destroys an enemy, and thereby augments his own power. True, there is beauty in acquiring land by putting down a weak enemy; but the land acquired will also be poor, and the king in the neighbourhood, who has hitherto been a friend, will now become an enemy.

The enemies being equally strong, he who acquires territory after beating a fortified enemy over-reaches the other; for the capture of a fort is conducive to the protection of territory and to the destruction of wild tribes.

As to the acquisition of land from a wandering enemy, there is the difference of having a powerful or powerless enemy close to the acquired territory;

for the land which is close to a powerless enemy is easily maintained, while that bordering upon the territory of a powerful enemy has to be kept at the expense of men and money.

Which is better, the acquisition of a rich land close to a constant enemy, or that of sterile land near to a temporary enemy?

My teacher says that a rich land with a constant enemy is better, inasmuch as it yields much wealth to maintain a strong army, by which the enemy can be put down.

Not so, says Kautilya: for, a rich land creates many enemies, and the constant enemy will ever be an enemy, whether or not he is helped [with men and money to conciliate him]; but a temporary enemy will be quiet either from fear or favour. That land, on the border of which there are a number of forts giving shelter to bands of thieves, Mlecchas [non-Indo-Aryan barbarians] and wild tribes, is a land with a constant enemy; and that which is of reverse character is one with a temporary enemy.

Which is better, a small piece of land, not far, or an extensive piece of land, very far?

A small piece of land, not far, is better, inasmuch as it can be easily acquired, protected, and defended, whereas the other is of a reverse nature.

Of the above two kinds of land, which is better, that which can be maintained by itself, or that which requires external armed force to maintain?

The former is better, as it can be maintained with the army and money produced by itself, whereas the latter is of a reverse character as a military station.

Which is better, acquisition of land from a stupid or a wise king?

That acquired from a stupid king is better, as it can be easily acquired and secured, and cannot be taken back, whereas that obtained from a wise king, beloved of his subjects, is of a reverse nature.

Of two enemies, of whom one can only be harassed and another is reducible, acquisition of land from the latter is better; for when the latter is attacked, he, having little or no help, begins to run away, taking his army and treasure with him, and he is deserted by his subjects, whereas the former does not do so, as he has the help of his forts and friends.

Of two fortified kings, one who has his forts on a plain is more easily reduced than the other owning a fort in the centre of a river; for a fort in a plain can be easily assailed, destroyed or captured along with the enemy in it, whereas a fort surrounded by a river requires twice as much effort to capture, and supplies the enemy with water and other necessaries of life.

Of two kings, one owning a fort surrounded by a river, and another having mountainous fortifications, seizing the former's land is better, for a fort in the centre of a river can be assailed by a bridge formed of elephants made to stand in a row in the river, or by wooden bridges, or by means of boats; and the river will not always be deep and can be emptied of its water, whereas a fort on a mountain is of a self defensive nature, and not easy to besiege or to ascend; and where one portion of the army defending it is routed out, the other portions can escape unhurt, and such a fort is of immense service, as it affords facilities to throw down heaps of stones and trees over the enemy.

Which is easier, seizing land from those who fight on plains, or from those who fight from low grounds?

Seizing the land from the latter is easier, inasmuch as they have to fight in time and space of adverse nature, whereas the former can fight anywhere and at any time.

Of the two enemies, one fighting from ditches and another from heights [khanakakashayodhibhyam], seizing land from the former is better; for they can be serviceable, inasmuch as they fight from ditches and with weapons in hand, whereas the latter can only fight with weapons in hand.

Whoever, well-versed in the science of polity, wrests land from such and other enemies will outshine both his allies in combination with him and enemies out of combination. . . .

Considerations about an Enemy in the Rear

When the conqueror and his enemy simultaneously proceed to capture the rear of their respective enemies who are engaged in an attack against others, he who captures the rear of one who is possessed of vast resources gains more advantage [atisandhatte]; for one who is possessed of vast resources has to put down the rear-enemy only after doing away with one's frontal enemy already attacked, but not one who is poor in resources and who has not realised the desired profits.

Resources being equal, he who captures the rear of one who has made vast preparations gains more advantages, for one who has made vast preparations has to put down the enemy in the rear only after destroying the frontal enemy, but not one whose preparations are made on a small scale and whose movements are, therefore, obstructed by the Circle of States.

Preparations being equal, he who captures the rear of one who has marched out with all the resources gains more advantages; for one whose base is undefended is easy to be subdued, but not one who has marched out with a part of the army after having made arrangements to defend the rear.

Troops taken being of equal strength, he who captures the rear of one who has gone against a wandering enemy gains more advantages: for one who has marched out against a wandering enemy has to put down the rear-enemy only after obtaining an easy victory over the wandering enemy; but not one who has marched out against an entrenched enemy, for one who has marched out against the entrenched enemy will be repelled in his attack against the enemy's forts and will, after his return, find himself between the rear-enemy and the frontal enemy who is possessed of strong forts.

This explains the cases of other enemies described before.

Enemies being of equal description, he who attacks the rear of one who has gone against a virtuous king gains more advantages, for one who has gone against a virtuous king will incur the displeasure of even his own people, whereas one who has attacked a wicked king will endear himself to all.

This explains the consequences of capturing the rear of those who have marched against an extravagant king, or a king living from hand to mouth, or a niggardly king.

The same reasons hold good in the case of those who have marched against their own friends.

When there are two enemies, one engaged in attacking a friend and another an enemy, he who attacks the rear of the latter gains more advantages: for one who has attacked a friend will, after easily making peace with the friend, proceed against the rear-enemy; for it is easier to make peace with a friend than with an enemy.

When there are two kings, one engaged in destroying a friend and another an enemy, he who attacks the rear of the former gains more advantages; for one who is engaged in destroying an enemy will have the support of his friends and will thereby put down the rear-enemy, but not the former who is engaged in destroying his own side.

When the conqueror and his enemy in their attack against the rear of an enemy mean to enforce the payment of what is not due to them, he whose enemy has lost considerable profits and has sustained a great loss of men and money gains more advantages: when they mean to enforce the payment of what is due to them, then he whose enemy has lost profits and army, gains more advantages.

When the assailable enemy is capable of retaliation and when the assailant's rear-enemy, capable of augmenting his army and other resources, has entrenched himself on one of the assailant's flanks, then the rear-enemy gains more advantages; for a rear enemy on one of the assailant's flanks will not only become a friend of the assailable enemy, but also attack the base of the assailant whereas a rear-enemy behind the assailant can only harass the rear.

Kings capable of harassing the rear of an enemy and of obstructing his movements are three: the group of kings situated behind the enemy, and the groups of kings on his two flanks.

He who is situated between a conqueror and his enemy is called an *antardhi* [one between two kings]; when such a king is possessed of forts, wild tribes, and other kinds of help, he proves an impediment in the way of the strong.

When the conqueror and his enemy are desirous of catching hold of a Madhyama king and attack the latter's rear, then he who in his attempt to enforce the promised payment separates the Madhyama king from the latter's friend, and obtains, thereby, an enemy as a friend, gains more advantages; for an enemy compelled to sue for peace will be of greater help than a friend compelled to maintain the abandoned friendship.

This explains the attempt to catch hold of a neutral king.

Of attacks from the rear and front, that which affords opportunities of carrying on a treacherous fight [mantrayuddha] is preferable.

My teacher says that in an open war, both sides suffer by sustaining a heavy loss of men and money; and that even the king who wins a victory will appear as defeated in consequence of the loss of men and money.

No, says Kautilya, even at considerable loss of men and money, the destruction of an enemy is desirable.

Loss of men and money being equal, he who entirely destroys first his frontal enemy, and next attacks his rear-enemy gains more advantages; when both the conqueror and his enemy are severally engaged in destroying their respective frontal enemies, he who destroys a frontal enemy of deep-rooted enmity and of vast resources, gains more advantages.

This explains the destruction of other enemies and wild tribes:

When an enemy in the rear and in the front, and an assailable enemy to be marched against happen together, then the conqueror should adopt the following policy:

The rear-enemy will usually lead the conqueror's frontal enemy to attack the conqueror's friend; then having set the *akranda* [the enemy of the rear-enemy] against the rear-enemy's ally.

And, having caused war between them, the conqueror should frustrate the rear-enemy's designs; likewise he should provoke hostilities between the allies of the *akranda* and of the rear-enemy;

he should also keep his frontal enemy's friend engaged in war with his own friend; and with the help of his friend's friend he should avert the attack, threatened by the friend of his enemy's friend;

he should, with his friend's help, hold his rear-enemy at bay; and with the help of his friend's friend he should prevent his rear-enemy attacking the *akranda* [his rear-ally];

thus the conqueror should, through the aid of his friends, bring the Circle of States under his own sway, both in his rear and front;

he should send messengers and spies to reside in each of the states composing the Circle, and having again and again destroyed the strength of his enemies, he should keep his counsels concealed, being friendly with his friends;

the works of him whose counsels are not kept concealed will, though they may prosper for a time, perish as undoubtedly as a broken raft on the sea.

Recruitment of Lost Power

When the conqueror is thus attacked by the combined army of his enemies, he may tell their leader: "I shall make peace with you; this is the gold, and I am the friend; your gain is doubled; it is not worthy of you to augment at your own expense the power of your enemies who keep a friendly appearance now; for gaining in power they will put you down in the long run."

Or he may tell the leader, so as to break the combination: "Just as an innocent person like myself is now attacked by the combined army of these kings, so the very same kings in combination will attack you in weal or woe; for power intoxicates the mind; hence break their combination."

The combination being broken, he may set the leader against the weak among his enemies; or, offering inducements, he may set the combined power of the weak against the leader; or in whatever way he may find it to be conducive to his own prosperity, in that way he may make the leader incur the displeasure of others, and thus frustrate their attempts; or showing the prospect of a larger profit, he may through intrigue make peace with their leader. Then the recipients of salaries from two states, exhibiting the acquisition of large profits [to the leader] may satirise the kings, saying, "You are all very well combined."

If some of the kings of the combination are wicked, they may be made to break the treaty; then the recipients of salaries from two states may again tell them, so as to break the combination entirely: "This is just what we have already pointed out."

When the enemies are separated, the conqueror may move forward by catching hold of any of the kings [as an ally].

In the absence of a leader, the conqueror may win him over who is the inciter of the combination; or who is of a resolute mind, or who has endeared himself to his people, or who, from greed or fear, joined the combination, or who is afraid of the conqueror, or whose friendship with the conqueror is based upon some consanguinity of royalty, or who is a friend, or who is a wandering enemy—in the order of enumeration.

Of these, one has to please the inciter by surrendering oneself, by conciliation and salutation: him who is of a resolute mind, by giving a daughter in marriage or by availing oneself of his youth [to beget a son on one's wife?]; him who is the beloved of his people, by giving twice the amount of profits; him who is greedy, by helping with men and money; him who is afraid of the combination, by giving a hostage to him who is naturally timid; by entering into a closer union with him whose friendship is based upon some consanguinity of royalty; by doing what is pleasing and beneficial to both or by abandoning hostilities against him who is a friend; and by offering help and abandoning hostilities against him who is a wandering enemy; one has to win over the confidence of any of the above kings by adopting suitable means or by means of conciliation, gifts, dissension, or threats. . . .

He who is in troubles and is apprehensive of an attack from his enemy should, on the condition of supplying the enemy with army and money, make peace with the enemy on definite terms with reference to place, time, and work; he should also set right any offence he might have given by the violation of a treaty; if he has no supporters, he should find them among his relatives and friends; or he may build an impregnable fortress, for he who is defended by forts and friends will be respected both by his own and his enemy's people.

Whoever is wanting in the power of deliberation should collect wise men around himself, and associate with old men of considerable learning; thus he would attain his desired ends.

He who is devoid of a good treasury and army should direct his attention towards the strengthening of the safety and security of the elements of his sovereignty; for the country is the source of all those works which are conducive to treasury and army; the haven of the king and of his army is a strong fort.

Irrigational works [setubandha] are the source of crops; the results of a good shower of rain are ever attained in the case of crops below irrigational works.

The roads of traffic are a means to over-reach an enemy, for it is through the roads of traffic that armies and spies are led [from one country to another]; and that weapons, armour, chariots, and draught animals are purchased; and that entrance and exit [in travelling] are facilitated.

Mines are the source of whatever is useful in battle.

Timber forests are the source of such materials as are necessary for building forts, conveyances and chariots.

Elephant forests are the source of elephants.

Pasture lands are the source of cows, horses, and camels to draw chariots.

In the absence of such sources of his own, he should acquire them from someone among his relatives and friends. If he is destitute of an army, he should, as far as possible, attract to himself the brave men of corporations, of thieves, of wild tribes, of Mlecchas, and of spies who are capable of inflicting injuries upon enemies.

He should also adopt the policy of a weak king towards a powerful king, in view of averting danger from enemies or friends.

Thus with the aid of one's own party, the power of deliberation, the treasury, and the army, one should get rid of the clutches of one's enemies.

Measures Conducive to Peace with a Strong and Provoked Enemy; and the Attitude of a Conquered Enemy

When a weak king is attacked by a powerful enemy, the former should seek the protection of one who is superior to his enemy, and whom his enemy's power of deliberation for intrigue cannot affect. Of kings who are equal in the power of deliberation, difference should be sought in unchangeable prosperity and in association with the aged.

In the absence of a superior king, he should combine with a number of his equals who are equal in power to his enemy and whom his enemy's power of purse, army, and intrigue cannot reach. Of kings who are equally possessed of the power of purse, army, and intrigue, difference should be sought in their capacity for making vast preparations.

In the absence of equals, he should combine with a number of inferior kings who are pure and enthusiastic, who can oppose the enemy, and whom his enemy's power of purse, army, and intrigue cannot reach. Of kings who are equally possessed of enthusiasm and capacity for action, difference should be sought in the opportunity of securing favourable battlefields. Of kings who are equally possessed of favourable battlefields, difference should be sought in their ever being ready for war. Of kings who are equally possessed of favourable battlefields and who are equally ready for war, difference should be sought in their possession of weapons and armour necessary for war.

In the absence of any such help, he should seek shelter inside a fort in which his enemy with a large army can offer no obstruction to the supply of foodstuff, grass, firewood and water, but would sustain a heavy loss of men and money. When there are many forts, difference should be sought in their affording facility for the collection of stores and supplies. Kautilya is of opinion that, one should entrench oneself in a fort inhabited by men and provided with stores and supplies. Also, for the following reasons, one should shelter oneself in such a fort:

"I shall oppose him [the enemy] with his rear-enemy's ally or with a Madhyama king, or with a neutral king, I shall either capture or devastate his kingdom with the aid of a neighbouring king, a wild tribe, a scion of his family, or an imprisoned prince; by the help of my partisans with him, I shall create troubles in his fort, country or camp; when he is near, I shall murder him with weapons, fire, or poison, or any other secret means at my pleasure; I shall cause him to sustain a heavy loss of men and money in works undertaken by himself or made to be undertaken at the instance of my spies; I shall easily sow the seeds of dissension among his friends or his army when they have suffered from loss of men and money; I shall catch hold of his camp by cutting off supplies and stores going to it; or by surrendering myself [to him], I shall create some weak points in him and put him down with all my resources; or having curbed his spirit, I shall compel him to make peace with me on my own terms; when I obstruct his movements troubles arise to him from all sides; when he is helpless, I shall slay him with the help of my hereditary army or with his enemy's army, or with wild tribes; I shall maintain the safety and security of my vast country by entrenching myself within my fort; the army of myself and of my friends will be invincible when collected together in this fort; my army, which is trained to fight from valleys, pits, or at night, will bring him into difficulties on his way, when he is engaged in an immediate work; owing to loss of men and money, he will make himself powerless when he arrives here at a bad place and in a bad time; owing to the existence of forts and of wild tribes [on the way], he will find this country accessible only at considerable cost of men and money; being unable to find positions favourable for the exercise of the armies of himself and of his friends, suffering from disease, he will arrive here in distress; or having arrived here, he will not return."

In the absence of such circumstances, or when the enemy's army is very strong, one may run away abandoning one's fort.

My teacher says that one may rush against the enemy like a moth against a flame; success in one way or other [i.e., death or victory] is certain for one who is reckless of life.

No, says Kautilya, having observed the conditions conducive to peace between himself and his enemy, he may make peace; in the absence of such conditions, he may, by taking recourse to threats, secure peace or a friend; or he may send a messenger to one who is likely to accept peace; or having pleased with wealth and honour the messenger sent by his enemy, he may tell the latter: "This is the king's manufactory; this is the residence of the queen and the prince; myself and this kingdom are at your disposal, as approved of by the queen and the princes."

Having secured his enemy's protection, he should behave himself like a servant to his master by serving the protector's occasional needs. Forts and other defensive works, acquisition of things, celebration of marriages, installation of the heir-apparent, trade in horses, capture of elephants, construction of covert places for battle [sattra], marching against an enemy, and holding sports—all these he should undertake only at the permission of his protector. He should also obtain his protector's permission before making any agreement with people settled in his country or before punishing those who may run away from country. If the citizens and country people living in his kingdom prove disloyal or inimical to him, he may request of his protector another good country; or he may get rid of wicked people by making use of such secret means as are employed against traitors. He should not accept the offer of a good country even from a friend. Unknown to his protector, he may see the protector's minister, high priest, commander of the army or heir-apparent. He should also help his protector as much as he can. On all occasions of worshipping gods and making prayers, he should cause his people to pray for the long life of his protector; and he should always proclaim his readiness to place himself at the disposal of his protector.

Serving him who is strong and combined with others, and being far away from the society of suspected persons, a conquered king should thus always behave himself towards his protector.

The Attitude of a Conquered King

In view of causing financial trouble to his protector, a powerful vassal king, desirous of making conquests, may, under the permission of his protector, march on countries where the formation of the ground and the climate are favourable for the maneuver of his army, his enemy having neither forts nor any other defensive works, and the conqueror himself having no enemies in the rear. Otherwise [in case of enemies in the rear], he should march after making provisions for the defence of his rear.

By means of conciliation and gifts, he should subdue weak kings; and by means of sowing the seeds of dissension and by threats, strong kings. By adopting a particular, or an alternative, or all of the strategic means, he should subdue his immediate and distant enemies.

He should observe the policy of conciliation by promising the protection of villages, of those who live in forests, of flocks of cattle, and of roads of traffic, as well as the restoration of those who have been banished or who have run away or who have done some harm.

Gifts of land, of things, and of girls in marriage, and absence of fear—by declaring these, he should observe the policy of gifts.

By instigating any one of a neighbouring king, a wild chief, a scion of the enemy's family, or an imprisoned prince, he should sow the seeds of dissension.

By capturing the enemy in an open battle, or in a treacherous fight, or through a conspiracy, or in the tumult of seizing the enemy's fort by strategic means, he should punish the enemy.

He may reinstate kings who are spirited and who can strengthen his army; likewise he may reinstate those who are possessed of a good treasury and army, and who can therefore help him with money; as well as those who are wise, and who can therefore provide him with lands.

Whoever among his friends helps him with gems, precious things, raw materials acquired from commercial towns, villages, and mines, or with conveyances and draught animals acquired from timber and elephant forests, and herds of cattle, is a friend affording a variety of enjoyment [chitrabhoga]; whoever supplies him with wealth and army is a friend affording vast enjoyment [mahabhoga]; whoever supplies him with army, wealth, and lands is a friend affording all enjoyments [sarvabhoga]; whoever safeguards him against a side-enemy is a friend affording enjoyments on one side [ekatobhogi]; whoever helps also his enemy and his enemy's allies is a friend affording enjoyment to both sides [ubhayatobhogi]; and whoever helps him against his enemy, his enemy's ally, his neighbour, and wild tribes, is a friend affording enjoyment on all sides [sarvatobhogi].

If he happens to have an enemy in the rear, or a wild chief, or an enemy, or a chief enemy capable of being propitiated with the gift of lands, he should provide such an enemy with a useless piece of land; an enemy possessed of forts with a piece of land not connected with his [the conqueror's] own territory; a wild chief with a piece of land yielding no livelihood; a scion of the enemy's family with a piece of land that can be taken back; an enemy's prisoner with a piece of land which is [not?] snatched from the enemy; a corporation of armed men with a piece of land constantly under troubles from an enemy; the combination of corporations with a piece of land close to the territory of a powerful king; a corporation invincible in war with a piece of land under both the above troubles; a spirited king desirous of war with a piece of land which affords no advantageous positions for the maneuver of the army; an enemy's partisan with waste lands; a banished prince with a piece of land exhausted of its resources; a king who has renewed the observance of a treaty of peace after breaking it, with a piece of land which can be colonized at considerable cost of men and money; a deserted prince with a piece of land which affords no protection; and his own protector with an uninhabitable piece of land.

[The king who is desirous of making conquests] should continue in following the same policy towards him, who, among the above kings, is most helpful and keeps the same attitude; should by secret means bring him round who is opposed; should favour the helpful with facilities for giving further help, besides bestowing rewards and honour at all costs upon him; should give relief to him who is under troubles; should receive visitors at their own choice and afford satisfaction to them; should avoid using contemptuous, threatening, defamatory, or harsh words towards them; should, like a father, protect those who are promised security from fear; should punish the guilty after publishing their guilt; and in order to avoid causing suspicion to the protector, the vassal king should adopt the procedure of inflicting secret punishments upon offenders.

He should never covet the land, things, and sons and wives of the king slain by him; he should reinstate in their own estates the relatives of the kings slain. He should install in the kingdom the heir-apparent of the king who has died while working [with the conqueror]; all conquered kings will, if thus treated, loyally follow the sons and grandsons of the conqueror.

Whoever covets the lands, things, sons,and wives of the kings whom he has either slain or bound in chains will cause provocation to the Circle of States and make it rise against himself; also his own ministers employed in his own territory will be provoked, and will seek shelter under the Circle of States, having an eye upon his life and kingdom.

Hence conquered kings preserved in their own lands in accordance with the policy of conciliation will be loyal to the conqueror and follow his sons and grandsons. . . .

THE WORK OF AN INVADER

The conqueror should know the comparative strength and weakness of himself and of his enemy; and having ascertained the power, place, time, the time of marching and of recruiting the army, the consequences, the loss of men and money, and profits and danger, he should march with his full force; otherwise, he should keep quiet.

My teacher says that of enthusiasm and power, enthusiasm is better: a king, himself energetic, brave, strong, free from disease, skilful in wielding weapons, is able with his army as a secondary power to subdue a powerful king; his army, though small, will, when led by him, be capable of turning out any work. But a king who has no enthusiasm in himself will perish, though he is powerful and possessed of a strong army.

No, says Kautilya, he who is possessed of power over-reaches, by the sheer force of his power, another who is merely enthusiastic. Having acquired, captured, or brought another enthusiastic king as well as brave soldiers, he can make his enthusiastic army of horses, elephants, chariots, and others to move anywhere without obstruction. Powerful kings, whether women, young men,

From Kautilya, *Arthashastra*, translated by R. Shamasastry (1915), 5th ed. (Mysore: Sri Raghuveer, 1956), [bk. 9,] 367–70.

lame, or blind, conquered the earth by winning over or purchasing the aid of enthusiastic persons.

My teacher says that of power [money and army] and skill in intrigue, power is better; for a king, though possessed of skill for intrigue [*mantrashakti*] becomes a man of barren mind if he has no power; for the work of intrigue is well defined. He who has no power loses his kingdom as sprouts of seeds in drought vomit their sap.

No, says Kautilya, skill for intrigue is better; he who has the eye of knowledge, and is acquainted with the science of polity, can, with little effort, make use of his skill for intrigue, and can succeed by means of conciliation, and other strategic means and by spies and chemical appliances in over-reaching even those kings who are possessed of enthusiasm and power. Thus of the three acquirements, viz., enthusiasm, power and skill for intrigue, he who possesses more of the quality mentioned later than the one mentioned first in the order of enumeration will be successful in over-reaching others.

Country [space] means the earth; in it the thousand yojanas of the northern portion of the country that stretches between the Himalayas and the ocean from the dominion of no insignificant emperor; in it there are such varieties of land, as forests, villages, mountains, level plains, and uneven grounds. In such lands he should undertake such work as he considers to be conducive to his power and prosperity. That part of the country in which his army finds a convenient place for its maneuver, and which proves unfavourable to his enemy, is the best; that part of the country which is of the reverse nature is the worst; and that which partakes of both the characteristics is a country of middling quality.

Time consists of cold, hot, and rainy periods. The divisions of time are: the night, the day, the fortnight, the month, the season, solstices, the year, and the yuga [cycle of five years]. In these divisions of time he should undertake such works as are conducive to the growth of his power and prosperity. That time which is congenial for the maneuver of his army, but which is of the reverse nature for his enemy, is the best; that which is of the reverse nature is the worst; and that which possesses both the characteristics is of middling quality.

My teacher says that of strength, place, and time, strength is the best; for a man who is possessed of strength can overcome the difficulties due either to the unevenness of the ground or to the cold, hot, or rainy periods of time. Some say that place is the best, for the reason that a dog, seated in a convenient place, can drag a crocodile, and that a crocodile in low ground can drag a dog.

Others say that time is the best, for the reason that during the day-time the crow kills the owl and that at night the owl the crow.

No, says Kautilya, of strength, place, and time, each is helpful to the other; whoever is possessed of these three things should, after having placed one-third or one-fourth of his army to protect his base of operations against his rear-enemy and wild tribes in his vicinity, and after having taken with him as much army and treasure as is sufficient to accomplish his work, march during the month of Margashirsha [December] against his enemy whose collection of foodstuffs is old and insipid, and who has not only not gathered fresh foodstuffs, but also not repaired his fortifications, in order to destroy the enemy's rainy crops and autumnal handfuls [*mushti*]. He should march during the month of Chaitra [March], if he means to destroy the enemy's autumnal crops and vernal handfuls. He should march during the month of Jyestha [May-June] against one whose storage of fodder, firewood and water has diminished and who has not repaired his fortifications, if he means to destroy the enemy's vernal crops and handfuls of the rainy season. Or he may march during the dewy season against a country which is of hot climate and in which fodder and water are obtained in little quantities. Or he may march during the summer against a country in which the sun is enshrouded by mist and which is full of deep valleys and thickets of trees and grass, or he may march during the rains against a country which is suitable for the maneuver of his own army and which is of the reverse nature for his enemy's army. He has to undertake a long march between the month of Margashirsha [December] and Taisha [January], a march of mean length between March and April, and a short march between May and June; and in order to be near, a fourth variety of march may be made against one in trouble. . . .

My teacher says that one should almost invariably march against an enemy in troubles.

But Kautilya says: that when one's resources are sufficient, one should march, since the troubles of an enemy cannot be properly recognised; or whenever one finds it possible to reduce or destroy an enemy by marching against him, then one may undertake a march.

When the weather is free from heat, one should march with an army mostly composed of elephants. Elephants with profuse sweat in hot weather are attacked by leprosy; and when they have no water for bathing and drinking, they lose their quickness and become obstinate. Hence, against a country containing plenty of water and during the rainy season, one should march with an army mostly composed of elephants. Against a country of the reverse description, i.e., which has little rain and muddy water, one should march with an army mostly composed of asses, camels, and horses.

Against a desert, one should march during the rainy season with all the four constituents of the army [elephants, horses, chariots and men]. One should prepare a program of short and long distance to be marched in accordance with the nature of the ground to be traversed, viz., even ground, uneven ground, valleys and plains.

When the work to be accomplished is small, march against all kinds of enemies should be of a short duration; and when it is great, it should also be of long duration; during the rains, encampments should be made abroad. . . .

CONCERNING A POWERFUL ENEMY

The Duties of a Messenger

When a king of poor resources is attacked by a powerful enemy, he should surrender himself together with his sons to the enemy and live like a reed [in the midst of a current of water].

Bharadvaja says that he who surrenders himself to the strong, bows down before Indra [the god of rain].

But Vishalaksha says that a weak king should rather fight with all his resources, for bravery destroys all troubles; this [fighting] is the natural duty of a Kshatriya, no matter whether he achieves victory or sustains defeat in battle.

No, says Kautilya, he who bows down to all like a crab on the banks [of a river] lives in despair; whoever goes with his small army to fight perishes like a man attempting to cross the sea without a boat. Hence, a weak king should either seek the protection of a powerful king or maintain himself in an impregnable fort.

Invaders are of three kinds: a just conqueror, a demon-like conqueror, and a greedy conqueror.

Of these, the just conqueror is satisfied with mere obeisance. Hence, a weak king should seek his protection.

Fearing his own enemies, the greedy conqueror is satisfied with what he can safely gain in land or money. Hence, a weak king should satisfy such a conqueror with wealth.

The demon-like conqueror satisfies himself not merely by seizing the land, treasure, sons and wives of the conquered, but by taking the life of the latter. Hence, a weak king should keep such a conqueror at a distance by offering him land and wealth.

When any one of these is on the point of rising against a weak king, the latter should avert the invasion by making a treaty of peace, or by taking recourse to the battle of intrigue [*mantrayuddha*], or by a treacherous fight in the battlefield. He may seduce the enemy's men either by conciliation or by giving gifts, and should prevent the treacherous proceedings of his own men either by sowing the seeds of dissension among them or by punishing them. Spies,

From Kautilya, *Arthashastra*, translated by R. Shamasastry (1915), 5th ed. (Mysore: Sri Raghuveer, 1956), [bk. 12,] 411–17.

under concealment, may capture the enemy's fort, country, or camp with the aid of weapons, poison, or fire. He may harass the enemy's rear on all sides; and he may devastate the enemy's country through the help of wild tribes. Or he may set up a scion of the enemy's family or an imprisoned prince to seize the enemy's territory. When all his mischief has been perpetrated, a messenger may be sent to the enemy (to sue for peace); or he may make peace with the enemy without offending the latter. If the enemy still continues the march, the weak king may sue for peace by offering more than one-fourth of his wealth and army, the payment being made after the lapse of a day and night.

If the enemy desires to make peace on condition of the weak king surrendering a portion of his army, he may give the enemy such of his elephants and cavalry as are uncontrollable or as are provided with poison; if the enemy desires to make peace on condition of his surrendering his chief men, he may send over to the enemy such portion of his army as is full of traitors, enemies and wild tribes under the command of a trusted officer, so that both his enemy and his own undesirable army may perish; or he may provide the enemy with an army composed of fiery spies, taking care to satisfy his own disappointed men (before sending them over to the enemy); or he may transfer to the enemy his own faithful and hereditary army that is capable to hurt the enemy on occasions of trouble; if the enemy desires to make peace on condition of his paying a certain amount of wealth, he may give the enemy such precious articles as do not find a purchaser or such raw products as are of no use in war; if the enemy desires to make peace on condition of his ceding a part of his land, he should provide the enemy with that kind of land which he can recover, which is always at the mercy of another enemy, which possesses no protective defences, or which can be colonised at considerable cost of men and money; or he may make peace, surrendering his whole state except his capital.

He should so contrive as to make the enemy accept that which another enemy is likely to carry off by force; and he should take care more of his person than of his wealth, for of what interest is perishing wealth? . . .

Slaying the Commander-in-Chief and Inciting a Circle of States

Spies in the service of the king [the enemy] or of his courtiers may, under the pretence of friendship, say in the presence of other friends that the king is angry with the chiefs of infantry, cavalry, chariots and elephants. When their men are collected together, fiery spies having guarded themselves against night watches, may, under the pretence of the king's [the enemy's] order, invite the chiefs to a certain house and slay the chiefs when returning from the house. Other spies in the vicinity may say that it has been the king's [the enemy's] order to slay them. Spies may also tell those who have been banished from the country: "This is just what we foretold; for personal safety, you may go elsewhere."

Spies may also tell those who have not received what they requested of the king [the enemy] that the officer in charge of waste lands has been told by the king: "Such and such a person has begged of me what he should not demand; I refused to grant his request; he is in conspiracy with my enemy. So make attempts to put him down." Then the spies may proceed in their usual way.

Spies may also tell those who have been granted their request by the king [the enemy] that the officer in charge of waste lands has been told by the king: "Such and such persons have demanded their due from me; I have granted them all their requests in order to gain their confidence. But they are conspiring with my enemy. So make attempts to put them down." Then the spies may proceed in their usual way.

Spies may also tell those who do not demand their due from the king that the officer in charge of waste lands has been told: "Such and such persons do not demand their due from me. What else can be the reason than their suspicion about my knowledge of their guilt? So make attempts to put them down." Then the spies may proceed in their usual way.

This explains the treatment of partisans.

A spy employed as the personal servant of the king [the enemy] may inform him that such and such ministers of his are being interviewed by the enemy's servants. When he comes to believe this, some treacherous persons may be represented as the messengers of the enemy, specifying as "this is that."

The chief officers of the army, the ministers and other officers may be induced by offering land and gold to fall against their own men and secede from the enemy [their king]. If one of the sons of the commander-in-chief is living near or inside the fort, a spy may tell him: "You are the most worthy son; still you are neglected; why are you indifferent? Seize your position by force; otherwise the heir-apparent will destroy you."

Or some one of the family [of the commander-in-chief of the king], or one who is imprisoned may be bribed in gold and told: "Destroy the internal strength of the enemy, or a portion of his force in the border of his country or any other army."

Or having seduced wild tribes with rewards of wealth and honour, they may be incited to devastate the enemy's country. Or the enemy's rear-enemy may be told: "I am, as it were, a bridge to you all; if I am broken like a rafter, this king will down you all; let us, therefore, combine and thwart the enemy in his march." Accordingly, a message may be sent to individual or combined states to the effect: "After having done with me, this king will do his work of you; beware of it. I am the best man to be relied upon."

In order to escape from the danger from an immediate enemy, a king should frequently send to a Madhyama or a neutral king (whatever would please him); or one may put one's whole property at the enemy's disposal. . . .

STRATEGIC MEANS TO CAPTURE
A FORTRESS

The Operation of a Siege

Reduction [of the enemy] must precede a siege. The territory that has been conquered should be kept so peacefully that it might sleep without any fear. When it is in rebellion, it is to be pacified by bestowing rewards and remitting taxes, unless the conqueror means to quit it. Or he may select his battlefields in a remote part of the enemy's territory, far from the populous centres; for, in the opinion of Kautilya, no territory deserves the name of a kingdom or country unless it is full of people. When a people resist the attempt of the conqueror, then he may destroy their stores, crops, and granaries, and trade.

By the destruction of trade, agricultural produce, and standing crops, by causing the people to run away, and by slaying their leaders in secret, the country will be denuded of its people.

When the conqueror thinks: "My army is provided with abundance of staple corn, raw materials, machines, weapons, dress, labourers, ropes and the like, and has a favourable season to act, whereas an enemy has an unfavourable season and is suffering from disease, famine and loss of stores and defensive force, while his hired troops as well as the army of his friend are in a miserable condition"—then he may begin the siege.

Having well guarded his camp, transports, supplies and also the roads of communication, and having dug up a ditch and raised a rampart round his camp, he may vitiate the water in the ditches round the enemy's fort, or empty the ditches of their water, or fill them with water if empty, and then he may assail the rampart and the parapets by making use of underground tunnels and iron rods. If the ditch is very deep, he may fill it up with soil. If it is defended by a number of men, he may destroy it by means of machines. Horse soldiers may force their passage through the gate into the fort and smite the enemy. Now and then, in the midst of tumult, he may offer terms to the enemy by taking recourse to one, two, three, or all of the strategic means.

Having captured the birds, such as the vulture, crow, *naptr, bhasa,* parrot, *maina,* and pigeon, which have their nests in the fort walls, and having tied to

From Kautilya, *Arthashastra,* translated by R. Shamasastry (1915), 5th ed. (Mysore: Sri Raghuveer, 1956), [bk. 13,] 433–39.

their tails inflammable powder [*agniyoga*], he may let them fly to the forts. If the camp is situated at a distance from the fort and is provided with an elevated post for archers and their flags, then the enemy's fort may be set on fire. Spies, living as watchmen of the fort, may tie inflammable powder to the tails of mongooses, monkeys, cats and dogs, and let them go over the thatched roofs of the houses. A splinter of fire kept in the body of a dried fish may be caused to be carried off by a monkey, or a crow, or any other bird [to the thatched roofs of the houses].

Small balls prepared from the mixture of *sarala* [*Pinus longifolia*], *devadaru* [deodar], *putitrna* [stinking grass], *guggulu* [bdellium], *shriveshtaka* [turpentine], the juice of *sajja* [*Vatica robusta*], and *laksha* [lac] combined with dungs of an ass, camel, sheep, and goat are inflammable [*agnidharanah*, i.e., such as keep fire].

The mixture of the powder of *priyala* [*Chironjia sapida*], the charcoal of *avalguja* [oanyza, serratula, anthelmintica], *madhuchchhishta* [wax], and the dung of a horse, ass, camel, and cow is an inflammable powder to be hurled against the enemy.

The powder of all the metals [*sarvaloha*] as red as fire, or the mixture of the powder of kumbhi [*Gmelia arberea*], *sisa* [lead] and *trapu* [zinc], mixed with the charcoal powder of the flowers of *paribhadraka* [deodar], *palasa* [*Butea frondosa*], and hair, and with oil wax, and turpentine, is also an inflammable powder.

A stick of *visvasaghati* painted with the above mixture and wound round with a bark made of hemp, zinc, and lead, is a fire-arrow [to be hurled against the enemy].

When a fort can be captured by other means, no attempt should be made to set fire to it; for fire cannot be trusted; it not only offends gods, but also destroys the people, grains, cattle, gold, raw materials and the like. Also the acquisition of a fort with its property all destroyed is a source of further loss. Such is the aspect of a siege.

When the conqueror thinks: "I am well provided with all necessary means and with workmen, whereas my enemy is diseased, with officers proved to be impure under temptations, with unfinished forts and deficient stores, allied with no friends, or with friends inimical at heart," then he should consider it as an opportune moment to take up arms and storm the fort.

When fire, accidental or intentionally kindled, breaks out; when the enemy's people are engaged in a sacrificial performance, or in witnessing spectacles or the troops, or in quarrel due to the drinking of liquor; or when the enemy's army is too much tired by daily engagements in battles and is reduced in strength in consequence of the slaughter of a number of its men in a number of battles; when the enemy's people wearied from sleeplessness have fallen asleep; or on the occasion of a cloudy day of floods, or of a thick fog or snow, general assault should be made.

Or having concealed himself in a forest after abandoning the camp, the conqueror may strike the enemy when the latter comes out.

A king, pretending to be the enemy's chief friend or ally, may make the friendship closer with the besieged, and send a messenger to say: "This is thy weak point; these are thy internal enemies; that is the weak point of the besieger; and this person [who, deserting the conqueror, is now coming to thee] is thy partisan." When this partisan is returning with another messenger from the enemy, the conqueror should catch hold of him, and having published the partisan's guilt, should banish him, and retire from the siege operations. Then the pretending friend may tell the besieged: "Come out to help me, or let us combine and strike the besieger." Accordingly, when the enemy comes out, he may be hemmed between the two forces [the conqueror's force and the pretending friend's force] and killed or captured alive to distribute his territory [between the conqueror and the friend]. His capital city may be razed to the ground; and the flower of his army be made to come out and be destroyed.

This explains the treatment of a conquered enemy or wild chief.

Either a conquered enemy or the chief of a wild tribe [in conspiracy with the conqueror] may inform the besieged: "With the intention of escaping from a disease, or from the attack in his weak point by his enemy in the rear, or from a rebellion in his army, the conqueror seems to be thinking of going elsewhere, abandoning the siege." When the enemy is made to believe this, the conqueror may set fire to his camp and retire. Then the enemy coming out may be hemmed . . . as before.

Or having collected merchandise mixed with poison, the conqueror may deceive the enemy by sending that merchandise to the latter.

Or a pretending ally of the enemy may send a messenger to the enemy, asking him: "Come out to smite the conqueror already struck by me." When he does so, he may be hemmed . . . as before.

Spies, disguised as friends or relatives and with passports and orders in their hands, may enter the enemy's fort and help to its capture.

Or a pretending ally of the enemy may send information to the besieged: "I am going to strike the besieging camp at such a time and place; then you should also fight along with me." When the enemy does so, or when he comes out of his fort after witnessing the tumult and uproar of the besieging army in danger, he may be slain as before.

Or a friend or a wild chief in friendship with the enemy may be induced and encouraged to seize the land of the enemy when the latter is besieged by the conqueror. When accordingly any one of them attempts to seize the enemy's territory, the enemy's people or the leaders of the enemy's traitors may be employed to murder him [the friend or the wild chief]; or the conqueror himself may administer poison to him. Then another pretending friend may inform the enemy that the murdered person was a fratricide [as he attempted to seize the territory of his friend in troubles]. After strengthening his intimacy with the enemy, the pretending friend may sow the seeds of dissension between the enemy and his officers and have the latter hanged. Causing the peaceful people of the enemy to rebel, he may put them down, unknown to the enemy. Then having taken with him a portion of his army composed of furious wild tribes, he may enter the enemy's fort and allow it to be captured by the conqueror. Or traitors, enemies, wild tribes and other persons who have deserted the enemy, may, under the plea of having been reconciled, honoured and rewarded, go back to the enemy and allow the fort to be captured by the conqueror.

Having captured the fort or having returned to the camp after its capture, he should give quarter to those of the enemy's army who, whether as lying prostrate in the field, or as standing with their back turned to the conqueror, or with their hair dishevelled, with their weapons thrown down or with their body disfigured and shivering under fear, surrender themselves. After the captured fort is cleared of the enemy's partisans and is well guarded by the conqueror's men, both within and without, he should make his victorious entry into it.

Having thus seized the territory of the enemy close to his country, the conqueror should direct his attention to that of the Madhyama king; this being taken, he should catch hold of that of the neutral king. This is the first way to conquer the world. In the absence of the Madhyama and neutral kings, he should, in virtue of his own excellent qualities, win the hearts of his enemy's subjects, and then direct his attention to other remote enemies. This is the second way. In the absence of a Circle of States [to be conquered], he should conquer his friend or his enemy by hemming each between his own force and that of his enemy or that of his friend respectively. This is the third way.

Or he may first put down an almost invincible immediate enemy. Having doubled his power by this victory, he may go against a second enemy: having trebled his power by this victory, he may attack a third. This is the fourth way to conquer the world.

Having conquered the earth with its people of distinct castes and divisions of religious life, he should enjoy it by governing it in accordance with the duties prescribed to kings.

Intrigue, spies, winning over the enemy's people, siege, and assault are the five means to capture a fort.

Restoration of Peace in a Conquered Country

The expedition which the conqueror has to undertake may be of two kinds: in wild tracts or in single villages and the like.

The territory which he acquires may be of three kinds: that which is newly acquired, that which is recovered [from an usurper], and that which is inherited.

Having acquired a new territory, he should cover the enemy's vices with his own virtues, and the enemy's virtues by doubling his own virtues, by strict observance of his own duties, by attending to his works, by bestowing rewards, by remitting taxes, by giving gifts, and by bestowing honours. He should follow the friends and leaders of the people. He should give rewards, as promised, to those who deserted the enemy for his cause; he should also offer rewards to them as often as they render help to him; for whoever fails to fulfil his promises becomes untrustworthy both to his own and his enemy's people. Whoever acts against the will of the people will also become unreliable. He should adopt the same mode of life, the same dress, language, and customs as those of the people. He should follow the people in their faith with which they celebrate their national, religious and congregational festivals or amusements. His spies should often bring home to the mind of the leaders of provinces, villages, castes, and corporations the hurt inflicted on the enemies in contrast with the high esteem and favour with which they are treated by the conqueror, who finds his own prosperity in theirs. He should please them by giving gifts, remitting taxes, and providing for their security. He should always hold religious life in high esteem. Learned men, orators, charitable and brave persons should be favoured with gifts of land and money and with remission of taxes. He should release all the prisoners, and afford help to miserable, helpless, and diseased persons. He should prohibit the slaughter of animals for half a month during the period of Chaturmasya [from July to September], for four nights during the full moon, and for a night on the day of the birth star of the conqueror or of the national star. He should also prohibit the slaughter of females and young ones [*yonibalavadham*] as well as castration. Having abolished those customs or transactions which he might consider either as injurious to the growth of his revenue and army or as unrighteous, he should establish righteous transactions. He should compel born thieves as well as the Mlechchhas to change their habitations often and reside in many places. Such of his chief officers in charge of the forts, country parts, and the army, and ministers and priests, as are found to have been in conspiracy with the enemy should also be compelled to have their habitations in different places on the borders of the enemy's country. Such of his men as are capable to hurt him, but are convinced of their own fall with that of their master, should be pacified by secret remonstrance. Such renegades of his own country as are captured along with the enemy should be made to reside in remote corners. Whoever of the enemy's family is capable to wrest the conquered territory and is taking shelter in a wild tract on the border, often harassing the conqueror, should be provided with a sterile portion of territory or with a fourth part of a fertile tract on the condition of supplying to the conqueror a fixed amount of money and a fixed number of troops, in raising which he may incur the displeasure of the people and may be destroyed by them. Whoever has caused excitement to the people or incurred their displeasure should be removed and placed in a dangerous locality.

Having recovered a lost territory, he should hide those vices of his, owing to which he lost it, and increase those virtues by which he recovered it.

With regard to the inherited territory, he should cover the vices of his father, and display his own virtues.

He should initiate the observance of all those customs, which, though righteous and practised by others, are not observed in his own country, and give no room for the practice of whatever is unrighteous, though observed by others.

PART 5

BYZANTIUM

PROCOPIUS
(C. A.D. 500–565?)

Procopius, who was born at Caesarea in Palestine, held high office at Con-
stantinople and rose to be Prefect of the City in A.D. 562. Earlier he had
served as Belisarius's secretary and accompanied him on his campaigns in
Iran, North Africa, and Italy. Procopius's history of Justinian's wars recounts
the campaigns of Belisarius and Narses; the counterattack against the
Persians in 530, the reconquest of North Africa in 552–54, and the struggle
with the Goths.

THE PERSIAN WAR

. . . In this engagement seven Persians fell, the Romans getting the bodies, and
after it both sides kept their positions. But one young Persian, riding his horse
very near to the Roman army, challenged them all to see if anyone would fight
him. No one dared to run the risk, except for a certain Andreas, one of Buzes'
entourage, not a soldier nor one who had ever engaged in warfare, but a teacher
of gymnastics in charge of a wrestling school in Byzantium. He was with the
army as Buzes' bath attendant. He was a Byzantine by birth. He alone had the
courage, without being ordered by Buzes or anyone else, voluntarily to take
on this man in single combat. He got in first while the barbarian was still wondering where to aim, and hit him in the right breast with his spear. The Persian could not withstand the blow from this very strong man, and he fell from
his horse onto the ground, whereupon Andreas slaughtered him with a short
knife as he lay flat on his back like a sacrificial victim, and a great shout broke
out from the city wall and from the Roman troops. The Persians were enraged
by this and dispatched another horseman to take up the task, a brave man

From Procopius, *History of the Wars,* translated by Averil Cameron (New York: Washington
Square Press, 1967), 33–39, 104–14. Copyright © 1967 by Washington Square Press, Inc. Reprinted
by permission of Pocket, a division of Simon & Schuster, Inc.

of splendid physique, and no youth, but one who actually showed some grey hair. This man rode up to the enemy army, and brandishing the whip which he used to strike his horse, he challenged to battle any Roman who was willing. When no one went out to meet him, Andreas came into the open, unnoticed by anyone, even though Hermogenes had forbidden him. Both men charged furiously with their spears, and the spears, crashing against their breastplates, were completely shattered, while the horses, cannoning headlong into each other, fell themselves and threw their riders. The two men, falling next to each other, both struggled hard to get up, but the Persian could not do this because of the hindrance of his size, and Andreas was the first to rise (for his wrestling-school practice enabled him to do it). He struck the other as he was getting up on his knee and killed him as he fell to the ground. Then a shout perhaps even greater than before broke out from the city wall and the Roman army, and the Persians broke up their phalanx and retreated to Ammodios, while the Romans came inside the city wall singing the pæan of victory, for it was already growing dark. And so both sides encamped for the night. . . .

. . . Belisarius and Hermogenes quickly arranged their soldiers in the former position, since they had seen the Persians advancing toward them. And the barbarians, coming up before them, took up their position in front. But the Mirranes did not station all the Persians against the Romans, but only half, allowing the others to remain behind. These were to relieve the fighters and be fresh when they attacked the enemy, so that they could all fight in continuous succession. He ordered only the troop known as the "Immortals" to remain where they were until he gave the signal. He stationed himself in the middle of the front line, and put Pityaxes in charge of those on the right, and Baresmanes in charge of those on the left wing. Thus both sides were drawn up. Pharas stood beside Belisarius and Hermogenes and said: "I do not think that if I stay here with the Eruls I can do much harm to the enemy, but if we hide on this slope and then, when the Persians are engaged in the battle, climb up through this ridge and suddenly advance on their rear, shooting at them from behind, we shall in all probability strike the fatal blow." These were his words, and since Belisarius and the generals approved, he acted accordingly.

Neither side began the battle until midday, but as soon as noon had passed, the barbarians started the engagement. They had put off the time of the encounter until this time of day because it was their custom to eat only in the evening, whereas the Romans ate before noon, and so they thought the Romans would never hold out so well if they attacked them while they were hungry. First of all each side shot arrows at the other, and the weapons made a great mist with their number. Many fell on both sides, but the barbarians' weapons fell far thicker, for they fought in succession and were always fresh, giving the enemy no hint of what they were doing. Yet even thus the Romans did not get the worst of it. They were favored by a wind which blew on the barbarians and would not allow their weapons to go far. When each side had used up all its arrows, they used their spears against each other, and the battle started at closer quarters. The Roman left wing was in the most serious trouble. The Cadiseni, who were fighting there under Pityaxes, coming up in great numbers suddenly turned the enemy and following closely on them as they fled killed many. The troops under Sunicas and Aigan saw this and came to them at a run. But first the three hundred Eruls with Pharas came down upon the enemy's rear from the high ground and gave a wonderful display of valor against the Cadiseni and others. And when the Cadiseni saw Sunicas' troops now coming against them from the flank, they turned to flight. The rout became complete, for the Romans there joined up with each other and slaughtered many barbarians. On the right wing no less than three thousand perished in this reversal, the rest just managing to find safety back in the phalanx. The Romans did not pursue them further, and each side took up its position opposite the other in battle order. Such was the course of these events.

But the Mirranes secretly sent troops to the left, including all the Immortals. When Belisarius and Hermogenes saw them they gave the command for Sunicas' and Aigan's men, six hundred in number, to proceed to the righthand angle, where Simmas' and Askan's men were positioned, and behind them they posted many of Belisarius' men. So the Persians who were holding the left wing under the leadership of Baresmanes advanced at a run with the Immortals against the Romans drawn up against them. The Romans could not withstand their attack and were made to flee. Then the Romans at the angle and those who were behind them charged against the pursuers with all their might, and since they met the barbarians from the flank, they divided their army into two, with the majority on the right, but also cutting some off on the left. Among these there happened to be Baresmanes' standard-bearer, and Sunicas made for him and hit him with his spear. Now the Persians who were at the front of the pursuit, realizing what danger they were in, wheeled around, abandoned the pursuit and set about them, exposing themselves as a result to enemy fire from both sides—for the Romans who were in flight realized what was happening and turned back. And the Immortals and the rest of the Persians saw that the standard had been knocked over and thrown to the ground. They made for the Romans near it with Baresmanes, and the Romans came to meet them. First Sunicas killed Baresmanes, knocking him from his horse on to the ground. At this the barbarians were filled with alarm and had no further thought of valor, but turned to flight in great confusion. The Romans encircled them and killed about five thousand. So the whole of each army was on the move, the Persians in retreat, the Romans in pursuit. While they were in these straits, such of the Persian army as were on foot threw down their shields and so were ignominiously killed by the enemy as they were caught. But the Romans' pursuit was short, for Belisarius and Hermogenes would not allow them to go any further. They were afraid that something might happen to make the Persians turn and rout them as they were in their reckless pursuit, and it seemed sufficient to them to keep their victory unspoiled. On that day the Persians had after many years been defeated in battle by the Romans. So the two sides separated. After this the Persians did not wish to fight the Romans openly, but there were surprise attacks on both sides, in which the Romans did not come off worst. This then was the fate of the armies in Mesopotamia. . . .

Chosroes [Khosru] himself moved with all his army and came up to the wall of Petra and there he pitched camp and began a siege. But on the following day after he had encircled the wall and suspected that it was not very defensible, he decided to storm the wall. He brought up the entire army there and set about it, ordering them all to shoot at the battlements. The Romans defended themselves with machines and every kind of missile. So at first the Persians did little damage to the Romans, even though they were shooting very thickly and were themselves hit very much by them, for they were shooting from a height. But it was fated that Petra should be taken by Chosroes; later John was by some chance fatally wounded in the throat and died, and after this the other Romans gave up hope of anything. Then the barbarians retreated to their camp, for it was already growing dark, and on the following day they devised an excavation against the wall in the following way.

The city of Petra is partly unapproachable because of the sea and partly because of sheer rocks which rise up there on all sides. It is from this that it got its name. It has one entrance on level ground, and even this is not a wide one, for precipitous crags overhang it on both sides. Here the builders of the city, with forethought to prevent that part of the wall from being assailable, had built long walls stretching for a considerable distance along each cliff at the entrance. On these walls they built two towers, one on either side, not in the usual way, but differently. They did not leave the space inside the building empty, but made the whole of the towers, from the ground up to a great height, of enormous stones fitting to each other, so that they could not be shaken down by a ram or any other machine. This was the nature of the fortifications at Petra.

But the Persians secretly made a trench and got beneath one of the towers. They removed many of the stones from there and put wood in their place, which shortly afterwards they set on fire. The flame gradually rose and broke down the strength of the stones, shaking the entire tower, and suddenly brought it all down to the ground. But the Romans who were inside the tower realized beforehand enough of what was happening not to fall to the ground with it, but to make their escape inside the city wall. Now the enemy who were storming the wall on the level ground could capture the city without any hindrance. And so the terrified Romans held a conference with the barbarians, and after receiving pledges from Chosroes for their lives and their wealth they made a voluntary surrender of themselves and their city. . . .

When Chosroes heard that Belisarius was encamped with the entire Roman army in Europum, he decided to go no further forward. He sent to Belisarius one of the royal secretaries called Abandanes, who had a high reputation for intelligence, to find out what sort of general he was, though ostensibly to complain that the Emperor Justinian had not sent envoys to Persia to treat for peace according to their agreement. When he heard this Belisarius did as follows. He chose six thousand tall, fine-looking men and set out for a hunt, some distance from the camp, telling Diogenes, the bodyguard, and Adolius, the son of Acacius, an Armenian who looked over the quiet for the Emperor in the palace (the Romans call the holders of this office "silentiaries"), but was at that time commanding some Armenians, to cross the river with a thousand horses and move about the bank there, giving the enemy the impression all the time that if they wanted to cross the Euphrates and go to their own country, they would never allow them. They did accordingly.

When Belisarius had heard that the enemy was very near, he made a tent of some thick cloth, of the sort which it is the custom to call a "pavilion," and sat there as if in a deserted spot, trying to show that he had come without any equipment. He arranged the soldiers like this. On either side of the tent were Thracians and Illyrians, and after them Goths, next to them Eruls, and then Vandals and Maurusii. They extended far over the plain. They did not wait standing in the same place all the time, but separated from each other and walked about carelessly and at random, watching Chosroes' envoy. None of them had either a cloak nor any other covering for their shoulders, but were strolling about in linen tunics and trousers, with their girdles on top. Each one had his horsewhip and for weapons one had a sword, another an ax, another an uncovered bow. They all gave the appearance of being intent upon the hunt and forgetful of anything else. So Abandanes came before Belisarius and said that King Chosroes was very angry because the Cæsar (for this is what the Persians called the Roman Emperor) had not sent him the envoys as he had previously agreed, and that as a result Chosroes had been forced to bear arms against Roman territory. And Belisarius was not afraid at the thought of so great a number of barbarians being encamped nearby. He was not thrown into confusion by what the man said, but answered him with a relaxed and laughing expression: "Men do not usually act in the way that Chosroes has just now done. For other men, if a dispute occurs between themselves and any of their neighbors, send spokesmen to them first, and only make war on them if they do not find them reasonable. But he comes into the midst of the Romans and then offers peace talks."

With this he dismissed the envoy.

The envoy came to Chosroes and told him to leave as quickly as possible, for the envoy said he had met a very brave general, one more shrewd than any other man, and soldiers such as he had never seen before and for whose orderly behavior he had the greatest admiration. Further, the stakes in the struggle were not equal for himself and for Belisarius, the difference being that if he himself won he would be conquering Cæsar's slave, whereas if he should chance to be defeated he would bring great shame on the monarchy and the Persian race. The victorious Romans could easily save themselves in strongholds and in their own land, while of the Persian troops, if they should meet with a reversal, not even a messenger could escape to Persia. Chosroes was convinced by this warning and decided to retreat to Persia, but was greatly puzzled as to how to do it, for he believed that the river crossing was guarded by the enemy. He could not go back along the same road, which was completely deserted, because all their provisions which they had earlier brought with them when they invaded Roman territory were already exhausted. Finally, after much pondering, it seemed best to him to risk a battle to get to the opposite bank and make their journey through country that was flourishing with every kind of good thing. But Belisarius knew very well that even one hundred thousand men could never check Chosroes' crossing, for the river can be crossed by boat in many places thereabouts for some distance, and in any case, the Persian army was too big to be prevented from crossing by a few enemy. He told Diogenes and Adolius with their men and the thousand men first to patrol the bank there, so as to send the barbarians into confusion and perplexity. But after he had frightened him in the way I have related, he was afraid that something might prevent him from leaving Roman territory. It seemed to him vital to drive out Chosroes' army without risking a battle against the myriads of barbarians with soldiers who were very few in number and absolutely terrified of the Medic army. Accordingly, he told Diogenes and Adolius to stay quiet.

Chosroes built a bridge with great speed and suddenly crossed the river Euphrates with the entire army. For the Persians can cross any river without trouble, since they have in their equipment on the march iron hooks with which they fit long beams to each other and improvise a bridge on the spot wherever they want it. As soon as he was on the other side, he sent to Belisarius, saying that he had done a favor to the Romans in the retreat of the Medic army, and that he was expecting the envoys from them, who ought to be present very shortly. And Belisarius, too, crossed the river Euphrates with the entire Roman army and immediately sent to Chosroes. When they reached him, they were full of gratitude for the retreat and promised that envoys would come to him from the Emperor immediately, who would ratify with him the previous agreement about the peace. . . .

THE GOTHIC WAR

. . . The armies came together and were drawn up in this way. They all stood facing each other on both sides, making the front of the battle line as long and as deep as possible. Of the Romans, Narses and John held the left wing near the mound and with them all the best part of the Roman army. Each of them, apart from the rest of the soldiers, was followed by a large number of body-guards and spearsmen and Hunnic barbarians chosen for valor. On the right, Valerian was posted and also John the Glutton, with Dagisthæus and the rest of the Romans. On both wings they posted infantry archers from the regular soldiers—about eight thousand in number. In the middle of the battle line Narses positioned the Lombards and the Eruls and all the other barbarians, making them dismount from their horses and fight on foot, so that they would not fail in the engagement, and in case they deserted, so that they would not be able to retreat very fast. The end of the left wing Narses put at an angle to the Roman front line, posting one thousand five hundred cavalry there. He had previously told the five hundred that as soon as any of the Romans were routed, they should make it their duty to assist them. He told the one thousand that when the enemy infantry began to join in the action, they should get behind them at once and shoot at them from the rear. In the same way Totila posted all his army opposite the enemy. He went around his battle formation, encouraging the soldiers, and by his expression and his words urged them to the fight. And Narses did the same, raising their hopes with bracelets and bangles and gold bridles on poles and showing them other inducements to make them fight. For some time neither side began the battle; both remained inactive, waiting for the enemy to attack.

After some time, however, one of the Gothic army, Coccas by name, who had a considerable reputation for boldness, rode his horse forward, came up to the Roman army and challenged any who would to come out and fight him in single combat. This Coccas happened to be one of the Roman soldiers who had earlier deserted to Totila. At once one of Narses' spearsmen went to meet him, an Armenian called Anzalas, also on horseback. So Coccas first charged

From Procopius, *History of the Wars,* translated by Averil Cameron (New York: Washington Square Press, 1967), 268–77. Copyright © 1967 by Washington Square Press, Inc. Reprinted by permission of Pocket, a division of Simon & Schuster, Inc.

the enemy to score a hit with his spear, aiming at the stomach. But Anzalas suddenly made his horse swerve and rendered the charge useless. In this way he got on his opponent's flank and thrust his spear into his left side. The other fell from his horse and lay on the ground, dead. A great shout was raised by the Roman army, but not even now did either side start any fighting. Totila came alone to the space between the armies, not to fight a single combat but to frustrate the enemy of this opportunity for attack. He had heard that the remaining two thousand Goths were coming somewhere near at hand, and he was trying to put off the engagement until they arrived. He did this, therefore—first, he deliberately showed the enemy his identity. He was wearing armor plentifully covered in gold, and the decoration on his cheek plates as well as on his helmet and spear was of purple—indeed a wonderful display of regal splendor. He rode a horse of immense size, on which he gave a most skillful performance of the war dance there in no-man's-land. He wheeled his horse around in a circle and turned it about with another circling movement. From his horse, he flung his spear to the breezes and caught it again as it spun, and he passed it from hand to hand many times, transferring it with great expertise. In this performance he took a great pride, leaning back and moving his seat and bending to either side, as if he had been well taught in dancing from his childhood. By this means he consumed all the early part of the evening. Wanting to put off the beginning of the battle as long as he could, he sent to the Roman army, saying that he wanted to have a meeting with them. But Narses said he was just playing about, for previously, when there was time for preliminary talks, he had wanted to fight, while now, when he was in no-man's-land, he was coming to parley.

In the meantime, however, the Goths were joined by the two thousand. Totila heard that they had reached the entrenchment, and as it was time for their meal, he went to his own tent. The Goths broke up their battle formation and returned. But when Totila reached his quarters, he found that the two thousand were already there. He told them all to have their meal, then changed his armor. And after arming them all carefully, he led out his army at once against the enemy, thinking that they would take them unawares and capture them. But even so, he did not find the Romans unprepared, for Narses was afraid that the enemy might try to take them unawares, as did actually happen, and had forbidden them all to take their meal or to sleep or to take off any of their armor or to release their horses from their bridles. He did not leave them without food altogether; he told them to eat in their ranks and in their armor and to keep a close watch for the enemy attack. However, they were not now drawn up in the same way.

The Roman wings, where the foot archers were stationed, about four thousand of them, were turned into a crescent shape at Narses' order. All the Gothic foot soldiers were posted together behind the cavalry, so that if the cavalry should happen to be routed they could turn back to them in their flight and find safety, and both could advance together at once. The Goths had all been told in advance not to use bows or any other weapon whatever in this engagement, except their spears. Because of this it came about that Totila was defeated by his own folly. He entered this battle, for what reason I cannot tell, and presented his army to the enemy unequal in armor, not drawn up in an opposing position, nor matched in other ways.

The Romans utilized every kind of ploy in the engagement as was called for, either shooting arrows or pushing with their spears or using their swords in their hands or wielding anything else that was available to them and suitable for the emergency, some of them on horses, others going into battle on foot, according to what would suit their need, and in some places managing to encircle the enemy, in others waiting for their attack and repulsing their onslaught with their shields. But the Gothic cavalry, leaving the foot soldiers behind, put all their trust in their spears and charged with an unconsidered rush, and when they were in the action, they reaped the fruits of their own folly. For by charging into the middle of the enemy, they did not notice that they were in the midst of eight thousand foot soldiers. And under fire from arrows on both sides, they quickly gave way, for the archers soon turned both wings of the front line into a crescent, as I said before. So the Goths lost many men and horses in this engagement, though they had not yet joined with the enemy and only reached the enemy battle line late and with difficulty, after suffering many terrible injuries. Here I cannot admire any of the Romans or their barbarian allies more than the rest. The zeal of them all and their valor and their energy was one, and all of them held the onrush of the enemy attack and repulsed it most courageously. It was already near evening, and both armies moved, the Goths to flight and the Romans to pursuit.

The Goths could not withstand the enemy and gave way before their attack and retreated headlong, overcome before their numbers and good discipline. They had no thoughts of valor; they were panic-stricken, as though ghosts had fallen upon them, or as though they were being fought from heaven. They soon reached their own infantry and the disaster increased and worsened. They did not reach them in an orderly retreat to rest and to renew the fight with them, in the usual way, either to repel their pursuers by making a push or to make an attempt on the palisade or to try any other form of fighting, but in so disorderly a fashion that some of them were actually killed by the onrush of the cavalry. For this reason the foot soldiers did not open ranks and receive them, or hold firm to save them. They all fled headlong with them, and even killed each other, as if they were fighting a battle in the dark. The Roman army reaped the benefits of their fright and kept killing whoever was in front of them without mercy, their victims neither defending themselves nor daring to look at them—offering themselves to the enemy to treat as they liked. In this way fear encompassed them, and they were overcome by terror. Six thousand of them died in this action, and many put themselves into the hands of the enemy. For the present they took them captive, but they soon killed them. Not only Goths were killed, but also many of the former Roman soldiers who had earlier been part of the Roman army but who had deserted to Totila and the Goths, as I mentioned earlier. Those of the Gothic army who were not killed and who did not fall into the hands of the enemy managed to escape and to flee as best they could, on horseback or on foot or by what chance or opportunity or place available.

So this is how the battle ended. It was now completely dark. Some of the Romans pursued Totila, who was fleeing in the dark with only five men, one of whom was Scipuar; the Romans, among whom was Asbadus, the Gepid, did not know that it was Totila. When Asbadus got near to Totila, he rushed at him to stab him in the back with his spear, but a young Goth from Totila's household, who was following his master as he fled, cried out loudly in his indignation: "Why have you come, dog, to strike your own master?" But Asbadus drove his spear into Totila with all his might, but was himself transfixed there, hit in the foot by Scipuar. Scipuar himself stood there, too, hit by one of the pursuers. Those in the chase with Asbadus gave up the pursuit to save him and turned back with him. But Totila's companions thought that they were still after them and rode on as fast as before. They took Totila with them, even though he was mortally wounded and certainly dying, for their speed was the result of necessity. They rode for ten and one-half miles, till they came to a place called Capræ. Here they stopped and went no further and tended Totila's wound. But not long afterwards, he came to the end of his days. There his companions buried him and returned. This was the end of Totila's rule and of his life. He had ruled the Goths for eleven years. His death was not worthy of his earlier achievements, for previously he had been successful, and his end did not match his deeds. Here again Fortune is revealed as playing cat and mouse and ridiculing human affairs while displaying her own irrationality and her inexplicable nature. She gave spontaneously, for no reason, good fortune to Totila for some time, but then wantonly dealt him this wretched death, far from what he deserved. But this, I suspect, has never been comprehensible to men, nor will it ever be. Men talk about it, and opinions are forever flying about to suit each man's taste, as he tries to assuage his ignorance with the explanation that seems most reasonable. But I will return to my former subject.

The Romans did not know that Totila had been killed like this until one woman, a Goth, told them and showed them the grave. At first, they did not believe the tale, but when they came to the place and at once dug up the grave, they removed from it Totila's corpse. And it is said that they recognized it. Thus satisfying their own curiosity, they reburied him and told Narses the whole story at once.

Some say, however, that what happened to Totila in this battle was not like this, and it did not seem to me to be out of place to record it. They say, then, that the Gothic army did not suffer an irrational or surprising defeat, but that while some Romans were firing, an arrow suddenly hit Totila, not through deliberate aim, for Totila was fighting in the ranks as an ordinary soldier, wearing armor and taking up a position anywhere in the battle line, not wanting to be seen by the enemy and not exposing himself to attack. Some chance, then, engineered this and directed the arrow to his body. They say he was mortally wounded—as much as a man can be—and left the battle line in great pain with a few men and retired a little way. He managed to ride his horse as far as Capræ in his suffering, but there, almost fainting, he stayed to tend his wound, and not long afterwards the last day of his life came to him. The Gothic army were not strong enough to fight the enemy in any case, and now their commander was unaccountably removed from the fighting. They were astounded that Totila alone should be fatally wounded, and not by a deliberate enemy attack. As a result they were very much afraid and disheartened, and thus fell into limitless terror and this shameful defeat. But let each man speak as he believes about this.

Narses was overjoyed at these events and kept referring it all to the agency of God, which was in fact the true explanation, while he settled what he had in hand. First of all, to be free of the wickedness of the Lombards among his troops (for in addition to their other lawless ways, they burned down all the houses they came upon and violated the women who had taken refuge in the churches), he endowed them with a large sum of money and released them to go back home, telling Valerian and Damian, his brother, to escort them as far as the borders of Roman territory to stop them harming anyone on their journey. When the Lombards had left Roman land, Valerian encamped near the city of Verona so as to besiege it and bring it over to the Emperor. The garrison there were afraid and held talks with Valerian, meaning to make an agreement to surrender themselves and the city. When the Franks holding the garrisons in Venetia heard of this, they did all they could to stop them and demanded the land, on the grounds that it belonged to them. So Valerian returned from there with all his army without success.

The Goths who had fled from the engagement and escaped crossed the river Po and got control of the city of Ticinum and the surrounding land and made Teias their ruler. He found all the money that Totila had deposited in Ticinum and decided to invite the Franks to an alliance. As best he could under the circumstances, he organized the Goths and collected them all around him with great energy. When Narses heard this, he told Valerian to hold guard with all his men near the Po, so that the Goths could not gather at will, while going himself to Rome with the whole army. When he reached Tuscany, he took Narnia by agreement and left a garrison for the people of Spolitium, who had no defenses, telling them to rebuild as soon as possible all the part of the wall which the Goths had destroyed. He also sent a party to test the garrison at Perusia. Two Romans who had deserted were in charge of the guards at Perusia, Meligidius and Uliphus, who had formerly been Cyprian's bodyguard but who had killed him (Cyprian was then in charge of the garrison there) under persuasion from Totila, who made him many promises. So on hearing from Narses, Meligidius took counsel with his Roman troops and decided to surrender the city. But when Uliphus' men heard what was going on, they joined against them openly. Uliphus and his supporters were killed, and Meligidius at once surrendered Perusia to the Romans. Uliphus, then, obviously met with vengeance from God, for he perished in the very place where he had himself killed Cyprian. So this is how this went.

But when the Goths manning the garrison in Rome heard that Narses and the Roman army were advancing against them and were not far away, they prepared to meet them as best they could. It so happened that Totila had burned down many of the buildings in the city when he took it for the first time [which he thought of rebuilding in their entirety when he took it for the second time], but after reflecting that if they were divided into small groups, the Goths would not be able to defend the whole wall, he ended by surrounding a small part of the city near the tomb of Hadrian with a small fortification and joining it onto the existing wall to make a kind of fortress. There the Goths deposited their most precious possessions and kept constant guard, not bothering about the rest of the wall. So now they left a few guards here while all the rest went on to the battlements of the city wall, anxious to counter the enemy's attempts to storm the wall.

But because of its exceptional length, the Romans could not surround the whole of the wall of Rome in their attack, nor could the Goths defend it. They scattered, and the one side attacked it wherever they could, while the others defended themselves as best they could. Narses brought up a large number of archers and set them against a part of the wall, while on the other side John, the nephew of Vitalian, attacked it with his men. In another place Philimuth and the Eruls caused trouble, and the rest followed a long way away. They all made attacks on the wall at great distances from each other. The barbarians, drawn up against them, received their attack. Where there was no Roman attack, those parts of the wall were deserted—all the Goths gathered wherever the enemy attacked, as I said before. But in the meantime, at Narses' order,

Dagisthæus, with a large force and with the standards of both Narses and John, brought up a large number of scaling ladders and made a sudden attack on a part of the wall that was completely undefended. He leaned the ladders against the wall at once, without encountering any opposition, and got inside the wall with his men, with no difficulty, so that they could open the gates at their leisure. The Goths heard of this at once and had no further thought for valor, but all fled where each man could. Some jumped into the fortress, others made for Portus at a run.

At this point in my narrative it occurs to me how Fortune scoffs at human affairs. She is not always the same to men, nor does she look at them with the same expression; she changes in time and place and plays a game with them, altering the worth of the wretches according to place, time, and method. This must be so if Bessas, who had earlier lost Rome, not long afterwards saved Petra, in Lazica, for the Romans and again if Dagisthæus, who had left Petra to the enemy, shortly afterwards recovered Rome for the Emperor. But this has always happened, and it will ever be so as long as Fortune is the same to men.

Then Narses went with all his men to attack the fortress. The barbarians, in terror, took guarantees of personal safety and immediately handed over themselves and the fortress, in the twenty-eighth year of the reign of the Emperor Justinian [A.D. 552]. In this way Rome was taken for the fifth time in his reign, and Narses at once sent its keys to the Emperor.

MAURIKIOS
(C. A.D. 539–602)

The Cappadocian general Maurikios (Maurice), who succeeded his father-in-law Tiberius II as emperor of Byzantium in 582, was the reputed author of a considerable treatise on military matters, the Strategikon, *which he is said to have composed c. A.D. 600. (It may, however, have been written by an entirely different Maurikios, or by Orbicius, or by someone named Rufus.) Apart from the writings of Sun Zi and the* Arthashastra, *Maurikios's* Strategikon *is probably the most remarkable compilation of military lore from antiquity and the early Middle Ages. Maurikios may have been the first to describe and analyze the military techniques of the peoples on the periphery of the Byzantine empire. The idea that there are an ethnology and a geography of war is missing from the strategic texts of antiquity; the enemy exists almost as an abstraction, since strategic principles and tactical solutions were held to be universally valid. The disastrous defeat inflicted on Crassus by the Parthians (see p. 457 above) is a striking illustration of this.*

The emperor Maurikios was brought down by an army mutiny, said to have been provoked by his severe military discipline and strict economic measures. He abdicated, but was subsequently put to death, together with his five sons, by his successor, Phocas.

STRATEGY

Before the Day of Battle

A ship cannot cross the sea without a helmsman, nor can one defeat an enemy without tactics and strategy. With these and the aid of God it is possible to overcome not only an enemy force of equal strength but even one greatly su-

From *Maurice's "Strategikon": Handbook of Byzantine Military Strategy,* translated by George T. Dennis (Philadelphia: University of Pennsylvania Press, 1984), [bk. 7,] 64–74. Reproduced by permission of the University of Pennsylvania Press.

perior in numbers. For it is not true, as some inexperienced people believe, that wars are decided by courage and numbers of troops, but, along with God's favor, by tactics and generalship, and our concern should be with these rather than wasting our time in mobilizing large numbers of men. The former provide security and advantage to men who know how to use them well, whereas the other brings trouble and financial ruin.

The leader must take advantage of favorable times and places in fighting against the enemy. First, he must guard against hostile attacks which can injure our men, and then he must attempt to launch the same against the enemy. Above all he must look for enemy ambushes, sending out frequent and far-ranging patrols in all directions in the area around the battlefield. He must avoid disordered and uncoordinated pursuits. We would not allow the general to take part personally in raids or other reckless attacks. These should be entrusted to other competent officers. For if one of the subordinate officers blunders or fails, the situation may be quickly straightened out. But if the leader of the whole army fails, his fall can open the way to complete disorder.

That general is wise who before entering into war carefully studies the enemy, and can guard against his strong points and take advantage of his weaknesses. For example, the enemy is superior in cavalry; he should destroy his forage. He is superior in number of troops; cut off their supplies. His army is composed of diverse peoples; corrupt them with gifts, favors, promises. There is dissension among them; deal with their leaders. This people relies on the spear; lead them into difficult terrain. This people relies on the bow; line up in the open and force them into close, hand-to-hand fighting. Against Scythians or Huns launch your assault in February or March when their horses are in wretched condition after suffering through the winter, and proceed as just suggested for attacking archers. If they march or make camp without proper precautions, make unexpected raids on them by night and by day. If they are reckless and undisciplined in combat and not inured to hardship, make believe you are going to attack, but delay and drag things out until their ardor cools, and when they begin to hesitate, then make your attack on them. The foe is superior in infantry; entice him into the open, not too close, but from a safe distance hit him with javelins.

Warfare is like hunting. Wild animals are taken by scouting, by nets, by lying in wait, by stalking, by circling around, and by other such stratagems rather than by sheer force. In waging war we should proceed in the same way, whether the enemy be many or few. To try simply to overpower the enemy in the open, hand to hand and face to face, even though you might appear to win, is an enterprise which is very risky and can result in serious harm. Apart from extreme emergency, it is ridiculous to try to gain a victory which is so costly and brings only empty glory. . . .

GATHERING INTELLIGENCE ABOUT THE ENEMY

Every effort should be made by continuously sending out keen-sighted scouts at appropriate intervals, by spies and patrols, to obtain information about the enemy's movements, their strength and organization, and thus be in a position to prevent being surprised by them. . . .

ENEMY PRISONERS TAKEN BY PATROLS

If some of the enemy are captured by a patrol or desert to us, then, if they are nicely armed and in good physical condition, they should not be shown to the army, but sent off secretly to some other place. But if they appear in miserable shape, make sure to show the deserters to the whole army; have the prisoners stripped and paraded around, and make them beg for their lives so that our men may think that all the enemy soldiers are that wretched.

PUNISHMENT OF OFFENDERS

In the vicinity of the enemy and with a pitched battle imminent, the commanding officers of the tagmas should be ordered to guard against punishing soldiers who have committed offenses for those few days and not to deal harshly with the soldiers at all. Instead, they should be careful in dealing with those who are suspected of harboring some grievance. But if they prove intractable, then use some plausible pretext to send them off to some other place for a while until after the battle so they will not go over to the enemy and provide him with some information he should not have. Men of the same race as the enemy should be sent away long before and should not be brought into battle against their own people.

MAINTENANCE OF THE SOLDIERS, THEIR HORSES, AND THEIR CAMPS

When battle is imminent, provisions should be made bearing in mind the possibility of defeat and steps taken to guard against its adverse effects. In particular, food for a few days for both men and horses should be collected. Fortified camps should be constructed in suitable places, according to the plan given below, in which water may be safely stored for emergencies. . . .

WAGING WAR AGAINST AN UNFAMILIAR PEOPLE

If we find ourselves at war with a powerful people and one whose ways are strange to us, and the army, not knowing what to expect becomes nervous, then we must be very careful to avoid getting into an open battle with them right away. Before any fighting the first and safest thing to do is to choose a few experienced and lightly armed soldiers and have them very secretly carry out attacks against some detachments of the enemy. If they succeed in killing or capturing some of them, then most of our soldiers will take this as evidence of our own superiority. They will get over their nervousness, their morale will pick up, and they will gradually become used to fighting against them.

SURPRISE ATTACKS BY THE ENEMY ON THE MARCH

If the enemy launches a surprise attack, and conditions are not favorable for battle because the terrain is rugged or thickly covered or because the time is not to our advantage, then we should not plan on fighting there. Instead, we should work on getting our forces together, occupy a position suitable for camp, and delay until the place and the time become more favorable and not be forced to fight when we do not want to. This does not mean that we are running away from the enemy, but only that we are avoiding a poor location.

CAMPS AND MAINTENANCE OF THE HORSES IN THEM

When the enemy is approaching our camp, and especially if it looks as though the fighting is to be done in the Scythian manner, our options are as follows. If the army is to stay within the fortifications and there await the enemy, enough hay or grass for the horses for one or two days should be gotten ready and stored. But if the army is to march out with the idea of moving to another camp and there lining up for battle, then it has to carry along a day's supply of hay or grass and deposit it in the new fortification. For it is not likely that the enemy will allow the servants to go out foraging on that day or to graze the horses. But if the enemy should come very close, it would be a good idea, as mentioned, for each man to collect the necessary forage on the march. For usually after they have set up camp the boys will not be able to go out and collect forage, especially if the enemy cavalry outnumbers ours. . . .

Points to be Observed on the Day of Battle

NOT OVERBURDENING THE GENERAL ON THE DAY OF BATTLE

On the actual day of battle the general should not take on too many tasks. He might exert himself too much, become worn out, and overlook some really essential matters. He should not look downcast or worried but should ride jauntily along the lines and encourage all the troops. He should not himself join in the actual fighting; this is not the role of the general but of the soldier. After making all the proper arrangements, he should station himself in a suitable spot from which he can observe which troops are exerting themselves and which might be slackening. When needed he should be ready to send assistance to a unit in trouble by making use of his reserves, that is, the flank and rear guards.

ENEMY ARCHERS

In combat against archers every effort should be made to guard against positioning our troops on the lower slopes of mountains and difficult terrain. Our troops should form high up in the hills or else come down from the mountains all the way and draw up on level, open ground. Otherwise, they may be suddenly overcome by hostile detachments lying in ambush under cover of the heights.

NOT ENGAGING THE ENEMY IN COMBAT OR SHOWING OUR OWN STRENGTH BEFORE LEARNING THE ENEMY'S INTENTIONS

Contact should not be made with the enemy's main body, nor should they be allowed to observe our own formation clearly, before reconnoitering their lines and finding out whether they are planning any ambushes.

CONCEALMENT OF THE SECOND LINE WHEN IT IS UNABLE TO FOLLOW BEHIND THE FIRST SO THAT THE TWO APPEAR AS ONE

If the site of the battle is in open and unobstructed country in which the second line cannot be easily hidden, then, to keep the enemy from accurately observing the army as it advances to combat, the second line should follow very closely behind the first so that the two will appear as one battle line to the enemy. About a mile away from them our second line should slow down, gradually drop behind the first line to the proper distance, and assume its normal formation. This makes it difficult for the enemy, or even for our own allies, to get a clear idea of how we are disposing our troops.

INTELLIGENCE AND METHOD OF MEETING A SURPRISE ENEMY ATTACK

If it is reported that an enemy detachment has gotten by our flank guards and our own ambushing parties and is launching an attack against our front line, then some of the bandons stationed on the flanks of our second line should come to their support. If they attack from one side, the support should come from that flank; if from both sides, then from both flanks. If the attack is directed against the rear of the second line, and the rear guard is not strong enough to deal with it, the same flank units should provide aid. In this way the rest of the troops can concentrate on their duty of supporting the first line.

THE WOUNDED

After the battle the general should give prompt attention to the wounded and see to burying the dead. Not only is this a religious duty, but it greatly helps the morale of the living.

APPARENT STRENGTH OF THE ENEMY

If the enemy's army is large and appears formidable by reason of the multitudes of men and horses, we should not draw up our army on high ground right away while the enemy is still at a distance. Apprehensive at the sight of such a large force, our men will quickly begin to lose courage. Instead, they should be formed on lower ground where they will not see the enemy or be seen by them. When the enemy approaches to about a mile or half a mile, then the army should move to high ground, so that the troops will not have time to lose confidence before the battle begins. But if the terrain will not allow this strategy, and the enemy can be clearly seen from a distance, then spread the report beforehand along the battle line that the opposing force consists mostly of horses and baggage trains, not of men. . . .

AFTER A DEFEAT

If the first day of battle ends in a defeat, it is, in our opinion, absolutely undesirable and useless to try to get those same troops who have been beaten in the field to go back into actual combat around the same time or within the next few days. We strongly advise any general against even thinking of doing this. It is an extremely difficult thing for anyone to bring off. Nobody makes a habit of immediately retrieving a defeat, except the Scythians, and it is particularly foreign to the Romans. For even if the general understands the mistake he has made and hopes to remedy it by means of a second battle, the soldiers as a whole are unable to grasp the reason for deliberately going right back into the fighting. They are more likely to look upon what happened as God's will and completely lose heart. So then, unless it is absolutely necessary, for a few days after a defeat in battle no attempt should be made to line up again and resume the offensive. It is better to rely on stratagems, deception, carefully timed surprise moves, and the so-called fighting while fleeing, until the troops come to forget their discouragement, and their morale picks up once more. . . .

When a battle ends in defeat there must be no indecision or delay, unless of course there is reason to hope for the arrival of allies or some other form of support, or unless, as may happen, overtures have been made by the enemy. These must not be made public without good reason, but should be dealt with privately. If the terms are lenient, and what is proposed can be done immediately, agreement should not be put off but should be confirmed with hostages or by oath. But if the terms are harsh and proposed with a view to delaying and getting our troops to let up their guard, this should be countered by circulating rumors making them even more unfavorable, so that when the men learn how harsh they are they will become angry and feel compelled to resist the enemy more forcefully and be more obedient to their own officers. The greater the delay, the more demoralized do the vanquished become and the more confident the victors. Therefore, before the men become utterly depressed, the general should have the tagmatic commanders, as well as the dekarchs and pentarchs, exhort the troops and point out that this is no time for despondency but rather for anger against the enemy and for courage for all to make up for the failure of a few. If there is cause to hope that the defeat may be retrieved in the open field, the formations described should be used. But even if such is not the case, it is very important to show a bold front before the dangers. If the victorious foe consists mostly of infantry, then we should withdraw without delay on horseback and in good order either to retreat or to establish camp safely someplace else. If the victors consist of cavalry, Persians or Scythians, for example, it is best to abandon superfluous property and the slower horses. Except for a small mounted force, all should take their stand on foot in two phalanxes or formations, or in one four-sided rectangular formation. In the middle should be the horses and baggage, with the soldiers on the outside, as described, and the archers on foot in front of them. In this way the army can move or retreat in safety.

AFTER A VICTORY IN BATTLE

. . . If the outcome of the battle is favorable, one should not be satisfied with merely driving the enemy back. This is a mistake made by inexperienced leaders who do not know how to take advantage of an opportunity, and who like to hear the saying: "Be victorious but do not press your victory too hard." By not seizing the opportunity, these people only cause themselves more trouble and place the ultimate results in doubt. There can be no rest until the enemy is completely destroyed. If they seek refuge behind fortifications, apply pressure by direct force or by preventing them from getting more supplies for men and horses until they are annihilated or else agree to a treaty to our advantage. One should not slacken after driving them back just a short distance, nor, after so much hard work and the dangers of war, should one jeopardize the success of the whole campaign because of lack of persistence. In war, as in hunting, a near-miss is still a complete miss.

LEO VI
(A.D. 865–912)

Leo VI, known as the Wise, reigned from 886 to 912. He belonged to the so-called Macedonian dynasty, which ruled from 867 to 1081, centuries during which Byzantium was at its zenith. Leo completed a legislative code, the Basilica, *begun by Basil I, that simplified and updated the laws promulgated by Justinian. The* Taktika *(Tactics) attributed to Leo, perhaps written c. 900, takes up and summarizes the science of war that runs from Onasander to the emperor Maurikios. Like the latter, Leo describes and analyzes the strategic cultures of the peoples on the periphery of the Byzantine empire, with advice, based on his own experience, as to how to fight them. He also examines the successes of Islam and suggests ways to counter them.*

TACTICS

On the Day of Battle

. . . If you are waging war against a people that fights with the bow, avoid rugged and mountainous places. Do not go near the foothills of mountains either: if the enemy were to take the higher ground, he would cause you a lot of trouble. Either you must take high ground yourself or stay away from mountains altogether by retiring into the plain.

Do not engage in combat, and avoid battle with the enemy altogether, unless you have carefully checked his deployment and fully reconnoitred all his dispositions.

If the terrain on which you are to fight is a level open plain, where it is difficult to conceal your second line from him on the march, make it join up with

From Leo VI, *Institutions militaires,* translated by Joly de Maizeroy, in *Bibliothèque historique et militaire,* edited by Liskenne and Sauvan, vol. 2 (Paris, 1840), bks. 1, 9, 16–20. Translated from the French by A. M. Berrett.

the first one so that the two look like a single one. When you are no more than a mile away from him, let the second slow down to allow the first to advance, and resume the proper distance.

Be very suspicious of any movement that looks like withdrawal or flight on the part of the enemy, which is often a feint to draw the other side into a trap. Do not follow him blindly, but in battle order, even when you are most confident of victory.

If the enemy army is very large, avoid taking yours along the high ground, from where the sight of such a large force might frighten your soldiers. Rather take them along low ground, where they can neither see nor be seen, until you are within range of the sound of the trumpet. Then move to higher ground, if there is any, and order a charge before they have been able to see anything that might dishearten them.

If you can join with the enemy before he is altogether formed up, you will certainly cause him a lot of damage.

If you have suffered a reverse in an action, it is neither prudent nor proper to get into a new engagement the same day. Even if you have not suffered a serious defeat, I would not advise it at all, unless in case of absolute necessity; this is because the troops may be disheartened by the first setback and regard it as a bad omen for the future. Instead of making it a point of honor to get your revenge in a general action, rather try and surprise the enemy, and give new heart to your soldiers by finding some opportunity where you are sure of winning but risk nothing. If, however, you do decide to resume fighting, make the second line move to the front, stiffened by a few from the first, which will take [the second's] place [by moving back].

If your infantry is defeated, sustain the retreat with the cavalry, which must also withdraw in good order to camp. If, on the contrary, it is the cavalry that is defeated, you should abandon the most cumbersome baggage, and form the infantry up into two phalanxes, or a square, in the middle of which you should put the beasts of burden and other impedimenta. Position the archers outside, and if you keep this formation throughout the march, it will be carried out safely.

If God has granted you victory, do not stop. . . . Use your advantage and push the enemy until he is totally crushed. . . .

After an action, make sure the wounded are given the necessary care: bury the dead honorably and with due respect. That much is due brave men who have sacrificed their lives for religion and the service of the state. Such respect for the dead comforts and encourages the living.

If the deceased leave wives and children, they must be given whatever consolation and help you can provide, but only if the fathers were killed fighting valiantly.

We see that [both] the Romans [i.e., Byzantines] and other nations set more store in impressing their enemies by adopting a ferocious barbaric appearance than in stunning them with the quality of their arms. Both are only illusions, which soon vanish; victory in battles come from God, from the valor of the troops and the skill of the general. Onasander claims that nothing is more apt to strike consternation in the enemy than the appearance of the army in battle and the glitter of its weapons; the wisest of the moderns hold the opposite opinion and feel that it is better to hide this glitter until the two sides are close. That is my feeling too. Thus, assuming that the terrain is flat and open, have the soldiers keep their helmets in their hands, put their shields on their backs, and lower their lances, so that those weapons do not glitter in the distance. But when you are only one or two signals away, if you suddenly bring them out, the appearance and surprise will overawe the enemy, who will long have thought they were dealing with a disordered army, and, struck by such a spectacle, will not have time to regain their composure.

Sudden Invasions

I shall now set out for you as briefly as possible what you must do to make a sudden invasion of enemy country, or to oppose one that he might want to make into yours, when peace is not altogether well established.

All the ancient captains and the best of the moderns have the maxim of seizing on favorable circumstances and forestalling the enemy by attacking him before he has had time to finish his preparations. You can derive a great deal of advantage from acting in this way if you are evenly matched, and even more if you are inferior to the enemy.

As I have already said, it is much better to use ruses than force, risking nothing and not getting caught up in the inevitable perils. You must use whatever means you find most suitable to the time, the place, the people involved, and the general state of things.

Therefore receive envoys from the enemy gently and honorably. Send them away politely; but follow them at once without postponing execution of your plan.

Examine the enemy's disposition and how his forces are positioned; if you find the occasion favorable, march on him during the night with many archers and surprise him an hour or two before dawn.

If his forces are dispersed and you arrive when they are still on the roads, you are sure to rout them completely. . . .

When, in order to enter the enemy's territory, you have to cross a river that is not fordable, build bridges with long, wide beams, of which there are [usually] many to be found; or make use of dugout canoes. At each end of the bridge, build towers of wood or stone, or an earthwork with a ditch behind it, so that, as required, you can cross safely to fight the enemy, and likewise withdraw and take up the bridge. In open warfare, these bridges are constructed in the same way, and you establish your camp close to the river so as to control the bank, and cross without danger to march on the enemy. Withdrawal into the camp will also [thus] be assured and unimpeded.

From the ancient commanders, we hear of a number of ways of achieving nocturnal surprises, which I shall relate to you. When you are only a short [day's march] away from the enemy, you can send him a deputation or two to beguile him with peace proposals; that gives him a sense of security, of which you can take advantage by attacking him the following night. At other times, you can appear to withdraw from the place where you are, and then suddenly come back at him; or you can hide somewhere with the bulk of your troops and then surprise him, charging before he has realized what is happening. Often herds of livestock are displayed as bait to draw the enemy; and while he is busy carrying them off, and so in great disorder, troops lying in ambush suddenly fall on him.

Or again you can approach the enemy as if you have decided to give battle. If, in that position, you then appear afraid to commit yourself, that makes him overconfident and negligent, which provides a wonderful opportunity of surprising him by attacking during the night.

It is important to have good guides who know the paths well, so that the army does not get lost. You must keep total silence, marching in absolute quiet. Transmit commands by word of mouth to halt your troops or make them advance, or by some signal, like a whistle or striking a shield: any other noise would reveal your arrival to the enemy. You must also make sure that the front of your deployment is not too extended; you should march in column, one division behind the other, always taking care to maintain adequate depth.

When you are within reach of the enemy, array your army in the light of the position on the ground and attack in two or three spots. In such a situation, you must not seek to surround him by attacking the four sides of his camp, because being thus driven together and pushed from all sides, the enemy would become a single compact mass and give you a great deal of trouble. You must leave a passage open and allow those who so wish to flee.

If you have a large army, you should sound only one or two trumpets to order the charge, so that the enemy believes you are few in number. If on the other hand your army is small, make sure you sound every trumpet you have, so as to make the enemy think your forces are more numerous than they really are. You should not fail to keep a good reserve force to use when necessary and to support those who have moved up to the front.

If the enemy has only infantry, and you attack him with cavalry, you are sure to defeat him, or else to be able to retreat without great loss, because he will be unable to pursue you. But if the enemy is made up of cavalry, you will have to take good measures to ensure your retreat in case you are not successful. If you, too, have only cavalry, you should make your disposition as if for a general action, so that if the enemy's cavalry is waiting for you in good order, you do not get involved in fighting without being formed up.

If you want to capture the baggage train, either by day or by night, you should detach a few squadrons for that purpose. The bulk of your army will stay with you. When larger-scale operations are called for, carry them out yourself, or, alternatively, put one of your [senior officers] in charge. Everything you do will always be undertaken with little risk on your part if you know how to choose a favorable opportunity; such as when the enemy has less strength than us or when he is not prepared to face you. . . .

If enemies invade your country, avoid a general encounter with them, even if your forces are equal to theirs. Rather use ruses, setting ambushes for them night and day. Make the roads impassable, occupy strongpoints, and cut down or spoil all the forage within their reach. If you want to attack them, it is better to choose the time when they are returning from collecting booty than when are setting off for it, because then they are burdened down and tired. Someone who is on his own ground should not be in a hurry to fight, because he will be able to find several opportunities to harass the enemy and ravage him without exposing himself.

Take good care to shelter yourself from all danger, while keeping yourself within range to foil the enemy's plans. Although you will not want to risk a general action, you should not omit anything to make it seem that you do and prepare everything to that end, which will certainly cause him a lot of concern.

If the country where the enemy has entered is suitable for his purpose, and you are unable to oppose him, you should fall back by another route before his forces are within sight of you, so as to invade their country. That is what our general Nicephorus [grandfather of the emperor Nicephorus II, Phocas (r. 963-69)?] did when Pulcher, the Saracen leader, was ravaging Cappadocia. He entered Cilicia, took Tarsus and caused them great damage.

As soon as you know the enemy's line of march, you must equip all your castles and fortresses with all things necessary for their defense. The inhabitants should withdraw their possessions and their livestock into them. You should increase the fortifications of the weakest positions so that they should be as well able to resist as the others. If the enemy decides to attack them, secretly get help to them; prevent him foraging and collecting provisions, and always have troops ready to fall on those who come out of his camp. By hemming him in from all sides in that way, you will reduce him to a most unhappy state.

That is what I have to say to you on the subject of invasions, as regards both offense and defense. Let us now move on to other things, which are of no less importance. . . .

It is essential, as far as you possibly can, to secure precise intelligence of the number of his cavalry and infantry. To that end, you must know their dispositions—that is, their method of forming up. For that is what makes an army. This is why those who do not have up-to-date information are invariably led into error when they want to make an estimate of them. . . .

Not everyone is in a position to know the various ways of forming up the troops of an army and to discern each disposition, so you must not rely solely on the examination of theorizers or guards, especially in regard to nations that keep their horse close together in battle order. You must use skilled and experienced men.

You must not judge the enemy's number by the extent of his army. In order not to be deceived, you must carefully examine its depth, and distinguish reality from what is simply appearance from the baggage that is placed in the rear.

Gather all the information you can for yourself, from deserters, from prisoners, from someone who can take advantage of the terrain to insinuate himself into a place from where he can get accurate information, or from a spy who will infiltrate the enemy camp. . . .

You must forbid all those who mount guard on foot to sit or lie down, so that they will be more alert and vigilant. However, as the stationary ones will nevertheless not have the endurance to keep watch all night, it is best to relieve them, which should be done at fixed times. To be sure that they remain on the alert, have them visited by prefects, who will punish anyone found at fault, since their negligence could place the general in great danger. . . .

Not only must the enemy not know where your guards are, but it is just as well that your own troops not know where they are either, so that any would-be deserters may run into them.

If you want to uncover any spies who may be in your camp, first confer with the commanders of the troops to be sure they carry out what you order them to do. Have them issue orders that at a trumpet call at two or three o'clock in the morning, everyone, whether soldiers or camp followers, should go into their tents. If there is a stranger, he too will enter a tent, where he will be recognized by the duty officer, of if he stays outside, he will be seen by the officers, who will have him arrested. That can be done either in a general encampment where all the troops are collected together or in a special camp where there are only a few bands.

Those who are found in the camp in this way and who are not known, whether Romans or strangers, must be examined until you have discovered why they are there. . . .

. . . When you capture spies, you should not always treat them the same way. If your army is weaker than that of the enemy, or you are short of something, have them put to death or keep them in prison; but if it is strong, fit, and rearing to go, made up of brave, obedient, well-disciplined men, let the spies go after you have let them see this. What they say will do you no harm; it will simply spread terror among the enemy. . . .

Methods of the Romans and Various Nations in the Disposition of Armies

We shall now discuss the various orders of battle adopted by ancient Roman generals and those of other nations, so that knowledge of them will enable you not only to use them when the opportunity arises but also to improve them and come up with something even better. . . .

If a mishap happens to you, act so as to ensure that the enemy does not get to know of it, and learn to be calm in adversity. In that way you will conceal the magnitude of the damage and people will not believe you lack resources. . . .

We have seen enemies of the Romans, such as the Persians, neither asking for quarter nor proposing any terms, even in the most desperate straits; rather, they have waited until we made offers to them, such was their strength and fortitude.

Let us summarize what I have said: you will arm your troops in the manner prescribed, and you will have many good archers. This arm is excellent and of great service, especially against the Saracens and the Turks, who put all their hope in them. We need archers, not only to oppose theirs, but also to shoot at their cavalry, which does them much harm, and discourages them when they see their best horses killed. . . .

If you know you are dealing with a warlike nation, it is as well to postpone combat as long as you can; camp in an advantageous place and fortify it. If the day you are to fight is one of the warmest days of summer, play for time until about midday so as to sap the ardor of the enemy, who will be exhausted by the great heat. . . .

The Scythians all have the same way of forming up in battle and a method of fighting, turning [in the saddle to loose their arrows behind them], which is peculiar to them. They are divided under different rulers, are brave and hardy, and live an altogether pastoral life. Each horde is led and governed by a single chief. The Turks and Bulgarians are the only ones who form up and fight in the same way, standing firmer and having more order than any of the other Scythian nations.

Since the Bulgarians have embraced the Christian faith, we do not wish to arm ourselves against them or to learn how to fight them, especially as they are now subject to our rule since God punished them for having violated the treaty that they had made with us.

As regards the Turkish nation, it is very numerous, sets little store by objects of luxury and ease, and devotes itself only to war and to making itself redoubtable in combat. As it is governed despotically by its prince, those of its officers who make a mistake are punished with extreme rigor. Its behavior is governed less by love and zeal than by fear. Moreover, it constantly endures fatigue and the vagaries of the weather and has few needs, like the other nomads. The Turks keep their plans very secret and are greedy for money; they are faithless in their engagements and have few scruples about breaking their word. It is vain to think of winning them over by presents. When they have received them, they do not set you any fewer traps. They skillfully take their time and never miss an opportunity when it appears favorable to them. They do not always attack openly, but use ruses when possible.

They are armed with cuirasses, swords, spears, and arrows. They throw their spears from behind the shoulder and use the bow, especially against pursuers. As soon as the opportunity offers, they take up the spear again and thus fight alternately with one or other weapon. The best horses have their fronts protected with iron or leather. They are much given to discharging arrows from horseback. They take with them a quantity of mares and cows, whose milk they drink. They do not camp, like the Romans, in redoubts; rather, up to the actual day of fighting, they are separated into tribes and families. They post their guards far away and so thickly that they cannot be easily taken by surprise. They carefully feed a large number of horses summer and winter. When they are at war they choose the best, and keep them near their tents with fetters on their feet, which they only remove to fight.

In their order of battle, they do not divide their army into three parts as the Romans do; rather, they form themselves up into several large troops, with small intervals between them, so that they seem to be a single body of men. In addition, they hold troops in reserve to support the places that need them, and others to surround the enemy if he has failed to take precautions. They put their baggage a mile or two away in the rear, to the right or left, with a guard. When they have spare horses, they put them behind the lines, as they do other animals, tying them together so as to make a barrier. In order to give an impression of greater depth, they make some formations deeper than others. The front is even and regular. They like to fight from a distance, set ambushes, simulate flight, disperse, and suddenly come back to charge. When their enemies flee, they are not content, like the Romans and other nations, to follow them casually and take their booty; instead they pursue them constantly to exterminate them, if they can, right down to the last man. If one takes refuge in a fort, they at once seek to know the quantity of provisions, munitions, men, and horses that it contains. They lay siege to it and put unrelenting pressure on it until they have reduced it. They make sweet proposals at first, and if these are accepted, they impose harsher ones.

They greatly fear infantry that maims their horses; and if they set foot on the ground, as they are not at all used to doing so, they suffer greatly. Nor do they like dealing with a tight line of cavalry in good order on an open plain.

Shortage of forage will always make them suffer greatly, because they have so many horses.

One means of getting the better of them is to come up with them so as to fight hand to hand at close quarters or surprise them at night. To do this, part of the troops should remain concealed while the rest attack. Nothing causes them more pain than if some of their own men desert. This sign of inconstancy and greed in their compatriots humiliates them and lowers the high opinion they have of their nation.

When you are warring against them, you must be very careful indeed; and if you propose to fight, make sure you have a fort to withdraw to where there are water, forage, and provisions for several days, in case you should be worsted. . . .

Pay special attention to your flanks and rear. Tell your runners to get within no more than three or four arrow shots at most from the defenders when pursuing the enemy. Arrange things so as to ensure that you fight on the open plain where there are no woods or ravines or valleys, for fear of traps, which the Turks are accustomed to setting in such spots. Post guards on the four sides, placed at a certain distance, to advise of their movements. If possible, try and put your back to a river that is unfordable, a lake, or a marsh.

If the outcome of battle is favorable, do not follow the enemy either too half-heartedly or too zealously. When the Turks come off worse in the first shock, they do not seek to repair it immediately, like other nations. They flee, but they then try to regain the upper hand by all sorts of means.

If I have spoken to you of these customs of the Turks, it is not that you necessarily have to fight them. At present they are neither our neighbors nor our enemies; on the contrary, they seem to want to become our allies. It is thus solely in order that you may be informed about the various orders of battle and all the stratagems of war that experience and study have invented. In that way you will be able to use them when suitable opportunities arise, or invent other means of opposing them. It is for the same reason that I will tell you about the methods and characters of some other peoples, such as the Franks and the Lombards, formerly infidels, but now Christians, some of whom have become our subjects and others our allies. I shall not omit the Slavs, who were formerly subject to the Romans when they lived beyond the Danube, where they lived a pastoral life.

The Franks and the Lombards cherish freedom. The latter have lost much of that virtue. With regard to the Franks, they are brave and daring almost to the point of foolhardiness. Cowardice is held in horror among them; the least backward movement is taken as flight and marked with infamy. This contempt for death drives them to fight courageously hand to hand, either as cavalry or as infantry. If their cavalry is caught in some defile, it dismounts, and forms up very well, just like infantry. They are armed with shields, lances, and very long swords, attached to baldrics. Some of them carry them attached to their belts. They do not form up for battle as the Romans do, by companies and battalions, but by tribes and families. Those bound by friendship, and by a sort of brotherhood, also join together. It has often been seen that if one of them is killed, the others will rush into danger to avenge his death.

Their battle formations are even and very closely spaced in front; they like above all to fight on foot, but on foot or on horseback, they run at the enemy impetuously and charge passionately. The Franks are least obedient to their chiefs. They willingly come to war, for a time, without needing to be pressured to do so; but if they have to stay longer, they become impatient and return home.

They are rather improvident in everything and very unreliable; they attach little importance to the disposition of armies, especially of the cavalry. We know from experience of their greed for money and how easy it is to corrupt them. They find it hard to bear suffering. Sharp and daring they may be in spirit, but their bodies are weak, delicate, and not well suited to hard work. Heat, rain, and cold lay them out; shortage of foodstuffs, and especially wine, upsets them enormously, as does a long war. Rugged and difficult country does not suit their cavalry, which charges rapidly with the lance. As they are rather neglectful about posting guards and maintaining reserves, they can easily be attacked from the flanks and the rear.

If you pretended to flee, they will certainly disband. If you then immediately turn back to charge them, you can do them a lot of damage. Another excellent tactic is to attack them at night with archers, because they camp separately and dispersed.

If you pay attention to their customs and their character, you will not fight them in a pitched battle, especially at the beginning of a war; rather, you will harass them with frequent attacks and ambushes. Make the war drag on and dangle peace proposals before them; by dragging out the negotiations, you will make them use up their provisions. The length of time and the inconvenience of the weather will cool their ardor and diminish their boldness. To succeed in such a plan of conduct, you must occupy strong places difficult of access, where the enemy cannot use his pikes.

The Slavs' way of life and customs are rather similar to those of the Franks: jealous of their freedom, they always refused to submit to the empire while they were living in their native land beyond the Danube; even after crossing over to this side, they preferred to obey a despot of their own nation rather than the Romans. As for those who have embraced the Christian faith, they retain as much as they can of their old freedom.

This nation is numerous, patient in its labors, and tireless. Heat, cold, hunger, and shortage of everything do not wear them down. Our august father, the emperor Basil, drew it out of barbarism and slavery; he gave it orderly government, gave it Roman-style governors, and caused it to receive holy baptism. He devoted himself to making it the friend of the Romans, to use against their enemies. The empire was delivered from its attacks from which it had suffered for years, having fought several wars against it. . . .

I now move on to the Saracens, ever our enemies; we must describe their genius and character, and tell of their customs, the weapons they use and the best way of making war against them.

The Saracens are Arabs by origin and used to live on the edge of the country known as Arabia Felix. Having received the laws of Muhammad, they spread into Syria and Palestine; they then took Mesopotamia and Egypt, taking advantage of the wars between the Roman empire and the Persians. They blaspheme against Christ, whom they do not regard as true God and Savior of the world. . . . They observe their laws very strictly, are carnal and much given to women. They gratify their senses and pollute their souls. We who follow a holy divine law detest their impiety and make war on them to support the faith.

They usually have camels to carry their baggage rather than oxen, asses, and mules. The appearance and smell of these animals terrify horses, which is one of the reasons why they prefer them. They further frighten their enemies' horses by the noise of drums and cymbals, to which theirs are accustomed. They usually put all their camels and other beasts of burden in the middle of their army; they tie pennants or flags to them to make them look like combatants, so as to appear more numerous.

They have a hot temperament, being born in a burning climate. Their infantry is made up of Ethiopians, who carry large bows. They place them in front of their cavalry, which greatly impresses those seeking to attack them. The infantry ride pillion behind the cavalry when the expedition is not far from the frontier. It uses swords, lances, battle-axes, and also arrows. They are protected by helmets, cuirasses, decorated boots, gauntlets, and other things that Romans use. They like to decorate their belts and swords and their horses' bridles with silver ornaments.

Once they are disorganized, it is difficult to rally them; they think only of saving their lives. Hope of victory makes them more daring; but reverses diminish their courage. They are convinced that evils come from God, like other things; that is why they accept misfortune without complaint, and await a more propitious time to fight. . . . To guarantee themselves against surprises, they barricade themselves in their camp and mount a good guard right through the night.

Their order of battle is a long square, set back everywhere and very difficult to break into. They use this pattern in marches as in battle. In fact, they imitate the Romans in many of the usages of war and methods of attack, which they have learned from us.

When they are arrayed and face to face, they are in no rush to mount a charge. They take the first shock with firmness and once combat is joined, they do not easily let go. When they see the enemy's ardor weakening, they spur themselves on to repel him vigorously.

In sea battles, they behave as they do in infantry combat: pressed up against one another, covered by shields, they withstand all the enemy's missiles; and when he has none left, and is tired, they begin fighting hand to hand; that is why you must treat them with a great deal of circumspection.

Their maxims and their methods in war are much better than those of other more experienced nations. We have learned this from reports sent to us, from the report of our generals, and from our most pious father, who was often at war with them.

The rigors of winter, cold and rain, cause them a great deal of suffering and deprive them of strength. That is why rainy and wet weather is the best time to attack them, as has often succeeded for us. It even happens that the strings of their bows become wet and stretched out so that they cannot use them. It is thus above all in the great heat of summer that they emerge from Tarsus and other towns in Cilicia to make their expeditions against the Romans.

It is very risky, as I have said, to have a general encounter with them, even though they may appear to be weaker in numbers. It is better to stay protected in a good position from where you can watch their movements. When they come during the winter, to overrun the country and plunder it, you may find the opportunity to fall on them by surprise, even when they are fully equipped for war.

They make up their army neither by enlistment nor by drawing lots; rather, masses of them come from Syria and Palestine to enroll as volunteers, the rich led on by zeal for the fatherland, the poor by hope of booty. This attraction brings in even young men who are not yet grown up, whom women are only too pleased to arm. . . .

If you occupy certain high positions with archers and slingers when they pass through the defiles of Mount Taurus on their raids, or rather when they are coming back tired, burdened with animals and other loot, you can attack their cavalry with considerable advantage. You can also roll large stones down on them . . . or ambush them.

They never break their formation, even when they are attacked on two or three sides at once. They fight together until they secure victory or, losing all hope, flee. You must first attack them with arrows; because their mounted archers, Ethiopians and others, whom they position in front, being naked, are easily wounded and immediately take flight. They are also very afraid of losing their horses, which are their lifeline. . . .

The Saracens are less greedy of glory than of booty. As they are not farmers, the poor have to seek a living by their swords. Those who live in Cilicia, being mostly foot soldiers, fight on land or sea, in vessels known as *cumbaria*. When they are not making raids by land, they embark on their ships, and come and infest all the coasts where they land to ravage the country. If you can win a victory over them, you will be free of them for a long time. That intimidates those of them who have stayed at home and makes them afraid to venture on new expeditions.

You must have spies and watchers attentive to what they are doing, so that you can make your preparations in the light of that information, in such a way as to counter their undertakings. If you are warned that they are embarking on a sea raid, have your land forces march into their country; if, on the contrary, they come by land, let our chief admiral descend on the coasts of Tarsus and Adonis. The peoples of Cilicia are not numerous enough to make war by land and sea at the same time. . . .

Actions at Sea

It remains to speak of actions at sea, about which we find nothing written by the ancient writers on tactics. What there is, scattered here and there, is at present of little use. The knowledge that we have comes from generals who transmitted it from one to the other. I shall explain to you in a few words what I have learned touching the management of triremes, now known as dromons.

First, you must know about piloting and steering vessels and learn to know the various winds, the movements and various aspects of the stars, and the revolutions of the sun and the moon, which influence the change of the seasons, and to predict shifts in the weather. You need to know about all these matters to protect yourself against storms and accidents at sea.

Your galleys must be well built and fit for action. They must neither be made of wood that is too thick and heavy, which would render them unwieldy and difficult to maneuver, nor have planks that are too thin, which would make them weak and expose them to being smashed by the shock of enemy ships. They need to be of such proportions as will at once be fast in sailing, solid enough to face the sea, and strong enough to withstand shock in combat.

The rigging and everything needed for the equipment of dromons must be kept ready. It is wise to have extras of some items, such as anchors; oars, with their rowlocks; sails; and all sorts of rope. You must also have a stock of a number of curved pieces of timber, planks, joists, tow, resin, nails, and all the tools needed for construction and repair—saws, drills, axes, and suchlike.

On front of the prow you should place a bronze-covered spout to pour [Greek] fire on the enemy. Above the spout, build a wooden platform surrounded by a parapet and planks. Soldiers will be positioned there to fight and discharge missiles.

In large dromons, wooden turrets can be erected in the middle of the deck. Soldiers positioned there throw large rocks onto the enemy vessels, or iron-spiked maces, which break the ship or crush those underneath as they fall; or they pour fire onto it to burn it. Each dromon must be oblong, of a breadth proportionate to its length, with two banks of oars, one above, the other below.

In each bank there will be at least twenty-five benches to seat the oarsmen: twenty-five below and twenty-five above, and on each there will be two oarsmen, one on the right and one on the left, which will make one hundred men in all, oarsmen and soldiers. Each galley will have its prefect, a lieutenant, a flame-thrower, and two pilots to steer. Of the last two oarsmen on the prow side, one should be appointed fireman and one to drop anchor. The pilot who steers in the prow must be seated in the highest position and well protected by defensive weapons. The prefect's seat will be in the poop, in a place where he is set apart and sheltered from missiles, and from where he can observe everything so as to give his orders and see to maneuvers.

You can always make bigger dromons that contain up to two hundred men; even more if necessary. Fifty will be for the benches below and one hundred and fifty for the benches above, who will all be armed to fight.

You can build smaller boats with a single bank of oars, known as galliots, which are very light in sailing; they can be used for guard duties, for reconnoitring and for all expeditions where speed is of the essence. . . .

You must have freight ships to carry not only the fleet's baggage and provisions but also supplies of weapons, such as bows, arrows, [other] missiles, and in general everything needed for war. As the soldiers on the dromons run short of an item, they can [thus] be resupplied. You should also carry mangonels [missile throwers] and other machines of that type to use when needed, so that you do not suffer a reverse for lack of this precaution.

The oarsmen on the upper benches and all those with the prefect must be armed from head to toe, with shields, helmets, cuirasses, armguards, and thighpieces, if not behind at least in front, so as not to be unprotected in hand-to-hand fighting. They will fight with pikes, javelins, and swords. Those who have no iron armor will make some from sinews woven onto leather doublets. The former will stay behind the cataphracts [heavy cavalry], from where they will discharge arrows.

But they must not exhaust their strength by discharging too many of them, because when the barbarians, who seek protection from arrows by overlapping their shields, see they are used up, they will attack with their swords and long pikes, so that they easily overcome men whom they find tired out. That is how the Saracens use them, and they always withstand the first shock. You should therefore be restrained in the number of missiles you discharge, husbanding military resources so that they last all through the action.

Make sure that no one lacks means of subsistence, so as to disarm seditious activities and prevent shortage from driving soldiers to decamp. . . .

If you camp on a shore in your own country, where there are no enemies to fear, take care that the soldiers do not mistreat the inhabitants; but when you land on an enemy coast, you must post guards on land and at sea and always be ready to fight. You must redouble your vigilance as you run more risks; for if the enemy knows you have landed, he will endeavor night and day to burn your ships. . . .

As there are propitious moments, and the hazards of war are uncertain, you must try and win through some stratagem, or some surprise, and not engage in a pitched battle except in extreme necessity. That is why you should take care not to get so close to the enemy that you cannot avoid combat, unless you have great confidence in the number and strength of your galleys and the courage of your soldiers. . . .

There are various methods of forming up, according to the circumstances. If your superiority makes you decide to give battle, avoid doing so close to your country, where, according to the old proverb, "The soldier thinks he is safe if he can plant his pike there." It is better that it be on the enemy's coasts, because, the enemy, seeing a safe haven, will show less firmness and resolution. . . .

Before the day of battle, assemble your prefects to deliberate with them and do what is judged best by the majority. If something happens that forces you to change your initial resolutions, warn all the galleys by a signal from yours, which will indicate your intention.

Since your galley acts as the head of the whole fleet, it should be distinguished from the others by its size and strength, and manned by an elite crew. At the same time, your squadron leaders should choose the best men in the dromons under their command to form their crews. Everyone will always keep an eye on the flagship, follow its lead, and watch for new orders.

For signals you can use a flame, a flag, or something else that is high and clearly visible, that can express all that you want to convey, whether to attack or to retreat; to surround the enemy or to set a trap for him; to rush to the help of a section in danger; to row faster or to sail more slowly.

At sea you cannot use the human voice or a trumpet because the noise of the waves and the oars, the cries of the combatants, and the sound and the fury of the clash of vessels would prevent them from being heard. Every order must be conveyed by a particular signal, which must be agreed upon in advance. You may keep the flag upright, slope it, raise it, lower it, replace it with another of different design, or simply change the color, as used to be done. The flag of combat was red, held aloft on a long pike. You must be well versed in the knowledge of different signals, and so must your counts and prefects, so that no one makes any mistakes and everyone clearly understands the orders you give, which is of the greatest importance.

When a well-founded hope of victory has made you resolve to fight, it will be the weather, the place, and the disposition of the enemy that will determine the order of battle; as to that, we can only give general rules.

You can range your fleet in a crescent, with the galleys on both ends, advancing like two horns or two hands. Take care to place the best, and the best armed especially, at the tips. The flagship should be in the middle of the crescent from where you will easily be able to see everything and give your orders. This semi-circular disposition is that best suited to surrounding the enemy. It also has many advantages for retreat, as a number of the ancients, who used this method, have taught us.

When your fleet encounters the enemy's, you can place it in a crescent formation by pulling your galleys from the center and then withdrawing the others one after another to form a semi-circle. This maneuver will look like flight, but it will actually simply be to fight with greater advantage, since your galleys will be quite ready to swing back against the enemy if he follows you and ventures into the crescent, which he will not dare do for fear of being surrounded.

You can also form up in a straight line. With this disposition, you will have your prow facing the enemy, so as to burn his vessels with the [Greek] fire that the spouts pour on them. Or you can form up in two or three lines, depending on how many vessels you have. When the first line is engaged and its galleys are grappling with the enemy's, the others dart to right and left to strike at the flanks or the rear, so that the enemy cannot sustain this new attack.

Another method is to let few vessels appear. When the enemy, spread out over the sea, sees this small number, he will come and attack them; then the others will appear and sow confusion in the whole fleet.

Or again you can have your lightest and fastest galleys advance. When these have initiated the fight, they will pretend to flee, and draw the enemy galleys to row hard after them. Then the others, which will be fresh, will fall on them, and, since their attack is unexpected, they are bound to take them; or they can let the strongest and best pass them, and throw themselves on the last ones, which are bound to be the worst equipped. When the enemy, full of confidence, launches a hot pursuit, his ships break their formation, become scattered, and often end up very far from one another. In that case, you can attack some of his galleys, setting two or three of yours against one of his; in that way you will take them without much trouble before they can be succored. If you have a larger fleet than the enemy's, keep a good part of it in reserve; make the engagement last till nightfall and when the enemy is worn out, unleash the fresh galleys that have not fought, which he will not have enough strength left to withstand.

The most favorable time to attack a fleet is when it is being beaten by a strong gale; you will find the vessels and crews tired. If they are on land, you can burn the ships during the night.

Both the ancients and the moderns tell of various expedients to destroy enemy vessels or harm their crews. Among these are [Greek] fire launched from spouts with a sound of thunder and flaming smoke, burning the vessels on which it lands.

You can also hurl pots of quicklime. The pot breaks and the quicklime is released as dust, suffocating those on deck. Large numbers of iron caltrops thrown into a vessel also cause a lot of trouble.

Above all you must prepare pots full of flammable matter that, when they break as they fall, are bound to set the vessel on fire.

Large caltrops are also used, or round blocks of wood with iron spikes stuck in them. They are coated with tar and sulphur-soaked cloths, and after they have been set alight, they are hurled into vessels, where they cause fires. The enemy finds them hard to put out; some have their feet burnt, others their hands; and those who are thus occupied reduce the number of combatants.

With cranes, or similar machines, turning on a pivot, you can lift large boulders and drop them on the vessel to which you are grappled. With a mangonel, you can also throw liquid burning pitch, or some other substance, prepared beforehand. . . .

There are several other methods listed by the ancients, not to mention those one can imagine, which it would be too long to record here. There are even some that it is not proper to divulge, for fear that enemies might get to hear of them and take precautions to protect themselves against them and use them themselves against us. . . .

You will therefore have [both] large and small dromons at your disposal, to use depending on the enemy's dispositions. Neither the Saracens nor the northern Scythians are thus equipped; the former use large ships, which are cumbrous and slow. The Scythians have smaller, lighter ones, with which they descend the rivers and enter the Black Sea.

Maxims and Sayings

In addition to the instructions I have just given you, you should heed the following maxims, which I have drawn from several ancient authors and record because of their brevity. . . .

Deliberate with all due care, and do not suspend the execution of what has been decided on for fear of any drawbacks that might occur to you. Excessive prudence is harmful.

Only communicate your plans to a few of the most discreet individuals and put about contrary rumors. Enemies told of them by their spies or your deserters will take mistaken measures if they believe them. If they do not believe them, they will not take proper precautions, and you will be able to catch them by surprise by carrying out what was initially only a feint on your part.

It is not safe always to use the same maneuvers and ruses, even if they have worked well for you. When the enemy sees you making a habit of them, he will inevitably take the opportunity of setting a trap, into which you will fall. A single pattern of behavior soon becomes known: he who varies his practice will embarrass his opponent and keep him in a permanent state of uncertainty. . . .

On the eve of action, if you order all the sick, the wounded, and those who have bad horses to stand aside, all the cowards will pretend to be ill, or that their horses are missing something. In that way, you will find out who they are and [can] send them to castles or leave them to guard the camp. . . .

Order your soldiers to be ready to fight at any time, in any weather, night or day, rain or shine. There is no moment when you can say: I have nothing to fear. . . .

If you are using foreign troops, it is prudent that they be fewer in number than your own, especially if you are defending your country, for if they are more numerous, they may seize it themselves. Those who sell their service for money may allow themselves to be corrupted by a larger sum to turn against you.

Make sure that you always have more of your nation's troops than there are auxiliaries. If you have many of the latter, make sure, if possible, that they are from different nations.

Do not mix allied troops with your own, especially if they are of a different religion; rather, let them camp and march separately. And do not entrust your secrets to their leaders, lest they misuse them if they become your enemies. . . .

If you wish to reach a good peace, prepare well for war. . . .

Deliberate with many, decide alone or with few, execute at once. . . .

It is fine to conquer without risking anything, by harassing or starving the enemy. Only the common herd admire the bold who succeed by strokes of luck. Rather imitate those who owe their success to their skill: they alone deserve to be praised. Always take every possible precaution to assure the success of your undertakings. . . .

Modesty and restraint are the qualities necessary in men of war. You must only take to the army what is absolutely essential; luxury softens and corrupts morals. . . .

When Scipio was chosen general, he did away with all the tables, beds, and multiple vessels used by the army. He allowed soldiers only a single cooking pot, one spit, and one wooden goblet apiece; officers, a silver one. He prohibited anointing oneself with scented oil; ordered that men dine standing, on dishes not cooked over a fire; that at supper they eat only boiled or roasted meat; and that each tribune only have a small tent to sleep in. Thus, throughout his generalship, he made himself famous by his victories. He put no faith in astrology, predictions, the appearance of ghosts, auguries, dreams, or divination. He scorned everything by which people claimed to be able to foretell the future and that put fear in people's minds, which a good general knows how to cure. By imitating him, you will raise immortal trophies to your glory. . . .

If you have a small army in comparison to your enemy's, camp in a narrow place, sufficient for however many you are, where the enemy cannot take advantage of his superiority.

Just as you must endeavor to know where enemy camps are and how many troops they contain, so also you must prevent them from reconnoitering yours as far as possible.

If your troops are marching in close order, they will appear to be fewer, as the eye will be deceived. If you want to make them seem more than you have, make them march in dispersed order, so that they take up more ground. In the camp, put two barrackfuls in one tent and put the weapons nearby if you want to make the army seem smaller than it is. If you want the opposite, divide one barrackful into two or three tents. This latter stratagem will prevent the enemy from underestimating you; but as he cannot long remain deceived, you must raise your camp and position yourself somewhere safe until you have got reinforcements.

You must feel out your enemy to try and get to know his character. If he is daring, do something to annoy him and get him to undertake some risky movement, for which you will punish him. If he is timid and fearful, astonish him by sharp, unexpected attacks.

When God has given you victory, if the enemy sues for peace, you must not impose excessively harsh conditions on him. Remember that fortune is inconstant; and that from one day to the next, the least circumstance can change the face of things. . . .

With money, you can often undo your enemies without fighting by engaging another people to attack them. They will weaken and destroy each other, while you retain all your forces and become superior to them.

If you surprise a fort or take it by scaling, have one of the gates opened to let the enemy escape freely. When they can see a way out, they will not think of defending themselves. You must always avoid fighting desperate men.

LIUTPRAND
(C. A.D. 920–972)

In about A.D. 950, Liutprand was sent on an embassy to Constantinople by Berengar, king of Italy. Later he was also an emissary to the Byzantine court for the Holy Roman Emperor Otto I, who made him bishop of Cremona in 961. Greek fire, an incendiary weapon, probably consisting of naphtha, sulfur, and quicklime, had been invented in the last quarter of the seventh century. It was used successfully in 674–78 when Constantinople was besieged by an Arab fleet, and then, on a larger scale, during a sea-borne Slav invasion from Kiev down the Dnieper and across the Black Sea. Liutprand describes the measures adopted by Emperor Romanus I to fight Prince Igor's fleet.

THE USE OF GREEK FIRE AGAINST THE RUS

After [Emperor] Romanus had spent some sleepless nights lost in thought while Igor was ravaging all the coastal regions, Romanus was informed that he possessed some dilapidated galleys which the government had left out of commission on account of their age. When he heard this, he ordered the *kalaphatai*—that is, the shipwrights—to come to him, and he said to them, "Hurry without delay, and prepare these remaining galleys for service. Place the devices which shoot out fire, not only in the prow but also in the stern and on both sides of each ship." When the galleys had been outfitted according to his orders, he manned them with his most competent sailors and ordered them to proceed against King Igor.

They set out, and when King Igor saw them out on the sea, he ordered his troops not to kill the sailors but to take them alive. But then God, merciful and

From Liutprand, *Antapodosis*, quoted in D. J. Geanakoplos, *Byzantium: Church, Society, and Civilization Seen through Contemporary Eyes* (Chicago: University of Chicago Press, 1984), 113. Reprinted by permission of the University of Chicago Press and D. J. Geanakoplos.

compassionate, wished not only to protect but to honor with victory those who served and worshiped him and sought his aid [i.e., the Byzantines]. Therefore, he quieted the winds and calmed the sea. For otherwise it would have been difficult for the Greeks to shoot their fire. Then, having become surrounded by the Rus, the Greeks hurled their fire all around them. When the Rus saw this, they at once threw themselves from their ships into the sea, choosing to be drowned by the waves rather than cremated by the fire. Some, weighted down by their breastplates and helmets (which they would never see again) sank to the bottom of the sea. Others were burned as they swam on the waves. No one escaped that day unless he was able to flee to the shore [in his vessel]. For the ships of the Rus, on account of their small size, can sail in very little water whereas the galleys of the Greeks, because of their greater draught, cannot do so.

KRITOVOULOS
(c. 1410–?)

In 1470 the Greek historian Kritovoulos wrote a five-volume History of
Sultan Mehmed II, *dealing with the period 1451–67. Kritovoulos himself
became governor of the island of Imbros, under Mehmed II. His account of
the fall of Constantinople in 1453 (at which he was not present) is that of a
historian who is being as impartial as possible.*

THE FALL OF CONSTANTINOPLE

Sultan Mehmed considered it necessary in preparation for his next move to
get possession of the harbor and open the Horn for his own ships to sail in.
So, since every effort and device of his had failed to force the entrance, he made
a wise decision, and one worthy of his intellect and power. It succeeded in accomplishing his purpose and in putting an end to all uncertainties.

He ordered the commanders of the vessels to construct as quickly as possible glideways leading from the outer sea to the inner sea, that is, from the
harbor to the Horn, near the place called Diplokion, and to cover them
with beams. This road, measured from sea to sea, is just about eight stadia.
It is very steep for more than half the way, until you reach the summit of the
hill, and from there again it descends to the inner sea of the Horn. And as the
glideways were completed sooner than expected, because of the large number
of workers, he brought up the ships and placed large cradles under them, with
stays against each of their sides to hold them up. And having under-girded
them well with ropes, he fastened long cables to the corners and gave them to
the soldiers to drag, some of them by hand, and others by certain machines
and capstans.

From Kritovoulos, *History of Mehmed the Conqueror,* translated by Charles T. Riggs (Princeton: Princeton University Press, 1954), §§ 172–82, 215–34. Copyright © 1954, renewed 1982, by
Princeton University Press. Reprinted by permission of Princeton University Press.

So the ships were dragged along very swiftly. And their crews, as they followed them, rejoiced at the event and boasted of it. Then they manned the ships on the land as if they were on the sea. Some of them hoisted the sails with a shout, as if they were setting sail, and the breeze caught the sails and bellied them out. Others seated themselves on the benches, holding the oars in their hands and moving them as if rowing. And the commanders, running along by the sockets of the masts with whistlings and shouting, and with their whips beating the oarsmen on the benches, ordered them to row. The ships, borne along over the land as if on the sea, were some of them being pulled up the ascent to the top of the hill while others were being hauled down the slope into the harbor, lowering the sails with shouting and great noise.

It was a strange spectacle, and unbelievable in the telling except to those who actually did see it—the sight of ships borne along on the mainland as if sailing on the sea, with their crews and their sails and all their equipment. I believe this was a much greater feat than the cutting of a canal across at Athos by Xerxes, and much stranger to see and to hear about. Furthermore, this event of but yesterday, before our very eyes, makes it easier to believe that the other also actually happened, for without this one, the other would have seemed a myth and sounded like idle talk.

Thus, then, there assembled in the bay called Cold Waters, a little beyond Galata, a respectable fleet of some sixty-seven vessels. They were moored there.

The Romans, when they saw such an unheard-of thing actually happen, and warships lying at anchor in the Horn—which they never would have suspected—were astounded at the impossibility of the spectacle, and were overcome by the greatest consternation and perplexity. They did not know what to do now, but were in despair. In fact they had left unguarded the walls along the Horn for a distance of about thirty stadia, and even so they did not have enough men for the rest of the walls, either for defense or for attack, whether citizens or men from elsewhere. Instead, two or even three battlements had but a single defender.

And now, when this sea-wall also became open to attack and had to be guarded, they were compelled to strip the other battlements and bring men there. This constituted a manifest danger, since the defenders were taken away from the rest of the wall while those remaining were not enough to guard it, being so few.

Not only was there this difficulty, but, the bridge being completed, heavy infantry and bowmen could cross against the wall. Hence that part also had to be guarded. And the ships near the mouth of the harbor and at the chain, galleons and triremes alike, as well as the other ships in the harbor had the greater need to be on guard since now they were subject to attack from within as well as from outside. Therefore in many directions they appeared to have, and actually had, difficulties. Still, they did not neglect anything that could be done.

Giustinianni [commander of the Genoese fleet aiding the Byzantines] removed one of his galleons from the mouth of the harbor plus three of the Italian triremes, and took them against the end of the gulf where the Sultan's ships were anchored. There he anchored so as to fight from them and prevent the [Ottoman] warships from going out anywhere in the gulf or being able to do any harm to the harbor or its shipping. This he thought was the best plan as a counter-measure. But it was only a temporary expedient.

For Sultan Mehmed, seeing this, made the following counter-moves: He ordered the cannon-makers to transfer the cannon secretly by night and place them near the shore, opposite to where the ships and the galleon were moored, and fire stones at them. This they did with great speed, and they hit one of the triremes in the middle and sank it with all on board, excepting a very few who swam to the other triremes. Then the crews quickly moved the ships away a good distance, and anchored there. If this had not been done quickly, the other triremes also would have been sunk, with their crews, as well as the galleon, for they seemed to have had no sense at all of their danger. They were thus very near to destruction, for the cannon were ready to fire the stone balls at them.

But when this failed, the Romans had nothing else they could do. They simply fired at the ships from the walls with catapults and javelins and prevented them from moving about. And from the triremes at the mouth of the harbor some attacked them every day and chased them back and prevented their injuring anything in the harbor. And they often pursued them till near the land, toward their own men. Then these ships would again turn and attack the triremes, and men would follow on foot, firing and being fired on, and so they had long-range exchanges daily.

Then the Sultan mounted his horse and went around to all the other divisions, reviewing them and giving his orders to all in general and each in particular. He encouraged them and stirred them up for the battle, especially the officers of the troops, calling each one by name. Then, having passed along the entire army, along the wall from sea to sea, and having given the necessary orders and encouraged and incited all for the fight, and having urged them to play the man, he ordered them to have their food and rest until the battle-cry should be given and they should see the signal. And after doing all this, he went back to his tent, had his meal, and rested.

Now the Romans, seeing the army so quiet and more tranquil than usual, marveled at the fact and ventured on various explanations and guesses. Some—not judging it aright—thought this was a preparation for withdrawal. Others—and this proved correct—believed that it was a preparation for battle and an alert, things which they had been expecting in the near future. So they passed the word along and then went in silence to their own divisions and made all sorts of preparations.

The hour was already advanced, the day was declining and near evening, and the sun was at the Ottoman's backs but shining in the faces of their enemies. This was just as the Sultan had wished; accordingly he gave the order first for the trumpets to sound the battle-signal, and the other instruments, the pipes and flutes and cymbals too, as loud as they could. All the trumpets of the other divisions, with the other instruments in turn, sounded all together, a great and fearsome sound. Everything shook and quivered at the noise. After that, the standards were displayed.

To begin, the archers and slingers and those in charge of the cannon and the muskets, in accord with the commands given them, advanced against the wall slowly and gradually. When they got within bowshot, they halted to fight. And first they exchanged fire with the heavier weapons, with arrows from the archers, stones from the slingers, and iron and leaden balls from the cannon and muskets. Then, as they closed with battleaxes and javelins and spears, hurling them at each other and being hurled at pitilessly in rage and fierce anger. On both sides there was loud shouting and blasphemy and cursing. Many on each side were wounded, and not a few died. This kept up till sunset, a space of about two or three hours.

Then, with fine insight, the Sultan summoned the shield-bearers, heavy infantry and other troops and said: "Go to it, friends and children mine! It is time now to show yourselves good fighters!" They immediately crossed the moat, with shouts and fearful yells, and attacked the outer wall. All of it, however, had been demolished by the cannon. There were only stockades of great beams instead of a wall, and bundles of vine-branches, and jars full of earth. At that point a fierce battle ensued close in and with the weapons of hand-to-hand fighting. The heavy infantry and shield-bearers fought to overcome the defenders and get over the stockade, while the Romans and Italians tried to fight these off and to guard the stockade. At times the infantry did get over the wall and the stockade, pressing forward bravely and unhesitatingly. And at times they were stoutly forced back and driven off.

The Sultan followed them up, as they struggled bravely, and encouraged them. He ordered those in charge of the cannon to put the match to the cannon. And these, being set off, fired their stone balls against the defenders and worked no little destruction on both sides, among those in the near vicinity.

So, then, the two sides struggled and fought bravely and vigorously. Most of the night passed, and the Romans were successful and prevailed not a little. Also, Giustinianni and his men kept their positions stubbornly, and guarded the stockade and defended themselves bravely against the aggressors.

Sultan Mehmed saw that the attacking divisions were very much worn out by the battle and had not made any progress worth mentioning, and that the Romans and Italians were not only fighting stoutly but were prevailing in the battle. He was very indignant at this, considering that it ought not to be endured any longer. Immediately he brought up the divisions which he had been reserving for later on, men who were extremely well armed, daring and brave, and far in advance of the rest in experience and valor. They were the elite of the army: heavy infantry, bowmen, and lancers, and his own bodyguard, and along with them those of the division called Yenitsari [Janissaries].

Calling to them and urging them to prove themselves now as heroes, he led the attack against the wall, himself at the head until they reached the moat. There he ordered the bowmen, slingers, and musketeers to stand at a distance and fire to the right, against the defenders on the palisade and on the battered wall. They were to keep up so heavy a fire that those defenders would be unable to fight, or to expose themselves because of the cloud of arrows and other projectiles falling like snowflakes.

To all the rest, the heavy infantry and the shieldbearers, the Sultan gave orders to cross the moat swiftly and attack the palisade. With a loud and terrifying war-cry and with fierce impetuosity and wrath, they advanced as if mad. Being young and strong and full of daring, and especially because they were fighting in the Sultan's presence, their valor exceeded every expectation. They attacked the palisade and fought bravely without any hesitation. Needing no further orders, they knocked down the turrets which had been built out in front, broke the yardarms, scattered the materials that had been gathered, and forced the defenders back inside the palisade.

Giustinianni with his men, and the Romans in that section fought bravely with lances, axes, pikes, javelins, and other weapons of offense. It was a hand-to-hand encounter, and they stopped the attackers and prevented them from getting inside the palisade. There was much shouting on both sides—the mingled sounds of blasphemy, insults, threats, attackers, defenders, shooters, those shot at, killers and dying, of those who in anger and wrath did all sorts of terrible things. And it was a sight to see there: a hard fight going on hand-to-hand with great determination and for the greatest rewards, heroes fighting valiantly, the one party struggling with all their might to force back the defenders, get possession of the wall, enter the City, and fall upon the children and women and the treasures, the other party bravely agonizing to drive them off and guard their possessions, even if they were not to succeed in prevailing and in keeping them.

Instead, the hapless Romans were destined finally to be brought under the yoke of servitude and to suffer its horrors. For although they had battled bravely, and though they lacked nothing of willingness and daring in the contest, Giustinianni received a mortal wound in the breast from an arrow fired by a crossbow. It passed clear through his breastplate, and he fell where he was and was carried to his tent in a hopeless condition. All who were with him were scattered, being upset by their loss. They abandoned the palisade and wall where they had been fighting, and thought of only one thing—how they could carry him on to the galleons and get away safe themselves.

But the Emperor Constantine besought them earnestly, and made promises to them if they would wait a little while, till the fighting should subside. They would not consent, however, but taking up their leader and all their armor, they boarded the galleons in haste and with all speed, giving no consideration to the other defenders.

The Emperor Constantine forbade the others to follow. Then, though he had no idea what to do next—for he had no other reserves to fill the places thus left vacant, the ranks of those who had so suddenly deserted, and meantime the battle raged fiercely and all had to see to their own ranks and places and fight there—still, with his remaining Romans and his bodyguard, which was so few as to be easily counted, he took his stand in front of the palisade and fought bravely.

Sultan Mehmed, who happened to be fighting quite near by, saw that the palisade and the other part of the wall that had been destroyed were now empty of men and deserted by the defenders. He noted that men were slipping away secretly and that those who remained were fighting feebly because they were so few. Realizing from this that the defenders had fled and that the wall was deserted, he shouted out: "Friends, we have the City! We have it! They are already fleeing from us! They can't stand it any longer! The wall is bare of defenders! It needs just a little more effort and the City is taken! Don't weaken, but on with the work with all your might, and be men and I am with you!"

So saying, he led them himself. And they, with a shout on the run and with a fearsome yell, went on ahead of the Sultan, pressing on up to the palisade. After a long and bitter struggle they hurled back the Romans from there and climbed by force up the palisade. They dashed some of their foe down into the ditch between the great wall and the palisade, which was deep and hard to get out of, and they killed them there. The rest they drove back to the gate.

PART 6

THE ARAB WORLD

THE KORAN
(seventh century)

ON HOLY WAR

Fight in the path of God against those who fight you, but do not transgress, for God does not love transgressors.

Kill them wherever you encounter them, and expel them from whence they have expelled you, for dissension [*fitna*] is worse than killing. But do not fight them by the Sacred Mosque unless they fight you first, and if they do fight you, then kill them. Such is the recompense of the unbelievers.

But if they desist, then God is forgiving and merciful.

Fight them until there is no more dissension, and religion is God's. If they desist, there is no enmity, save against the unjust. [2.190–93]

When you meet those who are infidels, strike their necks until you have overwhelmed them, tighten their bonds, and then release them, either freely or for ransom, when war lays down its burdens. Thus it is, and if God wished, He would crush them Himself, but He tests you against one another. Those who are killed in the path of God, He does not let their good deeds go for nothing. [47.4–5]

From *Islam: From the Prophet Muhammad to the Capture of Constantinople*, edited and translated by Bernard Lewis, vol. 1, *Politics and War* (New York: Harper Torchbooks, 1974), 209–10. Copyright © 1974 by Bernard Lewis. Reprinted by permission of HarperCollins Publishers.

AL-MUTTAQI' AL-HINDI
(1477–1567)

Al-Muttaqi' al-Hindi was born in Gujarat, India, into a respectable family. He at first belonged to the Cishti order at Burhanpur. In 1534 he left India for Mecca. He stayed there for thirty years, studied with Ibn-Hadjar al-'Askalani and entered the Kadiri and Shadhili orders. He died at Mecca, where his learning and spiritual discipline were highly respected.

SAYINGS ASCRIBED TO THE PROPHET

Jihad is incumbent upon you with every emir, whether he be godly or wicked and even if he commit major sins. Prayer is incumbent upon you behind every Muslim, be he godly or wicked and even if he commit major sins. Prayer is incumbent upon you for every Muslim who dies, be he godly or wicked and even if he commit major sins.

Paradise is under the shadow of swords.

Where the believer's heart shakes on the path of God, his sins fall away from him as the fruit falls off a date palm.

If anyone shoots an arrow at the enemy on the path of God and his arrow reaches his enemy, whether it hits him or misses, it is accounted equal in merit to liberating a slave.

He who draws his sword in the path of God has sworn allegiance to God.

If anyone ransoms a prisoner from the hands of the enemy, I am that prisoner.

He who fights so that the word of God may prevail is on the path of God.

He who dies fighting on the frontier in the path of God, God protects him from the testing of the tomb.

The unbeliever and the one who kills him will never meet in Hell.

From *Islam: From the Prophet Muhammad to the Capture of Constantinople*, edited and translated by Bernard Lewis, vol. 1, *Politics and War* (New York: Harper Torchbooks, 1974), 210–12. Copyright © 1974 by Bernard Lewis. Reprinted by permission of HarperCollins Publishers.

God sent me as a mercy and a portent; He did not send me as a trader or as a cultivator. The worst of the community on the Day of Resurrection are the traders and the cultivators, except for those who are niggardly with their religion.

A day and a night of fighting on the frontier is better than a month of fasting and prayer.

The best thing a Muslim can earn is an arrow in the path of God.

He who equips a warrior in the Holy War for God has the same reward as he, while the warrior's reward is not diminished.

He who when he dies has never campaigned or even intended to campaign dies in a kind of hypocrisy.

Fight against the polytheists with your property, your persons, and your tongues.

Swords are the keys of Paradise.

A sword is sufficient witness.

God wonders at people who are led to Heaven in chains.

A campaign by sea is like ten campaigns by land, and he who loses his bearings at sea is like one who sheds his blood in the path of God.

Every prophet has his monasticism, and the monasticism of this community is the Holy War in the path of God.

If a campaigner by sea is seasick, he has the reward of a martyr; if drowned, of two martyrs.

In Islam there are three dwellings, the lower, the upper, and the uppermost. The lower is the Islam of the generality of Muslims. If you ask any one of them he will answer, "I am a Muslim." In the upper their merits differ, some of the Muslims being better than others. The uppermost is the jihad in the cause of God, which only the best of them attain.

Will you not ask me why I laugh? I have seen people of my community who are dragged to Paradise against their will. They asked, "O Prophet of God, who are they?" He said, "They are non-Arab people whom the warriors in the Holy War have captured and made to enter Islam."

Shoot and ride! Of the two, I would rather have you shoot than ride. Anything in which a man passes his time is vain except for shooting with his bow, training his horse, or dallying with his wife. These three things are right. He who abandons archery after having learned it is ungrateful to the one who taught him.

Accursed be he who carries the Persian bow. Keep to the Arab bow and to the lances by which God gives you power in these lands and gives you victory over your enemy.

Learn to shoot, for what lies between the two marks is one of the gardens of Paradise.

Warfare is deception.

The Muslims are bound by their stipulations.

The Muslims are bound by their stipulations as long as these are lawful.

Of any village that you come to and stay in, you have a share, but of any village that is disobedient to God and His Prophet, one-fifth of it belongs to God and His Prophet and the rest is yours.

Treat an Arab as an Arab and a half-breed as a half-breed. The Arab has two shares and the half-breed one.

Kill the old polytheists but spare the young ones.

If you find a tithe collector, kill him.

Go in the name of God and in God and in the religion of the Prophet of God! Do not kill the very old, the infant, the child, or the woman. Bring all the booty, holding back no part of it. Maintain order and do good, for God loves those who do good.

Why are some people so bent on killing today that they even kill children? Are not the best of you the sons of idolators? Do not kill children! Do not kill children! Every soul is born with a natural disposition [to the true religion] and remains so until their tongue gives them powers of expression. Then their parents make Jews or Christians of them.

Expel the Jews and the Christians from the Arabian peninsula.

Accept advice to treat prisoners well.

Looting is no more lawful than carrion.

He who loots is not one of us.

He has forbidden looting and mutilation.

He has forbidden the killing of women and children.

He who flees is not one of us.

The bite of an ant is more painful to the martyr than the thrust of a weapon, which is more desirable to him than sweet, cold water on a hot summer day.

AL-BUKHARI
(810–870)

To know the Sunna and the hadiths—that is, all the sayings and deeds of the Prophet and his principal companions—the work of Al-Bukhari is essential. After the Koran, Al-Bukhari's Sahih *(Authentic) constitutes the chief source of Muslim law and ethics.*

SAYINGS ASCRIBED TO THE PROPHET

The Effort of Jihad

O Muslims, do not wish to meet the enemy; ask God for peace. But when you meet the enemy, be patient and remember that paradise lies in the shadow of swords.

Mastery of the Seas

'Umair bin al-Aswad al-'Ansi reported that he went to meet Ubada bin al-Samit when he was in his own house on the coast of Emesa. He had Umm-Haram with him. Umair said: "She told us that she had heard the Prophet say: 'The first group of my followers to undertake an expedition by sea will surely acquire merit.'" Umm-Haram went on: "I then said to him: 'O Messenger of God, shall I be among them?' 'You will be,' he replied; and he added: 'The first of my followers to attack Caesar's city will have their sins forgiven.'"

From *Principes de stratégie arabe*, edited by Jean-Paul Charnay (Paris: Editions de l'Herne, 1984). Translated from the French by A. M. Berrett. Reproduced by permission of Jean-Paul Charnay.

AL-TABARI
(c. 838–923)

*Al-Tabari was an exegetist of the Sunna. He traces not only the political
history of Islam down to 915 but universal history. The battle of Kadisaya in
636 or 637 between the Persians and the Arabs was won by the latter. (It was
invoked by Iraq during the recent conflict with Iran.) Al-Tabari also relates
the story of the battle of Karbala' in 680, where Husein, the Prophet's
grandson, and his family and supporters were defeated. This battle has the
greatest significance for the Shi'ites, and it is commemorated each year.*

*Abu Bakr was the second caliph; 'Umar (not to be confused with 'Umar,
son of Sa'd b. Abi Waqqas, the Umayyad commander at Karbala') was the
third.*

ABU BAKR ON THE RULES OF WAR

O people! I charge you with ten rules; learn them well!

Do not betray, or misappropriate any part of the booty; do not practice
treachery or mutilation. Do not kill a young child, an old man, or a woman.
Do not uproot or burn palms or cut down fruitful trees. Do not slaughter
a sheep or a cow or a camel, except for food. You will meet people who have
set themselves apart in hermitages; leave them to accomplish the purpose
for which they have done this. You will come upon people who will bring
you dishes with various kinds of foods. If you partake of them, pronounce
God's name over what you eat. You will meet people who have shaved
the crown of their heads, leaving a band of hair around it. Strike them with
the sword.

Go, in God's name, and may God protect you from sword and pestilence.

From *Islam: From the Prophet Muhammad to the Capture of Constantinople*, edited and translated by Bernard Lewis, vol. 1, *Politics and War* (New York: Harper Torchbooks, 1974), 213. Copyright © 1974 by Bernard Lewis. Reprinted by permission of HarperCollins Publishers.

CONQUEST

Isfahan

In the name of God, the Merciful and the Compassionate.

A letter from 'Abdallah ibn-Qays to the Fadhusafan and the inhabitants of Isfahan and its surroundings.

You are safe as long as you discharge your obligations, which are: to pay the *jizya*, which you must pay according to your capacity every year, paying it to whoever is the governor of your country, for every adult male; you must also guide the Muslim [traveler], keep his road in repair, lodge him for a day and a night, and provide the walker with a mount for one stage.

Do not assert your authority over any Muslim. What you owe to the Muslims is your goodwill and the payment of your dues; you have safe-conduct [*aman*] as long as you comply. But if you change anything, or if anyone among you changes anything and you do not hand him over, then you have no safe-conduct. If anyone insults a Muslim, he will be severely punished for it. If he strikes a Muslim, we shall kill him.

Tiflis

In the name of God, the Merciful and the Compassionate.

This is a letter from Habib ibn-Maslama for the inhabitants of Tiflis of the Georgians, in the land of Hurmuz, giving you safe-conduct for yourselves, your property, your convents, your churches, and your prayers, on the condition that you submit to the humiliation [?] of the *jizya* at the rate of a full dinar per household.

You owe us your goodwill and your help against the enemies of God and our enemies; lodging for the wayfarer for the night, with the food and drink permitted for the people of the book; and guidance on the road, as far as this causes no harm to any of you. If you become Muslims and perform the prayer and pay the *zakat*, then you are our brothers in religion and our *mawali*. But if anyone turns away from God and His Prophets and His books and His party, then we declare war against you without limit, for God does not love traitors.

From *Islam: From the Prophet Muhammad to the Capture of Constantinople,* edited and translated by Bernard Lewis, vol. 1, *Politics and War* (New York: Harper Torchbooks, 1974), 238–41. Copyright © 1974 by Bernard Lewis. Reprinted by permission of HarperCollins Publishers.

THE BATTLE OF KADISAYA

When Sa'd b. Abi Waqqas reviewed his army, he found that he had thirty-five thousand men under arms. [Rustem was encamped on the borders of lower Mesopotamia.] [Caliph] 'Umar wrote to Sa'd to tell him to go to Kadisaya, a city situated in that province. When the Muslim general arrived there, he learned that Rustem had asked the king for further forces, and that fifty thousand men were marching to join him, so that the Persian army would be made up of one hundred and fifty thousand men. Sa'd sent 'Umar a letter in which he spoke to him of how large the enemy forces were and how few the Muslims. The caliph replied: "I am going to have troops sent. Do not worry."

Rustem had arrayed his army in battle order and had elephants posted in front of the ranks. Sa'd, who was seriously ill, mounted his horse and said to the Muslims: "Fix your eyes on me; when you hear me proclaim the war cry 'God is great!' all attack at once." After a while, when Sa'd had given the signal, the Muslims all repeated the battle cry and began the attack. But their efforts were in vain because of the elephants that were in front of the Persian ranks. Then the Arabs dismounted, attacked the elephants with their sabers and lances and forced them to withdraw. . . .

. . . Next day combat was resumed and became very fierce. The elephants were in front of the Persian columns. The Arabs charged them, launched a hail of arrows at them, and struck their trunks with their sabers. This maddened the elephants and they turned tail and fled; they ran all the way to Madain without stopping and without the Persians running after them being able to bring them back. When he saw his troops moving back toward the rear, Rustem feared a general defeat and mounted his horse and cried out: "Soldiers, imagine that the elephants never existed." He thus got the soldiers to go on fighting. But night was approaching; Rustem reformed his battle lines and cried out: "We shall fight until day to finish it in one go!"

When Sa'd saw that the Persians were beginning to fight again and had reformed their lines, he caused the following orders to be published: "Let each Muslim go back to his place in the ranks. Be ready to carry on fighting all through the night. Put the infantry in front; lancers, archers, and those fighting with sabers must dismount." The Persians advanced in darkness, and a bitter struggle ensued. There was never a more murderous combat between Persians and Arabs. That night was called the "night of rumbling" because of the noise produced by the clash of fighters engaged in hand-to-hand combat and because of the cries they raised.

From *Principes de stratégie arabe,* edited by Jean-Paul Charnay (Paris: Editions de l'Herne, 1984). Translated from the French by A. M. Berrett. Reproduced by permission of Jean-Paul Charnay.

The struggle between Arabs and Persians continued to be ardently fought. The night was so dark that the combatants could not see each other. . . . This terrible struggle lasted until morning. Six thousand Muslims lay on the field of battle. Then, Sa'd, fearing that the battle would just go on and on, called together the chiefs of the various tribes and exhorted them to stir up the ardor of their troops for the struggle. "God will give us victory over the enemy," he said to them. "You know that it was the Persians who started this war. If we remain alive, we shall subjugate them. If you die, you have hope of paradise." When the chiefs of the tribes returned to their troops, they repeated what Sa'd had said to their soldiers, and the Muslims fought without letting up. . . .

. . . Just when the heat had reached its peak and the dust raised by the wind was blinding the Persian soldiers, the Muslims, focusing their efforts on a single point, broke through the center of the enemy army. From the place where he was seated, near the camels, Rustem saw the situation his troops were in.

An Arab named Hilal, getting to where the camels bearing Rustem's treasure were, struck out wildly with his saber; the blow happened to hit the camel on which Rustem was seated, whom the darkness produced by the dust prevented him from seeing. The rope holding the load of money on the camel having been cut, the load fell on Rustem's head; in spite of the pain he felt, he jumped to his feet and threw himself into the canal to swim to safety. Hilal, seeing a man fleeing, smelling the odors of musk and perfumes, and finally noticing the golden throne, realized that it was Rustem's throne. When he saw nobody on the throne, he was certain that the man who had just thrown himself into the water was Rustem. In jumping, Rustem had broken his leg and was unable to move. Hilal ran up, seized him by the leg, pulled him out of the water, and cut off his head, which he attached to the end of his lance. Then he got up on the throne and cried out: "Muslims, I have killed Rustem." The Muslims responded with a cry of triumph. When the Persians saw their general's head, they gave way and began to flee. Sa'd sent men in pursuit of them and ordered one of his officers to search the bodies of the Persians and gather together their baggage and weapons and all the booty.

THE BATTLE OF KARBALA'

Husein spent the whole night readying his weapons and chanting dirges. When his young son 'Ali, who was sick and lying in his tent, heard him chanting that way, he began to weep. Then all the women began to scream and sob. Husein

From *Principes de stratégie arabe,* edited by Jean-Paul Charnay (Paris: Editions de l'Herne, 1984). Translated from the French by A. M. Berrett. Reproduced by permission of Jean-Paul Charnay.

said to them: "Do not weep, for it would rejoice the enemy." Then, raising his eyes toward heaven, he cried out: "Lord, you know they swore an oath to me and have broken it. Grant me vengeance over them!" Then he called together his supporters who had followed him and spoke to them in these terms: "Whatever happens to you, it is you yourselves who have prepared it. It is not I who pushed you into war. We are few, and the enemy is strong. As for me, I have made the sacrifice of my life. Not only did I not lead you into war but I free you from your oath. Let all those who would like to leave go!" They replied: "O son of the apostle of God, what excuse could we give your grandfather on the day of resurrection for having abandoned his son in such a place, into the hands of his enemies? No, we have sworn our lives to you!" So Husein prepared himself for battle. . . .

'Umar, son of Sa'd [b. Abi Waqqas], having arrayed his troops, advanced to join battle. Husein dismounted from his horse, mounted a camel and presented himself before the enemy ranks in such a way as to be seen by the whole of 'Umar's army, and spoke in these terms: "People of Kufa, I know that my words will not save me; but I wish to speak, in order to make plain your responsibility before God and my own innocence, before battle is joined. You all know that I am the son of Fatima, daughter of the apostle of God, and the son of 'Ali, cousin of the Prophet and the first believer. Ja'afar of the two wings was my uncle; 'Hamza, the prince of martyrs, was my father's uncle; and Hasan was my brother, of whom the Prophet said that he was the lord of those who dwell in paradise. If you believe in God and in the mission of my grandfather, the apostle of God, tell me what crime I have committed that you should seek my life." . . .

When no one replied to this speech, Husein said: "I give thanks to God, who pronounces against you; for my charge against you is unanswerable and you have nothing to allege against me." Then, addressing a few individuals, Husein said: "So-and-so, did you not write to me to call me to your side, saying in your letter that you had sworn an oath to me? Did you summon me in order to kill me?" They replied: "We are disgusted with that oath." Husein cried out: "Thanks be to God! You no longer have any argument with God and the Prophet!" Then he said: "Lord, you are my consolation in every affliction, my succor in every adversity, my strength in every misfortune, my protector in every circumstance. You are the source of all grace and the end of every extremity; protect me, O most merciful one." Husein then made his camel kneel down and remounted his horse; he lined up his troops and calmly waited for the enemy to begin his attack. . . .

. . . Shamir said to 'Umar b. Sa'd: "Why are you hesitating? Begin the attack." 'Umar fitted an arrow to his bow and said: "You are all witnesses that it is I who am shooting the first arrow. . . ."

... The heat had become intense and Husein's friends were extremely thirsty. 'Amr b. 'Hajjaj, who commanded the right wing of 'Umar's army, said to him: "These men have made a pact with death; it is not possible to defeat them piecemeal; a general attack is necessary." 'Umar made his archers advance and ordered them all to fire at once. Twenty of Husein's men fell dead; all the rest were wounded, but they continued to fight.

It was now Husein's turn to fight, and he advanced. But his companions said to him: "Son of the apostle of God, so long as one single one of us remains alive, we will not allow you to go and fight." With tears in his eyes, Husein retorted: "May God reward you!" They set off one after the other, and as he advanced each said: "Peace be upon you; son of the apostle of God, hail"; and Husein replied: "Peace be upon you; go, I shall follow you." When all his friends were killed or wounded and there remained with him only his brothers, sons, and nephews and members of his household, Husein said: "My turn has come." They said: "So long as we are alive, it would not be right for you to go into battle." Then his son 'Ali, the eldest, the first of all the members of his family, advanced chanting: "I am 'Ali, son of Husein, son of 'Ali. By the Lord of the temple, we are the closest relatives of the Prophet. By God, never shall we allow the son of the bastard to be our master!"

And before his father's eyes, he charged the enemy ten times, and at each onslaught he killed two or three men. He was parched with thirst, and his tongue was dry. He came to Husein and said to him: "Father, I am thirsty." Husein replied: "Son, may my body be your ransom; what can I do?" Then he came up to him and put his tongue in his son's mouth. 'Ali returned to the fighting, and a man named Murra b. Sa'd came to meet him, slipped behind him, and felled him with a single sword blow. 'Ali fell and was immediately surrounded by a host of enemies, who cut his body to pieces. When he saw his son thus, Husein began to weep and sob (something he had never previously been heard to do), and Zainab came out of the tent and hurled herself on the body of 'Ali [her brother], screaming as she did so. ...

... Only his five brothers now remained with Husein: 'Abbas, 'Abdallah, 'Othman, Muhammad, and Ja'afar. His other two brothers, Muhammad, son of the 'Hanifite, and 'Umar, had remained in Mecca. Qasim, son of Hasan, who was only ten years old, came out of the tent sword in hand. Husein said to him: "Go back in, you are too young to fight." Qasim said: "Uncle, I adjure you in the name of the Prophet, let me go!" And he went off. A horseman threw himself on him and felled him with a sword blow that cleaved his head in two. Husein's brothers then threw themselves on the enemy, all five at once. They were surrounded and killed. Then Husein's horse fell, struck by an arrow. Husein dismounted. It was nearing the hour of afternoon prayer. Weakened by the pangs of thirst, Husein sat down on the ground. Several enemy soldiers closed in on him to kill him; but none dared strike him. They went away saying that they did not want to assume responsibility for his death. Husein had a child, named 'Abdallah, who was a year old. Deeply affected by his crying, he took him on his lap and wept. One of the Beni-Asads shot at him; the arrow penetrated the child's ear, and he died at once. Husein put him down and cried out: "We belong to God and to God we return! Lord, give me the strength to bear these hardships!" He got up. Completely worn out with thirst, he headed for the Euphrates and sought a spot where he could drink. Shamir cried out: "Woe on you! Do not let him drink! He is dead from the effects of thirst, and if he drinks he will come back to life!" Just as Husein was bending over to drink the water, an arrow was shot at him and entered his mouth. He spat out the mouthful of water that he had not yet swallowed, pulled the arrow out of his palate, left the banks of the river and reached the entrance to his tent, bleeding from the mouth. 'Umar b. Sa'd ran up to kill him. When he got close, Husein said to him: "Have you come to kill me?" 'Umar was ashamed. He went back to his foot soldiers: "Why are you just standing there hesitating to surround and kill him?" Then the soldiers fell on Husein from all sides, and he attacked and killed several of them. Shamir and 'Umar b. Sa'd looked on from a distance. Shamir said: "Have you ever seen a man who has lost every member of his house, received so many wounds, been so long deprived of water and assailed by so many soldiers, yet show so much valor?" Husein continued to defend himself against the soldiers; wounded in three or four parts of his body by cuts from swords, spears, and arrows, he lost a large quantity of blood, and his wounds increased his thirst. Then Shamir, with six of his retinue, fell on him. Husein received them with his sword. A man named Zor'a struck him with a sword blow that cut his arm clean off his shoulder. Husein fell, then got up again and sought to throw himself on the man, but he fell again. Zor'a slipped behind him and plunged his spear into his back, so that the point came out through his chest. Husein had fallen on his face, and as he withdrew his lance from Husein's body, Zor'a drew from him his last breath. Shamir came up and cut off his head; Qais b. Ash'ath removed his cloak; Ba'hr b. Ka'b, his trousers; Akhnas b. Mazyad, his turban, and 'Habib b. Bodsail, his sword. Shamir then had the tent sacked; the women even had their clothes taken off them. Hearing the women's cries, 'Umar b. Sa'd, arrived just as Shamir, sword in hand, was about to kill 'Ali the younger, the son of Husein, who was ill. 'Umar said to him: "Are you not ashamed to kill a child?" . . .

. . . Shamir then said to 'Umar: "The emir ['Ubaydallah, governor of Basra] has ordered that Husein's body be trampled under horses' hooves." He therefore commanded twenty horsemen, among whom were Ish'aq b. Haiwa and

Akhnas b. Mazyad, to ride their horses over Husein's body, which was torn to pieces. They spent the night at that spot. 'Umar sent a letter to 'Ubaydallah and sent him Husein's head by Khawali b. Yezid, of the Asba'h tribe. The next day, he buried the dead of his army, to the number of ninety-eight, leaving the corpses of Husein and his people unburied. The women were made to sit on camels, and they took the road for Kufa.

IBN AL-ATHIR
(1160–1233)

Like Al-Tabari, Ibn al-Athir was the author of a universal history, the Kamil
al tarikh *(Complete History). He was a contemporary of Saladin's and an
eyewitness of the Muslims' victorious counterattack against the crusaders in
the Third Crusade. Ibn al-Athir also describes the irruption of the Mongols
into the Muslim world of the Middle East in 1220–21, which he also witnessed.
His historical work, a compilation going back to the origins of history, is
considered of fundamental importance for the period between the tenth and
thirteenth centuries. It covers the whole of the Muslim world, from central
Asia to Spain.*

THE BATTLE OF HITTIN

While the reunited Franks were on their way to Saffuriyya, Saladin called a
council of his emirs. Most of them advised him not to fight, but to weaken the
enemy by repeated skirmishes and raids. Others however advised him to pillage the Frankish territories, and to give battle to any Frankish army that might
appear in their path, "Because in the East people are cursing us, saying that we
no longer fight the infidels but have begun to fight Muslims instead. So we
must do something to justify ourselves and silence our critics." But Saladin
said: "My feeling is that we should confront all the enemy's forces with all the
forces of Islam; for events do not turn out according to man's will and we do
not know how long a life is left to us, so it is foolish to dissipate this concentration of troops without striking a tremendous blow in the Holy War." So on

From *Arab Historians of the Crusades,* translated from the Italian by E. J. Costello (Berkeley:
University of California Press, 1984), 119–25. Originally published as *Storici Arabi delle Crociate,*
selected and translated by Francesco Gabrieli (Turin: Einaudi, 1957). Italian translation copyright
© 1957 by Giulio Einaudi Editore S.p.A., Turin. English translation copyright © 1969 by Routledge
and Kegan Paul Ltd. Reproduced by permission of Routledge and Kegan Paul Ltd.

Thursday, 2 July 1187, the fifth day after we encamped at Uqhuwana, he struck camp and moved off up the hill outside Tiberias, leaving the city behind him. When he drew near to the Franks, however, there was no one to be seen, for they had not yet left their tents. So he went back down the hill with his army. At night he positioned troops where they would prevent the enemy from giving battle and then attacked Tiberias with a small force, breached the wall and took the city by storm during the night. The inhabitants fled for refuge to the citadel, where the Countess and her children were, and defended themselves there while the lower town was sacked and burned.

When the Franks learned that Saladin had attacked Tiberias and taken it and everything in it, burning the houses and anything they could not remove, they met to take counsel. Some advised the King [Guy of Lusignan] to meet the Muslims in battle and chase them out of Tiberias, but the Count [Raymond of Tripoli] intervened to say: "Tiberias belongs to me and my wife. There is no question that Saladin is master there now and that only the citadel remains, where my wife is immured. For my part, if he takes the citadel, my wife and all my possessions there and then goes away I shall be happy enough. By God, I have observed the armies of Islam over the course of the years and I have never seen one equal to Saladin's army here in numbers or in fighting power. If he takes Tiberias he will not be able to stay there, and when he has left it and gone away we will retake it; for if he chooses to stay there he will be unable to keep his army together, for they will not put up for long with being kept away from their homes and families. He will be forced to evacuate the city, and we will free our prisoners." But Prince Arnat of al-Karak [Reginald of Châtillon] replied: "You have tried hard to make us afraid of the Muslims. Clearly you take their side and your sympathies are with them, otherwise you would not have spoken in this way. As for the size of their army, a large load of fuel will be good for the fires of Hell." "I am one of you," said the Count, "and if you advance then I shall advance with you, and if you retreat I shall retreat. You will see what will happen." The generals decided to advance and give battle to the Muslims, so they left the place where they had been encamped until now and advanced on the Muslim army. When Saladin received the news he ordered his army to withdraw from its position near Tiberias; his only reason for besieging Tiberias was to make the Franks abandon their position and offer battle. The Muslims went down to the water [of the lake]. The weather was blazingly hot and the Franks, who were suffering greatly from thirst, were prevented by the Muslims from reaching the water. They had drained all the local cisterns, but could not turn back for fear of the Muslims. So they passed that night tormented with thirst. The Muslims for their part had lost their first fear of the enemy and were in high spirits, and spent the night inciting one another to battle. They could smell victory in the air, and the more they saw of the unexpectedly low morale of the Franks the more aggressive and daring they became; throughout the night the cries "Allah akbar" (God is great) and "There is no God but Allah" rose up to heaven. Meanwhile the Sultan was deploying the vanguard of archers and distributing the arrows.

On Saturday, 4 July 1187, Saladin and the Muslims mounted their horses and advanced on the Franks. They too were mounted, and the two armies came to blows. The Franks were suffering badly from thirst, and had lost confidence. The battle raged furiously, both sides putting up a tenacious resistance. The Muslim archers sent up clouds of arrows like thick swarms of locusts, killing many of the Frankish horses. The Franks, surrounding themselves with their infantry, tried to fight their way toward Tiberias in the hope of reaching water, but Saladin realized their objective and forestalled them by planting himself and his army in the way. He himself rode up and down the Muslim lines encouraging and restraining his troops where necessary. The whole army obeyed his commands and respected his prohibitions. One of his young mamluks led a terrifying charge on the Franks and performed prodigious feats of valor until he was overwhelmed by numbers and killed, when all the Muslims charged the enemy lines and almost broke through, slaying many Franks in the process. The Count saw that the situation was desperate and realized that he could not withstand the Muslim army, so by agreement with his companions he charged the lines before him. The commander of that section of the Muslim army was Taqi ad-Din 'Umar, Saladin's nephew. When he saw that the Franks charging his lines were desperate and that they were going to try to break through, he sent orders for a passage to be made for them through the ranks.

One of the volunteers had set fire to the dry grass that covered the ground; it took fire and the wind carried the heat and smoke down on to the enemy. They had to endure thirst, the summer's heat, the blazing fire and smoke and the fury of battle. When the Count fled the Franks lost heart and were on the verge of surrender, but seeing that the only way to save their lives was to defy death they made a series of charges that almost dislodged the Muslims from their position in spite of their numbers, had not the grace of God been with them. As each wave of attackers fell back they left their dead behind them; their numbers diminished rapidly, while the Muslims were all around them like a circle about its diameter. The surviving Franks made for a hill near Hittin, where they hoped to pitch their tents and defend themselves. They were vigorously attacked from all sides and prevented from pitching more than one tent, that of the King. The Muslims captured their great cross, called the "True Cross," in which they say is a piece of the wood upon which, according to them, the Messiah was crucified. This was one of the heaviest blows that could be inflicted on them and made their death and destruction certain. Large numbers of their cavalry and infantry were killed or captured. The King stayed on the hillside with five hundred of the most gallant and famous knights.

I was told that al-Malik al-Afdal, Saladin's son, said: "I was at my father Saladin's side during that battle, the first that I saw with my own eyes. The Frankish King had retreated to the hill with his band, and from there he led a furious charge against the Muslims facing him, forcing them back upon my father. I saw that he was alarmed and distraught, and he tugged at his beard as he went forward crying: 'Away with the Devil's lie!' The Muslims turned to counterattack and drove the Franks back up the hill. When I saw the Franks retreating before the Muslim onslaught I cried out for joy: 'We have conquered them!' But they returned to the charge with undiminished ardour and drove our army back toward my father. His response was the same as before, and the Muslims counterattacked and drove the Franks back to the hill. Again I cried: 'We have beaten them!' but my father turned to me and said: 'Be quiet; we shall not have beaten them until that tent falls!' As he spoke the tent fell, and the Sultan dismounted and prostrated himself in thanks to God, weeping for joy." This was how the tent fell: the Franks had been suffering terribly from thirst during that charge, which they hoped would win them a way out of their distress, but the way of escape was blocked. They dismounted and sat down on the ground and the Muslims fell upon them, pulled down the King's tent and captured every one of them, including the King, his brother, and Prince Arnat of Karak, Islam's most hated enemy. They also took the ruler of Jubáil, the son of Humphrey [of Toron], the Grand Master of the Templars, one of the Franks' greatest dignitaries, and a band of Templars and Hospitallers. The number of dead and captured was so large that those who saw the slain could not believe that anyone could have been taken alive, and those who saw the prisoners could not believe that any had been killed. From the time of their first assault on Palestine in 1098 until now the Franks had never suffered such a defeat.

When all the prisoners had been taken Saladin went to his tent and sent for the King of the Franks and Prince Arnat of Karak. He had the King seated beside him and as he was half-dead with thirst gave him iced water to drink. The King drank, and handed the rest to the Prince, who also drank. Saladin said: "This godless man did not have my permission to drink, and will not save his life that way." He turned on the Prince, casting his crimes in his teeth and enumerating his sins. Then he rose and with his own hand cut off the man's head. "Twice," he said, "I have sworn to kill that man when I had him in my power: once when he tried to attack Mecca and Medina, and again when he broke the truce to capture the caravan." When he was dead and had been dragged out of the tent the King began to tremble, but Saladin calmed and reassured him. As for the ruler of Tripoli, when he escaped from the battle, as we have described, he went to Tyre and from there made his way to Tripoli. He was there only a few days before he died of rage and fury at the disaster that had befallen the Franks in particular, and all Christendom in general.

When Saladin had brought about the downfall of the Franks he stayed at the site of the battle for the rest of the day, and on the Sunday returned to the siege of Tiberias. The Countess sent to request safe-conducts for herself and her children, companions and possessions, and he granted her this. She left the citadel with all her train, and Saladin kept his word to her and let her escape unmolested. At the Sultan's command the King and a few of the most distinguished prisoners were sent to Damascus, while the Templars and Hospitallers were rounded up to be killed. The Sultan realized that those who had taken them prisoner were not going to hand them over, for they hoped to obtain ransoms for them, and so he offered fifty Egyptian *dinar* for each prisoner in these two categories. Immediately he got two hundred prisoners, who were decapitated at his command. He had these particular men killed because they were the fiercest of all the Frankish warriors, and in this way he rid the Muslim people of them. He sent orders to his commander in Damascus to kill all those found in his territory, whoever they belonged to, and this was done.

A year later I crossed the battlefield, and saw the land all covered with their bones, which could be seen even from a distance, lying in heaps or scattered around. These were what was left after all the rest had been carried away by storms or by the wild beasts of these hills and valleys.

BAHA' AD-DIN IBN SHADDAD
(1145–1234)

Baha' ad-Din ibn Shaddad entered the service of Saladin in 1188. After Saladin's death, he was appointed grand cadi of Aleppo in Syria in 1193. His biography of Saladin is considered an excellent historical account by an eyewitness, devoid of flattery. It gives a very lifelike picture of the great Kurdish fighter and a detailed chronicle of the Third Crusade.

THE FALL OF ACRE

The besiegers battered the walls ceaselessly with catapults, which was the only method of attack they used, and eventually the walls began to crumble, their structure collapsed, and exhaustion and vigilance wore the defenders out. There were few of them against a great number of enemy soldiers, and they underwent the most severe trial of endurance; in fact some of them went for several nights on end without closing their eyes, night or day, whereas the circle hemming them in consisted of a great number of men who took it in turns to fight. The defenders however were but few, and had had to share the duties of the wall, the trenches, the catapults and the galleys.

When the enemy realized this, and when the walls seemed to be tottering, their structure undermined, they began to attack on all sides, divided into groups and detachments that took it in turn to fight. Each time that a detachment exhausted itself it retired to rest and another took its place. On the seventh of the month [jumada II 586/12 July 1191] they began a great offensive, manning night and day all the mounds surrounding their trenches with

From *Arab Historians of the Crusades,* translated from the Italian by E. J. Costello (Berkeley: University of California Press, 1984), 215–22. Originally published as *Storici Arabi delle Crociate,* selected and translated by Francesco Gabrieli (Turin: Einaudi, 1957). Italian translation copyright © 1957 by Giulio Einaudi Editore S.p.A., Turin. English translation copyright © 1969 by Routledge and Kegan Paul Ltd. Reproduced by permission of Routledge and Kegan Paul Ltd.

infantry and combatants. The Sultan, who learnt of the assault from eye-witnesses and by an agreed signal from the garrison—a roll of drums—mounted his horse and ordered the army to mount and attack the enemy. A great battle was fought that day. As deeply concerned as a mother bereft of her child, Saladin galloped from battalion to battalion inciting his men to fight for the Faith. Al-Malik al-'Adil, they say, himself led two charges that day. The Sultan moved through the ranks crying: "For Islam!" his eyes swimming with tears. Every time he looked toward Acre and saw the agony she was in and the disaster looming for her inhabitants, he launched himself once more into the attack and goaded his men on to fight. That day he touched no food and drank only a cup or two of the potion prescribed for him by his doctor. I was left behind and could not take part in the attack because of an illness that afflicted me. I was in my tent at Tall al-'Ayadiyya, and all the battle was spread out before my eyes. Night fell, the Sultan returned to his tent after the final evening prayer, exhausted and in anguish, and slept fitfully. The next morning he had the drums beaten, marshalled his army and returned to the battle he had left the night before.

On that day a letter arrived from the beleaguered men in which they said: "We have reached such a pitch of exhaustion that we can do nothing but surrender. Tomorrow, the eighth of the month, if you can do nothing for us, we shall beg for our lives and hand over the city, securing only our personal safety." This was one of the saddest messages ever received by the Muslims, and it stabbed them to the heart; the more so since Acre contained all the military equipment from Palestine, Jerusalem, Damascus, Aleppo, Egypt and all the Muslim lands, as well as the army's greatest emirs, and such gallant champions of Islam as Saif ad-Din 'Ali al-Mashtub, Saif ad-Din Qaraqush, and others. Qaraqush in particular had directed the defense of the town since the enemy first besieged it. The Sultan was smitten by the news as by no other blow that had ever struck him, to such an extent that his life was feared for. But he continued his unceasing prayers to God and turned to Him throughout the crisis, with patience and pious abnegation and tenacious energy: "And God does not waste the hire of the doer of good." He wanted to try by assault to re-establish contact with the besieged men. The alarm sounded among the troops, the champions mounted their horses, cavalry and infantry assembled. But on that day the army did not support him in the attack on the enemy, for the enemy infantry stood like an unbreakable wall with weapons, ballistas and arrows, behind their bastions. Attacked on every side by the Muslims, they held firm and defended themselves most vigorously. A man who penetrated as far as their trenches told how there was a huge Frank there who leapt on to the parapet of the trench and chased back the Muslims; some men standing close to him handed him stones which he threw down on to the Muslims sheltering behind the parapet. More than fifty stones and arrows struck him without dislodging him from the defensive battle he had undertaken, until a Muslim pyrotechnician threw an incendiary bottle at him and burnt him alive. Another observant old soldier who penetrated the trenches that day told me that on the other side of the parapet was a woman dressed in a green mantle, who shot at us with a wooden bow and wounded many Muslims before she was overcome and killed. Her bow was taken and carried to the Sultan, who was clearly deeply impressed by the story. Thus the fighting continued until nightfall.

Acre, Incapable of Further Resistance, Negotiates with the Franks

The attack on the city from all sides was intensified, with troops taking turns to fight, and the defenders were reduced to a handful of infantry and cavalry as a result of the great losses they had suffered. The survivors lost heart at the thought of the imminence of death, and felt incapable of any further defiance. Meanwhile the enemy captured their trenches and the wall of the first bastion. The Franks had tunnelled under it, filled the mines with combustible material and set fire to it. Part of the bastion crumbled and the Franks got in. But they lost more than a hundred and fifty men there, dead or captured, including six of their leaders. One of these cried: "Do not kill me, and I will make the Franks retreat!" but a Kurd fell on him and killed him, and the other five were killed in the same way. The next day the Franks issued a proclamation: "Return those six men, and we will grant freedom to all the city!" But the Muslims replied that they were already dead, which caused great grief to the Franks, who suspended the offensive for three days after this.

It was said that Saif ad-Din al-Mashtub himself went out under safe-conduct to talk to the French King [Philip II], and said to him: "In the past we have taken many of your cities by storm. In every case, when the inhabitants asked for an amnesty it has been granted, and we have allowed them honorably to go into safety. Now we would surrender this city, and we hope that you will guarantee our lives." The King replied: "Those whom you captured in the past were our subjects, and in the same way you are our mamluks and slaves. We shall see what is to be done with you." To which al-Mashtub, they say, replied harshly and at length, saying among other things: "We shall not hand over the city until we are all dead, and not one of us will die before he has killed fifty of your leaders," and he went away. When al-Mashtub brought the news to the city some of the garrison were afraid, and climbing an embankment escaped to the Muslim camp by night. . . . among the distinguished men in the party were 'Izz ad-Din Arsil, Ibn al-Jawali and Sunqur al-Ushaqi. When Arsil and Sunqur reached the camp they vanished without leaving the faintest trace, for fear of Saladin's wrath. Ibn al-Jawali was taken and thrown into prison.

On the following morning the Sultan mounted, intending to take the enemy by surprise, and took with him spades and other equipment for bridging the trenches. But the troops refused to support him in carrying out his plan, and said rebelliously: "You want to place all Islam in jeopardy, but such a plan could not have a successful outcome." That day three messengers came from the English King [Richard I] asking Saladin for fruit and snow, and saying that the Grand Master of the Hospital would come out the next day to discuss peace. The Sultan treated the messengers with honor, and they went to the market and walked about there, and returned to their own camp at nightfall. That day the Sultan told Sarim ad-Din Qaimaz an-Najmi to take his men and penetrate the enemy lines. He took a group of Kurdish emirs such as al-Janah, (al-Mashtub's brother), and his friends, as far as the Frankish lines. Qaimaz himself raised the standard over the enemy trenches and fought a part of the day in defense of the oriflam. At the height of the battle that day 'Izz ad-Din Jurdik an-Nuri arrived, dismounted and fought vigorously alongside his men. On Friday, 5 July, the Frankish army took the initiative. They were completely surrounded by Muslims, who passed the night fully armed and in the saddle, looking for a chance to help their brothers in Acre, who, they hoped, would be able to attack some point of the enemy lines, break through and get out; the army outside helping them to hold their position, so that some would escape and some be taken, according to their fate. But the besieged men who had agreed to the plan, could not get out that night because an escaped slave had informed the enemy and precautions were taken and strict watch kept. On Friday 10th three enemy messengers spent an hour with al-Malik al-'Adil and returned without reaching any agreement. The day ended with the Muslim army holding the plain facing the enemy, and thus the night passed.

On Saturday the 11th the Franks, in full panoply, moved forward and it appeared that they wanted a pitched battle with the Muslims. When they were drawn up about forty men came out of the gate below the pavilion and invited certain mamluks, among them al-'Adl az-Zabdani of Sidon one of the Sultan's freedmen, to present themselves. Al-'Adl came up to them and began to negotiate for the garrison in Acre to be allowed to go free, but the terms were too stiff and the Saturday came to an end without any conclusion being reached.

Letters Arrive from the City

On Sunday the 12th letters reached us (from Acre) saying: "We have sworn an oath to one another to die. We shall fight until death. We shall not yield the city as long as we have a breath of life in us. See what you can do to distract the enemy from us and draw his fire. These are our decisions. Take care that you do not yield to the enemy. Our part is now over." The messenger who swam out with this letter said that from the great noise heard in the city during the night the Franks thought that a great army had entered Acre. "A Frank," he said, "came up to the wall and cried out to one of the guards: 'In the name of your Faith, tell me how many soldiers came into your city last night.' This was the night before the Saturday, during which a great uproar was heard that alarmed both sides, but its cause was not discovered. 'A thousand cavalry,' replied the other. 'No,' he returned, 'fewer than that; I saw them myself, and they were dressed in green robes'!"

Repeated attacks by Muslim contingents were still able at this stage to turn the enemy attack away from the siege, even after the city was wide open to be taken. But the defenders grew weaker, the number of breaches in the walls increased although the defenders built up in place of the broken wall another internal wall from which they fought when the vulnerable section finally collapsed. On Tuesday 14th of the month there arrived Sabiq ad-Din of Shaizar, on Wednesday Badr ad-Din Yildirim with a large band of Turcomans to whom the Sultan had sent a large sum of money to be distributed among them as pay, and on Thursday Asad ad-Din Shirkuh the younger. Through all this the Franks held firm, refusing to grant the besieged men their lives until every Frankish prisoner in Muslim hands had been returned, and all the cities of Palestine submitted to the Franks. They were offered the surrender of the town with everything in it except the defenders, and they refused it. They were offered the return of the True Cross, and still they refused, becoming increasingly greedy and more obstinate. No one knew any longer what expedient to use with them: "They play at being cunning, and God too plays at being cunning, and He is the better player."

The Garrison Agree to Surrender in Return for Their Lives

On Friday 17 jumada II a swimmer got out of the city with letters saying that the defenders were at their last gasp. The breaches had grown and the people, unable to resist any longer, saw that death was certain and were sure that when the city was taken by storm they would all be put to the sword. They had therefore made an agreement handing over the city with all its equipment, munitions, and ships, in addition to 200,000 *dinar*, 500 ordinary prisoners and 100 important ones nominated by the Franks themselves, and also the True Cross. In return they were allowed to leave the city freely with their personal possessions, women and children. They also guaranteed 400 *dinar* to the Marquis [of Montferrat] who had acted as intermediary in the negotiations. On this basis agreement was reached.

IBN HUDHAYL AL-ANDALUSI
(fourteenth century)

Ibn Hudhayl al-Andalusi, a contemporary of Ibn Khaldun's, who lived at the court of the Nasrid dynasty in Granada, originally wrote his Kitab Tuhfat al-anfus wa shi'ar sukkan al-Andalus, *a treatise on the jihad, or "holy war," at the request of Sultan Muhammad V. He subsequently revised it and prepared an abridged version at the request of the latter's grandson, Muhammad VII, at a time when the Moorish kingdom was weakening in the face of the Christian advance.*

PRINCIPLES OF WAR

The pillar of all science, the bond that strengthens every link, is the leader versed in the art of governing, ready to assume the burden of command. Therefore anyone with command of troops must be well up in this specialty, courageous when he is advancing, careful in the precautions he takes, sincere in his intentions, vigilant in all his movements, penetrating in his insights, indulgent to his subordinates.

If these qualities are combined in the commander of troops, they will enable his mind to summon up precisely those ruses and stratagems that will be decisive for victory when they are put into effect against the enemy.

The main qualities of command are gentleness without weakness, severity without harshness.

Authority comes from a wise admiration.

Prefer fear to blind hope.

From *Principes de stratégie arabe,* edited by Jean-Paul Charnay (Paris: Editions de l'Herne, 1984). Translated from the French by A. M. Berrett. Reproduced by permission of Jean-Paul Charnay.

Refrain from haste and you will avoid mistakes.

Going into battle with their head down makes men bold.

He who fears his enemy thereby fortifies the army of his soul.

Defeat softens resolve.

Ruses are more effective than action; a decision taken after careful consideration is better than an abrupt gesture.

Put out the opposite of what you have decided, and make it look as if you are going to do something different.

Put a quick end to the machinations of enemy spies.

Extreme endurance opens the door to victory.

Avoid consulting the ignorant or anyone likely to be influenced by personal ambition, or by fear.

Leave the enemy be until he moves on you.

Watch out for the opportunity to the point where you might be accused of slowness.

Procrastination when action is possible is a setback.

Being precipitate when you lack strength leads to collapse.

The slightest failing destroys the power of an army.

Win over hearts by telling them what they want to hear [?].

Be swifter to move on the enemy when he is advancing toward you [?].

Put men about whom you have suspicions in front; beware of the secret enemy.

Be watchful when you leave a post.

Do not let the danger that you have just escaped from make you shy of confronting another similar one.

Beware of the wiles of spies.

Obey the great man and the little man will obey you.

Beware of the woman who takes refuge under your protection.

Act as if all the people in your camp were your adversaries.

If you do the opposite of what pleases you, you will be getting it right.

Be conciliatory before things get too messy.

Put the bravest men in front of you.

Do not forget to set up an ambush at the moment of conflict; be on your guard against one set by the enemy in the same circumstances.

Do not be content with taking from the enemy as much as you give him.

Do not underestimate your enemy, or you will lower your guard.

Do not be contemptuous of your auxiliaries, or you will become an easy prey for your enemies.

If you show yourself greedy to your brothers, you are proportionately generous to your enemies.

Do not let defeated troops creep into your camp in secret.

Do not lead into battle men who do not fear you, have nothing to hope for from you, or do not need you.

Do not lead the pursuit yourself when you are on the track of the defeated.

Avoid turning aside to pillage before having fully dealt with the enemy.

Check your battle order when you make contact with the enemy.

Do not neglect your battle order at the moment of meeting: shifts in that order are one of the greatest causes of weakness.

Modify the conditions of *amàn* [giving mercy] when you seize a propitious opportunity against your opponent.

Fear discord among your companions.

Seek to win over the enemy leaders.

When you launch an attack, avoid being backed up against a river.

When you are at grips with the enemy, deem him capable of winning and exploiting your defeat, and then all you will have to do is gather up the booty.

Anyone escorting hostages is not safe.

Put off combat as long as possible—the only expense is in men; but if you cannot avoid it, ensure it happens at the end of the day.

Temporization is excellent, except when opportunity offers itself.

Often a stratagem is more effective than courage.

Often a word has undone an army.

Victory accompanies mature reflection.

Deliberation before destruction!

Assessment rather than illusion.

Mistrust is the wisest of your defenders and the most dependable of your troops, with the help of the Almighty!

Reflection on the possible consequences of an adventure before coming to grips is a sign of unease.

In combat, ignorance of the possible consequences gives more resolution than reasoning; reflection stiffens decision making before battle, but disturbs it during battle.

Conduct of Battle

Hostility and the enemy are like fire: if you master it from the beginning, it is easy to put it out, but if you allow it time to take hold, doing so becomes difficult, and the damage caused is multiplied. It is up to the determined judgment of the warrior not to scorn any enemy, however humble, nor to neglect him, however base he be. You are scorning an evil, which often gets worse.

The wisdom of Solomon son of David declared that war is sweet at the beginning, terrible in its ending: it is like fire, which although only a spark to start with becomes a blaze.

When you fight, do not be prodigal either with your blood or with your forces at the beginning of the affair, lest when it is at its height, you are already powerless and exhausted by fatigue. Do not join battle, even if you are sure of your strength, before knowing how you can get out of it. He who underestimates his enemy is deluded about his own strength, and that is already a weakness in itself. The resolute man is always on his guard against a sudden attack from his enemy if he is close by; against an incursion, if he is far away; against an ambush, if he shows himself; against a counterattack, if he flees. It has been said that the more you rely on your own strength and resources, the more you must be on your guard against the enemy, since the fact of being strong does not mean that you can neglect the precipice. Hudbat al-Adry said:

> I do not wish for war while it leaves me alone,
> but when I charge, I put everything into it!
> I do not rejoice excessively if fate smiles on me,
> but neither am I frightened by its overwhelming reverses.

Now in two verses of his great Book, God brought together all the directions relating to war when He said: "O you who believe! if you meet a small troop of infidels, be firm and call on God frequently, and perhaps you will attain felicity. Obey God and His Prophet and do not argue with each other, for you will weaken yourself and your power would leave you. Endure, for God is with the patient." . . .

. . . The ancients said: "To the great host, fear! To the few, victory!" God the Imposing said: "On the day of Honeyn, you will rejoice in your multitude, yet it has been of no help to you. The earth was not big enough to contain you, however large it might be, and here you have retraced your steps by fleeing!"

The truth is that the host always admires itself and that admiration leads to its ruin. The Prophet said: "The best number of companions is four; the best number of scouts is forty; the best detachment, four hundred; the best regiment, four thousand; an army of twelve thousand men will never be defeated for smallness, so long as those in it are well united." . . .

. . . According to the customs of all war leaders, the leaders of men and the bravest warriors are placed in the center of the battlefront, since if the two wings are broken, all eyes will turn to the center; if the leader's standard is flying in the wind there, and the drums are sounding, the center becomes a citadel for the two wings and the rallying point for all who are defeated. When the center is staved in, the two wings are destroyed. It is in this as with a bird in flight: if one of its wings is broken, it may nevertheless hope to get back to the nest in good time, while if it is struck in the head, both wings go down with it.

The defeat of both wings is of little importance if the center holds firm: stragglers endeavor to join the center and success goes with them. Conversely, it is rare that a force whose center has been defeated meets with success or reestablishes its situation, unless it be a feint on the part of the command, consisting in deliberately withdrawing troops from the center, leaving little there, until the enemy has penetrated it and become distracted with pillaging, when the two wings close up behind it. That is a stratagem that has been used by warriors. . . .

. . . But one of the most important ruses in fighting consists in ambush, and it is impossible to count how many soldiers have lost their lives or nicked their sabers in ambushes! Thus it is, for example, that the [front-rank] horseman, believing himself still far from the battle and the need to defend the honor [of his banner], happens to turn round and no longer sees any flag flying behind him or hears any drums sounding. Then he thinks of nothing but his own salvation. You must be very concerned about such situations: the very heart of war consists in using the brave, and putting heroes to the test. So bind the valiant, the daring, the true warriors, the intrepid to you, and you will have no reason to regret it, [even] if they are few in number. Do not forget what the poet says: "A thousand men are worth one and one is worth a thousand in such a difficult situation."

IBN KHALDUN
(1332–1406)

The peerless fourteenth-century political scientist, philosopher of history, and sociologist Ibn Khaldun was born in Tunis. As a young man, he lived at the court of the Marinid dynasty in Morocco and then served as chamberlain to the sultan of Tunis. Later he went to Granada in Spain. In 1378, after retiring to Tlemcen, he published his Kitab al-Ibar *(Universal History), in which he tentatively mapped out a cultural anthropology of Muslim civilization. Subsequently he taught in Cairo and was sent on a mission to Timur in Damascus.*

BEDOUINS AND SEDENTARY PEOPLE

Sedentary people have become used to laziness and ease. They are sunk in well-being and luxury. They have entrusted the defence of their property and their lives to the governor and ruler who rules them, and to the militia which has the task of guarding them. They find full assurance of safety in the walls that surround them, and the fortifications that protect them. No noise disturbs them, and no hunting occupies their time. They are carefree and trusting, and have ceased to carry weapons. Successive generations have grown up in this way of life. They have become like women and children, who depend upon the master of the house. Eventually, this has come to be a quality of character that replaces natural disposition.

The Bedouins, on the other hand, live apart from the community. They are alone in the country and remote from militias. They have no walls or gates. Therefore, they provide their own defence and do not entrust it to, or rely upon

From Ibn Khaldun, *The Muqaddimah: An Introduction to History,* translated by Franz Rosenthal, edited by N. J. Dawood (Princeton: Bollingen Series, Princeton University Press, 1967), 94–95. Copyright © 1967 by Princeton University Press. Reprinted by permission of Princeton University Press.

others for it. They always carry weapons. They watch carefully all sides of the road. They take hurried naps only when they are together in company or when they are in the saddle. They pay attention to the most distant barking or noise. They go alone into the desert, guided by their fortitude, putting their trust in themselves. Fortitude has become a character quality of theirs, and courage their nature. They use it whenever they are called upon or roused by an alarm. When sedentary people mix with them in the desert or associate with them on a journey, they depend on them. They cannot do anything for themselves without them. This is an observed fact. [Their dependence extends] even to knowledge of the country, the directions, watering places, and crossroads. Man is a child of the customs and the things he has become used to. He is not the product of his natural disposition and temperament. The conditions to which he has become accustomed, until they have become for him a quality of character and matters of habit and custom, have replaced his natural disposition. If one studies this in human beings, one will find much of it, and it will be found to be a correct observation. . . .

THE ADMIRALTY

The Byzantines, the European Christians, and the Goths lived on the northern shore of the Mediterranean. Most of their wars and most of their commerce [were] by sea. They were skilled in navigating [the Mediterranean] and in naval war. When these people coveted the possession of the southern shore, as the Byzantines [coveted] Ifriqiyah and as the Goths the Maghrib, they crossed over in their fleets and took possession of it. Thus, they achieved superiority over the Berbers and deprived them of their power. They had populous cities there, such as Carthage, Sbeitla, Jalula, Murnaq, Cherchel, and Tangier. The ancient master of Carthage used to fight the master of Rome and to send fleets loaded with armies and equipment to wage war against him. Thus, [seafaring] is a custom of the inhabitants of both shores of the Mediterranean, which was known in ancient as in modern times.

When the Muslims took possession of Egypt, 'Umar b. al-Khattab wrote to 'Amr b. al-'As and asked him to describe the sea to him. 'Amr replied: "The sea is a great creature upon which weak creatures ride—like worms upon a piece of wood." Thus, he recommended at that time that the Muslims be kept away from seafaring. No Arab travelled by sea save those who did so without

From Ibn Khaldun, *The Muqaddimah: An Introduction to History,* translated by Franz Rosenthal, edited by N. J. Dawood (Princeton: Bollingen Series, Princeton University Press, 1967), 208–13. Copyright © 1967 by Princeton University Press. Reprinted by permission of Princeton University Press.

'Umar's knowledge and were punished by him for it. Thus it remained until Mu'awiyah's reign. He permitted the Muslims to go by sea and to wage the holy war in ships. The reason for this was that on account of their Bedouin attitude, the Arabs were at first not skilled in navigation and seafaring, whereas the Byzantines and the European Christians, on account of their experience of the sea and the fact that they had grown up travelling in ships, were used to the sea and well trained in navigation.

The royal and governmental authority of the Arabs became firmly established and powerful at that time. The non-Arab nations became servants of the Arabs and were under their control. Every craftsman offered them his best services. They employed seagoing nations for their maritime needs. Their own experience of the sea and of navigation grew, and they turned out to be very expert. They wished to wage the holy war by sea. They constructed ships and galleys and loaded the fleet with men and weapons. They embarked the army and warriors to fight against the unbelievers across the sea. This was the special concern of the provinces and border regions closest to the shores of the Mediterranean, such as Syria, Ifriqiyah, the Maghrib, and Spain. The caliph 'Abd-al-Malik recommended to Hassan b. an-Nu'man, the governor of Ifriqiyah, that a shipyard be set up in Tunis for the production of maritime implements, as he was desirous of waging the holy war. From there, the conquest of Sicily was achieved.

Thereafter, under the [North African] Fatimids and the [Spanish] Umayyads, the fleets of Ifriqiyah and Spain constantly attacked each other's countries in civil war operations, and they thoroughly devastated the coastal regions. In the days of 'Abd-ar-Rahman an-Nasir, the Spanish fleet had grown to about two hundred vessels, and the African fleet to the same number, or close to it. The fleet admiral in Spain was Ibn Ramahis. The ports used by [the Spanish fleet] for docking and hoisting sail were Pechina and Almeria. The fleet was assembled from all the provinces. Each region where ships were used contributed one unit under the supervision of a commander in charge of everything connected with fighting, weapons and combatants alike. There also was a captain who directed the movement of the fleet, using either the wind or oars. He also directed its anchoring in port. When the whole fleet was assembled for a large-scale raid or for important government business, it was manned in its home port. The ruler loaded it with men from his best troops and clients, and placed them under the supervision of one commander, who belonged to the highest class of the people of his realm and to whom all were responsible. He then sent them off, and awaited their victorious return with booty.

During the time of the Muslim dynasty, the Muslims gained control over the whole Mediterranean. Their power and domination over it was vast. The Christian nations could do nothing against the Muslim fleets, anywhere in the Mediterranean. All the time, the Muslims rode its wave for conquest. There occurred then many well-known episodes of conquest and plunder. The Muslims took possession of all the islands that lie off its shores, such as Mallorca, Minorca, Ibiza, Sardinia, Sicily, Pantelleria, Malta, Crete, Cyprus, and of all the other [Mediterranean] provinces of the Byzantines and the European Christians. Abu l-Qasim ash-Shi'i and his descendants sent their fleets on raids against the island of Genoa from al-Mahdiyah. They returned victorious with booty. Mujahid al-'Amiri, the master of Denia, one of the *reyes de taifas,* conquered the island of Sardinia with his fleet in 1014–15. The Christians reconquered it in due course.

During all that time, the Muslims were gaining control over the largest part of the high sea. Their fleets kept coming and going, and the Muslim armies crossed the sea in ships from Sicily to the great mainland opposite Sicily, on the northern shore. They fell upon the European Christian rulers and made massacres in their realms. This happened in the days of the Banu Abi l-Husayn, the rulers of Sicily, who supported the Fatimid propaganda there. The Christian nations withdrew with their fleets to the northeastern side of the Mediterranean, to the coastal regions inhabited by the European Christians and the Slavs, and to the Aegean islands, and did not go beyond them. The Muslim fleet had pounced upon them as eagerly as lions upon their prey. They covered most of the surface of the Mediterranean with their equipment and numbers and travelled its lanes [on missions both] peaceful and warlike. Not a single Christian board floated on it.

Eventually, however, the Fatimid and Umayyad dynasties weakened and softened and were affected by infirmity. Then, the Christians reached out for the eastern islands of the Mediterranean, such as Sicily, Crete, and Malta, and took possession of them. They pressed on against the shores of Syria during this interval, and took possession of Tripoli, Ascalon, Tyre, and Acco. They gained control over all the seaports of Syria. They conquered Jerusalem and built there a church as an outward manifestation of their religion and worship. They deprived the Banu Khazrun of Tripolitania and [conquered] Gabès and Sfax, and imposed a poll tax upon their inhabitants. Then they took possession of al-Mahdiyah, the [original] seat of the Fatimids, and took it away from the descendants of Buluggin b. Ziri. In the fifth [eleventh] century, they had the lead in the Mediterranean. In Egypt and Syria, interest in the fleet weakened and eventually ceased to exist. Since then, they have shown no concern for the naval matters with which they had been so exceedingly concerned under the Fatimid dynasty. In consequence, the identity of the office of the admiralty was lost in those countries. It remained in Ifriqiyah and the Maghrib, but only there. At the present time, the western Mediterranean has large fleets and is very powerful. No enemy has trespassed on it or been able to do anything there.

In [Almoravid] times, the admirals of the fleet in [the West] were the Banu Maymun, chieftains from the peninsula of Cadiz, which they [later on] handed over to [the Almohad] 'Abd-al-Mu'min, to whom they paid obedience. Their fleets, from the countries on both shores, reached the number of one hundred.

In the twelfth century, the Almohad dynasty flourished and had possession of both shores. The Almohads organized their fleet in the most perfect manner ever known and on the largest scale ever observed. Their admiral was Ahmad as-Siqilli. The Christians had captured him, and he had grown up among them. The ruler of Sicily [Roger II] selected him for his service and employed him in it, but he died and was succeeded by his son, whose anger [Ahmad] somehow aroused. He feared for his life and went to Tunis, where he stayed with the chief of Tunis. He went on to Marrakech, and was received there by the caliph Yusuf al-'Ashri b. 'Abd-al-Mu'min with great kindness and honor. [The caliph] gave him many presents and entrusted him with command of his fleet. [As commander of the fleet] he went to wage the holy war against the Christian nations. He did noteworthy and memorable deeds during the Almohad dynasty.

In his time, the Muslim fleet was of a size and quality never, to our knowledge, attained before or since. When Salah-ad-din Yusuf b. Ayyub, the ruler of Egypt and Syria at this time, set out to recover the ports of Syria from the Christian nations and to cleanse Jerusalem of the abomination of unbelief and to rebuild it, one fleet of unbelievers after another came to the relief of the ports, from all the regions near Jerusalem which they controlled. They supported them with equipment and food. The fleet of Alexandria could not stand up against them. [The Christians] had had the upper hand in the eastern Mediterranean for so long, and they had numerous fleets there. The Muslims, on the other hand, had for a long time been too weak to offer them any resistance there, as we have mentioned. In this situation, Salah-ad-din sent 'Abd-al-Karim b. Munqidh, a member of the family of the Banu Munqidh, the rulers of Shayzar, as his ambassador to Ya'qub al-Mansur, the Almohad ruler of the Maghrib at that time, asking for the support of his fleets, to prevent the fleets of the unbelievers from achieving their desire of bringing relief to the Christians in the Syrian ports. Al-Mansur sent him back to Salah-ad-din, and did not comply with his request.

This is evidence that the ruler of the Maghrib alone possessed a fleet, that the Christians controlled the eastern Mediterranean, and that the dynasties in Egypt and Syria at that time and later were not interested in naval matters or in building up government fleets.

Ya'qub al-Mansur then died, and the Almohad dynasty became infirm. The Galician nations seized control of most of Spain. The Muslims sought refuge in the coastal region and took possession of the islands of the western

Mediterranean. They regained their former strength, and their power on the surface of the Mediterranean grew. Their fleets increased, and the strength of the Muslims became again equal to that of [the Christians]. This happened in the time of [the Marinid] Sultan, Abu l-Hasan, the Zanatah ruler in the Maghrib. When he desired to wage the holy war, his fleet was as well equipped and numerous as that of the Christians.

Then, the naval strength of the Muslims declined once more, because of the weakness of the ruling dynasty. Maritime habits were forgotten under the impact of the strong Bedouin attitude prevailing in the Maghrib, and as the result of the discontinuance of Spanish habits. The Christians resumed their former, famous maritime training, and [renewed] their constant activity in the Mediterranean and their experience with conditions there. [They again showed] their former superiority over others on the high seas and in [Mediterranean] shipping. The Muslims came to be strangers to the Mediterranean. The only exceptions are a few inhabitants of the coastal regions. They ought to have many assistants and supporters, or they ought to have support from the dynasties to enable them to recruit help and to work toward the goal of [increased seafaring activities].

The rank [of admiral] has been preserved to this day in the dynasties of the Maghrib. There, the identity [of the admiralty is still preserved], and how to take care of a fleet, how to build ships and navigate them, is known. Perhaps some political opportunity will arise in the coastal countries, and the Muslims will ask the wind to blow against unbelief and unbelievers. The inhabitants of the Maghrib have it on the authority of the books of predictions that the Muslims will yet have to make a successful attack against the Christians and conquer the lands of the European Christians beyond the sea. This, it is said, will take place by sea. . . .

METHODS OF WAGING WAR PRACTICED
BY THE VARIOUS NATIONS

Wars and different kinds of fighting have always occurred in the world since God created it. The origin of war is the desire of certain human beings to take revenge on others. Each [party] is supported by the people sharing in its group feeling. When they have sufficiently excited each other for the purpose and the two parties confront each other, one seeking revenge and the other trying to

From Ibn Khaldun, *The Muqaddimah: An Introduction to History,* translated by Franz Rosenthal, edited by N. J. Dawood (Princeton: Bollingen Series, Princeton University Press, 1967), 223–30. Copyright © 1967 by Princeton University Press. Reprinted by permission of Princeton University Press.

defend itself, there is war. It is something natural among human beings. No nation and no race [generation] is free from it.

The reason for such revenge is as a rule either jealousy and envy, or hostility, or zeal in behalf of God and His religion, or zeal in behalf of royal authority and the effort to found a kingdom.

The first [kind of war] usually occurs between neighbouring tribes and competing families.

The second [kind]—war caused by hostility—is usually found among savage nations living in the desert, such as the Arabs, the Turks, the Turkomans, the Kurds, and similar peoples. They earn their sustenance with their lances and their livelihood by depriving other people of their possessions. They declare war against those who defend their property against them. They have no further desire for rank and royal authority. Their minds and eyes are set only upon depriving other people of their possessions.

The third is the [kind] the religious law calls "the holy war."

The fourth [kind], finally, is dynastic war against seceders and those who refuse obedience.

These are the four kinds of war. The first two are unjust and lawless, the other two are holy and just wars.

Since the beginning of men's existence, war has been waged in the world in two ways. One is by advance in closed formation. The other is the technique of attack and withdrawal.

The advance in closed formation has been the technique of all the non-Arabs throughout their entire existence. The technique of attack and withdrawal has been that of the Arabs and of the Berbers of the Maghrib.

Fighting in closed formation is more steady and fierce than fighting with the technique of attack and withdrawal. That is because in fighting in closed formation, the lines are orderly and evenly arranged, like arrows or like rows of worshippers at prayers. People advanced in closed lines against the enemy. This makes for greater steadiness in assault and for better use of the proper tactics. It frightens the enemy more. A closed formation is like a long wall or a well-built castle which no one could hope to move.

It is obvious what great wisdom there is in requiring that the lines be kept steady and in forbidding anyone to fall back during an attack. Those who turn their backs to the enemy bring disorder into the line formation. They are guilty of the crime of causing a rout. Fighting in closed formation was more important [than any other kind] in the opinion of Muhammad.

Fighting with the technique of attack and withdrawal is not as fierce or as secure against the possibility of rout, as is fighting in closed formation, unless there is set up a steady line formation to the rear, to which the fighting men may fall back in attack and withdrawal throughout the fighting. Such a line formation would take the place of the closed formation.

The ancient dynasties had many soldiers and a vast realm. They subdivided their armies into smaller units. The reason for this was that their soldiers grew exceedingly numerous and were assembled from the most remote regions. This made it unavoidable that some of the soldiers would not know others, when they mingled on the field of battle and engaged the enemy in shooting and close fighting. It was feared lest, on such occasions, they would fall to fighting each other because of the existing confusion and their ignorance of each other. Therefore, they divided the armies into smaller units and put men who knew each other together. They arranged the units in an arrangement resembling the natural one of the four directions of the compass. The chief of all the armies, either the ruler himself or a general, was in the center. This arrangement was called "the battle order." It is mentioned in the history of the Persians, that of the Byzantines, and that of the [Umayyad and 'Abbasid) dynasties at the beginning of Islam. In front of the ruler stood one army with its own battle lines, its own general and its own flag. It was called "the advance guard." Then, to the right of the place where the ruler was, stood another army. It was called "the right flank." There was another army to the left, called "the left flank." Then, there was another army behind the main army, called "the rear guard." The ruler and his entourage stood at the middle of these four [armies]. The place where he was, was called the center. When this ingenious arrangement was completed— covering an area within the field of vision [of a single observer] or extending over a wider area but with at most one or two days' [journey] between each of the two armies, and utilizing the possibilities suggested by the greater or smaller number of soldiers—then, when the battle order was thus set up, the advance in closed formation could begin. This may be exemplified by the history of the [Muslim] conquests and the history of the [Umayyad and 'Abbasid] dynasties.

Much the same sort of arrangement was also to be found among the Spanish Umayyads. It is not known among us now, because we live in a time when dynasties possess small armies which cannot mistake each other on the field of battle. Most of the soldiers of both parties together could nowadays be assembled in a hamlet or a town. Everyone of them knows his comrade and calls him by his name and surname in the thick of battle. Therefore, this particular battle order can be dispensed with.

One of the techniques of the people who use the method of attack and withdrawal, is to set up, behind their armies, a [barricade] of solid objects and dumb animals to serve as a refuge for the cavalry during attack and withdrawal. It is intended to steady the fighters, so that they will fight more persistently and have a better chance of winning.

Those who fight in closed formation do the same, in order to increase their steadfastness and power. The Persians who fought in closed formation used to employ elephants in their wars. They made them carry wooden towers like castles, loaded with combatants, weapons, and flags. They disposed them in successive lines behind them in the thick of battle, as if they were fortresses. This fortified them psychologically and gave them added confidence.

In this connection, one may compare what happened at Kadisaya. On the third day, the Persians pressed the Muslims hard with [the elephants]. Eventually, some outstanding Arabs counterattacked, infiltrated among the elephants, and struck them on the trunk with their swords. [The elephants] fled and turned back to their stables in al-Mada'in. This paralysed the Persian camp, and they fled on the fourth day.

The Byzantines, the Gothic rulers in Spain, and most other non-Arab peoples used to employ thrones for the purpose of steadying the battle lines. A throne would be set up for the ruler in the thick of battle and surrounded by those of the ruler's servants, entourage, and soldiers who were thought to be willing to die for him. Flags were run up at the corners of the throne. A further wall of sharpshooters and foot soldiers was put around it. The throne thus assumed considerable dimensions. It became, for the fighters, a place to fall back upon and a refuge in attack and withdrawal. This was what the Persians did in the battle of Kadisaya. Rustum sat upon a throne that had been set up for him there. Finally, the Persian lines became disordered, and the Arabs penetrated to his throne. He abandoned it and went to the Euphrates, where he was killed.

The Arabs and most other Bedouin nations that move about and employ the technique of attack and withdrawal, dispose their camels and the pack animals carrying their litters in lines to steady the fighting men. [Such lines] become for them a place to fall back upon. Every nation that follows this technique can be observed to be more steady in battle and to be better protected against being surprised and routed. This is a well-attested fact, but it has been altogether neglected by the contemporary dynasties. Instead, they dispose the pack animals carrying their baggage and large tents behind them, as a rear guard. These animals cannot take the place of elephants and camels. Therefore, the armies are exposed to the danger of being routed, and they are always ready to flee in combat.

At the beginning of Islam, all battles were fought in closed formation, although the Arabs knew only the technique of attack and withdrawal. Two things at the beginning of Islam caused them to [fight in closed formation]. First, their enemies fought in closed formation, and they were thus forced to fight them in the same way. Second, they were willing to die in the holy war, because they wished to prove their endurance and were very firm in their belief. Now, the closed formation is the fighting technique most suitable for one willing to die.

When luxury penetrated the various dynasties, the use of the rally line behind the fighters was forgotten. This was because when they were Bedouins and lived in tents, they had many camels, and the women and children lived in camp with them. Then they achieved royal luxury and became used to living in palaces and in a sedentary environment and they abandoned the ways of the desert and waste regions. At that time, they forgot the period of camels and litters, and it was difficult for them to use them. When they travelled, they left their women behind. Royal authority and luxury caused them to use tents both large and small. They restricted themselves to pack animals carrying baggage and tents. They used these things to form their [protective] line in war. It was by no means sufficient. These things, unlike one's own family and property, do not inspire any willingness to die. People, therefore, have little endurance. The turmoil of the battle frightens them, and their lines crumble.

We have mentioned the strength that a line formation behind the army gives to the fighters who use the technique of attack and withdrawal. Therefore the Maghribi rulers have come to employ groups of European Christians in their army, and they are the only ones to have done that, for their compatriots know only the technique of attack and withdrawal. The position of the ruler is strengthened by establishing a line formation in support of the fighting men ahead of it. The men in such a line formation must be people who are used to hold firm in closed formation. If not, they will run away like the men who use the technique of attack and withdrawal, and, when they run away, the ruler and the army will be routed. Therefore, the rulers of the Maghrib had to use soldiers from a nation used to hold firm in closed formation. That nation was the European Christians. The Maghribi rulers do that despite the fact that it means utilizing the aid of unbelievers. They fear that their own line formation might run away, and [they know that] the European Christians know only how to hold firm, because it is their custom to fight in closed formation. They are, therefore, more suitable for the purpose than others. However, the Maghribi rulers employ [such European Christians] only in wars against Arab and Berber nations, in order to force them into submission. They do not use them for the holy war, because they are afraid that they might take sides against the Muslims. Such is the situation in the Maghrib at this time.

We hear that the fighting [technique] of the contemporary Turkish nations is the shooting of arrows. Their battle order consists of a line formation. They divide their army into three lines, one placed behind the other. They dismount from their horses, empty their quivers on the ground in front of them, and then shoot from a sitting position. Each line protects the one ahead of it against being overrun by the enemy, until victory is assured for one party. This is a very good and remarkable battle order.

In war, the ancients followed the method of digging trenches around their camps when they were about to attack, because they were afraid of treacherous night attacks and assaults by night upon the camp, since darkness and wildness multiply fear. Under such conditions, the soldiers might seek refuge in flight and would find in the darkness a psychological protection against the shame of [fleeing]. If all the soldiers were to do the same, the camp would be disorganized, and there would be a rout. Therefore, they were accustomed to dig trenches around the camp. They set up their tents and made trenches all around them on every side, lest the enemy be able to get through them in a night attack, in which case they would abandon each other.

Dynasties were able to do such things involving large concentrations of manpower, wherever they settled, because civilization was prosperous and royal authority impressive. But when civilization was ruined, and [strong dynasties] were succeeded by weak dynasties with few soldiers and no workers, the thing was altogether forgotten, as if it had never been.

One should think of the admonitions and encouragement that 'Ali gave his men on the day of Siffin. One will find in them a good deal of military knowledge. No one had better insight into military matters than 'Ali. He said in one of his speeches: "Straighten out your lines like a strongly constructed building.

"Place the armed men in front, and those who are not armed in the rear.

"Bite on your molars. This makes it harder for sword blows to harm the head.

"Keep something wrapped around the tips of your spears. This preserves the sharpness of their points.

"Keep your eyes down. This keeps the soul more concentrated and gives greater peace to the heart.

"Do not hold your flags inclined and do not remove them. Place them in the hands only of those among you who are brave.

"Call upon truth and endurance for aid, for 'after endurance there is victory'."

There is no certainty of victory in war, even when the equipment and the numerical [superiority] that cause victory exist. Victory and superiority in war come from luck and chance. This is explained by the fact that the causes of superiority are, as a rule, a combination of several factors. There are external factors, such as the number of soldiers, the perfection and good quality of weapons, the number of brave men, [skillful] arrangement of the line formation, the proper tactics, and similar things. Then, there are hidden factors.

These may be the result of human trickery, such as spreading alarming news and rumors to cause defections [in the ranks of the enemy]; occupying high points, so that one is able to attack from above, which surprises those below and causes them to abandon each other; hiding in thickets or depressions and concealing oneself from the enemy in rocky terrain, so that one's own armies suddenly appear when [the enemy] is in a precarious situation, and he must then flee to safety [instead of defending himself], and similar things. These hidden factors may also be celestial matters, which man has no power to produce for himself. They affect people psychologically, and thus generate fear in them. They cause confusion in the centers of armies, and there are routs. Routs very often are the result of hidden causes, because both parties make much use of [the opportunities offered by] them in their desire for victory. One of them must by necessity be successful in their use. Muhammad said: "War is trickery." An Arab proverb says: "Many a trick is worth more than a tribe."

It is thus clear that superiority in war is, as a rule, the result of hidden causes, not of external ones. The occurrence of opportunities as the result of hidden causes is what is meant by the word "luck." This explains Muhammad's victory with small numbers over the polytheists during his lifetime, and the victories of the Muslims during the Muslim conquests after Muhammad's death. Terror in the hearts of their enemies was why there were so many routs during the Muslim conquests, but it was a factor concealed from men's eyes.

At-Turtushi mentions that one of the reasons for victory in war is that one side may have a larger number of brave and famous knights than the other. For instance, one side may have ten or twenty famous heroes, and the other only eight or sixteen. The side that has more, even if only one more, will be victorious. He states this very emphatically. He is referring to the external causes we have mentioned before, but he is not right. What is the fact proven to make for superiority is the situation with regard to group feeling. If one side has a group feeling comprising all, while the other side is made up of numerous different groups, and if both sides are approximately the same in numbers, then the side with a united group feeling is stronger than, and superior to, the side that is made up of several different groups.

PART 7

PERSIA

KAI KA'US IBN ISKANDAR
(c. 1020–1085)

Kai Ka'us ibn Iskandar came from Guilan. He wrote the Qabus Namah
*(Mirror for the Princes) for his son in the middle of the eleventh century. Its
forty-four chapters cover a wide range of topics, with the emphasis on moral
precepts and rules of conduct. The prince for whom the book was written was
the last of his dynasty. In 1090, after a seven-year reign, he was assassinated
on the orders of Hasan Ibn al-Sabbah, the Old Man of the Mountain, leader
of the Order of the Assassins.*

ON GIVING BATTLE TO AN ENEMY

Once you engage in battle it is inexcusable to display any sloth or hesitation;
you must breakfast on the enemy before he dines on you. When you have arrived in the midst of the fray, be remiss in nothing but take no precautions for
your own life; he that is destined to sleep in the grave will never again sleep at
home. This I have expressed in the following quatrain:

> Though I should have a lion for foe I'd dare,
> Were he unseen or seen, my sword to bare,
>   Who's destined friendless in the tomb to lie,
> Can never sleep at home in friendship's care.

In the course of the battle, as long as you are able to advance a foot, never
take a step backward. Even when you are hemmed in amongst the enemy,
never cease the struggle; you may with your bare fist knock the enemy out of
the fight. And as long as they see activity, proving you to be in good fettle, they
will stand in awe of you. At a time like this reconcile your heart with death.

From Kai Ka'us ibn Iskandar, *A Mirror for the Princes,* translated by Reuben Levy (New York:
Dutton, 1951), 219–21. Translation copyright. Used by permission of the publisher, Dutton, an imprint of New American Library, a division of Penguin Books USA Inc.

[429]

Under no conditions be afraid, but be bold; for a short blade becomes elongated [grows longer] in the hands of the brave. Be remiss in nothing whilst you are in the battle, for if any mark of fear or cowardice is revealed in you, even if you had a thousand lives you would be unable to save a single one, and the humblest person could overwhelm you. Cowardice results either in your being slain or in the besmirching of your name. Once you become notorious amongst men for poltroonery and for a display of sloth and feebleness in such circumstances as these, and for failing your comrades, you will be disgraced amongst your friends and associates. Neither repute nor comfort will be left to you; amongst your contemporaries and companions you will be stricken with shame. Death is preferable to such a life, and it is far better to die in good odour than to spend one's life in disrepute.

Do not be over-hasty in shedding innocent blood, and regard no killing of Muslims to be lawful, unless they are brigands, thieves and grave-robbers or such whose execution is demanded by the law. Torment in both worlds is inflicted for the shedding of innocent blood; you will find retribution for it on the Day of Resurrection, but also in this world your name will be besmirched. None of your subjects will trust you, those who serve you will despair of reward from you, your people will conceive hatred for you and will in their hearts become your enemies. Retribution for the shedding of innocent blood will assuredly not be confined to the next world, for I have read in books and ascertained by experience that the punishment for evil may also be inflicted on men even in this world. When they are gone, even if their own stars chance to be favourable, misfortune will befall their children. Therefore spare yourself and your offspring by shedding no innocent blood.

Yet do not neglect your duty where blood must rightfully be shed, for the general welfare demands it and out of remissness evil is born. It is told of my grandfather Shams al-Ma'ali that he was a bloodthirsty man, never able to forgive an offence. He was a cruel man, and because of his cruelty his troops determined upon seeking vengeance. They accordingly entered into a conspiracy with my uncle, Falak al-Ma'ali, who came and seized his father, Shams al-Ma'ali, being compelled to that action by the army, which threatened to transfer the kingdom to a stranger if he did not agree to their terms. Realising that the sovereignty would thereby be lost to his family, he was thus driven by force to take the course he did.

Now comes the point of my story. The king, being seized and fettered, was placed in a palanquin and sent to the fort of Chanashak [in Astarabad]. Amongst the men charged with his custody was one called 'Abd Allah the Dromedary-guard. As they were proceeding on the way Shams al-Ma'ali asked this man, "Have you any knowledge of the person who directed this affair and how it was planned; for here is a matter about which, though of great importance, I could gather no information?" "Such-and-such persons did it," 'Abd Allah replied, mentioning five generals, "and they misled the army. I myself was at the center of the affair; I made them all swear an oath [of loyalty], and it was I who brought the matter to this stage. But do not hold me answerable for it. Blame yourself, because all this has come about through your many killings and not because the army has changed its character."

Shams al-Ma'ali's answer was that the other was mistaken. "This business has come upon me," he said, "through my failure to kill. If the possibility of such an affair had ever occurred to my mind, I should undoubtedly have slain you, together with the other five men. Had I done so, my affairs would have prospered and I should now have been in a place of security."

I relate this story to prevent you from being in any degree careless over the duties of justice and governmental control and from treating over-lightly anything essential to these matters.

(Do not practise castration to procure eunuchs; it is the equivalent of shedding blood, because, for the sake of your own lusts, you lessen the number of Muslim offspring in the world, and there can be no greater wrong than that. If you need a eunuch, acquire someone who has castrated himself; the benefit of his action will be yours, the sin will be another's and you will be relieved of the consequences of it.)

Howbeit, in the matter of your conduct in battle, behave as I have advised; do not spare yourself, for unless you expose your body to be meat for dogs how shall you acquire yourself a lion's name? Strive therefore to get fame and bread, and, having got them, endeavour to acquire wealth. When you have that, guard it and expend it only by measure. . . .

THE ART OF CONTROLLING AN ARMED FORCE

My son, if you come to have control of the army, deal generously both with your troops and the people, doing good for your own part and desiring it on your master's part. Be ever alert and acquire full knowledge of the art of leading troops and setting up battle-array. On the day when battle is to take place, appoint to the right and left of the line commanders who have been tried in war and possess experience of the world; station your most valorous commander and the choicest troops on the flank, where they are the main support of the force.

From Kai Ka'us ibn Iskandar, *A Mirror for the Princes,* translated by Reuben Levy (New York: Dutton, 1951), 219–21. Translation copyright. Used by permission of the publisher, Dutton, an imprint of New American Library, a division of Penguin Books USA Inc.

However weak the enemy may be, attribute no weakness to him and take as great precautions with him as you would with a powerful foe. Make no such display of valour in battle as will throw your forces to the winds; but, also, do not be so pusillanimous that by your cowardice you overthrow your own army. Never neglect to send out spies and to inform yourself of the dispositions of the enemy; let there be no neglect either by day or night in putting out sentinels.

On the day of battle, when the two armies confront each other, be of cheerful countenance and say to your own army, "Who may these be? What roots have they? Let us at once destroy them!" Do not launch your army all together. Send it forward standard by standard [of foot] and troop by troop of horse, assigning each separate commander and captain to his position, telling such a one to go to such-and-such a position with his men. Keep in front of you those that are to bear the brunt of the fighting and pay special regard to anyone who fights valiantly, overthrows or wounds one of the enemy, captures a horseman, seizes a horse or performs any other laudable deed. Reward such a man for his services by presentation of a robe of honour and increasing his pay; do not spare money at such a time. And in general do not be mean-spirited, that you may swiftly attain your object; for each of your troopers, seeing your open-handedness, will have his appetite for battle aroused and none will falter, and thus victory will be won as you desire.

If your objective is gained by the attack you launch, well and good. But do not then act with haste; remain in your place without further exerting yourself. Should the battle bear heavily on your commanders, so that danger threatens, then, when the fighting reaches you, act as the occasion demands and refuse to let the thought of defeat enter your mind. Fight to the death; he that reconciles his heart with death and can detach his mind from thought of life will not by any trivial means be dislodged from his position.

When you have won the victory, do not pursue too far after the defeated foeman, because many misunderstandings happen on the return and it becomes impossible to know how matters stand. That great emir, my father (Allah [be] compassionate [to] him!), never went in pursuit of a defeated enemy. He used to say that when defeated men become desperate they will renounce life and make a stand. If the enemy counter-attacks it is better not to persist against him, lest any mistake occur.

When you go to war, you will inevitably see with the eyes in your head the outward aspect of the situation and the way into the battle. But with the eye of the mind you must likewise have regard to the way by which you are to emerge, for it may be different from what you desire. Further, there is this one matter which you must not forget (even though I have spoken of it elsewhere, I repeat it): if, in the course of the battle your situation becomes difficult, let us suppose, and if one pace to the rear of you there is an easier position, beware against taking that one pace. If you retreat by a single span, you will be overthrown. Exert yourself always to advance from your position and never give way a single pace.

It is a matter of necessity that your troops should at all times be under an oath (sworn by your life and head) of loyalty to you, and you, for your part, must be generous towards your troops. If you cannot make lavish provision beforehand of robes of honour and presents, at all events allow yourself no niggardliness in promises, and take not a mouthful of bread or a cup of wine except in company with your troops; for what a trifle of food will accomplish cannot be accomplished by gold or silver or robes of honour. Keep your troops always contented and if you wish them not to grudge their lives on your behalf do not grudge them food.

Although all happenings are bound up with the destiny decreed by Allah, yet do you fulfil the obligation of planning in the manner most appropriate; what is destined will come about independently of you.

Therefore, if it should come about that God (May he be exalted!) has compassion upon you and bears you into the kingship, have a care for the rules of kingship and be noble of spirit after the fashion which I shall now describe.

NIZAM AL-MULK
(1018–1092)

*Abu Hassan Ali, Nizam al-Mulk, the founder of the university of Baghdad,
is typical of the Iranian scholars, or* diwani, *who by putting their knowledge
at the disposal of the Seljuk Turks succeeded in organizing a vast empire that
went beyond the historic borders of Iran and for centuries was responsible for
spreading Iranian traditions and methods of government all over the Middle
East. The eleventh century was a time of great changes for the region: the
Turks irrupted into Muslim lands and began to take charge of the fate of
Islam; Iran disengaged itself from the grip of Arabism, but Sunnism recovered
strongly against Shi'ism, thanks to the sword of the new Turkish converts.*

*In 1086, at the request of Sultan Malik Shah (r. 1072–92), Nizam
al-Mulk compiled the* Siyasat namah *(Book of Government), which
subsequently became the basic training manual for every administrator in
Iran and the Ottoman empire, as well as in Moghul India, until the coming
of Western political and administrative sciences. Nizam al-Mulk advocated
the political and religious reassertion of Sunnism. He was murdered in 1092
by the Ismailis.*

THE BOOK OF GOVERNMENT

On the Turn of Fortune's Wheel and in Praise of the Master
of the World—May Allah Confirm his Sovereignty

In every age and time God (be He exalted) chooses one member of the human
race and, having endowed him with goodly and kingly virtues, entrusts him
with the interests of the world and the well-being of His servants; He charges
that person to close the doors of corruption, confusion and discord, and He

From Nizam al-Mulk, *The Book of Government, or, Rules for Kings*, translated by Hubert Darke
(London and Boston: Routledge & Kegan Paul, 1978), 9, 74–75, 93–101, 121. Copyright © 1960, 1978
by Routledge and Kegan Paul. Reproduced by permission of Routledge and Kegan Paul Ltd.

[434]

imparts to him such dignity and majesty in the eyes and hearts of men, that under his just rule they may live their lives in constant security and ever wish for his reign to continue.

Whenever—Allah be our refuge!—there occurs any disobedience or disregard of divine laws on the part of His servants, or any failure in devotion and attention to the commands of The Truth (be He exalted), and He wishes to chasten them and make them taste the retribution for their deeds—may God not deal us such a fate, and keep us far from such a calamity!—verily the wrath of The Truth overtakes those people and He forsakes them for the vileness of their disobedience; kingship disappears altogether, opposing swords are drawn, blood is shed, and whoever has the stronger hand does whatever he wishes, until those sinners are all destroyed in tumults and bloodshed, and the world becomes free and clear of them; and through the wickedness of such sinners many innocent persons too perish in the tumults; just as, by analogy, when a reed-bed catches fire every dry particle is consumed and much wet stuff is burnt also, because it is near to that which is dry.

Then by divine decree one human being acquires some prosperity and power, and according to his deserts The Truth bestows good fortune upon him and gives him wit and wisdom, wherewith he may employ his subordinates every one according to his merits and confer upon each a dignity and a station proportionate to his powers. He selects ministers and their functionaries from among the people, and giving a rank and post to each, he relies upon them for the efficient conduct of affairs spiritual and temporal. . . .

On Sending Pages from the Court upon Important Business

Pages are frequently sent out from the court, some at the king's behest, mostly not. They are apt to cause trouble to the people and extort money from them. [Supposing there is] a case involving a sum of two hundred dinars, a page goes out and takes five hundred as a perquisite; this causes extreme embarrassment and poverty to the people. Pages should not be sent unless there is an urgent matter, and if they are sent it should be only at the Sublime Command; and they must be given to understand the exact amount due, and they are not to take any more than this by way of perquisite. Then everything will be in order.

On Sending Spies and Using Them for the Good of the Country and the People

Spies must constantly go out to the limits of the kingdom in the guise of merchants, travellers, sufis, pedlars, and mendicants, and bring back reports of everything they hear, so that no matters of any kind remain concealed, and if anything [untoward] happens it can in due course be remedied. In the past it has often happened that governors, assignees, officers and army-commanders have planned rebellion and resistance, and plotted mischief against the king; but spies forestalled them and informed the king, who was thus enabled to set out immediately with all speed and, coming upon them unawares, to strike them down and frustrate their plans; and if any foreign king or army was preparing to attack the country, the spies informed the king, and he took action and repelled them. . . .

Concerning Solitaries and Their Equipment
and Administration

There should be kept at the court two hundred men called solitaries, men chosen for good appearance and stature as well as for great manliness and bravery. A hundred of them should be Khurasani and a hundred from Dailam and their duty is to be in constant attendance upon the king both at home and abroad. They are permanently attached to the court and must be finely attired. Two hundred sets of weapons are to be kept ready for them and issued to them when duty commences and withdrawn when they are dismissed. Of those weapons twenty swordbelts and twenty shields should be [decorated] with gold, and a hundred and eighty belts and shields with silver, together with pikestaffs. They should be paid suitably high clothing allowances in addition to their regular pay. There should be a sergeant to every fifty men and his job is to know all about his men and to give them their orders. They must all be good horsemen and be provided with the necessary trappings, so that upon all important occasions they will not fail to perform their special functions.

The names of four thousand unmounted men of all races should always be kept on the rolls. One thousand picked men are exclusively for the king and the three thousand are to be attached to the retinues of governors and army-commanders so as to be ready for any emergency.

On the Provision and Use of Jeweled Weapons

Twenty special sets of arms, studded with gold, jewels and other ornaments, must always be kept ready and stored at the treasury, so that on feast days and whenever ambassadors arrive from distant parts of the world, twenty pages finely attired can take these weapons and stand round the throne. And although our sovereign (praise be to Allah The Mighty) has attained such a lofty state that he can do without such ceremonies, nevertheless the pomp and circumstance of the kingdom and kingship must be maintained, for every king's elegance and finery must accord with his exalted position and lofty ambition. Today there is no king on earth greater than the Master of the World (may Allah perpetuate his reign) and there is no kingdom more vast than his. So it is fitting that wherever other kings possess one of a thing, our sovereign should have ten; where they have ten he should have a hundred, for he has at his command all spiritual and material resources, coupled with a sound judgment. In fact he lacks nothing of majesty and dominion.

Concerning Ambassadors and Their Treatment

When ambassadors come from foreign countries nobody is aware of their movements until they actually arrive at the city gates; and nobody makes any preparation for them or gives them anything; and they will surely attribute this to our negligence and indifference. So officers at the frontiers must be told that whenever anyone approaches their stations they should at once despatch a rider [to the capital] and report who it is who is coming, how many men there are with him, mounted and unmounted, how much baggage and equipment he has, and what is his business. A trustworthy person must be appointed to accompany them and conduct them to the nearest big city; there he will hand them over to another agent who will likewise go with them to the next city or district, and so on until they reach the court. Whenever they arrive at a place where there is cultivation, it must be a standing order that officers, tax-collectors and assignees should give them hospitality at every stopping place and entertain them well so that they depart satisfied. When they return, the same procedure is to be followed. Whatever treatment is given to an ambassador, whether good or bad, it is as if it were done to the very king who sent him; and kings have always shewn the greatest respect to one another and treated envoys well, for by this their own dignity has been enhanced not diminished. And if at any time there has been disagreement or estrangement between kings, ambassadors have still come and gone as occasion requires, and discharged their missions according to their instructions; never have they been molested or treated with less than usual courtesy. Such a thing would be disgraceful, as God (to Him be power and glory) says in His incontrovertible book [Koran 24.53], "The messenger has only to deliver the message plainly." (This means that the messenger has only to convey the outward purport.)

It should also be realized that when kings send ambassadors to one another their purpose is not merely the message or the letter which they communicate openly, but secretly they have a hundred other points and objects in view. In fact they want to know about the state of roads, mountain-passes and rivers, to see whether an army can pass or not; where fodder is available and where not; who are the officers in every place; what is the size of that king's army and how well it is armed and equipped; what is the standard of his table and his company; what is the organization and etiquette of his court and audience-hall; does he play polo and hunt; what are his qualities and manners, his designs and intentions, his appearance and bearing; is he cruel or just, old or young; is his country flourishing or decaying; are his troops contented or complaining; are the peasants rich or poor; is he avaricious or generous; is he negligent in affairs; is his vizier competent, religious and righteous or the reverse; are his generals experienced and battle-tried or not; are his boon-companions polite and worthy; what are his likes and dislikes; in his cups is he jovial and good-natured or not; is he strict in religious matters and does he shew magnanimity and mercy or is he careless and slack; does he incline more to jesting or to gravity; and does he prefer boys or women. So that, if at any time they want to win over that king, or oppose his designs or criticize his faults, being informed of all his affairs they can think out their plan of campaign, and knowing what to do in all circumstances, they can take effective action. . . .

. . . ambassadors are generally censorious and always on the look out to see what faults there are in kingdom and kingship, and what virtues; then next time they will convey censure and criticism of those things from their kings. With this in mind past kings, when they have been intelligent and alert, have always refined their manners, and adopted good customs, and employed worthy men of pure faith, lest anyone should find fault with them.

For an embassy a man is required who has served kings, who is bold in speaking, who has travelled widely, who has a portion of every branch of learning, who is retentive of memory and farseeing, who is tall and handsome, and if he is old and wise, that is better. If a boon-companion is sent as an envoy he will be more reliable; and if a man is sent who is brave and manly, skilled in arms and horsemanship, and renowned as a duellist, it will be extremely good, for he will shew the world that our men are like him; and if an ambassador be a man of noble family that will be good too, for they will have respect for his ancestry and not do him any mischief; and he should not be a wine-bibber, a buffoon, a gambler, a babbler or a simpleton. Very often kings have sent envoys bearing gifts of money and valuables and sued for peace and shewn themselves weak and submissive; after giving this illusion they have followed up by sending prepared troops and picked men in to the attack and defeating the enemy. The conduct and good sense of an ambassador are a guide to the conduct, wisdom, judgment and greatness of his king. . . .

On Settling the Dues of All the Army

The troops must receive their pay regularly. Those who are assignees of course have their salaries to hand independently as assigned; but in the case of pages who are not fit for holding assignments, their pay must be made available. When the amount required has been worked out according to the number of troops, the money should be put into a special fund until the whole sum is in hand, and it must always be paid to them at the proper time. Alternatively the king may summon the men before him twice a year, and command that they be paid, not in such a way that the task be delegated to the treasury and they receive their money from there without seeing the king; rather the king should with his own hands put it into their hands (and skirts), for this increases their feelings of affection and attachment, so that they will strive more eagerly and steadfastly to perform their duties in war and peace.

The system of the kings of old was that they did not give assignments: every soldier was paid by the treasury four times a year in cash according to his rank, and they were always well supplied and provisioned, and whatever the emergency 2,000 or 20,000 horsemen instantly mounted and set out to meet it.

On Having Troops of Various Races

When troops are all of one race dangers arise; they lack zeal and they are apt to be disorderly. It is necessary that they should be of different races. Two thousand Dailamites and Khurasanis should be stationed at the court. Those that exist at present should be retained and the remainder be levied; and if some of these are from Gurjistan [Georgia] and Shabankara (in Pars), it will be suitable because men of these races are also good.

It was the custom of Sultan Mahmud to have troops of various races such as Turks, Khurasanis, Arabs, Hindus, men of Ghur and Dailam. When he was on an expedition, every night he used to detail several men of each group to go on guard and allotted each group their station; and for fear of one another no group dared to move from their places; they kept watch until daybreak in competition with one another and did not go to sleep. And when it was the day of battle, each race strove to preserve their name and honour, and fought all the more zealously lest anyone should say that such-and-such race showed slackness in battle. Thus all races endeavoured to surpass one another.

Since the fighting men were organized on this basis they were all valiant and intrepid. Consequently once they had taken up their arms they did not retreat one pace until they had defeated the enemy.

When once or twice an army has waxed valiant and gained victory over the enemy, thereafter a mere hundred of their horsemen will be a match for a thousand of the enemy and no force will ever again be able to oppose that triumphant army and all the armies of neighbouring countries will fear that king and submit to him. . . .

On Preparing Arms and Equipment
for Wars and Expeditions

Senior officers who receive large allowances must be told to have arms and equipment ready for war and to buy pages, for their grandeur and splendour consist in these things, not in the magnificence of their household decorations and furniture. The man who has more of the former will be more acceptable in the sight of the king, and will acquire greater prestige and power among his equals and his subordinates.

AL-RAWANDI
(thirteenth century)

Mohammad b. Ali b. Soleyman al-Rawandi, the historian of the Seljuks, wrote the Rahat al-Sadur *at the beginning of the thirteenth century at the court of the Seljuk sultan in Konya.*

CONDUCT OF WAR, CONDUCT OF BATTLE

If the king is not well informed about the enemy's affairs, he will be unable to deal with him. He must know the enemy's situation in detail, as well as he knows his own. A chess player must watch his opponent's game as much as his own. The reasons for and causes of a victory are numerous:

1. Hope of booty that takes hold of the army.
2. Hatred of the enemy, which inflames the heart of the fighter.
3. Fear and terror sown in the ranks of the enemy.
4. Hope of peace, which weakens their determination to fight us and reduces their hatred of us.
5. A well-informed and eloquent ambassador who goes to the enemy and, if he finds him disposed to compromise, unknown to the two armies, offers him peace.

Thus he undermines the enemy's determination and when he lets his guard fall and neglects his preparations, then the ambassador will be better able to learn his secrets. The envoy must not be easygoing, confused, a drunkard or covetous. He must be pious, eloquent, and faithful to the king. He must inform himself of the size of the enemy army, its strengths and weaknesses, its expenses and reserves. He must be able to inspire fear in the enemy by inter-

From Mohammad b. Ali b. Soleyman al-Rawandi, *Rahat al-sadur va ayat al sorure,* edited by M. Minawi (Tehran, 1954), translated by Ahmad Salamatian. Translated from the French by A. M. Berrett.

[441]

spersing his conversation with remarks such as "Our king says: 'I do not want to be the cause of the spilling of blood, I do not know who is the instigator of this idea that I am belligerent. The great sages have said: "Wicked is he who makes the enemy a friend and not he who makes his friend into an enemy." I am one of those whom one must not have as an enemy, as I have a victorious army, an immense fortune, well-informed ministers, and powerful warriors.'" Then if the enemy gets upset and loses patience on hearing such comments, do not be afraid of his ruses and skill. For anger clouds the intelligence, and it is intelligence that wins wars. Do not fear numbers, the great sages have said: "Fear the enemy that is united and not the enemy that is numerous."

... The dispositions of the battle lines on the day of confrontation are of several sorts. In each region and at each place, forces must be deployed adequately. The order of battle is generally of two sorts: compact or dispersed. Compact alignment can take only three forms: straight, curved, and triangular. All three need a left, a center, a right, and wings. Dispersed order is only possible when your army is made up of well-armed cavalry and the terrain is extensive enough for the men to be able to maneuver detachment by detachment. Each detachment must form into a triangle with three sides, one of which must always be the pivot of the two others that are fighting. The configuration of the battlefield and the disposition of the men must be such that the combatants can clearly see their companions and their enemy. It is by watching the enemy's maneuvers and the weapons he is using that one can see how and with what weapons to face him. The army must use its weapons skillfully and the men must already have had intensive training in the use of various weapons. If the enemy army is rather made up of infantry and the king's army has more horsemen, a large spread-out battlefield must be chosen. A curved alignment must be adopted, and at the two ends of the line, two detachments must be placed at a distance. They will be the pillars of the line, and by their movement they will prevent the enemy infantry from moving out to the left or right, both during the attack and when your army withdraws and at the time of their maneuvering for the general assault.

Conversely, if the enemy has more horsemen, a narrow terrain with fixed positions must be chosen. The infantry must be put on the right and left, with the cavalry behind it. A straight line must be formed, and the infantry must be prevented from chasing after the enemy horsemen. Detachments of infantry must be placed on guard to stop surprise attacks by horsemen to the right and left. If you want to launch a general assault, you must send your own horsemen to attack the right wing and the left wing of the enemy ranks and have the infantry advance in successive waves until the enemy's positions are taken. If the terrain is not suitable to set up fixed positions there, if it is flat and desert-like, then form the ranks in a circle and place the hardened fighters on the outside and keep the less experienced inside. In such a situation, success will only be a miracle from heaven. It is better to accept peace.

If the king's army is made up of horsemen and the enemy's of infantrymen, then you must disperse in small detachments with hardened fighters at their head. The camp must be set up away from the enemy lines and every precaution taken against attacks by night. Permanent harassment from all sides at once must be organized so as to prevent the enemy getting any rest, so that the exhausted infantrymen are also terrorized by the frequency and permanence of the attacks. If the two armies are made up of horsemen or infantrymen, then it is necessary to adapt to the terrain and form ranks in such a way as to be able to resist the enemy attacks and organize your own attacks. Sufficient forces must always be kept in the center to be able to reinforce the right or the left. Detachments of warriors must always be held in reserve to be sent immediately to points where the line shows signs of weakness, so as to prevent it being pierced. If there is a famous champion in the enemy army, several fighters must be assigned to him, who must not let him out of their sight and must go ahead of him wherever he is heading in the battle. In that way the impression of his power in the eyes of the army will be counterbalanced.

Experience has shown that if the king is patient and far-sighted, the army loyal, united, and contented, and the terrain well chosen, victory can be expected from God, who is just, even if the enemy is superior in numbers.

NASIR AL-DIN AL-TUSI
(1201–1274)

The Shi'ite Nasir al-Din al-Tusi was the wazir *of the Mongol khan Hülegü,
who put an effective end to the Abbasid caliphate with the conquest and sack
of Baghdad in 1258. His book on ethics, the* Akhlaq-i Nasiri, *was completed
at the end of the thirteenth century and is a reflection on the nature of
kingship and its organization.*

THE USE OF WAR

The prince must keep his secrets well so as to safeguard his room for maneuver and be able to avoid contradiction. If the enemy gets to know his secrets,
he must at once take appropriate countermeasures. . . . His spies and informers must constantly inform themselves about all that is covered by the seal of
secrecy, especially as regards enemies and their situation, their activities, their
state of mind, and their projects. The most effective weapon with which to
fight an enemy is knowledge of his projects and intentions. . . . To achieve this,
every scrap of information must be collected together concerning the decision-making process, preparations, equipment, accumulation of weapons and
munitions, the constitution of stocks, all the movements, concentration, and
dispersion of troops, every change in everyday habits and alterations in the enemy's routine . . . any unusual absence from or presence at court, every particular effort on his part to seek out information and discover secrets and to
establish eavesdropping on discussions and conversations, the least details of
insignificant affairs. It is by analyzing the banal and insignificant gestures and
sayings of children, slaves, retainers, and servants in the entourage of trusted
people close to the enemy and his harem that you can best gain access to his
best-guarded secrets. To achieve that result, the best means is to step up the

From Nasir al-Din al-Tusi, *Akhlaq-i Nasiri,* edited by M. Minawi and A. Heydari (Tehran,
1981), translated by Ahmad Salamatian. Translated from the French by A. M. Berrett.

number of meetings and conversations with everybody. You must know how to exploit your contacts. It is through increasing the number of these contacts that you can gain access to the innermost sanctum well disguised. . . .

The prince must first seek coexistence and concord with other princes by every possible means, so as to avoid war and killing as much as possible. If war proves inevitable, there are two hypotheses: either he launches war or he defends himself. To launch a war, the prince must have as his objective only good and religion. He must avoid the quest for hegemony and domination through ambition. He must fulfill all the conditions of prudence and vigilance. He should not launch war before being sure of his victory. He should only ever launch war with faithful and well-unified troops. The greatest danger is to be caught in a pincer between two enemies. So far as possible, the king must avoid leading his troops in person, for if he fails, his authority is irreparably harmed, and even if he is successful, the dignity, magnificence, and prosperity of the country will suffer. To command a military expedition, the officer must be courageous and valiant and already have acquired a great reputation for valor and bravery; have perfect aptitude for, judicious counsel in, and the knowledge and capacity to use all the ruses and tactics of war; and be experienced in and used to war.

It is not prudent to have recourse to arms so long as it is possible to disperse and annihilate the enemy through ruse and stratagem. Ardashir said: "Do not use a stick where a whip will do nor a sword where a mace suffices." War must be the last resort. . . . To break the unity of the enemy and disperse his troops, ruses, deceit, fabrication, and the use of lies are not reprehensible, but recourse to treachery is never permissible. The most important dispositions to take for any war are to be alert and send out spies and scouts.

In war it is also necessary to take into consideration the interests of commerce and not risk men's lives, goods, and equipment if there is not also the hope of large commercial profits. The ground where battle will be given must be carefully studied and men placed in position according to their capacities and the need to protect them. Only enclose yourself behind walls and trenches at times of distress and absolute necessity. For that sort of tactic gives the initiative to the enemy. If someone distinguishes himself during the fighting by some act of bravery, do not hesitate to honor him and do not stint on rewarding him with all sorts of honors and gifts. Remain serene and patient and avoid being impulsive and foolhardy. It is extremely unwise to underestimate an enemy, however weak he is, and not to take every precaution. . . .

So far as possible, taking prisoners is preferable to killing and has many advantages. You can keep prisoners as slaves or hostages to be exchanged for money or to force the enemy to do as we want, whereas there is no advantage in killing. Above all, do not give the order to kill after a victory. Do not be fanatical and commit excesses of belligerence. After victory, an enemy should enjoy the same status as a subject or a protected slave.

But if you are attacked, and if you are simply defending yourself by accepting war, the prince should, if he has the capacity to resist, combine all his forces and all his efforts to surprise the enemy by ambushes, night attacks, diversions, and other tactics. In general, the people of a city who let war unfold on their territory are defeated. But if there are no forces to resist by attack, take every precaution to strengthen the walls, dig trenches and expend all you have in the way of fortune, ruses, and tactics to obtain an armistice and peace.

MUBARAKSHAH
(c. 1150–1224)

Muhammad b. Mansur Mubarakshah dedicated his Adab al-harb wa-al-shaja'ah *(Rules of War and Bravery), a compilation of texts, maxims, and anecdotes dealing with the art of government and war, to Shams al-Din Iltutmish, a former slave who became sultan of Delhi (A.D. 1211–36).*

THE RULES OF WAR AND BRAVERY

If you want to preserve peace and friendship between two countries, you must clearly demarcate the borders and record them in treaties in which you swear in writing in the name of God, His Messenger, the angels, the revealed books, the prophets, and the apostles. These treaties must spell out the transit rights of pilgrims, and of expeditionary forces on their way to go and fight the infidels, public areas and open grazing areas, and every other exception to the common rules. In both countries the treaty thus drawn up must be read out loud and the judges, imams, nobles descended from the Prophet, sheikhs, competent authorities, heads of the army and the administration, the most important men of the two parties must countersign the treaties. Afterward, signed texts must be exchanged, and they must be scrupulously respected. If one of the signatories does not honor his commitments, the co-signatories and neighboring princes must be informed, and they must be taken as witnesses of this violation of the treaty, before responding to the hostilities thus embarked on. The one who breaks his word and commits perjury will surely be defeated by the one who keeps his word. . . .

On days when the armed forces march past and are reviewed, you must act to ensure that the number of horsemen, foot soldiers and matériel appears

From Muhammad b. Mansur b. Said Mubarakshah, *Adab al-harb wa-al-shaja'ah*, edited by A. Soheyli Khonsari (Eqbal, 1967), translated by Ahmad Salamatian. Translated from the French by A. M. Berrett.

much greater than it really is. In that way, the enemy's agents who have infiltrated will be impressed, and through their alarming reports will spread fear among the enemy, which will deter him from seeking war, so that peace will be preserved. Such a peace is preferable to an untimely war whose outcome cannot be foreseen. Winning the peace is better than winning a war because it spares the army, the country, and the population destruction, rapine, and massacre. . . .

The camp should be set up on land close to water and forage. Guards should be posted all round the camp in the desert and on the roads to bar the way to the enemy army. If the army is not very numerous, you should camp by a river, a stream or on the side of a mountain. You must never neglect ambushes. You should camp near places where cattle, horses, and forage can be found. . . . In the camp, everyone must know his preassigned place. The vanguard, which arrives first, establishes itself in a forward position, followed by the right wing and the left wing, which are themselves followed by the right and the left. Then it is the turn of the center, which puts itself in the middle. Just behind the center, you should set up the harem, the kitchen, the treasury, the vestiary, the arsenal, and the stirrup depot; behind these you should place the army supplies depot, hospitals, and prisons and their guards. And then on one side the horses and on the other the camels and the flocks. You should place both mounted and foot guards all round to the right and left. Thus the royal camp will be well surrounded and guarded by everybody who will be able to protect the king from the ruses and treachery of the enemy. . . .

Scouts mounted on well-trained, fast horses carrying light weapons, water, and food in sufficient quantity should be sent to meet the enemy. Their leaders must be experienced and skillful. They must advance in dispersed order, go up into the hills and, as soon as they see the enemy, pass information from one to another without making any noise, and intelligently, until it reaches the supreme command and the person of the king. They should avoid skirmishes, but if that becomes inevitable, they must fight withdrawing, while simultaneously sending one or two despatches to the king to inform him. . . .

The spy must be shrewd and frank in the reports he makes so as to avoid leading the army commanders into error. He must never underestimate the enemy. Each day he must send out new scouts and, during the night, the horsemen, formed into detachments of one hundred, must mount guard in turn around the camp. During the march, neither the population nor the king's subjects who live in regions the army is passing through must be disturbed. . . .

There are five sorts of war:

1. War against the infidels. This is a religious obligation. If you kill in it, you are a fighter of God, and if you are killed in it, you are a martyr in the way

of God. On the day of resurrection, the martyrs will be just behind the prophets and the apostles.

2. War by a section of Muslims who seek hegemony and domination over other Muslims. In this case, it is the duty of all the other Muslims to prevent them from continuing the war and killing each other, as God the All-Powerful said: "If two parties of believers take up arms the one against the other, make peace between them. If either of them commits aggression against the other, fight against the aggressors till they submit to Allah's judgment" [Koran 49.9].

3. War against the Kharejites, those who rebel against the sultan, cease to obey and lay claim to the kingdom and kingship and do so without the adhesion or allegiance of Muslims. This war too is permitted and legitimate.

4. War against those who refuse to pay taxes due to the sultan. This war too is permitted. . . .

5. War against bandits and pillagers who kill people in order to seize their goods. But while it is permitted to make war, it is illegitimate to kill the wounded, massacre a defeated army, and pursue people simply to pillage them. . . .

If the infidels besiege a Muslim city or attack the land of Islam to kill and pillage, you must sound the call to general mobilization. Then everybody must fight, even wives without the permission of their husbands and slaves without the permission of their masters. . . .

If the routed enemy asks for quarter, you must grant it, but remain alert and watch him. It may always be a ruse or treachery. You must not be in a hurry to kill prisoners, but if the king gives the order to kill a prisoner, you must shut his mouth before he is executed, because a desperate man may say anything. . . .

In the countryside, you must take just the quantity of weapons and provisions that you need. You must not overburden the men. Each soldier must have with him a sum of money in case he should find himself in distress. . . .

You can do nothing with an army that is an amalgam of a hundred people here, a hundred people there, and so on. What can be achieved with four thousand men, united and standing shoulder to shoulder, you cannot do with forty or even four hundred thousand men who are divided and pulled this way and that by internal conflicts. . . .

Keep your secrets well if you do not want to be stripped naked. Obey your superiors if you want to be obeyed by your subordinates. Do not rush if you do not want to be harassed. A good counsel of war and good tactics are worth more than an army that is too large. Be patient so as not to suffer remorse. Even if the enemy is insignificant, he should be taken seriously; even if he is weak, you must not let him be. You must never neglect your preparations, the training of soldiers and keeping the army's equipment in repair. Ruses are better in war than force. As far as possible, avoid being bellicose. The commander of an army is like the head: when it is well, the body follows, but when it is unwell, the whole body suffers the consequences. . . .

During the siege, the best ruse is to assail the hearts of the besieged by throwing [them] letters, sending [them] messages, formulating good words and alluring promises, as far as you can. Thus the wildest rumors must be put about, such as: "They are going to mount catapults capable of melting the walls through a discharge of fire. . . . They are going to flood the ditches with burning oil capable of completely burning the walls. . . ." Detachments must discreetly leave the camp during the night and return at daybreak with standards and drums, pretending that they are freshly arrived troops come for the final assault.

You must gather information of all sorts on the number of men fit for fighting, the quantity of forage, water, and weapons still available to the besieged and their defense tactics. Then you must put criers all along the walls to proclaim: "O poor people, do not be so cruel to yourselves. With the quantities of forage, water, and provisions that you have left, you can only hold out for a few days. . . ." Thus the besieged, realizing that you know all about their capacity to hold out, will prefer peace and will surrender. At the foot of the walls, carpenters must work during the day building new cranes and catapults; the well diggers and masons must go all round the walls acting as if they are going to dig tunnels or destroy the walls at a particular place. Thus you keep the besieged in a high state of anxiety. You must also put about lying letters addressed to this or that chief of the advanced posts of the defense of the walls. In these letters you can write: "You are our friend and our ally; now we are sure of it. We are grateful, and our reward in honors, money, and gifts is assured you at the end of the siege," and so on. In that way you can divide the besieged. . . . The most important tactic of all is that the enemy should know nothing of your plans and you should know his in detail. . . . You must not be ashamed to be prudent and alert. It is ignorance and negligence that are unforgivable, fatal faults. You must never underestimate the enemy; it is better to overestimate him, take him seriously, and never stint on the means; in that way you will be able to deter him and avoid a war. . . . You must avoid winning by massacre and spilling blood; rather you must try and win by political ruse. Getting the enemy to submit, instead of annihilating him, is the best booty.

SA'DI
(c. 1209–1291)

The Persian poet Muslih al-Din, known as Sa'di, traveled all over the
Muslim world, from Andalusia to India and from Armenia to Yemen,
during the thirteenth century and witnessed the invasion of the Mongol
armies. He left two collections of reflections, completed at Shiraz: Bustan
(Orchard), a poem in 4,000 distiches, which appeared in 1257, and, a year
later, Gulistan *(Rose Garden), made up of eight books in prose. With*
Firdausi, Hafiz, and Omar Khayyám, he is one of the greatest Iranian
writers.

ON WAR

Resolving a conflict by flattering the enemy is better than launching a war.
When you lack the strength to conquer, it is better to close the door of hostility and open the door of generosity and well-being. . . . When you lack the
strength to bite a hand, embrace it, for with the victor there is no recourse but
hypocrisy and fraud. . . . It is with patience that you can scorch the enemy, that
is why you must flatter him with the same care as you would a friend. . . . Even
if you have the strength of an elephant and the claws of a lion, I feel that peace
is better than war. If all political tactics prove useless, however, drawing the
sword becomes legitimate. Nonetheless, if the enemy asks for peace, be conciliatory, but if he persists in being bellicose, you must take up the challenge.
If he is the one who seeks an armistice, your authority is a thousand times
greater, and if it is he who unleashes war, you will have no accounts to render
to the supreme ruler of the universe on the day of resurrection. But, faced with
a vengeful enemy, you must prepare for war; kindness to a hate-filled man is
an error. When the enemy seeks quarter, grant him your pardon. . . . When

From *Boustan*, in *Sa'di namah*, edited by Gholan Hossein Youssofy (Tehran: Kharazmi, 1984),
translated by Ahmad Salamatian. Translated from the French by A. M. Berrett.

you find yourself between two enemies, even weak ones, do not stay with your arms crossed, their coming together could make them strong. Buy the neutrality of one of them by tactics long enough to crush the other by force. When you draw your sword to fight, always discreetly keep open a door to peace.

PART 8

THE OTTOMAN EMPIRE

OTTOMAN CHRONICLE
(fourteenth century)

The janissaries, the elite infantry of the Ottoman armies, were largely recruited from among the children of subject peoples. They were brought up as Muslims, trained from the earliest childhood to be soldiers, and formed a force of professionals. With the decline of the empire from the seventeenth century on, they intervened in political life with increasing frequency. They were dissolved as a body in 1826.

THE ORIGIN OF THE JANISSARIES

One day a scholar called Kara Rüstem came from the land of Karaman. This Kara Rüstem went to Çandarli Halil, who was military judge, and said, "Why do you let so much state income go waste?" The military judge Kara Halil asked, "What income is this that is going waste? Tell me at once." Kara Rüstem said, "Of these prisoners that the warriors in the holy war bring back, one-fifth, according to God's command, belongs to the Padishah. Why do you not take this share?" The military judge Kara Halil said, "I will submit the matter to the Padishah!" He submitted it to Gazi Murad [Murad I (r. 1362–89)], who said, "If it is God's command, then take it." They called Kara Rüstem and said, "Master, carry out God's command." Kara Rüstem went away and stayed in Gallipoli and collected twenty-five aspers from each prisoner. This innovation dates from the time of these two men. To collect a tax from the prisoners in Gallipoli has become the practice since. . . . After that he also instructed Gazi Evrenos to take one out of every five prisoners captured in the raids and, if anyone had only four prisoners, to take twenty-five aspers from him. They acted according to this rule. They collected the young men. They took one in

Excerpt from *Islam: From the Prophet Muhammad to the Capture of Constantinople*, edited and translated by Bernard Lewis, vol. 1, *Politics and War* (New York: Harper Torch-books, 1974), 226–27. Copyright © 1974 by Bernard Lewis. Reprinted by permission of Harper-Collins Publishers.

every five prisoners captured in the raids and delivered them to the Porte. Then they gave these young men to the Turks in the provinces so that they should learn Turkish, and then they sent them to Anatolia. The Turks let these young men work in the fields for a while and made use of them until they learned Turkish. After a few years they brought them to the Porte and made them janissaries, giving them the name *yeniçeri* [new troops]. Their origin goes back to this time.

BUSBECQ
(1522–1592)

Ogier Ghiselin de Busbecq was sent as ambassador from the Hapsburg empire to Constantinople, where he stayed from 1555 to 1562. He was received there by Sultan Suleiman I (1520–66), who, with the conquest of Hungary (battle of Mohács, 1526) had taken the empire to its greatest extent. Busbecq's Letters informed the Poles and Hapsburgs, who were rightly worried about the Ottoman empire's power, about its institutions and customs. In them he gave a perhaps rather overflattering portrait of the Ottoman army so as to incite the Christian rulers to promote reforms. Nonetheless, aside from the Spanish tercios, the Ottoman army was at the time the best and most disciplined in the world.

THE SULTAN IN THE FIELD

The Sultan, when he sets out on a campaign, takes as many as 40,000 camels with him, and almost as many baggage-mules, most of whom, if his destination is Persia, are loaded with cereals of every kind, especially rice. Mules and camels are also employed to carry tents and arms and warlike machines and implements of every kind. The territories called Persia . . . are much less fertile than our country; and, further, it is the custom of the inhabitants, when their land is invaded, to lay waste and burn everything, and so force the enemy to retire through lack of food. The latter, therefore, are faced with serious peril, unless they bring an abundance of food with them. They are careful, however, to avoid touching the supplies which they carry with them as long as they are marching against their foes, but reserve them, as far as possible, for their return journey, when the moment for retirement comes and they are forced to retrace their steps through regions which the enemy has laid waste,

From *The Turkish Letters of Ogier Ghiselin de Busbecq, Imperial Ambassador at Constantinople, 1554–1562*, translated by Edward E. Forster (Oxford: Clarendon Press, 1927), 58–62. Reproduced by permission of Oxford University Press.

or which the immense multitude of men and baggage animals has, as it were, scraped bare, like a swarm of locusts. It is only then that the Sultan's store of provisions is opened, and just enough food to sustain life is weighed out each day to the Janissaries and the other troops in attendance upon him. The other [irregular] soldiers are badly off, if they have not provided food for their own use; most of them, having often experienced such difficulties during their campaigns—and this is particularly true of the cavalry—take a horse on a leading-rein loaded with many of the necessities of life. These include a small piece of canvas to use as a tent, which may protect them from the sun or a shower of rain, also some clothing and bedding and a private store of provisions, consisting of a leather sack or two of the finest flour, a small jar of butter, and some spices and salt; on these they support life when they are reduced to the extremes of hunger. They take a few spoonfuls of flour and place them in water, adding a little butter, and then flavour the mixture with salt and spices. This, when it is put on the fire, boils and swells up so as to fill a large bowl. They eat of it once or twice a day, according to the quantity, without any bread, unless they have with them some toasted bread or biscuit. They thus contrive to live on short rations for a month or even longer, if necessary. Some soldiers take with them a little sack full of beef dried and reduced to a powder, which they employ in the same manner as the flour, and which is of great benefit as a more solid form of nourishment. Sometimes, too, they have recourse to horseflesh; for in a great army a large number of horses necessarily dies, and any that die in good condition furnish a welcome meal to men who are starving. I may add that men whose horses have died, when the Sultan moves his camp, stand in a long row on the road by which he is to pass with their harness or saddles on their heads, as a sign that they have lost their horses, and implore his help to purchase others. The Sultan then assists them with whatever gift he thinks fit.

All this will show you with what patience, sobriety, and economy the Turks struggle against the difficulties which beset them, and wait for better times. How different are our soldiers, who on campaign despise ordinary food and expect dainty dishes (such as thrushes and beccaficoes) and elaborate meals. If these are not supplied, they mutiny and cause their own ruin; and even if they are supplied, they ruin themselves just the same. For each man is his own worst enemy and has no more deadly foe than his own intemperance, which kills him if the enemy is slow to do so. I tremble when I think of what the future must bring when I compare the Turkish system with our own; one army must prevail and the other be destroyed, for certainly both cannot remain unscathed. On their side are the resources of a mighty empire, strength unimpaired, experience and practice in fighting, a veteran soldiery, habituation to victory, endurance of toil, unity, order, discipline, frugality, and watchfulness. On our side is public poverty, private luxury, impaired strength, broken spirit, lack of endurance and training; the soldiers are insubordinate, the officers avaricious; there is contempt for discipline; licence, recklessness, drunkenness, and debauchery are rife; and, worst of all, the enemy is accustomed to victory, and we to defeat. Can we doubt what the result will be? Persia alone interposes in our favour; for the enemy, as he hastens to attack, must keep an eye on this menace in his rear. But Persia is only delaying our fate; it cannot save us. When the Turks have settled with Persia, they will fly at our throats supported by the might of the whole East; how unprepared we are I dare not say!

PART 9

MONGOLIA AND CENTRAL ASIA

IBN AL-ATHIR
(1160–1233)

For a note on Ibn al-Athir, see p. 400.

THE COMING OF THE MONGOLS

These were a people who emerged from the confines of China, and attacked the cities of Turkistan, like Kashghar and Balasaghun, and thence advanced on the cities of Transoxiana, such as Samarqand, Bukhara and the like, taking possession of them, and treating their inhabitants in such wise as we shall mention; and of them one division then passed on into Khurasan, until they had made an end of taking possession, and destroying, and slaying, and plundering, and thence passing on to Ray, Hamadan and the Highlands, and the cities contained therein, even to the limits of Iraq, whence they marched on the towns of Adharbayjan and Arraniyya, destroying them and slaying most of their inhabitants, of whom none escaped save a small remnant; and all this in less than a year; this is a thing whereof the like hath not been heard. And when they had finished with Adharbayjan and Arraniyya, they passed on to Darband-i-Shirwan, and occupied its cities, none of which escaped save the fortress wherein was their King; wherefore they passed by it to the countries of the Lan and the Lakiz and the various nationalities which dwell in that region, and plundered, slew, and destroyed them to the full. And thence they made their way to the lands of Qipchaq, who are the most numerous of the Turks, and slew all such as withstood them, while the survivors fled to the fords and mountain-tops, and abandoned their country, which these Tartars overran. All this they did in the briefest space of time, remaining only for so long as their march required and no more.

Another division, distinct from that mentioned above, marched on Ghazna and its dependencies, and those parts of India, Sistan and Kirman which bor-

From *A Literary History of Persia,* edited by Edward G. Browne (Cambridge: Cambridge University Press, 1902), 2:427–31.

der thereon, and wrought therein deeds like unto the other, nay, yet more grievous. Now this is a thing the like of which ear hath not heard; for Alexander, concerning whom historians agree that he conquered the world, did not do so with such swiftness, but only in the space of about ten years; neither did he slay, but was satisfied that men should be subject to him. But these Tartars conquered most of the habitable globe, and the best, the most flourishing and most populous part thereof, and that whereof the inhabitants were the most advanced in character and conduct, in about a year; nor did any country escape their devastations which did not fearfully expect them and dread their arrival.

Moreover they need no commissariat, nor the conveyance of supplies, for they have with them sheep, cows, horses, and the like quadrupeds, the flesh of which they eat, [needing] naught else. As for their beasts which they ride, these dig into the earth with their hoofs and eat the roots of plants, knowing naught of barley. And so, when they alight anywhere, they have need of nothing from without.

JOHN OF PLANO CARPINO
(c. 1182–1252)

Giovanni of Plano Carpino, Franciscan monk from Umbria, was sent by
Pope Innocent IV as ambassador extraordinary to the Mongol great khan.
(In 1241 the Mongols had advanced as far as the neighborhood of Vienna.)
His mission lasted from 1245 to 1247. He reached Karakorum in July 1246
and left there in November the same year. He reached Lyon (where the papal
court had moved to escape Emperor Frederick II) a year later and brought
back a letter from the great khan that spelled out the Mongol threat. Plano
Carpino's embassy came a few years before that of Guillaume de Ruysbroek.
In my opinion, the analysis of the Mongols' warrior characteristics by Plano
Carpino is one of the masterpieces of military literature in terms of its detail
and intelligence.

HOW MONGOLS FIGHT

Having spoken of their empire, we will now deal with war in the following
manner; first we will tell of their battle array, second of their arms, thirdly of
their cunning in engagements, fourthly of the cruelty they show to captives,
fifthly of how they make assaults on forts and cities, and sixthly of the bad faith
they show to those who surrender to them.

Chingis Chan ordained that the army should be organised in such a way
that over ten men should be set one man and he is what we call a captain of
ten; over ten of these should be placed one, named a captain of a hundred; at
the head of ten captains of a hundred is placed a soldier known as a captain of
a thousand, and over ten captains of a thousand is one man, and the word they
use for this number means "darkness." [John has confused *duman*, darkness,

From *The Mongol Mission: Narratives and Letters of the Franciscan Missionaries in Mongolia*
and China in the Thirteenth and Fourteenth Centuries, edited by Christopher Dawson (London
and New York: Sheed & Ward, 1955), 32–38.

[465]

with *tümen,* which means 10,000.] Two or three chiefs are in command of the whole army, yet in such a way that one holds the supreme command.

When they are in battle, if one or two or three or even more out of a group of ten run away, all are put to death; and if a whole group of ten flees, the rest of the group of a hundred are all put to death, if they do not flee too. In a word, unless they retreat in a body, all who take flight are put to death. Likewise if one or two or more go forward boldly to the fight, then the rest of the ten are put to death if they do not follow and, if one or more of the ten are captured, their companions are put to death if they do not rescue them.

They all have to possess the following arms at least: two or three bows, or at least one good one, three large quivers full of arrows, an axe and ropes for hauling engines of war. As for the wealthy, they have swords pointed at the end but sharp only on one side and somewhat curved, and they have a horse with armour; their legs also are covered and they have helmets and cuirasses. Some have cuirasses, and protection for their horses, fashioned out of leather in the following manner: they take strips of ox-hide, or of the skin of another animal, a hand's breadth wide and cover three or four together with pitch, and they fasten them with leather thongs or cord; in the upper strip they put the lace at one end, in the next they put it in the middle and so on to the end; consequently, when they bend, the lower strips come up over the upper ones and thus there is a double or triple thickness over the body.

They make the covering for their horses in five sections, one on one side of the horse and one on the other, and these stretch from the tail to the head and are fastened to the saddle and behind the saddle on its back and also on the neck; another section they put over its hindquarters where the ties of the two parts are fastened and in this last-named piece they make a hole for the tail to come through; covering the breast there is another section. All these pieces reach down as far as the knees or joints of the leg. On its forehead they put an iron plate, which is tied to the aforementioned sections on each side of the neck.

The cuirass is made in four parts. One piece stretches from the thigh to the neck, but is shaped to fit the human figure, being narrow across the chest and curved round the body from the arms downwards; behind, over the loins, they have another piece, which reaches from the neck and meets the first piece encircling the body; these two sections, namely the front one and the back, are fastened with clasps to two iron plates, one on each shoulder; also on each arm they have a piece stretching from the shoulder to the hand and open at the bottom, and on each leg another piece. All these sections are fastened together by clasps.

The upper part of the helmet is of iron or steel, but the part affording protection to the neck and throat is of leather. All these leather sections are made in the manner described above.

Some of the Tartars [Mongols] have all the things we have mentioned made of iron in the following fashion: they make a number of thin plates of the metal, a finger's breadth wide and a hand's breadth in length, piercing eight little holes in each plate; as a foundation they put three strong narrow straps; they then place the plates one on top of the other so that they overlap, and they tie them to the straps by narrow thongs which they thread through the afore-mentioned holes; at the top they attach a thong, so that the metal plates hold together firmly and well. They make a strap out of these plates and then join them together to make sections of armour as has been described above. They make these into armour for horses as well as men and they make them shine so brightly that one can see one's reflection in them.

Some of them have lances which have a hook in the iron neck, and with this, if they can, they will drag a man from his saddle. The length of their arrows is two feet, one palm and two digits. Since feet are not all the same, we will give the measurement of a geometrical foot; the length of a digit is two grains of barley, and sixteen digits make a geometrical foot. The heads of the arrows are very sharp and cut on both sides like a two-edged sword—the Tartars always carry files at the side of their quiver for sharpening their arrows. The iron heads have a pointed tail, a digit's breadth in length and this they stick into the shaft.

They have a shield made of wicker or twigs, but I do not think they carry it except in camp and when guarding the Emperor and the princes, and this only at night. They also have other arrows for shooting birds and animals and unarmed men; these are three digits wide; in addition they have various other kinds of arrows for shooting birds and animals.

When they are going to make war, they send ahead an advance guard and these carry nothing with them but their tents, horses and arms. They seize no plunder, burn no houses and slaughter no animals; they only wound and kill men or, if they can do nothing else, put them to flight. They much prefer, however, to kill than to put to flight. The army follows after them, taking everything they come across, and they take prisoner or kill any inhabitants who are to be found. Not content with this, the chiefs of the army next send plunderers in all directions to find men and animals, and they are most ingenious at searching them out.

When they come to a river, they cross it in the following manner, even if it is wide. The nobles have a circular piece of light leather, round the edge of which they make numerous loops, through which they thread a rope; they draw this up so that it makes a pouch, which they fill with their clothes and other things, pressing them down very tightly together; on top of these, in the middle, they put their saddles and other hard things. The men also sit in the middle and they tie the boat they have made in this way to the tail of a horse. They make one man swim in front with the horse to guide it, or sometimes they have a couple of oars with which they row to the other side of the water and so cross the river. The horses, however, they drive into the water, and a man swims by the side of one horse, which he guides, and the others all follow it; in this way they cross both narrow and wide rivers. The poorer men have a leather bag securely sewn—everybody is expected to possess one of these—and into this bag or satchel they put their clothes and all their belongings; having tied the sack tightly at the top, they hang it on to a horse's tail and cross in the manner described above.

It should be known that when they come in sight of the enemy they attack at once, each one shooting three or four arrows at their adversaries; if they see that they are not going to be able to defeat them, they retire, going back to their own line. They do this as a blind to make the enemy follow them as far as the places where they have prepared ambushes. If the enemy pursues them to these ambushes, they surround and wound and kill them. Similarly if they see that they are opposed by a large army, they sometimes turn aside and, putting a day's or two days' journey between them, they attack and pillage another part of the country and they kill men and destroy and lay waste the land. If they perceive that they cannot even do this, then they retreat for some ten or twelve days and stay in a safe place until the army of the enemy has disbanded, whereupon they come secretly and ravage the whole land. They are indeed the most cunning in war, for they have now been fighting against other nations for forty years and more.

When however they are going to join battle, they draw up all the battle lines just as they are to fight. The chiefs or princes of the army do not take part in the fighting but take up their stand some distance away facing the enemy, and they have beside them their children on horseback and their womenfolk and horses; and sometimes they make figures of men and set them on horses. They do this to give the impression that a great crowd of fighting-men is assembled there. They send a detachment of captives and men of other nationalities who are fighting with them to meet the enemy head-on, and some Tartars may perhaps accompany them. Other columns of stronger men they dispatch far off to the right and the left so that they are not seen by the enemy and in this way they surround them and close in and so the fighting begins from all sides. Sometimes when they are few in number they are thought by the enemy, who are surrounded, to be many, especially when the latter catch sight of the children, women, horses and dummy figures described above, which are with the chief or prince of the army and which they think are combatants; and alarmed by this they are thrown into disorder. If it happens that the enemy fight well, the Tartars make a way of escape for them; then as soon as they begin to take flight and are separated from each other they fall upon them and more are slaughtered in flight than could be killed in battle. However, it should be known that, if they can avoid it, the Tartars do not like to fight hand to hand but they wound and kill men and horses with their arrows; they only come to close quarters when men and horses have been weakened by arrows.

They reduce fortresses in the following manner. If the position of the fortress allows it, they surround it, sometimes even fencing it round so that no one can enter or leave. They make a strong attack with engines and arrows and they do not leave off fighting by day or night, so that those inside the fortress get no sleep; the Tartars however have some rest, for they divide up their forces and they take it in turns to fight so that they do not get too tired. If they cannot capture it in this way they throw Greek fire; sometimes they even take the fat of the people they kill and, melting it, throw it on to the houses, and wherever the fire falls on this fat it is almost inextinguishable. It can however be put out, so they say, if wine or ale is poured on it. If it falls on flesh, it can be put out by being rubbed with the palm of the hand.

If they are still unsuccessful and the city or fort has a river, they dam it or alter its course and submerge the fortress if possible. Should they not be able to do this, they undermine the city and armed men enter it from underground; once inside, some of them start fires to burn the fortress while the rest fight the inhabitants. If however they are not able to conquer it even in this way, they establish a fort or fortification of their own facing the city, so as not to suffer any injury from the missiles of the enemy; and they stay for a long time over against the city, unless by chance it has outside help from an army which fights against the Tartars and removes them by force. While they are pitched before the fortification they speak enticing words to the inhabitants making them many promises to induce them to surrender into their hands. If they do surrender to them, they say: "Come out, so that we may count you according to our custom," and when they come out to them they seek out the artificers among them and keep these, but the others, with the exception of those they wish to have as slaves, they kill with the axe. If they do spare any others they never spare the noble and illustrious men, so we are told, and if by chance the unexpected happens and some nobles are kept, they can never afterwards escape from captivity either by entreaty or by bribe.

All those they take prisoner in battle they put to death unless they happen to want to keep some as slaves. They divide those who are to be killed among the captains of a hundred to be executed by them with a battle-axe; they in their turn divide them among the captives, giving each slave to kill ten or more or less as the officers think fit. . . .

HOW TO FIGHT MONGOLS

Having spoken of the countries subject to the Tartars [Mongols], I must now add a description of how to wage war against them, and it seems to me it should be dealt with in the following manner: first as to their plans, secondly, as to arms and army organisation, thirdly how to meet their cunning in engagements, fourthly of the fortification of camps and cities, fifthly of what ought to be done with prisoners.

It is the intention of the Tartars to bring the whole world into subjection if they can and, as has been mentioned above, on this point they have received a command from Chingis Chan. It is for this reason that their Emperor writes in his letters: "The strength of God, the Emperor of all men" and this is the inscription on his seal: "God in heaven and Cuyuc Chan on earth, the strength of God, the seal of the Emperor of all men." This also accounts for their refusing to make peace with any nation unless, as has been told, they surrender into their hands. Since there is no country on earth which they fear with the exception of Christendom, they are preparing to make war on us. Wherefore be it known unto everyone that, while we were in the land of the Tartars, we attended a solemn court, which had been announced several years back and at which, in our presence, they chose Cuyuc as Emperor, or Chan as it is in their language. The said Cuyuc Chan, together with all the princes, raised the standard to proceed against the Church of God and the Roman Empire, and against all Christian kingdoms and nations of the West, unless they carry out the instructions he is sending to the Lord Pope, the rulers and the Christian peoples of the West.

In my opinion, these instructions ought on no account to be observed, first because of the extreme, nay intolerable, hitherto unheard-of servitude to which they reduce all nations they conquer and which we have seen with our own eyes; then because they are not trustworthy and no nation can rely on their word—they break any promises they make as soon as they see that the tide is turned in their favour, and they are full of deceit in all their deeds and assurances; it is their object to wipe off the face of the earth all princes, nobles, knights and men of gentle birth, as has already been told, and they do this to those in their power in a sly and crafty manner: then because it is unfitting that Christians should be subject to them in view of the abominations they practise and seeing that the worship of God is brought to nought, souls are perishing and bodies are afflicted beyond belief in many ways; it is true at first

From *The Mongol Mission: Narratives and Letters of the Franciscan Missionaries in Mongolia and China in the Thirteenth and Fourteenth Centuries,* edited by Christopher Dawson (London and New York: Sheed & Ward, 1955), 43–49.

they speak fair words, but afterwards they sting and hurt like a scorpion; and lastly because they are fewer in number and weaker in body than the Christian peoples.

At the aforementioned court the fighting-men and chiefs of the army were given their appointments. Out of ten men they are sending three with their servants from every country under their sway. One army is to penetrate by way of Hungary, and a second by way of Poland, so we were told. They will come prepared to fight without a break for eighteen years, and they have been assigned their time for setting out. Last March we came upon an army which had been called up from among all the Tartars through whose territory we travelled after leaving Russia. In three or four years' time they will reach Comania. From there they will make an attack on the countries mentioned above; I do not know however whether they will come immediately after the third winter is over, or wait some time longer so that they have a better chance of coming unexpectedly.

All these things are sure and certain, unless God, in His mercy, places some hindrance in their way as He did when they went into Hungary and Poland. It was their plan to continue fighting for thirty years, but their Emperor was killed by poison and consequently they have rested from battle until the present time. But now, since an Emperor has been newly appointed, they are beginning to prepare for the fight once again. It should be known that the Emperor said with his own lips that he wanted to send an army into Livonia and Prussia. Since it is their object to overthrow the whole world and reduce it to slavery—a slavery, as has already been said, unbearable for men of our race—they must therefore be met in battle.

If one province is not prepared to help another, then the country the Tartars are attacking will be vanquished and they will fight against another country with the prisoners they take and these will be placed in the front line. If they fight badly the Tartars kill them, but if they fight well, then they keep them by means of promises and flattery, and to prevent them from running away they go so far as to promise to make them mighty lords. But after this, when they can feel sure that they will not leave them, they turn them into most wretched slaves and they do the same with the women they wish to keep as servants and concubines. And so, with the inhabitants of the district they have conquered, they destroy another country and, in my opinion, there is no province able to resist them by itself unless God fight on its side for, as has already been said, men are collected together from every country to fight under their dominion. Therefore if Christians wish to save themselves, their country and Christendom, then ought kings, princes, barons and rulers of countries to assemble together and by common consent send men to fight against the Tartars before they begin to spread over the land, for once they begin to be scattered throughout a country it is impossible for anyone to give any effective help to another, for troops of Tartars search out the inhabitants everywhere and slaughter them. If the latter shut themselves up in fortresses, the Tartars station three or four thousand or more men round the fort or city to besiege it, at the same time continuing to spread all over the country killing men.

Whoever wishes to fight against the Tartars ought to have the following arms: good strong bows, crossbows, of which they are much afraid, a good supply of arrows, a serviceable axe of strong iron or a battle-axe with a long handle; the heads of the arrows for both bows and cross-bows ought to be tempered after the Tartar fashion, in salt water when they are hot, to make them hard enough to pierce the Tartar armour. They should also have swords and lances with a hook to drag the Tartars from their saddle, for they fall off very easily; knives, and cuirasses of a double thickness, for the Tartar arrows do not easily pierce such; a helmet and armour and other things to protect the body and the horses from their weapons and arrows. If there are any men not as well armed as we have described, they ought to do as the Tartars and go behind the others and shoot at the enemy with their bows and crossbows. There ought to be no stinting of money when purchasing weapons for the defence of souls and bodies and liberty and other possessions.

The army should be organised in the same way as the Tartar army, under captains of a thousand, captains of a hundred, captains of ten and the chiefs of the army. The last named ought on no account to take part in the battle, just as the Tartar chiefs take no part, but they should watch the army and direct it. They should make a law that all advance together either to battle or elsewhere in the order appointed. Severe punishment ought to be meted out to anyone who deserts another either going into battle or fighting, or takes flight when they are not retreating as a body, for if this happens a section of the Tartar force follows those fleeing and kills them with arrows while the rest fight with those who have remained on the field, and so both those who stay and those who run away are thrown into confusion and killed. Similarly anyone who turns aside to take plunder before the army of the enemy has been completely vanquished ought to be punished with a very heavy sentence; among the Tartars such a one is put to death without any mercy. The chiefs of the army should choose their battle ground, if possible a flat plain, every part of which they can watch, and if they can they should have a large forest behind them or on their flank, so situated however that the Tartars cannot come between them and the wood. The army ought not to assemble into one body, but many lines should be formed, separated from each other, only not too far apart. One line ought to be sent to meet the first line of Tartars to approach; if the Tartars feign flight they ought not to pursue them very far, certainly not further than they can see, in case the Tartars lead them into ambushes they have prepared, which is what they usually do. And let another line be in readiness to help the first if occasion require it.

Moreover they ought to have scouts in every direction, behind, to the right and to the left, to see when the other lines of Tartars are coming, and one line ought always to be sent to meet each Tartar line, for the Tartars always strive to surround their enemies; the greatest precautions ought to be taken to prevent their doing this, for in this way an army is easily vanquished. Each line should take care not to pursue them for long, on account of the ambushes they are wont to prepare, for they fight with deceit rather than courage.

The leaders of the army ought always to be ready to send help to those who are fighting if they need it. Another reason for avoiding too long a pursuit after the Tartars is so as not to tire the horses, for we have not the great quantity which they have. The horses the Tartars ride on one day they do not mount again for the next three or four days, consequently they do not mind if they tire them out seeing they have such a great number of animals. Even if the Tartars retreat our men ought not to separate from each other or be split up, for the Tartars pretend to withdraw in order to divide the army, so that afterwards they can come without any let or hindrance and destroy the whole land. The Christians should also beware of their usual tendency of over-expenditure, lest they be obliged to go home on account of lack of money and the Tartars destroy the whole earth and the name of God be blasphemed on account of their extravagance. They should take care to see that if it come to pass that some fighting men return home, others take their place.

Our leaders ought also to arrange that our army is guarded day and night, so that the Tartars do not make a sudden and unexpected attack upon them for, like the devils, they devise many ways of doing harm. Indeed our men ought to be on the alert as much during the night as in the daytime, they should never undress to lie down, nor sit at table enjoying themselves, so that they cannot be taken unawares, for the Tartars are always on the watch to see how they can inflict some damage. The inhabitants of a country who are apprehensive and fear that the Tartars are coming to attack them should have secret pits in which they should put their corn as well as other things, and this for two reasons: namely so that the Tartars cannot get hold of them and also that, if God shows them His favour, they themselves will be able to find them afterwards. If they have to flee from their country, they ought to burn the hay and straw or hide it away in a safe place so that the horses of the Tartars will find less to eat.

If they wish to fortify cities or fortresses, let them first examine them from the point of view of position, for fortified places ought to be so situated that they cannot be reduced by engines and arrows; they should have a good supply of water and wood and, if possible, it should be impossible to deprive them of an entrance and exit, and they should have sufficient inhabitants for them to take it in turns in fighting. They ought to keep a careful watch to prevent the Tartars from taking the fortress by stealth, by means of cunning. They should have sufficient supplies to last for many years, and let them keep them carefully and eat them in moderation, for they do not know how long they will have to be shut up inside their fortress. When the Tartars once begin, they lay siege to a fortress for many years, for example at the present time in the land of the Alans they have been besieging a hill for the past twelve years, the inhabitants of which have manfully resisted and killed many Tartars and nobles.

Other fortresses and cities which have not the situation described above ought to be strongly protected by means of deep, walled ditches and well-built walls and they should have a good supply of bows and arrows and slings and stones. They must take great care not to allow the Tartars to place their engines in position, but they should drive them off with their own engines. If it happen that the Tartars by some device or cunning erect their engines, then the inhabitants ought to destroy them with theirs if they can; they should also use cross-bows, slings and engines against them to prevent them from drawing near to the city. In other respects they ought to be prepared as has already been described. As for fortresses and cities situated on rivers, they should be careful to see that they cannot be flooded out. Moreover, in regard to this point it should be known that the Tartars much prefer men to shut themselves into their cities and fortresses rather than fight with them in the open, for then they say they have got their little pigs shut in their sty, and so they place men to look after them as I have told above.

If any Tartars are thrown from their horse during the battle, they ought to be taken prisoner immediately, for when they are on the ground they shoot vigorously with their arrows, wounding and killing men and horses. If they are kept they can be the means of obtaining uninterrupted peace or a large sum of money would be given for them, for they have great love for each other. As to how Tartars may be recognised, it has been told above in the place where a description is given of their appearance. When they are taken prisoner, a strict guard must be kept over them if they are to be prevented from escaping. There are men of many other nations with them and these can be distinguished from them by means of the description set down above. It is important to know that there are many men in the Tartar army who, if they saw their opportunity and could rely on our men not to kill them, would fight against the Tartars in every part of the army, as they themselves told us, and they would do them worse harm than those who are their declared enemies.

ATA MALIK AL-JUWAYNI
(1226–1283)

'Alau' u' d-Din Ata Malik al-Juwayni, author of the Ta'rikh-i-Jahan-gusha, or History of the World Conqueror (i.e., Genghis Khan), was appointed governor of Baghdad by its Mongol conqueror Hülegü, founder of the dynasty of the Il-Khans, in 1259. He belonged to a titled Persian family, and his father, Baha' u' d-Din al-Juwayni, had served the Mongols before him. Al-Juwayni attended Hülegü at the capture of the Assassin stronghold of Alamut and carried off a selection of astronomical instruments and rare books as his share of the plunder.

THE MONGOLS IN IRAN

The reviewing and mustering of the army has been so arranged that they have abolished the registry of inspection . . . and dismissed the officials and clerks. For they have divided all the people into companies of ten, appointing one of the ten to be the commander of the nine others; while from among each ten commanders one has been given the title of "commander of the hundred," all the hundred having been placed under his command. And so it is with each thousand men and so also with each ten thousand, over whom they have appointed a commander whom they call "commander of the *tümen*." In accordance with this arrangement, if in an emergency any man or thing be required, they apply to the commanders of *tümen*; who in turn apply to the commanders of thousands, and so on down to the commanders of tens. There is a true equality in this; each man toils as much as the next, and no difference is made between them, no attention being paid to wealth or power. If there is

From *The History of the World Conqueror by 'Ala-ad-Din 'Ata-Malik Juvaini Translated from the Text of Mirza Muhammad Qazvini*, translated and edited by John Andrew Boyle (Manchester: Manchester University Press, 1958), 1: 159–64. Reprinted by permission of Manchester University Press.

a sudden call for soldiers an order is issued that so many thousand men must present themselves in such and such a place at such and such an hour of that day or night. "They shall not retard it [their appointed time] an hour; and they shall not advance it" [Koran 7.32]. And they arrive not a twinkling of an eye before or after the appointed hour. Their obedience and submissiveness is such that if there be a commander of a hundred thousand between whom and the Khan there is a distance of sunrise and sunset, and if he but commit some fault, the Khan dispatches a single horseman to punish him after the manner prescribed: if his head has been demanded, he cuts it off, and if gold be required, he takes it from him.

Another *yasa* [law] is that no man may depart to another unit than the hundred, thousand or ten to which he has been assigned, nor may he seek refuge elsewhere. And if this order be transgressed the man who transferred is executed in the presence of the troops, while he that received him is severely punished. For this reason no man can give refuge to another; if [for example] the commander be a prince, he does not permit the meanest person to take refuge in his company and so avoids a breach of the *yasa*. Therefore no man can take liberties with his commander or leader, nor can another commander entice him away....

Again, when the extent of their territories became broad and vast and important events fell out, it became essential to ascertain the activities of their enemies, and it was also necessary to transport goods from the West to the East and from the Far East to the West. Therefore throughout the length and breadth of the land they established [post stations], and made arrangements for the upkeep and expenses of each [post station], assigning thereto a fixed number of men and beasts as well as food, drink and other necessities. All this they shared out amongst the *tümen*, each two *tümen* having to supply one [post station]. Thus, in accordance with the census, they so distribute and exact the charge, that messengers need make no long detour in order to obtain fresh mounts while at the same time the peasantry and the army are not placed in constant inconvenience. Moreover strict orders were issued to the messengers with regard to the sparing of the mounts, etc., to recount all of which would delay us too long. Every year the [post stations] are inspected, and whatever is missing or lost has to be replaced by the peasantry....

Chingiz-Khan dispatched Toli to conquer the countries of Khorasan with men of action and lions of battle; and raising levies from the subject territories which lay across their path such as Abivard, Sarakhs, etc., they assembled an army of seven thousand men. Drawing near to Merv they sent four hundred horsemen across the ford by way of vanguard. These came by night to the bank where the Turcomans were encamped and watched their activities. Twelve thousand Turcoman horsemen were assembled there and used at every dawn to go to the gates in order to attack the town. . . . The Mongols laid an ambush in their pathway and waited in silence. The Turcomans were unable to recognize one another [in the dark] and as they arrived in small groups the Mongols cast them into the water and on to the wind of annihilation. Having thus broken their strength the Mongols came like the wind to their encampment and left the trace of the wolf upon the herd. And thus the Turcomans, whose numbers exceeded seventy thousand, were defeated by a mere handful of men. Most of them flung themselves into the water and were drowned, while the remainder took to flight. For since the Mongols were aided by Fortune and assisted by Fate, none was able to contend with them and he whose time was not yet come fled away casting down his arms.

The Mongols proceeded in this manner till nightfall and collected on the plain a herd of sixty thousand cattle (including sheep) which the Turcomans had driven from the gates, as well as other possessions, the amount of which was beyond computation. On the next day, which was [25 February 1221], and the last of the lives of most of the inhabitants of Merv, Toli, that furious lion, arrived with an army like unto a dark night and a raging sea and in multitude exceeding the sands of the desert, "all warriors of great renown."

He advanced in person to the Gate of Victory together with some five hundred horse and rode right round the town; and for six days they inspected the outworks, walls, moat and minaret [*sic*] and reached the conclusion that the townspeople's supplies would suffice to defend them and that the walls were a stout bastion that would withstand their attack.

On the seventh day, . . . the armies gathered together and halted before the Shahristan Gate. They joined battle, some two hundred men issuing from the gate and attacking. Toli dismounted in person . . . and advanced upon them. And the Mongols attacked in his company driving them back into the town. Others issued forth from another gate but the Mongols stationed there repelled the attack. And so the townspeople were nowhere able to achieve any result and could not even put their heads out of the gates. Finally the world donned garments of mourning, and the Mongols took up positions in several rings around the fortifications and kept watch throughout the night, so that none had any means of egress.

Mujir-al-Mulk [the governor] saw no way out save surrender and submission. In the morning, therefore, when the sun had raised the black veil from his moonlike face, he dispatched Jamal-ad-Din, one of the chief imams of Merv, as his ambassador and sued for quarter. Being reassured by fair words and promises, he got together presents from the quadrupeds in the town— horses, camels and mules—and went to Toli [in person]. Toli questioned him about the town and asked for details regarding the wealthy and notable. Mujir-al-Mulk gave him a list of two hundred persons, and Toli ordered them to be brought into his presence. . . .

The Mongols now entered the town and drove all the inhabitants, nobles and commoners, out on to the plain. For four days and nights the people continued to come out of the town; the Mongols detained them all, separating the women from the men. Alas! how many [fairylike] ones did they drag from the bosoms of their husbands! How many sisters did they separate from their brothers! How many parents were distraught at the ravishment of their virgin daughters!

The Mongols ordered that, apart from four hundred artisans whom they specified and selected from amongst the men and some children, girls and boys, whom they bore off into captivity, the whole population, including the women and children, should be killed, and no one, whether woman or man, be spared. The people of Merv were then distributed among the soldiers and levies, and, in short, to each man was allotted the execution of three or four hundred persons. . . .

When the army departed, those that had sought refuge in holes and cavities came out again, and there were gathered together some five thousand persons. A party of Mongols belonging to the rearguard then arrived and wished to have their share of slaughter. They commanded therefore that each person should bring a skirtful of grain out on to the plain for the Mongols; and in this way they cast into the well of annihilation most of those that had previously escaped. Then they proceeded along the road to Nishapur and slew all they found of those who had turned back from the plain and fled from the Mongols when half way out to meet them.

TIMUR
(1336–1405)

The Mongol conqueror Timur (called Timur-Leng, or Tamerlane) founded his short-lived empire, unlike that of Genghis Khan, on the basis of a system combining the yasa (law) drawn up by Genghis and the Shari'a (Islamic law). Many of his troops were Turkic-speaking. Starting from Transoxiana, Timur conquered the Mongol khanates of the Jagatai, the Il-Khans, and the Kipchak. He made systematic use of terror and warred ceaselessly between 1370 and 1405 in Khwarizm, eastern Turkestan, northern India (capture of Dehli, 1398), Afghanistan, Persia (massacre of Ispahan, 1387), Georgia, Armenia, Iraq (sack of Baghdad in 1394 and 1401), and Syria (massacre of Damascus, 1400). In 1402, near Ankara, he crushed the Ottomans. Timur patronized the arts, letters, and sciences, receiving many Islamic scholars in his capital, Samarkand. The great Persian poet Hafiz (c. 1320–89?) lived at Timur's court there.

THE CONQUEST OF DEHLI

Being satisfied as to my disposition of the forces, I began my march to Dehli. On the 22nd of Rabi-ul awwal I arrived and encamped at the fort of the village of Aspandi. In answer to my enquiries about this place I found that Samana was distant seven *kos*. The people of Samana, and Kaithal, and Aspandi are all heretics, idolaters, infidels, and misbelievers. They had now set fire to their houses and had fled with their children and property, and effects, towards Dehli, so that the whole country was deserted. Next day, the 23rd of the month, I started from the fort of Aspandi, and after marching six *kos* arrived at the village of Tughlik-pur. I encamped opposite the fort bearing that name. The people of the fort on hearing of the approach of my army, had abandoned it,

From *Tuzak-i-Timuri: The Autobiography of Timur,* translated by Henry Miers Elliot, edited by John Dowson (Lahore: Sind Sagar Academy), 44–61.

and had dispersed over the country. From the information supplied to me I learned that these people were called *sanawi* (fire-worshippers), [Zoroastrians]. Many of this perverse creed believe that there are two gods. One is called Yazdan [Ormazd], and whatever they have of good they believe to proceed from him. The other god they call Ahriman, and whatever sin and wickedness they are guilty of they consider Ahriman to be the author of. These misbelievers do not know that whatsoever there is of good or evil comes from God, and that man is the mere instrument of its execution. I ordered the houses of these heretics to be fired and their fort and buildings to be razed to the ground.

On the following day, the 24th of the month, I marched to Panipat, where I encamped. I there found that in obedience to orders received from the ruler of Dehli the people had deserted all their dwellings and had taken flight. . . . On the following day I marched from Panipat six *kos*, and encamped on the banks of a river which is on the road. I marched from this place on Friday, the 26th of the month, and I gave orders that the officers and soldiers of my army should put on their armour, and that every man should keep in his proper regiment and place in perfect readiness. We reached a village called Kanhigazin and there encamped. I issued my commands that on the morrow, the 28th of the month, a force of cavalry should proceed on a plundering excursion against the palace of Jahan-numa, a fine building erected by Sultan Firoz Shah on the top of a hill by the banks of the Jumna, which is one of the large rivers of Hindustan. Their orders were to plunder and destroy and to kill every one whom they met. Next day, in obedience to my commands, the division marched and proceeded to the palace of Jahan-numa, which is situated five miles from Dehli. They plundered every village and place they came to, killed the men, and carried off all the valuables and cattle, securing a great booty. They then returned, bringing with them a number of Hindu prisoners, both male and female.

On the 29th I again marched and reached the river Jumna. On the other side of the river I descried a fort, and upon making inquiry about it, I was informed that it consisted of a town and fort, called Loni and that it was held by an officer named Maimun as *kotwal* on behalf of Sultan Mahmud. I determined to take that fort at once, and as pasture was scant where I was, on the same day I crossed the river Jumna. I sent Emir Jahan Shah and Emir Shah Malik and Emir Allah-dad to besiege the fort of Loni, and I pitched my camp opposite to the fort. They invested the fort which was under the command of the *kotwal* named Maimun. He made preparations for resistance. At this time a holy *shaikh* who dwelt in the town came out very wisely and waited upon me. Although the *shaikh* was greatly honoured by the people, still, they would not listen to his advice, but determined to fight rather then surrender to me. These people were Hindus and belonged to the faction of Mallu Khan. They despised the counsels of the venerable father and resolved to resist. When I was informed of it, I ordered all the emirs and soldiers to assemble and invest the fort. They accordingly gathered with alacrity round the fort, and in the course of the one watch of the day they carried the place. It was situated in a *doab* between two rivers, one the Jumna, the other the Halin, the latter being a large canal, which was cut from the river Kalini and brought to Firozabad, and there connected with the Jumna by Sultan Firoz Shah. Many of the Rajputs placed their wives and children in their houses and burned them, then they rushed to the battle and were killed. Other men of the garrison fought and were slain, and a great many were taken prisoners. Next day I gave orders that the Musulman prisoners should be separated and saved, but that the infidels should all be despatched to hell with the proselyting sword. I also ordered that the houses of the *saiyids, shaikhs* and learned Musulmans should be preserved, but that all the other houses should be plundered and the fort destroyed. It was done as I directed and a great booty was obtained.

When my heart was satisfied with the conquest of Loni, I rode away from thence on the 1st Rabi'u-l akhir to examine the fords of the Jumna, and proceeded along the bank of the river. When I came opposite the palace Jahannuma, I found some places where the river was passable. At the time of midday prayer, I returned to the camp. I gave orders to the princes and emirs, and then held a council about the attack upon Dehli and the operations against Sultan Mahmud.

Council of War on the Attack of Dehli

After much discussion in the Council of War, where everyone had something to say and an opinion to offer, it appeared that the soldiers of my army had heard tales about the strength and prowess and appearance of the elephants of Hindustan. They had been told that in the fight one would take up a horseman and his horse with his trunk and hurl them in the air. These stories had been met by suitable answers from some of the bold troopers. The Council of War at length agreed that a plentiful supply of grain must first be secured, and stored in the fort of Loni as a provision for the army. After this was done, we might proceed to the attack of the fort and city of Dehli. When the Council was over, I ordered Emir Jahan Shah, Emir Sulaiman Shah, and other emirs to cross over the Jumna and to forage in the environs of Dehli, bringing off all the corn they could find for the use of the army.

It now occurred to me that I would cross over the Jumna with a small party of horse to examine the palace of Jahan-numa, and to reconnoitre the ground on which a battle might be fought. So I took an escort of 700 horsemen clad in armour and went off. I sent on 'Ali Sultan Tawachi and Junaid Bur-uldai as an advance guard. Crossing the Jumna I reached Jahan-numa and inspected the whole building, and I discovered a plain fit for a battlefield. 'Ali Sultan and Junaid, my advance-guard, each brought in a man belonging to the vanguard of the enemy. 'Ali Sultan's prisoner was named Muhammad Salaf. When I had interrogated him about the matters of Sultan Mahmud and Mallu Khan, I ordered him to be put to death as an augury of good. My scouts now brought me information that Mallu Khan with 4,000 horsemen in armour, 5,000 infantry, and twenty-seven fierce war elephants fully accoutred, had come out of the gardens of the city and had drawn up his array. I left Saiyid Khwajah and Mubashar Bahadur with 300 brave Turk horsemen on gray horses [*sufaid sawar-i Turk*] in the Jahan-numa and withdrew towards my camp. Mallu Khan advanced boldly towards the Jahan-numa and Saiyid Khwafah and Mubashar went forth to meet him. A conflict ensued, and my men fought valiantly. Immediately I heard of the action I sent Sunjak Bahadur and Emir Allah-dad with two regiments (*kushun*) to their support. As soon as practicable, they assailed the enemy with arrows and then charged them. At the second and third charge the enemy was defeated and fled towards Dehli in disorder. Many fell under the swords and arrows of my men. When the men fled, an extraordinary incident occurred; one of the great war elephants, called Bengális, fell down and died. When I heard of it I declared it to be a good omen. My victorious troops pursued the enemy to the vicinity of the city, and then returned to present themselves at my tent. I congratulated them on their victory and praised their conduct. Next day, Friday the 3rd of the month, I left that fort of Loni and marched to a position opposite to Jahan-numa where I encamped. The officers who had been sent out foraging brought in large quantities of grain and spoil.

Timur Instructs the Princes and Emirs about the Conduct of the War

I now held a court. I issued a summons to the princes, emirs, *nuyans*, commanders of *kushuns*, the commanders of *tumans*, of thousands and of hundreds, and to the braves of the advance-guard. They all came to my tent. All my soldiers were brave veterans, and had used their swords manfully under my own eyes. But there were none that had seen so many fights and battles as I had seen, and no one of the emirs or braves of the army that could compare with me in the amount of fighting I had gone through, and the experience I had gained. I therefore gave them instructions as to the mode of carrying on war; on making and meeting attacks; on arraying their men; on giving support to each other; and on all the precautions to be observed in warring with an enemy. I ordered the emirs of the right wing and the left wing, of the van and the centre, to take up their proper positions. Not to be too forward nor too backward, but to act with the utmost prudence and caution in their operations.

When I had finished, the emirs and others testified their approbation, and, carefully treasuring up my counsel, they departed expressing their blessings and thanks.

Massacre of 100,000 Hindus

At this court Emir Jahan Shah and Emir Sulaiman Shah, and other emirs of experience, brought to my notice that, from the time of entering Hindustan up to the present time, we had taken more than 100,000 infidels and Hindus prisoners, and that they were all in my camp. On the previous day, when the enemy's forces made the attack upon us, the prisoners made signs of rejoicing, uttered imprecations against us, and were ready, as soon as they heard of the enemy's success, to form themselves into a body, break their bonds, plunder our tents, and then to go and join the enemy, and so increase his numbers and strength. I asked their advice about the prisoners, and they said that on the great day of battle these 100,000 prisoners could not be left with the baggage, and that it would be entirely opposed to the rules of war to set these idolaters and foes of Islam at liberty. In fact, no other course remained but that of making them all food for the sword. When I heard these words I found them in accordance with the rules of war, and I directly gave my command . . . that every man who had infidel prisoners was to put them to death, and whoever neglected to do so should himself be executed and his property given to the informer. When this order became known to the *ghazis* of Islam, they drew their swords and put their prisoners to death. 100,000 infidels, impious idolaters, were on that day slain. Maulana Nasiru-d din 'Umar, a counsellor and man of learning, who, in all his life, had never killed a sparrow, now, in execution of my order, slew with his sword fifteen idolatrous Hindus, who were his captives.

After the whole of the vile idolators had been sent to hell, I gave orders that one man out of every ten should be told off to guard the property, and cattle and horses, which had been captured in the invasion; all the other soldiers were to march with me. At the time of mid-day prayer the signal was given for the march, and I proceeded to the spot selected for crossing the Jumna, and there encamped. The astrologers who accompanied the army consulted their books and almanacs as to the time propitious for battle, and they represented that the aspects of the stars made a short delay advisable. In all matters, small and great, I placed my reliance on the favour and kindness of God, and I knew that victory and conquest, defeat and flight, are each ordained by Him, so I placed no reliance on the words of the astrologers and star-gazer, but besought the giver of victory to favour my arms.

I did not wish the war to be of long continuance; so as soon as night was over and morning came, I arose to my devotions. I said the morning prayers in the congregation, and I repeated my private prayers, then I took the holy book, which I always carried with me, and sought a *fal* on the subject of the war. The verse which appeared was one in the chapter of the Bee. I immediately sought the interpretation of this verse from those who were present, and they replied that the manifest meaning of it was. . . . I received this *fal* as a propitious indication, and acted in full reliance on its command and on the favour of God.

On the 5th of Rabi'u-l akhir I passed the Jumna by a ford, and pitched my tents on the [other] side of the river. I gave orders to the emirs and other officers to station their men as close as possible round my tent; and I also directed that the ground round the camp should be parcelled out among them, and that each one should have a deep ditch dug in front of his allotment. All the soldiers, great and small, assembled en masse to dig the ditch. In two watches of the day the ditch round the whole camp was complete. I rode round to inspect it, and I ordered that the trees in the vicinity should be cut down, and brought within the ditch; that their branches should be formed into a strong abbatis, and that in some places planks should be set up.

It had been constantly dinned into the ears of my soldiers that the chief reliance of the armies of Hindustan was on their mighty elephants; that these animals, in complete armour, marched into battle in front of their forces, and that arrows and swords were of no use against them; that in height and bulk they were like small mountains, and their strength was such that at a given signal they could tear up great trees and knock down strongly built walls; that in the battle-field they could take up the horse and his rider with their trunks and hurl them into the air. Some of the soldiers, in the doubt natural to man, brought some little of what they had heard to my attention, so when I assigned their respective positions to the princes and emirs of the right and left wing and of the centre, I enquired of the learned and good men that accompanied my army, such as . . . where they would like to be placed in the day of battle. They had been with me in many campaigns, and had witnessed many a great battle, but the stories about the elephants of India had so affected them that they instantly replied that they would like to be placed with the ladies while the battle was in progress. So to allay the aprehensions of this class of men I gave orders that all the buffalos which had been taken and placed with the baggage should be brought up; I then had their heads and necks fastened to their legs and placed the animals inside the abattis.

Defeat of Sultan Mahmud of Dehli

I gave orders for the camp to be carefully guarded all night to prevent a nocturnal surprise by the enemy, and the night was passed with the caution and care which are necessary in war. When the morn of victory dawned I said my prayers in the congregation, and after I had discharged that duty I gave directions for the drums and other warlike instruments to be sounded. The princes, emirs and *nuyans*, armed themselves completely and marched with their respective forces in regular order. I mounted my horse and rode forth to marshal my array. . . . I took my own place with the centre. When all the forces were arrayed I ordered the advance-guard to go forward and obtain some knowledge of the enemy. One of the advance-guard captured a man belonging to the enemy's van and brought him in to me. When I enquired about the position of the enemy, he told me that Sultan Mahmud had drawn up his army with the intention of fighting. . . . The Sultan had taken up his own position with the centre and had appointed a body of troops to act as rear-guard. His whole force amounted to 10,000 veteran horse, and 40,000 warlike infantry. He had also 125 elephants covered with armour. Most of them carried howdahs in which were throwers of grenades [r'ad-andaz], fireworks [atash baz] and rockets [takhsh-andaz]. Thus they came up to battle.

The enemy's forces now made their appearance, and for better reconnoitring their order I rode to the top of a little hill which was hard by. There I carefully scrutinized their array, and I said to myself that with the favour of God I would defeat them and gain a victory. I alighted from my horse on the top of that hill and performed my devotions. I bowed my head to the ground and besought the Almighty for victory. As I did this I perceived signs that my prayers were heard. When I had finished, I mounted my horse in the full assurance of God's assistance. I returned to the centre and took up my position under the Imperial standard. . . .

The two armies now confronted each other, the drums were beaten on both sides, shouts and cries were raised, a trembling fell upon that field, and a great noise was heard. At this time Sunjak Bahadur, Saiyid Khwaja Allah-dad, and others, separated from the advance-guard, and when they perceived that Sultan Mahmud's forces had drawn near, they moved off to the right, and getting secretly behind the enemy's advance-guard as it came on unsuspecting, they rushed from their ambush, and falling upon them in the rear, sword in hand, they scattered them as hungry lions scatter a flock of sheep, and killed 600 of them in this one charge. Prince Pir Muhammad Jahangir, who commanded the right wing, moved forward his own forces, and with Emir Sulaiman Shah and his regiments of brave cavalry, fell upon the left wing of the enemy and poured down upon it a shower of arrows. They fell boldly upon this division of the enemy, which was commanded by Taghi Khan; and Prince Pir Muhammad Jahangir with great courage and determination attacked one of the fierce elephants and cut off its trunk with his sword, so that the severed part fell upon the ground. My brave soldiers pressing like furious elephants upon this wing of the enemy compelled it to take flight.

The left wing of my army, under Prince Sultan Husain, Emir Jahan Shah, Emir Ghiyasu-d din and other emirs, bravely attacked the enemy's right wing, which was commanded by Malik Mu'inud din and Malik Hadi. They so pressed it with the trenchant sword and piercing arrows that they compelled the enemy to break and fly. Jahan Shah pursued them, and attacked them again and again until they reached the gates of the city [of Dehli].

Simultaneously, Sultan Mahmud, with Mallu Khan and the army of the centre, with its officers and soldiers more numerous than ants or locusts, and with its strong war elephants, made its attack upon [my centre]. Prince Rustam, Emir Shaikh Nuru-d din etc. met it with a brave and resolute resistance. While they were thus engaged, Daulat Timur Tawachi, Mangali Khwaja and other emirs came up with their respective forces and assaulted the enemy. I now gave the order to a party of brave fellows who were in attendance upon me, and they cut their way to the sides of the emirs, who were fighting in the front of the battle. They brought the elephant drivers to the ground with their arrows and killed them. Then they attacked and wounded the elephants with their swords. The soldiers of Sultan Mahmud and Mallu Khan showed no lack of courage, but bore themselves manfully in the fight, still they could not withstand the successive assaults of my soldiers. Seeing their own plight and that of the soldiers and elephants around them, their courage fell, and they took to flight. Sultan Mahmud and Mallu Khan reached the city with a thousand difficulties, and shut themselves up close in the fortifications.

Prince Khalil Sultan captured one of the famous elephants of Sultan Mahmud, having brought down its driver with an arrow. He brought the animal to me and I embraced the lad, and gave him some fine presents, for he was only fifteen years old though he had exhibited such courage and manliness.

The whole of Sultan Mahmud's army was defeated; part was slain, and part had found refuge in the fort, and I, exalted with victory, marched towards the fort. When I reached its gates I carefully reconnoitred its towers and walls, and then returned to the side of the Hauz-i khass. This is a reservoir, which was constructed by Sultan Firoz Shah, and is faced all round with stone and cement [gach]. Each side of that reservoir is more than a bow-shot long, and there are buildings placed around it. This tank is filled by the rains in the rainy season, and it supplies the people of the city with water throughout the year. The tomb of Sultan Firoz Shah stands on its bank. When I had pitched my camp here, the princes and emirs and nuyans, and all the generals and officers, came to wait upon me to pay their respect and offer their congratulations on this great victory. I embraced the princes and emirs and I praised them all for their exertions and courage which I myself had seen. When I recounted the favours and mercies I had received from the Almighty, my excellent sons, the brave and renowned emirs, who served under me, and the great and glorious victories I had achieved, my heart melted, and the tears burst from my eyes. I cast myself upon the ground and poured forth my thanksgivings to the All-beneficent. All who were present raised their voices in prayer, and in wishes for the continuance of my prosperity and the prolongation of my reign.

... Sultan Mahmud and Mallu Khan. ... now repented of the course they had taken, and regretted that they had not made submission to me, and so avoided the evil which had befallen them. They saw that if they stayed in the fort they would be captured and made prisoners, so in the middle of that night, 7th Rabi'u-l akhir, Sultan Mahmud and Mallu Khan left the fort of Jahanpanah and fled towards the mountains and jungles. When I heard of this I immediately sent Emir Sa'id and ... other officers in pursuit. They followed with all speed, and, coming up with the fugitives, they killed many of them, and obtained great spoil. Malik Sharfu-d din and Malik Khudai-dad, sons of Rashid Mallu Khan were taken prisoners, with many others, and brought back to my camp. On the same night that I heard of the flight of the Sultan and his generals from Dehli, I sent Emir Allah-dad and other officers to watch the gate of Hauzrani, through which Mahmud had escaped; and that of Baraka, by which Mallu Khan had gone out. I also sent men to all the other gates, with orders not to let the people escape.

I mounted my horse and rode towards the gate of the *maidan.* I alighted at the 'id-gah, a lofty and extensive building, and I gave orders for my quarters to be moved there, and for my throne to be set up in the 'id-gah, I took my seat upon the throne and held a Court. The *saiyids,* the *ghazish,* the *'ulama* [learned Moslems], the *shaikhs,* and the great men and chiefs of the [Muhammadans of the] city assembled and came out to attend my Court. I had them introduced one by one, and they made their obeisances, and were admitted to the honour of kissing my throne. ...

I sent a party of men into the city to bring out the elephants which Sultan Mahmud had abandoned when he fled. They found 120 enormous elephants and several rhinoceroses, which they brought out to my court. As the elephants passed by me I was greatly amused to see the tricks which their drivers had taught them. Every elephant, at the sign of the driver, bowed his head to the ground, made his obeisance, and uttered a cry. At the direction of their drivers they picked up any object from the ground with their trunks and placed it in their driver's hand, or put it into their mouths and kept it. When I saw these mighty animals, so well trained and so obedient to weak man, I was greatly astonished, and I ordered that they should be sent to Turan and Iran, to Fars, and Azur, and Rum, so that the princes and nobles throughout my dominions might see these animals. Accordingly I sent five to Samarkand, two to Tabriz, one to Shiraz, five to Hirat, one to Sharwan, and one to Azurbaijan.

When Friday came, I sent Maulana Nasiru-d din 'Umar, with some other holy and learned men that accompanied my camp to the Masjid i jami', with directions to say the prayers for the Sabbath, and to repeat the *khutba* of my reign in the metropolis of Dehli. Accordingly, the *khutba,* with my name, was repeated in the pulpits of the mosques in the city of Dehli, and I rewarded the preachers with costly robes and presents.

When the preparations for holding a court in Dehli were complete I gave orders for the princes, the emirs, the *nuyans,* and other of my officers, and the *saiyids,* the *'ulama,* the *shaikhs,* and all the principal men of the city to attend my Court. When they had all arrived I entered and took my seat upon the throne. The Turk and Tajik musicians and singers began to play and sing. Wine [*sharab*] and sharbat, and sweetmeats, and all kinds of bread and meat were served; I bestowed rich robes, and caps, and girdles, and swords, and daggers and horses . . . upon the princes, and emirs and other leading men of my army, especially upon those braves who had distinguished themselves by deeds of valour under my own observation. To some I gave regiments and raised their dignity. Upon the *saiyids* and *'ulama* of the city I bestowed robes and presents. I ordered my secretaries to draw up despatches announcing my victories in Hindusthan, and to circulate them with all speed throughout my dominions. And I ordered my revenue officers to make provision for collecting the ransom-money assessed upon the city. . . .

Sack of the City of Dehli

On the 16th of the month some incidents occurred which led to the sack of the city of Dehli, and to the slaughter of many of the infidel inhabitants. One was this. A party of fierce Turk soldiers had assembled at one of the gates of the city to look about them and enjoy themselves, and some of them laid violent hands upon the goods of the inhabitants. When I heard of this violence, I sent some emirs who were present in the city, to restrain the Turks. A party of soldiers accompanied these emirs into the city. Another reason was that some of the ladies of my harem expressed a wish to go into the city and see the place of Hazar-sutun (thousand columns) which Malik Jauna built in the fort called Jahan-panah. I granted this request, and I sent a party of soldiers to escort the litters of the ladies. Another reason was that Jalal Islam and other *diwans* has gone into the city with a party of soldiers to collect the contribution laid upon the city. Another reason was that some thousand troopers with orders for grain, oil, sugar, and flour, had gone into the city to collect these supplies. Another reason was that it had come to my knowledge that great numbers of Hindus and *gabrs,* which their wives and children, and goods, and valuables, had come into the city from all the country round, and consequently I had sent some emirs with their regiments [*kushun*] into the city and directed them to pay no attention to the remonstrances of the inhabitants, but to seize and bring out these fugitives. For these several reasons a great number of fierce Turk soldiers were in the city. When the soldiers proceeded to apprehend the Hindus and *gabrs* who had fled to the city, many of them drew their swords and offered resistance. The flames of strife were thus lighted and spread through the whole city from Jahan-panah and Siri to Old Dehli, burning up all it reached. The savage Turks fell to killing and plundering. The Hindus set fire to their houses with their own hands, burned their wives and children in them, and rushed into the fight and were killed. The Hindus and *gabrs* of the city showed much alacrity and boldness in fighting. The emirs who were in charge of the gates prevented any more soldiers from going into the place, but the flames of war had risen too high for this precaution to be of any avail in extinguishing them. On that day, Thursday, and all the night of Friday, nearly 15,000 Turks were engaged in slaying, plundering, and destroying. When morning broke on Friday, all my army, no longer under control, went off to the city and thought of nothing but killing, plundering, and making prisoners. All that day the sack was general. The following day, Saturday, the 17th, all passed in the same way, and the spoil was so great that each man secured from fifty to a hundred prisoners, men, women and children. There was no man who took less than twenty. The other booty was immense in rubies, diamonds, garnets, pearls, and other gems; jewels of gold and silver; *ashrafis, tankas* of gold and silver of the celebrated 'Alai coinage; vessels of gold and silver; and brocades and silks of great value. Gold and silver ornaments of the Hindu women were obtained in such quantities as to exceed all account. Excepting the quarter of the *saiyids,* the *'ulama,* and the other Musulmans, the whole city was sacked. The pen of fate had written down this destiny for the people of this city. Although I was desirous of sparing them I could not succeed, for it was the will of God that this calamity should fall upon the city.

On the following day, Sunday, it was brought to my knowledge that a great number of infidel Hindus had assembled in the 'Masjid-i jami' of Old Dehli, carrying with them arms and provisions, and were preparing to defend themselves. Some of my people who had gone that way on business were wounded by them. I immediately ordered Emir Shah Malik, and 'Ali Sultan Tawachi to take a party of men and proceed to clear the house of God from infidels and idolators. They accordingly attacked these infidels and put them to death. Old Dehli then was plundered.

I ordered that all the artisans and clever mechanics, who were masters of their respective crafts, should be picked out from among the prisoners and set aside, and accordingly some thousands of craftsmen were selected to await my command. All these I distributed among the princes and emirs, who were present, or who were engaged officially in other parts of my dominions. I had determined to build a Masjid-i jami in Samarkand, the seat of my empire, which should be without a rival in any country; so I ordered that all builders and stonemasons should be set apart for my own special service.

By the will of God, and by no wish or direction of mine, all the three cities of Dehli, by name Siri, Jahan-panah, and Old Dehli, had been plundered. The *khutba* of my sovereignty, which is an assurance of safety and protection, had been read in the city. It was therefore my earnest wish that no evil might happen to the people of the place. But it was ordained by God that the city should be ruined. He therefore inspired the infidel inhabitants with a spirit of resistance, so that they brought on themselves that fate which was inevitable.

BABUR
(1483–1530)

Zahir ud-Din Muhammad Babur was a Jagataı Turk who claimed descent from both Timur and Genghis Khan. Driven out of Fergana in Turkestan by the Uzbeks (in one of those classic shock waves that precipitated conquests by yesterday's vanquished, nomads driven by the victor to occupy a new area), he seized Afghanistan, becoming ruler in Kabul in 1504. On 21 April 1526, the victory of Panipat, in which his adversary Sultan Ibrahim Lodi was killed, secured him possession of Delhi (on the access route for all invasions from the north of India) and effectively of the whole Indo-Gangetic basin. Babur was the founder of the Moghul dynasty, which reigned over virtually the whole of India from 1526 to 1858. Babur's Memoirs are written in Jagataı Turkic, in a straightforward lively style, very different from most Muslim writings of the time.

THE CONQUEST OF HINDUSTAN

We had information that Sultan Ibrahim, who lay on this side of Delhi, was advancing and that the *shekdar* of Hissar-Firozeh, had also advanced thirty miles towards us with the army of Hissar-Firozeh, and of the neighbouring districts. I sent on Kitteh Beg towards Ibrahim's camp to procure intelligence, and dispatched Momin Atkeh towards the army of Hissar-Firozeh to get notice of its motions.

On Sunday, the 13th of the first Jemadi, I marched from Ambala, and halted on the margin of a tank. The command of the whole right wing I gave to Humaiun. It was at this station, too, that Biban came and made his submission. These Afghans are provokingly rude and stupid. Although Dilawer Khan, who was his superior, both in the number of his retainers and in rank, did not sit

From *Memoirs of Babur*, translated by John Leyden and William Erskine (1826), edited and abridged by F. G. Talbot (1909; reprint, Lahore: National Book House, 1965), 178–88.

in the presence, and although the sons of Alim Khan stood, though they were princes, this man asked to be allowed to sit, and expected me to listen to his unreasonable demand.

Next morning, Humaiun [Babur's son] set out with his light force to attack Hamid Khan by surprise. Humaiun dispatched on before him a hundred or a hundred and fifty select men, by way of advanced guard. On coming near the enemy, this advanced body went close up to them, hung upon their flanks, and had one or two encounters, till the troops of Humaiun appeared in sight following them. No sooner were they perceived than the enemy took to flight. Our troops brought down one hundred or two hundred of their men, cut off the heads of the one half, and brought the other half alive into the camp, along with seven or eight elephants. Beg Mirak Moghul brought the news of this victory of Humaiun to the camp at this station. On the spot, I directed a complete dress of honour, a horse from my own stable, with a reward in money, to be given to him.

Humaiun reached the camp with a hundred prisoners, and seven or eight elephants, and waited on me. I ordered the matchlockmen to shoot all the prisoners as an example. This was Humaiun's first expedition, and the first service he had seen. It was a very good omen. Some light troops having followed the fugitives, took Hissar-Firozeh the moment they reached it, and returned after plundering it. . . .

Marching from that station we reached Shahabad. I sent fit persons towards Sultan Ibrahim's camp to procure intelligence, and halted several days in this station. From this place also I dispatched Rahmet Piadeh to Kabul, with letters announcing my victory. . . .

In this station, the sun entered Aries; we now began also to receive repeated information from Ibrahim's camp, that he was advancing slowly by a mile or two at a time, and halting two or three days at each station. I, on my side, likewise moved on to meet him, and encamped on the banks of the Jumna. Haider Kuli was sent out to procure intelligence. I crossed the Jumna by a ford. At Sirsaweh, there is a fountain, from which a small stream flows. It is rather a pretty place. Terdi Beg praised it highly. I said, "Yours be it"; and in consequence of these praises, I bestowed it on Terdi Beg. Having raised an awning in a boat, we sometimes sailed about on the broad stream of the river, and sometimes entered the creeks in the boat.

From this station we held down the river for two marches, keeping close along its banks, when Haider Kuli, who had been sent out to collect intelligence, returned, bringing information that Daud Khan and Hatim Khan had been seen across the river into the Doab with six or seven thousand horse, and had encamped five or six miles in advance of Ibrahim's position on the road towards us. I dispatched against this column, the whole left wing, as well as part of the centre under Yunis Ali, with instructions to advance rapidly and fall upon them by surprise. About noonday prayers, they crossed the river near our camp; and between afternoon and evening prayers set out from the opposite bank. Next morning, about the time of early prayers, they arrived close upon the enemy, who put themselves in some kind of order, and marched out to meet them: but our troops no sooner came up, than the enemy fled, and were followed in close pursuit, and slaughtered all the way to the limits of Ibrahim's camp. The detachment took one of the generals, with seventy or eighty prisoners, and six or eight elephants, all of which they brought in when they waited on me. Several of the prisoners were put to death, to strike terror into the enemy.

Marching thence, I arranged the whole army in order of battle, with right and left wing and centre, and after reviewing it, performed the *vim*. The custom of the *vim* is that, the whole army being mounted, the commander takes a bow or whip in his hand, and guesses at the number of the army, according to a fashion in use, and in conformity with which they affirm that the army may be so many. The number that I guessed was greater than the army turned out to be.

At this station I directed that, according to the custom of Rum [i.e., of the Ottomans], the gun-carriages should be connected together with twisted bull-hides as with chains. Between every two gun-carriages were six or seven breastworks. The matchlockmen stood behind these guns and breastworks, and discharged their matchlocks. I halted five or six days in this camp, for the purpose of getting this apparatus arranged. After every part of it was in order and ready, I called together all the emirs, and men of any experience and knowledge, and held a general council. It was settled that as Panipat was a considerable city, it would cover one of our flanks by its buildings and houses, while we might fortify our front by covered defences, and cannon, and that the matchlockmen and infantry should be placed in the rear of the guns and breastworks. With this resolution we moved, and in two marches reached Panipat. On our right, were the town and suburbs. In my front I placed the guns and breastworks which had been prepared. On the left, and in different other points, we dug ditches and made defences of the boughs of trees. At the distance of every bowshot, a space was left large enough for a hundred or a hundred and fifty men to issue forth. Many of the troops were in great terror and alarm. Trepidation and fear are always unbecoming. Whatsoever Almighty God has decreed from all eternity, cannot be reversed; though, at the same time, I cannot greatly blame them; they had some reason; for they had come two or three months' journey from their own country; we had to engage in

arms a strange nation, whose language we did not understand, and who did
not understand ours:

> We are all in difficulty, all in distraction,
> Surrounded by a people; by a strange people.

The army of the enemy opposed to us was estimated at one hundred thousand men; the elephants of the emperor and his officers were said to amount
to nearly a thousand. He possessed the accumulated treasures of his father and
grandfather, in current coin, ready for use. It is an usage in Hindustan, in situations similar to that in which the enemy now were, to expend sums of money
in bringing together troops who engage to serve for hire. Had he chosen to
adopt this plan, he might have engaged one or two hundred thousand more
troops. But God Almighty directed everything for the best. He had not the
heart to satisfy even his own army; and would not part with any of his treasure. Indeed, how was it possible that he should satisfy his troops, when he was
himself miserly to the last degree, and beyond measure avaricious in accumulating pelf? He was a young man of no experience. He was negligent in all his
movements; he marched without order; retired or halted without plan, and
engaged in battle without foresight. While the troops were fortifying their position in Panipat and its vicinity, with guns, branches of trees, and ditches,
Muhammed Sarban said to me, "You have fortified our ground in such a way
that it is not possible he should ever think of coming here." I answered, "You
judge of him by the khans and sultans of the Uzbeks." It is true that, the year in
which we left Samarkand and came to Hissar, a body of the Uzbek khans and
sultans having collected and united together, set out from Derbend in order
to fall upon us. I brought the families and property of all the moghuls and soldiers into the town and suburbs, and closing up all the streets, put them in a
defensible state. As these khans and sultans were perfectly versed in the proper
times and seasons for attacking and retiring, they perceived that we were resolved to defend Hissar to the last drop of our blood, and had fortified it under that idea; and seeing no hopes of succeeding in their enterprise, fell back
by Bundak. But you must not judge of our present enemies by those who were
then opposed to us. They have not ability to discriminate when it is proper to
advance and when to retreat. God brought everything to pass favourably. It
happened as I foretold. During the seven or eight days that we remained in Panipat, a very small party of my men, advancing close up to their encampment
and to their vastly superior force, discharged arrows upon them. They did not,
however, move, or make any demonstration of sallying out. At length, induced
by the persuasions of some Hindustani emirs, in my interest, I sent four or five
thousand men on a night attack. They did not assemble properly in the first

instance, and as they marched out in confusion, did not get on well. The day dawned, yet they continued lingering near the enemy's camp till it was broad daylight, when the enemy, on their side, beat their kettle-drums, got ready their elephants, and marched out upon them. Although our people did not effect anything yet, in spite of the multitude of troops that hung upon them in their retreat, they returned safe and sound, without the loss of a man. Muhammed Ali was wounded with an arrow, and though the wound was not mortal, yet it disabled him from taking his place in the day of battle. On learning what had occurred, I immediately detached Humaiun with his division two miles in advance, to cover their retreat, while I myself, remaining with the army, drew it out, and got it in readiness for action. The party which had marched to surprise the enemy fell in with Humaiun, and returned with him. As none of the enemy came near us, I drew off the army, and led it back to the camp. In the course of the night we had a false alarm; for nearly twenty-five minutes the call to arms and the uproar continued. Such of the troops as had never before witnessed an alarm of the kind, were in great confusion and dismay. In a short time, however, the alarm subsided.

By the time of early morning prayers, when the light was such that you could distinguish one object from another, notice was brought from the advanced patrols that the enemy were advancing, drawn up in order of battle. We too immediately braced on our helmets and our armour, and mounted. The right division was led by Humaiun, the left division was commanded by Muhammed Sultan Mirza. The right of the centre was commanded by Chin Taimur Sultan, the left of the centre by Khalifeh. The advance was led by Khosrou Gokultash. Abdul-Aziz, master of horse, had the command of the reserve. On the flank of the right division I stationed Wali Kazil, with their moghuls, to act as a flanking party. On the extremity of the left division I stationed Kara-Kuzi, to form the flankers, with instructions, that as soon as the enemy approached sufficiently near, they should take a circuit and come round upon their rear.

When the enemy first came in sight, they seemed to bend their force most against the right division. I therefore detached Abdul-Aziz, who was stationed with the reserve, to reinforce the right. Sultan Ibrahim's army, from the time it first appeared in sight, never made a halt, but advanced right upon us at a quick pace. When they came closer, and on getting a view of my troops, found them drawn up in the order and with the defences that have been mentioned, they were brought up and stood for a while, as if considering, "Shall we halt or not? shall we advance or not?" They could not halt, and they were unable to advance with the same speed as before. I sent orders to the troops stationed as flankers on the extremes of the right and left divisions, to wheel round the enemy's flank with all possible speed, and instantly to attack them in the rear; the right and left divisions were also ordered to charge the enemy. The flankers accordingly wheeled on the rear of the enemy, and began to make discharges of arrows on them. Mehdi Khwajeh came up before the rest of the left wing. A body of men with one elephant advanced to meet him. My troops gave them some sharp discharges of arrows, and the enemy's division was at last driven back. I dispatched from the main body Ahmedi Perwanchi to the assistance of the left division. The battle was likewise obstinate on the right. I ordered Muhammedi Gokultash to advance in front of the centre and engage. Ustad Ali also discharged his guns many times in front of the line to good purpose. Mustafa, the cannoneer, on the left of the centre, managed his artillery with great effect. The right and left divisions, the centre and flankers having surrounded the enemy and taken them in rear, were now engaged in hot conflict, and busy pouring in discharges of arrows on them. They made one or two very poor charges on our right and left divisions. My troops making use of their bows, plied them with arrows, and drove them in upon their centre. The troops on the right and left of their centre, being huddled together in one place, such confusion ensued, that the enemy, while totally unable to advance, found also no road by which they could flee. The sun had mounted spear-high when the onset of battle began, and the combat lasted till mid-day, when the enemy were completely broken and routed, and my friends victorious and exulting. By the grace and mercy of Almighty God, this arduous undertaking was rendered easy for me, and this mighty army, in the space of half a day, laid in the dust. Five or six thousand men were discovered lying slain, in one spot, near Ibrahim. We reckoned that the number lying slain, in different parts of this field of battle, amounted to fifteen or sixteen thousand men. On reaching Agra, we found, from the accounts of the natives of Hindustan, that forty or fifty thousand men had fallen in this field. After routing the enemy, we continued the pursuit, slaughtering, and making them prisoners. Those who were ahead, began to bring in the emirs and Afghans as prisoners. They brought in a very great number of elephants with their drivers, and offered them to me as *peshkesh*. Having pursued the enemy to some distance, and supposing that Ibrahim had escaped from the battle, I appointed a party of my immediate adherents, to follow him in close pursuit down as far as Agra. Having passed through the middle of Ibrahim's camp, and visited his pavilions and accommodations, we encamped on the banks of the Siah-ab.

It was now afternoon prayers when Tahir Taberi, the younger brother of Khalifeh, having found Ibrahim lying dead amidst a number of slain, cut off his head, and brought it in.

That very day I directed Humaiun Mirza to set out without baggage or encumbrances, and proceed with all possible expedition to occupy Agra, and take possession of the treasuries. I at the same time ordered Mehdi Khwajeh to leave the baggage behind, to push on by forced marches, to enter the Fort of Delhi, and seize the treasures.

Next morning we marched, and having proceeded about two miles, halted on the banks of the Jumna, in order to refresh our horses. After three marches, I encamped near Delhi, on the banks of Jumna. I bestowed the office of military collector of Delhi on Wali Kizil; I made Dost Diwan of Delhi, and directed the different treasuries to be sealed, and given into their charge. Moulana Mahmud, Sheikh Zin, and some others, went into Delhi, to Friday prayers, read the prayer in my name, distributed some money among the fakirs and beggars, and then turned back.

A few days later I halted in the suburbs of Agra, at the palace of Suliman. As this position was very far from the fort, I next morning moved and took up my quarters at the palace of Jilal Khan. The people of the fort had put off Humaiun, who arrived before me, with excuses; and he, on his part, considering that they were under no control, and wishing to prevent their plundering the treasure, had taken a position to shut up the issues from the place.

Bikermajit, a Hindu, who was raja of Gualiar, had governed that country for upwards of a hundred years. In the battle in which Ibrahim was defeated, Bikermajit was sent to hell. Bikermajit's family, and the heads of his clan, were at this moment in Agra. When Humaiun arrived, Bikermajit's people attempted to escape, but were taken by the parties which Humaiun had placed upon the watch, and put in custody. Humaiun did not permit them to be plundered. Of their own free will they presented to Humaiun a peace-offering, consisting of a quantity of jewels and precious stones. Among these was one famous diamond, the Koh-i-nor, which had been acquired by Sultan Alauddin. It is so valuable, that a judge of diamonds valued it at half of the daily expense of the whole world. It is about 320 ratis [1 rati = 2.171 Troy grains]. On my arrival, Humaiun presented it to me, and I gave it back to him as a present. . . .

On Thursday, the 28th of Rejeb, about the hour of afternoon prayers, I entered Agra, and took up my residence at Sultan Ibrahim's palace. From the time when I conquered the country of Kabul, which was in the year 1504, till the present time I had always been bent on subduing Hindustan. Sometimes, however, from the misconduct of my emirs and their dislike of the plan, sometimes from the cabals and opposition of my brothers, I was prevented from prosecuting any expedition into that country, and its provinces escaped being overrun. At length these obstacles were removed. There was now no one left, great or small, noble or private man, who could dare to utter a word in opposition to the enterprise. In the year 1519, I collected an army, and having taken the fort of Bajour by storm, put all the garrison to the sword. I next advanced into Behreh, where I prevented all marauding and plunder, imposed a contribution on the inhabitants, . . . in money and goods, divided the proceeds among the troops who were in my service, and returned back to Kabul. From that time till the year 1526, I attached myself in a peculiar degree to the affairs of Hindustan, and in the space of these seven or eight years entered it five times at the head of an army. The fifth time, the Most High God, of his grace and mercy, cast down and defeated an enemy so mighty as Sultan Ibrahim, and made me the master and conqueror of the powerful empire of Hindustan.

PART 10

LIMITED WARS IN THE WEST

JEAN FROISSART
(c. 1337–1404?)

*Jean Froissart, the chronicler of the Hundred Years' War, was a Frenchman
who lived in England from 1361 to 1369 and then retired to Valenciennes. He
was ordained a priest and secured a living near Mons; later he became a
canon at Chimay in Wallonia. He traveled in France, Italy, and the Low
Countries.*

THE BATTLE OF CRÉCY

That same Saturday, the King of France [Philip VI] rose early and heard mass
in the monastery of Saint Peter's at Abbéville, where he was lodging. With him
were the King of Bohemia, the Count of Alençon, the Count of Blois, the Count
of Flanders, the Duke of Lorraine and all the chief nobles. There was not
enough room for the whole army at Abbéville, and many of them were lodged
at Saint Riquier. The King set out with his army at sunrise, and when he had
advanced five miles was advised to form his army in battle order, and to let
those on foot go ahead, so as not to be trampled underfoot by the horses. The
King sent four valiant knights ahead, Lord Moyne of Bastelburg [in Bohemia],
the Lord of Noyers, the Lord of Beaujeu and the Lord of Anceris; they rode so
far ahead that they could easily make out the English position; and the English were aware that they had come to reconnoitre, but paid no attention and
let them return without attacking.

When King Philip saw them coming back, and pushing through the crowd
to reach him, he asked: "Sirs, what news?" They all looked at each other, none
liking to speak first. In the end the King asked Lord Moyne, who was attached
to King Charles of Bohemia, and who was acknowledged as one of the most

From *Froissart's Chronicles*, edited and translated by John Jolliffe (New York: Modern Library,
1968), 142–50. Copyright © 1967 by John Jolliffe. Reprinted by permission of the Peters Fraser &
Dunlop Group Ltd and of Random House, Inc.

valiant and chivalrous knights in Christendom, having performed many noble deeds.

"Sir," said Lord Moyne, "Since it is your wish, I will speak, but I do so under correction of my companions. We advanced far enough to reconnoitre your enemies. They are drawn up in three battalions, and are evidently awaiting you. If there is no better suggestion, my advice is that you should halt your army here for the rest of the day. For by the time your rearguard arrives and the army is properly drawn up, it will be late. Your troops will be tired, and in disarray, but you will find the enemy fresh and alert, and fully aware of what they must do. In the morning you can draw up your line of battle better, and reconnoitre more easily, and discover where you can most advantageously attack; for you may be sure that they will wait for you."

The King gave orders that this should be done, and his two marshals rode up and down giving the command "Halt banners, the King's command, in the name of God and Saint Denis." Those that were in front halted; those at the rear did not, but still pressed forward, saying that they would not halt until they were as far forward as the front, and those in front of them were pushed forward in their turn. This disorder was entirely caused by pride, every man wishing to surpass his neighbour, in spite of the marshal's words. Neither the King nor the marshals could stop them, since every lord was eager to show off his own power. So they advanced, in complete disorder, till they came in sight of the enemy. It would have been far better had the front rank stood firm: but on seeing the enemy they immediately retired, in complete disarray, which alarmed the rear, who thought they must have been fighting, and been turned back. There was then room for them to advance, had they so wished, and some did advance, while others held back. All the roads between Abbéville and Crécy were blocked with common people who, when they got within eight miles of the enemy, drew their swords and cried out "Kill, Kill." Nobody who was not present or has not had leisure to examine the whole affair can possibly imagine the confusion of that day, and in particular the chaotic state of the French. I owe my own knowledge of it mostly to the English, who were well able to observe the confusion, and to the men of Sir John of Hainault, who were always near the [French] King's person.

The English, who had been drawn up in three battalions, sitting quietly on the ground, calmly rose to their feet, when they saw the French approaching, and formed their ranks. The [Black] Prince's battalion was in front, with its archers drawn up in a triangular formation, with the men-at-arms behind. The Earls of Northampton and Arundel, who commanded the second battalion, were drawn up in good order on the Prince's flank, to support him if necessary.

You must realize that on the French side, the kings, dukes, counts and barons did not advance in any regular order, but one after another, as they pleased. As soon as King Philip came in sight of the English, his blood began to boil, such was his hatred. He cried out to his marshals: "Order the Genoese forward and let the battle begin, in the name of God and Saint Denis." There were about fifteen thousand Genoese crossbowmen; but they were quite unready for battle, being very tired and having marched over fifteen miles in full armour, carrying their crossbows. They told the constable that they were in no condition to fight, and the Count of Alençon, when he heard of it, said, "This is what one gets for employing such rabble; they fail us in the hour of need!" Meanwhile a violent storm broke from the heavens, with tremendous thunder and lightning. Before the rain came, an immense flight of crows had passed over both armies, indicating the severity of the coming storm. Several wiseacres explained that this was the sign of a great battle and of fearful bloodshed. The storm soon passed, and the sun came out, bright and clear, shining straight in the eyes of the French, whereas the English had it behind them.

When the Genoese were in some kind of order, and were ready to attack the English, they began to shout extremely loud in order to dismay the English, who, however, held their ground and paid no attention. They cried out a second time, loud and clear, and went forward a little, but the English did not move. A third time they shouted, extremely loud, and advanced, aimed their crossbows and began to shoot. The English archers then took a pace forward, and let fly their arrows in such unison that they were as thick as snow. The Genoese had never experienced such archery, and when they felt the arrows pierce their arms, heads, and coats of mail, they were much taken aback; some cut the cords of their crossbows, others flung them to the ground, and all turned tail and fled. The French had a large body of men-at-arms on horseback to supervise the Genoese. And when the latter tried to run away, they were prevented. For the King of France, seeing them turn back in disorder, cried out in a fury: "Kill all this rabble, kill them! They are getting in our way and they serve no purpose." Then you might have seen the men-at-arms laying about them, killing all they could of the runaways. The English kept up their hail of arrows as strongly as ever, shooting into the thick of the enemy; the arrows fell among the men-at-arms and their horses, bringing many of them down, horses and men together: once down, they were quite incapable of rising to their feet.

The valiant and noble King Charles of Bohemia was the son of the noble Emperor, Henry of Luxemburg; although the latter was nearly blind, he had the order of battle explained to him; and he enquired from his knights the whereabout of his son, the Lord Charles. They replied: "Sir, we do not know;

he is fighting in another part of the field." Then this valiant prince said: "Gentlemen, you are my men and my friends and my companions. I beg of you to lead me into the fight this day, that I may strike a blow with my sword." The knights nearest him did as he asked, though Lord Moyne and a number of good knights of Luxemburg wanted to leave him behind; but in order not to lose him, several knights tied their reins together, and advanced with their King at their head, to achieve his object. The truth is that in spite of the great number of lords and knights in the King of France's army, very few notable feats were achieved by them, for the battle began late in the day and the French arrived already weary. All the same they pressed on, preferring death to the dishonour of flight. Charles of Bohemia, who already called and signed himself King of Germany, and bore those arms, reached the field of battle in good order. But when he saw that the French were doing badly, he went away, by what road I do not know. Whereas the King his father advanced far into the fray, and struck four strokes or more with his sword, and fought as valiantly as his companions. So far forward did they advance that all were killed; their bodies were found next day, round the King their lord, with the reins of their horses knotted together.

King Philip was furious that his army was being cut down by a handful of Englishmen, and in spite of being advised by Sir John of Hainault to retreat, he advanced without a word to join his brother, the Count of Alençon, whose banner he could see on a little hill. There the Count of Alençon was advancing in good order against the English, and after riding past the archers, he succeeded in engaging the Prince of Wales's battalion, and fighting long and valiantly, as did the Count of Flanders in another part. The King of France was most anxious to join them, but there was a great hedge of archers and men-at-arms in front of him that remained unbroken. That morning, King Philip had given Sir John of Hainault a fine black charger, and he in turn had mounted Sir John de Fusselles on it, to carry his banner. This horse took the bit between its teeth and brought its rider, still carrying the banner of Hainault, right through the English army. And when he was at last able to turn, the horse stumbled and fell in a ditch, being hit by an arrow; there Sir John de Fusselles would have died had not his page followed him, making a detour round the battalions. The page found him in the ditch, unable to rise because of the horse but otherwise in no danger, for the English would not break their ranks to take prisoners. The page helped him up and they returned by a different way.

This battle, fought between Crécy and La Broye, was a very cruel and murderous affair, and many feats of arms went unrecorded. It was already late when the battle began, which hindered the French more than anything else, for towards nightfall many knights and squires lost their commanders, and they wandered about in small parties attacking the English, but before long they were all wiped out. For the English had decided that morning to take no prisoners and hold no one to ransom, so great were the numbers against them.

The Count of Blois, nephew of King Philip and of the Count of Alençon, came with his men under his banner to fight the English, and acquitted himself nobly, as did the Duke of Lorraine. Many people say that if the battle had begun in the morning, there would have been many notable feats of arms achieved on the French side. For a number of French knights and squires, as well as others from Germany and Savoy, broke the lines of archers in front of the Prince's battalion, and engaged, hand to hand, with the men-at-arms; upon which the second battalion, under the Earls of Northampton and Arundel, came to their aid, and none too soon, or they would have been hard pressed.

The first battalion, seeing the danger they were in, sent Sir Thomas Norwich to the King [Edward III], who had taken up a position on a little hill, by a windmill. "Sir," said Sir Thomas, "Lord Warwick and Lord Oxford and Sir Reginald Cobham, who are with your son, are hard pressed by the French; they beg you to come to their help with your battalion, for they think that if the numbers of the French increase, the Prince will be overwhelmed."

"Sir Thomas," replied the King, "is my son dead, or fallen, or so badly wounded that he cannot help himself?"

"No, sir, thank God, but he is so hard pressed that he needs your help."

"Well, Sir Thomas, go back to him and to those that sent you, and tell them not to ask for any help from me while my son is still alive. Say that I want them to let the boy win his spurs, for I am determined, please God, that the day shall be his, and that the honour and glory of it shall be won by him and by those to whom I have entrusted him."

Sir Thomas returned to his lords, and told them what the King had said. This answer gave them great encouragement, and they regretted having asked for help. They were inspired to even greater feats of valour than before, and held the position, to their great credit.

There were no doubt many great feats of arms of which I have no knowledge. But one thing is certain: Sir Godfrey of Harcourt, who was in the Prince's battalion, made every effort to save the life of his brother, having heard that his brother's banner had been seen engaged fighting for the French, against Sir Godfrey's side. But Sir Godfrey could not reach him in time: his brother was killed on the field, and so was the Count of Aumale, his nephew. Elsewhere, the Count of Alençon and the Count of Flanders fought fiercely under their banners, with their people round them, but they could not resist the might of the English. There they were slain, and with them many other knights and squires who attended and accompanied them. Louis Count of Blois and the

Duke of Lorraine, his brother-in-law, with their banners and troops, made a gallant stand in another part of the field; but they were surrounded by a troop of the English and Welsh, who showed them no mercy, and all their valour was in vain. The Count of Saint Pol and the Count of Auxerre were also killed, both gallant knights, and many others besides.

At the close of day, towards vespers, King Philip left the field utterly defeated, with only fifty barons round him in all; Sir John of Hainault was the chief among them, and nearest the King, with the Lords of Montmorency, Beaujeu, Aubigny, and Montfort. The King rode off, lamenting and bewailing, to the castle of La Broye. When they reached the gate, they found it locked, and the drawbridge up, for night had fallen—a dark, thick night. The King ordered the governor to be summoned, for he wished to enter. The governor was called, and appeared on the battlements, and asked who it was that called out at this time of night. King Philip heard his voice and called out; "Open, open, governor; it is the unhappy King of France." The governor recognized the King's voice, and already knew he had lost the day, from some fugitives who had passed below the castle. He lowered the bridge and opened the gate. The King entered, with his five companions, and they stayed till midnight. But the King would not shut himself up there or stay there; they drank a glass of wine, and then rode off, taking with them guides who knew the country. They left at midnight, and rode so hard that they reached Amiens at dawn. There the King stopped at a monastery, saying he would go no further till he found out which of his people lay dead on the field and who had escaped.

Now let us return to Crécy, and the position of the English. All that Saturday they never broke their ranks to pursue anybody, but held their position and repulsed the attacks that were made against them. This was the only reason why the King of France was not taken, for he stayed on the field till very late, as you have heard, with not more than sixty men around him, quite near the enemy. Then Sir John of Hainault had taken hold of the King's reins, having already remounted him once, when his horse was killed under him, and said: "Sir, come away, it is high time. Do not expose yourself. Today you have lost, but another day you will win." And he led the King forcibly from the field.

That day, the English archers brought a tremendous advantage to their side. Many people say that it was by their shooting that the day was won, although the knights achieved many noble deeds, fighting hand to hand, and rallying valiantly. But the archers certainly succeeded in one great achievement, for it was entirely by their fire at the beginning that the Genoese, and they were fifteen thousand in number, were turned back. And a great number of French men-at-arms, well armed and mounted and richly apparelled, were overthrown by the Genoese, who while running away, became entangled with them and brought them down so that they could not rise again. And on the English side there were a number of Cornishmen and Welshmen on foot, armed with large knives, who advanced between the archers and the men-at-arms (who made way for them) and came upon the French when they were in this plight; and they fell upon the earls, barons, knights, and squires and killed them mercilessly, great lords though they were. The King of England was afterwards much annoyed that these nobles had not been held to ransom.

By nightfall on Saturday, when there were no longer any shouts and battlecries to be heard, the English held the field, and their enemies were routed.

HERNÁN CORTÉS
(1485–1547)

Hernán Cortés was born in Estremadura, Spain, like most of the most outstanding conquistadores (among them Pizarro, Balboa, Valdivia, Alvarado, De Soto, and Orellana). After studying law at the university of Salamanca, he embarked for the New World in 1504. He became owner of an encomienda in Cuba but left on his expedition to Mexico in 1519, against the orders of the island's governor. Cortés prohibited pillaging, sought to negotiate alliances, and fought only when forced to. He pursued an indirect strategy that bordered on genius. After an initial setback, for which he was not responsible, he embarked on the siege of Tenochtitlán (now Mexico City), the Aztec capital, in a combined land and water operation in 1521 and took it. If the term has any political and military meaning, the capture of Tenochtitlán constituted a decisive battle.

THE SIEGE OF TENOCHTITLÁN

I sent messengers to the provinces of Tascalteca, Guaxocingo and Churultecal to inform them that the brigantines were ready and that I and all my people were prepared to surround the great city of Temixtitan [Tenochtitlán]. I requested them, therefore, that, as they had already been advised by me and had alerted their own people, they should come, as many and as well armed as possible, to Tesuico, where I would wait ten days for them; and that on no account should they exceed this, for it would most seriously disconcert my plans. When the messengers arrived the natives of these provinces were already prepared and eager to face the Culuans; those from Guaxocingo and Churultecal came to Calco, for so I had ordered them to do, as the siege was to begin

From *Hernán Cortés: Letters from Mexico*, rev. ed., translated and edited by Anthony Pagden (New Haven: Yale University Press, 1986), 206–58. Copyright © 1971 by Anthony Pagden; revised edition © 1986 by Yale University Press. Reprinted by permission of Yale University Press.

close by there. The captains from Tascalteca with all their men, well armed and in splendid array, arrived in Tesuico four or five days before Whitsunday, which was the time I had assigned to them. As I knew that they were arriving on that day, I went joyfully out to meet them; and they arrived so confident and well disciplined that none could be better. According to the count which the captains gave us, there were more than fifty thousand warriors, who were all very well received and well quartered by us.

On the day after Whitsun, I ordered all the foot soldiers and the horsemen to gather in the square of Tesuico, and there I allotted them to three captains who were to lead them to three cities close to Temixtitan. I made Pedro de Alvarado captain of one company, and gave him thirty horsemen and eighteen crossbowmen and harquebusiers, and 150 foot soldiers with swords and bucklers, and more than 25,000 warriors from Tascalteca; these were to encamp in the city of Tacuba.

I made Cristóbal de Olid captain of another company and gave him thirty-three horsemen, eighteen crossbowmen and harquebusiers, 160 foot soldiers with swords and bucklers and more than twenty thousand warriors of our allies; these were to quarter themselves in the city of Cuyoacán.

I made Gonzalo de Sandoval, the alguacil mayor, captain of the third company, and I gave him twenty-four horsemen, four harquebusiers and thirteen crossbowmen, and 150 foot soldiers with swords and bucklers, fifty of whom were chosen from those of my own company, together with all the people from Guaxocingo, Churultecal and Calco, who numbered more than thirty thousand men. They were to go by way of the city of Yztapalapa and destroy it, and thence continue along a causeway over the lake, supported by the brigantines, until they met with my garrison at Cuyoacan, so that after I had entered the lake with the brigantines the alguacil mayor might set up camp where he saw fit.

For the thirteen brigantines with which I was to cross the lake, I left three hundred men, most of whom were sailors and very able, so that there were twenty-five Spaniards in each brigantine, and each one had a captain, a lookout and six crossbowmen and harquebusiers.

When I had given these orders the two captains who were to go to Tacuba and Cuyoacan, after they had received their instructions, left Tesuico on the tenth of May. . . .

On the following morning the two captains arranged, as I had ordered them, to cut off the fresh water which flowed along the aqueducts to the city of Temixtitan. One of them, with twenty horsemen and some crossbowmen and harquebusiers, went to the source, which was a quarter of a league away, and destroyed the pipes, which were made of wood and stone and mortar. He fought and defeated the enemy, who tried to prevent him by land and from the water, thus succeeding in his purpose, which was to deprive the city of fresh water, which was a cunning stratagem.

That same day the captains had some bad places on the causeways, bridges and channels in the vicinity leveled, so that the horses might pass freely from one part to another.

This occupied them for three or four days, and during that time they had many encounters with the people of the city, in which some Spaniards were wounded and many of the enemy killed and many bridges and barricades taken. Many arguments and insults were exchanged between the Tascaltecans and the Culuans which were most remarkable and worthy of note. . . .

. . . On the day following the feast of Corpus Christi, on Friday at dawn, I sent Gonzalo de Sandoval, alguacil mayor, with all his men, out of Tesuico and ordered him to go straight to the city of Yztapalapa, which is rather less than six leagues from there. They arrived a little after midday and began to burn the city and to fight with the inhabitants. But when they saw the superior forces of the alguacil mayor, for more than thirty-five or forty thousand of our allies had gone with him, they took to the water in their canoes. The alguacil mayor, with all his forces, lodged in that city, remaining there that day to await my orders and discover what had happened to me.

When I had dispatched the alguacil mayor I immediately boarded one of the brigantines and we set out using both sail and oar. At the time the alguacil mayor was burning the city of Yztapalapa we came within sight of a large and well-fortified hill near the city, surrounded by water; on it were many people who had come from Temixtitan and all the villages around the lake; they knew that our first encounter would be with the people of Yztapalapa, and so they had gathered there to defend themselves and attack us if possible. When they saw the fleet approaching they began to shout and make smoke signals, so that the other cities by the lakes should know and be prepared. Although my intention had been to attack that part of the city which is in the water, we turned back to that hill or knoll, and I landed with 150 men, although it was very steep and high. With great difficulty we began to climb, and at last captured the fortifications which they had built for their defense on the top. We broke through them in such a manner that none of them escaped, save the women and children; in the struggle twenty-five Spaniards were wounded, but it was a most beautiful victory.

As the inhabitants of Yztapalapa had made smoke signals from some temple towers that stood on a very high hill close to the city, the people of Temixtitan and the other cities on the water knew that I was already crossing the lake in the brigantines and quickly gathered a large fleet of canoes to attack us and discover what sort of thing these brigantines were; as far as we could judge there were more than five hundred canoes. When I saw that they were sailing straight for us, I and all the men who were on the hill embarked with great haste, but I ordered the captains of the brigantines not to move, so that the canoes, thinking that we did not go out to them through fear, might themselves attack us; and indeed they began to direct their fleet toward us with considerable force. But when they had come within some two crossbowshots of us they stopped and remained motionless. I was anxious that this first encounter with them should result in a great victory, so that they would be inspired with a terror of the brigantines, for the key to the war lay with them, as both the Indians and ourselves were most exposed on water. And it pleased God that as we were watching one another a land breeze, very favorable to attacking them, sprang up, and I ordered the captain to break through the fleet of canoes and to drive them back into the city of Temixtitan. As the wind was good, we bore down through the middle of them, and although they fled as fast as they were able, we sank a huge number of canoes and killed or drowned many of the enemy, which was the most remarkable sight in the world. We then pursued them for three leagues or more until we had confined them among the houses of the city; and so it pleased Our Lord to grant us a greater and better victory than we could have asked or desired. . . .

We chased the canoes with the brigantines for fully three leagues, and those that escaped us sought refuge among the houses in the city. As it was late and already after vespers, I collected the brigantines together and sailed with them up to the causeway, and there I resolved to land with thirty men and seize two small temple towers which were surrounded by a low stone enclosure. When we landed, they fought most fiercely to defend those towers, but at last with great danger and much effort we captured them. I then ordered three heavy iron guns to be landed; and as the rest of the causeway from there to the city, which was half a league, was full of the enemy, and the water on either side of the causeway covered with canoes full of warriors, I had one of the guns loaded and discharged along the causeway, which did much damage to the enemy. Owing to the carelessness of our gunner, however, all the powder we had in that place was ignited. It was no great quantity, however, and that night I sent a brigantine some two leagues to Yztapalapa, where the alguacil mayor was, to bring all the powder that was there.

At first my intention, once I had embarked with the brigantines, had been to go to Cuyoacan and ensure that the garrison there was well protected and might do the enemy every possible harm, but, after I had landed that day on the causeway and captured those two towers, I decided to set up camp there and keep the brigantines close by the towers. I ordered half of the people at Cuyoacan together with fifty of the alguacil mayor's foot soldiers to come there the following day. Having made these provisions, we kept careful watch that night, for we were in great danger and all the people from the city had gathered there on the causeway and on the water. At midnight a great multitude of people arrived in canoes and poured along the causeway to attack our camp; this caused us great fear and consternation, especially as it was night, and never have they been known or seen to fight at such an hour unless they were certain of an easy victory. But as we were all well prepared, we began to fight with them, and the brigantines, each of which carried a small fieldpiece, began to fire at them and the crossbowmen and harquebusiers likewise. After this they dared advance no further, nor did they even come close enough to do us any harm; and so they left us in peace for what remained of the night and attacked us no more.

On the morning of the following day there arrived at my camp fifteen crossbowmen and harquebusiers and fifty soldiers with swords and bucklers and seven or eight horsemen from the garrison at Cuyoacan; and, even as they were arriving, the people from the city fought with us on the causeway and from their canoes. So great was the multitude that neither by land nor water could we see anything but people, shouting and screaming so it seemed the world was coming to an end. We began to fight with them up the causeway and gained a channel whose bridge they had removed and an earthwork which had been built behind it. We did them so much harm with the guns and from horseback that we drove them back almost as far as the first houses of the town. As on the far side of the causeway, where the brigantines could not go, there were many canoes from which they did us much harm with the arrows and javelins they hurled at us, I ordered a breach to be opened in the causeway near to our camp and sent four brigantines through. These drove the canoes in among the houses of the city so that in no place dared they come out into the open. On the other side of the causeway the remaining eight brigantines fought with the canoes and drove them in amongst the houses, even pursuing them there, which they had not dared do before, for there were so many stakes and shallows to hinder them. But as now they found canals by which they might enter in safety, they fought with those in the canoes, taking some of them and burning many houses in the suburbs of the city. We spent the whole day fighting the enemy in this manner.

On the following day the alguacil mayor, together with all the people he had in Yztapalapa, Spaniards as well as allies, departed for Cuyoacán, which is joined to the mainland by a causeway, a league and a half long. After the alguacil mayor had covered about a quarter of a league he reached a small town, which is also built on the water, but it is possible to ride through it in many places; the inhabitants began to attack him, but he routed them, killing many, and destroyed and burnt their town. When I learnt that the Indians had destroyed much of the causeway so that the men could not cross without difficulty, I sent two brigantines to help them cross, which they used as bridges for the foot soldiers. When they had crossed they set up camp at Cuyoacan, and the alguacil mayor with ten horsemen took the road to the causeway where we had pitched our camp, and when he arrived he found us fighting. He and his men then began to fight alongside us with the Indians on the causeway. While the aforementioned alguacil mayor was fighting he was pierced through the foot with a javelin; but although he and some others were wounded that day, we did so much harm to the enemy with the heavy ordnance, the crossbows and harquebuses, that neither those in the canoes nor those on the causeway dared approach us very close, and showed more fear and less arrogance than before. In this manner six days were spent, and on each day we fought them; the brigantines burnt all the houses they could around the city, having discovered a canal whereby they might penetrate the outskirts and suburbs. This was most advantageous and kept back the canoes, which now dared not come within a quarter of a league of our camp.

The following day Pedro de Alvarado, who was captain of the garrison at Tacuba, informed me how on the other side of the city the people of Temixtitan came and went as they chose along a causeway, and another smaller one which joined it, to some towns on the mainland. He believed that once they were hard pressed they would all abandon the city by these causeways. Although I desired them to leave more than they did themselves, for we could take greater advantage of them on the mainland than in that huge fortress on the water, I thought it wise to surround them on all sides so that they might avail themselves of nothing on the mainland. I ordered the alguacil mayor, wounded though he was, to move his camp to a small town at the end of one of these causeways. He left with twenty-three horsemen, a hundred foot soldiers and eighteen crossbowmen and harquebusiers, leaving me the other fifty foot soldiers which I kept in my company. On the following day, he arrived and set up camp as I had ordered, and thenceforth the city of Temixtitan was surrounded at all the points where it might be possible to escape along the causeways. . . .

I left the camp in the morning, and moved up the causeway on foot. There we found the enemy in defense of a breach in the causeway as wide and as deep as a lance, and they had built a barricade. We fought with them and they with us, both very courageously, but at last they were defeated and we proceeded up the causeway until we reached the entrance to the city, where there was a temple tower, at the foot of which had been a very large bridge which they had removed, over a broad channel of water, with another strong earthwork. When we arrived they began to fight with us, but as the brigantines attacked from both sides we were able to capture it without danger, which would have been impossible without them. As the enemy began to abandon the barricade, the men from the brigantines came ashore and we crossed the water together with the Indians of Tascalteca, Guaxocingo, Calco and Tesuico, who numbered more than eighty thousand men. While we filled in that broken bridge with stone and adobes, the Spaniards took another barricade on the principal and widest street in the city, and as there was no water nearby it was easier to capture. They then pursued the enemy up the street until they reached a bridge which had been destroyed save for a broad beam over which the Indians crossed, and, once they were on the other side and protected by the water, they drew it after them. On the far side of the bridge they had built another great earthwork with clay and adobes. When we arrived we found that we could not cross without throwing ourselves into the water, which was very dangerous as the enemy fought most bravely. On both sides of the street there was an infinite number of them, who attacked us very fiercely from the roof tops, but when the force of crossbowmen and harquebusiers arrived and we fired two guns up the street we were able to do them great harm. When we saw this certain of the Spaniards threw themselves into the water and struggled toward the other side, which took more than two hours to capture. But when the enemy saw them cross they abandoned the earthwork and the roof tops and fled up the street, whereupon all our people crossed over. I then ordered the earthworks to be destroyed and the channel filled up. Meanwhile the Spaniards and our Indian allies continued for about two crossbowshots, until they reached another bridge which was next to the square containing the principal dwellings of the city. But this bridge they had not removed nor had they built any earthwork in front of it, for they had not believed that we could have gained any part of what we had won that day, nor had we imagined that it would be even half as much.

At the entrance to the square I had a gun placed, and with it we did much harm to the enemy, who were so many that there was no room for them all in the square. When the Spaniards saw that there was no water there, the thing by which they were most endangered, they resolved to enter the square. When the inhabitants of the city saw them put this into effect and beheld the great multitude of our allies—although without us, they would have had no fear of them—they fled, and our allies pursued them until they were confined in the enclosure where they keep their idols, which is surrounded by a stone wall, and, as I explained in my earlier account, is large enough to hold a town of four hundred inhabitants. They soon abandoned it, and the Spaniards and our allies captured the place and remained inside it and inside the towers for a considerable while. But when the enemy saw that there were no horsemen they returned and drove the Spaniards out of the towers and the courtyard and the enclosure, where they found themselves hard pressed and in great danger; and as they were retreating rather too hastily, they turned and faced them beneath the arches of the forecourt. But the enemy attacked them so fiercely that they were forced to withdraw to the square, whence they were driven down the main street, abandoning the gun which was there. The Spaniards, as they were unable to resist the enemy, continued to retreat in great peril of their lives, and indeed they would have been much harmed had it not pleased God that at that moment three horsemen arrived. When the enemy saw them enter the square they thought that there were more and began to flee. The horsemen then killed some of them and regained the courtyard and enclosure that I have mentioned. Ten or twelve of the principal lords of the city barricaded themselves into the largest and highest of the towers, which has a hundred or more steps to the top; but four or five Spaniards fought their way up and killed them all, although they fought most bravely in their defense. Afterwards, another five or six horsemen arrived, and they and the others prepared an ambush in which they killed more than thirty of the enemy.

As it was already late I ordered my people to collect and withdraw, and in withdrawing we were assailed by such a multitude of the enemy that were it not for the horsemen the Spaniards would have been much injured. But as I had had all those dangerous crossings in the street and on the causeway, where we expected most danger, filled in and leveled by the time we withdrew, the horsemen could come and go with ease. When the enemy attacked us in our rear they charged them, killing some with the lances; as the street was very long they were able to do this four or five times. Although the enemy had witnessed the hurt they received, they came at us like mad dogs, and in no way could we halt them or prevent them from following us. The whole day would have been so spent had they not already recaptured many of the roof tops overlooking the street, and so placed the horsemen in great danger. For this reason we retreated up the causeway to our camp, and no Spaniard was endangered, although some were wounded. We set fire to most of the better houses in that street, so that when we next entered they might not attack us from the roof tops. This same day the alguacil mayor and Pedro de Alvarado fought very fiercely from their own positions. . . .

On the following morning, after I had heard Mass and instructed the captains in what they were to do, I left the camp with fifteen or twenty horsemen and three hundred Spaniards and all our Indian allies of whom there was an infinite number. When we had gone three crossbowshots along the causeway from the camp we found the enemy awaiting us with loud cries. As we had not attacked them for three days they had undone all we had achieved by filling up the breaches in the causeway, and had made them very much stronger and more dangerous to capture than before. But the brigantines arrived on both sides of the causeway, and as they could come in close to the enemy with their guns, crossbows and harquebuses they did them much harm. When our men saw this they landed and captured the first earthwork and the bridge; and we crossed over to the other side and began to pursue the enemy, who barricaded themselves in behind other breaches and earthworks which they had made. These we also captured, although with greater difficulty and danger than before, and we drove them from the street and the square containing the principal houses of the city. I then ordered the Spaniards to advance no farther, while I went with our allies filling in with stones and adobes the breaches in the causeway, which were so many that, although more than ten thousand Indians were engaged in this task, by the time we had finished it was already the hour of vespers. During all this time the Spaniards and our allies were fighting and skirmishing with the people of the city and setting ambushes for them in which many of them were killed.

I rode with the horsemen for a while through the city, and in the streets where there was no water we attacked with our lances all those whom we met, and drove them back so that they dared not venture onto dry land. When I saw how determined they were to die in their defense I deduced two things: that we would regain little, or none, of the riches which they had taken from us, and that they gave us cause, and indeed obliged us, to destroy them utterly. On this last I dwelt with more sorrow, for it weighed heavily on my soul, and thus I sought to find a way whereby I might frighten them and cause them to recognize their error and the harm they would receive from us; so for this reason I burnt and tore down the towers of their idols and their houses. In order that they should feel it the more, I commanded my men to set on fire those big houses in the square where the Spaniards and I had previously been quartered before we were expelled from the city. These were so large that a prince with more than six hundred people in his household and his retinue might be housed in them. There were also some others next to them which, though somewhat smaller, were very much prettier and more delicate; Mutezuma had kept in them every species of bird found in these parts. Although it distressed me, I determined to burn them, for it distressed the enemy very much more; and they showed great grief, as did their allies from the cities on the lakes, for they never believed that our force was sufficient to penetrate so far into the city, and this greatly dismayed them.

Once we had burnt these houses, I called together the men, as it was late, and returned to the camp; and when the people of the city saw that we were withdrawing, an infinite number fell upon us and attacked our rear guard with enormous force. But as the horsemen could gallop the whole length of the street we turned to attack them, killing many at every charge; but for all that they did not cease to come, shouting loudly at our backs. That day they showed great dismay, especially when they saw us enter their city, burning and destroying it, and with us the people of Tesuico, Calco and Suchimilco, and the Utumies, each calling out the name of his province, and in another part the

Tascaltecans, who all showed them their countrymen cut to pieces, saying that they would dine off them that night and breakfast off them the following morning, which in fact they did. Thus we returned to our camp to sleep, for we had labored hard that day; moreover the seven brigantines I had with me had sailed up the canals in the city and burnt a large part of it. The captains of the other camps and the six brigantines all fought very well, and I could speak at length of their exploits, but to avoid prolixity I will state only that they returned to their camps victorious and without having received any harm. . . .

As we had entered the city from our camp two or three days in succession, besides the three or four previous attacks, and had always been victorious, killing with crossbow, harquebus and field gun an infinite number of the enemy, we each day expected them to sue for peace, which we desired as much as our own salvation; but nothing we could do would induce them to do it. In order to put them in greater difficulties and to see if we might oblige them to surrender, I proposed to enter the city each day and to attack the inhabitants in three or four different places. I therefore commanded all the people from those cities on the water to come in their canoes; and on the morning of that day there gathered in the camp more than a hundred thousand of our allies. I then ordered that four brigantines with half the canoes, of which there were as many as fifteen hundred, should approach on one side, while the other three brigantines, with the same number of canoes, were to go to the other; and they were all to circle the city and burn and do all the damage they could. I entered along the main street and found it free from obstruction right up to the great houses in the square; nor had any of the breaches been reopened. I then advanced to the street which led to Tacuba, where there are six or seven bridges. From there I ordered a captain to enter another street with sixty or seventy men. Six horsemen went to guard his rear, and with them went more than ten or twelve thousand of our Indian allies. I then ordered another captain to do the same along another street, and I myself, with all the men who were left, proceeded up the road to Tacuba, where we won three bridges. These we filled in, but because it was already late we left the others for another day when they could be better taken, for I greatly desired to capture that street so that the people from Pedro de Alvarado's camp might communicate with ours and pass from one camp to the other, and the brigantines likewise. That day was one of great victory both on land and in the water, and we took some spoil from the city. The alguacil mayor and Pedro de Alvarado were also victorious.

On the following day I re-entered the city in the same order as before, and God granted us such a victory that in the places where I entered with my people there seemed to be no resistance, and the enemy retreated so swiftly that we appeared to have won three-quarters of the city. Pedro de Alvarado also drove them quickly back, and I was certain, on this day as on the previous one, that they would sue for peace, which, I assured them in every possible way, I greatly desired, with or without a victory; but, for all that, they never gave any sign of peace. That day we returned joyfully to our camp, although we could not but be saddened by their determination to die.

In these days past Pedro de Alvarado had won many bridges, and in order to hold them had placed a guard of foot soldiers and horsemen on them during the night, while the rest of his men returned to camp, which was three-quarters of a league from there. But because this task became intolerable, he decided to move his camp to the end of the causeway leading to the market-place of Temixtitan, which is a square much larger than that of Salamanca, and all surrounded by arcades. To reach this he had only to capture two or three bridges, but the channels there were very broad and dangerous, so he had to fight for several days, although he was always successful. On that day, of which I have already spoken, when he saw the enemy weaken, and saw how I constantly attacked them with great ferocity, he became so enamored of the taste of victory, with all those bridges and fortifications he had captured, that he resolved to cross and take a breach where more than seventy paces of causeway had been torn up and replaced by water to a depth of eight or nine feet. As they attacked that same day and were greatly assisted by the brigantines, they crossed the water, gained the bridges and pursued the enemy who fled. Pedro de Alvarado then made haste to fill in that breach so that the horses might also cross over, and because I had cautioned him each day, both in writing and in person, not to take an inch of ground without first making it safe for the horsemen, who were the mainstay of the fighting. When the people of the city saw that there were only forty or fifty Spaniards and some of our allies on the other side, and that the horsemen were unable to cross, they turned on them so swiftly that they drove them back into the water. Three or four Spaniards were taken alive to be sacrificed and some of our allies were killed.

Finally Pedro de Alvarado succeeded in retreating to his camp, and when that day I returned to mine and heard of all that had happened it distressed me more than anything else in the world, because it might have encouraged the enemy and led them to believe that we dared not enter the city again. The reason why Pedro de Alvarado wished to capture that dangerous breach was partly because, as I have said, he had defeated a great part of the enemy forces and they had shown some weakness; but above all he did it because his men were urging him to capture the marketplace, for, once that was taken, the city was almost won, as all the Indian forces had gathered there and placed all their hopes in it. As Alvarado's men saw how I continually defeated the Indians, they feared that I might capture the marketplace before they did, and, as they were closer to it than we, they held it a point of honor to take it first. For this reason Pedro de Alvarado was much importuned, and the same happened to me in my camp, for all the Spaniards greatly urged me to enter by one of the three streets leading to the marketplace, for we should meet with no resistance and, once it was captured, we would have less trouble thereafter. I made every possible excuse for not doing this, although I concealed the real reason, which was the disadvantages and dangers which I had observed; for in order to reach the marketplace we would have had to pass an infinite number of roof tops and broken roads and bridges, so that every house on our way would be like an island.

When I returned to my camp that afternoon and learned of Alvarado's defeat, I decided to go to his camp on the following morning to rebuke him, and to see what he had gained and where he had moved his camp, advising him as to what he must do for his own defense and for an attack on the enemy. When I reached his camp, however, I was truly astonished to see how far into the city he had gone and the dangerous bridges and passes which he had won, and I no longer blamed him as much as he had seemed to deserve. And when I had discussed with him what was to be done, I returned to my camp that same day.

Once this was over I made several sorties into the city in the usual places. The brigantines and canoes attacked in two places while I fought in the city in four others. We were always victorious and killed great numbers of the enemy, for every day a multitude of people came to join our forces. I hesitated, however, to advance farther into the city, because the enemy might still abandon their stubborn resistance; furthermore, our entry could not be effected without much danger, for they were all united, full of courage and determined to die. But when the Spaniards saw this delay, for they had been fighting without cease for more than twenty days, they urged me strongly, as I said above, to enter and take the marketplace; for once that was captured the Indians would have very little left to defend and would be forced, if they did not surrender, to die of hunger and thirst, there being nothing left to drink except salt water from the lake. When I excused myself, Your Majesty's treasurer told me that the whole camp demanded it and that I must therefore comply. To him and to the other good people who were there I replied that their intention and desire were commendable, and that no one wished to see this business finished so much as I; but I would not attempt it for the reason which his demands had forced me to reveal, namely, that although he was willing there would be others who, on account of the dangers, would not be. But finally they pressed me so much that I agreed to do all I could once I had spoken to the people in the other camps.

The following day I conferred with some of the officers among us, and we agreed to inform the alguacil mayor and Pedro de Alvarado that next day we would enter the city and attempt to take the marketplace. I wrote telling them what they were to do on the Tacuba side, and as well as writing, I sent two of my servants to inform them of the entire operation. The order they were to follow was that the alguacil mayor should go with ten horsemen, a hundred foot soldiers and fifteen crossbowmen and harquebusiers to Alvarado's camp, leaving ten horsemen behind in his own. With these he should arrange that on the following day they should lie in ambush behind some houses; he would then remove his baggage as if he were breaking camp; when the enemy began to pursue him, the horsemen would fall on them from behind. The alguacil mayor, with three of his brigantines and three of Pedro de Alvarado's, was to take that dangerous breach where Alvarado had been driven back, and fill it in with all haste, and then continue his advance; but on no account was he to leave a bridge which he had won without having it repaired and leveled. I also told them that if they could reach the marketplace without exposing themselves to extreme danger, they should make every effort to do so, for I would do the same. . . .

Everything having been arranged as mentioned, on the following day, after Mass, the seven brigantines left our camp with more than three thousand allied canoes; I, with twenty-five horsemen and the other men I had, together with those seventy from the camp at Tacuba, marched forward into the city. When we arrived I disposed my men in this manner: From where we were, three roads led into the marketplace, which the Mexicans call Tianguizco (and the whole place where it is located is called Tlatelulco). I told Your Majesty's treasurer and *contador* to take the principal one with seventy men and more than fifteen or twenty thousand of our allies and to place in the rear guard seven or eight horsemen. As soon as he captured the canals and earthworks he was to level them, for which purpose he took a dozen men with picks, as well as some of our allies whose task it was to fill up breaches. The other two streets, which ran from the Tacuba causeway to the marketplace, were narrower and consisted more of causeways, bridges and canals. I sent two captains with eighty men and more than ten thousand of our Indian allies along the broader of the two, at the entrance to which I placed two large guns with eight horsemen to guard them. With eight horsemen and some hundred foot soldiers, among whom were more than twenty-five crossbowmen and harquebusiers, and a huge number of our allies, I continued my march and moved as far up the other, narrower road as I was able. But at the entrance to it I halted the horsemen and ordered them on no account to move from there, nor to follow me unless I first ordered them to do so. I then dismounted and we arrived at a barricade they had built at the end of a bridge which we took with a small field gun, supported by the crossbowmen and harquebusiers. We then moved on along a street which they had breached in two or three places.

Apart from these three attacks which we made on the inhabitants of the city, our allies who attacked them on the roof tops and other places were so numerous it seemed that nothing could resist us. When we had taken these two

bridges, the barricades and the causeway, our allies followed up the street without any protection from us while I remained on a small island with some
twenty Spaniards, for I had seen that certain of our allies were engaged with
the enemy and were sometimes driven back into the water; with our help they
might return to the attack. In addition to this, we took care that the enemy was
prevented from attacking the Spaniards in the rear from certain side streets in
the city. These same Spaniards sent to inform me at this time that they had
gained much ground and were not far from the marketplace; they greatly
wished to press on, for they could already hear the attack being made by Sandoval and Alvarado on their side. I sent to tell them that on no account should
they advance a step until they had first made certain that all the bridges were
well filled in; thus, should they be obliged to retreat, the water would not hinder them at all, for it was there, as they knew, that the greatest danger lay. They
answered that all they had won was well repaired, and I might go there and see
for myself if it was so. And I, fearing that they might have been thoughtless
and not taken enough care in filling up the bridges, went there and discovered
that they had crossed a breach in the road ten or twelve paces wide, in which
the water was more than eight feet deep. When they crossed they had thrown
wood and reed grass into the breach, and because they had passed over one at
a time and with great care this had not sunk; now they were so drunk with the
joy of victory they imagined that they had made it quite safe. But at the very
moment I arrived at that feeble bridge I saw the Spaniards and many of our
allies in full retreat, with the enemy like hounds at their heels; and as I could
see the impending disaster I began to cry, "Stop! Stop!" But when I reached
the bank I found the water full of Spaniards and Indians as though not a straw
had been thrown into it. The enemy attacked so fiercely that in attempting to
kill the Spaniards they leapt into the water after them. Then some enemy canoes came up the canals and took some of the Spaniards away alive. As this affair happened so suddenly and I saw that my men were being killed, I determined to make a stand and die fighting. The best that I and my companions
could do was to help out some wretched Spaniards who were drowning; some
of these were wounded, some half-drowned and others had lost their weapons.
I sent them on ahead, at which point we were attacked by such a multitude of
the enemy that I and another twelve or fifteen were surrounded on all sides.
As I was so intent on rescuing the drowning, I neither saw nor gave a thought
to the harm I might receive. Certain Indians then came to seize me and would
have carried me off were it not for a captain of fifty men, who always accompanied me, and a youth in his company, who, after God, was the one to save
my life, and in doing so, like a valiant man, gave his own.

Meanwhile, the Spaniards who had escaped the rout were retreating along
the street, which was narrow and level with the water, the dogs having made
it so on purpose; as many of our allies were also fleeing that way, the road

was soon so blocked with people who moved so slowly that the enemy was able to attack them from the water on both sides and kill and capture as they chose. . . .

Now, after all our hardships, it pleased God that those of us who remained should reach the Tacuba causeway, which was very wide. There I mustered my men and took the rear guard myself with nine horsemen. The enemy came after us so swollen with the pride of victory that it seemed not one of us would escape alive; and withdrawing as best I could I sent word to the treasurer and contador to retire to the square in as orderly a fashion as possible. I sent the same orders to the other two captains who had gone along the street which led to the market; both parties had fought most bravely and captured many bridges and barricades, which they had also leveled very well, which was the cause of their being able to retreat unharmed. Before the treasurer and contador began to retreat, the people of the city had thrown, over the barricade where they were fighting, two or three of the heads of the captured Christians, although they did not at that time know whether they came from Pedro de Alvarado's camp or our own. When we had all gathered in the square, the enemy pressed upon us from every quarter, and in such numbers that it was all we could do to resist them, and in places where before our defeat they would never have dared attack. Then suddenly in a high temple tower close to the square they offered up to their gods as a sign of victory many perfumes and incense of a gummy substance which is found in these parts and resembles resin. And although we greatly desired to put a stop to this we were unable to do so, for our people were already retreating to the camp as fast as possible.

In this rout the enemy slew thirty-five or forty Spaniards, and more than a thousand of our Indian allies; more than twenty Christians were wounded, I myself being injured in the leg; we lost a small field gun and many harquebuses, crossbows and other arms.

Once they had gained their victory, the people of the city, in order to terrify the alguacil mayor and Pedro de Alvarado, took all the Spaniards they had captured dead or alive to Tlatelulco, which is the market, and on some high towers which are there sacrificed them naked, opening their chests and tearing out their hearts as an offering to the idols. The Spaniards of Alvarado's camp could see this clearly from where they were fighting, and recognized those who were being sacrificed as Christians by their white naked bodies. And, although they were grieved and greatly dispirited by the sight, they retreated to their camp, having fought very well that day and won through almost to the marketplace, which would have been taken if God, on account of our sins, had not permitted such a great disaster. We returned to our camp somewhat earlier than usual, and much saddened, for we had heard that the brigantines were lost, as the enemy canoes had fallen on us from behind, but, thank God, this was not true, although the brigantines and the canoes of our allies had been in great difficulties. So much so, indeed, that one brigantine was almost lost, and the captain and master were both wounded; the captain died within a week. All during that day and the following night the enemy celebrated with drums and trumpets so loudly it seemed as if the world was coming to an end. They opened all the streets and canals as before, and lit fires and posted sentries only two crossbowshots from our camp. And as we were so sorely defeated and wounded and without weapons, we needed to rest and recuperate.

In the meantime the people of the city sent messengers to many subject provinces, informing them of how they had won a great victory and had slain many Christians and that shortly they would have done with us, and advising them on no account to discuss terms with us. The proof they sent of their victory was the heads of those two horses which they had killed and of some Christians. These they carried about and displayed wherever they saw fit, which served further to confirm the rebels in their obstinacy. In order, however, that our enemies should not become too arrogant or perceive our own weakness, each day some Spaniards on horse and foot, together with many of our allies, went to fight in the city, although they could never gain more than a few bridges in the first street before reaching the square. . . .

That same day some Spaniards had been fighting in Temixtitan, and the enemy had sent asking for our interpreter to come because they wished to talk peace, which, however, it seemed, they wanted only on condition that we leave the entire land. They made this move only to gain a few days in which to rest and refurnish their supplies, for we never succeeded in breaking their will to fight. While we stood arguing through the interpreter, with nothing more than a fallen bridge between us and the enemy, an old man, in full view of everyone, very slowly extracted from his knapsack certain provisions and ate them, so as to make us believe that they were in no need of supplies, for we had told them they would all die of hunger. Our allies warned us that these talks were insincere and urged us to attack them, but we fought no more that day, for the lords had told the interpreter to convey their proposals to me.

Four days after Sandoval returned from Matalcingo the lords of that province and of Malinalco and of the province of Cuiscon, which is very large and important and had also rebelled, came to our camp and begged forgiveness for the past and offered to serve us well, which they did and have done until now.

While the alguacil mayor was at Matalcingo, the people of Temixtitan decided to attack Alvarado's camp by night, and struck shortly before dawn. When the sentries on foot and on horseback heard them they shouted, "To arms!" Those who were in that place flung themselves upon the enemy, who leapt into the water as soon as they saw the horsemen. Meanwhile the rest of our men came up and fought with them for more than three hours. We heard in our camp a field gun being fired, and, fearing that our men might be defeated, I ordered my own company to arm themselves and march into the city to weaken the offensive against Alvarado. And the Spanish attack was so fierce that the Indians decided to retreat. And that day we entered and fought in the city once more.

By this time those of us who had been wounded during our defeat were now healed. News arrived from Vera Cruz that a ship had arrived belonging to Juan Ponce de León, who had been defeated on the mainland or island of Florida; and with this news the citizens of Vera Cruz sent me some powder and crossbows, of which we were in dire need. Now, thanks be to God, all the lands round about had come over to our side. But when I saw how rebellious the people of this city were, and how they seemed more determined to perish than any race of man known before, I did not know by what means we might relieve ourselves of all these dangers and hardships, and yet avoid destroying them and their city which was indeed the most beautiful thing in the world. They paid no heed to us when we told them that we would not strike camp, nor would the brigantines cease to attack them from the water, that we had destroyed the peoples of Matalcingo and Malinalco and that there was no one in all the land who could help them, nor could they acquire maize or meat or fruit or water or any other provision. The more such things were told them, the less signs they showed of weakening; rather they seemed to attack each time with greater spirit. Then, seeing that the affair was continuing in this way, and that we had been besieging the city for more than forty-five days, I decided to take steps to ensure our greater safety and to place the enemy in further difficulties; my plan was to raze to the ground all the houses on both sides of the streets along which we advanced, so that we should move not a step without leaving everything behind us in ruins; and all the canals were to be filled in, no matter how long it took us. To this end I called together all the chiefs and principal persons among our allies and told them what I had decided, and asked them, in consequence, to call up many of their farm laborers, asking them to bring their *coas*, which are sticks which they use much as workmen in Spain dig with spades. They replied that they would willingly do as I asked, and that they welcomed my decision, for it seemed to them a way to destroy the city and this they desired more than anything else in the world.

Two or three days passed while arrangements were being made. The enemy were well aware that we were planning an offensive and they, as it afterwards appeared, were making every preparation for their defense, as we guessed they would. Having agreed with our allies, therefore, that we would fight the enemy on land and water, we left the next morning after Mass and took the road to the city. When we reached the bridge and barricade close to the great houses in the square the enemy called to us to advance no farther, for they desired peace. I ordered the men not to attack and told the enemy to call the lord of the city to come there and speak to me about terms. They then told me that they had sent for him and so detained me more than an hour, for in reality they had no wish for peace, and soon demonstrated the fact by beginning, as we stood quietly by, to hurl arrows, javelins and stones. When I saw this we attacked the barricade and captured it; but on entering the square we found it strewn with boulders to stop the horses crossing it, because on land it is they who carry the attack. Likewise we found a street walled up with stones and another covered with stones so that the horses could not pass up them. From that day forward we filled in that canal so thoroughly that the Indians never opened it again; and thenceforth we began, little by little, to destroy the houses and block all the canals we had won. As we were accompanied that day by more than 150,000 warriors, we made much progress. So we returned to our camp, and the brigantines and the canoes of our allies, which had likewise done much damage, also returned to rest.

On the following day we again entered the city in the same array, and when we reached that enclosure and the forecourt of the temple towers I ordered the captains and their men to do no more than block up the canals and level out the dangerous areas which we had won. Some of our allies I sent to burn and raze the houses and others to fight in the usual places while the horsemen were placed on guard in the rear. I myself climbed the highest of those towers, for the Indians recognized me and I knew it would distress them greatly to see me there. From there I encouraged our allies and sent them help when necessary; for, as they fought without pause, they sometimes forced the enemy to retreat and at other times were forced to retreat themselves. When this happened they were reinforced by three or four horsemen, which gave them immense courage to turn again upon our enemies. In this manner we entered the city five or six days in succession; and every time we withdrew we sent our allies out in front and positioned certain Spaniards in ambush in some houses while the horsemen remained behind and pretended to retreat suddenly, so as to bring the enemy out into the square. With these devices and the ambushes set by the foot soldiers we killed a number of them with our lances every afternoon. . . . That same evening I sent a messenger to the alguacil mayor asking him to appear at my camp before dawn with fifteen horsemen from his own and from Pedro de Alvarado's camp.

On the following morning the alguacil mayor arrived with fifteen horsemen. I had there another twenty-five from Cuyoacan, which made forty in all. Ten of them I sent out together with the rest of our people and the brigantines, ordering them to enter the city as before and to capture and destroy all they could. I would be there with the thirty horsemen when the time came to retreat, for as they knew that we had leveled much of the city I ordered them to pursue the enemy in force until they were confined in their canals and strongholds, and to hold them there until the hour came to retreat. Then I and the thirty horsemen, unobserved, would set an ambush in some large houses near to the other large ones on the square. The Spaniards did as I commanded, and half an hour after midday I set out for the city with the thirty horsemen. When we arrived I left my companions in the aforementioned houses and I myself climbed the high tower as I was accustomed to do. While I was present, some Spaniards opened a grave which contained more than fifteen hundred castellanos worth of gold ornaments.

When the time came I gave orders for my men to retreat in good order and for the horsemen to begin a charge when they reached the square, but to pretend to be afraid and stop short. This they were to do as soon as they saw a large force of people in and around the square; my men in ambush were eagerly awaiting the signal to begin their attack. They were keen to do a good job, and somewhat tired of waiting. I then joined them, and already the Spaniards, both on horse and on foot, and our Indian allies who knew of the ambush, were retreating across the square. The enemy pursued them with such wild cries that one might have thought they had conquered the world. The nine [sic] horsemen made as if to attack them across the square and then withdrew suddenly. When they had done this twice the enemy was so enraged that they attacked at the horses' flanks until they drove us into the entrance of the street where we were waiting in ambush. When we saw the Spaniards pass in front of us and heard a harquebus shot, which was the signal to attack, we knew it was time to emerge; and so with the cry of "Señor Santiago" we fell suddenly upon them, and charged up the square spearing them, cutting them down and overtaking many of them, who were then slain by our allies, so that in this ambush more than five hundred of their bravest and most notable men were lost. That night our allies dined sumptuously, for all those they had killed were sliced up and eaten. So great was the surprise and shock they received in seeing themselves so suddenly beaten, that not once did they shout or scream that evening nor dared they appear on the roof tops or in the streets unless they were quite certain of being safe. As it was almost dark when we finally withdrew, it seems that the enemy sent certain slaves to see whether we were retreating or what we were doing. When the appeared in the street ten or twelve horsemen attacked and pursued them so that not one escaped alive.

The enemy was so terrified by this victory of ours that never again during the whole course of the war dared they enter the square when we withdrew, even if there was only a single horseman there, nor dared they attack so much as one of our foot soldiers or Indian allies, thinking that an ambush would be sprung on them from beneath their very feet. And the victory which Our Lord

God gave us that day was the principal cause of the city being won the sooner, for the inhabitants were much dismayed by it and our allies greatly encouraged. So we returned to our camp resolved to bring a speedy end to the war, and not to let one day pass without entering the city. . . .

We already knew that the Indians in the city were very scared, and we now learnt from two wretched creatures who had escaped from the city and come to our camp by night that they were dying of hunger and used to come out at night to fish in the canals between the houses, and wandered through the places we had won in search of firewood, and herbs and roots to eat. And because we had already filled in many of the canals, and leveled out many of the dangerous stretches, I resolved to enter the next morning shortly before dawn and do all the harm we could. The brigantines departed before daylight, and I with twelve or fifteen horsemen and some foot soldiers and Indians entered suddenly and stationed several spies who, as soon as it was light, called us from where we lay in ambush, and we fell on a huge number of people. As these were some of the most wretched people and had come in search of food, they were nearly all unarmed, and women and children in the main. We did them so much harm through all the streets in the city that we could reach, that the dead and the prisoners numbered more than eight hundred; the brigantines also took many people and canoes which were out fishing, and the destruction was very great. When the captains and lords of the city saw us attack at such an unaccustomed hour, they were as frightened as they had been by the recent ambush, and none of them dared come out and fight; so we returned with much booty and food for our allies.

The following day we returned to the city, and, as our allies now saw how far we had advanced toward destroying it, they came to our camp in such multitudes we could no longer count them. That day we finally captured the Tacuba road and leveled the difficult stretches, so that the people in Alvarado's camp could communicate with us by way of the city; and on the main street which leads to the market two more bridges were captured and filled in. We also burnt the houses of the lord of the city, the second since Mutezuma's death, a boy of eighteen years of age called Guatimucin; these houses had been very strong, for they were large, well fortified and surrounded by water. Two other bridges on other streets which run close to the main road to the market were also captured, so that three-quarters of the city was now in our hands, and the Indians were forced to retreat to the strongest part of the city, which consisted of the houses farthest out over the water.

On the following day, which was that of St. James (Santiago), we entered the city in the same manner as before, following the main street which leads to the market, and we captured a very wide canal which they had thought a great safeguard, although, indeed, it took us a long time and was hard to win, and because it was so wide we were unable that day to fill it in so that the horses could cross over. As we were all on foot and the Indians saw that the horses had not crossed, they turned on us afresh and many of them were fine warriors. But we resisted their attack and, as we had many crossbowmen, forced them to retreat behind their barricades, although not before we had done them much injury with the bolts. In addition to this all the Spaniards carried pikes which I had ordered to be made after our defeat, and these proved most advantageous. That day we did nothing save burn and raze to the ground the houses on either side of that main street, which indeed was a sad sight; but we were obliged to do it, there being no other way of accomplishing our aims. . . .

On the following day, at nine o'clock, as we were preparing to re-enter the city, we saw from our camp smoke rising upward from the two very high towers in the Tlatelulco or market of the city; we could not guess what it meant, for it seemed to be more than that from the incense the Indians are accustomed to burn to their idols. We surmised, however, that Alvarado had reached there, which, though it later proved to be true, we hardly dared believe at the time. And in fact that day Alvarado and his men carried off a valiant achievement, for we still had many bridges and barricades to capture, and the greater part of the inhabitants continually came to defend them. When, however, he saw that we were harassing the enemy on our side, he made every effort to break through into the marketplace, which was their strongest point. But he only succeeded in coming within sight of it and in capturing those two towers and many others close to the market, which is in size almost equal to the whole area enclosed by the many towers of the city. The horsemen found themselves hard pressed and were forced to retreat, and in doing so three of their horses were wounded. Pedro de Alvarado and his men then withdrew to their camp; and we failed that day to take a canal and bridge, which was all that now stood between us and the market square, except for leveling off or filling in all the dangerous places. When we withdrew they pressed us hard, although it was to their cost.

The following morning we entered the city and launched an attack upon the last channel and barricade before the marketplace, next to the small tower, as I have said. An ensign [alférez] and two or three other Spaniards threw themselves into the water, whereupon the enemy fled the bridge and we began to fill in and level the ground so that the horses might cross. While this was being done, Pedro de Alvarado rode up along this same road with four horsemen, and both his men and mine rejoiced greatly at his arrival, for now we were together we might put a swift end to the war. Alvarado left sentries in the rear and on the flanks both for his own defense and to preserve all that we had won. As soon as the crossing had been repaired I took some of the horsemen and went to look at the market square, ordering the rest of my company, however, not to advance beyond the bridge. We then rode around the market square for a while and saw that the roofs above the archways were full of the enemy, but as the square was very large and we were mounted they dared not approach. I climbed that high tower which is close to the market, and there I found, as in other such towers, the heads of Christians as offerings to their idols, and also the heads of our Tascaltecan allies, for between them and the people of Culua there is a most ancient and bitter feud. . . .

. . . as we had not fought for three or four days we found the streets along which we passed full of women and children and other wretched people all starving to death, thin and exhausted; it was the most sorrowful of sights, and I ordered our allies to do them no harm. But not one of their effective warriors came near us, although we could see them on the roof tops, unarmed and wrapped in the cloaks they use. That day I again sued for peace, but their replies were evasive. For most of the day they kept us occupied in this fashion until at last I told them that I intended to attack and that they should withdraw their people, for, if they did not, I would give our allies permission to kill them. They then answered that they wanted peace; and I replied that I saw no chief with whom I might treat; once he came, and I would give him all the security he wished, we would talk of peace. We soon realized, however, that it was all a trick and that they were all prepared to fight us. Having then warned them many times, so as to press them into still greater straits, I ordered Pedro de Alvarado to take all his men and enter a large quarter still held by the enemy where there were more than a thousand houses; I entered by another place with the foot soldiers because there we could not make use of the horses. And although they fought fiercely with us we at last captured the whole quarter. So great was the slaughter that more than twelve thousand perished or were taken prisoner, and these were so cruelly used by our allies that not one was left alive, even though we severely censured and reprimanded them. . . .

When it was light I had all the men made ready and the guns brought out. On the previous day I had ordered Pedro de Alvarado to wait for me in the market square and not to attack before I arrived. When all the men were mustered and all the brigantines were lying in wait behind those houses where the enemy was gathered, I gave orders that when a harquebus was fired they should enter the little of the city that was still left to win and drive the defenders into the water where the brigantines were waiting. I warned them, however, to look with care for Guatimucin, and to make every effort to take him alive, for once that had been done the war would cease. I spoke with certain chieftains of the city whom I knew, and asked them for what reason their lord would not appear before me; for, although they were in the direst straits, they need not all perish; I asked them to call him, for he had no cause to be afraid. Two of those chieftains then appeared to go to speak with him. After a while they returned, bringing with them one of the most important persons in the city, whose name was Ciguacoacin, and he was captain and governor of them all and directed all matters concerning the war. I welcomed him openly, so that he should not be afraid; but at last he told me that his sovereign would prefer to die where he was rather than on any account appear before me, and that he personally was much grieved by this, but now I might do as I pleased. I now saw by this how determined he was, and so I told him to return to his people and to prepare them, for I intended to attack and slay them all; and so he departed after having spent five hours in such discussions.

The people of the city had to walk upon their dead while others swam or drowned in the waters of that wide lake where they had their canoes; indeed, so great was their suffering that it was beyond our understanding how they could endure it. Countless numbers of men, women and children came out toward us, and in their eagerness to escape many were pushed into the water where they drowned amid that multitude of corpses; and it seemed that more than fifty thousand had perished from the salt water they had drunk, their hunger and the vile stench. So that we should not discover the plight in which they were in, they dared neither throw these bodies into the water where the brigantines might find them nor throw them beyond their boundaries where the soldiers might see them; and so in those streets where they were we came across such piles of the dead that we were forced to walk upon them. I had posted Spaniards in every street, so that when the people began to come out they might prevent our allies from killing those wretched people, whose number was uncountable. I also told the captains of our allies that on no account should any of those people be slain; but they were so many that we could not prevent more than fifteen thousand being killed and sacrificed that day. . . .

. . . Thus, with this lord a prisoner, it pleased God that the war should cease, and the day it ended was Tuesday, the feast of Saint Hippolytus, the thirteenth of August, in the year 1521. Thus from the day we laid siege to the city, which was on the thirtieth of May of that same year, until it fell, there passed seventy-five days, during which time Your Majesty will have seen the dangers, hardships and misfortunes which these, Your vassals, endured, and in which they ventured their lives.

FRANCISCO DE JEREZ
(c. 1497–?)

Francisco de Jerez left Spain in 1515 and participated in the conquest of Peru from 1531 to 1533. He subsequently returned to Spain and settled in his birthplace, Seville. Jerez's Relación de la Conquista del Perú *was written in 1534.*

Atahuallpa, the last Inca ruler of Peru, died in 1533.

THE CAPTURE OF ATAHUALLPA

. . . [The Spaniards] took their leave, expecting Atahuallpa to come and see the governor [Pizarro] on the following morning. His camp was formed on the skirts of a small hill, the tents, which were of cotton, extending for a league, with that of Atahuallpa in the centre. All the men were on foot outside the tents, with their arms, consisting of long lances like pikes, stuck into the ground. There seemed to be upwards of thirty thousand men in the camp.

When the governor heard what had taken place, he ordered that a good watch should be kept that night in camp, and he commanded his captain-general to set the guards, and to see that the rounds were gone throughout the night, which was accordingly done. On the Saturday morning a messenger from Atahuallpa to the governor arrived and said: "My lord has sent me to tell you that he wishes to come and see you, and to bring his men armed; for the men whom you sent yesterday were armed; and he desires you to send a Christian with whom he may come." The governor answered: "Tell your lord to come when and how he pleases, and that, in what way soever he may come, I will receive him as a friend and brother. I do not send him a Christian, because it is not our custom so to send from one lord to another." The messenger set out with this answer, and, as soon as he reached the camp, the sentries saw

From *Reports on the Discovery of Peru,* translated and edited by Clements R. Markham (New York: Burt Franklin), 50–56.

that the Indians were in motion. In a short time another messenger arrived, and said to the governor: "Atahuallpa sends me to say that he has no wish to bring his troops armed, and, though they will come with him, many will come without arms, because he wishes to bring them with him and to lodge them in the town: and they are to prepare a lodging in the plaza, where he will rest, which is the house known as the house of the serpent, because there is a serpent of stone within it." The governor replied: "So let it be, and I pray that he may come quickly, for I desire to see him."

Very soon they saw the plain full of men, halting at intervals, to wait for those who were filing out of the camp. The march of the troops along the road continued until the afternoon; and they came in separate detachments. Having passed all the narrow places on the road, they reached the ground close to the camp of the Christians, and still troops kept issuing from the camp of the Indians. Presently the governor ordered all the Spaniards to arm themselves secretly in their lodgings, and to keep the horses saddled and bridled, and under the orders of three captains, but none were to show themselves in the open space. The captain of the artillery was ordered to have his guns pointed towards the enemy on the plain, and, when the time came, to fire. Men were stationed in the streets leading to the open space, and, taking twenty men with him, the governor went to his lodging. These had the duty entrusted to them of seizing the person of Atahuallpa, if he should come cautiously with so large a force as was coming; but the governor ordered that he should be taken alive. All the troops had orders not to leave their quarters, even if the enemy should enter the open space, until they should hear the guns fired off. The sentries were to be on the alert, and, if they saw that the enemy intended treachery, they were to give the signal; and all were to sally out of the lodgings, the cavalry mounted, when they heard the cry of *Santiago*.

Having made these arrangements, the governor waited for the appearance of Atahuallpa; but no Christian was in sight except the sentry, who gave notice of what was passing in the army of the Indians. The governor and captain-general visited the quarters of the Spaniards, seeing that they were ready to sally forth when it was necessary, saying to them all that they must be of good courage, and make fortresses of their hearts, for that they had no others, and no hope but in God, who would help those who worked in his service, even in their greatest need. He told them that though, for every Christian, there were five hundred Indians, yet they must have that reliance which good men find on such occasions, and they must trust that God would fight on their side. He told them that, at the moment of attacking, they must come out with desperate fury and break through the enemy, taking care that the horses do not hinder each other. These and similar exhortations were made by the governor and captain-general to the Christians, to raise their spirits, and they were more ready to come forth than to remain in their lodgings. Each man was ready to encounter a hundred, and they felt very little fear at seeing so great a multitude.

When the governor saw that it was near sunset, and that Atahuallpa did not move from the place to which he had repaired, although troops still kept issuing out of his camp, he sent a Spaniard to ask him to come into the square to see him before it was dark. As soon as the messenger came before Atahuallpa, he made an obeisance to him, and made signs that he should come to where the governor waited. Presently he and his troops began to move, and the Spaniard returned and reported that they were coming, and that the men in front carried arms concealed under their clothes, which were strong tunics of cotton, beneath which were stones and bags and slings; all which made it appear that they had a treacherous design. Soon the van of the enemy began to enter the open space. First came a squadron of Indians dressed in a livery of different colours, like a chess board. They advanced, removing the straws from the ground, and sweeping the road. Next came three squadrons in different dresses, dancing and singing. Then came a number of men with armour, large metal plates, and crowns of gold and silver. Among them was Atahuallpa in a litter lined with plumes of macaws' feathers, of many colours, and adorned with plates of gold and silver. Many Indians carried it on their shoulders on high. Next came two other litters and two hammocks, in which were some principal chiefs; and lastly, several squadrons of Indians with crowns of gold and silver.

As soon as the first entered the open space they moved aside and gave space to the others. On reaching the centre of the open space, Atahuallpa remained in his litter on high, and the others with him, while his troops did not cease to enter. A captain then came to the front and, ascending the fortress near the open space, where the artillery was posted, raised his lance twice, as for a signal. Seeing this, the governor asked the Father Friar Vicente if he wished to go and speak to Atahuallpa, with an interpreter? He replied that he did wish it, and he advanced, with a cross in one hand and the Bible in the other, and going amongst the troops up to the place where Atahuallpa was, thus addressed him: "I am a priest of God, and I teach Christians the things of God, and in like manner I come to teach you. What I teach is that which God says to us in this Book. Therefore, on the part of God and of the Christians, I beseech you to be their friend, for such is God's will, and it will be for your good. Go and speak to the governor, who waits for you."

Atahuallpa asked for the Book, that he might look at it, and the priest gave it to him closed. Atahuallpa did not know how to open it, and the priest was extending his arm to do so, when Atahuallpa, in great anger, gave him a blow on the arm, not wishing that it should be opened. Then he opened it himself, and, without any astonishment at the letters and paper, as had been shown by other Indians, he threw it away from him five or six paces, and, to the words which the monk had spoken to him through the interpreter, he answered with much scorn, saying: "I know well how you have behaved on the road, how you have treated my chiefs, and taken the cloth from my storehouses." The monk replied: "The Christians have not done this, but some Indians took the cloth without the knowledge of the governor, and he ordered it to be restored." Atahuallpa said: "I will not leave this place until they bring it all to me." The monk returned with this reply to the governor. Atahuallpa stood up on the top of the litter, addressing his troops and ordering them to be prepared. The monk told the governor what had passed between him and Atahuallpa, and that he had thrown the Scriptures to the ground. Then the governor put on a jacket of cotton, took his sword and dagger, and, with the Spaniards who were with him, entered amongst the Indians most valiantly; and, with only four men who were able to follow him, he came to the litter where Atahuallpa was, and fearlessly seized him by the arm, crying out *Santiago*. Then the guns were fired off, the trumpets were sounded, and the troops, both horse and foot, sallied forth. On seeing the horses charge, many of the Indians who were in the open space fled, and such was the force with which they ran that they broke down part of the wall surrounding it, and many fell over each other. The horsemen rode them down, killing and wounding, and following in pursuit. The infantry made so good an assault upon those that remained that in a short time most of them were put to the sword. The governor still held Atahuallpa by the arm, not being able to pull him out of the litter because he was raised so high. Then the Spaniards made such a slaughter amongst those who carried the litter that they fell to the ground, and, if the governor had not protected Atahuallpa, that proud man would there have paid for all the cruelties he had committed. The governor, in protecting Atahuallpa, received a slight wound in the hand. During the whole time no Indian raised his arms against a Spaniard. So great was the terror of the Indians at seeing the governor force his way through them, at hearing the fire of the artillery, and beholding the charging of the horses, a thing never before heard of, that they thought more of flying to save their lives than of fighting. All those who bore the litter of Atahuallpa appeared to be principal chiefs. They were all killed, as well as those who were carried in the other litters and hammocks. One of them was the page of Atahuallpa, and a great lord, and the others were lords of many vassals, and his councillors. The chief of Caxamalca was also killed, and others; but, the number being very great, no account was taken of them, for all who came in attendance on Atahuallpa were great lords. The governor went to his lodging, with his prisoner Atahuallpa, despoiled of his robes, which the Spaniards had torn off in pulling him out of the litter. It was a very wonderful thing to see so great a lord taken prisoner in so short a time, who came in such power.

NICCOLÒ MACHIAVELLI
(1469–1527)

Although not a major political figure in Florence, Niccolò Machiavelli mixed sufficiently with the city's ruling aristocracy to know the innermost workings of its politics. Machiavelli spent a period in disgrace, but when the Medicis were restored, he again played a role in Florentine political life. The Prince (1513) and the Discourses upon Livy (c. 1520) testify to his political genius. The Art of War (1521) is remarkable for the stress he puts on the need for militias rather than mercenaries; however, unlike his contemporary Francesco Guicciardini, but like many others, he underestimated the significance of artillery. The History of Florence (1525) was his last work.

OF DIFFERENT KINDS OF TROOPS

... The principal foundations that all states have, new ones as well as old or mixed, are good laws and good arms. And because there cannot be good laws where there are not good arms, and where there are good arms there must be good laws, I shall leave out the reasoning on laws and shall speak of arms.

I say, therefore, that the arms with which a prince defends his state are either his own or mercenary or auxiliary or mixed. Mercenary and auxiliary arms are useless and dangerous; and if one keeps his state founded on mercenary arms, one will never be firm or secure; for they are disunited, ambitious, without discipline, unfaithful; bold among friends, among enemies cowardly; no fear of God, no faith with men; ruin is postponed only as long as attack is postponed; and in peace you are despoiled by them, in war by the enemy. The cause of this is that they have no love nor cause to keep them in the field other than a small stipend, which is not sufficient to make them want to die for you.

From Niccolò Machiavelli, *The Prince*, translated by Harvey C. Mansfield, Jr. (Chicago: University of Chicago Press, 1985), 48–50. Copyright © 1985 by The University of Chicago. Reprinted by permission of the University of Chicago and Harvey C. Mansfield, Jr.

They do indeed want to be your soldiers while you are not making war, but when war comes, they either flee or leave. It should be little trouble for me to persuade anyone of this point, because the present ruin of Italy is caused by nothing other than its having relied for a period of many years on mercenary arms. These arms once made some headway for some, and may have appeared bold among themselves; but when the foreigner came, they showed what they were. Hence Charles [VIII], king of France, was allowed to seize Italy. . . . And he who said that our sins were the cause of it spoke the truth. But the sins were surely not those he believed, but the ones I have told of, and because these were the sins of princes, they too have suffered the punishment for them.

I want to demonstrate better the failure of these arms. Mercenary captains are either excellent men of arms or not: if they are, you cannot trust them because they always aspire to their own greatness, either by oppressing you, who are their patron, or by oppressing others contrary to your intention; but if the captain is not virtuous, he ruins you in the ordinary way. And if one responds that whoever has arms in hand will do this, mercenary or not, I would reply that arms have to be employed either by a prince or by a republic. The prince should go in person, and perform himself the office of captain. The republic has to send its citizens, and when it sends one who does not turn out to be a worthy man, it must change him; and if he is, it must check him with laws so that he does not step out of bounds. And by experience one sees that only princes and armed republics make very great progress; nothing but harm ever comes from mercenary arms. And a republic armed with its own arms is brought to obey one of its citizens with more difficulty than is a republic armed with foreign arms.

THE ART OF WAR

FABRIZIO. Since you are pleased to have it so, I intend to start my treatment of this material at the beginning, so that it may be better understood, for it is possible by that method to explain more at length. The purpose of him who wishes to make war is to be able to fight with any enemy in the field and to be able to win a battle. If he expects to do this, it is necessary to draw up an army. In order to draw up the army, it is necessary to find men, to arm them, to organize them, to train them both in small and in large bodies, to furnish them with quarters, and at last, either by remaining quiet or by marching, to bring them into the enemy's presence. These affairs comprise all the labor of field warfare,

From *Machiavelli: The Chief Works and Others,* translated by Allan Gilbert (Durham, N.C.: Duke University Press, 1965), 581–86. Reprinted by permission of Beverley Brian Gilbert.

which is the most necessary and the most honored. In a man who well understands how to offer battle to the enemy, the other errors he may make in affairs of war will be bearable; but he who lacks this knowledge, though in other particulars he may be very able, will never carry on a war with honor, because a single battle that you win cancels all your other bad actions. So in the same way if you lose one, all the good things you have earlier done have no value.

Since then the men must first be found, it is necessary to come to their selection, for so the ancients called it. We call it drafting, but in order to call it by a name more honored, I wish us to keep for it the name of selection. It is the opinion of those who have given rules for warfare that men should be chosen from temperate countries, in order that they may have spirit and prudence, because a hot country produces the prudent but not the spirited, a cold one the spirited but not the prudent. This rule is well given to one who is prince of all the world and therefore has the opportunity to take men from such places as seem good to him. But if we wish to give a rule that anybody will be able to use, we must say that every republic and every kingdom must draw its soldiers from its own countries, hot or cold or temperate as they happen to be. Because ancient examples show that in every country training can produce good soldiers, because where nature fails, the lack can be supplied by ingenuity, which in this case is more important than nature. And choosing them in other places is not to be called selection, because selection means taking the best from a region and having power to choose those who are not willing as well as those who are willing to serve. It is not, however, possible to make this selection except in places subject to you, because you cannot get those you wish in lands that are not yours, but you must take those who are willing.

Cosimo. Yet it is possible, even among those willing to come, to choose some and to omit some; and therefore it can be called selection.

Fabrizio. You speak the truth to a certain extent. But consider the defects that such selection has in itself, because many times we even discern that it is not selection. The first thing: those who are not your subjects and who serve willingly are not the best but rather the worst of a region; because if any there are of bad reputation, lazy, uncontrolled, without religion, fugitives from the authority of their fathers, swearers, gamblers, in every way badly brought up, they are the ones who are willing to serve as soldiers. Such habits are as contrary as possible to true and good soldiership. When so many such men offer themselves to you that they exceed the number you have designated, you can choose them, but when the material is bad, the selection cannot be good. Yet many times there are not enough to make up the number of which you have need, so that, since you are forced to take them all, it can no longer be called making a selection, but hiring infantry. With this bad method are formed today the armies in Italy and elsewhere, except in Germany, because nobody is hired by command of the prince but according to the desire of him who wishes to serve. Consider, then, what methods of these ancient armies can now be introduced into an army of men brought together in such a way.

COSIMO. What way can be used, then?

FABRIZIO. The one I mentioned: to select them from the prince's subjects and by his authority. . . .

As to fearing that [a citizen army] may take your state from you by means of one who will be made head of it, I answer that weapons borne by citizens or subjects, given by the laws and well regulated, never do damage; on the contrary they are always an advantage, and cities keep themselves uncorrupted longer by means of those weapons than without them. So Rome was free four hundred years and was armed; Sparta, eight hundred; many other cities have been unarmed and have been free less than forty years. Because cities have need of armies; when they do not have their own forces, they hire foreigners; and foreign forces sooner do injury to the public welfare than native ones, because they are easier to bribe, and a citizen who is trying to become powerful can sooner avail himself of them; and to some extent he has material easier to deal with, since he is to oppress men who are unarmed. Besides this, a city ought to fear two enemies more than one. A city that makes use of foreign armies fears at once the foreigner she hires and the citizen, and as to this fear being necessary, remember what I said a little earlier about Francesco Sforza. A city that uses its own forces, fears only its own citizen. But among all the reasons that can be given, I wish this to serve me: namely, that never did anybody establish a republic or a kingdom who did not suppose that the same persons who inhabited it would need with their weapons to defend it.

WAR AND POLITICAL STRATEGY

What Is Worthy of Note in the Case of the Three Roman Horatii and of the Three Alban Curiatii

Tullus, king of Rome, and Mettius, king of Alba, made a pact to the effect that whichever of these two sets of three men should win, their people would become lords over the other people. All the Alban Curiatii were killed, and of the Roman Horatii only one survived. Consequently Mettius, the Alban king, together with his people, became subject to the Romans. When the victorious Horatius returned to Rome he met one of his sisters who was married to one

From *The Discourses of Niccolò Machiavelli*, translated and edited by Leslie J. Walker (New Haven: Yale University Press, 1950), 267–68, 311–12, 392–95, 470–82. Copyright © 1950 by Yale University Press. Reprinted by permission of Yale University Press.

of the three Curiatii who had been slain. She was bewailing her husband's death, so he killed her. For this delinquency Horatius was brought to trial, and after much disputing was set free, not so much on account of his merits as on account of his father's intercession.

There are three things to be noted here:

(i) that never should one risk the whole of one's fortune on the success of but a part of one's forces;

(ii) that in assigning rewards and punishments in a well ordered city never should blameworthy actions be counterbalanced by deserts;

(iii) that it is never wise to adopt a course if there is reason to doubt, or if there be doubt, whether the other party will observe his engagements. For that one state should become subject to another is a matter of such consequence that it is incredible that any king or any people should rest content if the issue depend on three of their citizens being vanquished. This is illustrated by the conduct of Mettius, who, when the Romans won, at once admitted his own defeat and promised obedience to Tullus, yet in the first expedition which the Romans undertook against the Veientes, is found contriving how to let them down, like a man who comes to see too late how rash is the course he has adopted.

Those Who Fight for Glory's Sake Make Good and Faithful Soldiers

Another point to be considered in connection with the above discourse is what a difference there is between a contented army which fights for the glory of the thing and one that is ill disposed and fights to help on someone's ambition. For, whereas the Roman armies were accustomed to being victorious under the consuls, under the Decemviri they always lost.

This shows, amongst other things, the reason why mercenary troops are useless, for they have no cause to stand firm when attacked, apart from the small pay which you give them. And this reason is not sufficient to make them loyal, or to make them so much your friends that they should want to die for you. For in armies in which there is no affection for him for whom they are fighting such as would make them his partisans, it will be impossible for them ever to have valour enough to withstand even a moderately valorous foe. Since neither the requisite love nor the requisite enthusiasm can be aroused except in your own subjects, it is necessary if one desires to retain a form of government, i.e., desires to uphold either a republic or a kingdom, to arm oneself with one's own subjects, as it is manifest that all have done who by means of armies have reaped great profit.

Under the Ten the Roman armies had the same valour as before, but, because they had not the same disposition towards their rulers, they did not produce the same effect as usual. Whereas as soon as the administration of the Ten was abolished and they began to fight as free men, they recovered the same old spirit, and, in consequence, their attacks produced the same happy results as they had always done.

Men Rise from a Low to a Great Position by Means Rather of Fraud Than of Force

It is quite true, I think, that seldom, if ever, do men of low position obtain high rank except by force and by fraud, though there are, of course, others to whom rank comes merely by way of gift or inheritance. Nor do I think that force by itself ever suffices, whereas instances can easily be found in which fraud alone has sufficed. Anyone who has read the life of Philip of Macedon or that of Agathocles the Sicilian, for instance, or others of that ilk, will see that, from an extremely low, or at any rate a low position, they rose either to a kingdom or to very great power. Xenophon, in his Life of Cyrus, calls attention to the need for deceit. For in view of the amount of fraud used in the first expedition Cyrus made against the King of Armenia, and of the fact that it was by means of deceit, not by means of force, that he acquired his kingdom, one cannot but conclude from such actions that a prince who wishes to do great things must learn to practise deceit. Besides this, Xenophon also makes him deceive Cyaxares, king of the Medes, his maternal uncle, in various ways, and shows that without such frauds Cyrus could not have attained the greatness he did attain.

Nor do I think that anyone can be found whose position at the outset was humble, but who subsequently acquired vast power simply by the use of open and undisguised force: but it can quite well be done by using only fraud. . . . And what princes have to do at the outset of their career, republics also must do until such time as they become powerful and can rely on force alone.

Since in all her decisions, whether by chance or by choice, Rome took all steps necessary to make herself great, she did not overlook fraud. She could not at the start have been more deceitful than she was in the means she took, as we were saying just now, to acquire allies, since under this title she made them her servants, as was the case with the Latins and other peoples round about. For she first availed herself of their arms in order to subjugate neighbouring peoples and to build up her reputation as a state, and then, having subdued them, she increased to such an extent that she could beat anyone. Nor would the Latins ever have realised that in reality they were mere slaves, if they had not seen the Samnites twice defeated and forced to accept Rome's terms. Since this victory increased the already great reputation of the Romans with more distant rulers, who thus felt the impact of her name though not of her arms, envy and suspicion were aroused in those who did see and feel the weight of her arms, amongst them the Latins. . . .

Men Often Make the Mistake of Supposing That Pride Is Overcome by Humility

There are to be found numerous cases in which humility is not only no help, but is a hindrance, especially when used in dealing with arrogant men who, either out of envy or for some other cause, have come to hate you. . . .

A ruler, therefore, should never forget his dignity, nor, if he cares for his reputation, should he ever waive a point agreed upon unless he can enforce it, or thinks he can enforce it. For it is almost always better, when your position is such that you cannot in this way make the concession, to let it be extracted by force rather than by the threat of force; because, if you yield to a threat, you do so in order to avoid war, and more often than not, you do not avoid war. For those before whom you have thus openly demeaned yourself by yielding, will not stop there, but will seek to extort further concessions, and the less they esteem you the more incensed will they become against you. On the other hand, you will find your supporters growing cooler toward you, since they will look upon you as weak and pusillanimous. But if, as soon as you become aware of your adversary's intentions, you prepare to use force, even though your forces be inferior to his, he will begin to respect you, and, since the rulers with which you were allied will now esteem you, they will be ready to help when you begin to arm, which they would never have done had you given up.

This applies where you have but one enemy. If you have more, the wiser course is to hand over some of your possessions to one of them so as to win him to your side even after war has been declared, and that you may detach a member of the confederation which is hostile to you. . . .

On Conspiracies

Since conspiracies are of such dangerous consequence alike to princes and to private persons, I cannot well omit to discuss their nature, for it is plain that many more princes have lost their lives and their states in this way than by open war, because it is given to but few to make open war on a prince, whereas anyone can conspire against him. There is, on the other hand, no enterprise in which private persons can engage, more dangerous or more rash than is this, for it is both difficult and extremely dangerous in all its stages. Whence it comes about that, though many conspiracies have been attempted, very few have attained the desired end. . . .

The dangers involved in conspiracies, as I have said above, are considerable, and go on all the time, for in a conspiracy dangers crop up alike in forming the plot, in carrying it out, and as a result of its having been carried out. Plots may be formed by one conspirator, or by several. If by one person only, it cannot rightly be called a conspiracy. Rather is it a firm resolve on the part of some individual to kill the prince. Of the three dangers conspiracies entail, a one-man conspiracy lacks the first. For no danger can arise before the time for action comes, since no one else being privy to the secret, there is no danger of the plot being carried to the ears of the prince. To make a resolve of this kind lies within the competence of anybody whatsoever, be he great, small, noble, or insignificant, intimate or not intimate with the prince. For anyone is allowed at some time or other to speak to the prince, and anyone who gets the chance of speaking to him, gets a chance to relieve his feelings. . . . But let us leave these one-man plots and turn to conspiracies involving several people.

I maintain that one finds in history that all conspiracies have been made by men of standing or else by men in immediate attendance on a prince, for other people, unless they be sheer lunatics, cannot form a conspiracy; since men without power and those who are not in touch with a prince are devoid alike of any hope and of any opportunity of carrying out a conspiracy successfully. For, first of all, men without power cannot get hold of anyone who will keep faith with them, since no one can consent to do what they want under any of those prospects which induce men to take great risks, so that, once the plot has been communicated to two or three people, an informer will turn up and they are ruined. Moreover, should they actually be lucky enough to avoid informers, the carrying out of the plot will involve them in such difficulties, owing to the lack of easy access to the prince, that it will be impossible for them to escape disaster in carrying out their scheme. For, if men of standing and those who have easy access succumb to these difficulties, which will be dealt with presently, it is to be expected that in the case of these others such difficulties will be magnified without end. Consequently, since when their lives and property are not at stake, men do not entirely lose their heads, they become cautious when they recognise their weakness, and when they get sick of a prince confine themselves to cursing him, and wait for those of higher standing than they have, to avenge them. So that, should one in fact come across somebody of this kind who has attempted such a thing, one should praise his intention but not his prudence.

It would seem, then, that conspirators have all been men of standing or intimates of the prince, and, of these, those who have been moved to conspire by too many benefits are as numerous as those moved to conspire by too many injuries. . . .

And yet, if any conspiracies against a prince, made by men of standing, ought to have succeeded it should surely have been this, since it was made by another king, so to speak, who had every convenience requisite to satisfying his desire. But that lust for domination, which blinds men, blinds them yet again in the way they set about the business: for, if they knew but how to do their evil deeds with prudence, it would be impossible for them not to succeed.

A prince, therefore, who wants to guard against conspiracies, should fear those on whom he has conferred excessive favours more than those to whom he has done excessive injury. For the latter lack opportunity, whereas the former abound in it, and the desire is the same in both cases; for the desire to rule is as great as, or greater than, is the desire for vengeance. Consequently princes should confer on their friends an authority of such magnitude that between it and that of the prince there remains a certain interval, and between the two a something else to be desired. Otherwise it will be a strange thing if that does not happen to them which happened to the princes we have been talking about. But to return them to the lines of our discourse. . . .

Let us begin by discussing the dangers incurred at the outset. These are the more important, I maintain, since there is need of great discretion and one must have considerable luck if, in making one's plans, the plot is not to be discovered. Plots are discovered either from information received or by conjecture. Leakage of information is due either to lack of loyalty or to lack of discretion amongst those to whom you communicate the plot. Lack of loyalty may easily occur, because you can only communicate your plan to those in whom you have such confidence that you think they will risk death for your sake, or else to men who are discontented with the prince. Now there may be one or two persons whom you can trust, but it is impossible to find such men if you reveal your plans to many people, for the goodwill they bear you must indeed be great if the danger and the fear of punishment is not to outweigh it in their estimation. Men, too, quite frequently make mistakes about the affection another man has for them, nor can you be sure of it unless of it you have previously had experience, and to acquire experience in such a matter is a very risky business. Even should you have had experience of some other dangerous affair in which they have been loyal to you, you cannot infer from their loyalty in this case that they will be equally loyal in another which far exceeds it in dangers of all kinds. While if you judge of a person's loyalty by the degree of disaffection he has for the prince, here, too, you may easily be mistaken; for by the very fact of your having opened your mind to such a malcontent, you provide him with material with which to obtain contentment, so that, if he is to keep faith with you, either his hatred must be great or your influence over him must be very great indeed.

It thus comes about that conspiracies are frequently revealed and are crushed at the very start. Indeed, it is looked on as a marvel if a plot which has been communicated to many people, remains secret for any length of time. . . .

Against discovery due to such causes it is impossible so to guard as to prevent the plot being revealed, whether owing to malice, to indiscretion or to frivolous conversation, in all cases in which the number of those who are cognisant of it exceeds three or four. For, should more than one of the conspirators be arrested, it is impossible to prevent its coming out, because two cannot possibly agree as to every detail in the explanations they give. If only one man is arrested and he be a man of resolution, he may possibly have sufficient strength of mind to be silent about his fellow conspirators. It may well happen, however, that the other conspirators have less courage than he has, and that, instead of standing their ground, they may reveal the plot by running away, for the conspiracy will be discovered to whichever party courage is lacking, whether to the man who has been arrested or to those who are still at large. . . .

These, then, are the dangers to which a conspiracy is exposed in the course of its formation before the time comes for it to be carried out; and, if they are to be avoided, these are the remedies. The first, the safest, and, to tell the truth, the only one, is not to allow the conspirators time to give information against you, and to tell them of your plan only when you are ready to act, and not before. Those who have so acted, at any rate escape the dangers involved in contriving the plot, and more often than not, the others also. All of them, in fact, have been successful, and any prudent man should find it possible to conduct things in this fashion. . . .

A plot, then, should never be divulged unless one is driven to it and it is ripe for execution, and if you, perforce, have to divulge it, it should be told to but one other person, and this a man of whom you have had very considerable experience, or else one who is actuated by the same motives as you are. To find such a man is far easier than to find several, and for this very reason is less dangerous. Moreover, should you, in fact, make a mistake, you have here a chance of protecting yourself, which is not the case where many conspirators are involved. For I have heard a wise man say that you can talk about anything to one person alone, since, unless you allow yourself to be persuaded to commit yourself in writing, one man's "yes" will be worth just as much as the other man's "no". And against writing anything down everybody should be on his guard as against a rock, for nothing is more likely to convict you than is your own handwriting. . . .

As to the dangers which occur during the carrying out of a plot, these are due either to a change of plan, or to lack of courage on the part of the person who is to carry it out, or to the operative's making some mistake owing to carelessness, or to failure to complete the job in that there remain alive some of those who were to have been killed. I would here point out, therefore, that nothing so perturbs and interferes with anything undertaken by men as does their having suddenly and without due notice to change their plan and to give up that laid down at the start. And, if such a change of plan anywhere gives rise to disorder, it is in military operations and in affairs such as those of which we are speaking; because in a business of this kind what it is essential to do first and foremost is to get clearly into the heads of those concerned the part which each of them has to play, and, if men have for several days been picturing to themselves a certain course of action and a certain plan, and this is suddenly changed, it is impossible but that it should throw everything out of gear and spoil the whole scheme. So that it is much better to carry out the original plan, even if one sees in it certain inconveniences, than it is to cancel it and thereby to involve oneself in a host of inconveniences. This applies to cases in which there is no time to draw up a new plan, for, if there is time, a man can arrange matters as he pleases.

ON THE OBJECT OF WAR AND THE USE OF VICTORY

Those who make war have always and very naturally designed to enrich themselves and impoverish the enemy; neither is victory sought or conquest desirable, excepting to strengthen themselves and weaken the enemy. Hence it follows, that those who are impoverished by victory or debilitated by conquest, must either have gone beyond, or fallen short of, the end for which wars are made. A republic or a prince is enriched by the victories he obtains, when the enemy is crushed and possession is retained of the plunder and ransom. Victory is injurious when the foe escapes, or when the soldiers appropriate the booty and ransom. In such a case, losses are unfortunate, and conquests still more so; for the vanquished suffers the injuries inflicted by the enemy, and the victor those occasioned by his friends, which being less justifiable, must cause the greater pain, particularly from a consideration of his being thus compelled to oppress his people by an increased burden of taxation. A ruler possessing any degree of humanity, cannot rejoice in a victory that afflicts his subjects. The victories of the ancient and well organized republics, enabled them to fill their treasures with gold and silver won from their enemies, to distribute gratuities to the people, reduce taxation, and by games and solemn festivals, disseminate universal joy. But the victories obtained in the times of which we speak, first emptied the treasury, and then impoverished the people, without giving the victorious party security from the enemy. This arose entirely from the disorders inherent in their mode of warfare; for the vanquished soldiery, divesting themselves of their accoutrements, and being neither slain nor

From Niccolò Machiavelli, *The History of Florence and of the Affairs of Italy, from the Earliest Times to the Death of Lorenzo the Magnificent* (London: George Bell & Sons, 1882), 254–56.

detained prisoners, only deferred a renewed attack on the conqueror, till their leader had furnished them with arms and horses. Besides this, both ransom and booty being appropriated by the troops, the victorious princes could not make use of them for raising fresh forces, but were compelled to draw the necessary means from their subjects' purses, and this was the only result of victory experienced by the people, except that it diminished the ruler's reluctance to such a course, and made him less particular about his mode of oppressing them. To such a state had the practice of war been brought by the sort of soldiery then on foot, that the victor and the vanquished, when desirous of their services, alike needed fresh supplies of money; for the one had to re-equip them, and the other to bribe them; the vanquished could not fight without being re-mounted, and the conquerors would not take the field without a new gratuity. Hence it followed, that the one derived little advantage from the victory, and the other was the less injured by defeat; for the routed party had to be re-equipped, and the victorious could not pursue his advantage.

FRANCESCO GUICCIARDINI
(1483–1540)

Francesco Guicciardini was ambassador of the Florentine Republic to Ferdinand of Spain from 1511 to 1514, and subsequently governor of Modena in 1516. He organized the military defense of Parma and sought to form an alliance between the Italian states and the kingdom of France. Failing in 1527, he retired from political life in 1537 to write his major work, Storia d'Italia *(1537–40), which covers the period from 1492 to the death of Charles VIII of France. He paid great attention to the innovations in the area of mobility and artillery in Charles VIII's armies, which intervened victoriously in Italy in 1494. In the* Ricordi politici e civili, *which he began work on in 1525, he shows himself a dispassionate analyst of politics.*

THE PERFECTION OF THE FRENCH ARTILLERY

... Then there were 6,000 Swiss foot soldiers; 6,000 foot soldiers from [Charles VIII's] own kingdom—of which half came from Gascony, a province which in the opinion of the French is the best endowed with able infantrymen of any in France. To join up with this army there had been brought to Genoa by sea a great quantity of both siege and field artillery of a kind which had never been seen in Italy.

This pestilential armament—invented many years before in Germany—was first brought into Italy by the Venetians in the war which the Genoese had with them in about 1380. In this the Venetians, beaten on the sea and hard hit by the loss of Chioggia, would have accepted any conditions the victor liked to offer, if sober counsel had not been lacking on such an exceptional occasion. The name of the largest of these weapons was the bombard, which, after the

From *Guicciardini: History of Italy and History of Florence,* translated by Cecil Grayson, edited by John R. Hale (New York: Washington Square Press, 1964), 152–54. Copyright © 1964 by Washington Square Press, Inc. Reprinted by permission of Simon & Schuster, Inc.

invention had spread all over Italy, was used in sieges. Some were iron, some bronze, but they were all enormous; so that, because of the size of the machine, the lack of skill of the operators and the unsuitability of the apparatus, they were extremely slow and cumbersome to move. They were set up before towns with the same difficulties, and once set up there was so long an interval between shots that they used up a lot of time with relatively small effect compared with what came after. Hence the defenders of the besieged places had plenty of time to make repairs and fortifications inside. All the same the force of the explosion of the saltpeter with which the gunpowder is made, when it was lit, sent the cannon balls flying through the air with such a terrible noise and astonishing violence that this engine, even before it attained its later perfection, made all the siege instruments used by the ancients with so much fame to Archimedes and the other inventors look ridiculous. But the French made much more manageable pieces and only out of bronze, which they called cannons, and used iron balls where they used to be of stone and incomparably larger and heavier; and they moved them on cars which were drawn not by oxen as was the custom in Italy, but by horses. The men and equipment assigned to this work were so skillful that they could almost always keep up with the rest of the army; and when brought up to the walls they were set up with unbelievable rapidity. With only the briefest interval between shots they fired so rapidly and powerfully that they could do in a few hours what in Italy used to take days. And they employed this diabolical rather than human instrument no less in the field than at sieges, using the same cannon and other smaller pieces—built and transported according to their size with the same skill and speed.

This artillery made Charles' army most formidable to the whole of Italy; and it was formidable besides, not for the number but the caliber of the troops. The men-at-arms were nearly all from among the King's subjects, and not common people but gentlemen, not just taken on or laid off at the wish of the captains; and as the companies were paid not by them but by the King's ministers, they not only had their full numbers but were well set up and well provided with horses and arms—not being unable through poverty to equip themselves—and all competed to serve best from the instinct of honor which noble birth breeds in men's breasts as well as from the hopes they had of rewards for courageous deeds both inside and outside the service, which was arranged so that they could be promoted through various ranks up to captain. The captains had the same incentives, being nearly all barons and lords or at least of very noble birth, and nearly all subjects of the King of France. When they had their full complement of lancers—for according to the custom of the kingdom no one got more than 100 lancers to command—they had no other ambition than to earn their King's praise; so that there did not exist among them either the instability of changing masters out of ambition or greed, or rivalries with other captains for command of more troops.

In the Italian armies everything was just the opposite, for many of the men-at-arms, peasants or common citizens, were subjects of other rulers and entirely dependent on the captains with whom they agreed to serve, and who were responsible for recruiting and paying them, so that neither by nature nor circumstances had they any special incentive to give good service. The captains who were very seldom subjects of those who employed them—and often had very different ambitions and objects—were full of jealousy and hatred for one another; and having no agreed term to their commission and being entirely masters of their companies, they did not keep the number of soldiers they had been paid for; and not satisfied with reasonable conditions they imposed excessive terms on their employers. Unreliable in any service, they often passed into other employment, driven either by ambition or greed or other interests to be not only unreliable but treacherous. Nor was there less difference between the Italian infantry and that of Charles: for the Italians did not fight in firm and orderly squadrons but scattered throughout the field, usually withdrawing to the shelter of banks and ditches. But the Swiss, a most warlike nation, who had revived their ancient fame for ferocity in many brilliant victories and long practice of war, fought in squares arranged with an exact number in each line; and never breaking from this order they faced the enemy like a wall, firm and almost invincible where they could fight in a place large enough to deploy their squadrons. And the French and Gascon infantry fought with the same discipline and method, though not with the same courage.

WALTER RALEIGH
(1554–1618)

From 1578 on, Walter Raleigh was engaged in the privateering war waged by the English against Spanish galleons. Then, after 1580, he fought against the Irish rebels, which brought him to the attention of Queen Elizabeth, and he became one of her favorites. In 1584 he was in Virginia. He was disgraced and imprisoned in 1592. After his release, he set out on an expedition, which went part of the way up the Orinoco. In 1596 he took part in a raid on Cadiz, and in 1597 in one on the Azores. Imprisoned for thirteen years under James I, Raleigh wrote poetry and also a History of the World, *which remained unfinished. He was released in 1616 and, at the age of 60, embarked on an expedition to Guiana to search for gold. An attack on a Spanish settlement, carried out contrary to explicit orders, was his downfall. On his return to England, after a failed attempt to flee to France, Raleigh was executed.*

SEA WARFARE AND THE DEFENSE OF ENGLAND

Certainly, he that will happily perform a fight at sea, must be skilful in making choice of vessels to fight in; he must believe that there is more belonging to a good man of war, upon the waters, than great daring; and must know that there is a great deal of difference between fighting loose or at large, and grappling. The guns of a slow ship pierce as well, and make as great holes, as those in a swift. To clap ships together, without consideration, belongs rather to a mad man than to a man of war: for by such ignorant bravery was Peter Strozzi lost at the Azores, when he fought against the Marquess of Santa Cruz.

In like sort had the Lord Charles Howard, Admiral of England, been lost in the year 1588, if he had not been better advised than a great many malignant

From Walter Raleigh, *History of the World*, in Adrian Liddell Hart, *The Sword and the Pen* (New York: Crowell, 1976), 83–84.

fools were, that found fault with his demeanour. The Spaniards had an army aboard them; and he had none: they had more ships than he had, and of higher building and charging; so that, had he entangled himself with those great and powerful vessels, he had greatly endangered this Kingdom of England. For twenty men upon the defences are equal to an hundred that board and enter; whereas then, contrariwise, the Spaniards had an hundred, for twenty of ours, to defend themselves withal. But our Admiral knew his advantage, and held it: which had he not done, he had not been worthy to have held his head.

Here to speak in general of Seafight (for particulars are fitter for private hands than for the press), I say that a fleet of twenty ships, all good sailors, and good ships, have an advantage, on the open sea, of an hundred as good ships, and slower sailing. For if the fleet of an hundred sail keep themselves near together, in a gross squadron, the twenty ships, charging them upon any angle, shall force them to give ground, and to fall back upon their own next fellows, of which so many as entangle, are made unserviceable or lost. Force them they may easily, because the twenty ships, which give themselves scope, after they have given one broadside of artillery, by clapping into the wind and staying, they may give them the other: and so the twenty ships batter them in pieces with a perpetual volley: whereas those that fight in a troop have no room to turn, and can always use but one and the same beaten side.

If the fleet of an hundred sail give themselves any distance, then shall the lesser fleet prevail, either against those that are a-rear and hindmost, or against those that by advantage of oversailing their fellows keep the wind: and if upon a lee-shore, the ships next the wind be constrained to fall back into their own squadron, then it is all to nothing, the whole fleet must suffer shipwreck, or render itself.

It is impossible for any maritime country, not having the coasts admirably fortified, to defend itself against a powerful enemy that is master of the sea. Let us consider of the matter itself; what another nation might do, even against England, in landing an army, by advantage of a fleet, if we had none.

This question, whether an invading army may be resisted at their landing upon the coast of England, were there no fleet of ours at the sea to impeach it, is already handled by a learned gentleman of our nation, in his observations upon Caesar's *Commentaries,* that maintains the affirmative. This he holds only upon supposition, in absence of our shipping: and comparatively, as that it is a more safe and easy course to defend all the coast of England than to suffer any enemy to land, and afterwards to fight with him.

Surely I hold with him, that it is the best way, to keep our enemy from treading upon our ground; wherein, if we fail, then must we seek to make him wish that he had stayed at his own home. But making the question general, and positive, whether England, without help of her fleet, be able to debar an enemy from landing; I hold that it is unable so to do: and therefore I think it most dangerous to make the adventure.

RICHARD HAKLUYT
(c. 1553–1616)

*The English geographer Richard Hakluyt was adviser to the East India
Company and later became a member of the London Virginia Company,
working closely with Walter Raleigh, his patron.* He is mainly famous for his
The Principal Navigations, Voyages, Traffiques and Discoveries of the
English Nation *(1589; 1598–1600). In 1846 the Hakluyt Society, devoted to
the publication of "rare and valuable voyages, travels, and geographical
records," was formed.*

THE DESTRUCTION OF THE SPANISH ARMADA

Whenas therefore the Spanish fleet rode at anchor before Calais, the Lord Admiral of England took forthwith eight of his worst and basest ships which came next to hand, and disburdening them of all things which seemed to be of any value, filled them with gun-powder, pitch, brimstone, and with other combustible and fiery matter; and charging all their ordnance with powder, bullets, and stones, he sent the said ships upon the 28 of July being Sunday, about two of the clock after midnight, with the wind and tide against the Spanish fleet: which being forsaken of the pilots and set on fire, were directly carried upon the King of Spain's navy: which fire in the dead of the night put the Spaniards into such a perplexity and horror that cutting their cables whereon their anchors were fastened, and hoisting up their sails, they betook themselves very confusedly unto the main sea.

In this sudden confusion, the principal and greatest of the four galliasses falling foul of another ship, lost her rudder: for which cause when she could not be guided any longer, she was by the force of the tide cast into a certain

From Richard Hakluyt, *The Principal Navigations, Voyages, Traffiques and Discoveries of the English Nation,* excerpted in Adrian Liddell Hart, *The Sword and the Pen* (New York: Crowell, 1976), 78–81.

shoal upon the shore of Calais, where she was immediately assaulted by divers English pinnaces.

This huge and monstrous galliasse, wherein were contained three hundred slaves to lug at the oars, and four hundred soldiers, was in the space of three hours rifled in the same place; and there were found amongst divers other commodities 50,000 ducats of the Spanish king's treasure. At length the slaves were released out of their fetters.

Albeit there were many excellent and warlike ships in the English fleet, yet scarce were there 22 or 23 among them all which matched 90 of the Spanish ships in bigness, or could conveniently assault them. Wherefore the English ships using their prerogative of nimble steerage, whereby they could turn and wield themselves with the wind whichever way they listed, came often times very near upon the Spaniards, and charged them so sore, that now and then they were but a pike's length asunder: and so continually giving them one broad side after another, they discharged all their shot both great and small upon them, spending one whole day from morning till night in that violent kind of conflict, until such time as powder and bullets failed them.

The Spaniards that day sustained great loss and damage having many of their ships shot through and through, and they discharged likewise great store of ordnance against the English; who indeed sustained some hindrance, but not comparable to the Spaniards' loss; for they lost not any one ship or person of account. Albeit Sir Francis Drake's ship was pierced with shot above forty times, and his very cabin was twice shot through, and about the conclusion of the fight, the bed of a certain gentleman lying weary thereupon, was taken quite from under him with the force of a bullet. . . .

The 29 of July the Spanish fleet being encountered by the English lying close together under their fighting sails, with a southwest wind sailed past Dunkirk, the English ships still following the chase. The Lord Admiral of England despatched the Lord Henry Seymour with his squadron of small ships unto the coast of Flanders, where, with the help of the Dutch ships, he might stop the Prince of Parma his passage, if perhaps he should attempt to issue forth with his army. And he himself in the mean space pursued the Spanish fleet until the second of August, because he thought they had set sail for Scotland. And albeit he followed them very near, yet did he not assault them any more, for want of powder and bullets. But upon the fourth of August, the wind arising, when as the Spaniards had spread all their sails, betaking themselves wholly to flight, and leaving Scotland on the left hand, trended toward Norway.

The English seeing that they were now proceeded unto the latitude of 57 degrees, and being unwilling to participate that danger whereinto the Spaniards plunged themselves, and because they wanted things necessary, and especially powder and shot, returned back for England; leaving behind them certain pinnaces only, which they enjoined to follow the Spaniards aloof, and to observe their course.

The Spaniards seeing now that they wanted four or five thousand of their people and having divers maimed and sick persons, and likewise having lost 10 or 12 of their principal ships, they consulted among themselves, what they were best to do, being now escaped out of the hands of the English. They thought it good at length, so soon as the wind should serve them, to fetch a compass about Scotland and Ireland, and so to return for Spain.

They well understood, that commandment was given throughout all Scotland, that they should not have any succour or assistance there. Neither yet could they in Norway supply their wants. Fearing also lest their fresh water should fail them, they cast all their horses and mules overboard: and so touching nowhere upon the coast of Scotland; but being carried with a fresh gale between the Orkneys and Fair Isle, they proceeded far north, even unto 61 degrees of latitude, being distant from any land at the least 40 leagues. Here the Duke of Medina general of the fleet commanded all his followers to shape their course for Biscay: and he himself with twenty or five and twenty of his ships which were best provided of fresh water and other necessaries, holding on his course over the main ocean, returned safely home.

There arrived at Newhaven in Normandy, being by the tempest enforced to do so, one of the four great galliasses, where they found the ships with the Spanish women which followed the fleet at their setting forth. Two ships also were cast away upon the coast of Norway, one of them being of a great burthen; howbeit all the persons in the said great ship were saved: insomuch that of 134 ships, which set sail out of Portugal, there returned home 53 only small and great: namely of the four galliasses but one, and but one of the four galleys. Of the 91 great galleons and hulks there were missing 58, and 33 returned.

DUC DE RICHELIEU
(1585–1642)

Armand Jean du Plessis, duc de Richelieu, was appointed France's secretary of state in 1616 and made cardinal in 1622. Becoming chief minister in 1624, he restored royal authority and prepared the conditions for the establishment of French preponderance in Europe. He strengthened the army and navy and encouraged the development of commerce and a colonial empire. In the Thirty Years' War, he allied France with the Protestant powers against the Hapsburgs. Among other works, he wrote Mémoires (1600–1638) *and a* Testament politique, *both published after his death.*

ON SEA POWER

The power of arms requires not only that the king be strong on land, but also that he be powerful at sea. . . .

The sea is of all heritages the one over which rulers claim most, and yet it is one over which the rights of everybody are least clear.

The empire of that element was never clearly assured to anyone. It has been subject to various changes according to the inconstancy of its nature, so subject to the winds that it abandons itself to him who flatters it most and whose power is so unbounded that he holds himself ready to possess it with violence against all who might dispute his rule over it.

In short, the true titles of this dominion are force and not reason. One must be powerful to lay claim to that heritage.

In order to proceed in an orderly and methodical way, the ocean and the Mediterranean must be considered separately, and a distinction must be made between ordinary vessels that use both these seas and galleys, use of which is only good in the one that nature seems to have set aside expressly between the lands to expose it to fewer storms and give it more shelter.

From *Testament politique, ou les maximes d'état du cardinal de Richelieu* (Paris: Editions R. Laffont, 1948). Translated from the French by A. M. Berrett.

A great state should never be in a situation of receiving an insult without being able to avenge it.

And hence, England being situated where it is, if France was not powerful in vessels, England might do whatever it liked to harm France without fear of retribution.

It could obstruct our fisheries, disturb our trade, and, by blocking the mouths of our great rivers, force our merchants to pay whatever tolls it felt like asking.

It might raid our islands and even our coasts with impunity. Finally, the situation of the homeland of this proud nation relieving it of any grounds to fear the greatest powers on earth, which are powerless at sea, and the ancient envy it has of this kingdom would encourage it to risk everything, should our weakness not allow us any means of embarking on something to its detriment. . . .

It might be agreed that when French vessels meet English ones on the coasts of England, they shall salute first and lower the flag, and when English ships meet French ones on the coasts of France, they shall render them the same honors, provided that, when the English and French fleets meet somewhere other than on the coasts of the two kingdoms, each shall go on its way without ceremony, except to send a few tenders to reconnoitre each other, approaching no nearer than within cannon shot.

It could also be decided that, regardless of whether it were the coast of France or the coast of England, the fleet with the larger number of men of war will be saluted by the one with the smaller number, either by striking the flag or by not striking it.

Whatever expedient is adopted on this point, provided it is fair to everyone, it is right for Your Majesty to be strong at sea. I do not know whether what is reasonable will seem so to the English, so blinded are they on that subject that they know no equity but force.

The advantages that the Spaniards, who are proud to be our present enemies, derive from the Indies, oblige them to be strong on the ocean. Sound policy does not allow us to be weak there; rather, it requires that we be in a position to oppose any designs that they might have against us and to thwart their enterprises.

If Your Majesty is powerful at sea, the just apprehension that Spain will have of your attacking its fleets, the sole source of its subsistence, whether by a descent on its coasts, which stretch for over six hundred leagues, or an attack on some of its coastal forts, of which there are many, all weak, this apprehension, as I say, will compel it to be so powerful at sea and to maintain such strong garrisons that the bulk of the revenue of the Indies will be consumed by expense of keeping it all. And, if what remains is enough to preserve [Spain's domains], at least we shall have the advantage that it will no longer be enough to bother those of its neighbors, as it has been doing hitherto.

If Your Majesty had been as weak as his predecessors, he would not have reduced to ashes in the midst of the waters all the forces that Spain was able to put together on the ocean in 1638.

That proud and haughty nation would not have been forced to suffer the abasement of its pride, not only in the eyes of the whole of Italy, but of the whole of Christendom, which, seeing the islands of Sainte Marguerite and Saint Honorat, which [Spain] had only seized control of by surprise, snatched from its hands by naked force, at the same time and with the same eye saw the shame of that insolent nation and the glory and reputation of yours.

Finally, he would not have won that famous battle between galleys in the gulf of Genoa, which struck terror into his enemies and enhanced the esteem and the love of his allies and inspired so much respect among the indifferent that the weight of respect draws them altogether to his side.

Your Majesty having allies so far away from this kingdom that it is impossible to communicate with them except by sea, if they see France denuded of the necessary means to help them on certain occasions, it would be easy for those envious of the good fortune of both sides to sow the same division between men as there is between states, whereas if your seaborne forces are considerable, although scattered as to place, they will remain closely united by love and affection to this state.

Nature seems to have wanted to offer the empire of the sea to France by the advantageous situation of its two coasts, both equally provided with excellent ports, on the two seas, the ocean and the Mediterranean.

Brittany alone contains the finest ports on the ocean, and Provence, which is only twenty-eight miles long, has many more large and safe ones than Spain and Italy together.

The separation of the domains that make up the body of the Spanish monarchy makes communication between them so difficult that the sole means Spain has of keeping them together is to maintain a large number of vessels on the ocean, and galleys in the Mediterranean, whose continuous comings and goings, as it were, hold together the members and the head, carrying to and fro all the things required for their subsistence: orders for what must be undertaken, officers to command, soldiers to execute, and money, which is not only the sinew of war, but also the oil of peace. Whence it follows that, if we obstruct the freedom of such comings and goings, these domains, which cannot subsist by themselves, would be unable to avoid confusion, weakness, and all the desolation with which God threatens a divided kingdom. . . .

Thirty galleys will give that advantage to Your Majesty, and if to such a body he adds ten galleons, true citadels of the sea, a source of fear to galleys when they have a following wind, because their body bears no proportion to the weakness of those light vessels, and which do not in the least fear them even in the most absolute calm, because being equipped with cannon as good as those pursuing them, they are in a position to do them much harm, if they come too close. [This sentence has been altered in various ways in the manuscripts. It is probably to be read thus: "a source of fear to galleys when they have a following wind, *because of their size, which is out of all proportion to the weakness of these light vessels,* and which have no fear of them at all in absolute calm. With a following wind, the galleys can be crushed by the mass of galleons; in calm weather, they can do them damage with the cannon with which they are equipped."—ED.] Were the king of Spain to increase his forces on that sea by half, which he cannot do without great expense, he would not be in a position to repair the harm that we could inflict on him by reason of the union of our forces and the division of his. . . .

Italy is regarded as the center of the world, and, truth to tell, it is the most valuable part of the Spaniards' empire. It is the place where they most fear to be attacked and troubled, and the one where it is easiest to win great advantages over them provided that we go about it properly. And consequently, even if we had no design to do them harm, at least we should be in a position to give them a return blow so near the heart should they want to attempt anything against France, so that their arms may no longer have enough strength to carry out [Spain's] malicious designs against it. That strength will not only hold Spain in check, it will oblige the *grand seigneur* and his subjects, who measure the power of distant kings only by what they have at sea, to be more careful than they have been hitherto to honor the treaties made with them.

Algiers, Tunis, and the whole Barbary coast will respect and fear your power, instead of, as at present, scorning it with an unbelievable lack of faith.

In that case, either those barbarians will freely live in peace with Your Majesty's subjects or, if they are not so wise as to do so, they will be compelled to do by force what they have been unwilling to do by reason. Whereas at present we think we do not have war, we suffer all the evils of war and enjoy neither peace nor the harvest that it should bring us, we shall find calm and safety in war, which is very advantageous with men whose natural faithlessness is so great that protection from it can only be guaranteed by force.

SÉBASTIEN DE VAUBAN
(1633–1707)

Sébastien Le Prestre, seigneur de Vauban, was a military engineer and an architect. He took part in many campaigns. Along with the Netherlander Baron Menno van Coehoorn (1641–1704), Vauban was the great fortification engineer of his time. He was made general commissioner for fortifications in 1678, lieutenant-general of the armies in 1688, and marshal of France in 1705. In his lifetime, Vauban built thirty-three fortresses, laid out almost three hundred, and conducted over fifty sieges.

He wrote extensively on fortifications and sieges. He had a wide-ranging mind and he was also the author of a proposal for fiscal reform, which aroused the opposition of the nobility. It must be stressed that, between the sixteenth century and the mid eighteenth century, siegecraft and the art of building fortresses was certainly the most important part of the art of war. The short interlude that gave artillery superiority against high, relatively thin walls (Constantinople, 1453) was ended by the innovations of Italian engineers like Sangallo, Sanmichele, and Tartaglia, and Hollanders like Simon Stevinus (1548–1620) and, later, Coehoorn.

GENERAL RULES OR MAXIMS
FOR ATTACKING A FORTRESS

Always be well informed about the strength of garrisons before deciding to attack.

Always attack at the weakest points, and never at the strongest, unless forced to by higher considerations, which, compared to the particular ones, mean that what is stronger in ordinary cases is weaker in extraordinary ones: which

From Vauban, "De l'attaque et de la défense des places," in *Anthologie des classiques militaires français,* edited by L.-M. Chassain (Limoges-Paris-Nancy: Editions Charles-Lavauzelle, 1950). Translated from the French by A. M. Berrett.

depends on the sites, the weather, and the reasons why places are being attacked, and the various situations you may find yourself in.

When the king besieged Valenciennes, His Majesty was not unaware that the Aujain gate was the strongest in the whole fortress: however, he caused the attack to be made there:

(i) Because of the ease with which it could be approached by the Rhume causeway, which, being paved, brought all the munitions from Dunkirk, Ypres, Lille, Douai, and Tourcoing right up to the rear of the trenches, which could not be done anywhere else;

(ii) Because of the ease with which fascines could be had, there being large woods near there that could amply furnish everything needed;

(iii) So as to be able to contravallate, as we did, by a trench, the whole of that part between the flooded area below the fortress and the one above it; which being repeated at two *places d'armes* [rallying areas], one in front of the other, and along all the zigzags of the trench, the enemy was enclosed in the fortress and reduced to not letting out four men from his covered way from the Tournai gate to the Notre-Dame gate; such that if great help had arrived, the king, by strengthening the trench with two battalions and three or four squadrons, would have been able to take all the quarters on that side, which accounted for two-fifths of the full circuit of the lines, to strengthen his army with and face the enemy, without the attacks having ceased to do their job. These and other similar reasons sometimes prevail over everyday ones very advantageously, and that is why you must not hesitate to profit from them.

Similar reasons led Prince Eugene to attack Lille at the point where he did attack it, which is certainly one of the strongest sides of the fortress.

Open the trench only when the lines are well advanced, and the necessary munitions and equipment are in place, ready, and to hand; for you must not suffer for lack of them, but always have everything necessary to hand.

Always embrace the front of attacks so as to have the space required for batteries and rallying areas.

Always make three big lines parallel to the rallying areas, position and establish them well, making them as long as is required.

Linked attacks are preferable to all others.

Use the sap as soon as the trench becomes dangerous, and never do openly or by force what you can do by hard work; hard work always acts surely, and force does not always succeed and you risk much for little.

Never attack along narrow enclosed places or across marshes; even less along causeways when you can do so over dry, open ground.

Never attack by [way of] recessed angles, which may enable the enemy to envelop or fire over the heads of attackers; because instead of encircling [the enemy] the trench might later be enveloped [itself].

Never encumber the trench with troops, workers, or equipment; rather, keep them in the rallying areas to the right and left and leave the paths free for the working parties and comings and goings.

The surest means to carry through a successful siege is to have an army of observation.

Never push a work forward near the enemy, unless the man who has to support it is in a position to do so advantageously.

Make sure that the *batteries plongeantes* [firing from a superior position] known as "ricochets" are always situated on the enfilades and the outside of the pieces being attacked and not otherwise.

Use ricochet batteries and horsemen to take the covered way in preference to organized attacks wherever there is a possibility of doing so.

Observe the same attack maxim for all external positions and even for the main body of the fortress.

Never fire on the buildings of the fortress, which is a waste of time and consumes munitions uselessly on things that contribute nothing to its surrender and whose repair is always expensive after it is taken.

Haste in sieges does not hasten the taking of fortresses, in fact often delays it, and always causes more bloodshed, as witness Barcelona, Landau, and so on.

The season least suited to attacking fortresses is winter, because it is the time of bad weather and great cold, which make troops suffer a great deal.

Attack fortresses surrounded by marshes in the driest time of the year, because it is likely you will be less inconvenienced by the water.

With typical fortresses, typical attacks are in order; with atypical ones, attack as best you can, but stray from the rules as little as possible in any case.

In fortresses where there are a châteaux and a citadel, you must, wherever you can, attack by way of the citadel, if other considerations do not prevail, as often happens; because once the citadel is taken, the town necessarily follows; whereas if you attack the town first, you have two sieges to mount for one.

Never depart from or neglect observation of the rules on the pretext that a fortress is not good, for fear of causing a bad one to defend itself like a good one.

Attacks by [way of] narrow places are always difficult and subject to serious inconveniences, because you cannot always follow the rules there.

Unless the site is totally impossible, fortifications built by masters of the art invariably incorporate some standard, or almost standard, features. So it must be too with the conduct of well-mounted attacks.

Marshlands, which you can neither drain nor dry out, are only suitable for attacking fortresses if the weakness of their fortifications and garrisons make it so, and the width and height of the dikes by which you can approach [the fortress] are such as to enable you to drive a trench along the whole length, with the necessary returns, without being forced to enfilade; and there is some dry land alongside, higher than the level of the marsh, enabling you to establish batteries of all sorts usefully there to approximate in part the conditions ordinarily required.

Attack by day when the trench is so far advanced that there is no longer any point all along the front being attacked that is beyond range of [your] superiority in cannon, bombs, stones, and musketry; attack at night when many of these points are not in that position.

Every siege of any scale requires a man of experience, brains, and character to take the main responsibility for attacks under the authority of the commander. This man should direct the trench and everything to do with it; place all types of batteries, and give instructions to the artillery officers, who should obey him instantly, without adding or subtracting anything.

For the same reason, this director of attacks must command the engineers, sappers, and everything to do with attacks, for which he is accountable to the commander alone; for, when there are several individuals to whom account is due, it is impossible for there not to be confusion, after which everything, or almost everything, will go awry, to the great disadvantage of the siege and the troops.

TREATISE ON THE ATTACK AND DEFENSE OF FORTRESSES

Most fortresses that have been poorly defended have been so less because their commanders lacked courage than because they did not understand how to defend them. The reason is that commands are invariably either bestowed or bought; those that are bestowed are normally given to ex-officers as a reward for their services, without much attention being paid to their capacity.... Many of these officers whom a little favor has helped on their way think only of courting [their patrons] and turning their governorships to good account, so as to have something to live on part of the year in Paris and at court, where they reside as much as they can. Are they required to visit their fortresses? If so, it is on condition that they stay there as little as possible and on the

From Vauban, "Traité de l'attaque et de la défense des places fortes," in *Bibliothèque historique et militaire,* edited by Liskenne and Sauvan, vol. 5 (Paris, 1844). Translated from the French by A. M. Berrett.

understanding that they can gamble there, eat well, visit in the surrounding countryside on hunting parties, etc.; that is pretty much all that occupies them; there is not the least sign of them applying themselves to getting to know the strong and weak points of their fortresses, none at all, or so little that that little teaches them nothing. Very rarely do they bother to examine what has been entrusted to them, visit the positions, or make a few rounds; and were I to say that not one of them does so currently, it would be no more than the truth. I will go further: they do not do so either by day or by night, outside or inside, from close up or from far away. There is a general lack of application to studying their fortifications and how the whole thing works; the interrelationship of the parts that make up [the fortress] in general and in particular; how they can protect one another; the evasions they make possible; the harm they can do the enemy so long as we possess them; and the harm they may do us when we have lost them. These are all things that they ought to know perfectly well. However, I can say that of all the commanders [of fortresses] I have known, I have seen very few who have bothered to inform themselves about them. This is why few of them know the details of their defense, the uses to which they might put their fortifications, if they were properly understood, and how far a good defense can be taken. They never know how to assess clearly how strong or weak they are when a siege is getting under way. Not one understands the management of munitions, nor how much he needs, which means that they all make quite extraordinary demands and however much they may have, they are always short, because [munitions] are mostly wasted and very badly husbanded.

The same can be said of replacement weapons, to which they pay little attention until the need becomes urgent. They know even less about the numbers and quantity of troops they need and how to manage them during a siege so as not to expose them unnecessarily; the same goes for the use of cannon. All wait to work on their entrenchments until the enemy is upon them—that is, until there is no time left to do it because of the quantity of shot, bombs, and stones raining down on all sides on the pieces being attacked (which are the very ones that ought to have been protected early on), and that creates a handicap that they can no longer overcome. Governors who understand nothing about the defense of their fortresses, and hence make the most grievous errors, are thus the commonest thing in the world, and all because they have not prepared themselves, for lack of residence, study, and application. It necessarily follows from this that they are astonished and embarrassed when they find themselves besieged, which almost invariably produces a poor defense; whereas if they spent more time in their fortresses, applied themselves to getting to know them well, spending two or three hours a day to do so, often walked round them outside and in, consulted those who came to see them who have the reputation of knowing a thing or two about them, made notes for a good plan, etc., they might in a year or two make themselves very capable and well-informed. Without such application, a man might very well command a fortress for ten years without knowing it any better than he did the first day. What the governors [of fortresses] are being criticized for here goes also for the lieutenants of the king and majors who are normally second and third in command there. . . .

Among those who defend fortresses poorly, one could also put general officers and special commanders who are sent in anticipation of a siege to make up for the governor's lack of knowledge where it is a source of concern. Such men may well be seeing the fortress for the first time; as they cannot get to know it in such a short time, they are liable to commit grievous errors, which happens all too often. Moreover, the governor, who is always annoyed at having a master put over him, tells him as little as he can; he does not tell him very much about what he is thinking, and all this contributes to the loss of fortresses, in the defense of which both cut very poor figures. After which, once they are outside, they are to be seen waxing furious against the fortresses, decrying them and alleging defects in them that they do not have and that most do not know of. It is all just a feeble means of excusing their ignorance, not to say their cowardice!

It is desirable that the command of fortresses be given only to officers whose knowledge of fortification and service in the infantry is well known; they would then be defended better than they are today, when the best and most carefully fortified hardly put up more defense than the mediocre ones. When Menin, one of the kingdom's good fortresses, surrendered, I heard that there were still two demilunes to be taken and the descents of the fosse to be made, and that one flank of the fortress could not be taken, since the only way to achieve this was by flooding; this flank defended the bastion that was most damaged in the attack. The right flank was only slightly damaged: more thought and knowledge of fortification would have turned these demilunes to advantage, they both being very good and well-revetted, and would have spared us the shame of losing such a fine fortress in such a short time. To prevent similar cases occurring, governors should be required to produce a plan of defense after they have been in their fortresses a year or two; this plan would show whether they were capable of defense or not. The need to prepare it and give an account of it themselves would at least mean that they had to make some show of application to their trade and study fortification. If, after [submitting] several defense plans, they were seen to have no capacity, no knowledge of the good points of their fortresses, and the particular defense that each work can contribute, they should be removed. The good that would flow from such a measure is well enough known not to need explanation.

RAIMONDO DE MONTECUCCOLI
(1608–1681)

As generalissimo of the Austrian armies, Raimondo de Montecuccoli, an Italian in the service of the Hapsburgs, took part in campaigns in Silesia (1646) and Bohemia (1647). He also fought against the Turks, whom he crushed at St. Gotthard Abbey in 1664, and commanded the imperial forces against France. In his Memorie della guerra, *Montecuccoli advocates a number of innovations, among them fixing bayonets to muskets and forming companies of grenadiers. "He who thinks of too little is often deceived," he said; "he who thinks of everything, does nothing."*

MILITARY CONSIDERATIONS

On Disposition in Relation to Forces

Assess your forces and compare them to those of the enemy the way a disinterested judge compares the arguments of the parties in a civil case.

If the best part of your forces is made up of cavalry, seek out broad and open plains; if you rely more on your infantry, seek out mountains and narrow and obstructed places.

Infantry is good for sieges, cavalry for battles.

If your army is strong and battle-hardened, and the enemy's weak, recently raised, or softened by idleness, you should seek battle, as Alexander and Caesar did with their armies of veterans and victorious troops; if the enemy has the advantage in that area, avoid battles, camp where you have the advantage, fortify yourself in passes, and be content to prevent him from advancing. Imitate Fabius Maximus, whose forays against Hannibal are the most famous in

From Raimondo de Montecuccoli, *Mémoires militaires,* in *Bibliothèque historique et militaire,* edited by Liskenne and Sauvan, vol. 5 (Paris, 1844). Translated from the French by A. M. Berrett.

antiquity and won him very great renown among military commanders; for he must be seen in the context of a time when many lost battles, routs of the army, and other disgraces had sown fear in the hearts of the soldiers and the Roman people. Just look, I say, at how that dictator acted, and you see what to do in such circumstances: change the form of the war; temporize; seek a breathing space after a disgrace has occurred; and avoid risking the safety of the republic, because the least failure on the part of a weak army is considerable, as a slight illness has more impact on a broken and sick body than a serious one on a robust body, not because of the severity of the infirmity but because of the weakness of the patient.

Do not avoid combat, but seek to give it where you have the advantage.

Count more on advice than on chance.

Do not worry about grumbling among the people.

Camp opposite the enemy, shadow him as he marches by moving along the heights and through places where you have the advantage; seize castles and passages around his camp, and places through which he has to march; keep in line and do not let yourself be engaged at a disadvantage. It is always a great achievement simply to make him do nothing, waste his time, deceive him, ruin his plans, or halt or delay their advance and execution.

Strengthen fortresses; destroy bridges, abandon indefensible positions, withdraw troops from them and put them somewhere safe, lay waste the countryside through which the enemy must pass, burning houses and spoiling foodstuffs.

Have assured provisions behind you, draw the enemy into places where he will find none; harry his foragers with continual sallies; prevent him from sending out messages; observe his marches; shadow him; set ambushes for him. If you act like that, you can defeat the enemy without too much trouble. You are in your own country; you have all the help you need. The army you are dealing with does not have all that: it is in enemy country, far from home, with no fortresses, no stores, nowhere it can settle down, with no means of continuing the war; it sees its world, its forces, and its courage getting smaller and smaller all the time; so that, as I have said, it can be destroyed without too much trouble.

If you are much less strong than the enemy in troop numbers and quality, so that you cannot camp anywhere near him, you must abandon the countryside and withdraw into fortresses, as Byzantium's [forces] did against Philip [of Macedon] and Hannibal's against Scipio, so that the enemy, scouring the countryside, can be harassed and weakened by the garrisons of neighboring fortresses, without him being able to do anything much, or so that he tires of besieging and gives up, or lays several sieges one after another and uses up his time and his strength. . . .

Maxims for Offensive War

Be master of the countryside, and be stronger than the enemy, either in numbers or in the quality of your troops. Caesar said that two things are needed to conquer, preserve, and enlarge states: soldiers and money; that is what France does today; with money she buys some fortresses, with her arms she forces others.

Look out for special circumstances—for example, whether there is an internal war or factions in the country you wish to attack and you are called in by one of the parties.

Give battle, sow terror in the country, put it about that your forces are larger than they are, divide up your army into as many units as you can without risk, in order to be able to do several things at once.

Treat those who surrender well; treat those who resist harshly.

Make sure of your rear; leave things calm and well under control in your own country and on its borders.

Establish and secure yourself in some position to act as a fixed center and be capable of sustaining all the movements you make subsequently; make yourself master of the main rivers and crossings; make sure you have good lines of communication and correspondence.

Drive the enemy out of his forts by taking them, and out of the countryside by fighting. To imagine that you can achieve great things without fighting is an illusion.

Cut off his food supplies, take his storage depots, either by surprise or by force; press him closely and tighten your grip, put yourself between him and communication centers, garrison nearby places, surround him with fortifications, gradually destroy him by attacking his parties, his scouts, his convoys, burn his camp and munitions, send foul smoke over him, lay waste the countryside around towns, pull down windmills, pollute the water, spread contagious diseases among his troops, foster divisions among his men.

Make yourself master of the state:

by building new fortresses and citadels there and putting good garrisons in the old ones;

by winning over the hearts of the inhabitants;

by putting garrisons and colonies there;

by establishing alliances, leagues, and factions there;

by unsettling it through continuous raids, threats, and fires, thereby forcing it to pay tribute and submit;

by setting up your residence there;

by protecting weak neighbors and bringing down powerful ones; by not allowing powerful strangers to come and establish themselves there;

by taking the leading men with you as hostages, on the pretext of doing them honor;

by removing their will and power to act.

Maxims for Defensive War

Have one or more well-placed fortresses, in order to hold up the aggressor until you have got your forces together and have received help from some other power jealous of the attacker.

Support and encourage fortresses with a flying column, which is at the same time supported and encouraged by the fortresses.

To prevent sedition and internal divisions, keep the war abroad, where bad and upset feelings will evaporate and resolve themselves.

When you have no army, or your army is weak or consists entirely of cavalry, you must:

save whatever you can in fortresses, lay waste the rest, and particularly places where the enemy might position himself;

extend yourself with entrenchments when you see that the enemy is trying to hem you in; change position; do not stay in places where you can be enveloped, without being able to fight or withdraw, and for that [reason] have one foot on land and the other in the sea, or some major river;

forestall the enemy's designs, by passing help from hand to hand in places that he is approaching, distributing the cavalry in separated places so as to inconvenience him all the time, seize crossings, destroy bridges and windmills, dam rivers to swell them, cut down forests and turn them into barricades.

JEAN DE FOLARD
(1669–1752)

Chevalier Jean Charles de Folard was one of the outstanding military theoreticians of the eighteenth century. He was a soldier from the age of eighteen to the age of fifty, fighting in Italy, in Flanders, and in Malta against the Muslims, and then going into the service of Charles XII of Sweden, whom he greatly admired as a general. He took part in the War of the Spanish Succession in 1709. In his Traité de la colonne et de l'ordre profond *(1730), Folard advocates the formation of solid attack columns to make shock tactics effective. He argues that battle should be sought and asserts that a mass of troops will always succeed in piercing a thin line. In his* Découvertes sur la guerre *(1724), his most original work, he likewise opposes line order and the separation of arms and proposes a much deeper, checkerboard deployment of combined formations, linked by light elements. These ideas, expressed here and there in the eighteenth century (by Joly de Maizeroy and Guibert among others), were to be applied after the French Revolution, especially by Napoleon.*

ON COLUMN ORDER

There is no denying that column order is preferable to any other when you are resisting cavalry in a plain, attacking the enemy, breaking through his lines and destroying him in hand-to-hand combat, taking a trench, attacking a position, or finally undertaking some short, sharp action; it is the order easiest to maintain on the march and that best suited to moving forward with the most weight and impetus, which best keeps forces together.

The column must have a front two-thirds as long as its total depth, must be in close ranks and files, and have good reserves, which can be despatched wher-

From Jean Charles de Folard, *Traité de la colonne et de l'ordre profond*, in *Bibliothèque historique et militaire*, edited by Liskenne and Sauvan, vol. 4 (Paris, 1846). Translated from the French by A. M. Berrett.

ever they are needed, and be detached from the column without diminishing the strength of its order.

Troops must be so disposed in column order so that they can be maneuvered in every possible way without confusion—that is, you must be able to divide [the column] into several parts, get into battle, break it off and reform, move in every direction and change maneuvers without divisions or platoons getting mixed up with one another and without becoming disordered; all these changes of maneuver must also be prompt, it must be possible to execute them in the presence of the enemy, and they must also be supported and protected.

The column must be formed of only a single battalion, or at most two, except when circumstances or the terrain require that several be placed one behind the other, so as to be able to deploy them more easily and move your forces wherever they are felt to be needed.

When, in attacks, columns find themselves exposed to enemy fire, they must be supported in battle by battalions that oppose their fire to that of the enemy, so as to prevent their losing too many men before coming to grips with him; you may also leave a small gap between the two files in the center of the columns so as to be able to pass the wounded down it, from the head of the line to the tail.

When a column that is not supported by battalions in battle is attacked, either from the front or the sides, or, finding itself surrounded, is obliged to resist on all sides and fire from a stationary position . . . this must be done by ranks, beginning with the center, the other ranks kneeling, and so on from one rank to the next, or two ranks by two, until the first two on each wing, assuming that there are no grounds for fearing a sudden attack; in that case, these two ranks must hold their fire. As some clumsy men might fire too low, or break the heads of those kneeling in front of them, they must virtually touch the ground with their noses. . . .

ON DEFENSIVE WAR

A defensive posture is normally adopted when an enemy with infinitely superior forces is in a position to carry the war into your camp and you feel yourself too weak to carry the war into his; then you are forced into a position in which you must stay so long as it remains impossible to change the state of the war.

From Jean Charles de Folard, *Traité de la colonne et de l'ordre profond,* in *Bibliothèque historique et militaire,* edited by Liskenne and Sauvan, vol. 4 (Paris, 1846). Translated from the French by A. M. Berrett.

To be continually yielding ground to avoid an engagement is not to understand war. Covering a particular area that you feel it is important to hold on to and abandoning another that [you feel] is less so, and that reduces the enemy to very little, counts for a great deal when you are dealing with forces that no other would dare show himself before; but a great general will go farther; he will hold on to everything, he will keep his fortresses; he will prevent the enemy from laying his hands on any, and keeps him constantly in his sights along a border line that is always parallel, without him being able to pass beyond it and open a way into the country. If the enemy hastens and goes along his parallel, he must put himself in position to cover and go along his too, to face up to him and to reach the other positions just before his enemy, who might very well throw him off the scent by a countermarch. Extraordinary vigilance is required and perfect knowledge of the country one is defending to prevent entry into it, and to dispute the ground against a stronger enemy who is anxious not to lose time.

The important thing is to occupy advantageous positions. These are not always to be found in open and broken country, but they may be found in mountains. In all these sorts of wars, as in almost every other, the spade and the pick are the resource of the weak or of those who do not want to leave anything to chance; you dig trenches and put yourself in the position of having no fear of a sudden attack; you seize any opportunity that comes along to switch from timid defense—which you give the appearance of having adopted, to lull the enemy—to a bold and open offensive, although always ready to revert to the former if you do not meet the success you expected.

A general who is dealing with an enemy who stops him from carrying out his plans must try new ones, even ones that seem unworkable, because by so acting, you always find expedients that would remain unknown if you were to remain passive, not trying anything or doing anything; you must, as far as you can, create opportunities. An advantage of position on the part of one army, even though both sides have the same number of troops, makes for a very large disproportion; it is undeniable that a clumsy general with much larger forces than his enemy is weaker than the latter if he employs experience and skill against him.

If the enemy is engaged in a siege, you will outflank him and invest him from all sides with an army that forms, breaks up, and divides into several units that fly here and there around his camp and keep him continually on the alert, sometimes by day, more often by night, whichever is more convenient.

With this sort of war, you will soon have famine in a camp; forage will become very difficult and very dangerous [to find]; if they go foraging, it will only be as an army corps. The enemy disappears, comes together again where you are foraging, and falls with all his troops on your escorts, either to fight you piecemeal or, separated into several units, to pierce your chain or cut the line of your foragers; and precisely when he is harrying you in these places far from your base, where he weakens you and strips away your forces, he will smartly detach or embark troops to approach your lines and slip through the least-fortified and least-guarded places, and often through the strongest (which will be that much weaker for being denuded of men), on the generally accepted view that only the rash and imprudent would make an attempt from that side.

You prevent convoys from arriving; to do that, when there are some in the countryside, you place detachments in ambush; you try to surprise [the convoys] and scatter them, or get in front of them as quickly as you can with the largest possible force, and camp on the road in the most advantageous position. If the enemy marches on you to dislodge you, you leave him there, and by means of a forced march, you get out into his country, which you ravage. If the enemy comes back on you to drive you out, you let him come, and, after escaping him once again, you surprise him at his siege, attack lines where troops have been withdrawn, and send help into the fortress.

Since the maneuvers of small armies are always prompt and speedy and they get themselves moving easily, carrying out plans like this preempts whatever steps the enemy might take to oppose them, and secrecy is thereby better preserved. Everything is simple in a small army, whereas everything is organized, slow, and complicated in a large one.

You may also be thinking of cutting off the enemy's water, if possible, or starving him by keeping whatever you can in fortresses, and especially forage, victuals, and livestock; after that, you lay waste the length and breadth of the countryside, particularly the places where the enemy mainly intends to go; you occupy the castles capable of resisting a surprise attack, and that can only be taken by a siege in due and proper form, and the person in charge is ordered to surrender only when all is lost.

Flying camps are an admirable resource in defense, provided you know how to choose the positions and can dig in so advantageously that you cannot be forced out; from there you harry the enemy's forage and food supply and try to cut off his convoys.

You must try to position yourself advantageously and fortify your camp so that you will be safe from attack; if you see that the enemy is trying to hem you in, change position and, through well-concerted movements, seek to lure him into defiles or narrow places, difficult spots where you can cut him off or attack him from a better situation and with better weapons.

If the enemy decamps, follow him, shadow him, and harass him relentlessly, but do not enter into a decisive engagement; dispute some difficult passages; yield to him those that may lead him into a difficult situation; hold him there by the skill of your movements; divide your army into several units to prevent him from spreading out over the countryside; fall sometimes on his vanguard and sometimes on his rear; lay ambushes for him by night, by day, at any time; arm the peasants and set them on the foragers so as to deprive him of all means of sustenance; that, in short, is what is meant by active defense, and how to behave when you have such guests in your country. There is no better method to destroy an army without risking anything; it is the way of the great captains.

In countries that have deep valleys, mountain passes, and defiles, where a few men are enough to guard them, abandon the easiest ones and take the more difficult ones; position yourself in these places and fortify yourself there; establish a line of communication to ward off any movement by the enemy; advance your positions toward him; fortify them and back them up one after the other up to the army, so as to hold him up and dispute his every step. Finally try and envelop him on all sides, close in on his flanks, take his rear, fall on his convoys, harry him as he marches, and harass him relentlessly. . . .

ON MOUNTAIN WAR

Of all wars, none is more difficult, none requires more resort to strategems, and is at the same time more dangerous, than a war in mountains where there are high passes and deep valleys, with difficult paths, ravines, terrifying precipices, and a thousand other obstacles, which furnish an infinity of stratagems and resources. It is in these sorts of situations that a great captain can put to use all that is greatest and worthiest of his address and knowledge in the science of war. It is in these sorts of countries that nicely judged strokes are delivered, but for that one needs to be alert to seize the opportunity.

A keen, impetuous general who has a high opinion of his forces and his courage, and therefore thinks he can do anything, who wants only to fight, though the occasion be not ripe, soon meets ruin and shame, if his weaker but more resourceful and more patient antagonist disputes every inch of the country with him and often escapes him through sly, skillful movements; he thereby makes himself master of opportunities, and the stronger finds himself obliged to regulate himself by his movements if he wants to come up with him and fight him. He must be open and frank about his intentions, while the other, more refined and deeper in his, which only he knows, covers them from him and masks them with apparently fearful simulated retreats; through this pro-

From Jean Charles de Folard, *Traité de la colonne et de l'ordre profond*, in *Bibliothèque historique et militaire*, edited by Liskenne and Sauvan, vol. 4 (Paris, 1846). Translated from the French by A. M. Berrett.

found and deceptive behavior, he makes him less alert and less careful. The advantageous positions that are abandoned to us are often baits that lead us to our ruin. No stratagems are finer and more impenetrable than those based on the appearance of weakness and fear; they are only ever interpreted in favor of the weak after the event. Undertakings and behavior where you advance as you retreat, cover yourself, disguise yourself, hide your march, and take roundabout ways are always slow, but they are sure.

A general's conduct must have two main aspects: one looks to the security and preservation of his army, the other to the destruction of his enemy or his designs. With regard to the former, when you enter mountainous country, you must assure your rear or [see to it that there is] some other passage through which you have a way out available; you must not get too far from the routes along which your convoys pass; when you are obliged to get far away, the surest and wisest thing is to fortify yourself there. You must establish communications from one position to the next, block paths, keep the heights that seem least practicable, and equip them with an abatis; for even when there are no trees on the spot, there is nothing to stop them being taken from elsewhere and transported wherever you want. Post guards everywhere to warn each other by means of agreed signals—by night with fires, rockets, [etc.] and by day with smoke, and so on. Take care in everything not to do too little. You must do all you need and more; you can never take too many precautions, especially in mountainous country, which almost always lays you open to surprise, either from behind, or from crosspaths, valleys, or the heights that overlook you, if you do not take all the precautions necessary to protect yourself.

As for destroying your enemy or his designs, everything depends on the skill of the generals opposing one another. If the enemy general is careless and fails to take the precautions necessary for the safety and preservation of his army, you can deceive him, lead him from position to position, attack him in narrow places, cut off his retreat, and deprive him of food supplies by making yourself master of all the ways out and the heights. In this sort of favorable circumstance, you must fortify yourself strongly in the positions occupied, with [felled] trees as abatis, which you should extend lengthways, with the foot in, attached firmly to one another, and so close that the branches of one are interwoven with those of the next. You must also take precautions against attacks by those within, as well as against those of relieving forces arriving from without; above all, risk nothing and fear everything from the desperate boldness of an enemy who finds himself surrounded on all sides; for what it is best to do in such an unforeseen and extraordinary event is to lose no time in marching to the said occupied positions; concert [your movements], if possible, with relief forces; attack from both sides at once with no interval between one attack and the next, without breaking off, even though you are driven back, and have new units take the place of those who have been fighting, who re-assemble in the rear to return to the fighting if the others are driven back too.

Night is the best time for all these sorts of undertakings; you must not only tackle the positions that form the line of retreat but the whole enemy army, however advantageously positioned and entrenched it may be.

But if the general you are dealing with is vigilant, intelligent, and active; if he foresees all the traps you set for him; if he is infinitely superior to you in strength; if he reduces you to remaining tied up in the narrow limits of a strict defense, and to being wholly occupied with aborting his designs on you, then you must hold on to the most advantageous and strongest positions; there are some everywhere in mountainous country. You simply have to know them well and take advantage of them; you must fortify them one after the other; dispute the ground; try to gain some from the enemy, if you can; shut him in and spread out as you fortify your positions; and assure communications and the heights, forcing the enemy to fight you at a great disadvantage or be re-duced to remaining inactive. If he attacks you, especially by night, you must be careful not to move troops from the positions that can be forced most easily to the more difficult ones, despite the feints he might make there to get you to engage. You must, in these sorts of affairs, expect to be attacked wherever it is possible for the enemy to approach and, in consequence, be pre-pared for defense.

PETER THE GREAT
(1672–1725)

Peter the Great, tsar of Muscovy from 1682 and emperor of Russia from 1721,
tenaciously pursued the modernization of Russia in both civil and military
(army and navy) arenas. In 1703, as a "window on Europe," he established
a new capital, Saint Petersburg, on the river Neva. Charles XII was defeated
at Poltava in 1709, and the Baltic soon ceased to be a Swedish lake. Peter
the Great pursued an expansionist policy southward, toward the Black Sea
and the Sea of Azov. After Peter the Great, Russia, backward though it
was on many levels, became a great military power, which, with the help of
demography, weighed ever more heavily with each passing century. This
program for the domination of Europe is attributed to Peter the Great.

"TESTAMENT"

Keep the Russian nation constantly on a war footing, to keep the soldiers warlike and in good condition; never allow the soldiers to rest, except to improve
the state's finances, rebuild the army, or choose the favorable moment to attack. In that way, peace is made to serve war and war peace, in the interests of
the aggrandizement and increasing prosperity of Russia.

Endeavor by every possible means to bring in officers in wartime and scholars in peacetime from among the most educated peoples of Europe to enable
the Russian nation to benefit from the advantages that other nations enjoy
without it losing its own.

Whenever the occasion offers, get involved in the affairs and disputes of Europe, and especially those of Germany, which, being the closest, is of more direct interest.

Peter the Great, "Testament, ou plan de domination européenne laissé par lui à ses successeurs
au trône de Russie," in Gaston Bouthoul, *L'Art de la politique* (Paris: Editions Seghers, 1962).
Translated from the French by A. M. Berrett.

Divide Poland by stoking up trouble and constant jealousies there; win over the powerful with money; influence and corrupt the diets [Polish parliaments] so as to have a say in the election of kings; have your supporters appointed to office there, protect them, have Russian troops enter there, and stay there until such time as they can be established there permanently. If the neighboring powers put difficulties in the way, pacify them temporarily by dividing the country until we can take back what has been given up.

Take as much as you can from Sweden, and contrive that that country should attack you in order that you may have a pretext for subduing it. To do that, isolate it from Denmark and Denmark from Sweden, carefully nurturing their rivalries.

Always choose the wives of Russian princes from among the princesses of Germany in order to increase the number of family alliances, bring interests closer together, and thereby bind Germany to our cause by enhancing our influence.

Seek a trading alliance, preferably with England, as being the power that most needs us for its navy, and that can be the most useful to the development of ours. Exchange our wood and other products for England's gold and establish permanent contacts between its merchants and sailors and ours who will train this country's in navigation and trade.

Steadily expand northward, along the Baltic, and southward, along the Black Sea.

Approach as close to Constantinople and India as possible. He who rules there will be the real ruler of the world. Consequently, provoke constant wars, sometimes with the Turks, sometimes with Persia; establish dockyards on the Black Sea; get possession of that sea by degrees, and also of the Baltic *which is doubly necessary for the success of our plan:* hasten the decay of Persia; penetrate as far as the Persian Gulf; reestablish if possible, the ancient trade of the Levant, through Syria, and advance as far as the Indies, which are the emporium of the world.

Once there, you can do without England's gold.

Seek out and carefully maintain an alliance with Austria: appear to support Austria's ideas about the future kingship of Germany, and secretly rouse the jealousy of the princes against it.

Try to get Russia appealed to for help by one or the other and exercise a sort of protection over the country to lay the ground for future domination of it.

Get the house of Austria interested in driving the Turks out of Europe, and neutralize its jealousy when Constantinople is taken, either by getting it involved in a war with the old states of Europe or by giving it a portion of what has been conquered, which will be taken away from it later.

Win over and unite around you all the disunited or schismatic Greeks who are scattered either in Hungary or Turkey or southern Poland; make yourself their center, their support, and establish in advance a universal predominance through a sort of royalty or priestly supremacy; then you will have friends scattered among your enemies.

With Sweden dismembered, Persia defeated, Poland subjugated, Turkey conquered, our armies united, and the Black Sea and the Baltic guarded by our vessels, we shall then have to propose separately, and very secretly, first to the court of Versailles, then to that of Vienna, that we share the empire of the world with them. . . .

If one of them accepts, which is bound to happen, as a result of flattering their ambition or amour-propre, use it to crush the other; then crush the remaining one, by engaging in a struggle whose outcome is sure, Russia already possessing the whole of the East and much of Europe.

If—which is most unlikely—both reject the Russian offer, then you will have to provoke disputes between them and have them exhaust each other. Then, taking advantage of a decisive moment, Russia should throw her assembled troops on Germany, and at the same time two fleets should set out, one from the Sea of Azov, the other from the port of Archangel, loaded with Asiatic hordes [*sic!*], conveyed by the armed fleets of the Black Sea and the Baltic Sea. Advancing by way of the Mediterranean and the [Atlantic] Ocean, they will flood over France on the one side, while Germany will be on the other, and with these two countries defeated, the rest of Europe will easily fall under our yoke without striking a single blow.

MAURICE DE SAXE
(1696–1750)

Maurice de Saxe, the illegitimate son of Augustus II of Poland, fought under the command of Prince Eugene of Savoy against the Turks and in 1717 took part in the capture of Belgrade. In 1720 Maurice entered the service of France. A lieutenant-general in 1734, he fought in the War of the Austrian Succession and took Prague in 1741. Three years later, he was named marshal of France and was victorious in 1745 at the battle of Fontenoy; subsequently he conducted campaigns in Flanders and the Low Countries and won victories that led to the peace of Aix-la-Chapelle. He wrote Mes rêveries *when he was thirty-four, but they were published only posthumously, in 1757. "I am not for battles, especially at the beginning of a war; and I am convinced that a skillful general can make war all his life without being obliged to fight any," he said. By pursuing a war of attrition, he would seek to force the enemy to give up the struggle without having to fight a battle.*

REVERIES ON THE ART OF WAR

Raising Troops

Troops are raised by enlistment with a fixed term, without a fixed term, by compulsion sometimes, and most frequently by fraud.

When recruits are raised by enlistment it is unjust and inhuman not to observe the engagement. These men were free when they contracted the enlistment [that] binds them, and it is against all laws, human or divine, not to keep the promises made to them. What happens? The men desert. Can one, with

From "My Reveries upon the Art of War," translated by Thomas R. Phillips, in *Roots of Strategy: A Collection of Military Classics,* edited by Thomas R. Phillips (London: John Lane the Bodley Head, 1943; reprint, Stackpole Books, 1985), 19–94, 202–99. Reproduced by permission of Stackpole Books.

justice, proceed against them? The good faith upon which the conditions of enlistment were founded has been violated. Unless severe measures are taken, discipline is lost; and, if severe punishments are used, one commits odious and cruel actions. There are, however, many soldiers whose term of service is ended at the commencement of a campaign. The captains who wish to have their organizations full retain them by force. This results in the grievance of which I am speaking.

[The raising of troops by fraud is] also odious. Money is slipped secretly into the man's pocket and then he is told he is a soldier.

[Raising troops by force is] still worse. This is a public misfortune from which the citizens and the inhabitants can only save themselves by bribery and is founded on shameful means.

Would it not be better to prescribe by law that every man, whatever his condition in life, should be obliged to serve his prince and his country for five years. This law could not be objected to because it is natural and just that all citizens should occupy themselves with the defense of the nation. No inconvenience could result if they were chosen between the ages of twenty and thirty years. These are the years of libertinage, when youth seeks its fortune, travels the country, and is of little comfort to parents. This would not be a public calamity because one could be sure that, when five years had passed, discharge would be granted. This method of raising troops would provide an inexhaustible reservoir of fine recruits who would not be subject to desertion. In course of time, as a consequence, it would be regarded as an honor to have fulfilled one's service. But to produce this effect, it is essential to make no distinctions, to be immovable on this point, and to enforce the law particularly on the nobles and the rich. Then, no one will complain. Consequently, those who have served their time will scorn those who are reluctant to obey the law, and insensibly it will become an honor to serve. The poor bourgois will be consoled by the example of the rich, and the rich will not dare complain upon seeing the noble serve. Arms is an honorable profession. How many princes have borne arms! Witness M. de Turenne. And how many officers have I seen serve in the ranks rather than live in indolence! It is thus only effeminacy that will make this law appear hard to some. But everything has a good and a bad side. . . .

How to Form Troops for Combat

This is a broad subject, and I propose to deal with it in a manner so different from respected custom that I shall probably expose myself to ridicule. But to lessen the danger, I shall explain the present method. This is no small affair, for I could compose a big volume on it.

I shall begin with the march, and this makes it necessary to say something that will appear highly extravagant to the ignorant. No one knows what the ancients meant by the word *tactics*. Nevertheless, many military men use this word constantly and believe that it is drill or the formation of troops for battle. Everyone has the march played without knowing how to use it. And everyone believes that the noise is a military ornament.

We should have a better opinion of the ancients and of the Romans, who are our masters and who should be. It is absurd to imagine that the warlike sounds had no other purpose than to confuse each other.

But to return to the march, about which everyone bothers themselves to death but will never reach a conclusion unless I reveal the secret. Some wish to march slowly, others would march fast; but what about the troops whom no one knows how to make march fast or slowly, as they desire, or is necessary, and who require an officer at every corner to make them turn, some like snails and others running, or to advance this column [that] is always trailing. It is a comedy to see even a battalion commence movement! It is like a poorly constructed machine, about to fall apart at every moment and which staggers with infinite difficulty. Do you wish to hurry the head? Before the tail knows that the head is marching fast, intervals have been formed; to fill them promptly, the tail must run; the head that follows this tail must do the same; soon everything is in disorder, with the result that you are never able to march rapidly for fear of speeding up the head of the column.

The way to remedy all these inconveniences, and many others which follow and are of greater importance, is very simple, nevertheless, because it is dictated by nature. Shall I say it, this great word, which comprises all the mystery of the art, and which will no doubt seem ridiculous? Have them march in cadence. There is the whole secret, and it is the military step of the Romans. That is why these musical marches were instituted, and that is why one beats the drum; it is this which no one knows and which no one has perceived. With this you can march fast or slow as you wish; the tail will not lose distance; all your soldiers will start on the same foot; the changes of direction will be made together with speed and grace; the legs of your soldiers will not get tangled up; you will not be forced to halt after each turn in order to start off on the same foot; your soldiers will not exhaust themselves a quarter as much as at present. All this may seem extraordinary. Every one has seen people dancing all night. But take a man and make him dance for a quarter of an hour only without music, and see if he can bear it. This proves that tunes have a secret power over us, that they predispose out muscles to physical exercise and lighten the exercise.

If anyone asks me what tune should be played for men to march by, I should answer, without joking, that all marches in double or triple time are suitable for it, some more, others less, depending upon whether they are more or less accented, that all the tunes played on the tamborine or fife will do, likewise, and that one needs only to choose the more suitable.

I shall be told, perhaps, that many men have no ear for music. This is false; movement to music is natural and is automatic. I have often noticed, while beating for the colors, that all the soldiers went in cadence without intention and without realizing it. Nature and instinct did it for them. I shall go further: it is impossible to perform any evolution in close order without it, and I shall prove it in the proper place.

Considering what I have said superficially, it does not appear that this cadence is of such great importance. But, in a battle to be able to augment the rapidity of march, or to diminish it, has infinite consequences. The military step of the Romans was nothing else; with it they marched twenty-four miles in five hours, the equivalent of eight leagues. Let anyone try the experiment on a body of our infantry and see if it is possible to make them do eight leagues in five hours. Among the Romans this was the principal part of their drill. From this, one can judge the attention they gave to keeping their troops in condition, as well as the importance of cadence.

What will be said if I prove that it is impossible to charge the enemy vigorously without this cadence, and that without it one reaches the enemy always with ranks opened? What a monstrous defect! I believe, however, that no one has given it any attention for the past three or four hundred years.

It now becomes necessary to examine a little our method of forming battalions and of fighting. The battalions touch one another, since the infantry is all together and the cavalry also (for which, in truth, there is no common sense—but this will be covered in the proper place). The battalions, then, march ahead, and this very slowly because they are unable to do anything else. The majors cry: "Close," on which they press toward the center; insensibly the center gives way, which makes intervals between the battalions. There is no one who has had anything to do with these affairs but will agree with me. The majors' heads are turned because the general, whose head is turned also, cries after them when he sees the space between his battalions and is fearful of being taken in the flanks. He is thus obliged to call a halt, which should cost him the battle; but since the enemy is as badly disposed as he, the harm is slight. A man of intelligence would not stop to repair this confusion but would march straight ahead, for if the enemy moves he would be lost. What happens? Firing commences here and there, which is the height of misfortune. Finally they approach each other, and one of the two parties ordinarily takes to their heels at fifty or sixty paces, more or less. There you have what is called a charge. What is the cause of it all? Bad formations make it impossible to do better.

But I am going to suppose something impossible; I mean two battalions attacking to march toward each other without wavering, without doubling, and without breaking. Which will gain the advantage? The one that amuses itself shooting, or the one which will not have fired? The skillful soldiers tell me that it will be the one that has held its fire, and they are right. For besides being upset when he sees his opponent coming at him through the smoke, the one who has fired must halt to reload. And the one who stops while the other is marching toward him is lost.

If the previous war had lasted a little longer, indubitably everyone would have fought hand to hand. This was because the abuse of firing began to be appreciated; it causes more noise than harm, and those who depend on it are always beaten.

Powder is not as terrible as is believed. Few men, in these affairs, are killed from in front or fighting. I have seen entire salvos fail to kill four men. And I have never seen, and neither has anyone else, I believe, a single discharge do enough violence to keep the troops from continuing forward and avenging themselves with bayonet and shot at close quarters. It is then that men are killed, and it is the victorious who do the killing.

The Column

Notwithstanding the great regard I have for the Chevalier Follard, and that I think highly of his writings, I cannot agree with his opinion about the column. This idea seduced me at first; it looks dangerous to the enemy, but the execution of it reversed my opinion. It is necessary to analyze it to show its faults.

The Chevalier deceives himself in imagining that this column can be moved with ease. It is the heaviest body I know of, especially when it is twenty-four deep. If it happens that the files are once disordered, either by marching, the unevenness of the ground, or the enemy's cannon, no man alive can restore order. Thus it becomes a mass of soldiers who no longer have ranks or order, and where everything is confounded.

I have frequently been surprised that the column is not used to attack the enemy on the march. It is certain that a large army always takes up three or four times more ground on the march than is necessary to form it, even though marching in several columns. If, therefore, you get information of the enemy's route and the hour at which he is to begin his march, although he is at the distance of six leagues from you, you will always arrive in time to intercept him, for his head usually arrives in the new camp before his rear has left the old. It is impossible to form troops scattered over such a distance without making large intervals and dreadful confusion. I have often seen such a movement made without the enemy having thought of profiting by the occasion. And I thought they must have been bewitched.

This subject would furnish a useful chapter, for many diverse situations produce such marches. And in how many places may not one attack without risking anything? How frequently an army is separated on its march by bad roads, rivers, difficult passes? And how many such situations will enable you to surprise some part of it? How often do opportunities present themselves of separating it, so as to be able, although inferior, to attack one part with advantage and, at the same time, by the proper placement of a small number of troops, prevent its being relieved by the other? But all these circumstances are as various and intermediate as the situations which produce them, and nothing more is required than to keep well-informed, to acquire a knowledge of the country, and to dare. You risk nothing, for as these affairs are never decisive for you, they can be for the enemy. The heads of your columns attack as they arrive, and they are supported by the troops that follow them. This results from the formation itself. And you attack regiments which have no support. . . .

Small Arms

Fire should not be used against infantry where they can envelop you or you can envelop them. But where you are separated from an enemy by hedges, ditches, rivers, hollows, and such obstacles, then it is necessary to know how to aim and execute such terrible fire that it cannot be resisted.

I recommend the breech-loading musket. It can be loaded quicker, carries farther, is more accurate, and the effect is greater. In the excitement of battle, soldiers will not be able to put cartridges in the barrel without opening them. This often happens now and makes the muskets useless. They will not be able to insert two charges because the chamber will not hold them. Consequently, muskets will not burst as they often do [now].

To dislodge the enemy from a position on the other side of a river, from hedges, ditches, and such other places where the use of small arms is necessary, I would designate an officer or noncommissioned officer to every two files. He should advance the leader of the first a pace forward and show him where he is to direct his fire, allowing him to fire at will, that is, when he has found a target. The soldier behind him will then pass his gun forward, and the others in the same manner. The file leader will thus fire four shots in succession. It would be unusual if the second or third shot does not reach its mark. The commanding officer is close by him, watches his aim, directs him where to fire, and exhorts him not to hurry. This man is not hindered, nor crowded, nor hastened by the word of command. No one presses him; he can fire at ease and aim as long as he wishes, and he can fire four times in succession.

This file having fired, the officer withdraws it and advances the second[,] which performs in the same fashion. . . .

Artillery and Transport

I never would have an army composed of more than ten legions, eight regiments of cavalry, and sixteen of dragoons. This would amount to thirty-four thousand foot and twelve thousand horse, a total of forty-six thousand men. With such an army, one of a hundred thousand can be stopped if the general is clever and knows how to choose his camps. A greater army is only an embarrassment. I do not say that reserves are unnecessary, but only that the acting part of an army ought not to exceed such a number.

M. de Turenne was always victorious with armies infinitely inferior in numbers to those of his enemies because he moved more easily and knew how to select positions such that he could not be attacked while still always keeping near the enemy.

It is sometimes impossible to find a piece of ground in a whole province that will contain a hundred thousand men in order of battle. Thus the enemy is almost always forced to divide, in which case I can attack one of the parts; if I defeat it, I thereby intimidate the other and soon gain superiority. In short, I am convinced that the advantages which large armies have in numbers are more than lost in the encumbrance, the diversity of operations under the jarring conduct of different commanders, the deficiency of provisions, and many other inconveniences which are inseparable from them. . . .

The Defense of Places

I am always astonished that no one objects to the abuse of fortifying cities. These words may seem extraordinary, and I shall justify them. First examine the utility of fortresses. They cover a country, oblige the enemy to attack them or march around them, one can retire into them with troops and place them in security, they protect supplies, and, during the winter, troops, artillery, ammunition, etc., are kept in security.

If these considerations are examined, it will be found that fortresses are most advantageous when they are erected at the junction of two rivers. To invest them, when so placed, it is necessary to divide an army into three parts; the defender may defeat one of these three corps before the other two come to its aid. Before being invested, such a fortress always has two open sides, nor can the enemy completely surround the fortress in a day. He will need equipment for three bridges, and these often are hazards in themselves, due to storms and floods in the campaign season.

Besides this, in holding such a post and controlling the rivers, one is master of the country. Their course can be diverted if necessary, and they permit easy supply, formation of depots, and transport of munitions and all the other stores required in war.

Lacking rivers, places can be found fortified by nature so strongly that it is impossible to surround them, and which can be attacked only in spots. Small expense will make them impregnable. Others can be provided with locks and protected by extensive inundations. Everyone will admit that such situations can be found, and that, by aiding nature with art, they can be made impregnable. Nature is infinitely stronger than the works of man; why not profit from it?

Few cities have been founded for these purposes. Commerce has caused their growth, and their location was chosen by hazard. In the course of time they have grown and the inhabitants have surrounded them with walls for defense against the incursions of common enemies and for protection from internal disturbances in which nations are involved. All this was dictated by reason. The citizens fortified them for their own preservation, and they have defended them.

But what could be the inducement for rulers to fortify them? It could have some appearance of reason when Christianity lived in the midst of barbarism, when one city enslaved another, and when countries were devastated. But now that war is made with more moderation, what is there to fear? A town surrounded with a strong wall and capable of holding three or four hundred men, besides the inhabitants, together with some artillery, will be as secure as if the garrison consisted of as many thousands. For I maintain that these troops will not defend themselves longer than the four hundred and that the terms of surrender of the citizens will not be better.

But besides, what use will the enemy make of it after he has taken it? Will he fortify it? I think not. Thus he will be content with a contribution and will march on; perhaps he will not even besiege it because he will not be able to keep it. He will never hazard leaving a small garrison in it, and still less will he leave a large one because it will not be secure.

A still stronger reason persuades me that fortified cities are hard to defend. Suppose you have stored food supplies for three months for the garrison; after it is besieged you find that they last only eight days because you have not counted on twenty, thirty, or forty thousand mouths that must be fed. These are the peasants from the country who take refuge in the city and augment the number of the citizens. The wealth of a prince would not be able to establish such magazines in all the cities that might be attacked, and to renew them every year. And if he had the philosopher's stone, still he could not do it without creating a famine in the country.

I imagine some one will say: "I should expel the citizens who are unable to provide their own provisions." This would be a worse desolation than the enemy could cause, for how many are there in the cities who do not live from day to day? Besides, can you be sure that you will be besieged? And if you are, will the enemy tranquilly allow this multitude to withdraw? He will drive them back into the city. What will the governor do? Will he allow these unfortunates to die from hunger? Could he justify this conduct to his ruler? What can he do then? He will be forced to supply them with provisions and surrender in eight or fifteen days.

Suppose the garrison of a city consist of five thousand men and that there are forty thousand mouths besides that. The magazine is established for three months. But the forty-five thousand will eat in one day the supplies that would have lasted the five thousand for nine days. Thus the city cannot hold for more than eleven or twelve days. Even grant that it will last twenty days; in this case it will not even need to be attacked. It is obliged to surrender, and all the millions that have been spent in fortifying it are a useless expense.

It seems to me that what I have said should demonstrate the irremediable defects of fortified cities, and that it is more advantageous for a ruler to establish his strong points in localities aided by nature, and situated to cover the country, than to fortify cities at immense expense or to augment their fortifications. It is necessary, on the contrary, after having constructed others, to destroy the fortifications of cities down to the walls. At least no thought should be given to fortifying them further or of using the money to construct fortifications for such purposes.

Notwithstanding that what I have advanced is founded on reason, I expect hardly a single person to concur, so absolute is custom and such is its power over us. A fortified place, located as I have proposed, could hold out several months or even years, provided it can be supplied, because it is not encumbered with the civil population. . . .

Reflections upon War in General

Many persons believe that it is advantageous to take the field early. They are right when it is a question of seizing an important post; otherwise, it seems to me that there is no need to hasten and that one should remain in winter quarters longer than usual. What difference does it make if the enemy lays a few sieges? He will weaken himself by doing it, and, if you attack towards autumn with well-disciplined and well-ordered army, you will ruin him.

I have always noticed that a single campaign reduces an army by a third, at least, and sometimes by a half, and that the cavalry especially is in such a pitiable state by the end of October that they are no longer able to keep the field. I would prefer to continue in quarters until then, harass the enemy with detachments, and, towards the end of a good siege, fall on him with all my forces. I believe that I would have a good bargain and that he soon would think of withdrawing, although this might not be easy for him when opposed to troops that are well led and complete. He probably would be forced to abandon his baggage, cannon, part of his cavalry, together with all his wagons. This loss will not facilitate his going in the field so early next year. Perhaps he even might not dare to reappear. It is the affair of a month. And then one returns to winter quarters in good order, while the enemy is ruined. At this time of the year the barns are full, it is dry everywhere, and there is little sickness.

One can even turn in another direction and subsist all winter in the enemy's country. Winter need not be feared for troops so much as is commonly believed. I have made several winter campaigns in frightful climates; the men and horses kept well. There are no illnesses to fear, fevers are not prevalent as in summer, and the horses are in good condition.

There are situations which will permit you to place your troops in security in cantonments and with abundant food. The problem is to create these conditions. An experienced general does not live at the expense of his sovereign; on the contrary he will raise contributions for the subsistence of his army and for the ensuing campaign. Being well-lodged and warm, with an abundance of everything, the soldiers are contented and happy, and live at ease. In order to accomplish this it is necessary to know how to collect provisions and money from afar without fatiguing the troops. Large detachments are in danger of being attacked and cut off. They do not produce much and wear out the troops. To obviate this, the best way is to send circular letters to those places from which contributions are required, threatening them that parties will be sent out at a definite time to set fire to the houses of those who do not have quittances for the tax imposed. The tax should be moderate.

Following this, intelligent officers should be selected and assigned a certain number of villages to visit. They should be sent with detachments of twenty-five or thirty men and should be ordered to march only at night. The men should be ordered to refrain from pillage on pain of death. When they have arrived in the locality and it is time to determine if the villages have paid, they should send a sergeant with two men to the chief magistrate of the village to see if he has procured the quittance. If he has not, the leader of the detachment should show himself with his troops, set fire to a single house, and threaten to return and burn more. He should neither pillage, nor take the sum demanded, nor a larger one, but march away again.

All these detachments should be assembled at the same rendezvous before they are dismissed. There they should be searched and those who are found to have stolen the slightest thing should be hung without mercy. If, on the contrary, they have faithfully followed the orders given to them they should be rewarded. By such means, this method of raising contributions will become familiar to the troops, and the country a hundred leagues around will bring in food and money in abundance. The troops will not be exhausted, since twenty detachments a month can carry out the duty. These detachments will not be betrayed, whatever demand the enemy may make. And since it is a calamity that they feel and that they are unable to see until its effect are felt, their terror is increased, and no one sleeps in repose unless he has paid, regardless of any prohibitions the enemy may order.

A large body engaged in exacting contributions covers little of the country and causes trouble wherever it is. The inhabitants hide their goods and their cattle. In this state little is collected because they know the troops cannot remain long; they expect help—oftentimes they have gone for it themselves—with the result that the troops retire in haste without having accomplished much, and some are always lost. Even when things go best, the commander of the detachment, from fear or prudence, makes the best compromise he can with the inhabitants and only brings back worn-out troops in bad condition, some food, and little money. Such is the success that contributions ordinarily have. In place of this, in the fashion I propose, everything goes well and of itself.

Since only so much a month is required to be paid, the inhabitants will aid each other. They are able to furnish just so much more because they are not bothered by the presence of troops, because they have time, and because they do not see any recourse except to be burned out if they do not satisfy the demands. Finally, an immense extent of country is covered. The more distant inhabitants sell their supplies to bring in money, and those closer in bring in provisions. They should always be allowed to choose.

These detachments must be very unfortunate, or badly conducted, to be discovered. For a detachment of twenty-five men can cross a whole kingdom without being captured. They march off when they are discovered, and an army cannot take them. . . .

Spies and Guides

Too much attention cannot be paid to spies and guides. Montecuculli says that they are like eyes and are equally necessary to a general. He is right. Too much money cannot be spent to get good ones. These men should be chosen in the country where the war is being fought. They should be intelligent, cunning, and discreet. They should be placed everywhere, among the officers, the generals, the sutlers, and especially among purveyors of provisions, because their stores, magazines, and other preparations furnish the best intelligence concerning the real designs of the enemy.

Spies should not know one another. There should be several ranks of them. Some should associate with soldiers; others should follow the army under the guise of peddlers. These should know one of their companions of first rank from whom they receive anything that is to be conveyed to the general who pays them. This detail should be committed to one who is faithful and intelligent. He should report his activities every day, and it should be certain that he is incorruptible.

Signs

There are particular signs in war that must be studied and by which judgments can be formed with some certainty. The knowledge you have of the enemy and his customs will contribute a great deal to this. And there are signs common to all nations.

During a siege, for example, you discover towards the horizon and on the heights, as evening approaches, unorganized and idle groups of men looking at the city; this is a sure sign that a considerable attack is being prepared. This is because attacks are made with elements of different corps and thus are known to the whole army. Those who are not to take part in the attack gather on the heights to watch it at their ease.

When your camp is near that of the enemy and you hear much firing in it, you may expect an engagement the day following because the men are discharging and cleaning their arms.

When you are in the presence of the enemy under arms and you see the soldiers changing shirts, it is certain that you are going to be attacked, because they put on all their shirts, one over the other, in order not to lose any.

If there is any extensive movement in the enemy's army, this can be judged from several leagues by the dust which is never raised except for several reasons. The dust caused by foraging columns is not the same as that of columns on the march, but you should be able to distinguish the difference.

You also can judge the direction of the enemy's movement by the reflection of the sun on his arms. If the rays are perpendicular, he marches towards you; if they are varied and infrequent, he retreats; if they slant from right to left, he is moving towards the left; if, in the contrary, they slant left to right, his march is to the right. If there is a great amount of dust in his camp, not raised by foraging parties, he is sending off his sutlers and baggage, and you can be certain that he will march soon. This will give you time to make your dispositions to attack him on the march. You should know if it is practicable for him to march in your direction, whether that is his intention, and what way it is most probable that he will march. This can be judged from his position, his supplies, his depots, the terrain and, in short, his conduct in general.

Sometimes he places his ovens on his right or on his left. If you know the time and the quantity of his baking and if you are covered by a small stream, you can make a flank movement with your whole army. If he imitates you, as sometimes he is forced to do, you can return suddenly and attack the ovens

with ten or twelve thousand men. The expedition should be accomplished before he is aware of it because you always have several hours advantage of him,
exclusive of the time that may elapse between his receipt of intelligence and
the confirmation of it. He will undoubtedly wait before he puts his army in
motion, so that in all probability he will receive information of the attack of
his depot before he has given orders for the march.

There are an infinite number of such stratagems in war that can be employed
with little risk. Their consequences are often as great as those of a complete
victory. They may force the enemy to attack you at a disadvantage or even
to retreat shamefully with a superior army. And you will have risked little
or nothing.

The General Commanding

I have formed a picture of a general commanding[,] which is not chimerical—
I have seen such men.

The first of all qualities is COURAGE. Without this the others are of little
value, since they cannot be used. The second is INTELLIGENCE, which must be
strong and fertile in expedients. The third is HEALTH.

He should possess a talent for sudden and appropriate improvisation. He
should be able to penetrate the minds of other men, while remaining impenetrable himself. He should be endowed with the capacity of being prepared for
everything, with activity accompanied by judgment, with skill to make a
proper decision on all occasions, and with exactness of discernment.

He should have a good disposition free from caprice and be a stranger to
hatred. He should punish without mercy, especially those who are dearest
to him, but never from anger. He should always be grieved when he is forced
to execute the military rules and should have the example of Manlius constantly before his eyes. He should discard the idea that it is he who punishes
and should persuade himself and others that he only administers the military
laws. With these qualities, he will be loved, he will be feared, and, without
doubt, obeyed.

The functions of a general are infinite. He must know how to subsist his
army and how to husband it; how to place it so that he will not be forced
to fight except when he chooses; how to form his troops in an infinity of
different dispositions; how to profit from that favorable moment which occurs in all battles and which decides their success. All these things are of immense importance and are as varied as the situations and dispositions which
produce them.

In order to sell all these things the general should be occupied with nothing
else on the day of battle. The inspection of the terrain and the disposition of

his troops should be prompt, like the flight of an eagle. This done, his orders should be short and simple, as for instance: "The first line will attack and the second will be in support."

The generals under his command must be incompetent indeed if they do not know how to execute this order and to perform the proper maneuvers with their respective divisions. Thus the commander in chief will not be forced to occupy himself with it nor be embarrassed with details. For if he attempts to be a battle sergeant and be everywhere himself, he will resemble the fly in the fable that thought he was driving the coach.

Thus, on the day of battle, I should want the general to do nothing. His observations will be better for it, his judgment will be more sane, and he will be in better state to profit from the situations in which the enemy finds himself during the engagement. And when he sees an occasion, he should unleash his energies, hasten to the critical point at top speed, seize the first troops available, advance them rapidly, and lead them in person. These are the strokes that decide battles and gain victories. The important thing is to see the opportunity and to know how to use it.

Prince Eugene possessed this quality, which is the greatest in the art of war and which is the test of the most elevated genius. I have applied myself to the study of this great man and on this point can venture to say that I understand him.

Many commanding generals only spend their time on the day of battle in making their troops march in a straight line, in seeing that they keep their proper distances, in answering questions which their aides de camp come to ask, in sending them hither and thither, and in running about incessantly themselves. In short, they try to do everything and, as a result, do nothing. They appear to me like men with their heads turned, who no longer see anything and who only are able to do what they have done all their lives, which is to conduct troops methodically under the orders of a commander. How does this happen? It is because very few men occupy themselves with the higher problems of war. They pass their lives drilling troops and believe that this is the only branch of the military act. When they arrive at the command of armies they are totally ignorant, and, in default of knowing what should be done, they do what they know.

One of the branches of the art of war, that is to say drill and the method of fighting, is methodical; the other is intellectual. For the conduct of the latter it is essential that ordinary men should not be chosen.

Unless a man is born with talent of war, he will never be other than a mediocre general. It is the same with all talents; in painting, or in music, or in poetry, talent must be inherent for excellence. All sublime arts are alike in this respect. That is why we see so few outstanding men in a science. Centuries pass without producing one. Application rectifies ideas but does not furnish a soul, for that is the work of nature.

I have seen very good colonels become very bad generals. I have known others who were great takers of villages, excellent for maneuvers within an army, but who, outside of that, were not even able to lead a thousand men in war, who lost their heads completely and were unable to make any decision.

If such a man arrives at the command of an army, he will seek to save himself by his dispositions, because he has no other resources. In attempting to make them understood better he will confuse the spirit of his whole army with multitudinous messages. Since the least circumstances changes everything in war, he will want to change his arrangements, will throw everything in horrible confusion, and infallibly will be defeated.

One should, once for all, establish standard combat procedures which the troops, as well as the general who leads them, know. These are general rules, such as: preserving proper distances on the march; when charging to charge vigorously; to fill up intervals in the first line from the second. No written instructions are required for this; it is the A-B-C of the troops and nothing is simpler. And the generals should not give all their attention to these matters as most of them do.

But what the general should do, is to observe the attitude of the enemy, the movements he makes, or where he directs his troops. He should endeavor, by a feint at one point, to draw his troops from another, to confuse him, to seize every opportunity, and to know how to deliver the death thrust at the proper place. But, to be capable of all this, he should preserve an unfettered mind and not occupy himself with trifles.

I do not favor pitched battles, especially at the beginning of a war, and I am convinced that a skillful general could make war all his life without being forced into one.

Nothing so reduces the enemy to absurdity as this method; nothing advances affairs better. Frequent small engagements will dissipate the enemy until he is forced to hide from you.

I do not mean to say by this that when an opportunity occurs to crush the enemy that he should not be attacked, nor that advantage should not be taken of his mistakes. But I do mean that war can be made without leaving anything to chance. And this is the highest point of perfection and skill in a general. But when a battle is joined under favorable circumstances, one should know how to profit from victory and, above all, should not be contented to have won the field of battle in accordance with the present commendable custom.

The words of the proverb: "A bridge of gold should be made for the enemy," is followed religiously. This is false. On the contrary, the pursuit should be pushed to the limit. And the retreat which had appeared such a satisfactory solution will be turned into a route. A detachment of ten thousand men can destroy an army of one hundred thousand in flight. Nothing inspires so much terror or occasions so much damage, for everything is lost. Substantial efforts are required to restore the defeated army, and in addition you are rid of the enemy for a good time. But many generals do not worry about finishing the war so soon.

FREDERICK THE GREAT
(1712–1786)

Frederick II of Prussia led his first campaign at the age of twenty-eight, inheriting the useful military instrument forged by his father. His troops were highly disciplined and mobile; with fewer forces, Frederick often succeeded in carrying off victory through a flank attack (oblique order) backed up by cavalry. During his career, Frederick was initially an advocate of shock tactics (under the influence of Folard), but shifted and came out in favor of firepower over shock, which was very novel at the time. Oblique order enabled him to place his army in a flanking position at a right angle to the enemy's wing and unbalance his dispositions through a combination of firepower and shock. His victories over Austria at Leuthen in 1757 during the Seven Years' War and shortly afterward against Austria, Russia, and France at Rossbach are classic battles. With Marlborough (1650–1722) and Prince Eugene of Savoy, Frederick stands out as the great military figure of the eighteenth century in Europe. His teaching became dogma, which encountered its nemesis at Jena in 1806.

MILITARY INSTRUCTIONS FOR THE GENERALS

Prussian Troops

The discipline and the organization of Prussian troops demand more care and more application from those who command them than is demanded from a general in any other service.

If our discipline aids the most audacious enterprises, the composition of our troops requires attentions and precautions that sometimes are very trouble-

From "Military Instructions for the Generals," translated by Thomas R. Phillips, in *Roots of Strategy: A Collection of Military Classics*, edited by Thomas R. Phillips (London: John Lane the Bodley Head, 1943; reprint, Stackpole Books, 1985), 167–214. Reproduced by permission of Stackpole Books.

some. Our regiments are composed half of citizens and half of mercenaries. The latter, not attached to the state by any bonds of interest, become deserters at the first occasion. And since the numbers of troops is of great importance in war, the general should never lose sight of the importance of preventing desertion.

He can prevent it:

(1) By being careful to avoid camping too close to large woods.

(2) By having the soldiers visited frequently in their camps.

(3) By keeping them busy.

(4) By forming carefully a chain of guards around the camp so that no one can pass between them.

(5) By ordering patrols of hussars to watch the flanks and rear of the army.

(6) By examining, when desertion occurs in a regiment or in a company, whether it is not the fault of the captain, if the soldiers have received the pay and comforts which the King provides for them, or if the officer is guilty of some embezzlement.

(7) By observing strictly the orders that soldiers shall be led in ranks by an officer when they go to bathe or forage.

(8) By avoiding night marches unless they are required by the exigencies of war.

(9) By careful observance of order on marches with strict prohibition against a soldier leaving the ranks or his squad, by placing officers at the debouches of defiles or where roads traverse the route of march, and by having hussars patrol the flanks.

(10) By not withdrawing guards from villages until the whole army is under arms and ready to commence the march.

(11) By hiding carefully from the soldiers the movements we are forced to make to the rear or by endowing retreats with some specious reason which flatters the greed of the soldier.

(12) By preventing pillage, which is the source of the greatest disorders.

The greatest force of the Prussian army resides in their wonderful regularity, which long custom has made a habit, in exact obedience, and in the bravery of the troops.

The discipline of these troops, now evolved into habit, has such effect that in the greatest confusion of an action and the most evident perils their disorder still is more orderly than the good order of their enemies. Consequently, small confusions are redressed in a moment and all evolutions are made promptly. A general of other troops could be surprised in circumstances in which he would not be if commanding Prussians, since he will find resources in the speed with which they form and manoeuvre in the presence of the enemy.

Prussians' discipline renders these troops capable of executing the most difficult manoeuvres, such as traversing a wood in battle without losing their files or distances, advancing in close order at double time, forming with promptness, reversing their direction suddenly to fall on the flank of the enemy, gaining an advantage by a forced march, and finally in surpassing the enemy in constancy and fortitude.

Obedience to the officers and subordination is so exact that no one ever questions an order, hours are observed exactly, and however little a general knows how to make himself obeyed, he is always sure to be. No one ever reasons about the possibility of an enterprise and, finally, its accomplishment is never despaired of.

The Prussians are superior to their enemies in constancy since the officers, who have no other profession nor other fortune to hope from except their arms, animate themselves with an ambition and a gallantry beyond all test, because the soldier has confidence in himself, and because he makes it a point of honour never to give way. Many have been seen to fight even when wounded, since the organization in general, proud of its past brave engagements, considers that any soldier who has shown the least cowardice in action affronts it. . . .

Knowledge of the Country

Knowledge of the country is to a general what a rifle is to an infantryman and what the rules of arithmetic are to a geometrician. If he does not know the country he will do nothing but make gross mistakes. Without this knowledge his projects, be they otherwise admirable, become ridiculous and often impracticable. Therefore study the country where you are going to act! When it is desired to apply oneself to this essential part of war, the most detailed and exact maps of the country that can be found are taken and examined and re-examined frequently. If it is not in time of war, the places are visited, camps are chosen, roads are examined, the mayors of the villages, the butchers, and the farmers are talked to. One becomes familiar with the footpaths, the depth of the woods, their nature, the depth of the rivers, the practicable marshes and those which are not, and one observes in this study to distinguish carefully between the conditions of the marshes and the streams in the difficult seasons of the year. It cannot be said that a stream is impracticable in the month of August because it had been in the month of April. The road is chosen to be taken on such or such a march, the number of columns in which the march can be made, and all the strong camping places found on the route are examined to see if they can be used.

In reconnoitring these camps, they are examined to determine if the exits are numerous and easy, if they can be fortified by damming the streams and about what effect can be expected from this, if abatis can be made, and how large a number are required for this work to complete it in a certain time. Following this, the plans open to the enemy are considered, the marches he might make, and the camps he might occupy are examined, and an estimate is made if he could be attacked during his march or in his camp, if he could be turned, and all the movements that could be made against him are studied. The larger cities and the better cemeteries on the outskirts are reconnoitred to estimate likewise to what extent they could serve the one who occupies them.

This sort of knowledge can be obtained promptly in the plains but requires more skill and research in mountainous country where one of your first cares is to place your camp so that it will not be dominated but will be dominant over all the surrounding ground. The difficulty of procuring this advantage will perplex you, for you will be hindered in obtaining water, which must necessarily be close to camp, and you dare not place your troops in a locality more distant from your road than they should be. . . .

I assume that you have a map of it and that you will always estimate your projects, and what the enemy may be able to do, in this fashion. But in such reasoning it is essential to be objective and it is dangerous to delude oneself. To accomplish this put yourself in the place of your enemy, and all the hindrances which you will have imagined and which he will not make for you, when war comes, will be just so many things that will facilitate your operations. Good dancers often go through their steps in sabots, and they become more agile when they are in pumps. An examination of this nature needs to be made with reflection. As much time should be allotted to it as the matter requires; when this is done in a neighbouring country, it is necessary to hide your secret intention with the most specious pretexts that you are able to invent.

Coup d'Oeil

The *coup d'oeil* of a general is the talent which great men have of conceiving in a moment all the advantages of the terrain and the use that they can make of it with their army. When you are accustomed to the size of your army you soon form your *coup d'oeil* with reference to it, and habit teaches you the ground that you can occupy with a certain number of troops.

The *coup d'oeil* is of great importance on two occasions. The first is when you encounter the enemy on your march and are obliged to choose ground on which to fight instantly. As I have remarked, within a single square mile a hundred different orders of battle can be formed. The clever general perceives the advantages of the terrain instantly; he gains advantage from the slightest hillock, from a tiny marsh; he advances or withdraws a wing to gain superiority; he strengthens either his right or his left, moves ahead or to the rear, and profits from the merest bagatelles.

The *coup d'oeil* is required of the general when the enemy is found in position and must be attacked. Whoever has the best *coup d'oeil* will perceive at first glance the weak spot of the enemy and attack him there. I shall have occasion to extend myself concerning this in the article on battles. The judgment that is exercised about the capacity of the enemy at the commencement of a battle is also called *coup d'oeil.* This latter is the result only of experience.

The Dispositions of the Troops

It is on exact knowledge of the terrain that is regulated the dispositions of the troops and the order of battle of the army. Our modern formations for combat, for the most part, are defective because they all are cast in the same mould: the infantry in the centre and the cavalry on the wings. If an army is really to be camped according to the rules of war, it is essential that each arm should be placed in the locality where it can act. Infantry is most suitable for outposts; cavalry should always be in the plains or it becomes useless and cannot act. Thus, never encamp your cavalry near woods of which you are not the master, nor near impracticable marshes, nor in ravines parallel to your camp which prevent these troops from acting. For if the enemy intends to attack you and perceives your mistake, he will utilize these advantages.

He will oppose your cavalry with infantry and cannon, and he will rake them with rifle fire to the point that, provoked at seeing themselves killed uselessly, they take to flight. Therefore, without worrying about ordinary tricks, put all your cavalry on one wing! Put it all in the second line! Divide it equally between the two wings, or place it without observing the order of battle but according to the terrain that permits it to act.

As for Prussian infantry, it is superior to all rules. However, open country suits it best; I repeat it again. Never enclose it in villages and do not choose camps which are unassailable, but open enough so that you can attack the enemy. The power of the Prussians is in the attack, and I shall have farther on, when I speak of battles, occasion to give more illumination on this point. I observe that, regardless of circumstances, a corps of your army should always be destined for the reserve, even when you camp on two lines. The regiments which you intend to use for this purpose should be notified in advance. I shall have occasion to pluck this string in the article on battles, for rear guards are the safety of armies and often they carry victory away with them.

Detachments: How and Why They Should Be Made

There is an ancient rule of war that cannot be repeated often enough: hold your forces together, make no detachments and, when you want to fight the enemy, reassemble all your forces and seize every advantage to make sure of your success. This rule is so certain that most of the generals who have neglected it have been punished promptly. . . .

Thus the subject of detachments is extremely delicate. None should be made, except for good reasons, if you are acting offensively in open enemy country, and are only master of some strong point. If you are actually waging war never throw out detachments except for convoys. . . .

. . . Officers who command detachments should be determined men, intrepid and prudent. Light troops should never be able to excite them, but at the unexpected approach of a large army corps they must look out for themselves, and they should know how to withdraw before a superior force and to profit in turn of the advantage of numbers.

Ordinarily, most detachments are made in defensive wars. Petty geniuses attempt to hold everything; wise men hold fast to the most important resort. They parry the great blows and scorn the little accidents. There is an ancient apothegm: he who would preserve everything, preserves nothing. Therefore, always sacrifice the bagatelle and pursue the essential! The essential is to be found where the big bodies of the enemy are. Stick to defeating them decisively, and the detachments will flee by themselves or you can hunt them without difficulty. . . .

The Talents That a General Must Have, Ruses, Stratagems of War, Spies

A perfect general, like Plato's republic, is a figment of the imagination. Either would be admirable, but it is not characteristic of human nature to produce beings exempt from human weaknesses and defects. The finest medallions have a reverse side. But in spite of this awareness of our imperfections it is not less necessary to consider all the different talents that are needed by an accomplished general. These are the models that one attempts to imitate and which one would not try to approach if they were not presented to us. It is essential that a general should dissemble while appearing to be occupied, working with the mind and working with the body, ceaselessly suspicious while affecting tranquillity, saving of the blood of his soldiers and not squandering it except for the most important interests, informed of everything, always on the lookout to deceive the enemy and careful not to be deceived himself. In a word he should be more than an industrious, active, and indefatigable man, not forgetting one thing to execute another, and above all not despising those sorts of little details which pertain to great projects.

The above is too vague; I shall explain.

The dissimulation of the general consists of the important art of hiding his thoughts. He should be constantly on the stage and should appear most tranquil when he is most occupied, for the whole army speculates on his looks, on his gestures, and on his mood. If he is seen to be more thoughtful than customary, the officers will believe he is incubating some project of consequence. If his manner is uneasy, they believe that affairs are going badly, and they often imagine worse than the truth. These suppositions become the rumours of the army, and this army gossip is certain to pass over to the enemy's camp.

It is necessary, therefore, that the personal conduct of the general should be so well reasoned that his dissimulation will be so profound that no one can ever penetrate it. . . . While never despising his enemy in the bottom of his heart, he should never speak of him except with scorn and compare carefully the advantages of our troops over the others. If some detachment is unfortunate in the war, he should examine the cause; and, after having determined the reason for the fault, he should instruct his officers concerning it. In this fashion a few minor misfortunes will never discourage the troops, and they will always preserve the feeling of confidence in their ability.

Secrecy is so necessary for a general that the ancients have been said that there was not a human being able to hold his tongue. But here is the reason for that. If you form the finest plans in the world but divulge them, your enemy will learn about them, and then it will be very easy for him to parry them. The general plan of the campaign should be communicated at most to the officer responsible for supplies, and the rest of the details should not be told to officers except when the time has come to execute them. When there are generals detached and you must write to them, the letter should be completely in code. If the enemy intercepts one you will not have betrayed yourself.

Since there are prodigious preparations to be made for war and some must be started early, secrecy may be betrayed thereby. But in this case you must deceive your own officers and pretend to have designs you want the enemy to attribute to you. He will be notified by the indiscretion of your officers, and your real intention will remain hidden. And for surprises and sudden blows, well thought out instructions should be prepared, but they should not be delivered to the officers who are charged with the duty until the moment of execution. When you are planning to march, arrange everything in advance, so as to be able to act freely, always under other pretexts, and then do suddenly what you have proposed to yourself. It is absolutely necessary to change your methods often and to imagine new decoys. If you always act in the same manner you soon will be interpreted, for you are surrounded with fifty thousand curious who want to know everything that you think and how you are going to lead them.

The commander should practise kindness and severity, should appear friendly to the soldiers, speak to them on the march, visit them while they are cooking, ask them if they are well cared for, and alleviate their needs if they have any. Officers without experience in war should be treated kindly. Their good actions should be praised. Small requests should be granted them, and they should not be treated in an overbearing manner, but severity is maintained about everything regarding the service. The negligent officer is punished; the man who answers back is made to feel your severity by being reprimanded with the authoritative air that superiority gives; pillaging or argumentative soldiers, or those whose obedience is not immediate, should be punished.

The general even can discuss the war with some of his corps commanders who are most intelligent and permit them to express their sentiments freely in conversation. If you find some good things among what they say you should not remark about it then, but make use of it. When this has been done, you should speak about it in the presence of many others: it was so and so who had this idea; praise him for it. This modesty will gain the general the friendship of good thinking men, and he will more easily find persons who will speak their sentiments sincerely to him.

The principal task of the general is mental, large projects, and major arrangements. But since the best dispositions become useless if they are not executed, it is essential that the general should be industrious to see whether his orders are executed or not. He should select his encampment himself, so that thereby he may be the master of his position, that the plan of it may be profoundly impressed on his mind, that he may place the cavalry and infantry guards himself, and that he may order on the spot the manner in which villages should be occupied. Afterwards, no matter what happens, he is able to give his orders with knowledge, and he is able to make wise dispositions from his information of the ground. The more that all these minor details are well thought out, the more he will be able to estimate in each place what the enemy is able to do and the more tranquil he will be, having foreseen everything and provided in his mind for everything that might happen to him. But all this is not done except by his own energy. Thus be vigilant and indefatigable, and do not believe, having made one tour of your camp, that you have seen everything. Something new is uncovered every day, and sometimes it is only after having reflected two or three times on a subject that good ideas come to us.

Scepticism is the mother of security. Even though only fools trust their enemies, prudent persons never do. The general is the principal sentinel of his army. He should always be careful of its preservation and that it is never exposed to misfortune. One falls into a feeling of security after battles, when one is drunk with success, and when one believes the enemy completely disheartened. One falls into a feeling of security when a skilful enemy amuses you with pretended peace proposals. One falls into a feeling of security by mental laziness and through lack of calculation concerning the intentions of the enemy. To proceed properly it is necessary to put oneself in his place and say: what would I do if I were the enemy? What project could I form? Make as many as possible of these projects, examine them all, and above all reflect on the means to avert them. If you find yourself unable (either because your camp is badly defended or because it is not in the locality where it should be, or that it is necessary to make a movement), put it right at once! Often, through an hour's neglect, an unfortunate delay loses a reputation that has been acquired with a great deal of labour. Always presume that the enemy has dangerous designs and always be forehanded with the remedy. But do not let these calculations make you timid. Circumspection is good only to a certain point. A rule that I practice myself and which I have always found good is that in order to have rest oneself it is necessary to keep the enemy occupied. This throws them back on the defensive, and once they are placed that way they cannot rise up again during the entire campaign.

If you wish to be loved by our soldiers, husband their blood and do not lead them to slaughter. . . .

The Difference between Countries and the Precautions They Require of a General

I am writing this work only for Prussian officers. Consequently, I only speak of countries and of enemies where we may wage war. There are three sorts of countries: our own, neutral, and enemy, and in enemy country there are Catholics and Protestants. All of these things have their effect in war and require differences in conduct applicable to places and to circumstances. If one considers only glory there can be no war more favourable toward acquiring it than in our own country; since the least action of the enemy is known and discovered, detachments can be sent out boldly and, having the country on their side, are able to accomplish brilliant enterprises and are always successful; because in the larger operations of war you find more aid and can undertake bolder deeds, such as surprises of camps and cities; and since the people favour you, it will be due to your negligence or to an unpardonable ignorance if you do not succeed.

In neutral countries it is necessary to make friends. If you can win over the whole country so much the better. At least form a body of your partisans! The friendship of the neutral country is gained by requiring the soldiers to observe good discipline and by picturing your enemies as barbarous and bad intentioned. If the people there are Catholic, do not speak about religion; if they are Protestant, make the people believe that a false ardour for religion attaches you to them. Use priests and the devout for this purpose. Religion becomes a dangerous arm when one knows how to make use of it. However, move more carefully with your partisans and always play a sure game.

In countries which are both enemy and Catholic, such as Bohemia and Moravia, no partisan group should be attempted. They will all be lost, the country being hostile to them. If you are projecting some sudden blow, it must be done by detachments. You are obliged to wage a close-fisted war and to make use of your light troops on the defensive. My own experience has convinced me of this. . . .

What a General Can Expect from the Movements He Has His Army Make

Let no one imagine that it is sufficient just to move an army about to make the enemy regulate himself on your movements. A general who has a too presumptuous confidence in his skill runs the risk of being grossly duped. War is not an affair of chance. A great deal of knowledge, study, and meditation is necessary to conduct it well, and when blows are planned whoever contrives them with the greatest appreciation of their consequences will have a great advantage. However, to give a few rules on such a delicate matter, I would say that in general the first of two army commanders who adopts an offensive attitude almost always reduces his rival to the defensive and makes him regulate himself on his movements.

If you were to commence the campaign first and were to make some march which indicated an extensive plan, your enemy, who would be warned to oppose it, will be obliged to adjust himself to you; but if you make a march which gives him neither suspicions nor fears, or if he should be informed that you lack the resources to execute your project, he will pay no attention to you and on his part will undertake some better considered actions which will put you in a difficult place in turn.

Your first precaution should be to control your own subsistence. If this is well arranged you can undertake anything. The enemy likewise can be forced to make large detachments by harassing his rear with light troops, or by making demonstrations, as if you intended to make a diversion in some other province of his realm than that in which the war is being waged. Unskilful generals race to the first trap set before them. This is why a great advantage is drawn from knowledge of your adversary, and when you know his intelligence and character you can use it to play on his weaknesses.

Everything which the enemy least expects will succeed the best. If he relies for security on a chain of mountains that he believes impracticable, and you pass these mountains by roads unknown to him, he is confused to start with, and if you press him he will not have time to recover from his consternation. In the same way, if he places himself behind a river to defend the crossing and you find some ford above or below on which to cross unknown to him, this surprise will derange and confuse him. . . .

Why Most Entrenchments Are Taken

It is because whoever is enclosed in them is restricted to one ground and whoever attacks can manoeuvre freely; he who attacks is bolder than the one who defends himself; and because, furthermore, if a point in your entrenchment is forced, all the rest is lost on account of the discouragement that this occasions among the troops. However, I am of the opinion that the Prussians, with a resolute man at their head, could easily set right a misfortune of that type, especially if the general has conserved the resources of the reserves. Troops defending an entrenchment should fire continually, those attacking should not fire at all, but advance resolutely, gun on the shoulder.

Lines: How the Enemy Can Be Defeated with Unequal Forces When You Are the Weaker

A general should choose his ground with regard to the numbers and types of his troops and the strength of the enemy. If he is the stronger and has a great deal of cavalry he will seek the plains, primarily because his cavalry can act best there and, in second place, because his superiority gives him the means to envelop an enemy on open ground, something he would be unable to do in broken country. If, on the contrary, you are inferior in numbers, do not despair of winning, but do not expect any other success than that gained by your skill. It is necessary to seek mountainous country and use artifices, so that if you were to be forced to battle, the enemy would not be able to face you with a front superior to your own, and so that you may be able definitely to protect your flanks. . . .

There is the first remark which concerns only the terrain. The second relates to the manner of attacking. All weak armies attacking stronger ones should use the oblique order, and it is the best that can be employed in outpost engagements; for in setting yourself to defeat a wing and in taking a whole army in the flank, the battle is settled at the start. . . .

. . . I fortify my right with which I want to make my principal effort. I have placed a body of infantry on the flank of the cavalry to fire from the woods on the enemy cavalry. I have three lines of cavalry and three lines of infantry, and my left is only for the purpose of containing the enemy's right wing, while all my forces act on the right. By this means one part of my army defeats the other, I am victorious, and I execute with one part what others do with the whole. In this battle I prefer to attack with my right rather than with my left because I avoid an attack of a village, which would cause too many casualties. Whenever you engage in a battle with one flank, you are the master of your army; you can stimulate or slow down the combat as you deem appropriate, and the whole wing which is not fighting acts as a reserve for you. Never forget to husband all the resources you are able on every occasion and to have, in consequence, reserves always at hand to repair disorder, if it occurs at some point. . . .

Pursuit and What to Do after Battle

The enemy is pursued to the first defile; all the harm possible is done to him, but you should not allow yourself to become so drunk with success that you become imprudent. If the enemy is thoroughly defeated, make several marches after him, and you will gain a prodigious amount of territory. But always camp in accordance with regulations! Do not neglect the principles of foresight and know that often, puffed up with their success, armies have lost the fruit of their heroism through a feeling of false security. Think also of the poor wounded of the two armies. Especially have a paternal care for your own and do not be inhuman to those of the enemy. The wounded are disposed of by sending them to hospitals, and the prisoners by sending them to a neighbouring fortress under a strong escort. When an army has been defeated it is permissible to make detachments, especially when it is a question of cutting it off or of taking two or three of its cities at the same time. But it is the conditions of the time that should determine this operation, and there is no way to prescribe a general rule. . . .

Retreats of Defeated Bodies

A battle is lost less through the loss of men than by discouragement. I make my vows to Heaven that the Prussians never shall be obliged to make retreats but, since I should touch on this matter, I shall state my opinions. For small bodies, and in large plains, the infantry should form a square protecting the remaining cavalry, thus gaining the first defile or nearest wood. If it is a large body I should prefer retreat in chequerboard formation by entire lines which pass through each other; a general then can save his army if he seizes the first defile instantly, so that his troops posted there protect the retreat of the others through it. If his cavalry is discouraged, let it be sent away; for the rest of this day he will not be able to bring it against the enemy again.

How and Why Battle Should Be Accepted

The man who does things without motive or in spite of himself is either insane or a fool. War is decided only by battles, and it is not finished except by them. Thus they have to be fought, but it should be opportunely and with all the advantages on your side. I call it opportune when it is a question of chasing an enemy out of your country; or of driving him out of a position in a locality which prevents you from penetrating into his; when you want to force him to raise a siege; or when you are unable to make one until you have defeated him; or, when it is a question of gaining superiority for yourself for a whole campaign, and the enemy, committing a fault, gives you the opportunity to take it from him. Finally, when the enemy is to receive reinforcements, you should, if possible, defeat him before their junction.

Advantages are procured in battles every time that you are determined to fight, or when a battle that you have mediated upon for a long time is a consequence of the manoeuvres that you have made to bring it on. The best occasions that can be procured are when you cut the enemy off from his supplies and when you choose terrain favourable to the qualities of your troops and which forces the enemy to fight at the locality you choose. After this, what is most advantageous is to profit from a poor position of the enemy to push him out of it, but especially to occupy such positions yourself as enable you to cover a great deal of the country by small movements and so located that you will never be cut off from your own supplies nor from places which you should protect. The enemy should be attacked if he backs against a river, or if he has but a single bad defile behind him, because he risks a great deal and you risk little, even if you have bad luck.

Reflections on the Hazards and Misfortunes of War

When a general conducts himself with all prudence, he still can suffer ill fortune; for how many things do not co-operate at all with his labours! Weather, harvest, the officers, the health or sickness of his troops, blunders, the death of an officer on whom he counts, discouragement of the troops, exposure of your spies, negligence of the officers who should reconnoitre the enemy, and finally, betrayal. These are the things that should be kept continually before your eyes so as to be prepared for them and so that good fortune will not blind us.

HENRY LLOYD
(1729–1783)

*Henry Lloyd, a Briton, was successively in the service of the Hapsburgs
and Russia (as was quite normal at the time). Like Maurice de Saxe and
others, he observed that "the principle of democracy does not suffer from a
standing army made up of mercenaries." His* Military and Political Memoirs,
*published in 1801, gives the most complete view of conceptions of war in the
eighteenth century. Lloyd was able to see what he called "the sublime part"
of war, the appanage of great minds, the "just and rapid manner of applying
the principles to the infinite multitude of circumstances."*

ARMIES, ANCIENT AND MODERN

War is a state of action. An army is the instrument with which every species
of military action is performed: like all other machines it is composed of various parts, and its perfection will depend, first, on that of its several parts; and
second, on the manner in which they are arranged; so that the whole may have
the following properties, viz. strength, agility, and universality; if these are
properly combined, the machine is perfect. Care must be taken that not any
one of these properties be increased by diminishing another, but that the whole
may be in proportion.

By strength in an army, I do not mean that force which arises from numbers, but that which proceeds from the mode in which troops are ranged and
armed. This strength must be adequate to every purpose of war; equally proper
to resist or attack an enemy, whether cavalry or infantry, in an open or in a
close country.

By agility I mean, the celerity with which an army marches and performs
the various motions required in the conduct of a campaign. This property is

From Henry Lloyd, *Continuation of the History of the Late War in Germany between the King
of Prussia and the Empress of Germany and Her Allies*, pt. 2 (London, 1781), 1–6, 17–20, 26–37, 65–67.

the most essential, and cannot be acquired but by continual exercise, nor even then, unless the original constitution of the troops be calculated for a facility of motion.

The first problem in tactics should be this: how a given number of men ought to be ranged, so that they may move and act with the greatest velocity; for on this chiefly depends the success of all military operations.

An army superior in activity can always anticipate the motions of a less rapid enemy, and bring more men into action then they can in any given point, though inferior in number. This advantage must generally prove decisive, and insure success.

A battle is a changeable scene, in which every circumstance is instantaneous and transitory, without activity, those favourable opportunities, which always occur in days of action escape, and perhaps do not return in twenty campaigns.

By universality I mean, that the mode and form in which the troops are ranged, should be equally proper to act in different kinds of ground, and against every kind of troops, to attack or defend; because an army once formed into a line, and near the enemy, cannot without much difficulty change the order in which it is formed, or indeed make any motion, but forwards; therefore when any change is required, recourse must be had to the second line or reserve, and generally without success: it is therefore highly necessary that the first formation of the troops should be so general as to be applicable to every particular case, and require no change during the action, unless in employing more or fewer men against any given point.

If such are the properties (I mean strength, agility, and universality) which render an army perfect, it is evident that the arms made use of, the manual exercise, and the different evolutions in which the soldier is to be instructed, ought to be analogous to these principles, and whatever is not conformable to them should be exploded as vain and insignificant at least, if not, as very often happens, dangerous and impracticable.

I know that it is much more easy to conceive and point out the principles which ought to guide us in the construction of a machine than to put them in practice; for whatever passes through the hands of man participates of his imperfections. We should not however despair; if the perfection we aim at is not attainable, to approach it is a great merit, and will in some measure answer the end proposed.

For want of certain and known principles in the constitution of an army, caprice and imitation seem to have been our only guides; whence innumerable changes and novelties are continually introduced into our modern armies. Error and folly succeed each other like modes and fashion in dress; what is to-day an object of applause and admiration, is to-morrow exploded, and succeeded by some new chimera equally absurd and transient.

A certain great prince, in the course of his reign, has undoubtedly performed some very extraordinary acts; and therefore our military gentlemen have implicitly adopted the dress, exercise, evolutions, &c. used in his armies; I believe without sufficiently weighing the matter, or considering that the success of his operations ought principally to be attributed to his situation, as a sovereign of uncommon abilities at the head of his armies, and to the particular circumstances of his enemies; advantages which are but rarely combined so as to produce that unity and vigour on which success in war almost intirely depends.

The continual attention paid to the discipline of his troops, gives them a facility in manoeuvring superior to that of his enemies, which certainly contributed to his victories; his head and heart did the rest. Mode of dress, and a thousand insignificant objects with which he torments his army, had nothing to do in the matter. To obviate this phrenzy of imitation, and if possible to fix some certain principle for the composition and direction of any army, is the object of the following discourse.

Of the Composition of an Army

The different operations of war, and the variety of the ground in which they are performed, indicate a necessity of different species of arms as well as of troops; accordingly we find at all times armies composed of infantry and cavalry, and these armed with different kinds of weapons; some carried missile weapons, others hand-weapons: by missile weapons, I mean those instruments with which a man throws darts, stones, balls, &c. at an enemy when at a certain distance. By hand-weapons (I cannot otherwise translate what the French call *arme-blanche*) I mean those weapons which a man holds in his hand while he strikes the foe with the other end; such as swords, pikes, bayonets, &c.

It is needless to observe that there is a constant and invariable connexion, or at least there ought to be, between the species of arms made use of by the troops (infantry or cavalry) and the mode of ranging them; because they must be formed in such a manner as to be able to manage their arms with advantage: though this principle is self-evident, and essentially necessary to be observed in the composition of an army, yet we shall find in the sequel it has been almost neglected by the moderns.

The missile weapons of the antients were extremely weak, if compared with ours; the shield was sufficiently strong to parry, or at least diminish their effects; however they were found necessary, and generally adopted. It is evident that men armed with missile weapons could not be formed into one mass, or in a deep order of battle, because in that case they could not possibly have made use of their arms with any advantage; they were therefore left to themselves, that is, they chose the time, place, and object; and advanced or retreated only upon a general signal.

The use of such troops was very considerable; they could interrupt and harrass the motions of more massive bodies, though for want of consistency and strength they could not break them. No species of ground could be absolutely improper for those light troops, and a close country was particularly favourable to them; plains and cavalry were to be avoided; in every other circumstance they could act with advantage; but cavalry and massive bodies could neither move nor act but in plains and open countries.

No army could therefore be complete unless it was composed of three species of troops, viz. infantry, cavalry, and light troops; and accordingly we find the antients and moderns have adopted them in the constitution of their armies.

Of the antients the Tartars, and all the Asiatic people, thought that velocity was the peculiar advantage of the cavalry, and that this property might be exerted to advantage; it seems they fought pell-mell loosely, *à la debondade:* at least the Romans did so very often; for we are told that the cavalry dismounted in heat of action, and fought on foot, which they could not have done had it been formed into great squadrons, and attacked in a line in the modern European way.

A cavalry thus constituted was of great and general use, particularly in pursuing a broken enemy, who were necessarily exterminated, which is now the case with the Tartars and Spahi's. Their extreme activity and velocity prevent all disposition in the infantry for a retreat, unless they are favoured by a very broken ground, where cannon may be placed. As they move separately, and in very small bodies, they penetrate every where; and as no road is impervious to them, they in an instant surround their enemy, whom they generally cut to pieces.

We have endeavoured to unite mass and solidity to the velocity of the horse, but I think without success; activity, the peculiar property of the horse, is diminished, and almost totally destroyed by the mode in which our cavalry is formed; all bodies lose their velocity in proportion to the augmentation of their mass: though the advantages derived from cavalry and light troops, made the use of both absolutely necessary, yet as their manner of fighting was neither general nor decisive, the principal force of an army was thought to consist in a good body of infantry, and with reason if it is properly formed: its operations are, or may be more general, solid, and decisive, than those of the other bodies.

All troops, I believe, have been formed into squares, or parallelograms; because these are the only figures or forms in which a body of men united can move or act. The circle which was used by Caesar, and which is so much admired by Puysegur, could be proper only when it was surrounded, and confined to a particular spot, which was the case when it was used by Caesar.

Of the Advantages and Defects of Missile and Hand Weapons

Let us examine and compare the advantages and defects of missile and hand weapons: this will lead us to conclude, that both are absolutely necessary to form the institution of a complete body of men. Fire-arms are calculated for a defensive war, and to keep the enemy at a distance, which prevents a total overthrow; but are of no use when he can approach you.

Hand-weapons, on the contrary, can be of no use at a distance; but are absolutely necessary when the armies approach each other. The former are proper for a close country, the latter for an open one. The effects of the one are precarious and undecisive; those of the latter certain and complete. The musket is the resource of prudence and weakness; hand-weapons are the arms of valor and vigor.

An able general, at the head of troops armed with fire-arms, though inferior in number to the enemy, may protract a war many years, and finally prevail over a less able leader; which cannot be effected if the armies carry hand-weapons: for they must necessarily soon come to an action, and that action must, from the nature of the arms, be decisive: hence the art of war, among the ancients, was simple and decisive; and hence it is complicated and scientific among the moderns.

The art of war of the ancients was confined to what we call evolution, directed to the purpose of fighting only, which they considered as the sole means of finishing a war. In short, their whole attention was directed to discipline, to the exercise of the troops, and to the field of battle.

But we study camps, positions, and lines: our plans of operations are very extensive, and often embrace a hundred leagues, which we cover by occupying a given position: those of the ancients were contracted and confined within a narrow compass; seek the enemy, and fight him, was their favorite military maxim: they did not seem to think it possible to protract a war by skilful manoeuvres: accordingly, their wars were of very short duration, unless some exterior circumstances, arising from the nature of the ground, that of the troops, and finally, from the different political systems of the contending parties, tended to protract them; which we have shown to be the case in the Peloponnesian war, and which, we shall hereafter see, was the cause that made the Punic wars so long.

The principles of an active and defensive war were little known to the ancients. Jugurtha and Sertorius seem to have been the only generals of antiquity who understood and practised them: but none of these wars can be compared, for vigor and activity, with the late war in Germany; in which more battles were fought in two campaigns, than in any century among the ancients.

The result was very different from the usual effect of ancient wars. A great part of the globe changed masters during the sixth century of the Roman republic; whereas the empire of Germany remained in its former state, at the peace of Hubertsburg: this difference arose, we think, entirely from that of the ancient and modern arms, and consequently from the different mode of conducting a war.

We are often obliged to act a defensive part to cover and protect an immense tract of country against a superior enemy: prudence requires that we should avoid a general action; and when we think it adviseable to risk one, aided as we are with fire-arms, a thousand strong camps may be found where we may engage an enemy with advantage.

A given position will enable a good general to harrass and check the progress of an enemy during a whole campaign, whereas the ancients, armed with hand-weapons, came so near each other, that it was almost impossible to avoid a general action, which, from the nature of their arms, was decisive.

Fabius, aided by a very close and mountainous country, with difficulty protracted one campaign without coming to a battle, because Hannibal's forces consisted chiefly in cavalry, which, in such a country, could not act with advantage.

The result of what I have said is, that an army armed with fire-arms only, is slow in its motions, and undecisive in its actions; it is characterized with science and art, and particularly adapted to a defensive war.

Troops, armed with hand-weapons, are rapid in their motions, and decisive in their actions; less scientific than the former, but singularly proper for an attack.

It seems, therefore, that to render an army perfect, and adequate to every purpose of war, it should be provided with both kinds of weapons.

If one species of arms cannot be made so as to serve the purpose of a musket and a hand-weapon, which I believe is the case, a body of men must be so formed as to manage both kinds of arms; or, finally, different bodies of men armed differently, must be ranged in such a manner that they can aid and support each other. We shall examine this theory hereafter. How far modern armies are endowed with the perfection we aim at, will appear in the course of our investigation. . . .

Of the Modern Order of Battle

By order of battle, I mean the distribution of the different species of troops of which an army is composed, not including those which pass under the denomination of light troops, as they never enter the line.

In general, the whole is ranged in two or more lines; because, first, the being formed only in three ranks, it would take up so much ground, that it would be impossible to range or manage a numerous army. Secondly, to supply the defects and weakness of the first line, by supporting it, and replacing the whole or any part of it, which may be broken and thrown into disorder, by the second.

The cavalry and infantry form separate bodies; the former are generally placed on the flanks of the latter.

The perfection of an order of battle consists, as we apprehend, first, in placing each body of men, where they can act with most advantage. Secondly, in bodies of different species, being so placed as to be able to support each other that the victory may be complete; otherwise it often happens, that while your cavalry are victorious, the infantry are beat, and the battle lost, or vice versa. Thirdly, in your armies being so ranged as to be universally adapted to different species of ground, so as to require no material alteration in marching up to the enemy, or during the action.

First, it is evident, that if the cavalry are placed on the flanks of the infantry, they can neither support, nor be supported by it, which disposition I therefore conceive is a most capital defect.

Second, both in marching, camping, and fighting, it may and generally does happen, that the infantry and cavalry are placed on improper ground, where, however, they must so remain; because it is in general impossible to change the original disposition; therefore, upon the whole, it seems deficient in all the points, which constitute a solid and active order of battle.

Moreover, as both lines are formed in a close order, if the first is broke and vigorously pursued, it overthrows the second for want of sufficient openings. This cannot advance with celerity, and in a firm order to stop the enemy; so that both generally go off together, and the battle is lost. Whereas, if at least the second line had intervals to let the first pass through them, and at the same time advanced in good order, while the enemy is in some degree of confusion, they would not only check them, but probably would gain an easy victory.

The reason given for placing the cavalry on the wings is, to protect the flanks of the infantry, which I think is the most absurd reason that can be alledged, because this may in a moment fortify its flanks against infantry or cavalry, by forming a square or a column, which the cavalry cannot do; its flanks are naturally so weak, that they offer no kind of defence. . . .

Numbers, beyond a certain point, can add nothing to the force of an army, unless they can be made to act together; they increase its inactivity, and render it altogether unmanageable. By thus separating the cavalry from the infantry, it very seldom happens that they can be brought to act in a proper place, and in a proper moment: they really, in a day of action, form two different armies, and act separately, and very indirectly contribute, if at all, to the support and success of each other.

If either is beat, the other must fall back and retire: whereas if they were formed on other principles, the whole must be vanquished, or none, because they would form only one army, though composed of different species of troops, and mutually support each other. . . .

First, the general use of fire-arms, and of every kind of missile weapons, is not adapted to all the various operations of war, but is singularly proper for a defensive war, and consequently for a close country, where the troops being covered and protected by the obstacles which such a country offers, the enemy can with difficulty approach you.

Secondly, that the use of missile weapons has rendered the art of war much more scientific than it was among the ancients, when it was confined chiefly to the arrangement of the troops, the exercise, and evolutions: what we call manoeuvres, on an extensive line, seem to have been little known to them; and fighting was the only method adopted by them for finishing a war, which the nature of their arms soon brought to a conclusion.

Thirdly, that our battles neither are nor can be decisive, and may be considered rather as great skirmishes than general actions, very few being slain in comparison with what happened when hand-weapons alone were used.

Fourthly, though our infantry were formed three deep, with a view to the musket they carry; yet can they make but a very imperfect use of it, and the cavalry cannot use it at all.

Fifthly, that by forming both infantry and cavalry in three ranks, they are too weak to march with firmness and consistence, to attack or defend themselves against troops formed on more solid and active principles.

Sixthly, this method of forming the troops necessarily lengthens the line, so that it cannot march with any velocity in a plain, much less in a close country.

Seventhly, that a line of five or six miles, does of course meet with improper ground for the kind of troops which may happen to be placed there; yet no alteration can be made in the line, however necessary it may be.

Eighthly, that the whole front must advance together, which renders it totally inactive, and gives the enemy time to take their measures for fighting or retreating at their pleasure, which reduces the battle to an inconsiderable skirmish.

Ninthly, that the general cannot possibly see and conduct all the operations of such an extensive line, so that, by the neglect, ignorance, or malice of the officers under his command, the action is always very imperfectly carried on, and fails of success in more than one point; which may render that of the other attacks useless. It wants, in short, unity of action and activity in the execution.

Tenthly, to prevent the line from being protracted without end, we are obliged to form several; so that if we consider the few men who act together in the first, and that none at all act in the others, unless successively, and when it is commonly too late; we shall find, that not a sixth part of the army is engaged at one time, and of that sixth part not one, perhaps, at the most eligible point of attack or defence.

All these defects, and many more which could be enumerated, proceed originally from our making the musket the general instrument; and from our adapting both the formation of the troops and order of battle to that instrument. . . .

Of a Battle

I can no way better expose the defects of our military arrangements, than by relating in a few words, how this great machine, an army, is brought into action, how a battle is fought and concluded, and what are, in general, its consequences, which I have seen in the course of several campaigns.

After many marches and counter-marches, which often take up the most favourable part of a campaign, a battle is at length resolved on: all those who are informed of this resolution, and too many always are, put themselves in motion to solicit some command, or to carry the news of the expected victory; in obtaining which favour and intrigue generally prevail, to the prejudice of the truly brave and deserving officer.

Several days are employed in examining the position of the enemy, which might be done in five minutes; for a general who cannot, in one instant of time, see and determine the manner of attacking any camp, is unworthy to command an army: during such delay, the enemy prepare themselves to receive you, fortify themselves, change their position, or retire; so that you have fresh and great difficulties to encounter, or perhaps you lose your labour, and must follow the enemy to seek another opportunity, which may not offer in a whole campaign; especially if under an able general, who wishes to avoid an action.

The mode of attacking is at length fixed, which, ten to one, must be altered, because the enemy, while you lose your time in preparing yourself, have materially altered their position. If you are not apprized of this in time, and you march up to them, your original disposition is lost, and you are unable to form another that may be proper to answer the present circumstances, which may require that your cavalry or infantry should change the ground, and replace each other. Nothing of this can be executed before the enemy, without offering your flanks, and consequently exposing yourself to a total defeat. When any alteration in the order of battle is required, it should be done a day or two before you quit your camp, otherwise such confusion will ensue as cannot be remedied. . . .

The different brigades of artillery generally precede the columns, to favour their development; that is, to prevent the enemy from opposing the forming of the line, and because the general and the soldier think nothing can be done without it, though in truth it produces more noise than any real advantage. This prodigious train of cannon, and its concomitants, continually stop and retard the march of the troops by some accident or other, so that seldom or ever they arrive together, and in time, on the ground where the line is to be formed.

This is a very critical moment, if the enemy knew how to avail himself of it: for if he is perfectly acquainted with the ground between his camp, and that which you have left, he will know all the roads by which you march, and consequently by advancing to meet you, in order of battle, he can attack the heads of your columns, and defeat them all singly, without giving them an opportunity of ever forming the line, in the same manner as one attacks a rear-guard: but happily for you, he confides in the strength of his post, and suffers you to do what you please.

His army is like a set of china-ware on a chimney-piece, it must not be touched or moved, for fear of breaking it: after three or four hours cannonading and skirmishing your army is formed, and advances towards the enemy preceded by the artillery, which retards the march very much, and occasions the loss of many men, which could be avoided by marching rapidly to the enemy.

Supposing the army consists of sixty thousand men, the first line will occupy five or six miles; in this extent of ground a thousand obstacles both by art and nature occur, which necessarily retard your progress, because the whole line must advance together; for if some parts precede at any, though small distances, the others, a vigilant enemy, by marching rapidly through the intervals, cuts your army asunder, takes you in flank and gains the battle; which so happened exactly at the battle of Prague.

To avoid such an inconvenience, by keeping your army together, and advancing in a line parallel to that of the enemy, you are sometimes several hours in getting over a mile of ground, which ought to be executed in a few minutes. If by the firmness of your troops, and the inactivity of your enemy, you come up with him, and succeed in one or two points of attack only, the battle is won, though perhaps only two or three battalions have been displaced; and if you fail in what you suppose the principal attack, you retire almost unpursued, and you have lost the battle.

In the former case, the enemy has no resource in his first line, which can make no movement but forwards or backwards; so that if you can maintain yourself on the ground you have gained, the enemy retires successively, and goes off. This is a critical moment also, if the enemy knew what to do.

If instead of endeavouring to regain the points lost, he advanced part of his second line to prevent your going farther, and oblige you to bring the greatest part of your forces to maintain the ground gained, which is generally done; and if with the rest of his army he made some considerable effort on the rest of your line, in all probability he would succeed, and force you by this means to relinquish the advantages you had gained to prevent this part of your army from being cut off, which would certainly happen, if any other part of your line was driven back and defeated: sometimes, indeed, such a movement is made, but generally with a view only to favour a retreat, and seldom or ever to gain a victory.

As your attacks are successive, so must your advantages be, and you gain one part after another, or rather the enemy abandons them, you can make no general effort in attacking or pursuing the enemy, who has time to retire at his leisure.

Your army who have, perhaps, been twenty-four hours under arms, are so fatigued with that situation and with the combat, that they are unable to move, and much less to prosecute the advantages they have gained with any vigour.

The light troops are sent after the enemy, but with small success, for they are generally attentive only to plunder; and moreover, a few battalions thrown into a wood or village put an end to the pursuit; and the enemy, who probably have lost only a few cannon and prisoners, occupy a neighbouring hill, and your victory is reduced to nothing more than barely the field of battle.

Such have been the victories I have seen, and such the consequences, which I can attribute only to the natural slowness and inactivity of our armies, which proceed, as we have shewn, from the use of fire-arms, and from the consequent mode of ranging the troops.

Sometimes, indeed, a commander of very superior abilities may, from such an imperfect victory as I have described, draw great and signal advantages, as it happened after the battle of Lissa, where the Austrians, in the course of a month, lost successively the greater part of their army, without any apparent necessity for the loss.

But when the commanders are nearly equal in abilities, a whole war may pass in skirmishes, without their ever coming to a general and conclusive action, which happened on the Rhine when Montecuculi and Turenne were opposed to each other.

Indeed our battles, as we have seen, are commonly nothing more than great skirmishes; and therefore, as I have said before, wars are not now, as formerly, concluded by battles, but for want of means to protract them.

A New System

Having shewn, in the preceding chapters, that the use of fire-arms exclusively; the arrangement of our infantry and cavalry in three ranks in consequence of using those arms; and finally, the order of battle, are imperfect, and render an army inadequate to almost every operation of war; it remains, that we should examine, whether and how a given number of men, horse or foot, may be armed and formed, and the order of battle so contrived, that it may be free from those defects to which our modern institutions are subject; and that it possess strength, activity, and universality, in which we make the perfection of an army to consist.

While we make use of fire-arms alone, as is now the case in the infantry (for the bayonet and sword are of no use to the soldier) it is evident, that no system can be formed which will in any degree diminish the imperfections of our armies: if you range the men in two ranks, for example, that they may use the musket with more advantage, the line will be so extensive and weak, that it cannot be managed at all, or scarce be put in motion; much less will it be able to resist the shock of the enemy: and if, on the contrary, you range the troops in four or five ranks, all the arms they can carry will become totally useless.

It follows, therefore, that a certain number of men should be armed with pikes: this alone can enable us to form a number of men in such a manner, that they shall have strength to resist the shock of an enemy, horse or foot, and to act in every kind of ground with equal advantage; it must combine and unite the solidity of hand-weapons with the advantage of fire-arms. If this can be accomplished, we approach very near the perfection we aim at; and undoubtedly render an army, formed on these principles, superior to any other now existing.

The use of hand-weapons necessarily requires defensive weapons, sufficiently strong to parry or diminish their effects; they are so connected, that they ought never to be separated, particularly in the cavalry, where the action passes sword in hand.

Armour of any kind in the infantry, opposed to infantry, armed as it is at present, is less necessary, though always useful: it gives confidence to the men, and likewise diminishes, and sometimes destroys entirely the effects of a musket-ball when fired from a certain distance, or with a considerable angle, above or below the horizon and direct line. And as infantry may be, and very often is opposed to cavalry, and closes with infantry, I think it ought to be provided with such an armour as we shall propose hereafter.

It is well known, that a third or fourth part of an army, in the course of a few months, by death or sickness, goes off; of which diminution many causes may be assigned, as bad and scanty food, and neglect of the sick in the hospitals. The principal cause however is, I think, the dress, which does not cover the soldier against the inclemency of the weather, and seems calculated only for parade and shew, in a sunshiny day, before the ladies, like the dress of other petit-maitres. Whereas it is evident, that both the dress, arms, and exercise, should be made with a view only to health, and to the purposes of war: and it being impossible for the soldier to carry every thing which may, once in an age, be useful to him, we must fix upon such equipments only, as he will find always necessary and useful. . . .

General Reflection

What we have said regards an army in the field. It remains we should examine how such an army is to be prepared for action during peace, and how supported while in the field.

One of the greatest difficulties which occur, is in supporting the army in the field, I mean in furnishing recruits and cloathing. In a campaign or two, recruits are wanted, and the troops are almost naked.

The first are raised in the country, very often at a great distance from these at of war; so that many perish before they arrive; others are totally unfit for service, and the few remaining placed in regiments, are quite raw, and before these can be rendered useful, many go to the hospital; hence one may safely affirm, that not one fourth part ever arrives to a state of maturity and become real and useful soldiers. What a waste and destruction of men! Forty years peace and a good government will not atone for the calamities and losses of a six years war.

During the late war in Turkey, the Russians raised above three hundred thousand recruits, and yet the principal army under M. Romanzow, at the conclusion of it, did not amount to above thirty-six thousand; and that in Crimea, under Prince Dolgorouki, to about twelve thousand, and all were in want of many necessary articles, which is always the case, particularly if contractors are any way concerned.

What prevention of these evils can be found, it will be naturally asked? The best I can think of is as follows:

Let the regiments have what we call perpetual quarters; that is, they must always during the peace, remain in one fixed place: and these places must form a chain on that frontier, which most probably may hereafter be the seat of war. For each regiment must be built a small town in separate caserns, to prevent fire from communicating to the whole. A certain quantity of land must be assigned to them. If the frontier is subject to sudden attacks from small parties of the enemy, I would have a good intrenchment drawn about the caserns or barracks, with a good ditch well palisaded, where the peasants may remain in safety with their cattle, &c.

The recruits must be delivered to the regiments who are to take care to have them exercised. All the materials which serve to cloath the troops, must likewise be delivered into this depot, and there worked and made up by the soldiers and their wives, which would produce a vast saving to the sovereign, and the soldier would be better cloathed.

In time of war, a battalion remains here to train the recruits, and provide the cloathing for the whole regiment.

All the sick and invalids, wounded, &c. officers and soldiers, must be sent to this depot, where they can always be of service, though unfit for military duty in the field. If a sufficient quantity of land is assigned, it will maintain them comfortably with their pay; and the state is not burthened with half pay, or to turn numberless poor creatures adrift, which is now the case.

In this system, the soldier may and ought to be permitted to marry, that his children may supply the immense losses occasioned by the war. The women may help to cultivate the lands, and support the community, whereas they are now the pest of the army. The army will receive the recruits formed and healthy, and will be always complete and fit for action; whereas now half the campaign passes in exercising them, before you dare approach the enemy: and in case of a considerable defeat, a battalion may be sent to the depot, and replaced by that which was there.

Each male child, when he arrives at ten years of age, must have a portion of land allotted him, and he becomes a soldier. In short, by this method, the whole army becomes military colonies; and each soldier having, by this means, a certain, honourable and good retreat in his old age, serves cheerfully and well, becomes a member of the state, and has something to lose. No greater misfortune can happen to him than to be turned out of his regiment, which, in fact, is dispossessing him of his inheritance. Moreover, a man accustomed to live in a certain community, is more upon his guard than when he is continually strolling from one quarter to another; insomuch, that a regiment seldom passes through a village in its march, without leaving traces of insolence and disorder behind it.

JACQUES DE GUIBERT
(1743–1790)

Jacques Antoine Hippolyte, comte de Guibert, was a prophetic writer. In his Essai général de tactique *(General Essay on Tactics, 1770), he foresaw and welcomed the profound military transformation that was later brought about after 1792 by the French Revolution and subsequently continued by Napoleon. Guibert developed the idea of the citizen-soldier, advocated the divisional system, and recommended mobility and concentration. The* Essai général *became famous from its very first appearance. A few years later, in 1779, Guibert published* Défense du système de guerre moderne, *in which he revised some of the ideas expressed in the* Essai général. *His* De la force publique *(1790) crowned a creative, visionary, and impassioned corpus.*

INTRODUCTION TO THE *ESSAI GÉNÉRAL DE TACTIQUE*

. . . Would the philosopher find more satisfaction when he considered the military [as opposed to the political] state of Europe? There he would see each of its constitutions slavishly copied one from another; the peoples of the south subject to the same discipline as those of the north; the genius of nations directly contradicting the laws governing their soldiery; the profession of soldier abandoned to the lowest and most wretched class of citizens; the soldier on active service ever miserable and despised; the bigger states with bigger armies to maintain, burdensome to those nations in time of peace and yet insufficient to reassure them in time of war, because the rest of the people are simply a timid, pusillanimous mass. He would note in passing that some progress has been made in the area of tactics, and in a few other branches of military science. He would admire some petty details of our constitutions, the genius of

From Jacques de Guibert, *Ecrits militaires, 1772–1790* (Paris: Editions Copernic, 1977). Translated from the French by A. M. Berrett.

the king of Prussia, the temporary spurt of greatness he has given his nation. But where, he would wonder, was a military built on a firm foundation to be found? Where did there exist a warrior people that despised luxury, loved labor, and was drawn to glory by its laws?

What can result from our wars today? States that have neither treasure nor excess population, and whose peacetime expenditure already exceeds their receipts, nonetheless venture to declare war on one another. They embark on campaigns with armies they can neither recruit nor pay. Whether victor or vanquished, they are equally exhausted. The mass of national debts increases. Credit sinks. Money fails. Fleets no longer find seamen, nor armies soldiers. Ministers on both sides feel it is time to negotiate. Peace is made. A few colonies or provinces change hands. The source of quarrels is often left untouched, and each side settles down amid its ruins, preoccupied with paying its debts and preparing for war.

But suppose there were to arise in Europe a people that combined adherence to strict virtues and a national army with a set plan of aggrandizement, that did not lose sight of that plan, and that knew how to wage war at little cost and live on its victories, and so was not reduced to laying down its weapons for financial reasons. That people would be seen subjugating its neighbors and overthrowing our feeble constitutions, as the north wind bends frail reeds. . . .

Internal policy having thus prepared a nation, what scope foreign policy would have to settle on a system to advance its interests vis-à-vis the outside world and raise a formidable military force! How easy it would be to have invincible armies in a state where its subjects are citizens, where they cherish the government, love glory, and do not fear hard work. . . .

It is likewise the weakness of our governments that renders our military constitutions so imperfect and ruinous. It is that same weakness, not being able to create citizen armies, that makes them so numerous. It is that same weakness, not knowing how to reward them with honor, that pays them with money. It is that same weakness, not being able to count on the courage and fidelity of its people, because the people are enervated and discontented, that has mercenary soldiery bought abroad. It is that same weakness that puts forts all along the country's borders. Finally, it is that same weakness that is busy extinguishing every warrior virtue in a nation, not even so much as fostering them in the troops, because it is afraid they might spread from there among the citizenry and arm them one day against the abuses that oppress them. . . .

The state of which I am speaking will have possessions so put together, so well proportioned to its defensive means, that it will never have to fear its neighbors' hostility. In such a state, there will be no distinction between the center and the outlying areas. All parts will be equally flourishing and vigorous. There will be such easy communications between all of them, such a great commonality of interests, that wherever there is danger, all the forces will be quickly assembled there. It will have a watchful soldiery superior to its neighbors', and happy citizens, interested in the defense of that prosperity. Would they come and attack such men with mercenaries, with armies composed as all Europe's are today? . . .

I say that the science of modern war, compared with that of the ancients, is vaster and more difficult. That does not mean that it is more perfect and more luminous on every point. In regard to some things, it has made progress. In others, it has ramified and become complicated, at the expense of its perfection. Our firearms are superior to the missile weapons of the ancients. The science of artillery is superior to their ballistics, our fortifications to theirs: fortified places are now besieged and defended with more art. Such is the progress of the moderns. Such is the effect of mathematical enlightenment spread through the science of war. But armies have become too large. Artillery and light troops have increased too much. The borders of states bristle inappropriately with two or three lines of fortresses. These places are unnecessarily burdened with fortifications. The systems of engineers are for the most part too exclusive, too methodical, too poorly related to tactics. Armies are grossly inflated, as much by the increase in the number of fighting men as by the equipment and impedimenta that they trail in their wake, and are therefore difficult to set in motion. The details of their subsistence form a science of which ancient armies, smaller in numbers, more simple, and far better constituted, had no conception. Such are the errors and abuses that complicate modern military science, multiply the amount of knowledge composing it and make great generals so few and far between. . . .

As the science of modern war improves and gets closer to true principles, it might, then, become simpler and less difficult. Armies, being better constituted and more able to maneuver, would have fewer soldiers. Their various divisions would be carefully balanced and distributed according to the nature of the country and the kind of war to be fought there. They would follow simple, analogous tactics, capable of bringing about any movement that might be called for. In such an army, an officer from one arm of the service would be able to command in another arm. One would not see general officers, with no detailed knowledge of corps in which they have not served, giving the lie to the title they bear, a title that by giving them the power to command all arms, assumes them to have the universality of knowledge such leadership requires. Armies thus formed would be easier to move and lead. We would get away from the narrow, routinized way of doing things that hinders and detracts from operations. There would be great expeditions. There would be forced marches. They would know how to engage and win battles through maneuvers. They would be less often on the defensive. Less importance would be attached to what are called positions. Topographical details would cease to have the same importance, and would cease to overburden military science to the same degree. With fewer encumbrances, simplicity having replaced luxury, the details of subsistence would become less complicated and interfere less with operations. The science of the quartermaster would then consist in dragging the fewest possible impedimenta about and endeavoring to live on what the country has to offer. Artillery and fortifications would become increasingly enlightened. In each century, they would follow the advances of mathematics, which are their foundation. But neither would pretend to dominance or exclusivity or promote systems that complicate and make them more expensive. In armies and military calculations, they would simply hold the position they ought to have there. In the hands of generals, they would only be adjuncts usefully employed in strengthening and supporting the troops. In short, the branches of military science would together form a sheaf of illuminating rays, whose coming together in the mind of a single man would constitute him a general—that is to say, one capable of commanding armies.

PART 11

THE AGE OF TOTAL WARS

LAZARE CARNOT
(1753–1823)

Lazare Carnot specialized in military engineering and fortification at the Ecole de Mézières. After the French Revolution he was selected to the Legislative Assembly and then to the Convention. He was sent on missions to the Army of the Rhine (August 1792), the Army of the Pyrenees (September 1792–January 1793), and then the Army of the North, which he restored to order (March–August 1793). As a member of the Committee of Public Safety, he devoted himself to the struggle against the First Coalition (Austria, Prussia, Britain, Holland, and Spain) and internal revolts and reorganized the army. He generalized "amalgamation" and inaugurated new tactics: mass offensives with bayonets. At the end of 1793, on every border, the armies of the Coalition were driven back, and in 1794 the victory over the Austrians at Fleurus paved the way for the conquest of Belgium. The United Provinces and the Rhineland were soon conquered, and in the spring of 1795, Prussia, Spain, and Holland made peace.

Political intrigue forced Carnot to flee France in 1796, and he returned only in 1800. Napoleon made him minister of war. He resigned in July following disagreements with the First Consul. He was nominated to the Tribunate in 1802, but opposed its most important decisions, including the establishment of the Empire. At Napoleon's request, he wrote De la défense des places fortes *(1811). He was minister of the interior during the Hundred Days and was exiled after the Restoration, dying in Prussia.*

ON THE DEFENSE OF FORTIFIED PLACES

Fortresses are not distributed randomly along a frontier; they form a great whole, all the parts of which are linked to one another and to the general

From Lazare Carnot, *De la défense des places fortes*, in *Bibliothèque historique et militaire*, edited by Liskenne and Sauvan, vol. 4 (Paris, 1846). Translated from the French by A. M. Berrett.

system of war. Some have a special, determinate purpose, although still belonging to the general system in some respects, such as by protecting a seaport, a large arsenal, a major commercial or subsistence entrepôt, or a distant colony from attack. The importance of such positions needs no demonstrating.

Others are intended to halt an enemy invasion and guarantee against a surprise attack: such is the case with those built at strategic points; main roads linking the interior and the outside world; mountain gorges that may serve as [invasion] routes; the entrances to and exits from navigable waterways; places where rivers that flow along the frontier offer easy passage; points on the sea coast where enemy ships can easily land. Clearly the defense of all these points is so important that omissions regarding them might lead to disasters that would be felt at the heart of the state and spread alarm to the furthermost reaches of the empire.

There are fortresses whose principal purpose is to protect the flanks and rear of an active army going over its borders, confidently relying on such bases, sustained by garrisons proportionate to the services they demand. If such a place was taken, the active army would find itself caught between two fires, and its retreat would be cut off; and perhaps just when it was about to force an enemy to make a long-awaited peace, it would find itself facing the need to haggle for its own salvation, or to come out into the open, sword in hand, in the midst of great obstacles.

In other fortresses, stocks of provisions and munitions are established to meet the army's needs, either in the case of a defensive war or when it has to serve as a storage depot for an active army moving forward. When such a position is taken by the enemy, it is one of those unfortunate occurrences that is most difficult to put right. All the resources of the country will have been exhausted far and wide to be put in a secure place and to supply the army. The enemy arrives, obliged to draw his own subsistence with the greatest difficulty from his own storage depots, and one of the first aims of the war is to cut off his communications; instead of which, you abandon to him those that you yourself had taken such care to build up; you give him the means he lacked to move the war forward; you lose your means to operate; you are reduced to inaction and distress.

Other fortresses are intended to act as places for an army that has received a setback to retreat into, and to take in the survivors. If this refuge is taken, what will become of that army? It will be pursued without being able to reform; it will be scattered in all directions and destroyed piecemeal.

Finally, most fortresses fulfil several functions; everywhere they ensure communications, always of such importance in war, and make them very difficult for the enemy. They are always established [so as] to make them points where many roads, rivers, or canals meet; they are central points, from where movements start out in all directions; if these points are taken, the whole is broken and the breach made prevents help; the enemy penetrates to the heart of the state, and then you have to reconquer your own country.

Spread out evenly along a river that, like the Rhine, acts as a boundary of the empire, fortified places make an attack on that part of the frontier virtually impracticable and excessively dangerous for the enemy. Since they occupy the places where passage is most convenient, they make it very difficult for the enemy. Assuming that a successful crossing has been made, they still expose him—if he wishes to continue his invasion without first taking these fortresses—to being pursued from the rear and cut off from his own country, or to a diversion through those fortresses themselves, which are ready-made passages; and if the enemy wants first to take these fortresses, they pose great difficulties to him, because the river separating the various parts of the besieging army exposes them to being surprised and beaten one after the other.

When you can be sure they will hold out for a long time, fortresses in general offer excellent means of causing a diversion because, during the long siege operations undertaken by the enemy, you have the time to mount an expedition into his own country by way of another point, sowing terror there and coming back to make him raise the siege, if he has not already abandoned it to come and defend his own homeland.

He who has a good cordon of fortresses is always able to decide to accept or reject battle. He puts into it all that the surrounding countryside has been able to supply in the way of subsistence and withdraws with his army intact, under the protection of his inland fortresses, contenting himself with harassing the enemy. If the enemy wants to penetrate, he will be unable to collect together the provisions that he needs to keep his army together; he will be obliged to disperse so as to secure some from far away; then he can be attacked in detail, and although you are weaker than him, you will always be able to fight him with the advantage.

An enemy who wishes to invade a country surrounded by fortresses cannot conceal his plans for long; he cannot penetrate without first making a breach. The sieges that he has to embark on for that purpose require great preparations in terms of matériel and troop movements, which easily reveal his purpose. If he captures one of these frontline fortresses, it will take him the length of a campaigning season; and, at the beginning of the next one, he will find all the resources of the besieged focused on the breach he has begun. If the resistance he foresees make him try something different, the fortress he has taken will cease to be of any use to him; he will have consumed his time and resources to no purpose.

Fortresses save you from always having to keep the entire regular army in being, because by halting the enemy's first blow, they allow time for your forces to come together. It suffices for the men to be trained and their organization decided. From this angle, [fortresses] offer considerable ways of saving on manpower, consumption, and money; they even make newly raised men almost as useful as old troops, because the new militias may be used to garrison second- and third-rank fortresses, and get trained there during the respite won by the resistance of the frontline fortresses; they can even do much service in the fortresses under attack.

There are fortresses whose purpose is more circumscribed, but that are no less important for that reason in terms of their positions: such is the case with the town of Elsinore in Denmark, which, by the contributions that it obliges trading vessels passing through the Sound to pay, is a source of income for the king who possesses it; such too is the case with the fortress of Gibraltar, which enables the English to prevent any other power at war with them from passing through the Strait without a considerable escort and offers them a haven in bad weather and following a battle in these regions so far away from their home country.

Sometimes it is decided to fortify a place less because of the direct advantages that accrue than simply to deprive the enemy of it. On other occasions, there is a temptation to put a fort on a particular spot solely because it happens to be a good site, and as if to complete what nature has begun. But often it is precisely such a place that seems of little use that, as a result of some unforeseen development, becomes a point of the highest importance; such generally is the case with third-rank fortresses, which may save the state if the enemy, having exhausted all his resources in taking the protecting first- and second-rank ones finds himself unable to combat the last resources that the length of their defense has given the besieged time to accumulate there.

The construction, upkeep, and supply of fortresses involve the ruler in vast expense. This is money well spent, since it is a substitute for the far greater expenses that would be necessary to increase the size of the regular army sufficiently. It would be necessary to station units of soldiers at every outlet, every place where such positions are useful, who would do the job of a fortress—that is, eight or ten times the number of those making up the garrisons; for experience shows that a garrison can hold off a force ten times its size, which would have to be countered by a force of an equivalent size if there were no fortress to substitute for it.

The effect that a fortress produces is even surer, because, whatever the strength of the aggressor, it can always resist a sudden attack, whereas a detachment of troops can be attacked unexpectedly by a much larger force that has been hastily put together and find itself obliged to abandon the frontier, at least provisionally, thereby leaving it open to the enemy.

But the important services that fortresses can render assume that they are entrusted to reliable, capable, and determined people; otherwise they would produce a false sense of security, and would be more harmful than useful, since the enemy could seize them easily and then make use of them himself, as a base from which to carry the war forward.

The great expenditures involved in fortresses are made with a view to implementing the best principles of fortification known and constructing the defensive works recommended by the masters of the art; but what use will these works be if you surrender the fortress before the enemy has even made the least inroad into them? Now, generally, these works are the main part of the fortress itself, or virtually so; that is where the system of fortification proper lies. This system is encompassed by the covered way and the glacis. Up to that point, the layout does not matter; it is hardly even noticed. Whatever the layout, it is made up of flanking works whose fire intersects on the approaches as far as possible; but the difference between the best and the worst [such works] can produce at most a difference of two or three days in the progress of attacks up to the glacis.

It would thus be pure waste if such large-scale works had been prepared around and near the main part of the fortress, if, as soon as the enemy saw them, they had to be surrendered to him. An old central structure with ancient towers is as good at three hundred toises [1 toise = 1.949 meters] as Vauban's or Cormontaigne's fortifications; you can fire balls and bombs at [the enemy] from a rampart three centuries old just as well as you can from a bastion built on modern principles. It is only as he gets closer that the enemy gradually sees his difficulties increasing, finds that his movements are more hampered, his attacks more and more cramped. He is attacked from the flank, and sometimes from behind, and, being obliged to take cover from all sides, he finds himself forced to make never-ending detours, dig his trenches deeper, and even build underground galleries, where he meets other obstacles and other dangers that have been prepared in advance and linked with the system of fortification. All these difficulties disappear if you surrender before you have to because of the impossibility of putting up any further defense. Here, close to the main part [of the fortress], each minute costs the besieger more men than a whole day when he is at the beginning of the trench; each cannon shot from the besieged is more deadly than five hundred fired at the beginning of the siege. Sorties produce infinitely greater effects, and ones less dangerous for the garrison, because they enemy is farther away from the troops who should sustain him, while conversely the besieged is closer to the center of his resources. Sapping enterprises are much more frequent, much more speedily executed, and the disorder they occasion is much greater and much more difficult to repair. It is in the attack through breaches that the besieged, although inferior in numbers, is much stronger in terms of position; because he dominates, because he can only be attacked along a front equal to his own in the narrowness of the breach; because he cannot be outflanked; because cavalry cannot be used against him; because the enemy no longer has any artillery, while if he, the defender, has had the wit to profit from his advantages, he ought to have several pieces concealed, which he has saved for this decisive moment. In short, what the besieger has done up to now is child's play compared to what remains for him to do. He will soon be repulsed if the besieged holds out, and the moment comes for the besieged to enjoy the fruits of his labor.

A fortress that does not hold out as long as it might does not allow time for help to arrive. Often it is only attacked by the enemy to create a diversion and force a faraway army to abandon what it is doing to come and protect it. Then, to prevent the enemy from achieving his object, and so as not to weaken the regular army, you must have the time to assemble the depots in the interior, bring together neighboring garrisons, and even, if need be, raise new levies; if the fortress is surrendered before all that is done, far from having been useful, it will have occasioned difficult and costly movements; it will have inspired false confidence, which might become fatal if it provides the enemy with a fortress whose closeness will oblige you to deploy a force permanently watching him and permanently at the ready to prevent him from extending his conquest.

If, when the enemy makes such an attempt, he encounters more resistance than he had expected, he will be crushed to see that his sacrifices have been in vain; he will not dare try anything similar again. That is why he makes such tremendous efforts. When he sees that all is lost if he does not take the fortress at once, he pulls out all the stops; he neglects nothing: bombardment, surprise, sudden attack, corruption, terror, everything is put to work; he exposes himself to the most terrible risks, while the besieged only has to sustain an effort for a short while to cover himself with immortal glory.

A little reflection on the quantity of supplies of all sorts that a long siege requires, the difficulty of transport, and the sicknesses that occur in the late season soon indicates how troublesome and blameworthy a premature surrender is. It is in fact very rare that the besieger can bring together all the equipment that he needs, and even when he has the means to do so, he rarely does, because he counts on the defenders having no stamina. He often has enough troops neither for a besieging force nor for an army of observation; and, in the whole of the revolutionary war, there has perhaps not been a single case of an army being fully equipped to attack. Meanwhile, all that is needed here is a little tenacity [on the part of the defenders], as the enemy can only attack weakly, and his resources will be exhausted before he has half finished the job. He may call on the town to surrender with dire threats, but be ready to retreat himself if he is shown firm resolve. But he has counted on the weakness and ignorance of [the other side's] leaders, and he may well succeed in making them sign a capitulation that is really all the more shameful because it is couched in the most honorable terms; for it is precisely because he feels that the besieged can still defend themselves, and perhaps make him raise the siege, that he grants everything he is asked for.

The defenders ought to have held out longer, if only to get into the late season and consume the rest of [their] provisions, so as to prevent the enemy from enjoying them and make him consume his own. For with these combined provisions, he can, when the season is not yet very advanced, immediately attack a second-rank fortress before it has had the chance to stock itself, reduce it quickly, as with the first, and then move on to the third and take it by surprise, thus achieving a breakthrough in a single campaign, when all that was needed was a little constancy to make him fail or at least stop him for a few years and make him use up all the means of continuing offensive war.

The peoples of early antiquity were certainly forced to defend their towns to the very end; for everyone involved, what was at stake was all his worldly possessions: the whole empire was, so to speak, concentrated in a single fortress. . . .

The modern peoples of Europe have for the most part protected themselves from such terrible incursions by increasing the number of their fortresses. Today, the fate of these peoples no longer depends on the outcome of a single battle. A fortress taken involves only a partial and repairable misfortune; one may even lose one's capital and recover it, because the frontier offers many secure havens; three lines of fortresses, one behind the other, stop the excessive ambition of a conqueror and ruin him piecemeal.

But it may be that this great multiplicity of fortresses means that less importance is attached to each one individually, and that they are defended with less obstinacy. However, they only guarantee us against the scourges that the wars of old led to if, at the very least, the points attacked are defended as the ancient fortresses were. Otherwise the evil would only be postponed, not prevented; for, after taking three or four fortresses, the enemy would be in the heart of the state, and soon disasters of precisely the kind that fill ancient history would be happening. Our fortresses concentrate hostilities and limit them to a small area; that is their advantage. But it must be agreed that this small area is often hardly less unfortunate than invaded countries were in the past. This area is sacrificed temporarily for the salvation of all; but for all the rest to be saved, the enemy must encounter in this concentrated area the same resistance, the same obstinacy as would be shown if the whole nation had come together there and it was a matter of defending one's life, one's family, one's freedom. A robust defense is thus no small matter, and one of the chief causes of the light resistance that present-day fortresses put up may well be the fact that so far we have seemed to attach only a secondary importance to those senior officers who are responsible for it. These commands are often given as a sort of pension to former officers who can no longer stand up to the rigors of active campaigning; sometimes only old soldiers or newly raised troops are sent to garrison them; it seems to be assumed that looking after them properly is not as important as servicing mobile armies. This concatenation of circumstances too often diminishes the importance of the position that has to be defended. But if the best-trained and most active corps are generally employed in the line, it is because they are the only ones who can execute tactical maneuvers properly; while the others can very well serve in military towns provided that there is a nucleus of well-trained troops there; that itself is indeed one of the most striking advantages of fortresses. But if fewer tactics are required there, it requires just as much courage or perseverance to tolerate all the privations, besides merit that is all the more heroic because it is necessarily less noticed than on the field of battle under the eye of the ruler himself, or of a large number of his companions in glory, and in the presence of a whole grand army. . . .

General Conclusion

The art of defense is thus not in the least, as some have imagined, that of avoiding combat in favor of a rampart. On the contrary, it is the art of being able to fight successfully one against ten, the art of being constantly the aggressor when one had seemed condemned by circumstances to being constantly hunted down and pursued, and to being perpetually in search of some new retreat to avoid being overwhelmed by a superior enemy. The hard work lies in converting the general system of defense into a series of many limited attacks, combined in such a way as always to set the strong against the weak, without, however, ever compromising too large a part of one's forces.

If, to avoid the advantage given to the besieged by the attacks made by his adversary, the latter decides to proceed methodically and to take all the defenses of the fortress, inch by inch, which is M. de Vauban's grand principle of attack, the besieged will not thereby be forced to give up sudden attacks, which must always be the basis of his defensive system; but he will have to combine them with the employment of firearms in such a way that by alternating between the two, he prevents the enemy from ever establishing himself firmly in any one place.

The true spirit of defense consists neither in launching untimely and excessively unequal combats nor in making continual withdrawals, contenting oneself with slowing down the besiegers' advance by a series of small obstacles. It lies in watching out for every opportunity to catch him with an unexpected surprise attack when he weakens somewhere. It means extending oneself and making full use of the works of the fortress so as to leave him abruptly exposed to the most intense fire from the fortress, prepared for that very purpose, when he is seen to be massing his forces. In general, it can be said that against surprise attacks, one must defend oneself inch by inch; and against attacks made inch by inch, one must defend oneself by surprise attacks.

TO MICHAUD, COMMANDER OF THE ARMY
OF THE RHINE

Paris, 19 Germinal, Year II [30 March 1794]

Citizen general, you ask for a plan of operations for the coming campaign to be set out for you; at present we can give you only the outlines, the details of operations being necessarily subordinated to the forces and projects of the enemy; moreover, they have to be left to the zeal and wisdom of generals. We are not proposing any conquests at all on the Rhine frontiers, but to harass the enemy, to live at his expense, and to keep war away from our own hearths by means of continuous attacks. The means of achieving these aims are continual vigilance and tireless activity. You must encamp early and far from cities; leave in garrison-towns only what is strictly and rigorously necessary for [their] everyday maintenance; relieve these garrisons very frequently; change staff just as often; maintain strict discipline in the camps; train troops through daily exercises; not wear out the troops with useless exertion, but keep them always in tiptop form; get them used to looking after their weapons and equipment; make sure the generals see them every day and set them an example of activity, morality, and devotion to defeating the enemy.

Forces should be broken up as little as possible, posts relieved often, and two or three fifteen- or eighteen-thousand-man corps be held at various points on the frontier, always ready to move at once to the point being attacked. This method is greatly preferable to that of having each of these positions held with detachments, since such detachments, however large they may be, are always overcome, because the enemy always makes his means of attack proportionate to those of the defense, so as to defeat it. Moreover, experience shows that after a few days, detachments become sleepy, neglect to mount guard, and end up letting themselves be taken by surprise; it is therefore better to have only light posts there, with a larger body of troops behind them always ready to fall on any enemy that has penetrated one of them.

From *Anthologie des classiques militaires français,* edited by L.-M. Chassain (Limoges-Paris-Nancy: Editions Charles-Lavauzelle, 1950). Translated from the French by A. M. Berrett.

You must keep upsetting the enemy's arrangements by changes of position; that is also the way to render his spying useless, especially if these movements are made unexpectedly and kept to yourself until the moment they are put into execution. You must endeavor to make people think your forces are larger than they are, rather than endlessly complaining, as most generals do. The enemy, whose forces are much more depleted than ours, always has the wit to persuade us that he has enormous numbers of men. This reputation for strength encourages the troops, deters the ill-intentioned, and intimidates the enemy.

You must wear this enemy down by feints, sometimes at one point, sometimes at another, far removed from the first, to oblige him to make marches and countermarches, which weary his soldiers and sap his commanders of confidence by reason of the inconstancy of their operations. The frontiers of the Swiss are in your area; we recommend you especially as regards them to eliminate everything that might give them just grounds for concern; you cannot ignore the existence of a plan to put us at war with them; you must consult with the representatives of the people to repress by the most severe measures the malcontents who seek to make us an enemy of this loyal people.

Attack ceaselessly, and always with much larger forces, falling unexpectedly now on one post, now on another. We do not in the least like to be told that this or that weak position held out against an attack by a much larger force, as it turns out to show ignorance or lack of vigilance; the art of the general is to arrange things in such a way that wherever the enemy shows himself, he finds a force three times larger than his own.

Therefore harass the enemy without allowing him any rest; always be ahead of him, adopt the system of active defense, live at the enemy's expense, and sow terror in his country to keep him out of ours. By always standing ready to march, watching out for the enemy's mistakes, and skillfully grasping opportunities, you will fulfill the wish of the Committee and what it has the right to expect of a citizen entrusted with its confidence.

Carnot

THE CURRENT CAMPAIGN ON THE NORTHERN FRONTIERS

28 Messidor, Year II of the Republic one and indivisible [16 July 1794]

It is not enough that the arms of the Republic be everywhere triumphant; its victories must have a useful purpose and their outcome must not be aban-

From *Anthologie des classiques militaires français,* edited by L.-M. Chassain (Limoges-Paris-Nancy: Editions Charles-Lavauzelle, 1950). Translated from the French by A. M. Berrett.

doned to chance or enthusiasm, which could cause the loss in an instant of the fruit of so much work and heroism. It is thus absolutely essential to focus them in advance on the aim we seek to achieve.

The speed of our military successes and the fearlessness of the soldiers of the Republic make it impossible to doubt that we could, if we so wished, in the course of this campaign plant the tree of liberty on the banks of the Rhine, and reunite to France all the ancient territory of the Gauls. But, however seductive such a prospect might be, it may perhaps be thought wise to renounce it, and that France could only weaken itself thereby and lay itself open to an interminable war through such an enlargement.

Although the Rhine is a very formidable barrier, to advance up to it would mean a prodigious lengthening of our frontiers and lead to a grave overextension of the forces that have to defend them. Such a long frontier would require a large quantity of troops and constant vigilance to prevent a skillful enemy from taking a few crossing points by surprise, getting behind the armies, and forcing them hastily to abandon all their conquests and return to their former borders after enormous losses. If, therefore, it were decided to attempt such an invasion, we would have to be resolved to prolong the state of war, continue to maintain a large armed force, and expose ourselves to further reverses and successes, which would no longer permit hope of an end to political crises.

This proposal also has the drawback of going against the principle by which France renounces the spirit of conquest. It seems indeed that this principle requires that we should reject any aggrandizement not called for by the need to secure our own possessions, such as, for example, the fortresses of Ypres and Nieuwpoort, without which it is impossible to cover Dunkirk and the whole department of the Nord from the sea to the Lys effectively.

Let us add that most of the peoples that would have to be united for France to go as far as the banks of the Rhine are not ripe for our revolution, and the factions that would be formed within those areas would join with our external enemies to make us victims of our own successes.

Finally, by extending our borders further from the center of government action, and bringing them that much closer to the centers of action of foreign governments, we would weaken the drive of the former and open ourselves to a more immediate and intense shock from the latter, which would give them an enormous advantage.

It thus appears much wiser to restrain our proposals for aggrandizement to what is purely necessary to ensure maximum security for our own country, break the Coalition, assure our commerce, and render our enemies powerless to attack us later with any hope of success. It is thus from these considerations that I would like to establish the new barriers along the northern frontier.

The first line of defense would be established from Antwerp to Namur. . . .

... On the other side of the defense line of which I have just spoken, the citadel of Antwerp, which will have to be restored, will make us masters of navigation on the Scheldt above it, while below it, it will be protected by the Sluys and above all by the island of Walcheren, if it is possible to seize it. This island would be of the greatest importance to us, as it would give us a foothold in Zeeland and from there in Holland, from where our influence will inevitably drive out the *stadhouder* [William V of Orange], bring down the pro-England party, and take the heart out of the Coalition; for all the enemy powers are linked to Holland and the Bank of Amsterdam. If we have Holland, then British commerce is annihilated, both in the North Sea and in India! Prussia will no longer be able to pay its troops, and the emperor will be relegated to the back end of Bohemia and Austria. Nothing must therefore be neglected to ensure the success of this attempt on Walcheren, which appears as easy to carry out as it is decisive for the triumph of liberty.

We should nevertheless be very careful not to conquer Holland; the motives here are the same as those we have given above for not extending ourselves beyond Namur on the Meuse, and even much more powerful, since if we were to seek to conquer Holland, all the parties in that country would unite against us, and we would end up driving it into the enemy camp, destroying its dikes, stores, bank, and industry, and thereby depriving ourselves of the means to supply ourselves with basic necessities both for the navy and for consumption by the citizenry, means that will be inexhaustible provided Holland is prosperous. ...

Carnot

HORATIO NELSON
(1758–1805)

*Horatio Nelson, the greatest British admiral, fought France during the
French Revolution (Aboukir Bay, 1798) and the Empire. He won the outstanding victory at Trafalgar (1805) against the French and Spanish fleets
but died of wounds shortly after learning of his success. Trafalgar opened a
century and a half of absolute naval supremacy for Britain.*

THE TRAFALGAR MEMORANDUM

[H. M. S.] *Victory*, off Cadiz, 9th October 1805

Thinking it almost impossible to bring a Fleet of forty Sail of the Line into a
Line of Battle in variable winds, thick weather and other circumstances which
must occur, without such a loss of time that the opportunity would probably
be lost of bringing the Enemy to Battle in such a manner as to make the business decisive.

I have therefore made up my mind to keep the fleet in that position of sailing with the exception of the First and Second in Command that the order of
sailing is to be the Order of Battle, placing the fleet in two Lines of Sixteen ships
each with an advanced Squadron of Eight of the fastest sailing Two decked
ships which will always make if wanted a Line of Twenty Four Sail, on which
ever Line the Commander in Chief may direct.

The Second in Command will after my intentions are made known to him
have the entire direction of His Line to make the attack upon the Enemy and
to follow up the Blow until they are captured or destroyed.

The whole impression of the British must be, to overpower from two or
three Ships ahead of their Commander in Chief, supposed to be in the Centre, to the Rear of their fleet. I will suppose twenty Sail of the Enemy's Line to

Horatio Nelson, "The Trafalgar Memorandum," in Adrian Liddell Hart, *The Sword and the
Pen* (New York: Crowell, 1976), 147–48.

be untouched. It must be some time before they could perform a Manoeuvre to bring their force compact to attack any part of the British fleet engaged, or to succour their own ships which indeed would be impossible, without mixing with the ships engaged. Something must be left to chance, nothing is sure in a sea fight beyond all others, shot will carry away the mast and yards of friends as well as foes, but I look with confidence to a victory before the van of the Enemy could succour their Rear and then that the British Fleet would most of them be ready to receive their Twenty Sail of the Line or to pursue them should they endeavour to make off.

If the Van of the Enemy tacks, the captured Ships must run to Leeward of the British Fleet, if the Enemy wears, the British must place themselves between the Enemy and the captured and disabled British Ships and should the enemy close I have no fear as to the result.

The Second in Command will in all possible things direct the Movements of his Line by keeping them as compact as the nature of the circumstances will admit. Captains are to look to their particular Line as their rallying point. But in case signals can neither be seen or perfectly understood no Captain can do very wrong if he places his Ship alongside that of an Enemy. . . .

DUKE OF WELLINGTON
(1769–1852)

Arthur Wellesley, subsequently first duke of Wellington, served in India, where his brother was governor-general, from 1792 to 1805. He played a leading role in the Iberian peninsula at the head of a British expeditionary corps fighting Napoleon's forces. He defended Lisbon against Marshal Massena, held Marshal Soult in check in Spain, and defeated Marshal Jourdan at Vitoria. At the end of 1813, he penetrated into France and stayed there until the Bourbon Restoration. During the Hundred Days, he shared the triumph of the Waterloo campaign with the Prussian Field Marshal Blücher. He helped to install the second Restoration of Louis XVIII and commanded the occupation army from 1815 to 1818. Wellington, a conservative politically as well as militarily, played a key role in British politics during the first half of the nineteenth century.

TWO LETTERS

To Thomas Sydenham

Freneda [Portugal], 7 December 1811

... The principal point on which I wished to write to you is the disposal of this army, supposing that there should be a general breeze in Europe. I think that you have miscalculated the means and resources of France in men, and mistaken the objects of the French government in imagining that, under those circumstances, Buonaparte will be obliged or inclined to withdraw his army from Spain. He will not even reduce it considerably, but he will only not reinforce it. If I am right, the British army cannot be so advantageously employed as in

Arthur Wellesley, first duke of Wellington, in Adrian Liddell Hart, *The Sword and the Pen* (New York: Crowell, 1976), 157–61.

the Peninsula. Of that, I trust, there is no doubt. If the British army is not employed in the Peninsula, that part of the world would soon be conquered; and the army which would have achieved its conquest, reinforced by the levies in the Peninsula, would reduce to subjugation the rest of the world.

But that is not exactly the view which you have taken of the subject. You appear to think it probable that Buonaparte would be inclined or obliged to withdraw from the Peninsula; and you ask, what would I do in that case? I answer, attack the most vulnerable frontier of France, that of the Pyrenees. Oblige the French to maintain in that quarter 200,000 men for their defence; touch them vitally there, when it will certainly be impossible to touch them elsewhere, and form the nations of the Peninsula into soldiers, who would be allies of Great Britain for centuries. . . .

To Earl Bathurst

St. Jean de Luz [France], 21 November 1813

. . . All the powers of Europe require peace possibly more than France, and it would not do to found a new system of war upon the speculations of any individual on what he sees and learns in one corner of France. If Buonaparte becomes moderate, he is probably as good a Sovereign as we can desire in France; if he does not, we shall have another war in a few years; but if my speculations are well founded, we shall have all France against him; time will have been given for the supposed disaffection to his government to produce its effect; his diminished resources will have decreased his means of corruption, and it may be hoped that he will be engaged singlehanded against insurgent France and all Europe.

There is another view of this subject, however, and that is, the continuance of the existing war, and the line to be adopted in that case. At the present moment it is quite impossible for me to move at all: although the army was never in such health, heart, and condition as at present, and it is probably the most complete machine for its numbers now existing in Europe, the rain has so completely destroyed the roads that I cannot move; and, at all events, it is desirable, before I go farther forward, that I should know what the allies propose to do in the winter, which I conclude I shall learn from your Lordship as soon as the King's government shall be made acquainted with their intentions by the King's diplomatic servants abroad. As I shall move forward, whether in the winter or the spring, I can acquire and ascertain more fully the sentiments of the people, and the government can either empower me to decide to raise the Bourbon standard, or can decide the question hereafter themselves, after they shall have all the information before them which I can send them of the sentiments and wishes of the people.

I can only tell you that, if I were a Prince of the House of Bourbon, nothing should prevent me from now coming forward, not in a good house in London, but in the field in France; and if Great Britain would stand by him, I am certain he would succeed. This success would be much more certain in a month or more hence, when Napoleon commences to carry into execution the oppressive measures which he must adopt in order to try to retrieve his fortunes.

I must tell your Lordship, however, that our success, and every thing, depends upon your moderation and justice, and upon the good conduct and discipline of our troops. Hitherto these have behaved well, and there appears a new spirit among the officers, which I hope will continue, to keep the troops in order. But I despair of the Spaniards. They are in so miserable a state, that it is really hardly fair to expect that they will refrain from plundering a beautiful country, into which they enter as conquerors; particularly, adverting to the miseries which their own country has suffered from its invaders. I cannot, therefore, venture to bring them back into France, unless I can feed and pay them; and the official letter which will go to your Lordship by this post will show you the state of our finances, and our prospects. If I could now bring forward 20,000 good Spaniards, paid and fed, I should have Bayonne. If I could bring forward 40,000, I don't know where I should stop. Now I have both the 20,000 and the 40,000 at my command, upon this frontier, but I cannot venture to bring forward any for want of means of paying and supporting them. Without pay and food, they must plunder; and if they plunder, they will ruin us all. . . .

NAPOLEON
(1769–1821)

*Napoleon Bonaparte was born at Ajaccio, Corsica. After putting down
a serious insurrection against the leadership of the Convention in 1795, he
led a brilliant campaign in Italy in 1796–97 and then headed the French
expedition to Egypt in 1798–99. He became first consul in 1799, and had
himself proclaimed emperor in 1804. Perhaps the greatest Western military
genius since Alexander, Napoleon had an astonishing ability to take advantage of the particular conditions created by the French Revolution (levée en
masse, social mobility, proselytizing enthusiasm) at a time when France was
the greatest cultural, military, and economic power on the continent of Europe
and the nation with the largest population aside from Russia. Napoleon
allied mobility with concentration by combining movement, shock tactics,
and firepower directed at the enemy's weak point. Gradually, his lessons were
learned by his enemies, notably by Prussia. He suffered serious setbacks in
Spain after 1808 and then in Russia in 1812, and he had to abdicate in 1814.
He tried his luck again and was finally defeated at Waterloo in 1815. Like
many great generals, his genius was better expressed in his campaigns than
in his writings, but his instructions, orders of the day, and proclamations are
nonetheless noteworthy.*

MAXIMS (1)

In war, the commander alone understands the importance of certain things
and can alone, through his will and greater insight, conquer and overcome
all difficulties.

A collective government has less simple ideas and takes longer to make up
its mind.

From Napoleon Bonaparte, *Pensées politiques et sociales*, edited by A. Danserre (Paris: Flam-
marion, 1969) and *Comment faire la guerre* (Paris: Lébovici, 1973). Translated from the French by
A. M. Berrett.

Do not hold a council of war, but take the advice of each one individually.

A man of war must have as much character as spirit; men who have much spirit and little character are the least suited [to war; such a man resembles] a ship whose masting is disproportionate to its ballast; it is better to have much character and little spirit. Men who have only an average amount of spirit and a proportionate character often succeed in this profession; one needs as much base as height. Caesar, Hannibal, Prince Eugene, and Frederick [the Great] were generals who had a lot of spirit and character in proportion.

The art of war consists, with an inferior army, in always having more forces than one's enemy at the point where one is attacking or the point where one is being attacked; but this art is to be learned neither from books nor from habit; it is delicacy of touch that strictly speaking constitutes the genius of war.

The art of war lies in positioning one's troops so that they are everywhere at once. The art of positioning troops is the great art of war. Distribute your troops in such a way that, whatever the enemy does, you can reassemble them within a few days.

Do not frontally attack positions that you can secure by flanking them.

Do not do what the enemy wishes simply because he wishes it; avoid the field of battle that he has reconnoitred and studied. Be even more careful to avoid one that he has fortified and where he has entrenched himself.

What are the conditions that make an army superior? First, its organization; second, how much experience of war the officers and men have; third, how much self-confidence they all have—that is, how much boldness, patience, and all the moral resources supplied by the idea of self.

The passage from defense to offense is one of the most delicate operations of war.

You should never leave the defensive line where the troops reform and rest without having a definite plan that leaves no uncertainty about the operations to follow. It would be a great misfortune to leave this line only to be obliged later to resume it. Three-quarters of war is a matter of morale; the balance of forces counts as only one-quarter.

In mountain war, he who attacks is at a disadvantage; even in offensive war, the art consists in only fighting on the defensive and forcing the enemy to attack.

As for moral courage, it is very rare, the courage of two o'clock in the morning—the courage of the unexpected, which, even when something happens totally out of the blue, nevertheless retains freedom of spirit, judgment, and decision making.

Loss of time is irreparable in war; the reasons alleged are always bad, since operations only fail through delays.

In the occupation of a country, the principal points should be occupied, and from them mobile columns should set out to pursue brigands. The experience of the Vendée [uprisings against the French revolutionary regime] proved that it was best to have large numbers of mobile columns scattered everywhere, and not stationary units.

The falling out of a battle is the result of an instant, a thought; the two sides come closer in various combinations, they clash, they fight for a while, the decisive moment occurs, a spark of morale declares itself, and the smallest reserve finishes it.

Caesar's principles were the same as Hannibal's; keep your forces united; do not be vulnerable at any point; move speedily to the important points; rely on morale, the reputation of your arms, the fear you inspire, and also on political means to keep your allies faithful and conquered peoples submissive.

Military genius is a gift from heaven, but the essential quality of a commander is firmness of character and the resolve to conquer at any cost.

Commanders are guided by their own experience or by genius. Tactics, movements, the science of the engineer and the artilleryman can be learned from treatises, rather like geometry; but knowledge of the higher realms of war is only acquired by experience and by study of the wars and battles of the great generals. Does one learn in grammar to compose a book of the *Iliad* or a tragedy by Corneille?

Military science consists first in accurately calculating the odds and then weighing up exactly, almost mathematically, the contribution of chance. On this point there must be no mistake; a decimal point more or less can change everything. But this distinction between science and work can only be found in the head of a genius, for it is needed wherever there is creation, and, of course, the greatest improvisation of the human spirit is that which gives existence to what has none. Chance thus always remains a mystery for mediocre spirits and becomes a reality for superior men. . . .

The art of war does not require complicated maneuvers; the simpler ones are to be preferred. Above all, what is needed is common sense. In those terms, it is hard to see how generals make mistakes; it is because they want to be clever. The most difficult thing is to divine the enemy's plans, to see what is true in all the reports one receives. The rest only requires common sense, it is like a bout of fisticuffs: the more blows you give, the better it will be. . . .

Remember these three things: union of forces, activity, and firm resolution to perish with glory. These are the three great principles of the art of war that have always given me favorable fortune in all my undertakings. Death is nothing; but to live defeated and without glory is to die every day.

The whole art of war consists in a defense that is well thought out and extremely circumspect and an offense that is bold and rapid.

You must be slow in deliberation and swift in execution.

The art of war is a simple art and everything lies in the execution; there is nothing vague about it; everything in it is common sense, nothing is ideology.

Winning is nothing, you must know how to profit from your success.

At the beginning of a campaign, you must consider carefully whether to advance or not; but once you have taken the offensive, you must maintain it to the last extremity; for apart from the honor of arms and the morale of the army, which are lost in a retreat, and the courage it gives the enemy, retreats are more disastrous and cost more in men and equipment than the most bloody engagements, with this difference, that in a battle the enemy loses almost as much as you, while in a retreat you lose without him losing anything.

With a few exceptions, victory goes to the largest force. The art of war thus consists in being superior in numbers at the point where you want to fight. If your army is smaller than the enemy's, do not give him time to unite his forces; surprise him in his movements; fall rapidly on the various regiments you have taken care to isolate, and combine your maneuvers so as to be able in all encounters to have your whole army face divisions of the [enemy's] army. In that way, with an army half the size of the enemy's, you will always be stronger than him on the field of battle.

MAXIMS (2)

It is exceptional and difficult to find all the qualities of a great general combined in one man. What is most desirable and distinguishes the exceptional man, is the balance of intelligence and ability with character or courage. If courage is predominant, the general will hazard far beyond his conceptions; and on the contrary, he will not dare to accomplish his conceptions if his character or his courage are below his intelligence. . . .

In a battle like in a siege, skill consists in converging a mass of fire on a single point: once the combat is opened, the commander who is adroit will suddenly and unexpectedly open fire with a surprising mass of artillery on one of these points, and is sure to seize it. . . .

War is composed of nothing but accidents, and, although holding to general principles, a general should never lose sight of everything to enable him to profit from these accidents; that is the mark of genius.

In war there is but one favorable moment; the great art is to seize it. . . .

From "Military Maxims," in *Roots of Strategy: A Collection of Military Classics,* edited by Thomas R. Phillips (London: John Lane the Bodley Head, 1943; reprint, Stackpole Books, 1985), 433–41.

War on land, in general, consumes more men than naval warfare; it is more dangerous. The sailor in a fleet fights but once during a campaign; the ground soldier fights every day. The sailor, whatever may be the fatigues and dangers of the sea, suffers much less than the soldier: his is never hungry nor thirsty; he always has a place to sleep, his kitchen, his hospital and his pharmacy. There are fewer sick in the English and French fleets, where discipline maintains cleanliness and experience has discovered all the means of preserving health, than in armies. Besides the perils of battle, the sailor risks those of tempests; but seamanship has so much diminished the latter that it cannot be compared with those on land, such as popular uprisings, partial assassinations and surprises by hostile light troops.

An admiral commanding a fleet and a general commanding an army are men who need different qualities. One is born with the qualities proper to command an army, while the necessary qualities to command a fleet are acquired only by experience.

The art of war on land is an art of genius, of inspiration. On the sea everything is definite and a matter of experience. The admiral needs only one science, navigation. The general needs all or a talent equal to all, that of profiting by all experience and all knowledge. An admiral needs to divine nothing; he knows where his enemy is and he knows his strength. A general never knows anything with certainty, never sees his enemy clearly and never knows positively where he is. When armies meet, the least accident of the terrain, the smallest wood, hides a portion of the army. The most experienced eye cannot state whether he sees the entire enemy army or only three quarters of it. It is by the eyes of the mind, by reasoning over the whole, by a species of inspiration that the general sees, knows and judges. The admiral needs only an experienced glance; nothing of the enemy force is hidden from him. What makes the general's function difficult is the necessity of nourishing so many men and animals; if he permits himself to be guided by administrators, he will never budge and his expeditions will fail. The admiral is never bothered since he carries everything with him. An admiral has neither reconnaissances to make, terrain to examine nor fields of battle to study. Indian Ocean, American Ocean or North Sea—it is always a liquid plain. The most skillful will have no advantage over the least, except for his knowledge of prevailing winds in such and such coastal waters, by foresight of those which should prevail or by atmospheric signs: qualities which are acquired by experience and by experience only.

The general never knows the field of battle on which he may operate. His understanding is that of inspiration; he has no positive information; data to reach a knowledge of localities are so contingent on events that almost nothing is learned by experience. It is a faculty to understand immediately the relations of the terrain according to the nature of different countries; it is, finally, a gift, called a *coup d'oeil militaire* [the ability to take in the military situation at a glance] which great generals have received from nature. However the observations that can be made from topographic maps and the facility which education and habit give in reading maps, can be of some assistance.

An admiral depends more on the captains of his ships than a general on his generals. The latter has the opportunity to take direct command of the troops himself, to move to any point and to repair false movements. An admiral can influence personally only the men on the vessel on which he finds himself; smoke prevents signals from being seen and winds change or vary over the space occupied by his line. It is thus of all professions that in which subalterns should use the largest initiative.

GEOPOLITICS
(from the memoirs of Las Cases)

Emmanuel, Comte de Las Cases (1766–1842) was an aristocrat who rallied to Napoleon after being an emigré during the Revolution. He followed the Emperor to Saint Helena, where from June 1815 to November 1816 he re-corded what Napoleon did and said. The Mémorial *was published in 1823, two years after Napoleon's death.*

"The English were shaking when they saw us occupy Egypt [Napoleon said]. We showed Europe the real way of depriving them of India. They are still not altogether reassured; and they are right. If forty or fifty thousand European families ever settle their industry, their laws, and their administration in Egypt, India will soon be lost to the English, much more by force of circumstance than by force of arms. . . ."

. . . A major interest of the emperor's, and at the same time for Europe, is the establishment of Poland; without the restoration of that kingdom, Europe will be without frontiers on that side; Austria and Germany find themselves face to face with the strongest empire in the world [Russia].

In the evening, the emperor again returned to his love of geography. The emperor lingered particularly over Asia—the political situation of Russia, the ease with which it could make an attempt on India, and even China, and the alarm

From Emmanuel de Las Cases, *Mémorial de Sainte-Hélène*, in *Napoléon à Sainte-Hélène*, edited by Jean Tulard (Paris: Editions R. Laffont, 1981). Translated from the French by A. M. Berrett.

that the English must feel. He estimated the number of troops that Russia would have to use, where they would start from, which route they would be likely to take, and the treasure they would bring back. . . .

The emperor [spoke of] the admirable situation of Russia against the rest of Europe, and the enormous number it could summon up for an invasion. . . . Situated under the pole, backed by eternal ice, which in case of need would render it unassailable, Russia could only be attacked during three or four months, or a quarter of the year, while it had the whole twelve months in which to attack us. Its assailants would encounter only the rigors, suffering, and privations of a desert . . . while its peoples would be only too happy to fall on the delights of our southern lands.

To these physical characteristics, added the emperor, might be added the advantage of an immense settled population, brave, hardened, devoted, and passive, along with the vast numbers of peoples whose deprivation and wandering are their natural state of existence. "Who can avoid shuddering at the thought of such a mass, unassailable either from the flanks or from the rear, flooding down upon you with impunity, overwhelming everything in its path if triumphant, or if defeated withdrawing to its ice amid desolation and death. And it would do so with the facility of reappearing as soon as the occasion requires. Is that not the head of the Hydra, the Antaeus of fable, which can only be subdued by seizing its body and stifling it in an embrace. But where is Hercules? Only we dared try it, and, it must be confessed, we made rather a mess of it. . . ."

"Greece, the Peloponnesus at least, must go to the European power who has Egypt. That should be ours. . . . And then, to the north, an independent kingdom, Constantinople with its provinces, to act as a barrier to Russian power, as they claimed to do to France when they created Belgium. . . ."

"I was able to carve up the Turkish empire with Russia; we discussed it on more than one occasion. Constantinople always saved it. That capital was the great embarassment, the real sticking point. Russia wanted it; I would not grant it; it is too valuable a key; it alone is worth an empire; he who possesses it can rule the world. . . ."

DENIS DAVYDOV
(1784–1839)

Denis Vasilievich Davydov, a cavalry officer, suggested and secured the formation of a corps of Cossacks intended to harass the troops and logistics of Napoleon's army during the retreat from Russia in 1812. The results were significant. He wrote an important theoretical essay on partisan warfare, published in 1821 and translated into French in 1842. Unlike the Russian (and German) military leaders of the time, Davidov was conscious of the strategic importance of Russian territory.

ON GUERRILLA WARFARE

The concept of guerrilla warfare which still predominates is the result of a one-sided attitude or an apparently cautious view of the subject. Seizing prisoners and making them talk, committing to flames one or two enemy storehouses located near the army, suddenly smashing the advance guard, or viewing the multiplication of small detachments as the systematic and pernicious fragmentation of the army's effectiveness—these are usually the essential definitions of this type of warfare. All are erroneous! Guerrilla warfare consists neither of quite minor enterprises nor of those of the first order of magnitude, for it is not concerned with the burning of one or two granaries, nor with smashing pickets, nor with striking direct blows at the main forces of the enemy. Rather, it embraces and traverses the whole length of the enemy lines, from the opposing army's rear to the area of territory assigned for the stationing of troops, provisions, and weapons. Thus, guerrilla warfare stops up the source of the army's strength and continuing existence and puts it at the mercy of the guerrillas' own army while the enemy army is weakened, hungry,

From *The Guerrilla Reader: A Historical Anthology,* edited by Walter Laqueur (Philadelphia: Temple University Press, 1977), 53–57. Copyright © 1977 by Walter Laqueur. Reprinted by permission of Temple University Press.

disarmed, and deprived of the saving bonds of authority. This is guerrilla warfare in the fullest sense of the word!

There is no doubt that this kind of warfare would be less effective were it waged only between low-powered armies that did not require large quantities of food and supplies and that fought only with cold steel. However, the invention of gunpowder and firearms, the great increase in the size of military forces, and the preference for the concentration rather than fragmentation of forces posed impossible obstacles to the procurement of food supplies from the occupied territory. Also immense difficulties were encountered in the manufacture of charges in laboratories, the training of recruits, and the mustering of reserves amidst the alarms, engagements, and general accidents of war.

Under these circumstances, it became necessary to provide troops with all the necessities of war in a way that would not entail their procurement from the occupied area, something which would be impossible because of the disproportion between the number of consumers and the amount producible. The solution was to obtain the necessities from areas beyond the range of military operations. Hence there came about the division of the theater of war into two fields, the battlefield and the reserves field, the former being supplied by the produce of the latter. This produce would come not all at once or in bulk but as the army used up the provisions and military equipment it carried with it. Thus troops would not be burdened with excessive loads that would hamper their movement. Naturally, however, this invention led to the counter-invention with which the enemy could obstruct the delivery of supplies of the produce so vital to the efficiency of the opposing side. Two ways of achieving this aim were immediately obvious: action on the battlefield by detachments against the rear of the army where newly supplied ammunition and provisions are distributed and newly arrived reserve troops deployed, or action by these same detachments on the reserves field itself.

But then it was discovered that the first of these, the battlefield, was difficult of access owing to the close proximity of the enemy to the place appointed for the attack and that the second, the reserves field, was usually protected by fortifications enclosing the stores of provision, the ammunition factory, and the reserve formations. There remained the ground over which these three items were transported to the army. This is the field of guerrilla operations. It presents none of those obstacles that abound on both the battlefield and the reserves field because the enemy's main forces and fortifications, being located at its extremities, are in no position to defend it—the former because all their efforts are directed at fighting the main army of their adversary, the latter by reason of their natural immobility.

Hence it follows that guerrilla warfare cannot exist when the opposing army is situated on the reserves field itself. But the greater the distance separating the battlefield and the reserves field becomes, the more effective and decisive guerrilla warfare can be. . . .

As a definitive illustration of the great importance of guerrilla warfare in modern operations involving huge armies and concentrations of supplies, let us ask some questions and give the answers. First: by whom is war waged? By people, joined together in an army.

Second: can people do battle empty-handed? No. War is not like fist-fighting. These people need weapons. But now that gunpowder has been invented, even weapons alone are insufficient. Soldiers need cartridges and charges for their weapons. As these charges and cartridges are almost completely discharged during the course of each battle and since their manufacture is difficult during troop movements and operations, new supplies must be sent directly from the place where they are prepared. This is a clear demonstration that an army with weapons but without cartridges and charges is no better than an organized crowd of people who bear spears, a crowd which will scatter at the first shot from the enemy or, if it accepts battle, which will perish in so doing. In short, there is no strength in an army, for since the invention of gunpowder, an army without charges and cartridges is no army at all.

Third: does an army require reinforcement during the course of a war? Yes, it does. Men and horses are lost in battles, skirmishes, and exchange of fire; they become casualties to wounds received in battle or to diseases which run increasingly rampant because of the intense pressure of campaigns, inclement weather, and strains and shortages of all kinds. An army unable to refurbish itself will inevitably dwindle and disappear.

The fourth and final question seems superfluous: does the soldier need food? A man without food cannot exist, let alone fight. Because of its large size, the army of modern times cannot make do with the produce of the area it occupies. It therefore needs regular food supplies. Without these it will either die of hunger or scatter beyond the radius of military operations in search of sustenance, thereby degenerating into a corrupt horde of robbers and vagrants that will perish without protection or glory.

Thus, what method should be selected to deprive the enemy of these three fundamental elements of the vital strength and military might of his army? There is no other method than to destroy them by guerrilla warfare while they are being transported from the reserves field to the battlefield. What venture will an enemy embark upon without food, ammunition, or replacement troops? He will be compelled to cease his operations either by making peace, surrendering into captivity, or scattering with no hope of being reunited—

three dismal consequences totally opposed to those an army seeks when it opens hostilities. Besides the mortal threat that guerrilla warfare represents to these three fundamental elements of the strength and existence of an army, it poses danger to the secondary needs of an army that are so closely bound up with its welfare and no less exposed to danger than food, or ammunition, or transports of reserves. These secondary elements are clothing, footwear, and arms to replace those worn by excessive use or mislaid in the chaos of battle; surgical and hospital equipment; and messengers and aides-de-camp sometimes carrying vitally important orders to and from enemy headquarters and remote areas in the rear, command posts, and particular corps and detachments. The combined action of these units is disrupted and destroyed by guerrilla operations. Other targets may be transports of sick and wounded men on their way from the army to hospitals, teams of invalids who have recovered and are returning from hospital to the army, high-ranking officials traveling from one place to another to inspect particular units or take up a particular command, and so forth.

But this is not all. Guerrilla warfare can also have an effect upon the main operations of the opposing army. The army's strategic movements during the course of a campaign must inevitably encounter enormous difficulties when they can immediately be reported to the commander on the opposite side by guerrilla units or when they can be delayed by these same units building abatis or destroying fording-places. Also an army can be attacked by all the opposing forces when it has left one strategic point but not reached the next—a situation reminiscent of Seslavin at Maloyaroslavets. Similar obstacles are also a threat to the enemy during his retreat. Erected and defended by guerrilla detachments, these barriers allow the pursuing army to constrict the retreating one and exploit the advantages of the locality to bring about its final destruction—a spectacle we witnessed in 1812 during the retreat of the Napoleonic hordes from Moscow to the Nieman.

Still this is not all. Scarcely less important than the material aspect of this kind of operation is the moral one. Raising the lowered spirits of the inhabitants of areas in the enemy rear; distracting mercenary-minded troublemakers from giving assistance to the enemy by seizing all kinds of spoils from the enemy army and dividing them among the inhabitants; boosting the morale of one's own army by frequent deliveries and parades of captured soldiers and officials, transports and provisions, stock, and even guns; and, besides all this, stunning and disheartening the men in the opposing armies—such are the fruits of skillfully directed guerrilla warfare. What consequences will we not see when the success of guerrilla detachments leads to their winning over the entire population of regions in the enemy rear and when news of the horror sown along the enemy's lines of communication is broadcast among the ranks of its army? When the realization that there is no escape from the guerrilla bands robs each soldier of his reliance on the reserves field, the effect will be to cause timidity and circumspection and then looting, which is one of the chief reasons for a fall in discipline, and with it, the total destruction of an army.

WHY PARTISAN WAR SUITS RUSSIA

Each country's military organization must concord with the habits, customs, and natural disposition of its people; otherwise, army generals would be all the time getting their calculations wrong: nature is invincible. One would regret having sought to make a Turk a cuirassier and subjecting him to the rules of tactics, or feeling oneself quite secure in a camp guarded by central Europeans dressed as Cossacks. All armies are equal, since they are made up of men; and it is only their organization and the use made of them that can establish degrees of superiority among them. It can even be added with absolute certainty that such superiority can only be acquired by departing as little as possible from the fundamental dispositions, habits, and what might be called the speciality of each nation. What I am saying here may, I think, be applied to the government of nations in every part of the world.

Civilization, and with it knowledge of the rights that every individual has, commerce, luxury, and the relaxation of morals, are the main obstacles to the introduction of light troops in European armies. Peoples that are born horsemen transmit from one generation to the next the predisposition for small-scale war that they have acquired in their frequent excursions in search of booty and in continual wars with their neighbors, people who live in deserts or mountains. There is still something wild about the type of war we are dealing with, and the means to wage it have something of the mark of wild animals and uncivilized man.

Asia may serve as an example. Superstition rules even today in the minds of those peoples and halts any advance of civilization. Their wars involve simply sudden attacks, tireless activity, and rapid excursions across borders, undertaken by boisterous, fearless horsemen.

Their order of battle and the manner in which they launch attacks and pursuits are all unformed, unruly, and disordered, but at the same time rapid, fearless, and bold! How can there by any hope of establishing order among these warriors, crushed by servitude and breathing freely only on the field of battle?

From Denis Davydov, *Essai sur la guerre de partisans*, pt. 2, translated from the Russian by Henri de Polignac (Paris, 1842). Translated from the French by A. M. Berrett.

Where is the man who will try and pin down by discipline such an efferves-
cent host? Their Koran, with its prohibition on imitating Christians, their
scimitars, their deserts, and their light horse are all barriers against innovators.
. . . The highest degree of perfection to which the military forces of an empire
could attain would be to add Asiatic light troops to European armies. With the
latter one could wage war in the full strategic and tactical sense of that word;
and with the others one would deprive the enemy of all his means of subsistence and all his war communications. But how can the wild untrammeled
Asiatic be induced to act in concert with a regular army? To Russia alone, covering a third of Europe and part of Asia, was it given to possess one of the best-
organized armies in the world and rule over peoples who combine the warlike
habits of the men of Asia with the discipline and submissiveness of European
troops. I am referring to the Cossacks.

For centuries, continuous invasions by peoples from the east through the
Ukraine, [along] the banks of the Dnieper, Don, and Ural rivers, right into the
heart of Russia, gave the southern peoples of that empire many of the customs
and habits of their enemies and at the same time habituated them to this type
of warfare. All the territory between the southern banks of the Dnieper and
those of the Ural, which is inhabited only by different sorts of Cossacks, is living proof of what I have just argued. It is true that time, tranquillity, and the
yoke under which they live have made them lose some of their vigor in attack
and some of the individual agility of their masters from the East. But they still
retain enough to be the terror of all the light cavalry of Europe; and they are
also much superior to the Asiatics in terms of discipline. So that, led by skillful leaders, they can be employed in every service and make a useful contribution to the success of campaign plans. That is the true light cavalry, which
is not simply so by name and custom, but by innate disposition, and by being
constantly habituated to defending its land and its freedom, which is continually threatened by greedy neighbors. These troops, which belong to Russia
alone, have received little attention from writers on tactics, for the simple reason that the light troops of the rest of Europe, being made up of the same type
of men as the infantry, artillery, and heavy cavalry, do not and cannot have the
same importance as these three basic components of military force. But, surely,
when any of our generals is called to command in a European war, he will be
quite able to raise our light cavalry to the level of the abovementioned three
arms, and put to good use the advantage of having at his disposal one more
arm than all the other powers. The fact that Russia's superiority over the other
empires is not limited to the excellence of its light troops, but is enhanced by
the defensive position given it by the vastness of its territory, will make that
advantage all the greater. An enemy who advances deep into this endless country gets further and further away from his base of operations and all his military installations and is obliged, so as not to increase this enormous distance

further, to take the shortest route; and then he begins to face countless difficulties, both as regards getting supplies in the country invaded and as regards receiving foodstuffs from his distant installations. And the fact of this vast territory, so terrible for the enemy, is all to the advantage of our army. Acting in the heart of its broad, deep base of operations, it can, without moving too far away from it, direct its energies to any point being threatened and, through skillful or daring maneuvers, always retain free communication with those provinces that offer it most advantages as sources of supplies or carry the theater of war into them. I may add that it is relieved of any fear of being overwhelmed or driven over its borders.

It is, of course, true that this extraordinary size of the country means that the western border is greatly lengthened, and this has been regarded by men with old-fashioned ideas as exposing Russia to great dangers. But, if old prejudices are set aside, it is easy to see that any danger from this extension of frontiers disappears given the breadth and depth that go with it.

War normally begins in a country somewhere between two great belligerent powers; but there are few examples of it stopping there. In the present age, disputes between two states are not decided by combats between Horatii and Curiatii or a duel between two commanding generals; nor are these great disputes concluded by the taking of a few border fortresses, or the endless maneuvers of two small bodies of troops calling themselves armies. Today . . . whole nations rise up one against another, and it is speed of movement or force that decide which frontiers will be the ones attacked and where the war will be fought. From that angle, what difference does it make how long or short the frontiers are? Is not an invasion directed at the heart of the country, and is it not there that its defense can be organized? If the banks of the Rhine, dotted with so many first-class fortresses, were unable to prevent German troops from entering France or French troops from entering Germany, if the fate of these great powers was decided in Vienna, Berlin, and Paris, and not on the frontiers, and if, finally, to take another case, Russia and Spain, after their glorious struggles, were able, without the help of their frontiers, to drive out large French armies, what arguments can be made in favor of the prejudice I am rejecting?

Yet it must also be said that it is not equally without danger for every power to let its territory be invaded; I will even add that, for the invasion not to cause inevitable ruin, the empire attacked must not only be very large but, I repeat, its depth must be commensurate with its breadth. Otherwise, invasion would be wholly to the advantage of the attacking army; we can find an example in the not-too-distant past.

In 1806, the Prussian army, having suffered a severe setback on its borders, lost all communication with the center of the kingdom, was driven back to the sea, and laid down its weapons. One of the main causes of this unfortunate outcome was the fact that Prussia had little depth, particularly along the southern part of its frontier, which is where the enemy attacked. In the same year and the following one, in eastern Prussia, our army was twice exposed to the same danger, the first time when the French army tried to drive us back into Austrian Galicia and, above all, the second time, when this same army maneuvered between the Narva [Narew] and Königsberg to drive us back to the Frisches Haff. What exposed us to those dangers was the lack of space and depth of the theater of war, which, in retreat, gave so few means of escaping the enemy's pursuit and foiling his plans.

Russia is sheltered from such hazards, and I am quite convinced that, in the 1812 campaign, even if the enemy had taken . . . Orel or Tver, the independence of Russia would still have been unshakable. . . . and the French army would have experienced the same disasters. . . .

By what means can the goal be achieved without which wars can only be compared to the excursions of knights-errant, a goal that consists, not simply in chasing after an army that is withdrawing (perhaps with hidden intentions), or in briefly occupying a few provinces, but in totally annihilating all the enemy's forces and thereby obtaining the whole country's submission? What has to be done to attain that goal? Is it to be by a rapid, daring invasion that will strike terror into both nation and army? But that sort of undertaking can only succeed in cases where one can quickly in one fell swoop, so to speak, drive the enemy back to the remotest part of his territory, or pin him against one of those insurmountable obstacles that often form the frontiers of states.

I think that I have shown that the example of 1812 helps support what I am saying, that this way of waging war is not dangerous for Russia. If the enemy follows a slow and methodical plan, he will find just as many difficulties. It would all take too much time, and time is precious in an empire in which one can do nothing in the depths of winter, the deep mud of autumn, or the thaw of spring. In these various undertakings, it is always supplying the army that is the chief obstacle; for there are only two ways of providing for it: either the army feeds itself on what it can find in the towns or villages along its route or it is supplied by storage depots or transports of foodstuffs provided by all the inhabitants of the invaded provinces. But the sparseness of the population and the vastness of the distance between settlements in Russia, the burning of dwellings, and the flight of the inhabitants into the woods or to remote provinces totally rule out the first means and the tireless activity of light troops equally rules out the second. It is above all in this latter aspect that the true usefulness of [Cossack] troops stands out. Light teams, endlessly moving along the enemy's lines of communication and inserting themselves between army corps, fall on artillery parks, which they destroy as they do all convoys of foodstuffs, munitions, and so forth. Combining their excursions with the movements of their army, they facilitate and complement its successes. By making continuous attacks and turning up at different points, they distract both the enemy's attention and part of his forces and force him to follow one single route and to grope his way forward, with no hope of wiping out the indestructible swarm of light troops or even of catching up with it, cutting it off, or driving it up against some obstacle that would make it possible to surround it. He therefore has no choice but to retreat, preceded and surrounded by partisans, and closely shadowed by regular troops.

No doubt the means of defense I am suggesting are not easy ones; but it is equally true that the half-measures and flabbiness of action of most of the armies of Europe very often have disastrous consequences. Let us then take advantage of our nation's warrior spirit, our country's immense vastness, in whose deserts a countless army came and lost itself, and always prefer, as in 1812, losing our fortunes to losing our honor and our independence.

J. F. A. LE MIÈRE DE CORVEY
(1770–1832)

Jean Frédéric Auguste Le Mière de Corvey followed a series of French
theoreticians of "small wars," such as Augustin Grandmaison (La Petite
Guerre, ou Traité du service des troupes légères en campagne; *Paris, 1756)*
*and Julien de Jeney (*Le Partisan, ou l'Art de faire la petite guerre; *Paris,*
1772). The Vendée insurrection and the Peninsular War, in which he fought,
gave Le Mière de Corvey exceptional opportunities to observe and reflect on
the subject, however, and his Des partisans et des corps irréguliers *(Paris,*
1823) is undoubtedly, with Denis Davydov's, the most interesting contribution
of the period on the "small war."

ON PARTISANS AND IRREGULAR FORCES

Partisan and Guerrilla Units

When foreign armies invade the soil of the fatherland, you must expect to be
pillaged, ruined, and maltreated if you lack the courage to defend yourself.

If the national army is destroyed and you no longer have the means to put
sufficient forces in the field to face the enemy, form guerrilla or partisan units
at once. But if you want to fight this sort of war successfully, you must begin
by seizing the mountain gorges. It can also be fought successfully in well-
covered country full of defiles, woods, forests, hedges, and so forth. But never
adventure into flat country, especially when the enemy has plenty of cavalry,
which would be able to spread out there and would have a great advantage
over your companies of infantry, which, being used to fighting only as skirmishers, would be unable to put up any resistance to regular units on a plain.

From J. F. A. Le Mière de Corvey, *Des partisans et des corps irréguliers* (Paris, 1823), chs. 4, 5, 8,
11, and 12. Translated from the French by A. M. Berrett.

[662]

The aim of partisan units is always to have a force sufficiently large to worry the enemy; to be able to move it about anywhere in order to harass him relentlessly, gradually wear him down, prevent him getting supplies, destroy his convoys, seize them, take his dispatches, intercept his communications, and surprise all the stragglers you come across. This war, well fought, led by a skillful leader, will inspire terror in the enemy; it will be all very well for him to occupy the towns, but he will have to travel by road to communicate between one town and another, and he will be assailed on these roads. He will have to fight at each defile. He will not dare let a single carriage venture out without an escort. He will exhaust his troops, will be unable to recruit new ones, and will gradually be destroyed without ever having experienced one great loss on a single occasion.

In the war in Spain, the guerrillas harassed us so much on all the roads that, to protect our escorts from one stage to the next, small forts called blockhouses were put up at all the most dangerous road junctions; these were a sort of round tower made of wood, surrounded by a wide ditch; on the platform a small caliber cannon was placed on a movable base and turned to face the direction in which one wished to fire. Detachments were placed in these blockhouses; they protected the convoys and offered a haven to escorts mauled by the enemy.

It was of little use; the Spaniards found other roads, and outflanked these forts. We did not get what we expected out of them, and those of our troops obliged to garrison them had much better things to do.

Parties of guerrillas must avoid encounters in the plains against disciplined troops, unless they are in superior numbers or able to take the enemy by surprise; for, by limiting themselves to fighting such partisan war in mountains and wooded country, they do him extraordinary harm at little risk.

Suppose that there are one hundred and fifty companies in a country occupied by the enemy, and that each company has one hundred to one hundred and eighty men; that makes about eighteen to twenty thousand partisans. Well, if they avoid engagements with the regular forces and only attack them in isolated groups wherever they can, in a month there is not a single man who would not find a chance to get rid of one of the enemy. According to my calculations, that makes twelve men a year put out of action by each partisan. The eighteen thousand men scattered all over the invaded country will thus have made the enemy suffer a loss of over two hundred thousand men. This calculation is perhaps somewhat exaggerated; but if you add sickness, disputes with the inhabitants, and unforeseen events, enemy losses would certainly exceed that number by the end of the year, if the partisan leaders are good officers.

Such was the system Spain used against us. One hundred and fifty to two hundred guerrilla bands scattered all over Spain had sworn to kill thirty or forty Frenchmen a month each: that made six to eight thousand men a month for all the guerrilla bands together. The order was never to attack soldiers traveling as a body, unless the guerrillas outnumbered them. But they fired on all stragglers, attacked small escorts, and sought to lay hands on the enemy's funds, couriers, and especially convoys. As all the inhabitants acted as spies for their fellow citizens, the guerrillas knew when the convoys would leave and how strong their escorts would be, and the bands would make sure they were twice the size. They knew the country very well, and they would attack furiously in the most favorable spot. Success often crowned the undertaking; but they always killed a lot of men, and the goal was achieved. As there are twelve months in the year, we were losing about eighty thousand men a year, without any pitched battles. The war in Spain lasted seven years, so over five hundred thousand men were killed. . . . But that includes only those killed by the guerrillas. Add the battles of Salamanca, Talavera, and Vitoria, and several others that our troops lost; the sieges embarked on by Marshal Suchet; the defense of Saragossa; the fruitless attack on Cadiz; add too the invasion and evacuation of Portugal, the fevers and various illnesses that the temperature caused our soldiers to suffer, and you will see that we could add a further three hundred thousand men to that number during those seven years.

And who were these guerrilla chiefs who beat our brave captains? Were they distinguished former officers, well versed in military tactics? Not at all; the main leaders of these bands who put up such a stout resistance to the French army were a miller, a doctor, a shepherd, a priest, some monks, and a few deserters—not a single outstanding figure of the time among them.

From what has been said, it will be apparent that the prime aim of this sort of war is to bring about the destruction of the enemy almost without him noticing it, and as a drop of water dripping on a stone will eventually dig a hole in the stone, patience and perseverance are needed, always following the same system. In the long run, the enemy will suffer more from this than he would from losing pitched battles. Carefully avoid confrontations between masses of men and other masses in the plains and try to ensure that a group of partisans trained in one district never leaves it; the customs of the country sometimes differ from one side of a river to the other. In his own country, the guerrilla knows the views of all his neighbors; there are witnesses to everything that happens; everybody helps everybody else, and if someone wanted to do any harm, he would hide from his fellow citizens. Thus nowhere can one find more help for this sort of war than in the area where one normally lives; partisans from one district should accordingly never go and fight in another, unless it is temporarily on some important assignment. . . .

On the *Levée en Masse* in the Event of Invasion

ON THE CENTRAL COUNCIL AND THE MILITARY
DIVISION OF THE TERRITORY

If the invasion has only begun, the insurrection or *levée en masse* can hardly be general; but it will be that much stronger in country that can offer protection. So immediately form substantial nuclei of partisans in broken or mountainous country. As people generally have a good knowledge of the places where they normally live, try and make sure that your soldiers are from the area where they are to fight; they will fight all the better for it.

The insurrection will spread as the invasion develops, and so your partisan units must also increase in the same proportion. While awaiting the general uprising, I would limit myself to forming standing meetings in broken or mountainous country, and I would relentlessly harass the enemy from the minute he set foot on our territory.

Knowledge of the country would soon bring successes, as would the relations that you have with all the inhabitants. They could keep you informed of enemy movements, and if he were to try to destroy you, he would never succeed, because you could come upon him from all sides, and once his troops were engaged in the mountains, his cavalry and artillery would become useless, and he would be unable to get out without heavy losses.

A *levée en masse* can only be raised on government instructions; it is the government that gives orders for the creation of partisan forces, appoints generals to command regions, colonels to command districts, and all the serving officers. But if unforeseen circumstances suddenly paralyzed [the government's] forces and power, inasmuch as it is vital to start from a fixed point, to which everything must be linked, a junta or council should at once be summoned, which might be called the *central council,* since it would give overall directions for the *levée en masse* and all operations would emanate from it. This central council would thus be a sort of provisional government, which would replace the one temporarily paralyzed, and, as an invasion is always foreseen, if the head of government saw that it would be impossible to stop it in open combat, he ought to act in advance to appoint the members of the central council, charged with directing military operations during the invasion in his name. . . .

WHAT TRAINING SHOULD A PARTISAN SOLDIER HAVE?

A soldier who intends to engage in partisan warfare needs three things. To be sober, to march well, and to know how to fire a gun.

We assume, above all, that he is brave and filled with the desire to drive the enemy out or to do him as much harm as possible.

The partisan must regard rest and idleness as his most fearsome enemies.

Continuous drill makes good soldiers, because it fills them with ideas about their trade and teaches them to scorn dangers by making them familiar with hardship. . . .

Large-scale maneuvers are useless for irregular forces. They must attack boldly, and before attacking think carefully about what the outcome of the attack will be; but once they have started it, they must never look back.

Before embarking on an attack, the leader will designate the spot through which he will make his retreat in the event of failure, and each soldier will know where he has to withdraw to if fate does not smile on him.

The right way to fight advantageously against regular troops is the ambush. The man who lies in wait for his enemy is doubly strong, especially when he has an assured line of retreat.

Never attack regular troops en masse. The method of the people of the Vendée must be adopted: attack like marauders. As their leaders used to say when they saw republican forces: "Scatter, lads, here come the men in blue." These soldiers were undisciplined peasants, who spread out all over the plain to attack our armies and occupied too much territory for regular troops to be able to adjust and direct their attacks accurately, whereas, when you fire on a mass, a shot directed at one individual will always hit someone when there are several people close together in the same spot. If they were pursued too closely, they would run behind hedges to escape. There they would rally, await their enemies, and fire on them from the protection thus offered. When forced to, they would withdraw to a wood where no one dared follow them; the terrain protected them. For if they had not had ditches, hedges, and woods behind them, they would not have dared risk themselves on the plain against regular troops.

This boldness in attack and these men's perseverance often gave them the upper hand in this war against our armies. They counted on the unevenness of the terrain and their way of fighting, and there was also a dash of fanaticism mixed up in it. But if you really want to defend your country in the event of an invasion, then you must be decided to wage a war of extermination, and a dose of fanaticism is required, for the enemy armies use reprisals, and are all the more harsh in their judgments because they do not see a regular army facing them and want to treat as rebels and brigands those they are unable to overcome, whom they would treat on a nation-to-nation basis if they were waging a regular war against them. That is why wars of ideas, fired by religion or fought for some other cause that each side feels obliged to defend, are terrible wars. They are so because each looks upon his side as a particular cause to avenge, and often becomes cruel when he is the victor; the leaders even sometimes make use of this party spirit to inflame their soldiers. In the Vendée, we saw poorly armed peasants, without the least discipline, rush at heavy guns and seize them. Then they would turn them against the republican armies, and since artillery is only of use to a regular army, they would dismantle and spike them if the engagement had ended to their advantage. If the opposite happened, they would cut the traces and take the horses with them, or hamstring them.

This way of waging war is terrible; a regular force looks twice before pursuing an enemy into a position it does not know, since it does not know how strong it is and fears an ambush.

Although I suggest that these troops must follow no rule of tactics, that is not quite the right way to put it. Everything done in pursuit of a general order is a matter of tactics. What I mean is that they do not need to follow the rules of strategy or those of regular forces. But all that I offer here are tactics suitable for irregular units.

It will be very useful in moments of rest for corporals and sergeants who have served as regular soldiers to be able to teach uninformed peasants and workers belonging to partisan units a few simple maneuvers, which I limit to knowing how to charge one's rifle smartly, adjust properly, spread out quickly over a plain, and rally promptly: that is all it is necessary to know. When the leaders are good, and if the warrant officers have been regular soldiers, and the men have courage and patriotism (and you need some to leave your home, your possessions, and your family to fight voluntarily), nothing is impossible, and you are strong when you are defending your independence and your property.

On Attack and Defense in the Mountains

In the previous chapters we have established that partisans should always occupy the mountains; but as a good leader must know both attack and defense, I must here show how to defend the mountains where you have established yourself. You might be facing an experienced antagonist who, having fought this sort of war [before], harries you and wears you down, and sometimes ends up taking your heights.

Those who attack and defend in this sort of war must be very prudent. If I wanted to attack troops occupying the mountains, I would begin by trying to get control of the heights.

Nothing is more imprudent than to risk moving through gorges when you are not master of the heights; you may run into ambushes in any defile. The partisans must therefore pay particular attention to them, and so long as they occupy them, they need not fear their being taken by force; but once the heights have been taken, all ambushes cease. Conversely, so long as you control them, the enemy runs the risk, however many men he has, of being destroyed there or being obliged to return whence he has come, after suffering heavy losses.

If, then, a partisan leader finds the principal passages or the heights of the mountain chain where he has taken up position occupied by the enemy, whether by ruse or skill, and he wants to retake them, he must bring his troops together and make it appear that he is about to attack in force. This movement will attract the enemy's attention and hold him at bay for a while. Meanwhile, you must look for a pathway somewhere. However forbidding mountains seem, there are always ways over them if you look properly. Often the men who live in them do not know them themselves, because they have never needed to look for them. In this matter it is no use relying on the inhabitants, who normally only know their country from tradition or from their everyday use of a path; in such cases you must try and look for yourself or use alert, enterprising men who are not put off by difficulties. Ways out will almost always be found that would appear impracticable if necessity did not force people to use them. Then the enemy who does not know them does not know what to do and flees, fearful of being outflanked and attacked in several places, in a position where he would have no retreat if he needed one. The advantage is always with the inhabitant, who may be supposed to know the country in detail, and who has public opinion on his side. Sometimes you may find a traitor who sells himself to the enemy, but you have virtually all the inhabitants on your side, who give you all the information you might need. They know very well that an occupation can only be temporary and will be able to punish anyone who has helped the common enemy to the detriment of his fellow citizens later. But even if the law cannot touch him, public contempt would avenge honest people for the treason of the wretch who had sought to deliver his country to the enemy so as to keep his possessions and his job or to secure new ones. . . .

On the Defense of Broken Country;
How to Attack Large Units, Convoys, and Escorts;
Training for Forcing the Enemy at a River Crossing

If you are fighting in broken country, you have little to fear, and the enemy is in something of a pickle; he can only engage in minor skirmishes, which are never decisive. He is continually aware of the disadvantages of attacking troops under cover and protected by the terrain. Mass formations serve no purpose and obstinacy leads to the pointless loss of many men. Meanwhile, the dispersed partisans under cover fear nothing; all their blows strike true and, if the enemy does not have large forces, after sowing disorder in his ranks, they will vigorously pursue him. If he has not been careful to have his rear free to be able to form detachments and halt the partisans, he cannot withdraw without the risk of suffering heavy losses.

In well-covered country that is well broken up by hedges, ditches, patches of woods, side roads, barriers, marshes, and so on, such as are found in Brittany, for example, cannon are almost useless; they are impossible to maneuver, and the enemy risks seeing his horses killed, or his artillery pieces seized, without being able to defend them; neither is his cavalry of much use to him in such country, where he cannot make it maneuver and use it to advantage.

A detachment of partisans five or six hundred strong will stop an army in such country, because along lanes bordered by ditches and hedges, it is impossible to scout on one's flanks. A broad front is offered to the enemy, and marksmen hidden behind hedges can fire with the certainty of hitting a target. As they are scattered over a great length of ground, the enemy cannot know their strength and always thinks there are more of them than there really are. The least hut can be turned into a fortification, where the skirmishers gather; if the enemy wants to attack them there in regular order, and they are unable to sustain the shock, they withdraw into the woods, after causing the enemy many losses. The enemy gropes his way forward, no longer daring to leave the main road to pursue a unit whose strength he does not know. The partisan band withdraws along familiar paths and, marching faster than a regular unit, goes two or three leagues further on and resumes the attack all over again. The enemy is harassed at every step of his march; he dare not do anything, and even when he halts, he mounts a guard. This war wears him down; it tires him, his morale is affected, and he loses a lot of men. Meanwhile the partisans, always hidden, are experiencing no losses, or at least such light losses that they hardly realize they have been fighting.

With three or four hundred men, a sufficiently bold partisan leader can cause frightful disorder if he attacks an army on the march, especially if he knows the country well. . . .

Partisans have one other great advantage: in the event of a retreat, everyone helps and protects them, whereas if it is the enemy who suffers a setback, all the inhabitants will unite against him to finish him off and destroy him.

When a convoy is involved, you use the same means, but try and make sure you kill some horses belonging to the leading waggons; then the waggons stop, the convoy grinds to a halt, and all is chaos. If you see fit to break into it, do so, and you will manage to carry some [horses] off.

As the inhabitants will have told you both when the convoy is to leave and the route it is to take, nothing prevents a few men of goodwill from digging a few holes in a bad stretch of road during the night to slow down the movement of the waggons in the convoy. Or you can make good use of abatis of trees in the defiles. It will take quite a time to remove them; [meanwhile,] the sharpshooters concealed behind them open up a murderous fire. An abatis is the best possible barrier against the enemy.

Harry the enemy as he marches; pursue stragglers; always be ready in ambush; attack small escorts, and if your forces are not large enough to make a direct assault on a strong escort, harry it relentlessly. Attack it ten times in the same day if you can; keep trying to undermine it, and you will eventually succeed. If he puts up too spirited a resistance, withdraw in good order and reform further away; you will still march better than a regular unit. Moreover, you can take side roads without any need for scouts. Attack again, employ the same tactic, and if in the end you do not succeed in completely defeating the escort, you will do it a lot of damage.

It is hardly possible to prevent a crossing of a river by sheer force; how much less so with partisans. If the invasion has not come to an end, and you want to defend a river crossing, the best thing I can see to do, if you do not have an army to put against the enemy, is to wait to attack until some of his troops have crossed and are busy establishing a bridgehead. For if the enemy fears that his passage will be disputed, he will first make sure it is supported by his artillery, which will rain fire on the opposite bank, and he will cross with the help of pontoons. But as soon as part of his force has crossed, it will establish itself and begin the bridgehead to protect the rest of the crossing and hold out in the event of a setback. That is the right moment to attack. The enemy's cannon are of no use at all so long as he has troops on the opposite bank, and if it is nighttime, he will not know whether the men who are landing (for the crossing must always continue day and night until it is completed) are friends or enemies; once undecided, confusion will appear in his ranks, and if he is beaten, all who have crossed will be lost.

CARL VON CLAUSEWITZ
(1780–1831)

Carl von Clausewitz was present at the disastrous Prussian defeat at Jena in 1806. He was subsequently taken prisoner by the French and interned until 1809. Upon his release, he worked with Scharnhorst, Gneisenau, and Boyen on the reform of the Prussian army. He taught at the Military School in Berlin until 1812, when, like many other Prussian officers, he put himself at the service of the tsar of Russia out of Prussian patriotism, despite the attitude of the king of Prussia, who saved his dynasty by accepting a forced alliance with the emperor of the French. Clausewitz took part in the Russian campaign. Then, although in disgrace, he took part in the campaigns of 1814–15, in the Prussian service. Between 1818 and 1830, he headed the Berlin Military School. He died of cholera in 1831, leaving his major work, Vom Kriege *(*On War*), unfinished. It was published thanks to his widow; the erstwhile Countess Marie von Brühl. Only book 1, reprinted here, was finished. Books 3 and 8 (and chapter 26 of book 6, devoted to "small war") are also of great interest.*

ON THE NATURE OF WAR

What is War?

1. INTRODUCTION

We propose to consider first the single elements of our subject, then each branch or part, and, last of all, the whole, in all its relations—therefore to advance from the simple to the complex. But it is necessary for us to commence with a glance at the nature of the whole, because it is particularly necessary

Carl von Clausewitz, *On War*, translated by J. J. Graham (London: N. Trübner and Co., 1873) [bk. 1,] 1–42.

that in the consideration of any of the parts the whole should be kept constantly in view.

2. DEFINITION

We shall not enter into any of the abstruse definitions of war used by publicists. We shall keep to the element of the thing itself, to a duel. War is nothing but a duel on an extensive scale. If we would conceive as a unit the countless number of duels which make up a war, we shall do so best by supposing to ourselves two wrestlers. Each strives by physical force to compel the other to submit to his will: his first object is to throw his adversary, and thus to render him incapable of further resistance.

War therefore is an act of violence to compel our opponent to fulfil our will.

Violence arms itself with the inventions of Art and Science in order to contend against violence. Self-imposed restrictions, almost imperceptible and hardly worth mentioning, termed usages of International Law, accompany it without essentially imparing its power. Violence, that is to say physical force (for there is no moral force without the conception of states and law), is therefore the *means;* the compulsory submission of the enemy to our will is the ultimate *object.* In order to attain this object fully, the enemy must be disarmed; and this is, correctly speaking, the real aim of hostilities in theory. It takes the place of the final object, and puts it aside in a manner as something not properly belonging to war.

3. UTMOST USE OF FORCE

Now, philanthropists may easily imagine there is a skilful method of disarming and overcoming an enemy without causing great bloodshed, and that this is the proper tendency of the art of War. However plausible this may appear, still it is an error which must be extirpated; for in such dangerous things as war, the errors which proceed from a spirit of benevolence are just the worst. As the use of physical power to the utmost extent by no means excludes the co-operation of the intelligence, it follows that he who uses force unsparingly, without reference to the quantity of bloodshed, must obtain a superiority if his adversary does not act likewise. By such means the former dictates the law to the latter, and both proceed to extremities, to which the only limitations are those imposed by the amount of counteracting force on each side.

This is the way in which the matter must be viewed; and it is to no purpose, and even acting against one's own interest, to turn away from the consideration of the real nature of the affair, because the coarseness of its elements excites repugnance.

If the wars of civilised people are less cruel and destructive than those of savages, the difference arises from the social condition both of states in themselves and in their relations to each other. Out of this social condition and its relations war arises, and by it war is subjected to conditions, is controlled and modified. But these things do not belong to war itself; they are only given conditions; and to introduce into the philosophy of war itself a principle of moderation would be an absurdity.

The fight between men consists really of two different elements, the hostile *feeling* and the hostile *view*. In our definition of war, we have chosen as its characteristic the latter of these elements, because it is the most general. It is impossible to conceive the passion of hatred of the wildest description, bordering on mere instinct, without combining with it the idea of a hostile intention. On the other hand, hostile intentions may often exist without being accompanied by any, or at all events, by any extreme hostility of feeling. Amongst savages views emanating from the feelings, amongst civilised nations those emanating from the understanding, have the predominance; but this difference is not inherent in a state of barbarism, and in a state of culture in themselves it arises from attendant circumstances, existing institutions, etc., and therefore is not to be found necessarily in all cases, although it prevails in the majority. In short, even the most civilised nations may burn with passionate hatred of each other.

We may see from this what a fallacy it would be to refer the war of a civilised nation entirely to an intelligent act on the part of the Government, and to imagine it as continually freeing itself more and more from all feeling of passion in such a way that at last the physical masses of combatants would no longer be required; in reality, their mere relations would suffice—a kind of algebraic action.

Theory was beginning to drift in this direction until the facts of the last war taught it better. If war is an *act* of force, it belongs necessarily also to the feelings. If it does not originate in the feelings, it re-acts more or less upon them, and this more or less depends not on the degree of civilisation, but upon the importance and duration of the interests involved.

Therefore, if we find civilised nations do not put their prisoners to death, do not devastate towns and countries, this is because their intelligence exercises greater influence on their mode of carrying on war, and has taught them more effectual means of applying force than these rude acts of mere instinct. The invention of gunpowder, the constant progress of improvements in the construction of firearms are sufficient proofs that the tendency to destroy the adversary which lies at the bottom of the conception of war, is in no way changed or modified through the progress of civilisation.

We therefore repeat our proposition, that war is an act of violence, which in its application knows no bounds; as one dictates the law to the other, there arises a sort of reciprocal action, which in the conception, must lead to an extreme. This is the first reciprocal action, and the first extreme with which we meet (*first reciprocal action*).

4. THE AIM IS TO DISARM THE ENEMY

We have already said that the aim of the action in war is to disarm the enemy, and we shall now show that this in theoretical conception at least is necessary.

If our opponent is to be made to comply with our will, we must place him in a situation which is more oppressive to him than the sacrifice which we demand; but the disadvantages of this position must naturally not be of a transitory nature, at least in appearance, otherwise the enemy, instead of yielding, will hold out, in the prospect of a change for the better. Every change in this position which is produced by a continuation of the war, should therefore be a change for the worse, at least, in idea. The worst position in which a belligerent can be placed is that of being completely disarmed. If, therefore, the enemy is to be reduced to submission by an act of war, he must either be positively disarmed or placed in such a position that he is threatened with it according to probability. From this it follows that the disarming or overthrow of the enemy, whichever we call it, must always be the aim of warfare. Now war is always the shock of two hostile bodies in collision, not the action of a living power upon an inanimate mass, because an absolute state of endurance would not be making war; therefore what we have just said as to the aim of action in war applies to both parties. Here then is another case of reciprocal action. As long as the enemy is not defeated, I have to apprehend that he may defeat me, then I shall be no longer my own master, but he will dictate the law to me as I did to him. This is the second reciprocal action and leads to a second extreme (*second reciprocal action*).

5. UTMOST EXERTION OF POWERS

If we desire to defeat the enemy, we must proportion our efforts to his powers of resistance. This is expressed by the product of two factors which cannot be separated, namely, *the sum of available means* and *the strength of the will*. The sum of the available means may be estimated in a measure, as it depends (although not entirely) upon numbers; but the strength of volition, is more difficult to determine, and can only be estimated to a certain extent by the strength of the motives. Granted we have obtained in this way an approximation to the strength of the power to be contended with, we can then take a review of our own means, and either increase them so as to obtain a preponderance, or in case we have not the resources to effect this, then do our best by increasing our means as far as possible. But the adversary does the same; therefore there is a new mutual enhancement, which in pure conception, must create a fresh effort towards an extreme. This is the third case of reciprocal action, and a third extreme with which we meet (*third reciprocal action*).

6. MODIFICATION IN THE REALITY

Thus reasoning in the abstract, the mind cannot stop short of an extreme, because it has to deal with an extreme, with a conflict of forces left to themselves, and obeying no other but their own inner laws. If we should seek to deduce from the pure conception of war an absolute point for the aim which we shall propose and for the means which we shall apply, this constant reciprocal action would involve us in extremes, which would be nothing but a play of ideas produced by an almost invisible train of logical subtleties. If adhering closely to the absolute, we try to avoid all difficulties by a stroke of the pen, and insist with logical strictness that in every case the extreme must be the object, and the utmost effort must be exerted in that direction, such a stroke of the pen would be a mere paper law, not by any means adapted to the real world.

Even supposing this extreme tension of forces was an absolute which could easily be ascertained, still we must admit that the human mind would hardly submit itself to this kind of logical chimera. There would be in many cases an unnecessary waste of power, which would be in opposition to other principles of statecraft; an effort of will would be required disproportioned to the proposed object, and which therefore it would be impossible to realise, for the human will does not derive its impulse from logical subtleties.

But everything takes a different form when we pass from abstractions to reality. In the former everything must be subject to optimism, and we must imagine the one side as well as the other, striving after perfection and even attaining it. Will this ever take place in reality? It will if

1. War becomes a completely isolated act, which arises suddenly and is in no way connected with the previous history of the states;

2. If it is limited to a single solution, or to several simultaneous solutions;

3. If it contains within itself the solution perfect and complete, free from any reaction upon it, through a calculation beforehand of the political situation which will follow from it.

7. WAR IS NEVER AN ISOLATED ACT

With regard to the first point, neither of the two opponents is an abstract person to the other, not even as regards that factor in the sum of resistance, which does not depend on objective things, viz., the will. This will is not an entirely unknown quantity; it indicates what it will be to-morrow by what it is to-day. War does not spring up quite suddenly, it does not spread to the full in a moment; each of the two opponents can, therefore, form an opinion of the other, in a great measure, from what he is and what he does; instead of judging of him according to what he, strictly speaking, should be or should do. But, now, man with his incomplete organisation is always below the line of absolute perfection, and thus these deficiencies, having an influence on both sides, become a modifying principle.

8. IT DOES NOT CONSIST OF A SINGLE INSTANTANEOUS BLOW

The second point gives rise to the following considerations:—

If war ended in a single solution, or a number of simultaneous ones, then naturally all the preparations for the same would have a tendency to the extreme, for an omission could not in any way be repaired; the utmost, then, that the world of reality could furnish as a guide for us would be the preparations of the enemy, as far as they are known to us; all the rest would fall into the domain of the abstract. But if the result is made up from several successive acts, then naturally that which precedes with all its phases may be taken as a measure for that which will follow, and in this manner the world of reality here again takes the place of the abstract, and thus modifies the effort towards the extreme.

Yet every war would necessarily resolve itself into a single solution, or a sum of simultaneous results, if all the means required for the struggle were raised at once, or could be at once raised; for as one adverse result necessarily diminishes the means, then if all the means have been applied in the first, a second cannot properly be supposed. All hostile acts which might follow would belong essentially to the first, and form in reality only its duration.

But we have already seen that even in the preparation for war the real world steps into the place of mere abstract conception—a material standard into the place of the hypotheses of an extreme: that therefore in that way both parties, by the influence of the mutual reaction, reamin below the line of extreme effort, and therefore all forces are not at once brought forward.

It lies also in the nature of these forces and their application, that they cannot all be brought into activity at the same time. These forces are *the armies actually on foot, the country,* with its superficial extent and its population, *and the allies.*

In point of fact the country, with its superficial area and the population, besides being the source of all military force, constitutes in itself an integral part of the efficient quantities in war, providing either the theatre of war or exercising a considerable influence on the same.

Now it is possible to bring all the moveable military forces of a country into operation at once, but not all fortresses, rivers, mountains, people, etc., in short not the whole country, unless it is so small that it may be completely embraced by the first act of the war. Further, the co-operation of allies does not depend on the will of the belligerents; and from the nature of the political relations of states to each other, this co-operation is frequently not afforded until after the war has commenced, or it may be increased to restore the balance of power.

That this part of the means of resistance, which cannot at once be brought into activity, in many cases is a much greater part of the whole than might at first be supposed, and that it often restores the balance of power, seriously affected by the great force of the first decision, will be more fully shown hereafter. Here it is sufficient to show that a complete concentration of all available means in a moment of time, is contradictory to the nature of war.

Now this, in itself, furnishes no ground for relaxing our efforts to accumulate strength to gain the first result, because an unfavourable issue is always a disadvantage to which no one would purposely expose himself, and also because the first decision, although not the only one, still will have the more influence on subsequent events, the greater it is itself.

But the possibility of gaining a later result causes men to take refuge in that expectation owing to the repugnance, in the human mind, to making excessive efforts; and therefore forces are not concentrated and measures are not taken for the first decision with that energy which would otherwise be used. Whatever one belligerent omits from weakness, becomes to the other a real objective ground for limiting his own efforts, and thus again, through this reciprocal action, extreme tendencies are brought down to efforts on a limited scale.

9. THE RESULT IN WAR IS NEVER ABSOLUTE

Lastly, even the final decision of a whole war is not always to be regarded as absolute. The conquered state often sees in it only a passing evil, which may be repaired in after times by means of political combinations. How much this also must modify the degree of tension and the vigour of the efforts made is evident in itself.

10. THE PROBABILITIES OF REAL LIFE TAKE THE PLACE OF THE CONCEPTIONS OF THE EXTREME AND THE ABSOLUTE

In this manner the whole act of war is removed from under the rigorous law of forces exerted to the utmost. If the extreme is no longer to be apprehended, and no longer to be sought for, it is left to the judgment to determine the limits for the efforts to be made in place of it; and this can only be done on the data furnished by the facts of the real world by the *laws of probability*. Once the belligerents are no longer mere conceptions but individual states and governments, once the war is no longer an ideal, but a definite substantial procedure, then the reality will furnish the data to compute the unknown quantities which are required to be found.

From the character, the measures, the situation of the adversary, and the relations with which he is surrounded, each side will draw conclusions by the law of probability as to the designs of the other, and act accordingly.

11. THE POLITICAL OBJECT NOW REAPPEARS

Here, now, forces itself again into consideration a question which we had laid aside (see No. 2), that is, *the political object of the war*. The law of the extreme, the view to disarm the adversary, to overthrow him, has hitherto to a certain extent usurped the place of this end or object. Just as this law loses its force, the political object must again come forward. If the whole consideration is a calculation of probability based on definite persons and relations, then the political object, being the original motive, must be an essential factor in the product. The smaller the sacrifice we demand from our opponent, the smaller it may be expected will be the means of resistance which he will employ; but the smaller his are, the smaller will ours require to be. Further, the smaller our political object, the less value shall we set upon it, and the more easily shall we be induced to give it up altogether.

Thus, therefore, the political object, as the original motive of the war, will be the standard for determining both the aim of the military force, and also the amount of effort to be made. This it cannot be in itself; but it is so in relation to both the belligerent states, because we are concerned with realities, not with mere abstractions. One and the same political object may produce totally different effects upon different people, or even upon the same people at different times; we can, therefore, only admit the political object as the measure, by considering it in its effects upon those masses which it is to move, and consequently the nature of those masses also comes into consideration. It is easy to see that thus the result may be very different according as these masses are animated with a spirit which will infuse vigour into the action or otherwise. It is quite possible for such a state of feeling to exist between two states that a very trifling political motive for war may produce an effect quite disproportionate, in fact, a perfect explosion.

This applies to the efforts which the political object will call forth in the two states, and to the aim which the military action shall prescribe for itself. At times it may itself be that aim, as for example the conquest of a province. At other times, the political object itself is not suitable for the aim of military action; then such a one must be chosen as will be an equivalent for it, and stand in its place as regards the conclusion of peace. But, also, in this, due attention to the peculiar character of the states concerned is always supposed. There are circumstances in which the equivalent must be much greater than the political object in order to secure the latter. The political object will be so much the more the standard of aim and effort, and have more influence in itself, the more the masses are indifferent, the less that any mutual feeling of hostility prevails in the two states from other causes, and, therefore, there are cases where the political object almost alone will be decisive.

If the aim of the military action is an equivalent for the political object, that action will in general diminish as the political object diminishes, and that in a greater degree the more the political object dominates; and so is explained how, without any contradiction in itself, there may be wars of all degrees of importance and energy, from a war of extermination, down to the mere use of an army of observation. This, however, leads to a question of another kind which we have hereafter to develop and answer.

12. A SUSPENSION IN THE ACTION OF WAR
UNEXPLAINED BY ANYTHING SAID AS YET

However insignificant the political claims mutually advanced, however weak the means put forth, however small the aim to which military action is directed, can this action be suspended even for a moment? This is a question which penetrates deeply into the nature of the subject.

Every transaction requires for its accomplishment a certain time which we call its duration. This may be longer or shorter, according as the person acting throws more or less despatch into his movements.

About this more or less we shall not trouble ourselves here. Each person acts in his own fashion; but the slow person does not protract the thing because he wishes to spend more time about it, but because, by his nature, he requires more time, and if he made more haste, would not do the thing so well. This time, therefore, depends on subjective causes, and belongs to the length, so-called, of the action.

If we allow now to every action in war this, its length, then we must assume, at first sight at least, that any expenditure of time beyond this length, that is, every suspension of hostile action appears an absurdity; with respect to this it must not be forgotten that we now speak not of the progress of one or other of the two opponents, but of the general progress of the whole action of the war.

13. THERE IS ONLY ONE CAUSE WHICH CAN SUSPEND THE ACTION, AND THIS SEEMS TO BE ONLY POSSIBLE ON ONE SIDE IN ANY CASE

If two parties have armed themselves for strife, then a feeling of animosity must have moved them to it; as long now as they continue armed, that is do not come to terms of peace, this feeling must exist; and it can only be brought to a standstill by either side by one single motive alone, which is, *that he waits for a more favourable moment for action.* Now at first sight it appears that this motive can never exist except on one side, because it, *eo ipso,* must be prejudicial to the other. If the one has an interest in acting, then the other must have an interest in waiting.

A complete equilibrium of forces can never produce a suspension of action, for during this suspension he who has the positive object (that is the assailant) must continue progressing; for if we should imagine an equilibrium in this way, that he who has the positive object, therefore the strongest motive, can at the same time only command the lesser means, so that the equation is made up by the product of the motive and the power, then we must say, if no alteration in this condition of equilibrium is to be expected, the two parties must make peace; but if an alteration is to be expected, then it can only be favourable to one side, and therefore the other has a manifest interest to act without delay. We see that the conception of an equilibrium cannot explain a suspension of arms, but that it ends in the question of the *expectation of a more favourable moment.*

Let us suppose, therefore, that one of two states has a positive object, as, for instance, the conquest of one of the enemy's provinces—which is to be utilised in the settlement of peace. After this conquest his political object is accomplished, the necessity for action ceases, and for him a pause ensues. If the adversary is also contented with this solution he will make peace, if not he must act. Now, if we suppose that in four weeks he will be in a better condition to act, then he has sufficient grounds for putting off the time of action.

But from that moment the logical course for the enemy appears to be to act that he may not give the conquered party *the desired* time. Of course, in this mode of reasoning a complete insight into the state of circumstances on both sides, is supposed.

14. THUS A CONTINUANCE OF ACTION WILL ENSUE WHICH WILL ADVANCE TOWARDS A CLIMAX

If this unbroken continuity of hostile operations really existed, the effect would be that everything would again be driven towards the extreme; for irrespective of the effect of such incessant activity in inflaming the feelings and infusing into the whole a greater degree of passion, a greater elementary force, there would also follow from this continuance of action, a stricter continuity, a closer connection between cause and effect, and thus every single action would become of more importance, and consequently more replete with danger.

But we know that the course of action in war has seldom or never this unbroken continuity, and that there have been many wars in which action occupied by far the smallest portion of time employed, the whole of the rest being consumed in inaction. It is impossible that this should be always an anomaly, and suspension of action in war must be possible, that is no contradiction in itself. We now proceed to show this, and how it is.

15. HERE, THEREFORE, THE PRINCIPLE OF POLARITY IS BROUGHT INTO REQUISITION

As we have supposed the interests of one commander to be always antagonistic to those of the other, we have assumed a true *polarity*. We reserve a fuller explanation of this for another chapter, merely making the following observation on it at present.

The principle of polarity is only valid when it can be conceived in one and the same thing, where the positive and its opposite the negative, completely destroy each other. In a battle both sides strive to conquer; that is true polarity, for the victory of the one side destroys that of the other. But when we speak of two different things, which have a common relation external to themselves, then it is not the things but their relations which have the polarity.

16. ATTACK AND DEFENCE ARE THINGS DIFFERING IN KIND AND OF UNEQUAL FORCE. POLARITY IS, THEREFORE, NOT APPLICABLE TO THEM

If there was only one form of war, to wit the attack of the enemy, therefore no defence; or in other words, if the attack was distinguished from the defence merely by the positive motive, which the one has and the other has not, but the fight precisely one and the same: then in this sort of fight every advantage gained on the one side would be a corresponding disadvantage on the other, and true polarity would exist.

But action in war is divided into two forms, attack and defence, which, as we shall hereafter explain more particularly, are very different and of unequal strength. Polarity, therefore, lies in that to which both bear a relation, in the decision, but not in the attack or defence itself.

If the one commander wishes the solution put off, the other must wish to hasten it; but certainly only in the same form of combat. If it is A's interest not to attack his enemy at present but four weeks hence, then it is B's interest to be attacked, not four weeks hence, but at the present moment. This is the direct antagonism of interests, but it by no means follows that it would be for B's interest to attack A at once. That is plainly something totally different.

17. THE EFFECT OF POLARITY IS OFTEN DESTROYED BY THE SUPERIORITY OF THE DEFENCE OVER THE ATTACK, AND THUS THE SUSPENSION OF ACTION IN WAR IS EXPLAINED

If the form of defence is stronger than that of offence, as we shall hereafter show, the question arises, Is the advantage of a deferred decision as great on the one side as the advantage of the defensive form on the other? If it is not, then it cannot by its counter-weight overbalance the latter, and thus influence the progress of the action of the war. We see, therefore, that the impulsive force existing in the polarity of interests may be lost in the difference between the strength of the offensive and defensive, and thereby become ineffectual.

If, therefore, that side for which the present is favourable is too weak to be able to dispense with the advantage of the defensive, he must put up with the unfavourable prospects which the future holds out; for it may still be better to fight a defensive battle in the unpromising future than to assume the offensive or make peace at present. Now, being convinced that the superiority of the defensive (rightly understood) is very great, and much greater than may appear at first sight, we conceive that the greater number of those periods of inaction which occur in war are thus explained without involving any contradiction. The weaker the motives to action are, the more will those motives be absorbed and neutralised by this difference between attack and defence, the more frequently, therefore, will action in warfare be stopped, as indeed experience teaches.

18. A SECOND GROUND CONSISTS IN THE IMPERFECT
KNOWLEDGE OF CIRCUMSTANCES

But there is still another cause which may stop action in war, that is an incomplete view of the situation. Each commander can only fully know his own position; that of his opponent can only be known to him by reports, which are uncertain; he may, therefore, form a wrong judgment with respect to it upon data of this description, and, in consequence of that error, he may suppose that the initiative is properly with his adversary when it is really with himself. This want of perfect insight might certainly just as often occasion an untimely action as untimely inaction, and so it would in itself no more contribute to delay than to accelerate action in war. Still, it must always be regarded as one of the natural causes which may bring action in war to a standstill without involving a contradiction. But if we reflect how much more we are inclined and induced to estimate the power of our opponents too high than too low, because it lies in human nature to do so, we shall admit that our imperfect insight into facts in general must contribute very much to stop action in war, and to modify the principle of action.

The possibility of a standstill brings into the action of war a new modification, inasmuch as it dilutes that action with the element of Time, checks the influence or sense of danger in its course, and increases the means of reinstating a lost balance of force. The greater the tension of feelings from which the war springs, the greater, therefore, the energy with which it is carried on, so much the shorter will be the periods of inaction; on the other hand, the weaker the principle of warlike activity, the longer will be these periods: for powerful motives increase the force of the will, and this, as we know, is always a factor in the product of force.

19. FREQUENT PERIODS OF INACTION IN WAR REMOVE
IT FURTHER FROM THE ABSOLUTE, AND MAKE IT STILL
MORE A CALCULATION OF PROBABILITIES

But the slower the action proceeds in war, the more frequent and longer the periods of inaction, so much the more easily can an error be repaired; therefore so much the bolder a general will be in his calculations, so much the more readily will he keep them below the line of absolute, and build everything upon probabilities and conjecture. Thus, according as the course of the war is more or less slow, more or less time will be allowed for that which the nature of a concrete case particularly requires, calculation of probability based on given circumstances.

20. IT THEREFORE NOW ONLY WANTS THE ELEMENT OF CHANCE TO MAKE OF IT A GAME, AND IN THAT ELEMENT IT IS LEAST OF ALL DEFICIENT

We see from the foregoing how much the objective nature of war makes it a calculation of probabilities; now there is only one single element still wanting to make it a game, and that element it certainly is not without: it is chance. There is no human affair which stands so constantly and so generally in close connection with chance as war. But along with chance, the accidental, and along with it good luck, occupy a great place in war.

21. AS WAR IS A GAME THROUGH ITS OBJECTIVE NATURE, SO ALSO IS IT THROUGH ITS SUBJECTIVE

If we now take a look at the *subjective nature* of war, that is at those powers with which it is carried on, it will appear to us still more like a game. The element in which the operations of war are carried on is danger; but which of all the moral qualities is the first in danger? *Courage.* Now certainly courage is quite compatible with prudent calculation, but still they are things of quite a different kind, essentially different qualities of the mind; on the other hand, daring reliance on good fortune, boldness, rashness, are only expressions of courage, and all these propensities of the mind look for the fortuitous (or accidental), because it is their element.

We see therefore how from the commencement, the absolute, the mathematical as it is called, no where finds any sure basis in the calculations in the art of war; and that from the outset there is a play of possibilities, probabilities, good and bad luck, which spreads about with all the coarse and fine threads of its web, and makes war of all branches of human activity the most like a game of cards.

22. HOW THIS ACCORDS BEST WITH THE HUMAN MIND IN GENERAL

Although our intellect always feels itself urged towards clearness and certainty, still our mind often feels itself attracted by uncertainty. Instead of threading its way with the understanding along the narrow path of philosophical investigations and logical conclusions, in order almost unconscious of itself, to arrive in spaces where it feels itself a stranger, and where it seems to part from all well known objects, it prefers to remain with the imagination in the realms of chance and luck. Instead of living yonder on poor necessity, it revels here in the wealth of possibilities; animated thereby, courage then takes wings to itself, and daring and danger make the element into which it launches itself, as a fearless swimmer plunges into the stream.

Shall theory leave it here, and move on, self satisfied with absolute conclusions and rules? Then it is of no practical use. Theory must also take into account the human element; it must accord a place to courage, to boldness, even to rashness. The art of war has to deal with living and with moral forces; the consequence of which is that it can never attain the absolute and positive. There is therefore everywhere a margin for the accidental; and just as much in the greatest things as in the smallest. As there is room for this accidental on the one hand, so on the other there must be courage and self-reliance in proportion to the room left. If these qualities are forthcoming in a high degree, the margin left may likewise be great. Courage and self reliance are therefore principles quite essential to war; consequently theory must only set up such rules as allow ample scope for all degrees and varieties of these necessary and noblest of military virtues. In daring there may still be wisdom also, and prudence as well, only that they are estimated by a different standard of value.

23. WAR IS ALWAYS A SERIOUS MEANS FOR A SERIOUS OBJECT. ITS MORE PARTICULAR DEFINITION

Such is war; such the commander who conducts it; such the theory which rules it. But war is no pastime; no mere passion for venturing and winning; no work of a free enthusiasm; it is a serious means for a serious object. All that appearance which it wears from the varying hues of fortune, all that it assimilates into itself of the oscillations of passion, of courage, of imagination, of enthusiasm, are only particular properties of this means.

The war of a community—of whole nations and particularly of civilised nations—always starts from a political condition, and is called forth by a political motive. It is therefore a political act. Now if it was a perfect, unrestrained and absolute expression of force, as we had to deduce it from its mere conception, then the moment it is called forth by policy it would step into the place of policy, and as something quite independent of it would set it aside, and only follow its own laws, just as a mine at the moment of explosion cannot be guided into any other direction than that which has been given to it by preparatory arrangements. This is how the thing has really been viewed hitherto, whenever a want of harmony between policy and the conduct of a war has led to theoretical distinctions of the kind. But it is not so, and the idea is radically false. War in the real world, as we have already seen, is not an extreme thing which expends itself at one single discharge; it is the operation of powers which do not develop themselves completely in the same manner and in the same mea-

sure, but which at one time expand sufficiently to overcome the resistance opposed by inertia or friction, while at another they are too weak to produce an
effect; it is therefore, in a certain measure, a pulsation of violent force more or
less vehement, consequently making its discharges and exhausting its powers
more or less quickly, in other words conducting more or less quickly to the
aim, but always lasting long enough to admit of influence being exerted on it
in its course, so as to give it this or that direction, in short to be subject to the
will of a guiding intelligence. Now if we reflect that war has its root in a political object, then naturally this original motive which called it into existence
should also continue the first and highest consideration in the conduct of it.
Still the political object is not despotic lawgiver on that account; it must accommodate itself to the nature of the means, and through that is often completely changed, but it always remains that which has a prior right to consideration. Policy therefore is interwoven with the whole action of war, and must
exercise a continuous influence upon it as far as the nature of the forces
exploding in it will permit.

24. WAR IS A MERE CONTINUATION OF POLICY BY OTHER MEANS

We see, therefore, that war is not merely a political act, but also a real political instrument, a continuation of political commerce, a carrying out of the
same by other means. All beyond this which is strictly peculiar to war relates
merely to the peculiar nature of the means which it uses. That the tendencies
and views of policy shall not be incompatible with these means, the art of war
in general and the commander in each particular case may demand, and this
claim is truly not a trifling one. But however powerfully this may react on political views in particular cases, still it must always be regarded as only a modification of them; for the political view is the object, war is the means, and the
means must always include the object in our conception.

25. DIVERSITY IN THE NATURE OF WARS

The greater and more powerful the motives of a war, the more it affects the
whole existence of a people, the more violent the excitement which precedes
the war, by so much the nearer will the war approach to its abstract form, so
much the more will it be directed to the destruction of the enemy, so much
the nearer will the military and political ends coincide, so much the more
purely military and less political the war appears to be; but the weaker the motives and the tensions, so much the less will the natural direction of the military element—that is, force—be coincident with the direction which the po-

litical element indicates; so much the more must therefore the war become diverted from its natural direction, the political object diverge from the aim of an ideal war, and the war appear to become political.

But that the reader may not form any false conceptions, we must here observe that, but this natural tendency of war, we only mean the philosophical, the strictly logical, and by no means the tendency of forces actually engaged in conflict, by which would be supposed to be included all the emotions and passions of the combatants. No doubt in some cases these also might be excited to such a degree as to be with difficulty restrained and confined to the political road; but in most cases such a contradiction will not arise, because, by the existence of such strenuous exertions a great plan in harmony therewith would be implied. If the plan is directed only upon a small object, then the impulses of feeling amongst the masses will be also so weak, that these masses will require to be stimulated rather than repressed.

26. THEY MAY ALL BE REGARDED AS POLITICAL ACTS

Returning now to the main subject, although it is true that in one kind of war the political element seems almost to disappear, whilst in another kind it occupies a very prominent place, we may still affirm that the one is as political as the other; for if we regard the state policy as the intelligence of the personified state, then amongst all the constellations in the political sky which it has to compute, those must be included which arise when the nature of its relations imposes the necessity of a great war. It is only if we understand by policy not a true appreciation of affairs in general, but the conventional conception of a cautious, subtle, also dishonest craftiness, averse from violence, that the latter kind of war may belong more to policy than the first.

27. INFLUENCE OF THIS VIEW ON THE RIGHT UNDERSTANDING OF MILITARY HISTORY, AND ON THE FOUNDATIONS OF THEORY

We see, therefore, in the first place, that under all circumstances war is to be regarded not as an independent thing, but as a political instrument; and it is only by taking this point of view that we can avoid finding ourselves in opposition to all military history. This is the only means of unlocking the great book and making it intelligible. Secondly, just this view shows us how wars must differ in character according to the nature of the motives and circumstances from which they proceed.

Now, the first, the grandest, and most decisive act of judgment which the statesman and general exercises is rightly to understand in this respect the war in which he engages, not to take it for something, or to wish to make of it something which, by the nature of its relations, it is impossible for it to be. This is, therefore, the first, the most comprehensive of all strategical questions. We shall enter into this more fully in treating of the plan of a war.

For the present we content ourselves with having brought the subject up to this point, and having thereby fixed the chief point of view from which war and its theory are to be studied.

28. RESULT FOR THEORY

War is, therefore, not only a true chameleon, because it changes its nature in some degree in each particular case, but it is also, as a whole, in relation to the predominant tendencies which are in it, a wonderful trinity, composed of the original violence of its elements, hatred and animosity, which may be looked upon as blind instinct; of the play of probabilities and chance, which make it a free activity of the soul; and of the subordinate nature of a political instrument, by which it belongs purely to the reason.

The first of these three phases concerns more the people; the second more the general and his army; the third more the Government. The passions which break forth in war must already have a latent existence in the peoples. The range which the display of courage and talents shall get in the realm of probabilities and of chance depends on the particular characteristics of the general and his army; but the political objects belong to the Government alone.

These three tendencies, which appear like so many different lawgivers, are deeply rooted in the nature of the subject, and at the same time variable in degree. A theory which would leave any one of them out of account, or set up any arbitrary relation between them, would immediately become involved in such a contradiction with the reality, that it might be regarded as destroyed at once by that alone.

The problem is, therefore, that theory shall keep itself poised in a manner between these three tendencies, as between three points of attraction.

The way in which alone this difficult problem can be solved we shall examine in the book on the "Theory of War." In every case the conception of war, as here defined, will be the first ray of light which shows us the true foundation of theory, and which first separates the great masses, and allows us to distinguish them from one another.

End and Means in War

Having in the foregoing chapter ascertained the complicated and variable nature of war, we shall now occupy ourselves in examining into the influence which this nature has upon the end and means in war.

If we ask first of all for the aim upon which the whole war is to be directed, in order that it may be the right means for the attainment of the political object, we shall find that it is just as variable as are the political object and the particular circumstances of the war.

If, in the next place, we keep once more to the pure conception of war, then we must say that its political object properly lies out of its province, for if war is an act of violence to compel the enemy to fulfil our will, then in every case all depends on our overthrowing the enemy, that is, disarming him, and on that alone. This object, developed from abstract conceptions, but which is also the one aimed at in a great many cases in reality, we shall, in the first place, examine in this reality.

In connection with the plan of a campaign we shall hereafter examine more closely into the meaning of disarming a nation, but here we must at once draw a distinction between three things, which as three general objects comprise everything else within them. They are the *military power, the country,* and *the will of the enemy.*

The *military power* must be destroyed, that is, reduced to such a state as not to be able to prosecute the war. This is the sense in which we wish to be understood hereafter, whenever we use the expression "destruction of the enemy's military power."

The *country* must be conquered, for out of the country a new military force may be formed.

But if even both these things are done, still the war, that is, the hostile feeling and action of hostile agencies, cannot be considered as at an end as long as the *will* of the enemy is not subdued also; that is, its Government and its allies forced into signing a peace, or the people into submission; for whilst we are in full occupation of the country the war may break out afresh, either in the interior or through assistance given by allies. No doubt this may also take place after a peace, but that shows nothing more than that every war does not carry in itself the elements for a complete decision and final settlement.

But even if this is the case, still with the conclusion of peace a number of sparks are always extinguished, which would have smouldered on quietly, and the excitement of the passions abates, because all those whose minds are disposed to peace, of which in all nations and under all circumstances, there is always a great number, turn themselves away completely from the road to resistance. Whatever may take place subsequently, we must always look upon the object as attained, and the business of war as ended, by a peace.

As protection of the country is that one of these objects to which the military force is destined, therefore the natural order is that first of all this force should be destroyed; then the country subdued; and through the effect of these two results, as well as the position we then hold, the enemy should be forced to make peace. Generally the destruction of the enemy's force is done by degrees, and in just the same measure the conquest of the country follows immediately. The two likewise usually react upon each other, because the loss of provinces occasions a diminution of military force. But this order is by no means necessary, and on that account it also does not always take place. The enemy's army, before it is sensibly weakened, may retreat to the opposite side of the country, or even quite out of the country. In this case, therefore, the greater part or the whole of the country is conquered.

But this object of war in the abstract, this final means of attaining the political object in which all others are combined, the *disarming the enemy*, is by no means general in reality, is not a condition necessary to peace, and therefore can in no wise be set up in theory as a law. There are innumerable instances of treaties in which peace has been settled before either party could be looked upon as disarmed; indeed, even before the balance had undergone any sensible alteration. Nay, further, if we look at the case in the concrete, then we must say that in a whole class of cases the idea of a complete defeat of the enemy would be a mere imaginative flight, especially if the enemy is considerably superior.

The reason why the object deduced from the conception of war is not adapted in general to real war, lies in the difference between the two, which is discussed in the preceding chapter. If it was as pure conception gives it, then a war between two states of very unequal military strength would appear an absurdity; therefore would be impossible. At most, the inequality between the physical forces might be such that it could be balanced by the moral forces, and that would not go far with our present social condition in Europe. Therefore, if we have seen wars take place between states of very unequal power, that has been the case because there is a wide difference between war in reality and its original conception.

There are two considerations, which as motives, may practically take the place of inability to continue the contest. The first is the improbability, the second is the excessive price of success.

According to what we have seen in the foregoing chapter, war must always set itself free from the strict law of logical necessity, and seek aid from the calculation of probabilities: and as this is so much the more the case, the more the war has a bias that way, from the circumstances out of which it has arisen—the smaller its motives are and the excitement it has raised—so it is also conceivable how out of this calculation of probabilities even motives to peace may arise. War does not therefore always require to be fought out until one party is overthrown; and we may suppose that, when the motives and passions are slight, a weak probability will suffice to move that side to which it is unfavourable to give way. Now, were the other side convinced of this beforehand, it is natural that he would strive for this probability only instead of first trying and making the detour of a total destruction of the enemy's army.

Still more general in its influence on the resolution to peace is the consideration of the expenditure of force already made, and further required. As war is no act of blind passion, but is dominated over by the political object, therefore the value of that object determines the measure of the sacrifices by which it is to be purchased. This will be the case, not only as regards extent, but also as regards duration. As soon, therefore, as the required outlay becomes so great that the political object is no longer equal in value, the object must be given up, and peace will be the result.

We see, therefore, that in wars where one cannot completely disarm the other, the motives to peace on both sides will rise or fall on each side according to the probability of future success and the required outlay. If these motives were equally strong on both sides, they would meet in the centre of their political difference. Where they are strong on one side, they might be weak on the other. If their amount is only sufficient, peace will follow, but naturally to the advantage of that side which has the weakest motive for its conclusion. We purposely pass over here the difference which the *positive* and *negative* character of the political end must necessarily produce practically; for although that is, as we shall hereafter show, of the highest importance, still we are obliged to keep here to a more general point of view, because the original political views in the course of the war change very much, and at last may become totally different, *just because they are determined by results and probable events.*

Now comes the question how to influence the probability of success. In the first place, naturally by the same means which we use when the object is the subjugation of the enemy, by the destruction of his military force and the conquest of his provinces; but these two means are not exactly of the same import here as they would be in reference to that object. If we attack the enemy's army, it is a very different thing whether we intend to follow up the first blow with a succession of others until the whole force is destroyed, or whether we mean to content ourselves with a victory to shake the enemy's feeling of security, to convince him of our superiority, and to instil into him a feeling of apprehension about the future. If this is our object, we only go so far in the destruction of his forces as is sufficient. In like manner the conquest of the enemy's provinces is quite a different measure if the object is not the destruction of the enemy's army. In the latter case, the destruction of the army is the real effectual action, and the taking of the provinces only a consequence of it; to take them before the army had been defeated would always be looked upon only as a necessary evil. On the other hand, if our views are not directed upon the complete destruction of the enemy's force, and if we are sure that the enemy does not seek but fears to bring matters to a bloody decision, the taking possession of a weak or defenceless province is an advantage in itself, and if this advantage is of sufficient importance to make the enemy apprehensive about the general result, then it may also be regarded as a shorter road to peace.

But now we come upon a peculiar means of influencing the probability of the result without destroying the enemy's army, namely, upon the expeditions which have a direct connection with political views. If there are any enterprises which are particularly likely to break up the enemy's alliances or make them inoperative, to gain new alliances for ourselves, to raise political powers in our own favour, etc., etc., then it is easy to conceive how much these may increase the probability of success, and become a shorter way towards our aim than the routing of the enemy's army.

The second question is how to act upon the enemy's expenditure in strength, that is, to raise the price of success.

The enemy's outlay in strength lies in the *wear and tear* of his forces, consequently in the *destruction* of them on our part, and in the *loss* of *provinces*, consequently the *conquest* of them by us.

Here again, on account of the various significations of these means, so likewise it will be found that neither of them will be identical in its signification, in all cases if the objects are different. The smallness in general of this difference must not cause us perplexity, for in reality the weakest motives, the finest shades of difference, often decide in favour of this or that method of applying force. Our only business here is to show that certain conditions being supposed, the possibility of attaining the aim in different ways is no contradiction, absurdity, nor even error.

Besides these two means there are three other peculiar ways of directly increasing the waste of the enemy's force. The first is *invasion,* that is *the occupation of the enemy's territory, not with a view to keeping it,* but in order to levy contributions there, or to devastate it. The immediate object is here neither the conquest of the enemy's territory nor the defeat of his armed force, but merely to *do him damage in a general way.* The second way is to select for the object of our enterprises those points at which we can do the enemy most harm. Nothing is easier to conceive than two different directions in which our force may be employed, the first of which is to be preferred if our object is to defeat the enemy's army, while the other is more advantageous if the defeat of the enemy is out of the question. According to the usual mode of speaking we should say that the first is more military, the other more political. But if we take our view from the highest point, both are equally military, and neither the one nor the other can be eligible unless it suits the circumstances of the case. The third, by far the most important, from the great number of cases which it embraces, is the *wearying out* the enemy. We choose this expression not only to explain our meaning in few words but because it represents the thing exactly, and is not so figurative as may at first appear. The idea of wearying out in a struggle amounts in reality to *a gradual exhaustion of the physical powers and of the will produced through the long continuance of exertion.*

Now if we want to overcome the enemy by the duration of the contest we must content ourselves with as small objects as possible, for it is in the nature of the thing that a great end requires a greater expenditure of force than a small one; but the smallest object that we can propose to ourselves is simple passive resistance, that is a combat without any positive view. In this way, therefore, our means attain their greatest relative value, and therefore the result is best secured. How far now can this negative mode of proceeding be carried? Plainly not to absolute passivity, for mere endurance would not be fighting: and the defensive is an activity by which so much of the enemy's power must be destroyed, that he must give up his object. That alone is what we aim at in each single act, and therein consists the negative nature of our object.

No doubt this negative object in its single act is not so effective as the positive object in the same direction would be, supposing it successful; but there is this difference in its favour, that it succeeds more easily than the positive, and therefore it holds out greater certainty of success; what is wanting in the efficacy of its single act, must be gained through time, that is, through the duration of the contest, and therefore this negative intention, which constitutes the principle of the pure defensive, is also the natural means of overcoming the enemy by the duration of the combat, that is of wearing him out.

Here lies the origin of that difference of *Offensive* and *Defensive,* the influence of which prevails over the whole province of war. We cannot at present pursue this subject further than to observe that from this negative intention are to be deduced all the advantages and all the stronger forms of combat which are on the side of the *Defensive,* and in which that philosophical-dynamic law which exists between the greatness and the certainty of success is realised. We shall resume the consideration of all this hereafter.

If then the negative purpose, that is the concentration of all the means into a state of pure resistance, affords a superiority in the contest, and if this advantage is sufficient to *balance* whatever superiority in numbers the adversary may have, then the mere *duration* of the contest will suffice gradually to bring the loss of force on the part of the adversary to a point at which the political object can no longer be an equivalent, a point at which, therefore, he must give up the contest. We see then that this class of means, the wearying out of the enemy, includes the great number of cases in which the weaker resists the stronger.

Frederick the Great during the Seven Years' War was never strong enough to overthrow the Austrian monarchy; and if he had tried to do so after the fashion of Charles the Twelfth, he would inevitably have had to succumb himself.

But after his skilful application of the system of husbanding his resources had shown the powers allied against him, through a seven years' war, that the actual expenditure of strength far exceeded what they had at first anticipated, they made peace.

We see then that there are many ways to the aim in war; that the complete subjugation of the enemy is not essential in every case, that the destruction of the enemy's military force, the conquest of enemy's provinces, the mere occupation of them, the mere invasion of them—enterprises which are aimed directly at political objects—lastly a passive expectation of the enemy's blow, are all means which, each in itself, may be used to force the enemy's will just according as the peculiar circumstances of the case lead us to expect more from the one or the other. We could still add to these a whole category of shorter methods of gaining the end, which might be called arguments *ad hominem.* What branch of human affairs is there in which these sparks of individual spirit have not made their appearance, flying over all formal considerations? And least of all can they fail to appear in war, where the personal character of the combatants plays such an important part, both in the cabinet and in the field. We limit ourselves to pointing this out, as it would be pedantry to attempt to reduce such influences into classes. Including these, we may say that the number of possible ways of reaching the aim rises to infinity.

To avoid under-estimating these different short roads to the aim, either estimating them only as rare exceptions, or holding the difference which they cause in the conduct of war as insignificant, we must bear in mind the diversity of political objects which may cause a war,—measure at a glance the distance which there is between a death struggle for political existence, and a war which a forced or tottering alliance makes a matter of disagreeable duty. Between the two, gradations innumerable occur in reality. If we reject one of these gradations in theory, we might with equal right reject the whole, which would be tantamount to shutting the real world completely out of sight.

These are the circumstances in general connected with the aim which we have to pursue in war; let us now turn to the means.

There is only one single means, it is the *Fight.* However diversified this may be in form, however widely it may differ from a rough vent of hatred and animosity in a hand-to-hand encounter, whatever number of things may introduce themselves which are not actual fighting, still it is always implied in the conception of war, that all the effects manifested have their roots in the combat.

That this must also always be so in the greatest diversity and complication of the reality, is proved in a very simple manner. All that takes place in war takes place through armed forces, but where the forces of war, *i.e.,* armed men are applied, there the idea of fighting must of necessity be at the foundation.

All, therefore, that relates to forces of war—all that is connected with their creation, maintenance, and application, belongs to military activity.

Creation and maintenance are obviously only the means, whilst application is the object.

The contest in war is not a contest of individual against individual, but an organised whole, consisting of manifold parts; in this great whole we may distinguish units of two kinds, the one determined by the subject, the other by the object. In an army the mass of combatants ranges itself always into an order of new units, which again form members of a higher order. The combat of each of these members forms, therefore, also a more or less distinct unit. Further, the motive of the fight; therefore its object forms its unit.

Now to each of these units which we distinguish in the contest, we attach the name of combat.

If the idea of combat lies at the foundation of every application of armed power, then also the application of armed force in general, is nothing more than the determining and arranging a certain number of combats.

Every activity in war, therefore, necessarily relates to the combat either directly or indirectly. The soldier is levied, clothed, armed, exercised, he sleeps, eats, drinks and marches, all *merely to fight at the right time and place.*

If, therefore, all the threads of military activity terminate in the combat, we shall grasp them all when we settle the order of the combats. Only from this order and its execution proceed the effects; never directly from the conditions preceding them. Now, in the combat all the action is directed to the *destruction* of the enemy, or rather of *his fighting powers,* for this lies in the conception of combat. The destruction of the enemy's fighting power is, therefore, always the means to attain the object of the combat.

This object may likewise be the mere destruction of the enemy's armed force; but that is not by any means necessary, and it may be something quite different. Whenever, for instance, as we have shown, the defeat of the enemy is not the only means to attain the political object, whenever there are other objects which may be pursued, as the aim in a war, then it follows of itself that such other objects may become the object of particular acts of warfare, and, therefore, also the object of combats.

But even those combats which, as subordinate acts, are in the strict sense devoted to the destruction of the enemy's fighting force, need not have that destruction itself as their first object.

If we think of the manifold parts of a great armed force, of the number of circumstances which come into activity when it is employed, then it is clear that the combat of such a force must also require a manifold organisation, a subordinating of parts and formation. There may and must naturally arise for particular parts a number of objects which are not themselves the destruction of the enemy's armed force, and which, while they certainly contribute to increase that destruction, do so only in an indirect manner. If a battalion is ordered to drive the enemy from a rising ground, or a bridge, &c., then properly the occupation of any such locality is the real object, the destruction of the enemy's armed force, which takes place, only the means or secondary matter. If the enemy can be driven away merely by a demonstration, the object is attained all the same; but this hill or bridge is, in point of fact, only required as a means of increasing the gross amount of loss inflicted on the enemy's armed force. If this is the case on the field of battle, much more must it be so on the whole theatre of war, where not only one army is opposed to another, but one State, one nation, one whole country to another. Here the number of possible relations, and consequently possible combinations, is much greater, the diversity of measures increased, and by the gradation of objects each subordinate to another, the first means employed is further apart from the ultimate object.

It is, therefore, for many reasons possible that the object of a combat is not the destruction of the enemy's force, that is, of the force opposed to us, but that this only appears as a means. But in all such cases it is no longer a question of complete destruction, for the combat is here nothing else but a measure of strength—has in itself no value except only that of the present result, that is, of its decision.

But a measuring of strength may be effected in cases where the opposing sides are very unequal by a mere comparative estimate. In such cases no fighting will take place, and the weaker will immediately give way.

If the object of a combat is not always the destruction of the enemy's forces therein engaged—and if its object can often be attained as well without the combat taking place at all, by merely making a resolve to fight, and by the circumstances to which that gives rise—then that explains how a whole campaign may be carried on with great activity without the actual combat playing any notable part in it.

That this may be so, military history proves by a hundred examples. How many of those cases had a bloodless decision which can be justified, that is, without involving a contradiction; and whether some of the celebrities who rose out of them would stand criticism we shall leave undecided, for all we have to do with the matter is to show the possibility of such a course of events in war.

We have only one means in war—the battle; but this means, by the infinite variety of ways in which it may be applied, leads us into all the different ways which the multiplicity of objects allows of, so that we seem to have gained nothing; but that is not the case, for from this unity of means proceeds a thread which assists the study of the subject, as it runs through the whole web of military activity, and holds it together.

But we have considered the destruction of the enemy's force as one of the objects which may be pursued in war, and left undecided what importance should be given to it amongst other objects. In certain cases it will depend on circumstances, and as a general question we have left its value undetermined. We are once more brought back upon it, and we shall be able to get an insight into the value which must necessarily be accorded to it.

The combat is the single activity in war; in the combat the destruction of the enemy opposed to us is the means to the end; it is so even when the combat does not actually take place, because in that case there lies at the root of the decision the supposition at all events that this destruction is to be regarded as beyond doubt. It follows, therefore, that the destruction of the enemy's military force is the foundation-stone of all action in war, the great support of all combinations, which rest upon it like the arch on its abutments. All action, therefore, takes place on the supposition that if the solution by force of arms which lies at its foundation should be realised, it will be a favourable one. The decision by arms is, for all operations in war, great and small, what cash payment is in bill transactions. However remote from each other these relations, however seldom the realisation may take place, still it can never entirely fail to occur.

If the decision by arms lies at the foundation of all combinations, then it follows that the enemy can defeat each of them by gaining a successful decision with arms, not merely if it is that one on which our combination directly depends, but also by any other, if it is only important enough for every important decision by arms—that is, destruction of the enemy's forces reacts upon all preceding it, because, like a liquid element, they bring themselves to a level.

Thus, the destruction of the enemy's armed force appears, therefore, always as the superior and more effectual means, to which all others must give way.

But certainly it is only when there is a supposed equality in all other conditions that we can ascribe to the destruction of the enemy's armed force a greater efficacy. It would, therefore, be a great mistake to draw from it the conclusion that a blind dash must always gain the victory over skill and caution. An unskilful attack would lead to the destruction of our own and not of the enemy's force, and therefore is not what is here meant. The superior efficacy belongs not to the *means* but to the *end*, and we are only comparing the effect of one realised aim with the other.

If we speak of the destruction of the enemy's armed force, we must expressly point out that nothing obliges us to confine this idea to the mere physical force; on the contrary, the moral is necessarily implied as well, because both in fact are interwoven with each other even in the most minute details, and, therefore, cannot be separated. But it is just in connection with the inevitable effect which has been referred to, of a great act of destruction (a great victory) upon all other decisions by arms, that this moral element is most fluid, if we may use that expression, and, therefore, distributes itself the most easily through all the parts.

Against the far superior worth which the destruction of the enemy's armed force has over all other means, stands the expense and risk of this means, and it is only to avoid these that any other means are taken.

That this means must be costly stands to reason, for the waste of our own military forces must, *ceteris paribus,* always be greater the more our aim is directed upon the destruction of the enemy's.

But the danger of this means lies in this, that just the greater efficacy which we seek recoils on ourselves, and therefore has worse consequences in case we fail of success.

Other methods are, therefore, less costly when they succeed, less dangerous when they fail; but in this is necessarily lodged the condition that they are only opposed to similar ones, that is, that the enemy acts on the same principle; for if the enemy should choose the way of a great decision by arms, *our means must on that account be changed against our will, in order to correspond with his.* Then all depends on the issue of the act of destruction; but of course it is evident that, *ceteris paribus,* in this act we must be at a disadvantage in all respects because our views and our means had been directed in part upon other objects, which is not the case with the enemy. Two different objects of which one is not part of the other exclude each other; and, therefore, a force which may be applicable for the one, may not serve for the other. If, therefore, one of two belligerents is determined to take the way of the great decision by arms, then he has also a high probability of success, as soon as he is certain his opponent will not take that way, but follows a different object; and every one who sets before himself any such other aim only does so in a reasonable manner, provided he acts on the supposition that his adversary has as little intention as he has of resorting to the great decision by arms.

But what we have here said of another direction of views and forces relates only to other *positive objects,* which we may propose to ourselves in war besides the destruction of the enemy's force, not by any means to the pure defensive, which may be adopted with a view thereby to exhaust the enemy's forces. In the pure defensive, the positive object is wanting, and, therefore, while on the defensive, our forces cannot at the same time be directed on other objects; they can only be employed to defeat the intentions of the enemy.

We have now to consider the opposite of the destruction of the enemy's armed force, that is to say, the preservation of our own. These two efforts always go together, as they mutually act and re-act on each other; they are integral parts of one and the same view, and we have only to ascertain what effect is produced when one or the other has the predominance. The endeavour to destroy the enemy's force has a positive object and leads to positive results, of which the final aim is the conquest of the enemy. The preservation of our own forces has a negative object, leads therefore to the defeat of the enemy's intentions, that is to pure resistance, of which the final aim can be nothing more than to prolong the duration of the contest, so that the enemy shall exhaust himself in it.

The effort with a positive object calls into existence the act of destruction; the effort with the negative object awaits it.

How far this state of expectation should and may be carried we shall enter into more particularly in the theory of attack and defence, at the origin of which we again find ourselves. Here we shall content ourselves with saying that the awaiting must be no absolute endurance, and that in the action bound up with it the destruction of the enemy's armed force engaged in this conflict may be the aim just as well as anything else. It would, therefore, be a great error in the fundamental idea to suppose that the consequence of the negative course is that we are precluded from choosing the destruction of the enemy's military force as our object, and must prefer a bloodless solution. The advantage which the negative effort gives may certainly lead to that, but only at the risk of its not being the most advisable method, as that question is dependent on totally different conditions, resting not with ourselves but with our opponents. This other bloodless way cannot, therefore, be looked upon at all as the natural means of satisfying our great anxiety to spare our forces; on the contrary, when circumstances are not favourable to that way, it would be the means of completely ruining them. Very many Generals have fallen into this error, and been ruined by it. The only necessary effect resulting from the superiority of the negative effort is the delay of the decision, so that the party acting takes refuge in that way, as it were, in the expectation of the decisive moment. The consequence of that is generally *the postponement of the action* as much as possible in time and also in space, in so far as space is in connectiion with it. If the moment has arrived in which this can no longer be done without ruinous disadvantage, then the advantage of the negative must be considered as exhausted, and then comes forward unchanged the effort for the destruction of the enemy's force, which was kept back by a counterpoise, but never discarded.

We have seen, therefore, in the foregoing reflections, that there are many ways to the aim, that is, to the attainment of the political object; but that the only means is the combat, and that consequently everything is subject to a supreme law: which is the *decision by arms;* that where this is really demanded by one, it is a redress which cannot be refused by the other; that, therefore, a belligerent who takes any other way must make sure that his opponent will not take this means of redress, or his cause may be lost in that supreme court; that, therefore, in short, the destruction of the enemy's armed force amongst all the objects which can be pursued in war appears always as that one which over-rules all.

What may be achieved by combinations of another kind in war we shall only learn in the sequel, and naturally only by degrees. We content ourselves here with acknowledging in general their possibility, as something pointing to the difference between the reality and the conception, and to the influence of particular circumstances. But we would not avoid showing at once that the *bloody solution of the crisis,* the effort for the destruction of the enemy's force, is the firstborn son of war. If when political objects are unimportant, motives weak, the excitement of forces small, a cautious commander tries in all kinds of ways, without great crises and bloody solutions, to twist himself skilfully into a peace through the characteristic weaknesses of his enemy in the field and in the Cabinet, we have no right to find fault with him, if the premises on which he acts are well founded and justified by success; still we must require him to remember that he only travels on forbidden tracks, where the God of War may surprise him; that he ought always to keep his eye on the enemy, in order that he may not have to defend himself with a dress rapier if the enemy takes up a sharp sword.

The consequences of the nature of war, how end and means act in it, how in the modifications of reality it deviates sometimes more sometimes less from its strict original conception, plays backwards and forwards, yet always remains under that strict conception as under a supreme law: all this we must retain in idea, and bear constantly in mind in the consideration of each of the succeeding subjects, if we would rightly comprehend their true relations and proper importance, and not become involved incessantly in the most glaring contradictions with the reality, and at last with our own selves.

The Genius for War

Every special calling in life, if it is to be followed with success, requires peculiar qualifications of understanding and soul. Where these are of a high order, and manifest themselves by extraordinary achievements the mind to which they belong is termed *genius.*

We know very well that this word is used in many significations, which are very different both in extent and nature, and that with many of these significations it is a very difficult task to define the essence of Genius; but as we neither profess to be philosopher nor grammarian, we must be allowed to keep to the meaning usual in ordinary language, and to understand by "genius" a very high mental capacity for certain employments.

We wish to stop for a moment over this faculty and dignity of the mind, in order to vindicate its title, and to explain more fully the meaning of the conception. But we shall not dwell on that (genius) which has obtained its title through a very great talent, at genius properly so-called, that is a conception which has no defined limits, and what we have to do is to bring under consideration every common tendency of the powers of the mind and soul towards the business of war, the whole of which common tendencies we may look upon as the *essence of military genius.* We say "common," for just therein consists military genius, that it is not one single quality bearing upon war, as, for instance, courage, while other qualities of mind and soul are wanting, or have a direction which is unserviceable for war; but that it is an *harmonious association of powers,* in which one or other may predominate, but none must be in opposition.

If every combatant required to be more or less endowed with military genius, then our armies would be very weak; for as it implies a peculiar bent of the intelligent powers, therefore it can only rarely be found where the mental powers of a people are called into requisition, and trained in so many ways. The fewer the employments followed by a nation, the more that of arms predominates, so much the more prevalent military genius must also be found. But this merely applies to its prevalence, by no means to its degree, for that depends on the general state of intellectual culture in the country. If we look at a wild, warlike race, then we find a warlike spirit in individuals much more common than in a civilised people; for in the former almost every warrior possesses it; whilst in the civilised, whole masses are only carried away by it from necessity, never by inclination. But amongst uncivilised people we never find a really great general, and very seldom what we can properly call a military genius, because that requires a development of the intelligent powers which cannot be found in an uncivilised state. That a civilised people may also have a warlike tendency and development is a matter of course; and the more this is general, the more frequently also will military spirit be found in individuals in their armies. Now as this coincides in such case with the higher degree of civilisation, therefore from such nations have issued forth the most brilliant military exploits, as the Romans and the French have exemplified. The greatest names in these and in all other nations that have been renowned in war, belong strictly to epochs of higher culture.

From this we may infer how great a share the intelligent powers have in superior military genius. We shall now look more closely into this point.

War is the province of danger, and therefore courage above all things is the first quality of a warrior.

Courage is of two kinds; first, physical courage, or courage in presence of danger to the person: and next, moral courage, or courage before responsibility; whether it be before the judgment-seat of external authority, or of the inner power, the conscience. We only speak here of the first.

Courage before danger to the person, again, is of two kinds. First, it may be indifference to danger, whether proceeding from the organism of the individual, contempt of death, or habit: in any of these cases it is to be regarded as a permanent condition.

Secondly, courage may proceed from positive motives; such as personal pride, patriotism, enthusiasm of any kind. In this case courage is not so much a normal condition as an impulse.

We may conceive that the two kinds act differently. The first kind is more certain, because it has become a second nature, never forsakes the man: the second often leads him further. In the first there is more of firmness, in the second of boldness. The first leaves the judgment cooler, the second raises its power at times, but often bewilders it. The two combined make up the most perfect kind of courage.

War is the province of physical exertion and suffering. In order not to be completely overcome by them, a certain strength of body and mind is required, which, either natural or acquired, produces indifference to them. With these qualifications under the guidance of simply a sound understanding, a man is at once a proper instrument for war; and these are the qualifications so generally to be met with amongst wild and half-civilised tribes. If we go further in the demands which war makes on its votaries, then we find the powers of the understanding predominating. War is the province of uncertainty: three-fourths of those things upon which action in war must be calculated, are hidden more or less in the clouds of great uncertainty. Here, then, above all a fine and penetrating mind is called for, to grope out the truth by the tact of its judgment.

A common understanding may, at one time, perhaps hit upon this truth by accident: an extraordinary courage, at another time, may compensate for the want of this tact: but in the majority of cases the average result will always bring to light the deficient understanding.

War is the province of chance. In no sphere of human activity is such a margin to be left for this intruder, because none is so much in constant contact with him on all sides. He increases the uncertainty of every circumstance, and deranges the course of events.

From this uncertainty of all intelligence and suppositions, this continual interposition of chance, the actor in war constantly finds things different to his expectations; and this cannot fail to have an influence on his plans, or at least on the presumptions connected with these plans. If this influence is so great as to render the pre-determined plan completely nugatory, then, as a rule, a new one must be substituted in its place; but at the moment the necessary data are often wanting for this, because in the course of action circumstances press for immediate decision, and allow no time to look about for fresh data, often not enough for mature consideration. But it much more often happens that the correction of one premise, and the knowledge of chance events which have arisen, are not quite sufficient to overthrow our plans completely, but only suffice to produce hesitation. Our knowledge of circumstances has increased, but our uncertainty, instead of having diminished, has only increased. The reason of this is, that we do not gain all our experience at once, but by degrees; so our determinations continue to be assailed incessantly by fresh experience; and the mind, if we may use the expression, must always be under arms.

Now, if it is to get safely through this perpetual conflict with the unexpected, two qualities are indispensable: in the first place an understanding which, even in the midst of this intense obscurity, is not without some traces of inner light, which lead to the truth, and then the courage to follow this faint light. The first is figuratively expressed by the French phrase *coup d'œil*. The other is *resolution*. As the battle is the feature in war to which attention was originally chiefly directed, and as time and space are important elements in it, and were more particularly so when cavalry with their rapid decisions were the chief arm, the idea of rapid and correct decision related in the first instance to the estimation of these two elements, and to denote the idea an expression was adopted which actually only points to a correct judgment by eye. Many teachers of the art of war also then gave this limited signification as the definition of *coup d'œil*. But it is undeniable that all able decisions formed in the moment of action soon came to be understood by the expression, as for instance the hitting upon the right point of attack, etc. It is, therefore, not only the physical, but more frequently the mental eye which is meant in *coup d'œil*. Naturally, the expression, like the thing, is always more in its place in the field of tactics: still, it must not be wanting in strategy, inasmuch as in it rapid decisions are often necessary. If we strip this conception of that which the expression has given it of the over figurative and restricted, then it amounts simply to the rapid discovery of a truth, which to the ordinary mind is either not visible at all or only becomes so after long examination and reflection.

Resolution is an act of courage in single instances, and if it becomes a characteristic trait, it is a habit of the mind. But here we do not mean courage in face of bodily danger, but in face of responsibility, therefore to a certain extent against moral danger. This has been often called *courage d'esprit*, on the ground that it springs from the understanding; nevertheless, it is no act of the understanding on that account; it is an act of feeling. Mere intelligence is still not courage, for we often see the cleverest people devoid of resolution. The mind must, therefore, first awaken the feeling of courage, and then be guided and supported by it, because in momentary emergencies the man is swayed more by his feelings than his thoughts.

We have assigned to resolution the office of removing the torments of doubt, and the dangers of delay, when there are no sufficient motives for guidance. Through the unscrupulous use of language which is prevalent, this term is often applied to the mere propensity to daring, to bravery, boldness, or temerity. But, when there are *sufficient motives* in the man, let them be objective or subjective, true or false, we have no right to speak of his resolution; for, when we do so, we put ourselves in his place, and we throw into the scale doubts which did not exist with him.

Here, there is no question of anything but of strength and weakness. We are not pedantic enough to dispute with the use of language about this little misapplication, our observation is only intended to remove wrong objections.

This resolution now, which overcomes the state of doubting, can only be called forth by the intellect and in fact by a peculiar tendency of the same. We maintain that the mere union of a superior understanding and the necessary feelings are not sufficient to make up resolution. There are persons who possess the keenest perception for the most difficult problems, who are also not fearful of responsibility, and yet in cases of difficulty cannot come to a resolution. Their courage and their sagacity operate independently of each other, do not give each other a hand, and on that account do not produce resolution as a result. The forerunner of resolution is an act of the mind making evident the necessity of venturing, and thus influencing the will. This quite peculiar direction of the mind, which conquers every other fear in man by the fear of wavering or doubting, is what makes up resolution in strong minds: therefore, in our opinion, men who have little intelligence can never be resolute. They may act without hesitation under perplexing circumstances, but then they act without reflection. Now of course, when a man acts without reflection he cannot be at variance with himself by doubts, and such a mode of action may now and then lead to the right point; but we say now as before, it is the average result which indicates the existence of military genius. Should our assertion appear extraordinary to any one, because he knows many a resolute hussar-officer who is no deep thinker, we must remind him that the question here is about a peculiar direction of the mind, and not about great thinking powers.

We believe, therefore, that resolution is indebted to a special direction of the mind for its existence, a direction which belongs to a strong head, rather than to a brilliant one. In corroboration of this genealogy of resolution we may add that there have been many instances of men who have shown the greatest resolution in an inferior rank, and have lost it in a higher position. While on the one hand they are obliged to resolve, on the other they see the dangers of a wrong decision, and as they are surrounded with things new to them, their understanding loses its original force, and they become only the more timid the more they become aware of the danger of the irresolution into which they have fallen, and the more they have formerly been in the habit of acting on the spur of the moment.

From the *coup d'œil* and resolution, we are naturally led to speak of its kindred quality, *presence of mind,* which in a region of the unexpected like war must act a great part, for it is indeed nothing but a great conquest over the unexpected. As we admire presence of mind in a pithy answer to anything said unexpectedly, so we admire it in a ready expedient on sudden danger. Neither the answer nor the expedient need be in themselves extraordinary, if they only hit the point; for that which as the result of mature reflection would be nothing unusual, therefore insignificant in its impression on us, may as an instantaneous act of the mind produce a pleasing impression. The expression "presence of mind" certainly denotes very fitly the readiness and rapidity of the help rendered by the mind.

Whether this noble quality of a man is to be ascribed more to the peculiarity of his mind or to the equanimity of his feelings, depends on the nature of the case, although neither of the two can be entirely wanting. A telling repartee bespeaks rather a ready wit, a ready expedient on sudden danger implies more particularly a well-balanced mind.

If we take a general view of the four elements composing the atmosphere in which war moves, of *danger, physical efforts, uncertainty,* and *chance,* it is easy to conceive that a great force of mind and understanding are requisite to be able to make way with safety and success amongst such opposing elements, a force which, according to the different modifications arising out of circumstances, we find termed by military writers and annalists as *energy, firmness, staunchness, strength of mind and character.* All these manifestations of the heroic nature might be regarded as one and the same power of volition, modified according to circumstances; but nearly related as these things are to each other, still they are not one and the same, and it is desirable for us to distinguish here a little more closely at least the action of the powers of the soul in relation to them.

In the first place, to make the conception clear, it is essential to observe that the weight, burden, resistance, or whatever it may be called, by which that force of the soul in the general is brought to light, is only in a very small measure the enemy's activity, the enemy's resistance, the enemy's action directly. The enemy's activity only affects the general directly in the first place in relation to his person, without disturbing his action as commander. If the enemy, instead of two hours, resists for four, the commander instead of two hours is four hours in danger; this is a quantity which plainly diminishes the higher the rank of the commander. What is it for one in the post of commander-in-chief? It is nothing.

Secondly, although the opposition offered by the enemy has a direct effect on the commander through the loss of means arising from prolonged resistance, and the responsibility connected with that loss, and his force of will is first tested and called forth by these anxious considerations; still we maintain that this is not the heaviest burden by far which he has to bear, because he has only himself to settle with. All the other effects of the enemy's resistance act directly upon the combatants under his command, and through them re-act upon him.

As long as a troop full of good courage fights with zeal and spirit, it is seldom necessary for the chief to show great energy of purpose in the pursuit of his object. But, as soon as difficulties arise—and that must always happen when great results are at stake—then things no longer move on of themselves like a well-oiled machine, the machine itself then begins to offer resistance, and to overcome this, the commander must have a great force of will. By this resistance, we must not exactly suppose disobedience and murmurs, although these are frequent enough with particular individuals; it is the whole feeling of the dissolution of all physical and moral power, it is the heart-rending sight of the bloody sacrifice which the commander has to contend with in himself, and then, in all others who directly or indirectly transfer to him their impressions, feelings, anxieties and desires. As the forces in one individual after another become prostrated, and can no longer be excited and supported by an effort of his own will, the whole inertia of the mass gradually rests its weight on the will of the commander: by the spark in his breast, by the light of his spirit, the spark of purposes, the light of hope must be kindled afresh in others: in so far only as he is equal to this, he stands above the masses, and continues to be their master; whenever that influence ceases and his own spirit is no longer strong enough to revive the spirit of all others, the masses drawing him down with them sink into the lower region of animal nature, which shrinks from danger and knows not shame. These are the weights which the courage and intelligent faculties of the military commander have to overcome, if he is to make his name illustrious. They increase with the masses, and, therefore, if the forces in question are to continue equal to the burden, they must rise in proportion to the height of the station.

Energy in action expresses the strength of the motive through which the action is excited, let the motive have its origin in a conviction of the understanding, or in an impulse. But the latter can hardly ever be wanting where great force is to show itself.

Of all the noble feelings which fill the human heart in the exciting tumult of battle, none, we must admit, are so powerful and constant as the soul's thirst for honour and renown, which the German language treats so unfairly, and tends to depreciate by the unworthy associations in the words *Ehrgeiz* (greed of honour) and *Ruhmsucht* (hankering after glory). No doubt it is just in war that the abuse of these proud aspirations of the soul must bring upon the human race the most shocking outrages; but by their origin, they are certainly to be counted amongst the noblest feelings which belong to human nature, and in war they are the vivifying principle which gives the enormous body a spirit. Although other feelings may be more general in their influence, and many of them—such as love of country, fanaticism, revenge, enthusiasm of every kind may seem to stand higher, the thirst for honour and renown still remains indispensable. Those other feelings may rouse the great masses in general, and excite them more powerfully, but they do not give the leader a desire to will more than others, which is an essential requisite in his position, if he is to make himself distinguished in it. They do not, like a thirst for honour, make the military act specially the property of the leader, which he strives to turn to the best account; where he ploughs with toil, sows with care, that he may reap plentifully. It is through these aspirations we have been speaking of in commanders, from the highest to the lowest, this sort of energy, this spirit of emulation, these incentives, that the action of armies is chiefly animated and made successful. And now as to that which specially concerns the head of all, we ask, Has there ever been a great commander destitute of the love of honour, or is such a character even conceivable?

Firmness denotes the resistance of the will in relation to the force of a single blow, *staunchness* in relation to a continuance of blows. Close as is the analogy between the two, and often as the one is used in place of the other, still there is a notable difference between them which cannot be mistaken, inasmuch as firmness against a single powerful impression may have its root in the mere strength of a feeling, but staunchness must be supported rather by the understanding, for the greater the duration of an action the more systematic deliberation is connected with it, and from this staunchness partly derives its power.

If we now turn to *strength of mind or soul*, then the first question is, What are we to understand thereby?

Plainly it is not vehement expressions of feeling, nor easily excited passions, for that would be contrary to all the usage of language; but the power of listening to reason in the midst of the most intense excitement, in the storm of the most violent passions. Should this power depend on strength of understanding alone? We doubt it. The fact that there are men of the greatest intellect who cannot command themselves, certainly proves nothing to the contrary; for we might say that it perhaps requires an understanding of a powerful rather than of a comprehensive nature: but we believe we shall be nearer the truth if we assume that the power of submitting oneself to the control of the understanding, even in moments of the most violent excitement of the feelings, that power which we call *self-command,* has its root in the heart itself. It is, in point of fact, another feeling, which, in strong minds balances the excited passions without destroying them; and it is only through this equilibrium that the mastery of the understanding is secured. This counterpoise is nothing but a sense of the dignity of man, that noblest pride, that deeply-seated desire of the soul, always to act as a being endued with understanding and reason. We may, therefore, say that a strong mind is one which does not lose its balance even under the most violent excitement.

If we cast a glance at the variety to be observed in the human character in respect to feeling, we find, first, some people who have very little excitability, who are called phlegmatic or indolent.

Secondly, some very excitable, but whose feelings still never overstep certain limits, and who are therefore known as men full of feeling, but sober-minded.

Thirdly, those who are very easily roused, whose feelings blaze up quickly and violently like gunpowder, but do not last.

Fourthly, and lastly, those who cannot be moved by slight causes, and who generally are not to be roused suddenly, but only gradually; but whose feelings become very powerful, and are much more lasting. These are men with strong passions, lying deep and latent.

This difference of character lies, probably, close on the confines of the physical powers which move the human organism, and belongs to that amphibious organisation which we call the nervous system, which appears to be partly material, partly spiritual. With our weak philosophy, we shall not proceed further in this mysterious field. But it is important for us to spend a moment over the effects which these different natures have on action in war, and to see how far a great strength of mind is to be expected from them.

Indolent men cannot easily be thrown out of their equanimity; but we cannot certainly say there is strength of mind where there is a want of all manifestation of power. At the same time it is not to be denied that such men have a certain peculiar aptitude for war, on account of their constant equanimity. They often want the positive motive to action, impulse, and consequently activity, but they are not apt to throw things into disorder.

The peculiarity of the second class is, that they are easily excited to act on trifling grounds; but in great matters they are easily overwhelmed. Men of this kind show great activity in helping an unfortunate individual; but by the distress of a whole nation they are only inclined to despond, not roused to action.

Such people are not deficient in either activity or equanimity in war: but they will never accomplish anything great unless a great intellectual force furnishes the motive, and it is very seldom that a strong, independent mind is combined with such a character.

Excitable, inflammable feelings, are in themselves little suited for practical life, and therefore they are not very fit for war. They have certainly the advantage of strong impulses, but that cannot long sustain them. At the same time, if the excitability in such men takes the direction of courage, or a sense of honour; they may often be very useful in inferior positions in war, because the action in war over which commanders in inferior positions have control, is generally of shorter duration. Here one courageous resolution, one effervescence of the forces of the soul, will often suffice. A brave attack, a soul-stirring hurrah, is the work of a few moments; whilst a brave contest on the battle-field is the work of a day, and a campaign the work of a year.

Owing to the rapid movement of their feelings, it is doubly difficult for men of this description to preserve the equilibrium of the mind; therefore they frequently lose head, and that is the worst phase in their nature as respects the conduct of war. But it would be contrary to experience to maintain that very excitable spirits can never preserve a steady equilibrium, that is, to say that they cannot do so even under the strongest excitement. Why should they not have the sentiment of self-respect, for, as a rule, they are men of a noble nature? This feeling is seldom wanting in them, but it has not time to produce an effect. After an outburst they suffer most from a feeling of inward humiliation. If through education, self-observance, and experience of life, they have learned, sooner or later, the means of being on their guard, so that at the moment of powerful excitement they are conscious, betimes, of the counteracting force within their own breasts, then even such men may have great strength of mind.

Lastly, those who are difficult to move, but on that account susceptible of very deep feelings; men who stand in the same relation to the preceding as red heat to a flame are the best adapted by means of their Titanic strength to roll away the enormous masses, by which we may figuratively represent the difficulties which beset command in war. The effect of their feelings is like the movement of a great body, slower, but more irresistible.

Although such men are not so likely to be suddenly surprised by their feelings and carried away, so as to be afterwards ashamed of themselves like the preceding, still it would be contrary to experience to believe that they can never lose their equanimity, or be overcome by blind passion; on the contrary, this must always happen whenever the noble pride of self-control is wanting or as often as it has not sufficient weight. We see examples of this most frequently in men of noble minds belonging to savage nations, where the low degree of mental cultivation favours always the dominance of the passions. But even amongst the most civilised classes in civilised states, life is full of examples of this kind—of men carried away by the violence of their passions, like the poacher of old chained to the stag in the forest.

We, therefore, say once more a strong mind is not one that is merely susceptible of strong excitement, but one which can maintain its serenity under the most powerful excitement; so that, in spite of the storm in the breast, the perception and judgment can act with perfect freedom, like the needle of the compass in the storm-tossed ship.

By the term *strength of character*, or simply *character*, is denoted tenacity of conviction, let it be the result of our own or of others' views, and whether they are principles, opinions, momentary inspirations, or any kind of emanations of the understanding; but this kind of firmness certainly cannot manifest itself if the views themselves are subject to frequent change. This frequent change need not be the consequence of external influences; it may proceed from the continuous activity of our own mind, in which case it indicates a characteristic unsteadiness of mind. Evidently we should not say of a man who changes his views every moment, however much the motives of change may originate with himself, that he has character. Only those men therefore can be said to have this quality whose conviction is very constant, either because it is deeply rooted and clear in itself, little liable to alteration, or because, as in the case of indolent men, there is a want of mental activity, and therefore a want of motives to change; or lastly, because an explicit act of the will, derived from an imperative maxim of the understanding, refuses any change of opinion up to a certain point.

Now in war, owing to the many and powerful impressions to which the mind is exposed, and, in the uncertainty of all knowledge and of all science, more things occur to distract a man from the road he has entered upon, to make him doubt himself and others, than in any other human activity.

The harrowing sight of danger and suffering easily leads to the feelings gaining ascendancy over the conviction of the understanding; and in the twilight which surrounds everything, a deep clear view is so difficult, that a change of opinion is more conceivable and more pardonable. It is, at all times, only conjecture or guesses at truth which we have to act upon. This is why differences of opinion are nowhere so great as in war, and the stream of impressions acting counter to one's own convictions never ceases to flow. Even the greatest impassibility of mind is hardly proof against them, because the impressions are powerful in their nature, and always act at the same time upon the feelings.

When the discernment is clear and deep, none but general principles and views of action from a high standpoint can be the result; and on these principles the opinion in each particular case immediately under consideration lies, as it were, at anchor. But to keep to these results of bygone reflection in opposition to the stream of opinions and phenomena which the present brings with it is just the difficulty. Between the particular case and the principle there is often a wide space which cannot always be traversed on a visible chain of conclusions, and where a certain faith in self is necessary, and a certain amount of scepticism is serviceable. Here often nothing else will help us but an imperative maxim which, independent of reflection, at once controls it: that maxim is, in all doubtful cases to adhere to the first opinion, and not to give it up until a clear conviction forces us to do so. We must firmly believe in the superior authority of well-tried maxims, and under the dazzling influence of momentary events not forget that their value is of an inferior stamp. By this preference which is doubtful cases we give to first convictions, by adherence to the same our actions acquire that stability and consistency which make up what is called character.

It is easy to see how essential a well-balanced mind is to strength of character; therefore, men of strong minds generally have a great deal of character.

Force of character leads us to a spurious variety of it—*obstinacy.*

It is often very difficult in concrete cases to say where the one ends and the other begins; on the other hand, it does not seem difficult to determine the difference in idea.

Obstinacy is no fault of the understanding; we use the term as denoting a resistance against our better judgment, and it would be inconsistent to charge that to the understanding, as the understanding is the power of judgment. Obstinacy is *a fault of the feelings* or heart. This inflexibility of will, this impatience of contradiction, have their origin only in a particular kind of egotism, which sets above every other pleasure that of governing both self and others by its own mind alone. We should call it a kind of vanity were it not decidedly something better. Vanity is satisfied with mere show, but obstinacy rests upon the enjoyment of the thing.

We say therefore, force of character degenerates into obstinacy whenever the resistance to opposing judgment proceeds not from better convictions or a reliance upon a more trustworthy maxim, but from a feeling of opposition. If this definition, as we have already admitted, is of little assistance practically, still it will prevent obstinacy from being considered merely force of character intensified, whilst it is something essentially different—something which certainly lies close to it and is cognate to it, but is at the same time so little an intensification of it that there are very obstinate men who, from want of understanding, have very little force of character.

Having in these high attributes of a great military commander made ourselves acquainted with those qualities in which heart and head co-operate, we now come to a speciality of military activity which perhaps may be looked upon as the most marked if it is not the most important, and which only makes a demand on the power of the mind, without regard to the forces of feelings. It is the connection which exists between war and country or ground.

This connection is, in the first place, a permanent condition of war, for it is impossible to imagine our organised armies effecting any operation otherwise than in some given space; it is, secondly, of the most decisive importance, because it modifies, at times completely alters, the action of all forces; thirdly, while on the one hand it often concerns the most minute features of locality, on the other, it may apply to immense tracts of country.

In this manner a great peculiarity is given to the effect of this connection of war with country and ground. If we think of other occupations of man which have a relation to these objects, on horticulture, agriculture, on building houses and hydraulic works, on mining, on the chase, and forestry, they are all confined within very limited spaces which may be soon explored with sufficient exactness. But the commander in war must commit the business he has in hand to a corresponding space which his eye cannot survey, which the keenest zeal cannot always explore, and with which, owing to the constant changes taking place, he can also seldom become properly acquainted. Certainly the enemy generally is in the same situation; still, in the first place, the difficulty, although common to both, is not the less a difficulty, and he who by talent and practice overcomes it will have a great advantage on his side; secondly, this equality of the difficulty on both sides is merely an abstract supposition which is rarely realised in the particular case, as one of the two opponents (the defensive) usually knows much more of the locality than his adversary.

This very peculiar difficulty must be overcome by a natural mental gift of a special kind which is known by the—too restricted—term of (*Ortsinn*) sense of locality. It is the power of quickly forming a correct geometrical idea of any portion of country and consequently of being able to find one's place in it exactly at any time. This is plainly an act of the imagination. The perception no doubt is formed partly by means of the physical eye, partly by the mind, which fills up what is wanting with ideas derived from knowledge and experience, and out of the fragments visible to the physical eye forms a whole; but that this whole should present itself vividly to the reason, should become a picture, a mentally drawn map, that this picture should be fixed, that the details should never again separate themselves—all that can only be effected by the mental faculty which we call imagination. If some great Poet or Painter should feel hurt that we require from his goddess such as office; if he shrugs his shoulders at the notion that a sharp gamekeeper must necessarily excel in imagination, we readily grant that we only speak here of imagination in a limited snese, of its service in a really menial capacity. But however slight this service, still it must be the work of that natural gift, for if that gift is wanting, it would be difficult to imagine things plainly in all the completeness of the visible. That a good memory is a great assistance we freely allow; but whether memory is to be considered as an independent faculty of the mind in this case, or whether it is just that power of imagination which here fixes these things better on the memory, we leave undecided, as in many respects it seems difficult upon the whole to conceive these two mental powers apart from each other.

That practice and mental acuteness have much to do with it, is not to be denied. Puysegur, the famous Quartermaster-General of the famous Luxemburgh, used to say that he had very little confidence in himself in this respect at first, because if he had to fetch the Parole from a distance he always lost his way.

It is natural that scope for the exercise of this talent should increase along with rank. If the Hussar and Riflemen in command of a patrol, must know well all the highways and by-ways, and if for that a few marks, a few limited powers of observation are sufficient; so on the other hand the Chief of an army must make himself familiar with the general geographical features of a Province and of a Country; must always have vividly before his eyes the direction of the roads, rivers, and hills, without at the same time being able to dispense with the narrower "sense of locality" (Ortsinn). No doubt information of various kinds as to objects in general, Maps, Books, Memoirs, and for details the assistance of his Staff, are a great help to him; but it is nevertheless certain that if he has himself a talent for forming an ideal picture of a country quickly and distinctly, it lends to his action an easier and firmer step, saves him from a certain mental helplessness, and makes him less dependent on others.

If this talent then is to be ascribed to imagination, it is also almost the only service which military activity requires from that erratic goddess whose influence is more hurtful than useful in other respects.

We think we have now passed in review those manifestations of the powers of mind and soul which military activity requires from human nature. Everywhere Intellect appears as an essential co-operative force; and thus we can understand how the work of war, although so plain and simple in its effects, can never be conducted with distinguished success by people without distinguished powers of the understanding.

When we have reached this view, then we need no longer look upon such a natural thing as the turning an enemy's position, which has been done a thousand times, and a hundred other such like things, as the result of a great effort of genius.

Certainly one is accustomed to regard the plain honest soldier, as the very opposite of the man of reflection, full of inventions and ideas, or of the brilliant spirit shining in the ornaments of refined education of every kind. This antithesis is also by no means devoid of truth; but it does not show that the efficiency of the soldier consists only in his courage, and that there is no particular energy and capacity of the brain required in addition to make a man merely what is called a true soldier. We must again repeat that there is nothing more common than to hear of men losing their energy on being raised to a higher position, to which they do not feel themselves equal; but we must also remind our readers that we are speaking of pre-eminent services, of such as give renown in the branch of activity to which they belong. Each grade of command in War therefore forms its own stratum of requisite capacity of Fame and Honour.

An immense space lies between a general, that is, one at the head of a whole war, or of a theatre of war, and his second in command, for the simple reason that the latter is in more immediate subordination to a superior authority and supervision, consequently is restricted to a more limited sphere of independent thought. This is why common opinion sees no room for the exercise of high talent except in high places, and looks upon an ordinary capacity as sufficient for all beneath: this is why people are rather inclined to look upon a subordinate general grown grey in the service, and in whom constant discharge of routine duties has produced a decided poverty of mind as a man of failing intellect; and, with all respect for his bravery, to laugh at his simplicity. It is not our object to gain for these brave men a better lot; that would contribute nothing to their efficiency, and little to their happiness; we only wish to represent things as they are, and to expose the error of believing that a mere bravo without intellect can make himself distinguished in war.

As we consider distinguished talents requisite for those who are to attain distinction, even in inferior positions, it naturally follows that we think highly of those who fill with renown the place of second in command of any army; and their seeming simplicity of character as compared with a polyhistor, with ready men of business, or with Councillors of State, must not lead us astray as to the superior nature of their intellectual activity. It happens, sometimes, that men import the fame gained in an inferior position into a higher one, without, in reality, deserving it in the new position: and then if they are not much employed, and therefore not much exposed to the risk of showing their weak points, the judgment does not distinguish very exactly what degree of fame is really due to them; and thus such men are often the occasion of too low an estimate being formed of the characteristics required to shine in certain situations.

For each station, from the lowest upwards, to render distinguished services in war, there must be a particular genius. But the title of genius, history and the judgment of posterity only confer, in general, on those minds which have shone in the highest rank, that of commanders-in-chief. The reason is that here, in point of fact, the demand on the reasoning and intellectual powers generally is much greater.

To conduct a whole war, or its great acts, which we call campaigns, to a successful termination, there must be an intimate knowledge of state policy in its higher relations. The conduct of the war, and the policy of the State, here coincide; and the general becomes, at the same time, the statesman.

We do not give Charles XII the name of a great genius, because he could not make the power of his sword subservient to a higher judgment and philosophy—could not attain by it to a glorious object. We do not give that title to Henry IV, because he did not live long enough to set at rest the relations of different States by his military activity, and to occupy himself in that higher field where noble feelings and a chivalrous disposition have less to do in mastering the enemy than in overcoming internal dissension.

In order that the reader may appreciate all that must be comprehended and judged of correctly at a glance by a general, we refer to the first chapter. We say, the general becomes a statesman, but he must not cease to be the general. He takes into view all the relations of the State on the one hand; on the other he must know exactly what he can do with the means at his disposal.

As the diversity and undefined limits of all the circumstances bring a great number of things into consideration in war, as the most of these things can only be estimated according to probability, therefore if the chief of an army does not bring to bear upon all this a mind with an intuitive perception of the truth, a confusion of ideas and views must take place, in the midst of which the judgment will become bewildered. In this sense Buonaparte was right when he said that many of the questions which come before a general for decision would make problems for a mathematical calculation, not unworthy of the powers of Newton or Euler.

What is here required from the higher powers of the mind is a sense of unity, and a judgment raised to such a compass as to give the mind an extraordinary faculty of vision, which, in its range, allays and sets aside a thousand dim notions which an ordinary understanding could only bring to light with great effort, and over which it would exhaust itself. But this higher activity of the mind, this glance of genius would still not become matter of history if the qualities of temperament and character of which we have treated did not give it their support.

Truth alone is but a weak motive of action with men, and hence there is always a great difference between knowing and willing, between science and art. The man receives the strongest impulse to action through the feelings, and the most powerful succour, if we may use the expression, through those mixtures of heart and mind, which we have made acquaintance with, as resolution, firmness, perseverance, and force of character.

If, however, this elevated condition of heart and mind in the General did not manifest itself in the general effects resulting from it, and could only be accepted on trust and faith, then it would rarely become matter of history.

All that becomes known of the course of events in war is usually very simple, has a great sameness in appearance; no one on the mere relation of such events perceives the difficulties connected with them which had to be overcome. It is only now and again in the memoirs of Generals, or of those in their confidence, or by reason of some special historical inquiry directed to a particular circumstance that a portion of the many threads composing the whole web is brought to light. The reflections, mental doubts and conflicts which precede the execution of great acts are purposely concealed because they affect political interests, or the recollection of them is accidentally lost because they have been looked upon as mere scaffolding which had to be removed on the completion of the building.

If, now, in conclusion, without venturing upon a closer definition of the higher powers of the soul, we should admit a distinction in the intelligent faculties themselves according to the common ideas established by language, and ask ourselves what kind of mind comes closest to military genius? then a look at the subject as well as at experience will tell us that searching rather than inventive minds, comprehensive minds rather than such as have a special bent, cool rather than fiery heads are those to which in time of war we should prefer to trust the welfare of our brothers and children, the honour and the safety of our fatherland.

Of Danger in War

Usually before we have learnt what danger really is we form an idea of it which is rather attractive than repulsive. In the intoxication of enthusiasm, to fall upon the enemy at the charge—who cares then about bullets and men falling? The eyes shut for a moment, to throw oneself against cold death, uncertain whether we or another shall escape him, and all this close to the golden aim of victory, close to the rich fruit which ambition thirsts for—can this be difficult? It will not be difficult, and still less will it appear so. But such moments, which, however, are not the work of a single pulse-beat as is supposed, but rather like doctors' draughts, must be taken diluted and spoilt by mixture with time—such moments, we say, are but few.

Let us accompany the novice to the battle-field. As we approach, the thunder of the cannon becoming plainer and plainer is soon followed by the howling of shot, which attracts the attention of the inexperienced. Balls begin to strike the ground close to us, before and behind. We hasten to the hill where stands the General and his numerous Staff. Here the close striking of the cannon balls and the bursting of shells is so frequent that the seriousness of life makes itself visible through the youthful picture of imagination. Suddenly some one known to us falls—a shell makes its way into the crowd and causes some involuntary movements; we begin to feel that we are no longer perfectly at ease and collected, even the bravest is at least to some degree confused. Now, a step further into the battle which is raging before us like a scene in a theatre, we get to the nearest General of Division; here ball follows ball, and the noise of our own guns increases the confusion. From the General of Division to the

Brigadier. He a man of acknowledged bravery, keeps carefully behind a rising ground, a house, or a tree—a sure sign of increasing danger. Grape rattles on the roofs of the houses and in the fields; cannon balls howl over us, and plough the air in all directions, and soon there is a frequent whistling of musket balls; a step further towards the troops, to that sturdy Infantry which for hours has maintained its firmness under this heavy fire; here the air is filled with the hissing of balls which announce their proximity by a short sharp noise as they pass within an inch of the ear, the head, or the breast.

To add to all this, compassion strikes the beating heart with pity, at the sight of the maimed and fallen. The young soldier cannot reach any of these different strata of danger, without feeling that the light of reason does not move here in the same medium, that it is not refracted in the same manner as in speculative contemplation. Indeed, he must be a very extraordinary man who, under these impressions for the first time, does not lose the power of making any instantaneous decisions. It is true that habit soon blunts such impressions; in half-an-hour we begin to be more or less indifferent to all that is going on around us: but an ordinary character never attains to complete coolness, and the natural elasticity of mind; and so we perceive that here, again, ordinary qualities will not suffice; a thing which gains truth, the wider the sphere of activity which is to be filled. Enthusiastic, stoical, natural bravery, great ambition, or also long familiarity with danger, much of all this there must be if all the effects produced in this resistant medium are not to fall far short of that which, in the student's chamber, may appear only the ordinary standard.

Danger in war belongs to its friction; a correct idea of it is necessary for truth of perception, and therefore it is brought under notice here.

Of Bodily Exertion in War

If no one was allowed to pass an opinion on the events of war, except at a moment when he is benumbed by frost, sinking from heat and thirst, or dying with hunger and fatigue, we should certainly have fewer judgments correct objectively; but they would be so subjectively, at least; that is, they would contain in themselves the exact relation between the person giving the judgment and the object. We can perceive this by observing how modestly subdued, even spiritless and desponding, is the opinion passed upon the results of untoward events, by those who have been eye-witnesses, but especially if they have been parties concerned. This is, according to our view, a criterion of the influence which bodily fatigue exercises, and of the allowance to be made for it in matters of opinion.

Amongst the many things in war for which no tariff can be fixed, bodily effort may be specially reckoned. Provided there is no waste, it is a co-efficient of all the forces, and no one can tell exactly to what extent it may be carried. But what is remarkable is, that just as only a strong arm enables the archer to stretch the bowstring to the utmost extent, so also in war it is only by means of a great directing spirit, that we can expect the forces will be stretched to the utmost. For it is one thing if an army, in consequence of great misfortunes, surrounded with danger, falls all to pieces like a wall that has been thrown down, and can only find safety in the utmost exertion of its bodily strength; it is another thing entirely when a victorious army, drawn on by proud feelings only, is conducted at the will of its chief. The same effort which, in the one case, might at most excite our pity, must, in the other call forth our admiration, because it is much more difficult to sustain.

By this comes to light for the inexperienced eye, one of those things which put fetters in the dark, as it were, on the action of the mind, and wear out in secret the powers of the soul.

Although here strictly, the question is only respecting the extreme effort required by a commander from his army, by a leader from his followers, therefore of the spirit to demand it, of the art of getting it; still the personal physical exertion of generals and of the chief commander, must not be overlooked. Having brought the analysis of war conscientiously up to this point, we could not but take account also of the weight of this small remaining residue.

We have spoken here of bodily effort, chiefly because, like danger, it belongs to the fundamental causes of friction, and because its indefinite quantity makes it like an elastic body, the friction of which is well known to be difficult to calculate.

To check the abuse of these considerations, of such a survey of things which aggravate the difficulties of war, nature has given our judgment a guide in our sensibilities. Just as an individual cannot with advantage refer to his personal deficiencies if he is insulted and ill-treated, but may well do so if he has successfully repelled the affront, or has fully revenged it, so no Commander or army will lessen the impression of a disgraceful defeat by depicting the danger, the distress, the exertions, things which would immensely enhance the glory of a victory. Thus, our feeling, which after all is only a higher kind of judgment, forbids us to do what seems an act of justice to which our judgment would be inclined.

Information in War

By the word "Information," we denote all the knowledge which we have of the enemy and his country; therefore, in fact, the foundation of all our ideas and actions. Let us just consider the nature of this foundation, its want of trustworthiness, its changefulness, and we shall soon feel what a dangerous edifice war is, how easily it may fall to pieces and bury us in its ruins. For although it is a maxim in all books that we should trust only certain information, that we must be always suspicious; that is only a miserable book-comfort, belonging to that description of knowledge in which writers of systems and compendiums take refuge for want of anything better.

Great part of the information obtained in war is contradictory, a still greater part is false, and by far the greatest part is of a doubtful character. What is required of an officer is a certain power of discrimination, which only knowledge of men and things and good judgment can give. The law of probability must be his guide. This is not a trifling difficulty even in respect of the first plans, which can be formed in the chamber outside the real sphere of war; but it is enormously increased when in the thick of war itself one report follows hard upon the heels of another; it is then fortunate if these reports in contradicting each other, show a certain balance of probability, and thus themselves call forth a scrutiny. It is much worse for the inexperienced when accident does not render him this service, but one report supports another, confirms it, magnifies it, finishes off the picture with fresh touches of colour, until necessity in urgent haste forces from us a resolution which will soon be discovered to be folly, all those reports having been lies, exaggerations, errors, &c., &c. In a few words, most reports are false, and the timidity of men acts as a multiplier of lies and untruths. As a general rule every one is more inclined to lend credence to the bad than the good. Every one is inclined to magnify the bad in some measure, and although the alarms which are thus propagated, like the waves of the sea, subside into themselves, still, like them, without any apparent cause they rise again. Firm in reliance on his own better convictions, the chief must stand like a rock against which the sea breaks its fury in vain. The *rôle* is not easy; he who is not by nature of a buoyant disposition, or trained by experience in war, and matured in judgment, may let it be his rule to do violence to his own natural conviction by inclining from the side of fear to that of hope; only by that means will he be able to preserve his balance. This difficulty of seeing things correctly, which is one of the greatest frictions in war makes things appear quite different to what was expected. The impression of the senses is stronger than the force of the ideas resulting from methodical reflection, and this goes so far that no important undertaking was ever yet carried out without the Commander having to subdue new doubts in himself at the time of commencing the execution of his work. Ordinary men who follow the suggestions of others become, therefore, generally undecided on the spot; they think that they have found circumstances different to what they had expected, and this view gains strength by their again yielding to the suggestions of others. But even the man who has made his own plans when he comes to see things with his own eyes, will often think he has done wrong. Firm reliance on self must make him proof against the seeming pressure of the moment; his first conviction will in the end prove true, when the foreground scenery which fate has pushed on to the stage of war, with its accompaniments of terrific objects is drawn aside, and the horizon extended. This is one of the great chasms which separate *conception* from *execution.*

Friction in War

As long as we have no personal knowledge of war, we cannot conceive where those difficulties lie of which so much is said, and what that genius, and those extraordinary mental powers required in a general have really to do. All appears so simple, all the requisite branches of knowledge appear so plain, all the combinations so unimportant, that, in comparison with them, the easiest problem in higher mathematics impresses us with a certain scientific dignity. But if we have seen war, all becomes intelligible; and still, after all, it is extremely difficult to describe what it is which brings about this change, to specify this invisible and completely efficient Factor.

Everything is very simple in war, but the simplest thing is difficult. These difficulties accumulate and produce a friction, which no man can imagine exactly who has not seen war. Suppose now a traveller, who, towards evening, expects to accomplish the two stages at the end of his day's journey, four or five leagues, with post horses, on the high road—it is nothing. He arrives now at the last station but one, finds no horses, or very bad ones; then a hilly country, bad roads; it is a dark night, and he is glad when, after a great deal of trouble, he reaches the next station, and finds there some miserable accommodation. So in war, through the influence of an infinity of petty circumstances, which cannot properly be described on paper, things disappoint us, and we fall short of the mark. A powerful iron will overcomes this friction, it crushes the obstacles, but certainly the machine along with them. We shall often meet with this result. Like an obelisk, towards which the principal streets of a place converge, the strong will of a proud spirit, stands prominent and commanding, in the middle of the art of war.

Friction is the only conception which, in a general way, corresponds to that which distinguishes real war from war on paper. The military machine, the army and all belonging to it, is in fact simple; and appears, on this account, easy to manage. But let us reflect that no part of it is in one piece, that it is composed entirely of individuals, each of which keeps up its own friction in all directions. Theoretically all sounds very well; the commander of a battalion is responsible for the execution of the order given; and as the battalion by its discipline is glued together into one piece, and the chief must be a man of acknowledged zeal, the beam turns on an iron pin with little friction. But it is

not so in reality, and all that is exaggerated and false in such a conception manifests itself at once in war. The battalion always remains composed of a number of men, of whom, if chance so wills, the most insignificant is able to occasion delay, and even irregularity. The danger which war brings with it, the
bodily exertions which it requires, augment this evil so much, that they may
be regarded as the greatest causes of it.

This enormous friction, which is not concentrated, as in mechanics, at a few
points, is therefore everywhere brought into contact with chance, and thus
facts take place upon which it was impossible to calculate, their chief origin
being chance. As an instance of one such chance, take the weather. Here, the
fog prevents the enemy from being discovered in time, a battery from firing at
the right moment, a report from reaching the general; there, the rain prevents
a battalion from arriving, another from reaching in right time, because, instead of three, it had to march perhaps eight hours; the cavalry from charging
effectively because it is stuck fast in heavy ground.

These are only a few incidents of detail by way of elucidation, that the reader
may be able to follow the author, for whole volumes might be written on these
difficulties. To avoid this, and still to give a clear conception of the host of small
difficulties to be contended with in war, we might go on heaping up illustrations, if we were not afraid of being tiresome. But those who have already comprehended us will permit us to add a few more.

Activity in war is movement in a resistant medium. Just as a man in water
is unable to perform with ease and regularity the most natural and simplest
movement, that of walking, so in war, with ordinary powers, one cannot keep
even the line of mediocrity. This is the reason that the correct theorist is like
a swimming master, who teaches on dry land movements which are required
in the water, which must appear grotesque and ludicrous to those who forget
about the water. This is also why theorists, who have never plunged in themselves, or who cannot deduce any generalities from their experience, are un-
practical and even absurd, because they only teach what every one knows—
how to walk.

Further, every war is rich in particular facts; while, at the same time, each is
an unexplored sea, full of rocks, which the general may have a suspicion of,
but which he has never seen with his eye, and round which, moreover, he must
steer in the night. If a contrary wind also springs up, that is, if any great accidental event declares itself adverse to him, then the most consummate skill,
presence of mind and energy, are required; whilst to those who only look on
from a distance, all seems to proceed with the utmost ease. The knowledge of
this friction is a chief part of that so often talked of, experience in war, which
is required in a good general. Certainly, he is not the best general in whose
mind it assumes the greatest dimensions, who is the most overawed by it (this

includes that class of over-anxious generals, of whom there are so many amongst the experienced); but a general must be aware of it that he may overcome it, where that is possible; and that he may not expect a degree of precision in results which is impossible on account of this very friction. Besides, it can never be learnt theoretically; and if it could, there would still be wanting that experience of judgment which is called tact, and which is always more necessary in a field full of innumerable small and diversified objects, than in great and decisive cases, when one's own judgment may be aided by consultation with others. Just as the man of the world, through tact of judgment which has become habit, speaks, acts, and moves only as suits the occasion, so the officer, experienced in war, will always, in great and small matters, at every pulsation of war as we may say, decide and determine suitably to the occasion. Through this experience and practice, the idea comes to his mind of itself, that so and so will not suit. And thus he will not easily place himself in a position by which he is compromised, which, if it often occurs in war, shakes all the foundations of confidence, and becomes extremely dangerous.

It is, therefore, this friction, or what is so termed here, which makes that which appears easy in war difficult in reality. As we proceed, we shall often meet with this subject again, and it will hereafter become plain that, besides experience and a strong will, there are still many other rare qualities of the mind required to make a man a consummate general.

Concluding Remarks

Those things which as elements meet together in the atmosphere of war and make it a resistant medium for every activity, we have designated under the terms danger, bodily effort (exertion), information, and friction. In their impedient effects they may therefore be comprehended again in the collective notion of a general friction. Now is there, then, no kind of oil which is capable of diminishing this friction? Only one, and that one is not always available at the will of the Commander or his army. It is the habituation of an army to war.

Habit gives strength to the body in great exertion, to the mind in great danger, to the judgment against first impressions. By it a valuable circumspection is generally gained throughout every rank, from the Hussar and Rifleman, up to the General of Division, which facilitates the work of the chief Commander.

As the human eye in a dark room dilates its pupil draws in the little light that there is, partially distinguishes objects by degrees, and at last knows them quite well, so it is in war with the experienced soldier, whilst the novice is only met by pitch dark night.

Habituation to war no General can give his army at once; and the camps of manœuvre (peace exercises) furnish but a weak substitute for it, weak in comparison with real experience in war, but not weak in relation to other armies in which the training is limited to mere mechanical exercises of routine. So to regulate the exercises in peace time as to include some of these causes of friction, that the judgment, circumspection, even resolution of the separate leaders may be brought into exercise, is of much greater consequence than those believe who do not know the thing by experience. It is of immense importance that the soldier, high or low, whatever rank he has, should not have to encounter for the first time in war those things which, when seen for the first time, set him in astonishment and perplexity; if he has only met with them one single time before, even by that he is half acquainted with them. This relates even to bodily fatigues. They should be practised less to accustom the body than the mind to them. In war the young soldier is very apt to regard unusual fatigues as the consequence of faults, mistakes, and embarrassment in the conduct of the whole, and to become distressed by that. This would not happen if he had been prepared for that beforehand by exercises in peace.

Another less comprehensive but still very important means of gaining habituation to war in time of peace is to invite into the service officers of foreign armies, who have had experience in war. Peace seldom reigns over all Europe, and never in all quarters of the world. A State which has been long at peace should, therefore, always seek to procure some officers who have done good service at the different scenes of warfare; or to send there some of its own, that they may get a lesson in war.

However small the number of officers of this description may appear in proportion to the mass, still their influence is very sensibly felt. Their experience, the bent of their genius, the stamp of their character, influence their subordinates and comrades; and besides that, if they cannot be placed in positions of superior command, they may always be regarded as men acquainted with the country, who may be questioned on many special occasions.

HENRI JOMINI
(1779–1869)

Antoine Henri de Jomini, a Swiss from the canton of Vaud, worked for a bank in Paris before going on to become an officer in the army of the Helvetic Republic. He commanded a battalion at the age of twenty-one, and after the peace of Lunéville won attention with his Traité de grande tactique *(1803). He was appointed aide-de-camp to General Ney in the Austerlitz campaign and then promoted colonel by Napoleon. Jomini fought at Jena, Eylau, and in the early stages of the Peninsular War. He left the French army, but was recalled by Napoleon, becoming a brigadier at the age of twenty-eight. He took part in the Russian campaign, but after the battle of Bautzen clashed with Berthier, Napoleon's chief of staff, and went over to the Russians.*

Jomini was aide-de-camp to Emperor Alexander I at the battle of Leipzig in 1813 and subsequently attended the Congress of Vienna. He was named general in 1826 and in 1828 accompanied Emperor Nicholas I (who had been his pupil) during his campaign against the Turks. He helped found the Military Academy in Moscow in 1832. His major work, Précis de l'art de la guerre, *prepared for the czarevich Alexander, was published in Paris in 1837. Jomini retired in 1848; but he returned as adviser to the czar during the Crimean War (1853–56). He died in Paris in 1869. Although highly celebrated in his own lifetime, Jomini has been somewhat unfairly overshadowed by the posthumous glory of Clausewitz. He has in particular been criticized for seeking to formulate rules from Napoleon's successes. Such considerations aside, Jomini is one of the outstanding strategists of Western military history.*

STATESMANSHIP IN ITS RELATION TO WAR

Under this head are included those considerations from which a statesman concludes whether a war is proper, opportune, or indispensable, and determines the various operations necessary to attain the object of the war.

A government goes to war,

To reclaim certain rights or to defend them;

To protect and maintain the great interests of the state, as commerce, manufactures, or agriculture;

To uphold neighboring states whose existence is necessary either for the safety of the government or the balance of power;

To fulfill the obligations of offensive and defensive alliances;

To propagate political or religious theories, to crush them out, or to defend them;

To increase the influence and power of the state by acquisitions of territory;

To defend the threatened independence of the state;

To avenge insulted honor; or,

From a mania for conquest.

It may be remarked that these different kinds of war influence in some degree the nature and extent of the efforts and operations necessary for the proposed end. The party who has provoked the war may be reduced to the defensive, and the party assailed may assume the offensive; and there may be other circumstances which will affect the nature and conduct of a war, as,

1. A state may simply make war against another state.

2. A state may make war against several states in alliance with each other.

3. A state in alliance with another may make war upon a single enemy.

4. A state may be either the principal party or an auxiliary.

5. In the latter case a state may join in the struggle at its beginning or after it has commenced.

6. The theater of war may be upon the soil of the enemy, upon that of an ally, or upon its own.

7. If the war be one of invasion, it may be upon adjacent or distant territory: it may be prudent and cautious, or it may be bold and adventurous.

8. It may be a national war, either against ourselves or against the enemy.

9. The war may be a civil or a religious war.

From Henri de Jomini, *The Art of War,* translated by G. H. Mendell and W. P. Craighill (1862; reprint, Westport, Conn.: Greenwood Press, 1971), 14–38.

War is always to be conducted according to the great principles of the art; but great discretion must be exercised in the nature of the operations to be undertaken, which should depend upon the circumstances of the case.

For example: two hundred thousand French wishing to subjugate the Spanish people, united to a man against them, would not maneuver as the same number of French in a march upon Vienna, or any other capital, to compel a peace; nor would a French army fight the guerrillas of Mina as they fought the Russians at Borodino; nor would a French army venture to march upon Vienna without considering what might be the tone and temper of the governments and communities between the Rhine and the Inn, or between the Danube and the Elbe. A regiment should always fight in nearly the same way; but commanding generals must be guided by circumstances and events.

To these different combinations, which belong more or less to statesmanship, may be added others which relate solely to the management of armies. The name Military Policy is given to them; for they belong exclusively neither to diplomacy nor to strategy, but are still of the highest importance in the plans both of a statesman and a general.

Offensive Wars to Reclaim Rights

When a state has claims upon another, it may not always be best to enforce them by arms. The public interest must be consulted before action.

The most just war is one which is founded upon undoubted rights, and which, in addition, promises to the state advantages commensurate with the sacrifices required and the hazards incurred. Unfortunately, in our times there are so many doubtful and contested rights that most wars, though apparently based upon bequests, or wills, or marriages, are in reality but wars of expediency. . . .

In wars of this nature no rules can be laid down. To watch and to profit by every circumstance covers all that can be said. Offensive movements should be suitable to the end to be attained. The most natural step would be to occupy the disputed territory: then offensive operations may be carried on according to circumstances and to the respective strength of the parties, the object being to secure the cession of the territory by the enemy, and the means being to threaten him in the heart of his own country. Every thing depends upon the alliances the parties may be able to secure with other states, and upon their military resources. In an offensive movement, scrupulous care must be exercised not to arouse the jealousy of any other state which might come to the aid of the enemy. It is a part of the duty of a statesman to foresee this chance, and to obviate it by making proper explanations and giving proper guarantees to other states.

Of Wars Defensive Politically, and Offensive in a Military Point of View

A state attacked by another which renews an old claim rarely yields it without a war: it prefers to defend its territory, as is always more honorable. But it may be advantageous to take the offensive, instead of awaiting the attack on the frontiers.

There are often advantages in a war of invasion: there are also advantages in awaiting the enemy upon one's own soil. A power with no internal dissensions, and under no apprehension of an attack by a third party, will always find it advantageous to carry the war upon hostile soil. This course will spare its territory from devastation, carry on the war at the expense of the enemy, excite the ardor of its soldiers, and depress the spirits of the adversary. Nevertheless, in a purely military sense, it is certain that an army operating in its own territory, upon a theater of which all the natural and artificial features are well known, where all movements are aided by a knowledge of the country, by the favor of the citizens, and the aid of the constituted authorities, possesses great advantages.

These plain truths have their application in all descriptions of war; but, if the principles of strategy are always the same, it is different with the political part of war, which is modified by the tone of communities, by localities, and by the characters of men at the head of states and armies. The fact of these modifications has been used to prove that war knows no rules. Military science rests upon principles which can never be safely violated in the presence of an active and skillful enemy, while the moral and political part of war presents these variations. Plans of operations are made as circumstances may demand: to execute these plans, the great principles of war must be observed.

For instance, the plan of a war against France, Austria, or Russia would differ widely from one against the brave but undisciplined bands of Turks, which cannot be kept in order, are not able to maneuver well, and possess no steadiness under misfortunes.

Wars of Expediency

There are two kinds of wars of expediency: first, where a powerful state undertakes to acquire natural boundaries for commercial and political reasons; secondly, to lessen the power of a dangerous rival or to prevent his aggrandizement. These last are wars of intervention; for a state will rarely singly attack a dangerous rival: it will endeavor to form a coalition for that purpose.

These views belong rather to statesmanship or diplomacy than to war.

Of Wars with or without Allies

Of course, in a war an ally is to be desired, all other things being equal. Although a great state will more probably succeed than two weaker states in alliance against it, still the alliance is stronger than either separately. The ally not only furnishes a contingent of troops, but, in addition, annoys the enemy to a great degree by threatening portions of his frontier which otherwise would have been secure. All history teaches that no enemy is so insignificant as to be despised and neglected by any power, however formidable.

Wars of Intervention

To interfere in a contest already begun promises more advantages to a state than war under any other circumstances; and the reason is plain. The power which interferes throws upon one side of the scale its whole weight and influence; it interferes at the most opportune moment, when it can make decisive use of its resources.

There are two kinds of intervention: 1. Intervention in the internal affairs of neighboring states; 2. Intervention in external relations. . . .

Intervention in the external relations of states is more legitimate, and perhaps more advantageous. It may be doubtful whether a nation has the right to interfere in the internal affairs of another people; but it certainly has a right to oppose it when it propagates disorder which may reach the adjoining states.

There are three reasons for intervention in exterior foreign wars,—viz.: 1, by virtue of a treaty which binds to aid; 2, to maintain the political equilibrium; 3, to avoid certain evil consequences of the war already commenced, or to secure certain advantages from the war not to be obtained otherwise.

History is filled with examples of powers which have fallen by neglect of these principles. "A state begins to decline when it permits the immoderate aggrandizement of a rival, and a secondary power may become the arbiter of nations if it throw its weight into the balance at the proper time."

In a military view, it seems plain that the sudden appearance of a new and large army as a third party in a well-contested war must be decisive. Much will depend upon its geographical position in reference to the armies already in the field. . . .

There are several kinds of war resulting from these two different interventions:

1.   Where the intervention is merely auxiliary, and with a force specified by former treaties.

2. Where the intervention is to uphold a feeble neighbor by defending his territory, thus shifting the scene of war to other soil.

3. A state interferes as a principal party when near the theater of war,— which supposes the case of a coalition of several powers against one.

4. A state interferes either in a struggle already in progress, or interferes before the declaration of war.

When a state intervenes with only a small contingent, in obedience to treaty-stipulations, it is simply an accessory, and has but little voice in the main operations; but when it intervenes as a principal party, and with an imposing force, the case is quite different. . . .

It follows, then, that the safety of the army may be endangered by these distant interventions. The counterbalancing advantage is that its own territory cannot then be easily invaded, since the scene of hostilities is so distant; so that what may be a misfortune for the general may be, in a measure, an advantage to the state.

In wars of this character the essentials are to secure a general who is both a statesman and a soldier; to have clear stipulations with the allies as to the part to be taken by each in the principal operations; finally, to agree upon an objective point which shall be in harmony with the common interests. By the neglect of these precautions, the greater number of coalitions have failed, or have maintained a difficult struggle with a power more united but weaker than the allies.

The third kind of intervention, which consists in interfering with the whole force of the state and near to its frontiers, is more promising than the others. . . .

This double advantage is so decisive that it permits not only powerful monarchies, but even small states, to exercise a controlling influence when they know how to profit by it.

Aggressive Wars for Conquest and other Reasons

There are two very different kinds of invasion: one attacks an adjoining state; the other attacks a distant point, over intervening territory of great extent whose inhabitants may be neutral, doubtful, or hostile.

Wars of conquest, unhappily, are often prosperous,—as Alexander, Cæsar, and Napoleon during a portion of his career, have fully proved. However, there are natural limits in these wars, which cannot be passed without incurring great disaster. Cambyses in Nubia, Darius in Scythia, Crassus and the Emperor Julian among the Parthians, and Napoleon in Russia, furnish bloody proofs of these truths. The love of conquest, however, was not the only motive with Napoleon: his personal position, and his contest with England, urged him to enterprises the aim of which was to make him supreme. It is true that he loved war and its chances; but he was also a victim to the necessity of succeeding in his efforts or of yielding to England. It might be said that he was sent into this world to teach generals and statesmen what they should avoid. His victories teach what may be accomplished by activity, boldness, and skill; his disasters, what might have been avoided by prudence.

A war of invasion without good reason—like that of Genghis Khan—is a crime against humanity; but it may be excused, if not approved, when induced by great interests or when conducted with good motives. . . .

Let us hope that invasions may be rare. Still, it is better to attack than to be invaded; and let us remember that the surest way to check the spirit of conquest and usurpation is to oppose it by intervention at the proper time.

An invasion, to be successful, must be proportioned in magnitude to the end to be attained and to the obstacles to be overcome.

An invasion against an exasperated people, ready for all sacrifices and likely to be aided by a powerful neighbor, is a dangerous enterprise, as was well proved by the war in Spain (1808) and by the wars of the Revolution in 1792, 1793, and 1794. In these latter wars, if France was better prepared than Spain, she had no powerful ally, and she was attacked by all Europe upon both land and sea. . . .

When an invasion of a neighboring territory has nothing to fear from the inhabitants, the principles of strategy shape its course. The popular feeling rendered the invasions of Italy, Austria, and Prussia so prompt. . . . But when the invasion is distant and extensive territories intervene, its success will depend more upon diplomacy than upon strategy. The first step to insure success will be to secure the sincere and devoted alliance of a state adjoining the enemy, which will afford reinforcements of troops, and, what is still more important, give a secure base of operations, depots of supplies, and a safe refuge in case of disaster. The ally must have the same interest in success as the invaders, to render all this possible. . . .

Wars of Opinion

Although wars of opinion, national wars, and civil wars are sometimes confounded, they differ enough to require separate notice.

Wars of opinion may be intestine, both intestine and foreign, and, lastly, (which, however, is rare) they may be foreign or exterior without being intestine or civil.

Wars of opinion between two states belong also to the class of wars of intervention; for they result either from doctrines which one party desires to propagate among its neighbors, or from dogmas which it desires to crush,—in both cases leading to intervention. Although originating in religious or political dogmas, these wars are most deplorable; for, like national wars, they enlist the worst passions, and become vindictive, cruel, and terrible.

The wars of Islamism, the Crusades, the Thirty Years' War, the wars of the League, present nearly the same characteristics. Often religion is the pretext to obtain political power, and the war is not really one of dogmas. The successors of Mohammed cared more to extend their empire than to preach the Koran, and Philip II, bigot as he was, did not sustain the League in France for the purpose of advancing the Roman Church. . . .

The dogma sometimes is not only a pretext, but is a powerful ally; for it excites the ardor of the people, and also creates a party. For instance, the Swedes in the Thirty Years' War, and Philip II in France, had allies in the country more powerful than their armies. It may, however, happen, as in the Crusades and the wars of Islamism, that the dogma for which the war is waged, instead of friends, finds only bitter enemies in the country invaded; and then the contest becomes fearful.

The chances of support and resistance in wars of political opinions are about equal. It may be recollected how in 1792 associations of fanatics thought it possible to propagate throughout Europe the famous declaration of the rights of man, and how governments became justly alarmed, and rushed to arms probably with the intention of only forcing the lava of this volcano back into its crater and there extinguishing it. The means were not fortunate; for war and aggression are inappropriate measures for arresting an evil which lies wholly in the human passions, excited in a temporary paroxysm, of less duration as it is the more violent. Time is the true remedy for all bad passions and for all anarchical doctrines. A civilized nation may bear the yoke of a factious and unrestrained multitude for a short interval; but these storms soon pass away, and reason resumes her sway. To attempt to restrain such a mob by a foreign force is to attempt to restrain the explosion of a mine when the powder has already been ignited: it is far better to await the explosion and afterward fill up the crater than to try to prevent it and to perish in the attempt. . . .

In a military view these wars are fearful, since the invading force not only is met by the armies of the enemy, but is exposed to the attacks of an exasperated people. It may be said that the violence of one party will necessarily create support for the invaders by the formation of another and opposite one; but, if the exasperated party possesses all the public resources, the armies, the forts, the arsenals, and if it is supported by a large majority of the people, of what avail will be the support of the faction which possesses no such means?

What service did one hundred thousand Vendeans and one hundred thousand Federalists do for the Coalition in 1793?

History contains but a single example of a struggle like that of the Revolution; and it appears to clearly demonstrate the danger of attacking an intensely-excited nation. . . .

The military precepts for such wars are nearly the same as for national wars, differing, however, in a vital point. In national wars the country should be occupied and subjugated, the fortified places besieged and reduced, and the armies destroyed; whereas in wars of opinion it is of less importance to subjugate the country; here great efforts should be made to gain the end speedily, without delaying for details, care being constantly taken to avoid any acts which might alarm the nation for its independence or the integrity of its territory. . . .

National Wars

National wars, to which we have referred in speaking of those of invasion, are the most formidable of all. This name can only be applied to such as are waged against a united people, or a great majority of them, filled with a noble ardor and determined to sustain their independence: then every step is disputed, the army holds only its camp-ground, its supplies can only be obtained at the point of the sword, and its convoys are everywhere threatened or captured.

The spectacle of a spontaneous uprising of a nation is rarely seen; and, though there be in it something grand and noble which commands our admiration, the consequences are so terrible that, for the sake of humanity, we ought to hope never to see it. This uprising must not be confounded with a national defense in accordance with the institutions of the state and directed by the government.

This uprising may be produced by the most opposite causes. The serfs may rise in a body at the call of the government, and their masters, affected by a noble love of their sovereign and country, may set them the example and take the command of them; and, similarly, a fanatical people may arm under the appeal of its priests; or a people enthusiastic in its political opinions, or animated by a sacred love of its institutions, may rush to meet the enemy in defense of all it holds most dear.

The control of the sea is of much importance in the results of a national invasion. If the people possess a long stretch of coast, and are masters of the sea or in alliance with a power which controls it, their power of resistance is quintupled, not only on account of the facility of feeding the insurrection and of alarming the enemy on all the points he may occupy, but still more by the difficulties which will be thrown in the way of his procuring supplies by the sea.

The nature of the country may be such as to contribute to the facility of a national defense. In mountainous countries the people are always most formidable; next to these are countries covered with extensive forests. . . .

Defiles and large forests, as well as rocky regions, favor this kind of defense; and the Bocage of La Vendée, so justly celebrated, proves that any country, even if it be only traversed by large hedges and ditches or canals, admits of a formidable defense.

The difficulties in the path of an army in wars of opinions, as well as in national wars, are very great, and render the mission of the general conducting them very difficult. The events just mentioned, the contest of the Netherlands with Philip II and that of the Americans with the English, furnish evident proofs of this; but the much more extraordinary struggle of La Vendée with the victorious Republic, those of Spain, Portugal, and the Tyrol against Napoleon, and, finally, those of the Morea against the Turks, and of Navarre against the armies of Queen Christina, are still more striking illustrations.

The difficulties are particularly great when the people are supported by a considerable nucleus of disciplined troops. The invader has only an army: his adversaries have an army, and a people wholly or almost wholly in arms, and making means of resistance out of every thing, each individual of whom conspires against the common enemy; even the noncombatants have an interest in his ruin and accelerate it by every means in their power. He holds scarcely any ground but that upon which he encamps; outside the limits of his camp every thing is hostile and multiplies a thousandfold the difficulties he meets at every step.

These obstacles become almost insurmountable when the country is difficult. Each armed inhabitant knows the smallest paths and their connections; he finds everywhere a relative or friend who aids him; the commanders also know the country, and, learning immediately the slightest movement on the part of the invader, can adopt the best measures to defeat his projects; while the latter, without information of their movements, and not in a condition to send out detachments to gain it, having no resource but in his bayonets, and certain safety only in the concentration of his columns, is like a blind man: his combinations are failures; and when, after the most carefully-concerted movements and the most rapid and fatiguing marches, he thinks he is about to accomplish his aim and deal a terrible blow, he finds no signs of the enemy but his campfires: so that while, like Don Quixote, he is attacking windmills, his adversary is on his line of communications, destroys the detachments left to guard it, surprises his convoys, his depots, and carries on a war so disastrous for the invader that he must inevitably yield after a time. . . .

No army, however disciplined, can contend successfully against such a system applied to a great nation, unless it be strong enough to hold all the essential points of the country, cover its communications, and at the same time furnish an active force sufficient to beat the enemy wherever he may present himself. If this enemy has a regular army of respectable size to be a nucleus around which to rally the people, what force will be sufficient to be superior everywhere, and to assure the safety of the long lines of communication against numerous bodies? . . .

The immense obstacles encountered by an invading force in these wars have led some speculative persons to hope that there should never be any other kind, since then wars would become more rare, and, conquest being also more difficult, would be less a temptation to ambitious leaders. This reasoning is rather plausible than solid; for, to admit all its consequences, it would be necessary always to be able to induce the people to take up arms, and it would also be necessary for us to be convinced that there would be in the future no wars but those of conquest, and that all legitimate though secondary wars, which are only to maintain the political equilibrium or defend the public interests, should never occur again: otherwise, how could it be known when and how to excite the people to a national war? . . .

Civil Wars, and Wars of Religion

Intestine wars, when not connected with a foreign quarrel, are generally the result of a conflict of opinions, of political or religious sectarianism. In the Middle Ages they were more frequently the collisions of feudal parties. Religious wars are above all the most deplorable.

We can understand how a government may find it necessary to use force against its own subjects in order to crush out factions which would weaken the authority of the throne and the national strength; but that it should murder its citizens to compel them to say their prayers in French or Latin, or to recognize the supremacy of a foreign pontiff, is difficult of conception. Never was a king more to be pitied than Louis XIV, who persecuted a million of industrious Protestants, who had put upon the throne his own Protestant ancestor. Wars of fanaticism are horrible when mingled with exterior wars, and they are also frightful when they are family quarrels. The history of France in the times of the League should be an eternal lesson for nations and kings. It is difficult to believe that a people so noble and chivalrous in the time of Francis I should in twenty years have fallen into so deplorable a state of brutality.

To give maxims in such wars would be absurd. There is one rule upon which all thoughtful men will be agreed: that is, to unite the two parties or sects to drive the foreigners from the soil, and afterward to reconcile by treaty the conflicting claims or rights. Indeed, the intervention of a third power in a religious dispute can only be with ambitious views.

Governments may in good faith intervene to prevent the spreading of a political disease whose principles threaten social order; and, although these fears are generally exaggerated and are often mere pretexts, it is possible that a state may believe its own institutions menaced. But in religious disputes this is never the case. . . .

Double Wars, and the Danger of Undertaking
Two Wars at Once

The celebrated maxim of the Romans, not to undertake two great wars at the same time, is so well known and so well appreciated as to spare the necessity of demonstrating its wisdom.

A government may be compelled to maintain a war against two neighboring states; but it will be extremely unfortunate if it does not find an ally to come to its aid, with a view to its own safety and the maintenance of the political equilibrium. It will seldom be the case that the nations allied against it will have the same interest in the war and will enter into it with all their resources; and, if one is only an auxiliary, it will be an ordinary war.

Louis XIV, Frederick the Great, the Emperor Alexander, and Napoleon, sustained gigantic struggles against united Europe. When such contests arise from voluntary aggressions, they are proof of a capital error on the part of the state which invites them; but if they arise from imperious and inevitable circumstances they must be met by seeking alliances, or by opposing such means of resistance as shall establish something like equality between the strength of the parties. . . .

It follows, then, in general, that double wars should be avoided if possible, and, if cause of war be given by two states, it is more prudent to dissimulate or neglect the wrongs suffered from one of them, until a proper opportunity for redressing them shall arrive. The rule, however, is not without exception: the respective forces, the localities, the possibility of finding allies to restore, in a measure, equality of strength between the parties, are circumstances which will influence a government so threatened. We now have fulfilled our task, in noting both the danger and the means of remedying it. . . .

STRATEGY

Definition of Strategy and the Fundamental Principle
of War

The art of war, independently of its political and moral relations, consists of five principal parts, viz.: Strategy, Grand Tactics, Logistics, Tactics of the different arms, and the Art of the Engineer. We will treat of the first three branches, and begin by defining them. In order to do this, we will follow the order of procedure of a general when war is first declared, who commences with the points of the highest importance, as a plan of campaign, and afterward descends to the necessary details. Tactics, on the contrary, begins with details, and ascends to combinations and generalization necessary for the formation and handling of a great army.

We will suppose an army taking the field: the first care of its commander should be to agree with the head of the state upon the character of the war: then he must carefully study the theater of war, and select the most suitable base of operations, taking into consideration the frontiers of the state and those of its allies.

The selection of this base and the proposed aim will determine the zone of operations. The general will take a first objective point: he will select the line of operations leading to this point, either as a temporary or permanent line, giving it the most advantageous direction; namely, that which promises the greatest number of favorable opportunities with the least danger. An army marching on this line of operations will have a front of operations and a strategic front. The temporary positions which the corps d'armée will occupy upon this front of operations, or upon the line of defense, will be strategic positions.

When near its first objective point, and when it begins to meet resistance, the army will either attack the enemy or maneuver to compel him to retreat; and for this end it will adopt one or two strategic lines of maneuvers, which, being temporary, may deviate to a certain degree from the general line of operations, with which they must not be confounded.

To connect the strategic front with the base as the advance is made, lines of supply, depots, &c. will be established.

If the line of operations be long, and there be hostile troops in annoying proximity to it, these bodies may either be attacked and dispersed or be merely observed, or the operations against the enemy may be carried on without ref-

From Henri de Jomini, *The Art of War,* translated by G. H. Mendell and W. P. Craighill (1862; reprint, Westport, Conn.: Greenwood Press, 1971), 66–71.

erence to them. If the second of these courses be pursued, a double strategic front and large detachments will be the result.

The army being almost within reach of the first objective point, if the enemy oppose him there will be a battle; if indecisive, the fight will be resumed; if the army gains the victory, it will secure its objective point or will advance to attain a second. Should the first objective point be the possession of an important fort, the siege will be commenced. If the army be not strong enough to continue its march, after detaching a sufficient force to maintain the siege, it will take a strategic position to cover it. . . .

If the army be strong enough to make the best use of its victory, or if it have no siege to make, it will operate toward a second and more important objective point. If this point be distant, it will be necessary to establish an intermediate point of support. One or more secure cities already occupied will form an eventual base: when this cannot be done, a small strategic reserve may be established, which will protect the rear and also the depots by temporary fortifications. When the army crosses large streams, it will construct *têtes de pont;* and, if the bridges are within walled cities, earth-works will be thrown up to increase the means of defense and to secure the safety of the eventual base or the strategic reserve which may occupy these posts.

Should the battle be lost, the army will retreat toward its base, in order to be reinforced therefrom by detachments of troops, or, what is equivalent, to strengthen itself by the occupation of fortified posts and camps, thus compelling the enemy to halt or to divide his forces.

When winter approaches, the armies will either go into quarters, or the field will be kept by the army which has obtained decisive success and is desirous of profiting to the utmost by its superiority. These winter campaigns are very trying to both armies, but in other respects do not differ from ordinary campaigns, unless it be in demanding increased activity and energy to attain prompt success.

Such is the ordinary course of a war, and as such we will consider it, while discussing combinations which result from these operations.

Strategy embraces the following points:

1. The selection of the theater of war, and the discussion of the different combinations of which it admits.
2. The determination of the decisive points in these combinations, and the most favorable direction for operations.
3. The selection and establishment of the fixed base and of the zone of operations.
4. The selection of the objective point, whether offensive or defensive.
5. The strategic fronts, lines of defense, and fronts of operations.

6. The choice of lines of operations leading to the objective point or strategic front.

7. For a given operation, the best strategic line, and the different maneuvers necessary to embrace all possible cases.

8. The eventual bases of operations and the strategic reserves.

9. The marches of armies, considered as maneuvers.

10. The relation between the position of depots and the marches of the army.

11. Fortresses regarded as strategical means, as a refuge for an army, as an obstacle to its progress: the sieges to be made and to be covered.

12. Points for intrenched camps, *têtes de pont,* &c.

13. The diversions to be made, and the large detachments necessary.

These points are principally of importance in the determination of the first steps of a campaign; but there are other operations of a mixed nature, such as passages of streams, retreats, surprises, disembarkations, convoys, winter quarters, the execution of which belongs to tactics, the conception and arrangement to strategy.

The maneuvering of an army upon the battle-field, and the different formations of troops for attack, constitute Grand Tactics. Logistics is the art of moving armies. It comprises the order and details of marches and camps, and of quartering and supplying troops; in a word, it is the execution of strategical and tactical enterprises.

To repeat. Strategy is the art of making war upon the map, and comprehends the whole theater of operations. Grand Tactics is the art of posting troops upon the battlefield according to the accidents of the ground, of bringing them into action, and the art of fighting upon the ground, in contradistinction to planning upon a map. Its operations may extend over a field of ten or twelve miles in extent. Logistics comprises the means and arrangements which work out the plans of strategy and tactics. Strategy decides where to act; logistics brings the troops to this point; grand tactics decides the manner of execution and the employment of the troops.

It is true that many battles have been decided by strategic movements, and have been, indeed, but a succession of them; but this only occurs in the exceptional case of a dispersed army: for the general case of pitched battles the above definition holds good.

Grand Tactics, in addition to acts of local execution, relates to the following objects:

1. The choice of positions and defensive lines of battle.
2. The offensive in a defensive battle.

3. The different orders of battle, or the grand maneuvers proper for the attack of the enemy's line.
4. The collision of two armies on the march, or unexpected battles.
5. Surprises of armies in the open field.
6. The arrangements for leading troops into battle.
7. The attack of positions and intrenched camps.
8. *Coups de main.*

All other operations, such as relate to convoys, foraging-parties, skirmishes of advanced or rear guards, the attack of small posts, and any thing accomplished by a detachment or single division, may be regarded as details of war, and not included in the great operations.

The Fundamental Principle of War

It is proposed to show that there is one great principle underlying all the operations of war,—a principle which must be followed in all good combinations. It is embraced in the following maxims:

1. To throw by strategic movements the mass of an army, successively, upon the decisive points of a theater of war, and also upon the communications of the enemy as much as possible without compromising one's own.
2. To maneuver to engage fractions of the hostile army with the bulk of one's forces.
3. On the battle-field, to throw the mass of the forces upon the decisive point, or upon that portion of the hostile line which it is of the first importance to overthrow.
4. To so arrange that these masses shall not only be thrown upon the decisive point, but that they shall engage at the proper times and with energy.

This principle has too much simplicity to escape criticism: one objection is that it is easy to recommend throwing the mass of the forces upon the decisive points, but that the difficulty lies in recognizing those points.

This truth is evident; and it would be little short of the ridiculous to enunciate such a general principle without accompanying it with all necessary explanations for its application upon the field. . . .

The general theater of operations seldom contains more than three zones,— the right, the left, and the center; and each zone, front of operations, strategic position, and line of defense, as well as each line of battle, has the same subdivisions,—two extremities and the center. A direction upon one of these three will always be suitable for the attainment of the desired end. A direction upon one of the two remaining will be less advantageous; while the third direction will be wholly inapplicable. In considering the object proposed in connection with the positions of the enemy and the geography of the country, it will appear that in every strategic movement or tactical maneuver the question for decision will always be, whether to maneuver to the right, to the left, or directly in front. The selection of one of these three simple alternatives cannot, surely, be considered an enigma. The art of giving the proper direction to the masses is certainly the basis of strategy, although it is not the whole of the art of war. Executive talent, skill, energy, and a quick apprehension of events are necessary to carry out any combinations previously arranged. . . .

STRATEGIC COMBINATIONS

Of the System of Operations

War once determined upon, the first point to be decided is, whether it shall be offensive or defensive; and we will first explain what is meant by these terms. There are several phases of the offensive: if against a great state, the whole or a large portion of whose territory is attacked, it is an *invasion;* if a province only, or a line of defense of moderate extent, be assailed, it is the ordinary offensive; finally, if the offensive is but an attack upon the enemy's position, and is confined to a single operation, it is called the taking the *initiative.* In a moral and political view, the offensive is nearly always advantageous: it carries the war upon foreign soil, saves the assailant's country from devastation, increases his resources and diminishes those of his enemy, elevates the *morale* of his army, and generally depresses the adversary. It sometimes happens that invasion excites the ardor and energy of the adversary,—particularly when he feels that the independence of his country is threatened.

In a military point of view, the offensive has its good and its bad side. Strategically, an invasion leads to deep lines of operations, which are always dangerous in a hostile country. All the obstacles in the enemy's country, the mountains, rivers, defiles, and forts, are favorable for defense, while the inhabitants and authorities of the country, so far from being the instruments of the invading army, are generally hostile. However, if success be obtained, the enemy is struck in a vital point: he is deprived of his resources and compelled to seek a speedy termination of the contest.

For a single operation, which we have called the taking the *initiative,* the offensive is almost always advantageous, particularly in strategy. Indeed, if the

From Henri de Jomini, *The Art of War,* translated by G. H. Mendell and W. P. Craighill (1862; reprint, Westport, Conn.: Greenwood Press, 1971), 72–74.

art of war consists in throwing the masses upon the decisive points, to do this it will be necessary to take the initiative. The attacking party knows what he is doing and what he desires to do; he leads his masses to the point where he desires to strike. He who awaits the attack is everywhere anticipated: the enemy falls with large force upon fractions of his force: he neither knows where his adversary proposes to attack him nor in what manner to repel him.

Tactically, the offensive also possesses advantages, but they are less positive, since, the operations being upon a limited field, the party taking the initiative cannot conceal them from the enemy, who may detect his designs and by the aid of good reserves cause them to fail.

The attacking party labors under the disadvantages arising from the obstacles to be crossed before reaching the enemy's line; on which account the advantages and disadvantages of the tactical offensive are about equally balanced.

Whatever advantages may be expected either politically or strategically from the offensive, it may not be possible to maintain it exclusively throughout the war; for a campaign offensive in the beginning may become defensive before it ends.

A defensive war is not without its advantages, when wisely conducted. It may be passive or active, taking the offensive at times. The passive defense is always pernicious; the active may accomplish great successes. The object of a defensive war being to protect, as long as possible, the country threatened by the enemy, all operations should be designed to retard his progress, to annoy him in his enterprises by multiplying obstacles and difficulties, without, however, compromising one's own army. He who invades does so by reason of some superiority; he will then seek to make the issue as promptly as possible: the defense, on the contrary, desires delay till his adversary is weakened by sending off detachments, by marches, and by the privations and fatigues incident to his progress.

An army is reduced to the defensive only by reverses or by a positive inferiority. It then seeks in the support of forts, and in natural or artificial barriers, the means of restoring equality by multiplying obstacles in the way of the enemy. This plan, when not carried to an extreme, promises many chances of success, but only when the general has the good sense not to make the defense passive: he must not remain in his positions to receive whatever blows may be given by his adversary; he must, on the contrary, redouble his activity, and be constantly upon the alert to improve all opportunities of assailing the weak points of the enemy. This plan of war may be called the defensive-offensive, and may have strategical as well as tactical advantages. It combines the advantages of both systems; for one who awaits his adversary upon a prepared field, with all his own resources in hand, surrounded by all the advantages of being on his own ground, can with hope of success take the initiative, and is fully able to judge when and where to strike. . . .

EPITOME OF STRATEGY

The task which I undertook seems to me to have been passably fulfilled by what has been stated in reference to the strategic combinations which enter ordinarily into a plan of campaign. We have seen, from the definition at the beginning of this chapter, that, in the most important operations in war, *strategy* fixes the direction of movements, and that we depend upon *tactics* for their execution. Therefore, before treating of these mixed operations, it will be well to give here the combinations of grand tactics and of battles, as well as the maxims by the aid of which the application of the fundamental principle of war may be made.

By this method these operations, half strategic and half tactical, will be better comprehended as a whole; but, in the first place, I will give a synopsis of the contents of the preceding chapter.

From the different articles which compose it, we may conclude that the manner of applying the general principle of war to all possible theaters of operations is found in what follows:

1.   In knowing how to make the best use of the advantages which the reciprocal directions of the two bases of operations may afford. . . .

2.   In choosing, from the three zones ordinarily found in the strategic field, that one upon which the greatest injury can be done to the enemy with the least risk to one's self.

3.   In establishing well, and giving a good direction to, the lines of operations; adopting for defense the concentric system of the Archduke Charles in 1796 and of Napoleon in 1814; or that of Soult in 1814, for retreats parallel to the frontiers.

On the offensive we should follow the system which led to the success of Napoleon in 1800, 1805, and 1806, when he directed his line upon the extremity of the strategic front; or we might adopt his plan which was successful in 1796, 1809, and 1814, of directing the line of operations upon the center of the strategic front: all of which is to be determined by the respective positions of the armies, and according to the maxims presented. . . .

4.   In selecting judicious eventual lines of maneuver, by giving them such directions as always to be able to act with the greater mass of the forces, and to prevent the parts of the enemy from concentrating or from affording each other mutual support.

From Henri de Jomini, *The Art of War*, translated by G. H. Mendell and W. P. Craighill (1862; reprint, Westport, Conn.: Greenwood Press, 1971), 175–76.

5. In combining, in the same spirit of centralization, all strategic positions, and all large detachments made to cover the most important strategic points of the theater of war.

6. In imparting to the troops the greatest possible mobility and activity, so as, by their successive employment upon points where it may be important to act, to bring superior force to bear upon fractions of the hostile army.

The system of rapid and continuous marches multiplies the effect of an army, and at the same time neutralizes a great part of that of the enemy's, and is often sufficient to insure success; but its effect will be quintupled if the marches be skillfully directed upon the decisive strategic points of the zone of operations, where the severest blows to the enemy can be given.

However, as a general may not always be prepared to adopt this decisive course to the exclusion of every other, he must then be content with attaining a part of the object of every enterprise, by rapid and successive employment of his forces upon isolated bodies of the enemy, thus insuring their defeat. A general who moves his masses rapidly and continually, and gives them proper directions, may be confident both of gaining victories and of securing great results therefrom.

THOMAS BUGEAUD
(1784–1849)

Thomas Robert Bugeaud, marquis de La Piconnerie, duc d'Isly, was a
corporal at Austerlitz, but ended the Napoleonic wars a colonel. He rejoined
Napoleon during the Hundred Days and was dismissed from the army at
the Second Restoration. Bugeaud campaigned in North Africa in 1836–37,
was appointed governor-general of Algeria by Thiers in 1840, and became
marshal of France in 1843. In Algeria he adapted units to mobile warfare
and the counterinsurgency tactics used in colonial conquests, setting up
"Arab bureaus" and establishing agricultural settlements. His victory at
Isly in 1844 broke the power of Abd al-Qadir (1808–83), who had been
waging a war of resistance. In 1847 Bugeaud resigned as governor, feeling
himself insufficiently supported by the French government. He was asked
to be a candidate for the presidency, in opposition to Louis Napoleon,
but declined.

ON PACIFICATION

In making peace I was under no illusion that it would be eternal, or even that
it would last very long. Nor did I hope that the question of Africa would thereby
be completely resolved. I made peace because the government and much of
public opinion wanted it. If I threw myself into it with an ardor that had little
in common with my way of fighting, it is because I was indeed convinced that
a peace, even less good or more bad, as you prefer, was better for France than
an ill-fought war. I would say more: peace is better than a well-fought war; for
to fight war well in Africa, it would be necessary to deploy forces there whose
absence in Europe would be an immense danger for the country.

From T. R. Bugeaud de La Piconnerie, *Mémoire sur notre établissement dans la province d'Oran*
par suite de la paix, pt. 5 (Paris, 1837). Translated from the French by A. M. Berrett.

[744]

The longer peace lasts, the less difficult any future war will be, if we have foresight, if we know how to establish ourselves solidly on the territory we have definitively conquered, if we are wise enough to hold ourselves ever ready to make war, if we know how to open relations with the Arabs, which might imbue them with our customs, our tastes, and our habits, and, above all, if we know how to provide for the welfare of the Muslim populations living under our rule.

For his part, Abd al-Qadir will surely not remain inactive: he will create a small standing army; he will establish himself at Tlemcen; he will put down a few dissident tribes; he will build up a small artillery force. That will make him more powerful vis-à-vis the tribes but will not make him stronger against us than he is today. I would even say that he will be less strong when he has six thousand regular troops and guns.

Until now his strength has lain in his lightness, his freedom of movement, and the impossibility of getting at him. He did not have to protect depots, military towns, large population and commercial centers, lines, or bases of operations.

With peace for a few years and six to eight thousand men under arms (that is all he will be able to pay and maintain), he will have a little of all the encumbrances that I have just listed; it will no longer be impossible to get at him, because he will have towns and depots to guard. [When he has] infantry, battles will no longer be as inconclusive as they are today. The first action will be rougher, it is true, but we shall be able to make him suffer one of those great disasters that sow terror and discouragement all over the country, whereas hitherto it has been impossible to make any great impact on this host of horsemen, who may individually be excellent, but, lacking any overall strength together, lacking harmony, never engaged far enough for the action to be decisive. The unpredictability of their movements was rather embarassing for the generals and fascinating for our young soldiers. The troops taught the Arab commanders tactics, but it will be a long time before they learn the art properly. They will need a century before they learn how to harmonize the three arms on a battlefield. They will have the disadvantages of tactics without any of the benefits.

. . . But what above all will weaken the emir [Abd al-Qadir] is that, as the tribes are no longer warring amongst themselves, because they will be subject to a single prince, and as they become richer through trade and agriculture, relying on the standing army and gradually becoming familiar with our tastes and needs, they will soon become less warlike. Trade and day-to-day relations will make the hatred and repugnance that we inspire in them disappear. They will see that after all it is possible to live with Christians, and that we bring with us comfort and well-being. These ideas are already spreading; they will become general, and when war comes, they will work in our favor. [The Algerians] will submit with less difficulty.

It cannot be stressed enough, however, that for habits to change, for repugnance and prejudice to disappear, for ideas of civilization to penetrate, for us to be able to get something going and establish ourselves militarily and agriculturally, peace has to have some permanence. Even were we to have plans for total conquest in future, we would need this break to facilitate our future operations. It would be a break to gain new strength. Today, conquest is too difficult; it would require [France to] make exorbitant and almost permanent sacrifices. It would be necessary not only to conquer but to guard what is conquered, which would require almost as many men. But when I compare the sacrifices in men and money with the advantages that may result from possession of the whole country between the desert, Tunis, Morocco, and the sea, although I am a warrior by taste and by profession, I do not feel I can advise my country to embark on that conquest. I cannot flatter the nation's amourpropre at the expense of its highest interests; and I am convinced that the total conquest of Africa might compromise [France's] independence in Europe.

... Settling the Arabs by putting up permanent buildings would in my opinion be the best way to achieve our ends. Unfortunately, that is very difficult and very costly. In doing so we would bind them to the land; they would become less fierce, less warlike, easier to govern. Currently they cannot be reached either for war or for administration and it is really laughable, and painful at the same time to hear or read the tirades of our speakers and writers recommending that the way to achieve conquest and submission is to apply just laws, have a good distributive justice system, and make the Arabs feel the softness of our ways, and the advantages of our civilization. All that is doubtless fine and excellent, and I appreciate [these things] as much as anybody; but how can they be offered to people who run off when we approach, leaving only their warriors behind, who reply to sentimental words by firing their guns?

SHAKA
(c. 1787–1828)

One of the chief military innovations of the Zulu king Shaka was a heavy,
broad-bladed stabbing assegai (spear) called iklwa *(onomatopoeically*
mimicking the sucking sound it made when it was pulled out). Armed with
this weapon and trained in the tactics Shaka had taught them, his rigorously
drilled regiments (who are said to have been able to travel fifty miles in a
day) swept everything before them in southeastern Africa. Although Shaka
almost literally created the Zulu nation, his cruelties turned even his own
family against him in the end, and he was finally assassinated by his half-
brother Dingane.

Henry Francis Fynn (whom the Zulus called Mbulazi) was only twenty-
one when he met Shaka at his kraal, kwaBulawayo, in 1824. Fynn had had
some medical training in England, and he was able to treat Shaka's wounds
after an attempt to kill him, with the result that Shaka came to regard him as
a friend. Along with A. T. Bryant's Olden Times in Zululand and Natal, *
Fynn's journals, which he reconstructed in later life, are one of our main
sources of information about Shaka and the early history of the Zulus.

THE ZULU ARMY
(from the diary of Henry Francis Fynn)

When I next returned to Shaka's kraal, May 1826, I saw Somaphunga, brother
of Sikhunyana, then king of the Ndwandwe tribe. Somaphunga, afraid of being put to death by his brother, had escaped and come to tender his allegiance
to Shaka. He, moreover, gave such information to the King as could not possibly have been obtained by means of spies.

I had not been at the port many days before messengers arrived from Shaka
to call all hands, white as well as black, to resist an attack which was momen-

From *The Diary of Henry Francis Fynn*, edited by James Stuart and D. McK. Malcolm (Pieter-
maritzberg, South Africa: Shuter & Shooter, 1969), 122–31.

[747]

tarily expected on Shaka's kraal. This placed us in an awkward position, as we were far from being fit for active service. Powder was scarce, and our arms out of repair. Moreover, we were aware that, by complying, we should be violating the laws of our country, and embarking on a course which could in no way prove beneficial to us. On the other hand, we dreaded the consequences that might ensue from refusing to obey the order. After a general consultation, we decided to proceed to Shaka's residence. On arriving there, we found everything quiet and peaceful. A day or two after our arrival, however, the whole nation had been called to arms.

Shaka acquainted us with his intentions, and spoke of the necessity of our accompanying him, it being the custom, when the King proceeded in person to war, for every able-bodied man to accompany him. Attempts to explain the nature of the laws of our country and the duties they imposed on us, especially in regard to attacks on other nations, caused him to make some very unpleasant observations. We realised that the more we showed ourselves ready to accompany him, the better it would be for us. He showed us how dependent we were on him. He also pointed out that vessels seldom, or never, visited Natal; that he could destroy every one of us in such a way that there would be no one left to tell the tale; and that, if the English should seek to avenge our being massacred, they would be terror-struck at the magnitude of his army. . . . After these arguments, we proposed to retire to rest, seeing it was late. Shaka then remarked that there would be no necessity for our taking part in the actual fighting; all he wanted us to do was to accompany him, i.e., give him our moral support.

On the following morning we found out to our surprise that the whole army had already moved off during the night; two chiefs only being left to accompany us. We made all possible haste to overtake them, but were unable to do so until we had reached. . . . the general rendezvous of the forces. Thence the army was to proceed in separate divisions and by different routes. Here we rested two days, the divisions having been dispatched each with its orders and spies sent on ahead of the remaining forces (each regiment being headed by its chiefs), with heralds, in the meantime, loudly and repeatedly reciting the numerous heroic achievements and altogether wonderful characteristics of their sovereign. The day was exceedingly hot. Every man was ordered to roll up his shield and carry it on his back—a custom observed only when the enemy is known to be at a considerable distance. In the rear of the regiments were the baggage boys, few above the age of 12, and some not more than 6. These boys were attached to the chiefs and principal men, carrying their mats, headrests, tobacco, etc., and driving cattle required for the army's consumption. Some of the chiefs, moreover, were accompanied by girls carrying beer, corn and milk; and when their supply had been exhausted these carriers returned to their homes.

The whole body of men, boys and women amounted, as nearly as we could reckon, to 50,000. All proceeded in close formation, and when looked at from a distance nothing could be seen but a cloud of dust. We had not rested from the time we started, and were parched and almost perishing from thirst, when, coming to a marshy stream, about sunset, the craving to obtain water caused a general and excessive confusion. After the first regiment had passed, the whole of the swamp became nothing but mud, yet this mud was eaten and swallowed with avidity by the following regiments. Several men and boys were trampled to death; and although there was a cry of "shame" raised by many, and a call to help the victims, everyone was too much occupied to attempt to extricate them.

We travelled on until about nine at night, when we arrived at some kraals belonging to a once-powerful nation, the Iziyendane, of whom no more than 150 or 200 souls now remained. They were a different people from any we had yet seen. They were of a strong muscular build, more active than the Zulus, and not having their heads shaved, but wearing their hair about six or eight inches long and twisted in strings of the thickness of whip-cord. As these people had a perfect knowledge of the country, Shaka engaged them as guides and spies.

Next morning we proceeded at daylight, marching over extensive plains of hard and stony ground. At eleven we rested and Shaka employed the Hottentots in making sandals for himself. Cattle were killed for the use of the army. We ate the same food that Shaka did. Each day cattle were dealt out for the use of our Hottentots and natives. We had not been sitting more than an hour when Mr. Farewell was attacked by an ox and so severely injured as to be unable to proceed any further. The King left him in the care of the chiefs who had been directed to remain there, with a part of the seraglio women, until his return.

At one o'clock we proceeded on our march. The whole army was then made to form a single line across the plain, when we drove before us hartebeest, rhinoceros, pheasant and partridge in great numbers. We encamped at the end of the plain under stunted bushes that were dotted about here and there. The army rested here for two days. During the halt a force was detached and sent on ahead.

On resuming our march, Shaka requested me to join the detachment that had already gone on. He did this merely to please his own fancy. I accordingly went on. The frost of the preceding night had been so severe that many of the detachment, from the excessive cold, had slept, to wake no more. During the whole of this day's march not a tree or bush of any kind was to be seen; we were, therefore, obliged to roast our meat with dry grass. We encamped where we found the detachment, namely, in a cave of a mountain. This cave was shaped so as to form three sides of a square. . . .

The following day Shaka arrived with the remainder of the forces and next morning we proceeded in one body to a forest, where we rested for two days, awaiting the return of the spies. Several regiments were sent to kraals deserted by the hostile nation, the people having betaken themselves to a general rendezvous. They returned on the evening of the following day loaded with corn, a great luxury to us who had had nothing but meat for several days, and that extremely poor. To us, who were not used to such kind of living, it caused such pain in our teeth as prevented us from chewing.

When the spies returned, the army moved forward early in the morning and bivouacked at the foot of an immense forest, from which the enemy was not far distant. We had generally marched ahead to relieve ourselves from dust, and we had done so this morning till we came within sight of the enemy, when we thought that we ought to join Shaka, expecting him to be close at hand. We found that he was on the opposite mountain, and seeing a regiment carrying white shields, I diverted my course to it at once.

. . . When I had reached the bottom of the mountain and was ascending the opposite one, expecting to find Shaka there, I met one of his servants, who informed me that the King had remained at the forest, and advised me to go back, as, the ascent being difficult, the regiment would leave me a long way behind. Being a stranger to their mode of attack I determined to ascend the mountain and be a spectator of passing events.

The hill from which we had first seen the enemy presented to our view an extensive valley to the left of which was a hill separated by another valley from an immense mountain. On the upper part of this there was a rocky eminence, near the summit of which the enemy had collected all his forces, surrounding their cattle, and above them the women and children of the nation in a body. They were sitting down, awaiting the attack.

Shaka's forces marched slowly and with much caution, in regiments, each regiment divided into companies, till within 20 yards of the enemy, when they made a halt. Although Shaka's troops had taken up a position so near, the enemy seemed disinclined to move, till [they had been fired upon] three times. The first and second shots seemed to make no impression on them, for they only hissed and cried in reply: "That is a dog." At the third shot, both parties, with a tumultuous yell, clashed together, and continued stabbing each other for about three minutes, when both fell back a few paces.

Seeing their losses were about equal, both enemies raised a cry and this was followed by another rush, and they continued closely engaged about twice as long as in the first onset, when both parties again drew off. But the enemy's loss had now been the more severe. This urged the Zulus to a final charge. The shrieks now became terrific. The remnants of the enemy's army sought shelter in an adjoining wood, out of which they were soon driven. Then began a slaughter of the women and children. They were all put to death. The cattle being taken by the different regiments were driven to the kraal lately occupied by Sikhunyana. The battle, from the commencement to the close, did not last more than an hour and a half. The numbers of the hostile tribe, including women and children, could not have been less than 40,000. The number of cattle taken was estimated at 60,000. The sun having set while the cattle were being captured, the whole valley during the night was a scene of confusion. Parties of three, four, and five men each went about killing cattle and cutting off the tails of others to form part of their war dress. Many of Shaka's wounded managed to crawl on hands and knees in the hope of getting assistance, but for the enemy's wounded there was no hope.

Early next morning Shaka arrived, and each regiment, previous to its inspection by him, had picked out its cowards and put them to death. Many of these, no doubt, forfeited their lives only because their chiefs were in fear that, if they did not condemn some as being guilty, they would be suspected of seeking a pretext to save them and would incur the resentment of Shaka.

No man who had been actually engaged in the fight was allowed to appear in the King's presence until a purification by the doctor had been undergone. This doctor gave each warrior certain roots to eat, and to everyone who had actually killed one of the enemy an additional number. To make their bravery as public as possible, bits of wood are worn round the neck, each bit being supposed to reckon for an enemy slain. To the end of this necklace are attached bits of the root received from the doctor, part of which has been eaten. They then proceed to some river to wash their persons and, until this had been done, they may not eat any food, except the meat of cattle killed on the day of battle. Having washed, they appear before the King, when thanks or praise are the last thing they have to expect; censure being loudly expressed on account of something that had not been done as it should have been, and they get off well if one or two chiefs and a few dozen soldiers are not struck off the army list by being put to death.

During the afternoon a woman and child of the defeated tribe, the latter aged about 10 years, were brought before the King, and he made every enquiry respecting Sikhunyana; what had been his plans when he heard of the intended attack, and what was the general feeling as to its result. To induce her to set aside all fear, he gave her some beer and a dish of beef, which she ate, while giving all the information she was possessed of. When her recital was finished, both mother and child were sentenced to instant death. Being present, I begged the life of the child, that it might become my servant. An application to save the life of both was little likely to succeed. From her information, Shaka found that Sikhunyana, with a few men, had escaped. A regiment was ordered to pursue them, whilst another was detached to kill the wounded of the enemy. I now took the opportunity of writing Mr. Farewell an account of all that had taken place. The army, after clearing up, commenced its return home.

When we had been three days on the march orders were given for the army to be divided into three corps; one of which was to accompany Shaka; the other two were to attack two tribes under Mlotshwa and Beje. These chiefs had formerly been under Zwide, the late king of the defeated enemy. In an unsuccessful attack on Shaka these two tribes had been cut off from the main body and were induced to join Shaka. Believing that they had joined him only from motives of policy he dealt kindly with them at first, but the moment their former king had been subdued, and they could have no opportunity of revenge, they were attacked.

Mlotshwa took up his position on the Phondwane mountain, where his father had several times successfully defended himself. This was in the centre of a plain, and could only be ascended by two different passes guarded by men who hurled down masses of rock on their assailants. The women kept up the supply of these boulders for the men. This mountain hold was usually well stored with provisions. His provisions being exhausted, Mlotshwa submitted himself to Shaka and was again received into favour.

Beje's capabilities of defence were equally good. He, too, had a strong position among the rocks, and succeeded in cutting to pieces one of Shaka's regiments, raised only two months previously, and numbering two thousand men. This regiment had the name of the regiment of "Warmth," or in the Zulu "Motha." A few escaped and came to the army, now on its return homeward; but orders were given to put them to death at once, as men who had dared to fly.

Shaka now started on his return journey, leaving the regiments to attack the above-named chiefs. We accompanied him. . . .

I now proceeded to the Umzimkhulu River with a party of natives, who had learned the use of fire-arms in our service, for the purpose of elephant hunting. I had not long been established there before natives from the surrounding country, because of their distressed and famished state, flocked to me for protection from that death which those who had joined me in my former expeditions had escaped. It was not long before the remains of four tribes, with their chiefs—amounting to more than 2,000 of both sexes—came to live under me. Many of them were people who had made their escape when at the point of being put to death by the Zulus. By merely notifying such arrivals to

Shaka, the refugees were allowed to reside with us, a favour contrary to all former custom.

Messrs. Farewell, King, Isaacs, Cane and Ogle, as well as myself, have in this manner been the means of saving the lives of hundreds of people. The country for 25 miles round Natal was uninhabited except by the few previously mentioned. There are now more than 4,000 inhabitants under our protection, and our departure from the country would be the signal for their immediate destruction.

CHARLES ARDANT DU PICQ
(1821–1870)

*Charles Ardant du Picq became a lieutenant in the French army in 1842
and a captain in 1852. He had a brief spell in prison at Sebastopol in 1855.
He was promoted colonel in 1869 and was killed in action against the
Prussians a year later, near Gravelotte. His* Etudes sur le combat, *dealing
with both modern and ancient warfare, only appeared after his death. In it
he questioned—excessively systematically, some would say—the employment
of shock tactics in close combat in antiquity; conversely he stressed the
importance of the factor of morale in war.*

CONFIDENCE, THE SOUL OF VICTORY

Let us repeat now, what we said at the beginning of this study. Man does not
enter battle to fight, but for victory. He does everything that he can to avoid
the first and obtain the second. The continued improvement of all appliances
of war has no other goal than the annihilation of the enemy. Absolute bravery, which does not refuse battle even on unequal terms, trusting only to God
or to destiny, is not natural in man; it is the result of moral culture. It is infinitely rare, because in the face of danger the animal sense of self-preservation
always gains the upper hand. Man calculates his chances, with what errors we
are about to see.

Now, man has a horror of death. In the bravest, a great sense of duty, which
they alone are capable of understanding and living up to, is paramount. But
the mass always cowers at sight of the phantom, death. Discipline is for the
purpose of dominating that horror by a still greater horror, that of punishment or disgrace. But there always comes an instant when natural horror gets

From Charles Ardant du Picq, *Battle Studies*, translated by John N. Greely and Robert C.
Cotton (Harrisburg, Pa.: Stackpole Books, 1946), 120–28. Reproduced by permission of Stackpole Books.

an upper hand over discipline, and the fighter flees. "Stop, stop, hold out a few minutes, an instant more, and you are victor! You are not even wounded yet,— if you turn your back you are dead!" He does not hear, he cannot hear any more. He is full of fear. How many armies have sworn to conquer or perish? How many have kept their oaths? An oath of sheep to stand up against wolves. History shows, not armies, but firm souls who have fought unto death, and the devotion of Thermopylæ is therefore justly immortal.

Here we are again brought to the consideration of essential truths, enunciated by many men, now forgotten or unknown.

To insure success in the rude test of conflict, it is not sufficient to have a mass composed of valiant men like the Gauls or the Germans.

The mass needs, and we give it, leaders who have the firmness and decision of command proceeding from habit and an entire faith in their unquestionable right to command as established by tradition, law and society.

We add good arms. We add methods of fighting suitable to these arms and those of the enemy and which do not overtax the physical and moral forces of man. We add also a rational decentralization that permits the direction and employment of the efforts of all even to the last man.

We animate with passion, a violent desire for independence, a religious fanaticism, national pride, a love of glory, a madness for possession. An iron discipline, which permits no one to escape action, secures the greatest unity from top to bottom, between all the elements, between the commanding officers, between the commanding officers and men, between the soldiers.

Have we then a solid army? Not yet. Unity, that first and supreme force of armies, is sought by enacting severe laws of discipline supported by powerful passions. But to order discipline is not enough. A vigilance from which no one may escape in combat should assure the maintenance of discipline. Discipline itself depends on moral pressure which actuates men to advance from sentiments of fear or pride. But it depends also on surveillance, the mutual supervision of groups of men who know each other well.

A wise organization insures that the personnel of combat groups changes as little as possible, so that comrades in peace time maneuvers shall be comrades in war. From living together, and obeying the same chiefs, from commanding the same men, from sharing fatigue and rest, from coöperation among men who quickly understand each other in the execution of warlike movements, may be bred brotherhood, professional knowledge, sentiment, above all unity. The duty of obedience, the right of imposing discipline and the impossibility of escaping from it, would naturally follow.

And now confidence appears.

It is not that enthusiastic and thoughtless confidence of tumultuous or unprepared armies which goes up to the danger point and vanishes rapidly, giving way to a contrary sentiment, which sees treason everywhere. It is that intimate confidence, firm and conscious, which does not forget itself in the heat of action and which alone makes true combatants.

Then we have an army; and it is no longer difficult to explain how men carried away by passions, even men who know how to die without flinching, without turning pale, really strong in the presence of death, but without discipline, without solid organization, are vanquished by others individually less valiant, but firmly, jointly and severally combined.

One loves to picture an armed mob upsetting all obstacles and carried away by a blast of passion.

There is more imagination than truth in that picture. If the struggle depended on individuals, the courageous, impassioned men, composing the mob would have more chance of victory. But in any body of troops, in front of the enemy, every one understands that the task is not the work of one alone, that to complete it requires team work. With his comrades in danger brought together under unknown leaders, he feels the lack of union, and asks himself if he can count on them. A thought of mistrust leads to hesitation. A moment of it will kill the offensive spirit.

Unity and confidence cannot be improvised. They alone can create that mutual trust, that feeling of force which gives courage and daring. Courage, that is the temporary domination of will over instinct, brings about victory.

Unity alone then produces fighters. But, as in everything, there are degrees of unity. Let us see whether modern is in this respect less exacting than ancient combat.

In ancient combat there was danger only at close quarters. If the troops had enough morale (which Asiatic hordes seldom had) to meet the enemy at broadsword's length, there was an engagement. Whoever was that close knew that he would be killed if he turned his back; because, as we have seen, the victors lost but few and the vanquished were exterminated. This simple reasoning held the men and made them fight, if it was but for an instant.

Neglecting the exceptional and very rare circumstances, which may bring two forces together, action to-day is brought on and fought out from afar. Danger begins at great distances, and it is necessary to advance for a long time under fire which at each step becomes heavier. The vanquished loses prisoners, but often, in dead and in wounded, he does not lose more than the victor.

Ancient combat was fought in groups close together, within a small space, in open ground, in full view of one another, without the deafening noise of present day arms. Men in formation marched into an action that took place on the spot and did not carry them thousands of feet away from the starting point. The surveillance of the leaders was easy, individual weakness was immediately checked. General consternation alone caused flight.

To-day fighting is done over immense spaces, along thinly drawn out lines broken every instant by the accidents and the obstacles of the terrain. From the time the action begins, as soon as there are rifle shots, the men spread out as skirmishers or, lost in the inevitable disorder of a rapid march, escape the supervision of their commanding officers. A considerable number conceal themselves; they get away from the engagement and diminish by just so much the material and moral effect and confidence of the brave ones who remain. This can bring about defeat.

But let us look at man himself in ancient combat and in modern. In ancient combat:—I am strong, apt, vigorous, trained, full of calmness, presence of mind; I have good offensive and defensive weapons and trustworthy companions of long standing. They do not let me be overwhelmed without aiding me. I with them, they with me, we are invincible, even invulnerable. We have fought twenty battles and not one of us remained on the field. It is necessary to support each other in time; we see it clearly; we are quick to replace ourselves, to put a fresh combatant in front of a fatigued adversary. We are the legions of Marius, fifty thousand who have held out against the furious avalanches of the Cimbri. We have killed one hundred and forty thousand, taken prisoner sixty thousand, while losing but two or three hundred of our inexperienced soldiers.

To-day, as strong, firm, trained, and courageous as I am, I can never say; I shall return. I have no longer to do with men, whom I do not fear, I have to do with fate in the form of iron and lead. Death is in the air, invisible and blind, whispering, whistling. As brave, good, trustworthy, and devoted as my companions may be, they do not shield me. Only,—and this is abstract and less immediately intelligible to all than the material support of ancient combat,— only I imagine that the more numerous we are who run a dangerous risk, the greater is the chance for each to escape therefrom. I also know that, if we have that confidence which none of us should lack in action, we feel, and we are, stronger. We begin more resolutely, are ready to keep up the struggle longer, and therefore finish it more quickly.

We finish it! But in order to finish it, it is necessary to advance, to attack the enemy, and infantryman or troopers, we are naked against iron, naked against lead, which cannot miss at close range. Let us advance in any case, resolutely. Our adversary will not stand at the point-blank range of our rifle, for the attack is never mutual, we are sure of that. We have been told so a thousand times. We have seen it. But what if matters should change now! Suppose the enemy stands at point-blank range! What of that?

How far this is from Roman confidence!

In another place we have shown that in ancient times to retire from action was both a difficult and perilous matter for the soldier. To-day the temptation is much stronger, the facility greater and the peril less.

Now, therefore, combat exacts more moral cohesion, greater unity than previously. A last remark on the difficulty of obtaining it will complete the demonstration.

Since the invention of fire arms, the musket, the rifle, the cannon, the distances of mutual aid and support have increased among the different arms.

Besides, the facility of communications of all kinds permits the assembling on a given territory of enormous forces. For these reasons, as we have stated, battle fields have become immense.

Supervision becomes more and more difficult. Direction being more distant tends more often to escape from the supreme commanders and the subordinate leaders. The certain and inevitable disorder, which a body of troops always presents in action, is with the moral effect of modern appliances, becoming greater every day. In the midst of the confusion and the vacillation of firing lines, men and commanding officers often lose each other.

Troops immediately and hotly engaged, such as companies and squads, can maintain themselves only if they are well-organized and serve as supports or rallying points to those out of place. Battles tend to become now, more than they have ever been, the battles of men.

This ought not to be true! Perhaps. But the fact is that it is true.

Not all troops are immediately or hotly engaged in battle. Commanding officers always try to keep in hand, as long as possible, some troops capable of marching, acting at any moment, in any direction. To-day, like yesterday, like to-morrow, the decisive action is that of formed troops. Victory belongs to the commander who has known how to keep them in good order, to hold them, and to direct them.

That is incontrovertible.

But commanders can hold out decisive reserves only if the enemy has been forced to commit his.

In troops which do the fighting, the men and the officers closest to them, from corporal to battalion commander, have a more independent action than ever. As it is alone the vigor of that action, more independent than ever of the direction of higher commanders, which leaves in the hands of higher commanders available forces which can be directed at a decisive moment. That action becomes more preponderant than ever. Battles, now more than ever, are battles of men, of captains. They always have been in fact, since in the last analysis the execution belongs to the man in ranks. But the influence of the latter on the final result is greater than formerly. From that comes the maxim of to-day: The battles of men.

Outside of the regulations on tactics and discipline, there is an evident necessity for combating the hazardous predominance of the action of the soldier over that of the commander. It is necessary to delay as long as possible, that instant which modern conditions tend to hasten—the instant when the soldier gets from under the control of the commander.

This completes the demonstration of the truth stated before: Combat requires to-day, in order to give the best results, a moral cohesion, a unity more binding than at any other time. It is as true as it is clear, that, if one does not wish bonds to break, one must make them elastic in order to strengthen them.

WILLIAM T. SHERMAN
(1820–1891)

William Tecumseh Sherman, a graduate of West Point, was probably the greatest general on the Union side in the American Civil War. He fought in the Vicksburg and Chattanooga campaigns in 1863 and subsequently took Atlanta in September 1864. After burning Atlanta in November 1864, Sherman launched his historic "March to the Sea," splitting the Confederacy in two and leaving a trail of devastation behind him. He took Savannah on December 21 and then moved north through the Carolinas to come up behind Robert E. Lee's forces. In April 1865 Sherman received the surrender of the last major Confederate army from General Joseph E. Johnston.

Sherman was one of the first to grasp the changing nature of modern warfare and to pursue a deliberate policy of demoralizing the noncombatant enemy population as well as the opposing forces. "War is hell," he explained.

THE MARCH TO THE SEA

The two general orders made for this march appear to me, even at this late day, so clear, emphatic, and well-digested, that no account of that historic event is perfect without them, and I give them entire, even at the seeming appearance of repetition; and, though they called for great sacrifice and labor on the part of the officers and men, I insist that these orders were obeyed as well as any similar orders ever were, by an army operating wholly in an enemy's country, and dispersed, as we necessarily were, during the subsequent period of nearly six months.

From *Memoirs of General William T. Sherman* (New York: D. Appleton & Co., 1875), 2: 174–81.

[Special Field Orders, No. 119.]

Headquarters Military Division of the Mississippi,
in the Field, Kingston, Georgia, *November* 8, 1864.

The general commanding deems it proper at this time to inform the officers and men of the Fourteenth, Fifteenth, Seventeenth, and Twentieth Corps, that he has organized them into an army for a special purpose, well known to the War Department and to General Grant. It is sufficient for you to know that it involves a departure from our present base, and a long and difficult march to a new one. All the chances of war have been considered and provided for, as far as human sagacity can. All he asks of you is to maintain that discipline, patience, and courage, which have characterized you in the past; and he hopes, through you, to strike a blow at our enemy that will have a material effect in producing what we all so much desire, his complete overthrow. Of all things, the most important is, that the men, during marches and in camp, keep their places and do not scatter about as stragglers or foragers, to be picked up by a hostile people in detail. It is also of the utmost importance that our wagons should not be loaded with any thing but provisions and ammunition. All surplus servants, noncombatants, and refugees, should now go to the rear, and none should be encouraged to encumber us on the march. At some future time we will be able to provide for the poor whites and blacks who seek to escape the bondage under which they are now suffering. With these few simple cautions, he hopes to lead you to achievements equal in importance to those of the past.

By order of Major-General W. T. Sherman,

L. M. DAYTON, *Aide-de-Camp.*

[Special Field Orders, No. 120.]

Headquarters Military Division of the Mississippi,
in the Field, Kingston, Georgia, *November* 9, 1864.

1. For the purpose of military operations, this army is divided into two wings viz.:

The right wing, Major-General O. O. Howard commanding, composed of the Fifteenth and Seventeenth Corps; the left wing, Major-General H. W. Slocum commanding, composed of the Fourteenth and Twentieth Corps.

2. The habitual order of march will be, wherever practicable, by four roads, as nearly parallel as possible, and converging at points hereafter to be indicated

in orders. The cavalry, Brigadier-General Kilpatrick commanding, will receive special orders from the commander-in-chief.

3. There will be no general train of supplies, but each corps will have its ammunition-train and provision-train, distributed habitually as follows: Behind each regiment should follow one wagon and one ambulance; behind each brigade should follow a due proportion of ammunition-wagons, provision-wagons, and ambulances. In case of danger, each corps commander should change this order of march, by having his advance and rear brigades unencumbered by wheels. The separate columns will start habitually at 7 A.M., and make about fifteen miles per day, unless otherwise fixed in orders.

4. The army will forage liberally on the country during the march. To this end, each brigade commander will organize a good and sufficient foraging party, under the command of one or more discreet officers, who will gather, near the route traveled, corn or forage of any kind, meat of any kind, vegetables, corn-meal, or whatever is needed by the command, aiming at all times to keep in the wagons at least ten days' provisions for his command, and three days' forage. Soldiers must not enter the dwellings of the inhabitants, or commit any trespass; but, during a halt or camp, they may be permitted to gather turnips, potatoes, and other vegetables, and to drive in stock in sight of their camp. To regular foraging-parties must be intrusted the gathering of provisions and forage, at any distance from the road traveled.

5. To corps commanders alone is intrusted the power to destroy mills, houses, cotton-gins, etc.; and for them this general principle is laid down: In districts and neighborhoods where the army is unmolested, no destruction of such property should be permitted; but should guerrillas or bushwhackers molest our march, or should the inhabitants burn bridges, obstruct roads, or otherwise manifest local hostility, then army commanders should order and enforce a devastation more or less relentless, according to the measure of such hostility.

6. As for horses, mules, wagons, etc., belonging to the inhabitants, the cavalry and artillery may appropriate freely and without limit; discriminating, however, between the rich, who are usually hostile, and the poor and industrious, usually neutral or friendly. Foraging-parties may also take mules or horses, to replace the jaded animals of their trains, or to serve as jack-mules for the regiments or brigades. In all foraging, of whatever kind, the parties engaged will refrain from abusive or threatening language and may, where the officer in command thinks proper, give written certificates of the facts, but no receipts; and they will endeavor to leave with each family a reasonable portion for their maintenance.

7. Negroes who are able-bodied and can be of service to the several columns may be taken along; but each army commander will bear in mind that the ques-

tion of supplies is a very important one, and that his first duty is to see to those who bear arms.

8. The organization, at once, of a good pioneer battalion for each arm corps, composed if possible of negroes, should be attended to. This battalion should follow the advance-guard, repair roads and double them if possible, so that the columns will not be delayed after reaching bad places. Also, army commanders should practise the habit of giving the artillery and wagons the road, marching their troops on one side, and instruct the troops to assist wagons at steep hills or bad crossings of streams.

9. Captain O. M. Poe, chief-engineer, will assign to each wing of the army a pontoon-train, fully equipped and organized; and the commander thereof will see to their being properly protected at all times.

By order of Major-General W. T. Sherman,

L. M. Dayton, *Aide-de-Camp.*

The greatest possible attention had been given to the artillery and wagon trains. The number of guns had been reduced to sixty-five, or about one gun to each thousand men, and these were generally in batteries of four guns each.

Each gun, caisson, and forge, was drawn by four teams of horses. We had in all about twenty-five hundred wagons, with teams of six mules to each, and six hundred ambulances, with two horses to each. The loads were made comparatively light, about twenty-five hundred pounds net; each wagon carrying in addition the forage needed by its own team. Each soldier carried on his person forty rounds of ammunition, and in the wagons were enough cartridges to make up about two hundred rounds per man, and in like manner two hundred rounds of assorted ammunition were carried for each gun.

The wagon-trains were divided equally between the four corps, so that each had about eight hundred wagons, and these usually on the march occupied five miles or more of road. Each corps commander managed his own train; and habitually the artillery and wagons had the road, while the men, with the exception of the advance and rear guards, pursued paths improvised by the side of the wagons, unless they were forced to use a bridge or causeway in common.

I reached Atlanta during the afternoon of the 14th, and found that all preparations had been made—Colonel Beckwith, chief commissary, reporting one million two hundred thousand rations in possession of the troops, which was about twenty days' supply, and he had on hand a good supply of beef-cattle to be driven along on the hoof. Of forage, the supply was limited, being of oats and corn enough for five days, but I knew that within that time we would reach a country well stocked with corn, which had been gathered and stored in cribs, seemingly for our use, by Governor Brown's militia.

Colonel Poe, United States Engineers, of my staff, had been busy in his special task of destruction. He had a large force at work, had leveled the great depot, round-house, and the machine-shops of the Georgia Railroad, and had applied fire to the wreck. One of these machine-shops had been used by the rebels as an arsenal, and in it were stored piles of shot and shell, some of which proved to be loaded, and that night was made hideous by the bursting of shells, whose fragments came uncomfortably near Judge Lyon's house, in which I was quartered. The fire also reached the block of stores near the depot, and the heart of the city was in flames all night, but the fire did not reach the parts of Atlanta where the court-house was, or the great mass of dwelling-houses.

The march from Atlanta began on the morning of November 15th, the right wing and cavalry following the railroad southeast toward Jonesboro', and General Slocum with the Twentieth Corps leading off to the east by Decatur and Stone Mountain, toward Madison. These were divergent lines, designed to threaten both Macon and Augusta at the same time, so as to prevent a concentration at our intended destination, or "objective," Milledgeville, the capital of Georgia, distant southeast about one hundred miles. The time allowed each column for reaching Milledgeville was seven days. I remained in Atlanta during the 15th with the Fourteenth Corps, and the rear-guard of the right wing, to complete the loading of the trains, and the destruction of the buildings of Atlanta which could be converted to hostile uses, and on the morning of the 16th started with my personal staff, a company of Alabama cavalry, commanded by Lieutenant Snelling, and an infantry company, commanded by Lieutenant McCrory, which guarded our small train of wagons. . . .

About 7 A.M. of November 16th we rode out of Atlanta by the Decatur road, filled by the marching troops and wagons of the Fourteenth Corps; and reaching the hill, just outside of the old rebel works, we naturally paused to look back upon the scenes of our past battles. We stood upon the very ground whereon was fought the bloody battle of July 22d, and could see the copse of wood where McPherson fell. Behind us lay Atlanta, smouldering and in ruins, the black smoke rising high in air, and hanging like a pall over the ruined city. Away off in the distance, on the McDonough road, was the rear of Howard's column, the gun-barrels glistening in the sun, the white-topped wagons stretching away to the south; and right before us the Fourteenth Corps, marching steadily and rapidly, with a cheery look and swinging pace, that made light of the thousand miles that lay between us and Richmond. Some band, by accident, struck up the anthem of "John Brown's soul goes marching on"; the men caught up the strain, and never before or since have I heard the chorus of "Glory, glory, hallelujah!" done with more spirit, or in better harmony of time and place.

Then we turned our horses' heads to the east; Atlanta was soon lost behind the screen of trees, and became a thing of the past. Around it clings many a thought of desperate battle, of hope and fear, that now seem like the memory of a dream; and I have never seen the place since. The day was extremely beautiful, clear sunlight, with bracing air, and an unusual feeling of exhilaration seemed to pervade all minds—a feeling of something to come, vague and undefined, still full of venture and intense interest. Even the common soldiers caught the inspiration, and many a group called out to me as I worked my way past them, "Uncle Billy, I guess Grant is waiting for us at Richmond!" Indeed, the general sentiment was that we were marching for Richmond, and that there we should end the war, but how and when they seemed to care not; nor did they measure the distance, or count the cost in life, or bother their brains about the great rivers to be crossed, and the food required for man and beast, that had to be gathered by the way. There was a "devil-may-care" feeling pervading officers and men, that made me feel the full load of responsibility, for success would be accepted as a matter of course, whereas, should we fail, this "march" would be adjudged the wild adventure of a crazy fool. I had no purpose to march direct for Richmond by way of Augusta and Charlotte, but always designed to reach the sea-coast first at Savannah or Port Royal, South Carolina, and even kept in mind the alternative of Pensacola.

The first night out we camped by the road-side near Lithonia. Stone Mountain, a mass of granite, was in plain view, cut out in clear outline against the blue sky; the whole horizon was lurid with the bonfires of rail-ties, and groups of men all night were carrying the heated rails to the nearest trees, and bending them around the trunks. Colonel Poe had provided tools for ripping up the rails and twisting them when hot; but the best and easiest way is the one I have described, of heating the middle of the iron-rails on bonfires made of the cross-ties, and then winding them around a telegraph-pole or the trunk of some convenient sapling. I attached much importance to this destruction of the railroad, gave it my own personal attention, and made reiterated orders to others on the subject.

The next day we passed through the handsome town of Covington, the soldiers closing up their ranks, the color-bearers unfurling their flags, and the bands striking up patriotic airs. The white people came out of their houses to behold the sight, in spite of their deep hatred of the invaders, and the negroes were simply frantic with joy. Whenever they heard my name, they clustered about my horse, shouted and prayed in their peculiar style, which had a natural eloquence that would have moved a stone. I have witnessed hundreds, if not thousands, of such scenes; and can now see a poor girl, in the very ecstasy of the Methodist "shout," hugging the banner of one of the regiments, and jumping up to the "feet of Jesus."

I remember, when riding around by a by-street in Covington, to avoid the crowd that followed the marching column, that some one brought me an invitation to dine with a sister of Sam. Anderson, who was a cadet at West Point with me; but the messenger reached me after we had passed the main part of the town. I asked to be excused, and rode on to a place designated for camp, at the crossing of the Ulcofauhachee River, about four miles to the east of the town. Here we made our bivouac, and I walked up to a plantation-house close by, where were assembled many negroes, among them an old, gray-haired man, of as fine a head as I ever saw. I asked him if he understood about the war and its progress. He said he did; that he had been looking for the "angel of the Lord" ever since he was knee-high, and, though we professed to be fighting for the Union, he supposed that slavery was the cause, and that our success was to be his freedom. I asked him if all the negro slaves comprehended this fact, and he said they surely did. I then explained to him that we wanted the slaves to remain where they were, and not to load us down with useless mouths, which would eat up the food needed for our fighting-men; that our success was their assured freedom; that we could receive a few of their young, hearty men as pioneers; but that, if they followed us in swarms of old and young, feeble and helpless, it would simply load us down and cripple us in our great task. I think Major Henry Hitchcock was with me on that occasion, and made a note of the conversation, and I believe that old man spread this message to the slaves, which was carried from mouth to mouth, to the very end of our journey, and that it in part saved us from the great danger we incurred of swelling our numbers so that famine would have attended our progress. It was at this very plantation that a soldier passed me with a ham on his musket, a jug of sorghum-molasses under his arm, and a big piece of honey in his hand, from which he was eating, and, catching my eye, he remarked *sotto voce* and carelessly to a comrade, "Forage liberally on the country," quoting from my general orders. On this occasion, as on many others that fell under my personal observation, I reproved the man, explained that foraging must be limited to the regular parties properly detailed, and that all provisions thus obtained must be delivered to the regular commissaries, to be fairly distributed to the men who kept their ranks.

HELMUTH VON MOLTKE
(1800–1891)

Helmuth von Moltke belonged to the old German nobility of Mecklenburg. After serving in the Danish army, he entered the Berlin Military School, then headed by Clausewitz, in 1822. In 1835, with official authorization, he went into the Turkish service, in which he advised on the reorganization of the Ottoman army. In 1839 he took part in the Turkish campaign against Muhammad Ali's Egyptians in Syria. His war doctrine was based on the ideas of Clausewitz. He was made Prussian chief of staff in 1857 and worked with Bismarck and Albrecht von Roon, the minister of war, in the transformation of the Prussian military system, which enabled Prussia to win both against the Austrians in 1866 and against France in 1870–71.

Moltke was named field marshal in 1871. In the latter part of his life he was notably conscious of the dangers of the future. "The most redoubtable test that [can] threaten the existence of the new German empire would be a simultaneous war against France and Russia," he observed. A good strategist and a remarkable organizer, he knew how best to exploit the new logistical situation created by the introduction of railroads. He combined the inflexible determination of the leader with the capacity to delegate authority on the ground to subordinates. His influence on the German army was considerable. He was the supervising author of The Campaign of 1866 in Germany *(Berlin, 1867) and also wrote several other books, including* Questions of Applied Tactics *(n.d.).*

ON STRATEGY

Policy uses war to attain its objective. It has a decisive influence on the beginning and ending of war, and reserves the right either to raise the stakes in the course of operations or to be content with a slight success.

From Helmuth von Moltke, *Sur la stratégie: Mémoire de l'année 1871* (Paris: Ecole de guerre, 1909). Translated from the French by A. M. Berrett.

In such uncertainty, strategy can only direct its efforts toward the highest objective that it can attain with the means made available to it. It thus works for the best in the interest of policy, and to fulfill its objective, while remaining completely independent of it in how it acts.

The first duty of strategy is to prepare the means of fighting, the initial deployment of the army. In that, the most varied political, geographical, and national considerations come into play. A mistake in the original concentration of the armies is very difficult to rectify in the course of the campaign. But these dispositions can be worked on well in advance and, apart from the preparation of troops for war and the organization of the transport service, they ought infallibly to lead to the desired result.

It is not the same with the other duty of strategy—that is to say, the use in combat of the means prepared, their utilization during operations.

Here our will soon comes up against the independent will of the enemy. No doubt we can limit that will, if we are determined and ready to take the initiative; but we cannot break it by any other means than tactics, through combat.

The material and moral consequences of any major encounter are so far-reaching that they usually create an entirely different situation, requiring new measures. No plan of operations can with any certainty extend beyond the first encounter with the enemy's main forces. Only the uninformed imagine that a campaign can be developed and executed in accordance with a preordained plan, conceived in advance, settled in every detail, and adhered to the end.

The commander will surely always have in mind the grand objective that he is pursuing, without letting himself be sidetracked by the vicissitudes of events; but as for the means of attaining that objective, he will never be able to determine them with certainty and far in advance.

All through the campaign, he will have to take decisions based on circumstances impossible to predict. All the successive acts of war are thus not premeditated implementations of some plan but spontaneous actions, responding to the military situation of the moment. What is important, in each special, concrete case, is to see clearly through a mist of uncertainty, assess the facts accurately, guess the unknowns, reach a decision quickly, and then move to carry it out vigorously without letting oneself be sidetracked.

In addition to these factors, one known, one unknown, our own will and the enemy's, there are the temperature, sicknesses, railway accidents, misunderstandings, and mistakes, which are quite unpredictable, in short all the influences summed up by the words *chance, luck,* or *force majeure,* for which man is not responsible and which he does not control.

Yet it would be wrong to believe that the conduct of war is therefore subject to blind chance. A calculation of the probabilities would show that all these unforeseen happenings are in the end as often advantageous as harmful to either side, and the general who, in each particular case, makes his dispositions in the light of the situation, even if they are not ideal, always has the hope of attaining his objective. It is obvious that to achieve that result, theoretical knowledge is not enough; what need to come into play here are qualities of mind and character in terms of practical skill, and they are developed through an appropriate military training and the lessons of experience drawn from military history or everyday life.

It is certainly true that it is above all success that decides the reputation of a commander, but to determine where in that success his true merit lies is very difficult. The most capable man may fail in the face of the irresistible power of circumstances in which a man of modest worth may well triumph. In the long run, however, it is only the most skillful general who will succeed most of the time.

If, then, all is uncertain in war from the outset of operations, apart from the will and energy of the general, it is practically impossible to accord any value to a [particular] doctrine of strategy, the rules that might be deduced from it, and the system built up on that base.

Archduke Charles [(1771–1847), Austrian field marshal, son of Emperor Leopold II] declares that strategy is a science, tactics an art. He calls on "the science of commanders" to lay down how military operations will unfold, while art comes in only in the execution of strategic plans.

Conversely, General von Clausewitz says that "strategy is the use of combat for the objectives of war." And it is true that strategy gives tactics the means to fight and makes victory likely, by guiding armies and concentrating them on the battlefield. Moreover, it subsumes the successful outcome of each battle and uses it to design new plans. The pretensions of strategy dim in the face of tactical victory, and it has to be able to adapt to the newly created situation.

Strategy is a system of expedients. It is more than a science: it is the application of knowledge to practical life, the development of thought capable of modifying the original guiding idea in the light of ever-changing situations; it is the art of acting under the pressure of the most difficult conditions.

FRIEDRICH ENGELS
(1820–1895)

Friedrich Engels, a German Jew, was the companion, friend, and patron of Karl Marx, with whom he co-authored the Communist Manifesto *(1848), after having himself published an outstanding inquiry into* The Condition of the Working Class in England in 1844 *(1845). He settled in England permanently after 1850, where he was involved in the management of the Manchester branch of the firm of Ermen and Engels. In 1864, he co-founded the International Working Men's Association (First International) with Marx, and after Marx's death in 1883, he continued to be active in the socialist movement, playing a leading role in founding the Second International.*

*Engels followed the military developments of his time avidly. His writings on the subject (*Militarische Werke; *2 vols., Leipzig, 1956) show a constant concern to demonstrate the links between military changes and social situations.*

THE SPIRIT OF RESISTANCE

The last defeat of the French Army of the Loire and the retreat of Ducrot behind the Marne—supposing that movement to be as decisive as was represented . . . —finally settle the fate of the first combined operation for the relief of Paris. It has completely miscarried, and people begin again to ask whether this new series of misfortunes does not prove the inability of the French for further successful resistance—whether it would not be better to give up the game at once, surrender Paris, and sign the cession of Alsace and Lorraine.

Friedrich Engels, article in the *Pall Mall Gazette,* 8 December 1870, in Karl Marx and Friedrich Engels, *Collected Works,* vol. 22, *Marx and Engels, 1870–71* (New York: International Publishers, 1986), 193–97. Reprinted by permission of International Publishers.

The fact is, people have lost all remembrance of a real war. The Crimean, the Italian, and the Austro-Prussian war were all of them mere conventional wars—wars of Governments which made peace as soon as their military machinery had broken down or become worn out. A real war, one in which the nation itself participates, we have not seen in the heart of Europe for a couple of generations. We have seen it in the Caucasus, in Algeria, where fighting lasted more than twenty years with scarcely any interruption; we should have seen it in Turkey if the Turks had been allowed, by their allies, to defend themselves in their own home-spun way. But the fact is, our conventionalities allow to barbarians only the right of actual self-defence; we expect that civilized States will fight according to etiquette, and that the real nation will not be guilty of such rudeness as to go on fighting after the official nation has had to give in.

The French are actually committing this piece of rudeness. To the disgust of the Prussians, who consider themselves the best judges in military etiquette, they have been positively fighting for three months after the official army of France was driven from the field; and they have even done what their official army never could do in this campaign. They have obtained one important success and numerous small ones; and have taken guns, convoys, prisoners from their enemies. It is true they have just suffered a series of severe reverses; but these are as nothing when compared with the fate their late official army was in the habit of meeting with at the hands of the same opponents. It is true their first attempt to free Paris from the investing army, by an attack from within and from without at the same time, has signally failed; but is it a necessary sequel that there are no chances left for a second attempt?

The two French armies, that of Paris as well as that of the Loire, have both fought well, according to the testimony of the Germans themselves. They have certainly been beaten by inferior numbers, but that is what was to be expected from young and newly organized troops confronting veterans. Their tactical movements under fire, according to a correspondent in *The Daily News,* who knows what he writes about, were rapid and steady; if they lacked precision that was a fault which they had in common with many a victorious French army. There is no mistake about it: these armies have proved that they *are* armies, and will have to be treated with due respect by their opponents. They are no doubt composed of very different elements. There are battalions of the line, containing old soldiers in various proportions; there are Mobiles of all degrees of military efficiency, from battalions well officered, drilled, and equipped to battalions of raw recruits, still ignorant of the elements of the "manual and platoon"; there are francs-tireurs of all sorts, good, bad, and indifferent—probably most of them the latter. But there is, at all events, a nucleus of good fighting battalions, around which the others may be grouped;

and a month of desultory fighting, with avoidance of crushing defeats, will make capital soldiers out of the whole of them. With better strategy, they might even now have been successful; and all the strategy required for the moment is to delay all decisive fighting, and that, we think, can be done.

But the troops concentrated at Le Mans and near the Loire are far from representing the whole armed force of France. There are at least 200,000 to 300,000 more men undergoing the process of organization at points farther away to the rear. Every day brings these nearer to the fighting standard. Every day must send, for a time at least, constantly increasing numbers of fresh soldiers to the front. And there are plenty more men behind them to take their places. Arms and ammunition are coming in every day in large quantities: with modern gun factories and cannon foundries, with telegraphs and steamers, and the command of the sea, there is no fear of their falling short. A month's time will also make an immense difference in the efficiency of these men; and if two months were allowed them, they would represent armies which might well trouble Moltke's repose.

Behind all these more or less regular forces there is the great . . . mass of the people whom the Prussians have driven to that war of self-defence which, according to the father of King William, sanctions every means. When Fritz marched from Metz to Reims, from Reims to Sedan, and thence to Paris, there was not a word said about a rising of the people. The defeats of the Imperial armies were accepted with a kind of stupor; twenty years of Imperial régime had used the mass of the people to dull and passive dependence upon official leadership. There were here and there peasants who participated in actual fighting, as at Brazeilles, but they were the exception. But no sooner had the Prussians settled down round Paris, and placed the surrounding country under a crushing system of requisitions, carried out with no consideration whatever—no sooner had they begun to shoot francs-tireurs and burn villages which had given aid to the latter—and no sooner had they refused the French offers of peace and declared their intention to carry on a war of conquest, when all this changed. The guerrilla war broke out all around them, thanks to their own severities, and they have now but to advance into a new department in order to raise the [militia] far and wide. Whoever reads in the German papers the reports of the advance of Mecklenburg's and Frederick Charles's armies will see at a glance what an extraordinary effect this impalpable, ever disappearing and reappearing, but ever impeding insurrection of the people has upon the movements of these armies. Even their numerous cavalry, to which the French have scarcely any to oppose, is neutralized to a great extent by this general active and passive hostility of the inhabitants.

Now let us examine the position of the Prussians. Of the seventeen divisions before Paris, they certainly cannot spare a single one while Trochu may repeat any day his sorties en masse. Manteuffel's four divisions will have more work than they can execute in Normandy and Picardy for some time to come, and they may even be called away from them. Werder's two divisions and a half cannot get on beyond Dijon, except on raids, and this will last until at least Belfort shall have been reduced. The long thin line of communication marked by the railway from Nancy to Paris cannot send a single man out of those told off to guard it. The 7th Corps has plenty to do with garrisoning the Lorraine fortresses and besieging Longwy and Montmédy. There remain for field operations against the bulk of central and southern France the eleven infantry divisions of Frederick Charles and Mecklenburg, certainly not more than 150,000 men, including cavalry.

The Prussians thus employ about six-and-twenty divisions in holding Alsace, Lorraine, and the two long lines of communication to Paris and Dijon, and in investing Paris, and still they hold directly perhaps not one-eighth, and indirectly certainly not more than one-fourth, of France. For the rest of the country they have fifteen divisions left, four of which are under Manteuffel. How far these will be able to go depends entirely upon the energy of the popular resistance they may find. But with all their communications going by way of Versailles—for the march of Frederick Charles has not opened to him a new line viâ Troyes—and in the midst of an insurgent country, these troops will have to spread out on a broad front, to leave detachments behind to secure the roads and keep down the people; and thus they will soon arrive at a point where their forces become so reduced as to be balanced by the French forces opposing them, and then the chances are again favourable to the French; or else these German armies will have to act as large flying columns, marching up and down the country without definitely occupying it; and in that case the French regulars can give way before them for a time, and will find plenty of opportunities to fall on their flanks and rear.

A few flying corps, such as Blücher sent in 1813 round the flanks of the French, would be very effective if employed to interrupt the line of communication of the Germans. That line is vulnerable almost the whole of its length from Paris to Nancy. A few corps, each consisting of one or two squadrons of cavalry and some sharpshooters, falling upon that line, destroying the rails, tunnels, and bridges, attacking trains, &c., would go far to recall the German cavalry from the front where it is most dangerous. But the regular "Hussar dash" does certainly not belong to the French.

All this is on the supposition that Paris continues to hold out. There is nothing to compel Paris to give in, so far, except starvation. But the news we had in yesterday's *Daily News* from a correspondent inside that city would dispel many apprehensions if correct. There are still 25,000 horses besides those of the army in Paris, which at 500 kilos each would give 6 1/4 kilo, or 14 lb. of meat for every inhabitant, or nearly a 1/4 lb. per day for two months. With that, bread and wine *ad libitum,* and a good quantity of salt meat and other eatables, Paris may well hold out until the beginning of February. And that would give to France two months, worth more to her, now, than two years in time of peace. With anything like intelligent and energetic direction, both central and local, France, by then, ought to be in a position to relieve Paris and to right herself.

And if Paris should fall? It will be time enough to consider this chance when it becomes more probable. Anyhow, France has managed to do without Paris for more than two months, and may fight on without her. Of course, the fall of Paris may demoralize the spirit of resistance, but so may, even now, the unlucky news of the last seven days. Neither the one nor the other need do so. If the French entrench a few good maneuvering positions, such as Nevers, near the junction of the Loire and Allier—if they throw up advanced works round Lyons so as to make it as strong as Paris, the war may be carried on even after the fall of Paris; but it is not yet time to talk of that.

Thus we make bold to say that, if the spirit of resistance among the people does not flag, the position of the French, even after their recent defeats, is a very strong one. With the command of the sea to import arms, with plenty of men to make soldiers of, with three months—the first and worst three months—of the work of organization behind them, and with a fair chance of having one month more, if not two, of breathing-time allowed them—and that at a time when the Prussians show signs of exhaustion—with all that, to give in now would be rank treason. And who knows what accidents may happen, what further European complications may occur, in the meantime? Let them fight on, by all means.

EROSION BY THE WAVES
OF POPULAR WARFARE

The campaign on the Loire appears to have come to a momentary standstill, which allows us time to compare reports and dates, and to form the very confused and contradictory materials into as clear a narrative of actual events as can be expected under the circumstances.

The Army of the Loire began to exist as a distinct body on the 15th of November, when D'Aurelle de Paladines, hitherto commander of the 15th and

Friedrich Engels, article in the *Pall Mall Gazette,* 17 December 1870, in Karl Marx and Friedrich Engels, *Collected Works,* vol. 22, *Marx and Engels, 1870–71* (New York: International Publishers, 1986), 203–7. Reprinted by permission of International Publishers.

16th Corps, obtained command of the new organization formed under this name. What other troops entered into its composition at that date we cannot tell; in fact, this army received constant reinforcements, at least up to the end of November, when it consisted nominally of the following corps:—15th (Pallières), 16th (Chanzy), 17th (Sônis), 18th (Bourbaki), 19th (Barral, according to Prussian accounts), and 20th (Crouzat). Of these the 19th Corps never appeared either in the French or Prussian reports, and cannot therefore be supposed to have been engaged. Besides these, there were at Le Mans and the neighbouring camp of Conlie, the 21st Army Corps (Jaurès) and the Army of Brittany, which, on the resignation of Kératry, was attached to Jaurès' command. A 22nd Corps, we may add, is commanded by General Faidherbe in the North, with Lille for its base of operations. In the above we have omitted General Michel's corps of cavalry attached to the Army of the Loire: this body of horse, though said to be very numerous, cannot rank, from its recent formation and crude material, otherwise than as volunteer or amateur cavalry.

The elements of which this army was composed were of the most varied kinds, from old troopers recalled to the ranks, to raw recruits and volunteers averse to all discipline; from solid battalions such as the Papal Zouaves to crowds which were battalions only in name. Some kind of discipline, however, had been established, but the whole still bore the stamp of the great hurry which had presided at its formation. "Had this army been allowed four weeks more for preparation, it would have been a formidable opponent," said the German officers who had made its acquaintance on the field of battle. Deducting all those quite raw levies which were only in the way, we may set down the whole of D'Aurelle's five fighting corps (omitting the 19th) at somewhere about 120,000 to 130,000 men fit to be called combatants. The troops at Le Mans may have furnished about 40,000 more.

Against these we find pitted the army of Prince Frederick Charles, including the Grand Duke of Mecklenburg's command; their numbers we now know, through Capt. Hozier, to have been rather less than 90,000 all told. But these 90,000 were, by their experience of war, their organization, and the proved generalship of their leaders, quite competent to engage twice their number of such troops as were opposed to them. Thus, the chances were about even; and that they were so is immensely to the credit of the French people, who created this new army out of nothing in three months.

The campaign began, on the part of the French, with the attack on von der Tann at Coulmiers and the reconquest of Orléans, on November 9; the march of Mecklenburg to the aid of von der Tann; the maneuvering of D'Aurelle in the direction of Dreux, which drew off Mecklenburg's whole force in that direction, and made him enter upon a march towards Le Mans. This march was harassed by the French irregular troops in a degree hitherto unknown in the present war; the population showed a most determined resistance, francs-tireurs hovered round the flanks of the invaders; but the regular troops confined themselves to demonstrations, and could not be brought to bay. The letters of the German correspondents with Mecklenburg's army, their rage and indignation at those wicked French who insist upon fighting in the way most convenient to themselves and most inconvenient to the enemy, are the best proof that this short campaign about Le Mans was conducted exceedingly well by the defence. The French led Mecklenburg a perfect wild-goose chase after an invisible army up to about twenty-five miles from Le Mans: arrived thus far, he hesitated to go any farther, and turned south. The original plan had evidently been to deal a crushing blow at the Army of Le Mans, then to turn south upon Blois, and turn the left of the Army of the Loire; while Frederick Charles, just then coming up, attacked its front and rear. But this plan, and many others since, miscarried. D'Aurelle left Mecklenburg to his fate, marched against Frederick Charles, and attacked the 10th Prussian Corps on the 24th November at Ladon and Mézières, and a large body of Prussians on the 28th at Beaune-la-Rolande. It is evident that here he handled his troops badly. He had but a small portion of them in readiness, though this was his first attempt to break through the Prussian army and force his way to Paris. All he did was to inspire the enemy with respect for his troops. He fell back into entrenched positions in front of Orléans, where he concentrated all his forces. These he disposed, from right to left, as follows: the 18th Corps on the extreme right; then the 20th and 15th, all of them east of the Paris-Orléans railway; west of it the 16th; and on the extreme left the 17th. Had these masses been brought together in time, there is scarcely any doubt that they might have crushed Frederick Charles's army, then under 50,000 men. But by the time D'Aurelle was well established in his work, Mecklenburg had marched south again, and joined the right wing of his cousin, who now took the supreme command. Thus Mecklenburg's 40,000 men had now come up to join in the attack against D'Aurelle, while the French army of Le Mans, satisfied with the glory of having "repulsed" its opponent, quietly remained in its quarters, some sixty miles away from the point where the campaign was decided.

Then all of a sudden came the news of Trochu's sortie of the 30th of November. A fresh effort had to be made to support him. On the 1st D'Aurelle commenced a general advance against the Prussians, but it was too late. While the Germans met him with all their forces, his 18th Corps—on the extreme right—appeared to have been sent astray, and never to have been engaged. Thus he fought with but four corps, that is to say, with numbers (of actual combatants) probably little superior to those of his opponents. He was beaten; he appears to have felt himself beaten even before he was so. Hence the irresolution he displayed when, after having on the evening of the 3rd of December ordered a retreat across the Loire, he countermanded it next morning and resolved to defend Orléans. The usual result followed: order, counter-order, disorder. The Prussian attack being concentrated on his left and centre, his two right corps, evidently in consequence of the contradictory orders they had received, lost their line of retreat upon Orléans, and had to cross the river, the 20th at Jargeau and the 18th still further east, at Sully. A small portion of the latter appears to have been driven still more eastward, as it was found by the 3rd Prussian Corps on the 7th of December at Nevoy, near Gien, and thence pursued in the direction of Briare, always on the right bank of the river. Orléans fell into the hands of the Germans on the evening of the 4th, and the pursuit was at once organized. While the 3rd Corps was to skirt the upper course of the Loire on the right bank, the 10th was sent to Vierzon, and the Mecklenburg command on the right bank towards Blois. Before reaching that place, this latter force was met at Beaugency by at least a portion of the army of Le Mans, which now at last had joined Chanzy's command, and offered a pertinacious and partly successful resistance. But this was soon broken, for the 9th Prussian Corps was marching, on the left bank of the river, towards Blois, where it would have cut off Chanzy's retreat towards Tours. This turning movement had its effect. Chanzy retired out of harm's way, and Blois fell into the hands of the invaders. The thaw and heavy rains about this time broke up the roads, and thus stopped further pursuit.

Prince Frederick Charles has telegraphed to headquarters that the Army of the Loire is totally dispersed in various directions, that its centre is broken, and that it has ceased to exist as an army. All this sounds well, but it is far from being correct. There can be no doubt, even from the German accounts, that the seventy-seven guns taken before Orléans were almost all naval guns abandoned in the entrenchments. There may be 10,000, and, including the wounded, 14,000 prisoners, most of them very much demoralized; but the state of the Bavarians who on the 5th of December thronged the road from Artenay to Chartres, utterly disorganized, without arms or knapsacks, was not so much better. There is an utter absence of trophies gathered during the pursuit on and after the 5th; and if an army has broken up, its soldiery cannot fail to be brought in wholesale by an active and numerous cavalry such as we know the Prussians to possess. There is extreme inaccuracy here, to say the least of it. The thaw is no excuse; that set in about the 9th, and would leave four or five days of fine frozen roads and fields for active pursuit. It is not so much the thaw which stops the advance of the Prussians; it is the consciousness that the force of these 90,000 men, now reduced to about 60,000 by losses and garrisons left behind, is nearly spent. The point beyond which it is imprudent to follow up even a beaten enemy has very nearly been reached. There may be raids on a large scale further south, but there will be scarcely any further occupation of territory. The Army of the Loire, now divided into two armies under Bourbaki and Chanzy, will have plenty of time and room to re-form, and to draw towards it newly formed battalions. By its division it has ceased to exist as an army, but it is the first French army in this campaign which has done so not ingloriously. We shall probably hear of its two successors again.

In the meantime, Prussia shows signs of exhaustion. The men of the landwehr up to forty years and more—legally free from service after their thirty-second year—are called in. The drilled reserves of the country are exhausted. In January the recruits—about 90,000 from North Germany—will be sent out to France. This *may* give altogether the 150,000 men of whom we hear so much, but they are not yet there; and when they do come they will alter the character of the army materially. The wear and tear of the campaign has been terrible, and is becoming more so every day. The melancholy tone of the letters from the army shows it, as well as the lists of losses. It is no longer the great battles which make up the bulk of these lists, it is the small encounters where one, two, five men are shot down. This constant erosion by the waves of popular warfare in the long run melts down or washes away the largest army in detail, and, what is the chief point, without any visible equivalent. While Paris holds out, every day improves the position of the French, and the impatience at Versailles about the surrender of Paris shows best that that city may yet become dangerous to the besiegers.

WAR TO THE KNIFE

If the series of disasters to the French arms which mark the January campaign—the defeats of Faidherbe and Chanzy, the fall of Paris, the defeat and surrender to the Swiss of Bourbaki—if all these crushing events, concentrated in the short period of three weeks, may well be considered to have broken the spirit of resistance in France, it now seems not improbable that the Germans, by their extravagant demands, may rouse that spirit again. If the country is to be thoroughly ruined by peace as well as by war, why make peace at all? The propertied classes, the middle class of the towns and the larger landed proprietors, with part of the smaller peasantry, hitherto formed the peace party; they might have been reckoned upon to elect peace deputies for the National Assembly; but if such unheard-of demands are persisted in, the cry of war to the knife may rise from their ranks as well as from those of the workmen of the large towns. At any rate, it is well not to neglect whatever chance there may

Friedrich Engels, article in the *Pall Mall Gazette*, 8 February 1871, in Karl Marx and Friedrich Engels, *Collected Works*, vol. 22, *Marx and Engels, 1870–71* (New York: International Publishers, 1986), 251–54. Reprinted by permission of International Publishers.

be that the war may be resumed after the 19th of February; especially since the Germans themselves, if we may trust *The Daily News* of to-day, are not so satisfied with the prospect of affairs as to abstain from serious preparations for the resumption of hostilities. Let us, therefore, cast another glance at the military aspect of affairs.

The twenty-seven departments of France now occupied by the Prussians contain an area of 15,800,000 hectares, with a population (allowing for the fortresses still unsurrendered) of rather less than 12,500,000. The extent of all France comprises 54,240,000 hectares, and its population is 37,382,000. It thus appears that, in round numbers, thirty-eight and a half millions of hectares, with a population of 25,000,000, remain still unconquered,—fully two-thirds of the people, considerably more than two-thirds of the soil. Paris and Metz, the resistance of which so long retarded further hostile advance, have certainly fallen. The interior of the unconquered country contains no other entrenched camp—Lyons excepted—capable of playing the same part which these two fortresses have played. Rather less than 700,000 Frenchmen (not counting the National Guard of Paris) are prisoners of war or interned in Switzerland. But there are other circumstances which may make up for this deficiency, even if the three weeks' armistice should not be used for the creation of new camps, surrounded by field works; for which there is ample time.

The great bulk of unconquered France lies south of the line Nantes-Besançon; it forms a compact block, covered on three sides by the sea or by neutral frontiers, with only its northern boundary line open to the enemy's attack. Here is the strength of the national resistance; here are to be found the men and the material to carry on the war if it is resumed. To conquer and occupy this immense rectangle of 450 miles by 250 against a desperate resistance—regular and irregular—of the inhabitants, the present forces of the Prussians would not suffice. The surrender of Paris, leaving four corps for the garrison of that capital, will set free nine divisions; Bourbaki's surrender sets free Manteuffel's six line divisions; in all, fifteen divisions, or 150,000 to 170,000 additional soldiers for operations in the field, added to Goeben's four and Frederick Charles's eight divisions. But Goeben has plenty on his hands in the north, and Frederick Charles has shown by his halt at Tours and Le Mans that his offensive powers are exhausted to the full, so that for the conquest of the South there remain but the above fifteen divisions; and for some months to come no further reinforcements can arrive.

To these fifteen divisions the French will have to oppose in the beginning mostly new formations. There were about Nevers and Bourges the 15th and 25th Corps; there must have been in the same neighbourhood the 19th Corps, of which we have heard nothing since the beginning of December. Then there is the 24th Corps, escaped from Bourbaki's shipwreck, and Garibaldi's troops, recently reinforced to 50,000 men, but by what bodies and from what quarters we do not know. The whole comprises some thirteen or fourteen divisions, perhaps even sixteen, but quite insufficient as to quantity and quality to arrest the progress of the new armies which are sure to be sent against them if the armistice should expire without peace having been made. But the three weeks' armistice will not only give these French divisions time to consolidate themselves; it will also permit the more or less raw levies now in the camps of instruction, and estimated by Gambetta at 250,000 men, to transform at least the best of their battalions into useful corps fit to meet the enemy; and thus, if the war should be renewed, the French may be in a position to ward off any serious invasion of the South, not perhaps at the boundary line of the Loire or much north of Lyons, but yet at points where the presence of the enemy will not efficiently impair their force of resistance.

As a matter of course, the armistice gives ample time to restore the equipment, the discipline, and the morale of Faidherbe's and Chanzy's armies, as well as of all the other troops in Cherbourg, Havre, &. The question is whether the time will be so employed. While thus the strength of the French will be considerably increased, both as to numbers and quality, that of the Germans will scarcely receive any increment at all. So far, the armistice will be a boon to the French side.

But beside the compact block of southern France, there remain unconquered the two peninsulas of the Bretagne with Brest, and of the Cotentin with Cherbourg, and, moreover, the two northern departments with their fortresses. Havre, too, forms an unconquered, well-fortified spot on the coast. Every one of these four districts is provided with at least one well-fortified place of safety on the coast for a retreating army; so that the fleet, which at this moment has nothing, absolutely nothing, else to do, can keep up the communications between the South and all of them, transport troops from one place to another, as the case may require, and thereby all of a sudden enable a beaten army to resume the offensive with superior forces. Thus while these four western and northern districts are in a measure unassailable, they form so many weak points on the flanks of the Prussians. The line of actual danger for the French extends from Angers to Besançon; for the Germans it extends, in addition to this, from Angers by Le Mans, Rouen, and Amiens to the Belgian frontier. Advantages on this latter line gained over the French can never become decisive if moderate common sense be used by them; but those gained over the Germans may, under certain conditions, become so.

Such is the strategical situation. By using the fleet to advantage the French might move their men in the West and North, so as to compel the Germans to keep largely superior forces in that neighbourhood, and to weaken the forces sent out for the conquest of the South, which it would be their chief object to prevent. By concentrating their armies more than they have hitherto done, and, on the other hand, by sending out more numerous small partisan bands, they might increase the effect to be obtained by the forces on hand. There appear to have been many more troops at Cherbourg and Havre than were necessary for the defence; and the well executed destruction of the bridge of Fontenoy, near Toul, in the centre of the country occupied by the conquerors, shows what may be done by bold partisans. For, if the war is to be resumed at all after the 19th of February, it must be in reality a war to the knife, a war like that of Spain against Napoleon; a war in which no amount of shootings and burnings will prove sufficient to break the spirit of resistance.

FRIEDRICH RATZEL
(1844–1904)

Friedrich Ratzel, who taught at Munich (1876–86) and Leipzig (after 1886), was the founder of modern political geography. In 1902 he wrote presciently: "A vast area is taking on importance before our eyes, and the forces developing there are tranquilly awaiting the dawn of the Pacific age, the successor of the Atlantic age and the old, out-dated age of the little European region and the Mediterranean." Ratzel was the author of Anthropogeographie *(Munich, 1882),* Völker und Raüme *(Peoples and Spaces; Munich, 1894);* Politische Geographie *(Political Geography; Leipzig, 1897); and* Das Meer als ein Quelle des Völkergrösse *(The Sea, Source of the Power of Peoples; Leipzig, 1902). He had a major influence in an age of aggressive nationalisms and imperial geopolitics.*

THE SPATIAL GROWTH OF STATES

Spatial growth manifests itself as a peripheral phenomenon in pushing outward the frontier which must be crossed by the carriers of growth. The closer these carriers live to the boundary, the more intimately do they share an interest in this process; and the larger the frontier, the more pronouncedly peripheral will the growth be. A state which stretches out toward a desired district sends out at the same time growth nodes which exhibit more activity than does the rest of the periphery. This is discernible in the shape of countries and in the distribution of their inhabitants and other power media. The outcrops of Peshawar and Little Tibet, and those from Merv and Kokand permit immediate recognition of that which even their history does not show; that in their direction British India and Russia grow together, determined to envelop all the benefits of the lands which lie between them, just as Rome through conquering Gaul grew counter to the advancing Teutons. On its German and Ital-

From Friedrich Ratzel, *The Structure of Political Geography,* edited by Roger E. Kasperson and Julian V. Minghi, translated by Ronald Bolin (Chicago: Aldine, 1969), 23–25.

[782]

ian boundaries which for centuries were positions of particularly strong growth, France concentrates its power media in striving to resume repressed growth. It is characteristic of such segments that they attract a major portion of the activity of the state. The marches of eastwardly expanding Germany which, as they were conquered piece by piece, were fortified and colonized, are repeated along the growing edges of America in the west and in Argentina in the south. There, in a few years large cities have arisen from the primitive log cabins of the fortified frontier. Given the crowded conditions of states in Europe such excellent portions of the periphery are at once among the most dangerous and the most fortified: the wounds which they can receive are to be feared above all others.

Other portions of the periphery of a state are given a special character because they are made up of the outwardly oriented peripheral segments of once independent regions which have grown together with that state. In every large frontier area we find such fragments of former national, provincial, or municipal boundaries which are the less altered the less they are adjusted to the forward and backward pushes of historical movements and the more practically they are created, i.e. have been adjusted and adapted to the terrain. There is a difference as between the worn outer banks and the highly indented inner shore of a spit, between a centuries old and a continuously developing boundary. The western and southern boundaries of Saxony can be offered as examples of this.

The frontier undergoes the same development as does the area, the consolidation, and the continuity of the state. If we go back to the first states on earth we find an indeterminacy of boundaries to the point of effacement. Where the area is uncertain, its periphery cannot possibly be distinct. The mania for transferring our conception of the boundary as a precisely determined line to conditions where the state comprises only an ill-defined spot on the earth has led, in the Indian policy of the American powers as well as in Africa, to the most arrant misunderstandings. As [Dr. M. K. H.] Lichtenstein has said of the Kaffir boundary [in South Africa], the attempt was often made to fix a stable boundary which neither of the two parties should overstep without special permission from the sovereign; "in this, however, there has never been mutual consent." Not lines, but tiers are the important thing in this concept. In so far as a state is surrounded by politically empty space, the chances of encounter, of broad collision, are reduced and the state is drawn together. If its peoples, however, push beyond these limits, then it becomes more a matter of integration than of displacement. . . .

In its growth and evolution the state practices selection geographical benefits in that it occupies the good locations of a district before the poor. If its growth is related to the dispossession of other states, it victoriously captures the good areas and the dispossessed continue in the bad. Therefore in the younger lands (colonies) whose entire history is known to us, the new political structures lie pronouncedly tiered along the sea, on the rivers and lakes, and in the fertile plains, while the older political forms are driven into the initially less accessible and less desired interior, into the steppes and deserts, the mountains, and the swamps. The same has happened in North America, in Siberia, in Australia and in South Africa. By the advantages which such locations offer to the first colonists they early determine the fate of large lands for a long time to come. Even if political possession is changed the earlier coming population remains at a cultural advantage, and the cultural miscarriage of many politically successful invasions can be explained in this manner. Carriers of the same culture have, all in all, the same concept of the value of the land, and for this reason all European colonies of the last centuries have undergone corresponding spatial development. At other times other assessments predominated. The ancient Peruvians did not go down the Amazon, but rather extended their domination in the plateau along a slender strip nearly 4000 km. long. The ancient Greeks did not seek large fertile interiors, but rather, following in this regard the Phoenecians, sought islands and peninsulas between inlets. The Turks, on the other hand, occupied the high steppes of Asia Minor which the Greeks disdained, and the Magyars the puszta of the Danube lowland. Custom as well as the level of culture are reflected in this and it is for this reason that political growth continues as long as possible in regions where there are similar living and working conditions. The Phoenecians settled on the coasts, the Dutch on islands, and the Russians on rivers. How greatly the expansion of the Roman Empire was benefited by the closed natural character of the Mediterranean lands was well known to the ancients. For Greece as well as for Rome these lands therefore presented the most fortunate of colonial regions where they could feel almost everywhere even more at home than does a central European in North America between 35° and 45° north latitude.

THE SEA AND SEA-GOING PEOPLES

If, then, the Atlantic contributed to enlarging the stage of history in the North Atlantic, the same task will fall to the Pacific in the southern hemisphere. The most important and promising territories of the southern hemisphere are in the Pacific, and one day a great history peculiar to the antipodes will come

From Friedrich Ratzel, *La Géographie politique: Les Concepts fondamentaux*, translated by François Livald (Paris: Librairie Arthème Fayard, 1987), ch. 22. Translated from the French by A. M. Berrett. Reproduced by permission of Librairie Arthème Fayard.

about there. There is a second key fact: the predominance of Southeast Asia. The two formidable empires of China and Japan, where one-third of humanity lives, stand against the American territories caught between the cordillera and the ocean. Yet these two countries are only just beginning their extension into the ocean. Russia and the United States continue to dominate the northern Pacific and England the South Pacific, with France, Germany, and the United States setting up colonies in rivalry with England among the islands between the tropics. It is indeed just here that the canal at Panama or Nicaragua will provide a passage to the west. The journey to Lima or Valparaiso from Europe will take half the time; conversely, the Pacific states of the United States will be closer to the Atlantic. The United States will thus be the great beneficiary of the operation. Even though it can be said that humanity will reach its greatest development in the Pacific, what will remain decisive in the coming decades will be the strength with which a state can intervene in the Atlantic.

Control of the sea, with its infinite horizons, gives maritime peoples important character traits, such as daring, endurance, and foresightedness. They have made a major contribution to enlarging the scale of politics. Politics bound to small spaces is necessarily myopic; the vastnesses of the ocean enlarge the views of businessmen and statesmen alike. Athens always had a clearer idea of greater Greece than Sparta. The sea has the potential to make a state a world power. Rome's historical greatness began when it was recognized there that power necessarily involved the sea. Rome began to win when it combined land power and sea power, thus pitting a more lasting and solid force against the purely sea-based, and hence ephemeral, Greek and Punic monopolies. The sea is an international space, which borders national territories, is tied up with them, and gives isthmuses, capes, and even the smallest strips of land an international dimension. That does not mean any cosmopolitanism. On the contrary, given that the sea offers a larger space to the representation of national interests, it sharpens the intelligence, as witness all the commercial and maritime powers. That is owing essentially to the fact that political expansion by sea is always economic, and that control of the seas results from domination of sea-borne commerce. If control of the seas develops this gift of broad vision, related to the political sense of space and almost merging into it, the great political strength of maritime peoples arises from a combination of this faculty with awareness of their interests. These two factors make a whole that can only with difficulty be disentangled.

Launching and maintaining a maritime power demands much more strength of spirit than the domination of large countries. And its constant renewal. This cannot be the work either of an individual or of an army. Many bold, enterprising, adventurous, cunning men contribute to it. That is the reason why control of the seas is the best school for peoples who mobilize large forces. . . .

And each time we find the same characteristic: the rapid flowering of ideas and works over the space bounded by the movement of ships and merchandise.

The ease with which a country acquires influence and possessions in the most remote regions and the ease with which they can be held without large investments have enabled nations associated with the sea to win quick successes. If maritime nations develop so rapidly, it is not only because they are naturally limited to islands or coasts; they are able to make themselves powerful without annexing vast tracts of land. The Hansa merchants and the Netherlands are obvious examples. That the development of powers is abrupt and surprising is shown by the rapid progress of the Greeks, who had no sooner reached the western Mediterranean than they were establishing colonies on the coast of Iberia, or the almost miraculous expansion of the English between 1559 and 1650 on almost every coast of the globe.

This rapid expansion of maritime powers explains the sudden character of conflicts and their tendency to end in furthering hegemony. When the balance that has reigned among maritime powers is upset, one of them will have to secure for itself control of the maritime space involved. In time of peace, it is continental powers that aim at monopoly within their own territories, particularly in the area of trade; conversely, in time of war, it is maritime powers that tend toward monopoly.

ALFRED THAYER MAHAN
(1840–1914)

Alfred Thayer Mahan, a rear admiral in the U.S. navy and historian, was a prolix and sometimes contradictory writer, but in his books The Influence of Sea Power upon History, 1660–1783 *(1890) and* The Influence of Sea Power upon the French Revolution and Empire, 1793–1812 *(2 vols., 1892) he was the first to bring out clearly the importance of sea power. Through his writings and his influence, notably on President Theodore Roosevelt, he contributed to the growth of U.S. naval power. Mahan sought to identify the reasons for and conditions securing command of the sea and sketched a naval geopolitics for the United States (the Caribbean, for example, is regarded as "the American Mediterranean"). He predicted the defeat and surrender of the German navy in World War I.*

NAVAL STRATEGY

Steam has introduced a relative certainty and precision into the movements of fleets. Head winds and adverse currents now answer only to the miry and mountainous road, for which allowance can be made. The turns of the screw can be counted upon better even than the legs of the soldier. An Art of Naval War becomes possible; and it becomes imperative from the very fact that the rapid, many-sided activity in the development of weapons produces a confusion in the mind which must by all means be ended, if possible. Moreover, if we clear our own heads and settle our convictions, we may produce some effect on popular understanding, which sorely needs it; as was shown by the unintelligent clamor of sensible men during the Spanish War, and the demands then made as to the distribution of the fleet. If possible, we must get hold of the principles which, throughout all changes, underlie naval war; of the strongly marked outlines around which lesser details can be filled in and to

From A. T. Mahan, *Naval Strategy Compared and Contrasted with the Principles and Practice of Military Operations on Land* (Boston: Little, Brown, 1911), 115–79.

which they can be referred; by which this or that specious proposition can be judged and found to be sound or rotten, according as it fundamentally conforms to or conflicts with settled truth. . . .

The search for and establishment of leading principles—always few— around which considerations of detail group themselves, will tend to reduce confusion of impression to simplicity and directness of thought, with consequent facility of comprehension. It must be noted likewise that while steam has facilitated all naval movements, whether strategical or tactical, it has also brought in the element of communications to an extent which did not before exist. The communications are, perhaps, the most controlling feature of land strategy; and the dependence of steam ships upon renewing their limited supply of coal, contrasted with the independence of sailing ships as to the supply of their power of motion, is exactly equivalent to the dependence of an army upon its communications. It may be noted, too, that, taking one day with another, the wind in the long run would average the same for each of two opponents, so that in the days of sail there would be less of the inequality which results from the tenure of coaling stations, or from national nearness to the seat of war. Coal will last a little longer, perhaps, than the supplies an army can carry with it on a hurried march, but the anxiety about it is of the same character; and in the last analysis it is food and coal, not legs and engines, which are the motive powers on either element.

The days when fleets lay becalmed are gone, it is true; but gone also are the days when, with four or five months of food and water below, they were ready to follow the enemy to the other side of the world without stopping. . . .

Both the power and the difficulties due to steam call for a more comprehensive and systematic treatment of the art of war at sea, and for the establishment of definite principles upon which it reposes. To do this is simply a particular instance of the one object for which the War College exists. As the principles of the art of war are few, while embracing many features, so the principle of the War College is one; namely, the study of the art of war and the exposition of its principles. Like the body, it has but one backbone though many ribs. When these principles have been more or less successfully defined, the way is open to a clearer comprehension of naval history, a more accurate perception of the causes of success or failure in naval campaigns. Study of these, superimposed upon an adequate grasp of principles, contributes to the naval strategist the precise gain which the practice of a profession gives to a man— a lawyer, for instance—who has already mastered the principles. Extensive study of cases gives firmer grasp, deeper understanding, wider views, increased aptitude and quickness to apprehend the critical features in any suit, as distinct from details of less relative importance. . . .

. . . Land warfare has a much more extensive narrative development, because there has been very much more land fighting than sea; and also, perhaps because of this larger amount of material, much more effort has been made to elicit the underlying principles by formal analysis. Further, with the going of uncertainty and the coming of certainty into the motive power, a chief distinction between the movements of fleets and armies has disappeared. Unless, therefore, one is prepared to discard as useless what our predecessors have learned, it is in the study of the best military writers that we shall find the most ample foundations on which to build the new structure. Not attempting the vain, because useless, labor of starting on unbroken ground, we will accept what is already done as clear gain, and build. No doubt—and no fear—but we shall find differences enough; no one will mistake the new house for the old when it is finished; yet the two will have a strong resemblance, and the most marked contrasts will but bring out more clearly than ever the strong features common to both.

The definitions of strategy, as usually given, confine the applications of the word to military combinations, which embrace one or more fields of operations, either wholly distinct or mutually dependent, but always regarded as actual or immediate scenes of war. However this may be on shore, a French writer is unquestionably right in pointing out that such a definition is too narrow for naval strategy. "This," he says, "differs from military strategy, in that it is as necessary in peace as in war. Indeed, in peace it may gain its most decisive victories by occupying in a country, either by purchase or treaty, excellent positions which would perhaps hardly be got in war. It learns to profit by all opportunities of settling on some chosen point of a coast, and to render definitive an occupation which at first was only transient."

This particular differentiation of naval strategy is due to the unsettled or politically weak conditions of the regions to which navies give access, which armies can reach only by means of navies, and in which the operations of an army, if attempted, depend upon control of the sea. If a nation wishes to exert political influence in such unsettled regions it must possess bases suitably situated; and the needs of commerce in peace times often dictate the necessity of such possessions, which are acquired, as the French writer says, when opportunity offers.

In Europe, the great armies now prevent such acquisitions, except at the cost of war. . . .

. . . The diplomatist, as a rule, only affixes the seal of treaty to the work done by the successful soldier. It is not so with a large proportion of strategic points upon the sea. The above positions have all been acquired in peace, and without hostilities. The same is true of the acquisition of the Hawaiian Islands by the United States. . . . Such possessions are obtained so often without actual war, because the first owners on account of weakness are not able to make the resistance which constitutes war; or, for the same reason of weakness, feel the need of political connection with a powerful naval state. . . .

Another illustration of naval strategy in time of peace, which also depends in large measure upon the great distances which separate the strategic centers of interest—centers, for example, such as those of the Atlantic and Pacific coasts of the United States, or those of Great Britain in the Narrow Seas and in the Mediterranean—is to be seen in the changed disposition of navies at the present time. It would be interesting to estimate how much this is due to circumstances, to changes in international conditions, and how much to the greater attention to and comprehension of the principles and requirements of strategy, now to be found in naval officers, as compared with the placid acquiescence of former generations in routine traditions. I think it would be safe to say in this connection that the present recognition of the necessity for concentration is an advance due to study, to intellectual appreciation of a principle and of the military ineptness and danger of the former method of distributing the force of a nation in many quarters during peace; but that the particular methods in which this appreciation has shown itself are the result of international conditions. As an instance may be cited the present concentration of the British fleet in home waters. This is an immediate reflection of German naval development. . . .

The necessity for such sustained naval concentrations depends again upon the characteristic which above all differentiates naval strategy from that upon land. This characteristic is the mobility of navies as compared with armies, the outcome of the very different surfaces over which they respectively move. A properly disposed fleet is capable of movement to a required strategic position with a rapidity to which nothing on land compares. This necessitates a corresponding preparation on the other side, which at the least must be ready to get there equally rapidly and equally concentrated. All this is mobilization; a process common to land and sea, but differing both in the scale and in the rapidity with which it can be conducted. At sea, for navies, the process also is simple; which again means that it can be rapid. Complication means loss of time. For these reasons, while the disposition of armies in peace must be maintained with direct reference to war, the difficulty of mobilization for the other party permits a dispersion of the forces on land which is impolitic in naval dispositions. In the mobilization of a land force, concentration, militarily understood, is the prime object, as it is with navies; but it is the second step, that is, it follows the local activities which mobilize the several corps. With navies it should be less the first step than the condition at the instant war breaks out, however unexpected. Then again the impedimenta, the train, which constitutes so large a factor in military movements, exists for navies only in a very modified degree; and the train possesses substantially the same mobility as the battleships themselves, because the open field of the sea offers wider facilities than roads can do. All these advantages in mobility mean rapidity in time; and this reduction in the scale of time required for movement means expansion in the scale of distance that can be covered, in order to overpower a dispersed or an unwary enemy. Thus when the Japanese torpedo vessels surprised the unready Russian fleet before Port Arthur, they opened hostilities some hundreds of miles from their point of departure.

"The possession of the strategic points," says the Archduke Charles, "decides the success of the operations of war." This Napoleon also expressed in the words, "War is a business of positions." It is necessary, however, to guard against a mistake so common that it seems almost to be a permanent bias of the human mind in naval matters. It is one that has come home to myself gradually and forcibly throughout my reading; a result which illustrates aptly what I have just said of the gain by reading widely after principles are understood. I knew long ago, and quoted in these lectures, Jomini's assertion that it is possible to hold too many strategic points; but it is only by subsequent reading that I have come to appreciate how common is the opinion that the holding of each additional port adds to naval strength. Naval strength involves, unquestionably, the possession of strategic points, but its greatest constituent is the mobile navy. If having many ports tempts you to scatter your force among them, they are worse than useless. To this is to be added another remark, also due to Jomini, that if you cannot hope to control the whole field, it is an advantage to hold such points as give you control of the greater part of it. The farther toward an enemy you advance your tenable position by the acquisition of strategic points, or by the positions occupied in force by army or navy, the better; provided, in so doing, you do not so lengthen your lines of communication as to endanger your forces in the advanced positions.

An exceptionally strong illustration of the benefit of such advanced position is afforded by the Island of Cuba and the effect exercised upon the control of the Gulf of Mexico, according as a position in that island may be held or not by the United States. While Cuba was Spanish, the United States had to depend upon Pensacola and the Mississippi as points upon which to base naval operations. If, in such conditions, war arose with a European state, Cuba being neutral, the enemy venturing his battle-fleet into the Gulf of Mexico would not thereby expose his rear or his communications to attack in force to the same extent that he would now with the United States cruisers based upon Guantanamo, duly fortified. Between opponents of equal force this advanced position gives a decided advantage to the occupant by the facility it affords to molest and interrupt the supplies, and especially the coal supplies, of a hostile fleet attempting to maintain itself within the Gulf, or advanced in the Caribbean towards the Isthmus. As regards the Gulf coast alone, Key West to some extent would fulfil the office of Guantanamo. The two together are a better defence for our Gulf region as a whole than localized land defences at particular points of the region would be. As regards influence over the Canal Zone, the superiority in situation of Guantanamo over Key West is obvious. The deterrent effect of such positions upon a fleet does not apply to the same degree to single fast cruisers or small squadrons, because the loss of a few of them can be risked for the sake of annoying an enemy. . . .

From these instances the general reason for taking up such an advanced position is obvious. Behind your fleets, thus resting on secure positions and closely knit to the home country by well-guarded communications, the operations of commerce, transport, and supply can go on freely. Into such a sea the enemy cannot venture in force about equal to your own—Germany, in the instance just cited, into the Atlantic, or an enemy of the United States into the Gulf—because in the very act of venturing he exposes his communications, and, in case of reverse, he is too far away from his home ports. Cuba thus covers the Gulf of Mexico, but would not have an equal material effect upon operations against the North Atlantic Coast. The British blockades of a century ago, on the contrary, being pushed right up to the French shores, covered the entire ocean and all approaches to the British Islands, because so far advanced. In virtue of that advance, while maintained, they conferred upon the home country perfect security from invasion with substantial immunity to the commerce of the United Kingdom, the loss being less than three per cent per annum.

To-day, the British Islands by their geographical situation alone, as towards Germany, themselves occupy an advanced position; their control over the North Sea resembles closely that of Cuba over the Gulf of Mexico, and their defensive value to the communications of the country are the same. Even German cruisers—commerce destroyers—to reach the British commercial communications, must run the gauntlet of the North Sea, and act with diminished coal supply far from their bases of operation. The rear and its communications cannot, we know, be protected wholly from commerce destroyers in their attacks either upon supply ships or commerce. Such raids on the flanks and rear of an army were frequent in the American War of Secession. They can only be checked, not wholly prevented, by light bodies, or by cruisers similar to those who make them.

"Good partisan troops," says Jomini, whose experiences antedated the American War of Secession by half a century, "will always disturb convoys, whatever be the direction of the roads, even were that direction a perpendicular from the center of the base to the center of the front of operations—the case in which they are least open to the attacks of an enemy."

Such injuries, however, are not usually to be confounded with the cutting, or even threatening, the communications. They are the slight wounds of a campaign, not mortal blows; vexatious, not serious. It is a very different matter to have a powerful fleet in a strong port close to the communications.

Raiding operations against commerce, or against an enemy's communications, may proceed from remote colonial positions. . . .

The determination, therefore, of the strategic points of a maritime area, such as the Gulf and Caribbean, or as the Pacific, the two seas in which the United States is most critically interested, must be followed by a selection from among them, first, of those which have the most decisive effect upon the control of the theater of war; secondly, of those which represent the most advanced position which the United States, in case war unhappily arose, could occupy firmly, linked to it by intermediate positions or lines, such that the whole would form a well-knit, compact system from which she could not be dislodged by any but a greatly superior force.

Strategic Positions

The strategic value of any place depends upon three principal conditions:

1. Its position, or more exactly its situation. A place may have great strength, but be so situated with regard to the strategic lines as not to be worth occupying.

2. Its military strength, offensive and defensive. A place may be well situated and have large resources and yet possess little strategic value, because weak. It may, on the other hand, while not naturally strong, be given artificial strength for defense. The word "fortify" means simply to make strong.

3. The resources, of the place itself and of the surrounding country. It is needless to explain the advantages of copious resource or the disadvantages of the reverse. A conspicuous example of a place strong both for offense and defense, and admirably situated, yet without natural resources, is Gibraltar. The maintenance of this advanced post of Great Britain depended in the past wholly upon her control of the sea. Resources that are wanting naturally may be supplied artificially, and to a greater extent now than formerly. . . . From these considerations it follows that, other things being equal, a small island is of less strategic value than a large one; and a point like Key West, at the end of a long narrow peninsula of restricted access, is in so far inferior to Pensacola, and would be to Havana or Cienfuegos if Cuba were a thriving country.

As an illustration of the advantage of a large island over a small, or over several small ones, I will read you the opinion of the well-known Admiral Rodney, found in an official memorandum of the period of the War of American

Independence. Rodney had had a very long experience of the West Indies, both in peace and war.

> Porto Rico, in the hands of Great Britain, will be of infinite consequence, and of more value than all the Caribbee Islands united—will be easily defended, and with less expense than those islands; the defense of which divides the forces, and renders them an easier conquest to an active enemy: but this island will be such a check to both France and Spain, as will make their island of St. Domingo be in perpetual danger, and, in the hands of Great Britain, enable her to cut off all supplies from Europe bound to St. Domingo, Mexico, Cuba, or the Spanish Main; and, if peopled with British subjects, afford a speedy succour to Jamaica; and, when cultivated, employ more ships and seamen than all the Windward Islands united.

In this you have an example of the material which, as I have said before, naval history furnishes in abundance to the student of the art of war. All the advantages of a strategic point are here noted, though not quite in the orderly, systematic manner at which a treatise on the art of war would aim: Situation, relatively to Jamaica, Santo Domingo and other Spanish possessions; defensive strength, due to concentration, as compared with the dispersion of Lesser Antilles; offensive strength as against the communications of Spain with her colonies; and resources of numerous British subjects with their occupations, as well as of British ships and seamen.

Where all three conditions, situation, intrinsic strength, and abundant resources, are found in the same place, it becomes of great consequence strategically and may be of the very first importance, though not always. For it must be remarked that there are other considerations, lesser in the purely military point of view, which enhance the consequence of a seaport even strategically; such as its being a great mart of trade, a blow to which would cripple the prosperity of the country; or the capital, the fall of which has a political effect additional to its importance otherwise.

Of the three principal conditions, the first, situation, is the most indispensable; because strength and resources can be artificially supplied or increased, but it passes the power of man to change the situation of a port which lies outside the limits of strategic effect.

Generally, value of situation depends upon nearness to a sea route; to those lines of trade which, when drawn upon the ocean common, are as imaginary as the parallels of the chart, yet as really and usefully exist. If the position be on two routes at the same time, that is, near the crossing, the value is enhanced. A cross-roads is essentially a central position, facilitating action in as many directions as there are roads. Those familiar with works on the art of land war will recognize the analogies. The value becomes yet more marked if, by the lay of the land, the road to be followed becomes very narrow; as at the Straits of Gibraltar, the English Channel, and in a less degree the Florida Strait. Perhaps narrowing should be applied to every inlet of the sea, by which trade enters into and is distributed over a great extent of country; such as the mouth of the Mississippi, of the Dutch and German rivers, New York harbor, etc. As regards the sea, however, harbors or the mouths of rivers are usually *termini* or entrepôts, at which goods are transshipped before going farther. If the road be narrowed to a mere canal, or to the mouth of a river, the point to which vessels must come is reduced almost to the geometrical definition of a point and nearby positions have great command. Suez presents this condition now, and Panama soon will.

Analogously, positions in narrow seas are more important than those in the great ocean, because it is less possible to avoid them by a circuit. . . .

A radical difference underlying the conditions of land and sea strategy is to be found in the fact that the land is by nature full of obstacles, the removing or overcoming of which by men's hands opens communications or roads. By nature, the land is almost all obstacle, the sea almost all open plain. The roads which can be followed by an army are therefore of limited number, and are generally known, as well as their respective advantages; whereas at sea the paths by which a ship can pass from one point to another are innumerable, especially if a steamer, content to make a circuit. The condition of winds, currents, etc., certainly do combine with shortness of distance to tie ships down to certain general lines, but within these lines there is great scope for ingenuity in dodging the search of an enemy. . . .

For the reason that the open ocean offers such large opportunity for avoiding a position recognized as dangerous, first-rate strategic points will be fewer within a given area on sea than on land—a truth which naturally heightens the strategic value of such as do exist. For instance, Hawaii, in the general scheme of the Pacific, is a strategic point of singular importance. It is a great center of movement, an invaluable half-way house, an advanced position of great natural power of offense as a base of operations and for supply and repair; but in the control of commerce its effect is lessened by the wide sweep open to vessels wishing to avoid it. On the other hand, possession gives it defensive value additional to offensive, by excluding an enemy from using it, whether for war or for commerce. . . .

The *amount of trade* that passes enters into the question as well as the *nearness of the port* to the route. Whatever affects either affects the value of the position. It is the immense increase of German industry, commerce, and shipping that has made Great Britain, by the strategic position of the British Islands, the menacing object she has become in German eyes. The growth of

German trade, combined with the strategic position of Great Britain, has revolutionized the international relations of Europe. A similar new commercial condition, the Panama Canal, will change the strategic value of nearly every port in the Caribbean and of many in the Pacific, because of the consequent increase of trade passing that way. Imagine Suez closed again forever, and consider the twofold effect,—upon the Cape of Good Hope ports and upon those of the Mediterranean. Of this we have historical demonstration in the effect upon the fortunes of Venice and Genoa from the discovery of the Cape route. Sea power primarily depends upon commerce, which follows the most advantageous roads; military control follows upon trade for its furtherance and protection. Except as a system of highways joining country to country, the sea is an unfruitful possession. The sea, or water, is the great medium of circulation established by nature, just as money has been evolved by man for the exchanges of products. Change the flow of either in direction or amount, and you modify the political and industrial relations of mankind.

In general, however, it will be found that by sea, as by land, useful strategic points will be where highways pass, and especially where they cross or converge; above all, where obstacles force parallel roads to converge and use a single defile, such as a bridge. It may be remarked here that while the ocean is easier and has, generally, fewer obstacles than the land, yet the obstacles are more truly impassable. Ships cannot force their way over or through obstacles, but must pass round them—turn them. . . .

Military Strength

We come now to the second element in the strategic value of any position, namely, its military strength, offensive or defensive.

It is possible to imagine a point very well placed yet practically indefensible, because the cost of defensive works would be greater than the worth of the place when fortified. A much stronger site, although somewhat further off, would throw such a position out of consideration.

There are several elements, advantageous or disadvantageous, which enter into the characteristics making a port strong or weak, but they will all be found to range themselves under the two heads of defensive and offensive strength.

DEFENSIVE STRENGTH

The defense of seaports, as distinguished from the offensive use made of them, ranges under two heads: 1. Defense against attack from the sea; that is, by ships. 2. Defense against attack from the land; that is, by troops which in the absence of resistance may have landed at some near point of the coast and come up in the rear of the fortress.

As offensive efforts made from a fortified seaport, to facilitate which it has been fortified, are always by ships toward the sea, the sea may properly be spoken of as the front of such a port, while the land side is the rear....

... Napoleon said that no position can be permanently maintained if dependent upon defense only; if not prepared for offensive measures, or if it fails to use them. The enemy must be disturbed or he will succeed. At one time in the history of war this truth was so clearly apprehended, and the conditions of passive resistance so thoroughly appreciated, that the endurance of a besieged fortress could be calculated almost as exactly as a mathematical solution; that is, granting no attempt at relief. In a properly coördinated system of coast defense this counter-action, molestation, the offensive-defensive, belongs to the navy.

Coast defense in the restricted sense, when action is limited to repelling an immediate attack, is the part of the army chiefly; hence the scheme of preparations for such defense also belongs primarily to the army. That being the case, it is not for naval officers to distribute the preparations among the branches of the military service; but it is permissible to note that the duty of planning fortifications and superintending their constructions is by accepted tradition assigned to military engineers.

It should be noted also that such tactical considerations as the extent of the outer lines necessary to cover the landward defensive works of a place, and the consequent numbers of the garrison required to insure their maintenance, are questions of expert military knowledge. It follows, and will be still more evident as the naval requirements develop in the ensuing treatment, that sound decision in the selection of naval stations at home and abroad is for combined military and naval consultation. Indeed, every question and every preparation touching seacoast operations present this feature of combination between army and navy, working to a common end.

In all such coöperations there will be found conflicting conditions, as there will in most plans of campaign and in positions taken for battle—strong here, weak there. War in all its aspects offers a continual choice of difficulties and advantages. It is in reconciliation effected among these as far as possible, in allowance of due predominance to the most important, in disregard of difficulties where practicable, that the art of the commander consists. The one most demoralizing attitude is that which demands exemption from risks, or is daunted unduly by them....

Countries which are entirely surrounded by water, or whose land frontiers are bordered by communities of much less military strength, as is the case with Great Britain and the United States, may easily fall into the error of defending ports only against attack from the sea. For ports which are commercial only, not essential to naval activities, this must answer; for there is a limit to the money that can be spent upon coast fortifications. But any scheme of naval activity rests upon bases, as do all military operations. Bases are the indispensable foundations upon which the superstructure of offense is raised. Important naval stations, therefore, should be secured against attack by land as well as by sea. . . . Purely commercial cities are defended sufficiently by the condition that a large hostile expedition will be employed only in securing an adequate result, a decided military gain, such as the destruction of a great naval base; while a small landing force, though it conceivably might capture a commercial port, can do so only by a surprise, which in effect is a mere raid, liable to interception, and in any event productive of no decided military advantage. . . .

Skill and vigilance may now, as in all ages and conditions, enable the one party or the other to get the better; especially the one inside. I presume that a simple application of the three-point problem, to determining a straight channel through a presumed mine field, might be carried on by three lights placed at night for the observers; that such channel might be swept by night as well as by day; and that, once cleared, further laying of mines might be prevented by adequate scouting. Range lights will give pilotage for the channel cleared. Yet, granting that such means may be efficacious, the need for using them and the onerousness of their demands show how conditions have altered in twenty years. Obviously, too, the outsiders must try to stop such operations, with the result of a good deal of fighting corresponding to that which the army calls "outpost." . . .

. . . Now that bombardment of unfortified seaports is forbidden by international agreement, the question remains to what extent it will suit the policy of a nation by non-fortification to permit the tranquil occupation of its convenient harbors by an enemy's vessels; for the purpose, for instance, of coaling, or repairing, or demanding supplies. Of course any molestation of vessels so engaged is active war, and would at once deprive the port of the immunity attendant upon not being fortified. . . .

A moment's thought will show that one mode of coast defense by the navy to which attention is very largely directed nowadays, that by torpedo-vessels and submarine boats, is not strictly defensive in its action, but offensive. For harbor defense, torpedo-vessels are confined almost wholly to an offensive rôle—the offensive-defensive—because an attack by a fleet upon a port will usually be by daylight, while torpedo-vessels, in the general scheme of harbor defense, must limit their efforts mainly to the night. The chief rôle of the torpedo-vessels is in *attack* upon a hostile fleet which is trying to maintain its ground near the port.

The great extension and development given to torpedo-vessels since these lectures were written do not seem, as far as experience goes, to have affected the general principles here enunciated; nor in actual war has anything occurred to contradict the conclusions indicated to students of naval matters twenty years ago. Torpedo-vessels, when relying upon themselves alone, have always attacked by night. By day they have merely completed destruction already substantially achieved by the battleships; and this probably is the function that will fall to them in the unusual case of a fleet seriously attacking fortifications. . . .

Defenses, whether natural or artificial, covering strategic points such as coast fortresses, play a very important part in all warfare, because they interpose such passive resistance to the assailant as to enable smaller force to hold in check a larger. Their passive strength thus becomes equivalent to a certain number of men and allows the holder to let loose just so many to join the active army in the field. . . . Places so held serve many purposes and, in some proportion, are absolutely necessary to the control of any theater of war. They are as essential to sea as to land war; but, looked upon as conducive to the attainment of the objects of war, they are to be considered inferior to the army in the field. To take an extreme case, a *reductio ad absurdum*, if the number of such posts be so great that their garrisons swallow up the whole army of the state, it is evident that either some of them must be abandoned or the enemy's army be left unopposed. Thus Jomini says, "When a state finds itself reduced to throw the greater part of its force into its strong places, it is near touching its ruin." This received illustration in the war between Japan and Russia. Russia was reduced to shutting up her fleet in Port Arthur and Vladivostok; and persistence in this course, whether by choice or by necessity, prognosticated the ruin which overtook the naval predominance which at the beginning of the war she actually possessed over Japan.

In the sphere of maritime war, the navy represents the army in the field; and the fortified strategic harbors, upon which it falls back as ports of refuge after battle or defeat, for repairs or for supplies, correspond precisely to strongholds, like Metz, Strasburg, Ulm, upon which, systematically occupied with reference to the strategic character of the theater of war, military writers agree the defense of a country must be founded. The foundation, however, must not be taken for the superstructure for which it exists. In war, the defensive exists mainly that the offensive may act more freely. In sea warfare, the offensive is assigned to the navy; and if the latter assumes to itself the defensive, it simply locks up a part of its trained men in garrisons, which could be filled as well by forces that have not their peculiar skill. To this main proposition I must add a corollary, that if the defense of ports, many in number, be attributed to the navy, experience shows that the navy will be subdivided among them to an extent that will paralyze its efficiency. . . .

Every proposal to use a navy as an instrument of pure passive defense is found faulty upon particular examination; and these various results all proceed from the one fundamental fact that the distinguishing feature of naval force is mobility, while that of a passive defense is immobility. The only exception known to me is where permanent—that is, immobile—works cannot be constructed to command the surroundings, because of the extent and depth of the water area to be defended. . . .

I have now put before you reasons for rejecting the opinion that the navy is the proper instrument, generally speaking, for coast defense in the narrow sense of the expression, which limits it to the defense of ports. The reasons given may be summed up, and reduced to four principles, as follows:

1. That for the same amount of offensive power, floating batteries, or vessels of very little mobility, are less strong defensively against naval attack than land works are.

2. That by employing able-bodied seafaring men to defend harbors you lock up offensive strength in an inferior, that is, in a defensive, effort.

3. That it is injurious to the morale and skill of seamen to keep them thus on the defensive and off the sea. This has received abundant historical proof in the past.

4. That in giving up the offensive the navy gives up its proper sphere, which is also the most effective.

OFFENSIVE STRENGTH

The offensive strength of a seaport, considered independently of its strategic situation and of its natural and acquired resources, consists in its capacity:

1. To assemble and hold a large military force, of both ships of war and transports.

2. To launch such force safely and easily into the deep.

3. To follow it with a continued support until the campaign is ended. In such support are always to be reckoned facilities for docking, as the most important of all supports.

It may be urged justly that this continued support depends as much upon the strategic situation of the port and upon its resources as upon its strength. To this, however, must be replied that it was never meant that the division between the different elements which together make up the total value of a seaport was clear-cut and absolute. The division into heads is simply a convenient way by which the subject can be arranged and grasped more clearly. Some necessary conditions will affect, more or less, all three, strength, position, and resources, and will unavoidably reappear under different heads.

1. Assembling. It will be seen that depth of entrance, and the area of anchoring ground for large vessels, are elements of offensive strength. . . .
2. Launching. To launch a force safely and easily into the deep implies that when ready to start it can go out at once and take up its order of battle in the presence of an enemy, unmolested. . . .

If a fleet is able to steam out from port in line abreast, a change of course all together, when nearing the enemy, effects such deployment: but the channels by which harbors are left are usually too narrow for this. Ordinarily vessels must go out in column, and form line by a graduated movement. An outside enemy awaiting such issue would seek to deploy across the exit of the channel, out of range of the forts but within range of the exit, enabled thus to concentrate fire upon the leaders of the column before the vessels following can give support by deploying their batteries.

Belts of submarine mines, laid by the one party or the other, as was largely done by both the Japanese and Russians, may affect the conditions constituted by nature. Submarine mines may be said to introduce artificial hydrographic conditions. The inside party would aim to keep the enemy, by fear of mines, so far distant as to be out of range of its point of deployment; and the effect may be intensified by an energetic use of torpedo vessels and submarines. At Port Arthur, the Russian mines and the apprehension of torpedo attack did fix the Japanese fleet to the Elliott Islands, so that the Russians when they came out had no trouble about deploying.

An outside fleet, on the other hand, would wish by a like use of mines to prevent the issuing fleet from deploying until it had passed beyond support by the shore guns. The Japanese did not attempt this; that is, one-third of their battleship force having been lost early in the war, the exigencies of their case led them to seek the safety of a boom-protected anchorage, rather than expose their armored ships to torpedo attack by remaining continuously close to the port, in order to obtain the advantage of concentration on the head of the enemy's column. Their mine fields, by making the exit dangerous, enforced delay upon the enemy's fleet, enabling themselves to come up before it could escape; but this strategic advantage was not accompanied with the tactical advantage of concentration upon the leading enemies during the critical moment preceding deployment.

All these dispositions—boom anchorage, mine fields, concentration on enemy's leaders—are tactical. My subject is strategy. The excuse for the apparent digression is that the strength of a naval base of operations is a strategic consideration, affecting all the theater of war. Tactical facilities and disabilities are elements of strength or weakness, and as such a general consideration of them falls under the lawful scope of strategy. Mine fields, as used in the latest war, have introduced a new condition, affecting that element of offensive strength in a naval base which has been defined as the ability to launch a maritime force easily and safely into the deep.

These tactical considerations have a further very important bearing upon a strategic question of the gravest order; namely, the proper position for an outside fleet charged with the duty of checking the movements of a more or less equal enemy within a port. Hawke and St. Vincent in their day answered: Close to the port itself. Nelson, more inclined to take risks, said: Far enough off to give them a chance to come out; to tempt them to do so, for we want a battle. The difference was one of detail, for both aimed at interception, though by different methods. It may be mentioned in passing that Nelson paid for the deliberate looseness of his lines by some periods of agonizing suspense, touch with the enemy being lost. . . .

If a port have two outlets at a great distance from each other, the offensive power will be increased thereby, the enemy being unable to be before both in adequate force. . . .

In order that two outlets should confer fully the offensive advantage claimed, it is necessary that they should be so far apart that the enemy cannot concentrate before one, between the time that the fleet within indicates its intention of coming out and the time when it has formed its order of battle outside. With steam, few ports are so favorably situated; the dependence of sailing-ships upon the direction and force of the wind introduced a tactical and strategic element which can now be disregarded. . . .

The third element in the offensive strength of a strategic port has been stated as the capacity, after having covered the exit of a maritime force, to follow it with continued support throughout the intended operations.

Obviously, in any particular port, this capacity to support active operations will depend upon the scene and character of the operations. . . .

To follow a fleet with support means principally two things: (1) To maintain a stream of supplies out, and (2) to afford swift restoration to vessels sent back for that purpose.

"Supplies" is a comprehensive word. It embraces a large number of articles which are continuously being expended, and which must be renewed by means of storeships periodically dispatched. It applies also to maintaining the condition of a fleet by a system of reliefs. This involves a reserve, so that ships long out and worn are replaced by fresh vessels, and, yet more important, by refreshed crews. Of the capacity thus to refresh and thus to replace, numerous dry docks are the most important single constituent, because the most vital and the longest to prepare. . . .

Resources

The wants of a navy are so many and so varied that it would be time lost to name them separately. The resources which meet them may be usefully divided under two heads, natural and artificial. The latter, again, may be conveniently and accurately subdivided into resources developed by man in his peaceful occupation and use of a country, and those which are immediately and solely created for the maintenance of war.

Other things being equal, the most favorable condition is that where great natural resources, joined to a good position for trade, have drawn men to settle and develop the neighboring country. Where the existing resources are purely artificial and for war, the value of the port, in so far, is inferior to that of one where the ordinary occupations of the people supply the necessary resources. To use the phraseology of our subject, a seaport that has good strategic situation and great military strength, but to which all resources must be brought from a distance, is much inferior to a similar port having a rich and developed friendly region behind it. . . . The mutual dependence of commerce and the navy is nowhere more clearly seen than in the naval resources of a nation, the greatness of which depends upon peaceful trade and shipping. Compared with a merely military navy, it is the difference between a natural and a forced growth.

Among resources, dry docks occupy the place first in importance: (1) because to provide them requires the longest time; (2) because they facilitate various kinds of repairs; (3) because by the capacity to clean and repair several vessels at once, and so restore them with the least delay to the fleet, they maintain offensive energy.

Dry docks represent in condensed form the three requirements of a strategic seaport. In position they should be as near the scene of war as possible. Strength is represented by numbers; the more numerous the docks, the greater the offensive strength of the port. For resources, the illustration is obvious; docks are an immense resource. In contemplating the selection of a navy-yard site, it is evident that facility for excavating docks is a natural resource, while the subsequent construction is artificial. Evidently, also, a commercial port will supplement these resources in an emergency by the docks it may maintain for commerce, thus exemplifying what has been said as to the wide basis offered by resources developed by man in his peaceful occupation of a country.

Strategic Lines

The strategic points on a given theater of war are not to be looked upon merely separately and as disconnected. After determining their individual values by the test of position, military strength, and resources, it will remain to consider their mutual relations of bearing, distance, and the best routes from one to the other.

The lines joining strategic points are called by military writers strategic lines. On land there may be several lines, practicable roads, connecting the same two points; any one of which may at different times have different names, indicating the special use then being made of it, as, line of operation, line of retreat, line of communications, etc. At sea, other things being equal, the line that is shortest, measured by the time required to pass over it, is ordinarily the one to be chosen by a fleet; but this obvious remark, approaching a truism, is open to frequent modification by particular circumstances. . . .

The most important of strategic lines are those which concern the communications. Communications dominate war. This has peculiar force on shore, because an army is immediately dependent upon supplies frequently renewed. It can endure a brief interruption much less readily than a fleet can, because ships carry the substance of communications largely in their own bottoms. So long as the fleet is able to face the enemy at sea, communications mean essentially, not geographical lines, like the roads an army has to follow, but those necessaries, supplies of which the ships cannot carry in their own hulls beyond a limited amount. These are, first, fuel; second, ammunition; last of all, food. These necessaries, owing to the facility of water transportation as compared with land, can accompany the movements of a fleet in a way impossible to the train of an army. An army train follows rather than accompanies, by roads which may be difficult and must be narrow; whereas maritime roads are easy, and illimitably wide.

Nevertheless, all military organizations, land or sea, are ultimately dependent upon open communications with the basis of the national power; and the line of communications is doubly of value, because it usually represents also the line of retreat. Retreat is the extreme expression of dependence upon the home base. In the matter of communications, free supplies and open retreat are two essentials to the safety of an army or of a fleet. . . .

On the same sea frontier all the fortified ports will form parts of the base of operations, which itself may be properly called a strategic line. Provision should be made for safe and rapid communication between the ports; for while dissemination may be necessary to rapid preparation, concentration is essential to vigorous execution.

In conformity with this statement, of the need to provide for safe and rapid communication between the ports of a maritime frontier, in order to concentrate the forces when the moment for action arrives, we find mentioned among the needs of a base of operations ashore that of free movement and transport of troops and supplies behind the actual front. . . .

The problem of uniting a divided fleet, or of getting a separated ship safely to her main body may therefore be expected to recur; consequently the provision of methods to that end, by using the means of the day, is not of barren academic interest. Nor does the fact that the operation is very difficult, results doubtful, remove the consideration as impracticable. The very improbability of an effort has often been the cause of its success. In the case of a single armored ship, or of a small division, having to run for it in order to effect a junction with the main fleet in another port, the torpedo force could be assembled in such numbers as might be necessary to accompany the passage, which would commonly be made by night; for obscurity is a curtain that favors the weaker. Local familiarity, too, is a much stronger factor than the local knowledge given by charts, especially in the dark. This and the choice of time—all the elements, in short—favor the local navy in such measures. This, however, is not to say that they involve no risk. War cannot be made without running risks. . . .

So far, the strategic points of a theater of sea war have been considered only with reference to that particular theater—to their importance intrinsically, and to their relations to one another and to the fleet. The treatment of the subject would not be complete without a reference to the distance separating colonial possessions or outlying interests from a mother country, and to the effect of that distance upon their value to the holder. This is a branch of the subject which particularly concerns naval war as compared with that on land. The great military nations of the world being found almost wholly on the continent of Europe, with well-established frontiers, the distance of any point defended by them, or against which they move offensively in continental wars, is not very great, at least at first. There is also nothing on the Continent that corresponds to the common ground which all peoples find in the sea, when that forms one of their frontiers. As soon as a nation in arms crosses its land frontier it finds itself in the territory of a neutral or of the enemy. If a neutral, it cannot go on without the neutral's consent; if an enemy, advance must be gradual and measured, unless favored by overwhelming force or great immediate success. If the final objective is very distant, there will be one or more intermediate objectives, which must be taken and held as successive steps to the end in view; and such intermediate objectives will commonly represent just so many obstacles which will be seriously disputed by the defendant.

To push on regardless of such obstacles, and of the threat they hold out against the communications and lines of retreat, requires accurate knowledge of the enemy's condition and sound judgment as to the power of your own army to cover the distance to your distant objective, and to overcome its resistance, before the enemy can bring his own resources into play. This amounts to saying that the enemy is known to be much inferior in strength for the time being, and that you have good hope of striking him to the heart before he is ready to use his limbs and weapons. Thus struck at the very center of his strength, with the sinews of his military organization cut, the key of his internal communications perhaps seized, and concerted action thus hindered, the enemy may, by such a bold and well-timed movement, be brought to submit. This is the aim of modern war, and explains the great importance attached to rapid mobilization.

In naval operations such successes are wrought less by the tenure of a position than by the defeat of the enemy's organized force—his battle fleet. The same result will follow, though less conclusive and less permanent, if the fleet is reduced to inactivity by the immediate presence of a superior force; but decisive defeat, suitably followed up, alone assures a situation. As has been remarked before, the value of any position, sea or land, though very real, depends upon the use made of it; that is, upon the armed forces which hold it, for defense and offense. The sea is not without positions advantageous to hold; but peculiarly to it, above the land, is applicable the assertion that the organized force is the determining feature. The fleet, it may be said, is itself the position. A crushing defeat of the fleet, or its decisive inferiority when the enemy appears, means a dislocation at once of the whole system of colonial or other dependencies, quite irrespective of the position where the defeat occurs. Such a defeat of the British navy by the German in the North Sea would lay open all English colonies to attack, and render both them and the mother country unable to combine effort in mutual support. The fall of any coast position in the Empire would become then a question only of time and of the enemy's exertions, unless the British navy should be restored. Until then, there is no relieving force, no army in the field. Each separate position is left to its own resources, and when they are exhausted must succumb, as did Port Arthur; and as Gibraltar would have done in 1780 but for the navy of Great Britain, which was its army in the field. On the other hand, so long as the British fleet can maintain and assert superiority in the North Sea and around the British Islands, the entire Imperial system stands secure. The key of the whole is held, is within the hulls of the ships.

This is not to say that a powerful, although inferior, navy may not by successful evasion and subsequent surprise seize positions, one or more, in a distant part of the world, and there, so to say, entrench itself, to the discomfiture of the opponent and possibly to the attainment of some distinct ultimate national advantage. . . . This is one of the problems of war, the calculation of chances. Napoleon once said that the art of war consists in getting the most of the chances in your own favor. The superior fleet holds the strongest suit, but the strongest suit does not always win. The character and the skill of the player against you are important factors. For such reasons, the study of the chances, both in general elements of war and in the concrete cases of specific regions, is necessary; in order to fit an officer to consider broadly and to determine rapidly in particular contingencies which may arise.

Readiness and promptitude in action will of course give great advantages in such attempts, as they do in other military operations; and for the matter of that in all affairs of life. There is, however, a recognizable difference between the power of a great state either to attack or to defend a distant and isolated dependency, however strong, from which it is separated by hundreds or thousands of miles of sea, and the power of the same state to support a similar post in its interior or on its own frontier, whether sea or land. . . .

Other things being equal, the greater the distance the greater the difficulty of defense and of attack; and where there are many such points, the difficulty of defense increases in proportion to their distance, number, and dissemination. The situation of a nation thus encumbered, however unavoidably, is the reverse of that concentration, and maintenance of close communication, which are essential conditions of correct dispositions for war.

COLMAR VON DER GOLTZ
(1843–1916)

Baron Colmar von der Goltz took part in the Franco-Prussian war of 1870–71 and was subsequently appointed professor at the Potsdam military school, becoming one of the major military theoreticians of Wilhelmine Germany. In 1883 he was seconded to Turkey and put in charge of modernizing the Ottoman army. On returning to Germany, he rose eventually to the rank of field marshal and retired in 1913. In 1914 he became general aide-de-camp to the sultan of Turkey and the following year was given command of a Turkish army in Mesopotamia. He died in Baghdad in 1916. His writings include Das Volk in Waffen *(1883), translated as* The Nation in Arms *(1913).*

THE NATION IN ARMS

Modern Armies

It is absolutely natural that the great civilized nations of modern times should be continually improving their military organization to enable them in time of need to put the *totality* of their forces into action. The age of cabinet wars is over. A war can no longer be ended by reducing a single man at the head of a people or dominant political group to unconditional surrender; it requires the exhaustion of the nations fighting one another. The French people still to-day claim not to have wanted the war of 1870. But when the Empire, which had declared that war, had fallen, the same people at once showed themselves ready to continue the struggle to the bitter end. The same man [Adolphe Thiers] who in July 1870 had warned his country against an ill-thought-out declaration of war found himself governing it in September and took over as

From Colmar von der Goltz, *La Nation armée: Organisation militaire et méthodes de guerre modernes,* translated from the German by H. Monet (Paris, 1891). Translated from the French by A. M. Berrett.

head of the armies to become the most ardent advocate of bloody struggle. The fact is that wars have become wholly an affair of nations. The very same individual who is personally against warlike undertakings feels that it is his duty to devote himself wholly to them once the triumph or annihilation of his country is at stake. There is no one who does not recognize the moral beauty of that sentiment. It is the conflict of interests that leads to war, but the passions of peoples determine how far the war must be pushed outside all consideration of interest. As always, war serves policy to reach its objectives, but even for grievances of a lesser order, it must aim at the complete annihilation of the enemy. That necessarily leads to all material and moral means being brought to bear to bring down the enemy, and it is therefore natural and just to prepare the forces available in peacetime with a view to their deployment when the time comes.

A people that for humanitarian reasons would not like to go right to the bitter end, which had set itself a limit on the employment of force, would soon find itself being dragged along against its will. No enemy could be expected to observe the same reserve. On the contrary, the enemy would hasten to profit from this voluntary faint-heartedness by himself becoming more aggressive. . . .

Only nations that are constantly prepared to defend their independence sword in hand enjoy true security.

It is reasonable to think that the enormous sacrifices currently being asked will gradually lead to a state of exhaustion that will have an effect on the military organization and value of peoples. At the point where we are now, the problem lies in combining military life closely with national life in such a way that the former impedes the latter as little as possible, while exploiting the totality of its resources. Compulsory military service has best resolved the question, in the sense that since its adoption, the men under arms are not removed from the work force permanently, but only temporarily, and that all able men are nonetheless available to the army.

It is true that, since that time, the sacrifices imposed by the new system have reached levels previously thought impossible. . . .

. . . The French Revolution gave war back its original simplicity, which the previous century had replaced by a presumptuous and unintelligent pedantry.

Frederick the Great had shown the world what could be achieved with the limited means of past times. Napoleon, who opened the new era, showed from the very start how far war could go in its *unfettered* form. His principles still form the basis of our doctrine today. He reminded the world of arms of something the great king of Prussia had already taught it, but that it had since forgotten, which is that in war everything must be directed at destroying the enemy, and that the main place where decisions are reached is the battlefield.

The principle of conscription was applied with varying strictness depending on the needs of the moment; but it always weighed heaviest on the lower classes. Prussia replaced it with compulsory service, which spreads the burden of military obligations uniformly over the whole nation. The systematic training of the nation for war service is the consequence of that transformation.

Railroads, unknown in Napoleon's time, have made it possible to mass troops amazingly fast. They have had the effect of eliminating the long preliminary phases that preceded earlier wars, but, as a result, preparation for mobilization and mobilization itself have become considerably more important. Modern weaponry has also banished from the battlefield the columns of Napoleon's time; but their mobility has not been abandoned; it is to be found in the flexible articulation of present-day lines adapting themselves to all terrains. Finally, the new weaponry has considerably increased the importance of training in firepower.

Such is the path that has led us to modern armies, made up of all the living strength of nations, trained as best possible for war, provided with all that intelligence and money can supply, and equipped with such an organization that they can move from a peace footing to a war footing in just a few days.

It is this particular aspect of modern armies and the unlimited consumption of human raw material that typify modern war.

Conditions of Success in War

War is the continuation of policy by arms; whence the influence of the latter on the *manner* in which war is conducted. When this influence is criticized, it would normally be more accurate to criticize the policy itself. A bad policy will naturally have a bad impact on war.

Policy must not, of course, be understood in the narrow meaning of the word, in the sense of what we generally call "external policy"; domestic policy is important too; we are thus using the word *policy* in a broad sense.

The general state, public spirit, constitution, and moral and physical strength of a nation depend on policy, and these various factors in turn influence the manner in which war is conducted. . . .

The attitudes of certain states that, although not involved in any immediate participation in a war, are nevertheless directly interested in its outcome depend on policy. Their sympathy or hostility may be a matter of serious importance and greatly help or hamper things. It is again politics that generally decides the exact moment when war is declared, the choice of which can have a key bearing on success; in brief, it is policy that creates *the general situation within which the state goes to war,* and that situation will have a major influence on decisions, the conduct of the commander and even the army's morale.

War is such a decisive affair that, right from the first shot, politics begins to be much less important than previously. In the wars of the last century, the powers kept part of their armies in reserve, even after hostilities had started, and it was politics that decided whether the initial stakes should be raised or not. Today, *all* is thrown into the scales straight away, and it is the chance of battle that decides who wins.

Politics only recovers its rights when one side or the other begins to feel the need for peace more than the will to continue the struggle, as all hope of success by arms is finally abandoned. The role of politics is then to establish the basis for a mutual agreement. Sometimes, too, outside influences intervene and determine how far the victor can push his demands and the vanquished his concessions.

Toward the end of the war, when the outcome is no longer in doubt, the military element naturally increasingly gives way to the political. Often then politics even reacts to the commander's decisions. Political considerations may, in some cases, lead to a last battle that is militarily quite pointless, but is seen by one side as a last attempt at recovery and by the other as a last attempt to force the issue. . . .

This preponderant influence of politics in no way diminishes the importance of war or reduces the independence of its operations, provided the commander and the statesman in charge both subscribe to the principle that in all circumstances *the best service that war can render policy is to defeat the enemy utterly.* And by observing that dogma, you will have the double advantage of ensuring that policy has the greatest possible freedom of action and military operations have the greatest independence.

The need for close cooperation between policy and war is obvious. It is one more reason that bears out the principle that the advantage belongs to the state headed by a general and a politician combined in the person of a great king. . . .

The truth is that there can never be an absolute lack of congruence between the weaponry an army has and its morale, given that the latter includes intelligence, which seeks out good weapons. But untimely economy, technical errors, obstinacy, or false pride may not allow a weapon once thought good to be abandoned, and thus all these conditions may lead to marked inequalities in the weaponry of different armies, given the rapid advances of modern science. Weaponry that meets all the requirements of the moment is a necessity, because it involves the soldier's *confidence.* Soldiers must not feel themselves neglected in this respect, or inevitably condemned on the battlefield to be the victims of a superiority against which they are powerless. . . .

War requires money, more money, and still more money. Modern war, characterized by the principle of the unlimited use of all available resources, can hardly be conceived of without the modern principle of public loans. . . .

The ability to sustain war for a long time is a very precious guarantee of final success.

Money of itself will not, of course, be decisive; one must also know the limits within which one will be able to use it. A state that in the event of war retains free access to the sea will find that it has greater facilities for using its credit than a state to which all ports are closed as soon as the first shot is fired. The former is also in a position to appeal to foreign industry to arm and equip new units. . . . Command of the sea is thus indirectly a major component of power, even when the fleets are not in a position to give *direct* support to the operations of the land army.

Public wealth is a powerful help, but it will only bear fruit if the nation has the good sense to accept the necessary sacrifices *at the right time.* Tardy sacrifices cannot make up for early mistakes. . . . There again, material and moral factors both have an impact, as they do in every military question.

JOSEPH GALLIENI
(1849–1916)

*General Joseph Gallieni, who graduated from Saint-Cyr in 1870, was the
very model of a colonial officer, being both soldier and administrator. His
handling of operations and his implementation of reforms in Madagascar,
which he governed from 1896 to 1905, were remarkable. Only Louis Lyautey
in Morocco practised a similar policy. Gallieni was appointed military
governor of Paris in 1914, played a vital role in the initial stages of the battle
of the Marne, and in 1915 became minister of war. Among other books, he
published* Défense de Paris, 25 août–11 septembre 1914 *(Paris: Payot, 1920).*

THE CONQUEST OF MADAGASCAR

In the instructions I sent civil and military administrators and provincial heads
on 22 May 1898, before setting out for my second tour round the island, I reminded them all again in these terms of the principles to follow to ensure the
pacification of the still disturbed regions of the island:

> You only gain ground ahead after having completely organized the terrain
> behind you. It is yesterday's unsubdued natives who aid us and help us
> to win over the unsubdued of tomorrow. We march with a sure foot, and
> the last post occupied becomes the observation point from which the
> district or provincial officer examines the situation, seeks to make contact
> with the unknown people he finds in front of him by using those he has
> just subdued, decides on the new points to be occupied, and, in short,
> prepares the next step forward. This method never fails. It is the one that
> best handles the country and its inhabitants and best paves the way for

From Joseph Gallieni, *Rapport d'ensemble sur la pacification, l'organisation et la colonisation de
Madagascar (oct. 1896–mars 1899)* (Paris: Editions Charles-Lavauzelle, 1900). Translated from the
French by A. M. Berrett.

putting these new territories under our influence. It requires rare qualities on the part of our officers: initiative, intelligence, and activity, so that no opportunity of setting foot in areas still unknown and unsubdued is allowed to escape; prudence, calm, and perceptiveness, so as to avoid failures, which always have a harmful effect on our prestige; and knowing how to pick out from among the elements on the other side those they can use for the new advances to be made.

This method of gradually occupying a country that is in revolt or that has not been subdued can be contrasted with the method of pacification by military columns. But as, with that method, it is impossible to associate political action with military action, which must be used only exceptionally, as in the case of large and dangerous mobs fortified in redoubts, forests, or enclosures from which they threaten the security of the surrounding regions and prevent the submission and obedience of hesitant populations.

The use of columns has too often been synonymous with the systematic destruction of the enemy's villages and resources, because colonial war is treated as if it were war in Europe, in which the objective to be aimed at is the destruction of the enemy's main forces. In the colonies [as noted in the instructions referred to above]

it is necessary to treat the country and its inhabitants decently, since the former is intended to receive our future colonial enterprises and the latter will be our principle agents and collaborators to carry those enterprises to fruition. Every time that the incidents of war oblige one of our officers to take action against a village or an inhabited place, he must not lose sight of the fact that his first concern, once the submission of the inhabitants has been secured, is to rebuild the village [and] immediately set up a market and open a school there. He must thus take the utmost care to avoid all pointless destruction. . . .

Again, on 22 October 1896, I gave instructions to put an end to the burning of villages as a means of punishing inhabitants who had revolted:

It emerges from an examination of the reports prepared by the district, post, or reconnaissance officers that excessive and unjustified use has often been made of the burning of villages as a means of punishing their inhabitants.

The senior general commanding troops and military territories invites messieurs the district officers to give formal orders to put an end to such methods, which pointlessly ruin the country and can only increase the number of those who go and join the rebel bands.

In principle, they should rather tell the natives that the property of those who have thus abandoned their homes to take part in the uprising, and who have not returned by a date set by the district officer, will be confiscated and distributed among the loyal inhabitants.

It is only in absolutely exceptional cases that some villages may be burned as punishment; such a measure will never be taken except on the order of and under the responsibility of district officers, and a detailed report of the circumstances that gave rise to it will always be made.

... Also, with the benefit of the experience that we have already acquired in our attempts at colonization in other parts of the globe and in Madagascar itself, we should be able to avoid the dangers that arise from a false appreciation of the sort of relations that should exist between the natives and the newly arrived settlers in every new country. I have already given my views on this subject in detail in my last instructions of 22 January 1899, on the principles of colonization to be applied to Madagascar. We must above all treat these populations decently, but firmly, but at the same time with goodwill and above all a great spirit of justice. In the document [mentioned] above, I have shown that the natives of the Great Island [have] customs, perhaps shortcomings, which we [have] necessarily had to be take into account, and that it would be not only contrary to the interests of our settlers but even dangerous to tackle these customs head on. The education and training for work of races whose customs and needs are so different from ours can only be done over a long period and using extreme patience. If we go too fast, I am not afraid to say that we might expose ourselves to active discontent on the part of our subjects, and perhaps even new insurrectionary movements, as happened in 1878 in New Caledonia.

It is certainly our duty to encourage colonization in Madagascar by every means possible, and, as far as I am concerned, that encouragement has been the constant aim of all my efforts; but, I repeat, if our colonizing endeavors are to achieve sure results, they must seek to win over the confidence of the natives and not arouse their hostility.

ALFRED SCHLIEFFEN
(1833–1913)

Count Alfred von Schlieffen was assigned to the Prussian general staff in 1865 and fought in the battle of Sadowa in 1866. Promoted captain, he took part in the campaign against France in 1870–71. He became a brigadier in 1884, major-general in 1888, and deputy head of the general staff in 1889. On Moltke's death in 1890, he was appointed chief of staff. Schlieffen's influence was considerable; he trained Hindenburg, Arnim, Ludendorff, Seekt, and Litzmann, among others. He is particularly well known for the Schlieffen plan for the invasion of France, which he refined again and again between 1889 and 1905. Gambling on the slowness of Russian mobilization, this aimed at annihilating the French forces by a turning movement (the western wing violating Belgian neutrality), taking the French in a pincer movement. A version of the Schlieffen plan brought about the fall of France in 1940. Schlieffen's writings were collected in Gesammelte Schriften *(2 vols.; Berlin, 1910).*

PRESENT-DAY WAR

The Russo-Japanese War [of 1904–5] proved that simple attack on the enemy front can, despite all the difficulties, succeed. But the results of such an attack can only be meager, even in the most favorable case. Doubtless the enemy is repelled, but, later, on a different ground, he will renew the resistance he has only temporarily abandoned. The campaign drags on. But such wars have become impossible in an age when the nation's existence rests on the uninterrupted functioning of trade and industry, when a rapid decision is vital to get cogs that have stopped working moving again. It is not possible to carry on a strategy of attrition when the maintenance of millions of men involves billions

Alfred Schlieffen, "La Guerre actuelle," *Revue militaire générale* (Paris), April 1900. Translated from the French by A. M. Berrett.

in expenditure. To win a decisive, destructive success, it is necessary to make a simultaneous attack on two or three points at once—that is, on the front and against one or both flanks. An attack of this nature is relatively easy to execute for someone who has superior forces. But in present-day circumstances, it is difficult to count on such superiority. The means needed for a powerful flanking attack can only be obtained by reducing the forces deployed against the enemy front insofar possible. But even if these latter are used very stingily, they cannot see themselves as having as their sole mission to *occupy* the enemy, to use long-distance firepower to keep him where he is in sheltered positions. In *every case,* the front must be *attacked;* there must be an *advance* against the front. The rapid-firing long-range gun has been invented precisely so that a single weapon can replace many old weapons, so that it can suffice for all demands, provided the necessary munitions are available. Instead of massing reserves behind the front that are lacking at the decisive point, it is preferable to provide for resupply in munitions. Cartridges brought by motor vehicles are the best and most reliable reserves. All the troops that were formerly held in the rear to be used in the decisive attack must now, a priori, be used for the attack on the flank. The larger the forces intended for that attack, the more decisive the result of it will be.

But to attack an enemy flank you have to know where to find it. Determining exactly where it is used to be the mission of cavalry. It is likely that this task will in future fall to a fleet of dirigible balloons, which from the sky will have a better view than cavalry, whose own view is hampered by the very hills, forests, and topography within which it moves. But, just as cavalry had to drive the enemy cavalry from the field before it could devote itself to its reconnaissance mission, so dirigibles will have to anticipate giving battle in the skies to an enemy of equal strength. Happily, however, there are light balloons capable of rising higher than an adversary, firing destructive explosive projectiles, and then rising rapidly, so as not to be caught in the flames, which will shoot up very high.

Freed, in principle, from its reconnaissance role, the cavalry will endeavor to bring to bear on the enemy's rear the firepower of its artillery, machine guns, and long-range carbines. As in the past, it will meet the enemy cavalry in its path, which it will have to defeat before being able to carry out its proper mission; for—and the future will not alter this—the artillery will always, to some extent, first have to take care of the enemy artillery, the cavalry of the cavalry, and the balloons of the balloons, before being jointly able to help the infantry in the struggle for final victory.

Yet the battles of the future will not unfold quite so neatly. After the war of 1870–71, France and Germany built fortifications on their new common border to protect themselves, one against a new invasion and the other against a war of revenge. Whereas Germany limited itself to improving the newly acquired fortresses of Strasbourg and Metz, France built an almost continuous barrier along the upper reaches of the Moselle and the Meuse, designed to cover the whole of its eastern border from Switzerland to Belgium. [Germany] thus found itself in a difficult situation. While having no design for conquest, it could not remain indifferent and leave the enemy, who was pondering revenge, to watch in complete safety, from a sort of rallying ground, for the most favorable moment to launch forth from it.

The best defense is attack. Germany had to reserve the right to use this means if necessary. It therefore did not, as had been suggested, build a fortified line to counter a fortified line, but sought to secure a new means of attack. The heavy artillery was equipped with an explosive projectile of previously unknown power, which neither wall nor vault could withstand. The secret was not kept for long. The enemy invented similar destructive projectiles. Since then, both sides have seen a long, exasperated struggle, which has not yet died down, between the engineer and the artilleryman. The artilleryman endlessly invents new, bigger, more accurate guns, [and] more effective projectiles, which the engineer counters with works with an ever-greater capacity to withstand attack. This struggle, like the one over the rifle and the field gun, inevitably affected neighboring countries. It was accepted everywhere that peaceful Germany must constantly be thinking of some rapacious incursion into the smiling countryside of the Seine and the Loire. The direct route there being blocked, it could be taken that [the Germans] would seek to get round the unfortunate obstacle by way of Switzerland or Belgium. . . .

CHARLES CALLWELL
(1859–1928)

Charles Callwell, a British artillery officer who rose to be major-general, saw active service in Afghanistan and South Africa. He was director of military operations at the War Office in World War I and wrote Small Wars: Their Principles and Practice *(London, 1899), one of the key counterinsurgency manuals of the day.*

COUNTERINSURGENCY

The guerrilla mode of war must in fact be met by an abnormal system of strategy and tactics. The great principle which forms the basis of the art of war remains the combination of initiative with energy. But this is applied in a special form. The vigor and decision must be displayed in harassing the enemy and in giving him no rest. The hostile bands may elude the regular detachments, but their villages and flocks remain. The theater of war must be subdivided into sections, each to be dealt with by a given force or by a given aggregate of separate detachments. Defensive posts must be established where supplies can be collected, whither raided cattle can be brought, and which form independent bases. To each such base are attached one or more mobile or "flying" columns, organized to be ready to move out at a moment's notice, and equipped so as to penetrate to any part of the district told off to it and to return, certain of supplies for the task.

This question of flying columns deserves some further notice. The system which General Bugeaud introduced in Algeria was not new. General Hoche had worked on similar lines against the Chouans in Brittany with brilliant success. The principle of flying columns has since been used with great success

From Charles Callwell, *Small Wars: Their Principles and Practice* (London, 1899), reprinted in *The Guerrilla Reader: A Historical Anthology*, edited by Walter Laqueur (New York: New American Library, 1977), 114–18.

in the Western States against the Red Indians, in Afghanistan, and recently in Burma.

The troops forming such columns must be thoroughly equipped and must be able to travel light. Mobility is the first essential; for the guerrilla trusts to sudden strokes, and it is of the utmost importance that the marauding party should not have time to disperse, and that it should be attacked before it can withdraw and dissolve. Hoche urged the leaders of mobile columns to accustom their men to fatigue and hardships, and to keep them in condition. The strength of such columns depends upon the circumstances of the case. In Burma they seldom numbered more than three hundred men, with one or two guns. In Algeria where the enemy was brave and resolute small bodies would have been unsuitable, and General Bugeaud recommended three or four battalions with cavalry and two guns as a proper strength. Practically they should be as small as possible consistent with safety. Their composition, of course, depends upon the conditions of the campaign and upon the terrain. On open ground a large part of the force would often consist of mounted men. In the bush infantry alone can be used. . . .

In no class of warfare is a well-organized and well-served intelligence department more essential than in that against guerrillas. Hoche instituted an elaborate system of espionage in Brittany, paying especial attention to this very important subject. Guerrillas trust to secret and to sudden strokes, and if the secret is discovered, their plan miscarries. On the other hand all movements intended against them must be concealed. Guerrilla warfare means that the regular troops are spread about a hostile country where all their movements can be watched by the enemy and where their camps are full of spies. Partisan leaders seldom can be trusted, and in all dealings with them, great circumspection is essential. Hoche discouraged parleying with the rebels by subordinate officers, distrusting their chiefs. "Parle comme si tu avais confiance en tout le monde [Speak as though you trusted everyone]" was the motto of General Bugeaud "et agis comme si tu ne pouvais t'en rapporter à personne [and act as though you cannot rely on anyone]."

HALFORD J. MACKINDER
(1861–1947)

Halford J. Mackinder taught geography at Oxford from 1887 on and was director of the London School of Economics from 1903 to 1908. He was elected to Parliament in 1910 and served as British high commissioner in southern Russia in 1919–20. In 1904 he published The Geographical Pivot of History *in which he depicted a heartland (Germany) threatening a sea power (Britain). In 1943 he gave a new interpretation of this "pivot," now located much further east, in* The Round World and the Winning of the Peace.

THE GEOGRAPHICAL PIVOT OF HISTORY

The all-important result of the discovery of the Cape road to the Indies was to connect the western and eastern coastal navigations of Euro-Asia, even though by a circuitous route, and thus in some measure to neutralize the strategical advantage of the central position of the steppe nomads by pressing upon them in rear. The revolution commenced by the great mariners of the Columbian generation endowed Christendom with the widest possible mobility of power, short of a winged mobility. The one and continuous ocean enveloping the divided and insular lands is, of course, the geographical condition of ultimate unity in the command of the sea, and of the whole theory of modern naval strategy and policy as expounded by such writers as Captain Mahan and Mr. Spenser Wilkinson. The broad political effect was to reverse the relations of Europe and Asia, for whereas in the Middle Ages Europe was caged between an impassable desert to south, an unknown ocean to west, and icy forested wastes to north and north-east, and in the east and south-east was constantly threatened by the superior mobility of the horsemen and camelmen, she now emerged upon the world, multiplying more than thirty-fold the sea surface

From Halford J. Mackinder, *Democratic Ideals and Reality,* edited by Anthony J. Pearce (New York: Norton, 1962), 257–63. Reprinted by permission of W. W. Norton & Co., Inc.

and coastal lands to which she had access, and wrapping her influence round the Euro-Asiatic land-power which had hitherto threatened her very existence. New Europes were created in the vacant lands discovered in the midst of the waters, and what Britain and Scandinavia were to Europe in the earlier time, that have America and Australia, and in some measure even Trans-Saharan Africa, now become to Euro-Asia. Britain, Canada, the United States, South Africa, Australia, and Japan are now a ring of outer and insular bases for sea-power and commerce, inaccessible to the land-power of Euro-Asia.

But the land power still remains, and recent events have again increased its significance. While the maritime peoples of Western Europe have covered the ocean with their fleets, settled the outer continents, and in varying degree made tributary the oceanic margins of Asia, Russia has organized the Cossacks, and, emerging from her northern forests, has policed the steppe by setting her own nomads to meet the Tartar nomads. The Tudor century, which saw the expansion of Western Europe over the sea, also saw Russian power carried from Moscow through Siberia. The eastward swoop of the horsemen across Asia was an event almost as pregnant with political consequences as was the rounding of the Cape, although the two movements long remained apart.

It is probably one of the most striking coincidences of history that the seaward and the landward expansion of Europe should, in a sense, continue the ancient opposition between Roman and Greek. Few great failures have had more far-reaching consequences than the failure of Rome to Latinize the Greek. The Teuton was civilized and Christianized by the Roman, the Slav in the main by the Greek. It is the Romano-Teuton who in later times embarked upon the ocean; it was the Graeco-Slav who rode over the steppes, conquering the Turanian. Thus the modern land-power differs from the sea-power no less in the source of its ideals than in the material conditions of its mobility.

In the wake of the Cossack, Russia has safely emerged from her former seclusion in the northern forests. Perhaps the change of greatest intrinsic importance which took place in Europe in the last century was the southward migration of the Russian peasants, so that, whereas agricultural settlements formerly ended at the forest boundary, the centre of the population of all European Russia now lies to south of that boundary, in the midst of the wheat-fields which have replaced the more western steppes. Odessa has here risen to importance with the rapidity of an American city.

A generation ago steam and the Suez canal appeared to have increased the mobility of sea-power relatively to land-power. Railways acted chiefly as feeders to ocean-going commerce. But trans-continental railways are now transmuting the conditions of land-power, and nowhere can they have such effect as in the closed heart-land of Euro-Asia, in vast areas of which neither timber nor accessible stone was available for road-making. Railways work the greater wonders in the steppe, because they directly replace horse and camel mobility, the road stage of development having here been omitted.

In the matter of commerce it must not be forgotten that ocean-going traffic, however relatively cheap, usually involves the fourfold handling of goods—at the factory of origin, at the export wharf, at the import wharf, and at the inland warehouse for retail distribution; whereas the continental railway truck may run direct from the exporting factory into the importing warehouse. Thus marginal ocean-fed commerce tends, other things being equal, to form a zone of penetration round the continents, whose inner limit is roughly marked by the line along which the cost of four handlings, the oceanic freight, and the railway freight from the neighbouring coast, is equivalent to the cost of two handlings and the continental railway freight. English and German coals are said to compete on such terms midway through Lombardy.

The Russian railways have a clear run of 6,000 miles from Wirballen in the west to Vladivostok in the east. The Russian army in Manchuria is as significant evidence of mobile land-power as the British army in South Africa was of sea-power. True, that the Trans-Siberian railway is still a single and precarious line of communication, but the century will not be old before all Asia is covered with railways. The spaces within the Russian Empire and Mongolia are so vast, and their potentialities in population, wheat, cotton, fuel, and metals so incalculably great, that it is inevitable that a vast economic world, more or less apart, will there develop inaccessible to oceanic commerce.

As we consider this rapid review of the broader currents of history, does not a certain persistence of geographical relationship become evident? Is not the pivot region of the world's politics that vast area of Euro-Asia which is inaccessible to ships, but in antiquity lay open to the horse-riding nomads, and is to-day about to be covered with a network of railways? There have been and are here the conditions of a mobility of military and economic power of a far-reaching and yet limited character. Russia replaces the Mongol Empire. Her pressure on Finland, on Scandinavia, on Poland, on Turkey, on Persia, on India, and on China replaces the centrifugal raids of the steppe-men. In the world at large she occupies the central strategical position held by Germany in Europe. She can strike on all sides and be struck from all sides, save the north. The full development of her modern railway mobility is merely a matter of time. Nor is it likely that any possible social revolution will alter her essential relations to the great geographical limits of her existence. Wisely recognizing the fundamental limits of her power, her rulers have parted with Alaska; for it is as much a law of policy for Russia to own nothing over seas as for Britain to be supreme on the ocean.

Outside the pivot area, in a great inner crescent, are Germany, Austria, Turkey, India, and China, and in an outer crescent, Britain, South Africa,

Australia, the United States, Canada, and Japan. In the present condition of the balance of power, the pivot state, Russia, is not equivalent to the peripheral states, and there is room for an equipoise in France. The United States has recently become an eastern power, affecting the European balance not directly, but through Russia, and she will construct the Panama canal to make her Mississippi and Atlantic resources available in the Pacific. From this point of view the real divide between east and west is to be found in the Atlantic ocean.

The oversetting of the balance of power in favour of the pivot state, resulting in its expansion over the marginal lands of Euro-Asia, would permit of the use of vast continental resources for fleet-building, and the empire of the world would then be in sight. This might happen if Germany were to ally herself with Russia. The threat of such an event should, therefore, throw France into alliance with the over-sea powers, and France, Italy, Egypt, India, and Korea would become so many bridge heads where the outside navies would support armies to compel the pivot allies to deploy land forces and prevent them from concentrating their whole strength on fleets. On a smaller scale that was what Wellington accomplished from his sea-base at Torres Vedras in the Peninsular War. May not this in the end prove to be the strategical function of India in the British Imperial system? Is not this the idea underlying Mr. Amery's conception that the British military front stretches from the Cape through India to Japan?

The development of the vast potentialities of South America might have a decisive influence upon the system. They might strengthen the United States, or, on the other hand, if Germany were to challenge the Monroe doctrine successfully, they might detach Berlin from what I may perhaps describe as a pivot policy. The particular combinations of power brought into balance are not material; my contention is that from a geographical point of view they are likely to rotate round the pivot state, which is always likely to be great, but with limited mobility as compared with the surrounding marginal and insular powers.

I have spoken as a geographer. The actual balance of political power at any given time is, of course, the product, on the one hand, of geographical conditions, both economic and strategic, and, on the other hand, of the relative number, virility, equipment, and organization of the competing peoples. In proportion as these quantities are accurately estimated are we likely to adjust differences without the crude resort to arms. And the geographical quantities in the calculation are more measurable and more nearly constant than the human. Hence we should expect to find our formula apply equally to past history and to present politics. The social movements of all times have played around essentially the same physical features, for I doubt whether the progressive desiccation of Asia and Africa, even if proved, has in historical times vitally altered the human environment. The westward march of empire appears to me to have been a short rotation of marginal power round the south-western and western edge of the pivotal areas. The Nearer, Middle, and Far Eastern questions relate to the unstable equilibrium of inner and outer powers in those parts of the marginal crescent where local power is, at present, more or less negligible.

In conclusion, it may be well expressly to point out that the substitution of some new control of the inland area for that of Russia would not tend to reduce the geographical significance of the pivot position. Were the Chinese, for instance, organized by the Japanese, to overthrow the Russian Empire and conquer its territory, they might constitute the yellow peril to the world's freedom just because they would add an oceanic frontage to the resources of the great continent, an advantage as yet denied to the Russian tenant of the pivot region.

THE ROUND WORLD AND THE WINNING
OF THE PEACE

The particular events out of which sprang the idea of the Heartland were the British war in South Africa and the Russian war in Manchuria. The South African war ended in 1902, and in the spring of 1904 the Russo-Japanese war was clearly imminent. A paper which I read before the Royal Geographical Society early in the latter year, entitled "The Geographical Pivot of History," was therefore topical, but it had a background of many years of observation and thought.

The contrast presented by the British war against the Boers, fought 6,000 miles away across the ocean, and the war fought by Russia at a comparable distance across the land expanse of Asia, naturally suggested a parallel contrast between Vasco da Gama rounding the Cape of Good Hope on his voyage to the Indies, near the end of the fifteenth century, and the ride of Yermak, the Cossack, at the head of his horsemen, over the Ural range into Siberia early in the sixteenth century. That comparison in turn led to a review of the long succession of raids made by the nomadic tribes of Central Asia, through classical antiquity and the Middle Ages, upon the settled populations of the crescent of subcontinents: peninsular Europe, the Middle East, the Indies, and China proper. My conclusion was that

in the present decade we are for the first time in a position to attempt, with some degree of completeness, a correlation between the larger

From Halford J. Mackinder, *Democratic Ideals and Reality*, edited by Anthony J. Pearce (New York: Norton, 1962), 265–73. Reprinted by permission of W. W. Norton & Co., Inc.

geographical and the larger historical generalizations. For the first time we can perceive something of the real proportion of features and events on the stage of the whole world, and may seek a formula which shall express certain aspects, at any rate, of geographical causation in universal history. If we are fortunate, that formula should have a practical value as setting into perspective some of the competing forces in current international politics.

The word Heartland occurs once in the 1904 paper, but incidentally and as a descriptive and not a technical term. The expressions "pivot area" and "pivot state" were used instead, thus:

The oversetting of balance of power in favor of the pivot state, resulting in its expansion over the marginal lands of Euro-Asia, would permit of the use of vast continental resources for fleet-building, and the empire of the world would then be in sight. This might happen if Germany were to ally herself with Russia.

In conclusion, it may be well expressly to point out that the substitution of some new control of the inland area for that of Russia would not tend to reduce the geographical significance of the pivot position. Were the Chinese, for instance, organized by the Japanese, to overthrow the Russian Empire and conquer its territory, they might constitute the yellow peril to the world's freedom just because they would add an oceanic frontage to the resources of the great continent.

At the end of the First World War, my book *Democratic Ideals and Reality* was published in London and New York. Clearly the "pivot" label, which had been appropriate for an academic thesis at the beginning of the century, was no longer adequate to the international situation as it emerged from that first great crisis of our world revolution: hence "Ideals," "Realities" and the "Heartland." But the fact that, even when additional criteria were brought to bear, the thesis of 1904 still sufficed as the background for an estimate of the position fifteen years later, gave confidence that the formula sought had been found.

We turn now to the main object of the present article—the drafting of an interim estimate of the value of the Heartland concept in a survey of the world preliminary to the coming settlement. It must be understood that I am dealing with strategy, which, of course, is effective in peacetime no less than in wartime. I do not presume to join in the wide-sweeping debates already in progress which look forward over generations to come; I center my thoughts on the years during which the enemy is to be held down while, in the language of Casablanca, his philosophy of war is being killed.

The Heartland is the northern part and the interior of Euro-Asia. It extends from the Arctic coast down to the central deserts, and has as its western limits the broad isthmus between the Baltic and Black Seas. The concept does not admit of precise definition on the map for the reason that it is based on three separate aspects of physical geography which, while reinforcing one another, are not exactly coincident. First of all, we have in this region by far the widest lowland plain on the face of the globe. Secondly, there flow across that plain some great navigable rivers; certain of them go north to the Arctic Sea and are inaccessible from the ocean because it is cumbered with ice, while others flow into inland waters, such as the Caspian, which have no exit to the ocean. Thirdly, there is here a grassland zone which, until within the last century and a half, presented ideal conditions for the development of high mobility by camel and horse-riding nomads. Of the three features mentioned, the river basins are the easiest to present cartographically; the water divide which delimits the whole group of Arctic and "continental" rivers into a single unit does isolate neatly on the map a vast coherent area which is the Heartland according to that particular criterion. The mere exclusion of sea mobility and sea power, however, is a negative if important differential; it was the plain and the grassland belt which offered the positive conditions conducive to the other type of mobility, that proper to the prairie. As for the grassland, it traverses the whole breadth of the plain but does not cover its entire surface. Notwithstanding these apparent discrepancies, the Heartland provides a sufficient physical basis for strategical thinking. To go further and to simplify geography artificially would be misleading.

For our present purpose it is sufficiently accurate to say that the territory of the USSR is equivalent to the Heartland, except in one direction. In order to demarcate that exception—a great one—let us draw a direct line, some 5,500 miles long, westward from Bering Strait to Rumania. Three thousand miles from Bering Strait that line will cross the Yenisei River, flowing northward from the borders of Mongolia to the Arctic Ocean. Eastward of that great river lies a generally rugged country of mountains, plateaux and valleys, covered almost from end to end with coniferous forests; this I shall call Lenaland, from its central feature, the great River Lena. This is not included in Heartland Russia. Lenaland Russia has an area of three and three-quarter million square miles, but a population of only some six millions, of whom almost five millions are settled along the transcontinental railroad from Irkutsk to Vladivostok. In the remainder of this territory there are on the average over three square miles for every inhabitant. The rich natural resources—timber, water power and minerals—are as yet practically untouched.

West of the Yenisei lies what I have described as Heartland Russia, a plain extending 2,500 miles north and south, and 2,500 miles east and west. It contains four and a quarter million square miles and a population of more than 170 millions. The population is increasing at the rate of three millions a year.

The simplest and probably the most effective way of presenting the strategical values of the Russian Heartland is to compare them with those of France. In the case of France, however, the historical background is the First World War while in the case of Russia it is the Second World War.

France, like Russia, is a compact country, as long as it is broad, but not quite so well-rounded as the Heartland and therefore with a rather smaller area in proportion to the length of boundary to be defended. It is encompassed by sea and mountain, except to the northeast. In 1914–18 there were no hostile countries behind the Alps and the Pyrenees, and the fleets of France and her allies dominated the seas. The French and allied armies, deployed across the open northeastern frontier, were therefore well defended on either flank and were secure in the rear. The tragic lowland gateway in the northeast, through which so many armies have surged inward and outward, is 300 miles wide between the Vosges and the North Sea. In 1914, the line of battle, pivoting on the Vosges, wheeled backward to the Marne; and at the end of the war, in 1918, it wheeled forward on the same pivot. Through the four years' interval the elastic front sagged and bent but did not break even in the face of the great German attack in the spring of 1918. Thus, as it proved, there was space within the country sufficient both for defense in depth and for strategical retreat. Unfortunately for France, however, her principal industrial area was in that northeastern sector where the unceasing battle was waged.

Russia repeats in essentials the pattern of France, but on a greater scale and with her open frontier turned westward instead of northeastward. In the present war the Russian army is aligned across that open frontier. In its rear is the vast plain of the Heartland, available for defense in depth and for strategic retreat. Away back, this plain recedes eastward into the natural bulwarks constituted by the "inaccessible" Arctic coast, the Lenaland wilderness behind the Yenisei, and the fringe of mountains from the Altai to the Hindu Kush, backed by the Gobi, Tibetan and Iranian deserts. These three barriers have breadth and substance, and far excel in defensive value the coasts and mountains which engird France.

It is true that the Arctic shore is no longer inaccessible in the absolute sense that held until a few years ago. Convoys of merchant ships, assisted by powerful icebreakers and with airplanes reconnoitring ahead for water lanes through the ice pack, have traded to the Obi and Yenisei Rivers, and even to the Lena River; but a hostile invasion across the vast area of circum-polar ice and over the Tundra mosses and Targa forests of Northern Siberia seems almost impossible in the face of Soviet land-based air defense.

To complete the comparison between France and Russia, let us consider the relative scales of some parallel facts. Heartland Russia has four times the population, four times as wide an open frontier, and twenty times the area of France. That open frontier is not disproportionate to the Russian population; and to equal the breadth of the Soviet deployment Germany has had to eke out her more limited manpower by diluting it with less effective troops drawn from her subject countries. In one important respect, however, Russia began her second war with Germany in no better position than France occupied in 1914; as with France, her most developed agriculture and industries lay directly in the path of the invader. The second Five Year Plan would have remedied that situation had the German aggression been delayed a couple of years. Perhaps that was one of Hitler's reasons for breaking his treaty with Stalin in 1941.

The vast potentialities of the Heartland, however, to say nothing of the natural reserves in Lenaland, are strategically well placed. Industries are growing rapidly in such localities as the southern Urals, in the very pivot of the pivot area, and in the rich Kuznetsk coal basin in the lee of the great natural barriers east of the upper Yenisei River. In 1938 Russia produced more of the following foodstuffs than any other country in the world: wheat, barley, oats, rye and sugar beets. More manganese was produced in Russia than in any other country. It was bracketed with the United States in the first place as regards iron, and it stood second in production of petroleum. As for coal, ... the resources of the Kuznetsk and Krasnoyarsk coal basins are each estimated to be capable of supplying the requirements of the whole world for 300 years. The policy of the Soviet Government was to balance imports and exports during the first Five Year Plan. Except in a very few commodities the country is capable of producing everything which it requires.

All things considered, the conclusion is unavoidable that if the Soviet Union emerges from this war as conqueror of Germany, she must rank as the greatest land Power on the globe. Moreover, she will be the Power in the strategically strongest defensive position. The Heartland is the greatest natural fortress on earth. For the first time in history it is manned by a garrison sufficient both in number and quality.

JULIAN CORBETT
(1854–1922)

Julian S. Corbett began by writing novels after he left Cambridge. Subsequently he taught at the Naval War College, becoming a naval historian after 1900, and at Oxford (1903). Corbett published England in the Mediterranean: A Study in the Rise and Influence of British Power within the Straits, 1603–1719 *(1903–4) and studied the Spanish-American (1898) and Russo-Japanese (1904–5) naval wars. His major work was* Some Principles of Maritime Strategy *(1911) and his most original contribution* The Green Pamphlet *(1906).*

STRATEGICAL TERMS AND DEFINITIONS

Naval Strategy

Naval strategy does not exist as a separate branch of knowledge. It is only a section of a division of the art of war....

The true method of procedure then is to get hold of a general theory of war, and so ascertain the exact relations of naval strategy to the whole.

War is a form of political intercourse, a continuation of foreign politics which begins when force is introduced to attain our ends.

OBJECTS

We seek our ends by directing force upon certain objects, which may be ulterior or immediate.

Immediate objects (also called "Primary") are the ends of particular operations or movements. But it must be remembered that every primary object

From *Some Principles of Maritime Strategy* by Julian S. Corbett (Annapolis: Naval Institute Press, 1911), 307–24. Copyright © 1972 by U.S. Naval Institute, Annapolis, Maryland. Reproduced by permission of the U.S. Naval Institute.

has also its ulterior object; that is, every operation must be regarded, not only from the point of view of its special object, but also as a step to the end of the campaign or war.

Strategy is the art of directing force to the ends in view. Classified by the object it is Major Strategy, dealing with ulterior objects; Minor Strategy, with primary objects.

This also means that every operation of an army or fleet must be regarded in a double light, i.e., it must be planned and conducted in relation (1) to the general progress of the war; (2) to the object to which it is immediately directed.

Major Strategy (always regarding the ulterior object) has for its province the plan of the war, and includes: (1) Selection of the immediate or primary objects to be aimed at for attaining the ulterior object; (2) Selection of the force to be used, i.e., it determines the relative functions of the naval and military forces.

Minor Strategy has for its province the plans of operations. It deals with—

(1) The selection of the "objectives," that is, the particular forces of the enemy or the strategical points to be dealt with in order to secure the object of the particular operation.

(2) The directing of the force assigned for the operation.

Minor Strategy may be of three kinds:—

(1) Naval, where the immediate object is to be attained by a fleet only.

(2) Military, where the immediate object is to be attained by an army only.

(3) Combined, where the immediate object is to be attained by army and navy together.

NATURE OF OBJECT

The solution of every strategical problem, whether of Major or Minor Strategy, depends primarily on the nature of the object in view.

All objects, whether ulterior or not, may be positive or negative.

A positive object is where we seek to assert or acquire something for ourselves.

A negative object is where we seek to deny the enemy something or prevent his gaining something.

Where the object is positive, Strategy is offensive.

Where the object is negative, Strategy is defensive.

The Offensive, being positive in its aim is naturally the more effective form of war (i.e., it leads more directly to a final decision), and, as a rule, should be adopted by the stronger Power.

The Defensive, being negative in its aim, is naturally the stronger form of war; i.e., it requires less force, and, as a rule, is adopted by the weaker Power.[1]

The advantages of the Offensive are well known.
Its disadvantages are:—

(1)   That it grows weaker as it advances, by prolonging its communications.
(2)   That it tends to operations on unfamiliar ground.
(3)   That it continually increases the difficulty of retreat.

The advantages of Defence are chiefly:—

(1)   Proximity to base.
(2)   Familiar ground.
(3)   Facility for arranging surprise by counter attack.

GENERAL CHARACTERISTICS OF THE DEFENSIVE

True Defensive means waiting for a chance to strike.
    The strength and the essence of the defensive is the counter-stroke.
    A well designed defensive will always threaten or conceal an attack.
    A general defensive policy may consist of a series of minor offensive operations.
    The maxim is: If you are not relatively strong enough to assume the offensive, assume the defensive till you become so—

(1)   Either by inducing the enemy to weaken himself by attacks or otherwise;
(2)   Or by increasing your own strength, by developing new forces or securing allies.

Except as a preparation or a cover for offensive action the defensive is seldom or never of any use; for by the defensive alone we can never acquire anything, we can only prevent the enemy acquiring. But where we are too weak to assume the offensive it is often necessary to assume the defensive, and wait in expectation of time turning the scale in our favour and permitting us to ac-

---

1.   The general truth of this proposition is not affected by apparent exceptions where the contrary appears to be true. *The Offensive must not be confused with the Initiative.* It is possible to seize the Initiative, under certain conditions, by taking a defensive position from which the enemy is bound to dislodge us or abandon the operation.

cumulate strength relatively greater than the enemy's; we then pass to the offensive, for which our defensive has been a preparation.

As a cover or support for the offensive, the defensive will enable us to intensify the attack; for by assuming the defensive in one or more minor theatres of operation we can reduce our forces in those theatres to a minimum, and concentrate to a maximum for the offensive in the most important theatre.

OFFENSIVE OPERATIONS USED WITH A DEFENSIVE INTENTION

Counterattacks are those which are made upon an enemy who exposes himself anywhere in the theatre of his offensive operations. It is this form of attack which constitutes what Clausewitz calls the "surprise advantage of defence."

Diversions are similar operations undertaken against an enemy outside the limit of his theatre of offensive operations.

Diversions are designed to confuse his strategy, to distract his attention, and to draw off his forces from his main attack. If well planned, they should divert a force greater than their own. They should, therefore, be small. The nearer they approach the importance of a real attack the less likely they are to divert a force greater than their own.

It is only their power of diverting or containing a larger force than their own that justifies the breach of the law of concentration which they involve.

This power depends mainly on suddenness and mobility, and these qualities are most highly developed in combined expeditions.

NATURE OF ULTERIOR OBJECT

From the nature of the ulterior object we get an important classification of wars, according to whether such object is *limited* or *unlimited*.

(1)   *War with limited object* ("limited war") is where we merely seek to take from the enemy some particular part of his possessions, or interests; e.g., Spanish-American War, where the object was the liberation of Cuba.

(2)   *War with an unlimited object* is where we seek to overthrow the enemy completely, so that to save himself from destruction he must agree to do our will (become subservient); e.g., Franco-German War.

SYSTEM OF OPERATIONS

Having determined the nature of the war by the nature of its object (i.e., whether it is offensive or defensive and whether it is limited or unlimited), strategy has to decide on the system of operations or "plan of the war."

This depends upon:—

(1)   The theatre of the war.
(2)   The means at our disposal.

Theatre of the War Usually defined as "all the territory upon which the hostile parties may assail each other." This is insufficient. For an island power the theatre of war will always include sea areas. Truer definition: "geographical areas within which lie the ulterior objects of the war and the subordinate objects that lead up to them."

A "theatre of war" may contain several "theatres of operations."

Theatre of Operations Is generally used of the operations of one belligerent only.

An "operation" is any considerable strategical undertaking.

A "theatre of operations" is usually defined as embracing all the territory we seek to take possession of or to defend.

A truer definition is, "the area, whether of sea or land or both, within which the enemy must be overpowered before we can secure the object of the particular operation."

Consequently, since the nature of the war varies with the object, it may be defensive in one theatre of operations and offensive in another.

Where the operations are defensive in character any special movement or movements may be offensive.

OBJECTIVE

An objective is "any point or force against which an offensive movement is directed." Thus where the *object* in any theatre of operation is to get command of a certain sea in which the enemy maintains a fleet, that fleet will usually be the *objective*.

LINES OF OPERATION

A line of operation is "the area of land or sea through which we operate from our base or starting point to reach our objectives."

Lines of operation may be exterior or interior. We are said to hold the interior lines when we hold such a position, in regard to a theatre of operations, that we can reach its chief objective points, or forces, more quickly than the enemy can move to their defence or assistance. Such a position is called an interior position. "Exterior Lines" and "Exterior Position" are the converse of these.

LINES OF COMMUNICATION

This expression is used of three different things:—

(1) *Lines of supply,* running from the base of operations to the point which the operating force has reached.

(2) *Lines of lateral communication* by which several forces engaged in one theatre of operations can communicate with each other and move to each other's support.

(3) *Lines of retreat,* which are lines of supply reversed, *i.e.,* leading back to the base.

These three ideas are best described by the term "lines of passage and communication," which we had in use at the end of the eighteenth century.

Ashore, lines of passage and communication are roads, railways, waterways, &c.

At sea, they may be regarded as those waters over which passes the normal course of vessels proceeding from the base to the objective or the force to be supplied.

In Land Strategy the great majority of problems are problems of communication. Maritime Strategy has never been regarded as hinging on communications, but probably it does so even more than Land Strategy, as will appear from a consideration of maritime communications, and the extent to which they are the main preoccupation of Naval operations.

MARITIME COMMUNICATIONS

The various kinds of Maritime Communications for or against which a fleet may have to operate are:—

(1) Its own communications, or those of its adversary (which correspond to the communications of armies operating ashore). These tend to increase in importance strategically with the increasing hunger of modern fleets (for coal, ammunition, &c.).

(2) The communications of an army operating from an advanced oversea base, that is communication between the advanced and the main base.

(3)   Trade Routes, that is the communications upon which depend the national resources and the supply of the main bases, as well as the "lateral" or connecting communications between various parts of belligerents' possessions.

N.B.—Such "lines of passage and communication" are the preoccupation of Naval Strategy; that is to say, problems of Naval Strategy can be reduced to terms of "passage and communication" and this is probably the best method of solving them.

Naval Strategy Considered as a Question
of Passage and Communication

By "Naval Strategy" we mean the art of conducting the operations of the Fleet. Such operations must always have for their object "passage and communication"; that is, the Fleet is mainly occupied in guarding our own communications and seizing those of the enemy.

Proof I—Deductive We say the aim of Naval Strategy is to get command of the sea. What does this mean? It is something quite different from the Military idea of occupying territory, for the sea cannot be the subject of political dominion or ownership. We cannot subsist upon it (like an army on conquered territory), nor can we exclude neutrals from it. Admiral Colomb's theory of "conquest of water territory," therefore, involves a false analogy, and is not safe as the basis of a strategical system. What then is the value of the sea in the political system of the world? Its value is as a means of communication between States and parts of States. Therefore the "command of the sea" means the control of communications in which the belligerents are adversely concerned.[2]

Proof II—Inductive, from History or Past Experience History shows that the actual functions of the Fleet (except in purely maritime wars) have been threefold.

(1)   The prevention or securing of alliances (i.e., deterring or persuading neutrals as to participating in the war).

---

2.   Corollary: The command of the sea can never be, like the conquest of territory, the ulterior object of a war, unless it be a purely maritime war, as were approximately [England's] wars with the Dutch in the seventeenth century, but it may be a primary or immediate object, and even the ulterior object of particular operations.

(2)   The protection or destruction of commerce.

(3)   The furtherance or hindrance of military operations ashore.

Note.—The above is the best working "Definition of Naval Strategy," as emphasising its intimate connection with diplomatic, financial, and military aspects of major strategy.

These functions may be discharged in two ways:—

(1)   By direct territorial attacks, threatened or performed (bombardment, landing, raiding parties, &c.).

(2)   By getting command of the sea, i.e., establishing ourselves in such a position that we can control the maritime communications of all parties concerned, so that we can operate by sea against their territory, commerce, and allies, and they cannot operate against ours. [3]

COMMAND OF THE SEA

Command of the sea exists only in a state of war. If we say we have command of the sea in time of peace it is a rhetorical expression meaning that we have (a) adequate Naval positions; (b) an adequate Fleet to secure the command when war breaks out.

VARIOUS CONDITIONS OF COMMAND

1. It may be (a) general; (b) local.

(a) General command is secured when the enemy is no longer able to act dangerously against our line of passage and communication or to defend his own, or (in other words) when he is no longer able to interfere seriously with our trade or our military or diplomatic operations.

This condition exists practically when the enemy is no longer able to send squadrons to sea. [4]

(b) Local command implies a state of things in which we are able to prevent the enemy from interfering with our passage and communication in one or more theatres of operation.

3.   The power of this second method, by controlling communications, is out of all proportion to the first—direct attack. Indeed, the first can seldom be performed with any serious effect without the second. Thus, from this point of view also, it is clear that Naval Strategy is mainly a question of communications.

4.   Command of the sea does not mean that the enemy can do absolutely nothing, but that he cannot *seriously* interfere with the undertakings by which we seek to secure the object of the war, or to force our will upon him.

2. Both local and general command may be (*a*) temporary; (*b*) permanent.

(*a*) *Temporary command* is when we are able to prevent the enemy from interfering with our passage and communication in all or some theatres of operation during the period required for gaining the object in view (*i.e.*, the object of a particular operation or of a particular campaign). This condition existed after Togo's first action.

(*b*) *Permanent command* is when time ceases to be a vital factor in the situation, *i.e.*, when the possibility of the enemy's recovering his maritime position is too remote to be a practical consideration. This condition existed after Tsushima.

3. Command, whether general, local, or temporary, may be in three different states:—

(*a*) With us.
(*b*) With the enemy.
(*c*) In dispute.

If in dispute, it may be that:—

(1) We have preponderance.
(2) Our enemy has preponderance.
(3) Neither side preponderates.

COMMAND IN DISPUTE

The state of dispute is the most important for practical strategy, since it is the normal condition, at least in the early stages of the war, and frequently all through it.

The state of dispute continues till a final decision is obtained, i.e., till one side is no longer able to send a squadron to sea.

It is to the advantage of the preponderating Navy to end the state of dispute by seeking a decision. Hence the French tradition to avoid decisive actions as a rule when at war with England.

The truth of this appears from the fact that *general command of the sea is not essential to all oversea operations.*

In a state of dispute the preponderating Power may concentrate in one theatre of operations, and so secure the local or temporary command sufficient for obtaining the special object in view. The weaker Power may take advantage of such local concentration to operate safely elsewhere.

Rule 1. So long as a state of dispute can force the preponderating Power to concentrate, operating by evasion is possibly open to the weaker.

Rule 2. In a state of dispute although the weaker Power may not be able to obstruct the passage and communication of the stronger, it may be able to defend its own.

SHOULD COMMAND OF THE SEA ALWAYS BE THE PRIMARY OBJECT?

When the preponderating Power fails or neglects to get command (i.e., leaves the general command in dispute), the disadvantage to him is not so much the danger to his own operations as the facility given to the enemy for carrying out counter operations elsewhere.

Under certain conditions, therefore, it may not be the primary function of the fleet to seek out the enemy's fleet and destroy it, because general command may be in dispute while local command may be with us, and political or military considerations may demand of us an operation, for which such local command is sufficient, and which cannot be delayed until we have obtained a complete decision.

From the above it will appear "command of the sea" is too loose an expression for strategical discussion. For practical purposes should be substituted *"control of passage and communication."*

The question then in the consideration of any proposed operation or line of operations will be, not "Have we the command of the sea?" but "Can we secure the necessary lines of communication from obstruction by the enemy?"

METHODS OF SECURING CONTROL

1. *Permanent general control* can only be secured by the practical annihilation of the enemy's fleet by successful actions.

2. *Local and temporary control* may be secured by:—

(a) A defensive action not necessarily entirely successful (containing).

(b) Forcing concentration on the enemy elsewhere (diversion).

(c) Superior concentration so as to render impotent the enemy's force available in the special theatre of operations (masking or containing).

BLOCKADE

Blockades are of two natures, according to the object review. The object may be:—

(d) Blockade.

i. *Close blockade* to prevent the enemy putting to sea. The object being usually to secure local or temporary control.

ii. *Observation blockade,* to force the enemy to put to sea *by occupying the common lines of communications* (see below). In this case you are seeking a decision as a step towards general control.

Both natures are operations upon the lines of passage and communication, but in case (1) the primary intention is defensive, to secure our own line; in case (2) the primary intention is offensive, to seize the enemy's line and compel him to expose himself in an attempt to recover it.

GENERAL RULES FOR CONDUCTING BLOCKADES

In case (1) (defensive intention) blockade should be as close as is compatible with security from torpedo attack.

In case (2) (offensive intention) it should be as distant as is compatible with bringing enemy to action if he comes out.

THE PECULIARITY OF MARITIME COMMUNICATIONS

Since the whole idea of command of the sea and the whole theory of blockade rest on the control of communications, neither can be fully apprehended without a thorough understanding of the nature of maritime communications.

Ashore, the respective lines of communications of each belligerent tend to run more or less approximately in opposite directions, until they meet in the theatre of operations or the objective point.

At sea the reverse is the case; for in maritime warfare the great lines of communications of either belligerent tend to run approximately parallel, if, indeed, they are not identical.

Thus, in the case of a war with Germany, the object of which lay in the Eastern Mediterranean, or in America, or South Africa, our respective lines of communication would be identical.

This was also the case in all our imperial wars with France.

This peculiarity is the controlling influence of maritime warfare. Nearly all our current maxims of Naval strategy can be traced to the pressure it exerts on Naval thought.

It is at the root of the fundamental difference between Military and Naval strategy, and affords the explanation of much strategical error and confusion, which has arisen from applying the principles of land warfare to the sea without allowing for the antagonistic conditions of the communications and operations against them in each case.

On land the chief reason for not always striking the enemy's communications at once is that as a rule we cannot do so without exposing our own.

At sea, on the contrary, since the great lines are common to both, we cannot defend our own without striking at the enemy's.

Therefore, at sea, the obvious opening is to get your fleet into such a position that it controls the common lines, unless defeated or evaded.

Hence the maxim "that the proper place for our fleets is off the enemy's coast," "the enemy's coast is our true frontier," and the like.

But these maxims are not universally true, witness Togo's strategy against Rojesvensky, when he remained correctly upon his own coast.

Take again the maxim that the primary object of the fleet is to seek out the enemy's fleet and destroy it.

Here again Togo's practice was the reverse of the maxim.

The true maxim is "The primary object of the fleet is to secure communications, and if the enemy's fleet is in a position to render them unsafe it must be put out of action."

The enemy's fleet usually is in this position, but not always.

But nine times out of ten the maxim of seeking out the enemy's fleet, &c., is sound and applicable:—

(*a*) Because for us *general permanent command* is usually essential to ultimate success, and this cannot be obtained without destroying the enemy's fleet.

(*b*) Because usually the enemy's fleet opens with an attempt *to control the common communications*.

(*c*) Because usually the functions of the fleet are so complex (i.e., the calls upon it so numerous) that it will seek to strike a blow which solves all the difficulties. . . .

Also it must be remembered that nine times out of ten the most effective way of "seeking out the enemy's fleet" (i.e., forcing an action on him) is to seize a position which controls communications vital to his plan of campaign.

This was what happened in 1704. Rooke was unable to seek out the Toulon fleet, but by seizing Gibraltar he made it come to him (not intentionally, but by the operation of inevitable strategical law).

Compare Togo's strategy and that of the Americans in 1898.

Practically all great Naval actions have been brought about in this way, that is they have been the outcome on an effort to clear essential communications from the enemy's fleet, e.g., Gravelines, La Hogue, Quiberon, Trafalgar, Tsushima.

Similarly the great actions of the old Dutch wars were brought about because our geographical position placed us astride the Dutch trade communications, and they were forced to seek a decision against our fleet.

FINAL NOTE

In applying the maxim of "seeking out the enemy's fleet" it should be borne in mind:—

(1)   That if you seek it out with a superior force you will probably find it in a place where you cannot destroy it except at heavy cost.

(2)   That seeing that the defensive is a stronger form of war than the offensive, it is *prima facie* better strategy to make the enemy come to you than to go to him and seek a decision on his own ground.

FRIEDRICH VON BERNHARDI
(1849–1930)

Friedrich von Bernhardi, who fought in the Franco-Prussian War and subsequently rose to the rank of general, was one of the most original German military theoreticians of the 1871–1914 era. He analyzes the likely conditions of future wars in On War of Today *(London: H. Rees, 1912–13), probably his best book. Bernhardi believed that any future conflict would be short (a widespread opinion at the time). He shows how much "firepower dominates tactics today and imposes its laws on them" and argues that, in the last analysis, in modern war, it is the state with the greatest industrial and financial resources that is likely to win.*

ON WAR OF TODAY

Modern War

The nature of modern war is not a simple notion. It is subject to numerous modifications according to the character of the contending parties and of the various theatres of war. It is altogether different whether we are fighting in the Balkans or in Manchuria, whether Russians are fighting against Japanese, or Spaniards against Riff-Kabyles. The fundamental principles of war certainly remain the same, wherever it is waged; but special conditions cause in each case special methods of employment of the fighting forces, and these latter, again, will differ frequently.

If we are moving with forces of some size in a desolate, roadless, or mountainous country, we are obliged to adopt proceedings altogether different from those obtaining in a vast, slightly undulating plain, where railways and a well-built and extensive network of roads abound. Again, things will be otherwise

From Friedrich von Bernhardi, *On War of Today*, translated by Karl von Donat (New York: Garland Publishing, 1972), 1: 14–78.

if we carry on war with small armies in a country little cultivated, like the English in South Africa, or are operating with armies of the size as those of the Great European Military Powers in a richly cultivated and densely populated theatre of war.

It is this latter sort of war which we are concerned with most, for it is such a war we ourselves will have to wage, and this kind of war it is that stares us in the face like an inscrutable sphinx. There seems to be no doubt that, in a war like this, forces will assert themselves which we have no experience to gauge, and the effect of which we can scarcely properly realize. Whole nations are called up to take the field against each other. They are going to fight with arms of patterns, perfect as never before. The proportionate numbers of infantry, artillery, and cavalry are quite different from those of former times. Means of transport will be used to an extent and of a perfect type as we have never seen used before by any army in the field. Every technical means is pressed into the service to facilitate intercourse. Even the air must be conquered; dirigible balloons and flying machines will form quite a new feature in the conduct of war. The question also arises how modern permanent fortification will affect the combat. It seems that all trade and industry must stop, when every capable youth is called away from work. It has been said that the effect of modern arms is such as to incapacitate the weakened nervous system of the highly civilized nations of Mid-Europe to resist this effect for any length of time. And lastly, we must also weigh the influence of naval warfare on what is going on on land, and what its effect will be on the whole campaign. The course of events at sea may mean starvation for the population. In short, a future war will reveal to us a series of seemingly incalculable forces. One might almost come to think that success in war will be more or less a matter of chance, and could in no way be influenced by foresight or to any extent be forecast; that the will of the commander was, so to say, switched off in the incontrollable game of these tremendous forces; that we can only call up these forces, and then leave it to the elementary potentialities to produce whatever they choose from this turmoil.

I think it is not so, after all. If we closely examine the possible effect of all the new phenomena which in a future war must assert themselves, and then test them in their relation to the general laws of warfare, we must succeed in getting a general idea of the nature of modern war, and in ascertaining a method by which we can act most suitably.

It is true there are still experienced and prominent soldiers who think that, in spite of all changes in armaments, Moltke's strategy and conduct of war is the last word on the subject, and that it is now merely a question of finding out by what principles Moltke had acted so as to be prepared for successful military operations in future as well.

I do not think that such an interpretation comes up at all to Moltke's spirit and nature. The very way *he* acted seems to prove the truth that in every war we must make use of the lessons of the past only in so far as we can apply them to, or modify them in accordance with, the changed conditions of our time. He, of all men, was the one who worked with an open mind at all that concerns the conduct of war. He never disregarded the lessons of any war, nor was he satisfied with them alone. He was ever looking ahead to turn to account new developments.

That is the way he has shown us. We are not to rest satisfied with what he has thought and done, but to go on unfettered, turning to account fresh developments. We are to examine the conditions under which a future war must be conducted without blindly believing in authorities, and, from what Moltke and the German wars of unification have taught us, to develop new ideas and principles according to modern requirements.

"How the actual operations will turn out next," writes [Moltke] in a memorial of November, 1861, concerning a future campaign, "becomes more uncertain, indeed, the further we trace their progress. Yet we may consider the most likely contingencies, because they always start from given and permanently existing premises. Experience of former wars must not be neglected, but is no safe guide for our days. Half and whole centuries have since passed and changed the political and strategical situation. . . . To arrive at the result intended, the only way left to us is to trace the martial events of the future, and get thoroughly acquainted with the present conditions. Here we have to reckon partly with unknown and changeable factors, yet, on the other hand, often with known and permanent ones. We cannot arrive at a result *correct in all essentials,* but we can ascertain what is *probable,* and this, in war, is always the only basis on which we can found our measures."

What [Moltke] expresses here seems to be of a more general application, I think, than he meant it to be. What he says of the "actual operations" applies to war in general; for is not war experience the only possible foundation of military knowledge, the material, as it were, of which theory is in need for a scientific structure of a doctrine of war, whilst the changed conditions and new phenomena of the moment always create, by their supposed future development, new assets, which in actual warfare peremptorily demand to be considered? But the past, the present, and the future are invariably dominated by the general laws which are always and everywhere inherent in war as a social phenomenon.

If, therefore, we wish to recognize the probable character of a future war and the new demands it will make on its *conduct,* we must proceed from the two-fold point of view which Moltke considers necessary to adopt in weighing matters.

By the lessons which we learn from military history and our own experiences of war we must try to discern "the permanent factors" with which we have to reckon, and the laws of development. This is the only way we have for further guidance of what in war is altogether possible and feasible. War experience alone enables us to become aware of all the frictions, moral influences, chances, and personal elements in war, which all are of far-reaching importance, and almost completely beyond theoretical appreciation. But we must next closely examine under what external and internal conditions a future war must probably be conducted; how the conduct of war will be affected by the changes in military matters since we gained our last experiences in war; what effects these changes will produce. We must examine how far the results of our up-to-date war experiences will be influenced by these new phenomena, and we must try to find out in what directions this kind of influence is likely to assert itself. In this way alone can we succeed in ascertaining the conditions that will probably obtain in the next war, and in gaining some guiding rules for our action.

But that is just the point. It is not enough for us to discern the nature of modern war, and thus to some extent satisfy a theoretical want; we rather wish to be able to develop from this knowledge a doctrine for acting in the field—a law, as it were, of future victory.

If we survey the history of those wars, the course of which we can judge in some measure, we become aware of many instances where fighting dragged along without leading to a final and decisive issue. Neither side displays any special faculties that might turn the scale one way or the other. The result is then mostly some compromise between the belligerents which leaves matters pretty well as they were before, or the issue is brought about by the gradual bearing down of the weaker party. In other wars, on the contrary, a real issue is rapidly come to between two armies of apparently equal strength. Often it is the numerically weaker army which obtains the most decisive victory. When this happens, it is either a great Captain whose genius has turned the scale, or it is some particular circumstance which gave victory to the one party—a happy coincidence of favourable conditions; a numerical or tactical superiority; a special kind of armament; a moral superiority inherent in the character of an army; or a superior principle of acting. Where such peculiar advantages are placed in the hands of a great general who understands how to make a thorough use of them, success is, of course, all the greater. Our own Prussian history shows us repeatedly examples confirming the correctness of this view.

Under Frederic William I it was discerned that the fire of infantry was the decisive factor in action. Fire tactics were therefore brought up to an extraordinary degree of perfection. The introduction of the iron ramrod proved exceedingly advantageous to increasing the rapidity of fire. The Prussian infantry is said to have delivered ten rounds per minute even at that time. But rapidity of fire of that kind, and the precision of all movements as a *sine qua non* to it, were only possible with an iron discipline and a training which no other army could boast of to an equal degree of perfection. The Prussian infantry moved in rigid formations in an order which never failed even under the greatest stress, and thereby, as well as by its fire, proved superior to all its enemies.

Frederic the Great next recognized, immediately after the first battle he took part in, that fire and order alone would decide nothing if they were not accompanied by a resolute offensive. In further developing fire tactics, on the one hand by concentrating artillery at the decisive points, and, on the other, by making the power of fire everywhere subservient to the most determined offensive, he created a new factor of superiority over his adversaries, which asserted itself the more decisively, since he raised at the same time the manoeuvring power of his troops to such a height that no other hostile army could equal him therein. He further saw that cavalry was only of tactical value under the conditions then prevailing, if it understood how to make use of the velocity of the horse by a vigorous charge. By making this idea the leading principle of cavalry tactics, he made the Prussian cavalry the most victorious in the world. And, finally, in opposition to the learned strategists of his time, he saw the inexorable nature of war. Everywhere, wherever he possibly could, he tried, strategically as well as tactically, to bring matters to a most decisive issue, giving expression to this idea also in the form of his attack. Only by thus accumulating the actual factors of superiority did he succeed in fighting victoriously against a world in arms.

But the linear tactics which had developed in this way degenerated after Frederic's death into a system of artificialities, without any practical value. Over the mechanical art of leading troops the spirit of the principle and guiding idea was lost; strategy, too, set up the wildest systems. With this the Prussian army lost its all-conquering superiority. This became at once apparent in the wars of Frederic William II. The soundness of the troops, it is true, enabled them to be victorious on the battlefield, but the conduct of the war on the whole was wanting the great decisive features which result only from a clear perception of war's real nature. The conduct of war lost itself more and more in conventional forms, which were bound to have an effect all the more disadvantageous as the tactics were defective too and did not meet the new demands originating from the revolutionary wars.

In this way all the factors gradually disappeared which had made the Prussian army victorious. The wars dragged along without any decisive issue until Bonaparte appeared and brought into the conduct of war a new element of superiority. By opposing brute force to the learned and conventional mode of conducting war in his time, and by aiming at the utmost attainable with the simplest means, the great Corsican became irresistible to the armies of his age, until these in turn made use of his same principles against him, and until, by means of the Prussian army, recruited from the people by universal service, a new weapon was forged which, above all, proved superior through an idealism peculiar to that army.

This acquisition it was which led humiliated Prussia to renewed victories. By retaining universal service after the war, while all other States returned to the old system of professional armies, Prussia once more acquired a powerful superiority over her rivals. This superiority was enhanced by Prussia alone recognizing in time the importance of breech-loading arms and taking advantage of their greater efficiency. The result was the brilliant victories of 1866 and 1870–71.

It does not seem likely that under modern conditions we shall be favoured once more by Fortune in a similar manner. All the States on the Continent of Europe have introduced universal service, and have thus formed national armies; all over the world are in use the most modern and most effective weapons; everywhere a most prolific use is made of every technical appliance; everywhere in Europe the training of the troops is most zealously attended to, and the preparedness for war perfected to the utmost. A decided superiority of one army over any other can no longer be attained under these conditions. Nor can we count upon a stroke of good fortune as we had in our last wars, where a Bismarck conducted our policy, and a Moltke our armies; just as little dare we rely on the favour of special circumstances like, perhaps, a lucky political constellation, which statecraft might take advantage of with bold resolution. It may be we have, as a counterweight against the probable numerical superiority of our likely adversaries, other advantages to throw into the scale; above all an officers' corps, as no other army has, with an imperturbable offensive spirit and a uniformity of mind and feeling of duty which guarantee the steadfast and resolute action of everybody. Yet these are imponderable forces, which it is impossible to look upon as fixed factors in the reckoning, and against which must be set off the national advantages of our adversaries. Who is there that will deny, for instance, the high military qualities possessed by the French soldier, or the stubborn and often tried power of resistance of the Russians?

If it is thus impossible for us to gain a numerical or material superiority, and if, on the other hand, we have no right to claim a moral superiority for our army as a distinct asset of power, the question is forced upon us, whether it may not be possible to gain a start on our adversaries by some other means which might vouchsafe us the possibility of victory over these stronger enemies? . . .

He who fully sees and completely masters the difficulties arising from modern conditions in the conduct of war; he who has a clear and detailed insight into what can be done with modern war-appliances and what not, and how these must be used, therefore, to have the maximum effect; what, on the other hand, we must not do, so as not to upset the powerful mechanism of a modern army; he who by reason of such intelligence has arrived at clear and definite principles of acting, and is perfectly aware *of the decisive factors leading to success, particularly under modern conditions*—he will, at the outbreak of war, obtain a distinct superiority over an adversary, who from the outset either acts by wrong principles, or tries only in war itself to arrive at *that* clearness which he was unable to attain by his mental work in peace-time. This kind of superiority is, however, very much enhanced indeed if we can apply the knowledge we have obtained to the preparation for war, which, in fact, is already part of the conduct of war itself. The execution of what has been recognized as the most suitable is then greatly facilitated, and to the mental superiority, which reveals itself in the method of acting, a material superiority is added. *That* side will be superior in a way its opponent can scarcely retrieve, which, well aware of the decisive importance of the subject, has striven for, and has obtained, superiority by working at it in peace-time.

If, for instance, it should be proved that the command of the air will be the decisive factor in a future war, the army possessing the most effective aerial fleet would evidently have a decided advantage, though in other less important departments it may be inferior to its adversary.

It is, therefore, not a question of competing with our likely enemies in all the various branches without distinction, such as raising huge armies, increasing artillery and ammunition, improving heavy artillery and siege trains, extending the railway net, and employing every modern technical appliance. A competition like this would be ultimately decided by financial superiority, which we scarcely possess. We must rather exert ourselves in preparing for war in a distinct direction, and in gaining superiority not in every branch, but in the one we have recognized as the decisive one, whilst taking a correct view of all other important branches.

Much independence of thought and determination is required of him who is acting in this spirit in a responsible position and staking success in war, so to say, on one card. All depends, then, on whether a future war has been correctly estimated. Every error in decisive questions must prove fatal. Yet it is the only possible way for obtaining an unquestionable superiority, and almost every great captain has followed it.

All the more is it necessary to see perfectly clear in these matters after studying them thoroughly. We must resolutely get rid of the influence of conventional views and opinions, extend and thoroughly sift in every department the ideas we are forming about a future war, trace to their utmost limit the consequences of all that may be new in a coming war, and then try to discover with inexorable logic the weak and the decisive factors in the whole picture thus unfolded before our eyes. . . .

Constancy in War

If we review the whole of military history as far as we have access to it, we become aware of an infinite series of different forms of war; war we see constantly changing. "War," says Clausewitz, "is a perfect chameleon, because in each separate case it changes somewhat its nature."

The conditions under which wars are conducted are ever new ones. They result from the state of civilization of the nations and their social life; from the efficiency of their technical appliances, finances, and other resources of the States, and from the nature of their military institutions. They depend on the position and character of the theatres of war and of the belligerent States; they are influenced by historical traditions, and certainly a great deal by political circumstances—in short, by a countless number of all sorts of things constantly changing, and thus causing war also to appear in an ever varying form. We thus seem to move in war altogether in an absolutely unstable and ever changing element, with no fixed standard of opinion and norm for acting. This, however, is true only up to a certain point.

If we look closer into the military events, we perceive that in war, as in almost all other spheres of life, a certain constancy reigns supreme; that certain features constantly recur; that certain relations between mode of action and success often remain the same; that certain circumstances and moments have over and over again proved decisive, whilst no doubt the mass of individual incidents bears the character of the changeable or accidental.

If we try to account for the nature of this apparent contradiction, we soon come to recognize that, as with all things in the visible world, it is the form only which changes, while matter externally remains the same; so in war we must as well distinguish strictly between its outward appearance in form and its real nature. The former is mutable and ever transient, the latter is, however, always and under all conditions the same. Now, if we apply the term "Law" only to the relation of things to, and their effect on, each other, but the term "Principle" to a distinct mode of action resting on the lawfulness or constancy of things, then, in compliance with the nature and the form of war, there must be also two different kinds of laws and principles. A lasting validity can be attributed to constancy only in so far as it is part of the nature of war itself and independent of whatever form a war assumes. To the laws and principles of warfare, however, which are occasioned by the outward form of war, we cannot otherwise than assign but a transient validity. These laws and principles become worn out like the social conditions of which they are the outcome; they want, therefore, constantly to be checked and further developed to remain of practical use, and not hamper the freedom of proper action by dead routine.

It is evident how eminently important it is for practical purposes to recognize and correctly separate these two groups of laws. While the former represent *the constant norm of all acting* in war, the latter embrace *all progress* in military matters by rightly discerning and timely developing them.

It is exceedingly remarkable that neither the theorizers on war, nor the teachers of practical warfare, have hitherto become aware of this so striking difference in the laws on which the conduct of war is based.

It is true that Clausewitz also takes war in its simplest form when appreciating the fundamental principles of war, but then he does not draw all the conclusions from this correct elementary idea, the logical further development of which will necessarily lead to the separation of what is constant in war according to its nature and according to its form, and which must greatly facilitate the building up of a theory of war. It reduces to a system a subject hitherto altogether vague, and creates a sure foundation on which the doctrine of war must firmly rest so as not to become arbitrary.

That doctrine has now to solve a two-fold task.

Firstly—but once only—the task of exhaustively establishing the immutable laws of war, and then the perpetual task of incessantly adapting the practical doctrine of war to the transient forms of war within the limits prescribed by these laws. So long as we do not submit to this kind of system, the attempt of setting up a satisfactory doctrine of war must always fail, owing to its intrinsic impossibility.

In order to solve the first of the two tasks we must strip war of all its outward form, and rid it of all that is accidental, changeable, and dependent on special circumstances. In that case there remain, as far as I can see, *three* factors ruling war as such, no matter under what conditions it is waged, whether as a combat of individuals or of peoples, whether it is fought between savages or highly civilized nations.

Firstly, from its nature, the *object of war* is always the same: we wish, as Clausewitz has already defined it, to impose our will on that of the enemy, by either annihilating or damaging him, or warding him off; or, maybe, we want to force him to do, or to give up, what is to our advantage. Secondly, every combat is governed by the law of *attack and defence.* An action outside the limit of these two notions is altogether unthinkable. And, thirdly, all actions in war are *influenced by the physical, mental, and moral qualities of men.*

All laws and principles which can be derived directly and purely from these three factors must evidently be looked upon as permanent laws and of general application in war, which retain their decisive influence under all circumstances.

But in a certain sense the character of the theatre of war also accounts for some definite features of an invariable type.

In war on land, ground and the action of troops affect each other in many ways, always in the same manner. Defiles oblige us to decrease the front if we wish to pass them; steep gradients render upward movements difficult; eminences afford good view; ranges of hills cover from sight and direct fire; and similar instances of general application may be cited frequently. Naval warfare, on the other hand, is enacted on a storm-swept plain, and is subject to certain immutable laws from the nature of the sea. The same applies to the air and to the combats we shall see there in the future. The influence exercised by these conditions does not, of course, originate directly from the nature of war itself, but they create the modifications under which war is altogether proceeding. We must in many ways assign to these conditions also a permanent and systematic importance which we *cannot* disregard at all. But taking the theatre of war as given, there remain but the three factors—the *object*, the *form of action*, and *human nature*—which determine the permanent soul of war from which the immutable laws of the art of war must be deducted. . . .

The outward conditions determining war, we know, do not change by leaps and bounds, but do so gradually. Even the most momentous inventions and important social revolutions do not suddenly produce a change of all the factors influencing war. Thus it has taken centuries after the invention of gunpowder before fire-fight obtained its own, and it is scarcely possible to gauge to-day the probable effect of aerial navigation on the future conduct of war; for it is almost always impossible to discern the full significance of new inventions and innovations, and to account for them by suitable measures. In conformity with the slow change of the ruling factors, the laws governing the mutual relationship of things, and, jointly with these laws, the periodical principles of warfare as well, change but gradually. That which in the past was fundamentally right may therefore often be so in the present, in spite of certain developments having occurred, and form as a rule a reliable guide for recognizing the future, because things will develop lawfully, and, to a certain degree, can therefore be determined in advance, at least by reasoning. . . .

In the Napoleonic Wars the column tactics increased the infantry's capacity of resistance against cavalry charges; the whole mode of fighting in separate divisions and corps localized the success of cavalry more than did the linear tactics, where the army acted as an integer. The fact, too, affected cavalry unfavourably, that actions were much less than formerly restricted to the plain, and that portions of the infantry were extended into skirmishing lines, which did not present a favourable object to a charge; accordingly the tactical importance of cavalry decreased.

When next the firearms were still further improved, when the importance of skirmishing action increased, when the infantry in consequence looked more and more for ground affording cover, and when the battlefields became larger in extent, the cavalry stepped more and more into the background as a factor in battle. This was almost unconsciously acknowledged by reducing the strength of cavalry more and more in proportion to the other arms.

In this process we can evidently trace the lawful action of the force of circumstances, and we have a right to conclude that the cavalry, as an offensive weapon in the battles of the future, will lose still more of its importance than it has done hitherto. This is not only probable, but certain, since all the conditions impairing the success of a charge have further developed in a manner that could not be anticipated; but the circumstances which increase the chances of charging are not many. As regards the latter, the only point we can mention is that in future bodies of infantry, loosely organized and morally incapable of much resistance, will often be employed, and these will not always be able to make a proper use of their weapons. But as regards the former, the factors disadvantageous to a cavalry charge are almost overwhelming. The effect of firearms on cavalry is now simply destructive. The actions are fought in the main on ground rendering movements of cavalry difficult; in numbers the cavalry has been reduced to a mere fraction of the army; the battlefields have increased in size, and the infantry fighting formations nowhere present a suitable object for cavalry to charge on. These are facts with which we have to reckon. But we can, on the other hand, conclude from the past that in all those cases where, owing to favourable ground or the demoralization of the hostile troops, fire-effect is neutralized and tactical formations are disorganized, successful charges are still possible even to-day, though they can never again have the same decisive influence on the whole issue of the battle as in former days. It will be the same if we succeed in charging the flank of infantry deployed for action, but insufficiently secured in that direction, since modern battles are fought again, as in the days of Frederic the Great, in linear forms, with all their disadvantages. Nor must we forget that the great difference in the speed of infantry and cavalry is still unaltered, and that all the advantages accruing therefrom to cavalry are just the same as before.

If we sum up all these conditions in our verdict, we are justified, I think, in saying that we must, above all, make the fullest use of *that* superiority of the mounted arm—which is its strategic mobility—if we wish to derive real advantages from our cavalry. This argument is confirmed also by experience. We have seen already in the American War of Secession what effect the cavalry can produce in this direction, and also in the South African War the mounted

Boers always succeeded in meeting the turning movements of the English infantry, and the English, on the other hand, in making use of their mounted troops for constantly and successfully turning the Boer positions. The practical application of this is as obvious as the cognition that we are dealing here with a regular order of things, which is intelligible to anyone who is viewing the subject without bias.

Another example from the doctrines of strategy will explain still further my ideas about the regularity of development:

At the time of Frederic the Great the armies were greatly dependent on supplies from magazines, or, at least, they thought they were. Every pressure on their own lines of communication seemed to them a great danger, every threat on those of the enemy a great success. The pressure on the enemy's lines of communication became thus one of the most important maxims of operations. Napoleon, on the other hand, supplied his armies chiefly from the resources of the theatre of war. By this he made himself almost entirely independent of supplies from depots. A pressure on his lines of communication affected him little; tactical victory put an end to all anxiety caused by this pressure. His procedure was no doubt very advantageous so long as he was able to subsist on the country and sure of tactical victory. The moment he failed in both, as in Russia, the army perished from want of regular supplies from magazines. In the campaign of 1870–71 we used Napoleon's system in combination with supplies from depots, which answered well in opulent France. But we would grievously err should we think that this was the last word on the subject; and when Field-Marshal v. der Goltz lays it down as law that we need not mind a threat to our lines of communication, but must, by striking forward, force the enemy to abandon his threats, the validity of such a law is very limited, and rather applicable only if we are sure of victory and can live on the country without needing the lines of communication during the time before we gain the victory. But if in future, as will be most likely the case, situations arise in which armies are really dependent on supplies from depots, the strategic importance of the lines of communication will again assert itself to an enhanced degree, and similar principles in the conduct of war will prove necessary as they—*mutatis mutandis*—obtained at Frederic's time. . . .

Experience of War and Speculation

There are, above all, two modes of view from which errors arise.

The one method, it is true, starts from actualities. It takes the successful combats of victorious generals as the basis of its reflections; tries to prove a certain constancy in these combats; deduces from this constancy certain rules and principles, and then, attributing to them a general validity, frames on them a theory of war, which, seemingly built upon historical ground, fascinates the masses all the more readily when it claims for itself the authority of a great captain like Napoleon or Moltke. A classical example of this sort is Jomini. When we read him, there is apparently nothing problematical in war; rules and laws insuring success are laid down for every act, and we begin to think that the great Corsican gained his laurels merely by the fact that he conscientiously adhered to the rules construed from his wars by his critics after the events. Jomini actually does the worst possible violence to the deeds of Napoleon. He—often quite arbitrarily—presses them into a system which he foists on Napoleon, and, in doing so, completely fails to see what, above all, really constitutes the greatness of this captain—namely, the reckless boldness of his operations, where, scoffing at all theory, he always tried to do what suited each occasion best.

A like tendency has begun to assert itself also in reference to Moltke's conduct of war. On him, too, who conducted operations in the wars for a united Germany, people try to father a theory. One version has it that the strategy of the Field-Marshal rests on the relative dependency of the length of marches and the depth of columns; the other that Moltke had given preference to exterior lines as a matter of principle, and had imparted to us the knowledge that nothing but envelopment leads to success. In opposition to all previous great captains, he is also said to have made the doctrine law, that all forces must effect their junction on the battlefield and not be concentrated for battle beforehand.

In all these views there is, as in those of Jomini, a mixture of truth and fancy. They are often correct within a limited sense, yet are not in full accord with the actual facts, as an intimate critical investigation of Moltke's ideas and deeds will reveal. But even granted that Field-Marshal Moltke had thought as his critics have subsequently implied to him, it would, nevertheless, be inadmissible to generalize his ideas, and make them forthwith the guide for all future action.

The other method of viewing things, which is bound to lead to faulty results, I should like to call the purely theoretical and conventional method. It does not start exactly from military history; it rather tries to develop the theory of war from a series of conventional conditions and opinions gained *a priori*, which ultimately, it is true, rest on experience of war as well, but have lost their true meaning long ago through purely theoretical development. This method tries to regulate all martial action by lines and angles, or to rob it of its freedom by regular rules. It has led to systems which made operations in the midst of the most fertile countries dependent on the systematic movements of bread-waggons, which made operations subservient to geographical and topographical conditions, or tried to check their free scope by the strait-jacket of geometrical figures—systems certainly fascinating through the semblance of their profound scientific nature, but leading ultimately to a perfect misconception of what war itself really means. In this way the sword of the warrior—to use the same metaphor as Clausewitz—was exchanged for that of the courtier, which snapped, of course, when it came to actual blows.

Both methods are not altogether wrong, and if, in spite of that, they often went astray, and cannot be a safe guide in future, it is their one-sidedness and arbitrary restrictions which are at fault. The importance of theoretical speculation for the development of all that concerns war is not affected by the fact that it often arrived at one-sided results by defective methods. Speculation is a *preliminary* rather *necessary to all progress* in warfare, so long as it proceeds methodically, and is not advancing conclusions based on premises that are not and cannot be proved, and on which a logically arranged system may certainly be erected, but which is, for all that, built on sand.

Two points we must, above all, keep in view:

Firstly, we must strive to develop things as we find them, dismissing at the same time all arbitrariness. We must thoroughly examine them on their real merit, and endeavor to recognize the lawfulness of their origin, as well as the causes and limits of their efficiency. From these data we must try to deduce how things will naturally further develop under the influence of new achievements in the technical and social world, or of altered conditions for the conduct of war. Foreseeing, promoting, and making the most of natural developments to the advantage of the army, is the way to true progress. New inventions in the province of armaments or military mechanics generally must be thoroughly tested by trials in peace, under conditions as near to war as possible, before drawing conclusions as to their efficiency and importance for the conduct of war, and before making practical use of them. To misjudge the importance of momentous inventions is often more dangerous than overestimating new achievements.

The second demand to be satisfied by speculation consists in never allowing ourselves to be dominated by some individual manifestation, however important it may look in appearance, and thus to determine the future development of all that concerns war from a one-sided standpoint. So long as we approach things with a preconceived notion, or view them even, as it were, in the spirit of red tape, we can never form a true judgment of their real value. Every one-sided standpoint in regard to arms, for instance, which has done so much harm very often, cannot be condemned too strongly. We must strive rather to view every individual manifestation within the compass of military action as a whole, and tactical and strategical conditions in their mutual relationship; due regard we must also pay to the influence of social conditions on the army. We can but then determine *the relative value* of things, which is *the only real value* for purposes of war, and make a true estimate of their importance for the future.

Being thus warned by these circumstances to exercise the greatest circumspection and caution when speculating on the future development of things, we must, on the other hand, have the courage of thinking over the ideas and opinions recognized as correct as far as we can possibly go, and not be afraid of turning them into deeds, though our opinions may not be supported by experience, or are even contrary to the opinions prevailing. The greatest successes have often been enforced against public opinion, and even under the protest of so-called experts, who are often enthralled by tradition. . . .

Armies of Masses

Of all the features which are destined to influence the conduct of war under present conditions, and cause it to strike new lines, it is the levy of masses, above all, which no doubt will give its peculiar stamp to the next war.

In the Central European States the whole male population, as far as it is able to carry arms, will be called up, armed, and organized in tactical formations. In case of any hostile invasions, it is more likely than not that a "people's war" would be organized in the true sense of its meaning. The obligation of every citizen to serve is a generally accepted principle.

It is true, not all those obliged to serve are given a military training in peacetime. In Germany, for instance, this is far from being a fact for some time past. Yet everywhere enormous hosts are to be mobilized in case of war, not only for the defence of the native soil, but also for attack. It is right to some extent to speak of the armies of millions of modern times, the like of which have not been seen before in history.

It is, of course, out of the question that armies like these can be of a uniform character. We must distinguish various categories of them. There are in Europe militia armies and standing armies, which are absolutely different in character. In the latter the line regiments, augmented on mobilization by the latest annual contingents of reserves, and numbering in their ranks most of the regular officers and non-commissioned officers, are more efficient than troops of the second and third lines, which are composed of contingents of maturer ages, and which it is impossible to provide with officers fully competent.

The most efficient troops are called upon to face the enemy in first line, and to carry the war outside the country. The others are charged with the duty of furnishing the garrisons of fortresses, guarding railways, and occupying the districts conquered; or they serve to replace casualties suffered by the actual field army, or by any other fighting troops. All must *at least* be able to delay an enemy's attack by local defence, and to fight the enemy as guerilas should he cross the frontiers.

The consequence of this general levy is that the military value of the armies is very much more than formerly dependent on the character and nature of the nations themselves. The more of the population are enrolled into the fighting army, the more the spirit of the troops thus composed will be determined by the physical power as well as by the political and social spirit of the nation itself. An army with a discipline handed down from generation to generation, recruited from a vigorous folk accustomed to obedience, which has learned to limit its desires for the good of the common weal, and at the same time is trained to hard work and in the profession of arms, will give quite a different account of its power of resistance against demoralizing influences, as well as against the sufferings, fatigues, and privations of a campaign, than the army of another nation, which is physically weakened, infected by revolutions, or disused to arms owing to increasing opulence. Sound political training, preservation and strengthening of the spirit of discipline and subordination, readiness to make sacrifices in the interest of the community, which constitute the really loyal spirit of a citizen, are the necessary conditions for carrying on successfully the war of masses in our age. Where, however, the recruits who enter the army are accustomed to resistance and insubordination against all authority, the mechanism of a modern army runs the grave risk of breaking down even under the pressure of conditions which by themselves alone would not be decisive.

This development entails the further and, perhaps, still more important consequence, that the political importance of war has completely altered. Owing to the fact that all classes of the nation are affected, and that personal sacrifices are imposed on each individual family, wars for frivolous or dynastic purposes become impossible. We can and must uphold only by force of arms really vital interests of the country. The resolve to go to war is also rendered very difficult to-day, because war affects most deeply every member of the community. The sacrifice in wealth and blood that must be exacted will probably surpass everything we have experienced hitherto; and the dangers of such enterprise, moreover, as well as the evil consequences of defeat in war, will be far greater than ever. Prussia's crushing defeat at Jena in 1806, and her rising in the memorable year of 1813, give us, perhaps, an idea of what the sacrifices will be in a modern war, and the oppression a nation will have to suffer in all likelihood should the war bring on defeat and with it the conquest of the country by the enemy. That France did not suffer in a similar way in 1870–71 is due to the broadminded humanity with which the Germans have conducted the war. But it is not at all certain that other people will manifest an equally high moral standard.

Preparation of war in peace costs, as it is, large sums, and claims a considerable portion of the national revenue. If we mobilize, the necessary expenditure rises enormously, as the army must be supplied and kept efficient. As most of the labour will be withdrawn at the same time from the market, and all means of living be stopped thereby, the whole domestic life must be shaken to the core, which will prove all the more calamitous the more we are unfortunate in our operations.

It has been asserted and seemingly substantiated scientifically, that no State could carry through a war at all, waged with the masses levied in our days. It would not only mean absolute domestic ruin, but war itself would be completely paralyzed by the want of means that could not fail to be felt soon after its outbreak; the economic strength for maintaining such huge armies would simply fail. For this reason alone a war of that nature between two civilized nations would become impossible.

I think this view is going much too far. It is in the nature of human things that they regulate themselves automatically as it were. Economic impossibilities do not crop up suddenly and all at once; they assert themselves gradually and exercise an irresistible and pressing influence on the affairs of the belligerents as well. Owing to the stress of the situation acting in a similar manner in both camps, the belligerents will be obliged to adapt themselves gradually to the existing possibilities, and to intervene by adjusting domestic matters. We can, for instance, hand over workmen to some industrial and agricultural concerns from the second and third lines, when they are not immediately wanted for military operations. The victor in the first decisive battles may be able to demobilize altogether the echelons in rear of the army the moment the danger of hostile invasion has passed. The vanquished will sue for peace all the more readily the more impossible it appears to him, from an economical point of view, to re-establish the balance of power upset by defeat. But where in an indecisive struggle the adversaries keep each other in check, the standard of their performances will be gradually lowered, and success will ultimately fall to him who can boast of the highest moral energy and self-sacrificing spirit, or, where in both sides the moral motives are of an equally high standard, can hold out financially longest to finish the war. In this way the factors ruling the conduct of war will automatically adapt themselves, as it were, to the economic conditions, and a compromise between what was intended and what was possible will of necessity be the result.

If we have thus established that especially an unfortunate war *must* entail far more disastrous economic consequences than ever before, and *may* lead to complete economic ruin, yet the inference that wars with modern armies could not be carried to the bitter end from reasons of economy is indeed not justified.

Two points of practical import result, however, from these comments. Firstly, the economic superiority of a nation forms by itself an essential factor for success, and the way a State manipulates its finances must have a far-reaching influence on the conduct of war. Secondly, all special preparations for war must be carried out with the greatest seriousness, with the utmost consistency, and *without false economy*. There can be no doubt that nowhere will half or insufficient measures be punished more severely than in the sphere of armaments. The losses entailed by an unfortunate war are *so* great, the venture of risking these losses by insufficient preparation is so dangerous that even the greatest sacrifices for armaments seem justified by themselves and under all circumstances.

From a purely military point of view, the growth of the armies, looking merely at their proportionate numbers, renders all military action much more difficult. This difficulty is already felt when training soldiers. In order to raise the masses required for war without increasing the cost of peace training unduly, the terms of service had to be reduced considerably in recent times. The training of each man must therefore be completed in a very much shorter time than formerly, and this imposes in consequence a much severer task on officers and non-commissioned officers. A very great amount of labour is moreover thrown on them by the fact that a very much greater absolute number of recruits passes through their hands than in the smaller armies of the past, and that the numerous trained men must be retrained again and again and kept permanently efficient. The consequence is that the strength of the trainers is taxed already to the utmost in peace time.

Another effect of these conditions with which we have to reckon is, that with the growing size of the armies the tactical worth of the troops is gradually decreasing, even that of the line. The greater the numbers which must be raised for war, and the more men must be therefore trained in peace, the more difficult it becomes to have available suitable officers and non-commissioned officers to train the men and to lead them. In war, moreover, the line will be weakened by having to detail officers and non-commissioned officers to new formations, and the more there are of these new formations, the more this will weaken the line. This must impair the steadiness of the troops, and evidently cause a moment to arrive when the advantage of numbers is no longer of any value as compared with the tactical worth of the troops. It is just this point which the latest wars bring forcibly home to us. The levies of the French Republic, in spite of their numerical superiority, were of no avail in 1870–71 against the firmly-knit battalions of the Germans; and the Japanese, in spite of the notorious numerical inferiority of their army, invariably defeated the numerically superior Russians. In this respect the American War of Secession is also exceedingly instructive. Again and again the numerically superior armies of the Union succumbed to the tactically and morally better trained forces of the Confederates.

The conduct of war itself is further aggravated by the masses of men. It will, in the first instance, prove exceedingly difficult to move the various armies, which together form a modern army, by a uniform idea, and to direct them in such a way as to ensure the participation of every portion in the main issue, without wasting forces in minor operations. But the difficulties also grow with the number of troops, from a technical point of view. Railway transport, and the systematic movement of very large masses, their provisioning, the necessity of keeping them permanently efficient, and, therefore, of providing for the constant supply of ammunition, the evacuation of wounded and sick, the pushing forward of the necessary drafts of men, horses, and material, the guarding of all important roads and lines of communication of the army, all these necessities present problems in the technical conduct of war which are very difficult to solve.

The enormous number of troops raised obliges us to select large areas for assembling them, and to make a thorough use of the network of roads within those spaces so as to be altogether able to bring to the front as large a number of troops as possible. The same consideration will often oblige us to march on each road as many troops as possible. The number of troops on each road is again limited by the possibility of supplying them, and by the necessity of bringing into action—though perhaps not on the same day—the rearmost troops before the fighting strength of those in front is exhausted. The necessity of provisioning the troops and of replacing armaments demands at once that on all lines of advance, stores of equipments and provisions must be collected, pushed forward, and issued to the troops without this mechanism being allowed to stop for a single day. The difficulty is enhanced when, owing to the number of troops, living on the country becomes impossible, and all the wants have to be brought up from the rear.

The strategic mobility of the large modern armies is, under these circumstances, palpably far inferior to that of smaller armies, which, at least, in a rich theatre of war that provides supplies without difficulty, could move with much greater freedom. It is, moreover, evident that a large army, with numerous march columns moving parallel with each other, needs more time for wheeling, concentrating, and deploying than a smaller one, and has to contend with greater difficulties of supply. Topographical obstacles, too, are manifestly more difficult to overcome by large masses than by smaller bodies. Owing to the clumsiness of all movements, and the time they take, all decisions of headquarters must be prepared long beforehand; it is therefore impossible to make always constant use of the intelligence daily received about the enemy. This again obliges us to push reconnaissance very far ahead, so as to have as early as possible information about the enemy's measures. This increases the depth of the army on the march, and with depth grows the difficulty of operating. All these conditions must be thoroughly considered, if we wish to form a clear idea of modern warfare. Yet even they do not include all the difficulties of operating which arise from the number of troops alone.

In most cases, especially when we are obliged to fight against superior numbers of the enemy, we will have to apportion to the actual Field Army troops of the second line at least—therefore reserve formations in Germany. . . .

The mechanism of such an army is so enormous and complicated that it can only be kept going, and be directed, if all its parts work on the whole at least reliably, and if it is spared great and extensive moral shocks. We cannot, of course, count upon the fortunes of war keeping us free from manifestations of this kind, just as little as we can count upon being victorious in every action. These shocks can be got over if they are felt only locally. But when *large concentrated masses* are once out of hand, when panic has seized them, when supplies fail throughout, and the spirit of insubordination is rampant in those masses, they are not only powerless to resist the enemy, but become a positive danger to themselves and to their own commanders by breaking all bonds of discipline, upsetting the course of operations, and setting problems to the headquarters which are impossible for them to solve.

War conducted with large modern armies is therefore, in any case, a risky game, taxing to the utmost the resources of a State in men and money. Under such circumstances it is only natural, when measures are adopted everywhere to make it possible, should war break out, to finish it rapidly, and quickly relieve the tension which must arise when the whole nation is called to arms.

These efforts, together with the theoretical comprehension that it is as well to make, as much as possible effective use of all the existing forces at once, so as to make sure of success as far as it can be done, have caused arrangements to be made for the mobilization, immediately at the beginning of the war, of all the nation's fighting power, and for the strategic concentration of as many troops for simultaneous action as space and other conditions will permit. From this it follows that at the outbreak of war, a great and unexampled contest of millions of men will take place, which will impress on modern war, in its initial stage at least, its special feature.

But we cannot assume at all that the conditions as they will result from the calling up of a whole nation's strength, and from strategic concentration at the threatened frontier at the beginning of the war, will continue throughout its whole progress.

If in the Russo-Japanese War peculiar circumstances caused the armies to arrive in the theatre of war slowly and by degrees, and to grow constantly stronger in numbers as the struggle proceeded, it will probably be the reverse in a Central European War.

I have already pointed out that in the course of a long war the economic conditions must from physical necessity tend to reduce the employment of masses. But there are some other reasons tending in the same direction.

There will first and foremost be the natural waste, which will very rapidly reduce the masses in the field. Apart from the losses in action, the waste in men was very great already in 1870–71. The loss by marching alone, until the first actions took place, was 8 to 9 per cent, and during the war the companies especially became greatly reduced, often to half, and even less, their full establishments. The waste was also great, of course, in the drafts that had come out. All this will no doubt be far worse in future. In the vast numbers called up we must be prepared to find inferior men as well. The losses the troops of the first line will suffer when marching are therefore sure to be greater than formerly; they will enormously swell when we must operate with troops of inferior quality. We must also reckon with the fact that some men of the older contingents of reserves, fathers of families, and politically unreliable subjects, will try, by some pretext or other, to escape service, and often so, perhaps successfully. In 1870–71 in France, during the second phase of the war, the republican authorities were frequently obliged to use the most stringent measures to get the men to serve. Large numbers will be therefore lost from this cause too. The course of the war will probably produce altogether similar effects. The physical efforts made at the very beginning of the war are so great, that it is scarcely possible to increase them, at least in countries like France, which raises its last men on the first day of mobilization. If such an army is victorious, the inducement for further great exertion ceases, but if the war takes an unfavourable course, it will often seem hopeless to continue it when the supply of men has been exhausted, and the tension that gave rise to raising the masses will then give way.

All these circumstances will probably cause the size of the armies to dwindle away rapidly after the first decisive battles, especially when the physical and moral strength of a people does not come up to the high demands a modern war exacts. The war of masses will thus undoubtedly lose much of the character peculiar to it during the progress of events. In the conduct of war itself, conditions are also likely to arise, giving a different stamp to the combats after the first great decisive battles. It is quite a different thing when two intact armies meet on equal terms at the frontier, or when one army victoriously invades the enemy's country, and the other, beaten, but fighting in its own country, retreats. . . .

We must, rather, come to the final conclusion that, owing to the enormous size of the armies, a future war in Central Europe will be of a twofold nature. The *war at the time of concentration* will reveal the special features of a modern war with masses. The *operations afterwards,* however, which must result from the first great decisive battles, will be more like those we have witnessed hitherto. This latter period will be less distinguished by the special modern features due to the size of the combined forces in strategical and tactical operations, than by the achievements of modern military technics which will, of course, manifest their far-reaching influence also during, and immediately after, concentration for war. In addition to the effect of masses in future wars we must, therefore, also thoroughly investigate into these modern war appliances if we wish to gain a clear conception of the nature of the next war.

JEAN COLIN
(1864–1917)

*Jean Colin began his military career as an artillery officer. Following the
publication of* Etudes sur la campagne d'Italie en 1796, *he was seconded to
the French army's historical service (1900).* Les Transformations de la
guerre *(1911) is his chief work, although* Les Grandes Batailles de l'histoire
*(1915) is also excellent. Colin was promoted to lieutenant-colonel in 1914, and
subsequently to general, and fought in France and the East until his death,
which occurred at the front in late 1917.*

THE NEW CONDITIONS OF WAR

Progress of all sorts in war was much greater in the nineteenth century than
in any other. Everything was developed, transformed, and strengthened, not
only weapons, but also the means of subsistence, and above all the means of
communication.

Advances in weaponry modified combat and battles, but great as these have
been, they have not been enough to transform war as a whole. Let us imagine
an army equipped with the most modern weapons, but numbering only two
hundred thousand men and having only the means of communication available in 1806: the principles and procedures that it would be appropriate to
apply in military operations would be practically the same as they were a
hundred years ago.

The situation is quite different if we take into consideration the two great
changes that most concern the movement of armies, progress in the means of
communication and the increase in effectives.

The invention and development of railroads has had numerous and far-
reaching consequences: traffic and commercial and agricultural activity have

From Jean Colin, *Les Transformations de la guerre* (Paris: Economica, 1987), chs. 4 and 5. Translated from the French by A. M. Berrett.

reached an unheard-of intensity. The production of food commodities and the density of the road network have both increased dramatically. Combined with rapid rail transport, they have made possible the mobilization and revictualing of much larger armies than was possible at the beginning of the nineteenth century.

The fact that these armies must be revictualed by rail has led to new conditions of war. These conditions, which are inherent in the use of railroads, will no doubt disappear in future when further progress has brought the employment of road convoys back into use.

It has been noted that Napoleon put all his stores and hospitals into a field fortress—that is, a place safe from sudden attack. . . . Moreover, his armies were not so numerous as to be unable to live almost exclusively off the country. For all these reasons, they never ran the risk, except in the event of complete disaster, of being deprived of the necessary resources.

A modern army revictualed by rail is in a different situation. The troops are so numerous that the country in which they are operating can supply only a small part of their food requirements. Whereas in the nineteenth century it was usual to live off the country and hold the convoys in reserve, today it seems natural to depend entirely on the rear for supplies, leaving local resources intact to fall back on if rail transport should happen to be interrupted.

Whatever the case, generals ought not to allow themselves to be ruled by the rear services, any more than they were in earlier days by storage depots. In this respect, the freedom of action of the troops is preserved, as it always was, by convoys, horse-drawn or motorized, of which they must never be deprived. . . .

In 1859 and 1870, army movements were carried out by rail, but they were slow, being poorly organized. The railroads of today offer far more powerful resources, which we have become used to handling more methodically and scientifically. They lend themselves to rapid movements and make it possible to transport an army from one end of the theater of operations to the other in a few days. The long parallel lines that follow the course of the Rhine would enable the Germans, for example, to make rapid transports between Strasbourg and Cologne or Aachen. They might, after having apparently concentrated their troops and their efforts at one end of the theater of operations, and after making repeated attacks, thereby determining the concentration of our forces on one of their wings, suddenly bring their main strength to bear on the opposite end.

It is tempting to exaggerate the ease and speed with which transport by rail is carried out during operations, but often too one falls into the opposite excess. It takes two days to transport an army corps by a double-track line, and it is thus possible to move as many army corps in two days as there are lines going into the area where it is intended to operate. But troops transported by a single line are detrained on many platforms or sidings, often far apart. It takes a day, or even more, to reassemble them after detraining.

Finally, at least two days are required to prepare such a transport, but usually the movement will have been worked out and the orders for it given long beforehand.

When the use that can be made of rail transport, following the resources of the network, is known for certain, it only remains to develop these in the direction desired so as to facilitate maneuvers planned in accordance with studies made in peacetime.

Armies appear more cumbersome to move, but the means that they have at their disposal for their movements are more effective.

Similarly, although the number of troops seems to make it more difficult to exercise command, generals now have infinitely greater resources for transmitting orders than they did in the past.

By making possible command from a great distance, telegraphy has completely changed the conditions of war. . . .

To sum up, it is with war as it is with battle: operations will be as varied and as flexible and allow of and demand as much skill as in the past, provided that we make use of all the new means that allow us to obtain intelligence, issue orders instantaneously, and execute rapid maneuvers.

The latest transformations of war simply accentuate the evolution accomplished since the middle of the eighteenth century:

1.   Battle, formerly independent of operations, has become intimately linked up with operations since Napoleon, and now absorbs almost all operations.

2.   The line of communications, which was a matter of such little concern until Valmy [1792], and became very important in Napoleon's time, has now assumed vital importance.

3.   Following a natural law, recent industrial and military progress has favored defense in frontal engagements; but offense has more power to impose battle and make it decisive to one's advantage, since the attacking army occupies the whole breadth of the theater of operations and sweeps away everything in its passage.

FERDINAND FOCH
(1851–1929)

Ferdinand Foch began his career as a teacher of military history, strategy and applied tactics at the Ecole Supérieure de guerre (1894–1900), of which he subsequently became director in 1907, with the rank of general. He published Des principes de la guerre *(1903) and* Conduite de la guerre *(1904). In World War I, he came to the forefront after General Robert Nivelle's failure in the Aisne offensive. Foch replaced Henri Pétain as chief of the general staff in 1917, when the latter became commander in chief. After the German offensive of 1918, he was named generalissimo of the Allied armies and led the final counterattack. Foch was imbued with a belief in offense; his guiding principles were freedom of action and economy in the use of force. He was promoted marshal of France in 1918.*

PRINCIPLES OF WAR

Economy of Forces

This superior principle, which we shall call the principle of economy of forces, arose at the time of the [French] Revolution, along with the difficulties to which it was a response.

When then is the principle of economy of forces?

A simple definition will not suffice.

There is a proverb that says: "You cannot hunt two hares at the same time"; you would catch neither of them. There is also the old maxim of the Roman Senate: "You do not fight two wars at the same time. You must concentrate your efforts." It is the principle that Frederick [the Great] was recommending when he wrote: "You must know how to lose for a purpose, how to sacrifice a

From Ferdinand Foch, *Des principes de la guerre* (Paris: Berger Levrault, 1938), ch. 3. Translated from the French by A. M. Berrett.

province (he who wants to defend everything saves nothing) and how to march in the meantime with *all* your forces against the enemy's other forces, compel them to fight, make supreme efforts to destroy them, and then send detachments to meet the rest of his forces.

That is not all.

Those who say that it is the art of not expending your own forces, not dispersing your efforts, are telling only part of the truth. Those who see it as the art of knowing how to expend, to expend usefully and profitably, and to extract the maximum benefit from the resources you have, are closer to the truth.

It is easier to grasp what the principle is not.

"Suppose," as Rustow says, "someone who, to administer his fortune, divides it into four equal parts: one for housing, one for clothes, one for food, one for leisure. He would always have too much on one side and, above all, too little on another."

This is what in finance is known as *credit specialization,* which is incompatible with any kind of speculation and therefore with large profits. It is the theory of *fixed apportionment,* which is invariable; it will always be beaten by the theory of *available reserves.*

The principle of economy of forces, on the contrary, is the art of putting *all* your resources at a given moment into a *single* spot, of making use there of all your forces and, to make that possible, of ensuring that they always communicate with each other instead of dividing them up and assigning them to some fixed and invariable function. Then, once a result has been obtained, it is the art of making them once again converge and act against a new single objective.

It is the art of bringing *all* your forces to bear *successively* on the resistance you meet with, and, in order to do so, organizing these forces in a system.

The *necessity* of the principle made itself felt from the beginning of the [French] revolutionary wars, which were national wars involving large numbers. . . .

Freedom of Action

. . . Moreover, we shall see this notion of freedom of action, which is designed to protect our spirit of active discipline, and which results from the need for action by the main body to be supported by the combined acts of all involved, even detached units, generalize itself (like economy of forces) so as to become fundamental in all acts of war. This justifies the absolute nature of the principle: "In the last analysis, the art of war is the art of retaining one's freedom of action" (Xenophon).

Whether we are dealing with the means of war or operations, we have just seen that our constant concern is to keep that *freedom*. . . . But when, at the end of the war, there come to be a victor and a vanquished, in what will the difference between those two situations consist, if not in the fact that *one* will be free to do and demand from the other what he wills, and the *other* will be *compelled* to do and grant whatever the victor requires of him?

We must constantly keep in mind this need to preserve this idea of freedom if we wish, at the end of an operation (still more at the end of a series of operations), to find ourselves free, that is, victors, and not rules, that is, vanquished.

A constant concern, while we are preparing and combining an action against the enemy, must be to escape his will, to parry any undertaking of his by which he might prevent our action from succeeding. Every military idea, every scheme, every plan, must thus be accompanied by thoughts of *security*. As in fencing, we must attack without uncovering ourselves, or constantly parry to threaten the opponent.

V. I. LENIN
(1870–1924)

The revolutionary activist Vladimir Ilyich Ulyanov, known as Lenin, was imprisoned in 1895, exiled to Siberia in 1897 for three years, and then left Russia. In 1903 he formed the Bolshevik faction of the Russian Social Democratic Labor party. In the same year, he developed the theory of the vanguard party in What Is to Be Done? *Lenin returned to Russia at the time of the abortive 1905 revolution, but then went back into exile in Switzerland, where he engaged in polemics and wrote a great deal. In 1917, after the February revolution, the Germans facilitated his return to Russia (in order to neutralize the Russian war effort). In October, Lenin took the decision to seize power, against the advice of many members of the Central Committee, among them Zinoviev and Kamenev. Under his leadership, and with Trotsky at the head of the Red Army, the Soviet Union managed to survive a terrible civil war and foreign intervention (1918–20). Lenin then launched the New Economic Policy (NEP), designed to turn around a situation compromised by both war and nationalizations. He had a stroke in 1922 and died in 1924, but not without warning his colleagues against Stalin. His annotated reading of Clausewitz's* On War *contributed to the latter's reputation.*

ADVICE OF AN ONLOOKER

I am writing these lines on October 8 and have little hope that they will reach Petrograd comrades by the 9th. It is possible that they will arrive too late, since the Congress of the Northern Soviets has been fixed for October 10. Nevertheless, I shall try to give my "Advice of an Onlooker" in the event that the probable action of the workers and soldiers of Petrograd and of the whole "region" will take place soon but has not yet taken place.

From *Pravda*, 7 November 1920, reprinted in V. I. Lenin, *Collected Works* (Moscow: Progress Publishers, 1972), 26: 179–81.

It is clear that all power must pass to the Soviets. It should be equally indisputable for every Bolshevik that proletarian revolutionary power (or Bolshevik power—which is now one and the same thing) is assured of the utmost sympathy and unreserved support of all the working and exploited people all over the world in general, in the belligerent countries in particular, and among the Russian peasants especially. There is no need to dwell on these all too well known and long established truths.

What must be dealt with is something that is probably not quite clear to all comrades, namely, that in practice the transfer of power to the Soviets now means armed uprising. This would seem obvious, but not everyone has or is giving thought to the point. To repudiate armed uprising now would mean to repudiate the key slogan of Bolshevism (All Power to the Soviets) and proletarian revolutionary internationalism in general.

But armed uprising is a *special* form of political struggle, one subject to special laws to which attentive thought must be given. Karl Marx expressed this truth with remarkable clarity when he wrote that "*insurrection is an art quite as much as war.*"

Of the principal rules of this art, Marx noted the following:

(1) *Never play* with insurrection, but when beginning it realise firmly that you must *go all the way.*

(2) Concentrate a *great superiority of forces* at the decisive point and at the decisive moment, otherwise the enemy, who has the advantage of better preparation and organisation, will destroy the insurgents.

(3) Once the insurrection has begun, you must act with the greatest *determination,* and by all means, without fail, take the *offensive.* "The defensive is the death of every armed rising."

(4) You must try to take the enemy by surprise and seize the moment when his forces are scattered.

(5) You must strive for *daily* successes, however small (one might say hourly, if it is the case of one town), and at all costs retain "*moral superiority.*"

Marx summed up the lessons of all revolutions in respect to armed uprising in the words of "Danton, the greatest master of revolutionary policy yet known: *de l'audace, de l'audace, encore de l'audace.*"

Applied to Russia and to October 1917, this means: a simultaneous offensive on Petrograd, as sudden and as rapid as possible, which must without fail be carried out from within and from without, from the working-class quarters and from Finland, from Revel and from Kronstadt, an offensive of the *entire* navy, the concentration of a *gigantic superiority* of forces over the 15,000 or

20,000 (perhaps more) of our "bourgeois guard" (the officers' schools), our "Vendée troops" (part of the Cossacks), etc.

Our *three* main forces—the fleet, the workers, and the army units—must be so combined as to occupy without fail and to hold *at any cost:* (a) the telephone exchange; (b) the telegraph office; (c) the railway stations; (d) and above all, the bridges.

The *most determined* elements (our "shock forces" and *young workers,* as well as the best of the sailors) must be formed into small detachments to occupy all the more important points and to *take part* everywhere in all important operations, for example:

to encircle and cut off Petrograd; to seize it by a combined attack of the sailors, the workers, and the troops—a task which requires *art and triple audacity;*

to form detachments from the best workers, armed with rifles and bombs, for the purpose of attacking and surrounding the enemy's "centres" (the officers' schools, the telegraph office, the telephone exchange, etc.). Their watchword must be: *"Better die to a man than let the enemy pass!"*

Let us hope that if action is decided on, the leaders will successfully apply the great precepts of Danton and Marx.

The success of both the Russian and the world revolution depends on two or three days' fighting.

LEON TROTSKY
(1879–1940)

Lev Davidovich Bronstein, known as Leon Trotsky, was born into a Jewish family in the Ukraine. He embraced revolutionary ideas from the time he was in secondary school at Odessa (1888–95). He was deported to Siberia, but escaped in 1902 and went to London, where he met Lenin. He secretly returned to Russia in 1905 and was one of the movers of the Assembly of Workers' Deputies of Saint Petersburg. He was arrested and sentenced to deportation for life in 1906, but he escaped again and continued his activity in exile. In 1917 Trotsky returned to Russia and played a very active part in the Revolution in Saint Petersburg. Above all, in 1918 he set up the organization of the Red Army, which he headed as war commissar until the end of the Civil War. He was shunted aside by Stalin in 1927, deported to central Asia in 1928, and exiled in 1929. Trotsky was murdered in Mexico by an agent of Stalin's in 1940. See further How the Revolution Armed: The Military Writings and Speeches of Leon Trotsky *(5 vols; London: New Park Publications, 1979–81).*

THE ARMORED TRAIN

Now it is time to speak of "The train of the Predrevoyensoviet." During the most strenuous years of the revolution, my own personal life was bound up inseparably with the life of that train. The train, on the other hand, was inseparably bound up with the life of the Red Army. The train linked the front with the base, solved urgent problems on the spot, educated, appealed, supplied, rewarded, and punished.

An army cannot be built without reprisals. Masses of men cannot be led to death unless the army command has the death-penalty in its arsenal. So long

From Leon Trotsky, *My Life: An Attempt at Autobiography* (New York: Pathfinder Press, 1970), 411–20. Reprinted by courtesy of Pathfinder Press.

as those malicious tailless apes that are so proud of their technical achievements—the animals that we call men—will build armies and wage wars, the
command will always be obliged to place the soldiers between the possible
death in the front and the inevitable one in the rear. And yet armies are not
built on fear. The czar's army fell to pieces not because of any lack of reprisals.
In his attempt to save it by restoring the death-penalty, Kerensky only finished
it. Upon the ashes of the great war, the Bolsheviks created a new army. These
facts demand no explanation for any one who has even the slightest knowledge of the language of history. The strongest cement in the new army was
the ideas of the October revolution, and the train supplied the front with
this cement. . . .

Every regiment, every company, comprises men of different qualities. The
intelligent and self-sacrificing are in the minority. At the opposite pole is
an insignificant number of the completely demoralized, the skulkers, and
the consciously hostile. Between these two minorities is a large middle
group, the undecided, the vacillating. And when the better elements have
been lost in fighting or shoved aside, and the skulkers and enemies gain
the upper hand, the unit goes to pieces. In such cases, the large middle group
do not know whom to follow and, in the moment of danger, succumb
to panic. . . .

For two and a half years, except for comparatively short intervals, I lived in
a railway-coach that had formerly been used by one of the ministers of communication. The car was well fitted out from the point of view of ministerial
comfort, but it was scarcely adapted to work. There I received those who
brought reports, held conferences with local military and civil authorities,
studied telegraphic despatches, dictated orders and articles. From it I made
long trips along the front in automobiles with my co-workers. In my spare
time I dictated my book against Kautsky, and various other works. In those
years I accustomed myself, seemingly forever, to writing and thinking to
the accompaniment of Pullman wheels and springs.

My train was hurriedly organized in Moscow on the night of August 7, 1918.
In the morning I left in it for Sviyazhsk, bound for the Czecho-Slovak front.
The train was continually being reorganized and improved upon, and extended in its functions. As early as 1918, it had already become a flying apparatus of administration. Its sections included a secretariat, a printing-press, a
telegraph station, a radio station, an electric-power station, a library, a garage,
and a bath. The train was so heavy that it needed two engines; later it was divided into two trains. When we had to stop for some time at some one section
of the front, one of the engines would do service as courier, and the other was
always under steam. The front was shifting constantly, and one could take
no chances.

I haven't the history of the train at hand. It is buried in the archives of the war department. At one time it was painstakingly worked over by my young assistants. The diagram of the train's movements prepared for the civil-war exhibition used to attract a great many visitors, as the newspapers reported at the time. Later it was put in the civil-war museum. To-day it must be hidden away with hundreds and thousands of other exhibits, such as placards, proclamations, orders, flags, photographs, films, books and speeches reflecting the most important moments of the civil war and connected, in some way or other, with my part in it.

During the years of 1922 to 1924, that is, before repressions were begun against the opposition, the military publishing house managed to bring out five volumes of my works relating to the army and the civil war. The history of the train is not dealt with in these volumes. I can only partially reconstruct the orbit of the train's movements from the place names under the leading articles in the train newspaper, *En Route*—Samara, Chelyabinsk, Vyatka, Petrograd, Balashov, Smolensk, Samara again, Rostov-on-Don, Novocherkask, Kiev, Zhitomir, and so on, without end. I haven't even the exact figures of the total distance covered by the train during the civil war. One of the notes to my military books mentions 36 trips, with a total run of over 105,000 kilometers. One of my former fellow travellers writes that he reckons from memory that in three years we circled the earth five and a half times—he gives, that is, a figure twice as large as the one mentioned above. This does not include thousands of kilometres done by automobile from the railway line into the heart of the front lines. Since the train always went to the most critical points, the diagram of its journeyings gives a fairly exact and comprehensive picture of the relative importance of the different fronts. The greatest number of trips was in 1920, the last year of the war. My trips to the southern front were especially frequent, because all during that period it was the most stubborn, dangerous and extended of all the fronts.

What was the train of the chairman of the Revolutionary Military Council seeking on the civil-war fronts? The general answer is obvious: it was seeking victory. But what did it give the fronts? What methods did it follow? What were the immediate objects of its endless runs from one end of the country to the other? They were not mere trips of inspection. No, the work of the train was all bound up with the building-up of the army, with its education, its administration, and its supply. We were constructing an army all over again, and under fire at that. This was true not only at Sviyazhsk, where the train recorded its first month, but on all the fronts. Out of bands of irregulars, of refugees escaping from the Whites, of peasants mobilized in the neighboring districts, of detachments of workers sent by the industrial centres, of groups of communists and trades-unionists—out of these we formed at the front companies, battalions, new regiments, and sometimes even entire divisions. Even after defeats and retreats, the flabby, panicky mob would be transformed in two or three weeks into an efficient fighting force. What was needed for this? At once much and little. It needed good commanders, a few dozen experienced fighters, a dozen or so of communists ready to make any sacrifice, boots for the barefooted, a bath-house, an energetic propaganda campaign, food, underwear, tobacco and matches. The train took care of all this. We always had in reserve a few zealous communists to fill in the breaches, a hundred or so of good fighting men, a small stock of boots, leather jackets, medicaments, machine-guns, field-glasses, maps, watches and all sorts of gifts. Of course, the actual material resources of the train were slight in comparison with the needs of the army, but they were constantly being replenished.

But—what is even more important—tens and hundreds of times they played the part of the shovelful of coal that is necessary at a particular moment to keep the fire from going out. A telegraph station was in operation on the train. We made our connections with Moscow by direct wire. . . .

On all of my trips, I was accompanied by the chief workers in all the principal departments of the army, especially in those connected with the supply service. We had inherited from the old army supply service officers who tried to work in the old way or in even worse fashion, for the conditions became infinitely more difficult. On these trips, many of the old specialists had to learn new ways, and new ones received their training in live experience. After making the round of a division and ascertaining its needs on the spot, I would hold a conference in the staff-car or the dining-car, inviting as many representatives as possible, including those from the lower commanding force and from the ranks, as well as from the local party organizations, the Soviet administration, and the trades-unions. In this way I got a picture of the situation that was neither false nor highly colored. These conferences always had immediate practical results. No matter how poor the organs of the local administration might be, they always managed to squeeze a little tighter and cut down some of their own needs to contribute something to the army.

The most important sacrifices came from institutions. A new group of communists would be drawn from the institutions and put immediately into an unreliable regiment. Stuff would be found for shirts and for wrappings for the feet, leather for new soles, and an extra hundredweight of fat. But of course the local sources were not enough. After the conference, I would send orders to Moscow by direct wire, estimating our needs according to the resources of the centre, and, as a result, the division would get what it desperately needed, and that in good time. The commanders and commissaries of the front learned from their experience on the train to approach their own work—whether they were commanding, educating, supplying or administering justice—not from above, from the standpoint of the pinnacle of the staff, but from below, from the standpoint of the company or platoon, of the young and inexperienced new recruit.

Gradually, more or less efficient machinery for a centralized supply service for the front and the armies was established. But, alone, it did not and could not satisfy all needs. Even the most ideal organization will occasionally miss fire during a war, and especially during a war of manoeuvres based entirely on movement—sometimes, alas! in quite unforeseen directions. And one must not forget that we fought without supplies. As early as 1919, there was nothing left in the central depots. Shirts were sent to the front direct from the workshop. But the supply of rifles and cartridges was most difficult of all. The Tula munition factories worked for the needs of the current day. Not a carload of cartridges could be sent anywhere without the special authorization of the commander-in-chief. The supply of munitions was always as taut as a string. Sometimes the string would break, and then we lost men and territory.

Without constant changes and improvisations, the war would have been utterly impossible for us. The train initiated these, and at the same time regulated them. If we gave an impulse of initiative to the front and its immediate rear, we took care to direct it into the channels of the general system. I do not want to say that we always succeeded in this. But, as the civil war has demonstrated, we did achieve the principal thing—victory.

The trips to the sections of the front where often the treason of the commanding officers had created catastrophes were especially important. . . .

The war unrolled on the periphery of the country, often in the most remote parts of a front that stretched for eight thousand kilometres. Regiments and divisions were cut off from the rest of the world for months at a time. Very often they had not enough telephone equipment even for their own intercommunication, and would then succumb to hopelessness. The train, for them, was a messenger from other worlds. We always had a stock of telephone apparatus and wires. A wireless aerial had been arranged over a particular car in our train, so that we could receive radio messages from the Eiffel Tower, from Nauen, and from other stations, thirteen in all, with Moscow, of course, foremost. The train was always informed of what was going on in the rest of the world. The more important telegraphic reports were published in the train newspaper, and given passing comment, in articles, leaflets and orders. Kapp's raid, conspiracies at home, the English elections, the progress of grain collections, and feats of the Italian Fascismo were interpreted while the footprints of events were still warm, and were linked up with the fates of the Astrakhan or Archangel fronts.

These articles were simultaneously transmitted to Moscow by direct wire, and radioed from there to the press of the entire country. The arrival of the train put the most isolated unit in touch with the whole army, and brought it into the life not only of the country, but of the entire world. Alarmist rumors and doubts were dispelled, and the spirit of the men grew firm. This change of morale would last for several weeks, sometimes until the next visit of the train. In the intervals, members of the Revolutionary Military Council of the front or the army would make trips similar in character, but on a smaller scale. . . .

Part of the train was a huge garage holding several automobiles and a gasoline tank. This made it possible for us to travel away from the railway line for several hundred versts. A squad of picked sharpshooters and machine-gunners, amounting to from twenty to thirty men, occupied the trucks and light cars. A couple of hand machine-guns had also been placed in my car. A war of movement is full of surprises. On the steppes, we always ran the risk of running into some Cossack band. Automobiles with machine-guns insured one against this, at least when the steppe had not been transformed into a sea of mud. Once during the autumn of 1919, in the province of Voronezh, we could move at a speed of only three kilometres an hour. The automobiles sank deep into the black, rain-soaked earth. Thirty men had to keep jumping off their cars to push them along. . . .

The train was not only a military-administrative and political institution, but a fighting institution as well. In many of its features it was more like an armored train than a staff headquarters on wheels. In fact, it was armored, or at least its engines and machine-gun cars were. All the crew could handle arms. They all wore leather uniforms, which always make men look heavily imposing. On the left arm, just below the shoulder, each wore a large metal badge, carefully cast at the mint, which had acquired great popularity in the army. The cars were connected by telephone and by a system of signals. To keep the men on the alert while we were travelling, there were frequent alarms, both by day and by night. Armed detachments would be put off the train as "landing parties." The appearance of a leather-coated detachment in a dangerous place invariably had an overwhelming effect. When they were aware of the presence of the train just a few kilometres behind the firing-line, even the most nervous units, their commanding officers especially, would summon up all their strength. In the unstable poise of a scale, only a small weight is enough to decide. The role of that weight was played by the train and its detachments a great many times during its two and a half years of travel.

T. E. LAWRENCE
(1885–1935)

Thomas Edward Lawrence studied modern history at Oxford and subsequently took part in archaeological excavations in the Middle East. At the beginning of World War I, he joined British Military Intelligence in Cairo. In 1916 he was sent to the Hejaz, where the Arabs had launched a revolt against the Turks. In agreement with Emir Faisal (later Hashemite ruler of Iraq), he developed a strategy of the weak against the strong, based on harassment along the single railroad line, thus forcing the Ottoman command to immobilize large numbers of men. He took part in the capture of Damascus (with General Edmund Allenby) in 1918. With the appearance of Seven Pillars of Wisdom *(privately printed in 1926; published in 1935) the legend of Lawrence of Arabia began to grow. He and the German general Paul von Lettow-Vorbeck (1870–1934) who was undefeated in East Africa at the Armistice, were the only Europeans to think in terms, not of counterinsurgency, which had been practiced for decades in colonial wars, but of guerrilla war. Lawrence's reflections on this point are developed in chapter 33 of* Seven Pillars of Wisdom, *and especially the article "The Evolution of a Revolt" in the* Army Quarterly *(vol. 1, no. 1) in October 1920, as well as in the* Encyclopaedia Britannica *article reprinted here.*

GUERRILLA WARFARE

This study of the science of guerrilla, or irregular, warfare is based on the concrete experience of the Arab Revolt against the Turks 1916–1918. But the historical example in turn gains value from the fact that its course was guided by the practical application of the theories here set forth.

From *Encyclopaedia Britannica,* 14th edition (Chicago: Encyclopaedia Britannica, 1929), vol. 10, s.v. "Guerrilla." Copyright © 1929 by Encyclopaedia Britannica, Inc. Reprinted by permission of Encyclopaedia Britannica, Inc.

The Arab Revolt began in June, 1916, with an attack by the half-armed and inexperienced tribesmen upon the Turkish garrisons in Medina and about Mecca. They met with no success, and after a few days' effort withdrew out of range and began a blockade. This method forced the early surrender of Mecca, the more remote of the two centres. Medina, however, was linked by railway to the Turkish main army in Syria, and the Turks were able to reinforce the garrison there. The Arab forces which had attacked it then fell back gradually and took up a position across the main road to Mecca.

At this point the campaign stood still for many weeks. The Turks prepared to send an expeditionary force to Mecca, to crush the revolt at its source, and accordingly moved an army corps to Medina by rail. Thence they began to advance down the main western road from Medina to Mecca, a distance of about 250 miles. The first 50 miles were easy, then came a belt of hills 20 miles wide, in which were Feisal's Arab tribesmen standing on the defensive: next a level stretch, for 70 miles along the coastal plain to Rabegh, rather more than halfway. Rabegh is a little port on the Red Sea, with good anchorage for ships, and because of its situation was regarded as the key to Mecca. Here lay Sherif Ali, Feisal's eldest brother, with more tribal forces, and the beginning of an Arab regular army, formed from officers and men of Arab blood who had served in the Turkish Army. As was almost inevitable in view of the general course of military thinking since Napoleon, the soldiers of all countries looked only to the regulars to win the war. Military opinion was obsessed by the dictum of Foch that the ethic of modern war is to seek for the enemy's army, his centre of power, and destroy it in battle. Irregulars would not attack positions and so they were regarded as incapable of forcing a decision.

While these Arab regulars were still being trained, the Turks suddenly began their advance on Mecca. They broke through the hills in 24 hours, and so proved the second theorem of irregular war—namely, that irregular troops are as unable to defend a point or line as they are to attack it. This lesson was received without gratitude, for the Turkish success put the Rabegh forces in a critical position, and it was not capable of repelling the attack of a single battalion, much less of a corps.

In the emergency it occurred to the author that perhaps the virtue of irregulars lay in depth, not in face, and that it had been the threat of attack by them upon the Turkish northern flank which had made the enemy hesitate for so long. The actual Turkish flank ran from their front line to Medina, a distance of some 50 miles: but, if the Arab force moved towards the Hejas railway behind Medina, it might stretch its threat (and, accordingly, the enemy's flank) as far, potentially, as Damascus, 800 miles away to the north. Such a move would force the Turks to the defensive, and the Arab force might regain the initiative. Anyhow, it seemed the only chance, and so, in Jan. 1917, Feisal's tribesmen turned their backs on Mecca, Rabegh and the Turks, and marched away north 200 miles to Wejh.

This eccentric movement acted like a charm. The Arabs did nothing concrete, but their march recalled the Turks (who were almost into Rabegh) all the way back to Medina. There, one half of the Turkish force took up the entrenched position about the city, which it held until after the Armistice. The other half was distributed along the railway to defend it against the Arab threat. For the rest of the war the Turks stood on the defensive and the Arab tribesmen won advantage over advantage till, when peace came, they had taken 35,000 prisoners, killed and wounded and worn out about as many, and occupied 100,000 square miles of the enemy's territory, at little loss to themselves. However, although Wejh was the turning point its significance was not yet realized. For the moment the move thither was regarded merely as a preliminary to cutting the railway in order to take Medina, the Turkish headquarters and main garrison.

Strategy and Tactics

However, the author was unfortunately as much in charge of the campaign as he pleased, and lacking a training in command sought to find an immediate equation between past study of military theory and the present movements— as a guide to, and an intellectual basis for, future action. The text books gave the aim in war as "the destruction of the organized forces of the enemy" by "the one process battle." Victory could only be purchased by blood. This was a hard saying, as the Arabs had no organized forces, and so a Turkish Foch would have no aim: and the Arabs would not endure casualties, so that an Arab Clausewitz could not buy his victory. These wise men must be talking metaphors, for the Arabs were indubitably winning their war . . . and further reflection pointed to the deduction that they had actually won it. They were in occupation of 99% of the Hejaz. The Turks were welcome to the other fraction till peace or doomsday showed them the futility of clinging to the window pane. This part of the war was over, so why bother about Medina? The Turks sat in it on the defensive, immobile, eating for food the transport animals which were to have moved them to Mecca, but for which there was no pasture in their now restricted lines. They were harmless sitting there; if taken prisoner, they would entail the cost of food and guards in Egypt; if driven out northward into Syria, they would join the main army blocking the British in Sinai. On all counts they were best where they were, and they valued Medina and wanted to keep it. Let them!

This seemed unlike the ritual of war of which Foch had been priest, and so it seemed that there was a difference of kind. Foch called his modern war "absolute." In it two nations professing incompatible philosophies set out to try them in the light of force. A struggle of two immaterial principles could only end when the supporters of one had no more means of resistance. An opinion can be argued with: a conviction is best shot. The logical end of a war of creeds is the final destruction of one, and Salammbo the classical textbook-instance. These were the lines of the struggle between France and Germany, but not, perhaps, between Germany and England, for all efforts to make the British soldier hate the enemy simply made him hate war. Thus the "absolute war" seemed only a variety of war; and beside it other sorts could be discerned, as Clausewitz had numbered them, personal wars for dynastic reasons, expulsive wars for party reasons, commercial wars for trading reasons.

Now the Arab aim was unmistakably geographical, to occupy all Arabic-speaking lands in Asia. In the doing of it Turks might be killed, yet "killing Turks" would never be an excuse or aim. If they would go quietly, the war would end. If not, they must be driven out: but at the cheapest possible price, since the Arabs were fighting for freedom, a pleasure only to be tasted by a man alive. The next task was to analyse the process, both from the point of view of strategy, the aim in war, the synoptic regard which sees everything by the standard of the whole, and from the point of view called tactics, the means towards the strategic end, the steps of its staircase. In each were found the same elements, one algebraical, one biological, a third psychological. The first seemed a pure science, subject to the laws of mathematics, without humanity. It dealt with known invariables, fixed conditions, space and time, inorganic things like hills and climates and railways, with mankind in type-masses too great for individual variety, with all artificial aids, and the extensions given our faculties by mechanical invention. It was essentially formulable.

In the Arab case the algebraic factor would take first account of the area to be conquered. A casual calculation indicated perhaps 140,000 square miles. How would the Turks defend all that—no doubt by a trench line across the bottom, if the Arabs were an army attacking with banners displayed . . . but suppose they were an influence, a thing invulnerable, intangible, without front or back, drifting about like a gas? Armies were like plants, immobile as a whole, firm-rooted, nourished through long stems to the head. The Arabs might be a vapour, blowing where they listed. It seemed that a regular soldier might be helpless without a target. He would own the ground he sat on, and what he could poke his rifle at. The next step was to estimate how many posts they would need to contain this attack in depth, sedition putting up her head in every unoccupied one of these 100,000 square miles. They would have need of a fortified post every four square miles, and a post could not be less than 20 men. The Turks would need 600,000 men to meet the combined ill wills of all the local Arab people. They had 100,000 men available. It seemed that the assets in this sphere were with the Arabs, and climate, railways, deserts, technical weapons could also be attached to their interests. The Turk was stupid and would believe that rebellion was absolute, like war, and deal with it on the analogy of absolute warfare.

Humanity in Battle

So much for the mathematical element; the second factor was biological, the breaking-point, life and death, or better, wear and tear. Bionomics seemed a good name for it. The war-philosophers had properly made it an art, and had elevated one item in it, "effusion of blood," to the height of a principle. It became humanity in battle, an art touching every side of our corporal being. There was a line of variability (man) running through all its estimates. Its components were sensitive and illogical, and generals guarded themselves by the device of a reserve, the significant medium of their art. Goltz had said that when you know the enemy's strength, and he is fully deployed, then you know enough to dispense with a reserve. But this is never. There is always the possibility of accident, of some flaw in materials, present in the general's mind: and the reserve is unconsciously held to meet it. There is a "felt" element in troops, not expressible in figures, and the greatest commander is he whose intuitions most nearly happen. Nine-tenths of tactics are certain, and taught in books: but the irrational tenth is like the kingfisher flashing across the pool and that is the test of generals. It can only be ensued by instinct, sharpened by thought practising the stroke so often that at the crisis it is as natural as a reflex.

Yet to limit the art to humanity seemed an undue narrowing down. It must apply to materials as much as to organisms. In the Turkish Army materials were scarce and precious, men more plentiful than equipment. Consequently the cue should be to destroy not the army but the materials. The death of a Turkish bridge or rail, machine or gun, or high explosive was more profitable than the death of a Turk. The Arab army just then was equally chary of men and materials: of men because they being irregulars were not units, but individuals, and an individual casualty is like a pebble dropped in water: each may make only a brief hole, but rings of sorrow widen out from them. The Arab army could not afford casualties. Materials were easier to deal with. Hence its obvious duty to make itself superior in some one branch, guncotton or machine guns, or whatever could be most decisive. Foch had laid down the maxim, applying it to men, of being superior at the critical point and moment of attack. The Arab army might apply it to materials, and be superior in equipment in one dominant moment or respect.

For both men and things it might try to give Foch's doctrine a negative twisted side, for cheapness' sake, and be weaker than the enemy everywhere except in one point or matter. Most wars are wars of contact, both forces striving to keep in touch to avoid tactical surprise. The Arab war should be a war of detachment: to contain the enemy by the silent threat of a vast unknown desert, not disclosing themselves till the moment of attack. This attack need be only nominal, directed not against his men, but against his materials: so it should not seek for his main strength or his weaknesses, but for his most accessible material. In railway cutting this would be usually an empty stretch of rail. This was a tactical success. From this theory came to be developed ultimately an unconscious habit of never engaging the enemy at all. This chimed with the numerical plea of never giving the enemy's soldier a target. Many Turks on the Arab front had no chance all the war to fire a shot, and correspondingly the Arabs were never on the defensive, except by rare accident. The corollary of such a rule was perfect "intelligence," so that plans could be made in complete certainty. The chief agent had to be the general's head (de Feuquière said this first), and his knowledge had to be faultless, leaving no room for chance. The headquarters of the Arab army probably took more pains in this service than any other staff.

The Crowd in Action

The third factor in command seemed to be the psychological, that science (Xenophon called it diathetic) of which our propaganda is a stained and ignoble part. It concerns the crowd, the adjustment of spirit to the point where it becomes fit to exploit in action. It considers the capacity for mood of the men, their complexities and mutability, and the cultivation of what in them profits the intention. The command of the Arab army had to arrange their men's minds in order of battle, just as carefully and as formally as other officers arranged their bodies: and not only their own men's minds, though them first: the minds of the enemy, so far as it could reach them: and thirdly, the mind of the nation supporting it behind the firing-line, and the mind of the hostile nation waiting the verdict, and the neutrals looking on.

It was the ethical in war, and the process on which the command mainly depended for victory on the Arab front. The printing press is the greatest weapon in the armoury of the modern commander, and the commanders of the Arab army being amateurs in the art, began their war in the atmosphere of the 20th century, and thought of their weapons without prejudice, not distinguishing one from another socially. The regular officer has the tradition of 40 generations of serving soldiers behind him, and to him the old weapons are the most honoured. The Arab command had seldom to concern itself with what its men did, but much with what they thought, and to it the diathetic was more than half command. In Europe it was set a little aside and entrusted to men outside the General Staff. But the Arab army was so weak physically that it could not let the metaphysical weapon rust unused. It had won a province when the civilians in it had been taught to die for the ideal of freedom: the presence or absence of the enemy was a secondary matter.

These reasonings showed that the idea of assaulting Medina, or even of starving it quickly into surrender, was not in accord with the best strategy. Rather, let the enemy stay in Medina, and in every other harmless place, in the largest numbers. If he showed a disposition to evacuate too soon, as a step to concentrating in the small area which his numbers could dominate effectively, then the Arab army would have to try and restore his confidence, not harshly, but by reducing its enterprises against him. The ideal was to keep his railway just working, but only just, with the maximum of loss and discomfort to him.

The Turkish army was an accident, not a target. Our true strategic aim was to seek its weakest link, and bear only on that till time made the mass of it fall. The Arab army must impose the longest possible passive defence on the Turks (this being the most materially expensive form of war) by extending its own front to the maximum. Tactically it must develop a highly mobile, highly equipped type of force, of the smallest size, and use it successively at distributed points of the Turkish line, to make the Turks reinforce their occupying posts beyond the economic minimum of 20 men. The power of this striking force would not be reckoned merely by its strength. The ratio between number and area determined the character of the war, and by having five times the mobility of the Turks the Arabs could be on terms with them with one-fifth their number.

Range over Force

Success was certain, to be proved by paper and pencil as soon as the proportion of space and number had been learned. The contest was not physical, but moral, and so battles were a mistake. All that could be won in a battle was the ammunition the enemy fired off. Napoleon had said it was rare to find generals willing to fight battles. The curse of this war was that so few could do anything else. Napoleon had spoken in angry reaction against the excessive finesse of the 18th century, when men almost forgot that war gave licence to murder. Military thought had been swinging out on his dictum for 100 years, and it was time to go back a bit again. Battles are impositions on the side which believes itself weaker, made unavoidable either by lack of land-room, or by the need to defend a material property dearer than the lives of soldiers. The Arabs had nothing material to lose, so they were to defend nothing and to shoot nothing. Their cards were speed and time, not hitting power, and these gave them strategical rather than tactical strength. Range is more to strategy than force. The invention of bully-beef had modified land-war more profoundly than the invention of gunpowder.

The British military authorities did not follow all these arguments, but gave leave for their practical application to be tried. Accordingly the Arab forces went off first to Akaba and took it easily. Then they took Tafileh and the Dead Sea; then Azrak and Deraa, and finally Damascus, all in successive stages worked out consciously on these theories. The process was to set up ladders of tribes, which should provide a safe and comfortable route from the sea-bases (Yenbo, Wejh or Akaba) to the advanced bases of operation. These were sometimes 300 miles away, a long distance in lands without railways or roads, but made short for the Arab Army by an assiduous cultivation of desert-power, control by camel parties of the desolate and unmapped wilderness which fills up all the centre of Arabia, from Mecca to Aleppo and Baghdad.

The Desert and the Sea

In character these operations were like naval warfare, in their mobility, their ubiquity, their independence of bases and communications, in their ignoring of ground features, of strategic areas, of fixed directions, of fixed points. "He who commands the sea is at great liberty, and may take as much or as little of the war as he will": he who commands the desert is equally fortunate. Camel raiding-parties, self-contained like ships, could cruise securely along the enemy's land-frontier, just out of sight of his posts along the edge of cultivation, and tap or raid into his lines where it seemed fittest or easiest or most profitable, with a sure retreat always behind them into an element which the Turks could not enter.

Discrimination of what point of the enemy organism to disarrange came with practice. The tactics were always tip and run; not pushes, but strokes. The Arab army never tried to maintain or improve an advantage, but to move off and strike again somewhere else. It used the smallest force in the quickest time at the farthest place. To continue the action till the enemy had changed his dispositions to resist it would have been to break the spirit of the fundamental rule of denying him targets.

The necessary speed and range were attained by the frugality of the desert men, and their efficiency on camels. In the heat of summer Arabian camels will do about 250 miles comfortably between drinks: and this represented three days' vigorous marching. This radius was always more than was needed, for wells are seldom more than 100 miles apart. The equipment of the raiding parties aimed at simplicity, with nevertheless a technical superiority over the Turks in the critical department. Quantities of light machine guns were obtained from Egypt for use not as machine guns, but as automatic rifles, snipers' tools, by men kept deliberately in ignorance of their mechanism, so that the speed of action would not be hampered by attempts at repair. Another special feature was high explosives, and nearly every one in the revolt was qualified by rule of thumb experience in demolition work.

Armoured Cars

On some occasions tribal raids were strengthened by armoured cars, manned by Englishmen. Armoured cars, once they have found a possible track, can keep up with a camel party. On the march to Damascus, when nearly 400 miles off their base, they were first maintained by a baggage train of petrol-laden camels, and afterwards from the air. Cars are magnificent fighting machines, and decisive whenever they can come into action on their own conditions. But though each has for main principle that of "fire in movement," yet the tactical employments of cars and camel-corps are so different that their use in joint operations is difficult. It was found demoralizing to both to use armoured and unarmoured cavalry together.

The distribution of the raiding parties was unorthodox. It was impossible to mix or combine tribes, since they disliked or distrusted one another. Likewise the men of one tribe could not be used in the territory of another. In consequence, another canon of orthodox strategy was broken by following the principle of the widest distribution of force, in order to have the greatest number of raids on hand at once, and fluidity was added to speed by using one district on Monday, another on Tuesday, a third on Wednesday. This much reinforced the natural mobility of the Arab army, giving its priceless advantages in pursuit, for the force renewed itself with fresh men in every new tribal area, and so maintained its pristine energy. Maximum disorder was, in a real sense, its equilibrium.

An Undisciplined Army

The internal economy of the raiding parties was equally curious. Maximum irregularity and articulation were the aims. Diversity threw the enemy intelligence off the track. By the regular organization in identical battalions and divisions information builds itself up, until the presence of a corps can be inferred on corpses from three companies. The Arabs, again, were serving a common ideal, without tribal emulation, and so could not hope for any esprit de corps. Soldiers are made a caste either by being given great pay and rewards in money, uniform or political privileges: or, as in England, by being made outcasts, cut off from the mass of their fellow-citizens. There have been many armies enlisted voluntarily: there have been few armies serving voluntarily under such trying conditions, for so long a war as the Arab revolt. Any of the Arabs could go home whenever the conviction failed him. Their only contract was honour.

Consequently the Arab army had no discipline, in the sense in which it is restrictive, submergent of individuality, the Lowest Common Denominator of men. In regular armies in peace it means the limit of energy attainable by everybody present: it is the hunt not of an average, but of an absolute, a 100-per-cent standard, in which the 99 stronger men are played down to the level of the worst. The aim is to render the unit a unit, and the man a type, in order that their effort shall be calculable, their collective output even in grain and in bulk. The deeper the discipline, the lower the individual efficiency, and the more sure the performance. It is a deliberate sacrifice of capacity in order to reduce the uncertain element, the bionomic factor, in enlisted humanity, and its accompaniment is *compound* or social war, that form in which the fighting man has to be the product of the multiplied exertions of long hierarchy, from workshop to supply unit, which maintains him in the field.

The Arab war, reacting against this, was *simple* and individual. Every enrolled man served in the line of battle, and was self-contained. There were no lines of communication or labour troops. It seemed that in this articulated warfare, the sum yielded by single men would be at least equal to the product of a compound system of the same strength, and it was certainly easier to adjust to tribal life and manners, given elasticity and understanding on the part of the commanding officers. Fortunately for its chances nearly every young Englishman has the roots of eccentricity in him. Only a sprinkling were employed, not more than one per 1,000 of the Arab troops. A larger proportion would have created friction, just because they were foreign bodies (pearls if you please) in the oyster: and those who were present controlled by influence and advice, by their superior knowledge, not by an extraneous authority.

The practice was, however, not to employ in the firing line the greater numbers which the adoption of a "simple" system made available theoretically. Instead, they were used in relay: otherwise the attack would have become too extended. Guerrillas must be allowed liberal work-room. In irregular war if two men are together one is being wasted. The moral strain of isolated action makes this simple form of war very hard on the individual soldier, and exacts from him special initiative, endurance and enthusiasm. Here the ideal was to make action a series of single combats to make the ranks a happy alliance of commanders-in-chief. The value of the Arab army depended entirely on quality, not on quantity. The members had to keep always cool, for the excitement of a blood-lust would impair their science, and their victory depended on a just use of speed, concealment, accuracy of fire. Guerrilla war is far more intellectual than a bayonet charge.

The Exact Science of Guerrilla Warfare

By careful persistence, kept strictly within its strength and following the spirit of these theories, the Arab army was able eventually to reduce the Turks to helplessness, and complete victory seemed to be almost within sight when General Allenby by his immense stroke in Palestine threw the enemy's main forces into hopeless confusion and put an immediate end to the Turkish war. His too-greatness deprived the Arab revolt of the opportunity of following to the end the dictum of Saxe that a war might be won without fighting battles. But it can at least be said that its leaders worked by his light for two years, and the work stood. This is a pragmatic argument that cannot be wholly derided. The experiment, although not complete, strengthened the belief that irregular war or rebellion could be proved to be an exact science, and an inevitable success, granted certain factors and if pursued along certain lines.

Here is the thesis: Rebellion must have an unassailable base, something guarded not merely from attack, but from the fear of it: such a base as the Arab revolt had in the Red Sea ports, the desert, or in the minds of men converted to its creed. It must have a sophisticated alien enemy, in the form of a disciplined army of occupation too small to fulfil the doctrine of acreage: too few to adjust number to space, in order to dominate the whole area effectively from fortified posts. It must have a friendly population, not actively friendly, but sympathetic to the point of not betraying rebel movements to the enemy. Rebellions can be made by 2% active in a striking force, and 98% passively sympathetic. The few active rebels must have the qualities of speed and endurance, ubiquity and independence of arteries of supply. They must have the technical equipment to destroy or paralyze the enemy's organized communications, for irregular war is fairly Willisen's definition of strategy, "the study of communication," in its extreme degree, of attack where the enemy is not. In 50 words: Granted mobility, security (in the form of denying targets to the enemy), time, and doctrine (the idea to convert every subject to friendliness), victory will rest with the insurgents, for the algebraical factors are in the end decisive, and against them perfections of means and spirit struggle quite in vain.

GIULIO DOUHET
(1869–1930)

Giulio Douhet started out as an artillery officer but from 1912 to 1915 served as commander of the first Italian air unit. Having openly criticized Italian conduct of the war, he was court-martialed. After the Italian disaster at Caporetto in 1917, he was rehabilitated, however, and recalled to head the Italian air force; he was later promoted general. In 1921 he published Il dominio dell'aeria, *translated as* The Command of the Air *(Washington, D.C., 1942), in which he predicted, sometimes exaggeratedly, the importance that the air dimension of war might assume.*

COMMAND OF THE AIR

To have command of the air means to be in a position to prevent the enemy from flying while retaining the ability to fly oneself. Planes capable of carrying moderately heavy loads of bombs already exist, and the construction of enough of them for national defense would not require exceptional resources. The active ingredients of bombs or projectiles, the explosives, the incendiaries, the poison gases, are already being produced. An aerial fleet capable of dumping hundreds of tons of such bombs can easily be organized; therefore, the striking force and magnitude of aerial offensives, considered from the standpoint of either material or moral significance, is far more effective than those of any other offensive yet known. A nation which has command of the air is in a position to protect its own territory from enemy aerial attack and even to put a halt to the enemy's auxiliary actions in support of his land and sea operations, leaving him powerless to do much of anything. Such offensive actions can not only cut off an opponent's army and navy from their bases of

From Giulio Douhet, *The Command of the Air,* translated by Dino Ferrari, 2d ed. (New York: Coward-McCann, 1942), 24–31. Reproduced by permission of The Putnam-Berkley Group, Inc.

operations, but can also bomb the interior of the enemy's country so devastatingly that the physical and moral resistance of the people would also collapse.

All this is a present possibility, not one in the distant future. And the fact that this possibility exists, proclaims aloud for anyone to understand that to have command of the air is to have *victory*. Without this command, one's portion is defeat and the acceptance of whatever terms the victor is pleased to impose. Reasoning from the facts along the lines of logic, this is the conclusion we have reached. But since this conclusion applies to matters of very great practical importance, and since it is sharply at variance with the accepted way of looking at things, it behooves us to stop and amplify our statement before going on.

When conclusions are reached by reasoning with strict adherence to logic from actual verifiable facts, those conclusions ought to be accepted as valid even if they seem strange and radical, in direct contradiction to conventional thought patterns or fixed habits of mind based upon other facts, equally positive and verifiable to be sure, but entirely different in nature. To come to any other conclusion would be to deny reason itself. It would be like the reasoning of a peasant who insists upon cultivating his land exactly as his father and grandfather did before him, despite the fact that by using chemical fertilizers and modern machinery he could double or treble his harvest. Such old-fashioned, die-hard perverseness gets him nothing except a handicap in the market place.

Twelve years ago [in 1909], when the very first airplanes began to hedgehop between field and air, hardly what we would call flying at all today, I began to preach the value of command of the air. From that day to this I have done my level best to call attention to this new weapon of warfare. I argued that the airplane should be the third brother of the army and navy. I argued that the day would come when thousands of military planes would ply the air under an independent Ministry of the Air. I argued that the dirigible and other lighter-than-air ships would give way before the superiority of the plane. And everything I argued for then has come true just as I predicted it in 1909.

I did not prophesy then, and I do not prophesy now. All I did then was to examine the new problem posed by the existence of the new arm and reason from verifiable data; but I did not hesitate to follow up the implications of the conclusions I reached, in spite of the fact that then, as now, they may have sounded paradoxical. I was convinced with mathematical certainty that the facts would prove me right. . . .

What I have to say is this: In the preparations for national defense we have to follow an entirely new course because the character of future wars is going to be entirely different from the character of past wars. . . .

... For this reason clinging to the past will teach us nothing useful for the future, for that future will be radically different from anything that has gone before. The future must be approached from a new angle. ... In 1909 I wrote:

To us who until now have been inexorably bound to the surface of the earth; to us who have smiled superciliously, almost with compassion, at the efforts of a few intrepid pioneers whom we thought deluded with visions of the impossible, but who proved to be the real seers; to us who have only armies and navies, it must seem strange that the sky, too, is about to become another battlefield no less important than the battlefields on land and sea. But from now on we had better get accustomed to this idea and prepare ourselves for the new conflicts to come. If there are nations which can exist untouched by the sea, there are certainly none which exist without the breath of air. In the future, then, we shall have three instead of two separate and well-defined fields of battle; and, though in each of them the conflict will be carried on with different weapons, they will still have to be co-ordinated toward a common goal, which will always remain the same—namely, to win.

We are fully conscious today of the importance of having command of the seas, but soon the command of the air will be no less important because only by having such a command—and only then—can we make use of the advantages made possible by aerial observation and the ability to see targets clearly—advantages which we shall not be able fully to enjoy until we have the aerial power to keep the enemy grounded. The struggle for the command of the air will be bitter; and the so-called civilized nations will strive to forge the most telling means to wage the conflict. But any conflict, other things being equal, is ultimately decided by weight of numbers; so the race for supremacy will go on without cease, only checked now and then by economic contingencies. By virtue of this race for air supremacy, air fleets will grow in importance as they get larger.

The army and navy should not then see in the airplane merely an auxiliary arm of limited usefulness. They should rather see in the plane a third brother, younger of course, of the powerful family of War. ["I problemi dell'aeronavigazione," *La preparazione* (Rome), 1910.]

Now, after the experiences of the World War, I find no need to modify by a single word what I wrote eleven years ago. Time has confirmed my deductions, even though the concept of the command of the air has not yet been realized in practice. For that I am not to blame. But anyhow today—it could not possibly be otherwise—those ideas are rapidly gaining ground—especially outside of Italy.

The Extreme Consequences

To conquer the command of the air means victory; to be beaten in the air means defeat and acceptance of whatever terms the enemy may be pleased to impose. The truth of this affirmation, which for me is an axiom in itself, will become increasingly apparent to readers who will take the trouble to follow this study, wherein I hope to make it completely clear.

From this axiom we come immediately to this first corollary: In order to assure an adequate national defense, it is necessary—and sufficient—to be in a position in case of war to conquer the command of the air. And from that we arrive at this second corollary: All that a nation does to assure her own defense should have as its aim procuring for herself those means which, in case of war, are most effective for the conquest of the command of the air.

Any effort, any action, or any resources diverted from this essential aim makes conquering the command of the air that much less probable; and it makes defeat in case of war that much more probable. Any diversion from this primary purpose is an error. In order to conquer the air, it is necessary to deprive the enemy of all means of flying, by striking at him in the air, at his bases of operation, or at this production centers—in short, wherever those means are to be found. This kind of destruction can be accomplished only in the air or in the interior of the enemy's country. It can therefore be accomplished only by aerial means, to the exclusion of army and navy weapons. Therefore, the command of the air cannot be conquered except by an adequate aerial force. From this affirmation and the above-mentioned first corollary, we may draw an inference of practical value; namely: An adequate national defense cannot be assured except by an aerial force capable in case of war of conquering the command of the air. To be sure, this statement is directly opposed to the prevailing conception of national defense, and it puts the air arm first in order of importance. Nevertheless, to deny this affirmation, we must also deny the value of command of the air. To break away from the past is disturbing; but so is man's conquest of space disturbing.

As I have pointed out, this conclusion means the superseding of traditional values by new ones not yet fully realized. Up to this time the army and navy have been the predominant forces, and no one questioned that supremacy. Space was closed to man. But there is no *a priori* reason why the air arm cannot become the predominant power in its relations with surface forces. In examining these relations, we come to the conclusion that the air force is destined to predominate over both land and sea forces; this because their radius of offensive action is limited in comparison to the vastly greater radius of the air force.

As I said, we find ourselves now at a particular point in the curve of the evolution of war. After this point the curve drops off abruptly in a new direction, breaking off all continuity with the past. Therefore, if we have a tendency to deviate as little as possible from the beaten path, we will find ourselves diverging from reality, and we will wind up far removed from the realities of our time. To catch up with things as they are, we must change our course sharply and follow reality itself. If reason, common sense, and the facts themselves tell us that the army and navy are declining in importance as compared with air power, we are doing a disservice to our own defense preparations when we insist upon crediting the army and navy with fictitious values which have no basis in actual fact.

Nature does not progress by leaps and bounds—still less does man. I do not imagine that between today and tomorrow the army and navy will be abolished and only the air force increased.

For the present I ask only that we give the air arm the importance it deserves—in Italy we are far from doing that—and that during the transition period we adopt the following modest program: A progressive decrease of land and sea forces, accompanied by a corresponding increase of aerial forces until they are strong enough to conquer the command of the air. This is a program which will approach nearer and nearer reality as we grow firmer in promoting it.

Victory smiles upon those who anticipate the changes in the character of war, not upon those who wait to adapt themselves after the changes occur. In this period of rapid transition from one form to another, those who daringly take to the new road first will enjoy the incalculable advantages of the new means of war over the old. This new character of war, emphasizing the advantages of the offensive, will surely make for swift, crushing decisions on the battlefield. Those nations who are caught unprepared for the coming war will find, when war breaks out, not only that it is too late for them to get ready for it, but that they cannot even get the drift of it. Those who are ready first not only will win quickly, but will win with the fewest sacrifices and the minimum expenditure of means. So that, when this change is completed, though decisions in the field will be swift, the actual war will be fought with increasingly formidable air forces. But during the period of transition a limited force will be adequate to checkmate any opponent's army and navy.

If we must wait to be convinced of this until someone else sets us an example, we will be left behind; and to be left behind during this period means to be defeated in case of war. And, as I have already pointed out, that, ironically enough, is just what is happening now. In an effort to safeguard themselves against Germany's possible thirst for revenge, the Allies forced her along the surest road toward accomplishing it. It is a fact that Germany, forced to disarm on land and sea, will be driven to arm in the air. As we shall see, an air force capable of conquering the command of the air, especially during this transition period, requires comparatively limited means, a small personnel, and modest resources; and all of this can be quietly disposed without awakening the attention of potential enemies. At the slightest chafing of the yoke imposed upon her by the Allies, the inner drive to be free will surely push Germany along the new road.

This new road is an economic road which makes it feasible for us to provide for national defense with a limited expenditure of energy and resources once the respective weapons of air, land, and sea are properly evaluated. We remember that in England there have been Admirals of the Fleet who questioned the value of battleships versus airplanes; and we remember, too, that in America tests have been made which demonstrated that under certain conditions planes can sink armored ships.

Now we have reached the hour when we can no longer ignore this problem, which, in the interest of national defense, we should face squarely.

WILLIAM MITCHELL
(1879–1936)

*William Mitchell served in Cuba during the Spanish-American War of
1898 and in the Philippines at the beginning of the uprising against the
American occupation in 1899. He later graduated from the U.S. Army
Staff College. When the United States entered World War I in 1917, Mitchell
was in Spain, and he immediately went to Paris and placed himself at the
disposal of General Philippe Pétain. He was assigned to aviation and
eventually became commander of the U.S. expeditionary air force in Europe,
rising to the rank of brigadier general. After the war, Mitchell became
assistant chief of air service, in the U.S. army, but in 1925 he was court-
martialed and suspended from duty for criticizing official views on the subject
of the development of air power, after which he resigned. Mitchell was one of
the visionaries who foresaw the future role of aviation.*

THE AERONAUTICAL ERA

The world stands on the threshold of the "aeronautical era." During this epoch
the destinies of all people will be controlled through the air.

Our ancestors passed through the "continental era" when they consolidated
their power on land and developed their means of communication and intercourse over the land or close to it on the seacoast. Then came the "era of the
great navigators," and the competition for the great sea lanes of power, commerce, and communication, which were hitched up and harnessed to the land
powers created in the continental era. Now the competition will be for the possession of the unhampered right to traverse and control the most vast, the most
important, and the farthest reaching element of the earth, the air, the atmosphere that surrounds us all, that we breathe, live by, and which permeates
everything.

From William Mitchell, *Winged Defense: The Development and Possibilities of Modern Air
Power—Economic and Military* (New York: Putnam's, 1925), 3–24.

Air power has come to stay. But what, it may be asked, is air power? Air power is the ability to do something in or through the air, and, as the air covers the whole world, aircraft are able to go anywhere on the planet. They are not dependent on the water as a means of sustentation, nor on the land, to keep them up. Mountains, deserts, oceans, rivers, and forests, offer no obstacles. In a trice, aircraft have set aside all ideas of frontiers. The whole country now becomes the frontier and, in case of war, one place is just as exposed to attack as another place.

Aircraft move hundreds of miles in an incredibly short space of time, so that even if they are reported as coming into a country, across its frontiers, there is no telling where they are going to go to strike. Wherever an object can be seen from the air, aircraft are able to hit it with their guns, bombs, and other weapons. Cities and towns, railway lines and canals cannot be hidden. Not only is this the case on land, it is even more the case on the water, because on the water no object can be concealed unless it dives beneath the surface. Surface seacraft cannot hide, there are no forests, mountains, nor valleys to conceal them. They must stand boldly out on the top of the water.

Aircraft possess the most powerful weapons ever devised by man. They carry not only guns and cannon but heavy missiles that utilize the force of gravity for their propulsion and which can cause more destruction than any other weapon. One of these great bombs hitting a battleship will completely destroy it. Consider what this means to the future systems of national defense. As battleships are relatively difficult to destroy, imagine how much easier it is to sink all other vessels and merchant craft. Aerial siege may be laid against a country so as to prevent any communications with it, ingress or egress, on the surface of the water or even along railways or roads. In case of an insular power which is entirely dependent on its sea lanes of commerce for existence, an air siege of this kind would starve it into submission in a short time.

On the other hand, an attempt to transport large bodies of troops, munitions, and supplies across a great stretch of ocean, by seacraft, as was done during the World War from the United States to Europe, would be an impossibility. At that time aircraft were only able to go a hundred miles before replenishing their fuel; now they can go a thousand miles and carry weapons which were hardly dreamed of in the World War. For attacking cities that are producing great quantities of war munitions that are necessary for the maintenance of an enemy army and country in case of war, the air force offers an entirely new method of subduing them. Heretofore, to reach the heart of a country and gain victory in war, the land armies always had to be defeated in the field and a long process of successive military advances made against it. Broken railroad lines, blown up bridges, and destroyed roads, necessitated months of hardships, the loss of thousands of lives, and untold wealth to accomplish. Now an attack from an air force using explosive bombs and gas may cause the complete evacuation of and cessation of industry in these places. This would deprive armies, air forces, and navies even, of their means of maintenance. More than that, aerial torpedoes which are really airplanes kept on their course by gyroscopic instruments and wireless telegraphy, with no pilots on board, can be directed for over a hundred miles in a sufficiently accurate way to hit great cities. So that in future the mere threat of bombing a town by an air force will cause it to be evacuated, and all work in munitions and supply factories to be stopped.

A new set of rules for the conduct of war will have to be devised and a whole new set of ideas of strategy learned by those charged with the conduct of war. No longer is the making of war gauged merely by land and naval forces. Both of these old, well understood factors in conducting war are affected by air power which operates over both of them. Already, we have an entirely new class of people that we may call "the air-going people" as distinguished from the "land-going people" and the "sea-going people." The air-going people have a spirit, language, and customs of their own. These are just as different from those on the ground as those of seamen are from those of land men. In fact, they are much more so because our sea-going and land-going communities have been with us from the inception of time and everybody knows something about them, whereas the air-going people form such a new class that only those engaged in its actual development and the younger generation appreciate what it means.

The airmen fly over the country in all directions constantly, winter and summer they go, as well as by night and by day. The average dweller on the earth never knows that above him aircraft in the United States are speeding between the Atlantic and Pacific and from the northern frontier to the southern frontier, on regular scheduled trips. The pilots of these planes, from vantage points on high, see more of the country, know more about it, and appreciate more what the country means to them than any other class of persons.

Take, for instance, a trip from the east coast out to the Middle States, accomplished in four or five hours. One starts in the morning from the Atlantic. Looking out across it for miles along the coast, the shipping coming from Europe can be plainly seen entering the harbors. Back from the coast itself stretch the industrial cities with their great factories, pushing out to the West; numberless steel lines of railways searching for the gaps in the mountains to take them through to the Middle States; the strip of cities with their heavy populations is passed, then the small farms straggling into the Alleghany Mountains; with the white roads growing fewer and fewer as the Blue Ridge Mountains are approached. Once into the Alleghanies, the utter lack of development makes itself evident at once; as far as the eye can reach there is scarcely a habitation, a road, or a clearing. The inhabitants, deprived of the means of communication, are probably our least educated citizens, although largely the purest-blooded Americans in the country. Across the Alleghanies we reach the rich lands of the Middle States. The great farms seem to crowd themselves against each other in order to produce the largest crops. The country is traversed by well-made roads, railroads, electric power, telegraph, and telephone lines. Bright, clean cities are dotted with splendid schools, fine public works, parks, and hospitals. The development of the animal industry is tremendous; cattle, pigs and sheep are in abundance. While interspersed in this great agricultural country, we still find great cities with high chimneys belching black smoke, indicating the presence of great industries.

A few hours more and the airplane traverses the whole country to the Pacific Coast. Certainly no other class of men appreciate their country or know so much about it as the "air-going fraternity."

The absorbing interest in this new development is so great that the youth of the country everywhere is being inspired to make this their specialty. Bold spirits that before wanted to "go down to the sea in ships," now want to go "up in the air in planes."

The air force has ceased to remain a mere auxiliary service for the purpose of assisting an army or navy in the execution of its task. The air force rises into the air in great masses of airplanes. Future contests will see hundreds of them in one formation. They fight in line, they have their own weapons and their own way of using them, special means of communications, signalling, and of attacking.

Armies on the ground or ships on the water have always fought on one surface because they could not get off it. The air force fights in three dimensions—on the level, from up above, and from underneath. Every air attack on other aircraft is based on the theory of surrounding the enemy in the middle of a sphere with all our own airplanes around the whole periphery shooting at it. If we attack a city or locality, we send airplanes over it at various altitudes from two or three hundred feet up to thirty thousand, all attacking at once so that if any means of defense were devised which could hit airplanes or cause them to be destroyed from the ground, the efforts would be completely nullified, because they could neither see, hear, nor feel all of them. No missile-throwing weapons or any other devices have yet been created or thought of which can actually stop an air attack, so that the only defense against aircraft are other aircraft which will contest the supremacy of the air by air battles. Great contests for control of the air will be the rule in the future. Once supremacy of the air has been established, airplanes can fly over a hostile country at will.

How can a hostile air force be forced to fight, it may be asked, if they do not desire to leave the ground? The air strategist answers: "By finding a location of such importance to the enemy that he must defend it against a bombardment attack by airplanes."

Such a place as New York, for instance, would have to be defended if attacked by hostile bombers, and, as no anti-aircraft guns or other efforts, from the ground alone, would be of any particular avail, aircraft would have to be concentrated for its defense and a succession of great air battles would result. Putting an opponent on the defensive in the air is much more valuable comparatively than putting him on the defensive on the ground. Armies may dig trenches, live in them, or sit around in them waiting for an enemy to attack them. This cannot be done in the air for airplanes have to return to the ground periodically for refueling. If they are not in the air when the hostile air force appears, they will have no effect on it, because they cannot arise to a great altitude and catch it. Consequently, not more than about one-third of an air force can be kept constantly in the air, so that in the future, the country that is ready with its air force and jumps on its opponent at once will bring about a speedy and lasting victory. Once an air force has been destroyed it is almost impossible to build it up after hostilities commence, because the places capable of building aircraft will be bombed and the big air stations that train pilots and flyers will be destroyed. Even if the country on the defensive is able to create small parcels of aviation, they will be destroyed in detail, one after the other, by the victorious air force which not only has control of the air but is protecting its own interior cities that manufacture and turn out their equipment, airplanes, and supplies.

From an aeronautical standpoint, there are three different classes of countries: First, those which are composed of islands subject to air attack from the coast of a continent. In this case the insular country must completely dominate the air if it wishes to use an army against its neighbors so as to be able to transport and land it on the shores of the Continent. If its opponents on the Continent control the air, they can cut off all the insular country's supplies that come over the seas, they can bomb its ports and its interior cities, and, with their air force alone, bring the war to a close.

The second class of country is the one that has a land frontier directly facing and joining its opponent and which is partially self-sustaining and partially dependent on food and supplies from outside, either by railways, by sea, or by air. In this case, there is a possibility that armies might come into hostile contact if the air forces did not act quickly enough. Even then if the air forces of one or the other were ready at the start of the war, all the important cities would be laid waste, the railroads and bridges destroyed, roadways constantly bombed and torn up so as to prevent automobile transportation, and all seaports demolished. Again the air force might bring victory unaided to the side which was able to control the air.

The third class of country is one which is entirely self-sustaining but is out of the ordinary aircraft range. The United States comes under this category. No armed force of an European or Asiatic nation can come against the United States except through the air or over the water. An efficient air force in this instance would be able to protect the country from invasion and would insure its independence but would not be able to subject a hostile country to invasion, or to defeat it without leaving the country itself.

Consequently, an entirely new method of conducting war at a distance will come into being. We have seen that a superior air power will dominate all sea areas when they act from land bases and that no seacraft, whether carrying aircraft or not, is able to contest their aerial supremacy.

Strings of island bases will be seized by the strong powers as strategic points so that their aircraft may fly successively from one to the other and as aircraft themselves can hold these islands against seacraft, comparatively small detachments of troops on the ground will be required for their maintenance. An island, instead of being easily starved out, taken or destroyed by navies as was the case in the past, becomes tremendously strong because it cannot be gotten at by any land forces and, while supremacy of the air is maintained, cannot be taken by sea forces.

In the northern hemisphere there is no stretch of water greater than the present cruising range of airplanes that has to be crossed in going from America to Europe or from America to Asia. The farther north we go the narrower the intervals of water between the continents. The Behring Straits are only fifty-two miles wide, while in their center are two islands that make the widest stretch twenty-one miles, scarcely more distance than across the English Channel. The greatest straight line distance over the narrowest stretch of water between America and Europe is about four hundred miles, or four hours flight.

Cold is no impediment to the action of aircraft. In fact, the colder the weather, the clearer the sky and the better the flying conditions. The sun's rays are what make most of the trouble for the aviator. In the first place, they cause heat, which makes the air hold more water. When the air cools it causes fogs, clouds and haze, because the moisture congeals as the air can no longer hold it. The heat from the sun causes ascending currents of air and the air around rushes in to take the place of the ascending currents. This makes storms of all kinds—causes what we used to call holes in the air, which are merely up and down currents, and introduces much the same difficulties that storms at sea cause to ships. . . .

Our aerial routes between the continents will not follow the old land and water ways parallel to the equator which have been used heretofore, because our old means of transportation used to be confined to land and water in warm parts of the earth. The new routes will follow the meridians, straight over the top of the earth, which cut off hundreds of miles, save weeks of time, untold effort, dangers and expense.

What will this new element in warfare result in? Unquestionably, the amelioration and bettering of conditions in war because it will bring quick and lasting results. It will require much less expense as compared with that of the great naval and land armies which have heretofore been the rule and it will cause a whole people to take an increasing interest as to whether a country shall go to war or not, because they are all exposed to attack by aircraft, no matter if they live in the remotest interior of the country.

Now, much of a country's population thinks because it does not live near a seacoast or a land frontier, that its homes will be safe from attack and destruction. The worst that can happen to them, in case of defeat in war, would be higher taxes to pay, and war debts, because navies cannot reach them and armies only with the greatest difficulty. . . .

As air power can hit at a distance, after it controls the air and vanquishes the opposing air power, it will be able to fly anywhere over the hostile country. The menace will be so great that either a state will hesitate to go to war, or, having engaged in war, will make the contest much sharper, more decisive, and more quickly finished. This will result in a diminished loss of life and treasure and will thus be a distinct benefit to civilization. Air forces will attack centers of production of all kinds, means of transportation, agricultural areas, ports and shipping; not so much the people themselves. They will destroy the means of making war because now we cannot cut a limb from a tree, pick a stone from a hill and make it our principal weapon. Today to make war we must have great metal and chemical factories that have to stay in one place, take months to build, and, if destroyed, cannot be replaced in the usual length of a modern war. . . .

The air force is the great developing power in the world today. It offers not only the hope of increased security at home, but, also, on account of its speed of locomotion, of the greatest civilizing element in the future, because the essence of civilization is rapid transportation. It is probable that future wars again will be conducted by a special class, the air force, as it was by the armored knights in the Middle Ages. Again the whole population will not have to be called out in the event of a national emergency, but only enough of it to man the machines that are the most potent in national defense.

Each year the leading countries of the world are recognizing the value of air power more and more. All of the great nations, except the United States, have adopted a definite air doctrine as distinguished from their sea doctrine and their land doctrine. To develop anything, the underlying thought and reason must govern and then the organization must be built up to meet it. The doctrine of aviation of all of these great countries is that they must have sufficient air power to protect themselves in case they are threatened with war. Each one solves the matter in a way particularly adapted to its own needs. . . .

Great Britain leads the world in this conception of air power. She now has an Air Ministry which is co-equal with the Army and Navy. Her air force is designated by law as "the first line of defense" of the United Kingdom. The country is completely organized into aeronautical defense areas with the pursuit and bombardment aviation all under one command, so that the maximum power may be brought to bear anywhere desired, and not have it split up between the army and navy as it used to be. . . .

. . . The great nations of Europe and Asia are now approximating this organization more and more, as it becomes increasingly evident that air power, to be given its maximum chance, must be developed as a main arm instead of as an auxiliary.

HUGH TRENCHARD
(1873–1956)

Hugh Trenchard served in the South African war and commanded the Royal Flying Corps in World War I. As chief of air staff from 1919 to 1929, he was effectively the creator of the Royal Air Force. Giulio Douhet and William Mitchell were fellow visionaries of air war, but Trenchard, given his position, was able to put their common views into effect. He attained the rank of air marshal and was created Viscount Trenchard in 1936.

THE WAR OBJECT OF AN AIR FORCE

At a recent meeting of the Chiefs of Staff Sub-Committee the Report of the Commandant of the Imperial Defence College for the 1st Course (1927) was discussed. In that report the Commandant recommended that the principles of war should be described in identical terms in the Manuals of all three Services. He also expressed the view that at present the situation as regards air warfare was indeterminate. I suggested that the view had arisen from an unwillingness on the part of the other Services to accept the contention of the Air Staff that in future wars air attacks would most certainly be carried out against the vital centres of communication and of the manufacture of munitions of war of every sort no matter where these centres were situated.

It seems to me that the time is now ripe to lay down explicitly the doctrine of the Air Staff as to the object to be pursued by an Air Force in war.

The doctrine which in the past has determined and still determines the object to be pursued by Navies and Armies is laid down in the respective Service Manuals in these words:

Memorandum from Royal Air Force Chief of Air Staff Hugh Trenchard to chiefs of staff sub-committee on the War Object of an Air Force, 2 May 1928.

(i) *The Navy:* The Military aim of a Navy is to destroy in battle or to neutralise and to weaken the opposing navy including its directing will and morale.

(ii) *The Army:* The ultimate military aim in war is the destruction of the enemy's main forces on the battlefield.

I would state definitely that in the view of the Air Staff the object to be sought by air action will be to paralyse from the very outset the enemy's productive centres of munitions of war of every sort and to stop all communications and transportation.

In the new Royal Air Force War Manual this object will be stated in some such general terms as the following—the actual terms have not been defined: "The aim of the Air Force is to break down the enemy's means of resistance by attacks on objectives selected as most likely to achieve this end."

I will now proceed to examine this object from three viewpoints:

(i) Does this doctrine violate any true principle of war?

(ii) Is an air offensive of this kind contrary either to international law or to the dictates of humanity?

(iii) Is the object sought one which will lead to victory, and in that respect, therefore, a correct employment of air power?

Does This Doctrine Violate Any True Principle of War?

In my view the object of all three Services is the same, to defeat the enemy nation, not merely its army, navy or air force.

For any army to do this, it is almost always necessary as a preliminary step to defeat the enemy's army, which imposes itself as a barrier that must first be broken down.

It is not, however, necessary for an air force, in order to defeat the enemy nation, to defeat its armed forces first. Air power can dispense with that intermediate step, can pass over the enemy navies and armies, and penetrate the air defences and attack direct the centres of production, transportation and communication from which the enemy war effort is maintained.

This does not mean that air fighting will not take place. On the contrary, intense air fighting will be inevitable, but it will not take the form of a series of battles between the opposing air forces to gain supremacy as a first step before the victor proceeds to the attack of other objectives. Nor does it mean that attacks on air bases will not take place. It will from time to time certainly be found advantageous to turn to the attack of an enemy air base, but such attacks will not be the main operation.

For his main operation each belligerent will set out to attack direct those objectives which he considers most vital to the enemy. Each will penetrate the defences of the other to a certain degree.

The stronger side, by developing the more powerful offensive, will provoke in his weaker enemy increasingly insistent calls for the protective employment of aircraft. In this way he will throw the enemy on to the defensive and it will be in this manner that air superiority will be obtained, and not by direct destruction of air forces.

The gaining of air superiority will be incidental to this main direct offensive upon the enemy's vital centres and simultaneous with it.

There is no new principle involved in this attacking direct the enemy nation and its means and power to continue fighting. It is simply that a new method is now available for attaining the old object, the defeat of the enemy nation, and no principle of war is violated by it.

Is an Air Offensive of This Kind Contrary to International Law or to the Dictates of Humanity?

As regards the question of legality, no authority would contend that it is unlawful to bomb military objectives, wherever situated. There is no written international law as yet upon this subject, but the legality of such operations was admitted by the Commission of Jurists who drew up a code of rules for air warfare at The Hague in 1922–23. Although the code then drawn up has not been officially adopted it is likely to represent the practice which will be regarded as lawful in any future war. Among military objectives must be included the factories in which war material (including aircraft) is made, the depots in which it is stored, the railway termini and docks at which it is loaded or troops entrain or embark, and in general the means of communication and transportation of military *personnel* and *material.* Such objectives may be situated in centres of population in which their destruction from the Air will result in casualties also to the neighbouring civilian population, in the same way as the long-range bombardment of a defended coastal town by a naval force results also in the incidental destruction of civilian life and property. The fact that air attack may have that result is no reason for regarding the bombing as illegitimate provided all reasonable care is taken to confine the scope of the bombing to the military objective. Otherwise a belligerent would be able to secure complete immunity for his war manufactures and depots merely by locating them in a large city, which would, in effect, become *neutral* territory— a position which the opposing belligerent would never accept. What is illegitimate, as being contrary to the dictates of humanity, is the indiscriminate bombing of a city for the sole purpose of terrorising the civilian population.

It is an entirely different matter to terrorise munition workers (men and women) into absenting themselves from work or stevedores into abandoning the loading of a ship with munitions through fear of air attack upon the factory or dock concerned. Moral effect is created by the bombing in such circumstances but it is the inevitable result of a lawful operation of war—the bombing of a military objective. The laws of warfare have never prohibited such destruction as is "imperatively demanded by the necessities of war" (Hague Rules, 1907) and the same principle which allows a belligerent to destroy munitions destined to be used against him would justify him also in taking action to interrupt the manufacture and movement of such munitions and thus securing the same end at an earlier stage.

Is This Object One Which Will Lead to Victory, and a Correct Employment of Air Power?

Before I deal with the above heading I would like to state here that, in a war of the first magnitude with civilised nations, I do not for a moment wish to imply by the following remarks that the Air by itself can finish the war. But it will materially assist, and will be one of the many means of exercising pressure on the enemy, in conjunction with sea power and blockade and the defeat of his armies.

In pursuit of this object, air attacks will be directed against any objectives which will contribute effectively towards the destruction of the enemy's means of resistance and the lowering of his determination to fight.

These objectives will be military objectives. Among these will be comprised the enemy's great centres of production of every kind of war material, from battleships to boots, his essential munition factories, the centres of all his systems of communications and transportation, his docks and shipyards, railway workshops, wireless stations, and postal and telegraph systems.

There is no need to attack the enemy's organised air forces as a preliminary to this direct assault. It will be just as necessary in the future, as it has been in the past, for the Army, assisted by aircraft, to seek out and attack the enemy's Army, but the weight of the air forces will be more effectively delivered against the targets mentioned above rather than against the enemy's armed forces. These objectives are more vulnerable to the attack and generally exact a smaller toll from the attacker.

It will be harder to affect the morale of an Army in the field by air attack than to affect the morale of the Nation by air attacks on its centres of supply and communications as a whole; but to attack—let alone do serious damage—an Air Force in the field is even more difficult. Air bases can be well camouflaged; they can be prepared so that the personnel and material are well protected against bomb attack and their lay-out can be so arranged and spaced as to present a difficult target. An attacker can be induced to waste his strength by deception, such as by dummy aerodromes. Air units can be widely dispersed over the country-side so that it will be difficult to find them and do them extensive damage.

To attack the armed forces is thus to attack the enemy at his strongest point. On the other hand, by attacking the sources from which these armed forces are maintained infinitely more effect is obtained. In the course of a day's attack upon the aerodromes of the enemy perhaps 50 aeroplanes could be destroyed; whereas a modern industrial state will produce 100 in a day—and production will far more than replace any destruction we can hope to do in the forward zone. On the other hand, by attacking the enemy's factories, then output is reduced by a much greater proportion.

In the same way, instead of attacking the rifle and the machine gun in the trench where they can exact the highest price from us for the smallest gain we shall attack direct the factory where these are made.

We shall attack the vital centres of transportation and seriously impede these arms and munitions reaching the battlefield and, therefore, more successfully assist the Army in its direct attack on the enemy's Army. We shall attack the communications without which the national effort cannot be co-ordinated and directed.

These are the points at which the enemy is weakest. The rifleman or the sailor is protected, armed and disciplined, and will stand under fire. The great centres of manufacture, transport and communications cannot be wholly protected. The personnel, again, who man them are not armed and cannot shoot back. They are not disciplined and it cannot be expected of them that they will stick stolidly to their lathes and benches under the recurring threat of air bombardment.

The moral effect of such attacks is very great. Even in the last war ten years ago, before any of the heavier bombers or bombs had really been employed to any extent, the moral effect of such sporadic raids as were then practicable was considerable. With the greater numbers of aircraft, the larger carrying capacity and range, and the heavier bombs available to-day, the effect would seriously impede the work of the enemy's Navy, Army and Air Forces. Each raid spreads far outside the actual zone of the attack. Once a raid has been experienced false alarms are incessant and a state of panic remains in which work comes to a standstill. Of one town in the last war it is recorded that although attacked only seven times, and that by small formations, no less than 107 alarms were sounded, and work abandoned for the day. Each alarm by day brings the day's work to an end—while by night the mere possibility of a raid destroys the chance of sleep for thousands.

These effects, it must be remembered, were produced by occasional raids by very minor forces. The effect on the workers of a Nation of an intensive air campaign will again be infinitely greater than if the main part of that air attack was launched at the enemy's aerodromes and aeroplanes which may be many miles away from the vital points, and, if this air pressure is kept up, it will help to bring about the results that Marshal Foch summed up in the words "The potentialities of aircraft attacks on a large scale are almost incalculable, but it is clear that such attack, owing to its crushing moral effect on a Nation, may impress the public opinion to a point of disarming the Government and thus becoming decisive."

This Form of Warfare Is Inevitable

I have stated above the object which an Air Force should pursue in war, and the reasons on which the Air Staff base their contention that this object is in full accord with the principles of war, is in conformity with the laws of war, and is the best object by which to reach victory.

There is another side to the matter upon which I must lay stress. There can be no question, whatever views we may hold in regard to it, that this form of warfare will be used.

There may be many who, realising that this new warfare will extend to the whole community the horrors and suffering hitherto confined to the battle-field would urge that the Air offensive should be restricted to the zone of the opposing armed forces. If this restriction were feasible, I should be the last to quarrel with it; but it is not feasible. In a vital struggle all available weapons always have been used and always will be used. All sides made a beginning in the last war, and what has been done will be done.

We ourselves are especially vulnerable to this form of attack; and foreign thinkers on war have already shown beyond all doubt that our enemies will exploit their advantage over us in this respect and will thus force us to conform and to counter their attacks in kind.

Whatever we may wish or hope, and whatever course of action we may decide, whatever be the views held as to the legality, or the humanity, or the military wisdom and expediency of such operations, there is not the slightest doubt that in the next war both sides will send their aircraft out without scruple to bomb those objectives which they consider the most suitable.

I would, therefore, urge most strongly that we accept this fact and face it; that we do not bury our heads in the sand like ostriches; but that we train our officers and men, and organise our Services, so that they may be prepared to meet and to counter these inevitable air attacks.

JAMES CONNOLLY
(1868–1916)

James Connolly emigrated in 1903 from Ireland to the United States, where he worked for the Industrial Workers of the World (Wobblies). He returned to Ireland in 1910 and became a prominent labor organizer and leader of the Irish republican movement. Although a revolutionary syndicalist influenced by Marxism, he remained a Catholic. Connolly was one of the architects of the Easter Rebellion of 1916 and led the insurrectionary forces in Dublin as vice-president of the proclaimed Irish provisional government. He was wounded in the uprising, court-martialed, and executed by the British.

ON STREET FIGHTING

To traverse a mountain pass with any degree of safety the sides of the mountain must be cleared by flanking parties ahead of the main body; to pass over a bridge the banks of the river on each side must be raked with gun or rifle fire whilst the bridge is being rushed; to take a street properly barricaded and held on both sides by forces in the houses, these houses must be broken into and taken by hand-to-hand fighting. A street barricade placed in position where artillery cannot operate from a distance is impregnable to frontal attack. To bring artillery within a couple of hundred yards—the length of the average street—would mean the loss of the artillery if confronted by even imperfectly drilled troops armed with rifles.

The Moscow revolution, where only eighty rifles were in the possession of the insurgents, would have ended in the annihilation of the artillery had the number of insurgent rifles been eight hundred.

The insurrection of Paris in June, 1848, reveals how districts of towns, or villages, should be held. The streets were barricaded at tactical points *not on*

James Connolly, "On Street Fighting," *Workers' Republic,* 24 July 1915, reprinted in *The Guerrilla Reader: A Historical Anthology,* edited by Walter Laqueur (New York: New American Library, 1977), 169–71.

the main streets but commanding them. The houses were broken through so that passages were made inside the houses along the whole length of the streets. The party walls were loopholed, as were also the front walls, the windows were blocked by sandbags, boxes filled with stones and dirt, bricks, chests, and other pieces of furniture with all sorts of odds and ends piled up against them.

Behind such defenses the insurgents poured fire upon the troops through loopholes left for the purpose. . . .

The defense of a building in a city, town, or village is governed by the same rules. Such a building left unconquered is a serious danger even if its supports are all defeated. If it had been flanked by barricades, and these barricades were destroyed, no troops could afford to push on and leave the building in the hands of the enemy. If they did so, they would be running the danger of perhaps meeting a check farther on, which check would be disastrous if they had left a hostile building manned by an unconquered force in their rear. Therefore, the fortifying of a strong building, as a pivot upon which the defense of a town or village should hinge, forms a principal object of the preparations of any defending force, whether regular army or insurrectionary.

In the Franco-German War of 1870 the chateau, or castle, of Geissberg formed such a position in the French lines on 4 August. The Germans drove in all the supports of the French party occupying this country house and stormed the outer courts, but were driven back by the fire from the windows and loopholed walls. Four batteries of artillery were brought up to within nine hundred yards of the house and battered away at its walls, and battalion after battalion was hurled against it. The advance of the whole German army was delayed until this one house was taken. To take it caused a loss of twenty-three officers and three hundred twenty-nine men, yet it had only a garrison of two hundred.

In the same campaign the village of Bazeilles offered a similar lesson in the tactical strength of a well-defended line of houses. The German army drove the French off the field and entered the village without a struggle. But it took a whole army corps seven hours to fight its way through to the other end of the village.

A mountainous country has always been held to be difficult for military operations owing to its passes or glens. A city is a huge mass of passes or glens formed by streets and lanes. Every difficulty that exists for the operation of regular troops in mountains is multiplied a hundredfold in a city. And the difficulty of the commissariat, which is likely to be insuperable to an irregular or popular force taking to the mountains, is solved for them by the sympathies of the populace when they take to the streets.

The general principle to be deducted from a study of the examples we have been dealing with, is that the defense is of almost overwhelming importance in such warfare as a popular force like the Citizen Army might be called upon to participate in.

MIKHAIL TUKHACHEVSKY
(1893–1937)

Mikhail Nikolayevich Tukhachevsky, a lieutenant in the czarist forces during World War I, joined the Bolshevik party in April 1918 and subsequently took part in the creation of the Red Army. He fought in the First Army on the eastern front against Admiral Kolchak; in the Eighth Army on the southern front; in the Fifth Army on the eastern front, where he made a breakthrough in the Urals; and in the Thirteenth Army, where he drove the forces of General A. I. Denikin back. He advocated all-out attack, the formation of groups of partisans, and decentralization of command. He took part in the ill-fated invasion of Poland in 1920 and in 1921 put down the Kronstadt and Tambov revolts; he thereafter headed the Military Academy. Tukhachevsky became chief of staff of the Red Army and then commander of the Leningrad region in 1931. As vice-commissar for defense until 1936, he favored the development of tanks and military aviation. He was arrested in June 1937, accused of high treason, and executed at Stalin's behest.

COUNTERINSURGENCY

What are the general proposals for organizing the eradication of banditry? As was already noted, the basic question is the establishment of an indispensable political and economic union between the working class and the peasantry. From the national point of view, banditry . . . becomes even more complicated because of the necessity of outlining and putting into practice a correct national policy. Taking into account the cultural level of the native population, the Soviet power has to reckon not only with the national but also with the religious composition of the local population. When these questions, in addition to the formulation of a correct economic policy, are completely solved,

From *The Guerrilla Reader: A Historical Anthology*, edited by Walter Laqueur (Philadelphia: Temple University Press, 1977), 182–84. Copyright © 1977 by Walter Laqueur. Reprinted by permission of Temple University Press.

then the ground will be cut from under the feet of the banditry. . . . Thus prerequisites are essential for the ultimate liquidation of banditry. Banditry cannot be radically overcome without action of a political, national, and economic kind. We can see examples in imperialist colonies where, despite the enormous expenditure on fighting the local population and the colossal military forces employed against it, constant riots and insurrections still take place, the capitalist governments being completely unable to cope with them.

From the organizational point of view it is necessary to have a representative of the state or the party on the territory affected by banditry. This representation should encompass the military, political, and economic officials of the particular territory. The military struggle should be adopted to local conditions; representative bodies uniting the military and civil power ought to be set up. Due to the nature of national banditry this work should be carried out strictly within the national framework of the Soviet administration. The militia also ought to be composed of members of the local nationality.

Armed forces act in two ways: first, by carrying out the tasks of an army of occupation stationed in garrisons in order to safeguard the corresponding administrative Soviet bodies and their work; secondly, as a raiding force against the active bands. Apart from the occupying military units, a reinforced Soviet militia is to be set up in the localities. It is advisable that this militia should not be composed of locally born people. Basing themselves on this military nucleus, the Soviet authorities will carry out a purge of the peasant population. This purge entails the elimination of the bandit elements. While doing so, it is necessary to draw to our side wide segments of the peasantry and to create in the villages resistance to the further encouragement and spread of banditry.

Depending upon the degree to which the area has been pacified and the extent to which pro-Soviet elements have installed themselves in the countryside, it might be useful to arm these elements against the bandits. Thus an implacable opposition to banditry would be created in the countryside. It is necessary to give these organizations the responsibility for intelligence and for warning about the activities of the bandit detachments.

At the same time, one should practice large-scale repression and employ incentives. The most effective methods of repression are the eviction of the families of bandits who hide relatives and the confiscation and subsequent distribution among pro-Soviet peasants of their property. In the event of difficulty in organizing immediate eviction, the establishment of large-scale concentration camps is necessary.

A system of collective responsibility should be introduced and applied about harboring bandits or not reporting their location and activities.

The program of introducing repression and incentives should be planned in accordance with the available resources and the general plan of action.

Threats which are not implemented only undermine the authority of the administration and cause mistrust among the peasantry.

Before the start of the campaign of extirpation comes a preliminary period of organizational work to coordinate the measures of the Soviet administrative and military authorities. Only when everything is ready does it make sense to start decisive operations. Until this stage any action would only exhaust our troops.

The organs of the GPU and the intelligence detachments should establish the scope and composition of the bandit gangs, identify members of families involved in banditry, and ascertain the territorial origins of the bandit gangs. The origins of each gang must be established. Apart from this, one has to ascertain the composition of the personnel of the local bodies of the self-styled "peasant power." Once these conditions are met, the purge of the population will take place in complete congruence with the action of the Red army against these or other bandit gangs. The gangs either will be exterminated on the battlefield or will be detached from their territorial districts during the purge.

It is necessary to observe the promise of privileged treatment to those who surrender voluntarily with their arms. As the struggle against banditry succeeds, so will the number of those who surrender voluntarily increase. The general task of eradicating banditry will thereby be facilitated.

While occupying a territory, the garrisons should be of a numerical strength sufficient to enable them to beat off independently the attacks of bandit detachments. The raiding detachments should also be strong enough to enter independently into single combat with the bandits. There are particular advantages in the use of armored cars, which are the main scourge of the fast-moving bandits.

MOUNTING THREATS

I must remind you of the strategical views of the German General Staff, which is now being restored. At the celebrations in honor of the opening of the Military Academy of the German General Staff the inviolability was proclaimed of the strategical principles of the old German General Staff, from Scharnhorst to Count von Schlieffen. As you know, when Schlieffen was working on the preparations for the offensive against France, he in fact prepared to strike his main blow not where Germany had common frontiers with France, but pre-

Report delivered at a meeting of the Central Executive Committee of the USSR, 15 January 1936. Printed in M. N. Tukhachevsky, *Sentinel of Peace* (New York: International Publishers, 1936), 3–9.

cisely where Germany had no common frontiers with France. On the outbreak of the war the German army passed through the territory of Belgium, violating the latter's neutrality, and invaded France. It goes without saying that under present conditions, when between Germany and us lie certain states which have special relations with the Germans, the German army, if it really wants to, can find means of invading our territory. How it will end is another question, but of this allow me to speak a little later.

In preparing her imperialist plans, Germany is carrying on very intensive military work. It is not without good reason that Comrade Molotov stated that Germany has in point of fact been converted into a military camp.

Particularly intensive work is being carried on in the development of a powerful air force. Dorothy Woodman, in her book on Germany's air armaments, enumerates a large number of plants engaged in the production of airplanes and engines. Airplanes are being produced in more than 50 plants. In addition, there are a score of plants and more manufacturing airplane parts. More than 20 plants are producing airplane engines and parts, and about 20 plants are engaged in the production of various aircraft instruments and accessories. You therefore see that Germany is keeping her vast aviation industry fully employed, with the result that the development of the German air fleet is making gigantic strides.

This air threat affected British public opinion first of all. Baldwin stated that, owing to the achievements of modern aviation the frontiers of Great Britain lie not at Dover but on the Rhine. The British Parliament has sanctioned a vast increase in the air force. Last year an expansion of the air forces by 150 per cent was sanctioned. Great Britain has 52 squadrons and 71 more squadrons are to be formed.

France also was obliged to react to the development of German aviation. She supplemented her budget by an additional vote of 1,000,000,000 francs for the development of her air fleet.

Intense aviation development is also taking place in other countries bordering on our frontiers.

We observe in certain states, in Finland, for instance, an increase in the number of aerodromes, which is in excess of the requirements of the Finnish air fleet.

Germany is making great efforts to develop her artillery. General Spears of the British army declared last March in Parliament that according to available information German industry was producing 300 guns a month and that this figure was to be raised to 500 in the immediate future. I think the figures quoted by General Spears are not far from the mark.

Germany is not only intensively arming her infantry and cavalry units, but is creating a powerful tank force. According to data relating to the production of guns and certain other data which appeared in the world press, we may expect a production in Germany of no less than 200 tanks a month.

The program for the creation of 12 army corps and 36 divisions is being carried out at a feverish speed and far more rapidly than was at first intended. Attention must also be directed to the fact that this armed force consists very largely of regulars, and this means that the German army will be always prepared to carry out unexpected invasions. Its power of mobilization is very great. This fully corresponds with the statements made by General von Seeckt, the former chief of the Reichswehr. I should add to this that, with the object of increasing her ability to carry out sudden attacks, Germany is practising mass transfers of troops both by automobile and rail. For this purpose advantage is taken of the various fascist holidays and celebrations, which are also designed to facilitate preparations for war.

During the National-Socialist Party Congress held in Nuremberg from September 9 to September 18 last year, the Germans transferred 850,000 men to Nuremberg, utilizing 532 trains for this purpose. How intense this transfer of units was is shown by the following figures: on the outbreak of the war, in 1914, troop trains were dispatched to the French frontier on 13 railway lines at a rate of 40 trains per day on each line. During the war the intensity of these transfers reached 60 trains a day on each line. In the case of Nuremberg celebrations the transfers were as follows: on September 12 and 13, 140 trains arrived at Nuremberg each day. On September 17, 179 trains left Nuremberg. It should be mentioned, in addition, that certain military maneuvers were also going on in the vicinity of Nuremberg, which entailed additional movements of troops.

Similar exercises were observed during the celebrations of the harvest festival on October 6 last year at Mt. Bueckberg, to which 300,000 men were transported in the course of 12 hours, requiring 160 trains for the purpose.

Preparations no less intense and, I should say, even more noticeable, are being made in the case of automobile transport. This is proceeding, first, in the direction of building super-highways, that is to say, perfected roads which are free of intersecting roads and which provide tremendous opportunities for uninterrupted and unobstructed movements of troops. Plans have been drawn up for the construction of 7,000 kilometers of super-highways in the next few years. Three super-highways will run from West to East. Three thousand kilometers of motor way were in course of construction in the autumn of 1935. The first few hundred kilometers are already in operation. Three and a half billion marks have been assigned for this purpose, and about 30 per cent of this sum has already been spent.

If alongside of this you bear in mind that a motor corps of National-Socialists has been formed with 150,000 automobiles at its disposal, which carries on systematic training in mass transfers of men, you will understand the significance of this in case of war. At one time this corps concentrated 200,000 men at Tempelhof in the course of 17 hours. The automobile corps will, of course, play a tremendous role in a period of strategical concentration.

Germany's efforts in creating a powerful military force on land and in the air are being supplemented by an intense development of her naval forces. Since the conclusion of the agreement on naval armaments between Great Britain and Germany the latter has been laying down a large number of vessels, and by 1937 the size of her navy is to be double that of 1935. But this will be only half of what is provided for in the program.

One's attention is particularly drawn to the fact that Germany is now building vessels which she was forbidden to build under the Versailles Treaty. That treaty permitted her to build battleships of not more than 10,000 tons displacement, but now it is intended to build battleships up to 26,000 tons; formerly she was allowed to build cruisers of 6,000 tons, now 10,000 tons; destroyers correspondingly—800 tons and 1,650 tons. Formerly, Germany was not allowed to build submarines; she is building them now. Formerly, Germany was not allowed to build airplane carriers; she is building them now.

Such, comrades, are the vast preparations being made by the German militarists for war on land and sea and in the air which, considering the political views of the National-Socialists referred to by Comrade Molotov, cannot but compel us to pay serious attention to the protection of our Western frontiers, in order to create the necessary degree of defense.

The position is just as serious on our Far Eastern frontiers. The process here is of older date, and Japanese imperialism each year presents us with new proofs that its intentions are far from peaceful.

Today's *Pravda* prints extracts from an article by Sudzuki Mosaburo, a Japanese economist. This economist deals with the growth of the Japanese budget from 1931 to 1935, and we find that the appropriations for the development of airplane construction increased fivefold, and for the development of certain forms of artillery threefold. Appropriations for field artillery increased more than tenfold, and so on. This economist states that if the development of the Japanese munitions industry continues at the present rate it will definitely land Japan in war.

Today's *Pravda,* too, gives the contents of an article by a prominent commissary in the Japanese Ministry of War, Sigetomi, who says that the Japanese army must prepare for a protracted war and states that, in particular, preparations must be made to accustom Japanese soldiers to eat the food of Mongolia and Siberia, since the Japanese soldier is not accustomed to such a diet. Sigetomi openly speaks of a war of conquest and openly threatens the Soviet Union.

The development of the air force, artillery and tanks is proceeding at an extremely rapid rate in Japan. Even more significant are the preparations in the sphere of railway construction in Manchuria. It will be clear to anybody who glances at the map of Manchuria that it is not from economic considerations that railways are being constructed in that country. The railway construction is of a purely strategical character and is intended to facilitate attack on our Far East. The Japanese built 280 kilometers of railway line in Manchuria in 1932, 500 kilometers in 1933, 900 kilometers in 1934 and 1,200 kilometers in 1935. In addition, over 1,000 kilometers of railway line are still in the course of construction.

The development of Japanese naval forces is progressing extremely rapidly. The Japanese have replaced their navy during the past few years. Their first program, drawn up in 1930, is already almost completed, and they have already begun work on a second naval program.

The situation that has arisen both on our Eastern and Western frontiers has necessitated a most serious revision of our defensive measures. We are still in a situation in which we must be prepared for simultaneous and absolutely independent defense on both fronts, fronts which are 10,000 kilometers apart. But to this has been added the necessity of considerably increasing our permanent military preparedness, which has found expression in the energetic adoption of an enlarged form of the regular army system for infantry and other formations. There was also the necessity of further developing our armed forces in general. There has been considerable growth in our Western frontiers as well compared with former years.

J. F. C. FULLER
(1878–1966)

General J. F. C. Fuller, who had fought in the South African War and in India, became chief general staff officer of the newly formed British Tank Corps, whose potential was as yet unknown, in 1916. The surprise counterattack he organized at Cambrai in 1917 was the world's first notable tank engagement. After the war, Fuller taught at the British Staff College, where in 1926 he was made assistant to the chief instructor. Fuller left the army in 1930 in order to devote himself to writing about military affairs. At Hitler's invitation, he attended German maneuvers in 1936. He was one of the earliest advocates of mechanized force, which once again made the breakthrough and mobile warfare possible. His numerous books include Armament and History *(New York: Scribner, 1945) and* The Decisive Battles of the Western World *(3 vols.; London: Eyre & Spottiswoode, 1954–56).*

TANK WARFARE

The Influence of Tanks on Tactics

Tactics, or the art of moving armed men on the battlefield, change according to the weapons used and the means of transportation. Each new or improved weapon or method of movement demands a corresponding change in the art of war, and to-day the introduction of the tank entirely revolutionises this art in that:

From J. F. C. Fuller, *Memoirs of an Unconventional Soldier* (London: I. Nicholson and Watson, 1936), excerpted in *The Sword and the Pen: Selections from the World's Greatest Military Writings*, edited by Adrian Liddell Hart (New York: Thomas Y. Crowell, 1976). Reprinted by permission.

(i) It increases mobility by replacing muscular by mechanical power.

(ii) It increases security by using armour plate to cut out the bullet.

(iii) It increases offensive power by relieving the soldier from having to carry his weapons, and the horse from having to haul them, and it multiplies the destructive power of weapons by increasing ammunition supply.

Consequently, petrol enables an army to obtain greater effect from its weapons, in a given time and with less loss to itself than an army which relies upon muscular energy. Whilst securing a man dynamically, it enables him to fight statically; consequently, it super-imposes naval upon land tactics; that is, it enables men to discharge their weapons from a moving platform protected by a fixed shield.

The Influence of Tanks on Strategy

Strategy is woven upon communications; hitherto upon roads, railways, rivers and canals. To-day the introduction of a cross-country petrol-driven machine, tank or tractor, has expanded communications to include at least 75 per cent of the theatre of war over and above communications as we at present know them. The possibility to-day of maintaining supply and of moving weapons and munitions over the open, irrespective of roads and without the limiting factor of animal endurance, introduces an entirely new problem in the history of war. At the moment he who grasps the full meaning of this change, namely, that the earth has now become as easily traversable as the sea, multiplies his chances of victory to an almost unlimited extent. Every principle of war becomes easy to apply if movement can be accelerated and accelerated at the expense of the opposing side. To-day, to pit an overland mechanically moving army against one relying on roads, rails and muscular energy is to pit a fleet of modern battleships against one of wind-driven three-deckers. The result of such an action is not even within the possibilities of doubt; the latter will for a certainty be destroyed, for the highest form of machinery must win, because it saves time and time is the controlling factor in war.

The Present Tank Tactical Theory

Up to the present the theory of the tactical employment of tanks has been based on trying to harmonise their powers with existing methods of fighting, that is, with infantry and artillery tactics. In fact, the tank idea, which carries with it a revolution in the methods of waging war, has been grafted on to a system it is destined to destroy, in place of being given free scope to develop on its own lines. This has been unavoidable, because of the novelty of the idea, the uncertainty of the machine and ignorance in its use.

Knowledge can best be gained by practical experience, and at first this experience is difficult to obtain unless the new idea is grafted to the old system of war. Nevertheless, it behoves us not to forget that the tank (a weapon as different from those which preceded it as the armoured knight was from the unarmoured infantry who preceded him) will eventually, as perfection is gained and numbers are increased, demand a fundamental change in our tactical theory of battle.

The facts upon which this theory is based are now rapidly changing, and unless it changes with them, we shall not develop to the full the powers of the new machine; that is, the possibility of moving rapidly in all directions with comparative immunity to small-arm fire.

From this we can deduce the all-important fact that infantry, as at present equipped, will become first a subsidiary and later on a useless arm on all ground over which tanks can move. This fact alone revolutionises our present conception of war, and introduces a new epoch in tactics.

The Strategical Objective

Irrespective of the arm employed, the principles of strategy remain immutable, changes in weapons affecting their application only. The first of all strategical principles is "the principle of the object," the object being "the destruction of the enemy's fighting strength." This can be accomplished in several ways, the normal being the destruction of the enemy's field armies—his fighting personnel.

Now, the potential fighting strength of a body of men lies in its organisation; consequently, if we can destroy this organisation, we shall destroy its fighting strength and so have gained our object.

There are two ways of destroying an organisation:

(i)   By wearing it down (dissipating it).
(ii) By rendering it inoperative (unhinging it).

In war the first comprises the killing, wounding, capturing and disarming of the enemy's soldiers—body warfare. The second, the rendering inoperative of his power of command—brain warfare. Taking a single man as an example: the first method may be compared to a succession of slight wounds which will eventually cause him to bleed to death; the second—a shot through the brain.

The brains of an army are its Staff—Army, Corps and Divisional Head-quarters. Could we suddenly remove these from an extensive sector of the German front, the collapse of the personnel they control would be a mere matter of hours, even if only slight opposition were put up against it. Even if we put up no opposition at all, but in addition to the shot through the brain we fire a second shot through the stomach, that is, we dislocate the enemy's supply system behind his protective front, his men will starve to death or scatter.

Our present theory, based on our present weapons, weapons of limited range of action, has been one of attaining our strategical object by brute force; that is, the wearing away of the enemy's muscles, bone and blood. To accomplish this rapidly with tanks will demand many thousands of these machines, and there is little likelihood of our obtaining the requisite number by next year; therefore let us search for some other means, always remembering that probably, at no time in the history of war, has a difficulty arisen the solution of which has not at the time in question existed in some man's head, and frequently in those of several. The main difficulty has nearly always lurked, not in the solution itself, but in its acceptance by those who have vested interests in the existing methods.

As our present theory is to destroy "personnel," so should our new theory be to destroy "command," not after the enemy's personnel has been disorganised, but before it has been attacked, so that it may be found in a state of complete disorganisation when attacked. Here we have the highest application of the principle of surprise—surprise by novelty of action, or the impossibility of establishing security even when the unexpected has become the commonplace.

The Suggested Solution

In order to render inoperative the Command of the German forces on any given front, what are the requirements?

From the German front line the average distance to nine of their Army Headquarters is eighteen miles; to three Army Group Headquarters forty-five miles; and the distance away of their Western G.H.Q. is one hundred miles. For purposes of illustration the eighteen-mile belt or zone containing Army, Corps and Divisional Headquarters will prove sufficient.

Before reaching these Headquarters elaborate systems of trenches and wire entanglements, protected by every known type of missile-throwing weapon, have to be crossed.

To penetrate or avoid this belt of resistance, which may be compared to a shield protecting the system of command, two types of weapons suggest themselves:

(i)   The aeroplane.
(ii) The tank.

The first is able to surmount all obstacles; the second to traverse most.

The difficulties in using the first are very great; for even if landing-grounds can be found close to the various Headquarters, once the men are landed, they are no better armed than the men they will meet; in fact, they may be compared to dismounted cavalry facing infantry.

The difficulties of the second are merely relative. At present we do not possess a tank capable of carrying out the work satisfactorily, yet this is no reason why we should not have one nine months hence if all energies are devoted to design and production. The idea of such a tank exists, and it has already been considered by many good brains; it is known as the "medium D tank," and its specifications are as follows:

(i)   To move at a maximum speed of 20 miles an hour.
(ii)   To possess a circuit of action of 150 to 200 miles.
(iii) To be able to cross a 13- to 14-foot gap.
(iv)   To be sufficiently light to cross ordinary road, river and canal bridges.

The Tactics of the Medium D Tank

The tactics of the Medium D tank are based on the principles of movement and surprise, its tactical object being to accentuate surprise by movement, not so much through rapidity as by creating unexpected situations. We must never do what the enemy expects us to do; instead, we must mislead him, that is, control his brain by our own. We must suggest to him the probability of certain actions, and then, when action is demanded, we must develop it in a way diametrically opposite to the one we have suggested through our preparations.

Thus, in the past, when we massed men and guns opposite a given sector, he did the same and frustrated our attack by making his own defenses so strong that we could not break through them, or if we did, were then too exhausted to exploit our initial success. At the battle of Cambrai, when our normal method was set aside, our blow could not be taken advantage of, because the forces which broke through were not powerful enough to cause more than local disorganisation. The enemy's strength was not in his front line, but in rear of it; we could not, in the circumstances which we had not created, disorganise his reserves. Reserves are the capital of victory.

A study of Napoleon's tactics will show us that the first step he took in battle was not to break his enemy's front, and then when his forces were disorganised risk being hit by the enemy's reserves; but instead to draw the enemy's reserves into the fire fight, and directly they were drawn in to break through them or envelop them. Once this was done, security was gained; consequently, a pursuit could be carried out, a pursuit being more often then not initiated by troops disorganised by victory against troops disorganised by defeat.

BASIL LIDDELL HART
(1895–1970)

Basil Liddell Hart fought as a British infantry officer during World War I, was gassed on the Western front, and retired from the army in 1927. He proved to be an inestimable military historian; with J. F. C. Fuller, he belonged to the younger school that advocated mechanized force. He was the author of important books on the two world wars and a book on Strategy, the Indirect Approach *(New York: Praeger, 1954), which he identifies as the key to the victories of the great generals of history. At a time when frontal attack was universally favored, Liddell Hart's interpretation (notably of Britain's military history) had the enormous merit of reminding people of the importance of the strategy of indirect approach.*

THE STRATEGY OF INDIRECT APPROACH

The perfection of strategy would be, therefore, to produce a decision without any serious fighting. History, as we have seen, provides examples where strategy, helped by favourable conditions, has virtually produced such a result—among the examples being Caesar's Ilerda campaign, Cromwell's Preston campaign, Napoleon's Ulm campaign, Moltke's encirclement of MacMahon's army at Sedan in 1870, and Allenby's 1918 encirclement of the Turks in the hills of Samaria. The most striking and catastrophic of recent examples was the way that, in 1940, the Germans cut off and trapped the Allies' left wing in Belgium, following Guderian's surprise breakthrough in the centre at Sedan, and thereby ensured the general collapse of the Allied armies on the Continent.

From B. H. Liddell Hart, *The Decisive Wars of History* (1929), reprinted as *Strategy: The Indirect Approach* (London: Faber and Faber, 1954). Reproduced by permission of David Higham Associates.

While these were cases where the destruction of the enemy's armed forces was economically achieved through their disarming by surrender, such "destruction" may not be essential for a decision, and for the fulfilment of the war-aim. In the case of a state that is seeking, not conquest, but the maintenance of its security, the aim is fulfilled if the threat be removed—if the enemy is led to abandon his purpose.

The defeat which Belisarius incurred at Sura through giving rein to his troops' desire for a "decisive victory"—after the Persians had already given up their attempted invasion of Syria—was a clear example of unnecessary effort and risk. By contrast, the way that he defeated their more dangerous later invasion and cleared them out of Syria, is perhaps the most striking example on record of achieving a decision—in the real sense, of fulfilling the national object—by pure strategy. For in this case, the psychological action was so effective that the enemy surrendered his purpose without any physical action at all being required.

While such bloodless victories have been exceptional, their rarity enhances rather than detracts from their value—as an indication of latent potentialities, in strategy and grand strategy. Despite many centuries' experience of war, we have hardly begun to explore the field of psychological warfare.

It rests normally with the government, responsible for the grand strategy of a war, to decide whether strategy should make its contribution by achieving a military decision or otherwise. Just as the military means is only one of the means to the end of grand strategy—one of the instruments in the surgeon's case—so battle is only one of the means to the end of strategy. If the conditions are suitable, it is usually the quickest in effect, but if the conditions are unfavourable it is folly to use it.

Let us assume that a strategist is empowered to seek a military decision. His responsibility is to seek it under the most advantageous circumstances in order to produce the most profitable result. Hence his true aim is not so much to seek battle as to seek a strategic situation so advantageous that if it does not of itself produce the decision, its continuation by a battle is sure to achieve this. In other words, dislocation is the aim of strategy; its sequel may be either the enemy's dissolution or his easier disruption in battle. Dissolution may involve some partial measure of fighting, but this has not the character of a battle.

How is the strategic dislocation produced? In the physical, or "logistical," sphere it is the result of a move which (*a*) upsets the enemy's dispositions and, by compelling a sudden "change of front," dislocates the distribution and organization of his forces; (*b*) separates his forces; (*c*) endangers his supplies;

(*d*) menaces the route or routes by which he could retreat in case of need and reestablish himself in his base or homeland.

A dislocation may be produced by one of these effects, but is more often the consequence of several. Differentiation, indeed, is difficult because a move directed towards the enemy's rear tends to combine these effects. Their respective influence, however, varies and has varied throughout history according to the size of armies and the complexity of their organization.

In the psychological sphere, dislocation is the result of the impression on the commander's mind of the physical effects which we have listed. The impression is strongly accentuated if his realization of his being at a disadvantage is *sudden,* and if he feels that he is unable to counter the enemy's move. Psychological dislocation fundamentally springs from this sense of being trapped.

This is the reason why it has most frequently followed a physical move on the enemy's rear. An army, like a man, cannot properly defend its back from a blow without turning round to use its arms in the new direction. "Turning" temporarily unbalances an army as it does a man, and with the former the period of instability is inevitably much longer. In consequence, the brain is much more sensitive to any menace to its back.

In contrast, to move directly on an opponent consolidates his balance, physical and psychological, and by consolidating it increases his resisting power. For in the case of an army it rolls the enemy back towards their reserves, supplies, and reinforcements, so that as the original front is driven back and worn thin, new layers are added to the back. At the most, it imposes a strain rather than producing a shock.

Thus a move round the enemy's front against his rear has the aim not only of avoiding resistance on its way but in its issue. In the profoundest sense, it takes the *line of least resistance.* The equivalent in the psychological sphere is the *line of least expectation.* They are the two faces of the same coin, and to appreciate this is to widen our understanding of strategy. For if we merely take what obviously appears the line of least resistance, its obviousness will appeal to the opponent also; and this line may no longer be that of least resistance.

In studying the physical aspect we must never lose sight of the psychological, and only when both are combined is the strategy truly an indirect approach, calculated to dislocate the opponent's balance.

The mere action of marching indirectly towards the enemy and on to the rear of his dispositions does not constitute a strategic indirect approach. Strategic art is not so simple. Such an approach may start by being indirect in relation to the enemy's front, but by the very directness of its progress towards his rear may allow him to change his dispositions, so that it soon becomes a direct approach to his new front.

Because of the risk that the enemy may achieve such a change of front, it is usually necessary for the dislocating move to be preceded by a move, or moves, which can best be defined by the term "distract" in its literal sense of "to draw asunder." The purpose of this "distraction" is to deprive the enemy of his freedom of action, and it should operate in both the physical and psychological spheres. In the physical, it should cause a distension of his forces or their diversion to unprofitable ends, so that they are too widely distributed, and too committed elsewhere, to have the power of interfering with one's own decisively intended move. In the psychological sphere, the same effect is sought by playing upon the fears of, and by deceiving, the opposing command.

Superior weight at the intended decisive point does not suffice unless that point cannot be reinforced *in time* by the opponent. It rarely suffices unless that point is not merely weaker numerically but has been weakened morally. Napoleon suffered some of his worst checks because he neglected this guarantee—and the need for distraction has grown with the delaying power of weapons.

A deeper truth to which Foch and other disciples of Clausewitz did not penetrate fully is that in war every problem, and every principle, is a duality. Like a coin, it has two faces. Hence the need for a well-calculated compromise as a means to reconciliation. This is the inevitable consequence of the fact that war is a two-party affair, so imposing the need that while hitting one must guard. Its corollary is that, in order to hit with effect, the enemy must be taken off his guard. Effective concentration can only be obtained when the opposing forces are dispersed; and, usually, in order to ensure this, one's own forces must be widely distributed. Thus, by an outward paradox, true concentration is the product of dispersion.

A further consequence of the two-party condition is that to ensure reaching an objective one should have alternative objectives. Herein lies a vital contrast to the single-minded nineteenth century doctrine of Foch and his fellows—a contrast of the practical to the theoretical. For if the enemy is certain as to your point of aim he has the best possible chance of guarding himself—and blunting your weapon. If, on the other hand, you take a line that threatens alternative objectives, you distract his mind and forces. This, moreover, is the most economic method of distraction, for it allows you to keep the largest proportion of your force available on your real line of operation—thus reconciling the greatest possible concentration with the necessity of dispersion.

The absence of an alternative is contrary to the very nature of war. It sins against the light which Bourcet shed in the eighteenth century by his most penetrating dictum that "every plan of campaign ought to have several branches and to have been so well thought out that one or other of the said branches cannot fail of success." This was the light that his military heir, the young

Napoleon Bonaparte, followed in seeking always, as he said, to *"faire son thème en deux façons* [Do your task twice over]." Seventy years later Sherman was to relearn the lesson from experience, by reflection, and to coin his famous maxim about "putting the enemy on the horns of a dilemma." In any problem where an opposing force exists, and cannot be regulated, one must foresee and provide for alternative courses. Adaptability is the law which governs survival in war as in life—war being but a concentrated form of the human struggle against environment.

RAOUL CASTEX
(1878–1968)

The French admiral Raoul Castex first served in the Far East, where he saw the rise of Japan as a threat (1905). He became a commander in 1918 and commanded French aviation in the eastern Mediterranean until the end of World War I. Between 1926 and 1928, he was director of the Centre des hautes études navales. Between 1929 and 1935, he published his major work, Théories stratégiques *(6 vols.). Castex's views on geography and strategy are striking. He helped to create the* Collège des hautes études de défense nationale *in 1937 and was in charge of its courses until World War II. As commander-in-chief of maritime forces in the north, he expressed his disagreement as to the measures to be taken to deal with the situation in the Dunkirk sector. He was then placed on the reserve list.*

THE SIGNIFICANCE AND LIMITS
OF GEOGRAPHY

How geography has affected Russia depends on whether one is looking at offense or defense.

Defensively, nature made of Russia, or rather Russian Eurasia, a vast land mass, a supercontinental state provided with more or less everything it needed. From the angle of maintaining maritime communications, it has been relatively independent of hostile naval domination; its soil being deemed to be adequately protected, it was not accessible to any pressure from the sea. That was a considerable advantage in the area of naval and economic warfare.

As regards land war, [European] Russia has not been equipped with great physical obstacles, such as mountains, large lakes, or inland seas, and possesses

From Raoul Castex, "La Géographie," supplement to *Théories strategiques,* vol. 3, *Mélanges strategiques* (Paris: Académie de marine, 1976), pt. 2. Translated from the French by A. M. Berrett.

only a few large rivers, but it has derived considerable protection from its very size. Anyone seeking to overrun or invade it has had to face great distances, as well as the need to hold vast areas in his rear. Russia has demanded a great and exhausting effort of such an invader. In addition, territory here generally has less value than for other nations, and so the Russian defender could give up more to preserve his forces, and thus his room for maneuver was enhanced.

But a few reservations are in order. First (and it is a point to which we shall return), this aspect of things has been substantially changed in our time as a result of the considerable development of motorization. Again, the territory was not homogeneous: some parts of it were much more important than others, be it politically, industrially, or economically. They could not be treated merely as simple space, and they required a particular sort of defense that ruled out indefinite and systematic withdrawal. Finally, the precarious state of transportation and the low density of the rail and road network, which were notorious weaknesses of the country, meant that, for the maneuvers that it necessarily had to carry out, Russian defensive strategy itself suffered greatly from the large size of the national territory. Russia was as much the victim as the beneficiary of its size.

In the area of air defense, Russian vulnerability was low, a result not so much of distance (which was not in itself enough, given the range of action already attained by airplanes by 1940), as of the fact that the territory was so spread out, and the really sensitive and valuable points so few and far between. Here surface ruled everything. The country was like a gelatinous, amorphous mass, like an invertebrate, acephalous mollusc. An attacker from the air had inevitably to repeat the experience of Napoleon in 1812. The bombardment of Moscow brought him no more than the emperor had achieved from his occupation by land. A basic notion, always observed, was simply rediscovered from the air. Added to that is the feature that, of two neighboring countries, at equal distance by air from each other, the larger (Russia) is closer to the smaller (Germany), the whole of whose territory lies within its reach, than the smaller is to the larger, a large part of which is beyond its reach. Similarly, for other reasons, in the 1939–45 war, Germany was closer to England than England was to Germany, while the United States was closer to Germany than Germany was to America, and, thanks to its positions in Asia, closer to Japan than Japan was to it.

As regards offense, there is little to say about the land aspect except to stress how much Russia was hampered by geography here too—that is, by the great distances inadequately mastered as a result of poor transportation.

As regards naval war, offensives by sea, and, more generally, overseas political and military expansion, Russia was greatly hindered by several disadvantages.

First, the mediocrity of the instrument most necessary here, its fleet. In fact, this inferiority was not a matter of geography. But geography must be brought in, because it was, relative to the element of "forces," so important in modifying the influence of geography alone. It must also come in to illustrate once again the inaccuracy, in terms of offense, of the Soviet aphorism "Mastery of the seas is a bourgeois idea," which we have criticized before. This formula was radically false, even in the case of Russia, in the area of offensive-type external actions. In this regard, the country could not be uninterested in command of the sea, as it could when it was simply a matter of defense.

Second, in the more specifically geographical domain, for an offensive overseas, Russia suffered from having only bases and positions that were poorly sited in relation to the major areas of competition, the open ocean spaces, and its own center of power. Some were in the Baltic or the Black Sea, in closed basins controlled by other nations; others in peripheral regions like the Arctic Ocean or the far east of Siberia, whose remoteness prevented land power, weakened by distance, from backing up sea power as it ought to.

In modern times, Soviet Russia had deeply felt the impact of these two weaknesses, of forces and geography, at the time of the Spanish Civil War (1936–39). Russia had been unable adequately to ensure its ideological influence at the other end of Europe, sustain its Spanish co-religionists, and carry through its great plan for communism to take the West from the rear, because this offensive was almost totally maritime in character and was terribly handicapped in this respect in terms of both forces and geography.

Insularity

Technological advances have greatly enhanced the speed and range of action of vehicles and machines, as well as their independence of the elements. They also affect another geographical factor: the celebrated [state of] "insularity." Once upon a time, this had major strategic consequences, which now only exist when new conditions of space, very different from the old ones, come about.

Until our own day, England enjoyed this privilege of insularity. Given the domination of the seas that it had secured for itself, insularity gave it virtually total immunity from external attacks directed at its territory. It is to date the prototypical example of insularity, with all its military consequences.

This situation altered drastically when an enemy was established on the continental coast facing the island. The 1939–45 war proved that, and it was easily predictable. Continental air power, setting off from bases that were sufficiently close, had the whole of England within range—territory that had for so long been free of threat. Moreover, it also intervened very effectively against British sea communications, gravely compromising them. Submarines had similar capacities. Some surface vessels, such as small torpedo boats or launches could be used advantageously over these short distances and dangerously threaten the traffic through the waters south of the British Isles. [Hitler's] landing flotillas were no longer made up of lighters and gunboats like their predecessors [Napoleon's] at Boulogne; they had vessels enabling them to accomplish rapid crossings, easy landings, and tactical surprises, which gave a hostile land force an ease of movement that it had never possessed before.

In short, the vulnerability of the land [to attack], especially by way of the air, had increased in these changed times; England no longer enjoyed its peaceful insularity of the past. The distance separating it from the source of a continental attack had become too small, given the enemy's capacity. From this perspective, Great Britain's [geographic] situation in the twentieth century was scarcely better than that of Sicily, or the islands of Zeeland and Frisia, or the Channel Islands had once been. . . . A comparison of the distances involved in the two cases clearly shows what changes had occurred for England despite the fact that the geographical situation remained unchanged.

The sole remedy that can be used in such circumstances to recover the insularity of old is to increase the distances, to measure them against the enhanced mobility of the attacking craft and enlarge them in the same proportion. Something like the ocean must now be put between the continental threat and oneself to restore the physical protection and security of other days.

Thus the British Empire as a whole, and not simply Great Britain taken alone, for the time being enjoyed the insularity from which the original metropolitan core had benefited in bygone days. If we broaden the term widely, in its military sense, and regard a country as insular, *in the case of a specific war*, when it is very difficult or impossible to attack it by land, and when the enemy can only reach it by sea at the cost of a large-scale operation, requiring complete and prolonged control of the seas, then Canada, India, South Africa, Australia, and most British colonies were in effect insular in the conflict between England and its enemies in the years following 1939, and these countries were as protected as a result, at least until Japan entered the war, as the metropole was in the time of Cromwell or Nelson.

It was this virtually insular system that England made use of against its continental enemy, extending its rear, and the base of its resistance to the farthest reaches of the globe, to regions absolutely unassailable (so long as Japan remained outside the war) thanks to a surface naval superiority that had recovered its earlier advantages and was fully operational in this new framework, with no or almost no threat from the air. With that combination, the British Empire took the place of the British Isles. These were now no more than a forward outpost of the system, a segment of the front—to be revictualed, like any other forward element, with what was strictly necessary to sustain the struggle, and to be relieved by evacuation to the rear overseas of all impedimenta, everything unnecessary or valuable. The fall of that position, thus understood, would not have been a mortal danger for the rest, which could have held out indefinitely. The enemy was faced with an offensive problem just as insoluble as the one Napoleon had run up against in his geographical situation and with the means of his time. It was not enough for this enemy to conquer London, as under the First Empire; he also had to take Ottawa, the Cape [of Good Hope], Melbourne, and many other places.

Later, the incorporation of the United States into the arrangement completed it and broadened its base and defensive power. This is because, in our time, and in the particular case that arose, only countries like the United States were the heirs and possessors of true insularity in relation to the continental European enemy. That was where that insularity had taken refuge. The "Island," the "vast little island" of ages past, the nightmare of Napoleon's strategy, was now the whole American continent. To overcome it, the enemy had in addition to master the whole of that continent. And when it was said, as it was during that war, that the center of gravity of the Anglo-Saxon world had shifted from London to Washington, that was simply expressing the political repercussion of factors of material power, it is true, but also of the new fact that had arisen in the area of insularity, a geographical factor in war, under the impact of the profound transformation that technology had undergone. If in our times, the pole of sea power is now in Washington, that of land power is undeniably in Moscow, the United States and Russia being respectively the heirs, on vastly increased scales, of England and the European troublemaker of old, opposed to each other by the permanent conflict that already divided their predecessors and that meant that 1914 was already present in embryo in the frictions that arose between Wellington and Blücher in the midst of victory in 1815.

CHARLES DE GAULLE
(1890–1970)

Charles de Gaulle, the greatest Frenchman of the century, graduated from Saint-Cyr in 1913 and was promoted captain in 1915. He was taken prisoner at Verdun in 1916. He taught at the Ecole de guerre from 1924 to 1925. His unofficial views caused him problems. Marshal Pétain nevertheless had him give lectures at the Ecole, and he was sent on missions to Iraq, Iran, and Egypt. In 1934 he published Vers l'armée de métier *(translated as* The Army of the Future, *1943), a remarkable analysis of the new conditions of war, given the development of mechanized forces and air power.*

De Gaulle vainly advocated the creation of six French armored divisions at a time when in Germany the defeated were rethinking war. His November 1939 report on "the advent of mechanized force," which drew the necessary conclusions from the Polish campaign, was rejected. Yet it was sent to senior political and military figures (26 January 1940). De Gaulle was promoted general, a few months later, and on 6 June 1940, he was named undersecretary of state for war in Paul Raynaud's government. On 18 June, after the Franco-German armistice was signed, de Gaulle launched a call from London to continue the struggle, and on 7 August 1940, Churchill recognized him as leader of Free France. He became head of the provisional government of France in 1944, but resigned in 1946 when his policies were rejected. The Algerian revolt created the conditions for his return to power in 1958. In 1963, in order not to be heavily dependent on the United States in a militarily bipolar world, de Gaulle opted for a French nuclear force de frappe (strike force), and in 1966 he withdrew the French forces from NATO. He was also the author of Le Fil de l'épée *(1932),* La Discorde chez l'ennemi *(1944),* Mémoires de guerre *(3 vols.), and* Discours et Messages *(5 vols.).*

THE ARMY OF THE FUTURE

A weapon for repressive and preventive action—that is what we have to provide for ourselves. A weapon which can exert from the very outset extreme strength, and can hold the enemy in a state of chronic surprise. The internal combustion engine gives the means of satisfying these conditions of ruthlessness and of suddenness, since it will take whatever is required where it is needed and with all speed; provided, of course, that it is well handled.

To-morrow the professional army will move entirely on caterpillar wheels. Every element of troops and services will make its way across mountains and valleys on the appropriate vehicles. Not a man, not a gun, not a shell, not a piece of bread, will be transported in any other way. A large formation, striking camp at daybreak, will be a hundred miles away by night. It will need no more than one hour to come from a distance of ten miles, and across any kind of country, and take up its battle position against the enemy, or to disappear, in breaking off contact, out of range of fire and field-glasses. But this speed would be of little value if it could not be reinforced by such power of fire and assault that the rhythm of battle synchronized with that of movement. What would be the use of moving from place to place so rapidly behind the scenes of the battlefield, only to find oneself subsequently immobilized? But modern technique can solve that problem, thanks to the armoured car. By pursuing this ever-widening path, the stabilization of fronts by picked troops, which warped the last war from the point of view of military art, and, as a consequence, in the subsequent accounts of losses and results, will be avoided.

Six divisions of the line completely motorized and 'caterpillared,' and partly armoured, will constitute an army suitable for carrying through a campaign. It will be an organism whose front, depth and means of protection and supply will allow it to operate independently. Each one of the six larger units will, furthermore, be provided with all that it needs in the way of weapons and supply services to carry on the battle from beginning to end, even if it is encircled by others. One may picture as follows the composition of each division:

A heavily armoured brigade, moving across country as fast as a horse at the gallop, armed with 500 guns of medium calibre, 400 smaller pieces, and 600 machine-guns, crossing ditches three yards wide, climbing mounds thirty feet high, felling 40-year-old trees, knocking down walls twelve bricks wide, crushing all obstacles, barriers and hedge-rows—that is what industry to-day can provide for every professional division. This brigade of two regiments, one of heavy tanks, the other of medium tanks, with a reconnaissance battalion of very fast light machines, provided with improved equipment for liaison, observation and field work, will constitute the principal echelon of the larger unit.

From "The Necessary Modernization," in Charles de Gaulle, *The Army of the Future* (Philadelphia: J. B. Lippincott, 1941), 99–104. Copyright © 1940 by Hutchinson & Co. Ltd. Copyright © 1941 by Harper & Row, Publishers. Copyright renewed 1969 by Mrs. Vyvyan B. Holland. Reprinted by permission of HarperCollins Publishers.

A brigade of infantry consisting of two regiments of infantry and one battalion of riflemen, armed with 40 auxiliary pieces, the same number of anti-tank guns, 600 light and heavy machine-guns, provided with special tools for quickly digging trenches and shelters, equipped, as to clothes, painted sheets, trellises, etc., in such a way as to offer to the sight, and thus to attacks, only unrecognizable objects, will be devoted to the task of occupying, mopping up and organizing the territory which the terrible but temporary power of the tanks will have virtually secured. The mobile, but on the whole haphazard and short-range fire which will be operated in concert by the tanks and the infantry, must be covered, from as far away as possible, by another much more accurate system of fire. This is the task of the artillery, which will have at its disposal, in the division, all the various types of gun necessary for the preparation of attacks, for direct support, for distant or close protection, and for counter-battery work. Two artillery regiments, one consisting of heavy, short guns, the other of lighter long-range pieces, will form another strong unit, completed by an anti-aircraft group, and capable of discharging 100 tons of projectiles in a quarter of an hour, to a depth of six miles beyond the battle-front.

The division, consisting of three complementary brigades, reinforced by a battalion of engineers to deal with crossings and a battalion of communication troops, will have at its disposal a reconnaissance group for scouting purposes. This latter will be composed of very fast whippet tanks, of troops brought up in their train for fighting on foot, and of light vehicles for distant liaison; the whole designed to get into touch with the enemy, to hold a front temporarily, to cover a flank for the time being, to cover a retreat.

Aerial units, not intended for casual tasks at anyone's behest, but having a definite mission of keeping a single, specific general constantly informed, and always supporting the same comrades in battle and lengthening the effective range of familiar artillery, will be the eyes of the main unit.

Nevertheless, in spite of the speed, the protection, the wide dispersal afforded to the fighting troops by motor-vehicles, armed and caterpillared, the mass and the conspicuousness of troops so constituted will remain considerable.

The size of the machines, their noise and their tracks will be such that, without precautions, the enemy will have ample warning of their approach. But it is of paramount importance that he should be taken by surprise. Therefore, methodical camouflage must be put into effect. This art, as old as war, and one which, since the last conflict, has been made use of in many desultory ways, must become an essential element of manœuvre, as important as gunfire or mobility. It is impossible to exaggerate the results which can be achieved in this respect by research and discipline. In particular, the choice of disguise for fighting men and equipment according to the colour of the countryside, the creation of false landscapes and the alteration of the colours of objects considered with regard to distance, position and light are only at their crudest beginning. What about silence, particularly that of motor-engines, which could be obtained, if it was at all desired, by the adequate construction of the machines? What, especially, about smoke-screens, clouds and fogs, whose size, thickness and placing can be adapted to circumstances as required? But to make oneself visible and inaudible is not enough. There still remains the question of deceiving the enemy by means of false road indications, sham columns on the march, deceptive earthworks and lighting effects, artificial noises, misleading wireless messages. Each division will possess a camouflage battalion, specialising in these things, and provided with the necessary means of deceiving the enemy by simulating the presence of a large unit.

A light division will be attached to the ensemble formed by the six divisions of the line, for scouting purposes and to prevent surprise; this will be of the same general type as the others, but provided with faster and consequently more lightly armoured machines, light artillery, and with more mobile infantry, since they will not be armed with the same number of infantry guns. Finally, there will be the general reserves consisting of a brigade of very heavy tanks capable of attacking permanent fortifications, a brigade of artillery of very heavy calibre, a regiment of engineers, a regiment of signallers, a camouflage regiment, a regiment of reconnaissance aircraft, a regiment of riflemen and the usual supply services. These will complete the army of shock-troops.

As compared with the total number of troops that France sent into action in the month of August 1914, this army will possess a firing capacity three times larger, nearly ten times its speed and immeasurably greater degree of protection. When one adds that the whole will normally operate on one tenth of its front and that the professional soldiers get enormously increased results from their equipment, one can gather some idea of the power which the professional army of to-morrow will be able to wield.

WINSTON CHURCHILL
(1874–1965)

*After studying at the Royal Military College, Winston Churchill was
appointed to a cavalry regiment in 1895. He took part in the battle of
Omdurman (Sudan) against the forces of the Mahdi in 1898, and covered
the South African War (1899–1902) as a journalist. He was active thereafter
in British political life and held various cabinet posts. On 13 May 1940, he
became prime minister, making a speech on that occasion that has remained
a legend. Churchill was the very type of the national hero in time of crisis,
and perhaps the last heir of the imperial greatness of the Victorian age. He
was awarded the Nobel Prize for Literature and knighted in 1953.*

"BLOOD, TOIL, TEARS, AND SWEAT"

On Friday evening last I received His Majesty's Commission to form a new
Administration. It was the evident wish and will of Parliament and the nation
that this should be conceived on the broadest possible basis and that it should
include all Parties, both those who supported the late Government and also
the Parties of the Opposition. I have completed the most important part of
this task. A War Cabinet has been formed of five Members, representing, with
the Opposition Liberals, the unity of the nation. The three Party Leaders have
agreed to serve, either in the War Cabinet or in high executive office. The three
Fighting Services have been filled. It was necessary that this should be done in
one single day, on account of the extreme urgency and rigour of events. A number of other key positions were filled yesterday, and I am submitting a further
list to His Majesty tonight. I hope to complete the appointment of the principal Ministers during tomorrow. The appointment of the other Ministers usually takes a little longer, but I trust that, when Parliament meets again, this part

Prime Minister Winston S. Churchill, speech before the House of Commons, 13 May
1940.

of my task will be completed, and that the Administration will be complete in all respects.

I considered it in the public interest to suggest that the House should be summoned to meet today. Mr. Speaker agreed, and took the necessary steps, in accordance with the powers conferred upon him by the Resolution of the House. At the end of the proceedings today, the Adjournment of the House will be proposed until Tuesday, 21st May, with, of course, provision for earlier meeting if need be. The business to be considered during that week will be notified to Members at the earliest opportunity. I now invite the House, by the Resolution which stands in my name, to record its approval of the steps taken and to declare its confidence in the new Government.

To form an Administration of this scale and complexity is a serious undertaking in itself, but it must be remembered that we are in the preliminary stage of one of the greatest battles in history, that we are in action at many points in Norway and in Holland, that we have to be prepared in the Mediterranean, that the air battle is continuous, and that many preparations have to be made here at home. In this crisis I hope I may be pardoned if I do not address the House at any length today. I hope that any of my friends and colleagues, or former colleagues, who are affected by the political reconstruction, will make all allowance for any lack of ceremony with which it has been necessary to act. I would say to the House, as I said to those who have joined this Government: "I have nothing to offer but blood, toil, tears, and sweat."

We have before us an ordeal of the most grievous kind. We have before us many, many long months of struggle and of suffering. You ask, What is our policy? I will say: "It is to wage war, by sea, land and air, with all our might and with all the strength that God can give us: to wage war against a monstrous tyranny, never surpassed in the dark, lamentable catalogue of human crime. That is our policy." You ask, What is our aim? I can answer in one word: Victory—victory at all costs, victory in spite of all terror, victory however long and hard the road may be; for without victory there is no survival. Let that be realized; no survival for the British Empire; no survival for all that the British Empire has stood for; no survival for the urge and impulse of the ages, that mankind will move forward towards its goal. But I take up my task with buoyancy and hope. I feel sure that our cause will not be suffered to fail among men. At this time I feel entitled to claim the aid of all, and I say, "Come, then, let us go forward together with our united strength."

ADOLF HITLER
(1889–1945)

Adolf Hitler was born in Austria. During World War I, he was an infantry corporal. In 1920 he brought into being the National Socialist German Workers' (or Nazi) party. A putsch he organized in Munich with General Erich Ludendorff (1865–1937) failed in 1923. Hitler was sentenced to five years' imprisonment, but served only nine months, during which he wrote Mein Kampf (My Struggle), *a book articulating his ultranationalist, racist ideology. He rose to power democratically in the context of the crisis in 1933 and moved quickly to secure absolute power, including control of the military (1934). Through a bold policy that combined faits accomplis with piecemeal attrition and played on the democratic states' concern for security, he went from success to success between 1936 (remilitarization of the Rhineland) and 1938 (Anschluss with Austria and occupation of part of Czechoslovakia, endorsed by the Munich agreements with France and Britain). After invading Poland in the context of the German-Soviet pact of 1939, Hitler waged victorious campaigns in western Europe, including that against France in the spring of 1940, which were fought creatively with a highly mobile combination of mechanized forces (panzers) and air power (Blitzkrieg). Britain continued to resist, however, and Hitler opened a second front in the east by declaring war on the USSR in 1941, which brought the geostrategic situation back to the one the German high command had been seeking to avoid at the beginning of the century. On 30 April 1945, with the war hopelessly lost, Hitler committed suicide.*

WAR AND COLONIZATION IN THE EAST

27 July 1941

It should be possible for us to control this region to the East with two hundred and fifty thousand men plus a cadre of good administrators. Let's learn from the English, who, with two hundred and fifty thousand men in all, including fifty thousand soldiers, govern four hundred million Indians. This space in Russia must always be dominated by Germans. . . .

We'll take the southern part of the Ukraine, especially the Crimea, and make it an exclusively German colony. There'll be no harm in pushing out the population that's there now. The German colonist will be the soldier-peasant, and for that I'll take professional soldiers, whatever their line may have been previously. . . . The Reich will put at their disposal a completely equipped farm. The soil costs us nothing, we have only the house to build. . . . These soldier-peasants will be given arms, so that at the slightest danger they can be at their posts when we summon them. That's how the ancient Austria used to keep its Eastern peoples under control.

8–11 August 1941

The German colonists ought to live on handsome, spacious farms. The German services will be lodged in marvelous buildings, the governors in palaces. Beneath the shelter of the administrative services, we shall gradually organize all that is indispensable to the maintenance of a certain standard of living. Around the city, to a depth of thirty to forty kilometers, we shall have a belt of handsome villages connected by the best roads. What exists beyond that will be another world, in which we mean to let the Russians live as they like. It is merely necessary that we should rule them. In the event of a revolution, we shall only have to drop a few bombs on their cities, and the affair will be liquidated. Once a year we shall lead a troop of Kirghizes through the capital of the Reich, in order to strike their imaginations with the size of our monuments.

What India was for England, the territories of Russia will be for us.

17–18 September 1941

The struggle for the hegemony of the world will be decided in favor of Europe by the possession of the Russian space. Thus Europe will be an impregnable fortress, safe from all threat of blockade. All this opens up economic vistas which, one might think, will incline the most liberal of the Western democrats towards the New Order.

The essential thing, for the moment, is to conquer. After that everything will be simply a question of organization.

From *Hitler's Secret Conversations, 1941–1944*, edited by H. R. Trevor-Roper, translated by Norman Cameron and R. H. Stevens (New York: Farrar, Straus & Young, 1953). Reprinted by permission of George Weidenfeld & Nicolson Ltd.

When one contemplates this primitive world, one is convinced that nothing will drag it out of its indolence unless one compels the people to work. The Slavs are a mass of born slaves, who feel the need of a master. . . . If left to himself, the Slav would never have emerged from the narrowest of family communities. . . . The Slav peoples are not destined to live a cleanly life. They know it, and we would be wrong to persuade them of the contrary. It was we who, in 1918, created the Baltic countries and the Ukraine. But nowadays we have no interest in maintaining Baltic States, any more than in creating an independent Ukraine. We must likewise prevent them from returning to Christianity. That would be a grave fault, for it would be giving them a form of organization.

I am not a partisan, either, of a university at Kiev. It's better not to teach them to read. They won't love us for tormenting them with schools. Even to give them a locomotive to drive would be a mistake. And what stupidity it would be on our part to proceed to a distribution of land! In spite of that, we'll see to it that the natives live better than they've lived hitherto. We'll find among them the human material that's indispensable for tilling the soil.

We'll supply grain to all in Europe who need it. The Crimea will give us its citrus fruits, cotton and rubber (100,000 acres of plantation would be enough to insure our independence).

The Pripet marshes will keep us supplied with reeds.

We'll supply the Ukrainians with scarves, glass beads and everything that colonial peoples like.

The Germans—this is essential—will have to constitute amongst themselves a closed society, like a fortress. The least of our stable-lads must be superior to any native.

For German youth, this will be a magnificent field of experiment. We'll attract to the Ukraine Danes, Dutch, Norwegians, Swedes. The army will find areas for maneuvers there, and our aviation will have the space it needs.

PROCLAMATION TO THE GERMAN PEOPLE

German men and women! . . .

Since June 22 a battle of decisive importance for the entire world has been raging [the German invasion of the Soviet Union]. Only posterity will clearly recognize both the magnitude and the implications of this event. Only pos-

Adolf Hitler, speech at the Berlin Sportpalast, published in the *Völkischer Beobachter,* 5 October 1941, translated by G. H. Stein.

terity will realize that it marked the beginning of a new era. But even this struggle was not desired by me. . . .

The conspiracy of Democrats, Jews, and Free Masons was responsible for plunging Europe into war two years ago. Arms had to decide.

Since then a struggle has been taking place between truth and lies; and, as always, this war will end in victory for truth. In other words, no matter what lies British propaganda, international world Jewry, and their democratic accomplices may concoct, historical facts will not be changed. And the historical facts are not that the English are in Germany, not that other states have occupied Berlin, not that they have advanced in either the East or the West. Rather, the historical truth is that for the past two years Germany has been defeating one opponent after another. . . .

But in August and September of last year one thing was becoming clear: A showdown with England, which would have tied down the entire German Air Force, was no longer possible; for in my rear stood a state that was daily increasing its preparations for an attack against Germany at such a moment. . . . I finally decided to take the first step myself. When I see an enemy pointing his rifle at me I am not going to wait until he pulls the trigger. I would prefer to be the first to let loose.

Today I can tell you that it was the most difficult decision of my entire life, for such a step always involves risk, and only posterity will know the exact outcome. Thus one can rely only on one's conscience, on the confidence in one's people, on the strength of one's weapons, and, finally—as I have often said— on an appeal to Almighty God that He bless him who is himself ready and willing to fight and make sacrifices for his right to exist.

On the morning of June 22, the greatest battle in the history of the world began. Since then something like three and a half months have elapsed, and I can confirm one thing here today: Everything has gone according to plan. . . . Never during the entire period did we lose the initiative for even one second. On the contrary, right up to the present moment every action has developed just as much according to plan as was formerly the case in the East against Poland, then against Norway, and finally both against the West and in the Balkans. There is one more point I must make in this connection: We have not been mistaken either about the effectiveness of our plans or the efficiency and bravery of our soldiers. Nor have we been mistaken about the quality of our weapons. . . .

The course of this unique event is more or less known to you in outline. Two large army groups thrust forward to break open the center. One of the two flanking groups had the task of advancing against Leningrad; the other to occupy the Ukraine. These first tasks have been substantially completed. During this period of great and decisive struggle, the enemy often asked, "Why is nothing happening?" Well, something was happening all the time. It was precisely because something was happening that we could not speak.

If I were the British Prime Minister today, I would, under the circumstances, also imagine that peace reigned; for in fact nothing is happening over there. And that is precisely the difference. . . . We could not counter the enemy's claims, not because we did not sufficiently appreciate the constantly outstanding achievements of our soldiers, but because we did not want to give the enemy information which he—with his miserable intelligence service—would only find out about days, or even weeks, later. . . .

A German Armed Forces communiqué is a truthful report, even if some stupid British newspaper jerk [*Lümmel*] declares that it must first be confirmed. German Armed Forces communiqués have been thoroughly confirmed in the past.

There is after all no doubt that it was not the Poles but we who were victorious in Poland, although the British press reported it the other way around. There is also no doubt that we are sitting in Norway, and not the English. Nor is there any doubt that we were successful in Belgium and Holland, and not the British. There is also no doubt that Germany defeated France, and not the other way around. And finally, there is no doubt that we are in Greece, and once again not the British or the New Zealanders. And not they, but we are the victors. Thus the German army communiqués spoke the truth. . . .

And it is not different in the East now. According to the British version we have suffered one defeat after another for the last three months; yet we are 1,000 kilometers beyond our own frontiers; we are east of Smolensk; we are before Leningrad; we are on the Black Sea; we are near the Crimea—and the Russians are nowhere near the Rhine. Therefore, if the Russians have been continuously victorious they have made poor use of their victories, for after each of their victories they immediately marched back 100 or 200 kilometers— evidently to lure us deep into the area.

In addition, the following figures attest to the magnitude of this battle. . . . The number of Russian prisoners has now risen to roughly 2,500,000. The number of captured or destroyed artillery pieces in our hands is around 22,000. The number of captured or destroyed tanks in our possession amounts to over 18,000. The number of aircraft destroyed on the ground or shot down is over 14,500. And behind our troops lies an area of Russian territory twice as large as the German Reich at the time I took over its leadership in 1933, or four times as large as Great Britain.

German soldiers have covered 800 to 1,000 kilometers. This is as the crow flies! The distance they had to march on the ground is often one and a half or two times as great. All this on a fighting front of gigantic length, and against an enemy that, I must say, consists not of human beings but of animals or beasts. . . . And against this cruel, bestial, and animal-like opponent, armed with powerful weapons, our soldiers have won mighty victories. I cannot think of any words that would do justice to their performance. What they are continually achieving by their boldness, bravery, and immeasurable efforts cannot even be imagined. . . .

The events that I have spoken to you about here today have led me, an old National Socialist, to one inescapable conclusion. We are confronted by two extreme systems. One consists of the capitalist states, who by lies and trickery deny their people their natural rights, and who care only about their financial interests—for the preservation of which they are always prepared to sacrifice the lives of millions of human beings. On the other hand we have the communist extreme: a state that has brought indescribable misery to millions and a doctrine that would sacrifice everyone else to the same fate. In my opinion this imposes on us only one duty: to strive more than ever to fulfill our National Socialist ideals. For we must be clear on one point: When this war is finally over, it will be the German soldier who has won it; the German soldier who has come from the farm and factory, who really represents the masses of our nation.

It will have been won by the German homeland, with millions of male and female workers and farmers; it will have been won by the creative people in the offices and in the professions. All these millions of creative German people will have won it. And it is exclusively on these people that this state must be aligned in the future. . . .

Only when the entire German people becomes a single community of sacrifice [*Opfergemeinschaft*] can we hope and expect that Providence will stand by us in the future.

Almighty God has never helped a lazy man. Nor does he help a coward. Under no circumstances does he help those who do not help themselves. This principle applies here: German people, help yourselves and Almighty God will not deny you his assistance.

HEINZ GUDERIAN
(1888–1954)

Heinz Guderian was one of a handful of original thinkers, including the Britons Fuller and Liddell Hart, the Austrian Franz Eimannsberger, and the Frenchmen Maurice Etienne and de Gaulle, who were proponents of mechanized force. But in contrast to the conservatism of the victors of World War I, the defeated Germans sought to innovate. In 1937, in his book Achtung! Panzer, *Guderian proposed creating a large tank force. With him at its head, this was to prove decisive in 1940 in the invasion of France. The instrument created by Guderian was in reality a combination of tanks and aircraft specially suitable for Blitzkrieg and for offense in general. Guderian fought in Poland and Russia. He was the Third Reich's last army chief of staff.*

TANK ATTACK

The layman, when thinking of a tank attack, tends to envisage the steel monsters of Cambrai and Amiens as pictured in the war reports of that period. He thinks of vast wire entanglements being crushed like so much straw; he remembers how the tanks crashed through dug-outs, smashing machine-guns to splinters beneath their weight; he recalls the terror that they inspired as they ploughed through the battlefield, flames darting from their exhaust pipes, and how this "tank terror" was described as the cause of our collapse on the 8th of August 1918. Such steam-roller tactics are one—though not the most important—of the things tanks can do; but the events of the last war have so impressed themselves on the minds of many critics, that they have built up an entirely fanciful idea of a tank attack in which vast numbers of tanks massed together roll steadily forward to crush the enemy beneath their tracks (thus providing a magnificent target for artillery and anti-tank fire) whenever and

From Heinz Guderian, *Panzer Leader*, translated by Constantine Fitzgibbon (London: Michael Joseph; New York: Dutton, 1952), 39–46. Reprinted by permission of Heinz Guderian.

wherever ordered by the high command, regardless of the nature of the ground. The fire-power of the tanks is under-estimated: the tank is thought to be both blind and deaf: it is denied the ability to hold ground that it has captured. On the other hand every advantage is ascribed to anti-tank defence: it is alleged that the defence will no longer be susceptible to surprise by tanks; anti-tank guns and artillery always find their mark regardless of their own casualties, of smoke, fog, trees or other obstacles and ground contours; the defence, too, is always located exactly where the tanks are going to attack; with their powerful binoculars they can easily see through smoke screens and darkness, and despite their steel helmets they can hear every word that is said.

As a result of this picture it follows that tank attacks have no future. Should tanks therefore be scrapped and—as one critic has suggested—the tank period be simply by-passed? If this were done all our worries about new tactics for old arms of the service could be scrapped at the same time and we could settle down comfortably once again to positional warfare as practised in 1914–15. Only it is not very sensible to leap into the dark if you have no idea where you are going to land. It follows that until our critics can produce some new and better method of making a successful land attack other than self-massacre, we shall continue to maintain our belief that tanks—properly employed, needless to say—are today the best means available for a land attack. But in order to make it easier to judge the prospects of tank attacks, here are some of the significant characteristics of tanks today.

Armour Plating

All tanks intended for serious action are at least sufficiently armoured to be impervious to armour-piercing bullets fired from machine-guns. For fighting against anti-tank weapons and enemy tanks, such protection is insufficient; therefore the tanks so far ordered by the so-called victorious nations of the World War are considerably more strongly armoured. For example, to penetrate the shell of the French Char 2C a gun of at least 75 mm. calibre is required. If an army can in the first wave commit to the attack tanks which are invulnerable to the mass of the enemy's defensive weapons, then those tanks will inevitably overcome this their most dangerous adversary: and this must lead to the destruction of the enemy's infantry and engineers, since the latter, being shot at by tanks and with their defensive weapons eliminated, can easily be mopped up even by light tanks. However, should the defence succeed in producing a defensive weapon which can penetrate the armour of all the attacker's available tanks, and should he manage to deploy such weapons at the right time and in the decisive place, then the tanks will have to pay heavily for their successes or may even fail altogether if the defence is sufficiently concentrated and sufficiently deep. The struggle for mastery between missile and armour has been going on for thousands of years, and panzer troops have to reckon with it even as do fortress troops, sailors and, recently, airmen. The fact that such a struggle exists, with results that continually vary, is no reason for denigrating tanks as a land weapon: for if we do, we shall be reduced to sending men into the attack with no more protection than the woollen uniforms of the World War which, even then, were regarded as insufficient.

Movement

It has been said, "only movement brings victory." We agree with this proposition and wish to employ the technical means of our time to prove its truth. Movement serves to bring the troops in contact with the enemy: for this purpose one can use the legs of men or of horses, the railways or—recently—the automobile and the aeroplane engine. Once contact with the enemy has been made, movement is generally paralysed by hostile fire. In order to permit the relaxation of this paralysis, the enemy must either be destroyed or made inoperative or driven from his positions. This can be done by employing firepower so superior that his powers of resistance collapse. Fire-power from fixed positions has an effective range corresponding exactly to the observed range of the mass of the weapons employed. That is as far as the infantry can make use of its covering fire; when that point is reached the heavy weapons and the artillery must change their position in order to permit a further advance under cover of their fire-power. Vast numbers of weapons and an even vaster quantity of ammunition are needed to fight this sort of battle. The preparations for an attack of this sort require considerable time and are difficult to conceal. Surprise, that important element of success, is very hard to achieve. And even if the original attack does catch the enemy unawares, the moment it is launched the attacking force will have shown its hand, and the reserves of the defence will converge on the point of attack and block it; since reserve forces will now be motorised, the building up of new defensive fronts is easier than it used to be; the chances of an offensive based on the timetable of artillery and infantry cooperation are, as a result, even slighter today than they were in the last war.

Everything is therefore dependent on this: to be able to move faster than has hitherto been done: to keep moving despite the enemy's defensive fire and thus to make it harder for him to build up fresh defensive positions: and finally to carry the attack deep into the enemy's defences. The proponents of tank warfare believe that, in favourable circumstances, they possess the means for achieving this; the sceptics, on the other hand, say that since the element of surprise can no longer be produced as in 1918 "conditions for a successful tank attack can no longer be anticipated." But is it true that a tank attack can no longer take the enemy by surprise? How then does it happen that surprises have been achieved in warfare regardless of whether new or old methods were employed to bring them about? In 1916 General von Kuhl proposed to the High Command that in order to make a break-through primary importance must be attached to the element of surprise in launching the attack; and yet at that time he had no new methods or weapons at his disposal. As a result of surprise achieved, the March Offensive of 1918 was outstandingly successful, despite the fact that no new types of weapons were employed. If, in addition to the normal methods of achieving surprise, new weapons are also employed, then the effects of the surprise will be greatly increased; but the new weapons are not a prerequisite to those effects. We believe that by attacking with tanks we can achieve a higher rate of movement than has been hitherto obtainable, and—what is perhaps even more important—that we can keep moving once a break-through has been made. We believe that movement can be kept up if certain conditions, on which the success of a tank attack today depend, exist: these include among others, concentration of force in suitable terrain, gaps in the enemy's defence, and an inferior enemy tank force. When we are blamed because we cannot successfully attack in all and any conditions, because we cannot storm fortifications with tanks armed only with machine-guns, then we can only say that we are sorry and point out that other arms of the service possess in many respects even less attacking power than we do. We do not claim to be omnipotent.

It has been maintained that a weapon only achieves its maximum effectiveness while it is new and before it need fear defensive countermeasures. Pity the artillery! it is already hundreds of years old. Pity the air force! Age is creeping up on it in the form of anti-aircraft. We believe that the effectiveness of any weapon is a relative quality, depending on the effectiveness of the counter weapons employed against it. If tanks run into a superior enemy—whether in the form of hostile tanks or of anti-tank weapons—they will be beaten; their effectiveness will be reduced; if conditions are reversed, then they will achieve startling success. Every weapon is dependent not only on the strength of the opposition but also on its own willingness to make immediate, maximum use of the latest technical developments and thus to remain at the summit of its period. From this point of view the tank will not admit that it has been surpassed by any other weapon. It has been said: "The shells of the defensive artillery travel faster than the tanks that are attacking that artillery." Nobody, up to now, has questioned this fact. Yet as long ago as 1917 and 1918 hundreds of tanks could be moved up to a concentration area immediately behind the front lines of the infantry: could penetrate in their swarms the enemy's line of defensive fire: could clear a way for dozens of infantry and even of cavalry divisions: and what is more could do all this without any preliminary artillery bombardment, that is to say in the teeth of an intact enemy artillery. It is only in unusually unfavourable conditions that the hostile artillery can have any serious effect on the movement of tanks: and once the tanks have succeeded in breaking through to the gun lines, the batteries will soon fall silent and will thus be no longer capable even of hurting the following infantry. Even the immutable artillery tactics of having guns registered on all localities of possible danger proved a failure in the last war. The defensive fire will throw up columns of earth, dust, smoke and so on and this will limit the vision of the tank crews; but such limitation is not intolerable; even in peacetime we have learned how to overcome that. In fact tanks can now advance through night and fog on compass bearings.

In an attack that is based on a successful tank action the "architect of victory" is not the infantry but the tanks themselves, for if the tank attack fails then the whole operation is a failure, whereas if the tanks succeed, then victory follows.

Fire

Armour and movement are only two of the combat characteristics of the tank weapon; the third and the most important is fire-power.

Tank guns can be fired whether the tank is stationary or on the move. In both cases the gun is laid by direct observation. If the tank is stationary range can be quickly adjusted and the target destroyed with a minimum expenditure of ammunition. When the tank is in motion the recognition of targets becomes harder owing to difficulties in observation, but this is compensated for to a certain extent by the fact that the gun is situated comparatively high above ground, which is particularly useful if the terrain is overgrown; thus the high silhouette, which has been so frequently the cause of adverse comment as presenting the enemy with an easy target, is not without a certain advantage for the tank gunner. If it is necessary to shoot while in movement the chances of short-range accuracy are good; they decrease with longer range, higher speed and when travelling over uneven ground.

In any event, in land battles the tank possesses the unique quality of being able to bring its fire-power to bear while actually advancing against the enemy, and it can do this even though all the defence's guns and machine-guns have not been silenced. We do not doubt that guns fired from stationary positions are more accurate than guns fired in motion; we are well able to judge this, since we are capable of both types of engagement. However: "Only movement brings victory." Now should a tank attack be envisaged simply as a means of steam-rolling a path through thick and deep defensive positions held by infantry and artillery fully equipped with anti-tank weapons, as was done during the battles of matériel of the last war? Certainly not. A man who would attempt this would be thinking purely in terms of the infantry tank, a weapon whose sole function was the closest co-operation with the infantry, a weapon adjusted to the foot-soldier's scale of time and space values. This was a concept which we hung on to for far too long. We neither can nor wish to devote weeks or even months to reconnaissance; we have no desire to rely on an enormous expenditure of ammunition; what we do want to do is, for a short period of time, to dominate the enemy's defence in all its depth. We are well aware that with the limited fire-power of our tanks we cannot mount a "planned artillery preparation" or achieve a "concentrated artillery bombardment"; our intention is exactly the contrary, it is to knock out our targets with single, surely aimed shells. For we have not forgotten how during the war week-long barrages by the most powerful artillery on earth failed to enable the infantry to achieve victory. We have been taught by our enemies to believe that a successful, rapid tank attack, in sufficient width and depth to penetrate all the way through the opposing defence system, can achieve more towards ensuring victory than the system of limited advances as practised in the World War. Our shells, being aimed at specific targets, will not whistle over the enemy's heads as they did during those costly though pointless creeping barrages: rather if the attack is carried out with sufficient concentration, width and depth we shall destroy recognisable targets as they present themselves and thus drive a hole in the enemy's defences through which our reserves can follow more speedily than was possible in 1918. We want these reserves to be available in the form of Panzer Divisions, since we no longer believe that other formations have the fighting ability, the speed and the manœuvrability necessary for full exploitation of the attack and break-through. Therefore we do not regard the tank force as "an additional means for winning battles, which on many forseeable occasions could, in co-operation with other weapons, help the infantry to advance." If that were all that tanks were for, the situation would be the same now as in 1916; and if that were true then one might as well be resigned to positional warfare from the very beginning and give up all hope of quick decisions in the future. But neither the alleged superiority in armaments of our enemy in any future war, nor the increased accuracy and range of guns of all calibres, nor the technical advances made in the employment of artillery suffice to shake our beliefs. On the contrary! In the tank we see the finest weapon for the attack now available: we will not change our minds until such time as the technicians can show us something better. We will in no circumstances agree to time-wasting artillery preparation and the consequent danger of losing the element of surprise, simply because the old maxim says that "only fire can open the way to movement." We believe, on the contrary, that the combination of the internal combustion engine and armour plate enable us to take our fire to the enemy without any artillery preparation, provided always that the important conditions for such an operation are fulfilled: suitable terrain, surprise and mass commitment.

The idea of mass commitment gives our critics cold feet. They write: "There is also the question of organisation: of whether the massing of all tank strength in one striking force is a sound basic idea, or whether the alternative theory of allotting tanks organically to the infantry, in order to enable it to attack, is not worthy of equally serious consideration." We assume from this remark that the infantry without tanks is at present incapable of attacking; it follows that the weapon which can attack, and which can enable other arms of the service to advance, must indubitably be the principal weapon. The question of whether or not tanks should be allotted to infantry can be clarified by the following imaginary story:

Red and Blue are at war. Each side has 100 Infantry Divisions and 100 Tank Battalions. Red has split up its tanks among its Infantry Divisions: Blue has massed them in Panzer Divisions under direct control of supreme headquarters. On a front of, shall we say, 300 miles, 100 are tank-proof, 100 are difficult for tanks and 100 are good tank country. So in battle the following picture emerges: Red has deployed a sizeable proportion of its divisions, along with their tank components, opposite the Blue positions in country where tanks cannot operate and are therefore useless, while a further portion are in difficult tank country where, though not entirely wasted, their chances of successful action are small. Whatever happens, only a fraction of Red's tank forces can be employed in the country for which they are suited. Blue, on the other hand, has collected all its armour in the one place where a decision can be reached and where the ground can be made use of; he therefore has the opportunity of going into battle with at least double his adversary's tank strength while assuming the defensive along the rest of the front against Red's very small-scale tank attacks. An Infantry Division with, say, 50 anti-tank weapons can stand up far more easily to an attack by 50 tanks than to an attack by 200. We conclude that the suggestion that our tanks be divided among Infantry Divisions is nothing but a return to the original English tactics of 1916–17, which were even then a failure, for the English tanks were not successful until they were used in mass at Cambrai.

By carrying the attack quickly into the enemy's midst, by firing our motorised guns with their protective armour direct into the target, we intend to achieve victory. It is said: "The motor is not a new weapon: it is simply a new method of carrying old weapons forward." It is fairly well known that combustion engines do not fire bullets; if we speak of the tank as a new weapon, we mean thereby that it necessitates a new arm of the service, as happened for example in the navy in the case of the U-boat; that too is called a weapon. We are convinced that we are a weapon and one whose successes in the future will leave an indelible mark on battles yet to be fought. If our attacks are to succeed then the other weapons must be adjusted to fit in with our scale of time and space in those attacks. We therefore demand that in order to exploit our successes the necessary supporting arms be made as mobile as we are, and that even in peace-time those arms be placed under our command. For to carry out great decisive operations it is not the mass of the infantry but the mass of the tanks that must be on the spot.

ERWIN ROMMEL
(1891–1944)

Erwin Rommel was appointed commander of Hitler's headquarters bodyguard in 1939. He won prominence in France in 1940 and later with the Afrika Korps in Libya and Egypt, where he was eventually defeated by General Bernard Montgomery at El Alamein in 1942. In June 1944 he failed to halt the landing of Allied forces in Normandy. After the 20 July attempt on Hitler's life, he was allowed to commit suicide.

Marshal Rommel was perhaps more a tactician than a strategist. In his Lost Victories *(Chicago: Ragnery, 1958), Erich von Manstein shows himself more systematic. However, in his "Rules of Desert Warfare," Rommel, a practitioner of the highest talent, also reveals himself to be a military thinker.*

RULES OF DESERT WARFARE

Of all theatres of operations, it was probably in North Africa that the war took on its most advanced form. The protagonists on both sides were fully motorised formations, for whose employment the flat and obstruction-free desert offered hitherto undreamed-of possibilities. It was the only theatre where the principles of motorised and tank warfare, as they had been taught theoretically before the war, could be applied to the full—and further developed. It was the only theatre where the pure tank battle between major formations was fought. Even though the struggle may have occasionally hardened into static warfare, it remained—at any rate, in its most important stages (i.e., in 1941–42 during the Cunningham-Ritchie offensive, and in the summer

From "Rules of Desert Warfare," in *The Rommel Papers*, edited by B. H. Liddell Hart, translated by Paul Findlay (New York: Harcourt, Brace & Co., 1953), 197–201. Copyright © 1953 by B. H. Liddell Hart, renewed 1981 by Lady Kathleen Liddell Hart, Fritz Bayerlein-Dittmar, and Manfred Rommel. Reprinted by permission of Harcourt Brace Jovanovich, Inc., and Harper-Collins Publishers Ltd.

of 1942—Marmarica battles, capture of Tobruk)—based on the principle of complete mobility.

In military practice, this was entirely new, for our offensives in Poland and the West had been against opponents who, in all their operations, had still had to take account of their non-motorised infantry divisions and had thus had to suffer the disastrous limitation in their freedom of tactical decision which this imposes, especially in retreat. Often they had been forced into actions quite unsuited to the object of holding up our advance. After our break-through in France, the enemy infantry divisions had simply been overrun and outflanked by our motorised forces. Once this had happened they had had no choice but to allow their operational reserves to be worn away by our assault groups, often in tactically unfavourable positions, in an endeavour to gain time for the retreat of their infantry.

Non-motorised infantry divisions are only of value against a motorised and armoured enemy when occupying prepared positions. If these positions are pierced or outflanked, a withdrawal will leave them helpless victims of the motorised enemy, with nothing else to do but hold on in their positions to the last round. They cause terrible difficulties in a general retreat—for, as I have indicated, one has to commit one's motorised formations merely to gain time for them. I was forced to go through this myself during the Axis retreat from Cyrenaica in the winter of 1941–42, when the whole of the Italian infantry and a considerable part of the German, including the majority of what was to become 90th Light Division, were without vehicles and had either to be carried by a shuttle service of lorries, or to march. It was only the gallantry of my armour that enabled the retreat of the Italo-German infantry to be covered, for our fully motorised enemy was in hot pursuit. . . .

. . . Out of this pure motorised warfare, certain principles were established, principles fundamentally different from those applying in other theatres. These principles will become the standard for the future, in which the fully motorised formation will be dominant.

The envelopment of a fully motorised enemy in the flat and good-driving terrain of the desert has the following results:

(*a*) For a fully motorised formation, encirclement is the worst tactical situation imaginable, since hostile fire can be brought to bear on it from all sides; even envelopment on only three sides is a tactically untenable situation.

(*b*) The enemy becomes forced, because of the bad tactical situation in which the encirclement has placed him, to evacuate the area he is holding.

The encirclement of the enemy and his subsequent destruction in the pocket can seldom be the direct aim of an operation; more often it is only indirect, for any fully motorised force whose organisational structure remains intact will normally and in suitable country be able to break out at will through an improvised defensive ring. Thanks to his motorisation, the commander of the encircled force is in a position to concentrate his weight unexpectedly against any likely point in the ring and burst through it. This fact was repeatedly demonstrated in the desert.

It follows therefore that an encircled enemy force can only be destroyed

(*a*) when it is non-motorised or has been rendered immobile by lack of petrol, or when it includes non-mobile elements which have to be considered;

(*b*) when it is badly led or its command has decided to sacrifice one formation in order to save another;

(*c*) when its fighting strength has already been broken, and disintegration and disorganisation have set in.

Except for cases (*a*) and (*b*), which occurred very frequently in other theatres of war, encirclement of the enemy and his subsequent destruction in the pocket can only be attempted if he has first been so heavily battered in open battle that the organic cohesion of his force has been destroyed. I shall term all actions which have as their aim the wearing down of the enemy's power of resistance "battles of attrition." In motorised warfare, material attrition and the destruction of the organic cohesion of the opposing army must be the immediate aim of all planning.

Tactically, the battle of attrition is fought with the highest possible degree of mobility. The following points require particular attention:

(*a*) The main endeavour should be to concentrate one's own forces in space and time, while at the same time seeking to split the enemy forces spatially and destroy them at different times.

(*b*) Supply lines are particularly sensitive, since all petrol and ammunition, indispensable requirements for the battle, must pass along them. Hence, everything possible must be done to protect one's own supply lines and to upset, or better still, cut the enemy's. Operations in the enemy's supply area will lead immediately to his breaking off the battle elsewhere, since, as I have indicated, supplies are the fundamental premise of the battle and must be given priority of protection.

(*c*) The armour is the core of the motorised army. Everything turns on it, and other formations are mere auxiliaries. The war of attrition against the enemy armour must therefore be waged as far as possible by the tank destruction units. One's own armour should only be used to deal the final blow.

(*d*) Reconnaissance reports must reach the commander in the shortest possible time; he must take his decisions immediately and put them into effect as fast as he can. Speed of reaction decides the battle. Commanders of motorised forces must therefore operate as near as possible to their troops, and must have the closest possible signal communication with them.

(*e*) Speed of movement and the organisational cohesion of one's own forces are decisive factors and require particular attention. Any sign of dislocation must be dealt with as quickly as possible by reorganisation.

(*f*) Concealment of intentions is of the utmost importance in order to provide surprise for one's own operations and thus make it possible to exploit the time taken by the enemy command to react. Deception measures of all kinds should be encouraged, if only to make the enemy commander uncertain and cause him to hesitate and hold back.

(*g*) Once the enemy has been thoroughly beaten up, success can be exploited by attempting to overrun and destroy major parts of his disorganised formations. Here again, speed is everything. The enemy must never be allowed time to reorganise. Lightning regrouping for the pursuit and reorganisation of supplies for the pursuing forces are essential.

Concerning the technical and organisational aspect of desert warfare, particular regard must be paid to the following points:

(*a*) The prime requirements in the tank are maneuverability, speed and a long-range gun—for the side with the bigger gun has the longer arm and can be the first to engage the enemy. Weight of armour cannot make up for lack of gun-power, as it can only be provided at the expense of maneuverability and speed, both of which are indispensable tactical requirements.

(*b*) The artillery must have great range and must, above all, be capable of great mobility and of carrying with it ammunition in large quantities.

(*c*) The infantry serves only to occupy and hold positions designed either to prevent the enemy from particular operations, or to force him into other ones. Once this object has been achieved, the infantry must be able to get away quickly for employment elsewhere. It must therefore be mobile and be equipped to enable it rapidly to take up defence positions in the open at tactically important points on the battlefield.

It is my experience that bold decisions give the best promise of success. But one must differentiate between strategical or tactical boldness and a military gamble. A bold operation is one in which success is not a certainty but which in case of failure leaves one with sufficient forces in hand to cope with whatever situation may arise. A gamble, on the other hand, is an operation which can lead either to victory or to the complete destruction of one's force. Situations can arise where even a gamble may be justified—as, for instance, when in the normal course of events defeat is merely a matter of time, when the gaining of time is therefore pointless and the only chance lies in an operation of great risk.

The only occasion when a commander can calculate the course of a battle in advance is when his forces are so superior that victory is a foregone conclusion; then the problem is no longer one of "the means" but only of "the method." But even in this situation, I still think it is better to operate on the grand scale rather than to creep about the battlefield anxiously taking all possible security measures against every conceivable enemy move.

Normally, there is no ideal solution to military problems; every course has its advantages and disadvantages. One must select that which seems best from the most varied aspects and then pursue it resolutely and accept the consequences. Any compromise is bad.

ALEXANDER DE SEVERSKY
(1894–1974)

*Alexander de Seversky, who was born in Russia, became a lieutenant in
1914 and then an aviator in 1915 (Military Air School at Sebastopol); in 1917
he was made head of the Baltic fighter command. On a mission to the United
States in 1918, he offered his services to the U.S. government. In 1921 he acted
as adviser to General William E. Mitchell. In 1927, now a U.S. citizen, he
became a major in the U.S. Air Corps Specialist Reserve. In 1931 he started
Seversky Aircraft Corp., which built fighter planes. Seversky introduced
numerous technical innovations into military aviation.*

THE CHALLENGE TO AMERICA

The most significant single fact about the war now in progress is the emergence of aviation as the paramount and decisive factor in warmaking. There
is still some difference of opinion as to the precise role of aviation in the immediate future, its relation to the older military services, its role in this or that
specific battle or campaign. But there are no two opinions on the fundamental fact that aviation has altered the traditional textbook conceptions of strategy and tactics. All experts agree that air power will play an ever more decisive
part in determining the power balance among the nations of the earth. But it
does not need an expert to recognize this towering truth. It is inescapable in
the day-to-day news from every theater of conflict.

Since world empires have depended throughout history on the available
weapons of domination, the advent of this new weapon—swifter and more
destructive than any in the past, equally potent on land or at sea—must affect
fundamentally the pattern of life on our planet. It has already, indeed, gone

From Alexander P. de Seversky, *Victory through Air Power* (New York: Simon & Schuster, 1950),
3–7. Copyright © 1942 by Alexander P. de Seversky. Reprinted by permission of Simon & Schuster, Inc.

far toward smashing the accustomed power designs and toward sketching the future picture.

This process, it is self-evident, involves the United States as intimately as it does any other great nation. A realistic understanding of the new weapon, of its implications in terms of national security, of its challenge to America, is not a matter of choice. It is the very condition of national survival.

At the outbreak of the Second World War and for at least two years thereafter, the United States lagged dismally in military aviation—not only absolutely, considering the technical potentialities of aeronautics, but even relatively, compared with the achievements of other nations, especially Germany and Great Britain. Despite bureaucratic attempts to blur its outlines, the record is clear. American military aviation, when the European war started, was primitive and haphazard, whether measured by the yardstick of military performance—range, armament, fire power, speed—or by the yardstick of planned strategy, tactics, and organization.

As dramatically as though it had been staged by providence as a warning to the American people, our own entry into the war, on December 7, 1941, was signalized by a humiliating defeat through enemy air power. The tragedy at Pearl Harbor, on that day, underlined soon thereafter by the sinking of the British battleships *Prince of Wales* and *Repulse* from the air, cut through national complacency and brass-hat smugness. The terrific danger was exposed for all to see. That initial week shocked the American people even as the French people had been shocked when German aviation and Panzer divisions ignored their Maginot Line.

The challenge of air power cannot be met by merely "admitting" our failures and undertaking to "catch up" with more advanced countries. The tempo of air-power expansion is much too swift. A nation content to imitate and "catch up" must in the nature of the case remain backward, trailing foreign leaders. The method of trial-and-error is ruled out because the penalty for error may be loss of national independence. We cannot afford to wait and see, to suspend judgment; we may not have a second chance. The challenge can be met only by exploring the physical and psychological causes of our tardiness and weakness in the air, applying radical surgery rather than surface cures, and preparing for nothing less than undisputed first place in the epochal race for aerial supremacy.

The rapid obsolescence of aeronautical equipment, especially now under the impetus of a great war, enables us to overtake and outstrip other nations, provided we take advantage of it without delay. It offers us the chance to skip intermediary stages of development and reach out boldly beyond the present confines of aviation types. As far as the aircraft of tomorrow is concerned, all nations are starting from scratch. America is more richly endowed with the resources of brains, materials, personnel, and industrial efficiency than any other country on earth. Whether it utilizes these potentialities, or once more allows itself to trail along imitatively, depends on how quickly and thoroughly we comprehend the nature of the new weapon—and on how quickly and thoroughly we cleanse our air power from the accretions of conservatism, timidity, and astigmatic leadership.

In this book I hope to contribute toward that emancipation of American air power. I want to focus attention on the new principles of warfare shaped by the emergence of military aviation and demonstrated by the experience of the present war. Above all, I hope to convey the sense of air power as a dynamic, expanding force, the growth of which must be anticipated by courageous minds. It happens to be a force that eludes static, orthodox minds no matter how brilliant they may be. Air power speaks a strategic language so new that translation into the hackneyed idiom of the past is impossible. It calls not only for new machines and techniques of warmaking but for new men unencumbered by routine thinking.

We must not merely outbuild any potential enemy or combination of enemies—that is the lesser half of the job for a machine-age nation like the United States. We must outthink and outplan them, in a spirit of creative audacity. As long as aeronautics remains merely another industry, or just another adjunct of national defense, America will be foredoomed to a secondary position among the air-power nations. Aviation must be apprehended by the whole American people as the essential expression of the present-day world and given unbounded room for development. All those gifts of mechanical ingenuity, industrial efficiency, and, above all, imaginative daring which have made America the first nation of the industrial era must be given full play in American air power.

Let me at the outset summarize my basic convictions, in the simplest terms:

1. The rapid expansion of the range and striking power of military aviation makes it certain that the United States will be as exposed to destruction from the air, within a predictable period, as are the British Isles today.

2. Those who deny the practical possibility of a direct aerial attack on America are lulling the American people into an utterly false sense of safety which may prove as disastrous to us as the "Maginot Line mentality" proved to France.

3. To meet this threat to the existence and independence of our country we must begin immediately to prepare for the specific kind of war conditioned by the advent of air power. That can mean only an interhemispheric war direct across oceans, with air power fighting not over this or that locality, but by longitude and latitude anywhere in the uninterrupted "air ocean." Such pre-

paredness calls not merely for more aviation but for new military organization and new strategic conceptions.

4. Despite immediate shortcomings, there is no excuse for a defeatist approach to the problem. On the contrary, America has all the prerequisites for victory in the race for domination of the skies. It has all that is required to make it the dominant air-power nation, even as England in its prime was the dominant sea-power nation of the world.

The pressing immediate need is for a national awakening to the threat implicit in air power—and to the urgency of preparing not merely to meet it but to take the offensive initiative. Autonomous and specialized organization for air power, freed from the restraints and inertias of long-established army and naval organizations, is almost axiomatic. It will follow, I believe, just as soon as the American people break through their present lethargy.

If we continue to ignore these looming aeronautical facts, if we remain stubbornly committed to pure Army and Navy strategy, we shall be helpless when the interhemispheric aerial conflict catches up with us. I do not relinquish the hope that we shall be amply prepared long before that happens.

NICHOLAS SPYKMAN
(1893–1943)

Nicholas Spykman was professor of international relations and director of the Institute of International Studies at Yale University. His geopolitical theory of heartland and rimland (see map 7) was among the sources of the strategy of containment pursued by the United States during the Cold War.

HEARTLAND AND RIMLAND

The fundamental fact which is responsible for the conditions of this age of world politics is the development of ocean navigation and the discovery of sea routes to India and America. Maritime mobility is the basis for a new type of geopolitical structure, the overseas empire. Formerly, history had given us the pattern of great land powers based on the control of contiguous land masses such as the Roman, Chinese, and Russian empires. Now the sea has become a great artery of communication and we have been given a new structure of great power and enormous extent. The British, French, and Japanese empires and the sea power of the United States have all contributed to the development of a modern world which is a single field for the interplay of political forces. It is sea power which has made it possible to conceive of the Eurasian Continent as a unit and it is sea power which governs the relationships between the Old and the New Worlds.

The German geopolitician [Karl] Haushofer took over the interpretation of Mackinder and adapted it to his own peculiar needs. He has indicated the flow of rivers, a detail from which one accustomed to interpret maps can make some estimate of the location of mountain ranges. He has also sketched in certain areas of "political pressure" which illustrate the location of the centers of power Mackinder discussed but failed to locate on his map. Nevertheless, his

From Nicholas Spykman, *The Geography of the Peace* (New York: Harcourt, Brace & World, 1944). Reprinted by permission of Harcourt Brace Jovanovich, Inc.

chart fails also to afford a really adequate basis for discussion because it does not give the really important facts about topography which, in a geopolitical analysis, are indispensable.

We must, therefore, look at the topographical map and emphasize again the outlines of the land contours of the Eurasian Continent: the central lowland plain bounded by ice-covered waters to the north and by mountains in a great semicircle to the east, south, and west. Beyond the mountain belt lie the coastland regions consisting of plains separated by mountain spurs which stretch to the sea. In our further consideration of this picture of the earth, we shall have to refer again to these regions and it will be well to designate them by specific names. The central continental plain can continue to be called the heartland but we may note that it is, in effect, to be equated with the political extent of the Union of Soviet Socialist Republics. Beyond the mountain barrier, the coastland region, which is called by Mackinder the inner crescent, may more effectively be referred to as the rimland, a name which defines its character accurately. The surrounding string of marginal and mediterranean seas which separates the continent from the oceans constitutes a circumferential maritime highway which links the whole area together in terms of sea power. Beyond lie the off-shore islands and continents of Great Britain, Japan, Africa, and Australia which compose the outer crescent. The term "off-shore" describes so well their essential relationship to the central land mass that we shall use this terminology rather than that of Mackinder. The oceanic belt and the transoceanic New World complete the picture in terms of purely geographical factors. . . .

The Heartland

The importance of the heartland region was first suggested to Mackinder by his conception of the value of a central position with interior lines of communication made powerful and unified by the development of land transportation to a point where it could begin to compete with sea communication. He also envisaged the transformation of the steppe land from an area of low economic potential to one of high economic potential.

The actual facts of the Russian economy and geography make it not at all clear that the heartland is or will be in the very near future a world center of communication, mobility, and power potential. First of all, the distribution of climate in the world makes it certain that, in the absence of revolutionary developments in agricultural technique, the center of agrarian productivity will remain in western Russia rather than in the central Siberian region. A map plotting the cultivated land of the world emphasizes this fact. Although the

Russian state covers an area far larger than Canada, the United States, or Brazil, the actual extent of arable land is only a very small part of the total area. We must avoid the mistake of identifying all of Russia, or the heartland, as a region of great potential agrarian productivity.

Looking again at the geographic distribution of coal and iron deposits in the world as well as the oil fields and water power, we note that these essential elements of industrial power are located largely west of the Ural Mountains. It is true that there are reserves of coal and iron in Siberia, the exact extent of which are unknown but which undoubtedly constitute a sizeable quantity. Some reports say, also, that there are reserves of oil which can be important if developed. Certainly, the Soviet government has made and will continue to make constant and strenuous endeavors to shift the center of industrial production eastward. So far it has undoubtedly succeeded in developing factories and mines to an extent which has made it possible for Russia to provide herself with a large proportion of her vast war-time needs. The figures on the industrial production of the great area between the Urals and Novosibirsk remain vague and inaccurate and it is difficult to arrive at a complete estimate of the actual and potential importance of this region. It is, nevertheless, certain that it already supplements to an important extent the more fertile region to the west and southwest, although it must be remembered that it is not capable of supporting a large population from the produce of the land.

The railroad, the motor road, and the airplane have certainly created a new mobility in the center of the Eurasian land mass. It cannot, however, be ignored that this area is ringed to the north, east, south, and southwest by some of the greatest obstacles to transportation in the world. Ice and freezing temperatures for a large part of the year, and towering mountains pierced by only a few difficult passes, form its borders. A large part of the rimland areas which touch the heartland have even poorer transportation facilities. Afghanistan, Tibet, Sinkiang, and Mongolia are regions with no railroads, practically no motor roads, and only a few tortuous caravan routes of the most primitive sort. The law of the inverse ratio of power to distance remains valid within the same political unit as well as between political units. Within the immediate future, Central Asia will undoubtedly remain a region with a fairly low power potential.

The significance of this region was also defined by Mackinder in terms of position. The fact that the core of the heartland lies in the center of the Eurasian land mass gives it the advantage of interior communication with the lands of the inner crescent. It is obvious that the problems of an army which is working along the diameters of a circle of territory will be less difficult than those of forces which have to function along the circumference of that same region. In comparison with the exterior lines of British naval power running from

Great Britain through the circumferential highway around the Eurasian rimlands, Russia has interior lines of communication. The transportation lines between Russian Turkestan and Northwest India are certainly interior as compared with the sea route from Southampton to Karachi.

It must be pointed out, however, that interior lines function in terms of two points of reference rather than one. The relations between the center and the circumference may easily be changed if a point on the circumference becomes in turn the center of another circle of communication. Thus, the strategic implications of the position of the heartland in relation to the British Empire have meaning only if the military strength to be applied at the Indian frontier originates in Great Britain. The moment the defense of that frontier or the Persian frontier or the Chinese frontier rests on a locally developed war potential, the whole concept of interior and exterior lines is changed. What is true for India and China if they have to be defended by British sea power is no longer true if their military strength can be made a by-product of their own industrial development. In this case, unless the raw materials of power in the central Asiatic regions of Russia turn out to be great enough to balance those of the rimland regions, Soviet strength will remain west of the Urals and it will not be exerted overpoweringly against the coast lands to the east, south, and southwest.

The Rimland

In Mackinder's conception, the inner crescent of amphibian states surrounding the heartland consists of three sections: the European coast land, the Arabian-Middle Eastern desert land, and the Asiatic monsoon land. The first two regions are clearly defined as geographical areas but the third is a unit only from the special historical point of view represented by Great Britain. To the seaman, the Asiatic monsoon land looks like a single region. The similarities of climate and the easy accessibility of the area to sea power contribute to this impression. This territory is also well protected from the heartland by a string of barriers from the Himalayas and Tibet to the vast desert and mountain regions of Sinkiang and Mongolia. These mountains do not, however, make the monsoon lands behind them a single unit. The ranges of Burma and Indo-China extend down to the sea and interpose a great obstacle to contacts between the two great states. The fact that Buddhism reached China from India by way of Sinkiang and Thailand points to the difficulty of maintaining direct relations. Throughout their history, these two centers of oriental culture have remained fairly isolated from each other and their only contacts have been of a cultural and intellectual nature.

India and the Indian Ocean littoral, then, fall into a different geopolitical category from China, and it is scarcely accurate to classify them together as the Asiatic monsoon lands. The future will probably see the power of the two regions expressed as two distinct units connected only across the lower part of the Indo-China Peninsula by land or air power and around Singapore in terms of sea power. If this is true, then the Asiatic Mediterranean will continue to have great significance for the political strategy of the independent Asiatic world even as it has been of vital importance in the era of western sea power encirclement.

The rimland of the Eurasian land mass must be viewed as an intermediate region, situated as it is between the heartland and the marginal seas. It functions as a vast buffer zone of conflict between sea power and land power. Looking in both directions, it must function amphibiously and defend itself on land and sea. In the past, it has had to fight against the land power of the heartland and against the sea power of the off-shore islands of Great Britain and Japan. Its amphibious nature lies at the basis of its security problems.

The Off-shore Continents

Off the southeastern and southwestern shores of the Old World lie the two mediterranean seas beyond which stretch the continents of Australia and Africa. The position of these two off-shore continents is determined largely by the state which controls the European and Asiatic Mediterranean Seas. The Mackinder analysis defines the great desert region of Africa as a continental area inaccessible to sea power and therefore a southern heartland comparable to the northern one. This concept was perhaps of some value in understanding the political history of Africa before the penetration of that continent by the white man. It also had a certain validity in terms of British-Russian opposition as long as the circumferential envelopment of the Old World went by way of the Cape of Good Hope.

Since the completion of the Suez Canal, this interpretation has lost all practical significance. There is no sense using a term which connotes that an area is impenetrable to sea power when that area has actually been transformed by sea power penetration. It must also be remembered that, notwithstanding any geographic similarity that can be suggested between the two regions, the southern heartland differs in one basic and fundamental respect from the northern heartland. It contains no political power and has no power potential of its own. It is not and never has been the seat of outward pressure toward the crescent. It does not, therefore, function in the total global picture in any manner similar to the northern heartland.

The significance of both these off-shore continents in world politics is limited by climatic conditions which restrict their productive capacity and, consequently, their power potential. The greatest proportion of Africa lies in the tropical zone and is either extremely dry or extremely humid. In either case the continent does not contain, except at the extreme southern tip, the resources necessary for the building up of political units capable of exerting an important influence on the rest of the world. In the same way, the desert regions of Australia are so extensive that the remaining territory is left without the size and resources required for the formation of a power of the first rank.

The Dynamic Pattern
of Eurasian Politics

The general pattern of political action on the Eurasian Continent has been defined by Mackinder in terms of the pressure of nomadic peoples in the heartland outward against the states of the rimland. When the nomads who roamed the grasslands of the central lowland were replaced by the organized power of the Russian state, the same pattern was continued. The empire sought access to the sea and found its road blocked in the nineteenth century by British sea power which had expanded across the Eurasian littoral. The British imperial position rested on a maritime encirclement of the Eurasian land mass which was maintained by the predominance of her naval power along the circumferential maritime highway. This position could be threatened by the emergence of a competing sea power on the littoral of the continent, or by the penetration of Russian land power to the coast.

So convinced was Mackinder of the fact that any conflict in Europe must follow the pattern of land power-sea power opposition that he declared, in 1919, that the true character of the war which had just been concluded was not visible until after Russia had been defeated. British sea power could then be considered to be fighting against a land power which dominated the heartland. This interpretation would seem to be a little hard on the role of France as a land power, and it is strange to ignore the three years of Russian resistance on the eastern front.

Like all good geopolitical analyses, however, the Mackinder study represented a picture of the constellation of forces which existed at a particular time and within a particular frame of reference. It was first elaborated in 1904 before the conclusion of the British-Russian Entente of 1907 and was strongly influenced by the previous century of conflict between Russia and Great Britain. When, in 1919, his book *Democratic Ideals and Reality* was published, the conception of an inevitable historical opposition between Russian land power and

British sea power was reemphasized. The fallacy of this blanket application of a theory of history is seen when we realize that the opposition between these two states has never, in fact, been inevitable. Actually, in the three great world wars of the nineteenth and twentieth centuries, the Napoleonic Wars, the First World War, and the Second World War, the British and Russian empires have lined up together against an intervening rimland power as led by Napoleon, Wilhelm II, and Hitler.

In other words, there has never really been a simple land power–sea power opposition. The historical alignment has always been in terms of some members of the rimland with Great Britain against some members of the rimland with Russia, or Great Britain and Russia together against a dominating rimland power. The Mackinder dictum "Who controls eastern Europe rules the Heartland; who rules the Heartland rules the World Island; and who rules the World Island rules the World" is false. If there is to be a slogan for the power politics of the Old World, it must be "Who controls the rimland rules Eurasia; who rules Eurasia controls the destinies of the world."

Already the United States has gone to war twice within thirty years and the threat to our security each time has been the possibility that the rimland regions of the Eurasian land mass would be dominated by a single power. By the end of 1917, the success of the Germans in the east against Russia, which culminated in the Treaty of Brest-Litovsk of March 3, 1918, made it appear likely that the German bid for supremacy on the Atlantic littoral would be successful. At the same time, Japan, though ostensibly an ally of Great Britain and the United States, was also engaged in trying to achieve complete control over the Far East. In January of 1915 she began her campaign by pressing on China the Twenty-One Demands. Later, in 1918, she took part in the Allied invasion of Siberia and pushed her own interests there vigorously. Had she not been countered, she might have come out of the war with complete control over the Asiatic rimland.

The Washington Conference of 1921–22 achieved for us the partial withdrawal of Japan from the extreme claims of the Twenty-One Demands as well as a withdrawal from Siberia and from Shantung. Looking at the Washington treaties rather than the Treaty of Versailles as the end of the First World War we reduced our opponents to a relatively small area. It did not, however, take them long to resume their policies of expansion toward the control of the rimland and its vast power potential. The Second World War represents the continuation of that effort, begun in earnest by the Japanese in 1931 and by the Germans in 1936. At the point of maximum expansion this time, Germany reached indirectly to Dakar and Japan gained control as far as the Torres Strait between New Guinea and Australia.

The course of the Second World War has emphasized in no uncertain terms the importance of a power equilibrium in Europe to the peace and well-being of the world. The most recent expression of the heartland concept by Mackinder has recognized the predominant importance of the rimland and the necessity of British-Russian-United States collaboration to prevent the growth of German power in this area. He has modified his conception slightly by shifting the boundary of the heartland to the Yenisei River and lessening the emphasis on the Central Siberian grassland region. The focus of Soviet power is now located where its actual geographical concentration places it, west of the Urals. The heartland becomes less important than the rimland and it is the cooperation of British, Russian, and United States land and sea power that will control the European littoral and, thereby, the essential power relations of the world.

MOHANDAS K. GANDHI
(1869–1948)

*Mohandas K. Gandhi, known as the Mahatma (Great Soul), used the
principle of nonviolence and the weapon of passive noncooperation to win
India's independence from Britain, a democracy. These techniques have
proved ineffective against any other type of regime.*

THE WAY OF NONVIOLENCE

I would rather have India resort to arms in order to defend her honour than
that she should in a cowardly manner become or remain a helpless witness to
her own dishonour.

But I believe that nonviolence is infinitely superior to violence, forgiveness
is more manly than punishment. Forgiveness adorns a soldier. But abstinence
is forgiveness only when there is the power to punish; it is meaningless when
it pretends to proceed from a helpless creature. A mouse hardly forgives a cat
when it allows itself to be torn to pieces by her. I, therefore, appreciate the sentiment of those who cry out for the condign punishment of General Dyer and
his ilk. They would tear him to pieces if they could. But I do not believe India
to be a helpless creature. Only I want to use India's and my strength for a better purpose.

Let me not be misunderstood. Strength does not come from physical capacity. It comes from an indomitable will. An average Zulu is anyway more
than a match for an average Englishman in bodily capacity. But he flees from
an English boy, because he fears the boy's revolver or those who will use it for
him. He fears death and is nerveless in spite of his burly figure. We in India
may in a moment realize that one hundred thousand Englishmen need not

Mohandas K. Gandhi, speech, 11 August 1920, reprinted in *All Men Are Brothers: Life and
Thoughts of Mahatma Gandhi as Told in His Own Words* (New York: Columbia University Press,
1985), 94–96. Reproduced by permission of Columbia University Press.

frighten three hundred million human beings. A definite forgiveness would, therefore, mean a definite recognition of our strength. . . . It matters little to me that for the moment I do not drive my point home. We feel too downtrodden not to be angry and revengeful. But I must not refrain from saying that India can gain more by waiving the right of punishment. We have better work to do, a better mission to deliver to the world.

I am not a visionary. I claim to be a practical idealist. Religion of nonviolence is not meant merely for the *rishis* and saints. It is meant for the common people as well. Nonviolence is the law of our species as violence is the law of the brute. The spirit lies dormant in the brute, and he knows no law but that of physical might. The dignity of man requires obedience to a higher law, to the strength of the spirit.

I have ventured to place before India the ancient law of self-sacrifice. For *Satyagraha* and its offshoots, non-co-operation and civil resistance, are nothing but new names for the law of suffering. The *rishis*, who discovered the law of nonviolence in the midst of violence, were greater geniuses than Newton. They were themselves greater warriors than Wellington. Having themselves known the use of arms, they realized their uselessness and taught a weary world that its salvation lay not through violence but through nonviolence.

Nonviolence in its dynamic condition means conscious suffering. It does not mean meek submission to the will of the evil-doer, but it means putting one's whole soul against the will of the tyrant. Working under this law of our being, it is possible for a single individual to defy the whole might of an unjust empire to save his honour, his religion, his soul, and lay the foundation for that empire's fall or its regeneration.

And so I am not pleading for India to practise nonviolence because it is weak. I want her to practise nonviolence being conscious of her strength and power. No training in arms is required for realization of her strength. We seem to need it, because we seem to think that we are but a lump of flesh. I want to recognize that she has a soul that cannot perish and that can rise triumphant above every physical weakness and defy the physical combination of a whole world.

MAO ZE-DONG
(1893–1976)

Mao Ze-dong, a co-founder of the Chinese Communist party in 1921, carried out a study of the peasantry in 1928 that led him to exploit the revolutionary potential of the poor peasantry. In 1934, with Chu Te, he organized the "Long March," a retreat of almost 10,000 km, as well as the establishment of communist bases in northern China. His major military writings were Strategic Problems of the Revolutionary War in China *(1936),* Strategic Problems of the Partisan War against Japan *(1938), and* On Protracted War *(1938). Stalin had advised him to form a government of national unity with Chiang Kai-shek, but taking advantage of the Japanese invasion, he united the vanguard Communist party with the peasantry. His victory was nonetheless unexpected.*

STRATEGY IN CHINA'S REVOLUTIONARY WAR

The four principal characteristics of China's revolutionary war are: a vast semi-colonial country which is unevenly developed politically and economically and which has gone through a great revolution; a big and powerful enemy; a small and weak Red Army; and the agrarian revolution. These characteristics determine the line for guiding China's revolutionary war as well as many of its strategic and tactical principles. It follows from the first and fourth characteristics that it is possible for the Chinese Red Army to grow and defeat its enemy. It follows from the second and third characteristics that it is impossible for the Chinese Red Army to grow very rapidly or defeat its enemy quickly; in other words, the war will be protracted and may even be lost if it is mishandled. . . .

It is clear that we must correctly settle all the following matters of principle:

From *Selected Military Writings of Mao Tse-tung* (Beijing: Foreign Languages Press, 1963), 95–145.

Determine our strategic orientation correctly, oppose adventurism when on the offensive, oppose conservatism when on the defensive, and oppose flight-ism when shifting from one place to another.

Oppose guerrilla-ism in the Red Army, while recognizing the guerrilla character of its operations.

Oppose protracted campaigns and a strategy of quick decision, and uphold the strategy of protracted war and campaigns of quick decision.

Oppose fixed battle lines and positional warfare, and favour fluid battle lines and mobile warfare.

Oppose fighting merely to rout the enemy, and uphold fighting to annihilate the enemy.

Oppose the strategy of striking with two "fists" in two directions at the same time, and uphold the strategy of striking with one "fist" in one direction at one time.

Oppose the principle of maintaining one large rear area, and uphold the principle of small rear areas.

Oppose an absolutely centralized command, and favour a relatively centralized command.

Oppose the purely military viewpoint and the ways of roving rebels, and recognize that the Red Army is a propagandist and organizer of the Chinese revolution.

Oppose bandit ways, and uphold strict political discipline.

Oppose warlord ways, and favour both democracy within proper limits and an authoritative discipline in the army.

Oppose an incorrect, sectarian policy on cadres, and uphold the correct policy on cadres.

Oppose the policy of isolation, and affirm the policy of winning over all possible allies.

Oppose keeping the Red Army at its old stage, and strive to develop it to a new stage.

In the Chinese civil war, as in all other wars, ancient or modern, in China or abroad, there are only two basic forms of fighting, attack and defence. The special characteristic of China's civil war consists in the long-term repetition of "encirclement and suppression" campaigns and of our counter-campaigns together with the long-term alternation of the two forms of fighting, attack and defence, with the inclusion of the phenomenon of the great strategic shift of more than ten thousand kilometres (the Long March).

A defeat for the enemy is much the same. It is a strategic defeat for the enemy when his "encirclement and suppression" campaign is broken and our defensive becomes an offensive, when the enemy turns to the defensive and has to reorganize before launching another "encirclement and suppression" campaign. The enemy has not had to make a strategic shift of more than ten thousand kilometres such as we have, because he rules the whole country and is much stronger than we are. But there have been partial shifts of his forces. Sometimes, enemy forces in White strongholds encircled by the Red Army in some base areas have broken through our encirclement and withdrawn to the White areas to organize new offensives. If the civil war is prolonged and the Red Army's victories become more extensive, there will be more of this sort of thing. But the enemy cannot achieve the same results as the Red Army, because he does not have the help of the people and because his officers and men are not united. . . .

The Strategic Defensive

Our war began in the autumn of 1927, and at that time we had no experience at all. The Nanchang Uprising and the Canton Uprising failed, and in the Autumn Harvest Uprising the Red Army in the Hunan-Hupeh-Kiangsi border area also suffered several defeats and shifted to the Chingkang Mountains on the Hunan-Kiangsi border. In the following April the units which had survived the defeat of the Nanchang Uprising also moved to the Chingkang Mountains by way of southern Hunan. By May 1928, however, basic principles of guerrilla warfare, simple in nature and suited to the conditions of the time, had already been evolved, that is, the sixteen-character formula: "The enemy advances, we retreat; the enemy camps, we harass; the enemy tires, we attack; the enemy retreats, we pursue." This sixteen-character formulation of military principles was accepted by the Central Committee before the Li Lisan line. Later our operational principles were developed a step further. At the time of our first counter-campaign against "encirclement and suppression" in the Kiangsi base area, the principle of "luring the enemy in deep" was put forward and, moreover, successfully applied. By the time the enemy's third "encirclement and suppression" campaign was defeated, a complete set of operational principles for the Red Army had taken shape. This marked a new stage in the development of our military principles. . . . It covered the two stages of the strategic defensive and the strategic offensive, and within the defensive, it covered the two stages of the strategic retreat and the strategic counter-offensive. What came later was only a development of this formula.

But beginning from January 1932, after the publication of the Party's resolution entitled "Struggle for Victory First in One or More Provinces After Smashing the Third 'Encirclement and Suppression' Campaign," which contained serious errors of principle, the "Left" opportunists attacked these correct principles, finally abrogated the whole set and instituted a complete set of contrary "new principles" or "regular principles." From then on, the old principles were no longer to be considered as regular but were to be rejected as "guerrilla-ism." The opposition to "guerrilla-ism" reigned for three whole years. Its first stage was military adventurism, in the second it turned into military conservatism and, finally, in the third stage it became flight-ism. It was not until the Central Committee held the enlarged meeting of the Political Bureau at Tsunyi, Kweichow Province, in January 1935 that this wrong line was declared bankrupt and the correctness of the old line reaffirmed. But at what a cost! . . .

The object of strategic retreat is to conserve military strength and prepare for the counter-offensive. Retreat is necessary because not to retreat a step before the onset of a strong enemy inevitably means to jeopardize the preservation of one's own forces. In the past, however, many people were stubbornly opposed to retreat, considering it to be an "opportunist line of pure defence." Our history has proved that their opposition was entirely wrong.

To prepare for a counter-offensive, we must select or create conditions favourable to ourselves but unfavourable to the enemy, so as to bring about a change in the balance of forces, before we go on to the stage of the counter-offensive.

In the light of our past experience, during the stage of retreat we should in general secure at least two of the following conditions before we can consider the situation as being favourable to us and unfavourable to the enemy and before we can go over to the counter-offensive. These conditions are:

1. The population actively supports the Red Army.
2. The terrain is favourable for operations.
3. All the main forces of the Red Army are concentrated.
4. The enemy's weak spots have been discovered.
5. The enemy has been reduced to a tired and demoralized state.
6. The enemy has been induced to make mistakes.

The first condition, active support of the population, is the most important one for the Red Army. It means having a base area. Moreover, given this condition, it is easy to achieve conditions 4, 5 and 6. Therefore, when the enemy launches a full-scale offensive, the Red Army generally withdraws from the White area into the base area, because that is where the population is most active in supporting the Red Army against the White army. Also, there is a difference between the borders and the central district of a base area; in the latter the people are better at blocking the passage of information to the enemy, better at reconnaissance, transportation, joining in the fighting, and so on. Thus when we were combating the first, second and third "encirclement and suppression" campaigns in Kiangsi, all the places selected as "terminal points for the retreat" were situated where the first condition, popular support, was excellent, or rather good. This characteristic of our base areas made the Red Army's operations very different from ordinary operations and was the main reason why the enemy subsequently had to resort to the policy of blockhouse warfare.

One advantage of operating on interior lines is that it makes it possible for the retreating army to choose terrain favourable to itself and force the attacking army to fight on its terms. In order to defeat a strong army, a weak army must carefully choose favourable terrain as a battleground. But this condition alone is not enough and must be accompanied by other conditions. The first of these is popular support. The next is a vulnerable enemy, for instance, an enemy who is tired or has made mistakes, or an advancing enemy column that is comparatively poor in fighting capacity. In the absence of these conditions, even if we have found excellent terrain, we have to disregard it and continue to retreat in order to secure the desired conditions.

Another essential condition for a weak army fighting a strong one is to pick out the enemy's weaker units for attack. But at the beginning of the enemy's offensive we usually do not know which of his advancing columns is the strongest and which the second strongest, which is the weakest and which the second weakest, and so a process of reconnaissance is required. This often takes a considerable time. That is another reason why strategic retreat is necessary.

If the attacking enemy is far more numerous and much stronger than we are, we can accomplish a change in the balance of forces only when the enemy has penetrated deeply into our base area and tasted all the bitterness it holds for him. . . .

Finally, the object of retreat is to induce the enemy to make mistakes or to detect his mistakes. One must realize that an enemy commander, however wise, cannot avoid making some mistakes over a relatively long period of time, and hence it is always possible for us to exploit the openings he leaves us. The enemy is liable to make mistakes, just as we ourselves sometimes miscalculate and give him openings to exploit. In addition, we can induce the enemy to make mistakes by our own actions, for instance, by "counterfeiting an appearance," as Sun Tzu called it, that is, by making a feint to the east but attacking in the west. If we are to do this, the terminal point for the retreat cannot be rigidly limited to a definite area. Sometimes when we have retreated to the predetermined area and not yet found openings to exploit, we have to retreat farther and wait for the enemy to give us an opening.

The favourable conditions which we seek by retreating are in general those stated above. But this does not mean that a counter-offensive cannot be launched until all these conditions are present. The presence of all these conditions at the same time is neither possible nor necessary. But a weak force operating on interior lines against a strong enemy should strive to secure such conditions as are necessary in the light of the enemy's actual situation. . . .

Our army's experience in these five counter-campaigns against "encirclement and suppression" proves that the first battle in the counter-offensive is of the greatest importance for the Red Army, which is on the defensive, if it is to smash a large and powerful enemy "suppression" force. Victory or defeat in the first battle has a tremendous effect upon the entire situation, all the way to the final engagement. Hence we arrive at the following conclusions.

First, the first battle must be won. We should strike only when positively certain that the enemy's situation, the terrain and popular support are all in our favour and not in favour of the enemy. Otherwise we should rather fall back and carefully bide our time. There will always be opportunities; we should not rashly accept battle. . . .

Second, the plan for the first battle must be the prelude to, and an organic part of, the plan for the whole campaign. Without a good plan for the whole campaign it is absolutely impossible to fight a really good first battle. That is to say, even though victory is won in the first battle, if the battle harms rather than helps the campaign as a whole, such a victory can only be reckoned a defeat. . . . Hence, before fighting the first battle one must have a general idea of how the second, third, fourth, and even the final battle will be fought, and consider what changes will ensue in the enemy's situation as a whole if we win, or lose, each of the succeeding battles. Although the result may not—and, in fact, definitely will not—turn out exactly as we expect, we must think everything out carefully and realistically in the light of the general situation on both sides. Without a grasp of the situation as a whole, it is impossible to make any really good move on the chessboard.

Third, one must also consider what will happen in the next strategic stage of the war. Whoever directs strategy will not be doing his duty if he occupies himself only with the counter-offensive and neglects the measures to be taken after it succeeds, or in case it fails. In a particular strategic stage, he should take into consideration the succeeding stages, or, at the very least, the following one. Even though future changes are difficult to foresee and the farther ahead one looks the more blurred things seem, a general calculation is possible and an appraisal of distant prospects is necessary. In war as well as in politics, planning only one step at a time as one goes along is a harmful way of directing matters. After each step, it is necessary to examine the ensuing concrete changes and to modify or develop one's strategic and operational plans accordingly, or otherwise one is liable to make the mistake of rushing straight ahead regardless of danger. However, it is absolutely essential to have a long-term plan which has been thought out in its general outline and which covers an entire strategic stage or even several strategic stages. Failure to make such a plan will lead to the mistake of hesitating and allowing oneself to be tied down, which in fact serves the enemy's strategic objects and reduces one to a passive position. It must be borne in mind that the enemy's supreme command has some strategic insight. Only when we have trained ourselves to be a head taller than the enemy will strategic victories be possible. . . . In short, in the stage of retreat we must see ahead to the stage of the counter-offensive, in the stage of the counter-offensive we must see ahead to that of the offensive, and in the stage of the offensive we must again see ahead to a stage of retreat. Not to do so but to confine ourselves to considerations of the moment is to court defeat.

The first battle must be won. The plan for the whole campaign must be taken into account. And the strategic stage that comes next must be taken into account. These are the three principles we must never forget when we begin a counter-offensive, that is, when we fight the first battle.

Concentration of Troops

The concentration of troops seems easy but is quite hard in practice. Everybody knows that the best way is to use a large force to defeat a small one, and yet many people fail to do so and on the contrary often divide their forces up. The reason is that such military leaders have no head for strategy and are confused by complicated circumstances; hence, they are at the mercy of these circumstances, lose their initiative and have recourse to passive response.

No matter how complicated, grave and harsh the circumstances, what a military leader needs most of all is the ability to function independently in organizing and employing the forces under his command. He may often be forced into a passive position by the enemy, but the important thing is to regain the initiative quickly. Failure to do so spells defeat.

The initiative is not something imaginary but is concrete and material. Here the most important thing is to conserve and mass an armed force that is as large as possible and full of fighting spirit.

It is easy to fall into a passive position in defensive warfare, which gives far less scope for the full exercise of initiative than does offensive warfare. However, defensive warfare, which is passive in form, can be active in content, and can be switched from the stage in which it is passive in form to the stage in which it is active both in form and in content. In appearance a fully planned strategic retreat is made under compulsion, but in reality it is effected in order to conserve our strength and bide our time to defeat the enemy, to lure him in deep and prepare for our counter-offensive. On the other hand, refusal to retreat and hasty acceptance of battle . . . may appear a serious effort to gain the initiative, while in reality it is passive. Not only is a strategic counter-offensive active in content, but in form, too, it discards the passive posture of the period of retreat. In relation to the enemy, our counter-offensive represents our effort to make him relinquish the initiative and put him in a passive position.

Concentration of troops, mobile warfare, war of quick decision and war of annihilation are all necessary conditions for the full achievement of this aim. And of these, concentration of troops is the first and most essential.

Concentration of troops is necessary for the purpose of reversing the situation as between the enemy and ourselves. First, its purpose is to reverse the situation as regards advance and retreat. Previously it was the enemy who was advancing and we who were retreating; now we seek a situation in which we advance and he retreats. When we concentrate our troops and win a battle, then in that battle we gain the above purpose, and this influences the whole campaign.

Second, its purpose is to reverse the situation with regard to attack and defence. In defensive warfare the retreat to the prescribed terminal point belongs basically to the passive, or "defence," stage. The counter-offensive belongs to the active, or "attack," stage. Although the strategic defensive retains its defensive character throughout its duration, still as compared with the retreat the counter-offensive already represents a change not only in form but in content. The counter-offensive is transitional between the strategic defensive and the strategic offensive, and in the nature of a prelude to the strategic offensive; it is precisely for the purpose of the counter-offensive that troops are concentrated.

Third, its purpose is to reverse the situation with regard to interior and exterior lines. An army operating on strategically interior lines suffers from many disadvantages, and this is especially so in the case of the Red Army, confronted as it is with "encirclement and suppression." But in campaigns and battles we can and absolutely must change this situation. We can turn a big "encirclement and suppression" campaign waged by the enemy against us into a number of small, separate campaigns of encirclement and suppression waged by us against the enemy. We can change the converging attack directed by the enemy against us on the plane of strategy into converging attacks directed by us against the enemy on the plane of campaigns and battles. We can change the enemy's strategic superiority over us into our superiority over him in campaigns and battles. We can put the enemy who is in a strong position strategically into a weak position in campaigns and battles. At the same time we can change our own strategically weak position into a strong position in campaigns and battles. This is what we call exterior-line operations within interior-line operations, encirclement and suppression within "encirclement and suppression," blockade within blockade, the offensive within the defensive, superiority within inferiority, strength within weakness, advantage within disadvantage, and initiative within passivity. The winning of victory in the strategic defensive depends basically on this measure—concentration of troops. . . .

Mobile Warfare

Mobile warfare or positional warfare? Our answer is mobile warfare. So long as we lack a large army or reserves of ammunition, and so long as there is only a single Red Army force to do the fighting in each base area, positional warfare is generally useless to us. For us, positional warfare is generally inapplicable in attack as well as in defence.

One of the outstanding characteristics of the Red Army's operations, which follows from the fact that the enemy in powerful while the Red Army is deficient in technical equipment, is the absence of fixed battle lines.

The Red Army's battle lines are determined by the direction in which it is operating. As its operational direction often shifts, its battle lines are fluid. Though the main direction does not change in a given period of time, within its ambit the secondary directions may shift at any moment; when we find ourselves checked in one direction, we must turn to another. If, after a time, we find ourselves checked in the main direction too, then we must change even the main direction. . . .

Fluidity of battle lines leads to fluidity in the size of our base areas. Our base areas are constantly expanding and contracting, and often as one base area falls another rises. This fluidity of territory is entirely a result of the fluidity of the war.

Fluidity in the war and in our territory produces fluidity in all fields of construction in our base areas. Construction plans covering several years are out of the question. Frequent changes of plan are all in the day's work.

It is to our advantage to recognize this characteristic. We must base our planning on this characteristic and must not have illusions about a war of advance without any retreats, take alarm at any temporary fluidity of our territory or of the rear areas of our army, or endeavour to draw up detailed longterm plans. We must adapt our thinking and our work to the circumstances, be ready to sit down as well as to march on, and always have our marching rations handy. It is only by exerting ourselves in today's fluid way of life that we can secure relative stability tomorrow, and then full stability.

The exponents of the strategy of "regular warfare" which dominated our fifth counter-campaign denied this fluidity and opposed what they called "guerrilla-ism." Those comrades, who opposed fluidity, managed affairs as though they were the rulers of a big state, and the result was an extraordinary and immense fluidity—the 25,000-*li* Long March.

Our workers' and peasants' democratic republic is a state, but today it is not yet a full-fledged one. Today we are still in the period of strategic defensive in the civil war, the form of our political power is still far from that of a full-fledged state, our army is still much inferior to the enemy both in numbers and technical equipment, our territory is still very small, and our enemy is constantly out to destroy us and will never rest content till he has done so. In defining our policy on the basis of these facts, we should not repudiate guerrilla-ism in general terms but should honestly admit the guerrilla character of the Red Army. It is no use being ashamed of this. On the contrary, this guerrilla character is precisely our distinguishing feature, our strong point, and our means of defeating the enemy. We should be prepared to discard it, but we cannot do so today. In the future this guerrilla character would definitely become something to be ashamed of and to be discarded, but today it is invaluable and we must stick to it. . . .

Mobile warfare is primary, but we do not reject positional warfare where it is possible and necessary. It should be admitted that positional warfare should be employed for the tenacious defence of particular key points in a containing action during the strategic defensive, and when, during the strategic offensive, we encounter an enemy force that is isolated and cut off from help. We have had considerable experience in defeating the enemy by such positional warfare; we have cracked open many enemy cities, blockhouses and forts and broken through fairly well-fortified enemy field positions. In future we shall increase our efforts and remedy our inadequacies in this respect. We should by all means advocate positional attack or defence when circumstances require and permit it. At the present time, what we are opposed to is the general use of positional warfare or putting it on an equal footing with mobile warfare; that is impermissible. . . .

Guerrilla-ism has two aspects. One is irregularity, that is, decentralization, lack of uniformity, absence of strict discipline, and simple methods of work. These features stemmed from the Red Army's infancy, and some of them were just what was needed at the time. As the Red Army reaches a higher stage, we must gradually and consciously eliminate them so as to make the Red Army more centralized, more unified, more disciplined and more thorough in its work—in short, more regular in character. In the directing of operations we should also gradually and consciously reduce such guerrilla characteristics as are no longer required at a higher stage. Refusal to make progress in this respect and obstinate adherence to the old stage are impermissible and harmful, and are detrimental to large-scale operations.

The other aspect of guerrilla-ism consists of the principle of mobile warfare, the guerrilla character of both strategic and tactical operations which is still necessary at present, the inevitable fluidity of our base areas, flexibility in planning the development of the base areas, and the rejection of premature regularization in building the Red Army. In this connection, it is equally impermissible, disadvantageous and harmful to our present operations to deny the facts of history, oppose the retention of what is useful, and rashly leave the present stage in order to rush blindly towards a "new stage," which is as yet beyond reach and has no real significance at the present time. . . .

War of Quick Decision

A strategically protracted war and campaigns or battles of quick decision are two aspects of the same thing, two principles which should receive equal and simultaneous emphasis in civil wars and which are also applicable in anti-imperialist wars.

Revolutionary forces grow only gradually because the reactionary forces are very strong, and this fact determines the protracted nature of our war. Here impatience is harmful and advocacy of "quick decision" incorrect. To wage a revolutionary war for ten years, as we have done, might be surprising in other countries, but for us it is like the opening sections in an "eight-legged essay"— the "presentation, amplification and preliminary exposition of the theme"— and many exciting parts are yet to follow. No doubt developments in the future will be greatly accelerated under the influence of domestic and international conditions. As changes have already taken place in the international and domestic situation and greater changes are coming, it can be said that we have outgrown the past state of slow development and fighting in isolation. But we should not expect successes overnight. The aspiration to "wipe out the enemy before breakfast" is admirable, but it is bad to make concrete plans to do so. As China's reactionary forces are backed by many imperialist powers, our revolutionary war will continue to be a protracted one until China's revolutionary forces have built up enough strength to breach the main positions of our internal and external enemies, and until the international revolutionary forces have crushed or contained most of the international reactionary forces. To proceed from this point in formulating our strategy of long-term warfare is one of the important principles guiding our strategy.

The reverse is true of campaigns and battles—here the principle is not protractedness but quick decision. Quick decision is sought in campaigns and battles, and this is true at all times and in all countries. In a war as a whole, too, quick decision is sought at all times and in all countries, and a long drawn-out war is considered harmful. China's war, however, must be handled with the greatest patience and treated as a protracted war. . . . First, the Red Army has no sources from which to replenish its arms and especially its ammunition; second, the White forces consist of many armies while there is only one Red Army, which must be prepared to fight one operation after another in quick succession in order to smash each campaign of "encirclement and suppression"; and third, though the White armies advance separately, most of them keep fairly close to one another, and if we fail to gain a quick decision in attacking one of them, all the others will converge upon us. For these reasons we have to fight battles of quick decision. It is usual for us to conclude a battle in a few hours, or in a day or two. It is only when our plan is to "besiege the enemy in order to strike at his reinforcements" and our purpose is to strike not at the besieged enemy but at his reinforcements that we are prepared for a certain degree of protractedness in our besieging operations; but even then we seek a quick decision against the reinforcements. A plan of protracted operations is often applied in campaigns or battles when we are strategically on the defensive and are tenaciously defending positions on a holding front, or when, in a strategic offensive, we are attacking isolated enemy forces cut off from help, or are eliminating White strongholds within our base areas. But protracted operations of this kind help rather than hinder the main Red Army force in its battles of quick decision.

A quick decision cannot be achieved simply by wanting it, but requires many specific conditions. The main requirements are: adequate preparations, seizing the opportune moment, concentration of superior forces, encircling and outflanking tactics, favourable terrain, and striking at the enemy when he is on the move, or when he is stationary but has not yet consolidated his positions. Unless these requirements are satisfied, it is impossible to achieve quick decision in a campaign or battle.

The smashing of an enemy "encirclement and suppression" is a major campaign, but the principle of quick decision and not that of protractedness still applies. For the manpower, financial resources and military strength of a base area do not allow protractedness.

While quick decision is the general principle, we must oppose undue impatience. It is altogether necessary that the highest military and political leading body of a revolutionary base area, having taken into account the circumstances in its base area and the situation of the enemy, should not be overawed by the enemy's truculence, dispirited by hardships that can be endured, or dejected by setbacks, but should have the requisite patience and stamina. . . .

War of Annihilation

. . . For the Red Army which gets almost all its supplies from the enemy, war of annihilation is the basic policy. Only by annihilating the enemy's effective strength can we smash his "encirclement and suppression" campaigns and expand our revolutionary base areas. Inflicting casualties is a means of annihilating the enemy, or otherwise there would be no sense to it. We incur losses ourselves in inflicting casualties on the enemy but we replenish ourselves by annihilating his units, thereby not only making good our losses but adding to the strength of our army. A battle in which the enemy is routed is not basically decisive in a contest with an enemy of great strength. A battle of annihilation, on the other hand, produces a great and immediate impact on any enemy. . . .

Our policy for dealing with the enemy's first, second, third and fourth "encirclement and suppression" campaigns was war of annihilation. The forces annihilated in each campaign constituted only part of the enemy's total strength, and yet all these "encirclement and suppression" campaigns were smashed. In our fifth counter-campaign, however, the opposite policy was pursued, which in fact helped the enemy to attain his aims.

War of annihilation entails the concentration of superior forces and the adoption of encircling or outflanking tactics. We cannot have the former without the latter. Conditions such as popular support, favourable terrain, a vulnerable enemy force and the advantage of surprise are all indispensable for the purpose of annihilation.

Merely routing one enemy force or permitting it to escape has meaning only if, in the battle or campaign as a whole, our main force is concentrating its operations of annihilation against another enemy force, or otherwise it is meaningless. Here the losses are justified by the gains.

In establishing our own war industry we must not allow ourselves to become dependent on it. Our basic policy is to rely on the war industries of the imperialist countries and of our domestic enemy. We have a claim on the output of the arsenals of London as well as of Hanyang, and, what is more, it is delivered to us by the enemy's transport corps. This is the sober truth, it is not a jest.

PART 12

THE NUCLEAR ERA

BERNARD BRODIE
(1910–1978)

Bernard Brodie, one of the prime U.S. experts on strategic issues from World War II until his death, was professor of international relations at Yale University and senior staff member at the RAND Corporation in Santa Monica. He taught at the National War College and was later consultant to the military schools of the three services. His books include Sea Power in the Machine Age *(Princeton: Princeton University Press, 1941),* The Absolute Weapon *(co-author; New York: Harcourt, Brace, 1946), and* Strategy in the Missile Age *(Princeton: Princeton University Press, 1959).*

WAR IN THE ATOMIC AGE

Most of those who have held the public ear on the subject of the atomic bomb have been content to assume that war and obliteration are now completely synonymous, and that modern man must therefore be either obsolete or fully ripe for the millennium. No doubt the state of obliteration—if that should indeed be the future fate of nations which cannot resolve their disputes—provides little scope for analysis. A few degrees difference in nearness to totality is of relatively small account. But in view of man's historically-tested resistance to drastic changes in behavior, especially in a benign direction, one may be pardoned for wishing to examine the various possibilities inherent in the situation before taking any one of them for granted.

It is already known to us all that a war with atomic bombs would be immeasurably more destructive and horrible than any the world has yet known. The fact is indeed portentous, and to many it is overwhelming. But as a datum for the formulation of policy it is in itself of strictly limited utility. It

From Bernard Brodie, *The Absolute Weapon* (New York: Harcourt, Brace & Co., 1946), 21–76. Copyright © 1946 by Yale Institute of International Studies, renewed 1974 by Yale Concilium on International and Area Studies. Reprinted by permission of Harcourt Brace Jovanovich, Inc.

underlines the urgency of our reaching correct decisions, but it does not help us to discover which decisions are in fact correct.

Men have in fact been converted to religion at the point of the sword, but the process generally required actual use of the sword against recalcitrant individuals. The atomic bomb does not lend itself to that kind of discriminate use. The wholesale conversion of mankind away from those parochial attitudes bound up in nationalism is a consummation devoutly to be wished and, where possible, to be actively promoted. But the mere existence of the bomb does not promise to accomplish it at an early enough time to be of any use. The careful handling required to assure long and fruitful life to the Age of Atomic Energy will in the first instance be a function of distinct national governments, not all of which, incidentally, reflect in their behavior the will of the popular majority.

Governments are of course ruled by considerations not wholly different from those which affect even enlightened individuals. That the atomic bomb is a weapon of incalculable horror will no doubt impress most of them deeply. But they have never yet responded to the horrific implications of war in a uniform way. Even those governments which feel impelled to the most drastic self-denying proposals will have to grapple not merely with the suspicions of other governments but with the indisputable fact that great nations have very recently been ruled by men who were supremely indifferent to horror, especially horror inflicted by them on people other than their own.

Statesmen have hitherto felt themselves obliged to base their policies on the assumption that the situation might again arise where to one or more great powers war looked less dangerous or less undesirable than the prevailing conditions of peace. They will want to know how the atomic bomb affects that assumption. They must realize at the outset that a weapon so terrible cannot but influence the degree of probability of war for any given period in the future. But the degree of that influence or the direction in which it operates is by no means obvious. It has, for example, been stated over and over again that the atomic bomb is *par excellence* the weapon of aggression, that it weights the scales overwhelmingly in favor of surprise attack. That if true would indicate that world peace is even more precarious than it was before, despite the greater horrors of war. But is it inevitably true? If not, then the effort to make the reverse true would deserve a high priority among the measures to be pursued.

Thus, a series of questions present themselves. Is war more or less likely in a world which contains atomic bombs? If the latter, is it *sufficiently* unlikely—sufficiently, that is, to give society the opportunity it desperately needs to adjust its politics to its physics? What are the procedures for effecting that adjustment within the limits of our opportunities? And how can we enlarge our opportunities? Can we transmute what appears to be an immediate crisis into a long-term problem, which presumably would permit the application of more varied and better considered correctives than the pitifully few and inadequate measures which seem available at the moment?

It is precisely in order to answer such questions that we turn our attention to the effect of the bomb on the character of war. We know in advance that war, if it occurs, will be very different from what it was in the past, but what we want to know is: How different, and in what ways? A study of those questions should help us to discover the conditions which will govern the pursuit of security in the future and the feasibility of proposed measures for furthering that pursuit. At any rate, we know that it is not the mere existence of the weapon but rather its effects on the traditional pattern of war which will govern the adjustments which states will make in their relations with each other.

The Truman-Attlee-King statement of November 15, 1945, epitomized in its first paragraph a few specific conclusions concerning the bomb which had evolved as of that date: "We recognize that the application of recent scientific discoveries to the methods and practice of war has placed at the disposal of mankind means of destruction hitherto unknown, against which there can be no adequate military defense, and in the employment of which no single nation can in fact have a monopoly."

This observation, it would seem, is one upon which all reasonable people would now be agreed. But it should be noted that of the three propositions presented in it the first is either a gross understatement or meaningless, the second has in fact been challenged by persons in high military authority, and the third, while generally admitted to be true, has nevertheless been the subject of violently clashing interpretations. In any case, the statement does not furnish a sufficient array of postulates for the kind of analysis we wish to pursue.

It is therefore necessary to start out afresh and examine the various features of the bomb, its production, and its use which are of military importance. Presented below are a number of conclusions concerning the character of the bomb which seem to this writer to be inescapable. Some of the eight points listed already enjoy fairly universal acceptance; most do not. After offering with each one an explanation of why he believes it to be true, the writer will attempt to deduce from these several conclusions or postulates the effect of the bomb on the character of war.

The power of the present bomb is such that any city in the world can be effectively destroyed by one to ten bombs.

While this proposition is not likely to evoke much dissent, its immediate implications have been resisted or ignored by important public officials. These implications are twofold. First, it is now physically possible for air forces no greater than those existing in the recent war to wipe out all the cities of a great nation in a single day—and it will be shown subsequently that what is physically possible must be regarded as tactically feasible. Secondly, with our present industrial organization the elimination of our cities would mean the elimination for military purposes of practically the whole of our industrial structure. But before testing these extraordinary implications, let us examine and verify the original proposition.

The bomb dropped on Hiroshima completely pulverized an area of which the radius from the point of detonation was about one and one-quarter miles. However, everything to a radius of two miles was blasted with some burning and between two and three miles the buildings were about half destroyed. Thus the area of total destruction covered about four square miles, and the area of destruction and substantial damage extended over some twenty-seven square miles. The bomb dropped on Nagasaki, while causing less damage than the Hiroshima bomb because of the physical characteristics of the city, was nevertheless considerably more powerful. We have it on Dr. J. Robert Oppenheimer's authority that the Nagasaki bomb "would have taken out ten square miles, or a bit more, if there had been ten square miles to take out." From the context in which that statement appears it is apparent that Dr. Oppenheimer is speaking of an area of total destruction. . . .

It should be obvious that there is much more than a logistic difference involved between a situation where a single plane sortie can cause the destruction of a city like Hiroshima and one in which at least 500 bomber sorties are required to do the same job. Nevertheless, certain officers of the United States Army Air Forces, in an effort to "deflate" the atomic bomb, have observed publicly enough to have their comments reported in the press that the destruction wrought at Hiroshima could have been effected by two days of routine bombing with ordinary bombs. Undoubtedly so, but the 500 or more bombers needed to do the job under those circumstances would if they were loaded with atomic bombs be physically capable of destroying 500 or more Hiroshimas in the same interval of time. That observation discounts certain tactical considerations. These will be taken up in due course, but for the moment it is sufficient to point out that circumstances do arise in war when it is the physical carrying capacity of the bombing vehicles rather than tactical considerations which will determine the amount of damage done.

No adequate defense against the bomb exists, and the possibilities of its existence in the future are exceedingly remote.

This proposition requires little supporting argument in so far as it is a statement of existing fact. But that part of it which involves a prediction for the future conflicts with the views of most of the high-ranking military officers who have ventured opinions on the implications of the atomic bomb. No layman can with equanimity differ from the military in their own field, and the present writer has never entertained the once-fashionable view that the military do not know their business. But, apart from the question of objectivity concerning professional interests—in which respect the record of the military profession is neither worse nor better than that of other professions—the fact is that the military experts have based their arguments mainly on presumptions gleaned from a field in which they are generally not expert, namely, military *history*. History is at best an imperfect guide to the future, but when imperfectly understood and interpreted it is a menace to sound judgment.

The defense against hostile missiles in all forms of warfare, whether on land, sea, or in the air, has thus far depended basically on a combination of, first, measures to reduce the number of missiles thrown or to interfere with their aim (i.e., defense by offensive measures) and, secondly, ability to absorb those which strike. To take an obvious example, the large warship contains in itself and in its escorting air or surface craft a volume of fire power which usually reduces and may even eliminate the blows of the adversary. Unlike most targets ashore, it also enjoys a mobility which enables it to maneuver evasively under attack (which will be of little value under atomic bombs). But unless the enemy is grotesquely inferior in strength, the ship's ability to survive must ultimately depend upon its compartmentation and armor, that is, on its ability to absorb punishment. . . .

It is precisely this ability to absorb punishment, whether one is speaking of a warship or a city, which seems to vanish in the face of atomic attack. For almost any kind of target selected, the so-called "static defenses" are defenses no longer. For the same reason too, mere reduction in the number of missiles which strike home is not sufficient to save the target, though it may have some effect on the enemy's selection of targets. . . .

In his speech before the Washington Monument on October 5, 1945, Fleet Admiral Chester W. Nimitz correctly cautioned the American people against leaping to the conclusion that the atomic bomb had made armies and navies obsolete. But he could have based his cautionary note on better grounds than he in fact adopted. "Before risking our future by accepting these ideas at face value," he said, "let us examine the historical truth that, at least up to this time, there has never yet been a weapon against which man has been unable to devise a counterweapon or a defense."

Apart from the possible irrelevancy for the future of this observation—against which the phrase "at least up to this time" provides only formal protection—the fact is that it is not historically accurate. . . .

In so far as this doctrine becomes dogma and is applied to the atomic bomb, it becomes the most dangerous kind of illusion. . . .

. . . After five centuries of the use of hand arms with fire-propelled missiles, the large numbers of men killed by comparable arms in the recent war indicates that no adequate answer has yet been found for the bullet. . . . It has simply become customary to consider an "answer" satisfactory when it merely diminishes or qualifies the effectiveness of the weapon against which it is devised, and that kind of custom will not do for the atomic bomb.

Despite such statements as that of Canadian General A. G. L. McNaughton that means with which to counter the atomic bomb are already "clearly in sight," it seems pretty well established that there is no *specific* reply to the bomb. The physicists and chemists who produced the atomic bomb are apparently unanimous on this point: that while there was a scientific consensus long before the atomic bomb existed that it could be produced, no comparable opinion is entertained among scientists concerning their chances of devising effective countermeasures. . . .

Any active defense at all must be along the lines of affecting the carrier, and we have already noted that even when used with the relatively vulnerable airplane or V-1 the atomic bomb poses wholly new problems for the defense. A nation which had developed strong defenses against invading aircraft, which had found reliable means of interfering with radio-controlled rockets, which had developed highly efficient countersmuggling and countersabotage agencies, and which had dispersed through the surrounding countryside substantial portions of the industries and populations normally gathered in urban communities would obviously be better prepared to resist atomic attack than a nation which had either neglected or found itself unable to do these things. But it would have only a relative advantage over the latter; it would still be exposed to fearful destruction.

In any case, technological progress is not likely to be confined to measures of defense. The use of more perfect vehicles and of more destructive bombs in greater quantity might very well offset any gains in defense. And the bomb already has a fearful lead in the race. . . .

The atomic bomb not only places an extraordinary military premium upon the development of new types of carriers but also greatly extends the destructive range of existing carriers.

. . . The power of the new bomb completely alters the considerations which previously governed the choice of vehicles and the manner of using them. A rocket far more elaborate and expensive than the V-2 used by the Germans is still an exceptionally cheap means of bombarding a country if it can carry in its nose an atomic bomb. The relative inaccuracy of aim—which continued research will no doubt reduce—is of much diminished consequence when the radius of destruction is measured in miles rather than yards. And even with existing fuels such as were used in the German V-2, it is theoretically feasible to produce rockets capable of several thousands of miles of range, though the problem of controlling the flight of rockets over such distances is greater than is generally assumed.

Of more immediate concern than the possibilities of rocket development, however, is the enormous increase in effective bombing range which the atomic bomb gives to existing types of aircraft. That it has this effect becomes evident when one examines the various factors which determine under ordinary—that is, non-atomic bomb—conditions whether a bombing campaign is returning military dividends. . . .

With atomic bombs, however, the considerations described above which so severely limit bombing range tend to vanish. There is no question of increasing the number of bombs in order to make the sortie profitable. One per plane is quite enough. The gross weight of the atomic bomb is secret, but even if it weighed four to six tons it would still be a light load for a B-29. It would certainly be a sufficient pay load to warrant any conceivable military expenditure on a single sortie. The next step then becomes apparent. Under the callously utilitarian standards of military bookkeeping, a plane and its crew can very well be sacrificed in order to deliver an atomic bomb to an extreme distance. We have, after all, the recent and unforgettable experience of the Japanese kamikaze. Thus, the plane can make its entire flight in one direction, and, depending on the weight of the bomb and the ultimate carrying capacity of the plane, its range might be almost as great with a single atomic bomb as it would be with no bomb load whatever. The non-stop flight during November, 1945, of a B-29 from Guam to Washington, D.C., almost 8,200 statute miles, was in this respect more than a stunt. . . .

Under the conditions just described, any world power is able from bases within its own territories to destroy most of the cities of any other power. It is not *necessary*, despite the assertions to the contrary of various naval and political leaders including President Truman, to seize advanced bases close to enemy territory as a prerequisite to effective use of the bomb. The lessons of the recent Pacific war in that respect are not merely irrelevant but misleading, and the effort to inflate their significance for the future is only one example of the pre-atomic thinking prevalent today even among people who understand fully the power of the bomb. To recognize that power is one thing; to draw out its full strategic implications is quite another.

The facts just presented do not mean that distance loses all its importance as a barrier to conflict between the major power centers of the world. It would still loom large in any plans to consolidate an atomic bomb attack by rapid invasion and occupation. It would no doubt also influence the success of the bomb attack itself. Rockets are likely to remain of lesser range than aircraft and less accurate near the limits of their range, and the weather hazards which still affect aircraft multiply with distance. Advanced bases will certainly not be valueless. But it is nevertheless a fact that under existing technology the distance separating, for example, the Soviet Union from the United States offers no direct immunity to either with respect to atomic bomb attack, though it does so for all practical purposes with respect to ordinary bombs.

Superiority in air forces, though a more effective safeguard in itself than superiority in naval or land forces, nevertheless fails to guarantee security.

This proposition is obviously true in the case of very long range rockets, but let us continue to limit our discussion to existing carriers. In his *Third Report to the Secretary of War*, dated November 12, 1945, General H. H. Arnold, commanding the Army Air Forces, made the following statement: "Meanwhile [i.e., until very long range rockets are developed], the only known effective means of delivering atomic bombs in their present stage of development is the very heavy bomber, and that is certain of success only when the user has air superiority.". . .

. . . We know from the experience of the recent war that very inferior air forces can penetrate to enemy targets if they are willing to make the necessary sacrifices. The Japanese aircraft which raided Pearl Harbor were considerably fewer in number than the American planes available at Pearl Harbor. That, to be sure, was a surprise attack preceding declaration of hostilities, but such possibilities must be taken into account for the future. At any rate, the Japanese air attacks upon our ships off Okinawa occurred more than three years after the opening of hostilities, and there the Japanese, who were not superior in numbers on any one day and who did indeed lose over 4,000 planes in two months of battle, nevertheless succeeded in sinking or damaging no fewer than 253 American warships. For that matter, the British were effectively raiding targets deep in Germany, and doing so without suffering great casualties, long before they had overtaken the German lead in numbers of aircraft. The war has demonstrated beyond the shadow of a doubt that the sky is much too big to permit one side, however superior, to shut out enemy aircraft completely from the air over its territories.

The concept of "command of the air," which has been used altogether too loosely, has never been strictly analogous to that of "command of the sea." The latter connotes something approaching absolute exclusion of enemy surface craft from the area in question. The former suggests only that the enemy is suffering losses greater than he can afford, whereas one's own side is not. But the appraisal of tolerable losses is in part subjective, and is also affected by several variables which may have little to do with the number of planes downed. Certainly the most important of those variables is the amount of damage being inflicted on the bombing raids. An air force which can destroy the cities in a given territory has for all practical purposes the fruits of command of the air, regardless of its losses. . . .

That superiority which results in the so-called "command of the air" is undoubtedly necessary for successful strategic bombing with ordinary bombs, where the weight of bombs requires is so great that the same planes must be used over and over again. In a sense also (though one must register some reservations about the exclusion of other arms) General Arnold is right when he says of atomic bomb attack: "For the moment at least, absolute air superiority in being at all times, combined with the best antiaircraft ground devices, is the only form of defense that offers any security whatever, and it must continue to be an essential part of our security program for a long time to come." But it must be added that the "only form of defense that offers any security whatever" falls far short, even without any consideration of rockets, of offering the already qualified kind of security it formerly offered.

Superiority in numbers of bombs is not in itself a guarantee of strategic superiority in atomic bomb warfare.

Under the technical conditions apparently prevailing today, and presumably likely to continue for some time to come, the primary targets for the atomic bomb will be cities. One does not shoot rabbits with elephant guns, especially if there are elephants available. The critical mass conditions to which the bomb is inherently subject place the minimum of destructive energy of the individual unit at far too high a level to warrant its use against any target where enemy strength is not already densely concentrated. Indeed, there is little inducement to the attacker to seek any other kind of target. If one side can eliminate the cities of the other, it enjoys an advantage which is practically tantamount to final victory, provided always its own cities are not similarly eliminated.

The fact that the bomb is inevitably a weapon of indiscriminate destruction may carry no weight in any war in which it is used. Even in World War II, in which the bombs used could to a large extent isolate industrial targets from residential districts within an urban area, the distinctions imposed by international law between "military" and "nonmilitary" targets disintegrated entirely.

How large a city has to be to provide a suitable target for the atomic bomb will depend on a number of variables—the ratio of the number of bombs available to the number of cities which might be hit, the wastage of bombs in respect to each target, the number of bombs which the larger cities can absorb before ceasing to be profitable targets, and, of course, the precise characteristics and relative accessibility of the individual city. Most important of all is the place of the particular city in the nation's economy. We can see at once that it does not require the obliteration of all its towns to make a nation wholly incapable of defending itself in the traditional fashion. Thus, the number of *critical* targets is quite limited, and the number of hits necessary to win a strategic decision—always excepting the matter of retaliation—is correspondingly limited. That does not mean that additional hits would be useless but simply that diminishing returns would set in early; and after the cities of, say, 100,000 population were eliminated the returns from additional bombs expended would decline drastically. . . .

Regardless of American decisions concerning retention of its present secrets, other powers besides Britain and Canada will possess the ability to produce the bombs in quantity within a period of five to ten years hence.

This proposition by-passes the possibility of effective international regulation of bomb production being adopted within that period. A discussion of that possibility is left to subsequent chapters. One may anticipate, however, to the extent of pointing out that it is difficult to induce nations like the Soviet Union to accept such regulation until they can start out in a position of parity with the United States in ability to produce the bomb. The State Department Board of Consultant's report of March 16, 1946, acknowledges as much when it states that "acceleration" of the disappearance of our monopoly must be "inherent in the adoption of any plan of international control.". . .

At a public meeting in Washington on December 11, 1945, Major General Leslie R. Groves permitted himself the observation that the bomb was not a problem for us but for our grandchildren. What he obviously intended that statement to convey was the idea that it would take other nations, like Russia, many years to duplicate our feat. When it was submitted to him that the scientists who worked on the problem were practically unanimous in their disagreement, he responded that they did not understand the problem. The difficulties to be overcome, he insisted, are not primarily of a scientific but of an engineering character. And while the Soviet Union may have first-rate scientists, it clearly does not have the great resources in engineering talent or the industrial laboratories that we enjoy.

Perhaps so; but there are a few pertinent facts which bear on such a surmise. First of all, it has always been axiomatic in the armed services that the only way really to keep a device secret is to keep the fact of its existence secret. Thus, the essential basis of secrecy of the atomic bomb disappeared on August 6, 1945. . . .

The conviction that the bomb represents the apotheosis of aggressive instruments is especially marked among the scientists who developed it. They know the bomb and its power. They also know their own limitations as producers of miracles. They are therefore much less sanguine than many laymen or military officers of their capacity to provide the instrument which will rob the bomb of its terrors. One of the most outstanding among them, Professor J. Robert Oppenheimer, has expressed himself quite forcibly on the subject:

> The pattern of the use of atomic weapons was set at Hiroshima. They are weapons of aggression, of surprise, and of terror. If they are ever used again it may well be by the thousands, or perhaps by the tens of thousands; their method of delivery may well be different, and may reflect new possibilities of interception, and the strategy of their use may well be different from what it was against an essentially defeated enemy. But it is a weapon for aggressors, and the elements of surprise and of terror are as intrinsic to it as are the fissionable nuclei.

The truth of Professor Oppenheimer's statement depends on one vital but unexpressed assumption: that the nation which proposes to launch the attack will not need to fear retaliation. If it must fear retaliation, the fact that it destroys its opponent's cities some hours or even days before its own are destroyed may avail it little. It may indeed commence the evacuation of its own cities at the same moment it is hitting the enemy's cities (to do so earlier would provoke a like move on the opponent's part) and thus present to retaliation cities which are empty. But the success even of such a move would depend on the time interval between hitting and being hit. It certainly would not save the enormous physical plant which is contained in the cities and which over any length of time is indispensable to the life of the national community. Thus the element of surprise may be less important than is generally assumed.

If the aggressor state must fear retaliation, it will know that even if it is the victor it will suffer a degree of physical destruction incomparably greater than that suffered by any defeated nation of history, incomparably greater, that is, than that suffered by Germany in the recent war. Under those circumstances no victory, even if guaranteed in advance—which it never is—would be worth the price. The threat of retaliation does not have to be 100 per cent certain; it is sufficient if there is a good chance of it, or if there is belief that there is a good chance of it. The prediction is more important than the fact.

The argument that the victim of an attack might not know where the bombs are coming from is almost too preposterous to be worth answering, but it has been made so often by otherwise responsible persons that it cannot be wholly ignored. That the geographical location of the launching sites of long-range rockets may remain for a time unknown is conceivable, though unlikely, but that the identity of the attacker should remain unknown is not in modern times conceivable. The fear that one's country might suddenly be attacked in the midst of apparently profound peace has often been voiced, but, at least in the last century and a half, it has never been realized. As advancing technology makes war more horrible, it also makes the decision to resort to it more dependent on an elaborate psychological preparation. In international politics today few things are more certain than that an attack must have an antecedent hostility of obviously grave character. Especially today, when there are only two or three powers of the first rank, the identity of the major rival would be unambiguous. In fact, as Professor Jacob Viner has pointed out, it is the lack of ambiguity concerning the major rival which makes the bipolar power system so dangerous.

There is happily little disposition to believe that the atomic bomb by its mere existence and by the horror implicit in it "makes war impossible." In the sense that war is something not to be endured if any reasonable alternative remains, it has long been "impossible." But for that very reason we cannot hope that the bomb makes war impossible in the narrower sense of the word. Even without it the conditions of modern war should have been a sufficient deterrent but proved not to be such. If the atomic bomb can be used without fear of substantial retaliation in kind, it will clearly encourage aggression. So much the more reason, therefore, to take all possible steps to assure that multilateral possession of the bomb, should that prove inevitable, be attended by arrangements to make as nearly certain as possible that the aggressor who uses the bomb will have it used against him.

If such arrangements are made, the bomb cannot but prove in the net a powerful inhibition to aggression. It would make relatively little difference if one power had more bombs and were better prepared to resist them than its opponent. It would in any case undergo incalculable destruction of life and property. It is clear that there existed in the thirties a deeper and probably more generalized revulsion against war than in any other era of history. Under those circumstances the breeding of a new war required a situation combining dictators of singular irresponsibility with a notion among them and their general staffs that aggression would be both successful and cheap. The possibility of irresponsible or desperate men again becoming rulers of powerful states cannot under the prevailing system of international politics be ruled out in the future. But it does seem possible to erase the idea—if not among madmen rulers then at least among their military supporters—that aggression will be cheap.

Thus, the first and most vital step in any American security program for the age of atomic bombs is to take measures to guarantee to ourselves in case of attack the possibility of retaliation in kind. The writer in making that statement is not for the moment concerned about who will *win* the next war in which atomic bombs are used. Thus far the chief purpose of our military establishment has been to win wars. From now on its chief purpose must be to avert them. It can have almost no other useful purpose.

ALBERT WOHLSTETTER
(b. 1912)

In an important and contentious article on "The Delicate Balance of Terror,"
published in 1959, Albert Wohlstetter set out the principle that mutual
deterrence—and the balance underlying it—depends on the invulnerability
of each side's retaliatory capacity—its ability to survive an initial strike.
Whence the arms race, with each side seeking to retain an undeniable
second-strike capability.

THE DELICATE BALANCE OF TERROR

The first shock administered by the Soviet launching of sputnik has almost
dissipated. . . . Western defense policy has almost returned to the level of activity and the emphasis suited to the basic assumptions which were controlling before sputnik.

One of the most important of these assumptions—that a general thermonuclear war is extremely unlikely—is held in common by most of the critics of our defense policy as well as by its proponents. Because of its crucial role
in the Western strategy of defense, I should like to examine the stability of the
thermonuclear balance which, it is generally supposed, would make aggression irrational or even insane. The balance, I believe, is in fact precarious, and
this fact has critical implications for policy. Deterrence in the 1960s is neither
assured nor impossible but will be the product of sustained intelligent effort
and hard choices, responsibly made. . . .

The Presumed Automatic Balance

. . . Is deterrence a necessary consequence of both sides having a nuclear delivery capability, and is all-out war nearly obsolete? Is mutual extinction the

From Albert Wohlstetter, "The Delicate Balance of Terror," *Foreign Affairs* 37, no. 1 (1959):
211–34. Copyright © 1959 by the Council on Foreign Relations, Inc. Reprinted by permission of
Foreign Affairs (1959).

only outcome of a general war? This belief, frequently expressed by references to Mr. Oppenheimer's simile of the two scorpions in a bottle, is perhaps the prevalent one. It is held by a very eminent and diverse group of people—in England by Sir Winston Churchill, P. M. S. Blackett, Sir John Slessor, Admiral Buzzard and many others; in France by such figures as Raymond Aron, General Gallois and General Gazin; in this country by the titular heads of both parties as well as almost all writers on military and foreign affairs, by both Henry Kissinger and his critic, James E. King, Jr., and by George Kennan as well as Dean Acheson. . . .

Deterrence, however, is not automatic. While feasible, it will be much harder to achieve in the 1960s than is generally believed. One of the most disturbing features of current opinion is the underestimation of this difficulty. This is due partly to a misconstruction of the technological race as a problem in matching striking forces, partly to a wishful analysis of the Soviet ability to strike first.

Since sputnik, the United States has made several moves to assure the world (that is, the enemy, but more specifically our allies and ourselves) that we will match or overmatch Soviet technology and, specifically, Soviet offense technology. We have, for example, accelerated the bomber and ballistic missile programs, in particular the intermediate-range ballistic missiles. The problem has been conceived as more or better bombers—or rockets; or sputniks; or engineers. This has meant confusing deterrence with matching or exceeding the enemy's ability to strike first. Matching weapons, however, misconstrues the nature of the technological race. Not, as is frequently said, because only a few bombs owned by the defender can make aggression fruitless, but because even many might not. One outmoded A-bomb dropped from an obsolete bomber might destroy a great many supersonic jets and ballistic missiles. To deter an attack means being able to strike back in spite of it. It means, in other words, a capability to strike second. In the last year or two there has been a growing awareness of the importance of the distinction between a "strike-first" and a "strike-second" capability, but little, if any, recognition of the implications of this distinction for the balance of terror theory. . . .

The Quantitative Nature of the Problem
and the Uncertainties

In treating Soviet strategies it is important to consider Soviet rather than Western advantage and to consider the strategy of both sides quantitatively. The effectiveness of our own choices will depend on a most complex numerical interaction of Soviet and Western plans. Unfortunately, both the privileged and unprivileged information on these matters is precarious. As a result, competent people have been led into critical error in evaluating the prospects for deterrence. . . .

Perhaps the first stop in dispelling the nearly universal optimism about the stability of deterrence would be to recognize the difficulties in analyzing the uncertainties and interactions between our own wide range of choices and the moves open to the Soviets. On our side we must consider an enormous variety of strategic weapons which might compose our force, and for each of these several alternative methods of basing and operation. These are the choices that determine whether a weapons system will have any genuine capability in the realistic circumstances of a war. . . .

The difficulty of describing in a brief article the best mixture of weapons for the long-term future beginning in 1960, their base requirements, their potentiality for stabilizing or upsetting the balance among the great powers, and their implications for the alliance, is not just a matter of space or the constraint of security. The difficulty in fact stems from some rather basic insecurities. These matters are widely uncertain; we are talking about weapons and vehicles that are some time off and, even if the precise performances currently hoped for and claimed by contractors were in the public domain, it would be a good idea to doubt them. . . .

Some of the complexities can be suggested by referring to the successive obstacles to be hurdled by any system providing a capability to strike second, that is, to strike back. Such deterrent systems must have (a) a stable, "steady-state" peacetime operation within feasible budgets (besides the logistic and operational costs there are, for example, problems of false alarms and accidents). They must have also the ability (b) to survive enemy attacks, (c) to make and communicate the decision to retaliate, (d) to reach enemy territory with fuel enough to complete their mission, (e) to penetrate enemy active defenses, that is, fighters and surface-to-air missiles, and (f) to destroy the target in spite of any "passive" civil defense in the form of dispersal or protective construction or evacuation of the target itself.

Within limits the enemy is free to use his offensive and defensive forces so as to exploit the weaknesses of each of our systems. He will also be free, within limits, in the 1960s to choose that composition of forces which will make life as difficult as possible for the various systems we might select. It would be quite wrong to assume that we have the same degree of flexibility or that the uncertainties I have described affect a totalitarian aggressor and the party attacked equally. A totalitarian country can preserve secrecy about the capabilities and disposition of his forces very much better than a Western democracy. And the aggressor has, among other enormous advantages of the first strike, the ability to weigh continually our performance at each of the six barriers and to choose that precise time and circumstance for attack which will reduce uncertainty. It is important not to confuse our uncertainty with his. Strangely enough, some military commentators have not made this distinction and have founded their certainty of deterrence on the fact simply that there are uncertainties. . . .

The Delicacy of the Balance of Terror

The most important conclusion is that we must expect a vast increase in the weight of attack which the Soviets can deliver with little warning, and the growth of a significant Russian capability for an essentially warningless attack. As a result, strategic deterrence, while feasible, will be extremely difficult to achieve, and at critical junctures in the 1960s, we may not have the power to deter attack. Whether we have it or not will depend on some difficult strategic choices as to the future composition of the deterrent forces as well as hard choices on its basing, operations and defense.

Manned bombers will continue to make up the predominant part of our striking force in the early 1960s. None of the popular remedies for their defense will suffice—not, for example, mere increase of alertness (which will be offset by the Soviet's increasing capability for attack without significant warning), nor simple dispersal or sheltering alone or mobility taken by itself, nor a mere piling up of interceptors and defense missiles around SAC bases. . . .

On the other hand, it would be unwise to look for miracles in the new weapons systems, which by the mid 1960s may constitute a considerable portion of the United States force. After the Thor, Atlas and Titan there are a number of promising developments. The solid-fueled rockets, Minuteman and Polaris, promise in particular to be extremely significant components of the deterrent force. Today they are being touted as making the problem of deterrence easy to solve and, in fact, guaranteeing its solution. But none of the new developments in vehicles is likely to do that. For the complex job of deterrence, they all have limitations. The unvaryingly immoderate claims for each new weapons system should make us wary of the latest "technological breakthroughs." Only a very short time ago the ballistic missile itself was supposed to be intrinsically invulnerable on the ground. It is now more generally understood that its survival is likely to depend on a variety of choices in its defense.

It is hard to talk with confidence about the mid and late 1960s. A systematic study of an optimal or a good deterrent force which considered all the major factors affecting choice and dealt adequately with the uncertainties would be a formidable task. In lieu of this, I shall mention briefly why none of the many systems available or projected dominates the others in any obvious way. My comments will take the form of a swift run-through of the characteristic advantages and disadvantages of various strategic systems at each of the six successive hurdles mentioned earlier.

The first hurdle to be surmounted is the attainment of a stable, steady-state peacetime operation. Systems which depend for their survival on extreme decentralization of controls, as may be the case with large-scale dispersal and some of the mobile weapons, raise problems of accidents and over a long period of peacetime operation this leads in turn to serious political problems. Systems relying on extensive movement by land, perhaps by truck caravan, are an obvious example; the introduction of these on European roads, as is sometimes suggested, would raise grave questions for the governments of some of our allies. Any extensive increase in the armed air alert will increase the hazard of accident and intensify the concern already expressed among our allies. Some of the proposals for bombardment satellites may involve such hazards of unintended bomb release as to make them out of the question. . . .

After making allowance for the unreliability and inaccuracy of the missile, this means a ratio of some ten for one or better. To achieve safety by brute numbers in so unfavorable a competition is not likely to be viable economically or politically. However, a viable peacetime operation is only the first hurdle to be surmounted.

At the second hurdle—surviving the enemy offense—ground alert systems placed deep within a warning net look good against a manned bomber attack, much less good against intercontinental ballistic missiles, and not good at all against ballistic missiles launched from the sea. In the last case, systems such as the Minuteman, which may be sheltered and dispersed as well as alert, would do well. Systems involving launching platforms which are mobile and concealed, such as Polaris submarines, have particular advantage for surviving an enemy offense.

However, there is a third hurdle to be surmounted—namely that of making the decision to retaliate and communicating it. Here, Polaris, the combat air patrol of B-52s, and in fact all of the mobile platforms—under water, on the surface, in the air and above the air—have severe problems. Long distance communication may be jammed and, most important, communication centers may be destroyed.

At the fourth hurdle—ability to reach enemy territory with fuel enough to complete the mission—several of our short-legged systems have operational problems such as coördination with tankers and using bases close to the enemy. For a good many years to come, up to the mid 1960s in fact, this will be a formidable hurdle for the greater part of our deterrent force. . . .

The fifth hurdle is the aggressor's long-range interceptors and close-in missile defenses. To get past these might require large numbers of planes and missiles. (If the high cost of overcoming an earlier obstacle—using extreme dispersal or airborne alert or the like—limits the number of planes or missiles bought, our capability is likely to be penalized disproportionately here.) Or getting through may involve carrying heavy loads of radar decoys, electronic jammers and other aids to defense penetration. For example, vehicles like Minuteman and Polaris, which were made small to facilitate dispersal or mobility, may suffer here because they can carry fewer penetration aids.

At the final hurdle—destroying the target in spite of the passive defenses that may protect it—low-payload and low-accuracy systems, such as Minuteman and Polaris, may be frustrated by blast-resistant shelters. For example, five half-megaton weapons with an average inaccuracy of two miles might be expected to destroy half the population of a city of 900,000, spread over 40 square miles, provided the inhabitants are without shelters. But if they are provided with shelters capable of resisting over-pressures of 100 pounds per square inch, approximately 60 such weapons would be required; and deep rock shelters might force the total up to over a thousand.

Prizes for a retaliatory capability are not distributed for getting over one of these jumps. A system must get over all six. I hope these illustrations will suggest that assuring ourselves the power to strike back after a massive thermonuclear surprise attack is by no means as automatic as is widely believed.

In counteracting the general optimism as to the ease and, in fact, the inevitability of deterrence, I should like to avoid creating the extreme opposite impression. Deterrence demands hard, continuing, intelligent work, but it can be achieved. The job of deterring rational attack by guaranteeing great damage to an aggressor is, for example, very much less difficult than erecting a nearly airtight defense of cities in the face of full-scale thermonuclear surprise attack. Protecting manned bombers and missiles is much easier because they may be dispersed, sheltered or kept mobile, and they can respond to warning with greater speed. Mixtures of these and other defenses with complementary strengths can preserve a powerful remainder after attack. Obviously not all our bombers and missiles need to survive in order to fulfill their mission. To preserve the majority of our cities intact in the face of surprise attack is immensely more difficult, if not impossible. (This does not mean that the aggressor has the same problem in preserving his cities from retaliation by a poorly-protected, badly-damaged force. And it does not mean that *we* should not do more to limit the extent of the catastrophe to our cities in case deterrence fails. I believe we should.) Deterrence, however, provided we work at it, is feasible, and, what is more, it is a crucial objective of national policy.

What can be said, then, as to whether general war is unlikely? Would not a general thermonuclear war mean "extinction" for the aggressor as well as the defender? "Extinction" is a state that badly needs analysis. Russian casualties in World War II were more than 20,000,000. Yet Russia recovered extremely well from this catastrophe. There are several quite plausible circumstances in the future when the Russians might be quite confident of being able to limit damage to considerably less than this number—if they make sensible strategic choices and we do not. On the other hand, the risks of not striking might at some juncture appear very great to the Soviets, involving, for example, disastrous defeat in peripheral war, loss of key satellites with danger of revolt spreading—possibly to Russia itself—or fear of an attack by ourselves. Then, striking first, by surprise, would be the sensible choice for them, and from their point of view the smaller risk.

It should be clear that it is not fruitful to talk about the likelihood of general war without specifying the range of alternatives that are pressing on the aggressor and the strategic postures of both the Soviet bloc and the West. Deterrence is a matter of comparative risks. The balance is not automatic. First, since thermonuclear weapons give an enormous advantage to the aggressor, it takes great ingenuity and realism at any given level of nuclear technology to devise a stable equilibrium. And second, this technology itself is changing with fantastic speed. Deterrence will require an urgent and continuing effort.

The Uses and Risks of Bases Close to the Soviets

It may now be useful to focus attention on the special problems of deterrent forces close to the Soviet Union. First, overseas areas have played an important rôle in the past and have a continuing though less certain rôle today. Second, the recent acceleration of production of intermediate-range ballistic missiles and the negotiation of agreements with various NATO powers for their basing and operation have given our overseas bases a renewed importance in deterring attack on the United States—or so it would appear at first blush. Third, an analysis can throw some light on the problems faced by our allies in developing an independent ability to deter all-out attack on themselves, and in this way it can clarify the much agitated question of nuclear sharing. Finally, overseas bases affect in many critical ways, political and economic as well as military, the status of the alliance. . . .

Indeed nothing said here should suggest that deterrence is in itself an adequate strategy. The complementary requirements of a sufficient military policy cannot be discussed in detail here. Certainly they include a more serious development of power to meet limited aggression, especially with more advanced conventional weapons than those now available. They also include more energetic provision for active and passive defenses to limit the dimensions of the catastrophe in case deterrence should fail. For example, an economically feasible shelter program might make the difference between 50,000,000 survivors and 120,000,000 survivors.

But it would be a fatal mistake to suppose that because strategic deterrence is inadequate by itself it can be dispersed with. Deterrence is not dispensable. If the picture of the world I have drawn is rather bleak, it could none the less be cataclysmically worse. Suppose both the United States and the Soviet Union had the power to destroy each others' retaliatory forces and society, given the opportunity to administer the opening blow. The situation would then be something like the old-fashioned Western gun duel. It would be extraordinarily risky for one side *not* to attempt to destroy the other, or to delay doing so, since it not only can emerge unscathed by striking first but this is the sole way it can reasonably hope to emerge at all. Evidently such a situation is extremely unstable. On the other hand, if it is clear that the aggressor too will suffer catastrophic damage in the event of his aggression, he then has strong reason not to attack, even though he can administer great damage. A protected retaliatory capability has a stabilizing influence not only in deterring rational attack, but also in offering every inducement to both powers to reduce the chance of accidental war.

The critics who feel that deterrence is "bankrupt" sometimes say that we stress deterrence too much. I believe this is quite wrong if it means that we are devoting too much effort to protect our power to retaliate; but I think it is quite right if it means that we have talked too much of a strategic threat as a substitute for many things it cannot replace. . . .

Summary

Almost everyone seems concerned with the need to relax tension. However, relaxation of tension, which everyone thinks is good, is not easily distinguished from relaxing one's guard, which almost everyone thinks is bad. Relaxation, like Miltown, is not an end in itself. Not all danger comes from tension. To be tense where there is danger is only rational.

What can we say then, in sum, on the balance of terror theory of automatic deterrence? It is a contribution to the rhetoric rather than the logic of war in the thermonuclear age. The notion that a carefully planned surprise attack can be checkmated almost effortlessly, that, in short, we may resume our deep pre-sputnik sleep, is wrong and its nearly universal acceptance is terribly dangerous. Though deterrence is not enough in itself, it is vital. There are two principal points.

First, deterring general war in both the early and late 1960s will be hard at best, and hardest both for ourselves and our allies wherever we use forces based near the enemy.

Second, even if we can deter general war by a strenuous and continuing effort, this will by no means be the whole of a military, much less a foreign policy. Such a policy would not of itself remove the danger of accidental outbreak or limit the damage in case deterrence failed; nor would it be at all adequate for crises on the periphery.

A generally useful way of concluding a grim argument of this kind would be to affirm that we have the resources, intelligence and courage to make the correct decisions. That is, of course, the case. And there is a good chance that we will do so. But perhaps, as a small aid toward making such decisions more likely, we should contemplate the possibility that they may *not* be made. They *are* hard, *do* involve sacrifice, *are* affected by great uncertainties and concern matters in which much is altogether unknown and much else must be hedged by secrecy; and, above all, they entail a new image of ourselves in a world of persistent danger. It is by no means certain that we shall meet the test.

THOMAS C. SCHELLING
(b. 1921)

In the early 1950s, during the presidency of Dwight D. Eisenhower, Thomas C. Schelling was a member of the White House staff, the Executive Office of the President, and the Foreign Operations Administration. He was professor of economics and then director of the Center for International Affairs at Harvard University, and was for a long period co-chairman of the Harvard–MIT Faculty Seminar on Arms Control. Schelling greatly contributed to the debates on nuclear weapons.

THE DIPLOMACY OF VIOLENCE

The usual distinction between diplomacy and force is not merely in the instruments, words or bullets, but in the relation between adversaries—in the interplay of motives and the role of communication, understandings, compromise, and restraint. Diplomacy is bargaining; it seeks outcomes that, though not ideal for either party, are better for both than some of the alternatives. In diplomacy each party somewhat controls what the other wants, and can get more by compromise, exchange, or collaboration than by taking things in his own hands and ignoring the other's wishes. The bargaining can be polite or rude, entail threats as well as offers, assume a status quo or ignore all rights and privileges, and assume mistrust rather than trust. But whether polite or impolite, constructive or aggressive, respectful or vicious, whether it occurs among friends or antagonists and whether or not there is a basis for trust and goodwill, there must be some common interest, if only in the avoidance of mutual damage, and an awareness of the need to make the other party prefer an outcome acceptable to oneself.

With enough military force a country may not need to bargain. Some things a country wants it can take, and some things it has it can keep, by sheer

From Thomas C. Schelling, *Arms and Influence* (New Haven: Yale University Press, 1966), 1–34. Reprinted by permission of Yale University Press.

strength, skill and ingenuity. It can do this forcibly, accommodating only to opposing strength, skill, and ingenuity and without trying to appeal to an enemy's wishes. Forcibly a country can repel and expel, penetrate and occupy, seize, exterminate, disarm and disable, confine, deny access, and directly frustrate intrusion or attack. It can, that is, if it has enough strength. "Enough" depends on how much an opponent has. . . .

Hurting, unlike forcible seizure or self-defense, is not unconcerned with the interest of others. It is measured in the suffering it can cause and the victims' motivation to avoid it. Forcible action will work against weeds or floods as well as against armies, but suffering requires a victim that can feel pain or has something to lose. To inflict suffering gains nothing and saves nothing directly; it can only make people behave to avoid it. The only purpose, unless sport or revenge, must be to influence somebody's behavior, to coerce his decision or choice. To be coercive, violence has to be anticipated. And it has to be avoidable by accommodation. The power to hurt is bargaining power. To exploit it is diplomacy—vicious diplomacy, but diplomacy.

The Contrast of Brute Force with Coercion

. . . Brute force succeeds when it is used, whereas the power to hurt is most successful when held in reserve. It is the *threat* of damage, or of more damage to come, that can make someone yield or comply. It is *latent* violence that can influence someone's choice—violence that can still be withheld or inflicted, or that a victim believes can be withheld or inflicted. The threat of pain tries to structure someone's motives, while brute force tries to overcome his strength. Unhappily, the power to hurt is often communicated by some performance of it. Whether it is sheer terroristic violence to induce an irrational response, or cool premeditated violence to persuade somebody that you mean it and may do it again, it is not the pain and damage itself but its influence on somebody's behavior that matters. It is the expectation of *more* violence that gets the wanted behavior, if the power to hurt can get it at all.

To exploit a capacity for hurting and inflicting damage one needs to know what an adversary treasures and what scares him and one needs the adversary to understand what behavior of his will cause the violence to be inflicted and what will cause it to be withheld. The victim has to know what is wanted, and he may have to be assured of what is not wanted. The pain and suffering have to appear *contingent* on his behavior; it is not alone the threat that is effective—the threat of pain or loss if he fails to comply—but the corresponding assurance, possibly an implicit one, that he can avoid the pain or loss if he does comply. The prospect of certain death may stun him, but it gives him no choice.

Coercion by threat of damage also requires that our interests and our opponent's not be absolutely opposed. If his pain were our greatest delight and our satisfaction his greatest woe, we would just proceed to hurt and to frustrate each other. It is when his pain gives us little or no satisfaction compared with what he can do for us, and the action or inaction that satisfies us costs him less than the pain we can cause, that there is room for coercion. Coercion requires finding a bargain, arranging for him to be better off doing what we want—worse off not doing what we want—when he takes the threatened penalty into account. . . .

This difference between coercion and brute force is as often in the intent as in the instrument. To hunt down Comanches and to exterminate them was brute force; to raid their villages to make them behave was coercive diplomacy, based on the power to hurt. The pain and loss to the Indians might have looked much the same one way as the other; the difference was one of purpose and effect. If Indians were killed because they were in the way, or somebody wanted their land, or the authorities despaired of making them behave and could not confine them and decided to exterminate them, that was pure unilateral force. If *some* Indians were killed to make *other* Indians behave, that was coercive violence—or intended to be, whether or not it was effective. . . .

The contrast between brute force and coercion is illustrated by two alternative strategies attributed to Genghis Khan. Early in his career he pursued the war creed of the Mongols: the vanquished can never be the friends of the victors, their death is necessary for the victor's safety. This was the unilateral extermination of a menace or a liability. The turning point of his career, according to Lynn Montross, came later when he discovered how to use his power to hurt for diplomatic ends. "The great Khan, who was not inhibited by the usual mercies, conceived the plan of forcing captives—women, children, aged fathers, favorite sons—to march ahead of his army as the first potential victims of resistance." Live captives have often proved more valuable than enemy dead; and the technique discovered by the Khan in his maturity remains contemporary. . . .

Coercive Violence in Warfare

This distinction between the power to hurt and the power to seize or hold forcibly is important in modern war, both big war and little war, hypothetical war and real war. . . .

. . . It is the power to hurt, not military strength in the traditional sense, that inheres in our most impressive military capabilities at the present time. We have a Department of *Defense* but emphasize *retaliation*—"to return evil for evil" (synonyms: requital, reprisal, revenge, vengeance, retribution). And it is pain and violence, not force in the traditional sense, that inheres also in some of the least impressive military capabilities of the present time—the plastic bomb, the terrorist's bullet, the burnt crops, and the tortured farmer.

War appears to be, or threatens to be, not so much a contest of strength as one of endurance, nerve, obstinacy, and pain. It appears to be, and threatens to be, not so much a contest of military strength as a bargaining process— dirty, extortionate, and often quite reluctant bargaining on one side or both— nevertheless a bargaining process.

The difference cannot quite be expressed as one between the *use* of force and the *threat* of force. The actions involved in forcible accomplishment, on the one hand, and in fulfilling a threat, on the other, can be quite different. Sometimes the most effective direct action inflicts enough cost or pain on the enemy to serve as a threat, sometimes not. The United States threatens the Soviet Union with virtual destruction of its society in the event of a surprise attack on the United States; a hundred million deaths are awesome as pure damage, but they are useless in stopping the Soviet attack—especially if the threat is to do it all afterward anyway. So it is worth while to keep the concepts distinct—to distinguish forcible action from the threat of pain—recognizing that some actions serve as both a means of forcible accomplishment and a means of inflicting pure damage, some do not. Hostages tend to entail almost pure pain and damage, as do all forms of reprisal after the fact. Some modes of self-defense may exact so little in blood or treasure as to entail negligible violence; and some forcible actions entail so much violence that their threat can be effective by itself. . . .

To seek out and to destroy the enemy's military force, to achieve a crushing victory over enemy armies, was still the avowed purpose and the central aim of American strategy in both world wars. Military action was seen as an *alternative* to bargaining, not a *process* of bargaining.

The reason is not that civilized countries are so averse to hurting people that they prefer "purely military" wars. (Nor were all of the participants in these wars entirely civilized.) The reason is apparently that the technology and geography of warfare, at least for a war between anything like equal powers during the century ending in World War II, kept coercive violence from being decisive before military victory was achieved. Blockade indeed was aimed at the whole enemy nation, not concentrated on its military forces. . . . "Strategic bombing" of enemy homelands was also occasionally rationalized in terms of the pain and privation it could inflict on people and the civil damage it could do to the nation, as an effort to display either to the population or to the enemy leadership that surrender was better than persistence in view of the damage that could be done. It was also rationalized in more "military" terms, as a way of selectively denying war material to the troops or as a way of generally weakening the economy on which the military effort rested.

But as terrorism—as violence intended to coerce the enemy rather than to weaken him militarily—blockade and strategic bombing by themselves were not quite up to the job in either world war in Europe. . . .

The great exception was the two atomic bombs on Japanese cities. These were weapons of terror and shock. They hurt, and promised more hurt, and that was their purpose. The few "small" weapons we had were undoubtedly of some direct military value, but their enormous advantage was in pure violence. In a military sense the United States could gain a little by destruction of two Japanese industrial cities; in a civilian sense, the Japanese could lose much. The bomb that hit Hiroshima was a threat aimed at all of Japan. The political target of the bomb was not the dead of Hiroshima or the factories they worked in, but the survivors in Tokyo. . . .

. . . Earlier wars, like World Wars I and II or the Franco-Prussian War, were limited by termination, by an ending that occurred before the period of greatest potential violence, by negotiation that brought the threat of pain and privation to bear but often precluded the massive exercise of civilian violence. With nuclear weapons available, the restraint of violence cannot await the outcome of a contest of military strength; restraint, to occur at all, must occur during war itself.

This is a difference between nuclear weapons and bayonets. It is not in the number of people they can eventually kill but in the speed with which it can be done, in the centralization of decision, in the divorce of the war from political processes, and in computerized programs that threaten to take the war out of human hands once it begins.

That nuclear weapons make it possible to compress the fury of global war into a few hours does not mean that they make it inevitable. We have still to ask whether that is the way a major nuclear war would be fought, or ought to be fought. Nevertheless, that the whole war might go off like one big string of firecrackers makes a critical difference between our conception of nuclear war and the world wars we have experienced. . . .

There is another difference. In the past it has usually been the victors who could do what they pleased to the enemy. War has often been "total war" for the loser. With deadly monotony the Persians, Greeks, or Romans "put to death all men of military age, and sold the women and children into slavery," leaving the defeated territory nothing but its name until new settlers arrived sometime later. But the defeated could not do the same to their victors. . . .

Nuclear weapons make it possible to do monstrous violence to the enemy without first achieving victory. With nuclear weapons and today's means of delivery, one expects to penetrate an enemy homeland without first collapsing his military force. What nuclear weapons have done, or appear to do, is to promote this kind of warfare to first place. Nuclear weapons threaten to make war less military, and are responsible for the lowered status of "military victory" at the present time. Victory is no longer a prerequisite for hurting the enemy. And it is no assurance against being terribly hurt. One need not wait until he has won the war before inflicting "unendurable" damages on his enemy. One need not wait until he has lost the war. There was a time when the assurance of victory—false or genuine assurance—could make national leaders not just willing but sometimes enthusiastic about war. Not now.

Not only can nuclear weapons hurt the enemy before the war has been won, and perhaps hurt decisively enough to make the military engagement academic, but it is widely assumed that in a major war that is *all* they can do. Major war is often discussed as though it would be only a contest in national destruction. If this is indeed the case—if the destruction of cities and their populations has become, with nuclear weapons, the primary object in an all-out war—the sequence of war has been reversed. Instead of destroying enemy forces as a prelude to imposing one's will on the enemy nation, one would have to destroy the nation as a means or a prelude to destroying the enemy forces. If one cannot disable enemy forces without virtually destroying the country, the victor does not even have the option of sparing the conquered nation. He has already destroyed it. Even with blockade and strategic bombing it could be supposed that a country would be defeated before it was destroyed, or would elect surrender before annihilation had gone far. . . .

So nuclear weapons do make a difference, marking an epoch in warfare. The difference is not just in the amount of destruction that can be accomplished but in the role of destruction and in the decision process. Nuclear weapons can change the speed of events, the control of events, the sequence of events, the relation of victor to vanquished, and the relation of homeland to fighting front. Deterrence rests today on the threat of pain and extinction, not just on the threat of military defeat. . . .

In recent years there has been a new emphasis on distinguishing what nuclear weapons make possible and what they make inevitable in case of war. The American government began in 1961 to emphasize that even a major nuclear war might not, and need not, be a simple contest in destructive fury. Secretary McNamara gave a controversial speech in June 1962 on the idea that "deterrence" might operate even in war itself, that belligerents might, out of self-interest, attempt to limit the war's destructiveness. Each might feel the sheer destruction of enemy people and cities would serve no decisive military purpose but that a continued *threat* to destroy them might serve a purpose. The continued threat would depend on their not being destroyed yet. Each might reciprocate the other's restraint, as in limited wars of lesser scope. Even the worst of enemies, in the interest of reciprocity, have often not mutilated prisoners of war; and citizens might deserve comparable treatment. The fury of nuclear attacks might fall mainly on each other's weapons and military forces.

"The United States has come to the conclusion," said Secretary McNamara [in his commencement address at the University of Michigan on 16 June 1962],

> that to the extent feasible, basic military strategy in a possible general war should be approached in much the same way that more conventional military operations have been regarded in the past. That is to say, principal military objectives . . . should be the destruction of the enemy's military forces, not of his civilian population . . . giving the possible opponent the strongest imaginable incentive to refrain from striking our own cities.

This is a sensible way to think about war, if one has to think about it and of course one does. But whether the Secretary's "new strategy" was sensible or not, whether enemy populations should be held hostage or instantly destroyed, whether the primary targets should be military forces or just people and their source of livelihood, this is not "much the same way that more conventional military operations have been regarded in the past." This is utterly different, and the difference deserves emphasis.

In World Wars I and II one went to work on enemy military forces, not his people, because until the enemy's military forces had been taken care of there was typically not anything decisive that one could do to the enemy nation itself. . . .

To concentrate on the enemy's military installations while deliberately holding in reserve a massive capacity for destroying his cities, for exterminating his people and eliminating his society, on condition that the enemy observe similar restraint with respect to one's own society, is not the "conventional approach." In World Wars I and II the first order of business was to destroy enemy armed forces because that was the only promising way to make him surrender. To fight a purely military engagement "all-out" while holding in reserve a decisive capacity for violence, on condition the enemy do likewise, is not the way military operations have traditionally been approached. Secretary McNamara was proposing a new approach to warfare in a new era, an era in which the power to hurt is more impressive than the power to oppose.

From Battlefield Warfare to the Diplomacy of Violence

. . . When the Red Cross was founded in 1863, it was concerned about the disregard for noncombatants by those who made war; but in the Second World War noncombatants were deliberately chosen as targets by both Axis and

Allied forces, not decisively but nevertheless deliberately. The trend has been the reverse of what the International Committee hoped for.

In the present era noncombatants appear to be not only deliberate targets but primary targets, or at least were so taken for granted until about the time of Secretary McNamara's speech. In fact, noncombatants appeared to be primary targets at both ends of the scale of warfare; thermonuclear war threatened to be a contest in the destruction of cities and populations; and, at the other end of the scale, insurgency is almost entirely terroristic. We live in an era of dirty war.

Why is this so? Is war properly a military affair among combatants, and is it a depravity peculiar to the twentieth century that we cannot keep it within decent bounds? . . .

To answer this question it is useful to distinguish three stages in the involvement of noncombatants—of plain people and their possessions—in the fury of war. These stages are worth distinguishing; but their sequence is merely descriptive of Western Europe during the past three hundred years, not a historical generalization. The first stage is that in which the people may get hurt by inconsiderate combatants. This is the status that people had during the period of "civilized warfare" that the International Committee had in mind.

From about 1648 to the Napoleonic era, war in much of Western Europe was something superimposed on society. It was a contest engaged in by monarchies for stakes that were measured in territories and, occasionally, money or dynastic claims. The troops were mostly mercenaries and the motivation for war was confined to the aristocratic elite. Monarchs fought for bits of territory, but the residents of disputed terrain were more concerned with protecting their crops and their daughters from marauding troops than with whom they owed allegiance to. . . .

Hurting people was not a decisive instrument of warfare. Hurting people or destroying property only reduced the value of the things that were being fought over, to the disadvantage of both sides. Furthermore, the monarchs who conducted wars often did not want to discredit the social institutions they shared with their enemies. Bypassing an enemy monarch and taking the war straight to his people would have had revolutionary implications. Destroying the opposing monarchy was often not in the interest of either side; opposing sovereigns had much more in common with each other than with their own subjects, and to discredit the claims of a monarchy might have produced a disastrous backlash. It is not surprising—or, if it is surprising, not altogether astonishing—that on the European continent in that particular era war was fairly well confined to military activity. . . .

This was changed during the Napoleonic wars. In Napoleon's France, people cared about the outcome. The nation was mobilized. The war was a national effort, not just an activity of the elite. It was both political and military genius on the part of Napoleon and his ministers that an entire nation could be mobilized for war. Propaganda became a tool of warfare, and war became vulgarized.

That was the second stage in the relation of people to war, the second in Europe since the middle of the seventeenth century. In the first stage people had been neutral but their welfare might be disregarded; in the second stage people were involved because it was *their* war. Some fought, some produced materials of war, some produced food, and some took care of children; but they were all part of a war-making nation. . . .

This brings us to the third stage in the relation of civilian violence to warfare. If the pain and damage can be inflicted during war itself, they need not wait for the surrender negotiation that succeeds a military decision. If one can coerce people and their governments while war is going on, one does not need to wait until he has achieved victory or risk losing that coercive power by spending it all in a losing war. . . .

In the present era, since at least the major East-West powers are capable of massive civilian violence during war itself beyond anything available during the Second World War, the occasion for restraint does not await the achievement of military victory or truce. The principal restraint during the Second World War was a temporal boundary, the date of surrender. In the present era we find the violence dramatically restrained during war itself. . . .

A consequence of this third stage is that "victory" inadequately expresses what a nation wants from its military forces. Mostly it wants, in these times, the influence that resides in latent force. It wants the bargaining power that comes from its capacity to hurt, not just the direct consequence of successful military action. Even total victory over an enemy provides at best an opportunity for unopposed violence against the enemy population. How to use that opportunity in the national interest, or in some wider interest, can be just as important as the achievement of victory itself; but traditional military science does not tell us how to use that capacity for inflicting pain. And if a nation, victor or potential loser, is going to use its capacity for pure violence to influence the enemy, there may be no need to await the achievement of total victory.

Actually, this third stage can be analyzed into two quite different variants. In one, sheer pain and damage are primary instruments of coercive warfare and may actually be applied, to intimidate or to deter. In the other, pain and destruction *in* war are expected to serve little or no purpose but *prior threats* of sheer violence, even of automatic and uncontrolled violence, are coupled to military force. The difference is in the all-or-none character of deterrence and intimidation. Two acute dilemmas arise. One is the choice of making prospective violence as frightening as possible or hedging with some capacity for reciprocated restraint. The other is the choice of making retaliation as automatic as possible or keeping deliberate control over the fateful decisions. The choices are determined partly by governments, partly by technology. Both variants are characterized by the coercive role of pain and destruction—of threatened (not inflicted) pain and destruction. But in one the threat either succeeds or fails altogether, and any ensuing violence is gratuitous; in the other, progressive pain and damage may actually be used to threaten more. The present era, for countries possessing nuclear weapons, is a complex and uncertain blend of the two.

Coercive diplomacy, based on the power to hurt, was important even in those periods of history when military force was essentially the power to take and to hold, to fend off attack and expel invaders, and to possess territory against opposition—that is, in the era in which military force tended to pit itself against opposing force. Even then, a critical question was how much cost and pain the other side would incur for the disputed territory. . . .

The power to hurt is nothing new in warfare, but for the United States modern technology has drastically enhanced the strategic importance of pure, unconstructive, unacquisitive pain and damage, whether used against us or in our own defense. This in turn enhances the importance of war and threats of war as techniques of influence, not of destruction; of coercion and deterrence, not of conquest and defense; of bargaining and intimidation. . . .

War no longer looks like just a contest of strength. War and the brink of war are more a contest of nerve and risk-taking, of pain and endurance. Small wars embody the threat of a larger war; they are not just military engagements but "crisis diplomacy." . . .

Military strategy can no longer be thought of, as it could for some countries in some eras, as the science of military victory. It is now equally, if not more, the art of coercion, of intimidation and deterrence. The instruments of war are more punitive than acquisitive. Military strategy, whether we like it or not, has become the diplomacy of violence.

ANDRÉ BEAUFRE
(1902–1975)

André Beaufre was chief of operations at the headquarters of the French First Army in 1945, assistant to Marshal Jean de Lattre de Tassigny in Indochina, and then head of an interallied tactical study group stationed in Germany. He took part in the Algerian War (1955) and commanded the French army corps during the Suez intervention in 1956. He was deputy chief of staff at SHAPE in 1958 and French representative at the NATO standing group in Washington in 1960. Beaufre's Introduction à la strategie *appeared in 1963. In his preface, Basil Liddell Hart called the English translation,* An Introduction to Strategy, *"The fullest, most carefully formulated and up-to-date survey of strategy that has been published in this generation—on many points it outclasses all previous surveys."*

INDIRECT STRATEGY IN THE NUCLEAR AGE

Meaning of the Term

The term *indirect strategy* may appear ambiguous and confusing. Liddell Hart has brilliantly developed a theory of "the indirect approach," which he holds to be the best strategy. In the operational sphere the essence of this is not to "take the bull by the horns," in other words not to challenge the enemy to a direct trial of strength but to attack him only after he has been shaken, surprised and thrown off balance by an approach from an improbable direction, which he therefore did not expect. Examples are Alexander, who captured Palestine and Egypt before marching on Persia; Scipio, who conquered Spain before attacking Carthage, and so on. The allied landing in North Africa

From André Beaufre, *An Introduction to Strategy*, translated by R. H. Barry (New York: Praeger, 1965), 107–30. Translation copyright © 1965 by Faber and Faber Ltd. Reprinted by permission of Faber and Faber Ltd.

in 1942 and the Serbian campaign in 1918 come into the category of the indirect approach.

In fact the strategy of the indirect approach in a "must" for the side which cannot be certain of being strong enough to beat the enemy in battle on ground of the enemy's choosing. Liddell Hart rightly points out that no one can ever be certain of being strong enough and that, even if the strength is there, victory will be gained at reduced cost. For this reason he recommends systematic use of the indirect approach. In the majority of cases he is no doubt right; the fact remains, however, that the central feature of his theory is to redress the balance between the opposing forces before the test of battle and to do so by maneuver and not by fighting. Instead of confronting the enemy direct, he would play a more subtle game, the object of which is to compensate for inferiority in numbers.

In terms of conventional military strategy, this central thesis is translated into maneuver on the ground (the indirect approach); in terms of total strategy it has been applied in a somewhat different form whenever one side wished to achieve some result with military resources which for one reason or another were inferior to those by which it was likely to be opposed (resources available might be smaller overall or there might be some deterrent to the use of anything larger). For this reason I propose to give this strategy the general title "indirect strategy."

Because of the existence of the nuclear weapon and the agitation for decolonization, there is a wide field open to this strategy and, as we shall see, it has become extremely complex and frighteningly effective. Because it is indirect its insidious nature is frequently not understood, and it is for this reason that we have suffered a continuous series of defeats in this field. There can therefore be nothing more important than to try to understand how it works.

The essential difference between the indirect approach and indirect strategy is not merely that the former has a geographical connotation, as pointed out above. The object of the indirect approach is the attainment of military victory; it is only the preparatory maneuvering for this victory which is indirect. I therefore place the indirect approach in the category of direct strategy. The essential feature of indirect strategy is that it seeks to obtain a result by methods other than military victory.

A further characteristic of indirect strategy is that in it freedom of action appears in a very special guise. In this day and age (and this was the case even before the advent of the nuclear weapon) there is a definite area of freedom of action within which any conflict must be kept confined; the boundaries of this area are set by the repercussions which the course of the conflict may have upon the international situation. In 1912, for instance, the Balkan powers were prevented from pushing through to Constantinople lest Russia install herself there; in Morocco, France had to keep an eye on the interests of England and Spain and so on; [elsewhere] I have shown what an error the Germans made by invading Belgium in 1914 and initiating submarine warfare in 1916. The restraining factor in those days was fear of what Clausewitz meant by "escalation to the limit," in other words fear that a conflict about an issue of limited importance might light up a conflagration out of all proportion to the object in view. Between 1936 and 1939 Hitler's object was to reach his objectives without starting a world war. Now that the nuclear weapon exists, the danger of escalation has become so great that the area of freedom of maneuver is considerably reduced. That it still exists however, is proved by the number of limited conflicts which have taken place since 1950 (Korea, Indo-China, North Africa, Israel, Hungary, Suez, the Congo, Cuba, Berlin).

The more restricted the area of freedom of action becomes, the more important it is to make the best use of it, since it is then the only means of assaulting the status quo which the nuclear deterrent is supposed to maintain. The more restricted the area of freedom of action has become therefore, the more delicate have been the processes by which use was made of it, until these processes have become scarcely recognizable as aspects of warfare. The results achieved have nevertheless been great, greater than would have resulted from a major war: the West has been bundled out of China and almost all of South East Asia, there have been upheavals in the Middle East and Africa is in turmoil, even Central America and South America have been affected. All these events are not merely the inevitable product of historical evolution; they are the results of a very definite strategy which uses meticulously worked out maneuvers making judicious use of natural tendencies; I propose to call it indirect strategy. It is this strategy which has proved the best antidote to what has been called "the nuclear paralysis."

Indirect strategy is therefore the art of making the best use of the limited area of freedom of action left us by the deterrent effect of the existence of nuclear weapons and of gaining important and decisive victories in spite of the fact that the military resources which can be employed for the purpose must in general remain strictly limited.

Starting from this definition, we will now try to see what are the rules of this extremely delicate game.

The Concept of Indirect Strategy

The first essential in indirect strategy is to decide how great, in the existing situation, the area of freedom of action is and then to make sure that the extent of this area can be maintained or if possible increased, while at the same time reducing to the minimum that available to the enemy.

We come back here to the principle emphasized when analysing strategy in general. Any dialectical contest is a contest for freedom of action. The truly original feature of indirect strategy, however, is that the freedom of action available is dependent only to a small degree upon those operations which may be undertaken within the geographical area in question; it will be determined almost entirely by factors outside this area, e.g., an estimate of the validity of the nuclear deterrent, an estimate of international reactions, of the enemy's moral fibre and of his sensitivity both to external pressure and to any action which it is proposed to take and so on.

The likelihood of success of any particular operation is therefore dependent upon the success of action on the world-wide plane. I propose to call this the "exterior maneuver." All too often its importance has not been realized; people have not perceived that the focal point of the struggle was not in the area where fighting was taking place but outside it. It has been this serious mis-appreciation which has been at the root of the grave defeats we have suffered.

CONCEPT OF THE "EXTERIOR MANEUVER"

The central feature of the "exterior maneuver" is to assure for oneself the max-imum freedom of action while at the same time paralysing the enemy by a mul-titude of deterrent checks, somewhat as the Lilliputians tied up Gulliver. As with all operations designed to deter, action will of course be primarily psy-chological; political, economic, diplomatic and military measures will all be combined towards the same end.

The procedures employed to achieve this deterrent effect range from the most subtle to the most brutal: appeal will be made to the legal formulae of national and international law, play will be made with moral and humanitar-ian susceptibilities and there will be attempts to prick the enemy's conscience by making him doubtful of the justice of his cause. By these methods, oppo-sition from some section of the enemy's internal public opinion will be roused and at the same time some sector of international public opinion will be whipped up; the result will be a real moral coalition and attempts will be made to co-opt the more unsophisticated sympathizers by arguments based upon their own preconceived ideas. This climate of opinion will be exploited at the United Nations, for instance, or at other international gatherings; primarily, however, it will be used as a threat to prevent the enemy undertaking some particular action. There will be threatened or actual indirect intervention by the despatch of arms, specialists and volunteers. If necessary, play will be made with the threat of political and economic retaliation and finally there will be the threat of direct action, possibly even including the use of nuclear weapons.

This is no exhaustive list but the reader will recognize many well-known examples from recent history.

But procedures of this nature can only be successful if two conditions obtain: first the military deterrent force (whether nuclear or conventional) must pose a sufficient overall threat to prevent the enemy reacting on a major scale: second, all the actions envisaged must be in consonance with a definite line of policy so conceived that it forms a logical thesis. When, for instance, the United States, which is liberal by tradition, became involved in Cuba even though indirectly, as in the Bay of Pigs operation, they struck a psychologically false note; this would have been of little consequence in direct strategy (particularly if the operation had been successful), but in indirect strategy they had to pay dearly for it.

When France gave up her colonies in Black Africa and voluntarily evacuated Morocco and Tunisia, she struck a false note by clinging on to Algeria (alternatively the evacuation was the false note). Choice of the political line to be followed is therefore a decision fundamental to the success of the entire operation.

It is a point worth noting that, just as in military operations one captures a position on the ground and thereby denies it to the enemy, on the psychological plane it is possible to take over abstract positions and equally deny them to the other side. The Soviet Union for instance has succeeded in getting everyone to accept that the Iron Curtain is a water-tight political barrier in a West to East direction but that it presents no obstacle in an East-West direction; they have turned into their own preserve the peace platform, that of the abolition of atomic weapons (while themselves continuing to develop them) and that of anti-colonialism while themselves ruling the only colonial empire still in existence. There is no doubt that this phenomenon exists but it is in the realm of psychological tactics and will not be dealt with here. Be it noted in passing, however, that these "conquests" are in most cases based upon principles fully accepted by the other side. It may therefore be that these ideological positions occupied by the forces of Marxism may one day be "conquered" by the West; but this presupposes that the latter in their indirect strategy have learned the value of thinking and calculating instead of merely trying to apply juridical or moral principles which their enemy can use against them at every turn.

In choosing the political line to follow, account must of course be taken of the psychological urges of the moment (e.g., the longing for peace, decolonization, determination to raise living standards, etc.); additional factors are the enemy's vulnerable points and those of any allies of whom it is wished to make use. In most cases the result will be that the conflict will be conducted indirectly or "by proxy." This fiction deceives no one but psychologically it is important. In addition, of course, the possible reactions of the enemy must be forecast and effective counters to them prepared. The "political line" is in fact the general concept of a true operational plan in the psychological field; it must be worked out with the same precision as an operational plan in military strategy.

CONCEPT OF THE "INTERIOR MANEUVER"

Having thus made sure of a degree of freedom of action, the next step is to work out the maneuver to be employed in the geographical area where it is desired to obtain certain results. This I propose to call the "interior maneuver."

The main components of this problem are three variable but interconnected factors: material force, moral force and time. If the material force available is considerably superior to that of the enemy, moral pressure becomes less necessary and the operation can be completed in a very short time. If, on the other hand, the material forces available are small, moral pressure must be very great and the operation will inevitably be prolonged. There are therefore two forms of strategic procedure, one at each end of the scale.

In the first the object is to reach, very rapidly and using considerable superiority of material force, some intermediate objective within the limit of the external freedom of action available; a halt then appears to be made before proceeding to a further operation. This form of action therefore consists of a series of operations to capture relatively limited objectives, interspersed with negotiations; it may be called the "piecemeal" method. Hitler gave a remarkable demonstration of this method between 1936 and 1939. The USSR has tried it on several occasions with varying success (Czechoslovakia, Korea). The various Israeli campaigns in Sinai have been of the same type, though with a defensive objective.

In the second the idea is to reach the objective (which may be of considerable importance) not so much by military victory as by keeping up a prolonged conflict so designed and organized that it becomes more and more burdensome to the enemy. This is the "enervation" or "erosion" method and its main characteristic is protracted conflict; Mao Tse-tung is both its leading theorist and its most successful commander; the latest and perhaps the most complete example is Algeria; Berlin is in the same category, though the maneuver there is far more insidious.

There are, of course, any number of gradations between these two extremes. Korea was initially intended to be a "piecemeal" operation and ended in a struggle of attrition. The Indo-China campaign was based primarily on a strategy of erosion but almost ended in a military "piecemeal" operation.

THE EROSION METHOD

The concept of erosion is of great interest because it is in fact highly subtle. The problem is to cause an enemy who is far stronger than yourself to accept conditions which may be extremely severe, while employing only very limited resources against him. This is where full use must be made of the variable but interconnecting factors mentioned above: the longer the action continues, the more must moral pressure be brought into play in order to make up for inferiority in military force. The operation must therefore be conducted in two spheres at the same time, the material sphere, i.e., that of military force, and the moral sphere, i.e., that of psychological action.

The Material Sphere. The most important requirement in the material sphere is to hold out. In Raymond Aron's view this is the ultimate object of all strategy, but in any case it is clearly that of any operation based on erosion tactics. If one side is at a considerable material disadvantage it can only hope to survive by refusing battle and using harassing tactics to keep the conflict going; this means guerrilla action, which is as old as the hills but which each generation has nevertheless forgotten and had to learn afresh. In the last forty years, however, a most important set of strategic rules has been developed for this method of operation, as a result action on these lines can now be conducted on well-thought principles and therefore with considerably increased efficiency, thereby in large measure compensating for the disparity in material forces. Mao Tse-tung laid down seven rules as the basis for guerrilla operations: close co-operation between the population and the guerrillas; withdraw in face of an enemy advance in force; harass and attack if the enemy withdraws: strategically one to five suffices, tactically five to one is needed, the latter being achieved primarily by what he terms "converging withdrawal," i.e., concentrating during withdrawal (he had ample space available in China); his final rule was that for supply and equipment guerrillas must live off the enemy. These seven rules are the essential minimum for successful conduct of this form of warfare but it is frequently not recognized that they are a minimum; for instance, the O.A.S. [Organisation de l'Armée secrète] thought it could establish a "redoubt" in Algeria, the Americans approved the idea of a landing in Cuba in the form of a conventional "bridgehead."

In addition to these minimum desiderata there are two further basic concepts essential for the maintenance of freedom of action for guerrilla operations. The first originated with the Soviets, though it had earlier been employed by the Irish; it consists of systematic terrorism with the object of deterring the population from giving any information to the enemy, thereby hamstringing the security forces. We have seen both in Indo-China and in Algeria how efficient this method is; the savagery with which it was conducted never-theless raised no protest on the part of world opinion. The second concept was brilliantly exploited by Lawrence on the Hejaz railway; its principle is to extend the guerrilla threat over the widest possible area without provoking any enemy reaction but consequently facing him with a more and more difficult security problem. The result is that the enemy is forced to use far greater force guarding an ever-growing number of points and this can to a great extent redress the balance of forces available. In Algeria for instance more than 300,000 men were kept at full stretch by less than 30,000.

Lastly the number of guerrillas (whose expendability is very high) must be maintained and continuously increased so that the pressure mounts. For this purpose there must in the first instance be a system for arms smuggling (or parachuting as in France in 1944); this must be followed as soon as possible by the establishment of bases close to the territory to be attacked secured by the deterrent effect produced by the "exterior maneuver." This was the function of bases in China during the war in Indo-China, of the bases first in Egypt and then in Tunisia and Morocco during the war in Algeria, and of those in the ex-Belgian Congo during operations in Portuguese Angola. Some writers consider that the organization of these bases is the decisive factor in a war of this type. Even if it is not decisive, it is certainly of the greatest importance; it should be noted that the guerrilla movements which have failed, e.g., in Kenya and Malaya, were in fact those which were isolated. This last point also shows that the "exterior maneuver," in addition to its key role in assuring overall freedom of action, has a vital operational part to play.

The Psychological Sphere. In the psychological sphere the general concept is equally to hold out. To do this it is essential that the morale both of those fighting and of the population should be raised to and kept at a high level. Control of morale is therefore of vital importance. The object is still to cause the enemy to give up by a process of erosion. Psychological action will be essential in this case also, in order to draw the maximum advantage from any successes achieved.

This psychological action is a complex affair, since it is aimed at one and the same time at the men in the field and at the civil population, both friendly and enemy. It must be guided by two main factors: the basic "political line" and the psychological tactics selected.

The basic political line must be in consonance with that used in the "exterior maneuver." It must be capable of rousing in support of the struggle the dormant emotion of the population which it is desired to spur into action. These emotions (whether patriotic, religious, social, etc.) must be whipped up by arguments which at the same time should serve to show the righteousness of the cause they are being called on to support. Equally the success of the operation must be presented as assured—not, as in 1940, "because we are the stronger" (which is never the case initially in this type of war) but because "God [or some current of history] is on our side." The determinism of history should be presented as guiding events inexorably in the direction desired; it will thus fulfil the function which visions or sacred images played in whipping up enthusiasm for the crusades; it will produce a fatalistic attitude of mind but a fatalism coloured by optimism—conversely that of the enemy will be coloured by pessimism; it is an attitude of mind not unlike the fatalism of the Moslems, who alternated between being conquerors and slaves.

This last point is of major importance. We have never really realized how important a factor in the rapid conquest of the world by the white race was the feeling among the conquered peoples that we were borne on the wings of destiny and that nothing could stop us being the dictators of their future. That this was an illusion was proved to them by the reverses suffered by the West during the early part of the Second World War; we lost face and those moral factors which had previously worked in our favour now operate against us.

Psychological tactics clearly include the well-known techniques of today— propaganda, indoctrination, and organization of the civil population, all carried out by a close-knit and closely controlled cadre. It is essential in this type of war to grasp the fact that the only true successes are psychological successes and therefore action in the field is of value only in so far as it serves to raise the morale or the prestige of the fighting force or of the population. In general therefore guerrilla operations must be conducted with this end in view. On the other hand, if success eludes them or is very small, its place can be taken by bluff or, if necessary, complete falsification of the truth (think of the "heroic" defence of Port Said, the sinking of the *Suffren* by the Vietnamese or of the *Jean-Bart* by the Egyptians, the landing of an Egyptian Army in Kabylia, etc., etc.). Similarly the enemy will be able to double the psychological effect of any action he may take, even though it may be unoriginal and on a small scale, by issue of a stream of sensational news items such as the Western press loves to print. It should also be noted here that, although the political line must form a coherent whole, propaganda intended for external and internal consumption may be very different things.

Provided that there is full co-ordination between the exterior and interior "maneuvers," the conflict, which may start as a small-scale affair, will fester, grow and continue. Provided environmental action produces the necessary minimum deterrent effect and provided local action is not stifled at birth, there is every chance that the operation will ultimately be successful. At best the result will be that the enemy will give up the struggle (as in Tunisia, Morocco and Algeria). If the "exterior maneuver" fails to prevent the intervention of other powers, a compromise will be reached in the form of a partition (Israel and Indo-China). If the "exterior maneuver" does not give adequate support to the "interior maneuver," and if the enemy is sufficiently determined, the operation will be defeated (Kenya, Malaya). Nevertheless the seed sown during the struggle will grow later and at the very least the enemy will have been forced to make a very considerable effort for an insignificant expenditure of resources on our side.

This last point highlights the full importance of the erosion method; if the operation is well thought out and well conducted the risks involved are infinitesimal, whereas the possible dividends are high; even if the operation is defeated, the enemy will have been forced to expend considerable effort against an insignificant effort on our side. Twenty-three years ago, taking Hitler's tactics as the example, I forecast that this type of conflict was bound to develop in the future. Facts have more than borne out my prophecy. Today I believe that under the umbrella of the nuclear weapon this type of warfare will grow and go on growing until an effective counter to it has been developed and until there is some possibility of creating in this field a deterrent similar to that which we possess in others. We shall deal with this problem later, but first we must look at the "piecemeal" maneuver.

THE "PIECEMEAL" MANEUVER

"Piecemeal" tactics are simpler in that, as far as action on the spot is concerned, they are based primarily upon military strategic calculations. The part played by the "exterior maneuver," however, is just as important as in the case of the erosion method. This was clear in the case of Suez and Sinai; there military operations were completely successful but could not prevent the final defeat of the operation since it was completely without external cover.

This is not to say, however, that in a "piecemeal" operation military strategy is not subject to certain limitations. Freedom of action will invariably be small and, even if the "exterior maneuver" has been well thought out, there will be considerable risk either of defeat or escalation unless the local action achieves surprise and quickly produces an unarguable fait accompli which can serve as the basis for subsequent negotiations. The reason for the Soviet failure in Korea was that the operation did not produce a rapid result and got bogged down in a protracted campaign. If there had been no bridgehead at Fusan, the Inchon counteroffensive would never have taken place, nor would there have been any other subsequent American reaction. The Soviet plan did not provide for adequate speed or adequate strength. Similarly at Suez it was folly to carry out a "softening-up" air operation over the ten days prior to the landing; it merely presented the enemy with an opportunity to produce a fait accompli in his favour before the landing took place. As against this, Hitler's seizures of the left bank of the Rhine, of Austria and then of Czechoslovakia were in each case completed in forty-eight hours, the minimum reaction time for international diplomacy.

The local operation in this case must therefore be in the nature of a large-scale *coup de main;* its main features will be surprise, speed, rapid action in strength against weak points and immediate exploitation in force. It is eminently the job for airborne, motorized or armoured formations. Rapidity of action will of course be ensured not merely by accuracy of information and vigour of execution, but by the most careful preparation in all fields. An operation of this nature cannot be improvised.

The liberty of action gained by the "exterior maneuver" may be the vital prerequisite for success but there is another external factor almost equally essential; the objective must appear to be of a sufficiently limited nature to be acceptable to international opinion. Hitler was fairly successful in presenting each of his objectives as his sole and final demand. This game succeeded three times (up to and including Munich), but after Czechoslovakia no one was taken in by his "piecemeal" strategy. The next bite, Poland, started the escalation which ended in the Second World War, although there were many in the West who thought even then that there would be a further limited phase. This shows the limitations of this strategy; it is no good trying to use it to attain over-important objectives by a series of bounds, though possibly this might be done by spreading the operation out over a very long period of time. Since its methods are necessarily violent and it is naturally of a somewhat sensational character, it is far more dangerous to use than the erosion method. But in certain particular well-defined circumstances it may still be feasible and possibly extremely rewarding—particularly if, as Israel has done on several occasions, it can be presented as being defensive in character.

The Counters to Indirect Strategy

Ever since 1935 indirect strategy has been used almost continuously and almost invariably with success. Between 1936 and 1939 it was used by Hitler, employing primarily "piecemeal" tactics. From 1939 to 1945 there was a direct strategy interlude, but indirect strategy then took up the running once more, the protagonist being the Soviet Union, with emphasis this time more upon erosion tactics.

The fact that indirect strategy has been in fashion for so long and is apparently becoming even more fashionable stems from the conditions of modern war. Ever since 1918, but even more since Hiroshima, everyone has been clear that all-out war is an evil and everyone has tried to avoid it. Those, however, whose policy involves some change in the established order of things continue to use force to obtain their objectives. This leads inevitably to the delicate game of indirect strategy, which each of the great actors on the stage plays in accordance with his individual quirks of character; Hitler alternated over-rapidly between subtlety and violence; the Soviet Union has used the method of slow creeping diffusion of chaos under the umbrella of an insidious threat.

This is an ancient form of strategy (the Hundred Years' War was in reality nothing but a very long guerrilla campaign, the final scene of which was the psychological miracle of Joan of Arc) but each new manifestation of it has as a rule left people surprised and disconcerted. Men were blinded by the black and white theories of the nineteenth century and therefore believed that peace and war were two totally different things; in many cases they regarded indirect strategy as a game intimately connected with politics. Since people saw no alternative between all-out war or nothing, Hitler was allowed to go on unchecked for four years and then a world-wide conflict was let loose leading to the ruin of Europe; no one realized in time that Hitler could have been beaten by the very methods he was himself employing. After 1946 the Stalinist drive seemed to revive the danger; the United States reacted with a strategy which had certain indirect strategy aspects (particularly the Marshall Plan); their conscious effort, however, was in the direct strategy field and centred round the nuclear weapon. This produced the deterrent strategy, the result of which was to drive the Soviet Union (and others) to raise the tempo of their indirect strategy operations. The sequence is impressive: when blocked in Iran in 1946 they pushed forward in Greece, whence they were only ejected in 1950; in 1948 they scored a victory in China, in 1949 at Prague; in 1950 came Korea and intervention in Indo-China, in 1953–4 an indirect drive towards the Middle East; in 1954 North Africa went up in flames; in 1959 came Cuba; in 1960 the Congo and in 1961 Angola; and all the while Germany was kept under the pressure of a succession of Berlin crises. In fifteen years with certain ups and downs, the USSR has achieved results greater than she could have obtained by any major military victory.

Faced with this situation, the Western reaction has been disjointed and therefore ineffective, because the realities of the problem were not generally appreciated; the solutions adopted have usually only been palliatives and frequently actually played into the enemy's hands. It is vital that we should realize the true nature of indirect strategy and act accordingly.

I am not, of course, presumptuous enough to think that I can produce here a complete solution for the problem of developing a defence against indirect strategy. All I can hope to do is to point to some general ideas which may perhaps help us to find an effective answer to the challenge we face in these peculiar years of so-called "peace," during which so far all we have been able to do is to give up greater or smaller slices of territory. . . .

THE "EXTERIOR COUNTER-MANEUVER"

In strategy more than in any other field of activity, one must be able to sort out essentials from secondary factors. The essential element of direct strategy is force, in other words material resources, which, depending on their size, will enable us to obtain with greater or less ease the essential freedom of action. In indirect strategy freedom of action remains the essential feature but our main concern is with the indirect methods designed to ensure that we have it. The most important of these is the "exterior counter-maneuver." The overriding factor here is of course direct nuclear strategy with its global deterrent and there can therefore be no relaxation of effort in this field. But if this was all— as certain American theorists tend to say—the enemy would be left with complete freedom of action in indirect strategy. The converse is that if counter-action were completely successful, all indirect strategy problems would be solved. It is the "exterior maneuver" therefore which is decisive and it is here that our priority effort must be made.

The counter to the enemy's "exterior maneuver" consists of creating the largest possible number of deterrents to supplement the overall nuclear deterrent. Just as the original enemy action was based upon our vulnerable points, the choice of these deterrents must be based upon the vulnerable points in the enemy's system (public opinion at home, economy, the situation of the satellites and fellow-travellers, psychological taboos for the Marxist, for the Moslem or the black man, etc.). From these can be deduced the political line; in other words a choice can be made of those ideological and geographical positions which are to be defended and those which are to be threatened. Clearly a purely defensive line of policy would have little deterrent effect since the key to deterrence is the capacity to threaten. The political line must therefore definitely be offensive.

In the realm of ideology an offensive line of policy necessarily implies a capacity effectively to attack the weak points in the enemy's ideological system. It is therefore these weak points and not our own moral or philosophical ideas which must be the starting point. Our plan of attack, moreover, must take account of the requirements not of ourselves but of those we wish to convince. For instance we are at present completely without a "psychological striking force" because there is no body of liberal thought concentrated on the immediate requirements of the newly emerged states in the uncommitted world (their economy, social organization, political constitution, etc.). It must be admitted moreover that our ideas could well do with being adjusted, rejuvenated and co-ordinated to bring them into line with the facts of the present age (planned economy, social legislation and so on).

In the psychological sphere the essential component of deterrent capacity is to re-establish the prestige of Western civilization. Prestige is a complex compound of the present-day power and efficiency of the Western world together with an estimate of the power and efficiency it is likely to have in the future. The decline of the West sprang from the fact that it was blind enough to allow itself to be divided and its present inability to present a united front has merely confirmed this impression. The first essential in the re-establishment of the prestige of the West is to get it to agree that a closely co-ordinated overall strategy, or in other words a common policy, is a necessity. This is impossible so long as the system consists merely of NATO on the one hand, the aim of which is strictly military, and the United Nations on the other, which is nothing but a sounding board for international disagreement. It is essential that there should be a Western organization responsible for working out global strategy. Some solution such as that proposed by France (a global study by the world powers and regional studies by the powers concerned) might be the answer, but one thing is certain—if we cannot overcome the very real difficulties which exist in this matter, we have no hope of winning the struggle. The second essential factor in reviving our prestige is to re-establish world confidence in the future of our civilization. More use could be made for this purpose of the extraordinary economic progress made by Europe in recent years. But still more important is it to possess a dynamic and therefore a rejuvenated philosophy. Lastly prestige springs partly from the fear one is capable of instilling; particularly when dealing with emergent nations, "face" plays a considerable part. This means that we must arrange not to lose face again (as we did at Suez or the Bay of Pigs). We must try to regain face by efficient action based upon a carefully worked out program. The Cuba crisis in the autumn of 1962 demonstrated the effects which can be produced by doing so.

Turning to the geographic aspect, a choice must be made of those areas which we wish either to defend or to threaten or to attack. This choice will therefore be concerned on the one hand with those areas which protect points vital to us, on the other with those which threaten the enemy's vulnerable points, and if possible those in which action would be comparatively easy. We should try to choose areas which can form bases for further action (e.g., Cuba). We should not allow ourselves to be drawn into areas where the enemy can deploy considerable effort at little cost to himself while we are forced to expend resources on a large scale (e.g., South East Asia). Finally, difficult though this may be, high priority should be given to eliminating those peripheral bases from which the enemy can carry out indirect aggression.

THE "INTERIOR COUNTER-MANEUVER"

Turning now to the area in which indirect aggression has taken place, there are a number of differing forms of response. If aggression takes the form of a stage in a "piecemeal" operation and uses a considerable weight of armed force, it will be essential to have tactical forces available in the area to ensure that we are not rapidly faced with a fait accompli. The mere existence of these forces will usually be an adequate deterrent. If, on the other hand, the necessary forces are not available on the spot, we shall be forced to rely upon the effects of our "exterior counter-maneuver." The cases of Suez and Sinai showed that if there is lack of determination on the part of the aggressor, an "exterior maneuver" is quite capable of cancelling out any local success. Alternatively by speedy intervention, as in the case of the Americans in Korea, it may be possible to stop any decision being reached on the spot and so to checkmate the enemy's entire plan. This illustrates the valuable deterrent effect of highly mobile strategic reserves.

In the case of indirect aggression using "erosion" strategy, a number of alternative courses of action are open. The best, if it can be implemented, is to ensure retention of governmental control (the essential factor) without the use of large-scale resources and then to stifle the outbreak by efficient "exterior maneuver." If, however, this fails (as in the case of France in Algeria) we are forced back on to local counter-action, i.e., a direct counteroffensive.

In this case also the essential factor is the political line, the object of which must be to deprive the enemy of his trump cards. There are two facets to this: we must first maintain and increase our prestige, not merely by showing that we have adequate force available but also by showing that the future we hold out has possibilities (progress of our civilization, international aid, etc.); secondly, by thorough-going reforms, we must cut the ground from under the feet of the malcontents.

On the military side the essential is to foil the enemy's guerrilla strategy. In the first place there must be strict economy of force to avoid being swamped by any "Hejaz railway" type of maneuver. Only strictly limited areas will therefore be strongly garrisoned and only in these will persons and goods be fully protected; the areas must be carefully chosen having regard to their political and economic importance. In the rest of the country a certain degree of insecurity will have to be accepted; the task of the outposts left in these latter areas will be no more than to maintain an intelligence network to enable us to launch a series of operations to prevent the enemy establishing organized bases. In certain instances it may be right to allow the enemy to establish himself in these areas at his leisure in order to be able the more easily to destroy him later. The frontiers on the other hand must be hermetically sealed by barriers on the lines of those used in Libya by Fascist Italy and in Algeria. However well they may be carried out, these operations inevitably eat up considerable resources and this is their great disadvantage in a war which will inevitably be long. It will be the task of strategy to find the most economical solution and that of organization to devise a system (reliefs, etc.) which will enable the effort to be kept up long-term. In exceptionally favourable circumstances it may be worth while trying to force a decision against the guerrilla movement by the use of force on a large scale, always provided that the results are likely to pay off quickly. If they do not (as in Algeria in 1956) all that will be achieved is to reduce one's own ability to last out, in other words to play into the hands of the enemy's erosion strategy.

Finally, of course, all operations must be conducted with an eye to their psychological effect both on the enemy and on the civil population. In the heavily garrisoned areas, the latter will be completely protected and one ought therefore to be able favourably to compare its enviable existence with that of the population in the areas more or less controlled by the enemy. The protected areas will thus become refuge areas; in order to instil confidence they must under no circumstances be reduced and if they are extended there must be no subsequent withdrawal. Any reverses suffered must either be concealed or balanced by more spectacular successes on which suitable emphasis should be laid.

These are measures which must be taken. As they were listed the reader will have been reminded of many of the mistakes we have ourselves made, particularly in Algeria. However good these measures may be, it must always be remembered that in this type of warfare it is an exception for the defence to be successful; as pointed out above, this has only happened when there were no bases outside but adjacent to the theatre of operations from which the guerrillas could be supplied. An attempt to respond to an indirect strategy attack by direct defence is as foolish as the bull charging the red cloak rather than the toreador. It is the toreador, in other words the "exterior maneuver," which must be our target.

Conclusions on Indirect Strategy

Indirect strategy is therefore total war played in a minor key; it has in fact existed throughout the ages—as indeed has direct strategy. The forms it has assumed in the modern world and the frequency with which it is employed stem from the fact that all-out war today has for all thinking men become impractical. Indirect strategy is therefore truly complementary to direct nuclear strategy and is in many respects its antidote. The further nuclear strategy develops and the nearer it gets to establishing a balance, however precarious, of overall deterrence, the more will indirect strategy be used. Peace will become less and less peaceful and will get nearer and nearer to what in 1939 I called "war in peacetime" and which we now know as the Cold War.

The relationship between cold war and hot war is analogous to that between medicine and surgery. Instead of the bloody business of hot war, we now have "infections," which are none the less lethal for being insidious. Surgery is not as a rule effective against infection; there must be inoculation and counter-infection and the disease must be taken early. This is an incubator war; psychological infection is not unlike that produced by biological warfare and in just the same way, once launched, it is difficult to control; one of the principal causes of Germany's defeat in 1918 was that the virus of Bolshevism, which she had been largely instrumental in introducing into Russia a year earlier, rebounded upon her. Ever since 1921 the Soviet Union has made much play with the rush for decolonization but the process has often gone faster than she calculated and faced her with problems in Africa to which she had no ready response. Although it has been employed for centuries, we are not used to this clinical type of war.

Though its outward manifestations are of a specialized and frequently disconcerting nature, indirect strategy is no specialized form of strategy entirely divorced from direct strategy. The key to it, as with all strategy, is freedom of action; it is only the method by which this freedom is obtained which is different. It must be obtained by initiative combined with security and it is different because the area of freedom of action (and therefore the limits of security) depends upon what is done outside, not inside, the area at issue. This is its special feature and it is this which gives it its indirect character.

We must be quite clear on this point—that security depends upon the "exterior maneuver," the vital factors in which are the vulnerable points on each side. Any vulnerable point on our side offers the enemy a target; any vulnerable point on his side offers us an opportunity to threaten retaliation. This is the level on which the problem of security must be considered. Moreover some vulnerable points, particularly if created by a revolutionary movement, take a very long time to develop (the Congress of Baku was held in 1921 but decolonization only became a factor from 1945 to 196?; Cuba began to be a problem in 1956, etc.); both the indirect counters to ensure security and actions designed to counter the enemy's threats must therefore be initiated very early. The vital phase in indirect strategy takes place when the first symptoms appear. Anything later is too late.

Indirect strategy, therefore, is no more than a method of applying the universal strategic formula by raising to the nth degree certain of the variable factors; the factor of force being reduced to a minimum and the factor of time being largely increased. . . .

In fact the psychological factor, which invariably plays some part in any form of strategy, in indirect strategy becomes dominant. Material force not being available, its place must be taken by the force of some well-reasoned ideology and by the effectiveness of intelligently and meticulously worked out plans. Grey matter in fact takes over from brute force—and that is no bad thing.

It must not be forgotten, however, that in the game of indirect strategy the availability and the use of force are just as necessary as in direct strategy. Force may be used on a very reduced scale but this must not mislead us as to the importance of the part it plays. The nuclear force may be unseen, but it is always there and it is this which sets the boundaries of the battlefield, i.e., determines the touchlines of deterrence within which the game of indirect strategy must be played. Secondly, within indirect strategy itself, force is required to exploit (or threaten to exploit) the situations created by psychological maneuver. . . .

Some people have felt that in this delicate game, often so far removed from war on the traditional model, the use of force is a mortal offence. This is both dangerous and wrong. In itself force is neither good nor bad. It depends upon the cause for which it is used, in other words upon the policy which brings it into action. Throughout history force has played a cardinal role in conflict and to deplore this fact is simply to shut one's eyes to reality.

This delicate use of force is often thought to lie more in the realm of politics; people say that indirect strategy of the type I have just described is not "strategy" but "policy." This terminological argument is of little importance in itself, particularly since it is clear that indirect strategy will be conducted at heads of government level. The choice of the word, however, will reveal how far the problem is understood. Those who think indirect strategy is a form of policy are muddling up two different species of thing. The role of policy is to lay down objectives and decide the resources to be allocated to their attainment; it must therefore also decide if any particular objective is to be attained by indirect methods or not. The conduct of indirect strategy, however, is not policy; it is strategy; in other words within any policy there must be the most carefully worked out plans for the use of force.

The history of the last ten years has shown what fatal errors result from trying to deal with these problems empirically and by guesswork when faced with enemies fully conversant with the rules of the game. We must now learn to use these rules as they do—with the same realism, with the same alert intelligence; only thus can we avoid either seeing the successive collapse of all our positions or being forced to unleash as a last resort the catastrophe which the use of direct strategy would today inevitably bring in its train.

We must learn to live in this so-called peace and save what remains to us of true peace.

We must master the art of indirect strategy.

HENRY KISSINGER
(b. 1923)

*Henry Kissinger, a German-born professor of political science at Harvard
University, who contributed to the debate on nuclear weapons and "limited
war" in 1957 with the publication of* Nuclear Weapons and Foreign Policy,
*was adviser to Presidents Richard Nixon and Gerald Ford between 1969
and 1977. He was secretary of state from 1973 to 1977. Kissinger introduced
into U.S. diplomacy the classical views on interstate relations advocated by
Machiavelli, Clausewitz, and Raymond Aron. His memoirs* White House
Years *(Boston: Little, Brown, 1979) and* Years of Upheaval *(Boston: Little,
Brown, 1982) are a major contribution to an understanding of the period.*

DEFENSE POLICY AND STRATEGY

Defense and the Strategic Balance

Throughout history the political influence of nations has been roughly cor-
relative to their military power. While states might differ in the moral worth
and prestige of their institutions, diplomatic skill could augment but never
substitute for military strength. In the final reckoning weakness has invariably
tempted aggression and impotence brings abdication of policy in its train.
Some lesser countries have played significant roles on the world scale for brief
periods, but only when they were acting in the secure framework of an international equilibrium. The balance of power, a concept much maligned in
American political writing—rarely used without being preceded by the pejorative "outdated"—has in fact been the precondition of peace. A calculus of
power, of course, is only the beginning of policy; it cannot be its sole purpose.
The fact remains that without strength even the most elevated purpose risks
being overwhelmed by the dictates of others.

From Henry Kissinger, *White House Years* (Boston: Little, Brown & Co., 1979), 195–222. Copyright © 1979 by Henry A. Kissinger. Reprinted by permission of Little, Brown and Company.

This has been a hard lesson for Americans to learn. Protected by two oceans, we were persuaded for over a century that it was unnecessary for us to address issues of strategy. Alone among the great powers, we imagined that we could prevail through the purity of our motives and that our impact on the world was somehow unrelated to our physical power. We tended to oscillate between isolation and spurts of involvement, each conceived in moralistic terms. Even our military efforts had an abstract quality about them, focused more on logistics than on geopolitics. In our wars, we generally wore down our adversary by the weight of resources rather than by boldness or strategic conceptions.

By the late 1960s we were once again tempted by withdrawal. The frustrations of an inconclusive war encouraged some to ascribe our problems to being too heavily engaged around the world. Criticism originally aimed at the war in Vietnam was soon extended to the entire spectrum of our military programs and commitments. The informed opinion that had sustained a generation of enlightened postwar international involvement seemed to be turning sharply against it.

This threatened to put our nation and other free peoples into a precarious position. The political stability of Europe and Japan and the future evolution of the developing countries of Latin America, Africa, and Asia would turn on whether the United States possessed power relevant to its objectives and was perceived as able to defend its interests and those of its friends. If the war in Vietnam eroded our willingness to back the security of free peoples with our military strength, untold millions would be in jeopardy.

Unfortunately, our domestic travail was most acute at a moment when technology, combined with earlier deliberate decisions, was altering the nature of the strategic balance. Throughout the postwar period the Soviet Union had enjoyed an enormous advantage in conventional land forces. Soviet military capabilities suffered from two handicaps, however: the Soviet reach was relatively short; it was confined in effect to areas adjoining the Soviet Union. And the American preponderance in nuclear strategic forces was overwhelming. The Soviet Union could not press its local advantage for fear of being confronted by the nuclear superiority of the United States. This was the primary reason why the Soviet Union, despite its occasional bluster, never used its vast conventional forces against countries allied with the United States. It is one of the ironies of our time that since 1945 the Red Army has been employed in force only against *allies* of the Soviet Union (in East Berlin in 1953, in Hungary in 1956, in Czechoslovakia in 1968, and on the border with China in 1969).

By the late Sixties, however, the strategic nuclear balance was tending toward parity. This should have changed all the assumptions of our postwar strategy. Unfortunately, at the precise moment that our national debate should have concentrated on the implications of this new situation, *all* our defense programs were coming under increasing attack. They were decried as excessive, blamed on reckless leaders, and criticized as contributing to crises and conflicts.

The administrations in office in the Sixties decided consciously to accept a parity in strategic weapons they considered inevitable; by accepting it, however, they also accelerated it. In the Sixties the United States voluntarily halted its construction of land-based ICBMs and sea-based SLBMs. We had no programs to build additional strategic bombers. It was decided to maintain a strategic force consisting of 1,054 land-based ICBMs, 656 SLBMs, and about 400 B-52 bombers. We adopted these ceilings at a time when we far outnumbered the strategic forces of the Soviet Union. But these ceilings were not changed even when it became clear that the Soviet Union, reacting in part to its humiliation in the Cuban missile crisis of 1962 , had undertaken a massive effort to augment its military strength across the board.

In American folklore the Cuban crisis is remembered as a great American victory. And indeed it was. But the American and Soviet governments drew diametrically opposite conclusions from it. In American policy it led to the pursuit of arms control and détente, exemplified by the Test Ban and Non-Proliferation treaties and indeed in the decision to cease our missile construction once we had reached a fixed number. In the Soviet Union, by contrast, Khrushchev's humiliation in Cuba was one cause of his overthrow two years later. . . . The Soviet Union thereupon launched itself on a determined, systematic, and long-term program of expanding *all* categories of its military power—its missiles and bombers, its tanks and submarines and fighter planes—in technological quality and global reach. The 1962 Cuban crisis was thus an historic turning point—but not for the reason some Americans complacently supposed.

Three years after the Cuban confrontation, in 1965, the Soviet strategic arsenal comprised about 220 ICBMs and over 100 SLBMs. By 1968 the numbers had grown to nearly 860 ICBMs and over 120 SLBMs. By 1971 the Soviets had caught up with us—and they continued to build. Our estimates of their plans invariably turned out to be low. The brilliant analyst Albert Wohlstetter has demonstrated convincingly that the belief fashionable in the 1960s—that the Pentagon exaggerated Soviet programs to win higher appropriations—was exactly the opposite of the truth. American planners in the Fifties and Sixties consistently *underestimated* the Soviet buildup. The Soviet programs always were at the highest level of our estimates—not what was described as "most probable" but what was put forward as the "worst case." Instead of halting once they reached parity with us, as some expected, the Soviets continued to build—until stopped by the 1972 SALT accords, and then they switched to an energetic qualitative improvement.

The American response to the Soviet buildup in the Johnson Administration was twofold. There was a decision to build an antiballistic missile defense system (ABM), but it was forced on the Johnson Administration by an aroused Congress and it was left to Nixon to implement it. And on the offensive side, rather than match the numbers of Soviet missiles, our predecessors decided to develop MIRV warheads to multiply the offensive power of each of our existing missiles. The first US flight tests of MIRV'd missiles took place in 1968. Our predecessors had also decided to base our strategic force on light but highly accurate missiles, the Minuteman ICBM and Poseidon SLBM. (The Soviets had made the opposite decision, emphasizing missiles that were much larger than ours and therefore capable of delivering a far heavier payload. As Soviet technology improved, its advantage in numbers and payload would be enhanced by improved accuracy.) Thus decisions of the Johnson Administration determined the size as well as the numbers of our missiles throughout our period in office. This was because the lead time for most new weapons is at least six years between conception and production and because the Congress resisted new programs until the end of the Vietnam war. Hence no decision that we made could produce new weapons before the middle 1970s. And Congressional opposition threatened to delay this even further.

Thus, inexorably, the overwhelming preponderance that we had enjoyed in the Forties and Fifties was being eroded first into equality, eventually into vulnerability, of our land-based forces. The Soviets' heavier payload and imminent lead in numbers would be counterbalanced for a while by our technological lead. We were believed to be at least five years ahead in the development of MIRVs; the accuracy of our missiles was still superior, a crucial ingredient in any calculation about a hypothetical nuclear exchange. Our capacity to maintain a rough strategic balance was not yet endangered—provided our technological superiority was fully exploited. We could deploy an ABM to protect our cities or our missile sites. We could also speed up preliminary work on a more advanced bomber (later known as the B-1), a new submarine and submarine-launched missile (the Trident), and a new ICBM (the MX). After 1978 we would thus be in a strong position, provided all the programs started in the early 1970s were maintained. We took all these steps, but each was attacked both in the Congress and in the media. Our strategic dilemma was that without these future weapons systems our strategic forces would grow increasingly vulnerable; even with them our long-term security requirements were changing.

For *even with equality*, or a slight superiority, any new Administration would face an unprecedented challenge. Our defense strategies formed in the period of our superiority had to be reexamined in the harsh light of the new realities. Before too long an all-out nuclear exchange could inflict casualties on the United States amounting to tens of millions. A balance of destructiveness would then exist; and even if for a while our capacity to inflict casualties should exceed that of our adversaries, our reluctance to resort to nuclear war was certain to mount dramatically. The credibility of American pledges to risk Armageddon in defense of allies was bound to come into question. This raised critical issues: How could we maintain the independence and self-confidence of allied countries under the shadow of the Soviet Union's land armies (also growing) as well as its expanding nuclear arsenal? What should be our strategy for the use of our nuclear forces? If all-out thermonuclear war became too dangerous, would limited applications of nuclear forces still be feasible?

The Defense Debate

Such questions would have been difficult to answer in the best of circumstances. Unfortunately, the late 1960s and early 1970s were hardly a time for calm, rational analysis of strategic problems. The passionate critique of the war in Vietnam spread to an attack on the defense establishment as a whole; indeed, some saw in an assault on the defense budget a device for forcing an end to the war in Southeast Asia. "Reordering national priorities" from defense to domestic programs was the slogan of the period; it was a euphemism for severe cuts in the defense budget. Intellectuals who made fun of President Eisenhower's syntax and leadership when he was in office readily embraced as received truth his 1961 warning against permitting the so-called military-industrial complex to acquire a disproportionate influence on American life. Weapons—especially ours—were considered the cause rather than the symptoms of tension because it was alleged that our programs triggered Soviet responses rather than the other way around. The U.S. government's assertions that the Soviet buildup faced us with a genuine defense problem were ridiculed as standard output of the "Pentagon propaganda machine," regurgitated every year to influence budgetary decisions in the Congress. The valid perception that the strategic arms race was different from any that preceded it was turned into the proposition that *any* new expenditure for strategic forces was absurd because there already existed enough weapons to destroy humanity several times over. . . .

The most frequently cited "lesson" of Vietnam was that the United States had to reduce its overseas commitments. The impression was created that our deployments abroad, rather than deterring aggression, actually encouraged it. By withdrawing U.S. forces from overseas, it was said, the incidence of global conflict would go down, making lower defense expenditures possible. By the same token, reduced military budgets would force the government to curtail its foreign involvement. An additional benefit would be that funds would be freed for domestic welfare programs. . . .

Thus critics drew from the approaching nuclear parity the amazing conclusion that we should cut our *conventional* forces in which we were already vastly inferior. They saw in the end of the Vietnam war not an opportunity to make up for long-neglected procurement but an occasion for cutting our defense budget. . . .

From the beginning, Nixon was determined to resist these trends, believing that American power was not only morally defensible but crucial for the survival of free countries. But in the existing climate, strengthening our defenses proved no simple task. Not only the conduct of a war but the sinews of national security were under assault.

For me the debate brought much stress with old friends and former associates with whom I had served on arms control panels and study groups for over a decade. I agreed with them that nuclear weapons added a unique dimension to the arms race. To be sure, my reading of history did not support their view that all arms races caused tensions; arms buildups, historically, were more often a reflection rather than a cause of political conflicts and distrust. But I substantially agreed that what marked our time as a period of revolutionary change was the high state of readiness of strategic weapons and their destructiveness. Strategic forces, at once highly vulnerable and extremely powerful, could in a crisis tempt one side to strike first, especially if it feared that it might lose its means of retaliation to a first blow.

Like many in the academic community, I favored a conscious policy of stabilizing the arms race. I believed also that national leaders had a duty to disenthrall themselves of the simplistic notions that military power alone brought security, dating from a time when the penalties for misjudgment involved less catastrophic consequences. In my view it was in the interest of both sides to reduce the vulnerability of their retaliatory forces: by agreement on mutual restraint if possible, by unilateral actions if necessary. Even more important, I was convinced that a democratic society would never be able to brave the hazards of the nuclear age unless its people were convinced that its leaders responded rationally and soberly to the unprecedented existence of weapons of mass destruction. Given the dynamics of the Soviet system, I thought that military challenges were possible, perhaps even probable. I wanted the United States and its allies to be able to face them backed by a united public. One lesson of Vietnam was that firm counteractions, necessarily involving sacrifice, could always be undermined by domestic divisions if our people believed their governments needlessly sought or provoked confrontations.

Where I parted company with my friends and former colleagues was in my analysis of Soviet motivations. I did not accept the proposition that unilateral restraint in weapons procurement on our part would evoke a comparable response from the Kremlin. As believers in the predominance of "objective factors," the Soviet leaders were likely to interpret such steps less as gestures of conciliation than as weakness, caused by domestic or economic pressures. The Soviet Union after the Cuban missile crisis was going all out in its weapons procurement in every major category of arms. American abdication would tempt Soviet tendencies toward filling every vacuum; the USSR would accept a stabilization of the arms race only if convinced that it would not be allowed to achieve superiority. It was in our interest to demonstrate to the Soviet Union that given the inequality of resources it could not possibly win an arms race, that we would not stand by while the balance shifted against us, and that if sufficiently provoked we would simply outproduce them.

Nor did I agree with the military analysis so often advanced by critics of our defense programs. It was true that notions of military superiority had a different significance in the nuclear age; it did not follow that we could risk standing still while our adversaries built feverishly. Over the decades a growing imbalance against us was bound to deprive our pledges to defend our allies of *any* credibility; in extreme circumstances it might tempt an attack on the United States.

Even if the risks to the Soviet Union of an attempt to attack the United States would always seem exorbitant, an eroding strategic equilibrium was bound to have geopolitical consequences. It would accentuate our known inferiority in forces capable of regional defense. The countries around the Soviet periphery would be more and more tempted to seek security in accommodation. Nor were our dangers exhausted by deliberate acts of Soviet military pressure. In a revolutionary period many crises were conceivable that were not sought by either side; Soviet willingness to run risks was bound to grow as the strategic balance shifted against us. This could not fail to demoralize countries looking to us for protection, whether they were allied or technically nonaligned.

I therefore favored new strategic programs and a strengthened conventional defense, even while urging a major effort in negotiations to control arms. In time my views were to provoke the wrath of both conservatives and liberals, the former because they opposed any arms control, the latter because they opposed any arms buildup. By the same token, the 1969 debate on the military balance came to affect national decisions on both weapons procurement and SALT negotiations for all the years of the Nixon Administration.

The debate focused on two new weapons systems: the ABM program and the deployment of MIRVs on our missiles. The new Administration inherited both of these programs from its predecessor. But Nixon's victory had altered the political equation; it liberated Democratic critics of defense programs who had muted their views while their own party was in office. They were soon reinforced by some of the very Johnson Administration officials who had originated these programs and were eager to rejoin the mainstream of their party. Though Nixon had cut the defense budget submitted by Johnson by $ 1.1 billion, he was nevertheless abused almost immediately by an insistent chorus of Democratic critics. Some Republicans, believing the antimilitary sentiment to be the dominant public mood, joined them.

Antiballistic Missiles (ABM)

. . . We were being pressed to take two momentous steps: first, to abandon our ABM without reciprocity; and second, to postpone our MIRV deployment as a unilateral gesture—in short, to forgo both our missile defense and the means to defeat that already deployed by the Soviet Union. All this was being advocated while the Soviet missile arsenal was growing at the rate of two to three hundred missiles a year. If the Soviets were building while we abandoned our programs, what would be their incentive to negotiate limitations in an agreement? Our unilateral restraint would be an incentive for the Soviets not to settle but to procrastinate, to tilt the balance as much in their favor as possible while we paralyzed ourselves. To abandon ABM and MIRV together would thus not only have undercut the prospects for any SALT agreement but probably guaranteed Soviet strategic superiority for a decade.

And so it happened that when the SALT talks started in November, contrary to the dire predictions of arms controllers the Soviets proved eager to negotiate on ABM; they showed, on the other hand, interest only in limits on the *deployment* of MIRVs, leaving them free to test and thereby catch up to us technologically. Neither our ABM program nor MIRV testing created difficulties for SALT. On the contrary, they spurred it.

Strategic Doctrine

Amidst this turmoil, my staff and I—with the President's strong support— undertook a reexamination of military doctrine. The purpose was to enable us in time to plan and defend our military programs according to reasoned criteria, to adjust our strategy to new realities, and to try to lead the public debate away from emotionalism.

The first problem was to redefine the strategy for general nuclear war. According to the doctrine of "assured destruction," which had guided the previous Administration, we deterred Soviet attack by maintaining offensive forces capable of achieving a particular level of civilian deaths and industrial damage. The strategy did not aim at destroying the other side's missile or bomber forces; such an approach would have tied our force structure to the level of the other side's—which is precisely what the advocates of "assured destruction" sought to avoid. They preferred the apparent certainty of an absolute standard of destructiveness defined in economic terms (systems analysis was, after all, an economists' technique), which freed us from the need to match the growing Soviet power. The number of nuclear weapons needed to achieve a huge level of destruction was fixed and not large.

Remarkably, the doctrine of "assured destruction," espoused by liberal advocates of arms control who were supposedly most moved by humanitarian concerns, implied the most inhuman strategy for conducting a war. The reasoning was that the more horrible the consequences of war the less likely we were to resort to it; the more controllable its consequences the greater the risk that a war would actually occur. Therefore, for the United States and Soviet Union to aim at each other's population, rather than at each other's missile bases, was desirable; if mutual extermination was the only course, neither side would resort to nuclear weapons. What would happen in case of miscalculation was left to the future. How we would defend allies in these circumstances was not analyzed.

The dilemma never resolved by this doctrine was psychological. It was all very well to threaten mutual suicide for purposes of deterrence, particularly in case of a direct threat to national survival. But no President could make such a threat credible except by conducting a diplomacy that suggested a high irrationality—and that in turn was precluded by our political system, which requires us to project an image of calculability and moderation. And if deterrence failed and the President was finally faced with the decision to retaliate, who would take the moral responsibility for recommending a strategy based on the mass extermination of civilians? How could the United States hold its allies together as the credibility of its strategy eroded? How would we deal with Soviet conventional forces once the Soviets believed that we meant what we said about basing strategy on the extermination of civilians?

Carried a step farther, the doctrine of "assured destruction" led to the extraordinary conclusion that the vulnerability of our civilian population was an *asset* reassuring the Soviet Union and guaranteeing its restraint in a crisis. For the first time a major country saw an advantage in enhancing its *own* vulnerability. "Assured destruction" was one of those theories that sound impressive in an academic seminar but are horribly unworkable for a decision-maker in the real world and lead to catastrophe if they are ever implemented.

I was also concerned that as strategic equivalence between the United States and the Soviet Union approached, strategic forces might be used in less than an all-out attack. I pointed out to the President in June of 1969 the dilemma he would face if there was a limited Soviet nuclear attack and urged him to request the Pentagon to devise strategies to meet contingencies other than

all-out nuclear challenge. The President agreed. Orders to that effect were issued. But our military establishment resists intrusion into strategic doctrine
even when it comes from a White House seeking to be helpful. When I entered
office, former Defense Secretary Robert McNamara told me that he had tried
for seven years to give the President more options. He had finally given up, he
said, in the face of bureaucratic opposition and decided to improvise. I was
determined to do better; I succeeded only partially. Civilian defense planners
were reluctant because more options would require some new forces, com-
plicating budgetary decisions. The service chiefs were reluctant because they
prefer to negotiate their force levels by bargaining with each other, rather than
submitting them to the tender mercies of civilian analysts who, experience has
taught, are more likely to emasculate than to strengthen them. Since our military operations are planned by combined commands not subordinate to the
military services, the various chiefs of staff are more heads of procurement
enterprises than of organizations responsible for implementing strategy. They
are deeply suspicious of any doctrinal formulation that later might interfere
with their procurement decisions. So it happened that a specific Presidential
directive of 1969 inquiring into the rationale of naval programs was never answered satisfactorily in the eight years I served in Washington. The response
was always short of being insubordinate but also short of being useful. Despite
semiannual reminders it was listed as incomplete on the books when we left
office. The same attitude existed in other services.

Somewhat more progress was made in developing a more discriminating
strategy for all-out war, partly as a result of considerable White House pressure. The Joint Chiefs cooperated because they understood that the doctrine
of "assured destruction" would inevitably lead to political decisions halting or
neglecting the improvement of our strategic forces and in time reducing them.
We therefore developed in 1969 new criteria of "strategic sufficiency" that related our strategic planning to the destruction not only of civilians but of military targets as well. These criteria . . . gave us at least the theoretical capability to use forces for objectives other than the mass extermination of populations.

Translating these doctrinal innovations into operational plans proved far
more difficult. Planning started immediately, but it was not completed until
the incumbency of James R. Schlesinger as Secretary of Defense (1973–1975).
Some new targeting options were then produced. Unfortunately, by the time
they were developed they had been overtaken by advances in technology.
Expected casualties in a nuclear war had doubled even for minimum nuclear
options. Defense Secretary Harold Brown has pursued this effort in the Carter
Administration. Achieving a more discriminating nuclear strategy, preserving
at least some hope of civilized life, remains to this day one of the most dif-

ficult tasks to implement, requiring a substantial recasting of our military establishment. If unsolved, the problem will sooner or later paralyze our strategy and our foreign policy.

Tactical Nuclear Weapons

A similar problem existed with respect to tactical nuclear weapons. One might have thought that if our strategic forces tended toward parity with the USSR and if at the same time we were inferior in conventional military strength, greater emphasis would be placed on tactical nuclear forces. This indeed was NATO's proclaimed strategy of "flexible response." But there was little enthusiasm for this concept within our government. Civilian officials in the State Department and the Pentagon, especially systems analysis experts, were eager to create a clear "firebreak" between conventional and nuclear weapons and to delay the decision to resort to *any* nuclear weapons as long as possible. They were reluctant, therefore, to rely on tactical nuclear weapons, which they thought would tend to erode all distinctions between nuclear and conventional strategy.

A passage from a study on NATO's military options reflected this state of mind. This particular study was unable to find *any* use for nuclear weapons in NATO even though our stockpile there numbered in the thousands: The primary role of our nuclear forces in Europe, the study argued, is to raise the Soviet estimate of the expected costs of aggression and add great uncertainty to their calculations. Nuclear forces do not necessarily have a decisive impact on the likelihood or form of aggression, the study concluded. This was an astonishing statement from a country that had preserved the peace in Europe for over twenty years by relying on its nuclear preponderance. Nor was it clear how forces thought not to have a decisive impact could affect the calculations of a potential aggressor. It was a counsel of defeat to abjure both strategic and tactical nuclear forces, for no NATO country—including ours—was prepared to undertake the massive buildup in conventional forces that was the sole alternative.

To confuse matters further, while American civilian analysts deprecated the use of nuclear weapons as ineffective and involving a dangerous risk of escalation, our allies pressed a course contradicting the prevailing theory in Washington. They urged both a guaranteed early resort to tactical nuclear weapons and immunity of their territories from their use. Inevitably, discussions that had been going on since 1968 in the NATO Nuclear Planning Group began to produce serious differences of opinion.

This Group had been set up by Secretary McNamara as a device by which our allies could participate in nuclear decisions without acquiring nuclear weapons themselves. Denis Healey, then British Minister of Defense, had explained his government's view when Nixon visited London in February 1969. In Healey's judgment NATO's conventional forces would be able to resist for only a matter of days; hence early use of nuclear weapons was essential. Healey stressed the crucial importance of making the Soviets understand that the West would prefer to escalate to a strategic exchange rather than surrender. On the other hand, NATO should seek to reduce devastation to a minimum. The Nuclear Planning Group was working on solving this riddle; its "solution" was the use of a very small number of tactical weapons as a warning that matters were getting out of hand.

What Britain, supported by West Germany, was urging came to be called the "demonstrative use" of nuclear weapons. This meant setting off a nuclear weapon in some remote location, which did not involve many casualties—in the air over the Mediterranean, for example—as a signal of more drastic use if the warning failed. I never had much use for this concept. I believed that the Soviet Union would not attack Western Europe without anticipating a nuclear response. A reaction that was designed to be of no military relevance would show more hesitation than determination; it would thus be more likely to spur the attack than deter it. If nuclear weapons were to be used, we needed a concept by which they could stop an attack on the ground. A hesitant or ineffective response ran the risk of leaving us with no choices other than surrender or holocaust.

But what was an "effective" response? Given the political impossibility of raising adequate conventional forces, the Europeans saw nuclear weapons as the most effective deterrent. But they feared the use of them on their territories; what seemed "limited" to us could be catastrophic for them. The real goal of our allies—underlining the dilemma of tactical nuclear weapons—has been to commit the United States to the early use of *strategic* nuclear weapons, which meant a U.S.–Soviet nuclear war fought over their heads. This was precisely what was unacceptable to American planners. Our strategy—then and now—must envisage the ultimate use of strategic nuclear weapons if Europe can be defended in no other way. But it must also seek to develop other options, both to increase the credibility of the deterrent and to permit a flexible application of our power should deterrence fail.

In 1969, a temporary compromise emerged that in effect papered over the dispute. The Nuclear Planning Group kept open the possibility of both "demonstrative" and "operational" uses of tactical nuclear weapons. In other words, a decision was avoided. Laird was correct when he reported to the President: "The longer term problem of divergence between American and European views on strategy remains."

One and a Half Wars

While the nuclear issue was not resolved—and perhaps could not be—one major adaptation of our strategic doctrine did take place in 1969. It was destined to have profound consequences for our foreign policy. What started out as a highly esoteric discussion of military strategy turned into one of our most important signals to the People's Republic of China that we meant to improve our relations with it.

When the Nixon Administration came into office, the prevalent doctrine for conventional forces was the "two-and-one-half-war" strategy; according to it the United States needed forces sufficient to: (1) mount an initial (ninety-day) defense of Western Europe against a Soviet attack; (2) make a sustained defense against an all-out Chinese attack on either Southeast Asia or Korea; *and* (3) still meet a contingency elsewhere, for example, the Middle East. Our strategic planning assumed what was belied by the political facts: that we confronted a Communist monolith, that a general war would almost surely involve a simultaneous attack on our vital interests by both the Soviet Union and Communist China. To be sure, we never chose to build the conventional forces envisaged by this ambitious strategy. In military terms the two-and-one-half-war strategy was a paper exercise, in which certain divisions were earmarked for Europe and others for Asia. Its major result, however, was psychological. It connected the Soviet and Chinese threats in our thinking so inextricably that any analysis of possible use of nuclear weapons tended to presuppose that the Soviet Union and China were a single target area. Politically, it inhibited our understanding of the emerging split between the Communist giants and the opportunity this represented for the United States.

In one of my early initiatives as security adviser I launched a reexamination of the assumptions of the two-and-one-half-war concept. An Interdepartmental Group responded with five options, which my staff and I boiled down to three. Each alternative strategy was analyzed in terms of the contingencies it would enable us to meet and its budgetary implications. Strategies for NATO were matched in various combinations with strategies for Asia. These combinations were then related to projected domestic expenditures, so that the President could decide what level of risk he was running if he were to give up any particular strategic option for a specific domestic program. The three options were as follows:

Strategy 1 would maintain conventional forces for an initial (ninety-day) defense of Western Europe against a major Soviet attack, and for simultaneous assistance (by logistical support and limited US combat forces) to an Asian ally against threats short of a full-scale Chinese invasion.

Strategy 2 would maintain forces capable of either a NATO initial defense *or* a defense against a full-scale Chinese attack in Korea or Southeast Asia. That is, we would not maintain forces to fight on a large scale in Europe and Asia simultaneously.

Strategy 3 (essentially our strategy before the Vietnam war) would maintain US forces for a NATO initial defense *and* a defense of Korea or Southeast Asia against a full-scale Chinese attack. The forces would be capable of meeting the major Warsaw Pact and Chinese threats *simultaneously*.

On October 2, 1969, I wrote to the President summing up the options and their military and budgetary implications. The agencies had varying views, which I reported fairly, but in case of a split view the President as always wanted my recommendation. I urged that he approve Strategy 2: "I believe that a simultaneous Warsaw Pact attack in Europe and Chinese conventional attack in Asia is unlikely. In any event, I do not believe such a simultaneous attack could or should be met with ground forces."

Nixon accepted my recommendation. It was one of the more important decisions of his Presidency. First of all, it harmonized doctrine and capability. We had never generated the forces our two-and-one-half-war doctrine required; the gap between our declaratory and our actual policy was bound to create confusion in the minds of potential aggressors and to raise grave risks if we attempted to apply it. There was no realistic prospect that the Chinese and the Soviets would move against us at the same time. But if there *were* a joint assault by China and the Soviet Union, we would be faced with a threat to the global equilibrium; to pretend that in these circumstances we would confine our response to a conventional war in two widely separated areas would multiply our dangers.

The political implications were even more decisive. We had to give up the obsession with a Communist monolith. By linking Soviet and Chinese purposes we created presumptions that circumscribed the flexibility of our diplomacy and ran counter to the demonstrable antagonism between the two major Communist powers. The reorientation of our strategy signaled to the People's Republic of China that we saw its purposes as separable from the Soviet Union's, that our military policy did not see China as a principal threat. Although our change of doctrine was never acknowledged by Peking, it is inconceivable that it was ignored by those careful students of geopolitics who so meticulously monitored all American public statements. For not only did we begin to reflect the new strategic design in our military planning for both nuclear and conventional war; to leave no doubt about our intentions, we took the extraordinary step of spelling out our rationale in the President's first Foreign Policy Report to the Congress on February 18, 1970, along the lines of the analysis I have just described. The key sentences read:

> In the effort to harmonize doctrine and capability, we chose what is best described as the "1½-war" strategy. Under it we will maintain in peacetime general purpose forces adequate for simultaneously meeting a major Communist attack in *either* Europe or Asia, assisting allies against non-Chinese threats in Asia, and contending with a contingency elsewhere [emphasis added].

The choice of this strategy was based on the following considerations:

> —The nuclear capability of our strategic and theater nuclear forces serves as a deterrent to full-scale Soviet attack on NATO Europe or Chinese attack on our Asian allies;
> —The prospects for a coordinated two-front attack on our allies by Russia and China are low both because of the risks of nuclear war and the improbability of Sino-Soviet cooperation. . . .

And Western Europe—not Asia—was singled out as the theater in which the threat was most likely. We were, in short, concerned more with the danger of Soviet than of Chinese aggression.

We had sent an important signal to China. We would no longer treat a conflict with the USSR as automatically involving the People's Republic. We would treat our two adversaries on the basis of their actions toward us, not their ideology; we publicly acknowledged their differences and the unlikelihood of their cooperation. The Chinese had an option to move toward us.

LUCIEN POIRIER
(b. 1918)

Lucien Poirier, a general in the French army, specialized in nuclear issues, first at the Centre de prospective et d'évaluation du ministère des Armées and later as head of the military section of the Institut des hautes études de défense nationale. With General Pierre Gallois, he was one of the figures behind French nuclear strategy. He taught at the grandes écoles, *edited the journal* Stratégique, *and wrote* Des stratégies nucléaires *(1977),* Essais de stratégie théorique *(1982),* Les Voix de la stratégie. Généalogie de la stratégie militaire: Guibert, Jomini *(1985), and* Stratégie théorique II *(1987).*

ELEMENTS OF A THEORY OF CRISIS

The arrival of the nuclear age has given new prominence to two strategic modes: deterrence and indirect action. They in turn have revealed the importance of a hitherto neglected phenomenon of social and political activity that results from their combination: crisis.

Especially since the 1962 Cuban missile crisis, there has been much talk of crisis; that crisis has been studied in detail, and the most diverse lessons have been extracted from it. But, while there is much on which views differ, there is agreement that it marked a turning-point in the understanding of nuclear power and in international relations. Since then, crisis management has been one of the major components of strategic practice and a key focus of theoretical thinking.

The fact of crisis has, of course, always been manifest, in the most varied forms, in social and political history. But classical political and strategic theory was little concerned with it as a *fact of conflict* with its own specific char-

From Lucien Poirier, *Eléments pour une théorie de la crise* (Paris: Centre des hautes études militaires, 1975). Translated from the French by A. M. Berrett. Reproduced by permission of Lucien Poirier.

acteristics. It dealt with it only obliquely, as a hazy border zone between two clear and distinct objects: war and peace. For crisis, the period when armed conflicts incubate, there is not theoretical equivalent of what Clausewitz established for the truce that suspends them. . . .

To observe that crisis has become the *natural state* of the social and political community is not to give in to a pessimistic view of history. Physical violence, diffuse in one sensitive region, explicit in another, is everywhere and at all times present in the most diverse forms.

The problem of our time is neither to deny that reality nor simply to accept it as a fact of life; it lies in the capacity of the most powerful states, the ones most responsible for the fate of us all, to find the meaning of crises in their multiple manifestations; and then to invent the ways and means of controlling them so that they serve to construct a truly *universal* history.

. . . It is probably with *crisis strategy* that we can best grasp the interrelations between the three components—economic, cultural and military—of grand strategy.

The Concept of Crisis

Once we acknowledge that it has an identity independent of the war/peace dichotomy, crisis becomes one of the facts of conflict requiring particular political and strategic behavior. Assessments, decisions, and operations will necessarily be different, in their practice and in their spirit, from those required when the crisis was only an *amorphous* stage between peace and war.

Of course, this is only accurate for nuclear states. . . . We have seen that second-rank states only enter into crisis to emerge into open war or a settlement, whose terms they very rarely control: in most cases, the internationalization of regional disputes and the interested interference of the great powers resolve the crisis in ways, with means, and through a compromise that hardly satisfy the parties directly engaged on the ground.

I shall call *crisis management* a conflict strategy that is capable of developing into a war strategy for *some only* of the states involved. It summarizes a set of assessments, decisions, and intellectual and material operations through which the states involved in a crisis, whether directly or not:

(*a*) Define their various *interests* at stake in this particular situation and the dangers, actual or foreseeable, that threaten them. For each this amounts to assessing the likely effects of the disturbance on its relative position in the international system (power and vulnerability factors) (*b*)   Estimate and compare the *marginal values,* given their political project, of the hopes of benefit and the risks associated with the various crisis hypotheses

(*c*)   Infer from that assessment *the crisis goals* and the economic, cultural, and military strategies to be pursued according to the crisis hypotheses

(*d*)   *Guide their crisis action* and the operations that it combines, in the light of what the other side does and the gaps observed between the crisis goals and the actual results of the strategy pursued "on the ground" . . .

Understood like this, crisis management is something that can only be envisaged for states with the capacity to confirm, by their action, their special status as subjects of an autonomous policy. The rest remain, for various reasons and in varying degrees, the objects and instruments of these authentically sovereign policies and adapted grand strategies.

In other words, if nuclear capacity is the necessary condition for the autonomous decision making and freedom of action that are indispensable for carrying out a project, *crisis management is only a relevant and operational concept for the nuclear powers.* . . .

Crisis Control

ITS INITIAL PURPOSE

For the nuclear powers, and especially for the United States and the Soviet Union, their common interest and the status of adversaries/partners that flows from it dictate that they keep their crisis action within limits such that the probability of a direct war occurring between them remains zero. Crisis control thus consists in the dispositions and operations through which each of the superpowers signifies to and imposes on the other, and its clients, the limits on their freedom of action. These limits must not be transgressed on pain of dangerously increasing the risks of direct war and hence the nuclear risk.

The superpowers must constantly see to it that their allies and clients never take the initiative in a crisis, nor, *a fortiori,* in an armed conflict, without being given the green light.

Nevertheless, if a regional crisis is opened up by the careless initiative of an ally escaping the control of its patron or at its instigation, its development must not harm the regional interests of the other superpower to the point where the latter is tempted to intervene militarily, which would force the "patron" in turn to commit itself when it had no wish to.

Control, first preventive and then active, comes in at both the political and the strategic levels. For the United States and the USSR, it takes the form of political and, at the limit, military commitments alongside their allies, but these commitments must remain restrained so as not to lead the other great power to overreact. The American doctrine of flexible response reflects this circumspection.

Control thus acts in the first place as a *limiting and moderating factor* in the policy and military strategy of second-rank states in normal times, and especially, if they embark on open war; then as a *security factor* in the actions of the superpowers, insofar as it guarantees to each of them that the other is doing what it can to avoid the conditions for a direct armed conflict between them coming about. . . .

CRISIS CONTROL AND MASTERY OF CONFLICTS

Control operations, combining words and deeds, constitute the most novel aspect of crisis; it is what makes the strategy of external action of the nuclear powers diverge most, and visibly, from its conventional forms.

Control operations set as their objective permanent communication between the superpowers, but they are a striking affirmation that neither can any longer think of victory over the other. Crisis control thus performs a decisive function in the mastery of conflicts and arms control to which their undecided condition of being at once adversaries and partners condemns them, willy-nilly, so long as nuclear weaponry retains its rationalizing virtue. It is assuredly through the joint practice—if only by tacit consent—of crisis control that the United States and the Soviet Union best objectify their duopolistic subsystem to international society. It is through the tangible results of control, and the restrictions that it imposes, in sensitive regions, on the autonomous decision making and freedom of action of local states that their duopoly is often perceived as reflecting their desire for a shared hegemony over the rest of the world. . . .

PSYCHOLOGICAL ACTION AND WAR

Each [nation's] freedom of action requires first of all the consent of its public opinion. This support is vital to its political leadership, which cannot afford to be paralyzed by the reservations, or even fears, of the population when the time comes to take the decisions immediately called for by the first symptoms of crisis. Conversely, the political leadership must not be dragged into precipitate and overhasty decisions by the irrational impulses of bellicose groups or jingoistic masses. Similarly, it will seek to neutralize international opinion, or, better, win its sympathy by justifying its intervention.

This action will be complemented by a psychological war designed to have an impact on the freedom of action of the opposing political leadership and deprive it of the support of its domestic opinion. This always involves discrediting the other, giving him a bad conscience and sowing doubt in world opinion as to the well-foundedness of any intervention he might be contemplating.

Public opinion, domestic and external, thus today constitutes the first and constant objective of crisis management. Diplomacy and the mass media, backed by communications satellites, do their bit to persuade or dissuade, which often proves to be decisive in critical moments of the crisis. In addition, the big international organizations (UN, OAU, etc.) act as sounding boards for the accusations and defenses of the protagonists.

In other words, crisis action exploits all the resources of cultural strategy by playing on the sensitivity of national temperaments and the heterogeneity of the social and cultural fabric: ethnic, ideological, and religious cleavages; linguistic communities; historical memories; technological gaps; and so on. Anyone who claims an active role in crisis management must be equipped with the means of psychological warfare, which assumes a network of cultural influence and a permanent technical infrastructure capable of addressing both the elites and the masses, even remote ones, whose hostility has to be overcome or support retained. . . .

Summary: The Present Features of the Crisis

. . . That is why crisis management in the nuclear age falls within the competence of the political leadership, the supreme strategist. In order to control action, the political leadership has to be able to decide on military measures that are apparently minor but politically significant. We are witnessing the eviction of the military strategist, some of whose decisions, once considered to be simple matters of execution, will in future be taken by the political leadership. For the crisis aim can shift so rapidly that it may prove necessary to modify the ways and means by which this strategic aim is being pursued in the light of fleeting information—as varied as all the areas of activity concerned by the crisis—that the political center alone can collect and process with the necessary dispatch.

All this requires a politico-military organization and leadership centralized enough to respond to the demands and constraints of management. To manage this presupposes the capacity to think, calculate, and guide action in real time in order to compensate for the structural inertia of the economic and military apparatuses, which always leads to some lag in decisions—in short, the ability to respond to adversary initiatives. This notion of management in real time is vital in confused conflict situations that evolve rapidly and in which the lag in measures adopted, like the retardation of their effects, may be a source of serious misunderstandings. Such risks of error are all the more serious because it will always be difficult to make up for these gaps between the results aimed at and those obtained: any "visual flying" presupposes a high degree of behavioral flexibility and system response times that are as short as possible.

Furthermore, given the difficulties inherent in detecting and diagnosing a crisis and predicting its potential for aggravation, the ordinary conduct of politics and strategy must constantly count with the sudden eruption of these phenomena, even in the most settled climate of détente. That gives added strength to the centralizing function of a politico-military leadership permanently capable of reacting effectively to happenstance incidents whose potential for aggravation is unknown. We must therefore ask ourselves whether government structures, traditionally conceived to respond to the distinct necessities of peace and war, are suited to conceive and guide crisis strategies.

Crisis management is a transaction, a continuous negotiation imposed by the ambivalent adversarial/partnership status of the nuclear powers; it is an extremely complex matter, since it brings into play all the factors of power and reveals all the vulnerabilities of the protagonists; and, for the nuclear powers, it has to find its resolution in the crisis itself and not in its usual denouement, the payment in kind of war. Crisis theory might thus find models representative of its intellectual approaches in the analysis of commercial transactions.

It is a vast bargaining operation, and combines diplomatic word, economic action, and military deed, each sustaining and commenting on the others. It involves permanent communication among the parties, bluff, concessions, the development of forces so as to safeguard, or restore, and exploit freedom of political decision making and strategic action. It thus stresses psychological action and war, as well as the function of information media in a strategy that values exchanges of signs and speculates on semiotic calculations, as well as on those of physical forces.

Once one evokes freedom of decision making and capacity for action, the hierarchy of the powers determines the distribution of their effective roles in managing and settling crises.

Like any strategy, crisis strategy claims to be a goal-achievement system, and is based on a complex play of forces serving a will, itself sustained by the consciousness of a necessary political end. It thus rests on economic, cultural, and military potential and forces. And like any strategic management, it is an acid test of that potential and those forces; even if, for the nuclear powers, this test of truth must be carried out without actualizing the force between them directly. . . .

Finally, at the level of general military strategy, crisis management presupposes action and reaction capacities marked by an immediate and permanent availability of external action forces that are, par excellence, forces in being whose potentialities only have meaning if they are capable of being actualized "on demand." Their disposition must be flexible and open enough to favor the adoption of postures making it possible to respond instantly to the various crisis eventualities in sensitive regions (surveillance, alert, and information dispositions).

Quite clearly, air-sea and airborne forces remain the best adapted, on the one hand, to presence in sensitive regions, the modalities of which in terms of the nature and size of forces will be fine-tuned in the light of the rise of local negative tensions; and on the other hand, to the projection of force into the theater. Even then, these forces must be organized in such a way that the political power can use them freely, taking advantage of its decision-making autonomy in *significant actions,* which usually encapsulate crisis control and action. That presupposes, among other conditions of freedom of action, reliable links and transmissions between the political center and the military strategist engaged in the crisis theater, emphatically demonstrating the importance of the free use of space (satellites) and electronic warfare.

In addition, their equipment with tactical nuclear weapons will give external action forces a local persuasive or deterrent power (relations of force) that will enhance the scope of military actions decided on by the political leadership to have an impact on the other side's decision makers. However, these are all only theoretical perspectives since, *in the current state of things,* it is hard to imagine that the use of nuclear weapons, of any sort, can be credible for the defense of interests unconnected with the defense of the national space, treated as a sanctuary.

We should not forget that intervention in the crisis may lead to a limited local war. Doubtless the great power resigning itself to it would be leaving the crisis situation *stricto sensu;* but that eventuality not being improbable, whether deliberate or accidental, it must be retained among the hypotheses of management failure, and the lesson drawn: either to reject the prospect of limited war, with the political consequences of such an evasion (hopes of gain); or deliberately accept it (risks) and prepare for it. In that hypothesis the presence of tactical nuclear weaponry in a crisis-prone area would enhance the degree of freedom of the political leadership before the risks of a slippage of the crisis toward limited war—and that would be so even if, today, we do not know whether and how this local *ultima ratio* might be useful and effective. . . .

Finally, to remedy the natural inertia of its forces, the military must prepare its rapid mobilization while creating as little disturbance as possible to the normal life of the country. That is the purpose of *crisis plans* drawn up in "peacetime," in accordance with the political project, to which all sectors of national life should contribute. More than ever, military strategy must be thought and practiced in the framework of the grand strategy of which all crisis management is part and do so knowing that the dispositions taken and planned in ordinary times will often determine the decisions taken in time of crisis. . . .

Conclusion

Yet any crisis is above all history happening—a history perpetually undecided between the survivals of a past that is moribund, but refuses to die, and the incarnation of a future that is having great difficulty emerging from limbo; a history [now] more than ever hesitating between the prudent summation of an accumulation of small facts and the radical break, the great wager of war.

If war has always lurked on the horizon of crises, and the struggle to the death on the horizon of war, their image today is too terrifying to be innocently included in the calculations of political reason. Their irrationality thus invests the crisis, by way of compensation, and for a while, with a catalytic function, forcing history to make itself according to a new rationality.

To some states, armed force may still offer the means of precipitating their becoming, but in the nuclear age, war is no longer free either in its motives or in its acts: it is subject to rules of the game that are tyrannical enough for the protagonists to set limits to both its ends and the way in which it is fought, so as to call into question the too-common, because too-facile, concordance of paroxysmal violence and grand political designs.

With its specific operational logic, crisis takes over to impel states to express and resolve their conflicts in a new and more subtle language. For the more powerful, "major war" refers only to a situation that is ruled out in the dynamic of their subsystem, a limit fixed by reference to the absurd. What is left is the field of their conflict-laden relations and strategic solutions that obey the unavoidable rule of a political game that excludes direct war because it carries the risk of death for both players and spectators.

Weapons of instant mass destruction—deliberate genocide—thus restore, in a different form and with a more urgent necessity, the notion of *conflictual consensus* that governed relations between European monarchies in the eighteenth century. Conscious of their dynastic solidarity and the common destiny of a Europe unified by "a certain idea of man," the enlightened despots agreed to subject their necessary wars to no-less-necessary standards of moderation, which reflected their ambivalent status as adversaries/partners. . . .

For a century and a half, except for a few heretics, strategists sought, as the highest expression of the great art of war, to dominate the will of the adversary by disarming him, and by doing so exclusively through a decisive battle or campaign. There was nothing in the theories and doctrines of the time that sought scientifically to justify this approach to conflict resolution, this strategic paradigm. There was nothing in strategic practice that was not logically dictated by this radicalization of the aims of war, by what was posed axiomatically as a constant of the transformations forced on politico-strategic behavior by circumstances.

There was no military talent that was not judged by this criterion of effectiveness. Libraries are bursting with monographs on the campaigns of the past, whose analysis is based on the principles of an operational strategy organized around the concept of the decisive battle or the battle of annihilation. It took Lawrence of Arabia and Liddell Hart to secure the rehabilitation of limited war and indirect strategy, which the young [Jacques de] Guibert [1743–90] had pushed aside in favor of "grand-style war." It had been forgotten that Guibert only advocated that in application, to his time and country, of a general rule of consistency between policy and strategy. The most absolute among his disciples, and those of an excessively radicalized Clausewitz, did not see that the applications of this principle remained subject to circumstances, and that the geohistorical determinants of sociopolitical systems could impose a different rule on the strategic game.

The sudden appearance of weapons of unlimited violence in the area of forces ordinarily required by conflicts marks a new stage in the evolution of strategic thought and practice: it requires that emphasis now be put on indirect strategy in all its forms, as the strategy that complements nuclear deterrence; they are inseparable and must be thought of simultaneously, as an indivisible whole. Even better, nuclear weapons force us to see strategy in a different perspective and to observe that it makes the narrow confines of its original military domain break open and assume a new dimension. It penetrates all human activities involved in the dynamic of infra- and interstate systems, and the crisis phenomenon is supremely revealing of that extension.

But it is the demands and constraints of crisis management that suggest the combination and modulation of all social and political energies and forces so as to resolve conflicts that must be restrained from rising to the extreme of violence. It is in and through crisis that we ought to be able to observe most conveniently the mechanisms of grand strategy and its function of unifying economic, cultural, and military strategies. It is in and through crisis that we see why, after having long covered only big military operations, the concept of strategy must in future embrace war as one of the modes of the conflict dialectic and be understood as the practice of policy.

PIERRE M. GALLOIS
(b. 1911)

During World War II, Pierre M. Gallois served in the RAF until 1945. Subsequently, he was assigned to SHAPE (Supreme Headquarters, Allied Powers in Europe). In the course of many stays in the United States, he participated in strategic study groups specializing in nuclear weapons, making significant contributions to the theory of mutual deterrence. Gallois, who attained the rank of brigadier in the French air force, was the originator of the concepts that underlie France's nuclear force de frappe.

THE SOCIAL DIMENSION OF STRATEGY

The flow of new weapons resulting from abrupt scientific and technological innovation, which is a feature of our times, leaves the expert standing, catches the political leader short, and surpasses the understanding of the host of the uninitiated. For forty years, each decade has called into question the certainties painfully put together in the course of the preceding one. In 1945 the advent of the atomic bomb for the first time established a balance of forces notwithstanding the greatest numerical imbalance. For peoples, however, the prospect of using atomic weapons was unendurable. Ten years later, thanks to guided missiles, distances were suddenly shortened, geography effaced, and any defense other than the threat of reprisal rendered vain; the shield had disappeared, and only the sword remained. Almost simultaneously, in combination with the submarine, the new weapons now reversed the traditional objective of war; the decisive weapons, which good logic dictated should be neutralized, had become inaccessible, while any human and material property on which the belligerents might have designs lay open to annihilation. The trial of strength was absurd, and there had to be coexistence. Time passed, a mere few years, and a new mutation occurred; rockets were now so accurate that the

Translated from the French by A. M. Berrett.

destructive power they carried could be limited, making possible selective targeting, and the disarmament from a distance—even from a great distance—of an adversary with only conventional weapons, which are easy to destroy if taken by surprise where they are based. The gap between the great powers and the rest was widening. . . .

Contemporary military strategy is infatuated with the preponderance of the armed forces of the United States. Soviet studies are little known in the West, and treated with caution; American works rule the roost. But this American ethnocentrism is also the source of many distortions. Having conceived and realized the first nuclear weapons and built on them both the country's security and the ability to intervene abroad almost risk-free, the United States has been the scene of intense strategic research, naturally dominated by the new weapons. American experts, such as Bernard Brodie, Herman Kahn, Possony, Hans Morgenthau, Gary Snyder, Knorr, Waltz, Thomas Schelling, and thousands of others, have tried very hard to come up with a general theory of the use of force, but they have not been helped by the very fact that nuclear weapons are not among those actually used. In addition, almost all of them have overlooked the rapid evolution of weapons technology and the growing role of the people in the conduct of a nation's affairs. Impressed with the powers of the century's great decision makers, such as Stalin, Churchill, Roosevelt, Mao, and de Gaulle, they wrongly identified the wills of leaders with the confused, but increasingly decisive, wills of their peoples. Most of them see military strategy as a discipline that deals with the command of armed forces serving the state and executing its instructions. While apparently general, the definition is still too restrictive. It was inspired by the competition between the United States and the USSR, the contained confrontation of the two powers in Europe, the race for military supremacy and, more recently, expansionism under Brezhnev and the spread of antinomian doctrine even in the United States itself. The writings of [Nicholas] Spykman and [George] Kennan added a geopolitical dimension to strategy as it is perceived in the United States, the political design and the use—or threatened use—of force being combined into a single grand strategy that inspires and guides the actions of the state (whence the use of the new term *geostrategy*, which is in fact a tautology, since there is no strategy, including grand strategy, that does not take account of the features of the environment in which one or other intends to operate).

In the early 1960s, André Beaufre "modernized" ideas expressed by [Marshal Ferdinand] Foch when he was still a colonel and professor at the Ecole de guerre, writing: "The heart of strategy . . . is the art of the dialectic of forces, or more accurately the art of the dialectic of two opposing wills, using force to resolve their dispute." Although this definition of strategy was put forward eighteen years after Hiroshima, it did not fit the nuclear age. By the mid 1950s, with the new weaponry better assimilated, the political leaderships of the two superpowers—soon imitated by the governments of the other countries that were members of the "nuclear club"—were settling their conflicts, not by force, but through the mere existence of that force. This peculiarity of the nuclear age is vital: use belongs in the realm of the imaginary, and it is the display of the means of destruction respectively held by the various antagonists that is one of the foundations of their new grand strategy. Thus, in the age of the atomic bomb, and contrary to a widely expressed opinion, the "force" aspect of grand strategy includes only what you see. There is no complex dialectic, no subtlety in the strategic game when the nuclear card is there. If one knows what weapons there are, and how to assess the freedom of action of the other side, faced with the prospect of disaster, the dispute is immediately placed on an altogether different plane than that of an exchange of blows. It was thought proper to clothe the practice of deterrence with all the subtleties of which the most skillful diplomacy is capable. That is not the case at all. Deterrence goes without saying, so to speak. It does not rest on any learned or inspired dialectic, but on an observation so obvious that it is imprinted on the brain of future rulers even before they achieve power. Louis XI's strategy was altogether more complex than Eisenhower's against Khrushchev or Reagan's negotiating the denuclearization of Europe with Gorbachev. At grips with Charles the Bold; fighting the Aragonese, the English, the Flemings, and the papacy, besides his great feudatories; coveting Normandy and Burgundy, Genoa, Perpignan, and Calais; sweetening the Lombard bankers; and seeking the aid of Swiss infantry, the king of France was playing a hand more perilous and more difficult than that which any nuclear-backed political leadership faces.

Liddell Hart's thoughts about World War I and World War II led him, however, to make a distinction between the two strategies and rank them, military strategy being only one of the components of grand strategy. The conclusions he drew from the wars he had witnessed differed from those Clausewitz had been led to draw from the Napoleonic wars. Military strategy lies in the province of government policy and not that of the general; it is not designed to cover only a battle or an engagement, since fighting is not the only means of achieving the objectives sought by political leaderships. It is too simplistic to seek the annihilation of the enemy power without thinking about the aftermath of a victory won in such a way; a military strategy with successive limited objectives is more intelligent—if less immediate—and equally effective; it certainly gives fewer hostages to fortune. It is true that Liddell Hart confirms that military strategy is indeed the art of putting the available armed forces to work to do what the political leadership wants, but this strategy is only one of the elements of grand strategy: the permanent execution, according to circumstances, of the state's plans, using all [available] means, including, where necessary, force. The object of an intelligent military strategy is not to seek battle but to create a situation so advantageous that, if it does not itself bring about a favorable outcome, and if, in the last resort, it proves necessary to resort to arms, success is assured.

However "broad" Liddell Hart's strategy may seem, he fails to mention two new components of the antagonisms between powers, which are capable of subverting the state's plans: political propaganda and social agitation. They manifested themselves in 1917–18, when the czarist army collapsed from within rather than being defeated by the German armies; these latter in turn by contagion suffered the effects of the campaigns conducted by the new regime installed in Moscow. Before taking men from the Russian front to strengthen the French front, the German command was obliged to make many units won over to pacifism by Soviet propaganda undergo "patriotic reeducation." A few years later, Stalin set the priorities of "military science" thus: first, to ensure the stability of armies; next, to attend to the morale of the combatants; only then, and in this order, does Stalin mention the quality and quantity of fighting units, weapons performance, and the command structure.

Today, Stalin's views have been overtaken by the social and political evolution of populations and the profound transformation of the physical context that has occurred over the past three or four decades. . . .

. . . In general, people are now won over to the elimination of weapons of which they believe they would be the first victims. After the defeat of France, thus right from the early 1940s, the geographical situation of the belligerents abruptly put the "rear" in the front line. In the absence of a land front on which to fight, the Germans and the British, the latter followed by the Americans, turned their attention to the enemy's territory, and their strategic bombing destroyed civilian dwellings and installations supplying military logistics without distinction. In 1945 the victims of Hiroshima and Nagasaki, like the earlier ones of Dresden and Tokyo, were not combatants, and the two Japanese cities were not strictly speaking military targets. During World War II, there was a "reversal of vulnerabilities," civilian populations being taken as targets and hostilities wreaking their havoc in the rear as much as, if not more than, on the front.

This shift preceded a slow but inexorable spread of awareness of the unacceptable consequences of a conflict between nuclear powers. Every policy or action of the leaders that appeared to be leading to a trial of strength at once sparked a response from the masses. Vitally concerned, they [now] demand negotiation, compromise, even the unconditional acceptance of the demands of the threatening power (assuming the latter to possess freedom of action with respect to its own inhabitants that enables it to be threatening, which seems less and less likely because of the weakening of autocracies and the limits of authoritarian power).

Accelerated urbanization, another social phenomenon of our time, makes the human habitat an easy target—a "rewarding" one, as the staff officers say. In western Europe, three-quarters or even, in some countries, four-fifths of the population live in urban areas. That means that a nation's human and material assets are now concentrated in relatively small spaces, and their annihilation would require only a handful of missiles. The new importance of habitat has thus altered the vulnerability of industrialized countries. Feeling themselves being held hostage, populations no longer allow their leaders to pursue a warlike policy. When former Chancellor [Helmut] Schmidt said that the detonation of two nuclear warheads over the Federal Republic of Germany would be enough to make the Bundeswehr at once lay down its arms, he was reflecting very accurately a new situation as it actually is. He might have added that before this happened hundreds of thousands of demonstrators would have besieged the federal chancellery in Bonn to demand an immediate surrender. There is no longer any grand strategy—and hence how much less any military strategy—that can neglect the intervention of the masses in the face of peril, whether real or even imagined. Nor is it possible for the political leadership to ignore the limits that peoples put on its plans. Thus the strategic conceptions set out above, even the most recent ones, are already a thing of the past.

PRINCIPAL SUBJECTS COVERED

MARITIME STRATEGY

Thucydides: *The Dispute over Corcyra*
Julius Caesar: *The Battle of Pharsalus*
Cassius Dio: *The Battle of Actium*
Ibn Khaldun: *The Admiralty*
Walter Raleigh: *Sea Warfare and the Defense of England*
Richard Hakluyt: *The Destruction of the Spanish Armada*
Duc de Richelieu: *On Sea Power*
Horatio Nelson: *The Trafalgar Memorandum*
Friedrich Ratzel: *The Sea and Sea-going Peoples*
Alfred Thayer Mahan: *Naval Strategy*
Julian Corbett: *Strategical Terms and Definitions*
Raoul Castex: *The Significance and Limits of Geography*

GUERRILLA WARFARE

Sallust: *Guerrilla Warfare*
Denis Davydov: *On Guerrilla Warfare; Why Partisan War Suits Russia*
J. F. A. Le Mière de Corvey: *On Partisans and Irregular Forces*
Henri Jomini: *Statesmanship in Its Relation to War* (section entitled "National Wars")
Charles Callwell: *Counterinsurgency*
T. E. Lawrence: *Guerrilla Warfare*
James Connolly: *On Street Fighting*
Mikhail Tukhachevsky: *Counterinsurgency*
Mao Ze-dong: *Strategy in China's Revolutionary War*

AIR POWER

Giulio Douhet: *Command of the Air*
William Mitchell: *The Aeronautical Era*
Hugh Trenchard: *The War Object of an Air Force*
Alexander de Seversky: *The Challenge to America*

GEOPOLITICS

Napoleon: *Geopolitics*
Friedrich Ratzel: *The Spatial Growth of States*
Halford J. Mackinder: *The Geographical Pivot of History*
Nicholas Spykman: *Heartland and Rimland*

MECHANIZED GROUND WARFARE

J. F. C. Fuller: *Tank Warfare*
Charles de Gaulle: *The Army of the Future*
Heinz Guderian: *Tank Attack*
Erwin Rommel: *Rules of Desert Warfare*

Designer: Milenda Nan Ok Lee
Compositor: BookMasters
Text: 10/13 Minion
Display: Minion
Printer and Binder: Haddon Craftsmen